# Peterson's® Two-Year Colleges 2019

**PETERSON'S®**

**About Peterson's®**

Peterson's® has been your trusted educational publisher for over 50 years. It's a milestone we're quite proud of, as we continue to offer the most accurate, dependable, high-quality educational content in the field, providing you with everything you need to succeed. No matter where you are on your academic or professional path, you can rely on Peterson's for its books, online information, expert test-prep tools, the most up-to-date education exploration data, and the highest quality career success resources—everything you need to achieve your education goals. For our complete line of products, visit **www.petersons.com**.

For more information about Peterson's range of educational products, contact Peterson's, 8740 Lucent Blvd., Suite 400, Highlands Ranch, CO 80129, or find us online at **www.petersons.com**.

© 2018 Peterson's®

Previous editions published as *Peterson's Annual Guide to Undergraduate Study* © 1970, 1971, 1972, 1973, 1974, 1975, 1976, 1977, 1978, 1979, 1980, 1981, 1982 and as *Peterson's Two-Year Colleges* © 1983, 1984, 1985, 1986, 1987, 1988, 1989, 1990, 1991, 1992, 1993, 1994, 1995, 1996, 1997, 1998, 1999, 2000, 2001, 2002, 2003, 2004, 2005, 2006, 2007, 2008, 2009, 2010, 2011, 2012, 2013, 2014, 2015, 2016, 2017

ISSN 0894-9328
ISBN: 978-0-7689-4232-3

Printed in the United States of America

10  9  8  7  6  5  4  3  2  1      20  19  18

Forty-ninth Edition

# Contents

# A Note from the Peterson's® Editors

For more than 50 years, Peterson's has given students and parents the most comprehensive, up-to-date information on undergraduate institutions in the United States. Peterson's researches the data published in *Peterson's Two-Year Colleges* each year. The information is furnished by the colleges and is accurate at the time of publishing.

This guide also features advice and tips on the college search and selection process, such as how to decide if a two-year college is right for you, how to approach transferring to another college, and what's in store for adults returning to college. If you seem to be getting more, not less, anxious about choosing and getting into the right college, *Peterson's Two-Year Colleges* provides just the right help, giving you the information you need to make important college decisions and ace the admission process.

Opportunities abound for students, and this guide can help you find what you want in a number of ways:

"What You Need to Know About Two-Year Colleges" outlines the basic features and advantages of two-year colleges. "Surviving Standardized Tests" gives an overview of the common examinations students take prior to attending college. "Who's Paying for This? Financial Aid Basics" provides guidelines for financing your college education. "Frequently Asked Questions About Transferring" takes a look at the two-year college scene from the perspective of a student who is looking toward the day when he or she may pursue additional education at a four-year institution. "Returning to School: Advice for Adult Students" is an analysis of the pros and cons (mostly pros) of returning to college after already having begun a professional career. "Coming to America: Tips for International Students Considering Study in the U.S." is an article written particularly for students overseas who are considering a U.S. college education. "Community Colleges and the Green Economy" offers information on some exciting "green" programs at community colleges throughout the United States, as well as two insightful essays by Mary F. T. Spilde, President, Lane Community College and Tom Sutton, Director of Wind Energy and Technical Services, Kalamazoo Valley Community College. Finally, "How to Use This Guide" gives details

on the data in this guide: what terms mean and why they're here.

- If you already have specifics in mind, such as a particular institution or major, turn to the easy-to-use **Two-Year Colleges At-a-Glance Chart** or **Indexes.** You can look up a particular feature—location and programs offered—or use the alphabetical index and immediately find the colleges that meet your criteria.

- For information about particular colleges, turn to the **Profiles of Two-Year Colleges** section. Here, our comprehensive college profiles are arranged alphabetically by state. They provide a complete picture of need-to-know information about every accredited two-year college—from admission to graduation, including expenses, financial aid, majors, and campus safety. All the information you need to apply is placed together at the conclusion of each college **Profile.** Display ads, which appear near some of the institutions' profiles, have been provided and paid for by those colleges or universities that wished to supplement their profile data with additional information about their institution.

- In addition, two-page narrative descriptions, which appear in the **Featured Two-Year Colleges** section, are paid for and written by college officials and offer great detail about each college. They are edited to provide a consistent format across entries for your ease of comparison.

Peterson's publishes a full line of books—education exploration, test prep, financial aid, and career preparation. Peterson's publications can be found at high school guidance offices, college libraries and career centers, and your local bookstore and library. Peterson's books are also available at www.petersonsbooks.com.

We welcome any comments or suggestions you may have about this publication. Your feedback will help us make educational dreams possible for you—and others like you.

Colleges will be pleased to know that Peterson's helped you in your selection. Admissions staff members are more than happy to answer questions, address specific problems and help in any way they can. The editors at Peterson's wish you great success in your college search.

NOTICE: Certain portions of or information contained in this book have been submitted and paid for by the educational institution identified, and such institutions take full responsibility for the accuracy, timeliness, completeness and functionality of such content. Such portions or information include (i) each display ad in the "Profiles" section from pages 53 through 318 that comprises a half or full page of information covering a single educational institution, and (ii) each two-page description in the "Featured Two-Year Colleges" section from pages 322 through 327.

# The College Admissions Process: An Overview

# What You Need to Know About Two-Year Colleges

## David R. Pierce

Two-year colleges—better known as community colleges—are often called "the people's colleges." With their open-door policies (admission is open to individuals with a high school diploma or its equivalent), community colleges provide access to higher education for millions of Americans who might otherwise be excluded from higher education. Community college students are diverse and of all ages, races, and economic backgrounds. While many community college students enroll full-time, an equally large number attend on a part-time basis so they can fulfill employment and family commitments as they advance their education.

Community colleges can also be referred to as either technical or junior colleges, and they may either be under public or independent control. What unites two-year colleges is that they are regionally accredited, postsecondary institutions, whose highest credential awarded is the associate degree. With few exceptions, community colleges offer a comprehensive curriculum, which includes transfer, technical, and continuing education programs.

### IMPORTANT FACTORS IN A COMMUNITY COLLEGE EDUCATION

The student who attends a community college can count on receiving high-quality instruction in a supportive learning community. This setting frees the student to pursue his or her own goals, nurture special talents, explore new fields of learning, and develop the capacity for lifelong learning.

From the student's perspective, four characteristics capture the essence of community colleges:

1. They are community-based institutions that work in close partnership with high schools, community groups, and employers in extending high-quality programs at convenient times and places.

2. Community colleges are cost effective. Annual tuition and fees at public community colleges average approximately half those at public four-year colleges and less than 15 percent of private four-year institutions. In addition, since most community colleges are generally close to their students' homes, these students can also save a significant amount of money on the room, board, and transportation expenses traditionally associated with a college education.

3. Community colleges provide a caring environment, with faculty members who are expert instructors, known for excellent teaching and meeting students at the point of their individual needs, regardless of age, sex, race, current job status, or previous academic preparation. Community colleges join a strong curriculum with a broad range of counseling and career services that are intended to assist students in making the most of their educational opportunities.

4. Many offer comprehensive programs, including transfer curricula in such liberal arts programs as chemistry, psychology, and business management, that lead directly to a baccalaureate degree and career programs that prepare students for employment or assist those already employed in upgrading their skills. For those students who need to strengthen their academic skills, community colleges also offer a wide range of developmental programs in mathematics, languages, and learning skills, designed to prepare the student for success in college studies.

### GETTING TO KNOW YOUR TWO-YEAR COLLEGE

The first step in determining the quality of a community college is to check the status of its accreditation. Once you have established that a community college is appropriately accredited, find out as much as you can about the programs and services it has to offer. Much of that information can be found in materials the college provides. However, the best way to learn about a college is to visit in person.

During a campus visit, be prepared to ask a lot of questions. Talk to students, faculty members, administrators, and counselors about the college and its programs, particularly those in which you have a special interest. Ask about available certificates and associate degrees. Don't be shy. Do what you can to dig below the surface. Ask college officials about the transfer rate to four-year colleges. If a college emphasizes student services, find out what particular assistance is offered, such as educational or career guidance. Colleges are eager to provide you with the information you need to make informed decisions.

## COMMUNITY COLLEGES CAN SAVE YOU MONEY

If you are able to live at home while you attend college, you will certainly save money on room and board, but it does cost something to commute. Many two-year colleges offer you instruction in your own home through online learning programs or through home study courses that can save both time and money. Look into all the options, and be sure to add up all the costs of attending various colleges before deciding which is best for you.

## FINANCIAL AID

Many students who attend community colleges are eligible for a range of federal financial aid programs, state aid, and on-campus jobs. Your high school counselor or the financial aid officer at a community college will also be able to help you. It is in your interest to apply for financial aid months in advance of the date you intend to start your college program, so find out early what assistance is available to you. While many community colleges are able to help students who make a last-minute decision to attend college, either through short-term loans or emergency grants, if you are considering entering college and think you might need financial aid, it is best to find out as much as you can as early as you can.

## WORKING AND GOING TO SCHOOL

Many two-year college students maintain full-time or part-time employment while they earn their degrees. Over the years, a steadily growing number of students have chosen to attend community colleges while they fulfill family and employment responsibilities. To enable these students to balance the demands of home, work, and school, most community colleges offer classes at night and on weekends.

For the full-time student, the usual length of time it takes to obtain an associate degree is two years. However, your length of study will depend on the course load you take: the fewer credits you earn each term, the longer it will take you to earn a degree. To assist you in moving more quickly toward earning your degree, many community colleges now award credit through examination or for equivalent knowledge gained through relevant life experiences. Be certain to find out the credit options that are available to you at the college in which you are interested. You may discover that it will take less time to earn a degree than you first thought.

## PREPARATION FOR TRANSFER

Studies have repeatedly shown that students who first attend a community college and then transfer to a four-year college or university do at least as well academically as the students who entered the four-year institutions as freshmen. Most community colleges have agreements with nearby four-year institutions to make transfer of credits easier. If you are thinking of transferring, be sure to meet with a counselor or faculty adviser before choosing your courses. You will want to map out a course of study with transfer in mind. Make sure you also find out the credit-transfer requirements of the four-year institution you might want to attend.

## ATTENDING A TWO-YEAR COLLEGE IN ANOTHER REGION

Although many community colleges serve a specific county or district, they are committed (to the extent of their ability) to the goal of equal educational opportunity without regard to economic status, race, creed, color, sex, or national origin. Independent two-year colleges recruit from a much broader geographical area—throughout the United States and, increasingly, around the world.

Although some community colleges do provide on-campus housing for their students, most do not. However, even if on-campus housing is not available, most colleges do have housing referral services.

## NEW CAREER OPPORTUNITIES

Community colleges realize that many entering students are not sure about the field in which they want to focus their studies or the career they would like to pursue. Often, students discover fields and careers they never knew existed. Community colleges have the resources to help students identify areas of career interest and to set challenging occupational goals.

Once a career goal is set, you can be confident that a community college will provide job-relevant, technical education. About half of the students who take courses for credit at community colleges do so to prepare for employment or to acquire or upgrade skills for their current job. Especially helpful in charting a career path is the assistance of a counselor or a faculty adviser, who can discuss job opportunities in your chosen field and help you map out your course of study.

In addition, since community colleges have close ties to their communities, they are in constant contact with leaders in business, industry, organized labor, and public life. Community colleges work with these individuals and their organizations to prepare students for direct entry into the world of work. For example, some community colleges have established partnerships with local businesses and industries to provide specialized training programs. Some also provide the academic portion of apprenticeship training, while others offer extensive job-shadowing and cooperative education opportunities. Be sure to examine all of the career-preparation opportunities offered by the community colleges in which you are interested.

---

*David R. Pierce is the former President of the American Association of Community Colleges.*

# Surviving Standardized Tests

## WHAT ARE STANDARDIZED TESTS?

Colleges and universities in the United States use tests to help evaluate applicants' readiness for admission or to place them in appropriate courses. The tests that are most frequently used by colleges are the ACT® of American College Testing, Inc., and the College Board's SAT®. In addition, the Educational Testing Service (ETS) offers the TOEFL® test, which evaluates the English-language proficiency of nonnative speakers. The tests are offered at designated testing centers located at high schools and colleges throughout the United States and U.S. territories and at testing centers in various countries throughout the world.

Upon request, special accommodations for students with documented visual, hearing, physical, or learning disabilities are available. Examples of special accommodations include tests in Braille or large print and such aids as a reader, recorder, magnifying glass, or sign language interpreter. Additional testing time may be allowed in some instances. Contact the appropriate testing program or your guidance counselor for details on how to request special accommodations.

## THE ACT®

The ACT® is a standardized college entrance examination that measures knowledge and skills in English, mathematics, reading comprehension, and science reasoning and the application of these skills to future academic tasks. The ACT® consists of four multiple-choice tests.

### Test 1: English
- 75 questions, 45 minutes
- Usage and mechanics
- Rhetorical skills

### Test 2: Mathematics
- 60 questions, 60 minutes
- Pre-algebra
- Elementary algebra
- Intermediate algebra
- Coordinate geometry
- Plane geometry
- Trigonometry

### Test 3: Reading
- 40 questions, 35 minutes
- Prose fiction
- Humanities
- Social studies
- Natural sciences

### Test 4: Science
- 40 questions, 35 minutes
- Data representation
- Research summary
- Conflicting viewpoints

Each section is scored from 1 to 36 and is scaled for slight variations in difficulty. Students are not penalized for incorrect responses. The composite score is the average of the four scaled scores. The ACT® Plus Writing includes the four multiple-choice tests and a writing test, which measures writing skills emphasized in high school English classes and in entry-level college composition courses.

To prepare for the ACT®, ask your guidance counselor for a free guidebook, "Preparing for the ACT®," or download it at www.act.org/content/dam/act/unsecured/documents/Preparing-for-the-ACT.pdf. Besides providing general test-preparation information and additional test-taking strategies, this guidebook provides full-length practice tests, including a Writing test, information about the optional Writing Test, strategies to prepare for the tests, and what to expect on test day.

### DON'T FORGET TO . . .

- ❏ Take the SAT® or ACT® before application deadlines.
- ❏ Note that test registration deadlines precede test dates by about six weeks.
- ❏ Register to take the TOEFL® test if English is not your native language and you are planning on studying at a North American college.
- ❏ Contact the College Board or American College Testing, Inc., in advance if you need special accommodations when taking tests.

## THE SAT®

The redesigned SAT®, which saw its first test-takers in the spring of 2016, has these sections: Evidence-Based Reading and Writing, Math, and the Essay. It is based on 1,600 points—the top scores for the Math section and the Evidence-Based Reading and Writing section will be 800, and the Essay score is reported separately.

### Evidence-based Reading Test
- 52 questions; 65 minutes
- Passages in U.S. and world literature, history/social studies, and science
- Paired passages
- Lower and higher text complexities
- Words in context, command of evidence, and analysis

### Writing and Language Test
- 44 questions; 35 minutes
- Passages in careers, history/social studies, humanities, and science
- Argument, informative/explanatory, and nonfiction narrative passages

- Words in context, grammar, expression of ideas, and analysis

## Mathematics Test

- One no-calculator section (25 minutes)
- One calculator section (55 minutes)
- Content includes algebra, problem solving and data analysis, advanced math, area and volume calculations, trigonometric functions, and lines, triangles, and circles using theorems.

## Essay (Optional)

- 50 minutes
- Argument passage written for a general audience
- Analysis of argument in passage using text evidence
- Score: 3–12 (Reading: 1–4 scale, Analysis: 1–4 scale, Writing: 1–4 scale)

According to the College Board's website, the "Eight Key Changes" are the following:

- **Relevant Words in Context:** Students need to interpret the meaning of words based on the context of the passage in which they appear. The focus is on "relevant" words—not obscure ones.

- **Command of Evidence:** In addition to demonstrating writing skills, students need to show that they're able to interpret, synthesize, and use evidence found in a wide range of sources.

- **Essay Analyzing a Source:** Students read a passage and explain how the author builds an argument, supporting support their claims with actual data from the passage.

- **Math Focused on Three Key Areas:** Problem Solving and Data Analysis (using ratios, percentages, and proportional reasoning to solve problems in science, social science, and career contexts), the Heart of Algebra (mastery of linear equations and systems), and Passport to Advanced Math (more complex equations and the manipulation they require).

- **Problems Grounded in Real-World Contexts:** All of the questions are grounded in the real world, directly related to work performed in college.

- **Analysis in Science and in Social Studies:** Students need to apply reading, writing, language, and math skills to answer questions in contexts of science, history, and social studies.

- **Founding Documents and Great Global Conversation:** Students will find an excerpt from one of the Founding Documents—such as the Declaration of Independence, the Constitution, and the Bill of Rights—or a text from the "Great Global Conversation" about freedom, justice, and human dignity.

- **No Penalty for Wrong Answers:** Students earn points for the questions they answer correctly.

Check out the College Board's website at https://collegereadiness.collegeboard.org for the most up-to-date information.

---

## Top 10 Ways Not to Take the Test

1. Cramming the night before the test.
2. Not becoming familiar with the directions before you take the test.
3. Not becoming familiar with the format of the test before you take it.
4. Not knowing how the test is graded.
5. Spending too much time on any one question.
6. Second-guessing yourself.
7. Not checking spelling, grammar, and sentence structure in essays.
8. Writing a one-paragraph essay.
9. Forgetting to take a deep breath—
10. and finally—Don't lose it!

---

## SAT SUBJECT TESTS™

Subject Tests are required by some institutions for admission and/or placement in freshman-level courses. Each Subject Test measures one's knowledge of a specific subject and the ability to apply that knowledge. Students should check with each institution for its specific requirements. In general, students are required to take three Subject Tests (one English, one mathematics, and one of their choice).

Subject Tests are given in the following areas: biology, chemistry, Chinese, French, German, Italian, Japanese, Korean, Latin, literature, mathematics, modern Hebrew, physics, Spanish, U.S. history, and world history. These tests are one hour long and are primarily multiple-choice tests. Three Subject Tests may be taken on one test date.

Scored like the current SAT®, students gain a point for each correct answer and lose a fraction of a point for each incorrect answer. The raw scores are then converted to scaled scores that range from 200 to 800.

## THE TOEFL® INTERNET-BASED TEST (IBT)

The Test of English as a Foreign Language Internet-Based Test (TOEFL® iBT) is designed to help assess a student's grasp of English if it is not the student's first language. Performance on the TOEFL® test may help interpret scores on the critical reading sections of the SAT®. The test consists of four integrated sections: speaking, listening, reading, and writing. The TOEFL® iBT emphasizes integrated skills. The paper-based versions of the TOEFL® will continue to be administered in certain countries where the Internet-based version has not yet been introduced. For further information, visit www.toefl.org.

## WHAT OTHER TESTS SHOULD I KNOW ABOUT?

### The AP® Program

This program allows high school students to try college-level work and build valuable skills and study habits in the process. Subject matter is explored in more depth in AP courses than in other high school classes. A qualifying score on an AP test—which varies from school to school—can earn you college credit or advanced placement. Getting qualifying grades on enough exams can even earn you a full year's credit and sophomore standing at more than 1,500 higher-education institutions. There are more than thirty AP courses across multiple subject areas, including art history, biology, and computer science. Speak to your guidance counselor for information about your school's offerings.

### College-Level Examination Program (CLEP®)

The CLEP enables students to earn college credit for what they already know, whether it was learned in school, through independent study, or through other experiences outside of the classroom. More than 2,900 colleges and universities now award credit for qualifying scores on one or more of the 33 CLEP exams. The exams, which are 90 minutes in length and are primarily multiple choice, are administered at participating colleges and universities. For more information, check out the website at www.collegeboard.com/clep.

## WHAT CAN I DO TO PREPARE FOR THESE TESTS?

Know what to expect. Get familiar with how the tests are structured, how much time is allowed, and the directions for each type of question. Get plenty of rest the night before the test and eat breakfast that morning.

There are a variety of products, from books to software to videos, available to help you prepare for most standardized tests. Find the learning style that suits you best. As for which products to buy, there are two major categories— those created by the test-makers and those created by private companies. The best approach is to talk to someone who has been through the process and find out which product or products he or she recommends.

Some students report significant increases in scores after participating in coaching programs. Longer-term programs (40 hours) seem to raise scores more than short-term programs (20 hours), but beyond 40 hours, score gains are minor. Math scores appear to benefit more from coaching than critical reading scores.

### Resources

There is a variety of ways to prepare for standardized tests— find a method that fits your schedule and your budget. But you should definitely prepare. Far too many students walk into these tests cold, either because they find standardized tests frightening or annoying or they just haven't found the time to study. The key is that these exams are standardized. That means these tests are largely the same from administration to administration; they always test the same concepts. They have to, or else you couldn't compare the scores of people who took the tests on different dates. The numbers or words may change, but the underlying content doesn't.

So how do you prepare? At the very least, you should review relevant material, such as math formulas and commonly used vocabulary words, and know the directions for each question type or test section. You should take at least one practice test and review your mistakes so you don't make them again on the test day. Beyond that, you know best how much preparation you need. You'll also find lots of material in libraries or bookstores to help you: books and software from the test- makers and from other publishers (including Peterson's) or live courses that range from national test-preparation companies to teachers at your high school who offer classes.

# Who's Paying for This? Financial Aid Basics

A college education can be expensive—costing more than $150,000 for four years at some of the higher priced private colleges and universities. Even at the lower-cost state colleges and universities, the cost of a four-year education can approach $60,000. Determining how you and your family will come up with the necessary funds to pay for your education requires planning, perseverance, and learning as much as you can about the options that are available to you. But before you get discouraged, College Board statistics show that 53 percent of full-time students attend four-year public and private colleges with tuition and fees less than $9,000, while 20 percent attend colleges that have tuition and fees more than $36,000. College costs tend to be less in the western states and higher in New England.

Paying for college should not be looked at as a four-year financial commitment. For many families, paying the total cost of a student's college education out of current income and savings is usually not realistic. For families that have planned ahead and have financial savings established for higher education, the burden is a lot easier. But for most, meeting the cost of college requires the pooling of current income and assets and investing in longer-term loan options. These family resources, together with financial assistance from state, federal, and institutional sources, enable millions of students each year to attend the institution of their choice.

## FINANCIAL AID PROGRAMS

There are three types of financial aid:

1. Gift-aid—Scholarships and grants are funds that do not have to be repaid.

2. Loans—Loans must be repaid, usually after graduation; the amount you have to pay back is the total you've borrowed plus any accrued interest. This is considered a source of self-help aid.

3. Student employment—Student employment is a job arranged for you by the financial aid office. This is another source of self-help aid.

The federal government has four major grant programs—the Federal Pell Grant, the Federal Supplemental Educational Opportunity Grant, Academic Competitiveness Grants (ACG), and National SMART (Science and Mathematics Access to Retain Talent) grants. ACG and SMART grants are limited to students who qualify for a Pell Grant and are awarded to a select group of students. Overall, these grants are targeted to low-to-moderate income families with significant financial need. The federal government also sponsors a student employment program called the Federal Work-Study Program, which offers jobs both on and off campus, and several loan programs, including those for students and for parents of undergraduate students.

There are two types of student loan programs: subsidized and unsubsidized. The subsidized Federal Direct Loan and the Federal Perkins Loan are need-based, government-subsidized loans. Students who borrow through these programs do not have to pay interest on the loan until after they graduate or leave school. The unsubsidized Federal Direct Loan and the Federal Direct PLUS Loan Program are not based on need, and borrowers are responsible for the interest while the student is in school. These loans are administered by different methods. Once you choose your college, the financial aid office will guide you through this process.

After you've submitted your financial aid application and you've been accepted for admission, each college will send you a letter describing your financial aid award. Most award letters show estimated college costs, how much you and your family are expected to contribute, and the amount and types of aid you have been awarded. Most students are awarded aid from a combination of sources and programs. Hence, your award is often called a financial aid "package."

## SOURCES OF FINANCIAL AID

Millions of students and families apply for financial aid each year. Financial aid from all sources exceeds $143 billion per year. The largest single source of aid is the federal government, which will award more than $100 billion this year.

The next largest source of financial aid is found in the college and university community. Most of this aid is awarded to students who have a demonstrated need based on the Federal Methodology. Some institutions use a different formula, the Institutional Methodology (IM), to award their own funds in conjunction with other forms of aid. Institutional aid may be either need-based or non-need based. Aid that is not based on need is usually awarded for a student's academic performance (merit awards), specific talents or abilities, or to attract the type of students a college seeks to enroll.

Another source of financial aid is from state government. All states offer grant and/or scholarship aid, most of which is need-based. However, more and more states are offering substantial merit-based aid programs. Most state programs award aid only to students attending college in their home state.

Other sources of financial aid include:

- Private agencies
- Foundations
- Corporations
- Clubs
- Fraternal and service organizations

- Civic associations
- Unions
- Religious groups that award grants, scholarships, and low-interest loans
- Employers that provide tuition reimbursement benefits for employees and their children

More information about these different sources of aid is available from high school guidance offices, public libraries, college financial aid offices, directly from the sponsoring organizations, and online at www.petersons.com/college-search/scholarship-search.aspx.

## HOW NEED-BASED FINANCIAL AID IS AWARDED

When you apply for aid, your family's financial situation is analyzed using a government-approved formula called the Federal Methodology. This formula looks at five items:

1. Demographic information of the family
2. Income of the parents
3. Assets of the parents
4. Income of the student
5. Assets of the student

This analysis determines the amount you and your family are expected to contribute toward your college expenses, called your Expected Family Contribution, or EFC. If the EFC is equal to or more than the cost of attendance at a particular college, then you do not demonstrate financial need. However, even if you don't have financial need, you may still qualify for aid, as there are grants, scholarships, and loan programs that are not need-based.

If the cost of your education is greater than your EFC, then you do demonstrate financial need and qualify for assistance. The amount of your financial need that can be met varies from school to school. Some are able to meet your full need, while others can only cover a certain percentage of need. Here's the formula:

Cost of Attendance
− Expected Family Contribution
= Financial Need

The EFC remains constant, but your need will vary according to the costs of attendance at a particular college. In general, the higher the tuition and fees at a particular college, the higher the cost of attendance will be. Expenses for books and supplies, room and board, transportation, and other miscellaneous items are included in the overall cost of attendance. It is important to remember that you do not have to be low-income to qualify for financial aid. Many middle and upper-middle income families qualify for need-based financial aid.

## APPLYING FOR FINANCIAL AID

Every student must complete the Free Application for Federal Student Aid (FAFSA®) to be considered for financial aid. The FAFSA® is available from your high school guidance office, many public libraries, colleges in your area, or directly from the U.S. Department of Education.

Students are encouraged to apply for federal student aid on the Web. The electronic version of the FAFSA® can be accessed at http://www.fafsa.ed.gov.

## The NEW Federal Student Aid ID

In order for a student to complete the online FAFSA®, he or she will need a Federal Student Aid (FSA) ID. You can get this online at https://fsaid.ed.gov/npas/index.htm. Since May 2015, the FSA ID has replaced the previously used PIN system. Parents of dependent students also need to obtain their own FSA ID in order to sign their child's FAFSA® electronically online.

The FSA ID can be used to access several federal aid-related websites, including FAFSA.gov and StudentLoans.gov. It consists of a username and password and can be used to electronically sign Federal Student Aid documents, access your personal records, and make binding legal obligations. The FSA ID is beneficial in several ways:

- It removes your personal identifiable information (PII), such as your Social Security number, from your log-in credentials.
- It creates a more secure and efficient way to verify your information when you log in to access to your federal student aid information online.
- It gives you the ability to easily update your personal information.
- It allows you to easily retrieve your username and password by requesting a secure code be sent to your e-mail address or by answering challenge questions.

It's relatively simple to create an FSA ID and should only take a few minutes. In addition, you will have an opportunity to link your current Federal Student Aid PIN (if you already have one) to your FSA ID. The final step is to confirm your e-mail address. You will receive a secure code to the e-mail address you provided when you set up your FSA ID. Once you retrieve the code from your e-mail account and enter it—to confirm your e-mail address is valid—you will be able to use this e-mail address instead of your username to log in to any of the federal aid-related websites, making the log-in process EVEN simpler for you and your parents.

When you initially create your FSA ID, your information will need to be verified with the Social Security Administration. This process can take anywhere from one to three days. For that reason, it's a good idea to take care of setting up your FSA ID as early as possible, so it will be all set when you are ready to begin completing your FAFSA®.

IMPORTANT NOTE: Since your FSA ID provides access to your personal information and is used to sign online documents, it's imperative that you protect this ID. Don't share it with *anyone* or write it down in an insecure location—you could place yourself at great risk for identify theft.

### If Every College You're Applying to for Fall 2019 Requires the FAFSA®

. . . then it's pretty simple: Complete the FAFSA® after October 1, 2018, being certain to send it in before any college-imposed deadlines. (Students will now be permitted to send in the 2019–20 FAFSA® before January 1, 2018.) Students (and parents, as appropriate) are required to report income for an earlier tax year, so for the 2019–20 school year, you would report 2017 income information.

After you send in your FAFSA®, you'll receive a Student Aid Report (SAR) that includes all of the information you reported and shows your EFC. If you provided an e-mail address, the SAR is sent to you electronically; otherwise, you will receive a SAR or SAR Acknowledgment in the mail, which lists your FAFSA® information but may require you to make any corrections on the FAFSA® website. Be sure to review the SAR, checking to see if the information you reported is accurately represented. If you used estimated numbers to complete the FAFSA®, you may have to resubmit the SAR with any corrections to the data. The college(s) you have designated on the FAFSA® will receive the information you reported and will use that data to make their decision.

## The CSS/Financial Aid PROFILE®

To award their own funds, some colleges require an additional application, the CSS/Financial Aid PROFILE® form. The PROFILE asks supplemental questions that some colleges and awarding agencies feel provide a more accurate assessment of the family's ability to pay for college. It is up to the college to decide whether it will use only the FAFSA® or both the FAFSA® and the PROFILE. PROFILE applications are available from the high school guidance office and on the Web. Both the paper application and the website list those colleges and programs that require the PROFILE application.

### If a College Requires the PROFILE

**Step 1:** Register for the CSS/Financial Aid PROFILE in the fall of your senior year in high school. You can apply for the PROFILE online at http://profileonline.collegeboard.com/prf/index.jsp. Registration information with a list of the colleges that require the PROFILE is available in most high school guidance offices. There is a fee for using the Financial Aid PROFILE application ($25 for the first college, which includes the $9 application fee, and $16 for each additional college). You must pay for the service by credit card when you register. If you do not have a credit card, you will be billed. A limited number of fee waivers are automatically granted to first-time applicants based on the financial information provided on the PROFILE.

**Step 2:** Fill out your customized CSS/Financial Aid PROFILE. Once you register, your application will be immediately available online and will have questions that all students must complete, questions which must be completed by the student's parents (unless the student is independent and the colleges or programs selected do not require parental information), and *may* have supplemental questions needed by one or more of your schools or programs. If required, those will be found in Section Q of the application.

In addition to the PROFILE application you complete online, you may also be required to complete a Business/ Farm Supplement via traditional paper format. Completion of this form is not a part of the online process. If this form is required, instructions on how to download and print the supplemental form are provided. If your biological or adoptive parents are separated or divorced and your colleges and programs require it, your noncustodial parent may be asked to complete the Noncustodial PROFILE.

Once you complete and submit your PROFILE application, it will be processed and sent directly to your requested colleges and programs.

## IF YOU DON'T QUALIFY FOR NEED-BASED AID

If you are not eligible for need-based aid, you can still find ways to lessen your burden.

Here are some suggestions:

- Search for merit scholarships. You can start at the initial stages of your application process. College merit awards are increasingly important as more and more colleges award these to students they especially want to attract. As a result, applying to a college at which your qualifications put you at the top of the entering class may give you a larger merit award. Another source of aid to look for is private scholarships that are given for special skills and talents. Additional information can be found at www.finaid.org.

- Seek employment during the summer and the academic year. The student employment office at your college can help you locate a school-year job. Many colleges and local businesses have vacancies remaining after they have hired students who are receiving Federal Work-Study Program financial aid.

- Borrow through the unsubsidized Federal Direct Loan program. This is generally available to all students. The terms and conditions are similar to the subsidized loans. The biggest difference is that the borrower is responsible for the interest while still in college, although the government permits students to delay paying the interest right away and add the accrued interest to the total amount owed. You must file the FAFSA® to be considered.

- After you've secured what you can through scholarships, working, and borrowing, you and your parents will be expected to meet your share of the college bill (the Expected Family Contribution). Many colleges offer monthly payment plans that spread the cost over the academic year. If the monthly payments are too high, parents can borrow through the Federal Direct PLUS Loan Program, through one of the many private education loan programs available, or through home equity loans and lines of credit. Families seeking assistance in financing college expenses should inquire at the financial aid office about what programs are available at the college. Some families seek the advice of professional financial advisers and tax consultants.

# Frequently Asked Questions About Transferring

## Muriel M. Shishkoff

Among the students attending two-year colleges are a large number who began their higher education knowing they would eventually transfer to a four-year school to obtain their bachelor's degree. There are many reasons why students go this route. Upon graduating from high school, some simply do not have definite career goals. Although they don't want to put their education on hold, they prefer not to pay exorbitant amounts in tuition while trying to "find themselves." As the cost of a university education escalates—even in public institutions—the option of spending the freshman and sophomore years at a two-year college looks attractive to many students. Others attend a two-year college because they are unable to meet the initial entrance standards—a specified grade point average (GPA), standardized test scores, or knowledge of specific academic subjects—required by the four-year school of their choice. Many such students praise the community college system for giving them the chance to be, academically speaking, "born again." In addition, students from other countries often find that they can adapt more easily to language and cultural changes at a two-year school before transferring to a larger, more diverse four-year college.

If your plan is to attend a two-year college with the ultimate goal of transferring to a four-year school, you will be pleased to know that the increased importance of the community college route to a bachelor's degree is recognized by all segments of higher education. As a result, many two-year schools have revised their course outlines and established new courses in order to comply with the programs and curricular offerings of the universities. Institutional improvements to make transferring easier have also proliferated at both the two-and four-year levels. The generous transfer policies of the Pennsylvania, New York, and Florida state university systems, among others, reflect this attitude; these systems accept all credits from students who have graduated from accredited community colleges.

If you are interested in moving from a two-year college to a four-year school, the sooner you make up your mind that you are going to make the switch, the better position you will be to transfer successfully (that is, without having wasted valuable time and credits). The ideal point at which to make such a decision is **before** you register for classes at your two-year school; a counselor can help you plan your course work with an eye toward fulfilling the requirements needed for your major course of study.

Naturally, it is not always possible to plan your transferring strategy that far in advance, but keep in mind that the key to a successful transfer is **preparation,** and preparation takes time—time to think through your objectives and time to plan the right classes to take.

As students face the prospect of transferring from a two-year to a four-year school, many thoughts and concerns about this complicated and often frustrating process race through their minds. Here are answers to the questions that are most frequently asked by transferring students.

**Q** Does every college and university accept transfer students?

**A** Most four-year institutions accept transfer students, but some do so more enthusiastically than others. Graduating from a community college is an advantage at, for example, Arizona State University and the University of Massachusetts Boston; both accept more community college transfer students than traditional freshmen. At the University at Albany, SUNY, graduates of two-year transfer programs within the State University of New York System are given priority for upper-division (i.e., junior-and senior-level) vacancies.

Schools offering undergraduate work at the upper division only are especially receptive to transfer applications. On the other hand, some schools accept only a few transfer students; others refuse entrance to sophomores or those in their final year. Princeton University requires an "excellent academic record and particularly compelling reasons to transfer." Check the catalogs of several colleges for their transfer requirements before you make your final choice.

**Q** Do students who go directly from high school to a four-year college do better academically than transfer students from community colleges?

**A** On the contrary: some institutions report that transfers from two-year schools who persevere until graduation do *better* than those who started as freshmen in a four-year college.

**Q** Why is it so important that my two-year college be accredited?

**A** Four-year colleges and universities accept transfer credits only from schools formally recognized by a regional, national, or professional educational agency. This accreditation signifies that an institution or program of study meets or exceeds a minimum level of educational quality necessary for meeting stated educational objectives.

**Q** After enrolling at a four-year school, may I still make up necessary courses at a community college?

**A** Some institutions restrict credit after transfer to their own facilities. Others allow students to take a limited number of transfer courses after matriculation, depending on the subject matter. A few provide opportunities for cross-registration or dual enrollment, which means taking classes on more than one campus.

**Q** What do I need to do to transfer?

**A** First, send for your high school and college transcripts. Having chosen the school you wish to transfer to, check its admission requirements against your transcripts. If you find that you are admissible, file an application as early as possible before the deadline. Part of the process will be asking your former schools to send official transcripts to the admission office, i.e., not the copies you used in determining your admissibility.

Plan your transfer program with the head of your new department as soon as you have decided to transfer. Determine the recommended general education pattern and necessary preparation for your major. At your present school, take the courses you will need to meet transfer requirements for the new school.

**Q** What qualifies me for admission as a transfer student?

**A** Admission requirements for most four-year institutions vary. Depending on the reputation or popularity of the school and program you wish to enter, requirements may be quite selective and competitive. Usually, you will need to show satisfactory test scores, an academic record up to a certain standard, and completion of specific subject matter.

Transfer students can be eligible to enter a four-year school in a number of ways: by having been eligible for admission directly upon graduation from high school, by making up shortcomings in grades (or in subject matter not covered in high school) at a community college, or by satisfactory completion of necessary courses or credit hours at another postsecondary institution. Ordinarily, students coming from a community college or from another four-year institution must meet or exceed the receiving institution's standards for freshmen and show appropriate college-level course work taken since high school. Students who did not graduate from high school can present proof of proficiency through results

on the the GED® Test, the HiSET® Exam, or another state-approved high school equivalency test.

**Q** Are exceptions ever made for students who don't meet all the requirements for transfer?

**A** Extenuating circumstances, such as disability, low family income, refugee or veteran status, or athletic talent, may permit the special enrollment of students who would not otherwise be eligible but who demonstrate the potential for academic success. Consult the appropriate office—the Educational Opportunity Program, the disabled students' office, the athletic department, or the academic dean—to see whether an exception can be made in your case.

**Q** How far in advance do I need to apply for transfer?

**A** Some schools have a rolling admission policy, which means that they process transfer applications as they are received, all year long. With other schools, you must apply during the priority filing period, which can be up to a year before you wish to enter. Check the date with the admission office at your prospective campus.

**Q** Is it possible to transfer courses from several different institutions?

**A** Institutions ordinarily accept the courses that they consider transferable, regardless of the number of accredited schools involved. However, there is the danger of exceeding the maximum number of credit hours that can be transferred from all other schools or earned through credit by examination, extension courses, or correspondence courses. The limit placed on transfer credits varies from school to school, so read the catalog carefully to avoid taking courses you won't be able to use. To avoid duplicating courses, keep attendance at different campuses to a minimum.

**Q** What is involved in transferring from a semester system to a quarter or trimester system?

**A** In the semester system, the academic calendar is divided into two equal parts. The quarter system is more aptly named trimester, since the academic calendar is divided into three equal terms (not counting a summer session). To convert semester units into quarter units or credit hours, simply multiply the semester units by one and a half. Conversely, multiply quarter units by two thirds to come up with semester units. If you are used to a semester system of fifteen- to sixteen-week courses, the ten-week courses of the quarter system may seem to fly by.

**Q** Why might a course be approved for transfer credit by one four-year school but not by another?

**A** The beauty of postsecondary education in the United States lies in its variety. Entrance policies and graduation requirements are designed to reflect and serve each institution's mission. Because institutional policies vary so widely, schools may interpret the subject matter of a course from quite different points of view. Given that the granting of transfer credit indicates that a course is viewed as being, in effect, parallel to one offered by the receiving institution, it is easy to see how this might be the case at one university and not another.

**Q** Must I take a foreign language to transfer?

**A** Foreign language proficiency is often required for admission to a four-year institution; such proficiency also often figures in certain majors or in the general education pattern. Often, two or three years of a single language in high school will do the trick. Find out if scores received on Advanced Placement (AP®) examinations, placement examinations given by the foreign language department, or SAT Subject Tests™ will be accepted in lieu of college course work.

**Q** Will the school to which I'm transferring accept pass/no pass, pass/fail, or credit/no credit grades in lieu of letter grades?

**A** Usually, a limit is placed on the number of these courses you can transfer, and there may be other restrictions as well. If you want to use other-than-letter grades for the fulfillment of general education requirements or lower-division (freshman and sophomore) preparation for the major, check with the receiving institution.

**Q** Which is more important for transfer—my grade point average or my course completion pattern?

**A** Some schools believe that your past grades indicate academic potential and overshadow prior preparation for a specific degree program. Others require completion of certain introductory courses before transfer to prepare you for upper-division work in your major. In any case, appropriate course selection will cut down the time to graduation and increase your chances of making a successful transfer.

**Q** What happens to my credits if I change majors?

**A** If you change majors after admission, your transferable course credit should remain fairly intact. However, because you may need extra or different preparation for your new major, some of the courses you've taken may now be useful only as electives. The need for additional lower-level preparation may mean you're staying longer at your new school than you originally planned. On the other hand, you may already have taken courses that count toward your new major as part of the university's general education pattern.

Excerpted (and updated) from *Transferring Made Easy: A Guide to Changing Colleges Successfully,* by Muriel M. Shishkoff, © 1991 by Muriel M. Shishkoff (published by Peterson's).

# Returning to School: Advice for Adult Students

## Sandra Cook, Ph.D.
**Associate Vice President for Enrollment Management, San Diego State University**

Many adults think for a long time about returning to school without taking any action. One purpose of this article is to help the "thinkers" finally make some decisions by examining what is keeping them from action. Another purpose is to describe not only some of the difficulties and obstacles that adult students may face when returning to school but also tactics for coping with them.

If you have been thinking about going back to college, and believing that you are the only person your age contemplating college, you should know that approximately 7 million adult students are currently enrolled in higher education institutions. This number represents 50 percent of total higher education enrollments. The majority of adult students are enrolled at two-year colleges.

There are many reasons why adult students choose to attend a two-year college. Studies have shown that the three most important criteria that adult students consider when choosing a college are location, cost, and availability of the major or program desired. Most two-year colleges are public institutions that serve a geographic district, making them readily accessible to the community. Costs at most two-year colleges are far less than at other types of higher education institutions. For many students who plan to pursue a bachelor's degree, completing their first two years of college at a community college is an affordable means to that end. If you are interested in an academic program that will transfer to a four-year institution, most two-year colleges offer the "general education" courses that compose most freshman and sophomore years. If you are interested in a vocational or technical program, two-year colleges excel in providing this type of training.

## SETTING THE STAGE

There are three different "stages" in the process of adults returning to school. The first stage is uncertainty. Do I really want to go back to school? What will my friends or family think? Can I compete with those 18-year-old whiz kids? Am I too old? The second stage is choice. Once the decision to return has been made, you must choose where you will attend. There are many criteria to use in making this decision. The third stage is support. You have just added another role to your already-too-busy life. There are, however, strategies that

will help you accomplish your goals—perhaps not without struggle, but with grace and humor nonetheless. Let's look at each of these stages.

## UNCERTAINTY

Why are you thinking about returning to school? Is it to

- fulfill a dream that had to be delayed?
- become more educationally well-rounded?
- fill an intellectual void in your life?

These reasons focus on personal growth.

If you are returning to school to

- meet people and make friends
- attain and enjoy higher social status and prestige among friends, relatives, and associates
- understand/study a cultural heritage
- have a medium in which to exchange ideas

You are interested in social and cultural opportunities.

If you are like most adult students, you want to

- qualify for a new occupation
- enter or reenter the job market
- increase earnings potential
- qualify for a more challenging position in the same field of work

You are seeking career growth.

Understanding the reasons why you want to go back to school is an important step in setting your educational goals and will help you to establish some criteria for selecting a college. However, don't delay your decision because you have not been able to clearly define your motives. Many times, these aren't clear until you have already begun the process, and they may change as you move through your college experience.

Assuming you agree that additional education will benefit you, what is it that keeps you from returning to school? You may have a litany of excuses running through your mind:

- I don't have time.
- I can't afford it.
- I'm too old to learn.
- My friends will think I'm crazy.

- I'll be older than the teachers and other students.
- My family can't survive without me to take care of them every minute.
- I'll be X years old when I finish.
- I'm afraid.
- I don't know what to expect.

And that is just what these are—excuses. You can make school, like anything else in your life, a priority or not. If you really want to return, you can. The more you understand your motivation for returning to school and the more you understand what excuses are keeping you from taking action, the easier your task will be.

**If you think you don't have time:** The best way to decide how attending class and studying can fit into your schedule is to keep track of what you do with your time each day for several weeks. Completing a standard time-management grid (each day is plotted out by the half hour) is helpful for visualizing how your time is spent. For each 3-credit-hour class you take, you will need to find 3 hours for class plus 6 to 9 hours for reading-studying-library time. This study time should be spaced evenly throughout the week, not loaded up on one day. It is not possible to learn or retain the material that way. When you examine your grid, see where there are activities that could be replaced with school and study time. You may decide to give up your bowling league or some time in front of the TV. Try not to give up sleeping, and don't cut out every moment of free time. Here are some suggestions that have come from adults who have returned to school:

- Enroll in a time-management workshop. It helps you rethink how you use your time.
- Don't think you have to take more than one course at a time. You may eventually want to work up to taking more, but consider starting with one. (It is more than you are taking now!)
- If you have a family, start assigning to them those household chores that you usually do—and don't redo what they do.
- Use your lunch hour or commuting time for reading.

**If you think you cannot afford it:** As mentioned earlier, two-year colleges are extremely affordable. If you cannot afford the tuition, look into the various financial aid options. Most federal and state funds are available to full- and part-time students. Loans are also available. While many people prefer not to accumulate a debt for school, these same people will think nothing of taking out a loan to buy a car. After five or six years, which is the better investment? Adult students who work should look into whether their company has a tuition-reimbursement policy. There are also private scholarships, available through foundations, service organizations, and clubs, that are focused on adult learners. Your public library, the Web, and a college financial aid adviser are three excellent sources for reference materials regarding financial aid.

**If you think you are too old to learn:** This is pure myth. A number of studies have shown that adult learners perform as well as, or better than, traditional-age students.

**If you are afraid your friends will think you're crazy:** Who cares? Maybe they will, maybe they won't. Usually, they will admire your courage and be just a little jealous of your ambition (although they'll never tell you that). Follow your dreams, not theirs.

**If you are concerned because the teachers or students will be younger than you:** Don't be. The age differences that may be apparent in other settings evaporate in the classroom. If anything, an adult in the classroom strikes fear into the hearts of some 18-year-olds because adults have been known to be prepared, ask questions, be truly motivated, and be there to learn!

**If you think your family will have a difficult time surviving while you are in school:** If you have done everything for them up to now, they might struggle. Consider this an opportunity to help them become independent and self-sufficient. Your family can only make you feel guilty if you let them. You are not abandoning them; you are becoming an educational role model. When you are happy and working toward your goals, everyone benefits. Admittedly, it sometimes takes time for them to realize this. For single parents, there are schools that offer support groups, child care, and cooperative babysitting.

**If you're appalled at the thought of being X years old when you graduate in Y years:** How old will you be in Y years if you don't go back to school?

**If you are afraid or don't know what to expect:** Know that these are natural feelings when one encounters any new situation. Adult students find that their fears usually dissipate once they begin classes. Fear of trying is usually the biggest roadblock to the reentry process.

No doubt you have dreamed up a few more reasons for not making the decision to return to school. Keep in mind that what you are doing is making up excuses, and you are using these excuses to release you from the obligation to make a decision about your life. The thought of returning to college can be scary. Anytime anyone ventures into unknown territory, there is a risk, but taking risks is a necessary component of personal and professional growth. It is your life, and you alone are responsible for making the decisions that determine its course. Education is an investment in your future.

## CHOICE

Once you have decided to go back to school, your next task is to decide where to go. If your educational goals are well defined (e.g., you want to pursue a degree in order to change careers), then your task is a bit easier. But even if your educational goals are still evolving, do not defer your return. Many students who enter higher education with a specific major in mind change that major at least once.

Most students who attend a public two-year college choose the community college in the district in which they live. This is generally the closest and least expensive option if the school offers the programs you want. If you are planning to begin your education at a two-year college and then transfer to a four-year school, there are distinct advantages to choosing your four-year school early. Many community and four-year colleges have "articulation" agreements that designate what credits from the two-year school will transfer to the four-year college and how. Some four-year institutions accept an associate degree as equivalent to the freshman and sophomore years, regardless of the courses you have taken. Some four-year schools accept two-year college work only on a course-by-course basis. If you can identify which school you will transfer to, you can know in advance exactly how your two-year credits will apply, preventing an unexpected loss of credit or time.

Each institution of higher education is distinctive. Your goal in choosing a college is to come up with the best student-institution fit—matching your needs with the offerings and characteristics of the school. The first step in choosing a college is to determine what criteria are most important to you in attaining your educational goals. Location, cost, and program availability are the three main factors that influence an adult student's college choice. In considering location, don't forget that some colleges have conveniently located branch campuses. In considering cost, remember to explore your financial aid options before ruling out an institution because of its tuition. Program availability should include not only the major in which you are interested, but also whether or not classes in that major are available when you can take them.

Some additional considerations beyond location, cost, and programs are:

- Does the school have a commitment to adult students and offer appropriate services, such as child care, tutoring, and advising?

- Are classes offered at times when you can take them?

- Are there academic options for adults, such as credit for life or work experience, credit by examination (including CLEP), credit for military service, or accelerated programs?

- Is the faculty sensitive to the needs of adult learners?

Once you determine which criteria are vital in your choice of an institution, you can begin to narrow your choices. There are myriad ways for you to locate the information you desire. Many newspapers publish a "School Guide" several times a year in which colleges and universities advertise to an adult student market. In addition, schools themselves publish catalogs, class schedules, and promotional materials that contain much of the information you need, and they are yours for the asking. Many colleges sponsor information sessions and open houses that allow you to visit the campus and ask questions. An appointment with an adviser is a good way to assess the fit between you and the institution. Be sure to bring your questions with you to your interview.

## SUPPORT

Once you have made the decision to return to school and have chosen the institution that best meets your needs, take some additional steps to ensure your success during your crucial first semester. Take advantage of institutional support and build some social support systems of your own. Here are some ways of doing just that:

- Plan to participate in any orientation programs. These serve the threefold purpose of providing you with a great deal of important information, familiarizing you with the campus and its facilities, and giving you the opportunity to meet and begin networking with other students.

- Take steps to deal with any academic weaknesses. Take mathematics and writing placement tests if you have reason to believe you may need some extra help in these areas. It is not uncommon for adult students to need a math refresher course or a program to help alleviate math anxiety. Ignoring a weakness won't make it go away.

- Look into adult reentry programs. Many institutions offer adults workshops focusing on ways to improve study skills, textbook reading, test-taking, and time-management skills.

- Build new support networks by joining an adult student organization, making a point of meeting other adult students through workshops, or actively seeking out a "study buddy" in each class—that invaluable friend who shares and understands your experience.

- Incorporate your new status as "student" into your family life. Doing your homework with your children at a designated "homework time" is a valuable family activity and reinforces the importance of education.

- Make sure you take a reasonable course load in your first semester. It is far better to have some extra time on your hands and to succeed magnificently than to spend the entire semester on the brink of a breakdown. Also, whenever possible, try to focus your first courses not only on requirements, but also on areas of personal interest.

- Faculty members, advisers, and student affairs personnel are there to help you during difficult times—let them assist you as often as necessary.

After completing your first semester, you will probably look back in wonder at why you thought going back to school was so imposing. Certainly, it's not without its occasional exasperations. But, as with life, keeping things in perspective and maintaining your sense of humor make the difference between just coping and succeeding brilliantly.

# Coming to America: Tips for International Students Considering Study in the U.S.

## Introduction: Why Study in the United States?

Are you thinking about going to a college or university in the United States? If you're looking at this book, you probably are! All around the world, students like you, pursuing higher education, are considering that possibility. They envision themselves on modern, high-tech campuses in well-known cities, surrounded by American students, taking classes and having fun. A degree from a U.S. school would certainly lead to success and fortune, either back in your home country or perhaps even in the United States, wouldn't it?

It can be done—but becoming a student at a college or university in the U.S. requires academic talent, planning, time, effort, and money. While there may be only a small number of institutions of higher learning in your country, there are more than 2,900 four-year colleges and universities in the United States. Choosing one, being accepted, and then traveling and becoming a student in America is a big undertaking.

If this is your dream, here is some helpful information and expert tips from professionals who work with international students at colleges and universities throughout the United States.

## Timing and Planning

The journey to a college or university in the U.S. often starts years in advance. Most international students choose to study in the U.S. because of the high quality of academics. Your family may also have a lot of input on this decision, too.

"We always tell students they should be looking in the sophomore year, visiting in the junior year, and applying in the senior year," says Father Francis E. Chambers, OSA, D.Min., Associate Director of International Admission at Villanova University. He stresses that prospective students need to be taking challenging courses in the years leading up to college. "We want to see academic rigor. Most admission decisions are based on the first six semesters—senior year is too late."

Heidi Gregori-Gahan, Assistant Provost for International Programs at the University of Southern Indiana agrees that it's important to start early. "Plan ahead and do your homework. There is so much to choose from—so many schools, programs, degrees, and experiences. It can be overwhelming."

While students in some countries may pay an agent to help them get into a school in the United States, Gregori-Gahan often directs potential international students to EducationUSA (http://educationusa.state.gov), a U.S. State Department network of over 400 international student advising centers in more than 170 countries. "They are there to provide unbiased information about studying in the United States and help you understand the process and what you need to do."

Two to three years of advance planning is also recommended by Daphne Durham, who has been an international student adviser at Harvard, Suffolk University, Valdosta State University, and the University of Georgia. She points out that the academic schedule in other countries is often different than that of the United States, so you need to synchronize your calendar accordingly.

You will have to take several tests in order to gain admission to a U.S. school, so it's important to know when those tests are given in your country, then register and take them so your scores will be available when you apply. Even if you have taken English in school, you will probably have to take The Test of English as a Foreign Language (TOEFL®), but some schools also accept the International English Language Testing Sytem (IELTS). You will probably also have to take the SAT® or ACT® tests, which are achievement or aptitude tests, and are usually required of all students applying for admission, not just international students.

"Make sure you understand how the international admissions process works at the school or schools you want to attend," says Durham. "What test scores are needed and when? Does the school have a fixed calendar or rolling admissions?" Those are just some of the many factors that can impact your application and could make a difference in when you are able to start school.

"Every university is unique in what's required and what they need to do. Even navigating each school's different website can be challenging," explains Gregori-Gahan.

## Searching for Schools

This book contains information on thousands of four-year colleges and universities, and it will be a valuable resource for you in your search and application process. But with so many options, how do you decide which school you should attend?

"Where I find a big difference with international students is if their parents don't recognize the school, they don't apply to the school," says Fr. Chambers. "They could be overlooking a lot of great schools. They have to look outside the box."

The school Gregori-Gahan represents is in Evansville, Indiana, and it probably isn't familiar to students abroad. "Not many people have heard of anything beyond New York and California and maybe Florida. I like to tell students that this is 'real America.' But happy international students on our campus have recruited others to come here."

She points out that Internet technology has made a huge difference in the search process for international students. Websites full of information, live chat, webinars, virtual tours, and admission interviews via Skype have made it easier for potential students to connect with U.S. institutions, get more information, and be better able to visualize the campus.

One thing than will help narrow your search for a school is knowing specifically what you want to study. You need to know what the course of study is called in the United States, what it means, and what is required in order to study that subject. You also need to consider your future plans. What are your goals and objectives? What do you plan to do after earning your degree?

"If you're going to overcome the hurdles and get to a U.S. school, you have to have a directed path chosen," says Durham.

The other thing that could help your search process is finding a school that is a good fit.

## Fit Is Important

You want your clothing and shoes to fit you properly and be comfortable, so a place where you will spend four or more years of your life studying should also be comfortable and appropriate for you. So how can you determine if a particular school is a good fit?

"We really recommend international students visit first. Yes, there are websites and virtual tours, but there's still nothing that beats an in-person visit," says Fr. Chambers. He estimates that 50 to 60 percent of Villanova's international students visited the campus before enrolling.

"It can be hard to get a sense of a place—you're so far away and you're probably not going to set foot on campus until you arrive," says Gregori-Gahan. "There is a high potential for culture shock."

You need to ask yourself what is important to you in a campus environment, then do some homework to ensure that the schools you are considering meet those needs. Here are some things to consider when it comes to fit:

- **Location:** Is it important for you to be in a well-known city or is it a part of the United States that is unfamiliar a possibility? "Look at geographic areas, but also cost of living," recommends Durham. "Be sure to factor in transportation costs also, especially if you plan to return to your home country regularly."
- **Student population:** Some small schools have just 1,000 students while larger ones may have 30,000 students or more.
- **Familiar faces:** Is it important for you to be at a school with others from your home nation or region?

- **Climate:** Some students want a climate similar to where they live now, but others are open and curious about seasons and weather conditions they may not have ever experienced. "We do have four seasons here," says Gregori-Gahan. "Sometimes students who come here from tropical regions are concerned about the winters. The first snow is so exciting, but after that, students may not be aware of how cold it really is."
- **Amenities:** Do you want to find your own housing or choose a school where the majority of students live on campus? Is there public transportation available or is it necessary to walk or have a bicycle or car? Does the school or community have access to things that are important to you culturally and meet the traditions you want to follow?
- **Campus size:** Some campuses are tightly compacted into a few city blocks, but others cover hundreds of acres of land. "International students are amazed by how green and spacious our campus is, with blooming flowers, trees, and lots of grass," says Gregori-Gahan.
- **Academic offerings:** Does this school offer the program you want to study? Can you complete it in four years or perhaps sooner? What sort of internship and career services are available?
- **Finances:** Can you afford to attend this school? Is there any sort of financial assistance available for international students?
- **Support services:** Durham suggests students look carefully at each school's offerings for international students. "Does the school have online guidance for getting your visa? Is ESL tutoring available? Does the school offer host family or community friend programs?" She also suggests you look for campus support groups for students from your country or region.

Looking at the listings and reading the in-depth descriptions in this book can help you search for a school that is a good fit for you.

## Government Requirements

The one thing that every international student must have in order to study in the United States is a student visa. Having accurate advice and following all the necessary steps regarding the visa process is essential to being able to enter this country and start school.

As you schedule your tests and application deadlines, you must also consider how long it will take to get your visa. This varies depending on where you live; in some countries, extensive background checks are required. The subject you plan to study can also impact your visa status; it does help to have a major rather than be undeclared. The U.S. State Department website, http://travel.state.gov/content/visas/english/study-exchange.html, can give you an idea of how long it will take.

In addition to the visa, you will also need a Form I-20, which is a U.S. government immigration form. You must have that form when you get to the United States.

"It's very different from being a tourist. You need to be prepared to meet with an immigration officer and be interviewed about your college," explains Durham. "Where you are going, why you are going, where the school is located, what you are studying, and so on."

You also need to keep in mind that there are reporting requirements once you are a student in the U.S. Every semester, your adviser has to report to the government to confirm that you are enrolled in and attending school in order for you to stay in the United States.

## Finances

Part of the visa process includes having the funds to pay for the cost of your schooling and support yourself. Finances are a huge hurdle in the process of becoming a college student in the United States.

"It's crucial. So many foreign systems offer 'free' higher education to students. How is your family going to handle the ongoing expense of attending college for four years or longer in the United States?" Durham reiterates that planning ahead is key because there are so many details. Student loans require a U.S.-based cosigner. Each school has its own financial aid deadlines. You have to factor in your own government's requirements, such currency exchange and fund transfers.

The notion that abundant funds are available to assist international students is not true. Sometimes state schools may offer diversity waivers or there may be special scholarship opportunities for international students. But attending school in the U.S. is still a costly venture.

"We do offer financial aid to international students, but they still have to be able to handle a large portion of the costs. Full-need scholarships are not likely," explained Fr. Chambers. "Sometimes students think that once they get here, it will all work out and the funds will be there. But the scenario for the first year has to be repeated each year they are on campus."

## Once You Arrive...

You've taken your tests, researched schools, found a good fit, applied, got accepted, arranged the financing, gotten your visa and I-20, and made it to the campus in the United States. Now what?

You can expect the school where you have enrolled to be welcoming and helpful, but within reason. If you arrive on a weekend, or at a time outside of the time when international students are scheduled to arrive, the assistance you need may not be available to you.

Every school offers different levels of assistance to international students. For instance, Villanova offers a full-service office that can assist students with everything from visas, to employment, to finding a place for students to stay over breaks.

Fr. Chambers attends the international student orientation session to greet the students he's worked with through the recruitment and application process. "But I rarely see an international student after that. I think that bodes well for them being integrated into the entire university."

"Those of us who work with international students are really working to help them adjust," says Gregori-Gahan. "International students get here well before school starts so they can get over jet lag. We have orientation sessions and pair them with peer advisers who help them navigate the first few days, and we assure them that we are there for them."

Students should be open to their new setting, but they should be prepared that things may not be at all how they had envisioned during their planning and searching process. "While you may think you'll meet lots of Americans, don't underestimate the importance of community with your traditional home culture and people," says Durham.

## Don't Make These Mistakes

The journey to college attendance in the United States is a long one, with many steps. The experts warn about mistakes to avoid along the way.

"Not reading through everything thoroughly and not understanding what the program of study really is and what will it cost. You have to be really clear on the important details," says Gregori-Gahan.

"Every school does things differently," cautions Fr. Chambers. "International students must be aware of that as they are applying."

Durham stresses that going to school in the United States is too big a decision to leave to someone else. "Students need to know about their school—they have to be in charge of their application."

"It involves a lot of work to be successful and happy and not surprised by too many things," Gregori-Gahan says.

Hopefully now, you are more informed and better prepared to pursue your dream of studying at a college or university in the United States.

# Community Colleges and the Green Economy

Community colleges are a focal point for state and national efforts to create a green economy and workforce. As the United States transforms its economy into a "green" one, community colleges are leading the way—filling the need for both educated technicians whose skills can cross industry lines as well as those technicians who are able to learn new skills as technologies evolve.

President Obama extolled community colleges as "the unsung heroes of America's education system," essential to our country's success in the "global competition to lead in the growth of industries of the twenty-first century." With the support of state governments, and, more importantly, local and international business partners, America's community colleges are rising to meet the demands of the new green economy. Community colleges are training individuals to work in fields such as renewable energy, energy efficiency, wind energy, green building, and sustainability. The programs are as diverse as the campuses housing them.

Here is a quick look at just some of the exciting "green" programs available at community colleges throughout the United States.

At Mesalands Community College in Tucumcari, New Mexico, the North American Wind Research and Training Center provides state-of-the-art facilities for research and training qualified technicians in wind energy technology to help meet the need for an estimated 170,000 new positions in the industry by 2030. The Center includes a facility for applied research in collaboration with Sandia National Laboratories—the first-ever such partnership between a national laboratory and a community college. It also provides associate degree training for wind energy technicians, meeting the fast-growing demand for "windsmiths" in the western part of the country—jobs that pay $45,000–$60,000 per year. For more information, visit http://www.mesalands.edu.

Cape Cod Community College (CCCC) in Massachusetts has become one of the nation's leading colleges in promoting and integrating sustainability and green practices throughout all campus operations and technical training programs. Ten years ago, Cape Wind Associates, Cape Cod's first wind farm, provided $50,000 to jumpstart CCCC's wind technician program—considered a state model for community-based clean energy workforce development and education. In addition, hundreds of CCCC students have earned associate degrees in environmental technology and environmental studies, as well as certificate programs in coastal zone management, environmental site assessment, solar thermal tech-

nology, and more. Visit http://www.capecod.edu/web/natsci/env/programs for more information.

At Oakland Community College in Michigan, more than 350 students are enrolled in the college's Renewable Energies and Sustainable Living program and its related courses. Students gain field experience refurbishing public buildings with renewable materials, performing energy audits for the government, and working with small businesses and hospitals to reduce waste and pollution. To learn more, visit http://www.oaklandcc.edu/est/.

Portland Community College (PCC) in Portland, Oregon, offers associate degree and certificate options in Renewable Energy Systems (RES) training, preparing technicians for solar power, wind power, fuel cell, and other renewable energy fields. Students can earn an Associate in Applied Science (A.A.S.) degree or a One-Year Certificate in EET: Renewable Energy Systems. PCC's Microelectronic Technology Department offers an A.A.S. degree and a Certificate of Completion (COC) in Solar Voltaic Manufacturing Technology. The COC provides an orientation in solar manufacturing for those who have no prior education or experience in the field, which enables students to obtain entry-level jobs in this industry and eventually complete their A.A.S. degree.

Central Carolina Community College (CCCC) in Pittsboro, North Carolina, has been leading the way in "green" programs for more than a decade. It offered a sustainable agriculture class at its Chatham campus in 1996 and soon became the first community college in the nation to offer an Associate in Applied Science degree in sustainable agriculture and the first in North Carolina to offer an associate degree in biofuels. In addition, it was the first North Carolina community college to offer a North American Board of Certified Energy Practitioners (NABCEP)–approved solar PV panel installation course as part of its green building/renewable energy program. CCC also offers an associate degree in sustainable technology, a Natural Chef culinary arts program, an ecotourism certificate, and certificates in other green programs. For more information about Central Carolina Community College's green programs, visit http://www.cccc.edu/green.

At Metropolitan Community College in Omaha, Nebraska, the Continuing Education Department in partnership with ProTrain is offering green/renewable energy/sustainability online training courses. The courses are designed to provide students with the workforce skills necessary for many in-demand green-collar occupations. Green/Renewable Energy courses include Building Energy Efficient Level, Fundamentals of Solar Hot Water Heating, Green Building Sales (or Technical) Professional, and more. Sustainability Green Supply Chain Training courses include Alternative Energy Operations, Carbon Strategies, Green Building for Contractors, and Sustainability 101. Visit www.theknowledgebase.org/metropolitan/.

At Cascadia Community College in Bothell, Washington, thanks to a grant from Puget Sound Energy (PSE), students in the Energy Informatics class designed a kiosk screen that shows the energy usage and solar generation at the local 21 Acres Center for Local Food and Sustainable Living. The PSE grant supports the classroom materials for renewable energy education and the Web-based monitoring software that allows students and interested community members to track how much energy is being generated as the weather changes. For more information, visit http://www.cascadia.edu/Default.aspx.

At Grand Rapids Community College, the federally funded Pathways to Prosperity program has successfully prepared low-income residents for jobs in fields such as renewable energy. More than 200 people have completed the program, which began in 2010 thanks to a $4-million grant from the Department of Labor, and found jobs in industries ranging from energy-efficient building construction to alternative energy and sustainable manufacturing. For additional information, check out http://cms.grcc.edu/workforce-training/pathways-prosperity.

Established in 2008, the Green Institute at Heartland Community College in Normal, Illinois, supports a wide range of campus initiatives, educational programs, and community activities that are related to sustainability, energy conservation, renewable energy, recycling, retro-commissioning, and other environmental technologies. For more information, visit http://www.heartland.edu/greenInstitute/.

Most of California's 112 community colleges offer some type of green-tech classes. These include photovoltaic panel installation and repair, green construction practices, and biotechnology courses leading to careers in agriculture, medicine, and environmental forensics. Visit http://www.californiacommunity colleges.cccco.edu/ProgramstoWatch/MoreProgramstoWatch/GreenTechnology.aspx.

Linn-Benton Community College (LBCC) in Albany, Oregon, is now offering training for the Oregon Green Technology Certificate. Oregon Green Tech is a federally funded program that is designed to prepare entry-level workers with foundational skills for a variety of industries associated with or in support of green jobs. Students learn skills in green occupations that include green energy production; manufacturing, construction, installation, monitoring, and repair of equipment for solar, wind, wave, and bio-energy; building retro-fitting; process recycling; hazardous materials removal work; and more. LBCC is one of ten Oregon community colleges to provide training for the Green Technology Certificate, offered through the Oregon Consortium and Oregon Workforce Alliance. Visit http://www.linnbenton.edu for additional information.

The Santa Fe Community College Sustainable Technology Center in New Mexico offers several green jobs training programs along with various noncredit courses. It also provides credit programs from certificates in green building systems, environmental technology training, and solar energy training as well as an Associate in Applied Science (A.A.S.) degree in environmental technology. For more information, go online to http://www.sfcc.edu/sustainable_technologies_center.

In Colorado, Red Rocks Community College (RRCC) offers degree and certificate programs in renewable energy (solar photovoltaic, solar thermal, and wind energy technology), energy and industrial maintenance, energy operations and process technology, environmental technology, water quality management, and energy audit. RRCC has made a commitment to the national challenge of creating and sustaining a green workforce and instructs students about the issues of energy, environmental stewardship, and renewable resources across the college curriculum. For more information, visit http://www.rrcc.edu/green/.

At GateWay Community College in Phoenix, Arizona, graduates of the Environmental Science program now work for the U.S. Geological Survey (USGS), the Arizona Department of Environmental Quality (ADEQ), the Occupational Safety and Health Administration (OSHA), and municipalities across the state and region, as well as private consultants and environmental organizations. For additional information, check out http://www.gatewaycc.edu/environment.

During the past 4.5 years, 17 Illinois community colleges and their partners have created 35 certificate and degree programs to prepare students for careers in green industry sectors. Over 185 courses were created and piloted, online and on-site, in communities across Illinois. The courses were created using open-source materials, with the intent to be shared with other colleges and universities through the Department of Labor's Trade Adjustment Assistance Community College and Career Training (TAACCCT) Grant Program repository.

Next you'll find two essays about other green community college programs. The first essay was written by the president of Lane Community College in Eugene, Oregon, about the role Lane and other community colleges are playing in creating a workforce for the green economy. Then, read a first-hand account of the new Wind Turbine Training Program at Kalamazoo Valley Community College in Kalamazoo, Michigan—a program that has more applicants than spaces and one whose students are being hired BEFORE they even graduate. It's clear that there are exciting "green" programs at community colleges throughout the United States.

## The Role of Community Colleges in Creating a Workforce for the Green Economy

by Mary F.T. Spilde, President
Lane Community College

Community colleges are expected to play a leadership role in educating and training the workforce for the green economy. Due to close connections with local and regional labor markets, colleges assure a steady supply of skilled workers by developing and adapting programs to respond to the needs of business and industry. Further, instead of waiting for employers to create job openings, many colleges are actively engaged in local economic development to help educate potential employers to grow their green business opportunities and to participate in the creation of the green economy.

As the green movement emerges there has been confusion about what constitutes a green job. It is now clear that many of the green jobs span several economic sectors such as renewable energy, construction, manufacturing, transportation and agriculture. It is predicted that there will be many middle skill jobs requiring more than a high school diploma but less than a bachelor's degree. This is precisely the unique role that community colleges play. Community colleges develop training programs, including pre-apprenticeship, that ladder the curriculum to take lower skilled workers through a relevant and sequenced course of study that provides a clear pathway to career track jobs. As noted in *Going Green: The Vital Role of Community Colleges in Building a Sustainable Future and Green Workforce* by the National Council for Workforce Education and the Academy for Educational Development, community colleges are strategically positioned to work with employers to redefine skills and competencies needed by the green workforce and to create the framework for new and expanded green career pathways.

While there will be new occupations such as solar and wind technologists, the majority of the jobs will be in the energy management sector—retrofitting the built environment. For example, President Obama called for retrofitting more than 75 percent of federal buildings and more than 2 million homes to make them more energy-efficient. The second major area for growth will be the "greening" of existing jobs as they evolve to incorporate green practices. Both will require new knowledge, skills and abilities. For community colleges, this means developing new programs that meet newly created industry standards and adapting existing programs and courses to integrate green skills. The key is to create a new talent pool of environmentally conscious, highly skilled workers.

These two areas show remarkable promise for education and training leading to high wage/high demand jobs:

- Efficiency and energy management: There is a need for auditors and energy efficiency experts to retrofit existing buildings. Consider how much built environment we have in this country, and it's not difficult to see that this is where the vast amount of jobs are now and will be in the future.

- Greening of existing jobs: There are few currently available jobs that environmental sustainability will not impact. Whether it is jobs in construction, such as plumbers, electricians, heating and cooling technicians, painters, and building supervisors, or chefs, farmers, custodians, architects, automotive technicians and interior designers, all will need to understand how to lessen their impact on the environment.

Lane Community College offers a variety of degree and certificate programs to prepare students to enter the energy efficiency fields. Lane has offered an Energy Management program since the late 1980s—before it was hip to be green! Students in this program learn to apply basic principles of physics and analysis techniques to the description and measurement of energy in today's building systems, with the goal of evaluating and recommending alternative energy solutions that will result in greater energy efficiency and energy cost savings. Students gain a working understanding of energy systems in today's built environment and the tools to analyze and quantify energy efficiency efforts. The program began with an emphasis in residential energy efficiency/solar energy systems and has evolved to include commercial energy efficiency and renewable energy system installation technology.

The Renewable Energy Technician program is offered as a second-year option within the Energy Management program. Course work prepares students for employment designing and installing solar electric and domestic hot water systems. Renewable Energy students, along with Energy Management students, take a first-year curriculum in commercial energy efficiency giving them a solid background that includes residential energy efficiency, HVAC systems, lighting, and physics and math. In the second year, Renewable Energy students diverge from the Energy Management curriculum and take course work that starts with two courses in electricity fundamentals and one course in energy economics. In the following terms, students learn to design, install, and develop a thorough understanding of photovoltaics and domestic hot water systems.

Recent additions to Lane's offerings are Sustainability Coordinator and Water Conservation Technician degrees. Both programs were added to meet workforce demand.

Lane graduates find employment in a wide variety of disciplines and may work as facility managers, energy auditors, energy program coordinators, or control system specialists, for such diverse employers as engineering firms, public and private utilities, energy equipment companies, and departments of energy and as sustainability leaders within public and private sector organizations.

Lane Community College also provides continuing education for working professionals. The Sustainable Building Advisor (SBA) Certificate Program is a nine-month, specialized training program for working professionals. Graduate are able to advise employers or clients on strategies and tools for implementing sustainable building practices. Benefits from participating in the SBA program often include saving long-term building operating costs; improving the environmental, social, and economic viability of the region; and reducing environmental impacts and owner liability—not to mention the chance to improve one's job skills in a rapidly growing field.

The Building Operators Certificate is a professional development program created by The Northwest Energy Efficiency Council. It is offered through the Northwest Energy Education

Institute at Lane. The certificate is designed for operations and maintenance staff working in public or private commercial buildings. It certifies individuals in energy and resource-efficient operation of building systems at two levels: Level I–Building System Maintenance and Level II–Equipment Troubleshooting and Maintenance.

Lane Community College constantly scans the environment to assess workforce needs and develop programs that provide highly skilled employees. Lane, like most colleges, publishes information in its catalog on workforce demand and wages so that students can make informed decisions about program choice.

Green jobs will be a large part of a healthy economy. Opportunities will abound for those who take advantage of programs with a proven record of connecting with employers and successfully educating students to meet high skills standards.

## Establishing a World-Class Wind Turbine Technician Academy

### by Thomas Sutton, Director of Wind Energy and Technical Services
### Kalamazoo Valley Community College

When Kalamazoo Valley Community College (KVCC) decided it wanted to become involved in the training of utility-grade technicians for wind-energy jobs, early on the choice was made to avoid another "me too" training course.

Our program here in Southwest Michigan, 30 miles from Lake Michigan, had to meet industry needs and industry standards.

It was also obvious from the start that the utility-grade or large wind industry had not yet adopted any uniform training standards in the United States.

Of course, these would come, but why should the college wait when European standards were solidly established and working well in Germany, France, Denmark and Great Britain?

As a result, in 2009, KVCC launched its Wind Turbine Technician Academy, the first of its kind in the United States. The noncredit academy runs 8 hours a day, five days a week, for twenty-four weeks of intense training in electricity, mechanics, wind dynamics, safety, and climbing. The college developed this program rather quickly—in eight months—to fast-track individuals into this emerging field.

KVCC based its program on the training standards forged by the Bildungszentrum fur Erneuerebare Energien (BZEE)—the Renewable Energy Education Center. Located in Husum, Germany, the BZEE was created and supported by major wind-turbine manufacturers, component makers, and enterprises that provide operation and maintenance services.

As wind-energy production increased throughout Europe, the need for high-quality, industry-driven, international standards emerged. The BZEE has become the leading trainer for wind-turbine technicians across Europe and now in Asia.

With the exception of one college in Canada, the standards were not yet available in North America. When Kalamazoo Valley realized it could be the first college or university in the United States to offer this training program—that was enough motivation to move forward.

For the College to become certified by the BZEE, it needed to hire and send an electrical instructor and a mechanical instructor to Germany for six weeks of "train the trainer." The instructors not only had to excel in their respective fields, they also needed to be able to climb the skyscraper towers supporting megawatt-class turbines—a unique combination of skills to possess. Truly, individuals who fit this job description don't walk through the door everyday—but we found them! Amazingly, we found a top mechanical instructor who was a part-time fireman and comfortable with tall ladder rescues and a skilled electrical instructor who used to teach rappelling off the Rockies to the Marine Corps.

In addition to employing new instructors, the College needed a working utility-grade nacelle that could fit in its training lab that would be located in the KVCC Michigan Technical Education Center. So one of the instructors traveled to Denmark and purchased a 300-kilowatt turbine.

Once their own training was behind them and the turbine was on its way from the North Sea, the instructors quickly turned to crafting the curriculum necessary for our graduates to earn both an academy certificate from KVCC and a certification from the BZEE.

Promoting the innovative program to qualified potential students across the country was the next step. News releases were published throughout Michigan, and they were also picked up on the Internet. Rather quickly, KVCC found itself with more than 500 requests for applications for a program built for 16 students.

Acceptance into the academy includes a medical release, a climbing test, reading and math tests, relevant work experience, and, finally, an interview. Students in the academy's pioneer class, which graduated in spring 2010, ranged in age from their late teens to early 50s. They hailed from throughout Michigan, Indiana, Ohio, and Illinois as well as from Puerto Rico and Great Britain.

The students brought with them degrees in marketing, law, business, science, and architecture, as well as entrepreneurial experiences in several businesses, knowledge of other languages, military service, extensive travel, and electrical, computer, artistic, and technical/mechanical skills.

Kalamazoo Valley's academy has provided some high-value work experiences for the students in the form of two collaborations with industry that has allowed them to maintain and/or repair actual utility-grade turbines, including those at the 2.5 megawatt size. This hands-on experience will add to the attractiveness of the graduates in the market place. Potential employers were recently invited to an open house where they could see the lab and meet members of this pioneer class.

The College's Turbine Technician Academy has also attracted a federal grant for $550,000 to expand its program through additional equipment purchases. The plan is to erect our own climbing tower. Climbing is a vital part of any valid program, and yet wind farms cannot afford to shut turbines down just for climb-training. The funds were put to use engineering, fabricating, and erecting a wind training tower that incorporated all of the necessary components to teach competency-based work at heights safety training.

When the students are asked what best distinguishes the Kalamazoo Valley program, their answers point to the experienced instructors and the working lab, which is constantly changing to offer the best training experiences. Students also consistently report that the hands-on field experience operating and maintaining the five large turbines during the course has set them apart at companies where they work.

Industry continues to tell us that community colleges need to offer fast-track training programs of this caliber if the nation is to reach the U.S. Department of Energy's goal of 20 percent renewable energy by 2030. This would require more than 1,500 new technicians each year.

The Wind Turbine Technician Academy continues the process improvements as directed by industry input. The academy not only holds the BZEE certification, it is also one of the few American Wind Energy Association (AWEA) Seal of Approval schools in the nation.

With that in mind, KVCC plans to host several BZEE orientation programs for other community colleges in order to encourage them to consider adopting the European training standards and start their own programs.

Meanwhile, applications are continuing to stream in from across the country for the next Wind Turbine Technician Academy program at Kalamazoo Valley Community College. For more information about the program, visit http://www.kvccgrovescenter.com/career/wtta.

# How to Use This Guide

Peterson's *Two-Year Colleges 2019* contains a wealth of information for anyone interested in colleges offering associate degrees. This section details the criteria that institutions must meet to be included in this guide and provides information about research procedures used by Peterson's.

## QUICK-REFERENCE CHART

The **Two-Year Colleges At-a-Glance Chart** is a geographically arranged table that lists colleges by name and city within the state, or country in which they are located. Areas listed include the United States, Canada, and other countries; the institutions are included because they are accredited by recognized U.S. accrediting bodies (see **Criteria for Inclusion** section).

The At-a-Glance chart contains basic information that enables you to compare institutions quickly according to broad characteristics such as degrees awarded, enrollment, application requirements, financial aid availability, and numbers of sports and majors offered. A dagger (†) after the institution's name indicates that an institution has an entry in the **Featured Two-Year Colleges** section.

### Column 1: Degrees Awarded

C= *college transfer associate degree:* the degree awarded after a "university-parallel" program, equivalent to the first two years of a bachelor's degree.

T= *terminal associate degree:* the degree resulting from a one- to three-year program providing training for a specific occupation.

B= *bachelor's degree (baccalaureate):* the degree resulting from a liberal arts, science, professional, or preprofessional program normally lasting four years, although in some cases an accelerated program can be completed in three years.

M= *master's degree:* the first graduate (postbaccalaureate) degree in the liberal arts and sciences and certain professional fields, usually requiring one to two years of full-time study.

D= *doctoral degree* (research/scholarship, professional practice, or other)

### Column 2: Institutional Control

Private institutions are designated as one of the following:

Ind = *independent* (nonprofit)

I-R = *independent-religious:* nonprofit; sponsored by or affiliated with a particular religious group or having a nondenominational or interdenominational religious orientation.

Prop = *proprietary* (profit-making)

Public institutions are designated by the source of funding, as follows:

Fed = *federal*

St = *state*

Comm = *commonwealth* (Puerto Rico)

Terr = *territory* (U.S. territories)

Cou = *county*

Dist = *district:* an administrative unit of public education, often having boundaries different from units of local government.

City = *city*

St-L = *state and local:* local may refer to county, district, or city.

St-R = *state-related:* funded primarily by the state but administratively autonomous.

### Column 3: Student Body

M= *men only* (100% of student body)

PM = *coed, primarily men*

W= *women only* (100% of student body)

PW = *coed, primarily women*

M/W = *coeducational*

### Column 4: Undergraduate Enrollment

The figure shown represents the number of full-time and part-time students enrolled in undergraduate degree programs as of fall 2017.

### Columns 5–7: Enrollment Percentages

Figures are shown for the percentages of the fall 2017 undergraduate enrollment made up of students attending part-time (column 5) and students 25 years of age or older (column 6). Also listed is the percentage of students in the last graduating class who completed a college-transfer associate program and went directly on to four-year colleges (column 7).

For columns 8 through 15, the following letter codes are used: Y = yes; N = no; R = recommended; S = for some.

### Columns 8–10: Admission Policies

The information in these columns shows whether the college has an open admission policy (column 8) whereby virtually all applicants are accepted without regard to standardized test scores, grade average, or class rank; whether a high school equivalency certificate is accepted in place of a high school diploma for admission consideration (column 9); and whether a high school transcript (column 10) is required as part of the application process. In column 10, the combination of the codes R and S indicates that a high school transcript is recommended for all applicants (R) or required for some (S).

## Columns 11–12: Financial Aid

These columns show which colleges offer the following types of financial aid: need-based aid (column 11) and part-time jobs (column 12), including those offered through the federal government's Federal Work-Study program.

## Columns 13–15: Services and Facilities

These columns show which colleges offer the following: career counseling (column 13) on either an individual or group basis, job placement services (column 14) for individual students, and college-owned or -operated housing facilities (column 16) for noncommuting students.

## Column 16: Sports

This figure indicates the number of sports that a college offers at the intramural and/or intercollegiate levels.

## Column 17: Majors

This figure indicates the number of major fields of study in which a college offers degree programs.

## PROFILES OF TWO-YEAR COLLEGES AND SPECIAL MESSAGES

The **Profiles of Two-Year Colleges** contain basic data in capsule form for quick review and comparison. The following outline of the **Profile** format shows the section headings and the items that each section covers. Any item that does not apply to a particular college or for which no information was supplied is omitted from that college's **Profile.** Display ads, which appear near some of the institution's profiles, have been provided and paid for by those colleges that chose to supplement their profile with additional information. A star ★ next to the name of a school signifies that the school is one of the "Featured Two-Year Colleges," with a two-page in-depth description in that section of this guide and may also have an expanded profile on Peterson's website at www.petersons/com.

## Bulleted Highlights

The bulleted highlights section features important information, for quick reference and comparison. The number of possible bulleted highlights that an ideal **Profile** would have if all questions were answered in a timely manner follow. However, not every institution provides all of the information necessary to fill out every bulleted line. In such instances, the line will not appear.

## First Bullet

**Institutional control:** Private institutions are designated as independent (nonprofit), proprietary (profit-making), or independent, with a specific religious denomination or affiliation. Nondenominational or interdenominational religious orientation is possible and would be indicated.

Public institutions are designated by the source of funding. Designations include federal, state, province, commonwealth (Puerto Rico), territory (U.S. territories), county, district (an administrative unit of public education, often having boundaries different from units of local government), city, state and local (local may refer to county, district, or city), or state-related (funded primarily by the state but administratively autonomous).

**Religious affiliation is also noted here.**

**Institutional type:** Each institution is classified as one of the following:

> **Primarily two-year college:** Awards baccalaureate degrees, but the vast majority of students are enrolled in two-year programs.

> **Four-year college:** Awards baccalaureate degrees; may also award associate degrees; does not award graduate (postbaccalaureate) degrees.

> **Upper-level institution:** Awards baccalaureate degrees, but entering students must have at least two years of previous college-level credit; may also offer graduate degrees.

> **Comprehensive institution:** Awards baccalaureate degrees; may also award associate degrees; offers graduate degree programs, primarily at the master's, specialist's, or professional level, although one or two doctoral programs may be offered.

> **University:** Offers four years of undergraduate work plus graduate degrees through the doctorate in more than two academic or professional fields.

**Founding date:** If the year an institution was chartered differs from the year when instruction actually began, the earlier date is given.

**System or administrative affiliation:** Any coordinate institutions or system affiliations are indicated. An institution that has separate colleges or campuses for men and women but shares facilities and courses is termed a coordinate institution. A formal administrative grouping of institutions, either private or public, of which the college is a part, or the name of a single institution with which the college is administratively affiliated, is a system.

## Second Bullet

**Setting:** Schools are designated as urban (located within a major city), suburban (a residential area within commuting distance of a major city), small-town (a small but compactly settled area not within commuting distance of a major city), or rural (a remote and sparsely populated area). The phrase *easy access to...* indicates that the campus is within an hour's drive of the nearest major metropolitan area that has a population greater than 500,000.

## Third Bullet

**Endowment:** The total dollar value of funds and/or property donated to the institution or the multicampus educational system of which the institution is a part.

## Fourth Bullet

**Student body:** An institution is coed (coeducational—admits men and women), primarily (80 percent or more) women, primarily men, women only, or men only.

**Undergraduate students:** Represents the number of full-time and part-time students enrolled in undergraduate degree programs as of fall 2017. The percentage of full-time undergraduates and the percentages of men and women are given.

## Category Overviews

### Undergraduates

For fall 2017, the number of full- and part-time undergraduate students is listed. This list provides the number of states and U.S. territories, including the District of Columbia and Puerto Rico (or for Canadian institutions, provinces and territories), and other countries from which undergraduates come. Percentages of undergraduates who are part-time or full-time students; transfers in; live on campus; out-of-state; Black or African American, non-Hispanic/Latino; Hispanic/Latino; Asian, non-Hispanic/Latino; Native Hawaiian or other Pacific Islander, non-Hispanic/Latino; American Indian or Alaska Native, non-Hispanic/Latino are given.

**Retention:** The percentage of freshmen (or, for upper-level institutions, entering students) who returned the following year for the fall term.

### Freshmen

**Admission:** Figures are given for the number of students who applied for fall 2017 admission, the number of those who were admitted, and the number who enrolled. Freshman statistics include the average high school GPA; the percentage of freshmen who took the SAT® and received critical reading, writing, and math scores above 500, above 600, and above 700; as well as the percentage of freshmen taking the ACT® who received a composite score of 18 or higher.

### Faculty

**Total:** The total number of faculty members; the percentage of full-time faculty members as of fall 2017; and the percentage of full-time faculty members who hold doctoral/first professional/ terminal degrees.

**Student-faculty ratio:** The school's estimate of the ratio of matriculated undergraduate students to faculty members teaching undergraduate courses.

### Majors

This section lists the major fields of study offered by the college.

### Academics

**Calendar:** Most colleges indicate one of the following: 4-1-4, 4-4-1, or a similar arrangement (two terms of equal length plus an abbreviated winter or spring term, with the numbers referring to months); semesters; trimesters; quarters; 3-3 (three courses for each of three terms); modular (the academic year is divided into small blocks of time; courses of varying lengths are assembled according to individual programs); or standard year (for most Canadian institutions).

**Degrees:** This names the full range of levels of certificates, diplomas, and degrees, including prebaccalaureate, graduate, and professional, that are offered by this institution:

*Associate degree:* Normally requires at least two but fewer than four years of full-time college work or its equivalent.

*Bachelor's degree (baccalaureate):* Requires at least four years but not more than five years of full-time college-level work or its equivalent. This includes all bachelor's degrees in which the normal four years of work are completed in three years and bachelor's degrees conferred in a five-year cooperative (work-study plan) program. A cooperative plan provides for alternate class attendance and employment in business, industry, or government. This allows students to combine actual work experience with their college studies.

*Master's degree:* Requires the successful completion of a program of study of at least the full-time equivalent of one but not more than two years of work beyond the bachelor's degree.

*Doctoral degree (doctorate; research/scholarship, professional, or other):* The highest degree in graduate study. The doctoral degree classification includes Doctor of Education, Doctor of Juridical Science, Doctor of Public Health, Doctor of Philosophy, Doctor of Podiatry, Doctor of Veterinary Medicine, and many more.

*Post-master's certificate:* Requires completion of an organized program of study of 24 credit hours beyond the master's degree but does not meet the requirements of academic degrees at the doctoral level.

**Special study options:** Details are next given here on study options available at each college:

*Accelerated degree program:* Students may earn a bachelor's degree in three academic years.

*Academic remediation for entering students:* Instructional courses designed for students deficient in the general competencies necessary for a regular postsecondary curriculum and educational setting.

*Adult/continuing education programs:* Courses offered for nontraditional students who are currently working or are returning to formal education.

*Advanced placement:* Credit toward a degree awarded for acceptable scores on College Board Advanced Placement (AP®) tests.

*Cooperative (co-op) education programs:* Formal arrangements with off-campus employers allowing students to combine work and study in order to gain degree-related experience, usually extending the time required to complete a degree.

*Distance learning:* For-credit courses that can be accessed off-campus via cable television, the Internet, satellite, DVD, correspondence course, or other media.

*Double major:* A program of study in which a student concurrently completes the requirements of two majors.

*English as a second language (ESL):* A course of study designed specifically for students whose native language is not English.

*External* degree programs*:* A program of study in which students earn credits toward a degree through a combination of independent study, college courses, proficiency examinations, and personal experience. External degree programs require minimal or no classroom attendance.

*Freshmen honors college:* A separate academic program for talented freshmen.

*Honors programs:* Any special program for very able students offering the opportunity for educational enrichment, independent study, acceleration, or some combination of these.

*Independent study:* Academic work, usually undertaken outside the regular classroom structure, chosen or designed by the student with departmental approval and instructor supervision.

*Internships:* Any short-term, supervised work experience usually related to a student's major field, for which the student earns academic credit. The work can be full-or part-time, on or off-campus, paid or unpaid.

*Off-campus study:* A formal arrangement with one or more domestic institutions under which students may take courses at the other institution(s) for credit.

*Part-time degree program:* Students may earn a degree through part-time enrollment in regular session (daytime) classes or evening, weekend, or summer classes.

*Self-designed major:* Program of study based on individual interests, designed by the student with the assistance of an adviser.

*Services for LD students:* Special help for learning-disabled students with resolvable difficulties, such as dyslexia.

*Study abroad:* An arrangement by which a student completes part of the academic program studying in another country. A college may operate a campus abroad or it may have a cooperative agreement with other U.S. institutions or institutions in other countries.

*Summer session for credit:* Summer courses through which students may make up degree work or accelerate their program.

*Tutorials:* Undergraduates can arrange for special in-depth academic assignments (not for remediation)

working with faculty members one-on-one or in small groups.

**ROTC:** Army, Naval, or Air Force Reserve Officers' Training Corps programs offered either on campus, at a branch campus [designated by a (b)], or at a cooperating host institution [designated by (c)].

**Unusual degree programs:** Nontraditional programs such as a 3-2 degree program, in which three years of liberal arts study is followed by two years of study in a professional field at another institution (or in a professional division of the same institution), resulting in two bachelor's degrees or a bachelor's and a master's degree.

## Library

The name of the college's main library, plus the number of other libraries on campus will appear followed by: *Books:* number of physical and digital/electronic books; *Serial titles:* number of physical and digital/electronic serial titles; and the number of *Databases*. Also included here (if provided by the school) are the number of "Weekly public service hours" and study area information—the number of hours and days of the week open and if students can reserve study rooms.

## Student Life

**Housing options:** The institution's policy about whether students are permitted to live off-campus or are required to live on campus for a specified period; whether freshmen-only, coed, single-sex, cooperative, and disabled student housing options are available; whether campus housing is leased by the school and/or provided by a third party; whether freshman applicants are given priority for college housing. The phrase *college housing not available* indicates that no college-owned or -operated housing facilities are provided for undergraduates and that noncommuting students must arrange for their own accommodations.

**Activities and organizations:** Lists information on drama-theater groups, choral groups, marching bands, student-run campus newspapers, student-run radio stations, and social organizations (sororities, fraternities, eating clubs, etc.) and how many are represented on campus.

**Campus security:** Campus safety measures including 24-hour emergency response devices (telephones and alarms) and patrols by trained security personnel, student patrols, late-night transport-escort service, and controlled dormitory access (key, security card, etc.).

**Student services:** Information provided indicates services offered to students by the college, such as legal services, health clinics, personal-psychological counseling, and women's centers.

## Athletics

Membership in one or more of the following athletic associations is indicated by initials.

**NCAA:** National Collegiate Athletic Association

**NAIA:** National Association of Intercollegiate Athletics

**NCCAA:** National Christian College Athletic Association

**NJCAA:** National Junior College Athletic Association

**USCAA:** United States Collegiate Athletic Association

**CIS:** Canadian Interuniversity Sports

The overall NCAA division in which all or most intercollegiate teams compete is designated by a roman numeral I, II, or III. All teams that do not compete in this division are listed as exceptions.

Sports offered by the college are divided into two groups: intercollegiate (**M** or **W** following the name of each sport indicates that it is offered for men or women or **M/W** if the sport is offered for both men and women) and intramural. An **s** in parentheses following an **M, W or M/W** for an intercollegiate sport indicates that athletic scholarships (or grants-in-aid) are offered for men and/or women in that sport, and a **c** indicates a club team as opposed to a varsity team.

## Standardized Tests

The most commonly required standardized tests are the ACT®, SAT®, and SAT Subject Tests™. These and other standardized tests may be used for selective admission, as a basis for counseling or course placement, or for both purposes. This section notes if a test is used for admission or placement and whether it is required, required for some, or recommended.

In addition to the ACT and SAT, the following standardized entrance and placement examinations are referred to by their initials:

**ABLE:** Adult Basic Learning Examination

**ACT ASSET:** ACT Assessment of Skills for Successful Entry and Transfer

**ACT PEP:** ACT Proficiency Examination Program

**CAT:** California Achievement Tests

**CELT:** Comprehensive English Language Test

**CPAt:** Career Programs Assessment

**CPT:** Computerized Placement Test

**DAT:** Differential Aptitude Test

**LSAT:** Law School Admission Test

**MAPS:** Multiple Assessment Program Service

**MCAT:** Medical College Admission Test

**MMPI:** Minnesota Multiphasic Personality Inventory

**OAT:** Optometry Admission Test

**PAA:** Prueba de Aptitud Académica (Spanish-language version of the SAT)

**PCAT:** Pharmacy College Admission Test

**PSAT/NMSQT:** Preliminary SAT National Merit Scholarship Qualifying Test

**SCAT:** Scholastic College Aptitude Test

**SRA:** Scientific Research Association (administers verbal, arithmetical, and achievement tests)

**TABE:** Test of Adult Basic Education

**TASP:** Texas Academic Skills Program

**TOEFL:** Test of English as a Foreign Language (for international students whose native language is not English)

**WPCT:** Washington Pre-College Test

## Costs

Costs are given for the 2018–19 academic year or for the 2017–18 academic year if 2018–19 figures were not yet available. Annual expenses may be expressed as a comprehensive fee (including full-time tuition, mandatory fees, and college room and board) or as separate figures for full-time tuition, fees, room and board, or room only. For public institutions where tuition differs according to residence, separate figures are given for area or state residents and for nonresidents. Part-time tuition is expressed in terms of a per-unit rate (per credit, per semester hour, etc.) as specified by the institution.

The tuition structure at some institutions is complex in that freshmen and sophomores may be charged a different rate from that for juniors and seniors, a professional or vocational division may have a different fee structure from the liberal arts division of the same institution, or part-time tuition may be prorated on a sliding scale according to the number of credit hours taken. Tuition and fees may vary according to academic program, campus/location, class time (day, evening, weekend), course/credit load, course level, degree level, reciprocity agreements, and student level. Room and board charges are reported as an average for one academic year and may vary according to the board plan selected, campus/location, type of housing facility, or student level. If no college-owned or college-operated housing facilities are offered, the phrase *college housing not available* will appear in the Housing section of the Student Life paragraph.

Tuition payment plans that may be offered to undergraduates include tuition prepayment, installment payments, and deferred payment. A tuition prepayment plan gives a student the option of locking in the current tuition rate for the entire term of enrollment by paying the full amount in advance rather than year by year. Colleges that offer such a prepayment plan may also help the student to arrange financing.

The availability of full or partial undergraduate tuition waivers to minority students, children of alumni, employees or their children, adult students, and senior citizens may be listed.

## Financial Aid

The number of Federal Work Study and/or part-time jobs and average earnings are listed. Financial aid deadlines are given as well.

## Applying

Application and admission options include the following:

**Early admission:** Highly qualified students may matriculate before graduating from high school.

**Early action plan:** An admission plan that allows students to apply and be notified of an admission decision well in advance of the regular notification dates. If accepted, the candidate is not committed to enroll; students may reply to the offer under the college's regular reply policy.

**Early decision plan:** A plan that permits students to apply and be notified of an admission decision (and financial aid offer, if applicable) well in advance of the regular notification date. Applicants agree to accept an offer of admission and to withdraw their applications from other colleges. Candidates who are not accepted under early decision are automatically considered with the regular applicant pool, without prejudice.

**Deferred entrance:** The practice of permitting accepted students to postpone enrollment, usually for a period of one academic term or year.

**Application fee:** The fee required with an application is noted. This is typically nonrefundable, although under certain specified conditions it may be waived or returned.

**Requirements:** Other application requirements are grouped into three categories: required for all, required for some, and recommended. They may include an essay, standardized test scores, a high school transcript, a minimum high school grade point average (expressed as a number on a scale of 0 to 4.0, where 4.0 equals A, 3.0 equals B, etc.), letters of recommendation, an interview on campus or with local alumni, and, for certain types of schools or programs, special requirements such as a musical audition or an art portfolio.

**Application deadlines and notification dates:** Admission application deadlines and dates for notification of acceptance or rejection are given either as specific dates or as **rolling** and **continuous.** Rolling means that applications are processed as they are received, and qualified students are accepted as long as there are openings. Continuous means that applicants are notified of acceptance or rejection as applications are processed up until the date indicated or the actual beginning of classes. The application deadline and the notification date for transfers are given if they differ from the dates for freshmen. Early decision and early action application deadlines and notification dates are also indicated when relevant.

## Admissions Contact

The name, title, and phone number of the person to contact for application information are given at the end of the Profile. The admission office address is listed in most cases. Toll-free phone numbers may also be included. The admission office fax number and e-mail address, if available, are listed, provided the school wanted them printed for use by prospective students. Finally, the URL of the institution's Web site is provided.

## Additional Information

Each college that has a **Featured Two-Year College Close-Up** in the guide will have a cross-reference appended to the Profile, referring you directly to the page number of that **Featured Two-Year College Close-Up.**

## Institutional Changes Since *Peterson's®* *Two-Year Colleges 2018*

Here you will find an alphabetical listing of institutions that have recently closed, merged with other institutions, or changed their name or status.

## FEATURED TWO-YEAR COLLEGES

These narrative descriptions provide an inside look at certain colleges, shifting the focus to a variety of other factors that should also be considered. The descriptions provide a wealth of information that is crucial in the college decision-making equation—such as tuition, financial aid, academic programs, and life on campus. Prepared exclusively by college officials, the descriptions are designed to help give students a better sense of the individuality of each institution, in terms that include campus environment, student activities, and lifestyle. Such quality-of-life intangibles can be the deciding factors in the college selection process. The absence of any college or university does not constitute an editorial decision on the part of Peterson's. In essence, these descriptions are an open forum for colleges, on a voluntary basis, to communicate their particular message to prospective students. The colleges included have paid a fee to Peterson's to provide this information. The Close-Ups in the **Featured Two-Year Colleges** section are edited to provide a generally consistent format across entries for your ease of comparison.

## INDEXES

### Associate Degree Programs at Two- and Four-Year Colleges

These indexes present hundreds of undergraduate fields of study that are currently offered most widely according to the colleges' responses on *Peterson's Annual Survey of Undergraduate Institutions.* The majors appear in alphabetical order, each followed by an alphabetical list of the schools that offer an associate-level program in that field. Liberal Arts and Studies indicates a general program with no specified major. The terms used for the majors are those of the U.S. Department of Education Classification of Instructional Programs (CIPs). Many institutions, however, use different terms. Readers should refer to the **Featured Two-Year Colleges** two-page descriptions in this book for the school's exact terminology. In addition, although the term "major" is used in this guide, some colleges may use other terms, such as "concentration," "program of study," or "field."

## DATA COLLECTION PROCEDURES

The data contained in the **Profiles** of Two-Year Colleges and **Indexes** were researched in winter and spring 2018 through *Peterson's Annual Survey of Undergraduate Institutions*. Questionnaires were sent to the more than 1,700 colleges that meet the outlined inclusion criteria. All data included in this edition have been submitted by officials (usually admission and financial aid officers, registrars, or institutional research personnel) at the colleges themselves. All usable information received in time for publication has been included. The omission of any particular item from the **Profiles** of Two-Year Colleges and **Indexes** listing signifies either that the item is not applicable to that institution or that data were not available. Because of the comprehensive editorial review that takes place in our offices and because all material comes directly from college officials, Peterson's has every reason to believe that the information presented in this guide is accurate at the time of printing. However, students should check with a specific college or university at the time of application to verify such figures as tuition and fees, which may have changed since the publication of this volume.

## CRITERIA FOR INCLUSION IN THIS BOOK

*Peterson's Two-Year Colleges 2019* covers accredited institutions in the United States, U.S. territories, and other countries that award the associate degree as their most popular undergraduate offering (a few also offer bachelor's, master's, or doctoral degrees). The term two-year college is the commonly used designation for institutions that grant the associate degree, since two years is the normal duration of the traditional associate degree program. However, some programs may be completed in one year, others require three years, and, of course, part-time programs may take a consid-erably longer period. Therefore, "two-year college" should be understood as a conventional term that accurately describes most of the institutions included in this guide but which should not be taken literally in all cases. Also included are some non-degree-granting institutions, usually branch campuses of a multicampus system, which offer the equivalent of the first two years of a bachelor's degree, transferable to a bachelor's degree–granting institution.

To be included in this guide, an institution must have full accreditation or be a candidate for accreditation (preaccreditation) status by an institutional or specialized accrediting body recognized by the U.S. Department of Education or the Council for Higher Education Accreditation (CHEA). Institutional accrediting bodies, which review each institution as a whole, include the six regional associations of schools and colleges (Middle States, New England, North Central, Northwest, Southern, and Western), each of which is responsible for a specified portion of the United States and its territories. Other institutional accrediting bodies are national in scope and accredit specific kinds of institutions (e.g., Bible colleges, independent colleges, and rabbinical and Talmudic schools). Program registration by the New York State Board of Regents is considered to be the equivalent of institutional accreditation, since the board requires that all programs offered by an institution meet its standards before recognition is granted. This guide also includes institutions outside the United States that are accredited by these U.S. accrediting bodies. There are recognized specialized or professional accrediting bodies in more than forty different fields, each of which is authorized to accredit institutions or specific programs in its particular field. For specialized institutions that offer programs in one field only, we designate this to be the equivalent of institutional accreditation. A full explanation of the accrediting process and complete information on recognized, institutional (regional and national), and specialized accrediting bodies can be found online at www.chea.org or at www.ed.gov/admins/finaid/accred/index.html.

# Quick-Reference Chart

# Two-Year Colleges At-a-Glance

This chart includes the names and locations of accredited two-year colleges in the United States, Canada, and other countries and shows institutions' responses to the *Peterson's Annual Survey of Undergraduate Institutions*. If an institution submitted incomplete data, one or more columns opposite the institution's name is blank. A dagger after the school name indicates that the institution has one or more entries in the *Featured Two-Year Colleges* section. If a school does not appear, it did not report any of the information.

Y—Yes; N—No; R—Recommended; S—For Some

Column key: Degrees Awarded — College Transfer Associate (C), Terminal Associate (T), Bachelor's (B), Master's (M), Doctoral (D). Institutional Control — County/District/City, State and Local, State-Related (St-L); Federal, State and Commonwealth, Territory; Independent, Independent-Religious, Proprietary (Prop). Student Body — Men, Primarily Men, Women, Primarily Women, Coed (M/W).

| Name | Location | Degrees | Control | Student Body | Undergrad Enrollment | % Part-Time | % 25 or Older | % Grads to 4-Yr | HS Equiv Cert Accepted | Open Admissions | HS Transcript Required | Need-Based Aid | Part-Time Jobs | Job Placement | Career Counseling | College Housing | Sports | Majors |
|---|---|---|---|---|---|---|---|---|---|---|---|---|---|---|---|---|---|---|
| **UNITED STATES** | | | | | | | | | | | | | | | | | | |
| **Alabama** | | | | | | | | | | | | | | | | | | |
| Bevill State Community College | Jasper | C,T | St | M/W | 3,872 | 59 | 25 | 19 | Y | Y | Y | Y | Y | Y | Y | Y | | 14 |
| Community College of the Air Force | Maxwell Gunter Air Force Base | T | Fed | M/W | 268,763 | | | | | | | | | | | | | |
| George C. Wallace Community College | Dothan | C,T | St | M/W | 4,645 | 58 | 31 | | Y | Y | Y | Y | Y | Y | Y | N | 2 | 33 |
| H. Councill Trenholm State Community College | Montgomery | C | St | M/W | 1,845 | | 30 | | Y | Y | Y | Y | Y | Y | Y | N | N | 21 |
| Jefferson State Community College | Birmingham | C,T | St | M/W | 8,840 | 70 | 35 | | Y | Y | S | Y | Y | Y | Y | Y | N | 1 | 19 |
| Lurleen B. Wallace Community College | Andalusia | C,T | St | M/W | 1,838 | 48 | 18 | | Y | Y | Y | Y | Y | Y | Y | | N | 3 | 11 |
| Marion Military Institute | Marion | C | St | M/W | 446 | 1 | 1 | | N | | Y | Y | Y | Y | Y | Y | 13 | 2 |
| Northwest-Shoals Community College | Muscle Shoals | C | St | M/W | 3,440 | 58 | 20 | | Y | Y | | Y | Y | Y | Y | N | N | 17 |
| Reid State Technical College | Evergreen | T | St | M/W | 392 | 54 | 32 | | Y | | Y | Y | Y | Y | Y | N | | 2 |
| Snead State Community College | Boaz | C,T | St | M/W | 2,161 | 29 | | | | | | | | | | | | |
| **American Samoa** | | | | | | | | | | | | | | | | | | |
| American Samoa Community College | Pago Pago | C,T,B | Terr | M/W | 1,095 | 44 | 15 | 0 | Y | Y | | Y | Y | Y | Y | N | 8 | 36 |
| **Arizona** | | | | | | | | | | | | | | | | | | |
| Arizona Western College | Yuma | C,T | St-L | M/W | 7,557 | 71 | 62 | 21 | Y | | | Y | Y | Y | Y | Y | 7 | 70 |
| Carrington College–Mesa | Mesa | T | Prop | M/W | 599 | 6 | | | | | | | | | | | | |
| Carrington College–Phoenix East | Phoenix | T | Prop | M/W | 261 | 32 | | | | | | | | | | | | |
| Carrington College–Phoenix North | Phoenix | T | Prop | M/W | 653 | | | | | | | | | | | | | |
| Chandler-Gilbert Community College | Chandler | C,T | St-L | M/W | 14,906 | 72 | 19 | | Y | | | | Y | Y | Y | N | 6 | 37 |
| Cochise County Community College District | Douglas | C,T | St-L | M/W | 3,918 | 61 | 13 | 48 | Y | | R,S | Y | | | Y | Y | 3 | 49 |
| Coconino Community College | Flagstaff | C,T | St | M/W | 3,608 | 69 | | | | | | | | | | | | |
| Eastern Arizona College | Thatcher | C,T | St-L | M/W | 6,365 | 69 | 30 | 5 | Y | | R | Y | Y | Y | Y | Y | 10 | 54 |
| Estrella Mountain Community College | Avondale | C,T | St-L | M/W | 9,344 | 67 | | | | | | | | | | | | |
| Mesa Community College | Mesa | C | St-L | M/W | 20,424 | | | | Y | | | | Y | Y | Y | N | 11 | 53 |
| Mohave Community College | Kingman | C,T | St | M/W | 4,312 | 80 | 47 | | Y | | | | Y | Y | | N | | 34 |
| Penn Foster College | Scottsdale | C,T,B | Prop | M/W | 24,527 | | | | | | | | | | | | | |
| The Refrigeration School | Phoenix | T | Prop | PM | 688 | | | | | | | | | | | | | |
| Rio Salado College | Tempe | C,T | St-L | M/W | 20,865 | | | | | | | | | | | | | |
| Scottsdale Community College | Scottsdale | C,T | St-L | M/W | 9,458 | | 36 | | Y | | | Y | Y | Y | | N | 12 | 22 |
| Tohono O'odham Community College | Sells | C,T | Pub | M/W | 400 | 70 | 0 | 56 | Y | Y | Y | | | | Y | Y | 1 | 6 |
| **Arkansas** | | | | | | | | | | | | | | | | | | |
| Arkansas Northeastern College | Blytheville | C,T | St | M/W | 1,416 | 57 | | | | | | | | | | | | |
| Arkansas State University–Newport | Newport | C,T | St | M/W | 2,735 | 61 | 40 | | Y | Y | Y | | Y | Y | Y | N | | 15 |
| College of the Ouachitas | Malvern | C,T | St | M/W | 1,272 | 70 | 50 | | Y | Y | Y | Y | Y | Y | Y | N | | 17 |
| National Park College | Hot Springs | C,T | St-L | M/W | 2,996 | 59 | 63 | | Y | Y | Y | Y | Y | Y | Y | N | 5 | 31 |
| NorthWest Arkansas Community College | Bentonville | C,T | St | M/W | 7,715 | | | | Y | Y | Y | Y | Y | Y | Y | N | 6 | 23 |
| Southeast Arkansas College | Pine Bluff | C,T | St | M/W | 1,304 | 55 | 46 | | Y | Y | Y | Y | Y | Y | Y | N | 1 | 22 |
| Southern Arkansas University Tech | Camden | C,T | St | M/W | 1,650 | 70 | | | | | | | | | | | | |
| University of Arkansas Community College at Morrilton | Morrilton | C,T | St | M/W | 1,921 | 42 | 31 | 47 | Y | Y | Y | Y | Y | Y | Y | N | 5 | 16 |
| University of Arkansas Rich Mountain | Mena | C,T | St-L | M/W | 938 | 51 | 60 | | Y | Y | Y | Y | Y | Y | | N | | 7 |
| **California** | | | | | | | | | | | | | | | | | | |
| American Academy of Dramatic Arts–Los Angeles | Hollywood | C | Ind | M/W | 303 | | 11 | | N | Y | Y | Y | | | | Y | | 1 |
| Antelope Valley College | Lancaster | C,T,B | Dist | M/W | 14,125 | 71 | 37 | | Y | | | Y | Y | Y | Y | N | 12 | 66 |
| Cañada College | Redwood City | C,T | Dist | M/W | 5,433 | 93 | | | | | | | | | | | | |
| Carrington College–Citrus Heights | Citrus Heights | T | Prop | M/W | 448 | 4 | | | | | | | | | | | | |
| Carrington College–Pleasant Hill | Pleasant Hill | T | Prop | M/W | 437 | 18 | | | | | | | | | | | | |
| Carrington College–Pomona | Pomona | T | Prop | M/W | 356 | 23 | | | | | | | | | | | | |
| Carrington College–Sacramento | Sacramento | T | Prop | M/W | 1,186 | 21 | | | | | | | | | | | | |
| Carrington College–San Jose | San Jose | T | Prop | M/W | 715 | 9 | | | | | | | | | | | | |
| Carrington College–San Leandro | San Leandro | T | Prop | M/W | 416 | 4 | | | | | | | | | | | | |
| Carrington College–Stockton | Stockton | T | Prop | M/W | 545 | 2 | | | | | | | | | | | | |
| Cerritos College | Norwalk | C,T | Dist | M/W | 22,043 | 67 | | | | | | | | | | | | |
| Citrus College | Glendora | C | Dist | M/W | 12,780 | 61 | | | | | | | | | | | | |
| Coastline Community College | Fountain Valley | C | Dist | M/W | 11,431 | 78 | | | | | | | | | | | | |
| College of Marin | Kentfield | C,T | Dist | M/W | 5,749 | | | | Y | | | Y | Y | Y | Y | N | 8 | 55 |
| College of the Canyons | Santa Clarita | C,T | Dist | M/W | 26,171 | 64 | 37 | | Y | | R | Y | Y | Y | Y | N | 10 | 56 |
| College of the Desert | Palm Desert | C,T | Dist | M/W | 11,146 | 60 | 35 | | Y | | R | Y | Y | Y | | N | 11 | 88 |
| De Anza College | Cupertino | C,T | Dist | M/W | 20,808 | 52 | | | | | | Y | Y | Y | Y | N | 13 | 63 |
| Feather River College | Quincy | C,T,B | Dist | M/W | 2,079 | | 54 | 77 | Y | | | Y | Y | Y | Y | Y | 9 | 27 |
| FIDM/Fashion Institute of Design & Merchandising, Orange County Campus | Irvine | C,T | Prop | PW | 71 | 6 | 5 | | N | Y | Y | | | | | Y | | 6 |
| FIDM/Fashion Institute of Design & Merchandising, San Diego Campus | San Diego | C,T | Prop | PW | 66 | 8 | 9 | | N | Y | Y | | | Y | Y | Y | N | | 3 |
| Fullerton College | Fullerton | C,T | Dist | M/W | 24,588 | | 28 | | Y | | | Y | Y | Y | Y | N | 13 | 75 |
| Golden West College | Huntington Beach | C,T | Dist | M/W | 12,394 | 65 | | | | | | | | | | | | |
| Gurnick Academy of Medical Arts | San Mateo | C,T,B | Prop | M/W | | | | | | | | | | | | | | 5 |
| Imperial Valley College | Imperial | C,T | Dist | M/W | 7,828 | | | | | | | | | | | | | |

This chart includes the names and locations of accredited two-year colleges in the United States, Canada, and other countries and shows institutions' responses to the *Peterson's Annual Survey of Undergraduate Institutions*. If an institution submitted incomplete data, one or more columns opposite the institution's name is blank. A dagger after the school name indicates that the institution has one or more entries in the *Featured Two-Year Colleges* section. If a school does not appear, it did not report any of the information.

Legend: Y—Yes; N—No; R—Recommended; S—For Some

Column headers (diagonal): Degrees Awarded — College Transfer Associate (C); Terminal Associate (T); Bachelor's (B); Master's (M), Doctoral (D) · Institutional Control (County, District, City, Federal, State and Local, State-Related, Independent, Independent-Religious, Proprietary, Commonwealth, Territory) · Student Body (Men, Primarily Men, Women, Primarily Women, Coed) · Undergraduate Enrollment · Percent Attending Part-Time · Percent of Grads Going on to Four-Year Colleges · Percent 25 Years of Age or Older · Open Admissions · High School Equivalency Certificate Accepted · High School Transcript Required · Need-Based Aid Available · Part-Time Jobs Available · Career Counseling Available · Job Placement Services Available · College Housing Available · Number of Sports Offered · Number of Majors Offered

| Name | Location | Degrees | Control | Student Body | Undergrad Enrollment | % Part-Time | % to 4-Yr | % 25+ | Open Adm | HS Equiv Accepted | HS Transcript Req | Need-Based Aid | Part-Time Jobs | Career Counseling | Job Placement | College Housing | # Sports | # Majors |
|---|---|---|---|---|---|---|---|---|---|---|---|---|---|---|---|---|---|---|
| Los Angeles City College | Los Angeles | C,T | Dist | M/W | 16,556 | 72 | 62 | | Y | Y | R | | Y | Y | Y | N | 8 | 51 |
| Merced College | Merced | C,T | Dist | M/W | 11,552 | | 51 | | Y | | R | R | Y | Y | Y | N | 8 | 71 |
| Mission College | Santa Clara | C,T | Dist | M/W | 7,868 | | 60 | | Y | | | Y | Y | Y | Y | N | 6 | 24 |
| Mt. San Antonio College | Walnut | C,T | Dist | M/W | 4,568 | 43 | | | Y | | S | Y | Y | Y | Y | N | 14 | 81 |
| Orange Coast College | Costa Mesa | C,T | Dist | M/W | 21,731 | 61 | 28 | | Y | | | Y | Y | Y | Y | N | 14 | 89 |
| Palomar College | San Marcos | C | Dist | M/W | 25,244 | | 37 | | Y | | | Y | Y | Y | Y | N | 14 | 93 |
| Pasadena City College | Pasadena | C,T | Dist | M/W | 27,324 | 62 | 27 | | Y | | | Y | Y | Y | Y | N | 13 | 74 |
| Rio Hondo College | Whittier | C,T | Dist | M/W | | | | | Y | | | | Y | Y | Y | N | 11 | 4 |
| The Salvation Army College for Officer Training at Crestmont | Rancho Palos Verdes | C,T | I-R | M/W | 59 | | 88 | | N | Y | Y | | | | | Y | | 1 |
| San Joaquin Delta College | Stockton | C,T | Dist | M/W | 18,102 | | 31 | | Y | | | | Y | Y | Y | N | 18 | 57 |
| Santa Monica College | Santa Monica | C,T | Dist | M/W | 30,830 | 86 | | | | | | | | | | | | |
| Santa Rosa Junior College | Santa Rosa | C,T | Dist | M/W | 26,800 | | 46 | | Y | | | | Y | Y | Y | N | | 76 |
| Sierra College | Rocklin | C,T | Dist | M/W | 18,758 | 74 | | | | | | | | | | N | | |
| Southwestern College | Chula Vista | C,T | Dist | M/W | 18,413 | 60 | 31 | | Y | | | S | Y | Y | Y | N | 11 | 106 |
| **Colorado** | | | | | | | | | | | | | | | | | | |
| Arapahoe Community College | Littleton | C,T | St | M/W | 9,383 | 82 | | | | | | | | | | | | |
| Bel–Rea Institute of Animal Technology | Denver | T | Prop | M/W | 400 | | | | | | | | | | | | | |
| CollegeAmerica–Denver | Denver | T | Ind | M/W | 110 | | | | | | | | | Y | | | N | | 2 |
| CollegeAmerica–Fort Collins | Fort Collins | T,B | Ind | M/W | 120 | | | | | | | | | | | | | |
| Colorado Northwestern Community College | Rangely | C,T | St | M/W | 1,201 | 60 | 35 | | Y | Y | Y | | Y | Y | Y | Y | 9 | 14 |
| Community College of Aurora | Aurora | C,T | St | M/W | 7,379 | 80 | | | | | | | | | | | | |
| Front Range Community College | Westminster | C,T | St | M/W | 18,966 | 71 | 36 | | Y | | | Y | Y | Y | Y | N | | 30 |
| IBMC College | Fort Collins | T | Prop | M/W | 1,020 | | | | | | | | | | | | | |
| Lamar Community College | Lamar | C,T | St | M/W | 791 | 49 | 18 | | Y | Y | | | Y | Y | Y | Y | 7 | 11 |
| Morgan Community College | Fort Morgan | C,T | St | M/W | 1,474 | 78 | | | | | | | | | | | | |
| Northeastern Junior College | Sterling | C,T | St | M/W | 1,547 | 42 | 18 | 17 | Y | | R | Y | Y | Y | Y | Y | 8 | 44 |
| Otero Junior College | La Junta | C,T | St | M/W | 1,449 | | 32 | 12 | Y | | R | Y | Y | Y | Y | Y | 7 | 19 |
| Pueblo Community College | Pueblo | C,T,B | St | M/W | 5,993 | 66 | 49 | 21 | Y | | | | Y | Y | Y | N | | 36 |
| **Connecticut** | | | | | | | | | | | | | | | | | | |
| Asnuntuck Community College | Enfield | C,T | St | M/W | 1,945 | 66 | | | | | | | | | | | | |
| Housatonic Community College | Bridgeport | C,T | St | M/W | 5,138 | 66 | 41 | | Y | Y | Y | Y | Y | Y | | | | | 12 |
| Manchester Community College | Manchester | C,T | St | M/W | 6,321 | 69 | 32 | | Y | Y | Y | Y | Y | | | | N | 4 | 31 |
| Naugatuck Valley Community College | Waterbury | C,T | St | M/W | 6,378 | 66 | 35 | | Y | Y | Y | Y | Y | Y | | | N | | 32 |
| Norwalk Community College | Norwalk | C,T | St | M/W | 5,869 | 65 | | | | | | | | | | | | |
| St. Vincent's College | Bridgeport | C,T,B | I-R | M/W | 763 | 91 | | | | | | | | | | | | |
| Three Rivers Community College | Norwich | C,T | St | M/W | 4,187 | 68 | 40 | | Y | Y | R | Y | Y | Y | Y | N | 2 | 30 |
| **Florida** | | | | | | | | | | | | | | | | | | |
| Chipola College | Marianna | C,T,B | St | M/W | 2,104 | 59 | 37 | | Y | Y | Y | | Y | Y | | N | 4 | 19 |
| College of Business and Technology–Cutler Bay Campus | Cutler Bay | C | Prop | M/W | 137 | | 73 | | Y | Y | Y | | | Y | Y | N | | 3 |
| College of Business and Technology–Flagler Campus | Miami | C | Prop | M/W | 256 | | 83 | | Y | Y | Y | | | Y | Y | N | | 4 |
| College of Business and Technology–Hialeah Campus | Hialeah | C | Prop | PM | 200 | | 84 | | Y | Y | Y | | | Y | Y | N | | 2 |
| College of Business and Technology–Main Campus | Miami | C,B | Prop | M/W | 10 | | 70 | | Y | Y | Y | | | Y | Y | N | | 1 |
| College of Business and Technology–Miami Gardens | Miami Gardens | C,B | Prop | M/W | 91 | | 81 | | Y | Y | Y | | | Y | Y | N | | 4 |
| College of Central Florida | Ocala | C,T,B | St-L | M/W | 7,931 | 62 | 39 | | Y | Y | Y | Y | Y | Y | | N | 5 | 75 |
| Daytona State College | Daytona Beach | C,B | St | M/W | 13,141 | 61 | 39 | | Y | Y | Y | Y | Y | Y | Y | N | 8 | 52 |
| Florida Keys Community College | Key West | C,T,B | St | M/W | 1,030 | 65 | 37 | | Y | Y | S | Y | Y | Y | | Y | | 15 |
| Florida SouthWestern State College | Fort Myers | C,T,B | St-L | M/W | 16,616 | 66 | | | | | | | | | | | | |
| Gulf Coast State College | Panama City | C,T,B | St | M/W | 5,379 | 66 | 37 | | Y | Y | Y | | Y | Y | | N | 4 | 43 |
| Hillsborough Community College | Tampa | C,T | St | M/W | 27,061 | 60 | | | | | | | | | | | | |
| Miami Dade College† | Miami | C,T,B | St-L | M/W | 56,001 | 58 | 28 | | Y | Y | Y | Y | Y | Y | | N | 4 | 193 |
| Pensacola State College | Pensacola | C,B | St | M/W | 9,655 | 63 | 62 | 61 | Y | Y | Y | Y | Y | Y | Y | N | 10 | 106 |
| Seminole State College of Florida | Sanford | C,T,B | St-L | M/W | 17,706 | 65 | 43 | 32 | Y | Y | Y | Y | Y | Y | Y | N | 3 | 50 |
| Southeastern College–West Palm Beach | West Palm Beach | T | Prop | M/W | 558 | 52 | 70 | | Y | Y | Y | | | Y | Y | N | | 13 |
| South Florida State College | Avon Park | C,T,B | St | M/W | 2,885 | 66 | 44 | | Y | Y | Y | Y | Y | Y | Y | Y | 6 | 19 |
| Tallahassee Community College | Tallahassee | C,T,B | St-L | M/W | 11,782 | 51 | 19 | | Y | Y | Y | | Y | Y | | N | 6 | 38 |
| Ultimate Medical Academy Clearwater | Clearwater | T | Ind | M/W | 247 | | | | | | | | | | | | | |
| Ultimate Medical Academy Online | Tampa | T | Ind | M/W | 16,411 | 21 | | | | | | | | | | | | |
| **Georgia** | | | | | | | | | | | | | | | | | | |
| Albany Technical College | Albany | T | St | M/W | 3,251 | 57 | | | | | | | | | | | | |
| Athens Technical College | Athens | T | St | M/W | 4,210 | 75 | | | | | | | | | | | | |
| Atlanta Technical College | Atlanta | T | St | M/W | 3,775 | 63 | | | | | | | | | | | | |
| Augusta Technical College | Augusta | T | St | M/W | 4,370 | 61 | | | | | | | | | | | | |
| Central Georgia Technical College | Warner Robins | T | St | M/W | 7,762 | 69 | | | | | | | | | | | | |
| Chattahoochee Technical College | Marietta | T | St | M/W | 9,999 | 72 | | | | | | | | | | | | |
| Coastal Pines Technical College | Waycross | T | St | M/W | 2,775 | 78 | | | | | | | | | | | | |
| Columbus Technical College | Columbus | T | St | M/W | 3,228 | 72 | | | | | | | | | | | | |
| East Georgia State College | Swainsboro | C,T,B | St | M/W | 3,001 | 23 | | | | | | | | | | | | |
| Georgia Highlands College | Rome | C,T,B | St | M/W | 6,003 | 53 | 21 | | N | Y | Y | Y | Y | Y | | N | 12 | 6 |
| Georgia Military College | Milledgeville | C,B | Pub | M/W | 8,595 | 50 | 31 | | Y | Y | S | Y | Y | | | Y | 10 | 26 |
| Georgia Northwestern Technical College | Rome | T | St | M/W | 6,016 | 70 | | | | | | | | | | | | |
| Georgia Piedmont Technical College | Clarkston | T | St | M/W | 4,103 | 78 | | | | | | | | | | | | |
| Gordon State College | Barnesville | C,T,B | St | M/W | 3,986 | | 15 | | N | Y | Y | Y | Y | Y | | Y | 4 | 46 |
| Gupton-Jones College of Funeral Service | Decatur | T | Ind | M/W | 232 | | 77 | | Y | Y | Y | Y | | Y | Y | N | | 1 |
| Gwinnett Technical College | Lawrenceville | T | St | M/W | 7,479 | 78 | | | | | | | | | | | | |
| Lanier Technical College | Oakwood | T | St | M/W | 3,636 | 72 | | | | | | | | | | | | |
| North Georgia Technical College | Clarkesville | T | St | M/W | 2,838 | 68 | | | | | | | | | | | | |

This chart includes the names and locations of accredited two-year colleges in the United States, Canada, and other countries and shows institutions' responses to the *Peterson's Annual Survey of Undergraduate Institutions*. If an institution submitted incomplete data, one or more columns opposite the institution's name is blank. A dagger after the school name indicates that the institution has one or more entries in the *Featured Two-Year Colleges* section. If a school does not appear, it did not report any of the information.

Y—Yes; N—No; R—Recommended; S—For Some

Column key: **Degrees Awarded** — College Transfer Associate (C), Terminal Associate (T), Bachelor's (B), Master's (M), Doctoral (D). **Institutional Control** — County/District/City (Dist), State (St), State- and Locally-related (St-L), Federal, Territory (Terr), Independent (Ind), Independent-Religious (I-R), Proprietary (Prop). **Student Body** — Coed (M/W), Primarily Men (PM).

| College | Location | Degrees | Control | Student Body | Undergrad Enrollment | % Part-Time | % 25 or Older | % Grads to 4-Yr | HS Equiv Cert Accepted | Open Admissions | HS Transcript Required | Need-Based Aid | Career Counseling | Part-Time Jobs | Job Placement | College Housing | Sports Offered | Majors Offered |
|---|---|---|---|---|---|---|---|---|---|---|---|---|---|---|---|---|---|---|
| Oconee Fall Line Technical College | Sandersville | T | St | M/W | 1,404 | 74 | | | | | | | | | | | | |
| Ogeechee Technical College | Statesboro | T | St | M/W | 1,904 | 62 | | | | | | | | | | | | |
| Savannah Technical College | Savannah | T | St | M/W | 3,938 | 65 | | | | | | | | | | | | |
| Southeastern Technical College | Vidalia | T | St | M/W | 1,563 | 72 | | | | | | | | | | | | |
| Southern Crescent Technical College | Griffin | T | St | M/W | 4,703 | 66 | | | | | | | | | | | | |
| Southern Regional Technical College | Thomasville | T | St | M/W | 3,521 | 67 | | | | | | | | | | | | |
| South Georgia Technical College | Americus | T | St | M/W | 1,829 | 50 | | | | | | | | | | | | |
| West Georgia Technical College | Waco | T | St | M/W | 6,743 | 71 | | | | | | | | | | | | |
| Wiregrass Georgia Technical College | Valdosta | T | St | M/W | 3,940 | 76 | | | | | | | | | | | | |
| **Guam** | | | | | | | | | | | | | | | | | | |
| Guam Community College | Mangilao | T | Terr | M/W | 2,428 | 57 | | | | | | | | | | | | |
| **Hawaii** | | | | | | | | | | | | | | | | | | |
| Hawaii Tokai International College | Kapolei | C,T | Ind | M/W | 85 | | 1 | 75 | N | Y | Y | Y | | | | Y | | 1 |
| **Idaho** | | | | | | | | | | | | | | | | | | |
| Carrington College–Boise | Boise | T | Prop | M/W | 446 | 11 | | | | | | | | | | | | |
| College of Eastern Idaho | Idaho Falls | C,T | St | M/W | 791 | | 52 | | Y | Y | Y | Y | Y | Y | Y | N | | 14 |
| **Illinois** | | | | | | | | | | | | | | | | | | |
| Black Hawk College | Moline | C,T | St-L | M/W | 4,926 | 64 | 29 | 72 | Y | | R | Y | Y | Y | Y | N | 6 | 29 |
| City Colleges of Chicago, Kennedy-King College | Chicago | C,T | St-L | M/W | 2,818 | 44 | | | | | | | | | | | | |
| City Colleges of Chicago, Olive-Harvey College | Chicago | C,T | St-L | M/W | 2,882 | | | | Y | Y | S | Y | Y | Y | Y | N | 3 | 12 |
| Danville Area Community College | Danville | C,T | St-L | M/W | 2,645 | 62 | 32 | 58 | Y | Y | Y | Y | Y | Y | Y | N | 5 | 31 |
| Elgin Community College | Elgin | C,T | St-L | M/W | 9,949 | 68 | | | | | | | | | | | | |
| Harper College | Palatine | C,T | St-L | M/W | 13,749 | 64 | 29 | | Y | | Y | Y | Y | Y | | N | 12 | 66 |
| Highland Community College | Freeport | C,T | St-L | M/W | 1,678 | 51 | 30 | | Y | Y | R,S | Y | Y | Y | | N | 6 | 26 |
| Illinois Central College | East Peoria | C,T | St-L | M/W | 9,266 | 66 | 26 | 87 | Y | | Y | Y | Y | Y | | | 11 | 49 |
| Illinois Eastern Community Colleges, Frontier Community College | Fairfield | C,T | St-L | M/W | 1,791 | 84 | 51 | | Y | Y | Y | Y | Y | Y | Y | N | 4 | 16 |
| Illinois Eastern Community Colleges, Lincoln Trail College | Robinson | C,T | St-L | M/W | 933 | 57 | 35 | | Y | Y | Y | Y | Y | Y | Y | N | 4 | 14 |
| Illinois Eastern Community Colleges, Olney Central College | Olney | C,T | St-L | M/W | 1,142 | 54 | 47 | | Y | Y | Y | Y | Y | Y | Y | N | 3 | 16 |
| Illinois Eastern Community Colleges, Wabash Valley College | Mount Carmel | C,T | St-L | M/W | 3,662 | 87 | 39 | | Y | Y | Y | Y | Y | Y | Y | N | 3 | 22 |
| Illinois Valley Community College | Oglesby | C,T | Dist | M/W | 3,241 | 61 | 27 | 64 | Y | | Y | Y | Y | Y | Y | N | 7 | 40 |
| Kaskaskia College | Centralia | C,T | St-L | M/W | 3,107 | 61 | 20 | | Y | Y | Y | Y | Y | Y | Y | N | 9 | 41 |
| Kishwaukee College | Malta | C,T | St-L | M/W | 3,775 | 57 | 26 | | Y | | R,S | Y | Y | Y | | N | 5 | 29 |
| McHenry County College | Crystal Lake | C,T | St-L | M/W | 6,371 | 67 | 31 | | Y | | R | Y | Y | Y | | N | 6 | 27 |
| Morrison Institute of Technology | Morrison | C,T | Ind | PM | 144 | 1 | 11 | | Y | Y | Y | Y | Y | Y | | N | 3 | 6 |
| Morton College | Cicero | C,T | St-L | M/W | 3,913 | 65 | 25 | | Y | Y | Y | Y | Y | Y | | N | 6 | 29 |
| Oakton Community College | Des Plaines | C,T | Dist | M/W | 8,348 | | 36 | | Y | Y | R | Y | Y | Y | | N | 10 | 30 |
| Rend Lake College | Ina | C,T | St | M/W | 2,333 | 49 | 24 | | Y | Y | Y | Y | Y | Y | | N | 6 | 34 |
| Rock Valley College | Rockford | C | Dist | M/W | 6,378 | 56 | 26 | | Y | | Y | Y | Y | Y | | N | 9 | 32 |
| Sauk Valley Community College | Dixon | C,T | Dist | M/W | 2,220 | 55 | 37 | 78 | Y | | R | Y | Y | Y | | N | 5 | 45 |
| Shawnee Community College | Ullin | C,T | St-L | M/W | 1,505 | 55 | 22 | | Y | Y | Y | Y | Y | Y | | N | 3 | 19 |
| South Suburban College | South Holland | C,T | St-L | M/W | 4,115 | | 52 | | Y | Y | Y | Y | Y | | | N | 5 | 23 |
| Southwestern Illinois College | Belleville | C,T | Dist | M/W | | | | | | | | Y | | | Y | Y | | |
| Spoon River College | Canton | C,T | St | M/W | 1,560 | 52 | | | | | | | | | | | | |
| **Indiana** | | | | | | | | | | | | | | | | | | |
| Ancilla College | Donaldson | C,T | I-R | M/W | 548 | 18 | 11 | | Y | Y | Y | Y | Y | Y | Y | Y | 10 | 26 |
| Ivy Tech Community College–Bloomington | Bloomington | C,T | St | M/W | 6,198 | 73 | 41 | | Y | | | Y | Y | Y | Y | | | 44 |
| Ivy Tech Community College–Central Indiana | Indianapolis | C,T | St | M/W | 18,062 | 75 | 46 | | Y | | | Y | Y | Y | Y | N | 6 | 51 |
| Ivy Tech Community College–Columbus | Columbus | C,T | St | M/W | 2,653 | 75 | 45 | | Y | | | Y | Y | Y | Y | N | | 46 |
| Ivy Tech Community College–East Central | Muncie | C,T | St | M/W | 5,462 | 63 | 41 | | Y | | | Y | Y | Y | Y | N | | 55 |
| Ivy Tech Community College–Kokomo | Kokomo | C,T | St | M/W | 2,422 | 67 | 49 | | Y | | | Y | Y | Y | Y | N | | 49 |
| Ivy Tech Community College–Lafayette | Lafayette | C,T | St | M/W | 4,517 | 62 | 36 | | Y | | | Y | Y | Y | Y | N | | 55 |
| Ivy Tech Community College–North Central | South Bend | C,T | St | M/W | 4,805 | 71 | 49 | | Y | | | Y | Y | Y | Y | N | | 39 |
| Ivy Tech Community College–Northeast | Fort Wayne | C,T | St | M/W | 6,795 | 72 | 45 | | Y | | | Y | Y | Y | Y | N | | 39 |
| Ivy Tech Community College–Northwest | Gary | C,T | St | M/W | 8,314 | 71 | 48 | | Y | | | Y | Y | Y | Y | N | | 41 |
| Ivy Tech Community College–Richmond | Richmond | C,T | St | M/W | 1,527 | 73 | 53 | | Y | | | Y | Y | Y | Y | N | 1 | 46 |
| Ivy Tech Community College–Sellersburg | Sellersburg | C,T | St | M/W | 4,684 | 81 | 51 | | Y | | | Y | Y | Y | Y | N | | 47 |
| Ivy Tech Community College–Southeast | Madison | C,T | St | M/W | 2,334 | 73 | 40 | | Y | | | Y | Y | Y | Y | N | | 29 |
| Ivy Tech Community College–Southwest | Evansville | C,T | St | M/W | 4,076 | 77 | 53 | | Y | | | Y | Y | Y | Y | N | | 56 |
| Ivy Tech Community College–Wabash Valley | Terre Haute | C,T | St | M/W | 3,637 | 67 | 45 | | Y | | | Y | Y | Y | Y | N | 2 | 60 |
| Vincennes University | Vincennes | C,B | St | M/W | 18,904 | 72 | 31 | | Y | Y | Y | Y | Y | | | Y | 7 | 103 |
| **Iowa** | | | | | | | | | | | | | | | | | | |
| Des Moines Area Community College | Ankeny | C,T | St-L | M/W | 22,982 | 72 | 35 | | Y | | S | Y | Y | Y | Y | Y | 8 | 50 |
| Hawkeye Community College | Waterloo | C,T | St-L | M/W | 5,605 | 55 | 44 | | Y | Y | Y | Y | Y | Y | Y | N | 11 | 42 |
| Iowa Central Community College | Fort Dodge | C,T | St-L | M/W | 5,489 | | 14 | | Y | Y | R,S | Y | Y | Y | Y | Y | 16 | 35 |
| Northeast Iowa Community College | Calmar | C,T | St-L | M/W | 4,545 | 73 | 32 | | Y | | R | Y | Y | Y | Y | N | 7 | 29 |
| North Iowa Area Community College | Mason City | C | St-L | M/W | 2,947 | 54 | 18 | | Y | | Y | Y | Y | Y | Y | Y | 10 | 27 |
| St. Luke's College | Sioux City | C,T,B | Ind | M/W | 273 | 57 | 46 | 60 | N | Y | Y | Y | Y | Y | Y | N | | 4 |
| Southeastern Community College | West Burlington | C | St-L | M/W | 2,844 | 54 | | | | | | | | | | | | |
| Southwestern Community College | Creston | C,T | St | M/W | 1,680 | 50 | 29 | | Y | | Y | Y | Y | Y | Y | Y | 8 | 15 |
| Western Iowa Tech Community College | Sioux City | C,T | St | M/W | 6,152 | 63 | 21 | | Y | | R | Y | Y | Y | | Y | 8 | 56 |

This chart includes the names and locations of accredited two-year colleges in the United States, Canada, and other countries and shows institutions' responses to the *Peterson's Annual Survey of Undergraduate Institutions*. If an institution submitted incomplete data, one or more columns opposite the institution's name is blank. A dagger after the school name indicates that the institution has one or more entries in the *Featured Two-Year Colleges* section. If a school does not appear, it did not report any of the information.

**Legend:** Y—Yes; N—No; R—Recommended; S—For Some

**Column headings (left to right):**
- Degrees Awarded: College Transfer Associate (C), Terminal Associate (T), Bachelor's (B), Master's (M), Doctoral (D)
- Institutional Control: County, District, City, State and Local, State-Related / Independent, Independent-Religious, Proprietary / Federal, State, Commonwealth, Territory
- Student Body: Men, Primarily Men, Women, Primarily Women, Coed

| Name | Location | Degrees Awarded | Institutional Control | Student Body | Undergraduate Enrollment | Percent Attending Part-Time | Percent 25 Years of Age or Older | Percent of Grads Going on to Four-Year Colleges | Open Admissions | High School Equivalency Certificate Accepted | High School Transcript Required | Need-Based Aid Available | Part-Time Jobs Available | Career Counseling Services Available | Job Placement Services Available | College Housing Available | Number of Sports Offered | Number of Majors Offered |
|---|---|---|---|---|---|---|---|---|---|---|---|---|---|---|---|---|---|---|
| **Kansas** | | | | | | | | | | | | | | | | | | |
| Allen Community College | Iola | C,T | St-L | M/W | 2,379 | | | | | | | | | | | | | |
| Barton County Community College | Great Bend | C,T | St-L | M/W | 4,131 | 79 | | | Y | Y | R | Y | Y | Y | Y | Y | 15 | 101 |
| Cloud County Community College | Concordia | C,T | St-L | M/W | 1,873 | 57 | 25 | | Y | Y | R | Y | Y | Y | Y | Y | 11 | 24 |
| Dodge City Community College | Dodge City | C,T | St-L | M/W | 1,804 | | | | | | | | | | | | | |
| Donnelly College | Kansas City | C,T,B | I-R | M/W | 294 | 39 | 44 | | Y | Y | R | Y | Y | Y | Y | N | 3 | 4 |
| Hesston College | Hesston | C,T,B | I-R | M/W | 442 | 9 | 16 | | Y | Y | Y | Y | Y | Y | Y | Y | 10 | 13 |
| Hutchinson Community College | Hutchinson | C,T | St-L | M/W | 5,854 | 62 | 24 | 80 | Y | Y | Y | Y | Y | Y | Y | Y | 12 | 60 |
| Independence Community College | Independence | C,T | St | M/W | 897 | 43 | 17 | | | | Y | Y | Y | Y | Y | Y | 6 | 26 |
| Johnson County Community College | Overland Park | C,T | St-L | M/W | 19,110 | 68 | | | | | | | | | | | | |
| Manhattan Area Technical College | Manhattan | C,T | St-L | M/W | 825 | 58 | | | | | | | | | | | | |
| Salina Area Technical College | Salina | C,T | St-L | M/W | 582 | 63 | | | | | | | | | | | | |
| **Kentucky** | | | | | | | | | | | | | | | | | | |
| Gateway Community and Technical College | Florence | C,T | St | M/W | 4,215 | | 40 | | Y | Y | Y | | | Y | | N | | 13 |
| Hopkinsville Community College | Hopkinsville | C,T | St | M/W | 3,120 | 60 | | | Y | Y | R | Y | Y | Y | Y | N | 5 | 14 |
| Maysville Community and Technical College | Maysville | C,T | St | M/W | 3,495 | | | | Y | Y | Y | Y | Y | Y | Y | N | | 18 |
| Owensboro Community and Technical College | Owensboro | C,T | St | M/W | 3,789 | 60 | 36 | 8 | Y | Y | Y | Y | Y | Y | Y | N | | 27 |
| Somerset Community College | Somerset | C,T | St | M/W | 5,900 | 38 | | | Y | Y | Y | Y | Y | Y | | N | | 22 |
| Southcentral Kentucky Community and Technical College | Bowling Green | C,T | St | M/W | 4,953 | 54 | | | Y | | | | | | | | | 20 |
| Southeast Kentucky Community and Technical College | Cumberland | C,T | St | M/W | 3,125 | 53 | 32 | 45 | Y | Y | Y | Y | Y | Y | Y | N | 5 | 14 |
| Spencerian College | Louisville | T,B | Prop | M/W | 396 | 43 | 56 | | Y | Y | Y | Y | | Y | Y | Y | | 14 |
| Spencerian College–Lexington | Lexington | T | Prop | M/W | 74 | | | | | | | | | | | | | |
| West Kentucky Community and Technical College | Paducah | C,T | St | M/W | 6,088 | | 45 | | Y | Y | Y | Y | Y | Y | Y | N | 1 | 27 |
| **Louisiana** | | | | | | | | | | | | | | | | | | |
| Bossier Parish Community College | Bossier City | C | St | M/W | 6,042 | 62 | 43 | | Y | Y | | Y | Y | Y | Y | N | 10 | 35 |
| Central Louisiana Technical Community College | Alexandria | C | St | M/W | 2,432 | 54 | 25 | 30 | Y | Y | Y | Y | Y | Y | | | 3 | 9 |
| ITI Technical College | Baton Rouge | T | Prop | M/W | 622 | | 47 | | | | | Y | | Y | Y | N | | 9 |
| Louisiana State University at Eunice | Eunice | C,T | St | M/W | 2,906 | 52 | 25 | | Y | | Y | | Y | Y | | Y | 6 | 11 |
| Nunez Community College | Chalmette | C,T | St | M/W | 2,599 | 62 | 34 | | Y | | S | Y | Y | Y | Y | N | 1 | 8 |
| Southern University at Shreveport | Shreveport | C,T | St | M/W | 3,088 | 48 | 30 | | Y | Y | R | Y | Y | Y | Y | Y | 3 | 24 |
| Sowela Technical Community College | Lake Charles | C,T | St | M/W | 3,347 | 49 | 31 | | Y | Y | Y | Y | | Y | Y | N | | 16 |
| **Maine** | | | | | | | | | | | | | | | | | | |
| Beal College | Bangor | T | Prop | M/W | 464 | 22 | 53 | | Y | Y | Y | | Y | Y | Y | N | | 10 |
| Central Maine Community College | Auburn | C,T | St | M/W | 2,900 | 62 | 34 | | N | Y | Y | Y | Y | Y | Y | Y | 7 | 23 |
| Kennebec Valley Community College | Fairfield | C,T | St | M/W | 2,554 | 78 | 50 | | Y | Y | Y | Y | | Y | Y | N | 6 | 28 |
| Maine College of Health Professions | Lewiston | T,B | Ind | M/W | 188 | 77 | 44 | | N | Y | Y | Y | | | | Y | | 2 |
| Northern Maine Community College | Presque Isle | C,T | St | M/W | 955 | | 40 | | Y | Y | Y | Y | Y | Y | Y | Y | 2 | 17 |
| York County Community College | Wells | C,T | St | M/W | 1,708 | 77 | 31 | | Y | Y | Y | Y | Y | Y | | N | 5 | 21 |
| **Maryland** | | | | | | | | | | | | | | | | | | |
| Anne Arundel Community College | Arnold | C,T | St-L | M/W | 13,354 | 71 | 35 | | Y | | Y | | Y | Y | | N | 8 | 47 |
| Carroll Community College | Westminster | C,T | St-L | M/W | 3,020 | 67 | 24 | | Y | | Y | Y | Y | Y | | N | 3 | 35 |
| Cecil College | North East | C,B | Cou | M/W | 2,468 | 65 | 20 | | Y | Y | Y | Y | Y | Y | Y | | 8 | 42 |
| Chesapeake College | Wye Mills | C,T | St-L | M/W | 2,189 | | | | | Y | Y | Y | Y | Y | Y | N | 5 | 34 |
| Community College of Baltimore County | Baltimore | C,T | Cou | M/W | 19,349 | 72 | | | Y | Y | Y | | | Y | | N | 9 | 61 |
| Frederick Community College | Frederick | C,T | St-L | M/W | 6,220 | 67 | 25 | | Y | | R | Y | Y | Y | Y | N | 7 | 36 |
| Garrett College | McHenry | C,T | St-L | M/W | 754 | 31 | | | | | | | | | | | | |
| Hagerstown Community College | Hagerstown | C,T | St-L | M/W | 4,069 | 75 | 30 | | | | | S | | Y | Y | N | 9 | 29 |
| Harford Community College | Bel Air | C,T | St-L | M/W | 6,100 | | 28 | 50 | Y | | | | | | | | 13 | 70 |
| Howard Community College | Columbia | C,T | St-L | M/W | 9,726 | | 36 | | Y | | S | | Y | Y | Y | N | 6 | 48 |
| Montgomery College | Rockville | C,T | St-L | M/W | 22,875 | 65 | 29 | 51 | Y | | R | R | Y | Y | Y | N | 12 | 44 |
| Wor-Wic Community College | Salisbury | C,T | St-L | M/W | 3,110 | 74 | 43 | | Y | | R | | | Y | | N | | 20 |
| **Massachusetts** | | | | | | | | | | | | | | | | | | |
| Berkshire Community College | Pittsfield | C,T | St | M/W | 1,959 | 68 | | | | | | | | | | | | |
| Bristol Community College | Fall River | C,T | St | M/W | 7,637 | | 38 | | Y | Y | Y | Y | | Y | Y | N | 5 | 62 |
| Bunker Hill Community College | Boston | C,T | St | M/W | 12,996 | 65 | | | Y | Y | Y | Y | Y | Y | Y | N | 4 | 59 |
| FINE Mortuary College, LLC | Norwood | T | Prop | M/W | 99 | 85 | 68 | | | Y | Y | Y | | | Y | N | | 1 |
| Holyoke Community College | Holyoke | C,T | St | M/W | 5,565 | 55 | 33 | | Y | Y | Y | | Y | Y | Y | N | 8 | 26 |
| Massachusetts Bay Community College | Wellesley Hills | C,T | St | M/W | 4,629 | 67 | 36 | 55 | Y | Y | S | Y | Y | Y | Y | N | 6 | 35 |
| Middlesex Community College | Bedford | C,T | St | M/W | 8,745 | 64 | | | | | | | | | | | | |
| Mount Wachusett Community College | Gardner | C,T | St | M/W | 3,854 | 65 | | 29 | Y | Y | S | Y | Y | Y | Y | N | 8 | 38 |
| Northern Essex Community College | Haverhill | C,T | St | M/W | 5,726 | 66 | 35 | | Y | Y | Y | Y | Y | Y | Y | N | 10 | 57 |
| North Shore Community College | Danvers | C,T | St | M/W | 6,087 | | 39 | 45 | Y | Y | S | Y | Y | Y | Y | N | 2 | 40 |
| Quinsigamond Community College | Worcester | C,T | St | M/W | 7,370 | 63 | 40 | | Y | Y | Y | Y | Y | Y | Y | N | 7 | 57 |
| Springfield Technical Community College | Springfield | C,T | St | M/W | 5,343 | 57 | 39 | | Y | Y | Y | Y | Y | Y | Y | N | 6 | 53 |
| Urban College of Boston | Boston | T | Ind | PW | 812 | 93 | 85 | | Y | Y | S | | Y | | | N | | 3 |
| **Michigan** | | | | | | | | | | | | | | | | | | |
| Delta College | University Center | C,T | Dist | M/W | 9,132 | 64 | | | | | | | | | | | | |
| Grand Rapids Community College | Grand Rapids | C,T | Dist | M/W | 14,269 | 70 | 28 | | Y | Y | Y | Y | Y | Y | Y | N | 6 | 44 |
| Kellogg Community College | Battle Creek | C,T | St-L | M/W | 4,814 | 76 | | | | Y | Y | S | Y | Y | Y | N | 7 | 33 |
| Kirtland Community College | Roscommon | C,T | Dist | M/W | 1,528 | 67 | 37 | | Y | Y | Y | Y | Y | Y | Y | N | 3 | 20 |
| Lansing Community College | Lansing | C,T | St-L | M/W | 13,583 | 63 | | | | | | | | | | | | |
| Macomb Community College | Warren | C,T | Dist | M/W | 21,014 | 71 | 36 | | | | Y | | Y | Y | Y | N | 11 | 72 |
| Monroe County Community College | Monroe | C,T | Cou | M/W | 3,144 | | 25 | | Y | | Y | | Y | Y | Y | N | | 42 |
| Mott Community College | Flint | C,T | Dist | M/W | 7,689 | 74 | 40 | | | Y | Y | Y | Y | Y | Y | N | 7 | 46 |
| Muskegon Community College | Muskegon | C,T | St-L | M/W | 4,506 | 67 | | | | Y | Y | Y | Y | Y | Y | N | 8 | 43 |

This chart includes the names and locations of accredited two-year colleges in the United States, Canada, and other countries and shows institutions' responses to the *Peterson's Annual Survey of Undergraduate Institutions*. If an institution submitted incomplete data, one or more columns opposite the institution's name is blank. A dagger after the school name indicates that the institution has one or more entries in the *Featured Two-Year Colleges* section. If a school does not appear, it did not report any of the information.

Legend: Y—Yes; N—No; R—Recommended; S—For Some

Column key:
- **Degrees Awarded:** College Transfer Associate (C), Terminal Associate (T), Bachelor's (B), Master's (M), Doctoral (D)
- **Institutional Control:** County, District, City, Federal, State and Local, State-Related, Independent, Independent-Religious, Proprietary
- **Student Body:** Men, Primarily Men, Women, Primarily Women, Coed

| Institution | Location | Degrees | Control | Student Body | Undergrad Enroll | % 25 or Older | % Part-Time | % Grads to 4-Yr | Open Admissions | HS Equiv. Accepted | HS Transcript Req. | Need-Based Aid Req. | Part-Time Jobs | Career Counseling | Job Placement | College Housing | # Sports | # Majors |
|---|---|---|---|---|---|---|---|---|---|---|---|---|---|---|---|---|---|---|
| Saginaw Chippewa Tribal College | Mount Pleasant | C,T | Ind | M/W | 140 | 74 | 58 | | Y | | | | | Y | | | N | | 3 |
| St. Clair County Community College | Port Huron | C,T | | M/W | 3,625 | 61 | | | | | | | | | | | | | |
| Schoolcraft College | Livonia | C,T,B | Dist | M/W | 10,558 | 72 | 31 | | Y | Y | R,S | Y | Y | Y | Y | N | 8 | 41 |
| Southwestern Michigan College | Dowagiac | C,T | St-L | M/W | 2,330 | 56 | 19 | | Y | Y | Y | Y | Y | Y | | Y | 8 | 21 |
| Wayne County Community College District | Detroit | C,T | St-L | M/W | 14,806 | 86 | 40 | | Y | Y | Y | Y | Y | Y | Y | N | 5 | 43 |
| **Minnesota** | | | | | | | | | | | | | | | | | | |
| Alexandria Technical and Community College | Alexandria | C,T | St | M/W | 2,647 | 19 | | | Y | Y | S | Y | Y | | | N | 4 | 26 |
| Anoka-Ramsey Community College | Coon Rapids | C,T | St | M/W | 8,874 | 62 | | | | | | | | | | | | |
| Anoka Technical College | Anoka | C,T | St | M/W | 1,809 | 54 | | | | | | | | | | | | |
| Central Lakes College | Brainerd | C,T | St | M/W | 3,715 | 21 | | | Y | Y | Y | Y | Y | Y | | N | 7 | 30 |
| Century College | White Bear Lake | C,T | St | M/W | 8,442 | 57 | 38 | | Y | Y | Y | Y | Y | Y | | N | 12 | 49 |
| Dunwoody College of Technology | Minneapolis | T,B | Ind | PM | 1,302 | 18 | 45 | | N | Y | Y | Y | Y | Y | Y | N | | 27 |
| Hennepin Technical College | Brooklyn Park | C,T | St | M/W | 5,299 | | | | | | | | | | | | | |
| Lake Superior College | Duluth | C,T | St | M/W | 4,388 | 59 | 38 | | Y | | Y | Y | Y | Y | | N | 1 | 37 |
| Mesabi Range College | Virginia | C,T | St | M/W | 1,150 | 44 | | | | | | | | | | | | |
| Minnesota State College–Southeast Technical | Winona | C,T | St | M/W | 1,961 | 59 | | | | | | | | | | | | |
| Minnesota State Community and Technical College | Fergus Falls | C,T | St | M/W | 6,303 | 34 | | 68 | Y | Y | | Y | Y | Y | Y | Y | | 70 |
| Minnesota State Community and Technical College–Detroit Lakes | Detroit Lakes | C,T | St | M/W | 6,391 | 58 | | | | | | | | | | | | |
| Minnesota State Community and Technical College–Moorhead | Moorhead | C | St | M/W | 6,303 | 59 | | | | | | | | | | | | |
| Minnesota State Community and Technical College–Wadena | Wadena | C,T | St | M/W | 6,303 | 59 | | | | | | | | | | | | |
| Minnesota West Community and Technical College | Pipestone | C,T | St | M/W | 3,182 | | | | Y | Y | Y | Y | Y | Y | | | 7 | 42 |
| North Hennepin Community College | Brooklyn Park | C,T | St | M/W | 6,509 | | | | Y | Y | R | Y | Y | Y | Y | N | 10 | 31 |
| Northland Community and Technical College | Thief River Falls | C,T | St | M/W | 3,599 | 62 | | | Y | Y | Y | Y | Y | Y | | N | 13 | 33 |
| Rainy River Community College | International Falls | C,T | St | M/W | 241 | 54 | | | Y | Y | R | Y | Y | Y | Y | Y | 14 | 6 |
| Ridgewater College | Willmar | C,T | St | M/W | 3,366 | | | | Y | Y | Y | Y | Y | | | N | 9 | 51 |
| **Mississippi** | | | | | | | | | | | | | | | | | | |
| Copiah-Lincoln Community College | Wesson | C,T | St-L | M/W | 3,100 | 31 | 5 | | Y | Y | Y | Y | Y | Y | Y | Y | 8 | 64 |
| Hinds Community College | Raymond | C,T | St-L | M/W | 12,061 | 40 | 27 | | Y | | Y | Y | Y | Y | Y | Y | 14 | 61 |
| Meridian Community College | Meridian | C,T | St-L | M/W | 3,555 | | | | Y | Y | Y | Y | Y | Y | Y | Y | 10 | 13 |
| Northwest Mississippi Community College | Senatobia | C,T | St-L | M/W | 7,700 | | | | Y | Y | Y | Y | Y | | Y | Y | 7 | 14 |
| **Missouri** | | | | | | | | | | | | | | | | | | |
| Cottey College | Nevada | C,B | Ind | CW | 265 | 2 | 15 | 95 | N | Y | Y | Y | Y | Y | | Y | 6 | 13 |
| Crowder College | Neosho | C,T | St-L | M/W | 4,960 | 30 | | | Y | Y | Y | Y | Y | Y | Y | Y | 4 | 46 |
| East Central College | Union | C,T | Dist | M/W | 2,897 | 55 | 23 | | Y | Y | Y | Y | Y | Y | | N | 3 | 27 |
| Missouri State University–West Plains | West Plains | C,T | St | M/W | 1,918 | 51 | 29 | | Y | Y | S | Y | Y | Y | Y | Y | 2 | 16 |
| North Central Missouri College | Trenton | C,T | Dist | M/W | 1,505 | 47 | | | | | | | | | | | | |
| Ozarks Technical Community College | Springfield | C,T | Dist | M/W | 13,260 | | | | Y | Y | Y | Y | Y | Y | | N | | 45 |
| St. Charles Community College | Cottleville | C,T | St | M/W | 6,563 | 50 | 24 | | Y | Y | R,S | Y | Y | Y | | N | 3 | 27 |
| St. Louis Community College | St. Louis | C,T | Pub | M/W | 18,835 | 62 | 38 | | Y | Y | S | | Y | Y | Y | N | 5 | 39 |
| State Technical College of Missouri | Linn | T | St | PM | 1,256 | 17 | 7 | | | Y | Y | Y | Y | Y | Y | Y | 5 | 22 |
| Three Rivers College | Poplar Bluff | C,T | St-L | M/W | 3,226 | 45 | 29 | | Y | Y | R,S | Y | Y | Y | | Y | 3 | 28 |
| **Montana** | | | | | | | | | | | | | | | | | | |
| Aaniiih Nakoda College | Harlem | C,T | Fed | M/W | 236 | | | | | | | | | | | | | |
| Dawson Community College | Glendive | C,T | St-L | M/W | 329 | 38 | 189 | 31 | Y | Y | Y | Y | Y | | | Y | 10 | 13 |
| Great Falls College Montana State University | Great Falls | C,T | St | M/W | 1,690 | 62 | 53 | | Y | Y | Y | Y | Y | Y | | N | | 15 |
| **Nebraska** | | | | | | | | | | | | | | | | | | |
| CHI Health School of Radiologic Technology | Omaha | T | Ind | M/W | 15 | 27 | | | N | Y | Y | | | | | N | | 1 |
| Metropolitan Community College | Omaha | C,T | St-L | M/W | 17,003 | 58 | | | | | | | | | | | | |
| Mid-Plains Community College | North Platte | C,T | Dist | M/W | 2,222 | | 31 | | Y | Y | Y | Y | Y | Y | Y | Y | 5 | 19 |
| Nebraska Indian Community College | Macy | C,T | Fed | M/W | 180 | 74 | 44 | 100 | Y | Y | | Y | Y | Y | Y | N | | 7 |
| Northeast Community College | Norfolk | C,T | St-L | M/W | 5,075 | 58 | 31 | | Y | | | R,S | Y | Y | | Y | 9 | 73 |
| Southeast Community College, Lincoln Campus | Lincoln | C,T | Dist | M/W | 9,262 | 57 | | | | | | | | | | | | |
| Southeast Community College, Milford Campus | Milford | T | Dist | PM | 9,262 | 57 | | | | | | | | | | | | |
| **Nevada** | | | | | | | | | | | | | | | | | | |
| Career College of Northern Nevada | Sparks | T | Prop | M/W | 342 | | | 62 | Y | Y | | Y | Y | Y | Y | N | | 6 |
| Carrington College–Las Vegas | Las Vegas | T | Prop | M/W | 352 | 15 | | | | | | | | | | | | |
| Carrington College–Reno | Reno | T | Prop | M/W | 360 | 19 | | | | | | | | | | | | |
| Great Basin College | Elko | C,T,B | St | M/W | 3,362 | 73 | | | | | | | | | | | | |
| Truckee Meadows Community College | Reno | C,T,B | St | M/W | 10,720 | 74 | 37 | 46 | Y | | | | Y | Y | Y | N | | 54 |
| Western Nevada College | Carson City | C,T,B | St | M/W | 3,567 | 65 | | | | | | | | | | | | |
| **New Hampshire** | | | | | | | | | | | | | | | | | | |
| Lakes Region Community College | Laconia | C,T | St | M/W | 1,179 | 58 | 39 | | Y | Y | Y | Y | Y | Y | Y | Y | | 21 |
| NHTI, Concord's Community College | Concord | C | St | M/W | 3,700 | | | | | | | | | | | | | |
| St. Joseph School of Nursing | Nashua | C,T | Ind | M/W | 144 | 56 | 76 | | N | Y | Y | | | | | N | | 1 |
| White Mountains Community College | Berlin | C,T | St | M/W | 802 | 63 | 46 | | Y | Y | Y | Y | Y | Y | | Y | | 21 |
| **New Jersey** | | | | | | | | | | | | | | | | | | |
| Camden County College | Blackwood | C,T | St-L | M/W | 10,492 | 52 | 37 | | Y | Y | S | Y | Y | Y | Y | N | 8 | 46 |
| County College of Morris | Randolph | C,T | Cou | M/W | 7,949 | 52 | | | Y | Y | Y | Y | Y | Y | Y | N | 11 | 35 |
| Eastern International College | Belleville | C,T,B | Prop | M/W | | | | | | | | | | | | | | |
| Hudson County Community College | Jersey City | C,T | St-L | M/W | 8,864 | 42 | 33 | | Y | | | Y | Y | Y | Y | N | | 33 |
| Jersey College | Teterboro | C | Prop | PW | 2,743 | | | | | | | | | | | | | |

This chart includes the names and locations of accredited two-year colleges in the United States, Canada, and other countries and shows institutions' responses to the *Peterson's Annual Survey of Undergraduate Institutions*. If an institution submitted incomplete data, one or more columns opposite the institution's name is blank. A dagger after the school name indicates that the institution has one or more entries in the *Featured Two-Year Colleges* section. If a school does not appear, it did not report any of the information.

Y—Yes; N—No; R—Recommended; S—For Some

| Institution | Location | Degrees Awarded | Institutional Control | Student Body | Undergraduate Enrollment | Percent Attending Part-Time | Percent 25 Years of Age or Older | Percent of Grads Going on to Four-Year Colleges | Open Admissions | High School Equivalency Certificate Accepted | High School Transcript Required | Need-Based Aid Available | Part-Time Jobs Available | Career Counseling Available | Job Placement Services Available | College Housing Available | Number of Sports Offered | Number of Majors Offered |
|---|---|---|---|---|---|---|---|---|---|---|---|---|---|---|---|---|---|---|
| Mercer County Community College | Trenton | C,T | St-L | M/W | 7,979 | 61 | | | | | | | | | | | | | |
| Middlesex County College | Edison | C,T | Cou | M/W | 11,673 | | | | | | | | | | | | | |
| Raritan Valley Community College | Branchburg | C,T | St-L | M/W | 8,079 | 58 | 27 | 65 | Y | | Y | Y | Y | Y | | N | 7 | 47 |
| Sussex County Community College | Newton | C,T | St-L | M/W | 2,539 | 44 | | | | | | | | | | | | |
| Union County College | Cranford | C,T | St-L | M/W | 9,711 | 56 | 40 | | Y | Y | Y | Y | Y | Y | Y | N | 9 | 34 |
| **New Mexico** | | | | | | | | | | | | | | | | | | |
| Carrington College–Albuquerque | Albuquerque | T | Prop | M/W | 434 | 8 | | | | | | | | | | | | |
| Central New Mexico Community College | Albuquerque | C,T | St | M/W | 24,442 | 73 | 40 | | Y | | | Y | Y | Y | Y | N | | 60 |
| Mesalands Community College | Tucumcari | C,T | St | M/W | 1,005 | | 64 | | | | Y | | | | Y | | | 19 |
| New Mexico Junior College | Hobbs | C,T | St-L | M/W | 3,222 | | | | | | | | | | | | | |
| New Mexico State University&-Alamogordo | Alamogordo | C,T | St | M/W | 1,710 | 75 | | | Y | Y | Y | Y | Y | Y | Y | N | | 20 |
| San Juan College | Farmington | C,T | St | M/W | 5,172 | 54 | 55 | | Y | Y | Y | Y | Y | Y | Y | N | 4 | 51 |
| Santa Fe Community College | Santa Fe | C,T | St-L | M/W | 9,619 | 77 | | | | | | | | | | | | |
| Southwestern Indian Polytechnic Institute | Albuquerque | C,T | Fed | M/W | 402 | 14 | 39 | 1 | N | Y | Y | Y | Y | Y | Y | Y | 3 | 11 |
| **New York** | | | | | | | | | | | | | | | | | | |
| Adirondack Community College | Queensbury | C,T | St-L | M/W | 3,973 | 45 | 25 | | Y | Y | | Y | Y | Y | Y | Y | 10 | 25 |
| American Academy of Dramatic Arts&-New York | New York | T | Ind | M/W | 310 | | 20 | | N | Y | Y | Y | Y | Y | | Y | | 1 |
| The Belanger School of Nursing | Schenectady | C,T | Ind | M/W | 114 | 68 | 61 | 0 | N | Y | Y | Y | | | | N | | 1 |
| Borough of Manhattan Community College of the City University of New York | New York | C,T | St-L | M/W | 26,748 | 32 | | | | | | | | | | | | |
| Cayuga County Community College | Auburn | C,T | St-L | M/W | 4,921 | 68 | 40 | | Y | | Y | Y | Y | Y | | N | 8 | 37 |
| Clinton Community College | Plattsburgh | C,T | St-L | M/W | 1,913 | 50 | | | | | | | | | | | | |
| Cochran School of Nursing | Yonkers | T | Ind | PW | 120 | 78 | 88 | | N | Y | Y | Y | | | | N | | 1 |
| The College of Westchester | White Plains | C,T,B | Prop | M/W | 915 | 21 | 44 | | N | Y | Y | Y | Y | Y | Y | N | | 10 |
| Columbia-Greene Community College | Hudson | C,T | St-L | M/W | 1,624 | 63 | 28 | | Y | Y | Y | Y | Y | Y | Y | N | 7 | 15 |
| Dutchess Community College | Poughkeepsie | C,T | St-L | M/W | 9,061 | 58 | 13 | | Y | Y | Y | Y | Y | Y | Y | Y | 6 | 31 |
| Erie Community College | Buffalo | C,T | St-L | M/W | 2,417 | 24 | 40 | 54 | Y | Y | Y | Y | Y | Y | Y | N | 12 | 17 |
| Erie Community College, North Campus | Williamsville | C,T | St-L | M/W | 4,929 | 33 | 33 | 54 | Y | Y | Y | Y | Y | Y | Y | N | 12 | 32 |
| Erie Community College, South Campus | Orchard Park | C,T | St-L | M/W | 3,789 | 44 | 21 | 54 | Y | Y | Y | Y | Y | Y | Y | N | 12 | 19 |
| Fashion Institute of Technology&+ | New York | C,T,B,M | St-L | PW | 8,661 | 17 | 18 | | N | Y | Y | Y | Y | Y | Y | Y | 7 | 23 |
| Finger Lakes Community College | Canandaigua | C,T | St-L | M/W | 6,521 | 60 | | | | | | | | | | | | |
| Fiorello H. LaGuardia Community College of the City University of New York | Long Island City | C,T | St-L | M/W | 19,356 | 44 | 35 | 48 | Y | Y | Y | Y | Y | Y | | N | 7 | 43 |
| Genesee Community College | Batavia | C,T | St-L | M/W | 5,906 | | 27 | | Y | Y | Y | Y | Y | Y | | Y | 9 | 91 |
| Jamestown Business College | Jamestown | T,B | Prop | M/W | 311 | 2 | | | | | | | | | | | | |
| Jamestown Community College | Jamestown | C,T | St-L | M/W | 4,463 | 54 | 28 | 56 | Y | Y | Y | Y | Y | Y | | Y | 10 | 28 |
| Jefferson Community College | Watertown | C,T | St-L | M/W | 3,632 | 43 | | | N | Y | Y | Y | Y | Y | Y | Y | 6 | 35 |
| Kingsborough Community College of the City University of New York | Brooklyn | C,T | St-L | M/W | 15,280 | 46 | 23 | | Y | Y | Y | Y | Y | Y | Y | N | 7 | 43 |
| Long Island Business Institute | Flushing | C | Prop | M/W | 1,118 | 12 | | | | | | | | | | | | |
| Mohawk Valley Community College | Utica | C,T | St-L | M/W | 6,506 | 49 | 28 | | Y | | S | Y | Y | Y | Y | Y | 12 | 54 |
| Monroe Community College | Rochester | C,T | St-L | M/W | 12,907 | 39 | 39 | | Y | Y | Y | Y | Y | Y | Y | Y | 18 | 67 |
| Nassau Community College | Garden City | C,T | St-L | M/W | 20,267 | 43 | 23 | | Y | Y | Y | Y | Y | Y | Y | N | 18 | 53 |
| Niagara County Community College | Sanborn | C,T | St-L | M/W | 5,466 | 41 | 21 | | Y | Y | Y | Y | Y | Y | Y | Y | 10 | 42 |
| Queensborough Community College of the City University of New York | Bayside | C,T | St-L | M/W | 15,400 | 40 | 23 | 73 | Y | Y | Y | Y | Y | Y | Y | N | 11 | 46 |
| Schenectady County Community College | Schenectady | C,T | St-L | M/W | 6,634 | 67 | 30 | | Y | Y | Y | Y | Y | Y | Y | N | 6 | 21 |
| State University of New York College of Technology at Alfred | Alfred | C,T,B | St | M/W | 3,686 | 8 | 11 | | N | Y | Y | Y | Y | Y | Y | Y | 17 | 59 |
| Sullivan County Community College | Loch Sheldrake | C,T | St-L | M/W | 1,610 | 49 | 20 | 31 | Y | Y | Y | Y | Y | Y | Y | Y | 13 | 37 |
| Tompkins Cortland Community College | Dryden | C,T | St-L | M/W | 2,632 | 30 | 30 | | Y | Y | Y | Y | Y | Y | Y | Y | 22 | 35 |
| Ulster County Community College | Stone Ridge | C,T | St-L | M/W | 3,416 | 60 | | | | | | | | | | | | |
| Westchester Community College | Valhalla | C,T | St-L | M/W | 12,571 | 46 | 31 | | Y | Y | Y | Y | Y | Y | Y | N | 11 | 49 |
| **North Carolina** | | | | | | | | | | | | | | | | | | |
| Alamance Community College | Graham | C,T | St | M/W | 4,259 | 39 | 48 | | Y | Y | Y | Y | Y | Y | | N | | 28 |
| Asheville-Buncombe Technical Community College | Asheville | C,T | St | M/W | 7,542 | | 43 | | Y | Y | Y | Y | Y | Y | Y | N | | 44 |
| Caldwell Community College and Technical Institute | Hudson | C,T | St | M/W | 3,514 | 65 | 62 | | Y | Y | Y | | Y | Y | Y | N | 1 | 28 |
| Cape Fear Community College | Wilmington | C,T | St | M/W | 9,067 | 57 | | | | | | | | | | | | |
| Carolinas College of Health Sciences | Charlotte | T | Pub | M/W | 433 | 89 | | | | | | | | | | | | |
| Carteret Community College | Morehead City | C,T | St | M/W | 1,363 | 58 | 45 | | Y | Y | S | Y | Y | Y | Y | N | 3 | 24 |
| Cleveland Community College | Shelby | C,T | St | M/W | 2,700 | 63 | | | Y | Y | Y | Y | Y | Y | Y | N | | 28 |
| College of The Albemarle | Elizabeth City | C,T | St | M/W | 1,947 | 50 | 32 | | Y | Y | Y | Y | Y | Y | Y | N | 13 | 26 |
| Craven Community College | New Bern | C,T | St | M/W | 3,021 | 63 | | | Y | Y | Y | Y | Y | Y | Y | N | | 36 |
| Fayetteville Technical Community College | Fayetteville | C,T | St | M/W | 11,640 | 61 | 55 | 21 | Y | Y | Y | Y | Y | Y | Y | N | 2 | 46 |
| Halifax Community College | Weldon | C,T | St-L | M/W | 1,113 | 57 | 37 | | Y | Y | Y | Y | Y | Y | Y | N | | 17 |
| Haywood Community College | Clyde | C,T | St-L | M/W | | | 50 | | Y | Y | Y | Y | Y | Y | | N | 1 | 32 |
| James Sprunt Community College | Kenansville | C,T | St | M/W | 1,219 | 65 | 22 | 1 | Y | Y | Y | Y | Y | Y | | N | 2 | 21 |
| Johnston Community College | Smithfield | C,T | St | M/W | 4,152 | 63 | | | Y | Y | Y | Y | Y | Y | Y | N | 2 | 13 |
| Lenoir Community College | Kinston | C,T | St | M/W | 2,664 | 62 | 32 | | Y | Y | Y | Y | Y | Y | Y | N | 3 | 43 |
| Mitchell Community College | Statesville | C,T | St | M/W | 3,204 | 65 | 35 | 61 | Y | Y | Y | Y | Y | Y | Y | N | | 35 |
| Montgomery Community College | Troy | C,T | St | M/W | 925 | | 29 | | Y | Y | Y | | Y | Y | Y | N | | 15 |
| Piedmont Community College | Roxboro | C,T | St | M/W | 1,311 | | | | Y | Y | S | Y | Y | Y | Y | N | | 23 |
| Randolph Community College | Asheboro | C,T | St | M/W | 2,647 | 65 | 22 | | Y | Y | Y | Y | Y | Y | | N | | 25 |
| Richmond Community College | Hamlet | C,T | St | M/W | 2,528 | 59 | 32 | | Y | Y | Y | Y | Y | Y | | N | | 23 |
| Rockingham Community College | Wentworth | C,T | St | M/W | 1,779 | 62 | | | | | | | | | | | | |
| Rowan-Cabarrus Community College | Salisbury | C,T | St | M/W | 7,579 | | 30 | | Y | Y | Y | Y | Y | Y | Y | N | | 25 |
| Southwestern Community College | Sylva | C | St | M/W | 2,574 | 65 | | | Y | Y | | Y | Y | Y | Y | N | | 28 |
| Tri-County Community College | Murphy | C,T | St | M/W | 1,160 | | 65 | | Y | Y | Y | Y | Y | Y | Y | N | | 11 |

This chart includes the names and locations of accredited two-year colleges in the United States, Canada, and other countries and shows institutions' responses to the *Peterson's Annual Survey of Undergraduate Institutions.* If an institution submitted incomplete data, one or more columns opposite the institution's name is blank. A dagger after the school name indicates that the institution has one or more entries in the *Featured Two-Year Colleges* section. If a school does not appear, it did not report any of the information.

Legend: Y—Yes; N—No; R—Recommended; S—For Some

| Institution | Location | Degrees Awarded | Institutional Control | Student Body | Undergraduate Enrollment | Percent 25 Years of Age or Older | Percent Attending Part-Time | Percent of Grads Going on to Four-Year Colleges | High School Equivalency Certificate Accepted | Open Admissions | High School Transcript Required | Need-Based Aid Available | Career Counseling Available | Part-Time Jobs Available | Job Placement Services Available | College Housing Available | Number of Sports Offered | Number of Majors Offered |
|---|---|---|---|---|---|---|---|---|---|---|---|---|---|---|---|---|---|---|
| Wayne Community College | Goldsboro | C,T | St-L | M/W | 3,837 | 53 | 45 | | Y | Y | Y | Y | Y | Y | Y | N | | 33 |
| **North Dakota** | | | | | | | | | | | | | | | | | | |
| Bismarck State College | Bismarck | C,T,B | St | M/W | 3,976 | 44 | | | | | | | | | | | | |
| Dakota College at Bottineau | Bottineau | C,T | St | M/W | 811 | | | | | | | | | | | | | |
| Lake Region State College | Devils Lake | C,T | St | M/W | 1,972 | 73 | 20 | | Y | Y | S | Y | Y | Y | Y | Y | 7 | 14 |
| North Dakota State College of Science | Wahpeton | C,T | St | M/W | 2,985 | 43 | 14 | | Y | Y | Y | Y | Y | Y | Y | Y | 6 | 38 |
| Williston State College | Williston | C,T | St | M/W | 1,098 | 44 | 21 | | Y | Y | Y | Y | Y | Y | Y | Y | 5 | 15 |
| **Ohio** | | | | | | | | | | | | | | | | | | |
| AIC College of Design | Cincinnati | T,B | Ind | M/W | 34 | 12 | 22 | | N | Y | Y | | | Y | Y | N | | 1 |
| Bowling Green State University&-Firelands College | Huron | C,T,B | St | M/W | 1,970 | 52 | 28 | | Y | Y | Y | Y | Y | Y | Y | N | 5 | 20 |
| Central Ohio Technical College | Newark | T | St | M/W | 3,479 | 80 | 29 | | Y | Y | S | Y | Y | Y | Y | N | 7 | 29 |
| Columbus State Community College | Columbus | C,T | St | M/W | 27,109 | 74 | | | | | | | | | | | | |
| Eastern Gateway Community College | Steubenville | C,T | St-L | M/W | 8,546 | 79 | 35 | | Y | Y | S | Y | Y | Y | Y | N | 1 | 21 |
| Edison State Community College | Piqua | C,T | St | M/W | 3,248 | 77 | 43 | | Y | Y | Y | Y | Y | Y | Y | N | 4 | 40 |
| International College of Broadcasting | Dayton | C,T | Prop | M/W | | | | | | | | | | | | | | |
| Kent State University at Ashtabula | Ashtabula | C,T,B | St | M/W | 1,971 | 48 | 42 | | Y | Y | Y | Y | Y | Y | Y | N | 1 | 22 |
| Kent State University at East Liverpool | East Liverpool | C,T,B | St | M/W | 1,174 | 46 | 38 | | Y | Y | Y | Y | Y | Y | Y | N | | 13 |
| Kent State University at Salem | Salem | C,B | St | M/W | 1,694 | 37 | 32 | | Y | Y | Y | Y | Y | Y | Y | N | | 18 |
| Kent State University at Trumbull | Warren | C,B | St | M/W | 2,277 | | 35 | | Y | Y | Y | Y | Y | Y | Y | N | 1 | 22 |
| Kent State University at Tuscarawas | New Philadelphia | C,B | St | M/W | 2,131 | 39 | 27 | | Y | Y | Y | Y | Y | Y | Y | N | 8 | 21 |
| Lakeland Community College | Kirtland | C,T | St-L | M/W | 7,581 | 71 | | | Y | Y | Y | Y | Y | Y | Y | N | 6 | 39 |
| Lorain County Community College | Elyria | C,T | St-L | M/W | 11,042 | 73 | 31 | | Y | Y | S | Y | Y | Y | Y | N | 12 | 41 |
| The Ohio State University Agricultural Technical Institute | Wooster | C,T | St | M/W | 757 | 7 | 8 | 52 | Y | Y | Y | Y | Y | Y | Y | Y | 10 | 34 |
| Ohio Technical College | Cleveland | T | Prop | M/W | 883 | | 17 | | Y | Y | Y | | | | Y | | | 7 |
| Rosedale Bible College | Irwin | T | I-R | M/W | 89 | | | | | | | | | | | | | |
| School of Advertising Art | Kettering | T | Prop | M/W | 194 | 2 | 1 | | N | Y | Y | | | Y | Y | N | | 1 |
| Stark State College | North Canton | C,T | St-R | M/W | 11,028 | 72 | 46 | | Y | Y | Y | Y | Y | Y | | Y | | 28 |
| University of Cincinnati Blue Ash College | Cincinnati | C,T,B | St | M/W | 5,065 | 36 | | | | | | | | | | | | |
| University of Cincinnati Clermont College | Batavia | C,T,B | St | M/W | 2,883 | 45 | | | | | | | | | | | | |
| **Oklahoma** | | | | | | | | | | | | | | | | | | |
| Carl Albert State College | Poteau | C,T | St | M/W | 2,194 | 40 | 36 | | Y | | Y | Y | Y | Y | Y | Y | 6 | 24 |
| Clary Sage College | Tulsa | C | Prop | PW | 406 | | | | | | | | | | | | | |
| Community Care College | Tulsa | T | Ind | PW | 623 | | | | | | | | | | | | | |
| Murray State College | Tishomingo | C,T | St | M/W | 2,674 | | | | | | | | | | | | | |
| Oklahoma City Community College | Oklahoma City | C,T | St | M/W | 12,314 | 65 | 35 | | Y | | | S | Y | Y | Y | N | | 59 |
| Oklahoma State University Institute of Technology | Okmulgee | C,T,B | St | M/W | 2,502 | 30 | 25 | | Y | Y | Y | Y | Y | Y | Y | Y | 7 | 26 |
| Oklahoma State University&-Oklahoma City | Oklahoma City | C,T,B | St | M/W | 5,839 | 70 | 47 | 10 | Y | | S | Y | Y | Y | Y | N | | 36 |
| Oklahoma Technical College | Tulsa | C | Ind | M/W | 186 | | | | | | | | | | | | | |
| Seminole State College | Seminole | C,T | St | M/W | 1,633 | 41 | 32 | | Y | | R | Y | Y | Y | | Y | 7 | 27 |
| Tulsa Community College | Tulsa | C,T | St | M/W | 16,787 | 70 | 35 | | Y | | | Y | Y | Y | Y | N | 5 | 55 |
| **Oregon** | | | | | | | | | | | | | | | | | | |
| Central Oregon Community College | Bend | C,T | Dist | M/W | 5,205 | 54 | | | Y | Y | | Y | Y | Y | | Y | 12 | 56 |
| Oregon Coast Community College | Newport | C,T | Pub | M/W | 486 | 53 | | | | | | | | | | | | |
| Rogue Community College | Grants Pass | C,T | St-L | M/W | 4,901 | 61 | | | | | | | | | | | | |
| Tillamook Bay Community College | Tillamook | C,T | Dist | M/W | 261 | 51 | 45 | | Y | Y | R | Y | | | | Y | | 5 |
| Treasure Valley Community College | Ontario | C,T | St-L | M/W | 2,170 | 56 | 46 | | Y | | | Y | Y | | | Y | 9 | 33 |
| **Pennsylvania** | | | | | | | | | | | | | | | | | | |
| Bucks County Community College | Newtown | C,T | Cou | M/W | 7,783 | 66 | 27 | 53 | Y | | Y | Y | Y | Y | Y | N | 12 | 56 |
| Community College of Allegheny County | Pittsburgh | C,T | Cou | M/W | 16,147 | 65 | | | | | | R | Y | Y | | N | 15 | 135 |
| Community College of Philadelphia | Philadelphia | C,T | St-L | M/W | 30,194 | 54 | | 75 | Y | Y | S | Y | Y | Y | | N | 6 | 30 |
| Harrisburg Area Community College | Harrisburg | C,T | St-L | M/W | 18,681 | 70 | 32 | | Y | | | Y | Y | Y | Y | N | 4 | 69 |
| JNA Institute of Culinary Arts | Philadelphia | T | Prop | M/W | 59 | | | | | | | | | | | | | |
| Johnson College | Scranton | T | Ind | M/W | 376 | 3 | 20 | | N | Y | Y | Y | Y | Y | Y | Y | 7 | 19 |
| Lackawanna College | Scranton | C,T,B | Ind | M/W | 1,604 | 27 | 26 | | Y | Y | Y | Y | Y | Y | Y | Y | 11 | 42 |
| Lansdale School of Business | North Wales | C,T | Prop | M/W | 372 | | | | | | | | | | | | | |
| Lehigh Carbon Community College | Schnecksville | C,T | St-L | M/W | 6,953 | 64 | 36 | | Y | | | S | Y | Y | Y | N | 7 | 64 |
| Luzerne County Community College | Nanticoke | C,T | Cou | M/W | 5,669 | 55 | | | | | | | | | | | | |
| Manor College | Jenkintown | C,T | I-R | M/W | 632 | 32 | 31 | 60 | N | Y | Y | Y | Y | Y | | Y | 4 | 22 |
| Montgomery County Community College | Blue Bell | C,T | Cou | M/W | 10,392 | 66 | 33 | 55 | Y | Y | Y | Y | Y | Y | | Y | 13 | 64 |
| New Castle School of Trades | New Castle | T | Ind | PM | 503 | | | | N | Y | Y | | | Y | Y | N | | 7 |
| Northampton Community College | Bethlehem | C,T | St-L | M/W | 9,921 | 55 | 33 | | Y | | R,S | Y | Y | Y | Y | Y | 10 | 64 |
| Penn State DuBois | DuBois | C,T,B | St-R | M/W | 585 | 21 | 17 | | N | Y | Y | Y | | | | N | | 127 |
| Penn State Fayette, The Eberly Campus | Lemont Furnace | C,T,B | St-R | M/W | 652 | 10 | 13 | | N | Y | Y | Y | | | | N | 11 | 124 |
| Penn State Mont Alto | Mont Alto | C,T,B | St-R | M/W | 917 | 29 | 17 | | N | Y | Y | Y | | | | Y | 10 | 120 |
| Pennsylvania Highlands Community College | Johnstown | C,T | St-L | M/W | 2,784 | | 18 | | Y | | | Y | Y | Y | Y | N | 7 | 25 |
| Pennsylvania Institute of Technology | Media | C,T | Ind | M/W | 447 | | 60 | | Y | Y | Y | Y | Y | | | N | | 18 |
| Pittsburgh Career Institute | Pittsburgh | T | Prop | M/W | 200 | | | | | | | | | | | | | |
| Pittsburgh Institute of Aeronautics | Pittsburgh | C,T | Ind | PM | 368 | | | | | | | | | | | | | |
| Pittsburgh Institute of Mortuary Science, Incorporated | Pittsburgh | C,T | Ind | M/W | 193 | 56 | | | | | | | | | | | | |
| Pittsburgh Technical College | Oakdale | T,B | Prop | M/W | 1,835 | | 24 | | Y | Y | Y | | | Y | Y | Y | 5 | 18 |
| Thaddeus Stevens College of Technology | Lancaster | C,T | St | M/W | 1,142 | 1 | 4 | 0 | N | Y | Y | | | Y | Y | Y | 5 | 20 |
| University of Pittsburgh at Titusville | Titusville | C,T | St-R | M/W | 388 | 19 | | | | | | | | | | | | |
| Westmoreland County Community College | Youngwood | C,T | Cou | M/W | 5,554 | 58 | | | | | | | | | | | | |
| **Puerto Rico** | | | | | | | | | | | | | | | | | | |
| Humacao Community College | Humacao | T,B | Ind | M/W | 467 | 23 | 20 | | Y | | Y | Y | Y | Y | Y | N | | 14 |

This chart includes the names and locations of accredited two-year colleges in the United States, Canada, and other countries and shows institutions' responses to the *Peterson's Annual Survey of Undergraduate Institutions*. If an institution submitted incomplete data, one or more columns opposite the institution's name is blank. A dagger after the school name indicates that the institution has one or more entries in the *Featured Two-Year Colleges* section. If a school does not appear, it did not report any of the information.

Y—Yes; N—No; R—Recommended; S—For Some

| Institution | Location | Degrees Awarded | Institutional Control | Student Body | Undergrad Enrollment | % Attending Part-Time | % 25 or Older | % Grads to 4-Year | HS Equivalency Accepted | Open Admissions | HS Transcript Required | Need-Based Aid | Part-Time Jobs | Career Counseling | Job Placement Services | College Housing | Sports Offered | Majors Offered |
|---|---|---|---|---|---|---|---|---|---|---|---|---|---|---|---|---|---|---|
| **Rhode Island** | | | | | | | | | | | | | | | | | | |
| Community College of Rhode Island | Warwick | C | St | M/W | 15,101 | 71 | | | | | | | | | | | | |
| **South Carolina** | | | | | | | | | | | | | | | | | | |
| Greenville Technical College | Greenville | C,T | St | M/W | 11,745 | 59 | | | Y | Y | Y | Y | Y | Y | | Y | 8 | 36 |
| Horry-Georgetown Technical College | Conway | C,T | St-L | M/W | 7,018 | 57 | | | | | | | | | | | | |
| Northeastern Technical College | Cheraw | C,T | St-L | M/W | 976 | 54 | 43 | | Y | Y | Y | Y | Y | Y | Y | N | | 12 |
| Spartanburg Community College | Spartanburg | C,T | St | M/W | 4,715 | 54 | | | | | | | | | | | | |
| Spartanburg Methodist College | Spartanburg | C,T | I-R | M/W | 790 | 1 | 1 | | N | Y | Y | Y | Y | Y | Y | Y | 12 | 5 |
| Trident Technical College | Charleston | C,T | St-L | M/W | 13,271 | 58 | 27 | | Y | Y | S | Y | Y | Y | Y | N | | 39 |
| University of South Carolina Lancaster | Lancaster | C,T | St | M/W | 1,593 | | 13 | | Y | Y | Y | Y | Y | | | N | 4 | 4 |
| University of South Carolina Salkehatchie | Allendale | C,T | St | M/W | 1,076 | | | | | | | | | | | | | |
| University of South Carolina Union | Union | C,B | St | M/W | 905 | | 7 | 50 | N | Y | Y | Y | Y | | | N | 3 | 2 |
| Williamsburg Technical College | Kingstree | C,T | St | M/W | 732 | 73 | 25 | | Y | Y | Y | Y | Y | Y | | N | | 5 |
| **South Dakota** | | | | | | | | | | | | | | | | | | |
| Lake Area Technical Institute | Watertown | T | St | M/W | 2,055 | 26 | 12 | | Y | Y | Y | Y | Y | Y | Y | N | 6 | 28 |
| Mitchell Technical Institute | Mitchell | T | St | M/W | 1,253 | 33 | 24 | | Y | Y | Y | Y | Y | Y | Y | N | 6 | 28 |
| Sisseton-Wahpeton College | Sisseton | C,T | Fed | M/W | 175 | 27 | 21 | | Y | Y | Y | Y | Y | Y | Y | Y | 1 | 12 |
| Southeast Technical Institute | Sioux Falls | T | St | M/W | 2,244 | 36 | 30 | | N | Y | Y | Y | Y | Y | Y | Y | 3 | 52 |
| Western Dakota Technical Institute | Rapid City | T | St | M/W | 1,049 | 42 | 37 | | Y | Y | Y | Y | Y | Y | Y | N | | 23 |
| **Tennessee** | | | | | | | | | | | | | | | | | | |
| Cleveland State Community College | Cleveland | C,T | St | M/W | 3,005 | 46 | 24 | 33 | Y | Y | Y | | Y | Y | Y | N | 10 | 17 |
| Dyersburg State Community College | Dyersburg | C,T | St | M/W | 2,816 | 56 | 31 | | Y | Y | Y | Y | Y | Y | | N | 8 | 19 |
| Motlow State Community College | Tullahoma | C,T | St | M/W | 5,838 | | 16 | | Y | Y | Y | Y | Y | Y | | N | 9 | 7 |
| Nashville State Community College | Nashville | C,T | St | M/W | 8,914 | | | | | | | | | | | | | |
| North Central Institute | Clarksville | T | Prop | PM | 88 | | 73 | | Y | Y | R | Y | | | | N | | 1 |
| Northeast State Community College | Blountville | C,T | St | M/W | 6,088 | 44 | 25 | | Y | Y | Y | Y | | Y | | N | | 18 |
| Volunteer State Community College | Gallatin | C,T | St | M/W | 8,838 | 44 | 24 | | Y | Y | Y | Y | Y | Y | | N | 3 | 23 |
| Walters State Community College | Morristown | C,T | St | M/W | 6,075 | 46 | 16 | | Y | Y | Y | Y | Y | Y | | N | 5 | 20 |
| **Texas** | | | | | | | | | | | | | | | | | | |
| Alvin Community College | Alvin | C,T | St-L | M/W | 5,785 | 76 | 26 | | Y | | S | Y | Y | Y | | N | 2 | 55 |
| Amarillo College | Amarillo | C,T | St-L | M/W | | | 36 | | Y | | Y | Y | Y | Y | Y | N | 5 | 83 |
| Austin Community College District | Austin | C,T | St-L | M/W | 40,803 | | | | Y | Y | Y | Y | Y | Y | | N | 3 | 99 |
| Blinn College | Brenham | C,T | St-L | M/W | 18,747 | 44 | | | | | | | | | | | | |
| Brookhaven College | Farmers Branch | C,T | Cou | M/W | 13,284 | 83 | 40 | | Y | | Y | | | | | N | 4 | 27 |
| Cedar Valley College | Lancaster | C,T | St | M/W | 7,249 | | 43 | | Y | Y | Y | Y | Y | Y | | N | 4 | 21 |
| Central Texas College | Killeen | C,T | St-L | M/W | 15,672 | 77 | 52 | | Y | Y | Y | Y | Y | Y | | Y | 5 | 48 |
| Collin County Community College District | McKinney | C,T | St-L | M/W | 31,619 | 68 | 23 | 50 | Y | Y | S | Y | Y | Y | | N | 2 | 52 |
| Culinary Institute LeNotre | Houston | T | Prop | M/W | 320 | | | | Y | Y | Y | | | Y | Y | N | | 3 |
| Dallas Institute of Funeral Service | Dallas | C,T | Ind | M/W | 95 | | 59 | | Y | Y | Y | Y | | | | N | | 1 |
| Del Mar College | Corpus Christi | C,T | St-L | M/W | 11,833 | 77 | 44 | | Y | Y | Y | | Y | Y | | N | 10 | 102 |
| El Paso Community College | El Paso | C,T | Cou | M/W | 28,750 | 70 | 23 | | Y | | | Y | Y | Y | | N | 3 | 65 |
| Galveston College | Galveston | C,T | St-L | M/W | 2,208 | 74 | 37 | | Y | Y | S | Y | Y | Y | Y | Y | 7 | 28 |
| Hill College | Hillsboro | C,T | Dist | M/W | 4,075 | | 26 | | Y | Y | Y | Y | Y | Y | Y | Y | 5 | 62 |
| Houston Community College | Houston | C,T | St-L | M/W | 57,120 | 70 | 44 | | Y | | S | Y | Y | Y | | N | | 77 |
| KD Conservatory College of Film and Dramatic Arts | Dallas | C,T | Prop | M/W | 236 | | 44 | | Y | Y | Y | Y | | | | N | | 5 |
| Lone Star College–CyFair | Cypress | C,T | St-L | M/W | 21,636 | 69 | | | | | | | | | | | | |
| Lone Star College–Kingwood | Kingwood | C,T | St-L | M/W | 12,287 | 69 | | | | | | | | | | | | |
| Lone Star College–Montgomery | Conroe | C,T | St-L | M/W | 14,411 | 69 | | | | | | | | | | | | |
| Lone Star College–North Harris | Houston | C,T | St-L | M/W | 16,290 | 71 | | | | | | | | | | | | |
| Lone Star College–Tomball | Tomball | C,T | St-L | M/W | 9,013 | 70 | | | | | | | | | | | | |
| Lone Star College–University Park | Houston | C,T | St-L | M/W | 12,024 | 70 | | | | | | | | | | | | |
| McLennan Community College | Waco | C,T | Cou | M/W | 8,799 | | 32 | | Y | Y | Y | Y | Y | Y | Y | N | 5 | 26 |
| Mountain View College | Dallas | C,T | St-L | M/W | 9,068 | 77 | | | | | | | | | | | | |
| Navarro College | Corsicana | C,T | St-L | M/W | 8,968 | 66 | 19 | | Y | Y | Y | Y | Y | Y | Y | Y | 7 | 46 |
| North Central Texas College | Gainesville | C,T | St-L | M/W | 10,327 | 74 | 23 | 2 | Y | Y | Y | Y | Y | Y | | Y | 15 | 42 |
| Northwest Vista College | San Antonio | C,T | St-L | M/W | 13,115 | 69 | 27 | | Y | Y | Y | | | Y | | N | 4 | 19 |
| Odessa College | Odessa | C,T | St-L | M/W | 6,308 | 64 | 23 | | Y | Y | | Y | Y | Y | Y | Y | 11 | 55 |
| Panola College | Carthage | C,T | St-L | M/W | 2,646 | 50 | 8 | 15 | Y | Y | R,S | Y | Y | Y | Y | Y | 6 | 48 |
| Paris Junior College | Paris | C,T | St-L | M/W | 4,835 | 62 | 21 | | Y | Y | Y | Y | Y | Y | | Y | 7 | 62 |
| Richland College | Dallas | C,T | St-L | M/W | 19,736 | | 34 | | Y | | S | Y | Y | Y | | N | 14 | 15 |
| St. Philip's College | San Antonio | C,T | Dist | M/W | 12,050 | 87 | 35 | | Y | Y | Y | Y | Y | Y | | N | 5 | 66 |
| San Jacinto College District | Pasadena | C,T | St-L | M/W | 30,509 | 77 | 28 | 20 | Y | Y | Y | | | Y | | N | 8 | 81 |
| South Plains College | Levelland | C,T | St-L | M/W | 9,053 | 49 | | | | | | | | | | | | |
| Southwest Texas Junior College | Uvalde | C,T | St-L | M/W | | | 14 | | Y | Y | Y | Y | Y | Y | | N | 9 | 26 |
| Tarrant County College District | Fort Worth | C,T | Cou | M/W | 51,350 | 71 | 32 | | Y | | | | | | | N | 7 | 42 |
| Texarkana College | Texarkana | C,T | St-L | M/W | 4,251 | | 25 | | Y | Y | Y | Y | Y | Y | | Y | 5 | 40 |
| Texas State Technical College | Waco | C,T | St | M/W | 12,717 | 61 | 29 | | Y | Y | Y | Y | Y | Y | | Y | 7 | 38 |
| Trinity Valley Community College | Athens | C,T | St-L | M/W | 6,726 | | 28 | 19 | Y | Y | Y | Y | Y | Y | | Y | 7 | 55 |
| Tyler Junior College | Tyler | C,T,B | St-L | M/W | 11,478 | 49 | 24 | | Y | Y | Y | Y | Y | Y | | Y | 11 | 66 |
| Victoria College | Victoria | C,T | Cou | M/W | 4,000 | 74 | 37 | | Y | Y | Y | Y | Y | Y | Y | N | 3 | 10 |
| Wade College | Dallas | C,T,B | Prop | M/W | 238 | | 60 | | Y | Y | Y | | | Y | | N | | 4 |
| Weatherford College | Weatherford | C,T | St-L | M/W | 5,637 | | | | | | | | | | | | | |
| Western Texas College | Snyder | C,T | St-L | M/W | 2,250 | 74 | 11 | 32 | Y | Y | Y | Y | Y | Y | Y | Y | 12 | 34 |
| **Utah** | | | | | | | | | | | | | | | | | | |
| LDS Business College | Salt Lake City | C,T | I-R | M/W | | | | | Y | Y | | | Y | Y | | N | | 42 |
| Salt Lake Community College | Salt Lake City | C,T | St | M/W | 29,620 | 74 | 33 | | Y | | | Y | Y | Y | Y | N | 6 | 68 |

This chart includes the names and locations of accredited two-year colleges in the United States, Canada, and other countries and shows institutions' responses to the *Peterson's Annual Survey of Undergraduate Institutions*. If an institution submitted incomplete data, one or more columns opposite the institution's name is blank. A dagger after the school name indicates that the institution has one or more entries in the *Featured Two-Year Colleges* section. If a school does not appear, it did not report any of the information.

Legend: Y—Yes; N—No; R—Recommended; S—For Some

Degrees Awarded: College Transfer Associate (C); Terminal Associate (T); Bachelor's (B); Master's (M), Doctoral (D)
Institutional Control: County, District, City, State and Local; Federal; Independent; State, Commonwealth, Territory; Independent-Religious; Proprietary
Student Body: Men, Primarily Men; Women, Primarily Women; Coed

| Institution | Location | Degrees Awarded | Institutional Control | Student Body | Undergraduate Enrollment | Percent Attending Part-Time | Percent of Grads Going on to Four-Year Colleges | Percent 25 Years of Age or Older | Open Admissions | High School Equivalency Certificate Accepted | High School Transcript Accepted | Need-Based Aid Required | Part-Time Jobs Available | Career Counseling Available | Job Placement Services Available | College Housing Available | Number of Sports Offered | Number of Majors Offered |
|---|---|---|---|---|---|---|---|---|---|---|---|---|---|---|---|---|---|---|
| **Vermont** | | | | | | | | | | | | | | | | | | |
| Community College of Vermont | Montpelier | C,T | St | M/W | 6,351 | | | | | | | | | | | | | |
| New England Culinary Institute | Montpelier | C,B | Prop | M/W | 300 | 14 | | | | | | | | | | | | |
| **Virginia** | | | | | | | | | | | | | | | | | | |
| Central Virginia Community College | Lynchburg | C,T | St | M/W | 4,128 | | 22 | | Y | Y | | | Y | Y | Y | N | | 18 |
| Dabney S. Lancaster Community College | Clifton Forge | C,T | St | M/W | 1,186 | 64 | 23 | | Y | | | R | Y | Y | Y | N | 3 | 17 |
| Eastern Shore Community College | Melfa | C,T | St | M/W | 857 | | | | Y | Y | | R | Y | Y | Y | N | | 8 |
| John Tyler Community College | Chester | C,T | St | M/W | 10,380 | 76 | 24 | | Y | | | R | Y | Y | Y | N | 2 | 20 |
| J. Sargeant Reynolds Community College | Richmond | C,T | St | M/W | 9,334 | 72 | 39 | 7 | Y | Y | Y | Y | Y | Y | Y | N | | 39 |
| New River Community College | Dublin | C,T | St | M/W | 4,400 | | | | Y | | | R,S | Y | Y | Y | N | 4 | 27 |
| Patrick Henry Community College | Martinsville | C,T | St | M/W | 2,405 | 50 | | | Y | | | | | Y | Y | N | | |
| Piedmont Virginia Community College | Charlottesville | C,T | St | M/W | 5,608 | | | | Y | | | S | Y | Y | Y | N | 8 | 21 |
| Rappahannock Community College | Glenns | C,T | St-L | M/W | 3,463 | | | | Y | | | | Y | Y | Y | | 1 | 11 |
| Southwest Virginia Community College | Richlands | C,T | St | M/W | 2,304 | | 25 | 57 | Y | Y | Y | | Y | Y | Y | N | | 12 |
| Tidewater Community College | Norfolk | C,T | St | M/W | 22,776 | 45 | | | Y | | | | Y | Y | Y | N | 5 | 26 |
| Virginia Western Community College | Roanoke | C,T | St | M/W | 8,632 | 71 | | | Y | | | | Y | Y | Y | N | | 21 |
| Wytheville Community College | Wytheville | C,T | St | M/W | 2,745 | | 26 | | Y | | | | Y | Y | Y | N | | 21 |
| **Washington** | | | | | | | | | | | | | | | | | | |
| Carrington College–Spokane | Spokane | T | Prop | M/W | 407 | | | | | | | | | | | | | |
| Clark College | Vancouver | C,T,B | St | M/W | 10,477 | 52 | 34 | | | | | | Y | Y | Y | N | 8 | 30 |
| Northwest School of Wooden Boatbuilding | Port Hadlock | T | Ind | M/W | | | | | | | | | | | | | | |
| Olympic College | Bremerton | C,T,B | St | M/W | 7,253 | | | | | | | | | | | | | |
| Renton Technical College | Renton | C,T,B | St | M/W | 3,763 | 62 | 52 | | | | | S | Y | Y | Y | N | | 31 |
| **West Virginia** | | | | | | | | | | | | | | | | | | |
| Blue Ridge Community and Technical College | Martinsburg | C,T | St | M/W | 5,708 | 83 | 75 | | Y | Y | Y | | | Y | Y | N | | 25 |
| Potomac State College of West Virginia University | Keyser | C,T,B | St | M/W | 1,475 | 22 | 11 | | Y | Y | Y | Y | Y | | | Y | 10 | 54 |
| West Virginia Junior College–Bridgeport | Bridgeport | C,T | Prop | M/W | 150 | | | | | | | | | | | | | |
| **Wisconsin** | | | | | | | | | | | | | | | | | | |
| Blackhawk Technical College | Janesville | C,T | Dist | M/W | 2,034 | 60 | | | | | | | | | | | | |
| Chippewa Valley Technical College | Eau Claire | C,T | Dist | M/W | 7,134 | 70 | | | Y | | | Y | Y | Y | Y | N | | 35 |
| Fox Valley Technical College | Appleton | T | St-L | M/W | 11,658 | 81 | 44 | | Y | | | S | Y | Y | Y | N | | 54 |
| Gateway Technical College | Kenosha | T | St-L | M/W | 8,722 | 84 | 48 | | Y | | | | Y | Y | Y | | | 39 |
| Lakeshore Technical College | Cleveland | C,T | St-L | M/W | | | 54 | | Y | | | S | Y | | Y | N | | 20 |
| Madison Area Technical College | Madison | C,T | Dist | M/W | 16,537 | 70 | | | | | | | | | | | | |
| Mid-State Technical College | Wisconsin Rapids | C,T | St-L | M/W | 2,636 | 64 | 33 | | Y | | Y | | Y | Y | Y | N | 5 | 21 |
| Northcentral Technical College | Wausau | C,T | Dist | M/W | 5,167 | 74 | 44 | | Y | Y | S | Y | Y | Y | Y | Y | 5 | 37 |
| University of Wisconsin–Baraboo/Sauk County | Baraboo | C,T,B | St | M/W | 512 | | | | | Y | Y | Y | Y | Y | | N | 5 | 24 |
| University of Wisconsin–Barron County | Rice Lake | C,T,B | St | M/W | 505 | | | | | Y | Y | Y | Y | | | N | 5 | 24 |
| University of Wisconsin–Fond du Lac | Fond du Lac | C,T | St | M/W | 519 | | | | | Y | Y | Y | Y | Y | | N | 3 | 24 |
| University of Wisconsin–Fox Valley | Menasha | C,T | St | M/W | 1,364 | | 70 | | | Y | Y | Y | Y | Y | | N | 4 | 24 |
| University of Wisconsin–Manitowoc | Manitowoc | C,T | St | M/W | 354 | | | | | Y | Y | Y | Y | Y | Y | N | 3 | 24 |
| University of Wisconsin–Marathon County | Wausau | C,T | St | M/W | 838 | | | | | Y | Y | Y | Y | Y | | Y | 2 | 24 |
| University of Wisconsin–Marinette | Marinette | C,T | St | M/W | 286 | | | | | Y | Y | Y | Y | | | | 2 | 24 |
| University of Wisconsin–Marshfield/Wood County | Marshfield | C,T,B | St | M/W | 535 | | | | | Y | Y | Y | Y | | | Y | 4 | 24 |
| University of Wisconsin–Richland | Richland Center | C,T,B | St | M/W | 259 | | | | | Y | Y | Y | Y | | | Y | 4 | 24 |
| University of Wisconsin–Rock County | Janesville | C,T,B | St | M/W | 970 | | | | | Y | Y | Y | Y | | | N | 3 | 24 |
| University of Wisconsin–Sheboygan | Sheboygan | C,T | St | M/W | 602 | | | | | Y | Y | Y | Y | | | N | 3 | 24 |
| University of Wisconsin–Washington County | West Bend | C,T | St | M/W | 544 | | | | | Y | Y | Y | Y | Y | Y | N | 4 | 24 |
| University of Wisconsin–Waukesha | Waukesha | C,B | St | M/W | 1,782 | | | | | Y | Y | Y | Y | Y | | N | 5 | 24 |
| Waukesha County Technical College | Pewaukee | T | St-L | M/W | 7,696 | 80 | 50 | | Y | | | Y | Y | Y | | | | 39 |
| Wisconsin Indianhead Technical College | Shell Lake | C,T | Dist | M/W | 3,021 | 64 | 49 | | N | Y | | S | | Y | Y | N | | 23 |
| **Wyoming** | | | | | | | | | | | | | | | | | | |
| Casper College | Casper | C,T | St-L | M/W | 3,626 | 52 | | | | | | | | | | | | |
| Central Wyoming College | Riverton | C,T | St-L | M/W | 2,016 | 66 | | | | | | | | | | | | |
| Eastern Wyoming College | Torrington | C,T | St-L | M/W | 1,604 | 62 | | | | | | | | | | | | |
| Laramie County Community College | Cheyenne | C,T | Dist | M/W | 4,226 | 61 | 39 | | Y | Y | | S | Y | Y | | Y | 11 | 62 |
| Northwest College | Powell | C,T | St-L | M/W | 1,654 | 42 | 20 | | Y | Y | Y | Y | Y | Y | Y | Y | 9 | 53 |
| Western Wyoming Community College | Rock Springs | C,T | St-L | M/W | 3,390 | 68 | 36 | 8 | Y | Y | | R | Y | Y | Y | Y | 5 | 83 |
| **OTHER COUNTRIES** | | | | | | | | | | | | | | | | | | |
| **Marshall Islands** | | | | | | | | | | | | | | | | | | |
| College of the Marshall Islands | Majuro | T | St | M/W | 995 | 30 | | | | | | | | | | | | |

# Profiles
# of Two-Year
# Colleges

NOTICE: Certain portions of or information contained in this book have been submitted and paid for by the educational institution identified, and such institutions take full responsibility for the accuracy, timeliness, completeness and functionality of such content. Such portions or information include (i) each display ad in the "Profiles" section from pages 53 through 318 that comprises a half or full page of information covering a single educational institution, and (ii) each two-page description in the "Featured Two-Year Colleges" section from pages 322 through 327.

## ALABAMA

### Bevill State Community College
#### Jasper, Alabama

- **State-supported** 2-year, founded 1969, part of Alabama Community College System
- **Rural** 245-acre campus with easy access to Birmingham
- **Coed,** 3,872 undergraduate students, 41% full-time, 59% women, 41% men

**Undergraduates** 1,583 full-time, 2,289 part-time. Students come from 10 states and territories; 2% are from out of state; 15% Black or African American, non-Hispanic/Latino; 2% Hispanic/Latino; 0.3% Asian, non-Hispanic/Latino; 0.1% American Indian or Alaska Native, non-Hispanic/Latino; 1% Two or more races, non-Hispanic/Latino; 0.9% Race/ethnicity unknown; 7% transferred in. *Retention:* 59% of full-time freshmen returned.
**Freshmen** *Admission:* 820 enrolled.
**Faculty** *Total:* 283, 40% full-time, 12% with terminal degrees. *Student/faculty ratio:* 17:1.
**Majors** Administrative assistant and secretarial science; child-care and support services management; computer and information sciences; electrician; emergency medical technology (EMT paramedic); general studies; heating, ventilation, air conditioning and refrigeration engineering technology; industrial mechanics and maintenance technology; instrumentation technology; liberal arts and sciences/liberal studies; manufacturing engineering technology; registered nursing/registered nurse; tool and die technology; vehicle maintenance and repair technologies.
**Academics** *Calendar:* semesters. *Degree:* certificates and associate. *Special study options:* academic remediation for entering students, adult/continuing education programs, advanced placement credit, cooperative education, distance learning, honors programs, off-campus study, part-time degree program, services for LD students, summer session for credit.
**Library** Main Library plus 5 others. *Books:* 113,246 (physical); *Serial titles:* 3,563 (physical); *Databases:* 15. Weekly public service hours: 56.
**Student Life** *Housing Options:* coed. Campus housing is university owned. *Activities and Organizations:* drama/theater group, choral group, Student Government Association, Campus Ministries, Circle K, Outdoorsmen Club, Sigma Kappa Delta.
**Athletics** Member NJCAA.
**Costs (2018–19)** *Tuition:* state resident $3570 full-time, $121 per credit hour part-time; nonresident $7140 full-time, $242 per credit hour part-time. Full-time tuition and fees vary according to course load and program. Part-time tuition and fees vary according to course load and program. *Required fees:* $900 full-time, $29 per credit hour part-time. *Room and board:* room only: $1300. Room and board charges vary according to location. *Payment plan:* installment. *Waivers:* employees or children of employees.
**Financial Aid** Of all full-time matriculated undergraduates who enrolled in 2016, 2,711 applied for aid, 2,568 were judged to have need, 45 had their need fully met. 41 Federal Work-Study jobs (averaging $3494). In 2016, 62 non-need-based awards were made. *Average percent of need met:* 42%. *Average financial aid package:* $5291. *Average need-based gift aid:* $6235. *Average non-need-based aid:* $1937.
**Applying** *Options:* electronic application, early admission. *Required:* high school transcript. *Application deadlines:* rolling (freshmen), rolling (transfers). *Notification:* continuous (freshmen), continuous (transfers).
**Freshman Application Contact** Ms. Melissa Stowe, Dean of Students, Bevill State Community College, 1411 Indiana Avenue, Jasper, AL 35501. *Phone:* 205-387-0511 Ext. 5813. *E-mail:* melissa.stowe@bscc.edu. *Website:* http://www.bscc.edu/.

### Bishop State Community College
#### Mobile, Alabama

**Freshman Application Contact** Bishop State Community College, 351 North Broad Street, Mobile, AL 36603-5898. *Phone:* 251-405-7000. *Toll-free phone:* 800-523-7235. *Website:* http://www.bishop.edu/.

### Calhoun Community College
#### Decatur, Alabama

**Freshman Application Contact** Admissions Office, Calhoun Community College, PO Box 2216, Decatur, AL 35609-2216. *Phone:* 256-306-2593.

*Toll-free phone:* 800-626-3628. *Fax:* 256-306-2941. *E-mail:* admissions@calhoun.edu. *Website:* http://www.calhoun.edu/.

### Central Alabama Community College
#### Alexander City, Alabama

**Freshman Application Contact** Ms. Donna Whaley, Central Alabama Community College, 1675 Cherokee Road, Alexander City, AL 35011-0699. *Phone:* 256-234-6346 Ext. 6232. *Toll-free phone:* 800-634-2657. *Website:* http://www.cacc.edu/.

### Chattahoochee Valley Community College
#### Phenix City, Alabama

**Freshman Application Contact** Chattahoochee Valley Community College, 2602 College Drive, Phenix City, AL 36869-7928. *Phone:* 334-291-4929. *Website:* http://www.cv.edu/.

### Coastal Alabama Community College
#### Bay Minette, Alabama

**Freshman Application Contact** Ms. Carmelita Mikkelsen, Director of Admissions and High School Relations, Coastal Alabama Community College, 1900 Highway 31 South, Bay Minette, AL 36507. *Phone:* 251-580-2213. *Toll-free phone:* 800-381-3722. *Fax:* 251-580-2285. *E-mail:* cmikkelsen@faulknerstate.edu. *Website:* http://www.faulknerstate.edu/.

### Community College of the Air Force
#### Maxwell Gunter Air Force Base, Alabama

- **Federally supported** 2-year, founded 1972, part of Air University
- **Suburban** campus
- **Coed**

**Undergraduates** 268,763 full-time.
**Academics** *Calendar:* continuous. *Degrees:* certificates and associate (courses conducted at 125 branch locations worldwide for members of the U.S. Air Force). *Special study options:* academic remediation for entering students, adult/continuing education programs, advanced placement credit, distance learning, independent study, internships, off-campus study.
**Library** Air Force Library Service.
**Student Life** *Campus security:* 24-hour emergency response devices and patrols.
**Standardized Tests** *Required:* Armed Services Vocational Aptitude Battery (ASVAB) (for admission).
**Applying** *Options:* electronic application. *Required:* high school transcript, interview, military physical, good character, criminal background check.
**Freshman Application Contact** Ms. Gwendolyn Ford, Chief of Admissions Flight, Community College of the Air Force, 100 South Turner Boulevard, Maxwell Air Force Base, Maxwell - Gunter AFB, AL 36114-3011. *Phone:* 334-649-5081. *Fax:* 334-649-5015. *E-mail:* gwendolyn.ford@us.af.mil. *Website:* http://www.airuniversity.af.mil/Barnes/CCAF/.

### Enterprise State Community College
#### Enterprise, Alabama

**Director of Admissions** Mr. Gary Deas, Associate Dean of Students/Registrar, Enterprise State Community College, 600 Plaza Drive, Enterprise, AL 36330. *Phone:* 334-347-2623 Ext. 2233. *E-mail:* gdeas@eocc.edu. *Website:* http://www.escc.edu/.

### Fortis College
#### Mobile, Alabama

**Admissions Office Contact** Fortis College, 7033 Airport Boulevard, Mobile, AL 36608. *Toll-free phone:* 855-4-FORTIS. *Website:* http://www.fortis.edu/.

### Fortis College
#### Montgomery, Alabama

**Admissions Office Contact** Fortis College, 3470 Eastdale Circle, Montgomery, AL 36117. *Toll-free phone:* 855-4-FORTIS. *Website:* http://www.fortis.edu/.

# Fortis College
## Montgomery, Alabama

**Admissions Office Contact** Fortis College, 3736 Atlanta Highway, Montgomery, AL 36109. *Toll-free phone:* 855-4-FORTIS. *Website:* http://www.fortis.edu/.

# Fortis Institute
## Birmingham, Alabama

**Admissions Office Contact** Fortis Institute, 100 London Parkway, Suite 150, Birmingham, AL 35211. *Toll-free phone:* 855-4-FORTIS. *Website:* http://www.fortis.edu/.

# Gadsden State Community College
## Gadsden, Alabama

**Freshman Application Contact** Mrs. Jennie Dobson, Admissions and Records, Gadsden State Community College, PO Box 227, 1001 George Wallace Drive, Gadsden, AL 35902-0227. *Phone:* 256-549-8210. *Toll-free phone:* 800-226-5563. *Fax:* 256-549-8205. *E-mail:* info@gadsdenstate.edu. *Website:* http://www.gadsdenstate.edu/.

# George Corley Wallace State Community College
## Selma, Alabama

**Director of Admissions** Ms. Sunette Newman, Registrar, George Corley Wallace State Community College, PO Box 2530, Selma, AL 36702. *Phone:* 334-876-9305. *Website:* http://www.wccs.edu/.

# George C. Wallace Community College
## Dothan, Alabama

- **State-supported** 2-year, founded 1949, part of The Alabama Community College System
- **Rural** 258-acre campus
- **Coed,** 4,645 undergraduate students, 42% full-time, 65% women, 35% men

**Undergraduates** 1,929 full-time, 2,716 part-time. Students come from 7 states and territories; 0.7% are from out of state; 28% Black or African American, non-Hispanic/Latino; 3% Hispanic/Latino; 0.8% Asian, non-Hispanic/Latino; 0.1% Native Hawaiian or other Pacific Islander, non-Hispanic/Latino; 0.4% American Indian or Alaska Native, non-Hispanic/Latino; 2% Two or more races, non-Hispanic/Latino; 0.3% Race/ethnicity unknown; 7% transferred in.
**Freshmen** *Admission:* 922 enrolled.
**Faculty** *Total:* 226, 58% full-time. *Student/faculty ratio:* 17:1.
**Majors** Accounting; administrative assistant and secretarial science; autobody/collision and repair technology; automobile/automotive mechanics technology; automotive engineering technology; business administration and management; cabinetmaking and millwork; carpentry; child-care and support services management; clinical/medical laboratory technology; computer and information sciences; computer science; criminal justice/police science; drafting and design technology; electrical, electronic and communications engineering technology; electrician; emergency medical technology (EMT paramedic); general studies; heating, air conditioning, ventilation and refrigeration maintenance technology; heating, ventilation, air conditioning and refrigeration engineering technology; industrial mechanics and maintenance technology; liberal arts and sciences/liberal studies; licensed practical/vocational nurse training; machine tool technology; medical/clinical assistant; medical radiologic technology; nuclear/nuclear power technology; physical therapy technology; radiologic technology/science; registered nursing/registered nurse; respiratory care therapy; tool and die technology; welding technology.
**Academics** *Calendar:* semesters. *Degree:* certificates, diplomas, and associate. *Special study options:* academic remediation for entering students, adult/continuing education programs, advanced placement credit, cooperative education, distance learning, English as a second language, independent study, off-campus study, part-time degree program.
**Library** Learning Resources Centers. *Books:* 35,060 (physical), 659 (digital/electronic); *Serial titles:* 50 (physical), 8 (digital/electronic); *Databases:* 9.
**Student Life** *Housing:* college housing not available. *Activities and Organizations:* drama/theater group, student-run newspaper. *Campus security:* 24-hour patrols. *Student services:* personal/psychological counseling.

**Athletics** Member NJCAA. *Intercollegiate sports:* baseball M(s), softball W(s).
**Standardized Tests** *Recommended:* SAT or ACT (for admission).
**Costs (2018–19)** *Tuition:* state resident $3870 full-time, $129 per credit hour part-time; nonresident $7440 full-time, $248 per credit hour part-time. Full-time tuition and fees vary according to reciprocity agreements. Part-time tuition and fees vary according to reciprocity agreements. *Required fees:* $810 full-time, $27 per credit hour part-time. *Waivers:* senior citizens and employees or children of employees.
**Financial Aid** Of all full-time matriculated undergraduates who enrolled in 2016, 36 Federal Work-Study jobs (averaging $1391).
**Applying** *Options:* electronic application, early admission. *Required:* high school transcript. *Application deadlines:* rolling (freshmen), rolling (transfers).
**Freshman Application Contact** Mr. Keith Saulsberry, Director, Enrollment Services/Registrar, George C. Wallace Community College, 1141 Wallace Drive, Dothan, AL 36303. *Phone:* 334-983-3521 Ext. 2470. *Toll-free phone:* 800-543-2426. *Fax:* 334-983-3600. *E-mail:* ksaulsberry@wallace.edu. *Website:* http://www.wallace.edu/.

# H. Councill Trenholm State Community College
## Montgomery, Alabama

- **State-supported** 2-year, founded 1966, part of Alabama Community College System
- **Urban** 83-acre campus with easy access to Montgomery
- **Coed,** 1,845 undergraduate students
- **31%** of applicants were admitted

**Undergraduates** Students come from 2 states and territories; 68% Black or African American, non-Hispanic/Latino; 2% Hispanic/Latino; 1% Asian, non-Hispanic/Latino; 0.1% American Indian or Alaska Native, non-Hispanic/Latino; 0.2% Two or more races, non-Hispanic/Latino; 0.2% Race/ethnicity unknown; 0.1% international. *Retention:* 60% of full-time freshmen returned.
**Freshmen** *Admission:* 2,619 applied, 810 admitted.
**Faculty** *Total:* 142, 39% full-time, 11% with terminal degrees. *Student/faculty ratio:* 15:1.
**Majors** Accounting technology and bookkeeping; administrative assistant and secretarial science; automotive engineering technology; child-care and support services management; computer and information sciences; culinary arts; dental assisting; diagnostic medical sonography and ultrasound technology; drafting and design technology; electrician; emergency medical technology (EMT paramedic); general studies; graphic communications related; heating, ventilation, air conditioning and refrigeration engineering technology; industrial mechanics and maintenance technology; liberal arts and sciences/liberal studies; machine tool technology; manufacturing engineering technology; medical/clinical assistant; radiologic technology/science; respiratory care therapy.
**Academics** *Calendar:* semesters. *Degree:* certificates, diplomas, and associate. *Special study options:* academic remediation for entering students, adult/continuing education programs, advanced placement credit, cooperative education, distance learning, English as a second language, external degree program, independent study, internships, part-time degree program, services for LD students, summer session for credit.
**Library** Trenholm State Learning Resources plus 2 others. *Books:* 10,315 (physical), 36,943 (digital/electronic); *Serial titles:* 91 (physical), 59 (digital/electronic); *Databases:* 18. Weekly public service hours: 108.
**Student Life** *Housing:* college housing not available. *Activities and Organizations:* Student Government Association, Future Business Leaders of America, National Society of Leadership and Science, Phi Theta Kappa, Council of Peer Educators. *Campus security:* 24-hour patrols. *Student services:* personal/psychological counseling, veterans affairs office.
**Standardized Tests** *Required for some:* SAT or ACT (for admission).
**Costs (2017–18)** *Tuition:* state resident $2856 full-time, $119 per credit hour part-time; nonresident $5712 full-time, $238 per credit hour part-time. Full-time tuition and fees vary according to course load. Part-time tuition and fees vary according to course load. *Required fees:* $624 full-time, $26 per credit hour part-time. *Payment plan:* installment. *Waivers:* senior citizens and employees or children of employees.
**Applying** *Options:* electronic application, early admission. *Required:* high school transcript. *Application deadlines:* rolling (freshmen), rolling (transfers).
**Freshman Application Contact** Dr. Tennie McBryde, Director of Admissions/Records, H. Councill Trenholm State Community College, Montgomery, AL 36108. *Phone:* 334-420-4306. *Toll-free phone:* 866-753-4544. *Fax:* 334-420-4201. *E-mail:* tmcbryde@trenholmstate.edu. *Website:* http://www.trenholmstate.edu/.

## Jefferson State Community College
### Birmingham, Alabama

- **State-supported** 2-year, founded 1965, part of Alabama Community College System
- **Suburban** 351-acre campus with easy access to Birmingham
- **Endowment** $1.3 million
- **Coed,** 8,840 undergraduate students, 30% full-time, 61% women, 39% men

**Undergraduates** 2,647 full-time, 6,193 part-time. Students come from 30 states and territories; 52 other countries; 2% are from out of state; 25% Black or African American, non-Hispanic/Latino; 5% Hispanic/Latino; 2% Asian, non-Hispanic/Latino; 0.1% Native Hawaiian or other Pacific Islander, non-Hispanic/Latino; 0.3% American Indian or Alaska Native, non-Hispanic/Latino; 3% Two or more races, non-Hispanic/Latino; 3% international; 10% transferred in. *Retention:* 53% of full-time freshmen returned.
**Freshmen** *Admission:* 4,989 applied, 2,848 admitted, 1,716 enrolled. *Average high school GPA:* 3.0.
**Faculty** *Total:* 440, 33% full-time, 16% with terminal degrees. *Student/faculty ratio:* 19:1.
**Majors** Accounting technology and bookkeeping; administrative assistant and secretarial science; child-care and support services management; clinical/medical laboratory technology; computer and information sciences; construction engineering technology; criminal justice/police science; emergency medical technology (EMT paramedic); engineering technology; fire services administration; funeral service and mortuary science; general studies; hospitality administration; liberal arts and sciences/liberal studies; office management; physical therapy technology; radiologic technology/science; registered nursing/registered nurse; veterinary/animal health technology.
**Academics** *Calendar:* semesters. *Degree:* certificates and associate. *Special study options:* academic remediation for entering students, adult/continuing education programs, advanced placement credit, distance learning, English as a second language, honors programs, independent study, internships, part-time degree program, services for LD students, summer session for credit. *ROTC:* Army (c), Air Force (c).
**Library** Jefferson State Libraries plus 4 others. *Books:* 63,660 (physical), 193,910 (digital/electronic); *Serial titles:* 234 (physical), 296,861 (digital/electronic); *Databases:* 52. Weekly public service hours: 62.
**Student Life** *Housing:* college housing not available. *Activities and Organizations:* choral group, Student Government Association, Phi Theta Kappa, Sigma Kappa Delta, Jefferson State Ambassadors, Enactus. *Campus security:* 24-hour patrols. *Student services:* veterans affairs office.
**Athletics** Member NJCAA.
**Costs (2017–18)** *Tuition:* state resident $4500 full-time, $150 per semester hour part-time; nonresident $8070 full-time, $269 per semester hour part-time. Full-time tuition and fees vary according to course load. Part-time tuition and fees vary according to course load. *Waivers:* senior citizens and employees or children of employees.
**Applying** *Options:* electronic application, early admission, deferred entrance. *Required for some:* high school transcript. *Application deadlines:* rolling (freshmen), rolling (transfers). *Notification:* continuous (freshmen), continuous (transfers).
**Freshman Application Contact** Mrs. Lillian Owens, Director of Admissions and Retention, Jefferson State Community College, 2601 Carson Road, Birmingham, AL 35215-3098. *Phone:* 205-853-1200 Ext. 7990. *Toll-free phone:* 800-239-5900. *Fax:* 205-856-6070. *E-mail:* lowens@jeffstateonline.com.
*Website:* http://www.jeffersonstate.edu/.

## J. F. Drake State Community and Technical College
### Huntsville, Alabama

**Freshman Application Contact** Mrs. Kristin Treadway, Assistant Director of Admissions, J. F. Drake State Community and Technical College, Huntsville, AL 35811. *Phone:* 256-551-3111. *Toll-free phone:* 888-413-7253. *E-mail:* kristin.treadway@drakestate.edu. *Website:* http://www.drakestate.edu/.

## J. F. Ingram State Technical College
### Deatsville, Alabama

**Admissions Office Contact** J. F. Ingram State Technical College, 5375 Ingram Rd, Deatsville, AL 36022. *Website:* http://www.istc.edu/.

## Lawson State Community College
### Birmingham, Alabama

**Freshman Application Contact** Mr. Jeff Shelley, Director of Admissions and Records, Lawson State Community College, 3060 Wilson Road, SW, Birmingham, AL 35221-1798. *Phone:* 205-929-6361. *Fax:* 205-923-7106. *E-mail:* jshelley@lawsonstate.edu. *Website:* http://www.lawsonstate.edu/.

## Lurleen B. Wallace Community College
### Andalusia, Alabama

- **State-supported** 2-year, founded 2003, part of Alabama Community College System
- **Small-town** 200-acre campus
- **Coed,** 1,838 undergraduate students, 52% full-time, 57% women, 43% men

**Undergraduates** 957 full-time, 881 part-time. Students come from 10 states and territories; 9 other countries; 4% are from out of state; 21% Black or African American, non-Hispanic/Latino; 2% Hispanic/Latino; 0.4% Asian, non-Hispanic/Latino; 0.1% Native Hawaiian or other Pacific Islander, non-Hispanic/Latino; 0.8% American Indian or Alaska Native, non-Hispanic/Latino; 2% Two or more races, non-Hispanic/Latino; 0.3% Race/ethnicity unknown; 0.2% international.
**Freshmen** *Admission:* 465 enrolled.
**Faculty** *Total:* 103, 57% full-time, 6% with terminal degrees. *Student/faculty ratio:* 17:1.
**Majors** Administrative assistant and secretarial science; child-care and support services management; computer and information sciences; diagnostic medical sonography and ultrasound technology; diesel mechanics technology; emergency medical technology (EMT paramedic); forest technology; general studies; industrial electronics technology; liberal arts and sciences/liberal studies; registered nursing/registered nurse.
**Academics** *Calendar:* semesters. *Degree:* certificates and associate. *Special study options:* academic remediation for entering students, cooperative education, distance learning, honors programs, independent study, part-time degree program, summer session for credit.
**Library** Lurleen B. Wallace Library plus 3 others. Students can reserve study rooms.
**Student Life** *Housing:* college housing not available. *Activities and Organizations:* drama/theater group, choral group, Student Government Association, Student Ambassadors, Campus Civitan, Christian Student Ministries, Saints Angels. *Campus security:* security cameras. *Student services:* personal/psychological counseling.
**Athletics** Member NJCAA. *Intercollegiate sports:* baseball M(s), basketball M(s)/W(s), softball W(s).
**Costs (2017–18)** *Tuition:* state resident $3570 full-time, $119 per credit hour part-time; nonresident $7140 full-time, $238 per credit hour part-time. Full-time tuition and fees vary according to course load. Part-time tuition and fees vary according to course load. *Required fees:* $870 full-time, $29 per credit hour part-time. *Payment plan:* installment. *Waivers:* senior citizens and employees or children of employees.
**Financial Aid** Of all full-time matriculated undergraduates who enrolled in 2016, 86 Federal Work-Study jobs (averaging $903).
**Applying** *Options:* electronic application. *Required:* high school transcript. *Application deadlines:* rolling (freshmen), rolling (transfers).
**Freshman Application Contact** Lurleen B. Wallace Community College, PO Box 1418, Andalusia, AL 36420-1418. *Phone:* 334-881-2273. *Website:* http://www.lbwcc.edu/.

## Marion Military Institute
### Marion, Alabama

- **State-supported** 2-year, founded 1842, part of Alabama Community College System
- **Rural** 130-acre campus with easy access to Birmingham
- **Coed,** 446 undergraduate students, 99% full-time, 23% women, 77% men

**Undergraduates** 442 full-time, 4 part-time. Students come from 45 states and territories; 51% are from out of state; 17% Black or African American, non-Hispanic/Latino; 6% Hispanic/Latino; 3% Asian, non-Hispanic/Latino; 0.7% Native Hawaiian or other Pacific Islander, non-Hispanic/Latino; 1% American Indian or Alaska Native, non-Hispanic/Latino; 6% Two or more races, non-Hispanic/Latino; 4% transferred in; 100% live on campus. *Retention:* 40% of full-time freshmen returned.
**Freshmen** *Admission:* 1,065 applied, 595 admitted, 281 enrolled.
**Faculty** *Total:* 28, 71% full-time. *Student/faculty ratio:* 16:1.
**Majors** General studies; liberal arts and sciences/liberal studies.
**Academics** *Calendar:* semesters. *Degree:* associate. *Special study options:* academic remediation for entering students, English as a second language,

honors programs, services for LD students, study abroad. *ROTC:* Army (b), Air Force (c).

**Library** Baer Memorial Library. Weekly public service hours: 65; study areas open 24 hours, 5&-7 days a week.

**Student Life** *Housing:* on-campus residence required through sophomore year. *Options:* coed. Campus housing is university owned. *Activities and Organizations:* drama/theater group, choral group, marching band, Honor Guard, White Knights Precision Drill Team, Swamp Fox, Marching Band, Scabbard and Blade. *Campus security:* 24-hour patrols. *Student services:* health clinic, personal/psychological counseling, veterans affairs office.

**Athletics** Member NJCAA. *Intercollegiate sports:* baseball M(s), basketball M(s), cross-country running M(s)/W(s), golf M(s)/W(s), softball W(s), tennis M(s)/W(s). *Intramural sports:* basketball M/W, football M/W, riflery M/W, soccer M/W, softball M/W, table tennis M/W, ultimate Frisbee M/W, volleyball M/W, water polo M/W.

**Standardized Tests** *Required:* SAT or ACT (for admission).

**Costs (2018–19)** *One-time required fee:* $2470. *Tuition:* state resident $6000 full-time; nonresident $12,000 full-time. Full-time tuition and fees vary according to course load. *Required fees:* $948 full-time. *Room and board:* $4950. *Waivers:* employees or children of employees.

**Financial Aid** Of all full-time matriculated undergraduates who enrolled in 2016, 29 Federal Work-Study jobs (averaging $210).

**Applying** *Options:* electronic application, deferred entrance. *Application fee:* $30. *Required:* high school transcript, minimum 2.0 GPA. *Application deadlines:* rolling (freshmen), rolling (transfers). *Notification:* continuous (freshmen), continuous (transfers).

**Freshman Application Contact** Mrs. Brittany Crawford, Director of Admissions, Marion Military Institute, 1101 Washington Street, Marion, AL 36756. *Phone:* 800-664-1842. *Toll-free phone:* 800-664-1842. *Fax:* 334-683-2383. *E-mail:* bcrawford@marionmilitary.edu.
*Website:* http://www.marionmilitary.edu/.

# Northeast Alabama Community College
## Rainsville, Alabama

**Freshman Application Contact** Northeast Alabama Community College, PO Box 159, Rainsville, AL 35986-0159. *Phone:* 256-228-6001 Ext. 2325. *Website:* http://www.nacc.edu/.

# Northwest-Shoals Community College
## Muscle Shoals, Alabama

- **State-supported** 2-year, founded 1963, part of Alabama Community College System
- **Small-town** 210-acre campus
- **Endowment** $733,034
- **Coed,** 3,440 undergraduate students, 42% full-time, 59% women, 41% men

**Undergraduates** 1,436 full-time, 2,004 part-time. Students come from 3 states and territories; 2 other countries; 8% Black or African American, non-Hispanic/Latino; 6% Hispanic/Latino; 0.5% Asian, non-Hispanic/Latino; 0.9% American Indian or Alaska Native, non-Hispanic/Latino; 0.2% Two or more races, non-Hispanic/Latino; 2% Race/ethnicity unknown; 1% international; 3% transferred in.

**Freshmen** *Admission:* 1,833 applied, 1,833 admitted, 813 enrolled.

**Faculty** *Total:* 157, 46% full-time, 3% with terminal degrees. *Student/faculty ratio:* 20:1.

**Majors** Accounting technology and bookkeeping; administrative assistant and secretarial science; child-care and support services management; child development; computer and information sciences; criminal justice/police science; drafting and design technology; emergency medical technology (EMT paramedic); environmental engineering technology; general studies; industrial electronics technology; industrial mechanics and maintenance technology; liberal arts and sciences/liberal studies; medical/clinical assistant; multi/interdisciplinary studies related; registered nursing/registered nurse; salon/beauty salon management.

**Academics** *Calendar:* semesters. *Degree:* certificates and associate. *Special study options:* academic remediation for entering students, accelerated degree program, adult/continuing education programs, advanced placement credit, cooperative education, distance learning, double majors, honors programs, independent study, internships, off-campus study, part-time degree program, services for LD students, summer session for credit.

**Library** Larry W. McCoy Learning Resource Center. *Books:* 65,800 (physical), 27,000 (digital/electronic); *Databases:* 2. Weekly public service hours: 62.

**Student Life** *Housing:* college housing not available. *Activities and Organizations:* choral group, Student Government Association, Science Club, Phi Theta Kappa, Baptist Campus Ministry, Northwest-Shoals Singers. *Campus security:* 24-hour emergency response devices.

**Costs (2017–18)** *Tuition:* state resident $3570 full-time, $119 per credit hour part-time; nonresident $7080 full-time, $236 per credit hour part-time. Full-time tuition and fees vary according to course load. Part-time tuition and fees vary according to course load. *Required fees:* $841 full-time, $27 per credit hour part-time. *Waivers:* senior citizens and employees or children of employees.

**Financial Aid** Of all full-time matriculated undergraduates who enrolled in 2016, 21 Federal Work-Study jobs (averaging $1650). *Financial aid deadline:* 6/1.

**Applying** *Options:* electronic application. *Required:* high school transcript. *Application deadlines:* rolling (freshmen), rolling (transfers). *Notification:* continuous (transfers).

**Freshman Application Contact** Mr. Tom Carter, Assistant Dean of Recruitment, Admissions and Financial Aid, Northwest-Shoals Community College, PO Box 2545, Muscle Shoals, AL 35662. *Phone:* 256-331-5263. *Fax:* 256-331-5366. *E-mail:* tom.carter@nwscc.edu.
*Website:* http://www.nwscc.edu/.

# Reid State Technical College
## Evergreen, Alabama

- **State-supported** 2-year, founded 1966, part of Alabama Community College System
- **Rural** 26-acre campus
- **Coed,** 392 undergraduate students, 46% full-time, 56% women, 44% men

**Undergraduates** 181 full-time, 211 part-time. Students come from 3 states and territories; 1% are from out of state; 49% Black or African American, non-Hispanic/Latino; 0.8% Hispanic/Latino; 0.3% Native Hawaiian or other Pacific Islander, non-Hispanic/Latino; 0.3% American Indian or Alaska Native, non-Hispanic/Latino; 1% Two or more races, non-Hispanic/Latino.

**Freshmen** *Admission:* 59 applied, 59 admitted, 59 enrolled.

**Faculty** *Total:* 31, 61% full-time, 6% with terminal degrees. *Student/faculty ratio:* 12:1.

**Majors** Administrative assistant and secretarial science; electrical, electronic and communications engineering technology.

**Academics** *Calendar:* semesters. *Degree:* certificates and associate. *Special study options:* academic remediation for entering students, adult/continuing education programs, double majors, independent study, internships, part-time degree program, services for LD students, summer session for credit.

**Library** Edith A. Gray Library. *Books:* 6,392 (physical), 150,480 (digital/electronic); *Databases:* 2.

**Student Life** *Housing:* college housing not available. *Activities and Organizations:* Student Government Association, National Vocational-Technical Society, Who's Who. *Campus security:* 24-hour emergency response devices, day and evening security guard. *Student services:* personal/psychological counseling, veterans affairs office.

**Costs (2018–19)** *Tuition:* state resident $4356 full-time, $121 per credit hour part-time; nonresident $8712 full-time, $242 per credit hour part-time. Full-time tuition and fees vary according to course load and program. Part-time tuition and fees vary according to course load and program. *Required fees:* $1080 full-time, $30 per credit hour part-time. *Waivers:* senior citizens and employees or children of employees.

**Financial Aid** Of all full-time matriculated undergraduates who enrolled in 2016, 35 Federal Work-Study jobs (averaging $1500).

**Applying** *Options:* electronic application, early admission. *Required:* high school transcript. *Application deadlines:* rolling (freshmen), rolling (transfers).

**Freshman Application Contact** Ms. Mandy Godwin, Assistant to the Registrar, Reid State Technical College, Evergreen, AL 36401-0588. *Phone:* 251-578-1313 Ext. 148. *E-mail:* mwilson@rstc.edu.
*Website:* http://www.rstc.edu/.

# Remington College–Mobile Campus
## Mobile, Alabama

**Freshman Application Contact** Remington College–Mobile Campus, 828 Downtowner Loop West, Mobile, AL 36609. *Phone:* 251-343-8200. *Toll-free phone:* 800-323-8122. *Website:* http://www.remingtoncollege.edu/.

# Shelton State Community College
## Tuscaloosa, Alabama

**Freshman Application Contact** Ms. Sharon Chastine, Secretary to the Associate Dean of Student Services Enrollment, Shelton State Community College, 9500 Old Greensboro Road, Tuscaloosa, AL 35405. *Phone:* 205-391-2309. *Fax:* 205-391-3910. *E-mail:* schastine@sheltonstate.edu. *Website:* http://www.sheltonstate.edu/.

## Snead State Community College
Boaz, Alabama

- **State-supported** 2-year, founded 1898, part of Alabama College System
- **Small-town** 42-acre campus with easy access to Birmingham
- **Endowment** $2.6 million
- **Coed**

**Undergraduates** 1,538 full-time, 623 part-time. Students come from 11 states and territories; 1% are from out of state; 6% Black or African American, non-Hispanic/Latino; 11% Hispanic/Latino; 0.8% Asian, non-Hispanic/Latino; 0.2% Native Hawaiian or other Pacific Islander, non-Hispanic/Latino; 3% American Indian or Alaska Native, non-Hispanic/Latino; 0.6% Race/ethnicity unknown; 35% transferred in. *Retention:* 61% of full-time freshmen returned.
**Faculty** *Student/faculty ratio:* 23:1.
**Academics** *Calendar:* semesters. *Degree:* certificates and associate. *Special study options:* academic remediation for entering students, accelerated degree program, adult/continuing education programs, advanced placement credit, distance learning, independent study, internships, part-time degree program, services for LD students, student-designed majors, summer session for credit.
**Library** Learning Resource Center. *Books:* 6,430 (physical), 99,766 (digital/electronic); *Serial titles:* 15 (physical); *Databases:* 57.
**Student Life** *Campus security:* 24-hour patrols.
**Athletics** Member NJCAA.
**Financial Aid** Of all full-time matriculated undergraduates who enrolled in 2016, 45 Federal Work-Study jobs.
**Applying** *Options:* electronic application, early admission, deferred entrance. *Required:* high school transcript. *Required for some:* interview.
**Freshman Application Contact** Mr. Jason Cannon, Vice President Student Services, Snead State Community College, PO Box 734, Boaz, AL 35957-0734. *Phone:* 256-840-4150. *Fax:* 256-593-7180. *E-mail:* jcannon@snead.edu. *Website:* http://www.snead.edu/.

## Southern Union State Community College
Wadley, Alabama

**Freshman Application Contact** Admissions Office, Southern Union State Community College, PO Box 1000, Roberts Street, Wadley, AL 36276. *Phone:* 256-395-5157. *E-mail:* info@suscc.edu. *Website:* http://www.suscc.edu/.

## Virginia College in Huntsville
Huntsville, Alabama

**Freshman Application Contact** Director of Admission, Virginia College in Huntsville, 2021 Drake Avenue SW, Huntsville, AL 35801. *Phone:* 256-533-7387. *Fax:* 256-533-7785. *Website:* http://www.vc.edu/.

## Virginia College in Mobile
Mobile, Alabama

**Admissions Office Contact** Virginia College in Mobile, 3725 Airport Boulevard, Suite 165, Mobile, AL 36608. *Website:* http://www.vc.edu/.

## Virginia College in Montgomery
Montgomery, Alabama

**Admissions Office Contact** Virginia College in Montgomery, 6200 Atlanta Highway, Montgomery, AL 36117-2800. *Website:* http://www.vc.edu/.

## Wallace State Community College
Hanceville, Alabama

**Director of Admissions** Ms. Jennifer Hill, Director of Admissions, Wallace State Community College, PO Box 2000, 801 Main Street, Hanceville, AL 35077-2000. *Phone:* 256-352-8278. *Toll-free phone:* 866-350-9722. *Website:* http://www.wallacestate.edu/.

# ALASKA

## Alaska Career College
Anchorage, Alaska

**Freshman Application Contact** Alaska Career College, 1415 East Tudor Road, Anchorage, AK 99507. *Website:* http://www.alaskacareercollege.edu/.

## Alaska Christian College
Soldotna, Alaska

**Admissions Office Contact** Alaska Christian College, 35109 Royal Place, Soldotna, AK 99669. *Website:* http://www.alaskacc.edu/.

## Charter College
Anchorage, Alaska

**Director of Admissions** Ms. Lily Sirianni, Vice President, Charter College, 2221 East Northern Lights Boulevard, Suite 120, Anchorage, AK 99508. *Phone:* 907-277-1000. *Toll-free phone:* 888-200-9942. *Website:* http://www.chartercollege.edu/.

## Ilisagvik College
Barrow, Alaska

**Freshman Application Contact** Tennessee Judkins, Recruiter, Ilisagvik College, PO Box 749, Barrow, AK 99723. *Phone:* 907-852-1772. *Toll-free phone:* 800-478-7337. *Fax:* 907-852-1789. *E-mail:* tennessee.judkins@ilisagvik.edu. *Website:* http://www.ilisagvik.edu/.

## University of Alaska Anchorage, Kenai Peninsula College
Soldotna, Alaska

**Freshman Application Contact** Mrs. Julie Cotterell, Admission and Student Records Coordinator, University of Alaska Anchorage, Kenai Peninsula College, 156 College Road, Soldotna, AK 99669-9798. *Phone:* 907-262-0311. *Toll-free phone:* 877-262-0330. *E-mail:* jmcotterell@kpc.alaska.edu. *Website:* http://www.kpc.alaska.edu/.

## University of Alaska Anchorage, Kodiak College
Kodiak, Alaska

**Freshman Application Contact** University of Alaska Anchorage, Kodiak College, 117 Benny Benson Drive, Kodiak, AK 99615-6643. *Phone:* 907-486-1235. *Toll-free phone:* 800-486-7660. *Website:* http://www.koc.alaska.edu/.

## University of Alaska Anchorage, Matanuska-Susitna College
Palmer, Alaska

**Freshman Application Contact** Ms. Sandra Gravley, Student Services Director, University of Alaska Anchorage, Matanuska-Susitna College, PO Box 2889, Palmer, AK 99645-2889. *Phone:* 907-745-9712. *Fax:* 907-745-9747. *E-mail:* info@matsu.alaska.edu. *Website:* http://www.matsu.alaska.edu/.

## University of Alaska, Prince William Sound College
Valdez, Alaska

**Freshman Application Contact** Dr. Denise Runge, Academic Affairs, University of Alaska, Prince William Sound College, PO Box 97, Valdez, AK 99686-0097. *Phone:* 907-834-1600. *Toll-free phone:* 800-478-8800. *Fax:* 907-834-1691. *E-mail:* drunge@pwscc.edu. *Website:* http://www.pwsc.alaska.edu/.

# University of Alaska Southeast, Ketchikan Campus

## Ketchikan, Alaska

**Freshman Application Contact** Admissions Office, University of Alaska Southeast, Ketchikan Campus, 2600 7th Avenue, Ketchikan, AK 99901-5798. *Phone:* 907-225-6177. *Toll-free phone:* 888-550-6177. *Fax:* 907-225-3895. *E-mail:* ketch.info@uas.alaska.edu. *Website:* http://www.ketch.alaska.edu/.

# University of Alaska Southeast, Sitka Campus

## Sitka, Alaska

**Freshman Application Contact** Ms. Teal Gordon, Admissions Representative, University of Alaska Southeast, Sitka Campus, UAS Sitka, 1332 Seward Avenue, Sitka, AK 99835. *Phone:* 907-747-7726. *Toll-free phone:* 800-478-6653. *Fax:* 907-747-7731. *E-mail:* ktgordon@uas.alaska.edu. *Website:* http://www.uas.alaska.edu/.

# AMERICAN SAMOA

# American Samoa Community College

## Pago Pago, American Samoa

- **Territory-supported** primarily 2-year, founded 1969
- **Rural** 20-acre campus
- **Endowment** $3.1 million
- **Coed,** 1,095 undergraduate students, 56% full-time, 66% women, 34% men

**Undergraduates** 615 full-time, 480 part-time. Students come from 3 other countries; 0.8% Asian, non-Hispanic/Latino; 90% Native Hawaiian or other Pacific Islander, non-Hispanic/Latino; 9% international; 0.5% transferred in. *Retention:* 100% of full-time freshmen returned.
**Freshmen** *Admission:* 407 applied, 407 admitted, 382 enrolled.
**Faculty** *Total:* 87, 69% full-time, 8% with terminal degrees. *Student/faculty ratio:* 20:1.
**Majors** Accounting; agribusiness; agricultural business and management; agriculture; architectural drafting and CAD/CADD; art; autobody/collision and repair technology; automobile/automotive mechanics technology; automotive engineering technology; business administration and management; carpentry; civil engineering; computer technology/computer systems technology; construction trades; criminal justice/safety; education; electrical and electronic engineering technologies related; electrical, electronic and communications engineering technology; electrical, electronics and communications engineering related; elementary education; family and consumer economics related; forensic science and technology; health services/allied health/health sciences; human services; liberal arts and sciences/liberal studies; marine science/merchant marine officer; marine sciences; music; natural resources/conservation; nursing education; office occupations and clerical services; political science and government; practical nursing, vocational nursing and nursing assistants related; pre-law studies; public health/community nursing; welding technology.
**Academics** *Calendar:* semesters. *Degrees:* certificates, associate, and bachelor's. *Special study options:* academic remediation for entering students, adult/continuing education programs, cooperative education, double majors, independent study, internships, part-time degree program, services for LD students, summer session for credit. *ROTC:* Army (b).
**Library** ASCC Learning Resource Center/Library plus 1 other. *Books:* 33,000 (physical); *Serial titles:* 330 (physical). Weekly public service hours: 43.
**Student Life** *Housing:* college housing not available. *Activities and Organizations:* student-run newspaper, Student Government Association, Phi Theta Kappa, ASCC Research Foundation Student Club, Fa'aSamoa (Samoan culture) Club, Journalism Club. *Campus security:* 24-hour emergency response devices and patrols. *Student services:* health clinic, personal/psychological counseling, legal services, veterans affairs office.
**Athletics** *Intramural sports:* basketball M/W, football M/W, golf M/W, rugby M, soccer M, tennis M/W, track and field M/W, volleyball M/W.
**Standardized Tests** *Recommended:* SAT and SAT Subject Tests or ACT (for admission).
**Costs (2018–19)** *Tuition:* territory resident $3300 full-time, $110 per credit part-time; nonresident $3600 full-time, $120 per credit part-time. Full-time tuition and fees vary according to course level, course load, and degree level. Part-time tuition and fees vary according to course level, course load, and degree level. *Required fees:* $150 per term part-time. *Payment plan:* installment. *Waivers:* employees or children of employees.

**Financial Aid** Of all full-time matriculated undergraduates who enrolled in 2016, 499 applied for aid, 499 were judged to have need.
**Applying** *Options:* electronic application, early admission, deferred entrance. *Application deadline:* rolling (freshmen). *Notification:* continuous (freshmen).
**Freshman Application Contact** Elizabeth Leuma, Admissions Officer, American Samoa Community College, PO Box 2609, Pago Pago 96799, American Samoa. *Phone:* 684-699-9155 Ext. 411. *Fax:* 684-699-1083. *Website:* http://www.amsamoa.edu/.

# ARIZONA

# Arizona College

## Glendale, Arizona

**Freshman Application Contact** Admissions Department, Arizona College, 4425 West Olive Avenue, Suite 300, Glendale, AZ 85302-3843. *Phone:* 602-222-9300. *E-mail:* lhicks@arizonacollege.edu. *Website:* http://www.arizonacollege.edu/.

# Arizona Western College

## Yuma, Arizona

- **State and locally supported** 2-year, founded 1962, part of Arizona State Community College System
- **Rural** 640-acre campus
- **Coed,** 7,557 undergraduate students, 29% full-time, 58% women, 42% men

**Undergraduates** 2,221 full-time, 5,336 part-time. Students come from 32 states and territories; 29 other countries; 3% are from out of state; 2% Black or African American, non-Hispanic/Latino; 72% Hispanic/Latino; 0.9% Asian, non-Hispanic/Latino; 0.4% Native Hawaiian or other Pacific Islander, non-Hispanic/Latino; 1% American Indian or Alaska Native, non-Hispanic/Latino; 2% Two or more races, non-Hispanic/Latino; 4% Race/ethnicity unknown; 2% international; 6% live on campus.
**Freshmen** *Admission:* 1,710 enrolled.
**Faculty** *Total:* 378, 33% full-time, 11% with terminal degrees. *Student/faculty ratio:* 19:1.
**Majors** Accounting; agricultural business and management; agriculture; American Indian/Native American studies; architectural technology; automobile/automotive mechanics technology; automotive engineering technology; biology/biological sciences; business administration and management; CAD/CADD drafting/design technology; carpentry; chemistry; civil engineering technology; communication; community health and preventive medicine; computer and information sciences; computer graphics; construction engineering technology; construction management; criminal justice/law enforcement administration; crop production; culinary arts; data entry/microcomputer applications; dramatic/theater arts; early childhood education; electrical, electronic and communications engineering technology; elementary education; emergency medical technology (EMT paramedic); engineering; English; environmental science; family and consumer sciences/human sciences; fine/studio arts; fire science/firefighting; general studies; geology/earth science; health and physical education/fitness; heating, air conditioning, ventilation and refrigeration maintenance technology; heating, ventilation, air conditioning and refrigeration engineering technology; history; homeland security; hospitality administration; industrial technology; law enforcement investigation and interviewing; legal assistant/paralegal; logistics, materials, and supply chain management; manufacturing engineering technology; massage therapy; mathematics; music; parks, recreation and leisure facilities management; philosophy; physics; plant sciences; plumbing technology; political science and government; prenursing studies; psychology; radio and television broadcasting technology; radiologic technology/science; registered nursing/registered nurse; restaurant, culinary, and catering management; secondary education; social sciences; sociology; solar energy technology; Spanish; sport and fitness administration/management; water quality and wastewater treatment management and recycling technology; welding engineering technology.
**Academics** *Calendar:* semesters. *Degree:* certificates and associate. *Special study options:* academic remediation for entering students, adult/continuing education programs, advanced placement credit, cooperative education, distance learning, English as a second language, honors programs, independent study, part-time degree program, services for LD students, summer session for credit.
**Library** Arizona Western College and NAU-Yuma Library. *Books:* 58,607 (physical), 207,815 (digital/electronic); *Serial titles:* 406 (physical), 13,815 (digital/electronic); *Databases:* 49. Weekly public service hours: 68; students can reserve study rooms.

**Student Life** *Housing Options:* coed, men-only, women-only. Campus housing is university owned. *Activities and Organizations:* drama/theater group, student-run newspaper, radio and television station, choral group, Student Government Association, Spirit Squad, Dance Team, Matador Ambassadors, Presidential Leadership Society. *Campus security:* 24-hour emergency response devices and patrols, student patrols, late-night transport/escort service, controlled dormitory access. *Student services:* health clinic, personal/psychological counseling, veterans affairs office.

**Athletics** Member NJCAA. *Intercollegiate sports:* baseball M(s), basketball M(s)/W(s), football M(s), soccer M(s)/W(s), softball W(s), volleyball W(s). *Intramural sports:* cheerleading M(c)/W(c).

**Standardized Tests** *Required for some:* SAT or ACT (for admission).

**Costs (2018–19)** *Tuition:* state resident $2520 full-time, $84 per credit part-time; nonresident $9510 full-time, $317 per credit part-time. Full-time tuition and fees vary according to course load, program, and reciprocity agreements. Part-time tuition and fees vary according to course load, program, and reciprocity agreements. *Room and board:* $6570; room only: $2240. Room and board charges vary according to board plan and housing facility. *Payment plan:* installment. *Waivers:* senior citizens and employees or children of employees.

**Financial Aid** Of all full-time matriculated undergraduates who enrolled in 2016, 350 Federal Work-Study jobs (averaging $1500). 100 state and other part-time jobs (averaging $1800).

**Applying** *Options:* electronic application, early admission, deferred entrance. *Application deadlines:* rolling (freshmen), rolling (transfers).

**Freshman Application Contact** Nicole D. Harral, Director of Admissions/Registrar, Arizona Western College, PO Box 929, Yuma, AZ 85366. *Phone:* 928-344-7600. *Toll-free phone:* 888-293-0392. *Fax:* 928-344-7543. *E-mail:* nicole.harral@azwestern.edu. *Website:* http://www.azwestern.edu/.

## Carrington College–Mesa
### Mesa, Arizona

- **Proprietary** 2-year, founded 1977, part of Carrington Colleges Group, Inc.
- **Suburban** campus
- **Coed**

**Undergraduates** 565 full-time, 34 part-time. 2% are from out of state; 14% transferred in.

**Faculty** *Student/faculty ratio:* 41:1.

**Academics** *Degree:* certificates and associate.

**Costs (2017–18)** *Tuition:* $14,508 per degree program part-time. Full-time tuition and fees vary according to program. Part-time tuition and fees vary according to program.

**Applying** *Required:* essay or personal statement, high school transcript, interview.

**Freshman Application Contact** Carrington College–Mesa, 1001 West Southern Avenue, Suite 130, Mesa, AZ 85210. *Website:* http://www.carrington.edu/.

## Carrington College–Phoenix East
### Phoenix, Arizona

- **Proprietary** 2-year, part of Carrington Colleges Group, Inc.
- **Urban** campus
- **Coed**

**Undergraduates** 178 full-time, 83 part-time. 1% are from out of state; 8% Black or African American, non-Hispanic/Latino; 37% Hispanic/Latino; 6% Asian, non-Hispanic/Latino; 0.4% Native Hawaiian or other Pacific Islander, non-Hispanic/Latino; 3% American Indian or Alaska Native, non-Hispanic/Latino; 2% Two or more races, non-Hispanic/Latino; 6% Race/ethnicity unknown; 19% transferred in.

**Faculty** *Student/faculty ratio:* 8:1.

**Academics** *Degree:* certificates and associate.

**Costs (2017–18)** *Tuition:* $49,055 per degree program part-time. Full-time tuition and fees vary according to program. Part-time tuition and fees vary according to program.

**Applying** *Required:* essay or personal statement, high school transcript, interview.

**Freshman Application Contact** Carrington College–Phoenix East, 2149 West Dunlap Avenue, Suite 100, Phoenix, AZ 85021. *Website:* http://www.carrington.edu/.

## Carrington College–Phoenix North
### Phoenix, Arizona

- **Proprietary** 2-year, founded 1976, part of Carrington Colleges Group, Inc.
- **Urban** campus
- **Coed**

**Undergraduates** 653 full-time. 3% are from out of state; 7% Black or African American, non-Hispanic/Latino; 57% Hispanic/Latino; 0.9% Asian, non-Hispanic/Latino; 0.6% Native Hawaiian or other Pacific Islander, non-Hispanic/Latino; 7% American Indian or Alaska Native, non-Hispanic/Latino; 1% Two or more races, non-Hispanic/Latino; 2% Race/ethnicity unknown; 15% transferred in.

**Faculty** *Student/faculty ratio:* 35:1.

**Academics** *Degree:* certificates and associate.

**Costs (2017–18)** *Tuition:* $14,508 per degree program part-time. Full-time tuition and fees vary according to program. Part-time tuition and fees vary according to program.

**Applying** *Required:* essay or personal statement, high school transcript, interview.

**Freshman Application Contact** Carrington College–Phoenix North, 8503 North 27th Avenue, Phoenix, AZ 85051. *Website:* http://www.carrington.edu/.

## Central Arizona College
### Coolidge, Arizona

**Freshman Application Contact** Dr. James Moore, Dean of Records and Admissions, Central Arizona College, 8470 North Overfield Road, Coolidge, AZ 85128. *Phone:* 520-494-5261. *Toll-free phone:* 800-237-9814. *Fax:* 520-426-5083. *E-mail:* james.moore@centralaz.edu. *Website:* http://www.centralaz.edu/.

## Chandler-Gilbert Community College
### Chandler, Arizona

- **State and locally supported** 2-year, founded 1985, part of Maricopa County Community College District System
- **Suburban** 188-acre campus with easy access to Phoenix
- **Coed**, 14,906 undergraduate students, 28% full-time, 53% women, 47% men

**Undergraduates** 4,178 full-time, 10,728 part-time. Students come from 20 states and territories; 2% are from out of state; 4% Black or African American, non-Hispanic/Latino; 24% Hispanic/Latino; 6% Asian, non-Hispanic/Latino; 0.3% Native Hawaiian or other Pacific Islander, non-Hispanic/Latino; 2% American Indian or Alaska Native, non-Hispanic/Latino; 4% Two or more races, non-Hispanic/Latino; 9% Race/ethnicity unknown.

**Freshmen** *Admission:* 1,249 enrolled.

**Faculty** *Total:* 568, 25% full-time. *Student/faculty ratio:* 27:1.

**Majors** Accounting; accounting technology and bookkeeping; airline pilot and flight crew; business administration and management; business administration, management and operations related; business/commerce; business, management, and marketing related; computer and information sciences; computer and information sciences and support services related; computer programming; computer programming (vendor/product certification); computer systems analysis; computer systems networking and telecommunications; criminal justice/safety; data entry/microcomputer applications; data modeling/warehousing and database administration; dietetic technology; dietitian assistant; dramatic/theater arts; electromechanical technology; elementary education; fine/studio arts; general studies; information technology; kinesiology and exercise science; liberal arts and sciences and humanities related; liberal arts and sciences/liberal studies; lineworker; massage therapy; mechanic and repair technologies related; music management; organizational behavior; physical sciences; psychology; registered nursing/registered nurse; social work; visual and performing arts.

**Academics** *Calendar:* semesters. *Degree:* certificates, diplomas, and associate. *Special study options:* academic remediation for entering students, advanced placement credit, English as a second language, freshman honors college, honors programs, independent study, part-time degree program, services for LD students, study abroad, summer session for credit.

**Library** Chandler-Gilbert Community College Library.

**Student Life** *Housing:* college housing not available. *Activities and Organizations:* student-run radio station, choral group. *Campus security:* 24-hour emergency response devices and patrols, late-night transport/escort service. *Student services:* personal/psychological counseling, veterans affairs office.

**Athletics** Member NJCAA. *Intercollegiate sports:* baseball M, basketball M/W, golf M/W, soccer M/W, softball W, volleyball W.

**Costs (2018–19)** *Tuition:* area resident $2064 full-time, $86 per credit hour part-time; state resident $8832 full-time, $368 per credit hour part-time;

nonresident $7848 full-time, $327 per credit hour part-time. Full-time tuition and fees vary according to reciprocity agreements. Part-time tuition and fees vary according to reciprocity agreements. *Required fees:* $30 full-time. *Payment plans:* installment, deferred payment. *Waivers:* senior citizens and employees or children of employees.
**Applying** *Options:* electronic application.
**Freshman Application Contact** Alex Gadberry, Coordinator of Student Recruitment, Chandler-Gilbert Community College, 2626 East Pecos Road, Chandler, AZ 85225-2479. *Phone:* 480-726-4228. *E-mail:* alexander.gadberry@cgc.edu.
*Website:* http://www.cgc.maricopa.edu/.

## Cochise County Community College District

### Douglas, Arizona

- **State and locally supported** 2-year, founded 1962
- **Rural** 732-acre campus with easy access to Tucson
- **Coed,** 3,918 undergraduate students, 39% full-time, 56% women, 44% men

**Undergraduates** 1,519 full-time, 2,399 part-time. Students come from 17 states and territories; 2 other countries; 8% are from out of state; 5% Black or African American, non-Hispanic/Latino; 46% Hispanic/Latino; 2% Asian, non-Hispanic/Latino; 0.3% Native Hawaiian or other Pacific Islander, non-Hispanic/Latino; 0.7% American Indian or Alaska Native, non-Hispanic/Latino; 4% Two or more races, non-Hispanic/Latino; 1% Race/ethnicity unknown; 1% international; 3% transferred in; 2% live on campus. *Retention:* 63% of full-time freshmen returned.
**Freshmen** *Admission:* 1,412 applied, 1,412 admitted, 627 enrolled. *Average high school GPA:* 2.7.
**Faculty** *Total:* 296, 33% full-time. *Student/faculty ratio:* 16:1.
**Majors** Administrative assistant and secretarial science; adult and continuing education; agricultural business and management; air and space operations technology; airline pilot and flight crew; air transportation related; art; automobile/automotive mechanics technology; avionics maintenance technology; biology/biological sciences; building construction technology; business administration and management; chemistry; computer and information systems security; computer programming; computer science; computer systems networking and telecommunications; criminal justice/police science; crop production; culinary arts; digital communication and media/multimedia; dramatic/theater arts; early childhood education; economics; electrical, electronic and communications engineering technology; elementary education; emergency medical technology (EMT paramedic); engineering; English; equestrian studies; fire science/firefighting; general studies; health and physical education/fitness; humanities; information science/studies; intelligence; journalism; logistics, materials, and supply chain management; mathematics; mechatronics, robotics, and automation engineering; music; philosophy; physics; prenursing studies; registered nursing/registered nurse; respiratory care therapy; social sciences; speech communication and rhetoric; welding technology.
**Academics** *Calendar:* semesters. *Degrees:* certificates and associate (profile includes campuses in Douglas and Sierra Vista, AZ). *Special study options:* academic remediation for entering students, adult/continuing education programs, advanced placement credit, cooperative education, distance learning, English as a second language, honors programs, independent study, internships, part-time degree program, services for LD students, summer session for credit.
**Library** Andrea Cracchiolo plus 1 other. *Books:* 55,145 (physical), 40,945 (digital/electronic); *Serial titles:* 22 (physical), 7,401 (digital/electronic); *Databases:* 16. Weekly public service hours: 45.
**Student Life** *Housing Options:* coed, special housing for students with disabilities. Campus housing is university owned. *Activities and Organizations:* drama/theater group, choral group, Phi Theta Kappa, Student Nurses Association, Respiratory Therapy Student Association, Verses: Slam Poetry Club, Dance Club. *Campus security:* 24-hour emergency response devices and patrols, late-night transport/escort service. *Student services:* personal/psychological counseling, veterans affairs office.
**Athletics** Member NJCAA. *Intercollegiate sports:* baseball M(s), basketball M(s)/W(s), soccer W(s).
**Costs (2017–18)** *Tuition:* state resident $2460 full-time, $82 per credit hour part-time; nonresident $7800 full-time, $260 per credit hour part-time. Full-time tuition and fees vary according to course load, program, and reciprocity agreements. Part-time tuition and fees vary according to course load, program, and reciprocity agreements. *Room and board:* $6904. Room and board charges vary according to housing facility. *Payment plan:* installment. *Waivers:* senior citizens and employees or children of employees.
**Financial Aid** Of all full-time matriculated undergraduates who enrolled in 2014, 1,300 applied for aid, 1,121 were judged to have need. 72 Federal Work-Study jobs (averaging $5437). In 2014, 22 non-need-based awards were made.

*Average financial aid package:* $5876. *Average need-based loan:* $3658. *Average need-based gift aid:* $3730. *Average non-need-based aid:* $1666. *Financial aid deadline:* 6/15.
**Applying** *Options:* electronic application, deferred entrance. *Required for some:* high school transcript. *Recommended:* high school transcript. *Application deadlines:* rolling (freshmen), rolling (transfers). *Notification:* continuous (freshmen), continuous (transfers).
**Freshman Application Contact** Ms. Debbie Quick, Director of Admissions and Records, Cochise County Community College District, 4190 West Highway 80, Douglas, AZ 85607-6190. *Phone:* 520-515-3640. *Toll-free phone:* 800-593-9567. *Fax:* 520-515-5452. *E-mail:* quickd@cochise.edu.
*Website:* http://www.cochise.edu/.

## Coconino Community College

### Flagstaff, Arizona

- **State-supported** 2-year, founded 1991
- **Small-town** 5-acre campus
- **Endowment** $322,526
- **Coed**

**Undergraduates** 1,134 full-time, 2,474 part-time. 1% Black or African American, non-Hispanic/Latino; 18% Hispanic/Latino; 1% Asian, non-Hispanic/Latino; 0.2% Native Hawaiian or other Pacific Islander, non-Hispanic/Latino; 18% American Indian or Alaska Native, non-Hispanic/Latino; 4% Two or more races, non-Hispanic/Latino; 2% Race/ethnicity unknown; 22% transferred in. *Retention:* 58% of full-time freshmen returned.
**Faculty** *Student/faculty ratio:* 25:1.
**Academics** *Calendar:* semesters. *Degree:* certificates and associate. *Special study options:* academic remediation for entering students, adult/continuing education programs, distance learning, honors programs, independent study, internships, part-time degree program, study abroad, summer session for credit. *ROTC:* Air Force (b).
**Library** Information Resources and Library Services.
**Student Life** *Campus security:* 24-hour emergency response devices, student patrols, late-night transport/escort service, security patrols during hours of operation, electronic access throughout the campuses with security cards.
**Applying** *Options:* electronic application.
**Freshman Application Contact** Veronica Hipolito, Director of Student Services, Coconino Community College, 2800 South Lone Tree Road, Flagstaff, AZ 86001. *Phone:* 928-226-4334 Ext. 4334. *Toll-free phone:* 800-350-7122. *Fax:* 928-226-4114. *E-mail:* veronica.hipolito@coconino.edu.
*Website:* http://www.coconino.edu/.

## CollegeAmerica–Flagstaff

### Flagstaff, Arizona

**Freshman Application Contact** CollegeAmerica–Flagstaff, 399 South Malpais Lane, Flagstaff, AZ 86001. *Phone:* 928-213-6060 Ext. 1402. *Toll-free phone:* 800-622-2894. *Website:* http://www.collegeamerica.edu/.

## CollegeAmerica–Phoenix

### Phoenix, Arizona

**Admissions Office Contact** CollegeAmerica–Phoenix, 9801 North Metro Parkway East, Phoenix, AZ 85051. *Toll-free phone:* 800-622-2894. *Website:* http://www.collegeamerica.edu/.

## Diné College

### Tsaile, Arizona

**Freshman Application Contact** Mrs. Louise Litzin, Registrar, Diné College, PO Box 67, Tsaile, AZ 86556. *Phone:* 928-724-6633. *Toll-free phone:* 877-988-DINE. *Fax:* 928-724-3349. *E-mail:* louise@dinecollege.edu. *Website:* http://www.dinecollege.edu/.

## Eastern Arizona College

### Thatcher, Arizona

- **State and locally supported** 2-year, founded 1888, part of Arizona State Community College System
- **Small-town** campus
- **Endowment** $5.3 million
- **Coed,** 6,365 undergraduate students, 31% full-time, 55% women, 45% men

**Undergraduates** 1,957 full-time, 4,408 part-time. Students come from 25 states and territories; 24 other countries; 3% are from out of state; 3% Black or

African American, non-Hispanic/Latino; 20% Hispanic/Latino; 0.9% Asian, non-Hispanic/Latino; 0.8% Native Hawaiian or other Pacific Islander, non-Hispanic/Latino; 6% American Indian or Alaska Native, non-Hispanic/Latino; 1% Two or more races, non-Hispanic/Latino; 3% Race/ethnicity unknown; 1% international; 1% transferred in; 3% live on campus.

**Freshmen** *Admission:* 818 applied, 818 admitted, 597 enrolled.

**Faculty** *Total:* 340, 29% full-time, 8% with terminal degrees. *Student/faculty ratio:* 19:1.

**Majors** Anthropology; automobile/automotive mechanics technology; biology/biological sciences; business administration and management; business, management, and marketing related; business operations support and secretarial services related; business teacher education; chemistry; civil engineering technology; commercial and advertising art; cosmetology; criminal justice/law enforcement administration; criminal justice/police science; diesel mechanics technology; drafting and design technology; dramatic/theater arts; early childhood education; elementary education; emergency medical technology (EMT paramedic); environmental biology; fire science/firefighting; foreign languages and literatures; forestry; general studies; geology/earth science; graphic design; health and physical education/fitness; history; industrial electronics technology; industrial mechanics and maintenance technology; information science/studies; liberal arts and sciences/liberal studies; machine shop technology; mathematics; mining technology; multi/interdisciplinary studies related; music; pharmacy technician; photographic and film/video technology; physics; political science and government; pre-chiropractic; premedical studies; pre-pharmacy studies; pre-physical therapy; psychology; registered nursing/registered nurse; secondary education; small business administration; sociology; speech communication and rhetoric; welding technology; wildlife biology; writing.

**Academics** *Calendar:* semesters. *Degree:* certificates and associate. *Special study options:* academic remediation for entering students, adult/continuing education programs, advanced placement credit, cooperative education, distance learning, double majors, independent study, internships, part-time degree program, services for LD students, study abroad, summer session for credit.

**Library** Alumni Library plus 1 other. *Books:* 37,902 (physical), 968 (digital/electronic); *Serial titles:* 637 (physical); *Databases:* 41. Weekly public service hours: 80; students can reserve study rooms.

**Student Life** *Housing Options:* men-only, women-only. Campus housing is university owned. *Activities and Organizations:* drama/theater group, choral group, marching band, Latter-Day Saints Student Association, Criminal Justice Student Association, Multicultural Council, Phi Theta Kappa, Mark Allen Dorm Club. *Campus security:* 24-hour emergency response devices, late-night transport/escort service, controlled dormitory access, 20-hour patrols by trained security personnel. *Student services:* personal/psychological counseling.

**Athletics** Member NJCAA. *Intercollegiate sports:* baseball M(s), basketball M(s)/W(s), football M(s), golf M/W, softball W(s), volleyball W(s). *Intramural sports:* basketball M/W, racquetball M/W, swimming and diving M/W, table tennis M/W, tennis M/W, volleyball M/W.

**Costs (2018–19)** *Tuition:* state resident $2040 full-time, $85 per credit hour part-time; nonresident $9000 full-time, $375 per credit hour part-time. Full-time tuition and fees vary according to program. Part-time tuition and fees vary according to program. *Room and board:* $6595. Room and board charges vary according to board plan. *Waivers:* senior citizens and employees or children of employees.

**Financial Aid** Of all full-time matriculated undergraduates who enrolled in 2016, 1,105 applied for aid, 994 were judged to have need, 45 had their need fully met. In 2016, 99 non-need-based awards were made. *Average percent of need met:* 42%. *Average financial aid package:* $6372. *Average need-based gift aid:* $6122. *Average non-need-based aid:* $2635.

**Applying** *Options:* electronic application, early admission, deferred entrance. *Recommended:* high school transcript. *Application deadlines:* rolling (freshmen), rolling (transfers). *Notification:* continuous (freshmen).

**Freshman Application Contact** Suzette Udall, Records Assistant, Eastern Arizona College, 615 North Stadium Avenue, Thatcher, AZ 85552-0769. *Phone:* 928-428-8904. *Toll-free phone:* 800-678-3808. *Fax:* 928-428-3729. *E-mail:* admissions@eac.edu. *Website:* http://www.eac.edu/.

# Estrella Mountain Community College
## Avondale, Arizona

- **State and locally supported** 2-year, founded 1992, part of Maricopa County Community College District System
- **Urban** campus with easy access to Phoenix
- **Coed**

**Undergraduates** 3,124 full-time, 6,220 part-time. Students come from 1 other state; 8% Black or African American, non-Hispanic/Latino; 51% Hispanic/Latino; 4% Asian, non-Hispanic/Latino; 0.4% Native Hawaiian or other Pacific Islander, non-Hispanic/Latino; 2% American Indian or Alaska Native, non-Hispanic/Latino; 2% Two or more races, non-Hispanic/Latino; 3% Race/ethnicity unknown; 0.3% international; 7% transferred in.

**Faculty** *Student/faculty ratio:* 22:1.

**Academics** *Calendar:* semesters. *Degree:* certificates and associate. *Special study options:* academic remediation for entering students, adult/continuing education programs, advanced placement credit, cooperative education, distance learning, English as a second language, honors programs, independent study, part-time degree program, services for LD students, summer session for credit. *ROTC:* Air Force (c).

**Library** Estrella Mountain Library.

**Student Life** *Campus security:* 24-hour emergency response devices and patrols, late-night transport/escort service.

**Applying** *Options:* electronic application.

**Freshman Application Contact** Estrella Mountain Community College, 3000 North Dysart Road, Avondale, AZ 85392. *Phone:* 623-935-8812. *Website:* http://www.estrellamountain.edu/.

# Fortis College
## Phoenix, Arizona

**Admissions Office Contact** Fortis College, 555 North 18th Street, Suite 110, Phoenix, AZ 85006. *Toll-free phone:* 855-4-FORTIS. *Website:* http://www.fortis.edu/.

# GateWay Community College
## Phoenix, Arizona

**Freshman Application Contact** Director of Admissions and Records, GateWay Community College, 108 North 40th Street, Phoenix, AZ 85034. *Phone:* 602-286-8200. *Fax:* 602-286-8200. *E-mail:* enroll@gatewaycc.edu. *Website:* http://www.gatewaycc.edu/.

# Glendale Community College
## Glendale, Arizona

**Freshman Application Contact** Ms. Mary Blackwell, Dean of Enrollment Services, Glendale Community College, 6000 West Olive Avenue, Glendale, AZ 85302. *Phone:* 623-435-3305. *Fax:* 623-845-3303. *E-mail:* admissions.recruitment@gccaz.edu. *Website:* http://www.gc.maricopa.edu/.

# Golf Academy of America
## Chandler, Arizona

**Admissions Office Contact** Golf Academy of America, 2031 N. Arizona Avenue, Suite 2, Chandler, AZ 85225. *Website:* http://www.golfacademy.edu/.

# Mesa Community College
## Mesa, Arizona

- **State and locally supported** 2-year, founded 1965, part of Maricopa County Community College District System
- **Urban** 160-acre campus with easy access to Phoenix
- **Coed,** 20,424 undergraduate students, 31% full-time, 53% women, 47% men

**Undergraduates** 6,237 full-time, 14,187 part-time. 6% Black or African American, non-Hispanic/Latino; 28% Hispanic/Latino; 4% Asian, non-Hispanic/Latino; 0.4% Native Hawaiian or other Pacific Islander, non-Hispanic/Latino; 4% American Indian or Alaska Native, non-Hispanic/Latino; 3% Two or more races, non-Hispanic/Latino; 6% Race/ethnicity unknown; 2% international.

**Faculty** *Total:* 973, 31% full-time. *Student/faculty ratio:* 21:1.

**Majors** Administrative assistant and secretarial science; agroecology and sustainable agriculture; architectural drafting and CAD/CADD; automobile/automotive mechanics technology; biology/biotechnology laboratory technician; building/construction site management; business administration and management; business/commerce; computer and information sciences; computer systems analysis; computer systems networking and telecommunications; construction/heavy equipment/earthmoving equipment operation; criminal justice/police science; criminal justice/safety; dental hygiene; design and visual communications; drafting/design engineering technologies related; dramatic/theater arts; electrical, electronic and communications engineering technology; electromechanical technology; elementary education; emergency medical technology (EMT paramedic); fine/studio arts; food service systems administration; general studies; geography; health and physical education/fitness; insurance; interior design; journalism; kindergarten/preschool education; liberal arts and sciences/liberal studies; machine tool technology; manufacturing engineering; manufacturing engineering technology; marketing/marketing management; merchandising; music; music management; organizational behavior; ornamental horticulture; parks, recreation and leisure; physical sciences; public relations/image management; real estate; recording arts technology; registered nursing/registered nurse; system, networking, and LAN/WAN management; teacher assistant/aide; veterinary/animal health technology; visual and performing arts; web page, digital/multimedia and information resources design; welding technology.

**Academics** *Calendar:* semesters. *Degree:* certificates and associate. *Special study options:* academic remediation for entering students, adult/continuing education programs, advanced placement credit, cooperative education, distance learning, English as a second language, freshman honors college, honors programs, independent study, off-campus study, part-time degree program, services for LD students, student-designed majors, study abroad, summer session for credit. *ROTC:* Army (c), Air Force (c).

**Library** Information Commons. Students can reserve study rooms.

**Student Life** *Housing:* college housing not available. *Activities and Organizations:* drama/theater group, student-run newspaper, choral group, MECHA, International Student Association, American Indian Association, Asian/Pacific Islander Club. *Campus security:* 24-hour emergency response devices and patrols, student patrols. *Student services:* personal/psychological counseling, legal services, veterans affairs office.

**Athletics** Member NJCAA. *Intercollegiate sports:* baseball M(s), basketball M(s)/W(s), cheerleading W(s), cross-country running M(s)/W(s), golf M(s)/W(s), soccer M(s)/W(s), softball W(s), tennis M(s)/W(s), track and field M(s)/W(s), volleyball W(s). *Intramural sports:* basketball M/W, bowling M/W, cross-country running M/W, softball W, track and field M/W, volleyball M/W.

**Costs (2018–19)** *Tuition:* state resident $2064 full-time, $86 per credit hour part-time; nonresident $7848 full-time, $327 per credit hour part-time. Full-time tuition and fees vary according to course load and reciprocity agreements. Part-time tuition and fees vary according to course load and reciprocity agreements. *Required fees:* $30 full-time, $15 per term part-time. *Payment plan:* installment. *Waivers:* senior citizens and employees or children of employees.

**Applying** *Options:* electronic application, early admission, deferred entrance. *Application deadlines:* 9/1 (freshmen), 9/1 (transfers). *Notification:* continuous (freshmen).

**Freshman Application Contact** Carmen Newland, Dean, Enrollment Services, Mesa Community College, 1833 West Southern Avenue, Mesa, AZ 85202-4866. *Phone:* 480-461-7600. *Toll-free phone:* 866-532-4983. *Fax:* 480-844-3117. *E-mail:* admissionsandrecords@mesacc.edu. *Website:* http://www.mesacc.edu/.

## Mohave Community College
### Kingman, Arizona

- **State-supported** 2-year, founded 1971
- **Small-town** 160-acre campus
- **Coed,** 4,312 undergraduate students, 20% full-time, 65% women, 35% men

**Undergraduates** 841 full-time, 3,471 part-time. Students come from 19 states and territories; 5% are from out of state; 1% Black or African American, non-Hispanic/Latino; 24% Hispanic/Latino; 2% Asian, non-Hispanic/Latino; 0.6% Native Hawaiian or other Pacific Islander, non-Hispanic/Latino; 2% American Indian or Alaska Native, non-Hispanic/Latino; 3% Two or more races, non-Hispanic/Latino; 2% Race/ethnicity unknown.

**Freshmen** *Admission:* 499 enrolled.

**Faculty** *Total:* 300, 28% full-time. *Student/faculty ratio:* 13:1.

**Majors** Accounting; art; automobile/automotive mechanics technology; building/construction finishing, management, and inspection related; business administration and management; computer and information sciences related; computer programming (specific applications); computer science; criminal justice/police science; culinary arts; dental assisting; dental hygiene; drafting and design technology; education; emergency medical technology (EMT paramedic); English; fire science/firefighting; heating, air conditioning, ventilation and refrigeration maintenance technology; history; information technology; legal assistant/paralegal; liberal arts and sciences/liberal studies; mathematics; medical/clinical assistant; personal and culinary services related; pharmacy technician; physical therapy technology; psychology; registered nursing/registered nurse; sociology; substance abuse/addiction counseling; surgical technology; truck and bus driver/commercial vehicle operation/instruction; welding technology.

**Academics** *Calendar:* semesters. *Degree:* certificates and associate. *Special study options:* academic remediation for entering students, adult/continuing education programs, cooperative education, distance learning, English as a second language, independent study, part-time degree program, summer session for credit.

**Library** Mohave Community College Library.

**Student Life** *Housing:* college housing not available. *Activities and Organizations:* Art Club, Phi Theta Kappa, Computer Club (MC4), Science Club, Student Government. *Campus security:* late-night transport/escort service.

**Costs (2017–18)** *Tuition:* state resident $2430 full-time, $81 per credit hour part-time; nonresident $8505 full-time, $284 per credit hour part-time. Full-time tuition and fees vary according to program. Part-time tuition and fees vary according to program. *Required fees:* $210 full-time, $7 per credit hour part-time. *Payment plans:* installment, deferred payment. *Waivers:* employees or children of employees.

**Applying** *Options:* electronic application, early admission, deferred entrance. *Application deadlines:* rolling (freshmen), rolling (transfers). *Notification:* continuous (freshmen), continuous (transfers).

**Freshman Application Contact** Mrs. Ana Masterson, Dean of Student Services, Mohave Community College, 1971 Jagerson Avenue, Kingman, AZ 86409. *Phone:* 928-757-0803. *Toll-free phone:* 888-664-2832. *Fax:* 928-757-0808. *E-mail:* amasterson@mohave.edu. *Website:* http://www.mohave.edu/.

## Northland Pioneer College
### Holbrook, Arizona

**Freshman Application Contact** Ms. Suzette Willis, Coordinator of Admissions, Northland Pioneer College, PO Box 610, Holbrook, AZ 86025. *Phone:* 928-536-6271. *Toll-free phone:* 800-266-7845. *Fax:* 928-536-6212. *Website:* http://www.npc.edu/.

## Paradise Valley Community College
### Phoenix, Arizona

**Freshman Application Contact** Paradise Valley Community College, 18401 North 32nd Street, Phoenix, AZ 85032-1200. *Phone:* 602-787-7020. *Website:* http://www.pvc.maricopa.edu/.

## The Paralegal Institute at Brighton College
### Scottsdale, Arizona

**Freshman Application Contact** Patricia Yancy, Director of Admissions, The Paralegal Institute at Brighton College, 2933 West Indian School Road, Drawer 11408, Phoenix, AZ 85061-1408. *Phone:* 602-212-0501. *Toll-free phone:* 800-354-1254. *Fax:* 602-212-0502. *E-mail:* paralegalinst@mindspring.com. *Website:* http://www.theparalegalinstitute.edu/.

## Penn Foster College
### Scottsdale, Arizona

- **Proprietary** primarily 2-year
- **Coed**

**Undergraduates** Students come from 50 states and territories; 5 other countries.

**Academics** *Calendar:* continuous. *Degrees:* certificates, associate, and bachelor's. *Special study options:* academic remediation for entering students, accelerated degree program, distance learning, external degree program, independent study, off-campus study, part-time degree program, services for LD students.

**Library** Penn Foster College Online Library.

**Costs (2017–18)** *Tuition:* $79 per credit part-time. Part-time tuition and fees vary according to course load and program.

**Applying** *Options:* electronic application. *Application fee:* $75. *Required:* high school transcript.

**Freshman Application Contact** Admissions, Penn Foster College, 14300 North Northsight Boulevard, Suite 120, Scottsdale, AZ 85260. *Phone:* 888-427-1000. *Toll-free phone:* 800-471-3232. *Website:* http://www.pennfostercollege.edu/.

## Phoenix College
### Phoenix, Arizona

**Freshman Application Contact** Ms. Brenda Stark, Director of Admissions, Registration, and Records, Phoenix College, 1202 West Thomas Road, Phoenix, AZ 85013. *Phone:* 602-285-7503. *Fax:* 602-285-7813. *E-mail:* kathy.french@pcmail.maricopa.edu. *Website:* http://www.pc.maricopa.edu/.

# Pima Community College
## Tucson, Arizona

**Freshman Application Contact** Terra Benson, Director of Admissions and Registrar, Pima Community College, 4905B East Broadway Boulevard, Tucson, AZ 85709-1120. *Phone:* 520-206-4640. *Fax:* 520-206-4790. *E-mail:* tbenson@pima.edu. *Website:* http://www.pima.edu/.

# Pima Medical Institute
## Mesa, Arizona

**Freshman Application Contact** Pima Medical Institute, 2160 South Power Road, Mesa, AZ 85209. *Phone:* 480-898-9898. *Toll-free phone:* 800-477-PIMA. *Website:* http://www.pmi.edu/.

# Pima Medical Institute
## Mesa, Arizona

**Freshman Application Contact** Admissions Office, Pima Medical Institute, 957 South Dobson Road, Mesa, AZ 85202. *Phone:* 480-644-0267 Ext. 225. *Toll-free phone:* 800-477-PIMA. *Website:* http://www.pmi.edu/.

# Pima Medical Institute
## Phoenix, Arizona

**Admissions Office Contact** Pima Medical Institute, 13610 North Black Canyon Highway, Phoenix, AZ 85029. *Website:* http://www.pmi.edu/.

# Pima Medical Institute
## Tucson, Arizona

**Freshman Application Contact** Admissions Office, Pima Medical Institute, 3350 East Grant Road, Tucson, AZ 85716. *Phone:* 520-326-1600 Ext. 5112. *Toll-free phone:* 800-477-PIMA. *Website:* http://www.pmi.edu/.

# The Refrigeration School
## Phoenix, Arizona

- **Proprietary** 2-year, founded 1965
- **Urban** campus
- **Coed, primarily men**

**Undergraduates** 688 full-time. 6% are from out of state; 8% Black or African American, non-Hispanic/Latino; 20% Hispanic/Latino; 0.7% Asian, non-Hispanic/Latino; 0.6% Native Hawaiian or other Pacific Islander, non-Hispanic/Latino; 6% American Indian or Alaska Native, non-Hispanic/Latino; 2% Two or more races, non-Hispanic/Latino; 30% Race/ethnicity unknown. *Retention:* 72% of full-time freshmen returned.
**Faculty** *Student/faculty ratio:* 34:1.
**Academics** *Calendar:* continuous. *Degree:* certificates, diplomas, and associate.
**Costs (2017–18)** *Tuition:* $19,125 full-time. *Required fees:* $1900 full-time.
**Freshman Application Contact** Mr. John Palumbo, Regional Director of Admissions, The Refrigeration School, 4210 East Washington Street. *Phone:* 602-275-7133. *Toll-free phone:* 888-943-4822. *Fax:* 602-267-4811. *E-mail:* info@rsiaz.edu. *Website:* http://www.refrigerationschool.com/.

# Rio Salado College
## Tempe, Arizona

- **State and locally supported** 2-year, founded 1978, part of Maricopa County Community College District System
- **Urban** campus
- **Coed**

**Undergraduates** Students come from 38 other countries; 4% are from out of state.
**Faculty** *Student/faculty ratio:* 13:1.
**Academics** *Calendar:* semesters. *Degree:* certificates and associate. *Special study options:* academic remediation for entering students, accelerated degree program, adult/continuing education programs, advanced placement credit, cooperative education, distance learning, double majors, English as a second language, external degree program, honors programs, independent study, internships, part-time degree program, services for LD students, summer session for credit.
**Library** Rio Salado Library and Information Center.

**Student Life** *Campus security:* 24-hour emergency response devices, late-night transport/escort service.
**Costs (2017–18)** *Tuition:* state resident $2064 full-time, $86 per credit hour part-time; nonresident $5160 full-time, $215 per credit hour part-time. Full-time tuition and fees vary according to course load and reciprocity agreements. Part-time tuition and fees vary according to course load and reciprocity agreements. *Required fees:* $30 full-time, $15 per term part-time. *Payment plans:* installment, deferred payment.
**Applying** *Options:* electronic application, early admission, deferred entrance.
**Freshman Application Contact** Laurel Redman, Director of Admissions, Records and Registration, Rio Salado College, 2323 West 14th Street, Tempe 85281. *Phone:* 480-517-8563. *Toll-free phone:* 800-729-1197. *Fax:* 480-517-8199. *Website:* http://www.riosalado.edu/.

# Scottsdale Community College
## Scottsdale, Arizona

- **State and locally supported** 2-year, founded 1969, part of Maricopa County Community College District System
- **Urban** 160-acre campus with easy access to Phoenix
- **Coed,** 9,458 undergraduate students

**Undergraduates** Students come from 50 states and territories; 1% are from out of state; 4% Black or African American, non-Hispanic/Latino; 19% Hispanic/Latino; 3% Asian, non-Hispanic/Latino; 0.4% Native Hawaiian or other Pacific Islander, non-Hispanic/Latino; 5% American Indian or Alaska Native, non-Hispanic/Latino; 3% Two or more races, non-Hispanic/Latino; 6% Race/ethnicity unknown; 1% international.
**Faculty** *Total:* 489, 33% full-time, 15% with terminal degrees. *Student/faculty ratio:* 18:1.
**Majors** Accounting; administrative assistant and secretarial science; business administration and management; criminal justice/law enforcement administration; culinary arts; dramatic/theater arts; electrical, electronic and communications engineering technology; environmental design/architecture; equestrian studies; fashion merchandising; finance; hospitality administration; hotel/motel administration; information science/studies; interior design; mathematics; medical administrative assistant and medical secretary; photography; public administration; real estate; registered nursing/registered nurse; special products marketing.
**Academics** *Calendar:* semesters. *Degree:* certificates, diplomas, and associate. *Special study options:* academic remediation for entering students, adult/continuing education programs, advanced placement credit, cooperative education, English as a second language, honors programs, internships, off-campus study, part-time degree program, services for LD students, study abroad, summer session for credit.
**Library** Scottsdale Community College Library. *Books:* 44,599 (physical), 163,245 (digital/electronic); *Serial titles:* 608 (physical), 14 (digital/electronic); *Databases:* 66. Weekly public service hours: 62; students can reserve study rooms.
**Student Life** *Housing:* college housing not available. *Activities and Organizations:* drama/theater group, student-run newspaper, radio station, choral group, Student Leadership Forum, International Community Club, Phi Theta Kappa, Music Industry Club, SCC ASID-Interior Design group. *Campus security:* 24-hour emergency response devices and patrols, student patrols, late-night transport/escort service, 24-hour automatic surveillance cameras. *Student services:* personal/psychological counseling, veterans affairs office.
**Athletics** Member NCAA, NJCAA. All NCAA Division II. *Intercollegiate sports:* baseball M, basketball M/W, cross-country running M/W, football M, golf M/W, soccer M/W, softball W, volleyball W. *Intramural sports:* archery M/W, badminton M/W, basketball M/W, racquetball M/W, track and field M/W, volleyball M/W.
**Costs (2017–18)** *Tuition:* state resident $2580 full-time, $86 per credit hour part-time; nonresident $9810 full-time, $327 per credit hour part-time. Full-time tuition and fees vary according to program and reciprocity agreements. Part-time tuition and fees vary according to program and reciprocity agreements. *Required fees:* $30 full-time, $15 per term part-time. *Payment plans:* installment, deferred payment. *Waivers:* senior citizens and employees or children of employees.
**Financial Aid** Of all full-time matriculated undergraduates who enrolled in 2016, 75 Federal Work-Study jobs (averaging $2000). *Financial aid deadline:* 7/15.
**Applying** *Options:* electronic application, early admission. *Application deadline:* rolling (freshmen). *Notification:* continuous (freshmen).
**Freshman Application Contact** Ms. Laura Krueger, Director of Admissions and Records, Scottsdale Community College, 9000 East Chaparral Road, Scottsdale, AZ 85256. *Phone:* 480-423-6133. *Fax:* 480-423-6200. *E-mail:* laura.krueger@scottsdalecc.edu.
*Website:* http://www.scottsdalecc.edu/.

## Sessions College for Professional Design
### Tempe, Arizona

**Freshman Application Contact** Ms. Mhelanie Hernandez, Director of Admissions, Sessions College for Professional Design, 350 South Mill Avenue, Suite B-104, Tempe, AZ 85281. *Phone:* 480-212-1704. *Toll-free phone:* 800-258-4115. *E-mail:* admissions@sessions.edu. *Website:* http://www.sessions.edu/.

## South Mountain Community College
### Phoenix, Arizona

**Director of Admissions** Dean of Enrollment Services, South Mountain Community College, 7050 South Twenty-fourth Street, Phoenix, AZ 85040. *Phone:* 602-243-8120. *Website:* http://www.southmountaincc.edu/.

## Southwest Institute of Healing Arts
### Tempe, Arizona

**Director of Admissions** Katie Yearous, Student Advisor, Southwest Institute of Healing Arts, 1100 East Apache Boulevard, Tempe, AZ 85281. *Phone:* 480-994-9244. *Toll-free phone:* 888-504-9106. *E-mail:* joannl@swiha.net. *Website:* http://www.swiha.org/.

## Tohono O'odham Community College
### Sells, Arizona

- **Public** 2-year, founded 1998
- **Rural** 42-acre campus
- **Endowment** $314,747
- **Coed,** 400 undergraduate students, 31% full-time, 66% women, 34% men

**Undergraduates** 122 full-time, 278 part-time. 3% Black or African American, non-Hispanic/Latino; 1% Hispanic/Latino; 89% American Indian or Alaska Native, non-Hispanic/Latino; 0.5% Race/ethnicity unknown; 6% transferred in; 10% live on campus. *Retention:* 54% of full-time freshmen returned.
**Freshmen** *Admission:* 135 enrolled.
**Faculty** *Total:* 48, 35% full-time, 21% with terminal degrees. *Student/faculty ratio:* 10:1.
**Majors** Business administration and management; child development; computer systems analysis; early childhood education; human services; liberal arts and sciences/liberal studies.
**Academics** *Calendar:* semesters. *Degree:* certificates, diplomas, and associate. *Special study options:* academic remediation for entering students, adult/continuing education programs, cooperative education, double majors, part-time degree program, services for LD students, summer session for credit.
**Library** Tohono O'odham Community College Library plus 2 others. *Books:* 12,865 (physical), 54 (digital/electronic). Weekly public service hours: 40.
**Student Life** *Housing Options:* coed, men-only, women-only. Campus housing is university owned. *Activities and Organizations:* Student Senate, AISES, Archery Club. *Campus security:* 24-hour patrols. *Student services:* personal/psychological counseling.
**Athletics** Member NJCAA. *Intercollegiate sports:* basketball M(s)/W(s).
**Costs (2017–18)** *Tuition:* state resident $811 full-time, $35 per credit hour part-time; nonresident $811 full-time, $35 per credit hour part-time. Full-time tuition and fees vary according to class time, course level, course load, degree level, location, program, and student level. Part-time tuition and fees vary according to class time, course level, course load, degree level, location, program, and student level. *Required fees:* $110 full-time, $50 per term part-time. *Room and board:* $2400. *Payment plan:* installment. *Waivers:* employees or children of employees.
**Applying** *Options:* electronic application. *Required:* high school transcript. *Application deadlines:* rolling (freshmen), rolling (transfers). *Notification:* continuous (freshmen), continuous (transfers), rolling (early decision).
**Freshman Application Contact** Gloria Benevidez, Student Support Specialist, Tohono O'odham Community College, PO Box 3129, Sells, AZ 85634. *Phone:* 520-383-8401. *E-mail:* gbenevidez@tocc.edu. *Website:* http://www.tocc.edu/.

## Universal Technical Institute
### Avondale, Arizona

**Freshman Application Contact** Director of Admission, Universal Technical Institute, 10695 West Pierce Street, Avondale, AZ 85323. *Phone:* 623-245-4600. *Toll-free phone:* 800-510-5072. *Fax:* 623-245-4601. *Website:* http://www.uti.edu/.

## Yavapai College
### Prescott, Arizona

**Freshman Application Contact** Mrs. Sheila Jarrell, Admissions, Registration, and Records Manager, Yavapai College, 1100 East Sheldon Street, Prescott, AZ 86301-3297. *Phone:* 928-776-2107. *Toll-free phone:* 800-922-6787. *Fax:* 928-776-2151. *E-mail:* registration@yc.edu. *Website:* http://www.yc.edu/.

# ARKANSAS

## Arkansas Northeastern College
### Blytheville, Arkansas

- **State-supported** 2-year, founded 1975
- **Small-town** 80-acre campus with easy access to Memphis
- **Endowment** $187,500
- **Coed**

**Undergraduates** 610 full-time, 806 part-time. Students come from 5 states and territories; 18% are from out of state; 27% Black or African American, non-Hispanic/Latino; 3% Hispanic/Latino; 0.5% Asian, non-Hispanic/Latino; 0.1% Native Hawaiian or other Pacific Islander, non-Hispanic/Latino; 0.2% American Indian or Alaska Native, non-Hispanic/Latino; 0.8% Two or more races, non-Hispanic/Latino; 5% transferred in. *Retention:* 83% of full-time freshmen returned.
**Academics** *Calendar:* semesters. *Degree:* certificates and associate. *Special study options:* academic remediation for entering students, adult/continuing education programs, advanced placement credit, distance learning, double majors, part-time degree program, summer session for credit.
**Library** Adams/Vines Library.
**Student Life** *Campus security:* 24-hour patrols.
**Financial Aid** Of all full-time matriculated undergraduates who enrolled in 2016, 42 Federal Work-Study jobs (averaging $2500).
**Applying** *Options:* deferred entrance. *Recommended:* high school transcript.
**Freshman Application Contact** Arkansas Northeastern College, PO Box 1109, Blytheville, AR 72316. *Phone:* 870-762-1020. *Fax:* 870-763-1654. *Website:* http://www.anc.edu/.

## Arkansas State University–Beebe
### Beebe, Arkansas

**Freshman Application Contact** Mr. Ronald Hudson, Coordinator of Student Recruitment, Arkansas State University–Beebe, PO Box 1000, Beebe, AR 72012. *Phone:* 501-882-8860. *Toll-free phone:* 800-632-9985. *E-mail:* rdhudson@asub.edu. *Website:* http://www.asub.edu/.

## Arkansas State University Mid-South
### West Memphis, Arkansas

**Freshman Application Contact** Jeremy Reece, Director of Admissions, Arkansas State University Mid-South, 2000 West Broadway, West Memphis, AR 72301. *Phone:* 870-733-6786. *Toll-free phone:* 866-733-6722. *Fax:* 870-733-6719. *E-mail:* jreece@midsouthcc.edu. *Website:* http://www.asumidsouth.edu/.

## Arkansas State University–Mountain Home
### Mountain Home, Arkansas

**Freshman Application Contact** Ms. Delba Parrish, Admissions Coordinator, Arkansas State University–Mountain Home, 1600 South College Street, Mountain Home, AR 72653. *Phone:* 870-508-6180. *Fax:* 870-508-6287. *E-mail:* dparrish@asumh.edu. *Website:* http://www.asumh.edu/.

## Arkansas State University–Newport
### Newport, Arkansas

- **State-supported** 2-year, founded 1989, part of Arkansas State University System
- **Rural** 189-acre campus
- **Endowment** $2.0 million
- **Coed,** 2,735 undergraduate students, 39% full-time, 60% women, 40% men

**Undergraduates** 1,073 full-time, 1,662 part-time. Students come from 25 states and territories; 1% are from out of state; 15% Black or African

American, non-Hispanic/Latino; 5% Hispanic/Latino; 0.5% Asian, non-Hispanic/Latino; 0.1% American Indian or Alaska Native, non-Hispanic/Latino; 5% Two or more races, non-Hispanic/Latino; 2% Race/ethnicity unknown; 0.1% international; 4% transferred in.
**Freshmen** *Admission:* 1,209 applied, 806 admitted, 406 enrolled. *Average high school GPA:* 2.8.
**Faculty** *Student/faculty ratio:* 17:1.
**Majors** Autobody/collision and repair technology; automobile/automotive mechanics technology; business/commerce; computer technology/computer systems technology; criminal justice/law enforcement administration; education (multiple levels); emergency medical technology (EMT paramedic); forensic science and technology; general studies; health/medical preparatory programs related; heating, air conditioning, ventilation and refrigeration maintenance technology; middle school education; multi/interdisciplinary studies related; natural sciences; registered nursing/registered nurse.
**Academics** *Calendar:* semesters. *Degree:* certificates, diplomas, and associate. *Special study options:* academic remediation for entering students, adult/continuing education programs, advanced placement credit, cooperative education, distance learning, double majors, external degree program, independent study, internships, off-campus study, part-time degree program, services for LD students, summer session for credit.
**Library** Harryette M. Hodges and Kaneaster Hodges, Sr. Library plus 2 others. *Books:* 11,653 (physical), 27 (digital/electronic); *Databases:* 6. Weekly public service hours: 40.
**Student Life** *Housing:* college housing not available. *Activities and Organizations:* Phi Theta Kappa, Phi Beta Lambda, Service Veterans Organization. *Campus security:* text-based alert system; campus police 8-5 on-site. *Student services:* veterans affairs office.
**Standardized Tests** *Required:* SAT or ACT or ACT Compass (for admission).
**Costs (2017–18)** *Tuition:* state resident $2880 full-time, $96 per credit hour part-time; nonresident $4710 full-time, $157 per credit hour part-time. Full-time tuition and fees vary according to course load and program. Part-time tuition and fees vary according to course load and program. *Required fees:* $570 full-time, $19 per credit hour part-time. *Payment plan:* installment. *Waivers:* senior citizens and employees or children of employees.
**Financial Aid** Of all full-time matriculated undergraduates who enrolled in 2016, 19 Federal Work-Study jobs (averaging $4500).
**Applying** *Options:* electronic application. *Required:* high school transcript. *Application deadlines:* rolling (freshmen), rolling (transfers), rolling (early action). *Early decision deadline:* rolling (for plan 1), rolling (for plan 2). *Notification:* continuous (freshmen), continuous (transfers), rolling (early decision plan 1), rolling (early decision plan 2), rolling (early action).
**Freshman Application Contact** Arkansas State University–Newport, 7648 Victory Boulevard, Newport, AR 72112. *Phone:* 870-512-7800. *Toll-free phone:* 800-976-1676.
*Website:* http://www.asun.edu/.

## Baptist Health College Little Rock
### Little Rock, Arkansas
**Admissions Office Contact** Baptist Health College Little Rock, 11900 Colonel Glenn Road, Suite 100, Little Rock, AR 72210-2820. *Website:* http://www.bhclr.edu/.

## Black River Technical College
### Pocahontas, Arkansas
**Director of Admissions** Director of Admissions, Black River Technical College, 1410 Highway 304 East, Pocahontas, AR 72455. *Phone:* 870-892-4565. *Website:* http://www.blackrivertech.edu/.

## Bryan University
### Rogers, Arkansas
**Admissions Office Contact** Bryan University, 3704 West Walnut Street, Rogers, AR 72756. *Website:* http://www.bryanu.edu/.

## College of the Ouachitas
### Malvern, Arkansas
- **State-supported** 2-year, founded 1972
- **Small-town** 11-acre campus with easy access to Little Rock
- **Coed,** 1,272 undergraduate students, 30% full-time, 56% women, 44% men

**Undergraduates** 384 full-time, 888 part-time. Students come from 3 states and territories; 1% are from out of state; 14% Black or African American, non-

Hispanic/Latino; 5% Hispanic/Latino; 0.5% Asian, non-Hispanic/Latino; 0.2% Native Hawaiian or other Pacific Islander, non-Hispanic/Latino; 0.6% American Indian or Alaska Native, non-Hispanic/Latino; 4% Two or more races, non-Hispanic/Latino; 0.6% Race/ethnicity unknown; 0.1% international; 22% transferred in.
**Freshmen** *Admission:* 130 enrolled.
**Faculty** *Total:* 98, 40% full-time, 9% with terminal degrees.
**Majors** Accounting; administrative assistant and secretarial science; business administration and management; business/commerce; child-care and support services management; computer and information sciences; criminal justice/safety; early childhood education; electrician; electromechanical technology; industrial technology; liberal arts and sciences/liberal studies; medical administrative assistant and medical secretary; medical office management; multi/interdisciplinary studies related; office management; registered nursing/registered nurse.
**Academics** *Calendar:* semesters. *Degree:* certificates and associate. *Special study options:* academic remediation for entering students, accelerated degree program, advanced placement credit, cooperative education, distance learning, double majors, freshman honors college, honors programs, independent study, internships, part-time degree program, services for LD students, summer session for credit.
**Library** College of the Ouachitas Library/Learning Resource Center. Students can reserve study rooms.
**Student Life** *Housing:* college housing not available. *Campus security:* 24-hour emergency response devices and patrols. *Student services:* personal/psychological counseling, veterans affairs office.
**Costs (2017–18)** *Tuition:* state resident $2850 full-time, $95 per credit hour part-time; nonresident $5700 full-time, $190 per credit hour part-time. Full-time tuition and fees vary according to course load and program. Part-time tuition and fees vary according to course load and program. No tuition increase for student's term of enrollment. *Required fees:* $830 full-time, $28 per credit hour part-time. *Payment plan:* installment. *Waivers:* senior citizens and employees or children of employees.
**Financial Aid** Of all full-time matriculated undergraduates who enrolled in 2016, 18 Federal Work-Study jobs (averaging $2400).
**Applying** *Options:* electronic application, early admission, deferred entrance. *Required:* high school transcript, immunizations. *Application deadlines:* rolling (freshmen), rolling (transfers). *Notification:* continuous (freshmen), continuous (transfers).
**Freshman Application Contact** Janet Hunt, Student Success Coordinator, College of the Ouachitas, One College Circle, Malvern, AR 72104. *Phone:* 501-337-5000 Ext. 1194. *Toll-free phone:* 800-337-0266. *Fax:* 501-337-9382. *E-mail:* jhunt@coto.edu.
*Website:* http://www.coto.edu/.

## Cossatot Community College of the University of Arkansas
### De Queen, Arkansas
**Freshman Application Contact** Mrs. Tommi Cobb, Admissions Coordinator, Cossatot Community College of the University of Arkansas, 183 College Drive, DeQueen, AR 71832. *Phone:* 870-584-4471 Ext. 1158. *Toll-free phone:* 800-844-4471. *Fax:* 870-642-5088. *E-mail:* tcobb@cccua.edu. *Website:* http://www.cccua.edu/.

## East Arkansas Community College
### Forrest City, Arkansas
**Freshman Application Contact** Ms. Sharon Collier, Director of Enrollment Management/Institutional Research, East Arkansas Community College, 1700 Newcastle Road, Forrest City, AR 72335-2204. *Phone:* 870-633-4480. *Toll-free phone:* 877-797-3222. *Fax:* 870-633-3840. *E-mail:* dadams@eacc.edu. *Website:* http://www.eacc.edu/.

## Jefferson Regional Medical Center School of Nursing
### Pine Bluff, Arkansas
**Admissions Office Contact** Jefferson Regional Medical Center School of Nursing, 1600 West 40th Avenue, Pine Bluff, AR 71603. *Website:* http://www.jrmc.org/school-of-nursing/.

# National Park College
## Hot Springs, Arkansas

- **State and locally supported** 2-year, founded 1973, part of Arkansas Department of Higher Education
- **Suburban** 50-acre campus with easy access to Little Rock
- **Endowment** $11.3 million
- **Coed,** 2,996 undergraduate students, 41% full-time, 60% women, 40% men

**Undergraduates** 1,237 full-time, 1,759 part-time. Students come from 1 other state; 2% are from out of state; 17% transferred in. *Retention:* 100% of full-time freshmen returned.

**Freshmen** *Admission:* 4,969 applied, 4,969 admitted, 345 enrolled.

**Faculty** *Total:* 160, 63% full-time, 11% with terminal degrees. *Student/faculty ratio:* 18:1.

**Majors** Accounting; administrative assistant and secretarial science; art; business administration and management; child development; clinical laboratory science/medical technology; clinical/medical laboratory technology; commercial and advertising art; computer graphics; criminal justice/law enforcement administration; data processing and data processing technology; education; electrical, electronic and communications engineering technology; elementary education; emergency medical technology (EMT paramedic); finance; fire science/firefighting; health/health-care administration; health information/medical records administration; health professions related; industrial radiologic technology; information science/studies; liberal arts and sciences/liberal studies; medical administrative assistant and medical secretary; parks, recreation and leisure; parks, recreation and leisure facilities management; physical sciences; public administration; radiologic technology/science; registered nursing/registered nurse; trade and industrial teacher education.

**Academics** *Calendar:* semesters. *Degree:* certificates, diplomas, and associate. *Special study options:* academic remediation for entering students, adult/continuing education programs, advanced placement credit, cooperative education, distance learning, double majors, external degree program, honors programs, independent study, internships, part-time degree program, services for LD students, student-designed majors, study abroad, summer session for credit.

**Library** NATIONAL PARK COLLEGE LIBRARY.

**Student Life** *Housing:* college housing not available. *Activities and Organizations:* choral group, Student Government Association, Nighthawk Singers, Intramurals, Phi Theta Kappa, Anime Club. *Campus security:* 24-hour emergency response devices, Campus Resource Officer. *Student services:* personal/psychological counseling, veterans affairs office.

**Athletics** Member NJCAA. *Intercollegiate sports:* basketball M(s)/W(s), cheerleading M/W. *Intramural sports:* basketball M/W, football M/W, softball M/W, volleyball M/W.

**Standardized Tests** *Required:* ACT (for admission), SAT and SAT Subject Tests or ACT (for admission), ACCUPLACER (for admission).

**Applying** *Options:* early admission, deferred entrance. *Required:* high school transcript. *Application deadlines:* rolling (freshmen), rolling (transfers).

**Freshman Application Contact** National Park College, 101 College Drive, Hot Springs, AR 71913. *Phone:* 501-760-4202. *Website:* http://www.np.edu/.

# North Arkansas College
## Harrison, Arkansas

**Freshman Application Contact** Mrs. Charla Jennings, Director of Admissions, North Arkansas College, 1515 Pioneer Drive, Harrison, AR 72601. *Phone:* 870-391-3221. *Toll-free phone:* 800-679-6622. *Fax:* 870-391-3339. *E-mail:* charlam@northark.edu. *Website:* http://www.northark.edu/.

# NorthWest Arkansas Community College
## Bentonville, Arkansas

- **State-supported** 2-year, founded 1989
- **Suburban** 77-acre campus
- **Coed,** 7,715 undergraduate students

**Undergraduates** 2% Black or African American, non-Hispanic/Latino; 16% Hispanic/Latino; 3% Asian, non-Hispanic/Latino; 0.3% Native Hawaiian or other Pacific Islander, non-Hispanic/Latino; 2% American Indian or Alaska Native, non-Hispanic/Latino; 3% Two or more races, non-Hispanic/Latino; 3% Race/ethnicity unknown; 2% international. *Retention:* 59% of full-time freshmen returned.

**Faculty** *Total:* 475, 32% full-time. *Student/faculty ratio:* 18:1.

**Majors** Accounting; business administration and management; commercial and advertising art; computer programming; criminal justice/law enforcement administration; criminal justice/safety; culinary arts; data processing and data processing technology; drafting and design technology; early childhood education; education; electrical, electronic and communications engineering technology; emergency medical technology (EMT paramedic); environmental science; finance; fire services administration; health information/medical records technology; legal assistant/paralegal; liberal arts and sciences/liberal studies; occupational safety and health technology; physical therapy; registered nursing/registered nurse; respiratory care therapy.

**Academics** *Calendar:* semesters. *Degree:* certificates and associate. *Special study options:* academic remediation for entering students, accelerated degree program, adult/continuing education programs, advanced placement credit, cooperative education, distance learning, double majors, English as a second language, honors programs, independent study, internships, part-time degree program, services for LD students, student-designed majors, study abroad, summer session for credit. *ROTC:* Army (c), Air Force (c).

**Library** Pauline Whitaker Library plus 1 other.

**Student Life** *Housing:* college housing not available. *Activities and Organizations:* drama/theater group, student-run newspaper, choral group, Student Advisory Activity Council, Gamma Beta Phi, Phi Beta Lambda, Student Nurses Association, Enactus. *Campus security:* 24-hour emergency response devices and patrols. *Student services:* personal/psychological counseling, veterans affairs office.

**Athletics** *Intramural sports:* basketball M(c)/W(c), bowling M(c)/W(c), golf M(c), soccer M(c)/W(c), softball M(c)/W(c), volleyball W(c).

**Costs (2018–19)** *Tuition:* area resident $2250 full-time, $75 per credit hour part-time; state resident $3675 full-time, $123 per credit hour part-time; nonresident $3750 full-time, $125 per credit hour part-time. Full-time tuition and fees vary according to program. Part-time tuition and fees vary according to program. *Required fees:* $988 full-time, $29 per credit hour part-time, $55 per term part-time. *Payment plan:* installment. *Waivers:* senior citizens and employees or children of employees.

**Applying** *Options:* electronic application. *Required:* high school transcript. *Application deadlines:* rolling (freshmen), rolling (transfers). *Notification:* continuous (freshmen), continuous (transfers).

**Freshman Application Contact** NorthWest Arkansas Community College, One College Drive, Bentonville, AR 72712. *Phone:* 479-636-9222. *Toll-free phone:* 800-995-6922. *Fax:* 479-619-4116. *E-mail:* admissions@nwacc.edu. *Website:* http://www.nwacc.edu/.

# Ozarka College
## Melbourne, Arkansas

**Freshman Application Contact** Ms. Dylan Mowery, Director of Admissions, Ozarka College, PO Box 10, Melbourne, AR 72556. *Phone:* 870-368-7371 Ext. 2013. *Toll-free phone:* 800-821-4335. *E-mail:* dmmowery@ozarka.edu. *Website:* http://www.ozarka.edu/.

# Phillips Community College of the University of Arkansas
## Helena, Arkansas

**Director of Admissions** Mr. Lynn Boone, Registrar, Phillips Community College of the University of Arkansas, PO Box 785, Helena, AR 72342-0785. *Phone:* 870-338-6474. *Website:* http://www.pccua.edu/.

# Remington College–Little Rock Campus
## Little Rock, Arkansas

**Director of Admissions** Brian Maggio, Director of Recruitment, Remington College–Little Rock Campus, 10600 Colonel Glenn Road, Suite 100, Little Rock, AR 72204. *Phone:* 501-312-0007. *Toll-free phone:* 800-323-8122. *Fax:* 501-225-3819. *E-mail:* brian.maggio@remingtoncollege.edu. *Website:* http://www.remingtoncollege.edu/.

# Shorter College
## North Little Rock, Arkansas

**Director of Admissions** Mr. Keith Hunter, Director of Admissions, Shorter College, 604 Locust Street, North Little Rock, AR 72114-4885. *Phone:* 501-374-6305. *Website:* http://www.shortercollege.edu/.

# South Arkansas Community College
## El Dorado, Arkansas

**Freshman Application Contact** Dr. Stephanie Tully-Dartez, Director of Enrollment Services, South Arkansas Community College, PO Box 7010, El Dorado, AR 71731-7010. *Phone:* 870-864-7142. *Toll-free phone:* 800-955-2289. *Fax:* 870-864-7109. *E-mail:* dinman@southark.edu. *Website:* http://www.southark.edu/.

## Southeast Arkansas College
### Pine Bluff, Arkansas

- **State-supported** 2-year, founded 1991
- **Urban** 42-acre campus with easy access to Little Rock
- **Endowment** $559,963
- **Coed,** 1,304 undergraduate students, 45% full-time, 70% women, 30% men

**Undergraduates** 582 full-time, 722 part-time. Students come from 3 states and territories; 1 other country; 57% Black or African American, non-Hispanic/Latino; 2% Hispanic/Latino; 0.9% Asian, non-Hispanic/Latino; 0.1% Native Hawaiian or other Pacific Islander, non-Hispanic/Latino; 0.1% American Indian or Alaska Native, non-Hispanic/Latino; 0.8% Two or more races, non-Hispanic/Latino; 0.1% Race/ethnicity unknown; 0.1% international; 5% transferred in. *Retention:* 63% of full-time freshmen returned.
**Freshmen** *Admission:* 237 enrolled.
**Faculty** *Total:* 102, 54% full-time. *Student/faculty ratio:* 13:1.
**Majors** Business/commerce; cardiovascular technology; child-care provision; computer systems networking and telecommunications; criminal justice/law enforcement administration; criminal justice/safety; drafting and design technology; emergency medical technology (EMT paramedic); forensic science and technology; general studies; homeland security, law enforcement, firefighting and protective services related; industrial electronics technology; industrial mechanics and maintenance technology; legal assistant/paralegal; liberal arts and sciences/liberal studies; management information systems; medical radiologic technology; multi/interdisciplinary studies related; registered nursing/registered nurse; respiratory care therapy; science, technology and society; surgical technology.
**Academics** *Calendar:* semesters. *Degree:* certificates and associate. *Special study options:* academic remediation for entering students, accelerated degree program, advanced placement credit, cooperative education, distance learning, double majors, honors programs, independent study, internships, part-time degree program, services for LD students, summer session for credit.
**Library** Southeast Arkansas College Library. *Books:* 11,605 (physical), 94 (digital/electronic); *Serial titles:* 164 (physical), 8 (digital/electronic); *Databases:* 6.
**Student Life** *Housing:* college housing not available. *Activities and Organizations:* choral group, Phi Beta Lambda, HOSA, Phi Theta Kappa, Student Senate. *Campus security:* 24-hour patrols. *Student services:* personal/psychological counseling, veterans affairs office.
**Athletics** *Intramural sports:* softball M/W.
**Standardized Tests** *Required for some:* ACCUPLACER (if no other test scores are available, or test scores are older than 3 years). *Recommended:* SAT and SAT Subject Tests or ACT (for admission).
**Costs (2018–19)** *Tuition:* state resident $2820 full-time, $94 per credit hour part-time; nonresident $5640 full-time, $188 per credit hour part-time. Full-time tuition and fees vary according to location and program. Part-time tuition and fees vary according to location and program. *Required fees:* $640 full-time, $21 per credit hour part-time, $5 per term part-time. *Payment plan:* installment. *Waivers:* senior citizens and employees or children of employees.
**Financial Aid** Of all full-time matriculated undergraduates who enrolled in 2016, 704 applied for aid, 670 were judged to have need, 19 had their need fully met. 23 Federal Work-Study jobs (averaging $3071). In 2016, 9 non-need-based awards were made. *Average percent of need met:* 50%. *Average financial aid package:* $6296. *Average need-based loan:* $2991. *Average need-based gift aid:* $4668. *Average non-need-based aid:* $4721.
**Applying** *Options:* electronic application, early admission. *Required:* high school transcript. *Application deadline:* 8/21 (transfers). *Notification:* continuous (freshmen), continuous (transfers).
**Admissions Office Contact** Southeast Arkansas College, 1900 Hazel Street, Pine Bluff, AR 71603. *Toll-free phone:* 888-SEARK TC (in-state); 888-SEARC TC (out-of-state).
*Website:* http://www.seark.edu/.

## Southern Arkansas University Tech
### Camden, Arkansas

- **State-supported** 2-year, founded 1967, part of Southern Arkansas University System
- **Rural** 96-acre campus
- **Endowment** $1.7 million
- **Coed**
- **100% of applicants were admitted**

**Undergraduates** 501 full-time, 1,149 part-time. Students come from 12 states and territories; 2 other countries; 10% are from out of state; 36% Black or African American, non-Hispanic/Latino; 3% Hispanic/Latino; 0.5% Asian, non-Hispanic/Latino; 0.1% Native Hawaiian or other Pacific Islander, non-Hispanic/Latino; 0.4% American Indian or Alaska Native, non-Hispanic/Latino; 3% Two or more races, non-Hispanic/Latino; 0.1%

Race/ethnicity unknown; 0.1% international; 0.1% transferred in; 2% live on campus.
**Faculty** *Student/faculty ratio:* 17:1.
**Academics** *Calendar:* semesters. *Degree:* certificates and associate. *Special study options:* academic remediation for entering students, accelerated degree program, adult/continuing education programs, advanced placement credit, cooperative education, distance learning, double majors, external degree program, freshman honors college, honors programs, independent study, internships, off-campus study, part-time degree program, services for LD students, summer session for credit.
**Library** Southern Arkansas University Tech Learning Resource Center. *Books:* 17,910 (physical), 17,020 (digital/electronic); *Serial titles:* 964 (physical), 176 (digital/electronic); *Databases:* 9. Weekly public service hours: 45; students can reserve study rooms.
**Student Life** *Campus security:* 24-hour emergency response devices and patrols, late-night transport/escort service.
**Costs (2017–18)** *One-time required fee:* $75. *Tuition:* state resident $3240 full-time, $108 per credit hour part-time; nonresident $4680 full-time, $156 per credit hour part-time. Full-time tuition and fees vary according to course load and location. Part-time tuition and fees vary according to course load and location. *Required fees:* $1570 full-time, $50 per credit hour part-time, $75 per term part-time. *Room and board:* $5562; room only: $2800. Room and board charges vary according to housing facility and location.
**Applying** *Options:* electronic application, deferred entrance. *Application fee:* $50. *Required:* high school transcript.
**Freshman Application Contact** Mrs. Lisa Smith, Admissions Analyst, Southern Arkansas University Tech, PO Box 3499, Camden, AR 71711-1599. *Phone:* 870-574-4558. *Fax:* 870-574-4442. *E-mail:* lsmith@sautech.edu. *Website:* http://www.sautech.edu/.

## University of Arkansas Community College at Batesville
### Batesville, Arkansas

**Freshman Application Contact** Ms. Amy Foree, Enrollment Specialist, University of Arkansas Community College at Batesville, PO Box 3350, Batesville, AR 72503. *Phone:* 870-612-2113. *Toll-free phone:* 800-508-7878. *Fax:* 870-612-2129. *E-mail:* amy.foree@uaccb.edu. *Website:* http://www.uaccb.edu/.

## University of Arkansas Community College at Hope
### Hope, Arkansas

**Freshman Application Contact** University of Arkansas Community College at Hope, PO Box 140, Hope, AR 71802. *Phone:* 870-772-8174. *Website:* http://www.uacch.edu/.

## University of Arkansas Community College at Morrilton
### Morrilton, Arkansas

- **State-supported** 2-year, founded 1961, part of University of Arkansas System
- **Rural** 79-acre campus
- **Coed,** 1,921 undergraduate students, 58% full-time, 62% women, 38% men

**Undergraduates** 1,115 full-time, 806 part-time. Students come from 12 states and territories; 4 other countries; 0.6% are from out of state; 8% Black or African American, non-Hispanic/Latino; 7% Hispanic/Latino; 0.7% Asian, non-Hispanic/Latino; 0.1% Native Hawaiian or other Pacific Islander, non-Hispanic/Latino; 0.5% American Indian or Alaska Native, non-Hispanic/Latino; 6% Two or more races, non-Hispanic/Latino; 0.7% Race/ethnicity unknown; 2% international; 9% transferred in.
**Freshmen** *Admission:* 1,331 applied, 997 admitted, 521 enrolled. *Average high school GPA:* 3.0. *Test scores:* ACT scores over 18: 72%; ACT scores over 24: 12%.
**Faculty** *Total:* 79, 71% full-time, 11% with terminal degrees. *Student/faculty ratio:* 22:1.
**Majors** Autobody/collision and repair technology; automobile/automotive mechanics technology; business/commerce; child development; computer technology/computer systems technology; criminal justice/law enforcement administration; drafting and design technology; forensic science and technology; general studies; heating, air conditioning, ventilation and refrigeration maintenance technology; industrial mechanics and maintenance technology; liberal arts and sciences/liberal studies; machine shop technology;

middle school education; registered nursing/registered nurse; surveying technology.

**Academics** *Calendar:* semesters. *Degree:* certificates and associate. *Special study options:* academic remediation for entering students, advanced placement credit, cooperative education, distance learning, double majors, independent study, internships, part-time degree program, services for LD students, summer session for credit.

**Library** E. Allen Gordon Library. *Books:* 25,559 (physical), 162,609 (digital/electronic); *Serial titles:* 81 (physical); *Databases:* 24. Weekly public service hours: 66; students can reserve study rooms.

**Student Life** *Housing:* college housing not available. *Activities and Organizations:* Phi Theta Kappa, Student Activities Board, National Technical Honors Society, Thrive Student Ministries, Computer Information Systems Club. *Campus security:* 24-hour emergency response devices, late-night transport/escort service, campus alert system through phone call, text message, and/or e-mail. *Student services:* personal/psychological counseling.

**Athletics** *Intramural sports:* basketball M/W, football M/W, table tennis M/W, ultimate Frisbee M/W, volleyball M/W.

**Standardized Tests** *Recommended:* SAT or ACT (for admission), ACT Compass, ACCUPLACER.

**Costs (2017–18)** *Tuition:* area resident $2700 full-time, $90 per credit hour part-time; state resident $2970 full-time, $99 per credit hour part-time; nonresident $3840 full-time, $128 per credit hour part-time. Full-time tuition and fees vary according to course load and program. Part-time tuition and fees vary according to course load and program. *Required fees:* $932 full-time, $38 per credit hour part-time, $10 per term part-time. *Payment plan:* installment. *Waivers:* senior citizens and employees or children of employees.

**Financial Aid** Of all full-time matriculated undergraduates who enrolled in 2015, 1,178 applied for aid, 1,028 were judged to have need, 31 had their need fully met. In 2015, 45 non-need-based awards were made. *Average percent of need met:* 44%. *Average financial aid package:* $6082. *Average need-based loan:* $1686. *Average need-based gift aid:* $3161. *Average non-need-based aid:* $1033.

**Applying** *Options:* electronic application, early admission, deferred entrance. *Required:* high school transcript. *Required for some:* immunization records, prior college transcript(s). *Application deadlines:* rolling (freshmen), rolling (transfers). *Notification:* continuous (freshmen), continuous (transfers).

**Freshman Application Contact** Ms. Robin Jones, Administrative Specialist, University of Arkansas Community College at Morrilton, 1537 University Boulevard, Morrilton, AR 72110. *Phone:* 501-977-2053. *Toll-free phone:* 800-264-1094. *Fax:* 501-977-2123. *E-mail:* jonesr@uaccm.edu. *Website:* http://www.uaccm.edu/.

## University of Arkansas–Pulaski Technical College
### North Little Rock, Arkansas

**Freshman Application Contact** Mr. Clark Atkins, Director of Admissions, University of Arkansas–Pulaski Technical College, 3000 West Scenic Drive, North Little Rock, AR 72118. *Phone:* 501-812-2734. *Fax:* 501-812-2316. *E-mail:* catkins@pulaskitech.edu. *Website:* http://www.pulaskitech.edu/.

## University of Arkansas Rich Mountain
### Mena, Arkansas

- **State and locally supported** 2-year, founded 1983, part of University of Arkansas System
- **Small-town** 40-acre campus
- **Coed,** 938 undergraduate students, 49% full-time, 82% women, 18% men
- **100%** of applicants were admitted

**Undergraduates** 456 full-time, 482 part-time. 0.3% Black or African American, non-Hispanic/Latino; 4% Hispanic/Latino; 1% Asian, non-Hispanic/Latino; 0.2% Native Hawaiian or other Pacific Islander, non-Hispanic/Latino; 2% American Indian or Alaska Native, non-Hispanic/Latino; 1% Two or more races, non-Hispanic/Latino; 1% Race/ethnicity unknown; 1% international. *Retention:* 61% of full-time freshmen returned.

**Freshmen** *Admission:* 155 applied, 155 admitted, 155 enrolled.

**Majors** General studies; health information/medical records technology; information resources management; liberal arts and sciences/liberal studies; manufacturing engineering technology; multi/interdisciplinary studies related; registered nursing/registered nurse.

**Academics** *Calendar:* semesters. *Degree:* certificates and associate. *Special study options:* academic remediation for entering students, adult/continuing education programs, advanced placement credit, distance learning, double majors, English as a second language, part-time degree program, services for LD students, summer session for credit.

**Library** St. John Library. *Books:* 14,668 (physical), 13,747 (digital/electronic); *Databases:* 27. Students can reserve study rooms.

**Student Life** *Housing:* college housing not available. *Activities and Organizations:* drama/theater group. *Campus security:* campus security on duty during college hours. *Student services:* veterans affairs office.

**Costs (2018–19)** *Tuition:* area resident $1944 full-time, $81 per credit hour part-time; state resident $2280 full-time, $95 per credit hour part-time. Full-time tuition and fees vary according to course load and program. Part-time tuition and fees vary according to course load and program. *Required fees:* $936 full-time, $39 per credit hour part-time. *Payment plan:* installment. *Waivers:* senior citizens and employees or children of employees.

**Financial Aid** Of all full-time matriculated undergraduates who enrolled in 2016, 12 Federal Work-Study jobs (averaging $1500).

**Applying** *Options:* electronic application, early admission. *Required:* high school transcript. *Application deadlines:* rolling (freshmen), rolling (out-of-state freshmen), rolling (transfers). *Notification:* continuous (freshmen), continuous (out-of-state freshmen), continuous (transfers).

**Freshman Application Contact** Wendy McDaniel, Director of Admissions, University of Arkansas Rich Mountain, 1100 College Drive, Mena, AR 71953. *Phone:* 479-394-7622 Ext. 1440. *E-mail:* wmcdaniel@uarichmountain.edu. *Website:* http://www.uarichmountain.edu/.

# CALIFORNIA

## Advanced College
### South Gate, California

**Admissions Office Contact** Advanced College, 13180 Paramount Boulevard, South Gate, CA 90280. *Website:* http://www.advancedcollege.edu/.

## Advanced Computing Institute
### Los Angeles, California

**Admissions Office Contact** Advanced Computing Institute, 3470 Wilshire Boulevard 11th Floor, Los Angeles, CA 90010-3911. *Website:* http://www.advancedcomputinginstitute.edu/.

## Advanced Training Associates
### El Cajon, California

**Admissions Office Contact** Advanced Training Associates, 1810 Gillespie Way, Suite 104, El Cajon, CA 92020. *Toll-free phone:* 800-720-2125. *Website:* http://www.advancedtraining.edu/.

## Allan Hancock College
### Santa Maria, California

**Freshman Application Contact** Ms. Adela Esquivel Swinson, Director of Admissions and Records, Allan Hancock College, 800 South College Drive, Santa Maria, CA 93454-6399. *Phone:* 805-922-6966 Ext. 3272. *Toll-free phone:* 866-342-5242. *Fax:* 805-922-3477. *Website:* http://www.hancockcollege.edu/.

## ★ American Academy of Dramatic Arts–Los Angeles
### Hollywood, California

- **Independent** 2-year, founded 1974
- **Urban** 4-acre campus with easy access to Los Angeles
- **Endowment** $1.7 million
- **Coed,** 303 undergraduate students, 100% full-time, 60% women, 40% men

**Undergraduates** 303 full-time. Students come from 27 states and territories; 37 other countries; 53% are from out of state; 10% Black or African American, non-Hispanic/Latino; 8% Hispanic/Latino; 1% Asian, non-Hispanic/Latino; 0.3% Native Hawaiian or other Pacific Islander, non-Hispanic/Latino; 0.3% American Indian or Alaska Native, non-Hispanic/Latino; 6% Two or more races, non-Hispanic/Latino; 0.7% Race/ethnicity unknown; 33% international; 0.7% transferred in.

**Freshmen** *Admission:* 481 applied, 378 admitted, 139 enrolled.

**Faculty** *Total:* 50, 18% full-time, 2% with terminal degrees. *Student/faculty ratio:* 12:1.

**Majors** Dramatic/theater arts.

**Academics** *Calendar:* semesters. *Degree:* certificates, diplomas, and associate. *Special study options:* internships, services for LD students.

**Library** Bryn Morgan Library. *Books:* 15,000 (physical); *Serial titles:* 1,000 (physical). Weekly public service hours: 53.

**Student Life** *Housing Options:* Campus housing is university owned. *Activities and Organizations:* choral group. *Campus security:* 24-hour emergency response devices and patrols, controlled dormitory access. *Student services:* personal/psychological counseling, veterans affairs office.

**Costs (2018–19)** *Comprehensive fee:* $46,815 includes full-time tuition ($34,410), mandatory fees ($750), and room and board ($11,655). *Payment plan:* installment.

**Financial Aid** Of all full-time matriculated undergraduates who enrolled in 2016, 15 Federal Work-Study jobs (averaging $2000).

**Applying** *Options:* electronic application, deferred entrance. *Application fee:* $50. *Required:* essay or personal statement, high school transcript, 2 letters of recommendation, interview, audition. *Recommended:* minimum 2.0 GPA. *Application deadlines:* rolling (freshmen), rolling (transfers). *Notification:* continuous (freshmen), continuous (transfers).

**Freshman Application Contact** Steven Hong, Director of Admissions, American Academy of Dramatic Arts–Los Angeles, 1336 North La Brea Avenue, Los Angeles, CA 90028. *Phone:* 323-464-2777 Ext. 103. *Toll-free phone:* 800-222-2867. *E-mail:* shong@aada.edu. *Website:* http://www.aada.edu/.

# American Career College
## Anaheim, California

**Director of Admissions** Susan Pailet, Senior Executive Director of Admission, American Career College, 1200 North Magnolia Avenue, Anaheim, CA 92801. *Phone:* 714-952-9066. *Toll-free phone:* 877-832-0790. *E-mail:* info@americancareer.com. *Website:* http://americancareercollege.edu/.

# American Career College
## Los Angeles, California

**Director of Admissions** Tamra Adams, Director of Admissions, American Career College, 4021 Rosewood Avenue, Los Angeles, CA 90004. *Phone:* 323-668-7555. *Toll-free phone:* 877-832-0790. *E-mail:* info@americancareer.com. *Website:* http://americancareercollege.edu/.

# American Career College
## Ontario, California

**Director of Admissions** Juan Tellez, Director of Admissions, American Career College, 3130 East Sedona Court, Ontario, CA 91764. *Phone:* 951-739-0788. *Toll-free phone:* 877-832-0790. *E-mail:* info@americancareer.com. *Website:* http://americancareercollege.edu/.

# American Medical Sciences Center
## Glendale, California

**Admissions Office Contact** American Medical Sciences Center, 225 West Broadway, Suite 115, Glendale, CA 91204-5108. *Website:* http://www.amsc.edu/.

# American River College
## Sacramento, California

**Freshman Application Contact** American River College, 4700 College Oak Drive, Sacramento, CA 95841-4286. *Phone:* 916-484-8171. *Website:* http://www.arc.losrios.edu/.

# Antelope Valley College
## Lancaster, California

- **District-supported** primarily 2-year, founded 1929, part of California Community College System
- **Suburban** 135-acre campus with easy access to Los Angeles
- **Endowment** $4.6 million
- **Coed**, 14,125 undergraduate students, 29% full-time, 59% women, 41% men

**Undergraduates** 4,031 full-time, 10,094 part-time. Students come from 10 states and territories; 1 other country; 16% Black or African American, non-Hispanic/Latino; 53% Hispanic/Latino; 4% Asian, non-Hispanic/Latino; 0.2% Native Hawaiian or other Pacific Islander, non-Hispanic/Latino; 0.3% American Indian or Alaska Native, non-Hispanic/Latino; 5% Two or more races, non-Hispanic/Latino; 0.8% Race/ethnicity unknown; 0.1% international.

**Freshmen** *Admission:* 2,105 applied, 2,105 admitted, 2,105 enrolled.

**Faculty** *Total:* 622, 28% full-time, 8% with terminal degrees. *Student/faculty ratio:* 24:1.

**Majors** Accounting technology and bookkeeping; administrative assistant and secretarial science; aircraft powerplant technology; airframe mechanics and aircraft maintenance technology; American Sign Language (ASL); animation, interactive technology, video graphics and special effects; anthropology; apparel and textiles; applied horticulture/horticulture operations; art; autobody/collision and repair technology; automobile/automotive mechanics technology; biological and physical sciences; business administration and management; business/commerce; child-care provision; computer graphics; computer programming; computer systems networking and telecommunications; criminal justice/police science; data entry/microcomputer applications; desktop publishing and digital imaging design; drafting and design technology; electrical/electronics equipment installation and repair; electrician; engineering technology; English; family and consumer sciences/human sciences; fire prevention and safety technology; geography; geology/earth science; health and physical education/fitness; heating, air conditioning, ventilation and refrigeration maintenance technology; heating, ventilation, air conditioning and refrigeration engineering technology; history; humanities; industrial production technologies related; information technology; interior design; kinesiology and exercise science; landscaping and groundskeeping; liberal arts and sciences/liberal studies; mathematics; medical/clinical assistant; music; philosophy; photographic and film/video technology; photography; physical sciences; physics; political science and government; pre-engineering; radiologic technology/science; real estate; registered nursing/registered nurse; respiratory care therapy; sales, distribution, and marketing operations; sign language interpretation and translation; small business administration; social sciences; sociology; speech communication and rhetoric; teacher assistant/aide; visual and performing arts; welding technology; wildland/forest firefighting and investigation.

**Academics** *Calendar:* semesters. *Degrees:* certificates, associate, and bachelor's. *Special study options:* academic remediation for entering students, advanced placement credit, cooperative education, distance learning, English as a second language, external degree program, honors programs, independent study, part-time degree program, services for LD students, study abroad, summer session for credit. *ROTC:* Army (c), Navy (c), Air Force (c).

**Library** Antelope Valley College Library. *Books:* 54,721 (physical), 8,152 (digital/electronic); *Serial titles:* 10 (physical); *Databases:* 65. Weekly public service hours: 58; students can reserve study rooms.

**Student Life** *Housing:* college housing not available. *Activities and Organizations:* drama/theater group. *Campus security:* 24-hour emergency response devices and patrols, late-night transport/escort service. *Student services:* health clinic, personal/psychological counseling, veterans affairs office.

**Athletics** *Intercollegiate sports:* baseball M, basketball M/W, cross-country running M/W, football M, golf M, sand volleyball W, soccer W, softball W, tennis W, track and field M/W, volleyball W. *Intramural sports:* basketball M/W, golf M/W, swimming and diving M/W, tennis M/W, volleyball M/W, weight lifting M/W.

**Costs (2017–18)** *Tuition:* state resident $46 per unit part-time; nonresident $236 per unit part-time. *Required fees:* $20 per term part-time. *Payment plan:* installment.

**Applying** *Options:* electronic application, early admission. *Application deadlines:* rolling (freshmen), rolling (transfers). *Notification:* continuous (freshmen), continuous (transfers).

**Freshman Application Contact** Welcome Center, Antelope Valley College, 3041 West Avenue K, SSV Building, Lancaster, CA 93536. *Phone:* 661-722-6300 Ext. 6331. *Website:* http://www.avc.edu/.

# APT College
## Carlsbad, California

**Director of Admissions** Monica Hoffman, Director of Admissions/Registrar, APT College, 1939 Palomar Oaks Way, Suite A, Carlsbad, CA 92011. *Phone:* 800-431-8488. *Toll-free phone:* 800-431-8488. *Fax:* 888-431-8588. *E-mail:* aptc@aptc.com. *Website:* http://www.aptc.edu/.

# Bakersfield College
## Bakersfield, California

**Freshman Application Contact** Bakersfield College, 1801 Panorama Drive, Bakersfield, CA 93305-1299. *Phone:* 661-395-4301. *Website:* http://www.bakersfieldcollege.edu/.

# Barstow Community College

Barstow, California

**Freshman Application Contact** Barstow Community College, 2700 Barstow Road, Barstow, CA 92311-6699. *Phone:* 760-252-2411 Ext. 7236. *Website:* http://www.barstow.edu/.

# Berkeley City College

Berkeley, California

**Freshman Application Contact** Dr. May Kuang-chi Chen, Vice President of Student Services, Berkeley City College, 2050 Center Street, Berkeley, CA 94704. *Phone:* 510-981-2820. *Fax:* 510-841-7333. *E-mail:* mrivas@peralta.edu. *Website:* http://www.berkeleycitycollege.edu/.

# Beverly Hills Design Institute

Beverly Hills, California

**Freshman Application Contact** Beverly Hills Design Institute, 8484 Wilshire Boulevard, Suite 730, Beverly Hills, CA 90211. *Phone:* 310-360-8888. *Website:* http://www.bhdi.edu/.

# Brightwood College, Bakersfield Campus

Bakersfield, California

**Freshman Application Contact** Brightwood College, Bakersfield Campus, 1914 Wible Road, Bakersfield, CA 93304. *Phone:* 661-836-6300. *Toll-free phone:* 866-543-0208. *Website:* http://www.brightwood.edu/.

# Brightwood College, Chula Vista Campus

Chula Vista, California

**Freshman Application Contact** Brightwood College, Chula Vista Campus, 555 Broadway, Suite 144, Chula Vista, CA 91910. *Phone:* 877-473-3052. *Toll-free phone:* 866-543-0208. *Website:* http://www.brightwood.edu/.

# Brightwood College, Fresno Campus

Fresno, California

**Freshman Application Contact** Brightwood College, Fresno Campus, 44 Shaw Avenue, Fresno, CA 93612. *Phone:* 559-325-5100. *Toll-free phone:* 866-543-0208. *Website:* http://www.brightwood.edu/.

# Brightwood College, Los Angeles (Van Nuys) Campus

Van Nuys, California

**Freshman Application Contact** Ms. Renee Codner, Director of Admissions, Brightwood College, Los Angeles (Van Nuys) Campus, 15400 Sherman Way, Suite 101, Van Nuys, CA 91406. *Phone:* 818-763-2563 Ext. 240. *Toll-free phone:* 866-543-0208. *E-mail:* rcodner@mariccollege.edu. *Website:* http://www.brightwood.edu/.

# Brightwood College, Modesto Campus

Salida, California

**Freshman Application Contact** Brightwood College, Modesto Campus, 5172 Kiernan Court, Salida, CA 95368. *Phone:* 209-543-7000. *Toll-free phone:* 866-543-0208. *Website:* http://www.brightwood.edu/.

# Brightwood College, Palm Springs Campus

Palm Springs, California

**Freshman Application Contact** Brightwood College, Palm Springs Campus, 2475 East Tahquitz Canyon Way, Palm Springs, CA 92262. *Phone:* 760-778-3540. *Toll-free phone:* 866-543-0208. *Website:* http://www.brightwood.edu/.

# Brightwood College, Riverside Campus

Riverside, California

**Freshman Application Contact** Brightwood College, Riverside Campus, 4040 Vine Street, Riverside, CA 92507. *Phone:* 951-276-1704. *Toll-free phone:* 866-543-0208. *Website:* http://www.brightwood.edu/.

# Brightwood College, Sacramento Campus

Sacramento, California

**Freshman Application Contact** Brightwood College, Sacramento Campus, 4330 Watt Avenue, Suite 400, Sacramento, CA 95821. *Phone:* 916-649-8168. *Toll-free phone:* 866-543-0208. *Website:* http://www.brightwood.edu/.

# Brightwood College, San Diego Campus

San Diego, California

**Freshman Application Contact** Brightwood College, San Diego Campus, 9055 Balboa Avenue, San Diego, CA 92123. *Phone:* 858-279-4500. *Toll-free phone:* 866-543-0208. *Website:* http://www.brightwood.edu/.

# Brightwood College, Vista Campus

Vista, California

**Freshman Application Contact** Brightwood College, Vista Campus, 2022 University Drive, Vista, CA 92083. *Phone:* 760-630-1555. *Toll-free phone:* 866-543-0208. *Website:* http://www.brightwood.edu/.

# Bryan University

Los Angeles, California

**Admissions Office Contact** Bryan University, 3580 Wilshire Boulevard, Los Angeles, CA 90010. *Website:* http://losangeles.bryanuniversity.edu/.

# Butte College

Oroville, California

**Freshman Application Contact** Mr. Brad Zuniga, Director of Recruitment, Outreach and New Student Orientation, Butte College, 3536 Butte Campus Drive, Oroville, CA 95965-8399. *Phone:* 530-895-2948. *Website:* http://www.butte.edu/.

# Cabrillo College

Aptos, California

**Freshman Application Contact** Tama Bolton, Director of Admissions and Records, Cabrillo College, 6500 Soquel Drive, Aptos, CA 95003-3194. *Phone:* 831-477-3548. *Fax:* 831-479-5782. *E-mail:* tabolton@cabrillo.edu. *Website:* http://www.cabrillo.edu/.

# Cambridge Junior College

Yuba City, California

**Freshman Application Contact** Admissions Office, Cambridge Junior College, 990-A Klamath Lane, Yuba City, CA 95993. *Phone:* 530-674-9199. *Fax:* 530-671-7319. *Website:* http://www.cambridge.edu/.

# Cañada College

Redwood City, California

- **District-supported** 2-year, founded 1968, part of San Mateo County Community College District System
- **Suburban** 131-acre campus with easy access to San Francisco, San Jose
- **Endowment** $150,000
- **Coed**

**Undergraduates** 406 full-time, 5,027 part-time. 2% are from out of state; 3% Black or African American, non-Hispanic/Latino; 36% Hispanic/Latino; 10% Asian, non-Hispanic/Latino; 2% Native Hawaiian or other Pacific Islander, non-Hispanic/Latino; 0.2% American Indian or Alaska Native, non-Hispanic/Latino; 17% Two or more races, non-Hispanic/Latino; 2% Race/ethnicity unknown; 5% international.

**Faculty** *Student/faculty ratio:* 16:1.

**Academics** *Calendar:* semesters. *Degree:* certificates and associate. *Special study options:* academic remediation for entering students, accelerated degree program, adult/continuing education programs, advanced placement credit, cooperative education, distance learning, double majors, English as a second language, honors programs, independent study, internships, part-time degree program, services for LD students, study abroad, summer session for credit. *ROTC:* Army (c), Navy (c), Air Force (c).

**Library** *Books:* 25,000 (physical), 230,000 (digital/electronic); *Serial titles:* 40 (physical), 20,000 (digital/electronic); *Databases:* 45. Weekly public service hours: 64; students can reserve study rooms.

**Student Life** *Campus security:* 24-hour emergency response devices and patrols, late-night transport/escort service, 12-hour patrols by trained security personnel.

**Financial Aid** Of all full-time matriculated undergraduates who enrolled in 2014, 40 Federal Work-Study jobs (averaging $2026).

**Applying** *Options:* electronic application. *Recommended:* high school transcript.

**Freshman Application Contact** Cañada College, 4200 Farm Hill Boulevard, Redwood City, CA 94061-1099. *Phone:* 650-306-3125. *Website:* http://www.canadacollege.edu/.

## Carrington College–Citrus Heights
### Citrus Heights, California

- **Proprietary** 2-year, part of Carrington Colleges Group, Inc.
- **Coed**

**Undergraduates** 432 full-time, 16 part-time. 5% Black or African American, non-Hispanic/Latino; 22% Hispanic/Latino; 4% Asian, non-Hispanic/Latino; 0.9% Native Hawaiian or other Pacific Islander, non-Hispanic/Latino; 1% American Indian or Alaska Native, non-Hispanic/Latino; 8% Two or more races, non-Hispanic/Latino; 0.2% Race/ethnicity unknown; 0.2% international; 17% transferred in.

**Faculty** *Student/faculty ratio:* 24:1.

**Academics** *Degree:* certificates and associate.

**Costs (2017–18)** *Tuition:* $33,126 per degree program part-time. Full-time tuition and fees vary according to program. Part-time tuition and fees vary according to program.

**Applying** *Required:* essay or personal statement, high school transcript, interview.

**Freshman Application Contact** Carrington College–Citrus Heights, 7301 Greenback Lane, Suite A, Citrus Heights, CA 95621. *Website:* http://www.carrington.edu/.

## Carrington College–Pleasant Hill
### Pleasant Hill, California

- **Proprietary** 2-year, founded 1997, part of Carrington Colleges Group, Inc.
- **Coed**

**Undergraduates** 357 full-time, 80 part-time. 1% are from out of state; 11% Black or African American, non-Hispanic/Latino; 32% Hispanic/Latino; 16% Asian, non-Hispanic/Latino; 3% Native Hawaiian or other Pacific Islander, non-Hispanic/Latino; 0.5% American Indian or Alaska Native, non-Hispanic/Latino; 2% Two or more races, non-Hispanic/Latino; 3% Race/ethnicity unknown; 0.7% international; 24% transferred in.

**Faculty** *Student/faculty ratio:* 26:1.

**Academics** *Degree:* certificates and associate.

**Costs (2017–18)** *Tuition:* $33,126 per degree program part-time. Full-time tuition and fees vary according to program. Part-time tuition and fees vary according to program.

**Applying** *Required:* essay or personal statement, high school transcript, interview.

**Freshman Application Contact** Carrington College–Pleasant Hill, 380 Civic Drive, Suite 300, Pleasant Hill, CA 94523. *Website:* http://www.carrington.edu/.

## Carrington College–Pomona
### Pomona, California

- **Proprietary** 2-year
- **Coed**

**Undergraduates** 273 full-time, 83 part-time. 3% Black or African American, non-Hispanic/Latino; 63% Hispanic/Latino; 4% Asian, non-Hispanic/Latino; 0.8% Native Hawaiian or other Pacific Islander, non-Hispanic/Latino; 0.3% American Indian or Alaska Native, non-Hispanic/Latino; 2% Two or more races, non-Hispanic/Latino; 0.8% Race/ethnicity unknown; 16% transferred in.

**Faculty** *Student/faculty ratio:* 21:1.

**Academics** *Degree:* associate.

**Costs (2017–18)** *Tuition:* $33,126 per degree program part-time. Full-time tuition and fees vary according to program. Part-time tuition and fees vary according to program.

**Freshman Application Contact** Carrington College–Pomona, 901 Corporate Center Drive, Suite 300, Pomona, CA 91768. *Toll-free phone:* 877-206-2106. *Website:* http://www.carrington.edu/.

## Carrington College–Sacramento
### Sacramento, California

- **Proprietary** 2-year, founded 1967, part of Carrington Colleges Group, Inc.
- **Coed**

**Undergraduates** 935 full-time, 251 part-time. 11% are from out of state; 9% Black or African American, non-Hispanic/Latino; 31% Hispanic/Latino; 12% Asian, non-Hispanic/Latino; 2% Native Hawaiian or other Pacific Islander, non-Hispanic/Latino; 1% American Indian or Alaska Native, non-Hispanic/Latino; 3% Two or more races, non-Hispanic/Latino; 5% Race/ethnicity unknown; 0.3% international; 11% transferred in.

**Faculty** *Student/faculty ratio:* 14:1.

**Academics** *Degree:* certificates and associate.

**Costs (2017–18)** *Tuition:* $18,350 per degree program part-time. Full-time tuition and fees vary according to program. Part-time tuition and fees vary according to program.

**Applying** *Required:* essay or personal statement, high school transcript, interview.

**Freshman Application Contact** Carrington College–Sacramento, 8909 Folsom Boulevard, Sacramento, CA 95826. *Website:* http://www.carrington.edu/.

## Carrington College–San Jose
### San Jose, California

- **Proprietary** 2-year, founded 1999, part of Carrington Colleges Group, Inc.
- **Coed**

**Undergraduates** 654 full-time, 61 part-time. 2% Black or African American, non-Hispanic/Latino; 54% Hispanic/Latino; 16% Asian, non-Hispanic/Latino; 3% Native Hawaiian or other Pacific Islander, non-Hispanic/Latino; 4% Two or more races, non-Hispanic/Latino; 0.7% Race/ethnicity unknown; 0.8% international; 13% transferred in.

**Faculty** *Student/faculty ratio:* 24:1.

**Academics** *Degree:* certificates and associate.

**Costs (2017–18)** *Tuition:* $17,908 per degree program part-time. Full-time tuition and fees vary according to program. Part-time tuition and fees vary according to program.

**Applying** *Required:* essay or personal statement, high school transcript, interview.

**Freshman Application Contact** Carrington College–San Jose, 5883 Rue Ferrari, Suite 125, San Jose, CA 95138. *Website:* http://www.carrington.edu/.

## Carrington College–San Leandro
### San Leandro, California

- **Proprietary** 2-year, founded 1986, part of Carrington Colleges Group, Inc.
- **Coed**

**Undergraduates** 398 full-time, 18 part-time. 26% are from out of state; 19% Black or African American, non-Hispanic/Latino; 51% Hispanic/Latino; 9% Asian, non-Hispanic/Latino; 2% Native Hawaiian or other Pacific Islander, non-Hispanic/Latino; 0.5% American Indian or Alaska Native, non-Hispanic/Latino; 2% Two or more races, non-Hispanic/Latino; 0.7% Race/ethnicity unknown; 0.5% international; 16% transferred in.

**Faculty** *Student/faculty ratio:* 31:1.

**Academics** *Degree:* certificates and associate.

**Costs (2017–18)** *Tuition:* $15,868 per degree program part-time. Full-time tuition and fees vary according to program. Part-time tuition and fees vary according to program.

**Applying** *Required:* essay or personal statement, high school transcript, interview.

**Freshman Application Contact** Carrington College–San Leandro, 15555 East 14th Street, Suite 500, San Leandro, CA 94578. *Website:* http://www.carrington.edu/.

# Carrington College–Stockton
## Stockton, California

- **Proprietary** 2-year
- **Coed**

**Undergraduates** 533 full-time, 12 part-time. 9% Black or African American, non-Hispanic/Latino; 53% Hispanic/Latino; 10% Asian, non-Hispanic/Latino; 2% Native Hawaiian or other Pacific Islander, non-Hispanic/Latino; 0.4% American Indian or Alaska Native, non-Hispanic/Latino; 2% Two or more races, non-Hispanic/Latino; 2% Race/ethnicity unknown; 0.4% international; 16% transferred in.
**Faculty** *Student/faculty ratio:* 42:1.
**Academics** *Degree:* certificates and associate.
**Costs (2017–18)** *Tuition:* $17,908 per degree program part-time. Full-time tuition and fees vary according to program. Part-time tuition and fees vary according to program.
**Freshman Application Contact** Carrington College–Stockton, 1313 West Robinhood Drive, Suite B, Stockton, CA 95207. *Website:* http://www.carrington.edu/.

# Casa Loma College–Van Nuys
## Los Angeles, California

**Admissions Office Contact** Casa Loma College–Van Nuys, 6725 Kester Avenue, Los Angeles, CA 91405. *Website:* http://www.casalomacollege.edu/.

# Cerritos College
## Norwalk, California

- **District-supported** 2-year, founded 1956, part of California Community College System
- **Suburban** 140-acre campus with easy access to Los Angeles
- **Coed**

**Undergraduates** 7,209 full-time, 14,834 part-time. Students come from 32 other countries; 1% are from out of state; 3% Black or African American, non-Hispanic/Latino; 70% Hispanic/Latino; 8% Asian, non-Hispanic/Latino; 0.6% Native Hawaiian or other Pacific Islander, non-Hispanic/Latino; 5% American Indian or Alaska Native, non-Hispanic/Latino; 1% Two or more races, non-Hispanic/Latino; 7% Race/ethnicity unknown; 0.7% international; 2% transferred in.
**Academics** *Calendar:* semesters. *Degree:* certificates and associate. *Special study options:* academic remediation for entering students, advanced placement credit, distance learning, double majors, English as a second language, honors programs, independent study, part-time degree program, services for LD students, study abroad, summer session for credit.
**Library** Wilford Michael Library. *Books:* 117,647 (physical), 13,466 (digital/electronic); *Databases:* 66. Weekly public service hours: 71; students can reserve study rooms.
**Student Life** *Campus security:* 24-hour emergency response devices and patrols, student patrols, late-night transport/escort service.
**Athletics** Member NJCAA.
**Costs (2017–18)** *One-time required fee:* $29. *Tuition:* nonresident $263 per unit part-time. Full-time tuition and fees vary according to course load. Part-time tuition and fees vary according to course load. *Required fees:* $46 per unit part-time, $342 per term part-time.
**Financial Aid** Of all full-time matriculated undergraduates who enrolled in 2016, 180 Federal Work-Study jobs (averaging $3000). 89 state and other part-time jobs (averaging $2734).
**Applying** *Options:* electronic application, early admission, deferred entrance.
**Freshman Application Contact** Cerritos College, 11110 Alondra Boulevard, Norwalk, CA 90650-6298. *Phone:* 562-860-2451 Ext. 2102. *Website:* http://www.cerritos.edu/.

# Cerro Coso Community College
## Ridgecrest, California

**Freshman Application Contact** Mrs. Heather Ootash, Counseling/Matriculation Coordinator, Cerro Coso Community College, 3000 College Heights Boulevard, Ridgecrest, CA 93555. *Phone:* 760-384-6291. *Fax:* 760-375-4776. *E-mail:* hostash@cerrocoso.edu. *Website:* http://www.cerrocoso.edu/.

# Chabot College
## Hayward, California

**Director of Admissions** Paulette Lino, Director of Admissions and Records, Chabot College, 25555 Hesperian Boulevard, Hayward, CA 94545-5001. *Phone:* 510-723-6700. *Website:* http://www.chabotcollege.edu/.

# Chaffey College
## Rancho Cucamonga, California

**Freshman Application Contact** Erlinda Martinez, Coordinator of Admissions, Chaffey College, 5885 Haven Avenue, Rancho Cucamonga, CA 91737-3002. *Phone:* 909-652-6610. *E-mail:* erlinda.martinez@chaffey.edu. *Website:* http://www.chaffey.edu/.

# Citrus College
## Glendora, California

- **District-supported** 2-year, founded 1915, part of California Community College System
- **Small-town** 104-acre campus with easy access to Los Angeles
- **Coed**

**Undergraduates** 4,921 full-time, 7,859 part-time. 4% Black or African American, non-Hispanic/Latino; 61% Hispanic/Latino; 8% Asian, non-Hispanic/Latino; 0.1% Native Hawaiian or other Pacific Islander, non-Hispanic/Latino; 0.2% American Indian or Alaska Native, non-Hispanic/Latino; 3% Two or more races, non-Hispanic/Latino; 0.7% Race/ethnicity unknown; 4% international.
**Faculty** *Student/faculty ratio:* 30:1.
**Academics** *Calendar:* semesters. *Degree:* certificates, diplomas, and associate. *Special study options:* academic remediation for entering students, advanced placement credit, cooperative education, distance learning, double majors, English as a second language, honors programs, part-time degree program, services for LD students, study abroad, summer session for credit.
**Library** Hayden Library. Students can reserve study rooms.
**Student Life** *Campus security:* 24-hour patrols, student patrols, late-night transport/escort service.
**Costs (2017–18)** *Tuition:* state resident $1380 full-time, $46 per unit part-time; nonresident $8730 full-time, $245 per unit part-time. Full-time tuition and fees vary according to course load. Part-time tuition and fees vary according to course load. *Required fees:* $87 full-time.
**Financial Aid** Of all full-time matriculated undergraduates who enrolled in 2016, 141 Federal Work-Study jobs (averaging $5500).
**Applying** *Options:* electronic application, early decision. *Required:* high school transcript.
**Freshman Application Contact** Admissions and Records, Citrus College, Glendora, CA 91741-1899. *Phone:* 626-914-8511. *Fax:* 626-914-8613. *E-mail:* admissions@citruscollege.edu. *Website:* http://www.citruscollege.edu/.

# City College of San Francisco
## San Francisco, California

**Freshman Application Contact** Ms. Mary Lou Leyba-Frank, Dean of Admissions and Records, City College of San Francisco, 50 Phelan Avenue, San Francisco, CA 94112-1821. *Phone:* 415-239-3291. *Fax:* 415-239-3936. *E-mail:* mleyba@ccsf.edu. *Website:* http://www.ccsf.edu/.

# Clovis Community College
## Fresno, California

**Admissions Office Contact** Clovis Community College, 10309 North Willow Avenue, Fresno, CA 93730. *Website:* http://www.cloviscollege.edu/.

# Coastline Community College
## Fountain Valley, California

- **District-supported** 2-year, founded 1976, part of Coast Community College District System
- **Urban** campus with easy access to Orange County
- **Coed**

**Undergraduates** 2,488 full-time, 8,943 part-time. 12% Black or African American, non-Hispanic/Latino; 28% Hispanic/Latino; 22% Asian, non-Hispanic/Latino; 0.5% Native Hawaiian or other Pacific Islander, non-Hispanic/Latino; 0.8% American Indian or Alaska Native, non-Hispanic/Latino; 4% Two or more races, non-Hispanic/Latino; 2% Race/ethnicity unknown.
**Faculty** *Student/faculty ratio:* 32:1.
**Academics** *Calendar:* semesters. *Degree:* certificates and associate. *Special study options:* academic remediation for entering students, accelerated degree program, adult/continuing education programs, advanced placement credit, cooperative education, distance learning, double majors, English as a second language, external degree program, honors programs, independent study, internships, off-campus study, part-time degree program, services for LD students, study abroad, summer session for credit.

**Library** Coastline Virtual Library plus 1 other.

**Student Life** *Campus security:* 24-hour emergency response devices.

**Costs (2017–18)** *Tuition:* state resident $1104 full-time, $46 per unit part-time; nonresident $6648 full-time, $231 per unit part-time. Full-time tuition and fees vary according to course load. Part-time tuition and fees vary according to course load. *Required fees:* $32 full-time. *Payment plans:* installment, deferred payment.

**Financial Aid** Of all full-time matriculated undergraduates who enrolled in 2015, 12,392 applied for aid, 11,568 were judged to have need, 12 had their need fully met. *Average percent of need met:* 15. *Average financial aid package:* $3819. *Average need-based loan:* $3290. *Average need-based gift aid:* $3714. *Average indebtedness upon graduation:* $10,514. *Financial aid deadline:* 8/15.

**Applying** *Options:* electronic application, early admission. *Recommended:* high school transcript.

**Freshman Application Contact** Jennifer McDonald, Director of Admissions and Records, Coastline Community College, 11460 Warner Ave, Fountain Valley, CA 92708. *Phone:* 714-241-6163. *Website:* http://www.coastline.edu/.

# College of Alameda
## Alameda, California

**Freshman Application Contact** College of Alameda, 555 Ralph Appezzato Memorial Parkway, Alameda, CA 94501-2109. *Phone:* 510-748-2204. *Website:* http://alameda.peralta.edu/.

# College of Marin
## Kentfield, California

- **District-supported** 2-year, founded 1926, part of California Community College System
- **Suburban** 410-acre campus with easy access to San Francisco
- **Coed,** 5,749 undergraduate students, 23% full-time, 57% women, 43% men

**Undergraduates** 1,299 full-time, 4,450 part-time. 4% Black or African American, non-Hispanic/Latino; 31% Hispanic/Latino; 7% Asian, non-Hispanic/Latino; 0.2% Native Hawaiian or other Pacific Islander, non-Hispanic/Latino; 0.2% American Indian or Alaska Native, non-Hispanic/Latino; 6% Two or more races, non-Hispanic/Latino; 2% Race/ethnicity unknown; 1% international.

**Faculty** *Total:* 320, 38% full-time.

**Majors** Accounting technology and bookkeeping; animation, interactive technology, video graphics and special effects; architectural technology; art; autobody/collision and repair technology; automobile/automotive mechanics technology; biological and physical sciences; biology/biological sciences; business administration and management; business/commerce; chemistry; child-care provision; cinematography and film/video production; computer science; computer systems networking and telecommunications; court reporting; criminal justice/police science; dance; data modeling/warehousing and database administration; dental assisting; design and visual communications; dramatic/theater arts; engineering; engineering technology; English; ethnic, cultural minority, gender, and group studies related; film/cinema/video studies; foreign languages and literatures; French; geography; geology/earth science; health and physical education/fitness; history; humanities; interior design; international relations and affairs; landscaping and groundskeeping; liberal arts and sciences/liberal studies; machine tool technology; mass communication/media; mathematics; medical administrative assistant and medical secretary; medical/clinical assistant; music; office management; physical sciences; physics; plant nursery management; political science and government; psychology; real estate; registered nursing/registered nurse; social sciences; Spanish; speech communication and rhetoric.

**Academics** *Calendar:* semesters. *Degree:* certificates and associate. *Special study options:* academic remediation for entering students, advanced placement credit, cooperative education, distance learning, double majors, English as a second language, part-time degree program, services for LD students, summer session for credit.

**Library** Main Library plus 1 other.

**Student Life** *Housing:* college housing not available. *Activities and Organizations:* drama/theater group, student-run newspaper, choral group. *Campus security:* 24-hour emergency response devices and patrols, security cameras. *Student services:* health clinic, personal/psychological counseling, veterans affairs office.

**Athletics** *Intercollegiate sports:* baseball M, basketball M/W, soccer M/W, softball W, swimming and diving M/W, track and field M/W, volleyball W, water polo M/W.

**Costs (2018–19)** *Tuition:* state resident $1380 full-time, $46 per credit part-time; nonresident $9210 full-time, $307 per credit part-time. Full-time tuition and fees vary according to course load. Part-time tuition and fees vary

according to course load. *Required fees:* $110 full-time. *Payment plan:* installment.

**Applying** *Options:* electronic application. *Application deadlines:* rolling (freshmen), rolling (transfers).

**Admissions Office Contact** College of Marin, 835 College Avenue, Kentfield, CA 94904.

*Website:* http://www.marin.edu/.

# College of San Mateo
## San Mateo, California

**Director of Admissions** Mr. Henry Villareal, Dean of Admissions and Records, College of San Mateo, 1700 West Hillsdale Boulevard, San Mateo, CA 94402-3784. *Phone:* 650-574-6590. *E-mail:* csmadmission@smccd.edu. *Website:* http://www.collegeofsanmateo.edu/.

# College of the Canyons
## Santa Clarita, California

- **District-supported** 2-year, founded 1969, part of California Community College System
- **Suburban** 224-acre campus with easy access to Los Angeles
- **Coed,** 26,171 undergraduate students, 36% full-time, 52% women, 48% men

**Undergraduates** 9,525 full-time, 16,646 part-time. Students come from 51 other countries; 3% are from out of state; 20% transferred in.

**Freshmen** *Admission:* 2,349 enrolled.

**Faculty** *Total:* 748, 23% full-time. *Student/faculty ratio:* 17:1.

**Majors** Accounting technology and bookkeeping; administrative assistant and secretarial science; animation, interactive technology, video graphics and special effects; architectural drafting and CAD/CADD; art; athletic training; automobile/automotive mechanics technology; biological and physical sciences; building/construction site management; business administration and management; child-care provision; cinematography and film/video production; clinical/medical laboratory technology; computer science; computer systems networking and telecommunications; criminal justice/police science; dramatic/theater arts; English; fire prevention and safety technology; French; geography; geology/earth science; graphic design; history; hospitality administration; hotel/motel administration; humanities; interior design; journalism; kinesiology and exercise science; legal assistant/paralegal; liberal arts and sciences/liberal studies; library and archives assisting; mathematics; music; musical theater; parks, recreation and leisure; philosophy; photography; physics; political science and government; pre-engineering; psychology; real estate; registered nursing/registered nurse; restaurant, culinary, and catering management; sales, distribution, and marketing operations; sign language interpretation and translation; small business administration; social sciences; sociology; Spanish; speech communication and rhetoric; surveying technology; water quality and wastewater treatment management and recycling technology; welding technology.

**Academics** *Calendar:* semesters. *Degree:* certificates and associate. *Special study options:* academic remediation for entering students, accelerated degree program, adult/continuing education programs, advanced placement credit, cooperative education, distance learning, double majors, English as a second language, honors programs, internships, part-time degree program, services for LD students, study abroad, summer session for credit.

**Library** College of the Canyons Library. *Books:* 60,038 (physical), 157,512 (digital/electronic); *Serial titles:* 59 (physical); *Databases:* 36. Weekly public service hours: 120; students can reserve study rooms.

**Student Life** *Housing:* college housing not available. *Activities and Organizations:* drama/theater group, student-run newspaper, choral group. *Campus security:* 24-hour emergency response devices, late-night transport/escort service. *Student services:* health clinic, personal/psychological counseling, women's center, veterans affairs office.

**Athletics** *Intercollegiate sports:* baseball M, basketball M/W, cross-country running M/W, football M, golf M/W, soccer M/W, softball W, swimming and diving M/W, track and field M/W, volleyball W.

**Costs (2018–19)** *Tuition:* state resident $1104 full-time, $46 per credit hour part-time; nonresident $6984 full-time, $291 per credit hour part-time. Full-time tuition and fees vary according to course load. Part-time tuition and fees vary according to course load. *Required fees:* $50 full-time.

**Financial Aid** Of all full-time matriculated undergraduates who enrolled in 2015, 17,088 applied for aid, 12,026 were judged to have need. 104 Federal Work-Study jobs (averaging $2894).

**Applying** *Options:* electronic application. *Recommended:* high school transcript. *Application deadlines:* rolling (freshmen), rolling (transfers). *Notification:* continuous (freshmen), continuous (transfers).

**Freshman Application Contact** Dr. Jasmine Ruys, Dean, Enrollment Services, College of the Canyons, 26455 Rockwell Canyon Road, Santa

Clarita, CA 91355. *Phone:* 661-362-3280. *Fax:* 661-254-7996. *E-mail:* jasmine.ruys@canyons.edu.
*Website:* http://www.canyons.edu/.

# ★ College of the Desert
## Palm Desert, California

- **District-supported** 2-year, founded 1958, part of California Community College System
- **Small-town** 160-acre campus
- **Coed,** 11,146 undergraduate students, 40% full-time, 55% women, 45% men

**Undergraduates** 4,434 full-time, 6,712 part-time. Students come from 20 states and territories; 1% are from out of state; 3% Black or African American, non-Hispanic/Latino; 72% Hispanic/Latino; 3% Asian, non-Hispanic/Latino; 0.1% Native Hawaiian or other Pacific Islander, non-Hispanic/Latino; 0.4% American Indian or Alaska Native, non-Hispanic/Latino; 3% Two or more races, non-Hispanic/Latino; 0.6% Race/ethnicity unknown; 1% international; 3% transferred in. *Retention:* 71% of full-time freshmen returned.
**Freshmen** *Admission:* 2,599 applied, 2,599 admitted, 2,028 enrolled.
**Faculty** *Total:* 554, 28% full-time. *Student/faculty ratio:* 23:1.
**Majors** Accounting technology and bookkeeping; agribusiness; agriculture; alternative fuel vehicle technology; anthropology; applied horticulture/horticulture operations; architectural technology; art; athletic training; automobile/automotive mechanics technology; biological and physical sciences; biology/biological sciences; building/construction site management; building/home/construction inspection; business administration and management; business/commerce; business, management, and marketing related; chemistry; child-care and support services management; child-care provision; cinematography and film/video production; commercial and advertising art; computer and information sciences and support services related; computer graphics; computer programming; computer science; cooking and related culinary arts; creative writing; criminal justice/police science; crop production; culinary arts; dietetic technology; drafting and design technology; dramatic/theater arts; economics; engineering technologies and engineering related; English; environmental/environmental health engineering; environmental science; environmental studies; fire prevention and safety technology; fire science/firefighting; foods, nutrition, and wellness; French; geography; geology/earth science; golf course operation and grounds management; health and physical education/fitness; health/medical preparatory programs related; health services/allied health/health sciences; heating, air conditioning, ventilation and refrigeration maintenance technology; heating, ventilation, air conditioning and refrigeration engineering technology; history; hospitality administration; human development and family studies; humanities; information technology; Italian; journalism; kinesiology and exercise science; liberal arts and sciences/liberal studies; licensed practical/vocational nurse training; mass communication/media; mathematics; multi/interdisciplinary studies related; music; natural resources/conservation; office management; ornamental horticulture; parks, recreation and leisure; parks, recreation and leisure facilities management; parks, recreation, leisure, and fitness studies related; philosophy; physics; political science and government; pre-engineering; psychology; radio and television; registered nursing/registered nurse; resort management; social sciences; sociology; Spanish; speech communication and rhetoric; substance abuse/addiction counseling; turf and turfgrass management; vehicle maintenance and repair technologies; visual and performing arts.
**Academics** *Calendar:* semesters. *Degree:* certificates, diplomas, and associate. *Special study options:* academic remediation for entering students, adult/continuing education programs, cooperative education, distance learning, double majors, English as a second language, part-time degree program, services for LD students, study abroad, summer session for credit.
**Library** College of the Desert Library. Weekly public service hours: 56; students can reserve study rooms.
**Student Life** *Housing:* college housing not available. *Activities and Organizations:* drama/theater group, student-run newspaper, radio station. *Campus security:* 24-hour emergency response devices and patrols. *Student services:* health clinic, personal/psychological counseling, veterans affairs office.
**Athletics** Member NJCAA. *Intercollegiate sports:* baseball M, basketball M/W, cross-country running M/W, fencing M/W, football M, golf M/W, soccer M/W, softball W, tennis M/W, track and field M/W, volleyball W.
**Costs (2018–19)** *Tuition:* state resident $1297 full-time, $46 per credit hour part-time; nonresident $7625 full-time, $252 per credit hour part-time. *Required fees:* $38 full-time, $38 per term part-time. *Payment plan:* installment. *Waivers:* employees or children of employees.

**Applying** *Options:* electronic application. *Recommended:* high school transcript. *Application deadlines:* rolling (freshmen), rolling (transfers). *Notification:* continuous (freshmen), continuous (transfers).
**Freshman Application Contact** College of the Desert, 43-500 Monterey Avenue, Palm Desert, CA 92260-9305. *Phone:* 760-776-7441 Ext. 7441. *Website:* http://www.collegeofthedesert.edu/.

# College of the Redwoods
## Eureka, California

**Freshman Application Contact** Director of Enrollment Management, College of the Redwoods, 7351 Tompkins Hill Road, Eureka, CA 95501-9300. *Phone:* 707-476-4100. *Toll-free phone:* 800-641-0400. *Fax:* 707-476-4400. *Website:* http://www.redwoods.edu/.

# College of the Sequoias
## Visalia, California

**Freshman Application Contact** Ms. Lisa Hott, Director for Admissions, College of the Sequoias, 915 South Mooney Boulevard, Visalia, CA 93277-2234. *Phone:* 559-737-4844. *Fax:* 559-737-4820. *Website:* http://www.cos.edu/.

# College of the Siskiyous
## Weed, California

**Freshman Application Contact** Recruitment and Admissions, College of the Siskiyous, 800 College Avenue, Weed, CA 96094-2899. *Phone:* 530-938-5555. *Toll-free phone:* 888-397-4339. *E-mail:* admissions-weed@siskyous.edu. *Website:* http://www.siskiyous.edu/.

# Columbia College
## Sonora, California

**Freshman Application Contact** Admissions Office, Columbia College, 11600 Columbia College Drive, Sonora, CA 95370. *Phone:* 209-588-5231. *Fax:* 209-588-5337. *E-mail:* ccadmissions@yosemite.edu. *Website:* http://www.gocolumbia.edu/.

# Community Christian College
## Redlands, California

**Freshman Application Contact** Mr. Enrique D. Melendez, Assistant Director of Admissions, Community Christian College, 251 Tennessee Street, Redlands, CA 92373. *Phone:* 909-222-9556. *Fax:* 909-335-9101. *E-mail:* emelendez@cccollege.edu. *Website:* http://www.cccollege.edu/.

# Compton College
## Compton, California

**Director of Admissions** Ms. Stephanie Atkinson-Alston, Interim Associate Dean, Admissions and Records, Compton College, 1111 East Artesia Boulevard, Compton, CA 90221-5393. *Phone:* 310-900-1600 Ext. 2047. *Website:* http://www.compton.edu/.

# Concorde Career College
## Garden Grove, California

**Freshman Application Contact** Chris Becker, Director, Concorde Career College, 12951 South Euclid Street, Suite 101, Garden Grove, CA 92840. *Phone:* 714-703-1900. *Fax:* 714-530-4737. *E-mail:* cbecker@concorde.edu. *Website:* http://www.concorde.edu/.

# Concorde Career College
## North Hollywood, California

**Freshman Application Contact** Madeline Volker, Director, Concorde Career College, 12412 Victory Boulevard, North Hollywood, CA 91606. *Phone:* 818-766-8151. *Fax:* 818-766-1587. *E-mail:* mvolker@concorde.edu. *Website:* http://www.concorde.edu/.

# Concorde Career College
## San Bernardino, California

**Admissions Office Contact** Concorde Career College, 201 East Airport Drive, San Bernardino, CA 92408. *Website:* http://www.concorde.edu/.

## Concorde Career College
San Diego, California

**Admissions Office Contact** Concorde Career College, 4393 Imperial Avenue, Suite 100, San Diego, CA 92113. *Website:* http://www.concorde.edu/.

## Contra Costa College
San Pablo, California

**Freshman Application Contact** Admissions and Records Office, Contra Costa College, San Pablo, CA 94806. *Phone:* 510-235-7800 Ext. 7500. *Fax:* 510-412-0769. *E-mail:* ar@contracosta.edu. *Website:* http://www.contracosta.edu/.

## Copper Mountain College
Joshua Tree, California

**Freshman Application Contact** Greg Brown, Executive Vice President for Academic and Student Affairs, Copper Mountain College, 6162 Rotary Way, Joshua Tree, CA 92252. *Phone:* 760-366-3791. *Toll-free phone:* 866-366-3791. *Fax:* 760-366-5257. *E-mail:* gbrown@cmccd.edu. *Website:* http://www.cmccd.edu/.

## Cosumnes River College
Sacramento, California

**Freshman Application Contact** Admissions and Records, Cosumnes River College, 8401 Center Parkway, Sacramento, CA 95823-5799. *Phone:* 916-691-7411. *Website:* http://www.crc.losrios.edu/.

## Crafton Hills College
Yucaipa, California

**Director of Admissions** Larry Aycock, Admissions and Records Coordinator, Crafton Hills College, 11711 Sand Canyon Road, Yucaipa, CA 92399-1799. *Phone:* 909-389-3663. *E-mail:* laycock@craftonhills.edu. *Website:* http://www.craftonhills.edu/.

## Cuesta College
San Luis Obispo, California

**Freshman Application Contact** Cuesta College, PO Box 8106, San Luis Obispo, CA 93403-8106. *Phone:* 805-546-3130 Ext. 2262. *Website:* http://www.cuesta.edu/.

## Cuyamaca College
El Cajon, California

**Freshman Application Contact** Ms. Susan Topham, Dean of Admissions and Records, Cuyamaca College, 900 Rancho San Diego Parkway, El Cajon, CA 92019-4304. *Phone:* 619-660-4302. *Fax:* 619-660-4575. *E-mail:* susan.topham@gcccd.edu. *Website:* http://www.cuyamaca.edu/.

## Cypress College
Cypress, California

**Freshman Application Contact** Admissions Office, Cypress College, 9200 Valley View, Cypress, CA 90630-5897. *Phone:* 714-484-7346. *Fax:* 714-484-7446. *E-mail:* admissions@cypresscollege.edu. *Website:* http://www.cypresscollege.edu/.

## De Anza College
Cupertino, California

- **District-supported** 2-year, founded 1967, part of California Community College System
- **Suburban** 112-acre campus with easy access to San Francisco, San Jose
- **Coed,** 20,808 undergraduate students, 48% full-time, 50% women, 50% men

**Undergraduates** 9,940 full-time, 10,868 part-time. 4% Black or African American, non-Hispanic/Latino; 28% Hispanic/Latino; 46% Asian, non-Hispanic/Latino; 0.8% Native Hawaiian or other Pacific Islander, non-Hispanic/Latino; 0.5% American Indian or Alaska Native, non-Hispanic/Latino; 1% Race/ethnicity unknown.

**Freshmen** *Admission:* 166 enrolled.

**Faculty** *Total:* 845, 34% full-time. *Student/faculty ratio:* 25:1.

**Majors** Accounting; administrative assistant and secretarial science; art; art history, criticism and conservation; automobile/automotive mechanics technology; behavioral sciences; biology/biological sciences; business administration and management; business machine repair; ceramic arts and ceramics; child development; commercial and advertising art; computer graphics; computer programming; computer science; construction engineering technology; corrections; criminal justice/law enforcement administration; criminal justice/police science; developmental and child psychology; drafting/design engineering technologies related; dramatic/theater arts; drawing; economics; engineering; engineering technology; English; environmental studies; film/cinema/video studies; history; humanities; industrial technology; information science/studies; international relations and affairs; journalism; legal assistant/paralegal; liberal arts and sciences/liberal studies; licensed practical/vocational nurse training; machine tool technology; marketing/marketing management; mass communication/media; mathematics; medical/clinical assistant; music; philosophy; photography; physical education teaching and coaching; physical therapy; physics; political science and government; pre-engineering; printmaking; professional, technical, business, and scientific writing; psychology; purchasing, procurement/acquisitions and contracts management; radio and television; real estate; registered nursing/registered nurse; rhetoric and composition; sculpture; social sciences; sociology; Spanish.

**Academics** *Calendar:* quarters. *Degree:* certificates, diplomas, and associate. *Special study options:* academic remediation for entering students, adult/continuing education programs, distance learning, English as a second language, honors programs, independent study, internships, part-time degree program, services for LD students, student-designed majors, study abroad, summer session for credit. *ROTC:* Army (c), Air Force (c).

**Library** A. Robert DeHart Learning Center. Study areas open 24 hours, 5&-7 days a week; students can reserve study rooms.

**Student Life** *Housing:* college housing not available. *Activities and Organizations:* drama/theater group, student-run newspaper, choral group, Student Nurses Association, Phi Theta Kappa, Automotive Club, Vietnamese Club, Filipino Club. *Campus security:* 24-hour emergency response devices, student patrols, late-night transport/escort service. *Student services:* health clinic, personal/psychological counseling, legal services, veterans affairs office.

**Athletics** Member NCAA. All Division II. *Intercollegiate sports:* baseball M, basketball M/W, cross-country running M/W, football M, golf M/W, soccer M/W, softball W, swimming and diving M/W, tennis M/W, track and field M/W, volleyball M/W, water polo M. *Intramural sports:* badminton M/W, basketball M, soccer M/W, swimming and diving M/W, volleyball M/W.

**Applying** *Application deadlines:* rolling (freshmen), rolling (out-of-state freshmen), rolling (transfers). *Notification:* continuous (freshmen), continuous (out-of-state freshmen), continuous (transfers). **Freshman Application Contact** De Anza College, 21250 Stevens Creek Boulevard, Cupertino, CA 95014-5793. *Phone:* 408-864-8292. *Website:* http://www.deanza.fhda.edu/.

## Deep Springs College
Deep Springs, California

**Freshman Application Contact** Jack Davis, Chair, Applications Committee, Deep Springs College, HC 72, Box 45001, Dyer, NV 89010-9803. *Phone:* 760-872-2000. *Fax:* 760-874-0314. *E-mail:* apcom@deepsprings.edu. *Website:* http://www.deepsprings.edu/.

## Diablo Valley College
Pleasant Hill, California

**Freshman Application Contact** Ileana Dorn, Director of Admissions and Records, Diablo Valley College, Pleasant Hill, CA 94523-1529. *Phone:* 925-685-1230 Ext. 2330. *Fax:* 925-609-8085. *E-mail:* idorn@dvc.edu. *Website:* http://www.dvc.edu/.

## East Los Angeles College
Monterey Park, California

**Freshman Application Contact** Mr. Jeremy Allred, Associate Dean of Admissions, East Los Angeles College, 1301 Avenida Cesar Chavez, Monterey Park, CA 91754. *Phone:* 323-265-8801. *Fax:* 323-265-8688. *E-mail:* allredjp@elac.edu. *Website:* http://www.elac.edu/.

# East San Gabriel Valley Regional Occupational Program & Technical Center
## West Covina, California

**Admissions Office Contact** East San Gabriel Valley Regional Occupational Program & Technical Center, 1501 West Del Norte Avenue, West Covina, CA 91790. *Website:* http://www.esgvrop.org/.

# El Camino College
## Torrance, California

**Director of Admissions** Mr. William Mulrooney, Director of Admissions, El Camino College, 16007 Crenshaw Boulevard, Torrance, CA 90506-0001. *Phone:* 310-660-3418. *Toll-free phone:* 866-ELCAMINO. *Fax:* 310-660-6779. *E-mail:* wmulrooney@elcamino.edu. *Website:* http://www.elcamino.edu/.

# Empire College
## Santa Rosa, California

**Freshman Application Contact** Ms. Dahnja Barker, Admissions Officer, Empire College, 3035 Cleveland Avenue, Santa Rosa, CA 95403. *Phone:* 707-546-4000. *Toll-free phone:* 877-395-8535. *Website:* http://www.empcol.edu/.

# Evergreen Valley College
## San Jose, California

**Freshman Application Contact** Evergreen Valley College, 3095 Yerba Buena Road, San Jose, CA 95135-1598. *Phone:* 408-270-6423. *Website:* http://www.evc.edu/.

# Feather River College
## Quincy, California

- **District-supported** primarily 2-year, founded 1968, part of California Community College System
- **Rural** 420-acre campus
- **Endowment** $48,167
- **Coed,** 2,079 undergraduate students

**Undergraduates** Students come from 30 states and territories; 7 other countries; 8% are from out of state; 11% Black or African American, non-Hispanic/Latino; 30% Hispanic/Latino; 6% Asian, non-Hispanic/Latino; 1% Native Hawaiian or other Pacific Islander, non-Hispanic/Latino; 2% American Indian or Alaska Native, non-Hispanic/Latino; 6% Race/ethnicity unknown; 0.9% international.
**Faculty** *Total:* 98, 27% full-time, 12% with terminal degrees. *Student/faculty ratio:* 21:1.
**Majors** Accounting technology and bookkeeping; agriculture; anthropology; biology/biological sciences; business/commerce; child-care provision; computer programming; cooking and related culinary arts; corrections and criminal justice related; English; environmental studies; health and physical education/fitness; history; horse husbandry/equine science and management; humanities; kinesiology and exercise science; liberal arts and sciences/liberal studies; licensed practical/vocational nurse training; mathematics; natural resources/conservation; parks, recreation and leisure; physical sciences; political science and government; social sciences; sociology; visual and performing arts; wildlife, fish and wildlands science and management.
**Academics** *Calendar:* semesters plus summer and winter terms. *Degrees:* certificates, diplomas, associate, and bachelor's. *Special study options:* academic remediation for entering students, adult/continuing education programs, advanced placement credit, cooperative education, distance learning, double majors, English as a second language, independent study, part-time degree program, services for LD students, summer session for credit.
**Library** Feather River College Library. *Books:* 24,291 (physical), 350,000 (digital/electronic); *Serial titles:* 98 (physical), 28,376 (digital/electronic); *Databases:* 35. Weekly public service hours: 61; students can reserve study rooms.
**Student Life** *Housing Options:* coed. Campus housing is provided by a third party. *Activities and Organizations:* drama/theater group, choral group, Phi Theta Kappa Honor Society, International and Cultural Club, Horse Show Team, Student Environmental Association, Student Alliance for Equity. *Campus security:* student patrols, part-time private security company patrols. *Student services:* health clinic, personal/psychological counseling.
**Athletics** *Intercollegiate sports:* baseball M, basketball M/W, cross-country running W, equestrian sports M(s)/W(s), football M, sand volleyball W, soccer M/W, softball W, track and field W, volleyball W.

**Standardized Tests** *Recommended:* ACCUPLACER.
**Costs (2017–18)** *Tuition:* state resident $1380 full-time, $46 per credit part-time; nonresident $8430 full-time, $281 per credit part-time. Full-time tuition and fees vary according to course load. Part-time tuition and fees vary according to course load. *Required fees:* $81 full-time, $2 per credit part-time, $18 per term part-time. *Room and board:* room only: $5350. Room and board charges vary according to housing facility. *Payment plan:* installment.
**Financial Aid** Of all all full-time matriculated undergraduates who enrolled in 2016, 22 Federal Work-Study jobs (averaging $750). 103 state and other part-time jobs (averaging $1504).
**Applying** *Options:* electronic application.
**Freshman Application Contact** Mrs. Leslie Mikesell, Director of Admissions and Records, Feather River College, 570 Golden Eagle Avenue, Quincy, CA 95971. *Phone:* 530-283-0202 Ext. 285. *Toll-free phone:* 800-442-9799. *E-mail:* info@frc.edu. *Website:* http://www.frc.edu/.

# FIDM/Fashion Institute of Design & Merchandising, Orange County Campus
## Irvine, California

- **Proprietary** 2-year, founded 1981, part of FIDM/Fashion Institute of Design & Merchandising
- **Urban** campus with easy access to Los Angeles
- **Coed, primarily women,** 71 undergraduate students, 94% full-time, 87% women, 13% men

**Undergraduates** 67 full-time, 4 part-time. Students come from 11 states and territories; 5 other countries; 12% are from out of state; 24% transferred in.
**Freshmen** *Admission:* 127 applied, 72 admitted, 49 enrolled. *Average high school GPA:* 2.9.
**Faculty** *Total:* 11. *Student/faculty ratio:* 7:1.
**Majors** Apparel and textile marketing management; design and visual communications; fashion/apparel design; fashion merchandising; graphic design; interior design.
**Academics** *Calendar:* quarters. *Degree:* associate. *Special study options:* academic remediation for entering students, accelerated degree program, adult/continuing education programs, advanced placement credit, cooperative education, distance learning, English as a second language, independent study, internships, part-time degree program, services for LD students, study abroad, summer session for credit.
**Library** FIDM Orange County Campus Library. Students can reserve study rooms.
**Student Life** *Housing:* college housing not available. *Activities and Organizations:* Cross-Cultural Student Alliance, Fashion Industry Club, Phi Theta Kappa (national honor society), Student Council, FIDM MODE Magazine. *Campus security:* 24-hour emergency response devices, late-night transport/escort service, security guard escort. *Student services:* personal/psychological counseling, veterans affairs office.
**Standardized Tests** *Recommended:* SAT or ACT (for admission).
**Costs (2018–19)** *Tuition:* $32,075 full-time, $685 per credit hour part-time. Full-time tuition and fees vary according to degree level and program. Part-time tuition and fees vary according to degree level and program. *Required fees:* $1152 full-time. *Payment plan:* installment. *Waivers:* employees or children of employees.
**Applying** *Options:* electronic application, deferred entrance. *Application fee:* $225. *Required:* essay or personal statement, high school transcript, minimum 2.5 GPA, 3 letters of recommendation, interview, entrance project. *Application deadlines:* rolling (freshmen), rolling (transfers).
**Freshman Application Contact** Mr. Michael Mirabella, Admissions, FIDM/Fashion Institute of Design & Merchandising, Orange County Campus, 919 So Grand Ave, Los Angeles, CA 90015. *Phone:* 213-624-1200. *Toll-free phone:* 888-974-3436. *Website:* http://www.fidm.edu/.

# FIDM/Fashion Institute of Design & Merchandising, San Diego Campus
## San Diego, California

- **Proprietary** 2-year, founded 1985, part of FIDM/Fashion Institute of Design & Merchandising
- **Urban** campus with easy access to San Diego
- **Coed, primarily women,** 66 undergraduate students, 92% full-time, 91% women, 9% men

**Undergraduates** 61 full-time, 5 part-time. Students come from 17 states and territories; 4 other countries; 23% are from out of state; 50% transferred in. *Retention:* 82% of full-time freshmen returned.
**Freshmen** *Admission:* 110 applied, 50 admitted, 36 enrolled. *Average high school GPA:* 2.9.

**Faculty** *Total:* 12, 8% full-time. *Student/faculty ratio:* 5:1.

**Majors** Design and visual communications; fashion/apparel design; fashion merchandising.

**Academics** *Calendar:* quarters. *Degree:* associate. *Special study options:* academic remediation for entering students, accelerated degree program, adult/continuing education programs, advanced placement credit, cooperative education, distance learning, English as a second language, independent study, internships, part-time degree program, services for LD students, study abroad, summer session for credit.

**Library** FIDM San Diego Campus Library. Students can reserve study rooms.

**Student Life** *Housing:* college housing not available. *Activities and Organizations:* Cross-Cultural Student Alliance, Fashion Industry Club, Phi Theta Kappa (national honor society), Student Council, FIDM MODE Magazine. *Campus security:* 24-hour emergency response devices and patrols. *Student services:* personal/psychological counseling, veterans affairs office.

**Standardized Tests** *Recommended:* SAT or ACT (for admission).

**Costs (2018–19)** *Tuition:* $32,075 full-time. Full-time tuition and fees vary according to degree level and program. Part-time tuition and fees vary according to degree level and program. *Required fees:* $1152 full-time. *Payment plan:* installment. *Waivers:* employees or children of employees.

**Applying** *Options:* electronic application, deferred entrance. *Application fee:* $225. *Required:* essay or personal statement, high school transcript, minimum 2.5 GPA, 3 letters of recommendation, interview, major-determined project. *Application deadlines:* rolling (freshmen), rolling (transfers).

**Freshman Application Contact** Ms. Denise Baca, Campus Director, FIDM/Fashion Institute of Design & Merchandising, San Diego Campus, 350 Tenth Avenue, San Diego, CA 92101. *Phone:* 619-235-2049. *Toll-free phone:* 800-243-3436. *E-mail:* dbaca@fidm.edu. *Website:* http://www.fidm.edu/.

# Folsom Lake College
## Folsom, California

**Freshman Application Contact** Admissions Office, Folsom Lake College, 10 College Parkway, Folsom, CA 95630. *Phone:* 916-608-6500. *Website:* http://www.flc.losrios.edu/.

# Foothill College
## Los Altos Hills, California

**Freshman Application Contact** Ms. Shawna Aced, Registrar, Foothill College, Admissions and Records, 12345 El Monte Road, Los Altos Hills, CA 94022. *Phone:* 650-949-7771. *E-mail:* acedshawna@hda.edu. *Website:* http://www.foothill.edu/.

# Fremont College
## Cerritos, California

**Freshman Application Contact** Natasha Dawson, Director of Admissions, Fremont College, 18000 Studebaker Road, Suite 900A, Cerritos, CA 90703. *Phone:* 562-809-5100. *Toll-free phone:* 800-373-6668. *Fax:* 562-809-5100. *E-mail:* info@fremont.edu. *Website:* http://www.fremont.edu/.

# Fresno City College
## Fresno, California

**Freshman Application Contact** Office Assistant, Fresno City College, 1101 East University Avenue, Fresno, CA 93741-0002. *Phone:* 559-442-4600 Ext. 8604. *Fax:* 559-237-4232. *E-mail:* fcc.admissions@fresnocitycollege.edu. *Website:* http://www.fresnocitycollege.edu/.

# Fullerton College
## Fullerton, California

- **District-supported** 2-year, founded 1913, part of California Community College System
- **Suburban** 79-acre campus with easy access to Los Angeles
- **Coed,** 24,588 undergraduate students

**Undergraduates** Students come from 28 states and territories; 1% are from out of state; 4% Black or African American, non-Hispanic/Latino; 57% Hispanic/Latino; 17% Asian, non-Hispanic/Latino; 0.6% American Indian or Alaska Native, non-Hispanic/Latino; 1% Race/ethnicity unknown. *Retention:* 61% of full-time freshmen returned.

**Faculty** *Total:* 939, 37% full-time. *Student/faculty ratio:* 26:1.

**Majors** Accounting technology and bookkeeping; administrative assistant and secretarial science; anthropology; apparel and textile marketing management; apparel and textiles; applied horticulture/horticulture operations; architectural technology; area studies related; art; astronomy; automobile/automotive mechanics technology; biological and physical sciences; biology/biological sciences; biomedical technology; building/construction site management; building/home/construction inspection; business administration and management; carpentry; chemical technology; chemistry; child-care provision; computer science; construction trades related; cosmetology; criminal justice/police science; dance; drafting and design technology; dramatic/theater arts; economics; electrical/electronics equipment installation and repair; engineering; English; environmental studies; ethnic, cultural minority, gender, and group studies related; fashion/apparel design; foods, nutrition, and wellness; foreign languages and literatures; geography; geology/earth science; graphic and printing equipment operation/production; graphic design; hazardous materials management and waste technology; health and physical education/fitness; health/medical preparatory programs related; history; humanities; information technology; interior design; international business/trade/commerce; journalism; landscaping and groundskeeping; legal administrative assistant/secretary; legal assistant/paralegal; liberal arts and sciences/liberal studies; mass communication/media; mathematics; mechanical engineering/mechanical technology; microbiology; music; parks, recreation and leisure; philosophy; physics; plant nursery management; political science and government; psychology; radio and television; real estate; recording arts technology; religious studies; sales, distribution, and marketing operations; small business administration; sociology; speech communication and rhetoric; sport and fitness administration/management; technology/industrial arts teacher education.

**Academics** *Calendar:* semesters. *Degree:* certificates and associate. *Special study options:* academic remediation for entering students, adult/continuing education programs, advanced placement credit, cooperative education, English as a second language, honors programs, part-time degree program, services for LD students, study abroad, summer session for credit. *ROTC:* Army (c), Navy (c), Air Force (c).

**Library** William T. Boyce Library.

**Student Life** *Housing:* college housing not available. *Activities and Organizations:* drama/theater group, student-run newspaper, radio station. *Student services:* health clinic, personal/psychological counseling, women's center, legal services, veterans affairs office.

**Athletics** *Intercollegiate sports:* badminton W, baseball M, basketball M/W, cross-country running M/W, football M, golf W, soccer M/W, softball W, swimming and diving M/W, tennis M/W, track and field M/W, volleyball W, water polo M/W.

**Costs (2018–19)** *Tuition:* state resident $1148 full-time, $46 per credit hour part-time; nonresident $6010 full-time, $140 per credit hour part-time. Full-time tuition and fees vary according to course load. Part-time tuition and fees vary according to course load. *Required fees:* $24 full-time, $34 per year part-time.

**Financial Aid** Of all full-time matriculated undergraduates who enrolled in 2017, 29,579 applied for aid. *Financial aid deadline:* 6/30.

**Applying** *Options:* electronic application, early admission. *Application deadlines:* rolling (freshmen), rolling (transfers).

**Freshman Application Contact** Fullerton College, 321 East Chapman Avenue, Fullerton, CA 92832-2095. *Phone:* 714-992-7076. *Website:* http://www.fullcoll.edu/.

# Gavilan College
## Gilroy, California

**Freshman Application Contact** Gavilan College, 5055 Santa Teresa Boulevard, Gilroy, CA 95020-9599. *Phone:* 408-848-4754. *Website:* http://www.gavilan.edu/.

# Glendale Career College
## Glendale, California

**Admissions Office Contact** Glendale Career College, 240 North Brand Boulevard, Lower Level, Glendale, CA 91203. *Website:* http://www.glendalecareer.com/.

# Glendale Community College
## Glendale, California

**Freshman Application Contact** Ms. Sharon Combs, Dean, Admissions, and Records, Glendale Community College, 1500 North Verdugo Road, Glendale, CA 91208. *Phone:* 818-240-1000 Ext. 5910. *E-mail:* scombs@glendale.edu. *Website:* http://www.glendale.edu/.

# Golden West College
## Huntington Beach, California

- **District-supported** 2-year, founded 1966, part of Coast Community College District System
- **Suburban** 122-acre campus with easy access to Los Angeles
- **Endowment** $7.6 million
- **Coed**

**Undergraduates** 4,394 full-time, 8,000 part-time. 1% are from out of state; 2% Black or African American, non-Hispanic/Latino; 32% Hispanic/Latino; 28% Asian, non-Hispanic/Latino; 0.5% Native Hawaiian or other Pacific Islander, non-Hispanic/Latino; 0.3% American Indian or Alaska Native, non-Hispanic/Latino; 4% Two or more races, non-Hispanic/Latino; 1% Race/ethnicity unknown; 2% international. *Retention:* 71% of full-time freshmen returned.
**Faculty** *Student/faculty ratio:* 33:1.
**Academics** *Calendar:* semesters plus summer session. *Degree:* certificates and associate. *Special study options:* academic remediation for entering students, adult/continuing education programs, advanced placement credit, cooperative education, distance learning, English as a second language, external degree program, honors programs, independent study, internships, part-time degree program, services for LD students, student-designed majors, study abroad, summer session for credit. *ROTC:* Air Force (c).
**Library** Golden West College Library plus 1 other. Weekly public service hours: 48; students can reserve study rooms.
**Student Life** *Campus security:* 24-hour emergency response devices and patrols, late-night transport/escort service.
**Athletics** Member NJCAA.
**Costs (2017–18)** *Tuition:* state resident $1288 full-time, $46 per unit part-time; nonresident $8876 full-time, $302 per unit part-time. Full-time tuition and fees vary according to course load and program. Part-time tuition and fees vary according to course load and program. *Required fees:* $74 full-time, $20 per term part-time.
**Applying** *Options:* electronic application, early admission. *Required for some:* essay or personal statement. *Recommended:* high school transcript.
**Freshman Application Contact** Golden West College, PO Box 2748, 15744 Golden West Street, Huntington Beach, CA 92647-2748. *Phone:* 714-892-7711 Ext. 58965. *Website:* http://www.goldenwestcollege.edu/.

# Golf Academy of America
## Carlsbad, California

**Director of Admissions** Ms. Deborah Wells, Admissions Coordinator, Golf Academy of America, 1950 Camino Vida Roble, Suite 125, Carlsbad, CA 92008. *Phone:* 760-414-1501. *Toll-free phone:* 800-342-7342. *E-mail:* sdga@sdgagolf.com. *Website:* http://www.golfacademy.edu/.

# Grossmont College
## El Cajon, California

**Freshman Application Contact** Admissions Office, Grossmont College, 8800 Grossmont College Drive, El Cajon, CA 92020-1799. *Phone:* 619-644-7186. *Website:* http://www.grossmont.edu/.

# Gurnick Academy of Medical Arts
## San Mateo, California

- **Proprietary** primarily 2-year
- **Coed**

**Majors** Diagnostic medical sonography and ultrasound technology; magnetic resonance imaging (MRI) technology; nursing science; physical therapy; radiologic technology/science.
**Academics** *Degrees:* certificates, diplomas, associate, and bachelor's.
**Freshman Application Contact** Gurnick Academy of Medical Arts, 2121 South El Camino Real, Building C 2000, San Mateo, CA 94403. *Website:* http://www.gurnick.edu/.

# Hartnell College
## Salinas, California

**Director of Admissions** Director of Admissions, Hartnell College, 411 Central Avenue, Salinas, CA 93901. *Phone:* 831-755-6711. *Fax:* 831-759-6014. *Website:* http://www.hartnell.edu/.

# Imperial Valley College
## Imperial, California

- **District-supported** 2-year, founded 1922, part of California Community College System
- **Rural** 160-acre campus
- **Coed**
- 100% of applicants were admitted

**Undergraduates** 1% Black or African American, non-Hispanic/Latino; 91% Hispanic/Latino; 0.6% Asian, non-Hispanic/Latino; 0.1% American Indian or Alaska Native, non-Hispanic/Latino; 0.4% Two or more races, non-Hispanic/Latino; 3% Race/ethnicity unknown.
**Faculty** *Student/faculty ratio:* 28:1.
**Academics** *Calendar:* semesters. *Degree:* certificates and associate. *Special study options:* academic remediation for entering students, accelerated degree program, adult/continuing education programs, advanced placement credit, distance learning, double majors, English as a second language, part-time degree program, services for LD students, student-designed majors, summer session for credit.
**Library** Spencer Library. *Databases:* 45. Weekly public service hours: 57; students can reserve study rooms.
**Student Life** *Campus security:* student patrols, emergency phone poles on campus.
**Athletics** Member NJCAA.
**Costs (2017–18)** *Tuition:* state resident $1365 full-time, $46 per unit part-time; nonresident $7525 full-time, $209 per unit part-time. *Required fees:* $45 full-time.
**Applying** *Options:* electronic application. *Required for some:* high school transcript. *Recommended:* high school transcript.
**Freshman Application Contact** Imperial Valley College, 380 East Aten Road, PO Box 158, Imperial, CA 92251-0158. *Phone:* 760-355-6244. *Website:* http://www.imperial.edu/.

# Institute of Technology
## Clovis, California

**Admissions Office Contact** Institute of Technology, 564 West Herndon Avenue, Clovis, CA 93612. *Website:* http://www.iot.edu/.

# Irvine Valley College
## Irvine, California

**Director of Admissions** Mr. John Edwards, Director of Admissions, Records, and Enrollment Services, Irvine Valley College, 5500 Irvine Center Drive, Irvine, CA 92618. *Phone:* 949-451-5416. *Website:* http://www.ivc.edu/.

# Lake Tahoe Community College
## South Lake Tahoe, California

**Freshman Application Contact** Office of Admissions and Records, Lake Tahoe Community College, One College Drive, South Lake Tahoe, CA 96150. *Phone:* 530-541-4660 Ext. 211. *Fax:* 530-541-7852. *E-mail:* admissions@ltcc.edu. *Website:* http://www.ltcc.edu/.

# Laney College
## Oakland, California

**Freshman Application Contact** Mrs. Barbara Simmons, District Admissions Officer, Laney College, 900 Fallon Street, Oakland, CA 94607-4893. *Phone:* 510-466-7369. *Website:* http://www.laney.edu/.

# Las Positas College
## Livermore, California

**Director of Admissions** Mrs. Sylvia R. Rodriguez, Director of Admissions and Records, Las Positas College, 3000 Campus Hill Drive, Livermore, CA 94551. *Phone:* 925-373-4942. *Website:* http://www.laspositascollege.edu/.

# Lassen Community College
## Susanville, California

**Freshman Application Contact** Mr. Chris J. Alberico, Registrar, Lassen Community College, Highway 139, PO Box 3000, Susanville, CA 96130. *Phone:* 530-257-6181. *Website:* http://www.lassencollege.edu/.

# Laurus College
## San Luis Obispo, California

**Admissions Office Contact** Laurus College, 81 Higuera Street, Suite 110, San Luis Obispo, CA 93401. *Website:* http://www.lauruscollege.edu/.

# Learnet Academy
## Los Angeles, California

**Admissions Office Contact** Learnet Academy, 3251 West 6th Street, 2nd Floor, Los Angeles, CA 90020. *Website:* http://www.learnet.edu/.

# Long Beach City College
## Long Beach, California

**Director of Admissions** Mr. Ross Miyashiro, Dean of Admissions and Records, Long Beach City College, 4901 East Carson Street, Long Beach, CA 90808-1780. *Phone:* 562-938-4130. *Website:* http://www.lbcc.edu/.

# Los Angeles City College
## Los Angeles, California

- **District-supported** 2-year, founded 1929, part of Los Angeles Community College District (LACCD)
- **Urban** 42-acre campus
- **Coed,** 16,556 undergraduate students, 28% full-time, 56% women, 44% men

**Undergraduates** 4,671 full-time, 11,885 part-time. 9% Black or African American, non-Hispanic/Latino; 50% Hispanic/Latino; 15% Asian, non-Hispanic/Latino; 2% American Indian or Alaska Native, non-Hispanic/Latino; 3% Race/ethnicity unknown; 4% international; 6% transferred in.
**Freshmen** *Admission:* 33,147 applied, 25,210 admitted, 1,002 enrolled.
**Faculty** *Total:* 450, 41% full-time.
**Majors** Accounting; accounting technology and bookkeeping; administrative assistant and secretarial science; art; banking and financial support services; biological and physical sciences; business administration and management; chemistry; child development; Chinese; cinematography and film/video production; computer and information sciences and support services related; computer and information sciences related; computer engineering technology; computer science; criminal justice/law enforcement administration; criminal justice/police science; dental laboratory technology; dietetics; dietetic technology; dramatic/theater arts; electrical/electronics equipment installation and repair; engineering; English; finance; French; graphic design; humanities; human services; industrial radiologic technology; information technology; Japanese; journalism; Korean; legal administrative assistant/secretary; legal assistant/paralegal; liberal arts and sciences/liberal studies; marketing/marketing management; mathematics; medical administrative assistant and medical secretary; music; photographic and film/video technology; physics; political science and government; radio and television; radiologic technology/science; real estate; registered nursing/registered nurse; Spanish; speech communication and rhetoric; substance abuse/addiction counseling.
**Academics** *Calendar:* semesters. *Degree:* certificates, diplomas, and associate. *Special study options:* academic remediation for entering students, accelerated degree program, adult/continuing education programs, advanced placement credit, cooperative education, distance learning, double majors, English as a second language, freshman honors college, honors programs, internships, part-time degree program, services for LD students, study abroad, summer session for credit. *ROTC:* Army (c), Navy (c), Air Force (c).
**Library** Martin Luther King Jr. Library. *Books:* 155,954 (physical), 195,000 (digital/electronic); *Serial titles:* 87 (physical); *Databases:* 60. Weekly public service hours: 77; students can reserve study rooms.
**Student Life** *Housing:* college housing not available. *Activities and Organizations:* drama/theater group, student-run newspaper, choral group. *Campus security:* 24-hour emergency response devices and patrols, student patrols, late-night transport/escort service. *Student services:* health clinic, personal/psychological counseling, veterans affairs office.
**Costs (2018–19)** *Tuition:* state resident $1220 full-time, $46 per unit part-time; nonresident $7128 full-time, $297 per unit part-time. *Required fees:* $24 full-time, $12 per term part-time. *Payment plan:* installment.
**Applying** *Options:* electronic application. *Recommended:* high school transcript. *Application deadlines:* 9/5 (freshmen), 9/5 (transfers). *Notification:* continuous until 9/5 (freshmen), continuous until 9/5 (transfers).
**Freshman Application Contact** Dr. Terri Anderson, Office of Outreach and Recruitment, Los Angeles City College, 855 N. Vermont Ave., Los Angeles, CA 90029. *Phone:* 323-953-4000 Ext. 2598. *E-mail:* anderst@lacitycollege.edu.
*Website:* http://www.lacitycollege.edu/.

# Los Angeles County College of Nursing and Allied Health
## Los Angeles, California

**Freshman Application Contact** Admissions Office, Los Angeles County College of Nursing and Allied Health, 1237 North Mission Road, Los Angeles, CA 90033. *Phone:* 323-226-4911. *Website:* http://www.dhs.lacounty.gov/wps/portal/dhs/conah/.

# Los Angeles Harbor College
## Wilmington, California

**Freshman Application Contact** Los Angeles Harbor College, 1111 Figueroa Place, Wilmington, CA 90744-2397. *Phone:* 310-233-4091. *Website:* http://www.lahc.edu/.

# Los Angeles Mission College
## Sylmar, California

**Freshman Application Contact** Los Angeles Mission College, 13356 Eldridge Avenue, Sylmar, CA 91342-3245. *Website:* http://www.lamission.edu/.

# Los Angeles Pierce College
## Woodland Hills, California

**Director of Admissions** Ms. Shelley L. Gerstl, Dean of Admissions and Records, Los Angeles Pierce College, 6201 Winnetka Avenue, Woodland Hills, CA 91371-0001. *Phone:* 818-719-6448. *Website:* http://www.piercecollege.edu/.

# Los Angeles Southwest College
## Los Angeles, California

**Director of Admissions** Dan W. Walden, Dean of Academic Affairs, Los Angeles Southwest College, 1600 West Imperial Highway, Los Angeles, CA 90047-4810. *Phone:* 323-242-5511. *Website:* http://www.lasc.edu/.

# Los Angeles Trade-Technical College
## Los Angeles, California

**Freshman Application Contact** Los Angeles Trade-Technical College, 400 West Washington Boulevard, Los Angeles, CA 90015-4108. *Phone:* 213-763-7127. *Website:* http://www.lattc.edu/.

# Los Angeles Valley College
## Valley Glen, California

**Freshman Application Contact** Los Angeles Valley College, 5800 Fulton Avenue, Valley Glen, CA 91401. *Phone:* 818-947-5518. *Website:* http://www.lavc.edu/.

# Los Medanos College
## Pittsburg, California

**Freshman Application Contact** Ms. Gail Newman, Director of Admissions and Records, Los Medanos College, 2700 East Leland Road, Pittsburg, CA 94565-5197. *Phone:* 925-439-2181 Ext. 7500. *Website:* http://www.losmedanos.net/.

# Mendocino College
## Ukiah, California

**Freshman Application Contact** Mendocino College, 1000 Hensley Creek Road, Ukiah, CA 95482-0300. *Phone:* 707-468-3103. *Website:* http://www.mendocino.edu/.

# Merced College
## Merced, California

- **District-supported** 2-year, founded 1962, part of California Community College System
- **Small-town** 653-acre campus
- **Endowment** $3.2 million
- **Coed,** 11,552 undergraduate students

**Undergraduates** 2% are from out of state.

**Freshmen** *Admission:* 2,593 applied, 2,593 admitted.

**Faculty** *Total:* 516, 35% full-time. *Student/faculty ratio:* 26:1.

**Majors** Accounting technology and bookkeeping; administrative assistant and secretarial science; agribusiness; agricultural mechanics and equipment technology; agriculture; agronomy and crop science; animal/livestock husbandry and production; anthropology; applied horticulture/horticulture operations; architectural drafting and CAD/CADD; art; autobody/collision and repair technology; automobile/automotive mechanics technology; biology/biological sciences; biomedical technology; business administration and management; business/commerce; chemistry; child-care provision; computer installation and repair technology; computer science; cooking and related culinary arts; criminal justice/police science; crop production; diagnostic medical sonography and ultrasound technology; dramatic/theater arts; electrical/electronics equipment installation and repair; electrician; emergency medical technology (EMT paramedic); engineering technology; English; family and community services; fire prevention and safety technology; French; geography; geology/earth science; German; health and physical education/fitness; health/medical preparatory programs related; heating, ventilation, air conditioning and refrigeration engineering technology; history; horse husbandry/equine science and management; humanities; human services; information technology; instrumentation technology; international relations and affairs; kinesiology and exercise science; liberal arts and sciences/liberal studies; mathematics; mechanical drafting and CAD/CADD; mechanical engineering/mechanical technology; medical administrative assistant and medical secretary; music; office management; philosophy; photography; physics; pre-engineering; psychology; radiologic technology/science; real estate; registered nursing/registered nurse; sales, distribution, and marketing operations; small business administration; social sciences; sociology; Spanish; special education–early childhood; speech communication and rhetoric; welding technology.

**Academics** *Calendar:* semesters. *Degree:* certificates and associate. *Special study options:* academic remediation for entering students, accelerated degree program, adult/continuing education programs, advanced placement credit, cooperative education, distance learning, double majors, English as a second language, honors programs, independent study, off-campus study, part-time degree program, services for LD students, student-designed majors, summer session for credit.

**Library** Lesher Library plus 1 other. *Databases:* 76. Weekly public service hours: 56; students can reserve study rooms.

**Student Life** *Housing:* college housing not available. *Activities and Organizations:* drama/theater group, student-run newspaper, choral group. *Campus security:* 24-hour patrols. *Student services:* personal/psychological counseling, veterans affairs office.

**Athletics** Member NAIA. *Intercollegiate sports:* baseball M, cross-country running M/W, football M, softball W, swimming and diving M/W, track and field M/W, volleyball W, water polo M/W.

**Financial Aid** Of all full-time matriculated undergraduates who enrolled in 2014, 319 Federal Work-Study jobs (averaging $3456). 131 state and other part-time jobs (averaging $3456). *Financial aid deadline:* 7/15.

**Applying** *Options:* electronic application, early admission. *Recommended:* high school transcript. *Application deadlines:* rolling (freshmen), rolling (transfers). *Notification:* continuous (freshmen), continuous (transfers).

**Admissions Office Contact** Merced College, 3600 M Street, Merced, CA 95348-2898.

*Website:* http://www.mccd.edu/.

# Merritt College
## Oakland, California

**Freshman Application Contact** Ms. Barbara Simmons, District Admissions Officer, Merritt College, 12500 Campus Drive, Oakland, CA 94619-3196. *Phone:* 510-466-7369. *E-mail:* hperdue@peralta.cc.ca.us. *Website:* http://www.merritt.edu/.

# MiraCosta College
## Oceanside, California

**Freshman Application Contact** Jane Sparks, Interim Director of Admissions and Records, MiraCosta College, One Barnard Drive, Oceanside, CA 92057.

*Phone:* 760-795-6620. *Toll-free phone:* 888-201-8480. *E-mail:* admissions@miracosta.edu. *Website:* http://www.miracosta.edu/.

*See below for display ad and page 326 for the College Close-Up.*

## Mission College
### Santa Clara, California

- **District-supported** 2-year, founded 1977, part of California Community College System
- **Urban** 167-acre campus with easy access to San Francisco, San Jose
- **Endowment** $6.8 million
- **Coed,** 7,868 undergraduate students

**Undergraduates** Students come from 18 other countries; 0.3% are from out of state. *Retention:* 77% of full-time freshmen returned.
**Faculty** *Total:* 324, 43% full-time. *Student/faculty ratio:* 22:1.
**Majors** Accounting; administrative assistant and secretarial science; art; business administration and management; commercial and advertising art; computer engineering technology; computer programming; data processing and data processing technology; drafting and design technology; electrical, electronic and communications engineering technology; electrical/electronics drafting and CAD/CADD; fire science/firefighting; food technology and processing; graphic and printing equipment operation/production; health professions related; information science/studies; liberal arts and sciences/liberal studies; licensed practical/vocational nurse training; marketing/marketing management; mathematics; pre-engineering; real estate; social sciences; special products marketing.
**Academics** *Calendar:* semesters. *Degree:* certificates, diplomas, and associate. *Special study options:* academic remediation for entering students, adult/continuing education programs, advanced placement credit, cooperative education, distance learning, double majors, English as a second language, honors programs, independent study, internships, part-time degree program, services for LD students, summer session for credit. *ROTC:* Army (c), Air Force (c).
**Library** Mission College Library. *Books:* 65,071 (physical); *Serial titles:* 19,025 (digital/electronic); *Databases:* 59. Weekly public service hours: 55; students can reserve study rooms.
**Student Life** *Housing:* college housing not available. *Activities and Organizations:* choral group, Puente, Associated Student Government. *Campus security:* 24-hour emergency response devices, late-night transport/escort service, district police department, evening administrators. *Student services:* health clinic, personal/psychological counseling, legal services, veterans affairs office.
**Athletics** *Intercollegiate sports:* badminton M/W, baseball M, basketball W, softball W, tennis M/W, volleyball W.
**Costs (2018–19)** *Tuition:* state resident $46 per unit part-time; nonresident $234 per unit part-time. Full-time tuition and fees vary according to course load. *Required fees:* $61 per year part-time. *Payment plan:* installment.
**Applying** *Options:* electronic application. *Application deadlines:* rolling (freshmen), rolling (transfers). *Notification:* continuous (freshmen), continuous (transfers).
**Admissions Office Contact** Mission College, 3000 Mission College Boulevard, Santa Clara, CA 95054-1897.
*Website:* http://www.missioncollege.edu/.

## Modesto Junior College
### Modesto, California

**Freshman Application Contact** Ms. Martha Robles, Dean of Student Services and Support, Modesto Junior College, 435 College Avenue, Modesto, CA 95350. *Phone:* 209-575-6470. *Fax:* 209-575-6859. *E-mail:* mjcadmissions@mail.yosemite.cc.ca.us. *Website:* http://www.mjc.edu/.

## Monterey Peninsula College
### Monterey, California

**Director of Admissions** Ms. Vera Coleman, Registrar, Monterey Peninsula College, 980 Fremont Street, Monterey, CA 93940-4799. *Phone:* 831-646-4007. *E-mail:* vcoleman@mpc.edu. *Website:* http://www.mpc.edu/.

## Moorpark College
### Moorpark, California

**Freshman Application Contact** Ms. Katherine Colborn, Registrar, Moorpark College, 7075 Campus Road, Moorpark, CA 93021-2899. *Phone:* 805-378-1415. *Website:* http://www.moorparkcollege.edu/.

## Moreno Valley College
### Moreno Valley, California

**Freshman Application Contact** Jamie Clifton, Director, Enrollment Services, Moreno Valley College, 16130 Lasselle Street, Moreno Valley, CA 92551. *Phone:* 951-571-6293. *E-mail:* admissions@mvc.edu. *Website:* http://www.mvc.edu/.

## Mt. San Antonio College
### Walnut, California

- **District-supported** 2-year, founded 1946, part of California Community College System
- **Suburban** 421-acre campus with easy access to Los Angeles
- **Coed,** 29,960 undergraduate students, 9% full-time, 7% women, 8% men

**Undergraduates** 2,581 full-time, 1,987 part-time. 4% Black or African American, non-Hispanic/Latino; 63% Hispanic/Latino; 17% Asian, non-Hispanic/Latino; 0.3% Native Hawaiian or other Pacific Islander, non-Hispanic/Latino; 0.1% American Indian or Alaska Native, non-Hispanic/Latino; 3% Two or more races, non-Hispanic/Latino; 0.4% Race/ethnicity unknown; 2% international. *Retention:* 79% of full-time freshmen returned.
**Freshmen** *Admission:* 4,568 enrolled.
**Faculty** *Total:* 1,328, 32% full-time. *Student/faculty ratio:* 24:1.
**Majors** Accounting; administrative assistant and secretarial science; advertising; agricultural business and management; agriculture; airframe mechanics and aircraft maintenance technology; airline pilot and flight crew; air traffic control; animal/livestock husbandry and production; animal sciences; apparel and textiles; applied horticulture/horticulture operations; architectural engineering technology; avionics maintenance technology; biological and physical sciences; building/construction finishing, management, and inspection related; business administration and management; business teacher education; child development; civil engineering technology; commercial and advertising art; computer and information sciences; computer engineering technology; computer graphics; computer science; corrections; criminal justice/police science; dairy science; data processing and data processing technology; drafting and design technology; drafting/design engineering technologies related; electrical, electronic and communications engineering technology; emergency medical technology (EMT paramedic); engineering technology; English language and literature related; environmental studies; family and consumer sciences/human sciences; fashion merchandising; finance; fire science/firefighting; forest technology; health and physical education/fitness; heating, air conditioning, ventilation and refrigeration maintenance technology; horse husbandry/equine science and management; horticultural science; hotel/motel administration; humanities; industrial and product design; industrial radiologic technology; interior design; journalism; kindergarten/preschool education; landscape architecture; legal administrative assistant/secretary; legal assistant/paralegal; machine tool technology; marketing/marketing management; materials science; mathematics; medical administrative assistant and medical secretary; mental health counseling; music; occupational safety and health technology; ornamental horticulture; parks, recreation and leisure; parks, recreation and leisure facilities management; photography; physical sciences related; pre-engineering; quality control technology; radio and television; real estate; registered nursing/registered nurse; respiratory care therapy; sign language interpretation and translation; social sciences; surveying technology; transportation and materials moving related; visual and performing arts; welding technology; wildlife, fish and wildlands science and management.
**Academics** *Calendar:* semesters. *Degree:* certificates, diplomas, and associate. *Special study options:* academic remediation for entering students, adult/continuing education programs, advanced placement credit, cooperative education, distance learning, double majors, English as a second language, honors programs, independent study, part-time degree program, services for LD students, study abroad, summer session for credit. *ROTC:* Army (b), Air Force (b).
**Library** Learning Resources Center. *Books:* 75,587 (physical), 82,336 (digital/electronic); *Databases:* 113. Students can reserve study rooms.
**Student Life** *Housing:* college housing not available. *Activities and Organizations:* drama/theater group, student-run radio station, choral group, Alpha Gamma Sigma, Muslim Student Association, Student Government, Asian Student Association, Kasama-Filipino Student Organization. *Campus security:* 24-hour emergency response devices and patrols, late-night transport/escort service. *Student services:* health clinic, personal/psychological counseling, women's center.
**Athletics** *Intercollegiate sports:* baseball M, basketball M/W, cheerleading M/W, cross-country running M/W, football M, golf M/W, sand volleyball W, soccer M/W, softball W, swimming and diving M/W, tennis M/W, track and field M/W, volleyball W, water polo M/W, wrestling M.
**Costs (2017–18)** *Tuition:* state resident $1288 full-time, $46 per unit part-time; nonresident $8680 full-time, $310 per unit part-time. Full-time tuition and fees

vary according to course load and program. Part-time tuition and fees vary according to course load and program. *Required fees:* $61 full-time, $61 per term part-time.
**Applying** *Options:* electronic application, early admission, deferred entrance. *Required for some:* high school transcript. *Notification:* continuous (freshmen), continuous (transfers).
**Admissions Office Contact** Mt. San Antonio College, 1100 North Grand Avenue, Walnut, CA 91789-1399.
*Website:* http://www.mtsac.edu/.

## Mt. San Jacinto College
### San Jacinto, California

**Freshman Application Contact** Mt. San Jacinto College, 1499 North State Street, San Jacinto, CA 92583-2399. *Phone:* 951-639-5212. *Website:* http://www.msjc.edu/.

## MTI College
### Sacramento, California

**Freshman Application Contact** Director of Admissions, MTI College, 5221 Madison Avenue, Sacramento, CA 95841. *Phone:* 916-339-1500. *Fax:* 916-339-0305. *Website:* http://www.mticollege.edu/.

## Napa Valley College
### Napa, California

**Director of Admissions** Mr. Oscar De Haro, Vice President of Student Services, Napa Valley College, 2277 Napa-Vallejo Highway, Napa, CA 94558-6236. *Phone:* 707-253-3000. *Toll-free phone:* 800-826-1077. *E-mail:* odeharo@napavalley.edu. *Website:* http://www.napavalley.edu/.

## National Career College
### Panorama City, California

**Admissions Office Contact** National Career College, 14355 Roscoe Boulevard, Panorama City, CA 91402. *Website:* http://www.nccusa.edu/.

## National Polytechnic College
### Commerce, California

**Admissions Office Contact** National Polytechnic College, 6630 Telegraph Road, Commerce, CA 90040. *Website:* http://www.npcollege.edu/.

## Norco College
### Norco, California

**Freshman Application Contact** Mark DeAsis, Director, Enrollment Services, Norco College, 2001 Third Street, Norco, CA 92860. *E-mail:* admissionsnorco@norcocollege.edu. *Website:* http://www.norcocollege.edu/.

## North-West College
### West Covina, California

**Admissions Office Contact** North-West College, 2121 West Garvey Avenue, West Covina, CA 91790. *Toll-free phone:* 888-408-4211. *Website:* http://www.nw.edu/.

## Ohlone College
### Fremont, California

**Freshman Application Contact** Ohlone College, 43600 Mission Boulevard, Fremont, CA 94539-5884. *Phone:* 510-659-6107. *Website:* http://www.ohlone.edu/.

## Orange Coast College
### Costa Mesa, California

- **District-supported** 2-year, founded 1947, part of Coast Community College District System
- **Suburban** 164-acre campus with easy access to Los Angeles
- **Endowment** $18.2 million
- **Coed,** 21,731 undergraduate students, 39% full-time, 48% women, 52% men

**Undergraduates** 8,561 full-time, 13,170 part-time. Students come from 75 other countries; 2% are from out of state; 2% Black or African American, non-Hispanic/Latino; 34% Hispanic/Latino; 20% Asian, non-Hispanic/Latino; 0.2% American Indian or Alaska Native, non-Hispanic/Latino; 4% Two or more races, non-Hispanic/Latino; 1% Race/ethnicity unknown; 5% international; 10% transferred in.
**Freshmen** *Admission:* 4,063 enrolled.
**Faculty** *Total:* 691, 38% full-time. *Student/faculty ratio:* 32:1.
**Majors** Accounting; accounting technology and bookkeeping; aircraft powerplant technology; airframe mechanics and aircraft maintenance technology; airline flight attendant; animation, interactive technology, video graphics and special effects; anthropology; apparel and textile manufacturing; apparel and textile marketing management; applied horticulture/horticulture operations; architectural technology; art; audiology and speech-language pathology; aviation/airway management; biology/biological sciences; business administration and management; business/commerce; cardiovascular technology; chemistry; child-care and support services management; child-care provision; cinematography and film/video production; clinical/medical laboratory technology; commercial and advertising art; computer graphics; computer installation and repair technology; computer programming; computer science; construction trades; cooking and related culinary arts; culinary arts; dance; dance related; dental assisting; diagnostic medical sonography and ultrasound technology; dietetic technology; dramatic/theater arts; economics; electrical/electronics equipment installation and repair; electrocardiograph technology; electroneurodiagnostic/electroencephalographic technology; elementary education; engineering technologies and engineering related; family and consumer sciences/human sciences; fashion/apparel design; foods, nutrition, and wellness; foreign languages and literatures; geography; geology/earth science; health and physical education/fitness; health services/allied health/health sciences; history; hotel/motel administration; humanities; interior design; international business/trade/commerce; journalism; kinesiology and exercise science; liberal arts and sciences/liberal studies; machine tool technology; marine transportation related; mass communication/media; mathematics; medical/clinical assistant; mental health counseling; merchandising, sales, and marketing operations related (general); music; philosophy; photographic and film/video technology; photography; physical fitness technician; physics; political science and government; pre-engineering; psychology; real estate; recording arts technology; religious studies; respiratory care therapy; restaurant, culinary, and catering management; retail management; sales, distribution, and marketing operations; social sciences; sociology; Spanish; special education–early childhood; speech communication and rhetoric; tourism and travel services marketing; welding technology.
**Academics** *Calendar:* semesters plus summer session. *Degree:* certificates and associate. *Special study options:* academic remediation for entering students, adult/continuing education programs, advanced placement credit, cooperative education, distance learning, double majors, English as a second language, external degree program, freshman honors college, honors programs, internships, off-campus study, part-time degree program, services for LD students, student-designed majors, study abroad, summer session for credit. *ROTC:* Army (c), Air Force (c).
**Library** Main Library plus 1 other. *Books:* 108,078 (physical), 24,666 (digital/electronic); *Serial titles:* 91 (physical), 4 (digital/electronic); *Databases:* 59. Weekly public service hours: 64; students can reserve study rooms.
**Student Life** *Housing:* college housing not available. *Activities and Organizations:* drama/theater group, student-run newspaper, choral group, Architecture Club, Circle K, Doctors of Tomorrow, Speech, Theater, and Debate, Vietnamese Student Association. *Campus security:* 24-hour emergency response devices and patrols, student patrols, late-night transport/escort service. *Student services:* health clinic, personal/psychological counseling, legal services, veterans affairs office.
**Athletics** *Intercollegiate sports:* baseball M, basketball M/W, cheerleading M/W, crew M/W, cross-country running M/W, football M, golf M/W, soccer M/W, softball W, swimming and diving M/W, tennis M/W, track and field M/W, volleyball M/W, water polo M/W.
**Costs (2018–19)** *Tuition:* state resident $1288 full-time, $46 per unit part-time; nonresident $8876 full-time, $256 per unit part-time. *Required fees:* $900 full-time, $140 per term part-time. *Payment plan:* installment.
**Financial Aid** Of all full-time matriculated undergraduates who enrolled in 2016, 108 Federal Work-Study jobs (averaging $3000). *Financial aid deadline:* 5/28.
**Applying** *Options:* electronic application. *Application deadlines:* rolling (freshmen), rolling (transfers). *Notification:* continuous (freshmen), continuous (transfers).
**Admissions Office Contact** Orange Coast College, 2701 Fairview Road, Costa Mesa, CA 92626.
*Website:* http://www.orangecoastcollege.edu/.

# Oxnard College
## Oxnard, California

**Freshman Application Contact** Mr. Joel Diaz, Registrar, Oxnard College, 4000 South Rose Avenue, Oxnard, CA 93033-6699. *Phone:* 805-986-5843. *Fax:* 805-986-5943. *E-mail:* jdiaz@vcccd.edu. *Website:* http://www.oxnardcollege.edu/.

# Palomar College
## San Marcos, California

- **District-supported** 2-year, founded 1946, part of California Community College System
- **Suburban** 156-acre campus with easy access to San Diego
- **Coed,** 25,244 undergraduate students, 100% full-time, 47% women, 53% men

**Undergraduates** 25,244 full-time.
**Faculty** *Total:* 1,380, 22% full-time. *Student/faculty ratio:* 21:1.
**Majors** Accounting technology and bookkeeping; administrative assistant and secretarial science; advertising; animation, interactive technology, video graphics and special effects; apparel and textile marketing management; archeology; architectural drafting and CAD/CADD; architectural technology; art; astronomy; autobody/collision and repair technology; automobile/automotive mechanics technology; biological and physical sciences; biology/biological sciences; broadcast journalism; building/home/construction inspection; business administration and management; business/commerce; cabinetmaking and millwork; carpentry; ceramic arts and ceramics; chemistry; child-care and support services management; child-care provision; commercial and advertising art; computer graphics; computer programming; computer systems networking and telecommunications; construction trades related; dance; dental assisting; design and visual communications; desktop publishing and digital imaging design; diesel mechanics technology; drafting and design technology; dramatic/theater arts; drawing; drywall installation; economics; education; electrical/electronics drafting and CAD/CADD; electrician; emergency medical technology (EMT paramedic); English; family and community services; family and consumer sciences/human sciences; fashion/apparel design; film/cinema/video studies; fire prevention and safety technology; foreign languages and literatures; forensic science and technology; French; geography; geography related; geology/earth science; graphic and printing equipment operation/production; graphic design; homeland security; humanities; information technology; insurance; interior design; international business/trade/commerce; journalism; kinesiology and exercise science; legal studies; liberal arts and sciences/liberal studies; library and archives assisting; masonry; mathematics; medical administrative assistant and medical secretary; metal and jewelry arts; music; parks, recreation and leisure; photographic and film/video technology; pre-engineering; psychology; public administration; radio and television; real estate; registered nursing/registered nurse; sculpture; sheet metal technology; sign language interpretation and translation; social sciences; sociology; special education–early childhood; speech communication and rhetoric; substance abuse/addiction counseling; water quality and wastewater treatment management and recycling technology; web page, digital/multimedia and information resources design; welding technology; women's studies.
**Academics** *Calendar:* semesters. *Degree:* certificates and associate. *Special study options:* academic remediation for entering students, advanced placement credit, cooperative education, distance learning, English as a second language, internships, part-time degree program, services for LD students, summer session for credit. *ROTC:* Air Force (c).
**Library** Palomar College Library plus 1 other. *Books:* 100,000 (physical); *Serial titles:* 689 (physical). Weekly public service hours: 64.
**Student Life** *Housing:* college housing not available. *Activities and Organizations:* drama/theater group, student-run newspaper, radio and television station, choral group, SNAP (Student Nursing Association of Palomar College), Alpha Omega Rho Chapter of Phi Theta Kappa (international honor society), Active Minds, Student Veterans Organization, MEChA (Chicano organization). *Campus security:* 24-hour emergency response devices and patrols, late-night transport/escort service. *Student services:* health clinic, personal/psychological counseling, veterans affairs office.
**Athletics** *Intercollegiate sports:* baseball M, basketball M/W, football M, golf M, soccer M/W, softball W, swimming and diving M/W, tennis M/W, track and field M/W, volleyball M/W, water polo M/W, wrestling M. *Intramural sports:* basketball M/W, bowling M, golf M, skiing (downhill) M/W, soccer M, softball W, tennis M, volleyball M, water polo M, wrestling M.
**Costs (2018–19)** *Tuition:* state resident $1338 full-time, $46 per unit part-time; nonresident $8030 full-time, $285 per unit part-time. *Required fees:* $60 full-time, $1 per unit part-time, $19 per term part-time. *Payment plan:* installment.

**Applying** *Options:* electronic application. *Application deadlines:* rolling (freshmen), rolling (transfers). *Notification:* continuous (freshmen), continuous (transfers).
**Freshman Application Contact** Dr. Kendyl Magnuson, Senior Director of Enrollment Services, Palomar College, 1140 W Mission Road, San Marcos, CA 92069. *Phone:* 760-744-1150 Ext. 2171. *Fax:* 760-744-2932. *E-mail:* kmagnuson@palomar.edu.
*Website:* http://www.palomar.edu/.

# Palo Verde College
## Blythe, California

**Freshman Application Contact** Diana Rodriguez, Vice President of Student Services, Palo Verde College, 1 College Drive, Blythe, CA 92225. *Phone:* 760-921-5428. *Fax:* 760-921-3608. *E-mail:* diana.rodriguez@paloverde.edu. *Website:* http://www.paloverde.edu/.

# Pasadena City College
## Pasadena, California

- **District-supported** 2-year, founded 1924, part of California Community College System
- **Urban** 55-acre campus with easy access to Los Angeles
- **Coed,** 27,324 undergraduate students, 38% full-time, 52% women, 48% men

**Undergraduates** 10,422 full-time, 16,902 part-time. Students come from 28 states and territories; 20 other countries; 2% are from out of state; 4% Black or African American, non-Hispanic/Latino; 51% Hispanic/Latino; 23% Asian, non-Hispanic/Latino; 0.1% Native Hawaiian or other Pacific Islander, non-Hispanic/Latino; 0.1% American Indian or Alaska Native, non-Hispanic/Latino; 3% Two or more races, non-Hispanic/Latino; 0.9% Race/ethnicity unknown; 3% international; 92% transferred in. *Retention:* 74% of full-time freshmen returned.
**Freshmen** *Admission:* 4,861 enrolled.
**Faculty** *Total:* 1,077, 39% full-time. *Student/faculty ratio:* 25:1.
**Majors** Accounting; accounting technology and bookkeeping; administrative assistant and secretarial science; animation, interactive technology, video graphics and special effects; anthropology; architecture; art; audiology and speech-language pathology; automobile/automotive mechanics technology; biochemistry; biological and physical sciences; biology/biological sciences; broadcast journalism; building/home/construction inspection; business administration and management; business automation/technology/data entry; chemistry; child development; cinematography and film/video production; classics and classical languages; computer/information technology services administration related; computer science; computer technology/computer systems technology; construction trades; cosmetology; cosmetology, barber/styling, and nail instruction; criminal justice/law enforcement administration; dance; data entry/microcomputer applications related; dental assisting; dental hygiene; dental laboratory technology; desktop publishing and digital imaging design; digital communication and media/multimedia; drafting and design technology; dramatic/theater arts; electrical and electronic engineering technologies related; electrical and electronics engineering; engineering technology; fashion/apparel design; fashion merchandising; fire prevention and safety technology; food service and dining room management; graphic and printing equipment operation/production; graphic design; history; hospitality administration; humanities; industrial electronics technology; international business/trade/commerce; international/global studies; legal assistant/paralegal; liberal arts and sciences/liberal studies; library science related; licensed practical/vocational nurse training; machine shop technology; marketing/marketing management; mathematics; mechanical engineering; medical/clinical assistant; medical insurance/medical billing; medical office assistant; photography; photojournalism; psychology; radio and television; radio and television broadcasting technology; radiologic technology/science; registered nursing/registered nurse; sociology; Spanish; speech communication and rhetoric; theater design and technology; welding technology.
**Academics** *Calendar:* semesters. *Degree:* certificates, diplomas, and associate. *Special study options:* academic remediation for entering students, adult/continuing education programs, advanced placement credit, distance learning, double majors, English as a second language, honors programs, independent study, internships, part-time degree program, services for LD students, study abroad, summer session for credit.
**Library** Pasadena City College Library plus 1 other. *Books:* 133,975 (physical), 35,619 (digital/electronic); *Databases:* 56. Weekly public service hours: 54; students can reserve study rooms.
**Student Life** *Housing:* college housing not available. *Activities and Organizations:* drama/theater group, student-run newspaper, choral group, marching band, AGS Honor Society, TROPA, Candela Salsa, International Students, Ujima. *Campus security:* 24-hour emergency response devices and

patrols, late-night transport/escort service, cadet patrols. *Student services:* health clinic, personal/psychological counseling, legal services, veterans affairs office.

**Athletics** *Intercollegiate sports:* badminton M/W, baseball M, basketball M/W, cheerleading W(c), cross-country running M/W, football M, soccer M/W, softball W, swimming and diving M/W, tennis M/W, track and field M/W, volleyball W, water polo W. *Intramural sports:* water polo M(c).

**Costs (2018–19)** *Tuition:* state resident $1348 full-time, $46 per unit part-time; nonresident $6272 full-time, $280 per unit part-time. Full-time tuition and fees vary according to course load. Part-time tuition and fees vary according to course load. *Required fees:* $60 full-time, $24 per term part-time.

**Applying** *Options:* electronic application. *Application deadlines:* rolling (freshmen), rolling (transfers). *Notification:* continuous (freshmen), continuous (transfers).

**Admissions Office Contact** Pasadena City College, 1570 East Colorado Boulevard, Pasadena, CA 91106-2041.
*Website:* http://www.pasadena.edu/.

# Pima Medical Institute
## Chula Vista, California

**Freshman Application Contact** Admissions Office, Pima Medical Institute, 780 Bay Boulevard, Chula Vista, CA 91910. *Phone:* 619-425-3200. *Toll-free phone:* 800-477-PIMA. *Website:* http://www.pmi.edu/.

# Platt College
## Alhambra, California

**Director of Admissions** Mr. Detroit Whiteside, Director of Admissions, Platt College, 1000 South Fremont A9W, Alhambra, CA 91803. *Phone:* 323-258-8050. *Toll-free phone:* 888-866-6697 (in-state); 888-80-PLATT (out-of-state). *Website:* http://www.plattcollege.edu/.

# Platt College
## Ontario, California

**Director of Admissions** Ms. Jennifer Abandonato, Director of Admissions, Platt College, 3700 Inland Empire Boulevard, Ontario, CA 91764. *Phone:* 909-941-9410. *Toll-free phone:* 888-80-PLATT. *Website:* http://www.plattcollege.edu/.

# Porterville College
## Porterville, California

**Director of Admissions** Ms. Judy Pope, Director of Admissions and Records/Registrar, Porterville College, 100 East College Avenue, Porterville, CA 93257-6058. *Phone:* 559-791-2222. *Website:* http://www.pc.cc.ca.us/.

# Professional Golfers Career College
## Temecula, California

**Freshman Application Contact** Mr. Gary Gilleon, Professional Golfers Career College, 26109 Ynez Road, Temecula, CA 92591. *Phone:* 951-719-2994 Ext. 1021. *Toll-free phone:* 800-877-4380. *Fax:* 951-719-1643. *E-mail:* garygilleon@golfcollege.edu. *Website:* http://www.golfcollege.edu/.

# Reedley College
## Reedley, California

**Freshman Application Contact** Admissions and Records Office, Reedley College, 995 North Reed Avenue, Reedley, CA 93654. *Phone:* 559-638-0323. *Fax:* 559-637-2523. *Website:* http://www.reedleycollege.edu/.

# Rio Hondo College
## Whittier, California

- **District-supported** 2-year, founded 1960, part of California Community College System
- **Suburban** 128-acre campus with easy access to Los Angeles
- **Coed**

**Undergraduates** Students come from 5 states and territories; 0.2% are from out of state; 2% Black or African American, non-Hispanic/Latino; 77% Hispanic/Latino; 6% Asian, non-Hispanic/Latino; 0.1% Native Hawaiian or other Pacific Islander, non-Hispanic/Latino; 0.2% American Indian or Alaska Native, non-Hispanic/Latino; 0.9% Two or more races, non-Hispanic/Latino; 5% Race/ethnicity unknown; 0.3% international.
**Faculty** *Total:* 560, 34% full-time. *Student/faculty ratio:* 34:1.

**Majors** Business teacher education; criminal justice/law enforcement administration; liberal arts and sciences/liberal studies; registered nursing/registered nurse.

**Academics** *Calendar:* semesters. *Degree:* certificates and associate. *Special study options:* academic remediation for entering students, adult/continuing education programs, advanced placement credit, distance learning, English as a second language, honors programs, part-time degree program, services for LD students, study abroad, summer session for credit. *ROTC:* Army (c), Navy (c), Air Force (c).

**Library** Library and Learning Resource Center plus 1 other. *Books:* 88,245 (physical); *Serial titles:* 104 (physical); *Databases:* 12. Weekly public service hours: 68; students can reserve study rooms.

**Student Life** *Housing:* college housing not available. *Activities and Organizations:* drama/theater group, student-run newspaper, radio station, choral group. *Campus security:* 24-hour patrols, late-night transport/escort service. *Student services:* health clinic, personal/psychological counseling, women's center, legal services, veterans affairs office.

**Athletics** *Intercollegiate sports:* baseball M, basketball M/W, cross-country running M/W, soccer M/W, softball W, swimming and diving M/W, tennis M/W, track and field M/W, volleyball W, water polo M/W, wrestling M.

**Costs (2017–18)** *Tuition:* state resident $1380 full-time, $46 per credit part-time; nonresident $7380 full-time, $200 per credit part-time. Full-time tuition and fees vary according to course load. Part-time tuition and fees vary according to course load. *Required fees:* $72 full-time.

**Financial Aid** Of all full-time matriculated undergraduates who enrolled in 2017, 150 Federal Work-Study jobs (averaging $3200). 35 state and other part-time jobs (averaging $3200). *Financial aid deadline:* 5/1.

**Applying** *Application deadlines:* rolling (freshmen), rolling (transfers). *Notification:* continuous (freshmen), continuous (transfers).

**Freshman Application Contact** Rio Hondo College, 3600 Workman Mill Road, Whittier, CA 90601-1699. *Phone:* 562-692-0921 Ext. 3415. *Website:* http://www.riohondo.edu/.

# Riverside City College
## Riverside, California

**Freshman Application Contact** Joy Chambers, Dean of Enrollment Services, Riverside City College, Riverside, CA 92506. *Phone:* 951-222-8600. *Fax:* 951-222-8037. *E-mail:* admissionsriverside@rcc.edu. *Website:* http://www.rcc.edu/.

# Sacramento City College
## Sacramento, California

**Director of Admissions** Mr. Sam T. Sandusky, Dean, Student Services, Sacramento City College, 3835 Freeport Boulevard, Sacramento, CA 95822-1386. *Phone:* 916-558-2438. *Website:* http://www.scc.losrios.edu/.

# Saddleback College
## Mission Viejo, California

**Freshman Application Contact** Admissions Office, Saddleback College, 28000 Marguerite Parkway, Mission Viejo, CA 92692. *Phone:* 949-582-4555. *Fax:* 949-347-8315. *E-mail:* earaiza@saddleback.edu. *Website:* http://www.saddleback.edu/.

# The Salvation Army College for Officer Training at Crestmont
## Rancho Palos Verdes, California

- **Independent Salvation Army** 2-year, founded 1921
- **Suburban** 44-acre campus with easy access to Los Angeles
- **Coed,** 59 undergraduate students, 100% full-time, 63% women, 37% men

**Undergraduates** 59 full-time. Students come from 14 states and territories; 67% are from out of state; 7% Black or African American, non-Hispanic/Latino; 20% Hispanic/Latino; 5% Asian, non-Hispanic/Latino; 2% Native Hawaiian or other Pacific Islander, non-Hispanic/Latino; 8% Two or more races, non-Hispanic/Latino; 100% live on campus. *Retention:* 98% of full-time freshmen returned.
**Freshmen** *Admission:* 20 enrolled.
**Faculty** *Total:* 27, 78% full-time, 11% with terminal degrees. *Student/faculty ratio:* 3:1.
**Majors** Divinity/ministry.
**Academics** *Calendar:* quarters. *Degree:* associate. *Special study options:* academic remediation for entering students, accelerated degree program, cooperative education, distance learning, English as a second language, external degree program, independent study, internships, off-campus study, student-designed majors.

**Library** The Salvation Army Elfman Memorial Library plus 1 other. *Books:* 45,000 (physical).

**Student Life** *Housing:* on-campus residence required through sophomore year. *Options:* coed. Campus housing is university owned. *Activities and Organizations:* drama/theater group, choral group. *Campus security:* 24-hour emergency response devices and patrols. *Student services:* health clinic, personal/psychological counseling.

**Applying** *Application fee:* $15. *Required:* essay or personal statement, high school transcript, 2 letters of recommendation, interview. *Application deadline:* 6/1 (freshmen). *Notification:* 8/20 (freshmen).

**Freshman Application Contact** Capt. Brian Jones, Director of Curriculum, The Salvation Army College for Officer Training at Crestmont, 30840 Hawthorne Boulevard, Rancho Palos Verdes, CA 90275. *Phone:* 310-544-6442. *Fax:* 310-265-6520.
*Website:* http://www.crestmont.edu/.

## San Bernardino Valley College
### San Bernardino, California

**Director of Admissions** Ms. Helena Johnson, Director of Admissions and Records, San Bernardino Valley College, 701 South Mount Vernon Avenue, San Bernardino, CA 92410-2748. *Phone:* 909-384-4401. *Website:* http://www.valleycollege.edu/.

## San Diego City College
### San Diego, California

**Freshman Application Contact** Ms. Lou Humphries, Registrar/Supervisor of Admissions, Records, Evaluations and Veterans, San Diego City College, 1313 Park Boulevard, San Diego, CA 92101-4787. *Phone:* 619-388-3474. *Fax:* 619-388-3505. *E-mail:* lhumphri@sdccd.edu. *Website:* http://www.sdcity.edu/.

## San Diego Mesa College
### San Diego, California

**Freshman Application Contact** Ms. Cheri Sawyer, Admissions Supervisor, San Diego Mesa College, 7250 Mesa College Drive, San Diego, CA 92111. *Phone:* 619-388-2686. *Fax:* 619-388-2960. *E-mail:* csawyer@sdccd.edu. *Website:* http://www.sdmesa.edu/.

## San Diego Miramar College
### San Diego, California

**Freshman Application Contact** Ms. Dana Stack, Admissions Supervisor, San Diego Miramar College, 10440 Black Mountain Road, San Diego, CA 92126-2999. *Phone:* 619-536-7854. *E-mail:* dstack@sdccd.edu. *Website:* http://www.sdmiramar.edu/.

## San Joaquin Delta College
### Stockton, California

- **District-supported** 2-year, founded 1935, part of California Community College System
- **Urban** 165-acre campus with easy access to Sacramento
- **Coed,** 18,102 undergraduate students

**Undergraduates** Students come from 20 states and territories; 0.2% are from out of state; 13% Black or African American, non-Hispanic/Latino; 44% Hispanic/Latino; 17% Asian, non-Hispanic/Latino; 0.5% Native Hawaiian or other Pacific Islander, non-Hispanic/Latino; 0.3% American Indian or Alaska Native, non-Hispanic/Latino; 5% Two or more races, non-Hispanic/Latino; 0.5% Race/ethnicity unknown; 0.3% international. *Retention:* 77% of full-time freshmen returned.

**Faculty** *Total:* 544, 41% full-time. *Student/faculty ratio:* 27:1.

**Majors** Accounting; agricultural business and management; agricultural mechanization; agriculture; animal sciences; anthropology; art; automobile/automotive mechanics technology; biology/biological sciences; broadcast journalism; business administration and management; chemistry; civil engineering technology; commercial and advertising art; comparative literature; computer science; construction engineering technology; corrections; criminal justice/police science; crop production; culinary arts; dance; dramatic/theater arts; economics; electrical, electronic and communications engineering technology; engineering; engineering related; engineering technology; English; family and consumer sciences/human sciences; fashion merchandising; fire science/firefighting; geology/earth science; heating, air conditioning, ventilation and refrigeration maintenance technology; history; humanities; journalism; liberal arts and sciences/liberal studies; licensed practical/vocational nurse training; machine tool technology; mathematics; mechanical engineering/mechanical technology; music; natural resources management and policy; natural sciences; ornamental horticulture; philosophy; photography; physical education teaching and coaching; physical sciences; political science and government; psychology; registered nursing/registered nurse; religious studies; rhetoric and composition; social sciences; sociology.

**Academics** *Calendar:* semesters. *Degree:* certificates and associate. *Special study options:* academic remediation for entering students, adult/continuing education programs, advanced placement credit, cooperative education, distance learning, English as a second language, honors programs, independent study, part-time degree program, services for LD students, summer session for credit.

**Library** Goleman Library plus 1 other.

**Student Life** *Housing:* college housing not available. *Activities and Organizations:* drama/theater group, student-run newspaper, radio station, choral group. *Campus security:* 24-hour emergency response devices and patrols, late-night transport/escort service. *Student services:* personal/psychological counseling, legal services.

**Athletics** Member NJCAA. *Intercollegiate sports:* baseball M, basketball M/W, cross-country running M/W, fencing M/W, football M, golf M/W, soccer M/W, softball W, swimming and diving M/W, tennis M/W, track and field M/W, volleyball W, water polo M/W, wrestling M. *Intramural sports:* badminton M/W, basketball M/W, bowling M/W, soccer M/W, swimming and diving M/W, tennis M/W, ultimate Frisbee M/W, volleyball M/W, weight lifting M/W.

**Costs (2017–18)** *Tuition:* state resident $1288 full-time, $46 per unit part-time; nonresident $7840 full-time, $234 per unit part-time. Full-time tuition and fees vary according to course load. Part-time tuition and fees vary according to course load. *Waivers:* employees or children of employees.

**Financial Aid** Of all full-time matriculated undergraduates who enrolled in 2016, 11,009 applied for aid, 9,803 were judged to have need, 45 had their need fully met. 197 Federal Work-Study jobs (averaging $2304). *Average percent of need met:* 31%. *Average financial aid package:* $5450. *Average need-based loan:* $2603. *Average need-based gift aid:* $5197.

**Applying** *Options:* electronic application, early admission. *Application deadlines:* rolling (freshmen), rolling (transfers). *Notification:* continuous (freshmen), continuous (transfers).

**Freshman Application Contact** Ms. Karen Sea, Registrar, San Joaquin Delta College, 5151 Pacific Avenue, Stockton, CA 95207. *Phone:* 209-954-6127. *E-mail:* ksea@deltacollege.edu.
*Website:* http://www.deltacollege.edu/.

## San Joaquin Valley College
### Bakersfield, California

**Freshman Application Contact** Enrollment Services Director, San Joaquin Valley College, 201 New Stine Road, Bakersfield, CA 93309. *Phone:* 661-834-0126. *Toll-free phone:* 866-544-7898. *Fax:* 661-834-8124. *E-mail:* admissions@sjvc.edu. *Website:* http://www.sjvc.edu/campuses/central-california/bakersfield.

## San Joaquin Valley College
### Fresno, California

**Freshman Application Contact** Enrollment Services Director, San Joaquin Valley College, 295 East Sierra Avenue, Fresno, CA 93710. *Phone:* 559-448-8282. *Toll-free phone:* 866-544-7898. *Fax:* 559-448-8250. *E-mail:* admissions@sjvc.edu. *Website:* http://www.sjvc.edu/campuses/central-california/fresno/.

## San Joaquin Valley College
### Hanford, California

**Freshman Application Contact** San Joaquin Valley College, 215 West 7th Street, Hanford, CA 93230. *Toll-free phone:* 866-544-7898. *Website:* http://www.sjvc.edu/campuses/central-california/hanford/.

## San Joaquin Valley College
### Hesperia, California

**Freshman Application Contact** San Joaquin Valley College, 9331 Mariposa Road, Hesperia, CA 92344. *Toll-free phone:* 866-544-7898. *Website:* http://www.sjvc.edu/campuses/southern-california/victor-valley/.

# San Joaquin Valley College
Lancaster, California

**Freshman Application Contact** San Joaquin Valley College, 42135 10th Street West, Suite 147, Lancaster, CA 93534. *Toll-free phone:* 866-544-7898. *Website:* http://www.sjvc.edu/campuses/southern-california/antelope-valley/.

# San Joaquin Valley College
Ontario, California

**Freshman Application Contact** Enrollment Services Director, San Joaquin Valley College, 4580 Ontario Mills Parkway, Ontario, CA 91764. *Phone:* 909-948-7582. *Toll-free phone:* 866-544-7898. *Fax:* 909-948-3860. *E-mail:* admissions@sjvc.edu. *Website:* http://www.sjvc.edu/campuses/southern-california/ontario/.

# San Joaquin Valley College
Rancho Cordova, California

**Freshman Application Contact** Enrollment Services Director, San Joaquin Valley College, 11050 Olson Drive, Suite 210, Rancho Cordova, CA 95670. *Phone:* 916-638-7582. *Toll-free phone:* 866-544-7898. *Fax:* 916-638-7553. *E-mail:* admissions@sjvc.edu. *Website:* http://www.sjvc.edu/campuses/northern-california/rancho-cordova/.

# San Joaquin Valley College
Salida, California

**Freshman Application Contact** Enrollment Services Director, San Joaquin Valley College, 5380 Pirrone Road, Salida, CA 95368. *Phone:* 209-543-8800. *Toll-free phone:* 866-544-7898. *Fax:* 209-543-8320. *E-mail:* admissions@sjvc.edu. *Website:* http://www.sjvc.edu/campuses/northern-california/modesto/.

# San Joaquin Valley College
Temecula, California

**Freshman Application Contact** Ms. Robyn Whiles, Enrollment Services Director, San Joaquin Valley College, 27270 Madison Avenue, Suite 103, Temecula, CA 92590. *Phone:* 559-651-2500. *Toll-free phone:* 866-544-7898. *E-mail:* admissions@sjvc.edu. *Website:* http://www.sjvc.edu/campuses/southern-california/temecula/.

# San Joaquin Valley College
Visalia, California

**Freshman Application Contact** Susie Topjian, Enrollment Services Director, San Joaquin Valley College, 8400 West Mineral King Boulevard, Visalia, CA 93291. *Phone:* 559-651-2500. *Toll-free phone:* 866-544-7898. *Fax:* 559-734-9048. *E-mail:* admissions@sjvc.edu. *Website:* http://www.sjvc.edu/campuses/central-california/visalia/.

# San Joaquin Valley College–Fresno Aviation Campus
Fresno, California

**Freshman Application Contact** Enrollment Services Coordinator, San Joaquin Valley College–Fresno Aviation Campus, 4985 East Anderson Avenue, Fresno, CA 93727. *Phone:* 559-453-0123. *Toll-free phone:* 866-544-7898. *Fax:* 599-453-0133. *E-mail:* admissions@sjvc.edu. *Website:* http://www.sjvc.edu/campuses/central-california/fresno-aviation/.

# San Joaquin Valley College–Online
Visalia, California

**Freshman Application Contact** Enrollment Services Director, San Joaquin Valley College–Online, 8344 West Mineral King Avenue, Visalia, CA 93291. *Toll-free phone:* 866-544-7898. *E-mail:* admissions@sjvc.edu. *Website:* http://www.sjvc.edu/online-programs/.

# San Jose City College
San Jose, California

**Freshman Application Contact** Mr. Carlo Santos, Director of Admissions/Registrar, San Jose City College, 2100 Moorpark Avenue, San Jose, CA 95128-2799. *Phone:* 408-288-3707. *Fax:* 408-298-1935. *Website:* http://www.sjcc.edu/.

# Santa Ana College
Santa Ana, California

**Freshman Application Contact** Mrs. Christie Steward, Admissions Clerk, Santa Ana College, 1530 West 17th Street, Santa Ana, CA 92706-3398. *Phone:* 714-564-6053. *Website:* http://www.sac.edu/.

# Santa Barbara Business College
Bakersfield, California

**Admissions Office Contact** Santa Barbara Business College, 5300 California Avenue, Bakersfield, CA 93309. *Website:* http://www.sbbcollege.edu/.

# Santa Barbara Business College
Santa Maria, California

**Admissions Office Contact** Santa Barbara Business College, 303 East Plaza Drive, Santa Maria, CA 93454. *Website:* http://www.sbbcollege.edu/.

# Santa Barbara City College
Santa Barbara, California

**Freshman Application Contact** Ms. Allison Curtis, Director of Admissions and Records, Santa Barbara City College, Santa Barbara, CA 93109. *Phone:* 805-965-0581 Ext. 2352. *Fax:* 805-962-0497. *E-mail:* admissions@sbcc.edu. *Website:* http://www.sbcc.edu/.

# Santa Monica College
Santa Monica, California

- **District-supported** 2-year, founded 1929, part of California Community College System
- **Urban** 40-acre campus with easy access to Los Angeles
- **Coed**

**Undergraduates** 4,346 full-time, 26,484 part-time. 8% are from out of state; 10% Black or African American, non-Hispanic/Latino; 46% Hispanic/Latino; 7% Asian, non-Hispanic/Latino; 0.2% Native Hawaiian or other Pacific Islander, non-Hispanic/Latino; 0.1% American Indian or Alaska Native, non-Hispanic/Latino; 4% Two or more races, non-Hispanic/Latino; 0.8% Race/ethnicity unknown; 11% international; 96% transferred in.

**Academics** *Calendar:* semester plus optional winter and summer terms. *Degree:* certificates and associate. *Special study options:* academic remediation for entering students, adult/continuing education programs, advanced placement credit, cooperative education, distance learning, English as a second language, honors programs, independent study, internships, part-time degree program, services for LD students, study abroad, summer session for credit. *ROTC:* Army (c).

**Library** Santa Monica College Library.

**Student Life** *Campus security:* 24-hour emergency response devices and patrols, student patrols, late-night transport/escort service.

**Athletics** Member NJCAA.

**Financial Aid** Of all full-time matriculated undergraduates who enrolled in 2016, 450 Federal Work-Study jobs (averaging $3000).

**Applying** *Options:* early admission. *Required:* high school transcript.

**Freshman Application Contact** Santa Monica College, 1900 Pico Boulevard, Santa Monica, CA 90405-1628. *Phone:* 310-434-4774. *Website:* http://www.smc.edu/.

# Santa Rosa Junior College
Santa Rosa, California

- **District-supported** 2-year, founded 1918, part of California Community College System
- **Urban** 100-acre campus with easy access to San Francisco
- **Endowment** $41.3 million
- **Coed,** 26,800 undergraduate students

**Undergraduates** Students come from 36 other countries; 3% are from out of state; 2% Black or African American, non-Hispanic/Latino; 34% Hispanic/Latino; 5% Asian, non-Hispanic/Latino; 0.3% Native Hawaiian or other Pacific Islander, non-Hispanic/Latino; 0.7% American Indian or Alaska Native, non-Hispanic/Latino; 4% Two or more races, non-Hispanic/Latino; 7% Race/ethnicity unknown.

**Freshmen** *Admission:* 5,889 applied, 5,889 admitted.

**Majors** Agricultural business and management; agricultural communication/journalism; agroecology and sustainable agriculture; American Sign Language (ASL); animal sciences; anthropology; art; art history, criticism and conservation; automobile/automotive mechanics technology; behavioral sciences; biology/biological sciences; business administration and management; chemistry; child development; civil engineering technology; communication; community health services counseling; computer science; criminal justice/law enforcement administration; culinary arts; dance; dental hygiene; diesel mechanics technology; dietetic technology; digital communication and media/multimedia; dramatic/theater arts; early childhood education; economics; electrical, electronic and communications engineering technology; emergency medical technology (EMT paramedic); engineering; English; environmental studies; fashion/apparel design; fashion merchandising; fire science/firefighting; floriculture/floristry management; French; graphic design; health and physical education/fitness; history; horse husbandry/equine science and management; humanities; human resources management; human services; interior design; jazz/jazz studies; kinesiology and exercise science; landscaping and groundskeeping; Latin American studies; legal assistant/paralegal; liberal arts and sciences/liberal studies; licensed practical/vocational nurse training; mathematics; medical/clinical assistant; music related; natural resources/conservation; natural sciences; nutrition sciences; parks, recreation and leisure facilities management; pharmacy technician; philosophy; physics; political science and government; psychology; radiologic technology/science; real estate; registered nursing/registered nurse; religious studies; restaurant/food services management; social sciences; sociology; Spanish; surveying technology; viticulture and enology; women's studies.
**Academics** *Calendar:* semesters. *Degree:* certificates and associate. *Special study options:* academic remediation for entering students, adult/continuing education programs, advanced placement credit, cooperative education, distance learning, English as a second language, independent study, internships, off-campus study, part-time degree program, services for LD students, study abroad, summer session for credit.
**Library** Doyle Library plus 1 other. Students can reserve study rooms.
**Student Life** *Housing:* college housing not available. *Activities and Organizations:* drama/theater group, student-run newspaper, choral group, AG Ambassadors, MECHA, Alpha Gamma Sigma, Phi Theta Kappa, Puente. *Campus security:* 24-hour emergency response devices and patrols, student patrols. *Student services:* health clinic, personal/psychological counseling.
**Costs (2017–18)** *One-time required fee:* $40. *Tuition:* state resident $1280 full-time, $46 per unit part-time; nonresident $8608 full-time, $303 per unit part-time. Full-time tuition and fees vary according to course load. Part-time tuition and fees vary according to course load. *Room and board:* Room and board charges vary according to housing facility. *Payment plans:* installment, deferred payment.
**Financial Aid** Of all full-time matriculated undergraduates who enrolled in 2009, 135 Federal Work-Study jobs (averaging $2210). 43 state and other part-time jobs (averaging $7396).
**Applying** *Options:* electronic application, early admission. *Application deadlines:* rolling (freshmen), rolling (transfers). *Notification:* continuous (freshmen), continuous (transfers).
**Admissions Office Contact** Santa Rosa Junior College, 1501 Mendocino Avenue, Santa Rosa, CA 95401-4395.
*Website:* http://www.santarosa.edu/.

# Santiago Canyon College
## Orange, California

**Freshman Application Contact** Tuyen Nguyen, Admissions and Records, Santiago Canyon College, 8045 East Chapman Avenue, Orange, CA 92869. *Phone:* 714-628-4902. *Website:* http://www.sccollege.edu/.

# Shasta College
## Redding, California

**Director of Admissions** Dr. Kevin O'Rorke, Dean of Enrollment Services, Shasta College, PO Box 496006, 11555 Old Oregon Trail, Redding, CA 96049-6006. *Phone:* 530-242-7669. *Website:* http://www.shastacollege.edu/.

# Sierra College
## Rocklin, California

- **District-supported** 2-year, founded 1936, part of California Community College System
- **Suburban** 327-acre campus with easy access to Sacramento
- **Coed**

**Undergraduates** 4,874 full-time, 13,884 part-time. Students come from 27 states and territories; 10 other countries; 0.7% are from out of state; 3% Black or African American, non-Hispanic/Latino; 17% Hispanic/Latino; 5% Asian, non-Hispanic/Latino; 2% Native Hawaiian or other Pacific Islander, non-Hispanic/Latino; 0.7% American Indian or Alaska Native, non-Hispanic/Latino; 6% Two or more races, non-Hispanic/Latino; 2% Race/ethnicity unknown; 0.9% international; 18% transferred in; 1% live on campus. *Retention:* 68% of full-time freshmen returned.
**Faculty** *Student/faculty ratio:* 25:1.
**Academics** *Calendar:* semesters. *Degree:* certificates and associate. *Special study options:* academic remediation for entering students, accelerated degree program, advanced placement credit, distance learning, double majors, English as a second language, honors programs, independent study, internships, off-campus study, part-time degree program, services for LD students, study abroad, summer session for credit.
**Library** Leary Resource Center plus 1 other.
**Student Life** *Campus security:* 24-hour emergency response devices and patrols, late-night transport/escort service.
**Applying** *Options:* electronic application, early admission.
**Freshman Application Contact** Sierra College, 5100 Sierra College Boulevard, Rocklin, CA 95677. *Phone:* 916-660-7341. *Website:* http://www.sierracollege.edu/.

# Skyline College
## San Bruno, California

**Freshman Application Contact** Terry Stats, Admissions Office, Skyline College, 3300 College Drive, San Bruno, CA 94066-1698. *Phone:* 650-738-4251. *E-mail:* stats@smccd.net. *Website:* http://skylinecollege.edu/.

# Solano Community College
## Fairfield, California

**Freshman Application Contact** Solano Community College, 4000 Suisun Valley Road, Fairfield, CA 94534. *Phone:* 707-864-7000 Ext. 4313. *Website:* http://www.solano.edu/.

# South Coast College
## Orange, California

**Director of Admissions** South Coast College, 2011 West Chapman Avenue, Orange, CA 92868. *Toll-free phone:* 877-568-6130. *Website:* http://www.southcoastcollege.edu/.

# Southwestern College
## Chula Vista, California

- **District-supported** 2-year, founded 1961, part of California Community College system
- **Suburban** 158-acre campus with easy access to City of San Diego
- **Endowment** $1.2 million
- **Coed,** 18,413 undergraduate students, 40% full-time, 53% women, 47% men

**Undergraduates** 7,405 full-time, 11,008 part-time. 5% transferred in. *Retention:* 74% of full-time freshmen returned.
**Freshmen** *Admission:* 3,552 enrolled.
**Faculty** *Total:* 919, 23% full-time. *Student/faculty ratio:* 22:1.
**Majors** Accounting; accounting technology and bookkeeping; administrative assistant and secretarial science; animation, interactive technology, video graphics and special effects; anthropology; architectural technology; art; astronomy; automobile/automotive mechanics technology; banking and financial support services; biological and physical sciences; biology/biological sciences; biology/biotechnology laboratory technician; biomedical technology; building/construction site management; building/home/construction inspection; business administration and management; business/commerce; chemical technology; chemistry; child-care provision; child development; communications systems installation and repair technology; computer and information sciences; computer installation and repair technology; computer programming; computer science; computer systems networking and telecommunications; cooking and related culinary arts; crafts, folk art and artisanry; criminal justice/police science; dance; data entry/microcomputer applications related; dental hygiene; drafting and design technology; e-commerce; economics; electrical/electronics equipment installation and repair; emergency medical technology (EMT paramedic); engineering; English; ethnic, cultural minority, gender, and group studies related; fire prevention and safety technology; fire science/firefighting; floriculture/floristry management; forensic science and technology; French; general studies; geography; geology/earth science; graphic design; hazardous materials management and waste technology; health and physical education/fitness; health/medical preparatory programs related; history; hospitality administration; hotel/motel

administration; human services; industrial safety technology; information technology; insurance; international business/trade/commerce; Italian; journalism; landscaping and groundskeeping; language interpretation and translation; legal administrative assistant/secretary; legal assistant/paralegal; liberal arts and sciences/liberal studies; licensed practical/vocational nurse training; logistics, materials, and supply chain management; mathematics; medical/clinical assistant; medical insurance coding; music; music management; network and system administration; ornamental horticulture; parks, recreation and leisure; philosophy; photographic and film/video technology; photography; physical fitness technician; physical sciences; physics; plant nursery management; political science and government; psychology; public administration; public administration and social service professions related; radio and television; real estate; registered nursing/registered nurse; restaurant, culinary, and catering management; rhetoric and composition; sales, distribution, and marketing operations; small engine mechanics and repair technology; sociology; Spanish; surgical technology; tourism and travel services marketing; transportation and materials moving related; turf and turfgrass management; web/multimedia management and webmaster; web page, digital/multimedia and information resources design; women's studies.

**Academics** *Calendar:* semesters. *Degree:* certificates and associate. *Special study options:* academic remediation for entering students, adult/continuing education programs, advanced placement credit, cooperative education, distance learning, English as a second language, external degree program, honors programs, independent study, internships, part-time degree program, services for LD students, study abroad, summer session for credit.

**Library** Southwestern College Library/Learning Resource Center plus 3 others. *Books:* 104,784 (physical), 26,161 (digital/electronic); *Serial titles:* 191 (physical), 18 (digital/electronic); *Databases:* 58. Weekly public service hours: 126; students can reserve study rooms.

**Student Life** *Housing:* college housing not available. *Activities and Organizations:* drama/theater group, student-run newspaper, choral group. *Campus security:* 24-hour emergency response devices and patrols, late-night transport/escort service. *Student services:* health clinic, personal/psychological counseling, veterans affairs office.

**Athletics** *Intercollegiate sports:* baseball M, basketball M/W, cross-country running M/W, football M, soccer M/W, softball W, swimming and diving M/W, tennis W, track and field M/W, volleyball W, water polo M/W.

**Costs (2018–19)** *Tuition:* state resident $1288 full-time; nonresident $6552 full-time. Full-time tuition and fees vary according to course load. Part-time tuition and fees vary according to course load. *Required fees:* $100 full-time, $46 per unit part-time, $100 per year part-time.

**Applying** *Options:* electronic application, early admission. *Required for some:* high school transcript. *Application deadlines:* rolling (freshmen), rolling (out-of-state freshmen), rolling (transfers). *Notification:* continuous (freshmen), continuous (out-of-state freshmen), continuous (transfers).
**Freshman Application Contact** Admissions, Southwestern College, 900 Otay Lakes Road, Chula Vista, CA 91910-7299. *Phone:* 619-421-6700 Ext. 5215. *Fax:* 619-482-6489.
*Website:* http://www.swccd.edu/.

## Spartan College of Aeronautics and Technology
### Inglewood, California

**Freshman Application Contact** Admissions Office, Spartan College of Aeronautics and Technology, 8911 Aviation Boulevard, Inglewood, CA 90301. *Phone:* 866-451-0818. *Toll-free phone:* 800-879-0554. *Website:* http://www.spartan.edu/.

## Taft College
### Taft, California

**Freshman Application Contact** Nichole Cook, Admissions/Counseling Technician, Taft College, 29 Cougar Court, Taft, CA 93268. *Phone:* 661-763-7790. *Fax:* 661-763-7758. *E-mail:* ncook@taftcollege.edu. *Website:* http://www.taftcollege.edu/.

## Unitek College
### Fremont, California

**Admissions Office Contact** Unitek College, 4670 Auto Mall Parkway, Fremont, CA 94538. *Website:* http://www.unitekcollege.edu/.

## Valley College of Medical Careers
### West Hills, California

**Admissions Office Contact** Valley College of Medical Careers, 8399 Topanga Canyon Boulevard, Suite 200, West Hills, CA 91304. *Website:* http://www.vcmc.edu/.

## Ventura College
### Ventura, California

**Freshman Application Contact** Ms. Susan Bricker, Registrar, Ventura College, 4667 Telegraph Road, Ventura, CA 93003-3899. *Phone:* 805-654-6456. *Fax:* 805-654-6357. *E-mail:* sbricker@vcccd.net. *Website:* http://www.venturacollege.edu/.

## Victor Valley College
### Victorville, California

**Freshman Application Contact** Ms. Greta Moon, Interim Director of Admissions and Records, Victor Valley College, 18422 Bear Valley Road, Victorville, CA 92395. *Phone:* 760-245-4271. *Fax:* 760-843-7707. *E-mail:* moong@vvc.edu. *Website:* http://www.vvc.edu/.

## West Coast Ultrasound Institute
### Beverly Hills, California

**Admissions Office Contact** West Coast Ultrasound Institute, 291 S. La Cienega Boulevard, Suite 500, Beverly Hills, CA 90211. *Website:* http://wcui.edu/.

## West Hills College Coalinga
### Coalinga, California

**Freshman Application Contact** Sandra Dagnino, West Hills College Coalinga, 300 Cherry Lane, Coalinga, CA 93210-1399. *Phone:* 559-934-3203. *Toll-free phone:* 800-266-1114. *Fax:* 559-934-2830. *E-mail:* sandradagnino@westhillscollege.com. *Website:* http://www.westhillscollege.com/.

## West Hills College Lemoore
### Lemoore, California

**Admissions Office Contact** West Hills College Lemoore, 555 College Avenue, Lemoore, CA 93245. *Website:* http://www.westhillscollege.com/.

## West Los Angeles College
### Culver City, California

**Director of Admissions** Mr. Len Isaksen, Director of Admissions, West Los Angeles College, 9000 Overland Avenue, Culver City, CA 90230-3519. *Phone:* 310-287-4255. *Website:* http://www.lacolleges.net/.

## West Valley College
### Saratoga, California

**Freshman Application Contact** Ms. Barbara Ogilvie, Supervisor, Admissions and Records, West Valley College, 14000 Fruitvale Avenue, Saratoga, CA 95070-5698. *Phone:* 408-741-4630. *E-mail:* barbara_ogilvie@westvalley.edu. *Website:* http://www.westvalley.edu/.

## Woodland Community College
### Woodland, California

**Admissions Office Contact** Woodland Community College, 2300 East Gibson Road, Woodland, CA 95776. *Website:* http://wcc.yccd.edu/.

## Yuba College
### Marysville, California

**Director of Admissions** Dr. David Farrell, Dean of Student Development, Yuba College, 2088 North Beale Road, Marysville, CA 95901-7699. *Phone:* 530-741-6705. *Website:* http://yc.yccd.edu/.

# COLORADO

## Aims Community College
### Greeley, Colorado

**Freshman Application Contact** Ms. Susie Gallardo, Admissions Technician, Aims Community College, Box 69, 5401 West 20th Street, Greeley, CO 80632-0069. *Phone:* 970-330-8008 Ext. 6624. *E-mail:* wgreen@chiron.aims.edu. *Website:* http://www.aims.edu/.

## Arapahoe Community College
### Littleton, Colorado

- **State-supported** 2-year, founded 1965, part of Colorado Community College and Occupational Education System
- **Suburban** 52-acre campus with easy access to Denver
- **Coed**

**Undergraduates** 1,733 full-time, 7,650 part-time. 2% are from out of state; 3% Black or African American, non-Hispanic/Latino; 15% Hispanic/Latino; 4% Asian, non-Hispanic/Latino; 0.3% Native Hawaiian or other Pacific Islander, non-Hispanic/Latino; 0.7% American Indian or Alaska Native, non-Hispanic/Latino; 4% Two or more races, non-Hispanic/Latino; 6% Race/ethnicity unknown; 1% international. *Retention:* 47% of full-time freshmen returned.
**Faculty** *Student/faculty ratio:* 19:1.
**Academics** *Calendar:* semesters. *Degree:* certificates, diplomas, and associate. *Special study options:* academic remediation for entering students, accelerated degree program, adult/continuing education programs, advanced placement credit, cooperative education, distance learning, double majors, English as a second language, external degree program, independent study, internships, off-campus study, part-time degree program, services for LD students, study abroad, summer session for credit. *ROTC:* Army (c), Air Force (c).
**Library** Weber Center for Learning Resources plus 1 other.
**Student Life** *Campus security:* 24-hour emergency response devices and patrols, late-night transport/escort service.
**Costs (2017–18)** *Tuition:* state resident $4337 full-time, $145 per credit hour part-time; nonresident $17,793 full-time, $593 per credit hour part-time. Full-time tuition and fees vary according to program. Part-time tuition and fees vary according to program. *Required fees:* $207 full-time.
**Applying** *Options:* electronic application, early admission, deferred entrance.
**Freshman Application Contact** Arapahoe Community College, 5900 South Santa Fe Drive, PO Box 9002, Littleton, CO 80160-9002. *Phone:* 303-797-5623. *Website:* http://www.arapahoe.edu/.

## Bel–Rea Institute of Animal Technology
### Denver, Colorado

- **Proprietary** 2-year, founded 1971
- **Suburban** 6-acre campus with easy access to Denver
- **Coed**

**Undergraduates** Students come from 20 states and territories; 40% are from out of state.
**Academics** *Calendar:* quarters. *Degree:* associate. *Special study options:* academic remediation for entering students, internships, off-campus study, part-time degree program, services for LD students, summer session for credit.
**Library** Bel-Rea Institute Library. Weekly public service hours: 38.
**Applying** *Options:* electronic application, early admission, deferred entrance. *Required:* essay or personal statement, high school transcript, minimum 2.5 GPA, interview.
**Freshman Application Contact** Bel–Rea Institute of Animal Technology, 1681 South Dayton Street, Denver, CO 80247. *Phone:* 303-751-8700. *Toll-free phone:* 800-950-8001. *Website:* http://www.belrea.edu/.

## CollegeAmerica–Colorado Springs
### Colorado Springs, Colorado

**Freshman Application Contact** CollegeAmerica–Colorado Springs, 2020 North Academy Boulevard, Colorado Springs, CO 80909. *Phone:* 719-637-0600. *Toll-free phone:* 800-622-2894. *Website:* http://www.collegeamerica.edu/.

## CollegeAmerica–Denver
### Denver, Colorado

- **Independent** 2-year, founded 1962
- **Urban** campus
- **Coed,** 110 undergraduate students

**Faculty** *Student/faculty ratio:* 10:1.
**Majors** Accounting and business/management; medical/health management and clinical assistant.
**Academics** *Calendar:* continuous. *Degree:* associate. *Special study options:* academic remediation for entering students, accelerated degree program, cooperative education, distance learning.
**Student Life** *Housing:* college housing not available.
**Freshman Application Contact** Admissions Office, CollegeAmerica–Denver, 1385 South Colorado Boulevard, Denver, CO 80222. *Phone:* 303-300-8740 Ext. 7020. *Toll-free phone:* 800-622-2894. *Website:* http://www.collegeamerica.edu/.

## CollegeAmerica–Fort Collins
### Fort Collins, Colorado

- **Independent** primarily 2-year, founded 1962
- **Suburban** campus
- **Coed**

**Academics** *Calendar:* continuous. *Degrees:* associate and bachelor's. *Special study options:* cooperative education, distance learning, honors programs, independent study, internships.
**Applying** *Required:* essay or personal statement, high school transcript, interview. *Recommended:* minimum 2.0 GPA.
**Freshman Application Contact** CollegeAmerica–Fort Collins, 4601 South Mason Street, Fort Collins, CO 80525. *Phone:* 970-223-6060 Ext. 8002. *Toll-free phone:* 800-622-2894. *Website:* http://www.collegeamerica.edu/.

## Colorado Academy of Veterinary Technology
### Colorado Springs, Colorado

**Admissions Office Contact** Colorado Academy of Veterinary Technology, 2766 Janitell Road, Colorado Springs, CO 80906. *Website:* http://www.cavt.edu/.

## Colorado Northwestern Community College
### Rangely, Colorado

- **State-supported** 2-year, founded 1962, part of Colorado Community College and Occupational Education System
- **Rural** 150-acre campus
- **Coed,** 1,201 undergraduate students, 40% full-time, 57% women, 43% men

**Undergraduates** 480 full-time, 721 part-time. 23% are from out of state; 2% Black or African American, non-Hispanic/Latino; 13% Hispanic/Latino; 0.7% Asian, non-Hispanic/Latino; 0.2% Native Hawaiian or other Pacific Islander, non-Hispanic/Latino; 0.7% American Indian or Alaska Native, non-Hispanic/Latino; 2% Two or more races, non-Hispanic/Latino; 10% Race/ethnicity unknown; 2% international; 9% transferred in; 45% live on campus. *Retention:* 47% of full-time freshmen returned.
**Freshmen** *Admission:* 597 applied, 597 admitted, 171 enrolled.
**Faculty** *Total:* 93, 41% full-time, 6% with terminal degrees. *Student/faculty ratio:* 13:1.
**Majors** Accounting; aircraft powerplant technology; airline pilot and flight crew; automobile/automotive mechanics technology; business/commerce; cosmetology; dental hygiene; early childhood education; emergency medical technology (EMT paramedic); equestrian studies; general studies; liberal arts and sciences/liberal studies; registered nursing/registered nurse; small business administration.
**Academics** *Calendar:* semesters. *Degree:* certificates and associate. *Special study options:* academic remediation for entering students, adult/continuing education programs, advanced placement credit, distance learning, double majors, independent study, internships, part-time degree program, services for LD students, student-designed majors, summer session for credit.
**Library** Colorado Northwestern Community College Library–Rangely plus 1 other. *Books:* 22,558 (physical), 8,100 (digital/electronic); *Serial titles:* 10,875 (physical); *Databases:* 42. Students can reserve study rooms.
**Student Life** *Housing:* on-campus residence required for freshman year. *Options:* coed. Campus housing is university owned. Freshman campus housing is guaranteed. *Campus security:* student patrols, late-night

transport/escort service, controlled dormitory access. *Student services:* health clinic, personal/psychological counseling.

**Athletics** Member NJCAA. *Intercollegiate sports:* baseball M(s), basketball M(s)/W(s), softball W(s), volleyball W(s). *Intramural sports:* basketball M/W, racquetball M/W, rock climbing M/W, skiing (cross-country) M/W, skiing (downhill) M/W, softball M/W, table tennis M/W, volleyball M/W.

**Costs (2017–18)** *Tuition:* state resident $4337 full-time, $145 per credit hour part-time; nonresident $7229 full-time, $241 per credit hour part-time. Full-time tuition and fees vary according to course load, location, and program. Part-time tuition and fees vary according to course load, location, and program. *Required fees:* $474 full-time, $14 per credit hour part-time, $13 per term part-time. *Room and board:* $7106; room only: $2591. Room and board charges vary according to board plan, housing facility, and location. *Payment plan:* installment. *Waivers:* employees or children of employees.

**Financial Aid** Of all full-time matriculated undergraduates who enrolled in 2016, 424 applied for aid, 329 were judged to have need, 14 had their need fully met. In 2016, 39 non-need-based awards were made. *Average percent of need met:* 43%. *Average financial aid package:* $7372. *Average need-based loan:* $3568. *Average need-based gift aid:* $5277. *Average non-need-based aid:* $1540.

**Applying** *Options:* electronic application, early admission, deferred entrance. *Required:* high school transcript. *Required for some:* 3 letters of recommendation. *Application deadlines:* rolling (freshmen), rolling (transfers). *Notification:* continuous (freshmen), continuous (transfers).

**Freshman Application Contact** Colorado Northwestern Community College, 500 Kennedy Drive, Rangely, CO 81648-3598. *Phone:* 970-824-1129. *Toll-free phone:* 800-562-1105.

*Website:* http://www.cncc.edu/.

## Colorado School of Trades
### Lakewood, Colorado

**Freshman Application Contact** Colorado School of Trades, 1575 Hoyt Street, Lakewood, CO 80215-2996. *Phone:* 303-233-4697 Ext. 44. *Toll-free phone:* 800-234-4594. *Website:* http://www.schooloftrades.edu/.

## Community College of Aurora
### Aurora, Colorado

- **State-supported** 2-year, founded 1983, part of Colorado Community College System
- **Suburban** campus with easy access to Denver
- **Coed**

**Undergraduates** 1,465 full-time, 5,914 part-time. 21% Black or African American, non-Hispanic/Latino; 28% Hispanic/Latino; 8% Asian, non-Hispanic/Latino; 2% American Indian or Alaska Native, non-Hispanic/Latino; 6% Race/ethnicity unknown; 3% international.

**Faculty** *Student/faculty ratio:* 20:1.

**Academics** *Calendar:* semesters. *Degree:* certificates and associate. *Special study options:* academic remediation for entering students, adult/continuing education programs, cooperative education, distance learning, English as a second language, external degree program, independent study, internships, off-campus study, part-time degree program, services for LD students, summer session for credit.

**Library** Community College of Aurora Learning Resource Center. *Books:* 2,885 (physical), 151,126 (digital/electronic); *Serial titles:* 11,719 (digital/electronic); *Databases:* 29. Weekly public service hours: 63.

**Student Life** *Campus security:* late-night transport/escort service.

**Applying** *Required for some:* high school transcript.

**Freshman Application Contact** Community College of Aurora, 16000 East CentreTech Parkway, Aurora, CO 80011-9036. *Phone:* 303-360-4701. *Website:* http://www.ccaurora.edu/.

## Community College of Denver
### Denver, Colorado

**Freshman Application Contact** Mr. Michael Rusk, Dean of Students, Community College of Denver, PO Box 173363, Campus Box 201, Denver, CO 80127-3363. *Phone:* 303-556-6325. *Fax:* 303-556-2431. *E-mail:* enrollment_services@ccd.edu. *Website:* http://www.ccd.edu/.

## Concorde Career College
### Aurora, Colorado

**Admissions Office Contact** Concorde Career College, 111 North Havana Street, Aurora, CO 80010. *Website:* http://www.concorde.edu/.

## Ecotech Institute
### Aurora, Colorado

**Admissions Office Contact** Ecotech Institute, 1400 South Abilene Street, Aurora, CO 80012. *Website:* http://www.ecotechinstitute.com/.

## Front Range Community College
### Westminster, Colorado

- **State-supported** 2-year, founded 1968, part of Community Colleges of Colorado System
- **Suburban** 90-acre campus with easy access to Denver
- **Endowment** $407,436
- **Coed,** 18,966 undergraduate students, 29% full-time, 56% women, 44% men

**Undergraduates** 5,406 full-time, 13,560 part-time. Students come from 44 states and territories; 85 other countries; 2% are from out of state; 2% Black or African American, non-Hispanic/Latino; 17% Hispanic/Latino; 4% Asian, non-Hispanic/Latino; 0.2% Native Hawaiian or other Pacific Islander, non-Hispanic/Latino; 0.6% American Indian or Alaska Native, non-Hispanic/Latino; 4% Two or more races, non-Hispanic/Latino; 5% Race/ethnicity unknown; 2% international; 11% transferred in. *Retention:* 61% of full-time freshmen returned.

**Freshmen** *Admission:* 6,319 applied, 6,319 admitted, 2,474 enrolled.

**Faculty** *Total:* 1,125, 21% full-time. *Student/faculty ratio:* 19:1.

**Majors** Accounting technology and bookkeeping; animation, interactive technology, video graphics and special effects; applied horticulture/horticulture operations; architectural engineering technology; automobile/automotive mechanics technology; business administration and management; CAD/CADD drafting/design technology; computer and information sciences; computer systems networking and telecommunications; early childhood education; energy management and systems technology; general studies; geographic information science and cartography; health information/medical records technology; heating, ventilation, air conditioning and refrigeration engineering technology; holistic health; hospitality administration; interior design; legal assistant/paralegal; liberal arts and sciences and humanities related; liberal arts and sciences/liberal studies; medical office assistant; recording arts technology; registered nursing/registered nurse; science technologies related; sign language interpretation and translation; surgical technology; veterinary/animal health technology; welding technology; wildlife, fish and wildlands science and management.

**Academics** *Calendar:* semesters. *Degree:* certificates and associate. *Special study options:* academic remediation for entering students, advanced placement credit, cooperative education, distance learning, double majors, English as a second language, freshman honors college, honors programs, independent study, internships, off-campus study, part-time degree program, services for LD students, student-designed majors, study abroad, summer session for credit. *ROTC:* Army (c), Air Force (c).

**Library** College Hill Library plus 2 others. *Books:* 36,412 (physical), 447 (digital/electronic); *Databases:* 11. Weekly public service hours: 54; students can reserve study rooms.

**Student Life** *Housing:* college housing not available. *Activities and Organizations:* drama/theater group, student-run newspaper, Student Government Association, Student Colorado Registry of Interpreters for the Deaf, Students in Free Enterprise (SIFE), Gay-Straight Alliance, Recycling Club. *Campus security:* 24-hour emergency response devices and patrols, late-night transport/escort service. *Student services:* personal/psychological counseling, veterans affairs office.

**Costs (2017–18)** *Tuition:* state resident $3469 full-time, $145 per credit hour part-time; nonresident $14,234 full-time, $593 per credit hour part-time. Full-time tuition and fees vary according to program. Part-time tuition and fees vary according to program. *Required fees:* $325 full-time, $18 per credit part-time, $13 per term part-time. *Payment plan:* installment. *Waivers:* employees or children of employees.

**Applying** *Options:* electronic application, early admission, deferred entrance.

**Freshman Application Contact** Ms. Miori Gidley, Registrar, Front Range Community College, Westminster, CO 80031. *Phone:* 303-404-5000. *Fax:* 303-439-2614. *E-mail:* miori.gidley@frontrange.edu.

*Website:* http://www.frontrange.edu/.

## IBMC College
### Colorado Springs, Colorado

**Director of Admissions** Michelle Squibb, Admissions Representative, IBMC College, 6805 Corporate Drive, Suite 100, Colorado Springs, CO 80919. *Phone:* 719-596-7400. *Toll-free phone:* 800-748-2282. *Website:* http://www.ibmc.edu/.

# IBMC College

## Fort Collins, Colorado

- **Proprietary** 2-year, founded 1987
- **Suburban** campus with easy access to Denver
- **Coed**
- 92% of applicants were admitted

**Undergraduates** 1,020 full-time. 3% are from out of state; 1% Black or African American, non-Hispanic/Latino; 20% Hispanic/Latino; 0.5% Asian, non-Hispanic/Latino; 0.2% Native Hawaiian or other Pacific Islander, non-Hispanic/Latino; 0.6% American Indian or Alaska Native, non-Hispanic/Latino; 1% Two or more races, non-Hispanic/Latino. *Retention:* 69% of full-time freshmen returned.
**Faculty** *Student/faculty ratio:* 8:1.
**Academics** *Calendar:* continuous. *Degree:* certificates, diplomas, and associate. *Special study options:* accelerated degree program, adult/continuing education programs, cooperative education, honors programs, internships, summer session for credit.
**Library** IBMC College plus 8 others. *Books:* 834 (physical), 124,000 (digital/electronic).
**Costs (2017–18)** *One-time required fee:* $50. *Tuition:* $12,600 full-time. Full-time tuition and fees vary according to course load and program. Part-time tuition and fees vary according to course load and program. No tuition increase for student's term of enrollment. *Payment plans:* tuition prepayment, installment.
**Applying** *Options:* electronic application. *Application fee:* $50. *Required:* high school transcript, interview.
**Freshman Application Contact** Mr. Jeremy Shoup, Admissions and Marketing Coordinator, IBMC College, 3842 South Mason Street, Fort Collins, CO 80525. *Phone:* 970-223-2669. *Toll-free phone:* 800-495-2669. *E-mail:* jshoup@ibmc.edu. *Website:* http://www.ibmc.edu/.

# IntelliTec College

## Colorado Springs, Colorado

**Director of Admissions** Director of Admissions, IntelliTec College, 2315 East Pikes Peak Avenue, Colorado Springs, CO 80909. *Phone:* 719-632-7626. *Toll-free phone:* 800-748-2282. *Website:* http://www.intelliteccollege.edu/.

# IntelliTec College

## Grand Junction, Colorado

**Freshman Application Contact** Admissions, IntelliTec College, 772 Horizon Drive, Grand Junction, CO 81506. *Phone:* 970-245-8101. *Toll-free phone:* 800-748-2282. *Fax:* 970-243-8074. *Website:* http://www.intelliteccollege.edu/.

# IntelliTec College

## Pueblo, Colorado

**Admissions Office Contact** IntelliTec College, 3673 Parker Boulevard, Pueblo, CO 81008. *Toll-free phone:* 800-748-2282. *Website:* http://www.intelliteccollege.edu/.

# Lamar Community College

## Lamar, Colorado

- **State-supported** 2-year, founded 1937, part of Colorado Community College and Occupational Education System
- **Small-town** 125-acre campus
- **Coed,** 791 undergraduate students, 51% full-time, 53% women, 47% men

**Undergraduates** 404 full-time, 387 part-time. Students come from 29 states and territories; 9 other countries; 10% are from out of state; 5% Black or African American, non-Hispanic/Latino; 23% Hispanic/Latino; 0.1% Asian, non-Hispanic/Latino; 0.1% Native Hawaiian or other Pacific Islander, non-Hispanic/Latino; 0.9% American Indian or Alaska Native, non-Hispanic/Latino; 3% Two or more races, non-Hispanic/Latino; 2% Race/ethnicity unknown; 6% international; 5% transferred in; 20% live on campus. *Retention:* 49% of full-time freshmen returned.
**Freshmen** *Admission:* 455 applied, 455 admitted, 215 enrolled. *Average high school GPA:* 3.0.
**Faculty** *Total:* 46, 35% full-time. *Student/faculty ratio:* 21:1.
**Majors** Agricultural business and management; animal training; business automation/technology/data entry; construction trades; cosmetology; energy management and systems technology; liberal arts and sciences/liberal studies;

marketing/marketing management; registered nursing/registered nurse; science technologies related; system, networking, and LAN/WAN management.
**Academics** *Calendar:* semesters. *Degree:* certificates, diplomas, and associate. *Special study options:* academic remediation for entering students, adult/continuing education programs, advanced placement credit, cooperative education, distance learning, double majors, English as a second language, independent study, internships, part-time degree program, services for LD students, student-designed majors, summer session for credit.
**Library** Learning Resources Center. *Books:* 10,825 (physical); *Serial titles:* 23 (physical). Weekly public service hours: 53.
**Student Life** *Housing:* on-campus residence required for freshman year. *Options:* coed. Campus housing is university owned. *Campus security:* 24-hour emergency response devices and patrols, student patrols, late-night transport/escort service, controlled dormitory access. *Student services:* health clinic, personal/psychological counseling.
**Athletics** Member NJCAA. *Intercollegiate sports:* baseball M(s), basketball M(s)/W(s), equestrian sports M(s)/W(s), golf M(s), soccer M(c), softball W(s), volleyball W(s).
**Costs (2017–18)** *Tuition:* state resident $3470 full-time, $145 per credit hour part-time; nonresident $5783 full-time, $245 per credit hour part-time. Full-time tuition and fees vary according to course load, program, and reciprocity agreements. Part-time tuition and fees vary according to course load, program, and reciprocity agreements. *Required fees:* $438 full-time, $438 per year part-time. *Room and board:* $6340; room only: $2070. Room and board charges vary according to housing facility. *Payment plan:* installment. *Waivers:* employees or children of employees.
**Applying** *Options:* electronic application, early admission. *Application deadlines:* 9/16 (freshmen), 9/16 (transfers).
**Freshman Application Contact** Director of Admissions, Lamar Community College, 2401 South Main Street, Lamar, CO 81052-3999. *Phone:* 719-336-1592. *Toll-free phone:* 800-968-6920. *E-mail:* admissions@lamarcc.edu. *Website:* http://www.lamarcc.edu/.

# Lincoln College of Technology

## Denver, Colorado

**Freshman Application Contact** Lincoln College of Technology, 11194 East 45th Avenue, Denver, CO 80239. *Phone:* 800-347-3232 Ext. 43032. *Toll-free phone:* 844-215-1513. *Website:* http://www.lincolntech.edu/.

# Morgan Community College

## Fort Morgan, Colorado

- **State-supported** 2-year, founded 1967, part of Colorado Community College and Occupational Education System
- **Small-town** 20-acre campus with easy access to Denver
- **Endowment** $2.7 million
- **Coed**

**Undergraduates** 327 full-time, 1,147 part-time. Students come from 8 states and territories; 1% are from out of state; 3% Black or African American, non-Hispanic/Latino; 23% Hispanic/Latino; 0.5% Asian, non-Hispanic/Latino; 0.1% Native Hawaiian or other Pacific Islander, non-Hispanic/Latino; 0.7% American Indian or Alaska Native, non-Hispanic/Latino; 1% Two or more races, non-Hispanic/Latino; 6% Race/ethnicity unknown; 2% international; 2% transferred in. *Retention:* 62% of full-time freshmen returned.
**Faculty** *Student/faculty ratio:* 14:1.
**Academics** *Calendar:* semesters. *Degree:* certificates and associate. *Special study options:* academic remediation for entering students, adult/continuing education programs, advanced placement credit, distance learning, double majors, honors programs, independent study, internships, part-time degree program, services for LD students, summer session for credit.
**Library** Learning Resource Center. *Books:* 6,205 (physical), 205,240 (digital/electronic); *Serial titles:* 15 (physical), 18,964 (digital/electronic); *Databases:* 23.
**Student Life** *Campus security:* security cameras, local police patrols, free public phones.
**Costs (2017–18)** *Tuition:* state resident $3469 full-time, $145 per credit hour part-time; nonresident $14,234 full-time, $593 per credit hour part-time. Full-time tuition and fees vary according to course load, program, and reciprocity agreements. Part-time tuition and fees vary according to course load, program, and reciprocity agreements. *Required fees:* $353 full-time, $14 per credit hour part-time, $13 per term part-time.
**Applying** *Options:* electronic application, early admission, deferred entrance. *Recommended:* high school transcript.
**Freshman Application Contact** Ms. Kim Maxwell, Morgan Community College, 920 Barlow Road, Fort Morgan, CO 80701-4399. *Phone:* 970-542-3111. *Toll-free phone:* 800-622-0216. *Fax:* 970-867-6608. *E-mail:* kim.maxwell@morgancc.edu. *Website:* http://www.morgancc.edu/.

# Northeastern Junior College
## Sterling, Colorado

- **State-supported** 2-year, founded 1941, part of Colorado Community College and Occupational Education System
- **Small-town** 65-acre campus
- **Coed**, 1,547 undergraduate students, 58% full-time, 55% women, 45% men

**Undergraduates** 896 full-time, 651 part-time. Students come from 29 states and territories; 11 other countries; 7% are from out of state; 4% Black or African American, non-Hispanic/Latino; 14% Hispanic/Latino; 1% Asian, non-Hispanic/Latino; 0.1% Native Hawaiian or other Pacific Islander, non-Hispanic/Latino; 1% American Indian or Alaska Native, non-Hispanic/Latino; 3% Two or more races, non-Hispanic/Latino; 4% Race/ethnicity unknown; 5% international; 5% transferred in; 40% live on campus.

**Freshmen** *Admission:* 894 applied, 894 admitted, 446 enrolled. *Average high school GPA:* 3.0.

**Faculty** *Total:* 95, 52% full-time, 6% with terminal degrees. *Student/faculty ratio:* 16:1.

**Majors** Accounting; agricultural business and management; agricultural teacher education; agriculture; agronomy and crop science; animal sciences; anthropology; art; art history, criticism and conservation; automobile/automotive mechanics technology; biology/biological sciences; business administration and management; chemistry; child development; communication; cosmetology; criminal justice/police science; dramatic/theater arts; economics; elementary education; emergency medical technology (EMT paramedic); English; equestrian studies; farm and ranch management; fine/studio arts; geography; geology/earth science; history; journalism; liberal arts and sciences/liberal studies; licensed practical/vocational nurse training; marketing/marketing management; mathematics; music; natural sciences; philosophy; physical education teaching and coaching; physical sciences; political science and government; pre-engineering; psychology; registered nursing/registered nurse; social sciences; sociology.

**Academics** *Calendar:* semesters. *Degree:* certificates and associate. *Special study options:* academic remediation for entering students, accelerated degree program, adult/continuing education programs, advanced placement credit, cooperative education, distance learning, double majors, English as a second language, honors programs, internships, part-time degree program, services for LD students, summer session for credit.

**Library** Monahan Library. *Books:* 24,184 (physical), 105,876 (digital/electronic); *Serial titles:* 104 (physical), 86 (digital/electronic); *Databases:* 8. Weekly public service hours: 71.

**Student Life** *Housing:* on-campus residence required for freshman year. *Options:* coed, women-only. Campus housing is university owned. Freshman applicants given priority for college housing. *Activities and Organizations:* drama/theater group, choral group, Associated Student Government, Post Secondary Agriculture (PAS), Crossroads, NJC Ambassadors, Business Club. *Campus security:* 24-hour emergency response devices, late-night transport/escort service, controlled dormitory access. *Student services:* health clinic, personal/psychological counseling.

**Athletics** Member NJCAA. *Intercollegiate sports:* baseball M(s), basketball M(s)/W(s), equestrian sports M(s)/W(s), golf M(s)/W(s), soccer M(s)/W(s), softball W(s), volleyball W(s), wrestling M(s). *Intramural sports:* basketball M/W, volleyball M/W.

**Costs (2017–18)** *Tuition:* state resident $4337 full-time, $145 per credit hour part-time; nonresident $6506 full-time, $217 per credit hour part-time. Full-time tuition and fees vary according to course load and reciprocity agreements. Part-time tuition and fees vary according to course load and reciprocity agreements. *Required fees:* $604 full-time, $27 per credit hour part-time, $14 per term part-time. *Room and board:* $6860; room only: $3588. Room and board charges vary according to board plan and housing facility. *Payment plan:* installment. *Waivers:* senior citizens and employees or children of employees.

**Applying** *Options:* electronic application. *Recommended:* high school transcript. *Application deadlines:* rolling (freshmen), rolling (transfers). *Notification:* continuous (freshmen), continuous (transfers).

**Freshman Application Contact** Adam Kunkel, Director of Admission, Northeastern Junior College, Sterling, CO 80751. *Phone:* 970-521-7000. *Toll-free phone:* 800-626-4637. *Fax:* 970-521-6715. *E-mail:* adam.kunkel@njc.edu.

*Website:* http://www.njc.edu/.

# Otero Junior College
## La Junta, Colorado

- **State-supported** 2-year, founded 1941, part of Colorado Community College System
- **Rural** 40-acre campus
- **Endowment** $1.5 million
- **Coed**, 1,449 undergraduate students

**Undergraduates** Students come from 20 states and territories; 15 other countries; 10% are from out of state; 3% Black or African American, non-Hispanic/Latino; 32% Hispanic/Latino; 0.8% Asian, non-Hispanic/Latino; 0.5% Native Hawaiian or other Pacific Islander, non-Hispanic/Latino; 1% American Indian or Alaska Native, non-Hispanic/Latino; 6% Race/ethnicity unknown; 3% international. *Retention:* 53% of full-time freshmen returned.

**Faculty** *Total:* 75. *Student/faculty ratio:* 19:1.

**Majors** Administrative assistant and secretarial science; agricultural business and management; biological and physical sciences; biology/biological sciences; business administration and management; comparative literature; dramatic/theater arts; elementary education; history; humanities; kindergarten/preschool education; liberal arts and sciences/liberal studies; mathematics; modern languages; political science and government; pre-engineering; psychology; registered nursing/registered nurse; social sciences.

**Academics** *Calendar:* semesters. *Degree:* certificates and associate. *Special study options:* academic remediation for entering students, adult/continuing education programs, advanced placement credit, distance learning, external degree program, honors programs, internships, part-time degree program, summer session for credit.

**Library** Wheeler Library.

**Student Life** *Housing:* on-campus residence required for freshman year. *Options:* men-only, women-only. Campus housing is university owned. *Activities and Organizations:* drama/theater group, choral group. *Campus security:* 24-hour patrols, late-night transport/escort service, controlled dormitory access. *Student services:* veterans affairs office.

**Athletics** Member NJCAA. *Intercollegiate sports:* baseball M(s), basketball M(s)/W(s), golf M(s)/W(s), soccer M(s)/W(s), softball W(s), volleyball W(s), wrestling M(s). *Intramural sports:* basketball M/W, volleyball M/W.

**Costs (2017–18)** *Tuition:* state resident $3468 full-time, $145 per credit hour part-time; nonresident $5782 full-time, $241 per credit hour part-time. Full-time tuition and fees vary according to course load. Part-time tuition and fees vary according to course load. *Required fees:* $387 full-time, $13 per credit hour part-time. *Room and board:* $6578. Room and board charges vary according to board plan and housing facility. *Payment plans:* installment, deferred payment. *Waivers:* senior citizens.

**Financial Aid** Of all full-time matriculated undergraduates who enrolled in 2016, 30 Federal Work-Study jobs (averaging $2000). 100 state and other part-time jobs (averaging $2000).

**Applying** *Options:* electronic application, early admission. *Recommended:* high school transcript. *Application deadlines:* 8/15 (freshmen), 8/15 (transfers). *Notification:* continuous (freshmen), continuous (transfers).

**Freshman Application Contact** Mrs. Lauren Berg, Registrar, Otero Junior College, 1802 Colorado Avenue, La Junta, CO 81050. *Phone:* 719-384-6831. *Fax:* 719-384-6933. *E-mail:* lauren.berg@ojc.edu.

*Website:* http://www.ojc.edu/.

# Pikes Peak Community College
## Colorado Springs, Colorado

**Freshman Application Contact** Pikes Peak Community College, 5675 South Academy Boulevard, Colorado Springs, CO 80906-5498. *Phone:* 719-540-7041. *Toll-free phone:* 866-411-7722. *Website:* http://www.ppcc.edu/.

# Pima Medical Institute
## Aurora, Colorado

**Admissions Office Contact** Pima Medical Institute, 13750 East Mississippi Avenue, Aurora, CO 80012. *Toll-free phone:* 800-477-PIMA. *Website:* http://www.pmi.edu/.

# Pima Medical Institute
## Colorado Springs, Colorado

**Freshman Application Contact** Pima Medical Institute, 5725 Mark Dabling Boulevard, Colorado Springs, CO 80919. *Phone:* 719-482-7462. *Toll-free phone:* 800-477-PIMA. *Website:* http://www.pmi.edu/.

# Pima Medical Institute
## Denver, Colorado

**Freshman Application Contact** Admissions Office, Pima Medical Institute, 7475 Dakin Street, Denver, CO 80221. *Phone:* 303-426-1800. *Toll-free phone:* 800-477-PIMA. *Website:* http://www.pmi.edu/.

# Pueblo Community College
## Pueblo, Colorado

- **State-supported** primarily 2-year, founded 1933, part of Colorado Community College System
- **Urban** 35-acre campus
- **Endowment** $1.1 million
- **Coed,** 5,993 undergraduate students, 34% full-time, 58% women, 42% men

**Undergraduates** 2,041 full-time, 3,952 part-time. Students come from 23 states and territories; 0.8% are from out of state; 3% Black or African American, non-Hispanic/Latino; 32% Hispanic/Latino; 1% Asian, non-Hispanic/Latino; 0.3% Native Hawaiian or other Pacific Islander, non-Hispanic/Latino; 2% American Indian or Alaska Native, non-Hispanic/Latino; 3% Two or more races, non-Hispanic/Latino; 2% Race/ethnicity unknown; 0.8% international; 8% transferred in. *Retention:* 10% of full-time freshmen returned.
**Freshmen** *Admission:* 1,164 applied, 1,164 admitted, 701 enrolled.
**Faculty** *Total:* 427, 26% full-time. *Student/faculty ratio:* 16:1.
**Majors** Accounting technology and bookkeeping; animation, interactive technology, video graphics and special effects; autobody/collision and repair technology; automobile/automotive mechanics technology; business administration and management; business automation/technology/data entry; communications technology; computer and information sciences; cooking and related culinary arts; cosmetology; criminal justice/law enforcement administration; dental assisting; dental hygiene; early childhood education; electrical, electronic and communications engineering technology; electromechanical and instrumentation and maintenance technologies related; emergency medical technology (EMT paramedic); engineering technology; fire science/firefighting; general studies; liberal arts and sciences and humanities related; liberal arts and sciences/liberal studies; library and archives assisting; machine shop technology; manufacturing engineering technology; medical office management; occupational therapist assistant; physical therapy technology; psychiatric/mental health services technology; radiologic technology/science; registered nursing/registered nurse; respiratory care therapy; science technologies related; surgical technology; web page, digital/multimedia and information resources design; welding technology.
**Academics** *Calendar:* semesters. *Degrees:* certificates, associate, and bachelor's. *Special study options:* academic remediation for entering students, accelerated degree program, advanced placement credit, cooperative education, distance learning, double majors, English as a second language, honors programs, independent study, internships, part-time degree program, services for LD students, summer session for credit.
**Library** PCC Library. *Books:* 19,162 (physical), 33,004 (digital/electronic); *Serial titles:* 695 (physical), 7,707 (digital/electronic); *Databases:* 12. Weekly public service hours: 60.
**Student Life** *Housing:* college housing not available. *Activities and Organizations:* drama/theater group, choral group, Phi Theta Kappa, Welding Club, Culinary Arts Club, Performing Arts Club, Art Club. *Campus security:* 24-hour emergency response devices and patrols, late-night transport/escort service. *Student services:* health clinic, personal/psychological counseling, veterans affairs office.
**Costs (2018–19)** *Tuition:* state resident $7365 full-time, $180 per credit hour part-time; nonresident $17,858 full-time, $595 per credit hour part-time. Full-time tuition and fees vary according to course load, degree level, location, program, and reciprocity agreements. Part-time tuition and fees vary according to course load, degree level, location, program, and reciprocity agreements. *Required fees:* $733 full-time, $21 per credit hour part-time, $58 per term part-time. *Payment plans:* installment, deferred payment. *Waivers:* employees or children of employees.
**Applying** *Options:* electronic application, early admission, deferred entrance. *Application deadlines:* rolling (freshmen), rolling (transfers). *Notification:* continuous until 9/1 (freshmen), continuous until 9/1 (transfers).
**Freshman Application Contact** Mrs. Barbara Benedict, Director of Admissions and Records, Pueblo Community College, 900 West Orman Avenue, Pueblo, CO 81004. *Phone:* 719-549-3039. *Toll-free phone:* 888-642-6017. *Fax:* 719-549-3012. *E-mail:* barbara.benedict@pueblocc.edu. *Website:* http://www.pueblocc.edu/.

# Red Rocks Community College
## Lakewood, Colorado

**Freshman Application Contact** Admissions Office, Red Rocks Community College, 13300 West 6th Avenue, Lakewood, CO 80228-1255. *Phone:* 303-914-6360. *Fax:* 303-914-6919. *E-mail:* admissions@rrcc.edu. *Website:* http://www.rrcc.edu/.

# Spartan College of Aeronautics and Technology
## Broomfield, Colorado

**Freshman Application Contact** Spartan College of Aeronautics and Technology, 10851 West 120th Avenue, Broomfield, CO 80021. *Phone:* 303-466-7383. *Toll-free phone:* 800-510-3216. *Website:* http://www.spartan.edu/.

# Trinidad State Junior College
## Trinidad, Colorado

**Freshman Application Contact** Bernadine DeGarbo, Student Services Administrative Assistant, Trinidad State Junior College, 600 Prospect Street, Trinidad, CO 81082. *Phone:* 719-846-5621. *Toll-free phone:* 800-621-8752. *Fax:* 719-846-5620. *E-mail:* bernadine.degarbo@trinidadstate.edu. *Website:* http://www.trinidadstate.edu/.

# CONNECTICUT

# Asnuntuck Community College
## Enfield, Connecticut

- **State-supported** 2-year, founded 1972, part of Connecticut State Colleges & Universities (CSCU)
- **Suburban** 36-acre campus
- **Endowment** $137,046
- **Coed**

**Undergraduates** 652 full-time, 1,293 part-time. 8% are from out of state; 16% Black or African American, non-Hispanic/Latino; 13% Hispanic/Latino; 3% Asian, non-Hispanic/Latino; 0.3% American Indian or Alaska Native, non-Hispanic/Latino; 3% Two or more races, non-Hispanic/Latino; 2% Race/ethnicity unknown; 16% transferred in. *Retention:* 68% of full-time freshmen returned.
**Faculty** *Student/faculty ratio:* 17:1.
**Academics** *Calendar:* semesters. *Degree:* certificates and associate. *Special study options:* academic remediation for entering students, adult/continuing education programs, advanced placement credit, cooperative education, distance learning, double majors, English as a second language, independent study, internships, part-time degree program, services for LD students, student-designed majors, summer session for credit.
**Library** ACC Library plus 1 other.
**Student Life** *Campus security:* 24-hour emergency response devices, late-night transport/escort service.
**Applying** *Options:* deferred entrance. *Application fee:* $20. *Required:* high school transcript, interview.
**Freshman Application Contact** Jennifer Anilowski, Interim Director of Admissions, Asnuntuck Community College, 170 Elm Street, Enfield, CT 06082. *Phone:* 860-253-3090. *Fax:* 860-253-3014. *E-mail:* janilowski@asnuntuck.edu. *Website:* http://www.asnuntuck.edu/.

# Capital Community College
## Hartford, Connecticut

**Freshman Application Contact** Ms. Jackie Phillips, Director of the Welcome and Advising Center, Capital Community College, 950 Main Street, Hartford, CT 06103. *Phone:* 860-906-5078. *Toll-free phone:* 800-894-6126. *E-mail:* jphillips@ccc.commnet.edu. *Website:* http://www.ccc.commnet.edu/.

# Gateway Community College
## New Haven, Connecticut

**Freshman Application Contact** Mr. Joseph Carberry, Director of Enrollment Management, Gateway Community College, 20 Church Street, New Haven, CT 06510. *Phone:* 203-285-2011. *Toll-free phone:* 800-390-7723. *Fax:* 203-285-2018. *E-mail:* jcarberry@gatewayct.edu. *Website:* http://www.gwcc.commnet.edu/.

# Goodwin College
## East Hartford, Connecticut

**Freshman Application Contact** Mr. Nicholas Lentino, Assistant Vice President for Admissions, Goodwin College, One Riverside Drive, East Hartford, CT 06118. *Phone:* 860-727-6765. *Toll-free phone:* 800-889-3282. *Fax:* 860-291-9550. *E-mail:* nlentino@goodwin.edu. *Website:* http://www.goodwin.edu/.

# Housatonic Community College
## Bridgeport, Connecticut

- **State-supported** 2-year, founded 1967, part of Connecticut State Colleges & Universities (CSCU)
- **Urban** 4-acre campus with easy access to New York City
- **Coed,** 5,138 undergraduate students, 34% full-time, 61% women, 39% men

**Undergraduates** 1,729 full-time, 3,409 part-time. 31% Black or African American, non-Hispanic/Latino; 33% Hispanic/Latino; 3% Asian, non-Hispanic/Latino; 0.1% Native Hawaiian or other Pacific Islander, non-Hispanic/Latino; 0.2% American Indian or Alaska Native, non-Hispanic/Latino; 2% Two or more races, non-Hispanic/Latino; 1% Race/ethnicity unknown; 0.7% international; 7% transferred in. *Retention:* 57% of full-time freshmen returned.
**Freshmen** *Admission:* 3,606 applied, 3,606 admitted, 1,070 enrolled.
**Faculty** *Total:* 378, 21% full-time. *Student/faculty ratio:* 16:1.
**Majors** Accounting; administrative assistant and secretarial science; art; avionics maintenance technology; business administration and management; commercial and advertising art; criminal justice/law enforcement administration; humanities; human services; liberal arts and sciences/liberal studies; mathematics; physical therapy.
**Academics** *Calendar:* semesters. *Degree:* certificates and associate. *Special study options:* academic remediation for entering students, adult/continuing education programs, advanced placement credit, cooperative education, distance learning, double majors, English as a second language, honors programs, independent study, internships, off-campus study, part-time degree program, services for LD students, summer session for credit.
**Library** Housatonic Community College Library. *Books:* 55,000 (physical), 45,290 (digital/electronic); *Serial titles:* 104 (physical); *Databases:* 99. Students can reserve study rooms.
**Student Life** *Activities and Organizations:* drama/theater group, student-run newspaper, Student Senate, Association of Latin American Students, Community Action Network, Drama Club, Phi Theta Kappa. *Campus security:* 24-hour emergency response devices, late-night transport/escort service. *Student services:* personal/psychological counseling, women's center, veterans affairs office.
**Financial Aid** Of all full-time matriculated undergraduates who enrolled in 2016, 70 Federal Work-Study jobs (averaging $2850).
**Applying** *Options:* electronic application, deferred entrance. *Application fee:* $20. *Required:* high school transcript. *Application deadlines:* rolling (freshmen), rolling (transfers). *Notification:* continuous (freshmen), continuous (transfers).
**Admissions Office Contact** Housatonic Community College, 900 Lafayette Boulevard, Bridgeport, CT 06604-4704.
*Website:* http://www.housatonic.edu/.

# Manchester Community College
## Manchester, Connecticut

- **State-supported** 2-year, founded 1963, part of Connecticut State Colleges & Universities (CSCU)
- **Small-town** campus
- **Coed,** 6,321 undergraduate students, 31% full-time, 54% women, 46% men

**Undergraduates** 1,969 full-time, 4,352 part-time. 18% Black or African American, non-Hispanic/Latino; 22% Hispanic/Latino; 5% Asian, non-Hispanic/Latino; 0.1% Native Hawaiian or other Pacific Islander, non-Hispanic/Latino; 0.2% American Indian or Alaska Native, non-Hispanic/Latino; 2% Two or more races, non-Hispanic/Latino; 4% Race/ethnicity unknown; 13% transferred in. *Retention:* 62% of full-time freshmen returned.
**Freshmen** *Admission:* 2,536 applied, 2,532 admitted, 1,224 enrolled.
**Faculty** *Total:* 99. *Student/faculty ratio:* 16:1.
**Majors** Accounting; administrative assistant and secretarial science; business administration and management; clinical/medical laboratory technology; commercial and advertising art; criminal justice/law enforcement administration; dramatic/theater arts; engineering science; fine/studio arts; general studies; hotel/motel administration; human services; industrial engineering; industrial technology; information science/studies; journalism;

kindergarten/preschool education; legal administrative assistant/secretary; legal assistant/paralegal; liberal arts and sciences/liberal studies; management information systems; marketing/marketing management; medical administrative assistant and medical secretary; music; occupational therapist assistant; physical therapy technology; respiratory care therapy; social work; speech communication and rhetoric; surgical technology; teacher assistant/aide.
**Academics** *Calendar:* semesters. *Degree:* certificates and associate. *Special study options:* adult/continuing education programs, part-time degree program.
**Student Life** *Housing:* college housing not available.
**Athletics** Member NJCAA. *Intercollegiate sports:* baseball M, basketball M/W, soccer M/W, softball W.
**Costs (2018–19)** *Tuition:* state resident $3912 full-time, $159 per credit hour part-time; nonresident $11,736 full-time, $477 per credit hour part-time. Full-time tuition and fees vary according to program. Part-time tuition and fees vary according to program. *Required fees:* $472 full-time. *Payment plan:* installment. *Waivers:* senior citizens and employees or children of employees.
**Financial Aid** *Financial aid deadline:* 8/13.
**Applying** *Options:* electronic application. *Required:* high school transcript.
**Freshman Application Contact** Director of Admissions, Manchester Community College, PO Box 1046, Manchester, CT 06045-1046. *Phone:* 860-512-3210. *Fax:* 860-512-3221.
*Website:* http://www.manchestercc.edu/.

# Middlesex Community College
## Middletown, Connecticut

**Freshman Application Contact** Mensimah Shabazz, Director of Admissions, Middlesex Community College, Middletown, CT 06457-4889. *Phone:* 860-343-5742. *Fax:* 860-344-3055. *E-mail:* mshabazz@mxcc.commnet.edu. *Website:* http://www.mxcc.commnet.edu/.

# Naugatuck Valley Community College
## Waterbury, Connecticut

- **State-supported** 2-year, founded 1992, part of Connecticut State Colleges & Universities (CSCU)
- **Urban** 110-acre campus
- **Coed,** 6,378 undergraduate students, 34% full-time, 57% women, 43% men

**Undergraduates** 2,173 full-time, 4,205 part-time. Students come from 7 states and territories; 2 other countries; 0.3% are from out of state; 11% Black or African American, non-Hispanic/Latino; 30% Hispanic/Latino; 3% Asian, non-Hispanic/Latino; 0.2% Native Hawaiian or other Pacific Islander, non-Hispanic/Latino; 0.2% American Indian or Alaska Native, non-Hispanic/Latino; 3% Two or more races, non-Hispanic/Latino; 4% Race/ethnicity unknown; 0.3% international; 10% transferred in. *Retention:* 59% of full-time freshmen returned.
**Freshmen** *Admission:* 2,359 applied, 2,179 admitted, 1,336 enrolled.
**Faculty** *Total:* 431, 22% full-time. *Student/faculty ratio:* 17:1.
**Majors** Accounting technology and bookkeeping; aeronautics/aviation/aerospace science and technology; art; automobile/automotive mechanics technology; behavioral sciences; business administration and management; business/commerce; computer engineering technology; criminal justice/police science; digital communication and media/multimedia; early childhood education; electrical, electronic and communications engineering technology; engineering science; engineering technology; environmental engineering technology; finance; fire services administration; general studies; horticultural science; hospitality administration; hotel/motel administration; legal assistant/paralegal; liberal arts and sciences/liberal studies; marketing/marketing management; medical radiologic technology; physical sciences related; physical therapy technology; psychiatric/mental health services technology; registered nursing/registered nurse; respiratory care therapy; restaurant/food services management; substance abuse/addiction counseling.
**Academics** *Calendar:* semesters. *Degree:* certificates and associate. *Special study options:* academic remediation for entering students, accelerated degree program, adult/continuing education programs, advanced placement credit, cooperative education, distance learning, English as a second language, external degree program, honors programs, independent study, internships, off-campus study, part-time degree program, services for LD students, summer session for credit.
**Library** Max R. Traurig Learning Resource Center. *Books:* 38,400 (physical); *Serial titles:* 108 (physical); *Databases:* 12. Weekly public service hours: 65; students can reserve study rooms.
**Student Life** *Housing:* college housing not available. *Activities and Organizations:* drama/theater group, student-run newspaper, choral group, Student Senate, Choral Society, Automotive Technician Club, Human Service Club, Legal Assistant Club. *Campus security:* 24-hour emergency response

devices and patrols, late-night transport/escort service, security escort service. *Student services:* personal/psychological counseling, women's center, veterans affairs office.

**Standardized Tests** *Required:* ACCUPLACER (for admission).

**Costs (2017–18)** *Tuition:* state resident $4316 full-time, $253 per credit hour part-time; nonresident $12,868 full-time, $729 per credit hour part-time. Part-time tuition and fees vary according to course load. *Payment plan:* installment. *Waivers:* senior citizens and employees or children of employees.

**Financial Aid** Of all full-time matriculated undergraduates who enrolled in 2016, 70 Federal Work-Study jobs (averaging $1942). 16 state and other part-time jobs (averaging $1660).

**Applying** *Options:* electronic application, deferred entrance. *Application fee:* $20. *Required:* high school transcript. *Required for some:* interview. *Application deadlines:* rolling (freshmen), rolling (transfers). *Notification:* continuous (freshmen), continuous (transfers).

**Freshman Application Contact** Noel Rosamilio, Associate Dean of Enrollment Management, Naugatuck Valley Community College, Kinney Hall, K500, 750 Chase Parkway, Waterbury, CT 06708. *Phone:* 203-596-8780. *E-mail:* nrosamilio@nv.edu.
*Website:* http://www.nvcc.commnet.edu/.

# Northwestern Connecticut Community College
## Winsted, Connecticut

**Freshman Application Contact** Admissions Office, Northwestern Connecticut Community College, Park Place East, Winsted, CT 06098-1798. *Phone:* 860-738-6330. *Fax:* 860-738-6437. *E-mail:* admissions@nwcc.commnet.edu. *Website:* http://www.nwcc.commnet.edu/.

# Norwalk Community College
## Norwalk, Connecticut

- **State-supported** 2-year, founded 1961, part of Connecticut State Colleges & Universities (CSCU)
- **Suburban** 30-acre campus with easy access to New York City
- **Coed**

**Undergraduates** 2,047 full-time, 3,822 part-time. 1% are from out of state; 17% Black or African American, non-Hispanic/Latino; 37% Hispanic/Latino; 5% Asian, non-Hispanic/Latino; 0.2% Native Hawaiian or other Pacific Islander, non-Hispanic/Latino; 0.2% American Indian or Alaska Native, non-Hispanic/Latino; 1% Two or more races, non-Hispanic/Latino; 5% Race/ethnicity unknown; 2% international; 7% transferred in. *Retention:* 61% of full-time freshmen returned.

**Faculty** *Student/faculty ratio:* 18:1.

**Academics** *Calendar:* semesters. *Degree:* certificates and associate. *Special study options:* academic remediation for entering students, advanced placement credit, cooperative education, distance learning, English as a second language, independent study, internships, part-time degree program, services for LD students, summer session for credit.

**Library** Everett I. L. Baker Library.

**Student Life** *Campus security:* late-night transport/escort service, all buildings secured each evening, foot patrols and vehicle patrols by security from 7 am-11 pm.

**Applying** *Options:* electronic application, deferred entrance. *Required:* high school transcript, 4 math courses, 3 science courses, 2 labs, immunization form.

**Freshman Application Contact** Mr. Curtis Antrum, Admissions Counselor, Norwalk Community College, 188 Richards Avenue, Norwalk, CT 06854-1655. *Phone:* 203-857-7060. *Fax:* 203-857-3335. *E-mail:* admissions@ncc.commnet.edu. *Website:* http://www.ncc.commnet.edu/.

# Quinebaug Valley Community College
## Danielson, Connecticut

**Freshman Application Contact** Dr. Toni Moumouris, Director of Admissions, Quinebaug Valley Community College, 742 Upper Maple Street, Danielson, CT 06239. *Phone:* 860-774-1130 Ext. 318. *Fax:* 860-774-7768. *E-mail:* qu_isd@commnet.edu. *Website:* http://www.qvcc.edu/.

# St. Vincent's College
## Bridgeport, Connecticut

- **Independent** primarily 2-year, founded 1991, affiliated with Roman Catholic Church
- **Urban** campus with easy access to New York City
- **Endowment** $4.1 million
- **Coed**

**Undergraduates** 65 full-time, 698 part-time. Students come from 12 states and territories; 2% are from out of state; 15% Black or African American, non-Hispanic/Latino; 15% Hispanic/Latino; 2% Asian, non-Hispanic/Latino; 0.3% American Indian or Alaska Native, non-Hispanic/Latino; 21% Race/ethnicity unknown; 28% transferred in.

**Faculty** *Student/faculty ratio:* 14:1.

**Academics** *Calendar:* semesters. *Degrees:* certificates, associate, and bachelor's. *Special study options:* academic remediation for entering students, adult/continuing education programs, advanced placement credit, distance learning, internships, part-time degree program, summer session for credit.

**Library** Daniel T. Banks Health Science Library. *Books:* 1,500 (physical), 84,000 (digital/electronic); *Serial titles:* 81 (physical); *Databases:* 5. Weekly public service hours: 40; students can reserve study rooms.

**Student Life** *Campus security:* 24-hour emergency response devices and patrols, late-night transport/escort service.

**Standardized Tests** *Recommended:* SAT or ACT (for admission).

**Costs (2017–18)** *Tuition:* $14,520 full-time, $605 per credit hour part-time. Full-time tuition and fees vary according to course load. Part-time tuition and fees vary according to course load. *Required fees:* $1043 full-time, $1043 per year part-time.

**Financial Aid** Of all full-time matriculated undergraduates who enrolled in 2015, 45 applied for aid, 45 were judged to have need. *Average percent of need met:* 34. *Average financial aid package:* $8755. *Average need-based loan:* $4070. *Average need-based gift aid:* $5754. *Average indebtedness upon graduation:* $35,263.

**Applying** *Required:* high school transcript. *Recommended:* minimum 2.0 GPA.

**Freshman Application Contact** St. Vincent's College, 2800 Main Street, Bridgeport, CT 06606-4292. *Toll-free phone:* 800-873-1013. *Website:* http://www.stvincentscollege.edu/.

# Three Rivers Community College
## Norwich, Connecticut

- **State-supported** 2-year, founded 1963, part of Connecticut State Colleges & Universities (CSCU)
- **Suburban** 40-acre campus with easy access to Hartford
- **Coed**, 4,187 undergraduate students, 32% full-time, 59% women, 41% men

**Undergraduates** 1,340 full-time, 2,847 part-time. Students come from 5 states and territories; 1% are from out of state; 8% Black or African American, non-Hispanic/Latino; 17% Hispanic/Latino; 4% Asian, non-Hispanic/Latino; 0.3% Native Hawaiian or other Pacific Islander, non-Hispanic/Latino; 0.7% American Indian or Alaska Native, non-Hispanic/Latino; 5% Two or more races, non-Hispanic/Latino; 3% Race/ethnicity unknown; 0.2% international; 9% transferred in. *Retention:* 63% of full-time freshmen returned.

**Freshmen** *Admission:* 787 enrolled.

**Faculty** *Total:* 302, 23% full-time. *Student/faculty ratio:* 16:1.

**Majors** Accounting; accounting technology and bookkeeping; architectural drafting and CAD/CADD; architectural engineering technology; banking and financial support services; business/commerce; child-care and support services management; computer engineering technology; construction management; criminal justice/police science; education; electrical, electronic and communications engineering technology; engineering science; engineering technology; environmental engineering technology; fine/studio arts; general studies; graphic design; hospitality administration; kinesiology and exercise science; laser and optical technology; liberal arts and sciences/liberal studies; management information systems; manufacturing engineering technology; marketing/marketing management; mechanical engineering/mechanical technology; nuclear/nuclear power technology; psychiatric/mental health services technology; registered nursing/registered nurse; sport and fitness administration/management.

**Academics** *Calendar:* semesters. *Degrees:* certificates and associate (engineering technology programs are offered on the Thames Valley Campus; liberal arts, transfer and career programs are offered on the Mohegan Campus). *Special study options:* adult/continuing education programs, part-time degree program.

**Library** Three Rivers Community College Learning Resource Center plus 1 other.

**Student Life** *Housing:* college housing not available. *Activities and Organizations:* student-run newspaper. *Campus security:* 24-hour emergency response devices, late-night transport/escort service, 14-hour patrols by trained security personnel.

**Athletics** *Intramural sports:* baseball M(c)/W(c), golf M(c)/W(c).

**Costs (2017–18)** *One-time required fee:* $80. *Tuition:* state resident $3816 full-time, $159 per credit hour part-time; nonresident $11,448 full-time, $477 per credit hour part-time. Full-time tuition and fees vary according to course load and reciprocity agreements. Part-time tuition and fees vary according to course load and reciprocity agreements. *Required fees:* $460 full-time. *Payment plan:* installment. *Waivers:* senior citizens and employees or children of employees.

**Financial Aid** Of all full-time matriculated undergraduates who enrolled in 2010, 1,135 applied for aid, 967 were judged to have need, 266 had their need fully met. *Average percent of need met:* 48%. *Average financial aid package:* $2631. *Average need-based loan:* $3308. *Average need-based gift aid:* $2409.

**Applying** *Options:* electronic application, early admission, deferred entrance. *Recommended:* high school transcript. *Application deadlines:* rolling (freshmen), rolling (transfers). *Notification:* continuous (freshmen), continuous (transfers).

**Freshman Application Contact** Admissions Office, Three Rivers Community College, CT. *Phone:* 860-215-9296. *E-mail:* admissions@trcc.commnet.edu.

*Website:* http://www.threerivers.edu/.

## Tunxis Community College
### Farmington, Connecticut

**Freshman Application Contact** Ms. Tamika Davis, Director of Admissions, Tunxis Community College, 271 Scott Swamp Road, Farmington, CT 06032. *Phone:* 860-773-1494. *Fax:* 860-606-9501. *E-mail:* pmccluskey@tunxis.edu. *Website:* http://www.tunxis.edu/.

# DELAWARE

## Delaware College of Art and Design
### Wilmington, Delaware

**Freshman Application Contact** Ms. Allison Gullo, Delaware College of Art and Design, 600 North Market Street, Wilmington, DE 19801. *Phone:* 302-622-8867 Ext. 111. *Fax:* 302-622-8870. *E-mail:* agullo@dcad.edu. *Website:* http://www.dcad.edu/.

## Delaware Technical & Community College, Jack F. Owens Campus
### Georgetown, Delaware

**Freshman Application Contact** Ms. Claire McDonald, Admissions Counselor, Delaware Technical & Community College, Jack F. Owens Campus, PO Box 610, Georgetown, DE 19947. *Phone:* 302-856-5400. *Fax:* 302-856-9461. *Website:* http://www.dtcc.edu/.

## Delaware Technical & Community College, Stanton/George Campus
### Wilmington, Delaware

**Freshman Application Contact** Ms. Rebecca Bailey, Admissions Coordinator, Wilmington, Delaware Technical & Community College, Stanton/George Campus, 333 Shipley Street, Wilmington, DE 19713. *Phone:* 302-571-5343. *Fax:* 302-577-2548. *Website:* http://www.dtcc.edu/.

## Delaware Technical & Community College, Terry Campus
### Dover, Delaware

**Freshman Application Contact** Mrs. Maria Harris, Admissions Officer, Delaware Technical & Community College, Terry Campus, 100 Campus Drive, Dover, DE 19904. *Phone:* 302-857-1020. *Fax:* 302-857-1296. *E-mail:* terry-info@dtcc.edu. *Website:* http://www.dtcc.edu/.

# FLORIDA

## Academy for Nursing and Health Occupations
### West Palm Beach, Florida

**Admissions Office Contact** Academy for Nursing and Health Occupations, 5154 Okeechobee Boulevard, Suite 201, West Palm Beach, FL 33417. *Website:* http://www.anho.edu/.

## Advance Science College
### Hialeah, Florida

**Admissions Office Contact** Advance Science College, 3750 W. 12 Avenue, Hialeah, FL 33012. *Website:* http://www.asicollege.edu/.

## Altierus Career College
### Tampa, Florida

**Freshman Application Contact** Altierus Career College, 3319 West Hillsborough Avenue, Tampa, FL 33614. *Phone:* 813-879-6000 Ext. 129. *Website:* http://www.altierus.edu/.

## American Medical Academy
### Miami, Florida

**Admissions Office Contact** American Medical Academy, 12215 SW 112 Street, Miami, FL 33186-4830. *Website:* http://www.ama.edu/.

## ATA Career Education
### Spring Hill, Florida

**Admissions Office Contact** ATA Career Education, 7351 Spring Hill Drive, Suite 11, Spring Hill, FL 34606. *Website:* http://www.atafl.edu/.

## Aviator College of Aeronautical Science & Technology
### Fort Pierce, Florida

**Admissions Office Contact** Aviator College of Aeronautical Science & Technology, 3800 St. Lucie Boulevard, Fort Pierce, FL 34946. *Website:* http://aviator.edu/FlightSchool/.

## Broward College
### Fort Lauderdale, Florida

**Freshman Application Contact** Mr. Willie J. Alexander, Associate Vice President for Student Affairs/College Registrar, Broward College, 225 East Las Olas Boulevard, Fort Lauderdale, FL 33301. *Phone:* 954-201-7471. *Fax:* 954-201-7466. *E-mail:* walexand@broward.edu. *Website:* http://www.broward.edu/.

## Cambridge College of Healthcare & Technology
### Delray Beach, Florida

**Admissions Office Contact** Cambridge College of Healthcare & Technology, 5150 Linton Boulevard, Suite 340, Delray Beach, FL 33484. *Website:* http://www.cambridgehealth.edu/.

## Chipola College
### Marianna, Florida

- **State-supported** primarily 2-year, founded 1947
- **Rural** 105-acre campus
- **Coed,** 2,104 undergraduate students, 41% full-time, 61% women, 39% men

**Undergraduates** 859 full-time, 1,245 part-time. Students come from 7 states and territories; 6 other countries; 8% are from out of state; 15% Black or African American, non-Hispanic/Latino; 5% Hispanic/Latino; 0.7% Asian, non-Hispanic/Latino; 0.1% Native Hawaiian or other Pacific Islander, non-Hispanic/Latino; 1% American Indian or Alaska Native, non-Hispanic/Latino;

3% Two or more races, non-Hispanic/Latino; 1% Race/ethnicity unknown; 0.5% international; 7% transferred in.
**Freshmen** *Admission:* 264 enrolled. *Average high school GPA:* 2.5. *Test scores:* ACT scores over 18: 81%; ACT scores over 24: 25%; ACT scores over 30: 3%.
**Faculty** *Total:* 127, 31% full-time, 13% with terminal degrees. *Student/faculty ratio:* 24:1.
**Majors** Accounting; agriculture; agronomy and crop science; art; biological and physical sciences; business administration and management; clinical laboratory science/medical technology; computer and information sciences related; computer science; education; finance; liberal arts and sciences/liberal studies; mass communication/media; mathematics teacher education; pre-engineering; registered nursing/registered nurse; science teacher education; secondary education; social work.
**Academics** *Calendar:* semesters. *Degrees:* certificates, associate, and bachelor's. *Special study options:* academic remediation for entering students, adult/continuing education programs, advanced placement credit, distance learning, honors programs, independent study, part-time degree program, services for LD students, summer session for credit.
**Library** Chipola Library. *Books:* 30,000 (physical), 67,000 (digital/electronic); *Serial titles:* 150 (physical); *Databases:* 100. Weekly public service hours: 60; students can reserve study rooms.
**Student Life** *Housing:* college housing not available. *Activities and Organizations:* drama/theater group, student-run newspaper, choral group. *Campus security:* night security personnel. *Student services:* veterans affairs office.
**Athletics** Member NJCAA. *Intercollegiate sports:* baseball M(s), basketball M(s)/W(s), softball W(s).
**Costs (2018–19)** *Tuition:* state resident $104 per credit hour part-time; nonresident $298 per credit hour part-time. Full-time tuition and fees vary according to degree level. Part-time tuition and fees vary according to degree level. *Waivers:* senior citizens.
**Applying** *Options:* early admission. *Required:* high school transcript. *Application deadlines:* rolling (freshmen), rolling (transfers). *Notification:* continuous (freshmen), continuous (transfers).
**Freshman Application Contact** Mrs. Kathy L. Rehberg, Registrar, Chipola College, 3094 Indian Circle, Marianna, FL 32446-3065. *Phone:* 850-718-2233. *Fax:* 850-718-2287. *E-mail:* rehbergk@chipola.edu. *Website:* http://www.chipola.edu/.

# City College
## Altamonte Springs, Florida

**Director of Admissions** Ms. Kimberly Bowden, Director of Admissions, City College, 177 Montgomery Road, Altamonte Springs, FL 32714. *Phone:* 352-335-4000. *Fax:* 352-335-4303. *E-mail:* kbowden@citycollege.edu. *Website:* http://www.citycollege.edu/.

# City College
## Fort Lauderdale, Florida

**Freshman Application Contact** City College, 2000 West Commercial Boulevard, Suite 200, Fort Lauderdale, FL 33309. *Phone:* 954-492-5353. *Toll-free phone:* 866-314-5681. *Website:* http://www.citycollege.edu/.

# City College
## Gainesville, Florida

**Freshman Application Contact** Admissions Office, City College, 7001 Northwest 4th Boulevard, Gainesville, FL 32607. *Phone:* 352-335-4000. *Website:* http://www.citycollege.edu/.

# City College
## Hollywood, Florida

**Admissions Office Contact** City College, 6565 Taft Street, Hollywood, FL 33024. *Toll-free phone:* 866-314-5681. *Website:* http://www.citycollege.edu/.

# City College
## Miami, Florida

**Freshman Application Contact** Admissions Office, City College, 9300 South Dadeland Boulevard, Suite PH, Miami, FL 33156. *Phone:* 305-666-9242. *Fax:* 305-666-9243. *Website:* http://www.citycollege.edu/.

# College of Business and Technology–Cutler Bay Campus
## Cutler Bay, Florida

- **Proprietary** 2-year, founded 2009
- **Urban** campus with easy access to Miami
- **Coed,** 137 undergraduate students, 100% full-time, 38% women, 62% men

**Undergraduates** 137 full-time. Students come from 1 other state; 16% Black or African American, non-Hispanic/Latino; 92% Hispanic/Latino; 3% Asian, non-Hispanic/Latino; 2% Two or more races, non-Hispanic/Latino.
**Freshmen** *Admission:* 20 enrolled.
**Faculty** *Total:* 23, 22% full-time, 13% with terminal degrees. *Student/faculty ratio:* 13:1.
**Majors** Business administration and management; electrician; health information/medical records technology.
**Academics** *Calendar:* semesters. *Degree:* certificates, diplomas, and associate. *Special study options:* academic remediation for entering students, adult/continuing education programs, cooperative education, independent study, services for LD students.
**Library** CBT College–Cutler Bay Library. *Books:* 2,140 (physical); *Serial titles:* 20 (physical); *Databases:* 50.
**Student Life** *Housing:* college housing not available. *Campus security:* security guard patrol, local police department patrol.
**Costs (2018–19)** *Tuition:* $11,952 full-time. *Required fees:* $1500 full-time. *Payment plan:* installment.
**Applying** *Application fee:* $25. *Required:* high school transcript, interview.
**Freshman Application Contact** College of Business and Technology–Cutler Bay Campus, 19151 South Dixie Highway, Cutler Bay, FL 33157. *Phone:* 305-273-4499 Ext. 1100.
*Website:* http://www.cbt.edu/.

# College of Business and Technology–Flagler Campus
## Miami, Florida

- **Proprietary** 2-year, founded 1988
- **Urban** campus
- **Coed,** 256 undergraduate students, 100% full-time, 1% women, 99% men

**Undergraduates** 256 full-time. Students come from 1 other state; 0.4% Black or African American, non-Hispanic/Latino; 99% Hispanic/Latino.
**Freshmen** *Admission:* 28 enrolled.
**Faculty** *Total:* 33, 18% full-time. *Student/faculty ratio:* 17:1.
**Majors** Business administration and management; computer systems networking and telecommunications; electrician; heating, ventilation, air conditioning and refrigeration engineering technology.
**Academics** *Calendar:* semesters. *Degree:* certificates, diplomas, and associate. *Special study options:* academic remediation for entering students, adult/continuing education programs, cooperative education, English as a second language, independent study, services for LD students.
**Library** CBT College–Flagler Library. *Books:* 1,516 (physical); *Serial titles:* 6 (physical); *Databases:* 50.
**Student Life** *Housing:* college housing not available. *Campus security:* security guard patrol, local police department patrol.
**Costs (2018–19)** *Tuition:* $11,952 full-time. *Required fees:* $1500 full-time. *Payment plan:* installment.
**Applying** *Application fee:* $25. *Required:* high school transcript, interview.
**Freshman Application Contact** College of Business and Technology–Flagler Campus, 8230 West Flagler Street, Miami, FL 33144. *Phone:* 305-273-4499 Ext. 1100.
*Website:* http://www.cbt.edu/.

# College of Business and Technology–Hialeah Campus
## Hialeah, Florida

- **Proprietary** 2-year, founded 1988
- **Urban** campus with easy access to Miami
- **Coed, primarily men,** 200 undergraduate students, 100% full-time, 3% women, 97% men

**Undergraduates** 200 full-time. Students come from 1 other state; 0.5% Black or African American, non-Hispanic/Latino; 100% Hispanic/Latino.
**Freshmen** *Admission:* 30 enrolled.
**Faculty** *Total:* 32, 22% full-time, 9% with terminal degrees. *Student/faculty ratio:* 14:1.
**Majors** Electrician; heating, ventilation, air conditioning and refrigeration engineering technology.

**Academics** *Calendar:* semesters. *Degree:* certificates, diplomas, and associate. *Special study options:* academic remediation for entering students, adult/continuing education programs, cooperative education, English as a second language, independent study, services for LD students.
**Library** CBT College–Hialeah Library. *Books:* 897 (physical); *Serial titles:* 7 (physical); *Databases:* 50.
**Student Life** *Housing:* college housing not available. *Campus security:* local police department patrols.
**Costs (2018–19)** *Tuition:* $11,952 full-time. *Required fees:* $1500 full-time. *Payment plan:* installment.
**Applying** *Application fee:* $25. *Required:* high school transcript, interview.
**Freshman Application Contact** College of Business and Technology–Hialeah Campus, 935 West 49 Street, Hialeah, FL 33012. *Phone:* 305-273-4499 Ext. 1100.
*Website:* http://www.cbt.edu/.

# College of Business and Technology– Main Campus
## Miami, Florida

- **Proprietary** primarily 2-year, founded 1988
- **Urban** campus
- **Coed,** 10 undergraduate students, 100% full-time, 80% women, 20% men

**Undergraduates** 10 full-time. Students come from 1 other state; 100% Hispanic/Latino.
**Freshmen** *Admission:* 10 enrolled.
**Faculty** *Total:* 1, 100% full-time. *Student/faculty ratio:* 10:1.
**Majors** Business administration and management.
**Academics** *Calendar:* semesters. *Degrees:* certificates, diplomas, associate, and bachelor's. *Special study options:* academic remediation for entering students, adult/continuing education programs, cooperative education, English as a second language, independent study.
**Library** CBT College-Miami Branch Library (Use Flagler). *Books:* 590 (physical); *Serial titles:* 8 (physical); *Databases:* 50.
**Student Life** *Housing:* college housing not available. *Campus security:* security guard posted at main entrance, local police department.
**Costs (2018–19)** *Tuition:* $11,952 full-time. *Required fees:* $1500 full-time. *Payment plan:* installment.
**Applying** *Application fee:* $25. *Required:* high school transcript, interview.
**Freshman Application Contact** College of Business and Technology–Main Campus, 8700 West Flagler Street, Suite 420, Miami, FL 33174. *Phone:* 305-273-4499 Ext. 1100.
*Website:* http://www.cbt.edu/.

# College of Business and Technology– Miami Gardens
## Miami Gardens, Florida

- **Proprietary** primarily 2-year, founded 2012
- **Urban** campus with easy access to Miami
- **Coed,** 91 undergraduate students, 100% full-time, 33% women, 67% men

**Undergraduates** 91 full-time. Students come from 1 other state; 18% Black or African American, non-Hispanic/Latino; 81% Hispanic/Latino.
**Freshmen** *Admission:* 16 enrolled.
**Faculty** *Total:* 15, 20% full-time, 13% with terminal degrees. *Student/faculty ratio:* 15:1.
**Majors** Business administration and management; computer systems networking and telecommunications; electrician; health information/medical records technology.
**Academics** *Calendar:* semesters. *Degrees:* certificates, diplomas, associate, and bachelor's. *Special study options:* academic remediation for entering students, adult/continuing education programs, cooperative education, independent study, services for LD students.
**Library** CBT College–Miami Gardens Library. *Books:* 1,085 (physical); *Serial titles:* 18 (physical); *Databases:* 50.
**Student Life** *Housing:* college housing not available. *Campus security:* local police department.
**Costs (2018–19)** *Tuition:* $11,952 full-time. *Required fees:* $1500 full-time. *Payment plan:* installment.
**Applying** *Application fee:* $25. *Required:* high school transcript, interview.
**Freshman Application Contact** College of Business and Technology–Miami Gardens, 5190 NW 167 Street, Miami Gardens, FL 33014. *Phone:* 305-273-4499 Ext. 1100.
*Website:* http://www.cbt.edu/.

# College of Central Florida
## Ocala, Florida

- **State and locally supported** primarily 2-year, founded 1957, part of Florida Community College System
- **Small-town** 139-acre campus
- **Endowment** $65.4 million
- **Coed,** 7,931 undergraduate students, 38% full-time, 63% women, 37% men

**Undergraduates** 3,036 full-time, 4,895 part-time. 16% are from out of state.
**Freshmen** *Admission:* 4,416 applied, 2,430 admitted, 1,503 enrolled.
**Faculty** *Total:* 374, 37% full-time, 10% with terminal degrees.
**Majors** Accounting technology and bookkeeping; advertising; agribusiness; agriculture; animal sciences; architecture; art; biology/biological sciences; business administration and management; business administration, management and operations related; business/commerce; chemistry; clinical laboratory science/medical technology; computer and information sciences; construction engineering technology; criminal justice/law enforcement administration; criminology; dental assisting; drafting and design technology; dramatic/theater arts; early childhood education; economics; elementary education; emergency medical technology (EMT paramedic); engineering; engineering technology; English; environmental studies; equestrian studies; family and consumer sciences/human sciences; fire science/firefighting; foreign languages and literatures; forestry; health information/medical records technology; health/medical preparatory programs related; health services/allied health/health sciences; history; humanities; human services; information technology; interior architecture; journalism; landscaping and groundskeeping; legal assistant/paralegal; liberal arts and sciences and humanities related; liberal arts and sciences/liberal studies; library and information science; marketing/marketing management; mathematics; medical radiologic technology; music; music teacher education; occupational therapy; office management; parks, recreation and leisure; philosophy; physical education teaching and coaching; physical therapy; physical therapy technology; physics; pre-law studies; premedical studies; pre-pharmacy studies; pre-veterinary studies; psychology; registered nursing/registered nurse; religious studies; restaurant, culinary, and catering management; secondary education; social sciences; social work; sociology; special education; statistics; veterinary/animal health technology.
**Academics** *Calendar:* semesters. *Degrees:* certificates, diplomas, associate, and bachelor's. *Special study options:* academic remediation for entering students, adult/continuing education programs, advanced placement credit, cooperative education, distance learning, English as a second language, freshman honors college, honors programs, independent study, internships, part-time degree program, services for LD students, summer session for credit.
**Library** Clifford B. Stearns Learning Resources Center. *Books:* 75,935 (physical), 43,910 (digital/electronic); *Databases:* 152. Students can reserve study rooms.
**Student Life** *Housing:* college housing not available. *Activities and Organizations:* drama/theater group, student-run newspaper, choral group, Inspirational Choir, Model United Nations, Performing Arts, Phi Theta Kappa (PTK), Student Nurses Association. *Campus security:* 24-hour emergency response devices and patrols, student patrols, late-night transport/escort service. *Student services:* personal/psychological counseling.
**Athletics** Member NJCAA. *Intercollegiate sports:* baseball M(s), basketball M(s)/W(s), softball W(s), volleyball W(s). *Intramural sports:* bowling M/W.
**Costs (2017–18)** *Tuition:* state resident $5044 full-time, $107 per credit hour part-time; nonresident $20,252 full-time, $422 per credit hour part-time. Full-time tuition and fees vary according to course level, degree level, program, and student level. Part-time tuition and fees vary according to course level, degree level, program, and student level. *Waivers:* employees or children of employees.
**Financial Aid** Of all full-time matriculated undergraduates who enrolled in 2016, 1,203 applied for aid, 741 were judged to have need. *Average percent of need met:* 60%. *Average financial aid package:* $1863. *Average need-based loan:* $1371. *Average need-based gift aid:* $1942. *Average indebtedness upon graduation:* $2220.
**Applying** *Options:* electronic application, early admission. *Application fee:* $30. *Required:* high school transcript. *Application deadlines:* rolling (freshmen), rolling (transfers). *Notification:* continuous (freshmen), continuous (transfers).
**Freshman Application Contact** Ms. Devona Sewell, Registrar, Admission and Records, College of Central Florida, 3001 SW College Road, Ocala, FL 34474. *Phone:* 352-237-2111 Ext. 1398. *Fax:* 352-873-5882. *E-mail:* sewelld@cf.edu.
*Website:* http://www.cf.edu/.

## Concorde Career Institute
### Jacksonville, Florida

**Admissions Office Contact** Concorde Career Institute, 7259 Salisbury Road, Jacksonville, FL 32256. *Website:* http://www.concorde.edu/.

## Concorde Career Institute
### Miramar, Florida

**Admissions Office Contact** Concorde Career Institute, 10933 Marks Way, Miramar, FL 33025. *Website:* http://www.concorde.edu/.

## Concorde Career Institute
### Orlando, Florida

**Admissions Office Contact** Concorde Career Institute, 3444 McCrory Place, Orlando, FL 32803. *Website:* http://www.concorde.edu/.

## Concorde Career Institute
### Tampa, Florida

**Admissions Office Contact** Concorde Career Institute, 4202 West Spruce Street, Tampa, FL 33607. *Website:* http://www.concorde.edu/.

## Daytona College
### Ormond Beach, Florida

**Admissions Office Contact** Daytona College, 469 South Nova Road, Ormond Beach, FL 32174-8445. *Website:* http://www.daytonacollege.edu/.

## Daytona State College
### Daytona Beach, Florida

- **State-supported** primarily 2-year, founded 1957, part of Florida College System
- **Suburban** 115-acre campus with easy access to Orlando
- **Endowment** $12.9 million
- **Coed,** 13,141 undergraduate students, 39% full-time, 60% women, 40% men

**Undergraduates** 5,185 full-time, 7,956 part-time. Students come from 38 states and territories; 27 other countries; 1% are from out of state; 12% Black or African American, non-Hispanic/Latino; 17% Hispanic/Latino; 2% Asian, non-Hispanic/Latino; 0.2% Native Hawaiian or other Pacific Islander, non-Hispanic/Latino; 0.2% American Indian or Alaska Native, non-Hispanic/Latino; 3% Two or more races, non-Hispanic/Latino; 1% Race/ethnicity unknown; 0.4% international; 4% transferred in.
**Freshmen** *Admission:* 1,346 enrolled.
**Faculty** *Total:* 916, 31% full-time, 16% with terminal degrees. *Student/faculty ratio:* 16:1.
**Majors** Accounting technology and bookkeeping; aeronautical/aerospace engineering technology; architecture; biology teacher education; business administration and management; business administration, management and operations related; chemistry teacher education; community health services counseling; computer engineering technology; computer graphics; computer/information technology services administration related; computer programming; computer programming (specific applications); construction engineering technology; criminal justice/law enforcement administration; culinary arts; dental hygiene; digital communication and media/multimedia; drafting and design technology; early childhood education; electrical, electronic and communications engineering technology; elementary education; emergency medical technology (EMT paramedic); engineering technologies and engineering related; engineering technology; environmental science; fire prevention and safety technology; health information/medical records technology; hospitality administration; information technology; interior design; legal assistant/paralegal; liberal arts and sciences/liberal studies; mathematics teacher education; medical radiologic technology; music technology; network and system administration; occupational therapist assistant; office management; operations management; photographic and film/video technology; photography; physical therapy technology; physics teacher education; radio and television; registered nursing/registered nurse; respiratory care therapy; restaurant, culinary, and catering management; science teacher education; special education; special education–early childhood; web page, digital/multimedia and information resources design.
**Academics** *Calendar:* semesters. *Degrees:* certificates, diplomas, associate, and bachelor's. *Special study options:* academic remediation for entering students, adult/continuing education programs, advanced placement credit, cooperative education, distance learning, English as a second language, external degree program, freshman honors college, honors programs, independent study, internships, off-campus study, part-time degree program, services for LD students, study abroad, summer session for credit. *ROTC:* Army (c), Air Force (c).
**Library** Mary Karl Memorial Learning Resources Center plus 1 other. *Books:* 40,415 (physical), 185,001 (digital/electronic); *Serial titles:* 221 (physical), 46,685 (digital/electronic); *Databases:* 100. Weekly public service hours: 68; students can reserve study rooms.
**Student Life** *Housing:* college housing not available. *Activities and Organizations:* drama/theater group, student-run newspaper, choral group, Phi Theta Kappa International Honors Society, Student Government Association, Student Occupational Therapy Club, Business Club, Student Paralegal Club, national fraternities, national sororities. *Campus security:* 24-hour emergency response devices and patrols, late-night transport/escort service, emergency alert system capable of delivering text messages, voice calls, and email messages to college email accounts. *Student services:* personal/psychological counseling, women's center, veterans affairs office.
**Athletics** Member NJCAA. *Intercollegiate sports:* baseball M(s), basketball M(s)/W(s), golf W(s), soccer M(s)/W(s), softball W(s), volleyball W(s). *Intramural sports:* basketball M/W, football M/W, soccer M/W, table tennis M/W, volleyball M/W.
**Costs (2018–19)** *Tuition:* state resident $3071 full-time, $102 per credit hour part-time; nonresident $11,960 full-time, $399 per credit hour part-time. Full-time tuition and fees vary according to course level and course load. Part-time tuition and fees vary according to course level and course load. *Required fees:* $38 full-time, $1 per credit hour part-time. *Payment plan:* installment. *Waivers:* employees or children of employees.
**Financial Aid** Of all full-time matriculated undergraduates who enrolled in 2016, 131 Federal Work-Study jobs (averaging $1978). *Average need-based gift aid:* $1870.
**Applying** *Options:* electronic application, early admission, deferred entrance. *Required:* high school transcript. *Application deadlines:* rolling (freshmen), rolling (transfers). *Notification:* continuous (freshmen), continuous (transfers).
**Freshman Application Contact** Dr. Karen Sanders, Director of Admissions and Recruitment, Daytona State College, 1200 International Speedway Boulevard, Daytona Beach, FL 32114. *Phone:* 386-506-3050. *E-mail:* karen.sanders@daytonastate.edu.
*Website:* http://www.daytonastate.edu/.

## Eastern Florida State College
### Cocoa, Florida

**Freshman Application Contact** Ms. Stephanie Burnette, Registrar, Eastern Florida State College, 1519 Clearlake Road, Cocoa, FL 32922-6597. *Phone:* 321-433-7271. *Fax:* 321-433-7172. *E-mail:* cocoaadmissions@brevardcc.edu. *Website:* http://www.easternflorida.edu/.

## Florida Career College
### Boynton Beach, Florida

**Admissions Office Contact** Florida Career College, 1749 North Congress Avenue, Boynton Beach, FL 33426. *Website:* http://www.floridacareercollege.edu/.

## Florida Career College
### Hialeah, Florida

**Admissions Office Contact** Florida Career College, 3750 West 18th Avenue, Hialeah, FL 33012. *Toll-free phone:* 888-852-7272. *Website:* http://www.floridacareercollege.edu/.

## Florida Career College
### Jacksonville, Florida

**Admissions Office Contact** Florida Career College, 6600 Youngerman Circle, Jacksonville, FL 32244. *Website:* http://www.floridacareercollege.edu/.

## Florida Career College
### Lauderdale Lakes, Florida

**Admissions Office Contact** Florida Career College, 3383 North State Road 7, Lauderdale Lakes, FL 33319. *Website:* http://www.floridacareercollege.edu/.

## Florida Career College
### Margate, Florida

**Admissions Office Contact** Florida Career College, 3271 North State Road 7, Margate, FL 33063. *Website:* http://www.floridacareercollege.edu/.

# Florida Career College
## Miami, Florida

**Director of Admissions** Mr. David Knobel, President, Florida Career College, 1321 Southwest 107th Avenue, Suite 201B, Miami, FL 33174. *Phone:* 305-553-6065. *Toll-free phone:* 888-852-7272. *Website:* http://www.floridacareercollege.edu/.

# Florida Career College
## Orlando, Florida

**Admissions Office Contact** Florida Career College, 989 North Semoran Boulevard, Orlando, FL 32807. *Website:* http://www.floridacareercollege.edu/.

# Florida Career College
## Pembroke Pines, Florida

**Admissions Office Contact** Florida Career College, 7891 Pines Boulevard, Pembroke Pines, FL 33024. *Toll-free phone:* 888-852-7272. *Website:* http://www.floridacareercollege.edu/.

# Florida Career College
## Tampa, Florida

**Admissions Office Contact** Florida Career College, 9950 Princess Palm Avenue, Tampa, FL 33619. *Website:* http://www.floridacareercollege.edu/.

# Florida Career College
## West Palm Beach, Florida

**Admissions Office Contact** Florida Career College, 6058 Okeechobee Boulevard, West Palm Beach, FL 33417. *Toll-free phone:* 888-852-7272. *Website:* http://www.floridacareercollege.edu/.

# Florida Gateway College
## Lake City, Florida

**Freshman Application Contact** Admissions, Florida Gateway College, 149 SE College Place, Lake City, FL 32025-8703. *Phone:* 386-755-4236. *E-mail:* admissions@fgc.edu. *Website:* http://www.fgc.edu/.

# Florida Keys Community College
## Key West, Florida

- **State-supported** primarily 2-year, founded 1965, part of Florida College System
- **Small-town** 20-acre campus
- **Coed,** 1,030 undergraduate students, 35% full-time, 58% women, 42% men

**Undergraduates** 363 full-time, 667 part-time. 9% Black or African American, non-Hispanic/Latino; 27% Hispanic/Latino; 2% Asian, non-Hispanic/Latino; 0.4% Native Hawaiian or other Pacific Islander, non-Hispanic/Latino; 0.3% American Indian or Alaska Native, non-Hispanic/Latino; 3% Two or more races, non-Hispanic/Latino; 4% Race/ethnicity unknown; 0.9% international; 10% transferred in.

**Freshmen** *Admission:* 198 enrolled.

**Faculty** *Total:* 28. *Student/faculty ratio:* 12:1.

**Majors** Business administration and management; business administration, management and operations related; computer programming; computer systems analysis; diesel mechanics technology; diving, professional and instruction; fishing and fisheries sciences and management; hospitality administration; information technology; liberal arts and sciences/liberal studies; mechanical engineering technologies related; parks, recreation and leisure; registered nursing/registered nurse; restaurant, culinary, and catering management; wildlife, fish and wildlands science and management.

**Academics** *Calendar:* semesters. *Degrees:* certificates, associate, and bachelor's. *Special study options:* academic remediation for entering students, adult/continuing education programs, advanced placement credit, cooperative education, distance learning, double majors, English as a second language, independent study, internships, part-time degree program, services for LD students, student-designed majors, summer session for credit.

**Library** Florida Keys Community College Library. Students can reserve study rooms.

**Student Life** *Housing Options:* coed. Campus housing is university owned. *Activities and Organizations:* choral group. *Campus security:* 24-hour patrols. *Student services:* personal/psychological counseling, veterans affairs office.

**Costs (2018–19)** *Tuition:* state resident $109 per credit hour part-time; nonresident $439 per credit hour part-time. Full-time tuition and fees vary according to degree level. Part-time tuition and fees vary according to degree level. *Room and board:* room only: $10,508. Room and board charges vary according to board plan. *Payment plan:* installment. *Waivers:* employees or children of employees.

**Financial Aid** Of all full-time matriculated undergraduates who enrolled in 2016, 30 Federal Work-Study jobs (averaging $2000).

**Applying** *Options:* electronic application, early admission, deferred entrance. *Application fee:* $30. *Required for some:* essay or personal statement, high school transcript, letters of recommendation. *Application deadlines:* rolling (freshmen), rolling (transfers). *Notification:* continuous (freshmen), continuous (transfers).

**Freshman Application Contact** Florida Keys Community College, 5901 College Road, Key West, FL 33040-4397. *Phone:* 305-296-9081 Ext. 237. *Website:* http://www.fkcc.edu/.

# The Florida School of Traditional Midwifery
## Gainseville, Florida

**Freshman Application Contact** Admissions Office, The Florida School of Traditional Midwifery, 810 East University Avenue, 2nd Floor, Gainseville, FL 32601. *Phone:* 352-338-0766. *Fax:* 352-338-2013. *E-mail:* info@midwiferyschool.org. *Website:* http://www.midwiferyschool.org/.

# Florida SouthWestern State College
## Fort Myers, Florida

- **State and locally supported** primarily 2-year, founded 1962, part of Florida College System
- **Urban** 413-acre campus
- **Endowment** $731,365
- **Coed**

**Undergraduates** 5,708 full-time, 10,908 part-time. Students come from 46 states and territories; 27 other countries; 4% are from out of state; 10% Black or African American, non-Hispanic/Latino; 28% Hispanic/Latino; 2% Asian, non-Hispanic/Latino; 0.2% Native Hawaiian or other Pacific Islander, non-Hispanic/Latino; 0.4% American Indian or Alaska Native, non-Hispanic/Latino; 2% Two or more races, non-Hispanic/Latino; 6% Race/ethnicity unknown; 2% international; 4% transferred in; 2% live on campus. *Retention:* 66% of full-time freshmen returned.

**Faculty** *Student/faculty ratio:* 31:1.

**Academics** *Calendar:* semesters. *Degrees:* certificates, associate, and bachelor's. *Special study options:* academic remediation for entering students, accelerated degree program, advanced placement credit, cooperative education, distance learning, double majors, English as a second language, honors programs, independent study, internships, off-campus study, part-time degree program, services for LD students, study abroad, summer session for credit.

**Library** Richard H. Rush Library. *Books:* 45,355 (physical), 28,410 (digital/electronic); *Databases:* 128. Weekly public service hours: 79.

**Student Life** *Campus security:* 24-hour emergency response devices and patrols, late-night transport/escort service, controlled dormitory access, Rave Guardian app for students, faculty, and staff.

**Athletics** Member NJCAA.

**Financial Aid** Of all full-time matriculated undergraduates who enrolled in 2014, 3,887 applied for aid, 3,311 were judged to have need, 68 had their need fully met. In 2014, 166. *Average percent of need met:* 47. *Average financial aid package:* $6172. *Average need-based loan:* $3461. *Average need-based gift aid:* $5119. *Average non-need-based aid:* $2588.

**Applying** *Options:* electronic application, early admission, deferred entrance. *Application fee:* $30. *Required:* high school transcript.

**Freshman Application Contact** FSW Admissions, Florida SouthWestern State College, 8099 College Parkway, Fort Myers, FL 33919. *Phone:* 239-489-9054. *Fax:* 239-489-9094. *E-mail:* admissions@fsw.edu. *Website:* http://www.fsw.edu/.

# Florida State College at Jacksonville
## Jacksonville, Florida

**Freshman Application Contact** Dr. Peter Biegel, Registrar, Florida State College at Jacksonville, 501 West State Street, Jacksonville, FL 32202. *Phone:* 904-632-5112. *Toll-free phone:* 888-873-1145. *E-mail:* pbiegel@fscj.edu. *Website:* http://www.fscj.edu/.

## Florida Technical College
### Orlando, Florida

**Director of Admissions** Ms. Jeanette E. Muschlitz, Director of Admissions, Florida Technical College, 12900 Challenger Parkway, Orlando, FL 32826. *Phone:* 407-678-5600. *Toll-free phone:* 888-574-2082. *Website:* http://www.ftccollege.edu/.

## Fortis College
### Cutler Bay, Florida

**Admissions Office Contact** Fortis College, 19600 South Dixie Highway, Suite B, Cutler Bay, FL 33157. *Toll-free phone:* 855-4-FORTIS. *Website:* http://www.fortis.edu/.

## Fortis College
### Orange Park, Florida

**Admissions Office Contact** Fortis College, 700 Blanding Boulevard, Suite 16, Orange Park, FL 32065. *Toll-free phone:* 855-4-FORTIS. *Website:* http://www.fortis.edu/.

## Fortis Institute
### Pensacola, Florida

**Admissions Office Contact** Fortis Institute, 4081 East Olive Road, Suite B, Pensacola, FL 32514. *Toll-free phone:* 855-4-FORTIS. *Website:* http://www.fortis.edu/.

## Fortis Institute
### Port St. Lucie, Florida

**Admissions Office Contact** Fortis Institute, 9022 South US Highway 1, Port St. Lucie, FL 34952. *Toll-free phone:* 855-4-FORTIS. *Website:* http://www.fortis.edu/.

## Galen College of Nursing
### St. Petersburg, Florida

**Admissions Office Contact** Galen College of Nursing, 11101 Roosevelt Boulevard North, St. Petersburg, FL 33716. *Toll-free phone:* 877-223-7040. *Website:* http://www.galencollege.edu/.

## Golf Academy of America
### Apopka, Florida

**Admissions Office Contact** Golf Academy of America, 510 South Hunt Club Boulevard, Apopka, FL 32703. *Website:* http://www.golfacademy.edu/.

## Gulf Coast State College
### Panama City, Florida

- **State-supported** primarily 2-year, founded 1957, part of Florida College System
- **Urban** 80-acre campus
- **Endowment** $30.5 million
- **Coed,** 5,379 undergraduate students, 34% full-time, 60% women, 40% men

**Undergraduates** 1,840 full-time, 3,539 part-time. Students come from 13 states and territories; 3% are from out of state; 12% Black or African American, non-Hispanic/Latino; 7% Hispanic/Latino; 3% Asian, non-Hispanic/Latino; 0.9% American Indian or Alaska Native, non-Hispanic/Latino; 4% Two or more races, non-Hispanic/Latino; 3% Race/ethnicity unknown; 0.6% international; 3% transferred in.
**Freshmen** *Admission:* 950 enrolled.
**Faculty** *Total:* 329, 43% full-time. *Student/faculty ratio:* 19:1.
**Majors** Accounting technology and bookkeeping; animation, interactive technology, video graphics and special effects; automation engineer technology; business administration and management; business administration, management and operations related; CAD/CADD drafting/design technology; child-care provision; civil engineering technology; communications technology; computer/information technology services administration related; computer programming; computer programming (vendor/product certification); computer systems networking and telecommunications; construction engineering technology; criminal justice/law enforcement administration; dental hygiene; diagnostic medical sonography and ultrasound technology; digital arts; digital communication and media/multimedia; early

childhood education; electrical, electronic and communications engineering technology; emergency medical technology (EMT paramedic); engineering technology; fire prevention and safety technology; forensic science and technology; health services/allied health/health sciences; hospitality administration; liberal arts and sciences/liberal studies; management information systems; manufacturing engineering technology; medical administrative assistant and medical secretary; medical radiologic technology; music technology; network and system administration; nuclear medical technology; office management; physical therapy technology; registered nursing/registered nurse; respiratory care therapy; restaurant, culinary, and catering management; surgical technology; transportation/mobility management; web page, digital/multimedia and information resources design.
**Academics** *Calendar:* semesters. *Degrees:* certificates, associate, and bachelor's. *Special study options:* academic remediation for entering students, accelerated degree program, adult/continuing education programs, advanced placement credit, cooperative education, distance learning, double majors, English as a second language, external degree program, honors programs, independent study, off-campus study, part-time degree program, services for LD students, study abroad, summer session for credit.
**Library** Gulf Coast State College Library. *Books:* 32,529 (physical), 57,578 (digital/electronic); *Serial titles:* 43 (physical), 55,302 (digital/electronic); *Databases:* 176.
**Student Life** *Housing:* college housing not available. *Activities and Organizations:* drama/theater group, student-run newspaper, radio and television station, choral group, Student Government Association. *Campus security:* 24-hour patrols, late-night transport/escort service, patrols by trained security personnel during campus hours. *Student services:* personal/psychological counseling, veterans affairs office.
**Athletics** Member NJCAA. *Intercollegiate sports:* baseball M(s), basketball M(s)/W(s), softball W(s), volleyball W(s).
**Costs (2017–18)** *Tuition:* state resident $2370 full-time, $99 per credit hour part-time; nonresident $8633 full-time, $360 per credit hour part-time. Full-time tuition and fees vary according to degree level. Part-time tuition and fees vary according to degree level. *Required fees:* $620 full-time, $26 per credit hour part-time.
**Financial Aid** Of all full-time matriculated undergraduates who enrolled in 2016, 145 Federal Work-Study jobs (averaging $3200). 60 state and other part-time jobs (averaging $2600).
**Applying** *Options:* electronic application, early admission, deferred entrance. *Application fee:* $20. *Required:* high school transcript. *Application deadlines:* rolling (freshmen), rolling (transfers). *Notification:* continuous (freshmen).
**Freshman Application Contact** Mrs. Sam Wagner, Application Process Specialist, Gulf Coast State College, 5230 West U.S. Highway 98, Panama City, FL 32401. *Phone:* 850-769-1551 Ext. 2936. *Fax:* 850-913-3308. *E-mail:* swagner1@gulfcoast.edu.
*Website:* http://www.gulfcoast.edu/.

## Gwinnett Institute
### Orlando, Florida

**Admissions Office Contact** Gwinnett Institute, 1900 North Alafaya Trail, Orlando, FL 32826. *Website:* http://www.gwinnettcollege.edu/locations/orlando/.

## Hillsborough Community College
### Tampa, Florida

- **State-supported** 2-year, founded 1968, part of Florida College System
- **Urban** campus with easy access to Tampa, Clearwater, St. Petersburg
- **Coed**

**Undergraduates** 10,924 full-time, 16,137 part-time. Students come from 42 states and territories; 128 other countries; 1% are from out of state; 18% Black or African American, non-Hispanic/Latino; 29% Hispanic/Latino; 3% Asian, non-Hispanic/Latino; 0.2% Native Hawaiian or other Pacific Islander, non-Hispanic/Latino; 0.4% American Indian or Alaska Native, non-Hispanic/Latino; 3% Two or more races, non-Hispanic/Latino; 7% Race/ethnicity unknown; 3% international; 26% transferred in.
**Faculty** *Student/faculty ratio:* 24:1.
**Academics** *Calendar:* semesters. *Degree:* certificates and associate. *Special study options:* academic remediation for entering students, advanced placement credit, cooperative education, distance learning, English as a second language, honors programs, independent study, internships, off-campus study, part-time degree program, services for LD students, study abroad, summer session for credit. *ROTC:* Army (c), Air Force (c).
**Library** Dale Mabry Library plus 4 others. *Books:* 109,428 (physical), 44,898 (digital/electronic); *Serial titles:* 578 (physical), 47,889 (digital/electronic); *Databases:* 124.
**Student Life** *Campus security:* 24-hour emergency response devices and patrols, late-night transport/escort service.

**Athletics** Member NJCAA.

**Applying** *Options:* electronic application, early admission. *Required:* high school transcript.

**Freshman Application Contact** Ms. Jennifer Young, College Registrar, Hillsborough Community College, PO Box 31127, Tampa, FL 33631-3127. *Phone:* 813-259-6565. *E-mail:* jyoung92@hccfl.edu. *Website:* http://www.hccfl.edu/.

## Hope College of Arts and Sciences
### Pompano Beach, Florida

**Admissions Office Contact** Hope College of Arts and Sciences, 1200 SW 3rd Street, Pompano Beach, FL 33069. *Website:* http://www.hcas.edu/.

## Jones Technical Institute
### Jacksonville, Florida

**Admissions Office Contact** Jones Technical Institute, 8813 Western Way, Jacksonville, FL 32256. *Website:* http://www.jtech.org/.

## Key College
### Dania Beach, Florida

**Director of Admissions** Mr. Ronald H. Dooley, President and Director of Admissions, Key College, 225 East Dania Beach Boulevard, Dania Beach, FL 33004. *Phone:* 954-581-2223 Ext. 23. *Toll-free phone:* 877-421-6149. *Website:* http://www.keycollege.edu/.

## Lake-Sumter State College
### Leesburg, Florida

**Freshman Application Contact** Ms. Bonnie Yanick, Enrollment Specialist, Lake-Sumter State College, 9501 U.S. Highway 441, Leesburg, FL 34788-8751. *Phone:* 352-365-3561. *Fax:* 352-365-3553. *E-mail:* admissinquiry@lscc.edu. *Website:* http://www.lssc.edu/.

## Med-Life Institute
### Kissimmee, Florida

**Admissions Office Contact** Med-Life Institute, 4727 West Irlo Bronson Memorial Highway, Kissimmee, FL 34746. *Website:* http://www.medlifeinstitute.com/.

## Med-Life Institute
### Lauderdale Lakes, Florida

**Admissions Office Contact** Med-Life Institute, 4000 North State Road 7, Lauderdale Lakes, FL 33319. *Website:* http://www.medlifeinstitute.com/.

## Med-Life Institute
### Naples, Florida

**Admissions Office Contact** Med-Life Institute, 4995 East Tamiami Trail, Naples, FL 34112. *Website:* http://www.medlifeinstitute.com/.

## Meridian College
### Sarasota, Florida

**Admissions Office Contact** Meridian College, 7020 Professional Parkway East, Sarasota, FL 34240. *Website:* http://www.meridian.edu/.

## ★ Miami Dade College
### Miami, Florida

- **State and locally supported** primarily 2-year, founded 1960, part of Florida College System
- **Urban** campus
- **Endowment** $137.1 million
- **Coed,** 56,001 undergraduate students, 42% full-time, 57% women, 43% men

**Undergraduates** 23,589 full-time, 32,412 part-time. Students come from 37 states and territories; 165 other countries; 0.4% are from out of state; 14% Black or African American, non-Hispanic/Latino; 70% Hispanic/Latino; 1%

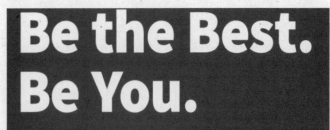

non-Hispanic/Latino; 0.1% American Indian or Alaska Native, non-Hispanic/Latino; 0.6% Two or more races, non-Hispanic/Latino; 2% Race/ethnicity unknown; 6% international; 0.1% transferred in.

**Freshmen** *Admission:* 44,910 applied, 44,910 admitted, 12,173 enrolled.

**Faculty** *Total:* 2,355, 30% full-time, 25% with terminal degrees. *Student/faculty ratio:* 26:1.

**Majors** Accounting technology and bookkeeping; aeronautics/aviation/aerospace science and technology; agriculture; airline pilot and flight crew; air traffic control; American studies; animation, interactive technology, video graphics and special effects; anthropology; architectural drafting and CAD/CADD; architectural engineering technology; architectural technology; art; Asian studies; audiology and speech-language pathology; automation engineer technology; aviation/airway management; banking and financial support services; behavioral sciences; biology/biological sciences; biology teacher education; biomedical technology; biotechnology; business administration and management; business administration, management and operations related; business automation/technology/data entry; CAD/CADD drafting/design technology; chemistry; chemistry teacher education; child-care provision; child development; cinematography and film/video production; civil engineering technology; clinical/medical laboratory technology; commercial and advertising art; community health services counseling; comparative literature; computer and information sciences; computer engineering technology; computer graphics; computer installation and repair technology; computer programming; computer programming (specific applications); computer programming (vendor/product certification); computer science; computer software technology; computer support specialist; computer systems networking and telecommunications; computer technology/computer systems technology; construction engineering technology; cooking and related culinary arts; corrections; corrections and criminal justice related; court reporting; criminal justice/law enforcement administration; criminal justice/police science; culinary arts; customer service support/call center/teleservice operation; dance; dental hygiene; diagnostic medical sonography and ultrasound technology; dietetics; dietetic technology; drafting and design technology; dramatic/theater arts; early childhood education; economics; education; education related; education (specific levels and methods) related; electrical and electronic engineering technologies related; electrical, electronic and communications engineering technology; electrician; elementary education; emergency medical technology (EMT paramedic); engineering; engineering related; engineering technology; English; entrepreneurship; environmental engineering technology; environmental science; finance; fire prevention and safety technology; fire science/firefighting; food science; forensic science and technology; forestry; French; funeral service and mortuary science; game and interactive media design; general studies; geology/earth science; German; health information/medical records administration; health information/medical records technology; health/medical preparatory programs related; health professions related; health services/allied health/health sciences; heating, air conditioning, ventilation and refrigeration maintenance technology; heating, ventilation, air conditioning and refrigeration engineering technology; histologic technician; histologic technology/histotechnologist; history; homeland security, law enforcement, firefighting and protective services related; horticultural science; hospitality administration; hotel/motel administration; humanities; human services; industrial technology; information science/studies; information technology; interior design; international relations and affairs; Italian; journalism; kindergarten/preschool education; landscaping and groundskeeping; Latin American studies; legal administrative assistant/secretary; legal assistant/paralegal; liberal arts and sciences/liberal studies; logistics, materials, and supply chain management; management information systems; manufacturing engineering technology; marketing/marketing management; massage therapy; mass communication/media; mathematics; mathematics teacher education; medical/clinical assistant; medical radiologic technology; middle school education; music; music performance; music teacher education; music technology; natural sciences; network and system administration; nonprofit management; nuclear medical technology; office management; operations management; ophthalmic technology; opticianry; ornamental horticulture; parks, recreation and leisure; pharmacy technician; philosophy; phlebotomy technology; photographic and film/video technology; photography; physical education teaching and coaching; physical sciences; physical therapy technology; physician assistant; physics; physics teacher education; pipefitting and sprinkler fitting; plant nursery management; plumbing technology; political science and government; Portuguese; pre-engineering; psychology; public administration; radio and television; radio and television broadcasting technology; radiologic technology/science; real estate; recording arts technology; registered nursing/registered nurse; respiratory care therapy; respiratory therapy technician; restaurant, culinary, and catering management; restaurant/food services management; science teacher education; security and loss prevention; sheet metal technology; sign language interpretation and translation; social sciences; social work; sociology; Spanish; special education; special education–individuals with hearing impairments; substance abuse/addiction counseling; teacher assistant/aide; telecommunications technology; theater design and technology; tourism and travel services management; veterinary/animal health technology; web page, digital/multimedia and information resources design.

**Academics** *Calendar:* 16-16-6-6. *Degrees:* certificates, associate, bachelor's, and postbachelor's certificates. *Special study options:* academic remediation for entering students, accelerated degree program, adult/continuing education programs, advanced placement credit, cooperative education, distance learning, English as a second language, freshman honors college, honors programs, independent study, internships, off-campus study, part-time degree program, services for LD students, study abroad, summer session for credit. *ROTC:* Army (b), Air Force (c).

**Library** Miami Dade College Learning Resources plus 9 others. *Books:* 185,820 (physical), 60,221 (digital/electronic); *Serial titles:* 708 (physical), 46,482 (digital/electronic); *Databases:* 126. Weekly public service hours: 69; students can reserve study rooms.

**Student Life** *Housing:* college housing not available. *Activities and Organizations:* drama/theater group, student-run newspaper, radio and television station, choral group, Student Government Association, Phi Theta Kappa, Phi Beta Lambda (business), Future Educators of America Professional, Kappa Delta Pi Honor Society (education). *Campus security:* 24-hour emergency response devices and patrols, student patrols, late-night transport/escort service, Emergency Mass Notification System (EMNS), campus public address systems, LiveSafe mobile safety App for students/employees. *Student services:* health clinic, personal/psychological counseling, veterans affairs office.

**Athletics** Member NCAA, NJCAA. All NCAA Division I. *Intercollegiate sports:* baseball M(s), basketball M(s)/W(s), softball W(s), volleyball W(s).

**Costs (2017–18)** *One-time required fee:* $30. *Tuition:* state resident $1987 full-time, $83 per credit hour part-time; nonresident $7947 full-time, $331 per credit hour part-time. Full-time tuition and fees vary according to course load, degree level, and program. Part-time tuition and fees vary according to course load, degree level, and program. *Required fees:* $851 full-time, $35 per credit hour part-time. *Waivers:* employees or children of employees.

**Financial Aid** Of all full-time matriculated undergraduates who enrolled in 2016, 800 Federal Work-Study jobs (averaging $5000). 125 state and other part-time jobs (averaging $5000).

**Applying** *Options:* electronic application, early admission. *Application fee:* $30. *Required:* high school transcript. *Application deadlines:* rolling (freshmen), rolling (transfers). *Notification:* continuous (freshmen), continuous (transfers).

**Freshman Application Contact** Ms. Elisabet Vizoso, Interim College Registrar, Miami Dade College, 11011 SW 104th Street, Miami, FL 33176. *Phone:* 305-237-2206. *Fax:* 305-237-2532. *E-mail:* evizoso@mdc.edu. *Website:* http://www.mdc.edu/.

*See below for display ad and page 324 for the College Close-Up.*

# North Florida Community College
## Madison, Florida

**Freshman Application Contact** Mr. Bobby Scott, North Florida Community College, 325 Northwest Turner Davis Drive, Madison, FL 32340. *Phone:* 850-973-9450. *Toll-free phone:* 866-937-6322. *Fax:* 850-973-1697. *Website:* http://www.nfcc.edu/.

# Northwest Florida State College
## Niceville, Florida

**Freshman Application Contact** Ms. Karen Cooper, Director of Admissions, Northwest Florida State College, 100 College Boulevard, Niceville, FL 32578. *Phone:* 850-729-4901. *Fax:* 850-729-5206. *E-mail:* cooperk@nwfsc.edu. *Website:* http://www.nwfsc.edu/.

# Orion College
## Plantation, Florida

**Admissions Office Contact** Orion College, 3500 North State Road 7, Plantation, FL 33319. *Toll-free phone:* 888-331-9957. *Website:* http://www.orioncollege.org/.

# Pasco-Hernando State College
## New Port Richey, Florida

**Freshman Application Contact** Ms. Estela Carrion, Director of Admissions and Student Records, Pasco-Hernando State College, 10230 Ridge Road, New Port Richey, FL 34654-5199. *Phone:* 727-816-3261. *Toll-free phone:* 877-TRY-PHSC. *Fax:* 727-816-3389. *E-mail:* carrioe@phsc.edu. *Website:* http://www.phsc.edu/.

# Pensacola State College
## Pensacola, Florida

- **State-supported** primarily 2-year, founded 1948, part of Florida College System
- **Urban** 130-acre campus with easy access to Mobile, Alabama
- **Endowment** $11.3 million
- **Coed,** 9,655 undergraduate students, 37% full-time, 61% women, 39% men

**Undergraduates** 3,583 full-time, 6,072 part-time. Students come from 37 states and territories; 5% are from out of state; 15% Black or African American, non-Hispanic/Latino; 7% Hispanic/Latino; 3% Asian, non-Hispanic/Latino; 0.4% Native Hawaiian or other Pacific Islander, non-Hispanic/Latino; 0.8% American Indian or Alaska Native, non-Hispanic/Latino; 6% Two or more races, non-Hispanic/Latino; 2% Race/ethnicity unknown; 0.4% international; 7% transferred in. *Retention:* 72% of full-time freshmen returned.
**Freshmen** *Admission:* 2,892 applied, 2,892 admitted, 1,049 enrolled. *Average high school GPA:* 3.0.
**Faculty** *Total:* 599, 30% full-time, 6% with terminal degrees. *Student/faculty ratio:* 19:1.
**Majors** Accounting; accounting technology and bookkeeping; administrative assistant and secretarial science; agricultural business and management; agriculture; architectural technology; art; art teacher education; biochemistry; biology/biological sciences; botany/plant biology; building/property maintenance; business administration and management; business administration, management and operations related; business/commerce; chemical technology; chemistry; child-care and support services management; child-care provision; civil engineering technology; commercial and advertising art; communications technology; computer and information sciences; computer and information sciences related; computer and information systems security; computer engineering; computer graphics; computer programming; computer programming (specific applications); computer programming (vendor/product certification); computer science; computer systems analysis; construction engineering technology; consumer services and advocacy; cooking and related culinary arts; criminal justice/law enforcement administration; cyber/computer forensics and counterterrorism; dental hygiene; diagnostic medical sonography and ultrasound technology; dietetics; drafting and design technology; dramatic/theater arts; early childhood education; education; education (specific levels and methods) related; electrical, electronic and communications engineering technology; elementary education; emergency medical technology (EMT paramedic); engineering; engineering technology; English; fire prevention and safety technology; food service systems administration; foods, nutrition, and wellness; forensic science and technology; geology/earth science; graphic design; hazardous materials management and waste technology; health/health-care administration; health information/medical records administration; health information/medical records technology; history; homeland security related; hospitality administration; hotel/motel administration; hotel, motel, and restaurant management; information science/studies; information technology; journalism; landscaping and groundskeeping; legal administrative assistant/secretary; legal assistant/paralegal; liberal arts and sciences/liberal studies; management information systems; management information systems and services related; management science; mathematics; medical radiologic technology; music; music teacher education; natural resources management and policy; nursing assistant/aide and patient care assistant/aide; nursing science; office management; operations management; ornamental horticulture; pharmacy technician; philosophy; photography; physical fitness technician; physical therapy technology; physics; pre-dentistry studies; pre-law studies; premedical studies; prenursing studies; pre-pharmacy studies; pre-veterinary studies; psychology; registered nursing/registered nurse; restaurant, culinary, and catering management; sociology; special education; telecommunications technology; veterinary/animal health technology; web page, digital/multimedia and information resources design.
**Academics** *Calendar:* semesters. *Degrees:* certificates, diplomas, associate, and bachelor's. *Special study options:* academic remediation for entering students, adult/continuing education programs, advanced placement credit, cooperative education, distance learning, double majors, English as a second language, external degree program, honors programs, independent study, internships, part-time degree program, services for LD students, summer session for credit. *ROTC:* Army (b).
**Library** Edward M. Chadbourne Library plus 3 others. Students can reserve study rooms.
**Student Life** *Housing:* college housing not available. *Activities and Organizations:* drama/theater group, student-run newspaper, choral group, Student Government Association, Health Occupations Students of America (HOSA), SkillsUSA, African-American Student Association, Forestry Club. *Campus security:* 24-hour emergency response devices and patrols, late-night transport/escort service. *Student services:* personal/psychological counseling, veterans affairs office.

**Athletics** Member NJCAA. *Intercollegiate sports:* baseball M(s), basketball M(s)/W(s), softball W(s), volleyball W(s). *Intramural sports:* archery M/W, badminton M/W, basketball M/W, bowling M/W, racquetball M/W, soccer M/W, softball W, tennis M/W, volleyball M/W.
**Costs (2018–19)** *One-time required fee:* $30. *Tuition:* state resident $3137 full-time, $105 per credit hour part-time; nonresident $12,593 full-time, $420 per credit hour part-time. Full-time tuition and fees vary according to course level and degree level. Part-time tuition and fees vary according to course level and degree level. *Payment plan:* deferred payment. *Waivers:* senior citizens and employees or children of employees.
**Financial Aid** Of all full-time matriculated undergraduates who enrolled in 2016, 120 Federal Work-Study jobs (averaging $3000).
**Applying** *Options:* electronic application, early admission. *Application fee:* $30. *Required:* high school transcript. *Application deadlines:* 8/30 (freshmen), 8/30 (transfers). *Notification:* continuous until 8/30 (freshmen), continuous until 8/30 (transfers).
**Freshman Application Contact** Ms. Kathy Dutremble, Registrar, Pensacola State College, 1000 College Boulevard, Pensacola, FL 32504. *Phone:* 850-484-2076. *Fax:* 850-484-1020. *E-mail:* kdutremble@pensacolastate.edu. *Website:* http://www.pensacolastate.edu/.

# Praxis Institute
## Miami, Florida

**Admissions Office Contact** Praxis Institute, 1850 SW 8th Street, 4th Floor, Miami, FL 33135. *Website:* http://www.praxis.edu/.

# Professional Hands Institute
## Miami, Florida

**Admissions Office Contact** Professional Hands Institute, 10 NW 42 Avenue, Suite 200, Miami, FL 33126. *Website:* http://prohands.edu/.

# Remington College–Heathrow Campus
## Lake Mary, Florida

**Admissions Office Contact** Remington College–Heathrow Campus, 7131 Business Park Lane, Lake Mary, FL 32746. *Toll-free phone:* 800-323-8122. *Website:* http://www.remingtoncollege.edu/.

# SABER College
## Miami, Florida

**Admissions Office Contact** SABER College, 3990 W. Flagler Street, Suite 103, Miami, FL 33134. *Website:* http://www.sabercollege.edu/.

# St. Johns River State College
## Palatka, Florida

**Director of Admissions** Dean of Admissions and Records, St. Johns River State College, 5001 Saint Johns Avenue, Palatka, FL 32177-3897. *Phone:* 386-312-4032. *Fax:* 386-312-4289. *Website:* http://www.sjrstate.edu/.

# Seminole State College of Florida
## Sanford, Florida

- **State and locally supported** primarily 2-year, founded 1966, part of Florida College System
- **Small-town** 200-acre campus with easy access to Orlando
- **Endowment** $24.6 million
- **Coed,** 17,706 undergraduate students, 35% full-time, 55% women, 45% men

**Undergraduates** 6,137 full-time, 11,569 part-time. Students come from 21 states and territories; 68 other countries; 3% are from out of state; 16% Black or African American, non-Hispanic/Latino; 24% Hispanic/Latino; 3% Asian, non-Hispanic/Latino; 0.3% Native Hawaiian or other Pacific Islander, non-Hispanic/Latino; 0.3% American Indian or Alaska Native, non-Hispanic/Latino; 3% Two or more races, non-Hispanic/Latino; 3% Race/ethnicity unknown; 2% international; 7% transferred in. *Retention:* 52% of full-time freshmen returned.
**Freshmen** *Admission:* 4,587 applied, 2,941 admitted, 2,670 enrolled.
**Faculty** *Total:* 798, 26% full-time, 22% with terminal degrees. *Student/faculty ratio:* 26:1.
**Majors** Accounting; administrative assistant and secretarial science; architectural engineering technology; automobile/automotive mechanics technology; banking and financial support services; building/construction finishing, management, and inspection related; business administration and

management; child development; civil engineering technology; computer and information sciences and support services related; computer and information sciences related; computer and information systems security; computer engineering related; computer engineering technology; computer graphics; computer hardware engineering; computer/information technology services administration related; computer programming; computer programming related; computer programming (specific applications); computer programming (vendor/product certification); computer software and media applications related; computer software engineering; computer systems networking and telecommunications; construction engineering technology; criminal justice/law enforcement administration; data entry/microcomputer applications; data entry/microcomputer applications related; data modeling/warehousing and database administration; data processing and data processing technology; drafting and design technology; electrical, electronic and communications engineering technology; emergency medical technology (EMT paramedic); finance; fire science/firefighting; industrial technology; information science/studies; information technology; interior design; legal assistant/paralegal; liberal arts and sciences/liberal studies; marketing/marketing management; network and system administration; physical therapy; registered nursing/registered nurse; respiratory care therapy; telecommunications technology; web/multimedia management and webmaster; web page, digital/multimedia and information resources design; word processing.

**Academics** *Calendar:* semesters. *Degrees:* certificates, diplomas, associate, bachelor's, and postbachelor's certificates. *Special study options:* academic remediation for entering students, accelerated degree program, adult/continuing education programs, advanced placement credit, cooperative education, distance learning, double majors, English as a second language, external degree program, honors programs, independent study, internships, part-time degree program, services for LD students, study abroad, summer session for credit. *ROTC:* Army (b).

**Library** Seminole State Library at Sanford Lake Mary plus 3 others. *Books:* 67,023 (physical), 145,374 (digital/electronic); *Serial titles:* 520 (physical), 18,003 (digital/electronic); *Databases:* 130. Weekly public service hours: 60; students can reserve study rooms.

**Student Life** *Housing:* college housing not available. *Activities and Organizations:* drama/theater group, student-run newspaper, choral group, Phi Beta Lambda, Phi Theta Kappa, Student Government Association, Sigma Phi Gamma, Hispanic Student Association. *Campus security:* 24-hour emergency response devices and patrols, late-night transport/escort service. *Student services:* personal/psychological counseling, veterans affairs office.

**Athletics** Member NJCAA. *Intercollegiate sports:* baseball M(s), golf W(s), softball W(s).

**Costs (2018–19)** *Tuition:* state resident $3131 full-time, $104 per credit hour part-time; nonresident $12,739 full-time, $382 per credit hour part-time. Full-time tuition and fees vary according to degree level. Part-time tuition and fees vary according to degree level. *Payment plan:* deferred payment. *Waivers:* senior citizens and employees or children of employees.

**Applying** *Options:* electronic application, early admission, deferred entrance. *Required:* high school transcript, minimum 2.0 GPA. *Application deadlines:* rolling (freshmen), rolling (transfers). *Notification:* continuous (freshmen), continuous (transfers).

**Admissions Office Contact** Seminole State College of Florida, 100 Weldon Boulevard, Sanford, FL 32773-6199.
*Website:* http://www.seminolestate.edu/.

## Southeastern College–West Palm Beach
### West Palm Beach, Florida

- **Proprietary** 2-year, founded 1988
- **Urban** campus
- **Coed,** 558 undergraduate students, 48% full-time, 83% women, 17% men

**Undergraduates** 269 full-time, 289 part-time. Students come from 6 states and territories; 2% are from out of state; 36% Black or African American, non-Hispanic/Latino; 36% Hispanic/Latino; 2% Asian, non-Hispanic/Latino; 0.2% American Indian or Alaska Native, non-Hispanic/Latino; 1% Two or more races, non-Hispanic/Latino; 7% Race/ethnicity unknown.

**Freshmen** *Admission:* 429 enrolled.

**Majors** Aesthetician/esthetician and skin care; business, management, and marketing related; computer and information sciences and support services related; computer systems networking and telecommunications; emergency medical technology (EMT paramedic); health professions related; licensed practical/vocational nurse training; massage therapy; medical/clinical assistant; medical insurance coding; medical insurance/medical billing; pharmacy technician; surgical technology.

**Academics** *Degree:* certificates, diplomas, and associate. *Special study options:* accelerated degree program, adult/continuing education programs, advanced placement credit, cooperative education, distance learning, English as a second language, internships, off-campus study, part-time degree program, services for LD students, summer session for credit.

**Library** Southeastern College Library. *Books:* 1,728 (physical); *Serial titles:* 26 (physical); *Databases:* 5. Weekly public service hours: 50.

**Student Life** *Housing:* college housing not available. *Campus security:* 24-hour patrols, late-night transport/escort service.

**Standardized Tests** *Required:* Wonderlic Assessment, TEAS (for admission).

**Costs (2018–19)** *Tuition:* $18,224 full-time, $621 per credit hour part-time. Full-time tuition and fees vary according to course load and program. Part-time tuition and fees vary according to course load and program. *Required fees:* $1500 full-time.

**Applying** *Application fee:* $55. *Required:* high school transcript, interview. *Required for some:* essay or personal statement, letters of recommendation. *Application deadlines:* rolling (freshmen), rolling (transfers), rolling (early action). *Early decision deadline:* rolling (for plan 1), rolling (for plan 2). *Notification:* continuous (freshmen), continuous (transfers), rolling (early decision plan 1), rolling (early decision plan 2), rolling (early action).

**Freshman Application Contact** Admissions Office, Southeastern College–West Palm Beach, 1756 North Congress Avenue, West Palm Beach, FL 33409. *Website:* http://www.sec.edu/.

## Southern Technical College
### Orlando, Florida

**Freshman Application Contact** Mr. Robinson Elie, Director of Admissions, Southern Technical College, 1485 Florida Mall Avenue, Orlando, FL 32809. *Phone:* 407-438-6000. *Toll-free phone:* 877-347-5492. *E-mail:* relie@southerntech.edu. *Website:* http://www.southerntech.edu/.

## Southern Technical College
### Tampa, Florida

**Director of Admissions** Admissions, Southern Technical College, 3910 Riga Boulevard, Tampa, FL 33619. *Phone:* 813-630-4401. *Toll-free phone:* 877-347-5492. *Website:* http://www.southerntech.edu/locations/tampa/.

## South Florida State College
### Avon Park, Florida

- **State-supported** primarily 2-year, founded 1965, part of Florida State College System
- **Rural** 228-acre campus with easy access to Tampa, St. Petersburg, Orlando
- **Endowment** $6.2 million
- **Coed,** 2,885 undergraduate students, 34% full-time, 64% women, 36% men

**Undergraduates** 975 full-time, 1,910 part-time. 3% are from out of state; 11% Black or African American, non-Hispanic/Latino; 37% Hispanic/Latino; 2% Asian, non-Hispanic/Latino; 0.3% Native Hawaiian or other Pacific Islander, non-Hispanic/Latino; 0.2% American Indian or Alaska Native, non-Hispanic/Latino; 2% Two or more races, non-Hispanic/Latino; 2% Race/ethnicity unknown; 1% international; 4% transferred in.

**Freshmen** *Admission:* 673 applied, 413 enrolled. *Average high school GPA:* 3.1.

**Faculty** *Total:* 156, 38% full-time, 16% with terminal degrees. *Student/faculty ratio:* 16:1.

**Majors** Business administration, management and operations related; computer engineering technology; computer programming; criminal justice/law enforcement administration; dental hygiene; elementary education; emergency medical technology (EMT paramedic); engineering technology; fire prevention and safety technology; health teacher education; horticultural science; landscaping and groundskeeping; liberal arts and sciences and humanities related; medical radiologic technology; network and system administration; office management; operations management; registered nursing/registered nurse; transportation/mobility management.

**Academics** *Calendar:* semesters. *Degrees:* certificates, diplomas, associate, and bachelor's. *Special study options:* academic remediation for entering students, adult/continuing education programs, advanced placement credit, cooperative education, distance learning, English as a second language, independent study, internships, part-time degree program, services for LD students, summer session for credit.

**Library** Library Services.

**Student Life** *Housing Options:* Campus housing is provided by a third party. *Activities and Organizations:* Phi Theta Kappa, Phi Beta Lambda, Art Club, Anime and Gaming Club, Basketball Club. *Campus security:* 24-hour emergency response devices and patrols, late-night transport/escort service. *Student services:* personal/psychological counseling.

**Athletics** Member NJCAA. *Intercollegiate sports:* baseball M(s), cross-country running W(s), softball W(s), volleyball W(s). *Intramural sports:* basketball M(c)/W(c), soccer M(c)/W(c).

Costs (2018–19) *One-time required fee:* $15. *Tuition:* state resident $2593 full-time, $105 per credit hour part-time; nonresident $9722 full-time, $394 per credit hour part-time. Full-time tuition and fees vary according to course level, course load, degree level, and program. Part-time tuition and fees vary according to course level, course load, degree level, and program. *Room and board:* $6040; room only: $2040. *Payment plan:* installment. *Waivers:* employees or children of employees.

Financial Aid *Average need-based gift aid:* $4666. *Average indebtedness upon graduation:* $3083.

Applying *Options:* electronic application, early admission, deferred entrance. *Application fee:* $15. *Required:* high school transcript. *Application deadline:* rolling (freshmen). *Notification:* continuous (freshmen).

Freshman Application Contact Ms. Brenda Desantiago, Admissions, South Florida State College, 600 West College Drive, Avon Park, FL 33825. *Phone:* 863-784-7416.

*Website:* http://www.southflorida.edu/.

## Sullivan and Cogliano Training Center
### Miami Gardens, Florida

Admissions Office Contact Sullivan and Cogliano Training Center, 4760 North West 167th Street, Miami Gardens, FL 33014. *Website:* http://www.sctrain.edu/.

## Tallahassee Community College
### Tallahassee, Florida

- **State and locally supported** primarily 2-year, founded 1966, part of Florida College System
- **Suburban** 214-acre campus
- **Endowment** $9.3 million
- **Coed**, 11,782 undergraduate students, 49% full-time, 54% women, 46% men

Undergraduates 5,830 full-time, 5,952 part-time. Students come from 15 states and territories; 78 other countries; 6% are from out of state; 30% Black or African American, non-Hispanic/Latino; 13% Hispanic/Latino; 2% Asian, non-Hispanic/Latino; 0.1% Native Hawaiian or other Pacific Islander, non-Hispanic/Latino; 0.3% American Indian or Alaska Native, non-Hispanic/Latino; 3% Two or more races, non-Hispanic/Latino; 3% Race/ethnicity unknown; 1% international; 6% transferred in. *Retention:* 56% of full-time freshmen returned.

Freshmen *Admission:* 2,562 admitted, 2,510 enrolled.

Faculty *Total:* 724, 24% full-time, 69% with terminal degrees. *Student/faculty ratio:* 22:1.

Majors Accounting technology and bookkeeping; CAD/CADD drafting/design technology; commercial and advertising art; computer graphics; computer programming; computer programming (specific applications); computer systems networking and telecommunications; construction engineering technology; corrections; criminal justice/law enforcement administration; criminal justice/police science; dental assisting; dental hygiene; diagnostic medical sonography and ultrasound technology; drafting and design technology; early childhood education; emergency medical technology (EMT paramedic); entrepreneurship; environmental science; fire science/firefighting; health information/medical records technology; homeland security related; information technology; legal assistant/paralegal; liberal arts and sciences/liberal studies; manufacturing engineering technology; masonry; medical radiologic technology; nursing assistant/aide and patient care assistant/aide; office management; pharmacy technician; physical fitness technician; registered nursing/registered nurse; respiratory care therapy; security and loss prevention; surgical technology; web page, digital/multimedia and information resources design; welding technology.

Academics *Calendar:* semesters. *Degrees:* certificates, associate, and bachelor's. *Special study options:* academic remediation for entering students, accelerated degree program, adult/continuing education programs, advanced placement credit, distance learning, English as a second language, external degree program, honors programs, independent study, off-campus study, part-time degree program, services for LD students, study abroad, summer session for credit. *ROTC:* Army (c), Navy (c), Air Force (c).

Library Tallahassee Community College Library. *Books:* 82,774 (physical), 53,129 (digital/electronic); *Serial titles:* 59 (physical), 42,687 (digital/electronic); *Databases:* 105. Weekly public service hours: 68; students can reserve study rooms.

Student Life *Housing:* college housing not available. *Activities and Organizations:* drama/theater group, student-run newspaper, choral group, Student Government Association, International Student Organization, Phi Theta Kappa, Model United Nations, Honors Council. *Campus security:* 24-hour emergency response devices and patrols, late-night transport/escort service. *Student services:* personal/psychological counseling, veterans affairs office.

Athletics Member NJCAA. *Intercollegiate sports:* baseball M(s), basketball M(s)/W(s), softball W(s). *Intramural sports:* basketball M/W, football M/W, soccer M/W, softball M/W, volleyball M/W.

Costs (2018–19) *Tuition:* state resident $2002 full-time, $101 per credit hour part-time; nonresident $7982 full-time, $387 per credit hour part-time. Full-time tuition and fees vary according to course load. Part-time tuition and fees vary according to course load. *Required fees:* $24 full-time, $24 per year part-time. *Payment plans:* installment, deferred payment. *Waivers:* employees or children of employees.

Financial Aid Of all full-time matriculated undergraduates who enrolled in 2016, 3,920 applied for aid, 2,778 were judged to have need. 110 Federal Work-Study jobs (averaging $2217). *Average financial aid package:* $3840. *Average need-based gift aid:* $3656.

Applying *Options:* electronic application, early admission, deferred entrance. *Required:* high school transcript. *Application deadlines:* 8/1 (freshmen), 8/1 (transfers).

Freshman Application Contact Student Success Center, Tallahassee Community College, 444 Appleyard Drive, Tallahassee, FL 32304-2895. *Phone:* 850-201-8555. *E-mail:* admissions@tcc.fl.edu. *Website:* http://www.tcc.fl.edu/.

## Ultimate Medical Academy Clearwater
### Clearwater, Florida

- **Independent** 2-year, founded 1994
- **Urban** campus with easy access to Tampa
- **Coed**

Undergraduates 247 full-time. 44% Black or African American, non-Hispanic/Latino; 11% Hispanic/Latino; 0.7% Asian, non-Hispanic/Latino; 1% American Indian or Alaska Native, non-Hispanic/Latino; 3% Two or more races, non-Hispanic/Latino; 9% Race/ethnicity unknown.

Academics *Calendar:* continuous. *Degree:* diplomas and associate. *Special study options:* distance learning, part-time degree program, services for LD students.

Applying *Required:* high school transcript.

Freshman Application Contact Ultimate Medical Academy Clearwater, 1255 Cleveland Street, Clearwater, FL 33755. *Toll-free phone:* 888-205-2510. *Website:* http://www.ultimatemedical.edu/.

## Ultimate Medical Academy Online
### Tampa, Florida

- **Independent** 2-year
- **Urban** campus
- **Coed**

Undergraduates 13,017 full-time, 3,394 part-time. Students come from 50 states and territories; 54% Black or African American, non-Hispanic/Latino; 8% Hispanic/Latino; 0.5% Asian, non-Hispanic/Latino; 0.4% Native Hawaiian or other Pacific Islander, non-Hispanic/Latino; 1% American Indian or Alaska Native, non-Hispanic/Latino; 2% Two or more races, non-Hispanic/Latino; 1% Race/ethnicity unknown. *Retention:* 80% of full-time freshmen returned.

Academics *Calendar:* continuous. *Degree:* diplomas and associate. *Special study options:* distance learning, part-time degree program, services for LD students.

Applying *Options:* electronic application. *Required:* high school transcript.

Freshman Application Contact Online Admissions Department, Ultimate Medical Academy Online, 3101 West Dr. Martin Luther King Jr. Boulevard, Tampa, FL 33607. *Phone:* 888-209-8848. *Toll-free phone:* 888-205-2510. *E-mail:* onlineadmissions@ultimatemedical.edu. *Website:* http://www.ultimatemedical.edu/.

## Universal Career School
### Sweetwater, Florida

Admissions Office Contact Universal Career School, 10720 W. Flagler Street, Suite 21, Sweetwater, FL 33174. *Website:* http://www.ucs.edu/.

## Virginia College in Fort Pierce
### Fort Pierce, Florida

Admissions Office Contact Virginia College in Fort Pierce, 2810 South Federal Highway, Fort Pierce, FL 34982-6331. *Website:* http://www.vc.edu/.

## Virginia College in Jacksonville
### Jacksonville, Florida

Admissions Office Contact Virginia College in Jacksonville, 5940 Beach Boulevard, Jacksonville, FL 32207. *Website:* http://www.vc.edu/.

# Virginia College in Pensacola
## Pensacola, Florida

**Admissions Office Contact** Virginia College in Pensacola, 312 East Nine Mile Road, Suite 34, Pensacola, FL 32514. *Website:* http://www.vc.edu/.

# WyoTech Daytona
## Ormond Beach, Florida

**Admissions Office Contact** WyoTech Daytona, 470 Destination Daytona Lane, Ormond Beach, FL 32174. *Toll-free phone:* 800-881-2AMI. *Website:* http://www.wyotech.edu/.

# GEORGIA

## Albany Technical College
### Albany, Georgia

- **State-supported** 2-year, founded 1961, part of Technical College System of Georgia
- **Coed**

**Undergraduates** 1,401 full-time, 1,850 part-time. 0.7% are from out of state; 79% Black or African American, non-Hispanic/Latino; 1% Hispanic/Latino; 0.4% Asian, non-Hispanic/Latino; 0.1% American Indian or Alaska Native, non-Hispanic/Latino; 0.9% Two or more races, non-Hispanic/Latino. *Retention:* 52% of full-time freshmen returned.
**Academics** *Calendar:* quarters. *Degree:* certificates, diplomas, and associate. *Special study options:* distance learning.
**Library** Albany Technical College Library and Media Center.
**Costs (2017–18)** *Tuition:* state resident $89 per credit hour part-time; nonresident $178 per credit hour part-time.
**Applying** *Options:* early admission. *Application fee:* $25. *Required:* high school transcript.
**Freshman Application Contact** Albany Technical College, 1704 South Slappey Boulevard, Albany, GA 31701. *Phone:* 229-430-3520. *Toll-free phone:* 877-261-3113. *Website:* http://www.albanytech.edu/.

## Andrew College
### Cuthbert, Georgia

**Freshman Application Contact** Ms. Bridget Kurkowski, Director of Admission, Andrew College, 413 College Street, Cuthbert, GA 39840. *Phone:* 229-732-5986. *Toll-free phone:* 800-664-9250. *Fax:* 229-732-2176. *E-mail:* admissions@andrewcollege.edu. *Website:* http://www.andrewcollege.edu/.

## Athens Technical College
### Athens, Georgia

- **State-supported** 2-year, founded 1958, part of Technical College System of Georgia
- **Suburban** campus
- **Coed**

**Undergraduates** 1,036 full-time, 3,174 part-time. 0.4% are from out of state; 20% Black or African American, non-Hispanic/Latino; 7% Hispanic/Latino; 3% Asian, non-Hispanic/Latino; 0.1% Native Hawaiian or other Pacific Islander, non-Hispanic/Latino; 0.1% American Indian or Alaska Native, non-Hispanic/Latino; 0.4% Two or more races, non-Hispanic/Latino; 5% Race/ethnicity unknown. *Retention:* 63% of full-time freshmen returned.
**Academics** *Calendar:* quarters. *Degree:* certificates, diplomas, and associate. *Special study options:* distance learning.
**Costs (2017–18)** *Tuition:* state resident $89 per credit hour part-time; nonresident $178 per credit hour part-time.
**Financial Aid** Of all full-time matriculated undergraduates who enrolled in 2016, 34 Federal Work-Study jobs (averaging $3090).
**Applying** *Options:* early admission. *Application fee:* $25. *Required:* high school transcript.
**Freshman Application Contact** Athens Technical College, 800 US Highway 29 North, Athens, GA 30601-1500. *Phone:* 706-355-5008. *Website:* http://www.athenstech.edu/.

## Atlanta Metropolitan State College
### Atlanta, Georgia

**Freshman Application Contact** Ms. Audrey Reid, Director, Office of Admissions, Atlanta Metropolitan State College, 1630 Metropolitan Parkway, SW, Atlanta, GA 30310-4498. *Phone:* 404-756-4004. *Fax:* 404-756-4407. *E-mail:* admissions@atlm.edu. *Website:* http://www.atlm.edu/.

## Atlanta Technical College
### Atlanta, Georgia

- **State-supported** 2-year, founded 1945, part of Technical College System of Georgia
- **Coed**

**Undergraduates** 1,406 full-time, 2,369 part-time. 0.2% are from out of state; 91% Black or African American, non-Hispanic/Latino; 3% Hispanic/Latino; 1% Asian, non-Hispanic/Latino; 0.1% Native Hawaiian or other Pacific Islander, non-Hispanic/Latino; 0.1% American Indian or Alaska Native, non-Hispanic/Latino; 2% Two or more races, non-Hispanic/Latino; 0.2% Race/ethnicity unknown. *Retention:* 55% of full-time freshmen returned.
**Academics** *Calendar:* quarters. *Degree:* certificates, diplomas, and associate. *Special study options:* distance learning, study abroad.
**Costs (2017–18)** *Tuition:* state resident $89 per credit hour part-time; nonresident $178 per credit hour part-time.
**Applying** *Options:* early admission. *Application fee:* $25. *Required:* high school transcript.
**Freshman Application Contact** Atlanta Technical College, 1560 Metropolitan Parkway, SW, Atlanta, GA 30310. *Phone:* 404-225-4455. *Website:* http://www.atlantatech.edu/.

## Augusta Technical College
### Augusta, Georgia

- **State-supported** 2-year, founded 1961, part of Technical College System of Georgia
- **Urban** campus
- **Coed**

**Undergraduates** 1,721 full-time, 2,649 part-time. 5% are from out of state; 48% Black or African American, non-Hispanic/Latino; 4% Hispanic/Latino; 1% Asian, non-Hispanic/Latino; 0.1% Native Hawaiian or other Pacific Islander, non-Hispanic/Latino; 0.4% American Indian or Alaska Native, non-Hispanic/Latino; 3% Two or more races, non-Hispanic/Latino; 2% Race/ethnicity unknown. *Retention:* 57% of full-time freshmen returned.
**Academics** *Calendar:* quarters. *Degree:* certificates, diplomas, and associate. *Special study options:* distance learning.
**Library** Information Technology Center.
**Costs (2017–18)** *Tuition:* state resident $89 per credit hour part-time; nonresident $176 per credit hour part-time.
**Applying** *Options:* early admission. *Application fee:* $25. *Required:* high school transcript.
**Freshman Application Contact** Augusta Technical College, 3200 Augusta Tech Drive, Augusta, GA 30906. *Phone:* 706-771-4150. *Website:* http://www.augustatech.edu/.

## Brown College of Court Reporting
### Atlanta, Georgia

**Admissions Office Contact** Brown College of Court Reporting, 1900 Emery Street NW, Suite 200, Atlanta, GA 30318. *Website:* http://www.bccr.edu/.

## Central Georgia Technical College
### Warner Robins, Georgia

- **State-supported** 2-year, founded 1966, part of Technical College System of Georgia
- **Suburban** campus
- **Coed**

**Undergraduates** 2,380 full-time, 5,382 part-time. 1% are from out of state; 52% Black or African American, non-Hispanic/Latino; 3% Hispanic/Latino; 1% Asian, non-Hispanic/Latino; 0.1% Native Hawaiian or other Pacific Islander, non-Hispanic/Latino; 0.3% American Indian or Alaska Native, non-Hispanic/Latino; 1% Two or more races, non-Hispanic/Latino; 0.8% Race/ethnicity unknown. *Retention:* 51% of full-time freshmen returned.
**Academics** *Calendar:* quarters. *Degree:* certificates, diplomas, and associate. *Special study options:* distance learning.
**Costs (2017–18)** *Tuition:* state resident $89 per credit hour part-time; nonresident $178 per credit hour part-time.
**Financial Aid** Of all full-time matriculated undergraduates who enrolled in 2016, 175 Federal Work-Study jobs (averaging $2000). *Financial aid deadline:* 9/1.

Applying *Options:* early admission. *Application fee:* $25. *Required:* high school transcript.
**Freshman Application Contact** Central Georgia Technical College, 80 Cohen Walker Drive, Warner Robins, GA 31088. *Phone:* 770-531-6332. *Toll-free phone:* 866-430-0135. *Website:* http://www.centralgatech.edu/.

# Chattahoochee Technical College
## Marietta, Georgia

- **State-supported** 2-year, founded 1961, part of Technical College System of Georgia
- **Suburban** campus
- **Coed**

**Undergraduates** 2,813 full-time, 7,186 part-time. 0.2% are from out of state; 30% Black or African American, non-Hispanic/Latino; 12% Hispanic/Latino; 3% Asian, non-Hispanic/Latino; 0.1% Native Hawaiian or other Pacific Islander, non-Hispanic/Latino; 0.5% American Indian or Alaska Native, non-Hispanic/Latino; 2% Two or more races, non-Hispanic/Latino; 1% Race/ethnicity unknown. *Retention:* 52% of full-time freshmen returned.
**Academics** *Calendar:* quarters. *Degree:* certificates, diplomas, and associate. *Special study options:* distance learning.
**Costs (2017–18)** *Tuition:* state resident $89 per credit hour part-time; nonresident $178 per credit hour part-time.
**Financial Aid** Of all full-time matriculated undergraduates who enrolled in 2016, 40 Federal Work-Study jobs (averaging $2500).
**Applying** *Options:* early admission. *Application fee:* $25. *Required:* high school transcript.
**Freshman Application Contact** Chattahoochee Technical College, 980 South Cobb Drive, SE, Marietta, GA 30060. *Phone:* 770-757-3408. *Website:* http://www.chattahoocheetech.edu/.

# Coastal Pines Technical College
## Waycross, Georgia

- **State-supported** 2-year, part of Technical College System of Georgia
- **Small-town** campus
- **Coed**

**Undergraduates** 615 full-time, 2,160 part-time. 0.3% are from out of state; 27% Black or African American, non-Hispanic/Latino; 4% Hispanic/Latino; 1% Asian, non-Hispanic/Latino; 0.1% Native Hawaiian or other Pacific Islander, non-Hispanic/Latino; 0.3% American Indian or Alaska Native, non-Hispanic/Latino; 1% Two or more races, non-Hispanic/Latino; 0.3% Race/ethnicity unknown. *Retention:* 68% of full-time freshmen returned.
**Academics** *Calendar:* quarters. *Degree:* certificates, diplomas, and associate. *Special study options:* distance learning.
**Costs (2017–18)** *Tuition:* state resident $89 per credit hour part-time; nonresident $178 per credit hour part-time.
**Applying** *Options:* early admission. *Application fee:* $25. *Required:* high school transcript.
**Freshman Application Contact** Coastal Pines Technical College, 1701 Carswell Avenue, Waycross, GA 31503. *Phone:* 912-338-5251. *Toll-free phone:* 877-ED-AT-OTC. *Website:* http://www.coastalpines.edu/.

# Columbus Technical College
## Columbus, Georgia

- **State-supported** 2-year, founded 1961, part of Technical College System of Georgia
- **Urban** campus
- **Coed**

**Undergraduates** 910 full-time, 2,318 part-time. 13% are from out of state; 44% Black or African American, non-Hispanic/Latino; 6% Hispanic/Latino; 2% Asian, non-Hispanic/Latino; 0.3% Native Hawaiian or other Pacific Islander, non-Hispanic/Latino; 0.3% American Indian or Alaska Native, non-Hispanic/Latino; 3% Two or more races, non-Hispanic/Latino; 2% Race/ethnicity unknown. *Retention:* 53% of full-time freshmen returned.
**Academics** *Calendar:* quarters. *Degree:* certificates, diplomas, and associate. *Special study options:* distance learning.
**Library** Columbus Technical College Library.
**Costs (2017–18)** *Tuition:* state resident $89 per credit hour part-time; nonresident $178 per credit hour part-time.
**Financial Aid** Of all full-time matriculated undergraduates who enrolled in 2016, 6 Federal Work-Study jobs (averaging $2000).
**Applying** *Options:* early admission. *Application fee:* $25. *Required:* high school transcript.
**Freshman Application Contact** Columbus Technical College, 928 Manchester Expressway, Columbus, GA 31904-6572. *Phone:* 706-649-1901. *Website:* http://www.columbustech.edu/.

# East Georgia State College
## Swainsboro, Georgia

- **State-supported** primarily 2-year, founded 1973, part of University System of Georgia
- **Rural** 207-acre campus
- **Coed**

**Undergraduates** 2,308 full-time, 693 part-time. Students come from 5 states and territories; 1 other country; 0.2% are from out of state; 44% Black or African American, non-Hispanic/Latino; 4% Hispanic/Latino; 0.9% Asian, non-Hispanic/Latino; 0.1% Native Hawaiian or other Pacific Islander, non-Hispanic/Latino; 0.2% American Indian or Alaska Native, non-Hispanic/Latino; 3% Two or more races, non-Hispanic/Latino; 0.9% Race/ethnicity unknown; 0.3% international; 9% transferred in; 12% live on campus. *Retention:* 1% of full-time freshmen returned.
**Faculty** *Student/faculty ratio:* 26:1.
**Academics** *Calendar:* semesters. *Degrees:* certificates, associate, and bachelor's. *Special study options:* academic remediation for entering students, adult/continuing education programs, advanced placement credit, distance learning, honors programs, independent study, off-campus study, part-time degree program, services for LD students, study abroad, summer session for credit.
**Library** East Georgia College Library. Students can reserve study rooms.
**Student Life** *Campus security:* 24-hour patrols, late-night transport/escort service, controlled dormitory access.
**Athletics** Member NJCAA.
**Costs (2017–18)** *One-time required fee:* $35. *Tuition:* state resident $2726 full-time, $91 per credit hour part-time; nonresident $10,320 full-time, $344 per credit hour part-time. Full-time tuition and fees vary according to class time, course load, location, and student level. Part-time tuition and fees vary according to class time, course load, location, and student level. *Required fees:* $886 full-time, $443 per term part-time. *Room and board:* $8504; room only: $5960. Room and board charges vary according to location.
**Financial Aid** Of all full-time matriculated undergraduates who enrolled in 2016, 43 Federal Work-Study jobs (averaging $1560).
**Applying** *Options:* early admission, deferred entrance. *Application fee:* $20. *Required:* high school transcript.
**Freshman Application Contact** East Georgia State College, 131 College Circle, Swainsboro, GA 30401-2699. *Phone:* 478-289-2112. *Website:* http://www.ega.edu/.

# Fortis College
## Smyrna, Georgia

**Admissions Office Contact** Fortis College, 2140 South Cobb Drive, Smyrna, GA 30080. *Toll-free phone:* 855-4-FORTIS. *Website:* http://www.fortis.edu/.

# Georgia Highlands College
## Rome, Georgia

- **State-supported** primarily 2-year, founded 1970, part of University System of Georgia
- **Suburban** 226-acre campus with easy access to Atlanta
- **Endowment** $39,054
- **Coed,** 6,003 undergraduate students, 47% full-time, 62% women, 38% men

**Undergraduates** 2,828 full-time, 3,175 part-time. Students come from 23 states and territories; 1% are from out of state; 16% Black or African American, non-Hispanic/Latino; 14% Hispanic/Latino; 2% Asian, non-Hispanic/Latino; 0.1% Native Hawaiian or other Pacific Islander, non-Hispanic/Latino; 0.2% American Indian or Alaska Native, non-Hispanic/Latino; 3% Two or more races, non-Hispanic/Latino; 0.1% Race/ethnicity unknown; 6% transferred in. *Retention:* 67% of full-time freshmen returned.
**Freshmen** *Admission:* 1,374 enrolled. *Average high school GPA:* 3.0.
**Faculty** *Total:* 277, 47% full-time, 25% with terminal degrees. *Student/faculty ratio:* 21:1.
**Majors** Dental hygiene; health/health-care administration; human services; liberal arts and sciences and humanities related; logistics, materials, and supply chain management; registered nursing/registered nurse.
**Academics** *Calendar:* semesters. *Degrees:* associate and bachelor's. *Special study options:* academic remediation for entering students, advanced placement credit, cooperative education, distance learning, double majors, honors programs, independent study, part-time degree program, services for LD students, study abroad, summer session for credit.
**Library** Georgia Highlands College Library–Floyd Campus plus 4 others. *Books:* 79,592 (physical), 178,561 (digital/electronic); *Serial titles:* 48 (physical), 4,380 (digital/electronic); *Databases:* 382. Weekly public service hours: 58; students can reserve study rooms.

**Student Life** *Housing:* college housing not available. *Activities and Organizations:* student-run newspaper, Association of Nursing Students, Green Highlands, Brother 2 Brother, Student Government Association, Phi Theta Kappa. *Campus security:* 24-hour emergency response devices and patrols, emergency phone/email alert system. *Student services:* personal/psychological counseling, veterans affairs office.

**Athletics** Member NJCAA. *Intercollegiate sports:* baseball M(s), basketball M(s)/W(s), softball W(s). *Intramural sports:* basketball M/W, cheerleading M/W, football M/W, golf M/W, skiing (downhill) M/W, table tennis M/W, tennis M/W, ultimate Frisbee M/W, volleyball M/W, weight lifting M/W.

**Costs (2018–19)** *Tuition:* state resident $2780 full-time, $93 per credit hour part-time; nonresident $10,526 full-time, $351 per credit hour part-time. Full-time tuition and fees vary according to course load and location. Part-time tuition and fees vary according to course load and location. *Required fees:* $1064 full-time, $412 per term part-time. *Payment plan:* installment. *Waivers:* senior citizens.

**Financial Aid** Of all full-time matriculated undergraduates who enrolled in 2016, 50 Federal Work-Study jobs (averaging $3500).

**Applying** *Options:* electronic application, deferred entrance. *Application fee:* $30. *Required:* high school transcript, minimum 2.0 GPA. *Application deadlines:* 7/15 (freshmen), 7/15 (transfers). *Notification:* continuous (freshmen), continuous (transfers).

**Freshman Application Contact** Charlene Graham, Assistant Director of Admissions, Georgia Highlands College, 3175 Cedartown Highway, Rome, GA 30161. *Phone:* 706-295-6339. *Toll-free phone:* 800-332-2406. *Fax:* 706-295-6341. *E-mail:* cgraham@highlands.edu. *Website:* http://www.highlands.edu/.

# Georgia Military College
## Milledgeville, Georgia

- **Public** primarily 2-year, founded 1879
- **Small-town** campus
- **Endowment** $1.5 million
- **Coed,** 8,595 undergraduate students, 50% full-time, 61% women, 39% men

**Undergraduates** 4,270 full-time, 4,325 part-time. Students come from 36 states and territories; 12 other countries; 4% are from out of state; 42% Black or African American, non-Hispanic/Latino; 7% Hispanic/Latino; 2% Asian, non-Hispanic/Latino; 0.4% Native Hawaiian or other Pacific Islander, non-Hispanic/Latino; 3% American Indian or Alaska Native, non-Hispanic/Latino; 0.2% Two or more races, non-Hispanic/Latino; 2% Race/ethnicity unknown; 0.2% international; 29% transferred in; 3% live on campus. *Retention:* 46% of full-time freshmen returned.

**Freshmen** *Admission:* 3,475 applied, 2,717 admitted, 1,492 enrolled.

**Faculty** *Total:* 890, 14% full-time. *Student/faculty ratio:* 15:1.

**Majors** Biology/biological sciences; business administration and management; business/commerce; computer and information systems security; computer science; criminal justice/law enforcement administration; early childhood education; English; general studies; health services/allied health/health sciences; health teacher education; history; homeland security; information technology; legal assistant/paralegal; logistics, materials, and supply chain management; management information systems; mass communication/media; mathematics; middle school education; political science and government; prenursing studies; psychology; secondary education; social work; sociology.

**Academics** *Calendar:* quarters. *Degrees:* associate and bachelor's. *Special study options:* academic remediation for entering students, advanced placement credit, cooperative education, distance learning, double majors, independent study, off-campus study, part-time degree program, services for LD students, student-designed majors, study abroad, summer session for credit. *ROTC:* Army (b).

**Library** Sibley Cone Library plus 1 other. *Books:* 38,125 (physical), 57,769 (digital/electronic); *Serial titles:* 52 (physical); *Databases:* 331. Weekly public service hours: 68.

**Student Life** *Housing:* on-campus residence required through sophomore year. *Options:* coed. Campus housing is university owned. Freshman campus housing is guaranteed. *Activities and Organizations:* drama/theater group, student-run newspaper, choral group, Student Government Association, Alpha Phi Omega National Service Fraternity, Phi Theta Kappa, Drama Club, Biology Club. *Campus security:* 24-hour emergency response devices and patrols, controlled dormitory access. *Student services:* health clinic, veterans affairs office.

**Athletics** Member NJCAA. *Intercollegiate sports:* cross-country running M/W, football M(s), golf M/W, riflery M/W, soccer M(s)/W(s), softball W(s). *Intramural sports:* badminton M/W, basketball M/W, golf M/W, softball M/W, tennis M/W, volleyball M/W.

**Costs (2018–19)** *Tuition:* state resident $5445 full-time, $121 per credit hour part-time; nonresident $5445 full-time, $121 per credit hour part-time. Full-time tuition and fees vary according to location. Part-time tuition and fees vary

according to location. *Required fees:* $679 full-time, $15 per credit hour part-time. *Room and board:* $7500; room only: $3150. Room and board charges vary according to location. *Waivers:* senior citizens and employees or children of employees.

**Financial Aid** Of all full-time matriculated undergraduates who enrolled in 2012, 6,554 applied for aid, 6,132 were judged to have need, 282 had their need fully met. 121 Federal Work-Study jobs (averaging $1614). In 2012, 61 non-need-based awards were made. *Average percent of need met:* 47%. *Average financial aid package:* $9567. *Average need-based loan:* $3189. *Average need-based gift aid:* $4626. *Average non-need-based aid:* $2226.

**Applying** *Options:* electronic application, early admission, deferred entrance. *Application fee:* $35. *Required for some:* high school transcript, interview. *Application deadlines:* rolling (freshmen), rolling (transfers).

**Freshman Application Contact** Georgia Military College, 201 East Greene Street, Old Capitol Building, Milledgeville, GA 31061-3398. *Phone:* 478-387-4890. *Toll-free phone:* 800-342-0413. *Website:* http://www.gmc.edu/.

# Georgia Northwestern Technical College
## Rome, Georgia

- **State-supported** 2-year, founded 1962, part of Technical College System of Georgia
- **Small-town** campus with easy access to Atlanta
- **Coed**

**Undergraduates** 1,809 full-time, 4,207 part-time. 1% are from out of state; 10% Black or African American, non-Hispanic/Latino; 13% Hispanic/Latino; 0.6% Asian, non-Hispanic/Latino; 0.2% American Indian or Alaska Native, non-Hispanic/Latino; 2% Two or more races, non-Hispanic/Latino. *Retention:* 64% of full-time freshmen returned.

**Academics** *Calendar:* quarters. *Degree:* certificates, diplomas, and associate. *Special study options:* distance learning.

**Costs (2017–18)** *Tuition:* state resident $89 per credit hour part-time; nonresident $178 per credit hour part-time.

**Applying** *Options:* early admission. *Application fee:* $25. *Required:* high school transcript.

**Freshman Application Contact** Georgia Northwestern Technical College, One Maurice Culberson Drive, Rome, GA 30161. *Phone:* 706-295-6933. *Toll-free phone:* 866-983-GNTC. *Website:* http://www.gntc.edu/.

# Georgia Piedmont Technical College
## Clarkston, Georgia

- **State-supported** 2-year, founded 1961, part of Technical College System of Georgia
- **Suburban** campus
- **Coed**

**Undergraduates** 897 full-time, 3,206 part-time. 0.1% are from out of state; 82% Black or African American, non-Hispanic/Latino; 3% Hispanic/Latino; 2% Asian, non-Hispanic/Latino; 0.1% Native Hawaiian or other Pacific Islander, non-Hispanic/Latino; 0.1% American Indian or Alaska Native, non-Hispanic/Latino; 2% Two or more races, non-Hispanic/Latino; 0.5% Race/ethnicity unknown. *Retention:* 59% of full-time freshmen returned.

**Academics** *Calendar:* quarters. *Degree:* certificates, diplomas, and associate. *Special study options:* distance learning.

**Costs (2017–18)** *Tuition:* state resident $89 per credit hour part-time; nonresident $178 per credit hour part-time.

**Financial Aid** Of all full-time matriculated undergraduates who enrolled in 2010, 7,200 applied for aid, 7,100 were judged to have need. 145 Federal Work-Study jobs (averaging $4000). *Average financial aid package:* $4500. *Average need-based gift aid:* $4500.

**Applying** *Options:* early admission. *Application fee:* $25. *Required:* high school transcript.

**Freshman Application Contact** Georgia Piedmont Technical College, 495 North Indian Creek Drive, Clarkston, GA 30021-2397. *Phone:* 404-297-9522 Ext. 1229. *Website:* http://www.gptc.edu/.

# Gordon State College
## Barnesville, Georgia

- **State-supported** primarily 2-year, founded 1852, part of University System of Georgia
- **Small-town** 235-acre campus with easy access to Atlanta
- **Coed,** 3,986 undergraduate students
- 83% of applicants were admitted

**Undergraduates** 0.8% are from out of state; 38% Black or African American, non-Hispanic/Latino; 4% Hispanic/Latino; 1% Asian, non-Hispanic/Latino;

0.1% American Indian or Alaska Native, non-Hispanic/Latino; 4% Two or more races, non-Hispanic/Latino; 0.5% Race/ethnicity unknown.

**Freshmen** *Admission:* 2,982 applied, 2,475 admitted.

**Faculty** *Total:* 197, 62% full-time. *Student/faculty ratio:* 21:1.

**Majors** Art; astronomy; biological and biomedical sciences related; biology teacher education; business administration and management; chemistry; computer science; criminal justice/safety; dental services and allied professions related; dramatic/theater arts; early childhood education; elementary education; engineering; English; English as a second/foreign language (teaching); English/language arts teacher education; environmental science; foreign languages and literatures; forestry; general studies; health and physical education/fitness; health information/medical records administration; health/medical preparatory programs related; history; history teacher education; human services; information technology; liberal arts and sciences/liberal studies; mass communication/media; mathematics; mathematics teacher education; middle school education; music; physics; political science and government; pre-engineering; pre-occupational therapy; pre-pharmacy studies; pre-physical therapy; psychology; radiologic technology/science; registered nursing/registered nurse; secondary education; social work; sociology; visual and performing arts.

**Academics** *Calendar:* semesters. *Degrees:* associate and bachelor's. *Special study options:* academic remediation for entering students, accelerated degree program, adult/continuing education programs, advanced placement credit, cooperative education, distance learning, double majors, honors programs, internships, off-campus study, part-time degree program, services for LD students, study abroad, summer session for credit.

**Library** Dorothy W. Hightower Collaborative Learning Center and Library. *Books:* 103,423 (physical), 35,999 (digital/electronic); *Serial titles:* 401 (physical), 87,985 (digital/electronic); *Databases:* 325. Weekly public service hours: 73.

**Student Life** *Housing:* on-campus residence required for freshman year. *Options:* coed. Campus housing is university owned. Freshman applicants given priority for college housing. *Activities and Organizations:* drama/theater group, student-run newspaper, choral group, Campus Activity Board, Student Government Association, Earth Wind Fire (science club), Student African American Brotherhood (SAAB), Swazi Step Team. *Campus security:* 24-hour emergency response devices and patrols, student patrols, controlled dormitory access, Resident Assistants and Resident Directors in housing, parking patrol. *Student services:* health clinic, personal/psychological counseling, veterans affairs office.

**Athletics** Member NJCAA. *Intercollegiate sports:* baseball M, basketball M, soccer M/W, softball W.

**Standardized Tests** *Required:* SAT or ACT (for admission).

**Costs (2018–19)** *Tuition:* state resident $3126 full-time, $104 per credit hour part-time; nonresident $11,548 full-time, $385 per credit hour part-time. *Required fees:* $1166 full-time, $550 per term part-time. *Room and board:* $8408. Room and board charges vary according to board plan and housing facility. *Payment plan:* installment.

**Financial Aid** Of all full-time matriculated undergraduates who enrolled in 2016, 75 Federal Work-Study jobs (averaging $1850).

**Applying** *Options:* electronic application, early admission. *Application fee:* $30. *Required:* high school transcript. *Application deadlines:* rolling (freshmen), rolling (transfers).

**Freshman Application Contact** Gordon State College, 419 College Drive, Barnesville, GA 30204-1762. *Phone:* 678-359-5021. *Toll-free phone:* 800-282-6504.

*Website:* http://www.gordonstate.edu/.

## Gupton-Jones College of Funeral Service
### Decatur, Georgia

- **Independent** 2-year, founded 1920, part of Pierce Mortuary Colleges, Inc.
- **Suburban** 3-acre campus with easy access to Atlanta
- **Coed**, 232 undergraduate students, 100% full-time, 59% women, 41% men

**Undergraduates** 232 full-time. Students come from 15 states and territories; 2 other countries; 86% are from out of state; 70% Black or African American, non-Hispanic/Latino; 0.9% Two or more races, non-Hispanic/Latino; 13% transferred in. *Retention:* 84% of full-time freshmen returned.

**Freshmen** *Admission:* 232 admitted, 232 enrolled. *Average high school GPA:* 2.0.

**Faculty** *Total:* 9, 78% full-time. *Student/faculty ratio:* 28:1.

**Majors** Mortuary science and embalming.

**Academics** *Calendar:* quarters. *Degree:* associate. *Special study options:* accelerated degree program, advanced placement credit, services for LD students.

**Library** Russell Millison Library. *Books:* 4,000 (physical).

**Student Life** *Housing:* college housing not available. *Activities and Organizations:* Student Council, national fraternities. *Campus security:* 24-hour emergency response devices. *Student services:* veterans affairs office.

**Costs (2017–18)** *One-time required fee:* $50. *Tuition:* $23,400 full-time, $260 per quarter hour part-time. Full-time tuition and fees vary according to course load and program. Part-time tuition and fees vary according to course load and program. No tuition increase for student's term of enrollment. *Required fees:* $170 full-time. *Payment plan:* installment.

**Applying** *Options:* electronic application. *Application fee:* $50. *Required:* high school transcript, health questionnaire. *Application deadline:* rolling (freshmen).

**Freshman Application Contact** Gupton-Jones College of Funeral Service, 5141 Snapfinger Woods Drive, Decatur, GA 30035-4022. *Phone:* 770-593-2257. *Toll-free phone:* 800-848-5352.

*Website:* http://www.gupton-jones.edu/.

## Gwinnett College
### Lilburn, Georgia

**Admissions Office Contact** Gwinnett College, 4230 Lawrenceville Highway, Suite 11, Lilburn, GA 30047. *Website:* http://www.gwinnettcollege.edu/.

## Gwinnett College
### Marietta, Georgia

**Admissions Office Contact** Gwinnett College, 1130 Northchase Parkway, Suite 100, Marietta, GA 30067. *Website:* http://www.gwinnettcollege.edu/locations/marietta/.

## Gwinnett College
### Sandy Springs, Georgia

**Admissions Office Contact** Gwinnett College, 6690 Roswell Road NE, Suite 2200, Sandy Springs, GA 30328. *Website:* http://www.medtech-atlanta.com/sandy-springs-ga/.

## Gwinnett Technical College
### Lawrenceville, Georgia

- **State-supported** 2-year, founded 1984, part of Technical College System of Georgia
- **Suburban** 88-acre campus
- **Coed**

**Undergraduates** 1,636 full-time, 5,843 part-time. 0.2% are from out of state; 33% Black or African American, non-Hispanic/Latino; 15% Hispanic/Latino; 8% Asian, non-Hispanic/Latino; 0.2% Native Hawaiian or other Pacific Islander, non-Hispanic/Latino; 0.2% American Indian or Alaska Native, non-Hispanic/Latino; 4% Two or more races, non-Hispanic/Latino; 6% Race/ethnicity unknown. *Retention:* 56% of full-time freshmen returned.

**Academics** *Calendar:* semesters. *Degree:* certificates, diplomas, and associate. *Special study options:* distance learning, English as a second language, part-time degree program, services for LD students, summer session for credit.

**Library** Gwinnett Technical College Library plus 1 other.

**Student Life** *Campus security:* 24-hour emergency response devices and patrols.

**Costs (2017–18)** *Tuition:* state resident $89 per credit hour part-time; nonresident $178 per credit hour part-time.

**Financial Aid** Of all full-time matriculated undergraduates who enrolled in 2016, 20 Federal Work-Study jobs (averaging $2100).

**Applying** *Options:* electronic application, early admission. *Application fee:* $25. *Required:* high school transcript.

**Freshman Application Contact** Gwinnett Technical College, 5150 Sugarloaf Parkway, Lawrenceville, GA 30043-5702. *Phone:* 678-762-7580 Ext. 434. *Website:* http://www.gwinnetttech.edu/.

## Interactive College of Technology
### Chamblee, Georgia

**Freshman Application Contact** Director of Admissions, Interactive College of Technology, 5303 New Peachtree Road, Chamblee, GA 30341. *Phone:* 770-216-2960. *Toll-free phone:* 800-447-2011. *Fax:* 770-216-2988. *Website:* http://ict.edu/.

## Interactive College of Technology
### Gainesville, Georgia

**Freshman Application Contact** Interactive College of Technology, 2323 Browns Bridge Road, Gainesville, GA 30504. *Website:* http://ict.edu/.

## Interactive College of Technology
### Morrow, Georgia

**Admissions Office Contact** Interactive College of Technology, 1580 Southlake Parkway, Suite C, Morrow, GA 30260. *Website:* http://ict.edu/.

## Lanier Technical College
### Oakwood, Georgia

- **State-supported** 2-year, founded 1964, part of Technical College System of Georgia
- **Coed**

**Undergraduates** 1,034 full-time, 2,602 part-time. 0.1% are from out of state; 9% Black or African American, non-Hispanic/Latino; 16% Hispanic/Latino; 3% Asian, non-Hispanic/Latino; 0.3% Native Hawaiian or other Pacific Islander, non-Hispanic/Latino; 0.5% American Indian or Alaska Native, non-Hispanic/Latino; 2% Two or more races, non-Hispanic/Latino; 0.1% Race/ethnicity unknown. *Retention:* 60% of full-time freshmen returned.
**Academics** *Calendar:* quarters. *Degree:* certificates, diplomas, and associate. *Special study options:* distance learning.
**Costs (2017–18)** *Tuition:* state resident $89 per credit hour part-time; nonresident $178 per credit hour part-time.
**Applying** *Options:* early admission. *Application fee:* $25. *Required:* high school transcript.
**Freshman Application Contact** Lanier Technical College, 2990 Landrum Education Drive, PO Box 58, Oakwood, GA 30566. *Phone:* 770-531-6332. *Website:* http://www.laniertech.edu/.

## Lincoln College of Technology
### Marietta, Georgia

**Admissions Office Contact** Lincoln College of Technology, 2359 Windy Hill Road, Marietta, GA 30067. *Toll-free phone:* 844-215-1513. *Website:* http://www.lincolntech.edu/.

## Miller-Motte Technical College
### Augusta, Georgia

**Admissions Office Contact** Miller-Motte Technical College, 621 Frontage Road NW, Augusta, GA 30907. *Toll-free phone:* 800-705-9182. *Website:* http://www.miller-motte.edu/.

## Miller-Motte Technical College
### Columbus, Georgia

**Admissions Office Contact** Miller-Motte Technical College, 1800 Box Road, Columbus, GA 31907. *Toll-free phone:* 800-705-9182. *Website:* http://www.miller-motte.edu/.

## Miller-Motte Technical College
### Macon, Georgia

**Admissions Office Contact** Miller-Motte Technical College, 175 Tom Hill Sr. Boulevard, Macon, GA 31210. *Toll-free phone:* 800-705-9182. *Website:* http://www.miller-motte.edu/.

## North Georgia Technical College
### Clarkesville, Georgia

- **State-supported** 2-year, founded 1943, part of Technical College System of Georgia
- **Coed**

**Undergraduates** 918 full-time, 1,920 part-time. 0.7% are from out of state; 8% Black or African American, non-Hispanic/Latino; 5% Hispanic/Latino; 1% Asian, non-Hispanic/Latino; 0.1% Native Hawaiian or other Pacific Islander, non-Hispanic/Latino; 0.5% American Indian or Alaska Native, non-Hispanic/Latino; 2% Two or more races, non-Hispanic/Latino; 1% Race/ethnicity unknown. *Retention:* 61% of full-time freshmen returned.

**Academics** *Calendar:* quarters. *Degree:* certificates, diplomas, and associate. *Special study options:* distance learning.
**Costs (2017–18)** *Tuition:* state resident $89 per credit hour part-time; nonresident $178 per credit hour part-time.
**Applying** *Options:* early admission. *Application fee:* $25. *Required:* high school transcript.
**Freshman Application Contact** North Georgia Technical College, 1500 Georgia Highway 197, North, PO Box 65, Clarkesville, GA 30523. *Phone:* 706-754-7724. *Website:* http://www.northgatech.edu/.

## Oconee Fall Line Technical College
### Sandersville, Georgia

- **State-supported** 2-year, part of Technical College System of Georgia
- **Coed**

**Undergraduates** 362 full-time, 1,042 part-time. 45% Black or African American, non-Hispanic/Latino; 2% Hispanic/Latino; 0.5% Asian, non-Hispanic/Latino; 0.1% American Indian or Alaska Native, non-Hispanic/Latino; 2% Two or more races, non-Hispanic/Latino; 0.4% Race/ethnicity unknown. *Retention:* 52% of full-time freshmen returned.
**Academics** *Calendar:* quarters. *Degree:* certificates, diplomas, and associate. *Special study options:* distance learning.
**Costs (2017–18)** *Tuition:* state resident $89 per credit hour part-time; nonresident $178 per credit hour part-time.
**Applying** *Options:* early admission. *Application fee:* $25. *Required:* high school transcript.
**Freshman Application Contact** Oconee Fall Line Technical College, 1189 Deepstep Road, Sandersville, GA 31082. *Phone:* 478-553-2050. *Toll-free phone:* 877-399-8324. *Website:* http://www.oftc.edu/.

## Ogeechee Technical College
### Statesboro, Georgia

- **State-supported** 2-year, founded 1989, part of Technical College System of Georgia
- **Small-town** campus
- **Coed**

**Undergraduates** 732 full-time, 1,172 part-time. 0.9% are from out of state; 33% Black or African American, non-Hispanic/Latino; 4% Hispanic/Latino; 0.5% Asian, non-Hispanic/Latino; 0.2% Native Hawaiian or other Pacific Islander, non-Hispanic/Latino; 0.2% American Indian or Alaska Native, non-Hispanic/Latino; 2% Two or more races, non-Hispanic/Latino. *Retention:* 58% of full-time freshmen returned.
**Academics** *Calendar:* quarters. *Degree:* certificates, diplomas, and associate. *Special study options:* distance learning.
**Costs (2017–18)** *Tuition:* state resident $89 per credit hour part-time; nonresident $178 per credit hour part-time.
**Applying** *Options:* early admission. *Application fee:* $25. *Required:* high school transcript.
**Freshman Application Contact** Ogeechee Technical College, One Joe Kennedy Boulevard, Statesboro, GA 30458. *Phone:* 912-871-1600. *Toll-free phone:* 800-646-1316. *Website:* http://www.ogeecheetech.edu/.

## SAE Institute Atlanta
### Atlanta, Georgia

**Admissions Office Contact** SAE Institute Atlanta, 215 Peachtree Street NE, Atlanta, GA 30303. *Website:* http://www.sae.edu/.

## Savannah Technical College
### Savannah, Georgia

- **State-supported** 2-year, founded 1929, part of Technical College System of Georgia
- **Urban** campus
- **Coed**

**Undergraduates** 1,393 full-time, 2,545 part-time. 2% are from out of state; 45% Black or African American, non-Hispanic/Latino; 7% Hispanic/Latino; 3% Asian, non-Hispanic/Latino; 0.2% Native Hawaiian or other Pacific Islander, non-Hispanic/Latino; 0.5% American Indian or Alaska Native, non-Hispanic/Latino; 3% Two or more races, non-Hispanic/Latino. *Retention:* 60% of full-time freshmen returned.
**Academics** *Calendar:* quarters. *Degree:* certificates, diplomas, and associate. *Special study options:* distance learning.
**Costs (2017–18)** *Tuition:* state resident $89 per credit hour part-time; nonresident $178 per credit hour part-time.

**Applying** *Options:* early admission. *Application fee:* $25. *Required:* high school transcript.
**Freshman Application Contact** Savannah Technical College, 5717 White Bluff Road, Savannah, GA 31405. *Phone:* 912-443-5711. *Toll-free phone:* 800-769-6362. *Website:* http://www.savannahtech.edu/.

## Southeastern Technical College
### Vidalia, Georgia

- **State-supported** 2-year, founded 1989, part of Technical College System of Georgia
- **Coed**

**Undergraduates** 435 full-time, 1,128 part-time. 0.1% are from out of state; 27% Black or African American, non-Hispanic/Latino; 8% Hispanic/Latino; 0.2% Asian, non-Hispanic/Latino; 0.6% Two or more races, non-Hispanic/Latino. *Retention:* 53% of full-time freshmen returned.
**Academics** *Calendar:* quarters. *Degree:* certificates, diplomas, and associate. *Special study options:* distance learning.
**Costs (2017–18)** *Tuition:* state resident $89 per credit hour part-time; nonresident $178 per credit hour part-time.
**Applying** *Options:* early admission. *Application fee:* $25. *Required:* high school transcript.
**Freshman Application Contact** Southeastern Technical College, 3001 East First Street, Vidalia, GA 30474. *Phone:* 912-538-3121. *Website:* http://www.southeasterntech.edu/.

## Southern Crescent Technical College
### Griffin, Georgia

- **State-supported** 2-year, founded 1965, part of Technical College System of Georgia
- **Small-town** campus
- **Coed**

**Undergraduates** 1,601 full-time, 3,102 part-time. 0.1% are from out of state; 44% Black or African American, non-Hispanic/Latino; 5% Hispanic/Latino; 1% Asian, non-Hispanic/Latino; 0.2% American Indian or Alaska Native, non-Hispanic/Latino; 1% Two or more races, non-Hispanic/Latino; 0.9% Race/ethnicity unknown. *Retention:* 58% of full-time freshmen returned.
**Academics** *Calendar:* quarters. *Degree:* certificates, diplomas, and associate. *Special study options:* distance learning.
**Library** Griffin Technical College Library.
**Costs (2017–18)** *Tuition:* state resident $89 per credit hour part-time; nonresident $178 per credit hour part-time.
**Applying** *Options:* early admission. *Application fee:* $25. *Required:* high school transcript.
**Freshman Application Contact** Southern Crescent Technical College, 501 Varsity Road, Griffin, GA 30223. *Phone:* 770-646-6160. *Website:* http://www.sctech.edu/.

## Southern Regional Technical College
### Thomasville, Georgia

- **State-supported** 2-year, founded 1963, part of Technical College System of Georgia
- **Coed**

**Undergraduates** 1,164 full-time, 2,357 part-time. 1% are from out of state; 33% Black or African American, non-Hispanic/Latino; 6% Hispanic/Latino; 0.4% Asian, non-Hispanic/Latino; 0.3% American Indian or Alaska Native, non-Hispanic/Latino; 0.6% Two or more races, non-Hispanic/Latino; 1% Race/ethnicity unknown. *Retention:* 61% of full-time freshmen returned.
**Academics** *Calendar:* quarters. *Degree:* certificates, diplomas, and associate. *Special study options:* distance learning.
**Costs (2017–18)** *Tuition:* state resident $89 per credit hour part-time; nonresident $178 per credit hour part-time.
**Applying** *Options:* electronic application, early admission. *Application fee:* $25. *Required:* high school transcript.
**Freshman Application Contact** Southern Regional Technical College, 15689 US 19 North, Thomasville, GA 31792. *Phone:* 229-225-5089. *Website:* http://www.southwestgatech.edu/.

## South Georgia State College
### Douglas, Georgia

**Freshman Application Contact** South Georgia State College, 100 West College Park Drive, Douglas, GA 31533-5098. *Phone:* 912-260-4409. *Toll-free phone:* 800-342-6364. *Website:* http://www.sgc.edu/.

## South Georgia Technical College
### Americus, Georgia

- **State-supported** 2-year, founded 1948, part of Technical College System of Georgia
- **Coed**

**Undergraduates** 917 full-time, 912 part-time. 4% are from out of state; 54% Black or African American, non-Hispanic/Latino; 3% Hispanic/Latino; 0.5% Asian, non-Hispanic/Latino; 0.1% American Indian or Alaska Native, non-Hispanic/Latino; 0.5% Race/ethnicity unknown. *Retention:* 64% of full-time freshmen returned.
**Academics** *Calendar:* quarters. *Degree:* certificates, diplomas, and associate. *Special study options:* distance learning.
**Costs (2017–18)** *Tuition:* state resident $89 per credit hour part-time; nonresident $178 per credit hour part-time.
**Applying** *Options:* early admission. *Application fee:* $25. *Required:* high school transcript.
**Freshman Application Contact** South Georgia Technical College, 900 South Georgia Tech Parkway, Americus, GA 31709. *Phone:* 229-931-2299. *Website:* http://www.southgatech.edu/.

## Virginia College in Augusta
### Augusta, Georgia

**Admissions Office Contact** Virginia College in Augusta, 2807 Wylds Road Extension, Suite B, Augusta, GA 30909. *Website:* http://www.vc.edu/.

## Virginia College in Columbus
### Columbus, Georgia

**Admissions Office Contact** Virginia College in Columbus, 5601 Veterans Parkway, Columbus, GA 31904. *Website:* http://www.vc.edu/.

## Virginia College in Macon
### Macon, Georgia

**Admissions Office Contact** Virginia College in Macon, 1901 Paul Walsh Drive, Macon, GA 31206. *Website:* http://www.vc.edu/.

## Virginia College in Savannah
### Savannah, Georgia

**Admissions Office Contact** Virginia College in Savannah, 14045 Abercorn Street, Suite 1503, Savannah, GA 31419. *Website:* http://www.vc.edu/.

## West Georgia Technical College
### Waco, Georgia

- **State-supported** 2-year, founded 1966, part of Technical College System of Georgia
- **Coed**

**Undergraduates** 1,931 full-time, 4,812 part-time. 2% are from out of state; 32% Black or African American, non-Hispanic/Latino; 5% Hispanic/Latino; 1% Asian, non-Hispanic/Latino; 0.1% Native Hawaiian or other Pacific Islander, non-Hispanic/Latino; 0.4% American Indian or Alaska Native, non-Hispanic/Latino; 2% Two or more races, non-Hispanic/Latino; 0.6% Race/ethnicity unknown. *Retention:* 59% of full-time freshmen returned.
**Academics** *Calendar:* quarters. *Degree:* certificates, diplomas, and associate. *Special study options:* distance learning.
**Costs (2017–18)** *Tuition:* state resident $89 per credit hour part-time; nonresident $178 per credit hour part-time.
**Financial Aid** Of all full-time matriculated undergraduates who enrolled in 2016, 68 Federal Work-Study jobs (averaging $800).
**Applying** *Options:* early admission. *Application fee:* $25. *Required:* high school transcript.
**Freshman Application Contact** West Georgia Technical College, 176 Murphy Campus Boulevard, Waco, GA 30182. *Phone:* 770-537-5719. *Website:* http://www.westgatech.edu/.

## Wiregrass Georgia Technical College
### Valdosta, Georgia

- **State-supported** 2-year, founded 1963, part of Technical College System of Georgia
- **Suburban** campus
- **Coed**

**Undergraduates** 947 full-time, 2,993 part-time. 0.7% are from out of state; 32% Black or African American, non-Hispanic/Latino; 5% Hispanic/Latino; 0.8% Asian, non-Hispanic/Latino; 0.2% Native Hawaiian or other Pacific Islander, non-Hispanic/Latino; 0.4% American Indian or Alaska Native, non-Hispanic/Latino; 2% Two or more races, non-Hispanic/Latino; 0.2% Race/ethnicity unknown. *Retention:* 59% of full-time freshmen returned.
**Academics** *Calendar:* quarters. *Degree:* certificates, diplomas, and associate. *Special study options:* distance learning.
**Costs (2017–18)** *Tuition:* state resident $89 per credit hour part-time; nonresident $178 per credit hour part-time.
**Applying** *Options:* early admission. *Application fee:* $25. *Required:* high school transcript.
**Freshman Application Contact** Wiregrass Georgia Technical College, 4089 Val Tech Road, Valdosta, GA 31602. *Phone:* 229-468-2278. *Website:* http://www.wiregrass.edu/.

# GUAM

## Guam Community College
### Mangilao, Guam

- **Territory-supported** 2-year, founded 1977
- **Small-town** 33-acre campus
- **Endowment** $8.8 million
- **Coed**

**Undergraduates** 1,038 full-time, 1,390 part-time. 1% Black or African American, non-Hispanic/Latino; 0.5% Hispanic/Latino; 41% Asian, non-Hispanic/Latino; 54% Native Hawaiian or other Pacific Islander, non-Hispanic/Latino; 0.5% Race/ethnicity unknown; 1% international; 1% transferred in. *Retention:* 62% of full-time freshmen returned.
**Faculty** *Student/faculty ratio:* 15:1.
**Academics** *Calendar:* semesters. *Degree:* certificates, diplomas, and associate. *Special study options:* academic remediation for entering students, adult/continuing education programs, advanced placement credit, cooperative education, double majors, English as a second language, honors programs, independent study, internships, off-campus study, part-time degree program, services for LD students, summer session for credit. *ROTC:* Army (c).
**Library** Learning Resource Center. *Books:* 21,379 (physical), 157,000 (digital/electronic); *Databases:* 40. Weekly public service hours: 60; students can reserve study rooms.
**Student Life** *Campus security:* 12-hour patrols by trained security personnel.
**Financial Aid** Of all full-time matriculated undergraduates who enrolled in 2016, 83 Federal Work-Study jobs (averaging $940).
**Applying** *Options:* early admission. *Required:* high school transcript.
**Freshman Application Contact** Dr. Julie Ulloa-Heath, Registrar, Guam Community College, PO Box 23069 GMF, Barrigada, GU 96921. *Phone:* 671-735-5561. *Fax:* 671-735-5531. *E-mail:* julie.ulloaheath@guamcc.edu. *Website:* http://www.guamcc.edu/.

# HAWAII

## Hawaii Community College
### Hilo, Hawaii

**Director of Admissions** Mrs. Tammy M. Tanaka, Admissions Specialist, Hawaii Community College, 1175 Manono Street, Hilo, HI 96720-5096. *Phone:* 808-974-7661. *Website:* http://www.hawcc.hawaii.edu/.

## Hawaii Tokai International College
### Kapolei, Hawaii

- **Independent** 2-year, founded 1992, part of Tokai University Educational System
- **Suburban** 7-acre campus with easy access to Honolulu
- **Coed,** 85 undergraduate students, 100% full-time, 35% women, 65% men

**Undergraduates** 85 full-time. Students come from 2 states and territories; 2 other countries; 5% are from out of state; 2% Hispanic/Latino; 6% Asian, non-Hispanic/Latino; 4% Native Hawaiian or other Pacific Islander, non-Hispanic/Latino; 5% Two or more races, non-Hispanic/Latino; 81% international; 30% live on campus. *Retention:* 86% of full-time freshmen returned.
**Freshmen** *Admission:* 35 applied, 30 admitted, 24 enrolled. *Average high school GPA:* 3.0.
**Faculty** *Total:* 22, 32% full-time, 41% with terminal degrees. *Student/faculty ratio:* 7:1.
**Majors** Liberal arts and sciences/liberal studies.
**Academics** *Calendar:* quarters. *Degree:* certificates, diplomas, and associate. *Special study options:* academic remediation for entering students, advanced placement credit, English as a second language, internships, part-time degree program, services for LD students, study abroad, summer session for credit.
**Library** Library and Learning Center plus 1 other. *Books:* 7,807 (physical); *Serial titles:* 30 (physical); *Databases:* 48. Weekly public service hours: 68; students can reserve study rooms.
**Student Life** *Housing Options:* men-only, women-only, special housing for students with disabilities. Campus housing is university owned. Freshman applicants given priority for college housing. *Activities and Organizations:* Basketball Club, International Friendship Association, Hiking Club, Hula Club, Phi Theta Kappa International Honor Society. *Campus security:* 24-hour emergency response devices and patrols, controlled dormitory access. *Student services:* health clinic, personal/psychological counseling.
**Costs (2018–19)** *One-time required fee:* $20. *Comprehensive fee:* $22,485 includes full-time tuition ($12,750), mandatory fees ($735), and room and board ($9000). Part-time tuition and fees vary according to course load. *Room and board:* Room and board charges vary according to board plan. *Waivers:* employees or children of employees.
**Applying** *Options:* electronic application, deferred entrance. *Application fee:* $50. *Required:* essay or personal statement, high school transcript, minimum 2.5 GPA. *Required for some:* interview. *Recommended:* letters of recommendation. *Application deadlines:* rolling (freshmen), rolling (transfers). *Notification:* continuous (freshmen), continuous (transfers).
**Freshman Application Contact** Mr. Darrell Kicker, Director of Admissions, Hawaii Tokai International College, 91-971 Farrington Highway, Kapolei, HI 96707. *Phone:* 808-983-4202. *Fax:* 808-983-4107. *E-mail:* admissions@tokai.edu.
*Website:* http://www.htic.edu/.

## Honolulu Community College
### Honolulu, Hawaii

**Freshman Application Contact** Admissions Office, Honolulu Community College, 874 Dillingham Boulevard, Honolulu, HI 96817. *Phone:* 808-845-9129. *E-mail:* honcc@hawaii.edu. *Website:* http://www.honolulu.hawaii.edu/.

## Kapiolani Community College
### Honolulu, Hawaii

**Freshman Application Contact** Kapiolani Community College, 4303 Diamond Head Road, Honolulu, HI 96816-4421. *Phone:* 808-734-9555. *Website:* http://www.kapiolani.hawaii.edu/.

## Kauai Community College
### Lihue, Hawaii

**Freshman Application Contact** Mr. Leighton Oride, Admissions Officer and Registrar, Kauai Community College, 3-1901 Kaumualii Highway, Lihue, HI 96766. *Phone:* 808-245-8225. *Fax:* 808-245-8297. *E-mail:* arkauai@hawaii.edu. *Website:* http://kauai.hawaii.edu/.

## Leeward Community College
### Pearl City, Hawaii

**Freshman Application Contact** Ms. Sheryl Higa, Assistant Registrar, Leeward Community College, 96-045 Ala Ike, Pearl City, HI 96782-3393. *Phone:* 808-455-0643. *Website:* http://www.leeward.hawaii.edu/.

## Remington College–Honolulu Campus
### Honolulu, Hawaii

**Director of Admissions** Louis LaMair, Director of Recruitment, Remington College–Honolulu Campus, 1111 Bishop Street, Suite 400, Honolulu, HI 96813. *Phone:* 808-942-1000. *Toll-free phone:* 800-323-8122. *Fax:* 808-533-3064. *E-mail:* louis.lamair@remingtoncollege.edu. *Website:* http://www.remingtoncollege.edu/.

## University of Hawaii Maui College
### Kahului, Hawaii

**Freshman Application Contact** Mr. Stephen Kameda, Director of Admissions and Records, University of Hawaii Maui College, 310 Kaahumanu Avenue, Kahului, HI 96732. *Phone:* 808-984-3267. *Toll-free phone:* 800-479-6692. *Fax:* 808-984-3872. *E-mail:* skameda@hawaii.edu. *Website:* http://maui.hawaii.edu/.

## Windward Community College
### Kaneohe, Hawaii

**Director of Admissions** Geri Imai, Registrar, Windward Community College, 45-720 Keaahala Road, Kaneohe, HI 96744-3528. *Phone:* 808-235-7430. *E-mail:* gerii@hawaii.edu. *Website:* http://www.windward.hawaii.edu/.

# IDAHO

## Carrington College–Boise
### Boise, Idaho

- **Proprietary** 2-year, founded 1980, part of Carrington Colleges Group, Inc.
- **Coed**

**Undergraduates** 395 full-time, 51 part-time. 16% are from out of state; 4% Black or African American, non-Hispanic/Latino; 17% Hispanic/Latino; 7% Asian, non-Hispanic/Latino; 0.2% Native Hawaiian or other Pacific Islander, non-Hispanic/Latino; 0.9% American Indian or Alaska Native, non-Hispanic/Latino; 2% Two or more races, non-Hispanic/Latino; 0.5% Race/ethnicity unknown; 18% transferred in.
**Faculty** *Student/faculty ratio:* 14:1.
**Academics** *Degree:* certificates and associate.
**Standardized Tests** *Required:* institutional entrance exam (for admission).
**Costs (2017–18)** *Tuition:* $54,810 per degree program part-time. Full-time tuition and fees vary according to program. Part-time tuition and fees vary according to program.
**Applying** *Required:* essay or personal statement, high school transcript, interview.
**Freshman Application Contact** Carrington College–Boise, 1122 North Liberty Street, Boise, ID 83704. *Website:* http://www.carrington.edu/.

## College of Eastern Idaho
### Idaho Falls, Idaho

- **State-supported** 2-year, founded 1969
- **Small-town** 60-acre campus
- **Coed,** 791 undergraduate students, 36% full-time, 19% women, 81% men

**Undergraduates** 285 full-time, 506 part-time. Students come from 7 states and territories; 1% are from out of state; 0.1% Black or African American, non-Hispanic/Latino; 15% Hispanic/Latino; 0.6% Asian, non-Hispanic/Latino; 0.3% Native Hawaiian or other Pacific Islander, non-Hispanic/Latino; 0.6% American Indian or Alaska Native, non-Hispanic/Latino; 0.9% Two or more races, non-Hispanic/Latino; 1% Race/ethnicity unknown. *Retention:* 40% of full-time freshmen returned.
**Faculty** *Student/faculty ratio:* 8:1.
**Majors** Accounting; administrative assistant and secretarial science; automobile/automotive mechanics technology; computer systems networking and telecommunications; diesel mechanics technology; electrician; fire science/firefighting; legal assistant/paralegal; marketing/marketing management; medical/clinical assistant; registered nursing/registered nurse; surgical technology; web page, digital/multimedia and information resources design; welding technology.
**Academics** *Calendar:* semesters. *Degree:* certificates and associate. *Special study options:* academic remediation for entering students, adult/continuing education programs, advanced placement credit, English as a second language, part-time degree program, services for LD students, summer session for credit.

**Library** Richard and Lila Jordan Library plus 1 other.
**Student Life** *Housing:* college housing not available. *Campus security:* 24-hour emergency response devices and patrols, late-night transport/escort service. *Student services:* veterans affairs office.
**Standardized Tests** *Required for some:* ACT Compass, ACT ASSET, or CPT.
**Costs (2017–18)** *Tuition:* state resident $2464 full-time, $108 per credit part-time; nonresident $9026 full-time, $216 per credit part-time. Full-time tuition and fees vary according to class time, course level, course load, degree level, location, program, and student level. Part-time tuition and fees vary according to class time, course level, course load, degree level, location, program, and student level. *Required fees:* $30 full-time, $30 per year part-time. *Waivers:* employees or children of employees.
**Financial Aid** Of all full-time matriculated undergraduates who enrolled in 2016, 37 Federal Work-Study jobs (averaging $1176). 11 state and other part-time jobs (averaging $1619).
**Applying** *Options:* electronic application, deferred entrance. *Required:* high school transcript. *Required for some:* essay or personal statement, interview. *Application deadline:* rolling (freshmen).
**Freshman Application Contact** Hailey Mack, Career Placement and Recruiting Coordinator, College of Eastern Idaho, 1600 South 25th East, Idaho Falls, ID 83404. *Phone:* 208-524-5337 Ext. 35337. *Toll-free phone:* 800-662-0261. *Fax:* 208-524-0429. *E-mail:* hailey.mack@cei.edu. *Website:* http://www.eitc.edu/.

## College of Southern Idaho
### Twin Falls, Idaho

**Freshman Application Contact** Director of Admissions, Registration, and Records, College of Southern Idaho, PO Box 1238, Twin Falls, ID 83303-1238. *Phone:* 208-732-6232. *Toll-free phone:* 800-680-0274. *Fax:* 208-736-3014. *Website:* http://www.csi.edu/.

## College of Western Idaho
### Nampa, Idaho

**Freshman Application Contact** College of Western Idaho, 6056 Birch Lane, Nampa, ID 83687. *Website:* http://cwidaho.cc/.

## North Idaho College
### Coeur d'Alene, Idaho

**Freshman Application Contact** North Idaho College, 1000 West Garden Avenue, Coeur d Alene, ID 83814-2199. *Phone:* 208-769-3303. *Toll-free phone:* 877-404-4536 Ext. 3311. *E-mail:* admit@nic.edu. *Website:* http://www.nic.edu/.

# ILLINOIS

## Ambria College of Nursing
### Hoffman Estates, Illinois

**Admissions Office Contact** Ambria College of Nursing, 5210 Trillium Boulevard, Hoffman Estates, IL 60192. *Website:* http://www.ambria.edu/.

## Black Hawk College
### Moline, Illinois

- **State and locally supported** 2-year, founded 1946
- **Urban** 232-acre campus
- **Coed,** 4,926 undergraduate students, 36% full-time, 59% women, 41% men

**Undergraduates** 1,753 full-time, 3,173 part-time. Students come from 16 states and territories; 22 other countries; 8% are from out of state; 12% Black or African American, non-Hispanic/Latino; 13% Hispanic/Latino; 4% Asian, non-Hispanic/Latino; 0.2% American Indian or Alaska Native, non-Hispanic/Latino; 4% Two or more races, non-Hispanic/Latino; 2% Race/ethnicity unknown; 0.1% international; 4% transferred in.
**Freshmen** *Admission:* 859 applied, 859 admitted, 769 enrolled.
**Faculty** *Total:* 223, 45% full-time, 14% with terminal degrees. *Student/faculty ratio:* 20:1.
**Majors** Accounting; administrative assistant and secretarial science; agricultural mechanics and equipment technology; agricultural production; agriculture; applied horticulture/horticulture operations; art; automobile/automotive mechanics technology; biological and physical sciences; child-care provision; criminal justice/police science; crop

production; design and visual communications; emergency medical technology (EMT paramedic); equestrian studies; fire services administration; general studies; health information/medical records technology; horse husbandry/equine science and management; information technology; liberal arts and sciences/liberal studies; manufacturing engineering technology; physical therapy technology; radiologic technology/science; registered nursing/registered nurse; retailing; small business administration; surgical technology; veterinary/animal health technology.

**Academics** *Calendar:* semesters. *Degree:* certificates and associate. *Special study options:* academic remediation for entering students, advanced placement credit, distance learning, English as a second language, independent study, internships, part-time degree program, services for LD students, summer session for credit.

**Library** Quad City Campus Library plus 1 other. *Books:* 28,372 (physical), 182,963 (digital/electronic); *Serial titles:* 140 (physical), 48,679 (digital/electronic); *Databases:* 15,675. Students can reserve study rooms.

**Student Life** *Housing:* college housing not available. *Activities and Organizations:* drama/theater group, student-run newspaper, choral group, National Student Nurses Association, Wellness Club, Phi Theta Kappa, Association of Lation American Students, Clean Sphere. *Campus security:* 24-hour patrols. *Student services:* personal/psychological counseling, veterans affairs office.

**Athletics** Member NJCAA. *Intercollegiate sports:* baseball M(s), basketball M(s)/W(s), golf M(s), softball W(s), volleyball W(s). *Intramural sports:* soccer M.

**Costs (2018–19)** *Tuition:* area resident $4470 full-time, $149 per credit hour part-time; state resident $7500 full-time, $250 per credit hour part-time; nonresident $7650 full-time, $255 per credit hour part-time. *Payment plan:* installment. *Waivers:* employees or children of employees.

**Financial Aid** Of all full-time matriculated undergraduates who enrolled in 2016, 157 Federal Work-Study jobs (averaging $1437). 176 state and other part-time jobs (averaging $1023).

**Applying** *Options:* electronic application, early admission, deferred entrance. *Application fee:* $20. *Recommended:* high school transcript. *Application deadlines:* rolling (freshmen), rolling (out-of-state freshmen), rolling (transfers), rolling (early action). *Early decision deadline:* rolling (for plan 1), rolling (for plan 2). *Notification:* continuous (freshmen), continuous (out-of-state freshmen), continuous (transfers), rolling (early decision plan 1), rolling (early decision plan 2), rolling (early action).

**Freshman Application Contact** Ms. Gabriella Hurtado, Recruitment Coordinator/Admissions Advisor, Black Hawk College, 6600-34th Avenue, Moline, IL 61265. *Phone:* 309-796-5341. *Toll-free phone:* 800-334-1311. *E-mail:* ghurtado@bhc.edu. *Website:* http://www.bhc.edu/.

# Carl Sandburg College
## Galesburg, Illinois

**Director of Admissions** Ms. Carol Kreider, Dean of Student Support Services, Carl Sandburg College, 2400 Tom L. Wilson Boulevard, Galesburg, IL 61401-9576. *Phone:* 309-341-5234. *Website:* http://www.sandburg.edu/.

# City Colleges of Chicago, Harold Washington College
## Chicago, Illinois

**Freshman Application Contact** Admissions Office, City Colleges of Chicago, Harold Washington College, 30 East Lake Street, Chicago, IL 60601-2449. *Phone:* 312-553-6010. *Website:* http://hwashington.ccc.edu/.

# City Colleges of Chicago, Harry S. Truman College
## Chicago, Illinois

**Freshman Application Contact** City Colleges of Chicago, Harry S. Truman College, 1145 West Wilson Avenue, Chicago, IL 60640-5616. *Phone:* 773-907-4000 Ext. 1112. *Website:* http://www.trumancollege.edu/.

# City Colleges of Chicago, Kennedy-King College
## Chicago, Illinois

- **State and locally supported** 2-year, founded 1935, part of City Colleges of Chicago
- **Urban** 40-acre campus with easy access to Chicago
- **Coed**

**Undergraduates** 1,584 full-time, 1,234 part-time. Students come from 20 states and territories; 8 other countries; 1% are from out of state; 78% Black or African American, non-Hispanic/Latino; 14% Hispanic/Latino; 1% Asian, non-Hispanic/Latino; 0.1% American Indian or Alaska Native, non-Hispanic/Latino; 3% Two or more races, non-Hispanic/Latino; 0.6% Race/ethnicity unknown; 1% transferred in. *Retention:* 34% of full-time freshmen returned.

**Faculty** *Student/faculty ratio:* 30:1.

**Academics** *Calendar:* semesters. *Degree:* certificates and associate. *Special study options:* academic remediation for entering students, adult/continuing education programs, advanced placement credit, cooperative education, distance learning, English as a second language, honors programs, internships, part-time degree program, summer session for credit.

**Library** Harold Washington College Library.

**Student Life** *Campus security:* late-night transport/escort service.

**Athletics** Member NJCAA.

**Costs (2017–18)** *Tuition:* area resident $1753 full-time, $1069 per term part-time; state resident $4603 full-time, $3159 per term part-time; nonresident $5953 full-time, $4149 per term part-time. Full-time tuition and fees vary according to course load and program. Part-time tuition and fees vary according to course load and program. *Payment plans:* installment, deferred payment.

**Financial Aid** Of all full-time matriculated undergraduates who enrolled in 2016, 148 Federal Work-Study jobs (averaging $1539).

**Applying** *Options:* electronic application. *Required:* high school transcript.

**Freshman Application Contact** Nicholas Ambrose, Assistant Registrar, City Colleges of Chicago, Kennedy-King College, 6301 South Halsted Street, W-110, Chicago, IL 60621. *Phone:* 773-602-5090. *Fax:* 773-602-5055. *E-mail:* nambrose1@ccc.edu. *Website:* http://www.ccc.edu/colleges/kennedy/.

# City Colleges of Chicago, Malcolm X College
## Chicago, Illinois

**Freshman Application Contact** Ms. Kimberly Hollingsworth, Dean of Student Services, City Colleges of Chicago, Malcolm X College, 1900 West Van Buren Street, Chicago, IL 60612-3145. *Phone:* 312-850-7120. *Fax:* 312-850-7119. *E-mail:* khollingsworth@ccc.edu. *Website:* http://malcolmx.ccc.edu/.

# City Colleges of Chicago, Olive-Harvey College
## Chicago, Illinois

- **State and locally supported** 2-year, founded 1970, part of City Colleges of Chicago
- **Urban** 67-acre campus with easy access to Chicago
- **Coed,** 2,882 undergraduate students, 35% full-time, 63% women, 37% men

**Undergraduates** 1,013 full-time, 1,869 part-time. 69% Black or African American, non-Hispanic/Latino; 24% Hispanic/Latino; 1% Asian, non-Hispanic/Latino; 0.2% American Indian or Alaska Native, non-Hispanic/Latino; 2% Two or more races, non-Hispanic/Latino; 0.6% Race/ethnicity unknown; 0.3% international. *Retention:* 52% of full-time freshmen returned.

**Faculty** *Total:* 126, 39% full-time. *Student/faculty ratio:* 22:1.

**Majors** Automobile/automotive mechanics technology; biological and physical sciences; business administration and management; child-care provision; criminal justice/safety; diesel mechanics technology; general studies; information technology; liberal arts and sciences/liberal studies; logistics, materials, and supply chain management; transportation/mobility management; web/multimedia management and webmaster.

**Academics** *Calendar:* semesters. *Degree:* certificates and associate. *Special study options:* academic remediation for entering students, accelerated degree program, adult/continuing education programs, advanced placement credit, cooperative education, distance learning, English as a second language, independent study, internships, part-time degree program, services for LD students, summer session for credit.

**Library** Olga-Haley Library-Learning Resource Center. *Books:* 70,820 (physical), 447,725 (digital/electronic); *Serial titles:* 50 (physical), 23,684 (digital/electronic); *Databases:* 81. Students can reserve study rooms.
**Student Life** *Housing:* college housing not available. *Activities and Organizations:* drama/theater group. *Campus security:* 24-hour emergency response devices and patrols. *Student services:* personal/psychological counseling, women's center, veterans affairs office.
**Athletics** Member NJCAA. *Intercollegiate sports:* baseball M, basketball M/W, volleyball W.
**Costs (2018–19)** *Tuition:* area resident $3504 full-time, $146 per credit hour part-time; state resident $9216 full-time, $384 per credit hour part-time; nonresident $11,444 full-time, $481 per credit hour part-time. Full-time tuition and fees vary according to program. Part-time tuition and fees vary according to course load and program. *Payment plan:* installment. *Waivers:* senior citizens and employees or children of employees.
**Financial Aid** Of all full-time matriculated undergraduates who enrolled in 2016, 150 Federal Work-Study jobs (averaging $3900).
**Applying** *Options:* electronic application, early admission, deferred entrance. *Required for some:* high school transcript. *Application deadlines:* rolling (freshmen), rolling (out-of-state freshmen), rolling (transfers). *Notification:* continuous (freshmen), continuous (out-of-state freshmen), continuous (transfers).
**Freshman Application Contact** Nailah Alexandar, Assistant Registrar, City Colleges of Chicago, Olive-Harvey College, 10001 South Woodlawn Avenue, Room 1405, Chicago, IL 60628. *Phone:* 773-291-6384. *E-mail:* nalexander17@ccc.edu.
*Website:* http://oliveharvey.ccc.edu/.

## City Colleges of Chicago, Richard J. Daley College
### Chicago, Illinois

**Freshman Application Contact** City Colleges of Chicago, Richard J. Daley College, 7500 South Pulaski Road, Chicago, IL 60652-1242. *Phone:* 773-838-7606. *Website:* http://daley.ccc.edu/.

## City Colleges of Chicago, Wilbur Wright College
### Chicago, Illinois

**Freshman Application Contact** Ms. Amy Aiello, Assistant Dean of Student Services, City Colleges of Chicago, Wilbur Wright College, Chicago, IL 60634. *Phone:* 773-481-8207. *Fax:* 773-481-8185. *E-mail:* aaiello@ccc.edu. *Website:* http://wright.ccc.edu/.

## College of DuPage
### Glen Ellyn, Illinois

**Freshman Application Contact** College of DuPage, IL. *E-mail:* admissions@cod.edu. *Website:* http://www.cod.edu/.

## College of Lake County
### Grayslake, Illinois

**Freshman Application Contact** Director, Student Recruitment, College of Lake County, Grayslake, IL 60030-1198. *Phone:* 847-543-2383. *Fax:* 847-543-3061. *Website:* http://www.clcillinois.edu/.

## Coyne College
### Chicago, Illinois

**Freshman Application Contact** Coyne College, 1 North State Street, Suite 400, Chicago, IL 60602. *Phone:* 773-577-8100 Ext. 8102. *Toll-free phone:* 800-707-1922. *Website:* http://www.coynecollege.edu/.

## Danville Area Community College
### Danville, Illinois

- **State and locally supported** 2-year, founded 1946, part of Illinois Community College Board
- **Small-town** 50-acre campus
- **Endowment** $14.8 million
- **Coed,** 2,645 undergraduate students, 38% full-time, 57% women, 43% men

**Undergraduates** 1,013 full-time, 1,632 part-time. Students come from 5 states and territories; 3 other countries; 7% are from out of state; 15% Black or African American, non-Hispanic/Latino; 5% Hispanic/Latino; 1% Asian, non-Hispanic/Latino; 0.1% Native Hawaiian or other Pacific Islander, non-Hispanic/Latino; 0.3% American Indian or Alaska Native, non-Hispanic/Latino; 9% Race/ethnicity unknown; 26% transferred in. *Retention:* 52% of full-time freshmen returned.
**Freshmen** *Admission:* 404 enrolled.
**Faculty** *Total:* 128, 50% full-time, 13% with terminal degrees. *Student/faculty ratio:* 18:1.
**Majors** Accounting technology and bookkeeping; agricultural business and management; art; art teacher education; automobile/automotive mechanics technology; biological and physical sciences; business automation/technology/data entry; CAD/CADD drafting/design technology; child-care provision; computer programming (specific applications); computer systems networking and telecommunications; corrections; criminal justice/police science; energy management and systems technology; engineering; executive assistant/executive secretary; fire science/firefighting; floriculture/floristry management; general studies; health information/medical records technology; industrial electronics technology; industrial mechanics and maintenance technology; juvenile corrections; liberal arts and sciences/liberal studies; manufacturing engineering technology; medical administrative assistant and medical secretary; radiologic technology/science; registered nursing/registered nurse; selling skills and sales; teacher assistant/aide; turf and turfgrass management.
**Academics** *Calendar:* semesters. *Degree:* certificates and associate. *Special study options:* academic remediation for entering students, adult/continuing education programs, advanced placement credit, cooperative education, distance learning, double majors, English as a second language, independent study, internships, off-campus study, part-time degree program, services for LD students, summer session for credit.
**Student Life** *Housing:* college housing not available. *Activities and Organizations:* drama/theater group, student-run newspaper, choral group, Phi Theta Kappa International Honor Society, The Guild, Powerhouse Campus Ministry, Rad Tech Club, Ag Club. *Campus security:* 24-hour emergency response devices and patrols. *Student services:* personal/psychological counseling, veterans affairs office.
**Athletics** Member NJCAA. *Intercollegiate sports:* baseball M(s), basketball M(s)/W(s), cheerleading W, cross-country running M(s)/W(s), softball W(s).
**Costs (2017–18)** *Tuition:* area resident $4500 full-time, $150 per credit hour part-time; state resident $7500 full-time, $250 per credit hour part-time; nonresident $7500 full-time, $250 per credit hour part-time. Full-time tuition and fees vary according to program. Part-time tuition and fees vary according to program. *Required fees:* $700 full-time, $45 per credit hour part-time. *Payment plan:* installment. *Waivers:* senior citizens and employees or children of employees.
**Financial Aid** Of all full-time matriculated undergraduates who enrolled in 2016, 52 Federal Work-Study jobs (averaging $3000). 60 state and other part-time jobs (averaging $3000).
**Applying** *Options:* early admission, deferred entrance. *Required:* high school transcript. *Application deadlines:* rolling (freshmen), rolling (transfers).
**Freshman Application Contact** Mr. Nick Catlett, Coordinator of Recruitment, Danville Area Community College, 2000 East Main Street, Danville, IL 61832-5199. *Phone:* 217-443-8864. *Fax:* 217-443-8337. *E-mail:* ncatlett@dacc.edu.
*Website:* http://www.dacc.edu/.

## Elgin Community College
### Elgin, Illinois

- **State and locally supported** 2-year, founded 1949, part of Illinois Community College Board
- **Suburban** 145-acre campus with easy access to Chicago
- **Coed**

**Undergraduates** 3,209 full-time, 6,740 part-time. Students come from 4 states and territories; 15 other countries; 0.2% are from out of state; 4% Black or African American, non-Hispanic/Latino; 42% Hispanic/Latino; 7% Asian, non-Hispanic/Latino; 0.1% Native Hawaiian or other Pacific Islander, non-Hispanic/Latino; 0.8% American Indian or Alaska Native, non-Hispanic/Latino; 3% Race/ethnicity unknown; 0.5% international; 4% transferred in. *Retention:* 77% of full-time freshmen returned.
**Academics** *Calendar:* semesters. *Degree:* certificates, diplomas, and associate. *Special study options:* academic remediation for entering students, accelerated degree program, advanced placement credit, cooperative education, distance learning, double majors, English as a second language, honors programs, independent study, internships, off-campus study, part-time degree program, services for LD students, study abroad, summer session for credit.
**Library** Renner Academic Library & Learning Resources.
**Student Life** *Campus security:* grounds patrolled daily 7 am-11 pm during the academic year.
**Athletics** Member NJCAA.

**Costs (2017–18)** *Tuition:* area resident $3870 full-time, $129 per credit hour part-time; state resident $13,035 full-time, $434 per credit hour part-time; nonresident $14,934 full-time, $498 per credit hour part-time. *Required fees:* $6 per term part-time.

**Applying** *Options:* electronic application. *Required for some:* high school transcript, specific departmental requirements.

**Freshman Application Contact** Admissions, Recruitment, and Student Life, Elgin Community College, 1700 Spartan Drive, Elgin, IL 60123. *Phone:* 847-214-7414. *E-mail:* admissions@elgin.edu. *Website:* http://www.elgin.edu/.

## Fox College
### Bedford Park, Illinois

**Freshman Application Contact** Admissions Office, Fox College, 6640 South Cicero, Bedford Park, IL 60638. *Phone:* 708-444-4500. *Website:* http://www.foxcollege.edu/.

## Harper College
### Palatine, Illinois

- **State and locally supported** 2-year, founded 1965, part of Illinois Community College Board
- **Suburban** 200-acre campus with easy access to Chicago
- **Coed**, 13,749 undergraduate students, 36% full-time, 55% women, 45% men

**Undergraduates** 4,882 full-time, 8,867 part-time. 4% Black or African American, non-Hispanic/Latino; 26% Hispanic/Latino; 12% Asian, non-Hispanic/Latino; 0.2% American Indian or Alaska Native, non-Hispanic/Latino; 2% Two or more races, non-Hispanic/Latino; 2% Race/ethnicity unknown; 0.9% international; 12% transferred in. *Retention:* 70% of full-time freshmen returned.

**Freshmen** *Admission:* 2,196 enrolled.

**Faculty** *Total:* 671, 30% full-time, 17% with terminal degrees. *Student/faculty ratio:* 19:1.

**Majors** Accounting; administrative assistant and secretarial science; architectural drafting and CAD/CADD; architectural engineering technology; art; banking and financial support services; biology/biological sciences; business administration and management; cardiovascular technology; chemistry; child-care provision; computer and information sciences; computer programming; computer programming (specific applications); computer science; criminal justice/law enforcement administration; cyber/computer forensics and counterterrorism; dental hygiene; diagnostic medical sonography and ultrasound technology; dietetics; dietetic technology; early childhood education; electrical, electronic and communications engineering technology; elementary education; emergency medical technology (EMT paramedic); engineering; English; environmental studies; fashion and fabric consulting; fashion/apparel design; fashion merchandising; finance; fine/studio arts; fire science/firefighting; food service systems administration; health teacher education; heating, air conditioning, ventilation and refrigeration maintenance technology; history; homeland security; hospitality administration; humanities; human services; interior design; international business/trade/commerce; legal administrative assistant/secretary; legal assistant/paralegal; liberal arts and sciences/liberal studies; marketing/marketing management; mathematics; medical administrative assistant and medical secretary; medical/clinical assistant; music; nanotechnology; philosophy; physical education teaching and coaching; physical sciences; psychology; public relations, advertising, and applied communication related; radiologic technology/science; registered nursing/registered nurse; sales, distribution, and marketing operations; small business administration; sociology and anthropology; speech communication and rhetoric; theater/theater arts management; web page, digital/multimedia and information resources design.

**Academics** *Calendar:* semesters. *Degree:* certificates and associate. *Special study options:* academic remediation for entering students, accelerated degree program, adult/continuing education programs, advanced placement credit, cooperative education, distance learning, English as a second language, freshman honors college, honors programs, independent study, internships, part-time degree program, services for LD students, study abroad, summer session for credit.

**Library** Harper College Library.

**Student Life** *Housing:* college housing not available. *Activities and Organizations:* drama/theater group, student-run newspaper, radio station, choral group, Student Radio Station, Program Board, Student Senate, Nursing Club, Phi Theta Kappa. *Campus security:* 24-hour emergency response devices and patrols, late-night transport/escort service. *Student services:* health clinic, personal/psychological counseling, women's center, legal services.

**Athletics** Member NJCAA. *Intercollegiate sports:* baseball M, basketball M/W, cross-country running M/W, soccer M/W, softball W, track and field M/W, volleyball W, wrestling M. *Intramural sports:* baseball M, basketball

M, football M, racquetball M/W, softball M/W, table tennis M/W, tennis M/W, volleyball M/W.

**Costs (2017–18)** *Tuition:* area resident $3750 full-time, $125 per credit hour part-time; state resident $11,460 full-time, $382 per credit hour part-time; nonresident $13,725 full-time, $458 per credit hour part-time. Full-time tuition and fees vary according to course load and program. Part-time tuition and fees vary according to course load and program. No tuition increase for student's term of enrollment. *Required fees:* $594 full-time, $16 per credit hour part-time. *Payment plans:* installment, deferred payment. *Waivers:* senior citizens and employees or children of employees.

**Financial Aid** Of all full-time matriculated undergraduates who enrolled in 2016, 2,598 applied for aid, 2,112 were judged to have need, 73 had their need fully met. In 2016, 66 non-need-based awards were made. *Average percent of need met:* 46%. *Average financial aid package:* $5218. *Average need-based loan:* $2987. *Average need-based gift aid:* $4956. *Average non-need-based aid:* $2626.

**Applying** *Options:* electronic application. *Application fee:* $25. *Required:* high school transcript. *Application deadlines:* rolling (freshmen), rolling (transfers). *Notification:* continuous (freshmen), continuous (transfers).

**Freshman Application Contact** Admissions Office, Harper College, 1200 West Algonquin Road, Palatine, IL 60067. *Phone:* 847-925-6700. *Fax:* 847-925-6044. *E-mail:* admissions@harpercollege.edu. *Website:* http://goforward.harpercollege.edu/.

## Heartland Community College
### Normal, Illinois

**Freshman Application Contact** Ms. Candace Brownlee, Director of Student Recruitment, Heartland Community College, 1500 West Raab Road, Normal, IL 61761. *Phone:* 309-268-8041. *Fax:* 309-268-7992. *E-mail:* candace.brownlee@heartland.edu. *Website:* http://www.heartland.edu/.

## Highland Community College
### Freeport, Illinois

- **State and locally supported** 2-year, founded 1962, part of Illinois Community College Board
- **Rural** 240-acre campus
- **Coed**, 1,678 undergraduate students, 49% full-time, 61% women, 39% men

**Undergraduates** 828 full-time, 850 part-time. 3% are from out of state; 8% Black or African American, non-Hispanic/Latino; 3% Hispanic/Latino; 1% Asian, non-Hispanic/Latino; 0.1% Native Hawaiian or other Pacific Islander, non-Hispanic/Latino; 0.7% American Indian or Alaska Native, non-Hispanic/Latino; 3% Two or more races, non-Hispanic/Latino; 3% Race/ethnicity unknown; 0.7% international; 3% transferred in.

**Freshmen** *Admission:* 655 applied, 655 admitted, 266 enrolled.

**Faculty** *Total:* 123, 38% full-time, 7% with terminal degrees. *Student/faculty ratio:* 15:1.

**Majors** Accounting; administrative assistant and secretarial science; autobody/collision and repair technology; automobile/automotive mechanics technology; biological and physical sciences; business administration and management; child-care provision; early childhood education; emergency medical technology (EMT paramedic); engineering; equestrian studies; general studies; graphic design; health information/medical records technology; heavy equipment maintenance technology; hospitality administration; industrial technology; information technology; liberal arts and sciences/liberal studies; mathematics teacher education; medical/clinical assistant; registered nursing/registered nurse; special education; teacher assistant/aide; web page, digital/multimedia and information resources design; welding technology.

**Academics** *Calendar:* semesters. *Degree:* certificates and associate. *Special study options:* academic remediation for entering students, adult/continuing education programs, advanced placement credit, cooperative education, distance learning, English as a second language, external degree program, honors programs, independent study, internships, part-time degree program, services for LD students, student-designed majors, summer session for credit.

**Library** Clarence Mitchell Library.

**Student Life** *Housing:* college housing not available. *Activities and Organizations:* drama/theater group, student-run newspaper, radio and television station, choral group, Phi Theta Kappa, Royal Scots, Prairie Wind, Intramurals, Collegiate Choir. *Campus security:* 24-hour emergency response devices and patrols. *Student services:* personal/psychological counseling, veterans affairs office.

**Athletics** Member NJCAA. *Intercollegiate sports:* baseball M(s), basketball M(s)/W(s), bowling M(s)/W(s), golf M(s)/W(s), softball W(s), volleyball W(s). *Intramural sports:* basketball M/W, volleyball M/W.

**Costs (2017–18)** *Tuition:* area resident $4230 full-time, $141 per credit hour part-time; state resident $7020 full-time, $234 per credit hour part-time;

nonresident $7080 full-time, $236 per credit hour part-time. Full-time tuition and fees vary according to program and reciprocity agreements. Part-time tuition and fees vary according to program and reciprocity agreements. *Required fees:* $780 full-time, $25 per credit hour part-time, $15 per term part-time. *Payment plans:* installment, deferred payment. *Waivers:* minority students, senior citizens, and employees or children of employees.

**Financial Aid** Of all full-time matriculated undergraduates who enrolled in 2016, 678 applied for aid, 594 were judged to have need. 51 Federal Work-Study jobs (averaging $1571). 28 state and other part-time jobs (averaging $1914). In 2016, 35 non-need-based awards were made. *Average percent of need met:* 36%. *Average financial aid package:* $6120. *Average need-based loan:* $3098. *Average need-based gift aid:* $5484. *Average non-need-based aid:* $3455.

**Applying** *Options:* electronic application, early admission, deferred entrance. *Required for some:* high school transcript, 1 letter of recommendation. *Recommended:* high school transcript. *Application deadlines:* rolling (freshmen), rolling (transfers).

**Freshman Application Contact** Mr. Jeremy Bradt, Director, Enrollment and Records, Highland Community College, 2998 West Pearl City Road, Freeport, IL 61032. *Phone:* 815-235-6121 Ext. 3500. *Fax:* 815-235-6130. *E-mail:* jeremy.bradt@highland.edu.
*Website:* http://www.highland.edu/.

# Illinois Central College
## East Peoria, Illinois

- **State and locally supported** 2-year, founded 1967, part of Illinois Community College Board
- **Suburban** 430-acre campus
- **Coed,** 9,266 undergraduate students, 34% full-time, 56% women, 44% men

**Undergraduates** 3,115 full-time, 6,151 part-time. Students come from 20 states and territories; 13 other countries; 1% are from out of state; 12% Black or African American, non-Hispanic/Latino; 4% Hispanic/Latino; 2% Asian, non-Hispanic/Latino; 0.1% Native Hawaiian or other Pacific Islander, non-Hispanic/Latino; 0.3% American Indian or Alaska Native, non-Hispanic/Latino; 3% Two or more races, non-Hispanic/Latino; 0.2% Race/ethnicity unknown; 1% international; 2% transferred in; 3% live on campus. *Retention:* 66% of full-time freshmen returned.
**Freshmen** *Admission:* 1,844 applied, 1,844 admitted, 875 enrolled.
**Faculty** *Total:* 531, 31% full-time, 11% with terminal degrees. *Student/faculty ratio:* 18:1.
**Majors** Accounting; administrative assistant and secretarial science; agricultural business and management; agricultural/farm supplies retailing and wholesaling; agricultural mechanics and equipment technology; animal/livestock husbandry and production; applied horticulture/horticulture operations; automobile/automotive mechanics technology; banking and financial support services; business administration and management; childcare provision; clinical/medical laboratory technology; computer programming; computer systems networking and telecommunications; construction engineering technology; criminal justice/police science; crop production; culinary arts; dental hygiene; diesel mechanics technology; electrical, electronic and communications engineering technology; emergency medical technology (EMT paramedic); energy management and systems technology; engineering; fire science/firefighting; general studies; graphic design; health and physical education/fitness; heating, air conditioning, ventilation and refrigeration maintenance technology; industrial technology; legal assistant/paralegal; liberal arts and sciences/liberal studies; library and archives assisting; manufacturing engineering technology; mechanical engineering/mechanical technology; occupational therapist assistant; physical therapy technology; platemaking/imaging; radiologic technology/science; registered nursing/registered nurse; respiratory care therapy; retailing; robotics technology; sign language interpretation and translation; substance abuse/addiction counseling; surgical technology; web/multimedia management and webmaster; web page, digital/multimedia and information resources design; welding technology.
**Academics** *Calendar:* semesters. *Degree:* certificates and associate. *Special study options:* academic remediation for entering students, adult/continuing education programs, advanced placement credit, distance learning, English as a second language, honors programs, independent study, internships, part-time degree program, services for LD students, study abroad, summer session for credit.
**Library** Illinois Central College Library plus 1 other. *Books:* 45,000 (physical), 67,809 (digital/electronic); *Serial titles:* 101 (physical), 11,251 (digital/electronic); *Databases:* 186. Weekly public service hours: 72.
**Student Life** *Housing Options:* coed, men-only, women-only, special housing for students with disabilities. Campus housing is provided by a third party.

*Activities and Organizations:* drama/theater group, student-run newspaper, radio station, choral group. *Campus security:* 24-hour emergency response devices and patrols, late-night transport/escort service, controlled dormitory access. *Student services:* health clinic, personal/psychological counseling.
**Athletics** Member NJCAA. *Intercollegiate sports:* baseball M(s), basketball M(s)/W(s), cross-country running M(s)/W(s), golf M(s), soccer M(s)/W(s), softball W(s), volleyball W(s), weight lifting M/W. *Intramural sports:* basketball M/W, bowling M/W, football M/W, softball M/W, ultimate Frisbee M/W, volleyball M/W.
**Costs (2017–18)** *Tuition:* area resident $3432 full-time, $143 per credit hour part-time; state resident $7320 full-time, $305 per credit hour part-time; nonresident $8640 full-time, $360 per credit hour part-time. Full-time tuition and fees vary according to course load and reciprocity agreements. Part-time tuition and fees vary according to course load and reciprocity agreements. *Room and board:* Room and board charges vary according to housing facility. *Payment plan:* installment. *Waivers:* senior citizens and employees or children of employees.
**Financial Aid** Of all full-time matriculated undergraduates who enrolled in 2011, 6,521 applied for aid, 5,525 were judged to have need.
**Applying** *Options:* electronic application, early admission. *Required:* high school transcript. *Application deadlines:* rolling (freshmen), rolling (transfers). *Notification:* continuous (freshmen), continuous (transfers).
**Freshman Application Contact** Emily Points, Dean of Students, Illinois Central College, 1 College Drive, East Peoria, IL 61635. *Phone:* 309-694-8501. *E-mail:* emily.points@icc.edu.
*Website:* http://www.icc.edu/.

# Illinois Eastern Community Colleges, Frontier Community College
## Fairfield, Illinois

- **State and locally supported** 2-year, founded 1976, part of Illinois Eastern Community Colleges System
- **Rural** 8-acre campus
- **Coed,** 1,791 undergraduate students, 16% full-time, 62% women, 38% men

**Undergraduates** 290 full-time, 1,501 part-time. 1% are from out of state; 1% Black or African American, non-Hispanic/Latino; 1% Hispanic/Latino; 0.3% Asian, non-Hispanic/Latino; 0.2% American Indian or Alaska Native, non-Hispanic/Latino; 0.1% Race/ethnicity unknown.
**Freshmen** *Admission:* 135 enrolled.
**Faculty** *Total:* 143, 4% full-time. *Student/faculty ratio:* 27:1.
**Majors** Automobile/automotive mechanics technology; biological and physical sciences; business automation/technology/data entry; construction trades; corrections; emergency care attendant (EMT ambulance); engineering; executive assistant/executive secretary; fire science/firefighting; general studies; health information/medical records technology; information technology; liberal arts and sciences/liberal studies; registered nursing/registered nurse; sport and fitness administration/management; web page, digital/multimedia and information resources design.
**Academics** *Calendar:* semesters. *Degree:* certificates and associate. *Special study options:* academic remediation for entering students, adult/continuing education programs, advanced placement credit, cooperative education, distance learning, double majors, English as a second language, external degree program, independent study, part-time degree program, services for LD students, student-designed majors, summer session for credit.
**Library** Learning Resource Center plus 1 other.
**Student Life** *Housing:* college housing not available. *Student services:* veterans affairs office.
**Athletics** Member NJCAA. *Intercollegiate sports:* baseball M, golf M/W, softball W, volleyball W.
**Costs (2017–18)** *Tuition:* area resident $2656 full-time, $83 per semester hour part-time; state resident $8589 full-time, $268 per semester hour part-time; nonresident $10,580 full-time, $331 per semester hour part-time. *Required fees:* $1154 full-time, $32 per semester hour part-time, $5 per term part-time. *Payment plan:* installment. *Waivers:* senior citizens and employees or children of employees.
**Applying** *Options:* electronic application, early admission, deferred entrance. *Required:* high school transcript. *Application deadlines:* rolling (freshmen), rolling (transfers). *Notification:* continuous (freshmen), continuous (transfers).
**Freshman Application Contact** Ms. Amy Loss, Coordinator of Registration and Records, Illinois Eastern Community Colleges, Frontier Community College, 2 Frontier Drive, Fairfield, IL 62837. *Phone:* 618-842-3711 Ext. 4114. *Toll-free phone:* 877-464-3687. *Fax:* 618-842-6340. *E-mail:* lossa@iecc.edu.
*Website:* http://www.iecc.edu/fcc/.

# Illinois Eastern Community Colleges, Lincoln Trail College

## Robinson, Illinois

- **State and locally supported** 2-year, founded 1969, part of Illinois Eastern Community Colleges System
- **Rural** 120-acre campus
- **Coed,** 933 undergraduate students, 43% full-time, 54% women, 46% men

**Undergraduates** 399 full-time, 534 part-time. 6% are from out of state; 5% Black or African American, non-Hispanic/Latino; 1% Hispanic/Latino; 1% Asian, non-Hispanic/Latino; 0.1% Native Hawaiian or other Pacific Islander, non-Hispanic/Latino; 0.6% American Indian or Alaska Native, non-Hispanic/Latino; 0.5% Race/ethnicity unknown.

**Freshmen** *Admission:* 174 enrolled.

**Faculty** *Total:* 82, 17% full-time. *Student/faculty ratio:* 19:1.

**Majors** Biological and physical sciences; business automation/technology/data entry; computer systems networking and telecommunications; construction trades; corrections; general studies; health information/medical records administration; liberal arts and sciences/liberal studies; mechanical engineering/mechanical technology; medical/clinical assistant; quality control technology; sport and fitness administration/management; teacher assistant/aide; telecommunications technology.

**Academics** *Calendar:* semesters. *Degree:* certificates and associate. *Special study options:* academic remediation for entering students, adult/continuing education programs, advanced placement credit, cooperative education, distance learning, double majors, English as a second language, external degree program, independent study, internships, part-time degree program, services for LD students, student-designed majors, summer session for credit.

**Library** Eagleton Learning Resource Center plus 1 other.

**Student Life** *Housing:* college housing not available. *Activities and Organizations:* drama/theater group, choral group, national fraternities.

**Athletics** Member NJCAA. *Intercollegiate sports:* baseball M(s), basketball M(s)/W(s), softball W(s), volleyball W(s). *Intramural sports:* baseball M, basketball M, softball W, volleyball W.

**Costs (2017–18)** *Tuition:* area resident $2656 full-time, $83 per semester hour part-time; state resident $8589 full-time, $268 per semester hour part-time; nonresident $10,580 full-time, $331 per semester hour part-time. *Required fees:* $1154 full-time, $32 per semester hour part-time, $5 per term part-time. *Payment plan:* installment. *Waivers:* senior citizens and employees or children of employees.

**Applying** *Options:* electronic application, early admission, deferred entrance. *Required:* high school transcript. *Application deadlines:* rolling (freshmen), rolling (transfers). *Notification:* continuous (freshmen), continuous (transfers).

**Freshman Application Contact** Ms. Megan Scott, Director of Admissions, Illinois Eastern Community Colleges, Lincoln Trail College, 11220 State Highway 1, Robinson, IL 62454. *Phone:* 618-544-8657 Ext. 1137. *Toll-free phone:* 866-582-4322. *Fax:* 618-544-7423. *E-mail:* scottm@iecc.edu. *Website:* http://www.iecc.edu/ltc/.

# Illinois Eastern Community Colleges, Olney Central College

## Olney, Illinois

- **State and locally supported** 2-year, founded 1962, part of Illinois Eastern Community Colleges System
- **Rural** 128-acre campus
- **Coed,** 1,142 undergraduate students, 46% full-time, 58% women, 42% men

**Undergraduates** 522 full-time, 620 part-time. 2% Black or African American, non-Hispanic/Latino; 1% Hispanic/Latino; 1% Asian, non-Hispanic/Latino; 0.2% American Indian or Alaska Native, non-Hispanic/Latino.

**Freshmen** *Admission:* 242 enrolled.

**Faculty** *Total:* 101, 41% full-time. *Student/faculty ratio:* 12:1.

**Majors** Accounting; autobody/collision and repair technology; automobile/automotive mechanics technology; biological and physical sciences; business administration and management; business automation/technology/data entry; culinary arts; engineering; general studies; human resources management; industrial mechanics and maintenance technology; information technology; liberal arts and sciences/liberal studies; medical administrative assistant and medical secretary; medical radiologic technology; registered nursing/registered nurse.

**Academics** *Calendar:* semesters. *Degree:* certificates and associate. *Special study options:* academic remediation for entering students, adult/continuing education programs, advanced placement credit, cooperative education, distance learning, double majors, English as a second language, external

degree program, independent study, internships, part-time degree program, services for LD students, student-designed majors, summer session for credit.

**Library** Anderson Learning Resources Center plus 1 other.

**Student Life** *Housing:* college housing not available. *Activities and Organizations:* drama/theater group, student-run newspaper, choral group.

**Athletics** Member NJCAA. *Intercollegiate sports:* baseball M(s), basketball M(s)/W(s), softball W(s). *Intramural sports:* baseball M, basketball M/W, softball W.

**Costs (2017–18)** *Tuition:* area resident $2656 full-time, $83 per semester hour part-time; state resident $8589 full-time, $268 per semester hour part-time; nonresident $10,580 full-time, $331 per semester hour part-time. *Required fees:* $1154 full-time, $32 per semester hour part-time, $5 per term part-time. *Payment plan:* installment. *Waivers:* senior citizens and employees or children of employees.

**Applying** *Options:* electronic application, early admission, deferred entrance. *Required:* high school transcript. *Application deadlines:* rolling (freshmen), rolling (transfers). *Notification:* continuous (freshmen), continuous (transfers).

**Freshman Application Contact** Ms. Andrea Pampe, Assistant Dean for Student Services, Illinois Eastern Community Colleges, Olney Central College, 305 North West Street, Olney, IL 62450. *Phone:* 618-395-7777 Ext. 2005. *Toll-free phone:* 866-622-4322. *Fax:* 618-392-5212. *E-mail:* pampea@iecc.edu. *Website:* http://www.iecc.edu/occ/.

# Illinois Eastern Community Colleges, Wabash Valley College

## Mount Carmel, Illinois

- **State and locally supported** 2-year, founded 1960, part of Illinois Eastern Community Colleges System
- **Rural** 40-acre campus
- **Coed,** 3,662 undergraduate students, 13% full-time, 36% women, 64% men

**Undergraduates** 458 full-time, 3,204 part-time. 7% are from out of state; 5% Black or African American, non-Hispanic/Latino; 0.7% Hispanic/Latino; 1% Asian, non-Hispanic/Latino; 0.2% American Indian or Alaska Native, non-Hispanic/Latino.

**Freshmen** *Admission:* 202 enrolled.

**Faculty** *Total:* 129, 24% full-time. *Student/faculty ratio:* 33:1.

**Majors** Agricultural business and management; agricultural production; biological and physical sciences; business administration and management; business automation/technology/data entry; child development; diesel mechanics technology; energy management and systems technology; engineering; executive assistant/executive secretary; general studies; industrial technology; legal assistant/paralegal; liberal arts and sciences/liberal studies; machine tool technology; manufacturing engineering technology; mining technology; radio and television; recording arts technology; social work; sport and fitness administration/management; sports communication.

**Academics** *Calendar:* semesters. *Degree:* certificates and associate. *Special study options:* academic remediation for entering students, adult/continuing education programs, advanced placement credit, cooperative education, distance learning, double majors, English as a second language, external degree program, independent study, internships, part-time degree program, services for LD students, student-designed majors, summer session for credit.

**Library** Bauer Media Center plus 1 other.

**Student Life** *Housing:* college housing not available. *Activities and Organizations:* drama/theater group, student-run newspaper, radio and television station, choral group.

**Athletics** Member NJCAA. *Intercollegiate sports:* baseball M(s), basketball M(s)/W(s), softball W(s). *Intramural sports:* baseball M, basketball M/W, softball W.

**Costs (2017–18)** *Tuition:* area resident $2656 full-time, $83 per semester hour part-time; state resident $8589 full-time, $268 per semester hour part-time; nonresident $10,580 full-time, $331 per semester hour part-time. *Required fees:* $1154 full-time, $32 per semester hour part-time, $5 per term part-time. *Payment plan:* installment. *Waivers:* senior citizens and employees or children of employees.

**Applying** *Options:* electronic application, early admission, deferred entrance. *Required:* high school transcript. *Application deadlines:* rolling (freshmen), rolling (transfers). *Notification:* continuous (freshmen), continuous (transfers).

**Freshman Application Contact** Mrs. Tiffany Cowger, Assistant Dean for Student Services, Illinois Eastern Community Colleges, Wabash Valley College, 2200 College Drive, Mt. Carmel, IL 62863. *Phone:* 618-262-8641 Ext. 3101. *Toll-free phone:* 866-982-4322. *Fax:* 618-262-8647. *E-mail:* cowgert@iecc.edu. *Website:* http://www.iecc.edu/wvc/.

# Illinois Valley Community College
## Oglesby, Illinois

- **District-supported** 2-year, founded 1924, part of Illinois Community College Board
- **Rural** 410-acre campus with easy access to Chicago
- **Endowment** $3.7 million
- **Coed,** 3,241 undergraduate students, 39% full-time, 57% women, 43% men

**Undergraduates** 1,259 full-time, 1,982 part-time. Students come from 1 other state; 1 other country; 2% Black or African American, non-Hispanic/Latino; 5% Hispanic/Latino; 1% Asian, non-Hispanic/Latino; 0.3% American Indian or Alaska Native, non-Hispanic/Latino; 10% Race/ethnicity unknown; 3% transferred in. *Retention:* 59% of full-time freshmen returned.

**Freshmen** *Admission:* 1,435 applied, 672 admitted, 487 enrolled.

**Faculty** *Total:* 270, 34% full-time. *Student/faculty ratio:* 16:1.

**Majors** Accounting; automobile/automotive mechanics technology; biological and physical sciences; business administration and management; business automation/technology/data entry; CAD/CADD drafting/design technology; child-care provision; child development; computer programming; computer systems networking and telecommunications; corrections; criminal justice/law enforcement administration; criminal justice/police science; data processing and data processing technology; drafting and design technology; drafting/design engineering technologies related; early childhood education; education; electrical, electronic and communications engineering technology; electrician; elementary education; engineering; English; forensic science and technology; general studies; graphic design; industrial technology; information technology; journalism; juvenile corrections; liberal arts and sciences/liberal studies; marketing/marketing management; massage therapy; mechanical engineering/mechanical technology; network and system administration; pre-engineering; registered nursing/registered nurse; selling skills and sales; social work; teacher assistant/aide.

**Academics** *Calendar:* semesters. *Degree:* certificates and associate. *Special study options:* academic remediation for entering students, advanced placement credit, distance learning, English as a second language, honors programs, independent study, internships, off-campus study, part-time degree program, services for LD students, student-designed majors, study abroad, summer session for credit.

**Library** Jacobs Library.

**Student Life** *Housing:* college housing not available. *Activities and Organizations:* drama/theater group, student-run newspaper, choral group, Chemistry Club, Student Embassadors, Phi Theta Kappa, Illinois Valley Leaders for Service, Student Veterans Association. *Campus security:* 24-hour emergency response devices and patrols, late-night transport/escort service. *Student services:* personal/psychological counseling, veterans affairs office.

**Athletics** Member NJCAA. *Intercollegiate sports:* baseball M, basketball M/W, golf M, soccer M/W, softball W, tennis M/W. *Intramural sports:* basketball M, volleyball W.

**Standardized Tests** *Recommended:* ACT (for admission).

**Costs (2017–18)** *Tuition:* $123 per credit hour part-time; state resident $353 per credit hour part-time; nonresident $382 per credit hour part-time. Full-time tuition and fees vary according to course load and reciprocity agreements. Part-time tuition and fees vary according to course load and reciprocity agreements. *Required fees:* $7 per credit hour part-time, $5 per term part-time. *Payment plan:* deferred payment. *Waivers:* senior citizens and employees or children of employees.

**Financial Aid** Of all full-time matriculated undergraduates who enrolled in 2016, 81 Federal Work-Study jobs (averaging $955).

**Applying** *Options:* electronic application, early admission, deferred entrance. *Required:* high school transcript. *Application deadlines:* rolling (freshmen), rolling (transfers). *Notification:* continuous (freshmen), continuous (transfers).

**Freshman Application Contact** Mr. Quintin Overocker, Director of Admissions and Records, Illinois Valley Community College, Oglesby, IL 61348. *Phone:* 815-224-0437. *Fax:* 815-224-3033. *E-mail:* quintin_overocker@ivcc.edu. *Website:* http://www.ivcc.edu/.

# John A. Logan College
## Carterville, Illinois

**Director of Admissions** Mr. Terry Crain, Dean of Student Services, John A. Logan College, 700 Logan College Road, Carterville, IL 62918-9900. *Phone:* 618-985-3741 Ext. 8382. *Fax:* 618-985-4433. *E-mail:* terrycrain@jalc.edu. *Website:* http://www.jalc.edu/.

# John Wood Community College
## Quincy, Illinois

**Freshman Application Contact** Mr. Lee Wibbell, Director of Admissions, John Wood Community College, Quincy, IL 62305-8736. *Phone:* 217-641-4339. *Fax:* 217-224-4208. *E-mail:* admissions@jwcc.edu. *Website:* http://www.jwcc.edu/.

# Joliet Junior College
## Joliet, Illinois

**Freshman Application Contact** Ms. Jennifer Kloberdanz, Director of Admissions and Recruitment, Joliet Junior College, 1215 Houbolt Road, Joliet, IL 60431. *Phone:* 815-729-9020 Ext. 2414. *E-mail:* admission@jjc.edu. *Website:* http://www.jjc.edu/.

# Kankakee Community College
## Kankakee, Illinois

**Freshman Application Contact** Ms. Kim Harpin, Director of Support Services, Kankakee Community College, 100 College Drive, Kankakee, IL 60901. *Phone:* 815-802-8472. *Fax:* 815-802-8472. *E-mail:* kharpin@kcc.edu. *Website:* http://www.kcc.edu/.

# Kaskaskia College
## Centralia, Illinois

- **State and locally supported** 2-year, founded 1966, part of Illinois Community College Board
- **Rural** 195-acre campus with easy access to St. Louis
- **Endowment** $7.7 million
- **Coed,** 3,107 undergraduate students, 39% full-time, 61% women, 39% men

**Undergraduates** 1,212 full-time, 1,895 part-time. Students come from 14 states and territories; 1% are from out of state; 5% Black or African American, non-Hispanic/Latino; 1% Hispanic/Latino; 0.6% Asian, non-Hispanic/Latino; 0.7% American Indian or Alaska Native, non-Hispanic/Latino; 2% Two or more races, non-Hispanic/Latino; 0.2% Race/ethnicity unknown; 1% transferred in.

**Freshmen** *Admission:* 202 enrolled.

**Faculty** *Total:* 150, 43% full-time, 7% with terminal degrees. *Student/faculty ratio:* 19:1.

**Majors** Accounting; agriculture; animal sciences; applied horticulture/horticulture operations; architectural drafting and CAD/CADD; automobile/automotive mechanics technology; biological and physical sciences; business automation/technology/data entry; business/commerce; carpentry; child-care provision; clinical/medical laboratory technology; construction management; cosmetology; criminal justice/law enforcement administration; culinary arts; dental assisting; electrical, electronic and communications engineering technology; emergency medical technology (EMT paramedic); engineering; executive assistant/executive secretary; food service and dining room management; general studies; health information/medical records technology; heating, air conditioning, ventilation and refrigeration maintenance technology; industrial mechanics and maintenance technology; juvenile corrections; liberal arts and sciences/liberal studies; library and archives assisting; music; network and system administration; occupational therapist assistant; physical therapy technology; radiologic technology/science; registered nursing/registered nurse; respiratory care therapy; robotics technology; teacher assistant/aide; veterinary/animal health technology; web/multimedia management and webmaster; welding technology.

**Academics** *Calendar:* semesters. *Degree:* certificates and associate. *Special study options:* academic remediation for entering students, accelerated degree program, adult/continuing education programs, cooperative education, distance learning, double majors, English as a second language, honors programs, independent study, internships, off-campus study, part-time degree program, services for LD students, summer session for credit. *ROTC:* Army (c).

**Library** Kaskaskia College Library. *Books:* 17,285 (physical), 24,433 (digital/electronic); *Serial titles:* 24 (physical); *Databases:* 86. Weekly public service hours: 47.

**Student Life** *Housing:* college housing not available. *Activities and Organizations:* drama/theater group, choral group, Phi Theta Kappa, Student Radiography Club, LPN Club, Physical Therapy Club, Fellowship of Christian Athletes. *Campus security:* 24-hour emergency response devices and patrols, late-night transport/escort service. *Student services:* personal/psychological counseling, veterans affairs office.

**Athletics** Member NJCAA. *Intercollegiate sports:* baseball M(s), basketball M(s)/W(s), cheerleading M(s)/W(s), cross-country running M(s)/W(s), golf M(s)/W(s), soccer W(s), softball W(s), tennis M(s), volleyball W(s).

**Standardized Tests** *Recommended:* SAT or ACT (for admission).

**Costs (2018–19)** *Tuition:* area resident $3990 full-time, $133 per credit hour part-time; state resident $7050 full-time, $235 per credit hour part-time; nonresident $11,850 full-time, $395 per credit hour part-time. Full-time tuition and fees vary according to program. Part-time tuition and fees vary according to program. *Required fees:* $480 full-time, $16 per credit hour part-time. *Payment plan:* installment. *Waivers:* senior citizens and employees or children of employees.

**Financial Aid** Of all full-time matriculated undergraduates who enrolled in 2016, 912 applied for aid, 704 were judged to have need, 46 had their need fully met. 22 Federal Work-Study jobs (averaging $2502). 8 state and other part-time jobs (averaging $1793). In 2016, 28 non-need-based awards were made. *Average percent of need met:* 46%. *Average financial aid package:* $6437. *Average need-based gift aid:* $3913. *Average non-need-based aid:* $4621.

**Applying** *Options:* electronic application, early admission, deferred entrance. *Required:* high school transcript. *Required for some:* interview. *Application deadlines:* rolling (freshmen), rolling (transfers). *Notification:* continuous (freshmen), continuous (transfers).

**Freshman Application Contact** Jenna Lammers, Registrar, Kaskaskia College, 27210 College Road, Centralia, IL 62801. *Phone:* 618-545-3044. *Toll-free phone:* 800-642-0859. *Fax:* 618-532-1990. *E-mail:* jlammers@kaskaskia.edu.

*Website:* http://www.kaskaskia.edu/.

# Kishwaukee College
## Malta, Illinois

- **State and locally supported** 2-year, founded 1967, part of Illinois Community College Board
- **Rural** 120-acre campus with easy access to Chicago
- **Coed,** 3,775 undergraduate students, 43% full-time, 53% women, 47% men

**Undergraduates** 1,634 full-time, 2,141 part-time. 15% Black or African American, non-Hispanic/Latino; 15% Hispanic/Latino; 2% Asian, non-Hispanic/Latino; 0.1% Native Hawaiian or other Pacific Islander, non-Hispanic/Latino; 0.5% American Indian or Alaska Native, non-Hispanic/Latino; 3% Two or more races, non-Hispanic/Latino; 2% Race/ethnicity unknown. *Retention:* 59% of full-time freshmen returned.

**Freshmen** *Admission:* 614 enrolled.

**Faculty** *Total:* 236, 32% full-time, 6% with terminal degrees. *Student/faculty ratio:* 16:1.

**Majors** Administrative assistant and secretarial science; agricultural mechanization; airline pilot and flight crew; applied horticulture/horticulture operations; art; autobody/collision and repair technology; automobile/automotive mechanics technology; biological and physical sciences; business administration and management; CAD/CADD drafting/design technology; child-care and support services management; child-care provision; criminal justice/police science; criminal justice/safety; diesel mechanics technology; education (multiple levels); electrical, electronic and communications engineering technology; emergency medical technology (EMT paramedic); engineering; fine/studio arts; forensic science and technology; information technology; landscaping and groundskeeping; liberal arts and sciences/liberal studies; network and system administration; ornamental horticulture; radiologic technology/science; registered nursing/registered nurse; teacher assistant/aide.

**Academics** *Calendar:* semesters. *Degree:* certificates, diplomas, and associate. *Special study options:* academic remediation for entering students, adult/continuing education programs, advanced placement credit, cooperative education, distance learning, double majors, English as a second language, external degree program, freshman honors college, honors programs, independent study, internships, off-campus study, part-time degree program, services for LD students, study abroad, summer session for credit.

**Library** Kishwaukee College Library. Students can reserve study rooms.

**Student Life** *Housing:* college housing not available. *Activities and Organizations:* drama/theater group, student-run newspaper, choral group. *Campus security:* 24-hour emergency response devices and patrols. *Student services:* health clinic, personal/psychological counseling, veterans affairs office.

**Athletics** Member NJCAA. *Intercollegiate sports:* baseball M(s), basketball M(s)/W(s), cross-country running M/W, softball W(s), volleyball W(s).

**Costs (2018–19)** *Tuition:* area resident $4260 full-time, $142 per credit hour part-time; state resident $8520 full-time, $284 per credit hour part-time; nonresident $12,780 full-time, $426 per credit hour part-time. Full-time tuition and fees vary according to program and reciprocity agreements. Part-time tuition and fees vary according to program and reciprocity agreements. *Required fees:* $570 full-time, $17 per credit hour part-time. *Payment plans:*

installment, deferred payment. *Waivers:* senior citizens and employees or children of employees.

**Financial Aid** *Average indebtedness upon graduation:* $4375.

**Applying** *Options:* electronic application, early admission, deferred entrance. *Required for some:* high school transcript. *Recommended:* high school transcript, transcripts from all other colleges or universities previously attended. *Application deadlines:* rolling (freshmen), rolling (transfers). *Notification:* continuous (freshmen), continuous (transfers).

**Freshman Application Contact** Ms. Graciela Horta, Coordinator, Student Outreach, Kishwaukee College, 21193 Malta Road, Malta, IL 60150. *Phone:* 815-825-1711. *E-mail:* ghorta@kish.edu.

*Website:* http://www.kish.edu/.

# Lake Land College
## Mattoon, Illinois

**Freshman Application Contact** Mr. Jon VanDyke, Dean of Admissions Services, Lake Land College, Mattoon, IL 61938-9366. *Phone:* 217-234-5378. *E-mail:* admissions@lakeland.cc.il.us. *Website:* http://www.lakelandcollege.edu/.

# Lewis and Clark Community College
## Godfrey, Illinois

**Freshman Application Contact** Lewis and Clark Community College, 5800 Godfrey Road, Godfrey, IL 62035-2466. *Phone:* 618-468-5100. *Toll-free phone:* 800-YES-LCCC. *Website:* http://www.lc.edu/.

# Lincoln College of Technology
## Melrose Park, Illinois

**Admissions Office Contact** Lincoln College of Technology, 8317 West North Avenue, Melrose Park, IL 60160. *Toll-free phone:* 844-215-1513. *Website:* http://www.lincolntech.edu/.

# Lincoln Land Community College
## Springfield, Illinois

**Freshman Application Contact** Mr. Ron Gregoire, Executive Director of Admissions and Records, Lincoln Land Community College, 5250 Shepherd Road, PO Box 19256, Springfield, IL 62794-9256. *Phone:* 217-786-2243. *Toll-free phone:* 800-727-4161. *Fax:* 217-786-2492. *E-mail:* ron.gregoire@llcc.edu. *Website:* http://www.llcc.edu/.

# MacCormac College
## Chicago, Illinois

**Director of Admissions** Mr. David Grassi, Director of Admissions, MacCormac College, 506 South Wabash Avenue, Chicago, IL 60605-1667. *Phone:* 312-922-1884 Ext. 102. *Website:* http://www.maccormac.edu/.

# McHenry County College
## Crystal Lake, Illinois

- **State and locally supported** 2-year, founded 1967, part of Illinois Community College Board
- **Suburban** 168-acre campus with easy access to Chicago
- **Coed,** 6,371 undergraduate students, 33% full-time, 54% women, 46% men

**Undergraduates** 2,097 full-time, 4,274 part-time. 0.4% are from out of state; 2% Black or African American, non-Hispanic/Latino; 16% Hispanic/Latino; 2% Asian, non-Hispanic/Latino; 0.2% Native Hawaiian or other Pacific Islander, non-Hispanic/Latino; 0.1% American Indian or Alaska Native, non-Hispanic/Latino; 3% Two or more races, non-Hispanic/Latino; 6% Race/ethnicity unknown; 0.2% international; 10% transferred in.

**Freshmen** *Admission:* 1,750 applied, 1,750 admitted, 1,024 enrolled. *Average high school GPA:* 2.3.

**Faculty** *Total:* 323, 30% full-time, 67% with terminal degrees. *Student/faculty ratio:* 21:1.

**Majors** Accounting; administrative assistant and secretarial science; animation, interactive technology, video graphics and special effects; applied horticulture/horticulture operations; biological and physical sciences; business administration and management; child-care provision; commercial photography; computer systems networking and telecommunications; construction management; criminal justice/police science; emergency medical technology (EMT paramedic); engineering; fine/studio arts; fire science/firefighting; general studies; health and physical education/fitness;

information technology; liberal arts and sciences/liberal studies; music; occupational therapist assistant; operations management; registered nursing/registered nurse; restaurant, culinary, and catering management; robotics technology; selling skills and sales; special education.

**Academics** *Calendar:* semesters. *Degree:* certificates and associate. *Special study options:* academic remediation for entering students, accelerated degree program, adult/continuing education programs, advanced placement credit, cooperative education, distance learning, English as a second language, independent study, internships, part-time degree program, services for LD students, study abroad, summer session for credit.

**Library** McHenry County College Library. *Books:* 42,019 (physical), 1,272 (digital/electronic); *Serial titles:* 52 (physical), 23,384 (digital/electronic); *Databases:* 106.

**Student Life** *Housing:* college housing not available. *Activities and Organizations:* drama/theater group, student-run newspaper, radio station, choral group, Phi Theta Kappa, Student Senate, Equality Club, Writer's Block, Latinos Unidos. *Campus security:* 24-hour emergency response devices and patrols, late-night transport/escort service.

**Athletics** Member NJCAA. *Intercollegiate sports:* baseball M(s), basketball M(s)/W(s), soccer M(s), softball W(s), tennis M(s)/W(s), volleyball W(s).

**Costs (2018–19)** *Tuition:* area resident $3120 full-time, $104 per credit hour part-time; state resident $11,862 full-time, $395 per credit hour part-time; nonresident $14,319 full-time, $477 per credit hour part-time. Full-time tuition and fees vary according to course load. Part-time tuition and fees vary according to course load. *Required fees:* $284 full-time, $9 per credit hour part-time, $7 per term part-time. *Payment plan:* installment. *Waivers:* senior citizens and employees or children of employees.

**Financial Aid** Of all full-time matriculated undergraduates who enrolled in 2016, 200 Federal Work-Study jobs (averaging $3700). 130 state and other part-time jobs (averaging $2000).

**Applying** *Options:* electronic application, early admission, deferred entrance. *Application fee:* $15. *Recommended:* high school transcript. *Application deadlines:* rolling (freshmen), rolling (transfers). *Notification:* continuous (freshmen), continuous (transfers).

**Freshman Application Contact** Kellie Carper-Sowiak, Manager of New Student Transitions, McHenry County College, 8900 US Highway 14, Crystal Lake, IL 60012-2761. *Phone:* 815-455-8670. *E-mail:* admissions@mchenry.edu.

*Website:* http://www.mchenry.edu/.

## Midwestern Career College
### Chicago, Illinois

**Admissions Office Contact** Midwestern Career College, 20 North Wacker Drive #3800, Chicago, IL 60606. *Website:* http://www.mccollege.edu/.

## Moraine Valley Community College
### Palos Hills, Illinois

**Freshman Application Contact** Mr. Andrew Sarata, Director, Admissions and Recruitment, Moraine Valley Community College, 9000 West College Parkway, Palos Hills, IL 60465-0937. *Phone:* 708-974-5357. *Fax:* 708-974-0681. *E-mail:* sarataa@morainevalley.edu. *Website:* http://www.morainevalley.edu/.

## Morrison Institute of Technology
### Morrison, Illinois

- **Independent** 2-year, founded 1973
- **Small-town** 17-acre campus
- **Endowment** $76,000
- **Coed, primarily men,** 144 undergraduate students, 99% full-time, 9% women, 91% men

**Undergraduates** 142 full-time, 2 part-time. Students come from 4 states and territories; 5% are from out of state; 7% transferred in; 55% live on campus.

**Freshmen** *Admission:* 94 applied, 94 admitted, 71 enrolled. *Average high school GPA:* 2.2.

**Faculty** *Total:* 15, 93% full-time. *Student/faculty ratio:* 13:1.

**Majors** CAD/CADD drafting/design technology; construction engineering technology; drafting and design technology; engineering technology; mechanical drafting and CAD/CADD; surveying technology.

**Academics** *Calendar:* semesters. *Degree:* associate. *Special study options:* academic remediation for entering students, double majors, internships, part-time degree program.

**Library** Morrison Tech Learning Center plus 1 other. Study areas open 24 hours, 5&-7 days a week.

**Student Life** *Housing:* on-campus residence required for freshman year. *Options:* coed. Campus housing is university owned. Freshman applicants

given priority for college housing. *Campus security:* late-night transport/escort service, controlled dormitory access.

**Athletics** *Intramural sports:* basketball M, bowling M/W, softball M/W, table tennis M/W, volleyball M/W.

**Financial Aid** Of all full-time matriculated undergraduates who enrolled in 2009, 20 Federal Work-Study jobs (averaging $2000).

**Applying** *Options:* deferred entrance. *Application fee:* $30. *Required:* high school transcript, proof of immunization. *Application deadline:* rolling (freshmen). *Notification:* continuous until 9/1 (freshmen), continuous (transfers).

**Admissions Office Contact** Morrison Institute of Technology, 701 Portland Avenue, Morrison, IL 61270-0410.

*Website:* http://www.morrisontech.edu/.

## Morton College
### Cicero, Illinois

- **State and locally supported** 2-year, founded 1924, part of Illinois Community College Board
- **Suburban** 25-acre campus with easy access to Chicago
- **Coed,** 3,913 undergraduate students, 35% full-time, 55% women, 45% men

**Undergraduates** 1,366 full-time, 2,547 part-time. Students come from 15 states and territories; 1% are from out of state; 3% Black or African American, non-Hispanic/Latino; 84% Hispanic/Latino; 1% Asian, non-Hispanic/Latino; 0.2% American Indian or Alaska Native, non-Hispanic/Latino; 4% Race/ethnicity unknown; 40% transferred in.

**Freshmen** *Admission:* 613 admitted, 613 enrolled.

**Faculty** *Total:* 240, 22% full-time, 16% with terminal degrees. *Student/faculty ratio:* 17:1.

**Majors** Accounting; administrative assistant and secretarial science; art; automobile/automotive mechanics technology; biological and physical sciences; business administration and management; CAD/CADD drafting/design technology; child-care provision; computer support specialist; criminal justice/police science; data processing and data processing technology; drafting and design technology; early childhood education; finance; fine/studio arts; fire science/firefighting; health information/medical records technology; heating, air conditioning, ventilation and refrigeration maintenance technology; information technology; legal administrative assistant/secretary; liberal arts and sciences/liberal studies; marketing/marketing management; massage therapy; medical administrative assistant and medical secretary; music; physical therapy; physical therapy technology; registered nursing/registered nurse; web/multimedia management and webmaster.

**Academics** *Calendar:* semesters. *Degree:* certificates and associate. *Special study options:* academic remediation for entering students, adult/continuing education programs, advanced placement credit, distance learning, English as a second language, internships, part-time degree program, services for LD students, student-designed majors, summer session for credit.

**Library** Learning Resource Center. Students can reserve study rooms.

**Student Life** *Housing:* college housing not available. *Activities and Organizations:* drama/theater group, student-run newspaper, radio station, Morton Ambassador Program, Campus Activities Board, Student Government Association, Nursing Club. *Campus security:* 24-hour patrols, security cameras.

**Athletics** Member NJCAA. *Intercollegiate sports:* baseball M(s), basketball M(s)/W(s), cross-country running M(s)/W(s), soccer M/W(s), softball W(s), volleyball W(s).

**Costs (2018–19)** *Tuition:* area resident $2112 full-time, $88 per credit hour part-time; state resident $5184 full-time, $216 per credit hour part-time; nonresident $6720 full-time, $280 per credit hour part-time. *Required fees:* $980 full-time, $40 per credit hour part-time, $10 per term part-time. *Payment plan:* installment. *Waivers:* senior citizens and employees or children of employees.

**Applying** *Options:* electronic application. *Application fee:* $10. *Required:* high school transcript. *Application deadlines:* rolling (freshmen), rolling (transfers).

**Admissions Office Contact** Morton College, 3801 South Central Avenue, Cicero, IL 60804-4398.

*Website:* http://www.morton.edu/.

## Northwestern College–Bridgeview Campus
### Bridgeview, Illinois

**Admissions Office Contact** Northwestern College–Bridgeview Campus, 7725 South Harlem Avenue, Bridgeview, IL 60645. *Toll-free phone:* 888-205-2283. *Website:* http://www.nc.edu/locations/bridgeview-campus/.

## Northwestern College–Chicago Campus
### Chicago, Illinois

**Freshman Application Contact** Northwestern College–Chicago Campus, 4829 North Lipps Avenue, Chicago, IL 60630. *Phone:* 708-233-5000. *Toll-free phone:* 888-205-2283. *Website:* http://www.nc.edu/locations/chicago-campus/.

## Oakton Community College
### Des Plaines, Illinois

- **District-supported** 2-year, founded 1969, part of Illinois Community College Board
- **Suburban** 193-acre campus with easy access to Chicago
- **Coed,** 8,348 undergraduate students

**Majors** Accounting technology and bookkeeping; administrative assistant and secretarial science; architectural drafting and CAD/CADD; automobile/automotive mechanics technology; banking and financial support services; biological and physical sciences; building/construction finishing, management, and inspection related; child-care provision; clinical/medical laboratory technology; computer programming; criminal justice/police science; electrical, electronic and communications engineering technology; engineering; fire science/firefighting; graphic design; health information/medical records administration; heating, ventilation, air conditioning and refrigeration engineering technology; information technology; liberal arts and sciences/liberal studies; manufacturing engineering technology; marketing/marketing management; mechanical engineering/mechanical technology; music; operations management; physical therapy technology; real estate; registered nursing/registered nurse; sales, distribution, and marketing operations; social work; substance abuse/addiction counseling.

**Academics** *Calendar:* semesters. *Degree:* certificates and associate. *Special study options:* academic remediation for entering students, adult/continuing education programs, advanced placement credit, distance learning, English as a second language, honors programs, independent study, internships, off-campus study, part-time degree program, services for LD students, study abroad, summer session for credit.

**Library** Oakton Community College Library plus 1 other.

**Student Life** *Housing:* college housing not available. *Activities and Organizations:* drama/theater group, student-run newspaper, choral group. *Campus security:* 24-hour emergency response devices and patrols, student patrols, late-night transport/escort service. *Student services:* health clinic, personal/psychological counseling, veterans affairs office.

**Athletics** Member NJCAA. *Intercollegiate sports:* baseball M, basketball M/W, cross-country running M/W, soccer M/W, softball W, tennis M/W, track and field M/W, volleyball W. *Intramural sports:* basketball M/W, cheerleading M, soccer M, table tennis M/W, volleyball M/W.

**Costs (2018–19)** *Tuition:* area resident $2958 full-time; state resident $8208 full-time; nonresident $9960 full-time. Full-time tuition and fees vary according to course load. Part-time tuition and fees vary according to course load. *Required fees:* $188 full-time. *Payment plans:* installment, deferred payment. *Waivers:* senior citizens and employees or children of employees.

**Applying** *Options:* electronic application. *Application fee:* $25. *Required for some:* interview. *Recommended:* high school transcript. *Application deadlines:* rolling (freshmen), rolling (transfers). *Notification:* continuous (freshmen), continuous (transfers).

**Freshman Application Contact** Ms. Nicci Cisarik, Admissions Specialist, Oakton Community College, 1600 East Golf Road, Des Plaines, IL 60016-1268. *Phone:* 847-635-1913. *Fax:* 847-635-1890. *E-mail:* ncisarik@oakton.edu.
*Website:* http://www.oakton.edu/.

## Parkland College
### Champaign, Illinois

**Freshman Application Contact** Mr. Tim Wendt, Director of Enrollment Services, Parkland College, Champaign, IL 61821-1899. *Phone:* 217-351-2482. *Toll-free phone:* 800-346-8089. *Fax:* 217-353-2640. *E-mail:* admissions@parkland.edu. *Website:* http://www.parkland.edu/.

## Prairie State College
### Chicago Heights, Illinois

**Freshman Application Contact** Jaime Miller, Director of Admissions, Prairie State College, 202 South Halsted Street, Chicago Heights, IL 60411. *Phone:* 708-709-3513. *E-mail:* jmmiller@prairiestate.edu. *Website:* http://www.prairiestate.edu/.

## Rend Lake College
### Ina, Illinois

- **State-supported** 2-year, founded 1967, part of Illinois Community College Board
- **Rural** 350-acre campus
- **Coed,** 2,333 undergraduate students, 51% full-time, 54% women, 46% men

**Undergraduates** 1,182 full-time, 1,151 part-time. Students come from 5 states and territories; 6 other countries; 0.5% are from out of state; 4% Black or African American, non-Hispanic/Latino; 0.9% Hispanic/Latino; 0.7% Asian, non-Hispanic/Latino; 0.1% Native Hawaiian or other Pacific Islander, non-Hispanic/Latino; 0.1% American Indian or Alaska Native, non-Hispanic/Latino; 2% transferred in.

**Freshmen** *Admission:* 589 admitted, 589 enrolled.

**Faculty** *Total:* 148, 39% full-time, 7% with terminal degrees. *Student/faculty ratio:* 18:1.

**Majors** Administrative assistant and secretarial science; agricultural business and management; agricultural mechanics and equipment technology; agricultural mechanization; agricultural production; architectural drafting and CAD/CADD; automobile/automotive mechanics technology; barbering; biological and physical sciences; biomedical technology; business/commerce; child-care provision; computer programming; computer technology/computer systems technology; cosmetology; criminal justice/police science; culinary arts; emergency medical technology (EMT paramedic); engineering; fine/studio arts; graphic design; health information/medical records technology; heavy equipment maintenance technology; industrial mechanics and maintenance technology; liberal arts and sciences/liberal studies; manufacturing engineering technology; medical/clinical assistant; medical radiologic technology; medical staff services technology; music; petroleum technology; registered nursing/registered nurse; surveying technology; welding technology.

**Academics** *Calendar:* semesters. *Degree:* certificates and associate. *Special study options:* academic remediation for entering students, adult/continuing education programs, advanced placement credit, cooperative education, distance learning, double majors, English as a second language, honors programs, independent study, internships, off-campus study, part-time degree program, services for LD students, study abroad, summer session for credit.

**Library** Learning Resource Center. *Books:* 12,794 (physical), 46,844 (digital/electronic); *Serial titles:* 69 (physical), 22,796 (digital/electronic); *Databases:* 33. Weekly public service hours: 54; students can reserve study rooms.

**Student Life** *Housing:* college housing not available. *Activities and Organizations:* drama/theater group, choral group, Agriculture Club, Automotive Club, Art League, College Bowl, Musical Notes Society. *Campus security:* 24-hour emergency response devices and patrols, late-night transport/escort service. *Student services:* personal/psychological counseling, veterans affairs office.

**Athletics** Member NJCAA. *Intercollegiate sports:* baseball M(s), basketball M(s)/W(s), golf M(s)/W(s), softball W(s), tennis W(s), volleyball W(s).

**Costs (2018–19)** *Tuition:* area resident $3300 full-time, $110 per credit hour part-time; state resident $5250 full-time, $175 per credit hour part-time; nonresident $6000 full-time, $200 per credit hour part-time. Full-time tuition and fees vary according to course level, course load, program, and reciprocity agreements. Part-time tuition and fees vary according to course level, course load, program, and reciprocity agreements. *Required fees:* $600 full-time, $20 per credit hour part-time. *Payment plan:* installment. *Waivers:* senior citizens and employees or children of employees.

**Financial Aid** Of all full-time matriculated undergraduates who enrolled in 2016, 133 Federal Work-Study jobs (averaging $1000). 174 state and other part-time jobs (averaging $940).

**Applying** *Options:* electronic application, deferred entrance. *Required:* high school transcript. *Application deadlines:* 8/18 (freshmen), 8/18 (transfers).

**Freshman Application Contact** Mrs. Jena Jensik, Director of Advisement, Rend Lake College, 468 North Ken Gray Parkway, Ina, IL 62846-9801. *Phone:* 618-437-5321 Ext. 1293. *Toll-free phone:* 800-369-5321. *Fax:* 618-437-5677. *E-mail:* jensikj@rlc.edu.
*Website:* http://www.rlc.edu/.

## Richland Community College
### Decatur, Illinois

**Freshman Application Contact** Ms. Catherine Sebok, Director of Admissions and Records, Richland Community College, Decatur, IL 62521. *Phone:* 217-875-7200 Ext. 558. *Fax:* 217-875-7783. *E-mail:* csebok@richland.edu. *Website:* http://www.richland.edu/.

# Rockford Career College
Rockford, Illinois

Director of Admissions Ms. Barbara Holliman, Director of Admissions, Rockford Career College, 1130 South Alpine Road, Suite 100, Rockford, IL 61108. *Phone:* 815-965-8616 Ext. 16. *Website:* http://www.rockfordcareercollege.edu/.

# Rock Valley College
Rockford, Illinois

- **District-supported** 2-year, founded 1964, part of Illinois Community College Board
- **Suburban** 217-acre campus with easy access to Chicago
- **Coed,** 6,378 undergraduate students, 44% full-time, 54% women, 46% men

Undergraduates 2,796 full-time, 3,582 part-time. 8% Black or African American, non-Hispanic/Latino; 20% Hispanic/Latino; 3% Asian, non-Hispanic/Latino; 0.1% Native Hawaiian or other Pacific Islander, non-Hispanic/Latino; 0.4% American Indian or Alaska Native, non-Hispanic/Latino; 2% Two or more races, non-Hispanic/Latino; 2% Race/ethnicity unknown; 0.6% international; 3% transferred in.
Freshmen *Admission:* 1,041 enrolled.
Faculty *Student/faculty ratio:* 17:1.
Majors Accounting; administrative assistant and secretarial science; automobile/automotive mechanics technology; avionics maintenance technology; business administration and management; child development; computer engineering technology; computer science; computer systems networking and telecommunications; construction engineering technology; criminal justice/law enforcement administration; dental hygiene; drafting/design engineering technologies related; electrical, electronic and communications engineering technology; electrician; energy management and systems technology; fire science/firefighting; graphic and printing equipment operation/production; human services; industrial and product design; industrial technology; liberal arts and sciences/liberal studies; marketing/marketing management; pre-engineering; quality control technology; registered nursing/registered nurse; respiratory care therapy; sheet metal technology; sport and fitness administration/management; surgical technology; tool and die technology; welding technology.
Academics *Calendar:* semesters. *Degree:* certificates, diplomas, and associate. *Special study options:* academic remediation for entering students, adult/continuing education programs, advanced placement credit, cooperative education, distance learning, English as a second language, honors programs, independent study, internships, part-time degree program, services for LD students, student-designed majors, study abroad, summer session for credit.
Library Educational Resource Center.
Student Life *Housing:* college housing not available. *Activities and Organizations:* drama/theater group, student-run newspaper, choral group, Black Student Alliance, Phi Theta Kappa, Adults on Campus, Inter-Varsity Club, Christian Fellowship. *Campus security:* 24-hour emergency response devices and patrols, late-night transport/escort service. *Student services:* personal/psychological counseling.
Athletics Member NJCAA. *Intercollegiate sports:* baseball M, basketball M/W, golf M, soccer M/W, softball W, squash W, tennis M/W, volleyball W. *Intramural sports:* skiing (downhill) M/W.
Costs (2018–19) *Tuition:* area resident $3450 full-time, $115 per credit hour part-time; state resident $8610 full-time, $287 per credit hour part-time; nonresident $15,000 full-time, $500 per credit hour part-time. Full-time tuition and fees vary according to course load. Part-time tuition and fees vary according to course load. *Required fees:* $314 full-time. *Payment plans:* installment, deferred payment. *Waivers:* employees or children of employees.
Financial Aid Of all full-time matriculated undergraduates who enrolled in 2016, 120 Federal Work-Study jobs (averaging $1800).
Applying *Required:* high school transcript.
Freshman Application Contact Mr. Melvin Allen, Executive Director of Recruitment and Admissions, Rock Valley College, 3301 North Mulford Road, Rockford, IL 61008. *Toll-free phone:* 800-973-7821. *E-mail:* m.allen@rockvalleycollege.edu.
*Website:* http://www.rockvalleycollege.edu/.

# SAE Institute Chicago
Chicago, Illinois

Admissions Office Contact SAE Institute Chicago, 820 North Orleans Street #125, Chicago, IL 60610. *Website:* http://www.sae.edu/.

# Sauk Valley Community College
Dixon, Illinois

- **District-supported** 2-year, founded 1965, part of Illinois Community College Board
- **Rural** 165-acre campus
- **Endowment** $2.0 million
- **Coed,** 2,220 undergraduate students, 45% full-time, 60% women, 40% men

Undergraduates 998 full-time, 1,222 part-time. 4% Black or African American, non-Hispanic/Latino; 8% Hispanic/Latino; 0.7% Asian, non-Hispanic/Latino; 0.2% Native Hawaiian or other Pacific Islander, non-Hispanic/Latino; 0.3% American Indian or Alaska Native, non-Hispanic/Latino; 0.1% Two or more races, non-Hispanic/Latino; 2% Race/ethnicity unknown. *Retention:* 59% of full-time freshmen returned.
Freshmen *Admission:* 585 applied, 585 admitted, 471 enrolled.
Faculty *Total:* 145; 30% full-time, 11% with terminal degrees. *Student/faculty ratio:* 21:1.
Majors Accounting; administrative assistant and secretarial science; agricultural business and management; agriculture; art; athletic training; biology/biological sciences; business administration and management; chemistry; communication; computer and information sciences related; corrections; criminal justice/law enforcement administration; criminal justice/police science; dramatic/theater arts; early childhood education; economics; education; electrical, electronic and communications engineering technology; elementary education; English; fire science/firefighting; foreign languages related; heating, air conditioning, ventilation and refrigeration maintenance technology; history; legal administrative assistant/secretary; management science; marketing/marketing management; mathematics; medical office assistant; music; occupational therapy; physical education teaching and coaching; physics; political science and government; premedical studies; pre-physical therapy; psychology; radiologic technology/science; registered nursing/registered nurse; secondary education; social work; sociology; special education; speech communication and rhetoric.
Academics *Calendar:* semesters. *Degree:* certificates and associate. *Special study options:* academic remediation for entering students, accelerated degree program, adult/continuing education programs, cooperative education, distance learning, English as a second language, honors programs, independent study, internships, off-campus study, part-time degree program, services for LD students, summer session for credit.
Library Learning Resource Center plus 1 other.
Student Life *Housing:* college housing not available. *Activities and Organizations:* drama/theater group, student-run newspaper, choral group, Phi Theta Kappa, Criminal Justice Club, Health Careers Club, Association of Latin American Students. *Campus security:* 24-hour emergency response devices and patrols, late-night transport/escort service. *Student services:* personal/psychological counseling.
Athletics Member NJCAA. *Intercollegiate sports:* baseball M(s), basketball M(s)/W(s), cross-country running M(s)/W(s), softball W(s), tennis M(s)/W(s). *Intramural sports:* basketball M/W.
Standardized Tests *Recommended:* ACT (for admission).
Financial Aid Of all full-time matriculated undergraduates who enrolled in 2016, 642 applied for aid, 409 were judged to have need. 55 Federal Work-Study jobs (averaging $2534). 5 state and other part-time jobs (averaging $2076). *Average percent of need met:* 32%. *Average financial aid package:* $4827. *Average need-based loan:* $2917. *Average need-based gift aid:* $4294.
Applying *Options:* electronic application, early admission, deferred entrance. *Recommended:* high school transcript. *Application deadlines:* rolling (freshmen), rolling (transfers). *Notification:* continuous (freshmen), continuous (transfers).
Freshman Application Contact Sauk Valley Community College, 173 Illinois Route 2, Dixon, IL 61021. *Phone:* 815-288-5511 Ext. 378. *Website:* http://www.svcc.edu/.

# Shawnee Community College
Ullin, Illinois

- **State and locally supported** 2-year, founded 1967, part of Illinois Community College Board
- **Rural** 163-acre campus
- **Coed,** 1,505 undergraduate students, 45% full-time, 64% women, 36% men

Undergraduates 680 full-time, 825 part-time. Students come from 3 states and territories; 2% are from out of state; 14% Black or African American, non-Hispanic/Latino; 4% Hispanic/Latino; 0.5% Asian, non-Hispanic/Latino; 0.1% Native Hawaiian or other Pacific Islander, non-Hispanic/Latino; 0.1% American Indian or Alaska Native, non-Hispanic/Latino; 2% Race/ethnicity unknown; 4% transferred in. *Retention:* 55% of full-time freshmen returned.
Freshmen *Admission:* 992 applied, 992 admitted, 239 enrolled.

**Faculty** *Total:* 90, 37% full-time, 4% with terminal degrees. *Student/faculty ratio:* 19:1.

**Majors** Accounting; agricultural business and management; automobile/automotive mechanics technology; biological and physical sciences; business administration and management; business automation/technology/data entry; child-care provision; clinical/medical laboratory technology; executive assistant/executive secretary; forensic science and technology; general studies; information technology; logistics, materials, and supply chain management; occupational therapist assistant; registered nursing/registered nurse; sheet metal technology; social work; veterinary/animal health technology; wildlife, fish and wildlands science and management.

**Academics** *Calendar:* semesters. *Degree:* certificates, diplomas, and associate. *Special study options:* academic remediation for entering students, accelerated degree program, adult/continuing education programs, advanced placement credit, cooperative education, distance learning, double majors, English as a second language, external degree program, independent study, internships, off-campus study, part-time degree program, services for LD students, summer session for credit.

**Library** Shawnee Community College Library. Students can reserve study rooms.

**Student Life** *Housing:* college housing not available. *Activities and Organizations:* drama/theater group, choral group, Phi Theta Kappa, Phi Beta Lambda, Music Club, Student Senate, Future Teachers Organization. *Campus security:* 24-hour patrols. *Student services:* personal/psychological counseling, veterans affairs office.

**Athletics** Member NJCAA. *Intercollegiate sports:* baseball M(s), basketball M(s)/W(s), softball W(s).

**Standardized Tests** *Required for some:* SAT (for admission). *Recommended:* SAT (for admission).

**Costs (2017–18)** *Tuition:* area resident $2760 full-time, $115 per credit hour part-time; state resident $4224 full-time, $176 per credit hour part-time; nonresident $4608 full-time, $192 per credit hour part-time. *Required fees:* $120 full-time, $5 per credit hour part-time. *Payment plans:* installment, deferred payment. *Waivers:* senior citizens and employees or children of employees.

**Financial Aid** Of all full-time matriculated undergraduates who enrolled in 2016, 60 Federal Work-Study jobs (averaging $2000). 50 state and other part-time jobs (averaging $2000).

**Applying** *Options:* electronic application, early admission, deferred entrance. *Required:* high school transcript. *Application deadlines:* rolling (freshmen), rolling (transfers). *Notification:* continuous (freshmen), continuous (transfers), rolling (early decision).

**Freshman Application Contact** Mrs. Erin King, Recruiter/Advisor, Shawnee Community College, 8364 Shawnee College Road, Ullin, IL 62992. *Phone:* 618-634-3200. *Toll-free phone:* 800-481-2242. *Fax:* 618-634-3300. *E-mail:* erink@shawneecc.edu. *Website:* http://www.shawneecc.edu/.

## Solex College
### Wheeling, Illinois

**Freshman Application Contact** Solex College, 350 East Dundee Road, Wheeling, IL 60090. *Website:* http://www.solex.edu/.

## Southeastern Illinois College
### Harrisburg, Illinois

**Freshman Application Contact** Dr. David Nudo, Director of Counseling, Southeastern Illinois College, 3575 College Road, Harrisburg, IL 62946-4925. *Phone:* 618-252-5400 Ext. 2430. *Toll-free phone:* 866-338-2742. *Website:* http://www.sic.edu/.

## South Suburban College
### South Holland, Illinois

- **State and locally supported** 2-year, founded 1927, part of Illinois Community College Board
- **Suburban** 5-acre campus with easy access to Chicago
- **Coed,** 4,115 undergraduate students, 29% full-time, 65% women, 35% men

**Undergraduates** 1,191 full-time, 2,924 part-time. 3% are from out of state; 54% Black or African American, non-Hispanic/Latino; 20% Hispanic/Latino; 1% Asian, non-Hispanic/Latino; 0.2% Native Hawaiian or other Pacific Islander, non-Hispanic/Latino; 0.3% American Indian or Alaska Native, non-Hispanic/Latino; 3% Two or more races, non-Hispanic/Latino; 0.8% Race/ethnicity unknown; 0.9% international. *Retention:* 20% of full-time freshmen returned.

**Freshmen** *Average high school GPA:* 2.3.

**Faculty** *Total:* 513, 22% full-time. *Student/faculty ratio:* 13:1.

**Majors** Accounting; accounting technology and bookkeeping; architectural drafting and CAD/CADD; biological and physical sciences; building/home/construction inspection; CAD/CADD drafting/design technology; child-care provision; construction engineering technology; court reporting; criminal justice/safety; electrical, electronic and communications engineering technology; executive assistant/executive secretary; fine/studio arts; information technology; kinesiology and exercise science; legal assistant/paralegal; liberal arts and sciences/liberal studies; nursing administration; occupational therapist assistant; office management; radiologic technology/science; small business administration; social work.

**Academics** *Calendar:* semesters. *Degree:* certificates and associate. *Special study options:* academic remediation for entering students, adult/continuing education programs, advanced placement credit, cooperative education, distance learning, English as a second language, honors programs, internships, off-campus study, part-time degree program, services for LD students, study abroad, summer session for credit.

**Library** South Suburban College Library plus 1 other. *Books:* 25,563 (physical); *Serial titles:* 56 (physical); *Databases:* 25. Weekly public service hours: 60; students can reserve study rooms.

**Student Life** *Housing:* college housing not available. *Activities and Organizations:* drama/theater group, choral group. *Campus security:* 24-hour emergency response devices and patrols.

**Athletics** Member NJCAA. *Intercollegiate sports:* baseball M, basketball M/W, soccer M/W, softball W, volleyball W.

**Costs (2017–18)** *Tuition:* area resident $4350 full-time, $145 per credit hour part-time; state resident $10,290 full-time, $343 per credit hour part-time; nonresident $11,940 full-time, $398 per credit hour part-time. Full-time tuition and fees vary according to course load and reciprocity agreements. Part-time tuition and fees vary according to course load and reciprocity agreements. *Required fees:* $533 full-time. *Payment plan:* installment. *Waivers:* senior citizens and employees or children of employees.

**Financial Aid** Of all full-time matriculated undergraduates who enrolled in 2015, 4,111 applied for aid, 3,901 were judged to have need. 128 Federal Work-Study jobs (averaging $1678). In 2015, 59 non-need-based awards were made. *Average percent of need met:* 59%. *Average financial aid package:* $4850. *Average need-based gift aid:* $2350. *Average non-need-based aid:* $611.

**Applying** *Options:* early admission, deferred entrance. *Required:* high school transcript. *Required for some:* essay or personal statement. *Recommended:* essay or personal statement, minimum 2.0 GPA. *Application deadlines:* rolling (freshmen), rolling (transfers). *Notification:* continuous (freshmen), continuous (transfers).

**Freshman Application Contact** Ms. Tiffane Jones, Admissions, South Suburban College, 15800 South State Street, South Holland, IL 60473. *Phone:* 708-596-2000 Ext. 2158. *E-mail:* admissionsquestions@ssc.edu. *Website:* http://www.ssc.edu/.

## Southwestern Illinois College
### Belleville, Illinois

- **District-supported** 2-year, founded 1946, part of Illinois Community College Board
- **Suburban** campus with easy access to St. Louis
- **Coed**

**Academics** *Calendar:* semesters. *Degree:* certificates, diplomas, and associate.

**Costs (2017–18)** *Tuition:* area resident $3390 full-time, $113 per credit hour part-time; state resident $11,970 full-time, $399 per credit hour part-time; nonresident $15,600 full-time, $520 per credit hour part-time. *Required fees:* $270 full-time, $9 per credit hour part-time.

**Financial Aid** Of all full-time matriculated undergraduates who enrolled in 2016, 170 Federal Work-Study jobs (averaging $1537). 179 state and other part-time jobs (averaging $1004).

**Freshman Application Contact** Southwestern Illinois College, 2500 Carlyle Avenue, Belleville, IL 62221-5899. *Toll-free phone:* 866-942-SWIC. *Website:* http://www.swic.edu/.

## Spoon River College
### Canton, Illinois

- **State-supported** 2-year, founded 1959, part of Illinois Community College Board
- **Rural** 160-acre campus
- **Endowment** $2.4 million
- **Coed**

**Undergraduates** 751 full-time, 809 part-time. Students come from 10 states and territories; 0.6% are from out of state; 11% Black or African American, non-Hispanic/Latino; 2% Hispanic/Latino; 0.8% Asian, non-Hispanic/Latino;

1% American Indian or Alaska Native, non-Hispanic/Latino; 0.5% Two or more races, non-Hispanic/Latino; 0.6% Race/ethnicity unknown; 0.1% international; 4% transferred in. *Retention:* 47% of full-time freshmen returned.

**Faculty** *Student/faculty ratio:* 13:1.

**Academics** *Calendar:* semesters. *Degree:* certificates and associate. *Special study options:* academic remediation for entering students, accelerated degree program, adult/continuing education programs, advanced placement credit, distance learning, English as a second language, independent study, internships, part-time degree program, services for LD students, summer session for credit. *ROTC:* Army (c).

**Library** Library/Learning Resource Center. *Books:* 12,647 (physical), 135,000 (digital/electronic); *Serial titles:* 4,560 (digital/electronic); *Databases:* 31. Weekly public service hours: 40.

**Student Life** *Campus security:* 24-hour emergency response devices, night patrol by trained security personnel.

**Athletics** Member NJCAA.

**Costs (2017–18)** *Tuition:* area resident $4160 full-time; state resident $9856 full-time; nonresident $10,688 full-time. Full-time tuition and fees vary according to location. Part-time tuition and fees vary according to location. *Required fees:* $640 full-time.

**Financial Aid** Of all full-time matriculated undergraduates who enrolled in 2016, 20 Federal Work-Study jobs (averaging $1525).

**Applying** *Options:* electronic application, early admission, deferred entrance. *Required:* high school transcript.

**Freshman Application Contact** Ms. Missy Wilkinson, Dean of Student Services, Spoon River College, 23235 North County 22, Canton, IL 61520-9801. *Phone:* 309-649-6305. *Toll-free phone:* 800-334-7337. *Fax:* 309-649-6235. *E-mail:* info@src.edu. *Website:* http://www.src.edu/.

## Taylor Business Institute
### Chicago, Illinois

**Director of Admissions** Mr. Rashed Jahangir, Taylor Business Institute, 318 West Adams, Chicago, IL 60606. *Website:* http://www.tbiil.edu/.

## Tribeca Flashpoint College
### Chicago, Illinois

**Admissions Office Contact** Tribeca Flashpoint College, 28 North Clark Street, Chicago, IL 60602. *Website:* http://www.tribecaflashpoint.edu/.

## Triton College
### River Grove, Illinois

**Freshman Application Contact** Ms. Mary-Rita Moore, Dean of Admissions, Triton College, 2000 Fifth Avenue, River Grove, IL 60171. *Phone:* 708-456-0300 Ext. 3679. *Fax:* 708-583-3162. *E-mail:* mpatrice@triton.edu. *Website:* http://www.triton.edu/.

## Vatterott College
### Fairview Heights, Illinois

**Admissions Office Contact** Vatterott College, 110 Commerce Lane, Fairview Heights, IL 62208. *Toll-free phone:* 888-202-2636. *Website:* http://www.vatterott.edu/.

## Vatterott College
### Quincy, Illinois

**Admissions Office Contact** Vatterott College, 3609 North Marx Drive, Quincy, IL 62305. *Website:* http://www.vatterott.edu/.

## Vet Tech Institute at Fox College
### Tinley Park, Illinois

**Freshman Application Contact** Admissions Office, Vet Tech Institute at Fox College, 18020 South Oak Park Avenue, Tinley Park, IL 60477. *Phone:* 888-884-3694. *Toll-free phone:* 888-884-3694. *Website:* http://chicago.vettechinstitute.edu/.

## Waubonsee Community College
### Sugar Grove, Illinois

**Freshman Application Contact** Joy Sanders, Admissions Manager, Waubonsee Community College, Route 47 at Waubonsee Drive, Sugar Grove, IL 60554. *Phone:* 630-466-7900 Ext. 5756. *Fax:* 630-466-6663. *E-mail:* admissions@waubonsee.edu. *Website:* http://www.waubonsee.edu/.

## Worsham College of Mortuary Science
### Wheeling, Illinois

**Director of Admissions** President, Worsham College of Mortuary Science, 495 Northgate Parkway, Wheeling, IL 60090-2646. *Phone:* 847-808-8444. *Website:* http://www.worsham.edu/.

# INDIANA

## Ancilla College
### Donaldson, Indiana

- **Independent Roman Catholic** 2-year, founded 1937
- **Rural** 63-acre campus
- **Endowment** $5.8 million
- **Coed,** 548 undergraduate students, 82% full-time, 53% women, 47% men

**Undergraduates** 451 full-time, 97 part-time. Students come from 19 states and territories; 7 other countries; 12% are from out of state; 18% Black or African American, non-Hispanic/Latino; 10% Hispanic/Latino; 0.4% American Indian or Alaska Native, non-Hispanic/Latino; 5% Two or more races, non-Hispanic/Latino; 3% international; 11% transferred in; 35% live on campus. *Retention:* 41% of full-time freshmen returned.

**Freshmen** *Admission:* 1,125 applied, 771 admitted, 228 enrolled. *Average high school GPA:* 2.5.

**Faculty** *Total:* 54, 35% full-time, 4% with terminal degrees. *Student/faculty ratio:* 16:1.

**Majors** Agriculture; animal sciences; behavioral sciences; biological and physical sciences; business administration and management; business administration, management and operations related; computer and information sciences; criminal justice/safety; culinary arts related; early childhood education; elementary education; English; environmental studies; general studies; health/medical preparatory programs related; health services/allied health/health sciences; history; hospitality administration related; kinesiology and exercise science; logistics, materials, and supply chain management; mass communication/media; registered nursing/registered nurse; religious studies related; secondary education; speech communication and rhetoric; theology and religious vocations related.

**Academics** *Calendar:* semesters. *Degree:* associate. *Special study options:* academic remediation for entering students, adult/continuing education programs, advanced placement credit, cooperative education, distance learning, double majors, independent study, internships, part-time degree program, services for LD students, student-designed majors, summer session for credit.

**Library** Gerald J. Ball Library. *Books:* 15,692 (physical), 3,767 (digital/electronic); *Serial titles:* 39 (physical); *Databases:* 84. Weekly public service hours: 66.

**Student Life** *Housing Options:* coed. Campus housing is university owned. Freshman applicants given priority for college housing. *Activities and Organizations:* Student Government Association, Ancilla Student Ambassadors, FFA, Phi Theta Kappa, Leaders for Life. *Campus security:* 24-hour emergency response devices and patrols, late-night transport/escort service, controlled dormitory access. *Student services:* personal/psychological counseling.

**Athletics** Member NJCAA. *Intercollegiate sports:* baseball M(s), basketball M(s)/W(s), bowling M(s)/W(s), cheerleading M(s)/W(s), golf M(s)/W(s), lacrosse M(s), soccer M(s)/W(s), softball W(s), volleyball W(s), wrestling M(s).

**Costs (2018–19)** *Comprehensive fee:* $26,830 includes full-time tuition ($17,100), mandatory fees ($230), and room and board ($9500). Full-time tuition and fees vary according to course load and program. Part-time tuition: $575 per credit hour. Part-time tuition and fees vary according to course load and program. *Required fees:* $55 per term part-time. *Payment plan:* installment. *Waivers:* employees or children of employees.

**Financial Aid** Of all full-time matriculated undergraduates who enrolled in 2016, 23 Federal Work-Study jobs (averaging $2000). *Financial aid deadline:* 4/15.

**Applying** *Options:* electronic application. *Required:* high school transcript. *Application deadlines:* rolling (freshmen), rolling (transfers).

**Freshman Application Contact** Ms. Ericka Taylor-Joseph, Executive Director of Admissions, Ancilla College, PO Box 1, 9601 Union Road, Donaldson, IN 46513. *Phone:* 574-936-8898 Ext. 326. *Toll-free phone:* 866-ANCILLA. *Fax:* 574-935-1773. *E-mail:* admissions@ancilla.edu. *Website:* http://www.ancilla.edu/.

## Brightwood College, Indianapolis Campus
### Indianapolis, Indiana

**Freshman Application Contact** Director of Admissions, Brightwood College, Indianapolis Campus, 4200 South East Street, Indianapolis, IN 46227. *Phone:* 317-782-0315. *Toll-free phone:* 866-543-0208. *Website:* http://www.brightwood.edu/.

## College of Court Reporting
### Valparaiso, Indiana

**Freshman Application Contact** Ms. Nicky Rodriquez, Director of Admissions, College of Court Reporting, 455 West Lincolnway, Valparaiso, IN 46385. *Phone:* 219-942-1459 Ext. 222. *Toll-free phone:* 866-294-3974. *Fax:* 219-942-1631. *E-mail:* nrodriquez@ccr.edu. *Website:* http://www.ccr.edu/.

## Fortis College
### Indianapolis, Indiana

**Freshman Application Contact** Mr. Alex Teitelbaum, Vice President Systems and Administration, Fortis College, 9001 North Wesleyan Road, Suite 101, Indianapolis, IN 46268. *Phone:* 410-633-2929. *Toll-free phone:* 855-4-FORTIS. *E-mail:* kbennett@edaff.com. *Website:* http://www.fortis.edu/.

## International Business College
### Indianapolis, Indiana

**Freshman Application Contact** Admissions Office, International Business College, 7205 Shadeland Station, Indianapolis, IN 46256. *Phone:* 317-813-2300. *Toll-free phone:* 800-589-6500. *Website:* http://www.ibcindianapolis.edu/.

## Ivy Tech Community College–Bloomington
### Bloomington, Indiana

- **State-supported** 2-year, founded 2001, part of Ivy Tech Community College System
- **Coed,** 6,198 undergraduate students, 27% full-time, 62% women, 38% men

**Undergraduates** 1,656 full-time, 4,542 part-time. 1% are from out of state; 3% Black or African American, non-Hispanic/Latino; 1% Hispanic/Latino; 2% Asian, non-Hispanic/Latino; 0.2% Native Hawaiian or other Pacific Islander, non-Hispanic/Latino; 0.2% American Indian or Alaska Native, non-Hispanic/Latino; 3% Two or more races, non-Hispanic/Latino; 19% Race/ethnicity unknown; 5% transferred in. *Retention:* 50% of full-time freshmen returned.
**Freshmen** *Admission:* 2,141 applied, 2,141 admitted, 696 enrolled.
**Faculty** *Total:* 318, 31% full-time. *Student/faculty ratio:* 19:1.
**Majors** Accounting technology and bookkeeping; administrative assistant and secretarial science; biotechnology; building/property maintenance; business administration and management; business automation/technology/data entry; cabinetmaking and millwork; computer and information sciences; computer science; computer systems networking and telecommunications; criminal justice/safety; data modeling/warehousing and database administration; drafting and design technology; early childhood education; education; electrical, electronic and communications engineering technology; electrician; emergency medical technology (EMT paramedic); engineering technology; executive assistant/executive secretary; fine/studio arts; general studies; heating, air conditioning, ventilation and refrigeration maintenance technology; hospitality administration; human services; industrial technology; informatics; information science/studies; information technology; legal assistant/paralegal; liberal arts and sciences/liberal studies; library and archives assisting; logistics, materials, and supply chain management; machine tool technology; manufacturing engineering technology; mechanic and repair technologies related; mechanics and repair; medical/health management and clinical assistant; medical radiologic technology; network and system administration; pipefitting and sprinkler fitting; psychiatric/mental health services technology; registered nursing/registered nurse; tool and die technology.
**Academics** *Calendar:* semesters. *Degree:* certificates and associate. *Special study options:* academic remediation for entering students, adult/continuing education programs, advanced placement credit, distance learning, external degree program, internships, part-time degree program, services for LD students, summer session for credit.

**Student Life** *Activities and Organizations:* Student Government, Phi Theta Kappa. *Campus security:* late-night transport/escort service.
**Costs (2017–18)** *Tuition:* state resident $4135 full-time, $138 per credit hour part-time; nonresident $8091 full-time, $270 per credit hour part-time. *Required fees:* $120 full-time, $60 per term part-time. *Payment plans:* installment, deferred payment. *Waivers:* senior citizens and employees or children of employees.
**Financial Aid** Of all full-time matriculated undergraduates who enrolled in 2016, 51 Federal Work-Study jobs (averaging $3259).
**Applying** *Options:* electronic application, deferred entrance. *Required:* high school transcript. *Required for some:* interview. *Application deadlines:* rolling (freshmen), rolling (transfers). *Notification:* continuous (freshmen), continuous (transfers).
**Freshman Application Contact** Mr. Neil Frederick, Assistant Director of Admissions, Ivy Tech Community College–Bloomington, 200 Daniels Way, Bloomington, IN 47404. *Phone:* 812-330-6026. *Toll-free phone:* 888-IVY-LINE. *Fax:* 812-332-8147. *E-mail:* nfrederi@ivytech.edu. *Website:* http://www.ivytech.edu/.

## Ivy Tech Community College–Central Indiana
### Indianapolis, Indiana

- **State-supported** 2-year, founded 1963, part of Ivy Tech Community College System
- **Urban** 10-acre campus
- **Coed,** 18,062 undergraduate students, 25% full-time, 53% women, 47% men

**Undergraduates** 4,604 full-time, 13,458 part-time. 1% are from out of state; 22% Black or African American, non-Hispanic/Latino; 5% Hispanic/Latino; 4% Asian, non-Hispanic/Latino; 0.2% Native Hawaiian or other Pacific Islander, non-Hispanic/Latino; 0.2% American Indian or Alaska Native, non-Hispanic/Latino; 4% Two or more races, non-Hispanic/Latino; 3% Race/ethnicity unknown; 7% transferred in. *Retention:* 46% of full-time freshmen returned.
**Freshmen** *Admission:* 3,207 enrolled.
**Faculty** *Total:* 946, 20% full-time. *Student/faculty ratio:* 23:1.
**Majors** Accounting technology and bookkeeping; automobile/automotive mechanics technology; biotechnology; business administration and management; business automation/technology/data entry; cabinetmaking and millwork; carpentry; child development; computer and information sciences; computer science; criminal justice/safety; data modeling/warehousing and database administration; design and visual communications; drafting and design technology; early childhood education; education; electrical, electronic and communications engineering technology; electrician; executive assistant/executive secretary; general studies; health information/medical records technology; heating, air conditioning, ventilation and refrigeration maintenance technology; hospitality administration related; human services; industrial production technologies related; industrial technology; informatics; information science/studies; information technology; legal assistant/paralegal; liberal arts and sciences/liberal studies; logistics, materials, and supply chain management; machine shop technology; machine tool technology; manufacturing engineering technology; masonry; mechanics and repair; medical/clinical assistant; medical/health management and clinical assistant; medical radiologic technology; network and system administration; occupational safety and health technology; painting and wall covering; pipefitting and sprinkler fitting; psychiatric/mental health services technology; registered nursing/registered nurse; respiratory care therapy; sheet metal technology; surgical technology; tool and die technology; transportation/mobility management.
**Academics** *Calendar:* semesters. *Degree:* certificates and associate. *Special study options:* academic remediation for entering students, adult/continuing education programs, advanced placement credit, cooperative education, distance learning, English as a second language, internships, off-campus study, part-time degree program, services for LD students, summer session for credit.
**Student Life** *Housing:* college housing not available. *Activities and Organizations:* student-run newspaper, Student Government, Phi Theta Kappa, Human Services Club, Administrative Office Assistants Club, Radiology Club. *Campus security:* 24-hour emergency response devices and patrols, late-night transport/escort service. *Student services:* personal/psychological counseling.
**Athletics** *Intramural sports:* baseball M, basketball M/W, cheerleading W, golf M/W, softball W, volleyball M/W.
**Costs (2017–18)** *Tuition:* state resident $4135 full-time, $138 per credit hour part-time; nonresident $8091 full-time, $270 per credit hour part-time. *Required fees:* $120 full-time, $60 per term part-time. *Payment plans:* installment, deferred payment. *Waivers:* senior citizens and employees or children of employees.
**Financial Aid** Of all full-time matriculated undergraduates who enrolled in 2016, 92 Federal Work-Study jobs (averaging $3766).

**Applying** *Options:* electronic application, early admission, deferred entrance. *Required:* high school transcript. *Required for some:* interview. *Application deadlines:* rolling (freshmen), rolling (transfers). *Notification:* continuous (freshmen), continuous (transfers).
**Freshman Application Contact** Ms. Tracy Funk, Director of Admissions, Ivy Tech Community College–Central Indiana, 50 West Fall Creek Parkway North Drive, Indianapolis, IN 46208-4777. *Phone:* 317-921-4371. *Toll-free phone:* 888-IVYLINE. *Fax:* 317-917-5919. *E-mail:* tfunk@ivytech.edu. *Website:* http://www.ivytech.edu/.

## Ivy Tech Community College–Columbus
### Columbus, Indiana

- **State-supported** 2-year, founded 1963, part of Ivy Tech Community College System
- **Small-town** campus with easy access to Indianapolis
- **Coed,** 2,653 undergraduate students, 25% full-time, 60% women, 40% men

**Undergraduates** 652 full-time, 2,001 part-time. 1% are from out of state; 2% Black or African American, non-Hispanic/Latino; 3% Hispanic/Latino; 1% Asian, non-Hispanic/Latino; 0.1% Native Hawaiian or other Pacific Islander, non-Hispanic/Latino; 0.2% American Indian or Alaska Native, non-Hispanic/Latino; 2% Two or more races, non-Hispanic/Latino; 9% Race/ethnicity unknown; 5% transferred in.
**Freshmen** *Admission:* 373 enrolled.
**Faculty** *Total:* 196, 27% full-time. *Student/faculty ratio:* 15:1.
**Majors** Accounting technology and bookkeeping; administrative assistant and secretarial science; agriculture; automobile/automotive mechanics technology; business administration and management; business automation/technology/data entry; cabinetmaking and millwork; computer and information sciences; computer science; criminal justice/safety; data modeling/warehousing and database administration; dental assisting; design and visual communications; drafting and design technology; early childhood education; education; electrical and power transmission installation; electrical, electronic and communications engineering technology; emergency medical technology (EMT paramedic); engineering technology; executive assistant/executive secretary; general studies; heating, air conditioning, ventilation and refrigeration maintenance technology; hospitality administration; human services; industrial technology; informatics; information science/studies; information technology; interior design; legal assistant/paralegal; liberal arts and sciences/liberal studies; library and archives assisting; logistics, materials, and supply chain management; machine tool technology; manufacturing engineering technology; masonry; mechanic and repair technologies related; mechanics and repair; medical/clinical assistant; medical radiologic technology; pipefitting and sprinkler fitting; pre-engineering; psychiatric/mental health services technology; surgical technology; tool and die technology.
**Academics** *Calendar:* semesters. *Degree:* certificates and associate. *Special study options:* academic remediation for entering students, adult/continuing education programs, advanced placement credit, distance learning, internships, part-time degree program, services for LD students, summer session for credit.
**Student Life** *Housing:* college housing not available. *Activities and Organizations:* Student Government, Phi Theta Kappa, LPN Club. *Campus security:* late-night transport/escort service, trained evening security personnel, escort service.
**Costs (2017–18)** *Tuition:* state resident $4135 full-time, $138 per credit hour part-time; nonresident $8091 full-time, $270 per credit hour part-time. *Required fees:* $120 full-time, $60 per term part-time. *Payment plans:* installment, deferred payment. *Waivers:* senior citizens and employees or children of employees.
**Financial Aid** Of all full-time matriculated undergraduates who enrolled in 2016, 26 Federal Work-Study jobs (averaging $1694).
**Applying** *Options:* electronic application, early admission, deferred entrance. *Required:* high school transcript. *Required for some:* interview. *Application deadlines:* rolling (freshmen), rolling (transfers). *Notification:* continuous (freshmen), continuous (transfers).
**Freshman Application Contact** Alisa Deck, Director of Admissions, Ivy Tech Community College–Columbus, 4475 Central Avenue, Columbus, IN 47203-1868. *Phone:* 812-374-5129. *Toll-free phone:* 888-IVY-LINE. *Fax:* 812-372-0331. *E-mail:* adeck@ivytech.edu. *Website:* http://www.ivytech.edu/.

## Ivy Tech Community College–East Central
### Muncie, Indiana

- **State-supported** 2-year, founded 1968, part of Ivy Tech Community College System
- **Suburban** 15-acre campus with easy access to Indianapolis
- **Coed,** 5,462 undergraduate students, 37% full-time, 61% women, 39% men

**Undergraduates** 2,030 full-time, 3,432 part-time. 1% are from out of state; 7% Black or African American, non-Hispanic/Latino; 2% Hispanic/Latino; 0.7% Asian, non-Hispanic/Latino; 0.1% Native Hawaiian or other Pacific Islander, non-Hispanic/Latino; 0.3% American Indian or Alaska Native, non-Hispanic/Latino; 4% Two or more races, non-Hispanic/Latino; 4% Race/ethnicity unknown; 6% transferred in. *Retention:* 48% of full-time freshmen returned.
**Freshmen** *Admission:* 1,032 enrolled.
**Faculty** *Total:* 468, 25% full-time. *Student/faculty ratio:* 15:1.
**Majors** Accounting technology and bookkeeping; administrative assistant and secretarial science; agriculture; automobile/automotive mechanics technology; building/property maintenance; business administration and management; carpentry; computer and information sciences; computer science; computer systems networking and telecommunications; construction trades; construction trades related; criminal justice/safety; data modeling/warehousing and database administration; dental assisting; dental hygiene; drafting and design technology; early childhood education; education; electrical, electronic and communications engineering technology; electrician; energy management and systems technology; engineering technology; executive assistant/executive secretary; general studies; health information/medical records technology; hospitality administration; hospitality administration related; human services; industrial mechanics and maintenance technology; industrial production technologies related; industrial technology; informatics; information science/studies; information technology; interior design; kinesiology and exercise science; legal assistant/paralegal; liberal arts and sciences/liberal studies; library and archives assisting; logistics, materials, and supply chain management; machine shop technology; machine tool technology; manufacturing engineering technology; masonry; medical/clinical assistant; medical/health management and clinical assistant; medical radiologic technology; network and system administration; painting and wall covering; physical therapy technology; pipefitting and sprinkler fitting; registered nursing/registered nurse; surgical technology; tool and die technology.
**Academics** *Calendar:* semesters. *Degree:* certificates and associate. *Special study options:* academic remediation for entering students, adult/continuing education programs, advanced placement credit, distance learning, internships, part-time degree program, services for LD students.
**Student Life** *Housing:* college housing not available. *Activities and Organizations:* Business Professionals of America, SkillsUSA–VICA, Student Government, Phi Theta Kappa, Human Services Club.
**Costs (2017–18)** *Tuition:* state resident $4135 full-time, $138 per credit hour part-time; nonresident $8091 full-time, $270 per credit hour part-time. *Required fees:* $120 full-time, $60 per term part-time. *Payment plans:* installment, deferred payment. *Waivers:* senior citizens and employees or children of employees.
**Financial Aid** Of all full-time matriculated undergraduates who enrolled in 2016, 65 Federal Work-Study jobs (averaging $2666).
**Applying** *Options:* electronic application, early admission, deferred entrance. *Required:* high school transcript. *Required for some:* interview. *Application deadlines:* rolling (freshmen), rolling (transfers). *Notification:* continuous (freshmen), continuous (transfers).
**Freshman Application Contact** Ms. Mary Lewellen, Ivy Tech Community College–East Central, 4301 South Cowan Road, Muncie, IN 47302-9448. *Phone:* 765-289-2291 Ext. 1391. *Toll-free phone:* 888-IVY-LINE. *Fax:* 765-289-2292. *E-mail:* mlewelle@ivytech.edu. *Website:* http://www.ivytech.edu/.

## Ivy Tech Community College–Kokomo
### Kokomo, Indiana

- **State-supported** 2-year, founded 1968, part of Ivy Tech Community College System
- **Small-town** 20-acre campus with easy access to Indianapolis
- **Coed,** 2,422 undergraduate students, 33% full-time, 58% women, 42% men

**Undergraduates** 804 full-time, 1,618 part-time. 6% Black or African American, non-Hispanic/Latino; 4% Hispanic/Latino; 2% Asian, non-Hispanic/Latino; 0.7% American Indian or Alaska Native, non-Hispanic/Latino; 4% Two or more races, non-Hispanic/Latino; 2% Race/ethnicity unknown; 5% transferred in. *Retention:* 55% of full-time freshmen returned.

**Freshmen** *Admission:* 392 enrolled.
**Faculty** *Total:* 221, 27% full-time. *Student/faculty ratio:* 12:1.
**Majors** Accounting technology and bookkeeping; administrative assistant and secretarial science; agriculture; automobile/automotive mechanics technology; building/construction site management; building/property maintenance; business administration and management; communication and journalism related; computer and information sciences; computer science; computer systems networking and telecommunications; construction trades related; criminal justice/safety; data modeling/warehousing and database administration; dental assisting; dental hygiene; design and visual communications; drafting and design technology; early childhood education; education; electrical, electronic and communications engineering technology; electrician; emergency medical technology (EMT paramedic); engineering technology; executive assistant/executive secretary; general studies; health aide; health information/medical records technology; heating, air conditioning, ventilation and refrigeration maintenance technology; human services; industrial production technologies related; industrial technology; informatics; information science/studies; information technology; legal assistant/paralegal; liberal arts and sciences/liberal studies; library and archives assisting; machine shop technology; machine tool technology; manufacturing engineering technology; mechanic and repair technologies related; mechanics and repair; medical/clinical assistant; network and system administration; physical therapy technology; registered nursing/registered nurse; surgical technology; tool and die technology.
**Academics** *Calendar:* semesters. *Degree:* certificates and associate. *Special study options:* academic remediation for entering students, adult/continuing education programs, advanced placement credit, distance learning, internships, part-time degree program, services for LD students, summer session for credit.
**Student Life** *Housing:* college housing not available. *Activities and Organizations:* student-run newspaper, Student Government, Collegiate Secretaries International, Licensed Practical Nursing Club, Phi Theta Kappa. *Campus security:* 24-hour emergency response devices, late-night transport/escort service. *Student services:* personal/psychological counseling.
**Costs (2017–18)** *Tuition:* state resident $4135 full-time, $138 per credit hour part-time; nonresident $8091 full-time, $270 per credit hour part-time. *Required fees:* $120 full-time, $60 per term part-time. *Payment plans:* installment, deferred payment. *Waivers:* senior citizens and employees or children of employees.
**Financial Aid** Of all full-time matriculated undergraduates who enrolled in 2016, 45 Federal Work-Study jobs (averaging $1829).
**Applying** *Options:* electronic application, early admission. *Required:* high school transcript. *Required for some:* interview. *Application deadlines:* rolling (freshmen), rolling (transfers). *Notification:* continuous (freshmen), continuous (transfers).
**Freshman Application Contact** Mr. Mike Federspill, Director of Admissions, Ivy Tech Community College–Kokomo, 1815 East Morgan Street, Kokomo, IN 46903-1373. *Phone:* 765-459-0561 Ext. 233. *Toll-free phone:* 888-IVY-LINE. *Fax:* 765-454-5111. *E-mail:* mfedersp@ivytech.edu. *Website:* http://www.ivytech.edu/.

# Ivy Tech Community College–Lafayette
## Lafayette, Indiana

- **State-supported** 2-year, founded 1968, part of Ivy Tech Community College System
- **Suburban** campus with easy access to Indianapolis
- **Coed**, 4,517 undergraduate students, 38% full-time, 55% women, 45% men

**Undergraduates** 1,698 full-time, 2,819 part-time. 1% are from out of state; 5% Black or African American, non-Hispanic/Latino; 6% Hispanic/Latino; 2% Asian, non-Hispanic/Latino; 0.2% Native Hawaiian or other Pacific Islander, non-Hispanic/Latino; 0.4% American Indian or Alaska Native, non-Hispanic/Latino; 3% Two or more races, non-Hispanic/Latino; 9% Race/ethnicity unknown; 7% transferred in. *Retention:* 53% of full-time freshmen returned.
**Freshmen** *Admission:* 797 enrolled.
**Faculty** *Total:* 397, 22% full-time. *Student/faculty ratio:* 15:1.
**Majors** Accounting technology and bookkeeping; agriculture; automobile/automotive mechanics technology; biotechnology; building/property maintenance; business administration and management; business automation/technology/data entry; cabinetmaking and millwork; carpentry; chemical technology; clinical/medical laboratory technology; computer and information sciences; computer science; computer systems networking and telecommunications; criminal justice/safety; data modeling/warehousing and database administration; dental assisting; drafting and design technology; early childhood education; education; electrical, electronic and communications engineering technology; electrician; executive assistant/executive secretary; general studies; health aide; health information/medical records technology; heating, air conditioning, ventilation and refrigeration maintenance technology; human services; industrial

production technologies related; industrial technology; informatics; information science/studies; information technology; legal assistant/paralegal; liberal arts and sciences/liberal studies; library and archives assisting; lineworker; machine tool technology; manufacturing engineering technology; masonry; mechanical engineering/mechanical technology; mechanic and repair technologies related; mechanics and repair; medical/clinical assistant; medical/health management and clinical assistant; painting and wall covering; pipefitting and sprinkler fitting; pre-engineering; psychiatric/mental health services technology; quality control and safety technologies related; registered nursing/registered nurse; respiratory care therapy; sheet metal technology; surgical technology; telecommunications technology.
**Academics** *Calendar:* semesters. *Degree:* certificates and associate. *Special study options:* academic remediation for entering students, advanced placement credit, distance learning, internships, part-time degree program, services for LD students, summer session for credit.
**Student Life** *Housing:* college housing not available. *Activities and Organizations:* student-run newspaper, Student Government, Phi Theta Kappa, LPN Club, Accounting Club, Student Computer Technology Association. *Student services:* personal/psychological counseling.
**Costs (2017–18)** *Tuition:* state resident $4135 full-time, $138 per credit hour part-time; nonresident $8091 full-time, $270 per credit hour part-time. *Required fees:* $120 full-time, $60 per term part-time. *Payment plans:* installment, deferred payment. *Waivers:* senior citizens and employees or children of employees.
**Financial Aid** Of all full-time matriculated undergraduates who enrolled in 2016, 65 Federal Work-Study jobs (averaging $2222). 1 state and other part-time job (averaging $2436).
**Applying** *Options:* electronic application. *Required:* high school transcript. *Required for some:* interview. *Application deadlines:* rolling (freshmen), rolling (transfers). *Notification:* continuous (freshmen), continuous (transfers).
**Freshman Application Contact** Mr. Ivan Hernanadez, Director of Admissions, Ivy Tech Community College–Lafayette, 3101 South Creasy Lane, PO Box 6299, Lafayette, IN 47903. *Phone:* 765-269-5116. *Toll-free phone:* 888-IVY-LINE. *Fax:* 765-772-9293. *E-mail:* ihernand@ivytech.edu. *Website:* http://www.ivytech.edu/.

# Ivy Tech Community College–North Central
## South Bend, Indiana

- **State-supported** 2-year, founded 1968, part of Ivy Tech Community College System
- **Suburban** 4-acre campus
- **Coed**, 4,805 undergraduate students, 29% full-time, 62% women, 38% men

**Undergraduates** 1,407 full-time, 3,398 part-time. 2% are from out of state; 14% Black or African American, non-Hispanic/Latino; 11% Hispanic/Latino; 1% Asian, non-Hispanic/Latino; 0.2% Native Hawaiian or other Pacific Islander, non-Hispanic/Latino; 0.4% American Indian or Alaska Native, non-Hispanic/Latino; 4% Two or more races, non-Hispanic/Latino; 3% Race/ethnicity unknown; 8% transferred in. *Retention:* 47% of full-time freshmen returned.
**Freshmen** *Admission:* 881 enrolled.
**Faculty** *Total:* 374, 28% full-time. *Student/faculty ratio:* 14:1.
**Majors** Accounting technology and bookkeeping; biotechnology; building/property maintenance; business administration and management; business automation/technology/data entry; cabinetmaking and millwork; carpentry; child-care and support services management; clinical/medical laboratory technology; computer and information sciences; criminal justice/safety; design and visual communications; early childhood education; educational/instructional technology; electrical, electronic and communications engineering technology; electrician; emergency medical technology (EMT paramedic); executive assistant/executive secretary; general studies; heating, air conditioning, ventilation and refrigeration maintenance technology; hospitality administration; human services; industrial production technologies related; industrial technology; interior design; ironworking; legal assistant/paralegal; liberal arts and sciences/liberal studies; library and archives assisting; machine tool technology; mechanic and repair technologies related; mechanics and repair; medical/clinical assistant; painting and wall covering; pipefitting and sprinkler fitting; registered nursing/registered nurse; sheet metal technology; telecommunications technology; tool and die technology.
**Academics** *Calendar:* semesters. *Degree:* certificates and associate. *Special study options:* academic remediation for entering students, adult/continuing education programs, advanced placement credit, distance learning, English as a second language, internships, off-campus study, part-time degree program, services for LD students, summer session for credit.
**Student Life** *Housing:* college housing not available. *Activities and Organizations:* Phi Theta Kappa, Student Government, LPN Club. *Campus*

*security:* 24-hour emergency response devices and patrols, late-night transport/escort service, security during hours of operation. *Student services:* personal/psychological counseling, women's center.

**Costs (2017–18)** *Tuition:* state resident $4135 full-time, $138 per credit hour part-time; nonresident $8091 full-time, $270 per credit hour part-time. *Required fees:* $120 full-time, $60 per term part-time. *Payment plans:* installment, deferred payment. *Waivers:* senior citizens and employees or children of employees.

**Financial Aid** Of all full-time matriculated undergraduates who enrolled in 2016, 100 Federal Work-Study jobs (averaging $1538).

**Applying** *Options:* electronic application, early admission, deferred entrance. *Required:* high school transcript. *Required for some:* interview. *Application deadlines:* rolling (freshmen), rolling (transfers). *Notification:* continuous (freshmen), continuous (transfers).

**Freshman Application Contact** Darryl Williams, Bi-Regional Director of Admissions, Ivy Tech Community College–North Central, 220 Dean Johnson Boulevard, South Bend, IN 46601-3415. *Toll-free phone:* 888-IVY-LINE. *E-mail:* dwilliams770@ivytech.edu. *Website:* http://www.ivytech.edu/.

# Ivy Tech Community College–Northeast
## Fort Wayne, Indiana

- **State-supported** 2-year, founded 1969, part of Ivy Tech Community College System
- **Urban** 22-acre campus
- **Coed,** 6,795 undergraduate students, 28% full-time, 54% women, 46% men

**Undergraduates** 1,869 full-time, 4,926 part-time. 1% are from out of state; 11% Black or African American, non-Hispanic/Latino; 5% Hispanic/Latino; 3% Asian, non-Hispanic/Latino; 0.2% Native Hawaiian or other Pacific Islander, non-Hispanic/Latino; 0.5% American Indian or Alaska Native, non-Hispanic/Latino; 4% Two or more races, non-Hispanic/Latino; 6% Race/ethnicity unknown; 7% transferred in. *Retention:* 50% of full-time freshmen returned.

**Freshmen** *Admission:* 1,504 enrolled.

**Faculty** *Total:* 449, 31% full-time. *Student/faculty ratio:* 16:1.

**Majors** Accounting technology and bookkeeping; agriculture; automobile/automotive mechanics technology; building/property maintenance; business administration and management; business automation/technology/data entry; cabinetmaking and millwork; computer and information sciences; computer science; construction trades; construction trades related; criminal justice/safety; data modeling/warehousing and database administration; drafting and design technology; early childhood education; electrical, electronic and communications engineering technology; electrician; executive assistant/executive secretary; heating, air conditioning, ventilation and refrigeration maintenance technology; hospitality administration; hospitality administration related; human services; industrial production technologies related; industrial technology; ironworking; legal assistant/paralegal; liberal arts and sciences/liberal studies; library and archives assisting; masonry; massage therapy; mechanics and repair; medical/clinical assistant; painting and wall covering; pipefitting and sprinkler fitting; psychiatric/mental health services technology; registered nursing/registered nurse; respiratory care therapy; sheet metal technology; tool and die technology.

**Academics** *Calendar:* semesters. *Degree:* certificates and associate. *Special study options:* adult/continuing education programs, advanced placement credit, distance learning, English as a second language, internships, part-time degree program, services for LD students, summer session for credit.

**Student Life** *Housing:* college housing not available. *Activities and Organizations:* student-run newspaper, Student Government, LPN Club, Phi Theta Kappa. *Campus security:* 24-hour emergency response devices and patrols, late-night transport/escort service.

**Costs (2017–18)** *Tuition:* state resident $4135 full-time, $138 per credit hour part-time; nonresident $8091 full-time, $270 per credit hour part-time. *Required fees:* $120 full-time, $60 per term part-time. *Payment plans:* installment, deferred payment. *Waivers:* senior citizens and employees or children of employees.

**Financial Aid** Of all full-time matriculated undergraduates who enrolled in 2016, 40 Federal Work-Study jobs (averaging $4041).

**Applying** *Options:* early admission. *Required:* high school transcript. *Required for some:* interview. *Application deadlines:* rolling (freshmen), rolling (transfers). *Notification:* continuous (freshmen), continuous (transfers).

**Freshman Application Contact** Robyn Boss, Director of Admissions, Ivy Tech Community College–Northeast, 3800 North Anthony Boulevard, Ft. Wayne, IN 46805-1489. *Phone:* 260-480-4211. *Toll-free phone:* 888-IVY-LINE. *Fax:* 260-480-2053. *E-mail:* rboss1@ivytech.edu. *Website:* http://www.ivytech.edu/.

# Ivy Tech Community College–Northwest
## Gary, Indiana

- **State-supported** 2-year, founded 1963, part of Ivy Tech Community College System
- **Urban** 13-acre campus with easy access to Chicago
- **Coed,** 8,314 undergraduate students, 29% full-time, 57% women, 43% men

**Undergraduates** 2,399 full-time, 5,915 part-time. 1% are from out of state; 21% Black or African American, non-Hispanic/Latino; 10% Hispanic/Latino; 0.9% Asian, non-Hispanic/Latino; 0.2% Native Hawaiian or other Pacific Islander, non-Hispanic/Latino; 0.4% American Indian or Alaska Native, non-Hispanic/Latino; 4% Two or more races, non-Hispanic/Latino; 5% Race/ethnicity unknown; 9% transferred in.

**Freshmen** *Admission:* 1,435 enrolled.

**Faculty** *Total:* 495, 26% full-time. *Student/faculty ratio:* 18:1.

**Majors** Accounting technology and bookkeeping; automobile/automotive mechanics technology; building/property maintenance; business administration and management; business automation/technology/data entry; cabinetmaking and millwork; carpentry; child-care and support services management; computer and information sciences; construction trades; criminal justice/safety; drafting and design technology; early childhood education; electrical, electronic and communications engineering technology; electrician; executive assistant/executive secretary; funeral service and mortuary science; general studies; heating, air conditioning, ventilation and refrigeration maintenance technology; hospitality administration; human services; industrial technology; ironworking; legal assistant/paralegal; liberal arts and sciences/liberal studies; library and archives assisting; machine tool technology; masonry; mechanic and repair technologies related; mechanics and repair; medical/clinical assistant; occupational safety and health technology; painting and wall covering; pipefitting and sprinkler fitting; psychiatric/mental health services technology; registered nursing/registered nurse; respiratory care therapy; sheet metal technology; surgical technology; telecommunications technology; tool and die technology.

**Academics** *Calendar:* semesters. *Degree:* certificates and associate. *Special study options:* academic remediation for entering students, adult/continuing education programs, advanced placement credit, distance learning, internships, part-time degree program, services for LD students, summer session for credit.

**Student Life** *Housing:* college housing not available. *Activities and Organizations:* Phi Theta Kappa, LPN Club, Computer Club, Student Government, Business Club. *Campus security:* 24-hour emergency response devices, late-night transport/escort service.

**Costs (2017–18)** *Tuition:* state resident $4135 full-time, $138 per credit hour part-time; nonresident $8091 full-time, $270 per credit hour part-time. *Required fees:* $120 full-time, $60 per term part-time. *Payment plans:* installment, deferred payment. *Waivers:* senior citizens and employees or children of employees.

**Financial Aid** Of all full-time matriculated undergraduates who enrolled in 2016, 74 Federal Work-Study jobs (averaging $2131).

**Applying** *Options:* electronic application, deferred entrance. *Required:* high school transcript. *Required for some:* interview. *Application deadlines:* rolling (freshmen), rolling (transfers). *Notification:* continuous (freshmen), continuous (transfers).

**Freshman Application Contact** Darryl Williams, Bi-Regional Director of Admissions, Ivy Tech Community College–Northwest, 1440 East 35th Avenue, Gary, IN 46409-499. *Phone:* 219-981-1111. *Toll-free phone:* 888-IVY-LINE. *E-mail:* dwilliams770@ivytech.edu. *Website:* http://www.ivytech.edu/.

# Ivy Tech Community College–Richmond
## Richmond, Indiana

- **State-supported** 2-year, founded 1963, part of Ivy Tech Community College System
- **Small-town** 23-acre campus with easy access to Indianapolis
- **Coed,** 1,527 undergraduate students, 27% full-time, 64% women, 36% men

**Undergraduates** 415 full-time, 1,112 part-time. 1% are from out of state; 4% Black or African American, non-Hispanic/Latino; 0.6% Hispanic/Latino; 0.5% Asian, non-Hispanic/Latino; 0.1% Native Hawaiian or other Pacific Islander, non-Hispanic/Latino; 0.6% American Indian or Alaska Native, non-Hispanic/Latino; 2% Two or more races, non-Hispanic/Latino; 3% Race/ethnicity unknown; 7% transferred in. *Retention:* 50% of full-time freshmen returned.

**Freshmen** *Admission:* 300 enrolled.

**Faculty** *Total:* 127, 31% full-time. *Student/faculty ratio:* 13:1.

**Majors** Accounting technology and bookkeeping; agriculture; automobile/automotive mechanics technology; building/property maintenance; business administration and management; business automation/technology/data entry; cabinetmaking and millwork; computer and information sciences; computer science; construction trades; construction trades related; criminal justice/safety; data modeling/warehousing and database administration; early childhood education; education; electrical, electronic and communications engineering technology; electrician; emergency medical technology (EMT paramedic); engineering technology; executive assistant/executive secretary; general studies; heating, air conditioning, ventilation and refrigeration maintenance technology; human services; industrial production technologies related; industrial technology; informatics; information science/studies; information technology; legal assistant/paralegal; liberal arts and sciences and humanities related; liberal arts and sciences/liberal studies; library and archives assisting; logistics, materials, and supply chain management; machine shop technology; machine tool technology; manufacturing engineering technology; mechanics and repair; medical/clinical assistant; medical/health management and clinical assistant; medical radiologic technology; network and system administration; pipefitting and sprinkler fitting; psychiatric/mental health services technology; registered nursing/registered nurse; respiratory care therapy; tool and die technology.

**Academics** *Calendar:* semesters. *Degree:* certificates and associate. *Special study options:* academic remediation for entering students, adult/continuing education programs, advanced placement credit, distance learning, independent study, internships, off-campus study, part-time degree program, services for LD students, summer session for credit.

**Student Life** *Housing:* college housing not available. *Activities and Organizations:* student-run newspaper, Student Government, Phi Theta Kappa, LPN Club, CATS 2000, Business Professionals of America. *Campus security:* 24-hour emergency response devices, late-night transport/escort service. *Student services:* personal/psychological counseling.

**Athletics** *Intramural sports:* softball M/W.

**Costs (2017–18)** *Tuition:* state resident $4135 full-time, $138 per credit hour part-time; nonresident $8091 full-time, $270 per credit hour part-time. *Required fees:* $120 full-time, $60 per term part-time. *Payment plans:* installment, deferred payment. *Waivers:* senior citizens and employees or children of employees.

**Financial Aid** Of all full-time matriculated undergraduates who enrolled in 2016, 14 Federal Work-Study jobs (averaging $3106). 1 state and other part-time job (averaging $3380).

**Applying** *Options:* electronic application, early admission. *Required:* high school transcript. *Required for some:* interview. *Application deadlines:* rolling (freshmen), rolling (transfers). *Notification:* continuous (freshmen), continuous (transfers).

**Freshman Application Contact** Linda Przybysz, Director of Admissions, Ivy Tech Community College–Richmond, 2325 Chester Boulevard, Richmond, IN 47374-1298. *Phone:* 765-966-2656 Ext. 1246. *Toll-free phone:* 888-IVY-LINE. *E-mail:* lprzybys@ivytech.edu.
*Website:* http://www.ivytech.edu/.

## Ivy Tech Community College–Sellersburg
### Sellersburg, Indiana

- **State-supported** 2-year, founded 1968, part of Ivy Tech Community College System
- **Small-town** 63-acre campus with easy access to Louisville
- **Coed,** 4,684 undergraduate students, 19% full-time, 52% women, 48% men

**Undergraduates** 867 full-time, 3,817 part-time. 9% are from out of state; 7% Black or African American, non-Hispanic/Latino; 2% Hispanic/Latino; 0.8% Asian, non-Hispanic/Latino; 0.1% Native Hawaiian or other Pacific Islander, non-Hispanic/Latino; 0.3% American Indian or Alaska Native, non-Hispanic/Latino; 3% Two or more races, non-Hispanic/Latino; 14% Race/ethnicity unknown; 8% transferred in. *Retention:* 55% of full-time freshmen returned.

**Freshmen** *Admission:* 964 enrolled.

**Faculty** *Total:* 203, 27% full-time. *Student/faculty ratio:* 20:1.

**Majors** Accounting technology and bookkeeping; administrative assistant and secretarial science; automobile/automotive mechanics technology; building/property maintenance; business administration and management; business automation/technology/data entry; cabinetmaking and millwork; carpentry; clinical/medical laboratory technology; computer and information sciences; computer science; computer systems networking and telecommunications; data modeling/warehousing and database administration; design and visual communications; drafting and design technology; early childhood education; education; electrical, electronic and communications engineering technology; electrician; energy management and systems technology; engineering technology; executive assistant/executive secretary; general studies; heating, air conditioning, ventilation and refrigeration maintenance technology; human services; industrial technology; informatics; information science/studies; information technology; kinesiology and exercise

science; legal assistant/paralegal; liberal arts and sciences/liberal studies; library and archives assisting; logistics, materials, and supply chain management; machine tool technology; mechanics and repair; medical/clinical assistant; medical/health management and clinical assistant; network and system administration; physical therapy technology; pipefitting and sprinkler fitting; psychiatric/mental health services technology; registered nursing/registered nurse; respiratory care therapy; sheet metal technology; telecommunications technology; tool and die technology.

**Academics** *Calendar:* semesters. *Degree:* certificates and associate. *Special study options:* academic remediation for entering students, adult/continuing education programs, advanced placement credit, cooperative education, distance learning, internships, part-time degree program, services for LD students, summer session for credit.

**Student Life** *Housing:* college housing not available. *Activities and Organizations:* Phi Theta Kappa, Practical Nursing Club, Medical Assistant Club, Accounting Club, Student Government. *Campus security:* late-night transport/escort service.

**Costs (2017–18)** *Tuition:* state resident $4135 full-time, $138 per credit hour part-time; nonresident $8091 full-time, $270 per credit hour part-time. *Required fees:* $120 full-time, $60 per term part-time. *Payment plans:* installment, deferred payment. *Waivers:* senior citizens and employees or children of employees.

**Financial Aid** Of all full-time matriculated undergraduates who enrolled in 2016, 20 Federal Work-Study jobs (averaging $5007). 1 state and other part-time job (averaging $6080).

**Applying** *Options:* electronic application, early admission, deferred entrance. *Required:* high school transcript. *Required for some:* interview. *Application deadlines:* rolling (freshmen), rolling (transfers). *Notification:* continuous (freshmen), continuous (transfers).

**Freshman Application Contact** Ben Harris, Director of Admissions, Ivy Tech Community College–Sellersburg, 8204 Highway 311, Sellersburg, IN 47172-1897. *Phone:* 812-246-3301 Ext. 4137. *Toll-free phone:* 888-IVY-LINE. *Fax:* 812-246-9905. *E-mail:* bharris88@ivytech.edu.
*Website:* http://www.ivytech.edu/.

## Ivy Tech Community College–Southeast
### Madison, Indiana

- **State-supported** 2-year, founded 1963, part of Ivy Tech Community College System
- **Small-town** 5-acre campus with easy access to Louisville
- **Coed,** 2,334 undergraduate students, 27% full-time, 64% women, 36% men

**Undergraduates** 635 full-time, 1,699 part-time. 1% are from out of state; 1% Black or African American, non-Hispanic/Latino; 0.7% Hispanic/Latino; 0.5% Asian, non-Hispanic/Latino; 0.4% American Indian or Alaska Native, non-Hispanic/Latino; 2% Two or more races, non-Hispanic/Latino; 7% Race/ethnicity unknown; 5% transferred in. *Retention:* 63% of full-time freshmen returned.

**Freshmen** *Admission:* 326 enrolled.

**Faculty** *Total:* 183, 30% full-time. *Student/faculty ratio:* 13:1.

**Majors** Accounting technology and bookkeeping; administrative assistant and secretarial science; business administration and management; business automation/technology/data entry; computer and information sciences; computer science; criminal justice/safety; data modeling/warehousing and database administration; drafting and design technology; early childhood education; education; electrical, electronic and communications engineering technology; executive assistant/executive secretary; general studies; human services; industrial technology; informatics; information science/studies; information technology; legal assistant/paralegal; liberal arts and sciences/liberal studies; logistics, materials, and supply chain management; manufacturing engineering technology; medical/clinical assistant; medical/health management and clinical assistant; medical radiologic technology; network and system administration; psychiatric/mental health services technology; registered nursing/registered nurse.

**Academics** *Calendar:* semesters. *Degree:* certificates and associate. *Special study options:* academic remediation for entering students, advanced placement credit, distance learning, internships, part-time degree program, services for LD students, summer session for credit.

**Student Life** *Housing:* college housing not available. *Activities and Organizations:* Student Government, Phi Theta Kappa, LPN Club. *Campus security:* 24-hour emergency response devices.

**Costs (2017–18)** *Tuition:* state resident $4135 full-time, $138 per credit hour part-time; nonresident $8091 full-time, $270 per credit hour part-time. *Required fees:* $120 full-time, $60 per term part-time. *Payment plans:* installment, deferred payment. *Waivers:* senior citizens and employees or children of employees.

**Financial Aid** Of all full-time matriculated undergraduates who enrolled in 2016, 26 Federal Work-Study jobs (averaging $1696).

Applying *Options:* electronic application. *Required:* high school transcript. *Required for some:* interview. *Application deadlines:* rolling (freshmen), rolling (transfers). *Notification:* continuous (freshmen), continuous (transfers).
**Freshman Application Contact** Shakira Grubbs, Director Express Enrollment Center, Ivy Tech Community College–Southeast, 590 Ivy Tech Drive, Madison, IN 47250-1881. *Phone:* 812-537-4010. *Toll-free phone:* 888-IVY-LINE. *E-mail:* sgrubbs5@ivytech.edu.
*Website:* http://www.ivytech.edu/.

# Ivy Tech Community College–Southwest
## Evansville, Indiana

- **State-supported** 2-year, founded 1963, part of Ivy Tech Community College System
- **Suburban** 15-acre campus
- **Coed,** 4,076 undergraduate students, 23% full-time, 57% women, 43% men

**Undergraduates** 928 full-time, 3,148 part-time. 1% are from out of state; 7% Black or African American, non-Hispanic/Latino; 0.9% Hispanic/Latino; 0.9% Asian, non-Hispanic/Latino; 0.1% Native Hawaiian or other Pacific Islander, non-Hispanic/Latino; 0.3% American Indian or Alaska Native, non-Hispanic/Latino; 3% Two or more races, non-Hispanic/Latino; 6% Race/ethnicity unknown; 7% transferred in. *Retention:* 52% of full-time freshmen returned.
**Freshmen** *Admission:* 523 enrolled.
**Faculty** *Total:* 290, 27% full-time. *Student/faculty ratio:* 17:1.
**Majors** Accounting technology and bookkeeping; administrative assistant and secretarial science; agriculture; automobile/automotive mechanics technology; biotechnology; boilermaking; building/property maintenance; business administration and management; business automation/technology/data entry; cabinetmaking and millwork; carpentry; computer and information sciences; computer science; construction/heavy equipment/earthmoving equipment operation; criminal justice/safety; data modeling/warehousing and database administration; design and visual communications; drafting and design technology; early childhood education; education; electrical, electronic and communications engineering technology; electrician; emergency medical technology (EMT paramedic); energy management and systems technology; engineering technology; executive assistant/executive secretary; general studies; heating, air conditioning, ventilation and refrigeration maintenance technology; hospitality administration; human services; industrial production technologies related; industrial technology; informatics; information science/studies; information technology; interior design; ironworking; legal assistant/paralegal; library and archives assisting; logistics, materials, and supply chain management; machine tool technology; manufacturing engineering technology; masonry; mechanic and repair technologies related; mechanics and repair; medical/clinical assistant; medical/health management and clinical assistant; network and system administration; painting and wall covering; pre-engineering; psychiatric/mental health services technology; registered nursing/registered nurse; sheet metal technology; surgical technology; telecommunications technology; tool and die technology.
**Academics** *Calendar:* semesters. *Degree:* certificates and associate. *Special study options:* academic remediation for entering students, advanced placement credit, cooperative education, distance learning, independent study, internships, part-time degree program, services for LD students, summer session for credit.
**Student Life** *Housing:* college housing not available. *Activities and Organizations:* Student Government, Phi Theta Kappa, LPN Club, National Association of Industrial Technology, Design Club. *Campus security:* late-night transport/escort service.
**Costs (2017–18)** *Tuition:* state resident $4135 full-time, $138 per credit hour part-time; nonresident $8091 full-time, $270 per credit hour part-time. *Required fees:* $120 full-time, $60 per term part-time. *Payment plans:* installment, deferred payment. *Waivers:* senior citizens and employees or children of employees.
**Financial Aid** Of all full-time matriculated undergraduates who enrolled in 2016, 65 Federal Work-Study jobs (averaging $2264).
**Applying** *Options:* electronic application, early admission, deferred entrance. *Required:* high school transcript. *Required for some:* interview. *Application deadlines:* rolling (freshmen), rolling (transfers). *Notification:* continuous (freshmen), continuous (transfers).
**Freshman Application Contact** Ms. Denise Johnson-Kincade, Director of Admissions, Ivy Tech Community College–Southwest, 3501 First Avenue, Evansville, IN 47710-3398. *Phone:* 812-429-1430. *Toll-free phone:* 888-IVY-LINE. *Fax:* 812-429-9878. *E-mail:* ajohnson@ivytech.edu.
*Website:* http://www.ivytech.edu/.

# Ivy Tech Community College–Wabash Valley
## Terre Haute, Indiana

- **State-supported** 2-year, founded 1966, part of Ivy Tech Community College System
- **Suburban** 55-acre campus with easy access to Indianapolis
- **Coed,** 3,637 undergraduate students, 33% full-time, 56% women, 44% men

**Undergraduates** 1,216 full-time, 2,421 part-time. 1% are from out of state; 4% Black or African American, non-Hispanic/Latino; 0.7% Hispanic/Latino; 0.5% Asian, non-Hispanic/Latino; 0.4% American Indian or Alaska Native, non-Hispanic/Latino; 2% Two or more races, non-Hispanic/Latino; 5% Race/ethnicity unknown; 7% transferred in. *Retention:* 55% of full-time freshmen returned.
**Freshmen** *Admission:* 544 enrolled.
**Faculty** *Total:* 287, 34% full-time. *Student/faculty ratio:* 19:1.
**Majors** Accounting technology and bookkeeping; agricultural mechanization; agriculture; airframe mechanics and aircraft maintenance technology; automobile/automotive mechanics technology; building/property maintenance; business administration and management; cabinetmaking and millwork; carpentry; chemical technology; clinical/medical laboratory technology; computer and information sciences; computer science; computer systems networking and telecommunications; construction/heavy equipment/earthmoving equipment operation; criminal justice/safety; data modeling/warehousing and database administration; design and visual communications; drafting and design technology; early childhood education; education; electrical, electronic and communications engineering technology; electrician; emergency medical technology (EMT paramedic); energy management and systems technology; engineering technology; executive assistant/executive secretary; general studies; health aide; health information/medical records technology; heating, air conditioning, ventilation and refrigeration maintenance technology; human services; industrial production technologies related; industrial technology; informatics; information science/studies; information technology; ironworking; legal assistant/paralegal; liberal arts and sciences/liberal studies; library and archives assisting; logistics, materials, and supply chain management; machine shop technology; machine tool technology; manufacturing engineering technology; masonry; mechanics and repair; medical/clinical assistant; medical/health management and clinical assistant; medical radiologic technology; network and system administration; occupational safety and health technology; painting and wall covering; pipefitting and sprinkler fitting; quality control and safety technologies related; registered nursing/registered nurse; respiratory care therapy; sheet metal technology; surgical technology; tool and die technology.
**Academics** *Calendar:* semesters. *Degree:* certificates and associate. *Special study options:* academic remediation for entering students, adult/continuing education programs, advanced placement credit, distance learning, internships, part-time degree program, services for LD students, summer session for credit.
**Student Life** *Housing:* college housing not available. *Activities and Organizations:* Student Government, Phi Theta Kappa, LPN Club, National Association of Industrial Technology. *Campus security:* 24-hour emergency response devices. *Student services:* personal/psychological counseling, women's center.
**Athletics** *Intramural sports:* basketball M/W, volleyball M/W.
**Costs (2017–18)** *Tuition:* state resident $4135 full-time, $138 per credit hour part-time; nonresident $8091 full-time, $270 per credit hour part-time. *Required fees:* $120 full-time, $60 per term part-time. *Payment plans:* installment, deferred payment. *Waivers:* senior citizens and employees or children of employees.
**Financial Aid** Of all full-time matriculated undergraduates who enrolled in 2016, 51 Federal Work-Study jobs (averaging $2110). 1 state and other part-time job (averaging $2963).
**Applying** *Options:* electronic application, early admission, deferred entrance. *Required:* high school transcript. *Required for some:* interview. *Application deadlines:* rolling (freshmen), rolling (transfers). *Notification:* continuous (freshmen), continuous (transfers).
**Freshman Application Contact** Nina Storey, Director of Admissions, Ivy Tech Community College–Wabash Valley, 7999 U.S. Highway 41 South, Terre Haute, IN 47802-4898. *Phone:* 812-298-2288. *Toll-free phone:* 888-IVY-LINE. *E-mail:* nstorey@ivytech.edu.
*Website:* http://www.ivytech.edu/.

# Lincoln College of Technology
## Indianapolis, Indiana

**Director of Admissions** Ms. Cindy Ryan, Director of Admissions, Lincoln College of Technology, 7225 Winton Drive, Building 128, Indianapolis, IN

46268. *Phone:* 317-632-5553. *Toll-free phone:* 844-215-1513. *Website:* http://www.lincolntech.edu/.

## Mid-America College of Funeral Service
### Jeffersonville, Indiana

**Freshman Application Contact** Mr. Richard Nelson, Dean of Students, Mid-America College of Funeral Service, 3111 Hamburg Pike, Jeffersonville, IN 47130-9630. *Phone:* 812-288-8878. *Toll-free phone:* 800-221-6158. *Fax:* 812-288-5942. *E-mail:* macfs@mindspring.com. *Website:* http://www.mid-america.edu/.

## Vet Tech Institute at International Business College
### Fort Wayne, Indiana

**Freshman Application Contact** Admissions Office, Vet Tech Institute at International Business College, 5699 Coventry Lane, Fort Wayne, IN 46804. *Phone:* 800-589-6363. *Toll-free phone:* 800-589-6363. *Website:* http://ftwayne.vettechinstitute.edu/.

## Vet Tech Institute at International Business College
### Indianapolis, Indiana

**Freshman Application Contact** Admissions Office, Vet Tech Institute at International Business College, 7205 Shadeland Station, Indianapolis, IN 46256. *Phone:* 800-589-6500. *Toll-free phone:* 800-589-6500. *Website:* http://indianapolis.vettechinstitute.edu/.

## Vincennes University
### Vincennes, Indiana

- **State-supported** primarily 2-year, founded 1801
- **Small-town** 160-acre campus
- **Coed,** 18,904 undergraduate students, 28% full-time, 45% women, 55% men

**Undergraduates** 5,359 full-time, 13,545 part-time. Students come from 40 states and territories; 15 other countries; 18% are from out of state; 10% Black or African American, non-Hispanic/Latino; 10% Hispanic/Latino; 0.6% Asian, non-Hispanic/Latino; 0.2% Native Hawaiian or other Pacific Islander, non-Hispanic/Latino; 0.3% American Indian or Alaska Native, non-Hispanic/Latino; 2% Two or more races, non-Hispanic/Latino; 5% Race/ethnicity unknown; 0.7% international; 1% transferred in; 40% live on campus. *Retention:* 52% of full-time freshmen returned.
**Freshmen** *Admission:* 5,486 applied, 4,346 admitted, 2,332 enrolled.
**Faculty** *Total:* 1,351, 15% full-time. *Student/faculty ratio:* 16:1.
**Majors** Accounting technology and bookkeeping; administrative assistant and secretarial science; agricultural business and management; aircraft powerplant technology; airline pilot and flight crew; American Sign Language (ASL); applied horticulture/horticulture operations; architectural drafting and CAD/CADD; art; art teacher education; art therapy; autobody/collision and repair technology; automation engineer technology; automobile/automotive mechanics technology; behavioral sciences; biological and biomedical sciences related; building/construction finishing, management, and inspection related; business administration and management; business/commerce; business teacher education; carpentry; chemistry related; chemistry teacher education; child-care and support services management; commercial and advertising art; communications technologies and support services related; computer/information technology services administration related; computer programming; computer systems networking and telecommunications; cosmetology; costume design; criminal justice/police science; culinary arts; design and applied arts related; diesel mechanics technology; dietetics; dramatic/theater arts; early childhood education; education; electrical and power transmission installation related; electrical, electronic and communications engineering technology; electrician; elementary education; emergency medical technology (EMT paramedic); engineering science; English; environmental studies; family and consumer sciences/home economics teacher education; family and consumer sciences/human sciences; fashion merchandising; fire science/firefighting; foreign languages and literatures; funeral service and mortuary science; health and physical education/fitness; health information/medical records technology; health teacher education; heating, air conditioning, ventilation and refrigeration maintenance technology; history; hotel/motel administration; industrial technology; information technology; journalism; legal assistant/paralegal; liberal arts and sciences and humanities related; liberal arts and sciences/liberal studies; lineworker; logistics, materials, and supply chain management; manufacturing engineering technology; marketing/marketing management; mathematics teacher education; mechanical drafting and CAD/CADD; medical radiologic technology; mining technology; music; natural resources/conservation; occupational therapy; pharmacy technician; philosophy; photojournalism; physical education teaching and coaching; physical therapy technology; pipefitting and sprinkler fitting; plumbing technology; pre-law studies; public relations/image management; radio and television broadcasting technology; recording arts technology; registered nursing/registered nurse; rehabilitation and therapeutic professions related; restaurant, culinary, and catering management; science teacher education; secondary education; securities services administration; sheet metal technology; social work; special education; surgical technology; surveying technology; technology/industrial arts teacher education; theater design and technology; tool and die technology; web/multimedia management and webmaster; welding technology.
**Academics** *Calendar:* semesters. *Degrees:* certificates, associate, and bachelor's. *Special study options:* academic remediation for entering students, accelerated degree program, adult/continuing education programs, advanced placement credit, distance learning, double majors, English as a second language, external degree program, freshman honors college, honors programs, independent study, internships, off-campus study, part-time degree program, services for LD students, student-designed majors, summer session for credit. *ROTC:* Army (b).
**Library** Shake Learning Resource Center.
**Student Life** *Housing:* on-campus residence required for freshman year. *Options:* coed, men-only, women-only. Campus housing is university owned. Freshman campus housing is guaranteed. *Activities and Organizations:* drama/theater group, student-run newspaper, radio and television station, choral group, national fraternities, national sororities. *Campus security:* 24-hour emergency response devices and patrols, student patrols, late-night transport/escort service, controlled dormitory access, surveillance cameras. *Student services:* health clinic, personal/psychological counseling.
**Athletics** Member NJCAA. *Intercollegiate sports:* baseball M, basketball M/W, bowling M, cross-country running M/W, golf M, track and field M/W, volleyball W.
**Costs (2017–18)** *Tuition:* state resident $5270 full-time; nonresident $13,100 full-time. Full-time tuition and fees vary according to course level, course load, location, program, reciprocity agreements, and student level. Part-time tuition and fees vary according to course level, course load, location, program, reciprocity agreements, and student level. *Required fees:* $467 full-time. *Room and board:* $9702. Room and board charges vary according to board plan, gender, and housing facility. *Payment plan:* installment. *Waivers:* senior citizens and employees or children of employees.
**Applying** *Options:* electronic application, deferred entrance. *Application fee:* $20. *Required:* high school transcript. *Required for some:* interview. *Application deadlines:* rolling (freshmen), rolling (transfers). *Notification:* continuous until 8/1 (freshmen), continuous (transfers).
**Freshman Application Contact** Vincennes University, 1002 North First Street, Vincennes, IN 47591. *Phone:* 812-888-4313. *Toll-free phone:* 800-742-9198.
*Website:* http://www.vinu.edu/.

# IOWA

## Clinton Community College
### Clinton, Iowa

**Freshman Application Contact** Mr. Gary Mohr, Executive Director of Enrollment Management and Marketing, Clinton Community College, 1000 Lincoln Boulevard, Clinton, IA 52732-6299. *Phone:* 563-336-3322. *Toll-free phone:* 800-462-3255. *Fax:* 563-336-3350. *E-mail:* gmohr@eicc.edu. *Website:* http://www.eicc.edu/ccc/.

## Des Moines Area Community College
### Ankeny, Iowa

- **State and locally supported** 2-year, founded 1966, part of Iowa Area Community Colleges System
- **Small-town** 362-acre campus
- **Endowment** $7.0 million
- **Coed,** 22,982 undergraduate students, 28% full-time, 55% women, 45% men

**Undergraduates** 6,476 full-time, 16,506 part-time. Students come from 52 states and territories; 12 other countries; 7% are from out of state; 6% Black or African American, non-Hispanic/Latino; 8% Hispanic/Latino; 4% Asian, non-Hispanic/Latino; 0.1% Native Hawaiian or other Pacific Islander, non-

Hispanic/Latino; 0.3% American Indian or Alaska Native, non-Hispanic/Latino; 2% Two or more races, non-Hispanic/Latino; 10% Race/ethnicity unknown; 0.9% international; 9% transferred in. *Retention:* 59% of full-time freshmen returned.

**Freshmen** *Admission:* 3,645 enrolled.

**Faculty** *Total:* 1,145, 30% full-time. *Student/faculty ratio:* 20:1.

**Majors** Accounting; accounting and business/management; accounting technology and bookkeeping; agricultural/farm supplies retailing and wholesaling; apparel and accessories marketing; applied horticulture/horticultural business services related; architectural drafting and CAD/CADD; autobody/collision and repair technology; automobile/automotive mechanics technology; biomedical technology; business administration and management; child-care provision; civil engineering technology; clinical/medical laboratory technology; commercial and advertising art; communications systems installation and repair technology; computer and information sciences and support services related; computer engineering technology; computer programming (specific applications); criminal justice/law enforcement administration; culinary arts; dental hygiene; desktop publishing and digital imaging design; diesel mechanics technology; electrical, electronic and communications engineering technology; fire prevention and safety technology; funeral service and mortuary science; health/health-care administration; heating, air conditioning, ventilation and refrigeration maintenance technology; hospitality administration; industrial electronics technology; industrial mechanics and maintenance technology; information technology; language interpretation and translation; legal assistant/paralegal; liberal arts and sciences/liberal studies; licensed practical/vocational nurse training; machine tool technology; marketing/marketing management; mechanical drafting and CAD/CADD; medical administrative assistant and medical secretary; medical/clinical assistant; office management; registered nursing/registered nurse; respiratory care therapy; sales, distribution, and marketing operations; sport and fitness administration/management; surveying engineering; tool and die technology; veterinary/animal health technology.

**Academics** *Calendar:* semesters. *Degrees:* certificates, diplomas, and associate (profile also includes information from the Boone, Carroll, Des Moines, and Newton campuses). *Special study options:* academic remediation for entering students, adult/continuing education programs, advanced placement credit, cooperative education, distance learning, English as a second language, honors programs, off-campus study, part-time degree program, services for LD students, student-designed majors, summer session for credit.

**Library** DMACC District Library plus 4 others.

**Student Life** *Housing Options:* coed. Campus housing is university owned. *Activities and Organizations:* drama/theater group, student-run newspaper, choral group, Agri-Business Club, Horticulture Club, Hospitality Arts Club, Iowa Delta Epsilon Chi, Dental Hygienist Club. *Campus security:* 24-hour emergency response devices and patrols, late-night transport/escort service. *Student services:* health clinic, personal/psychological counseling.

**Athletics** Member NJCAA. *Intercollegiate sports:* baseball M(s), basketball M(s)/W(s), cross-country running W(s), golf M(s)/W(s), volleyball W(s). *Intramural sports:* badminton M/W, basketball M/W, football M/W, golf M/W, soccer M/W, volleyball M/W.

**Standardized Tests** *Required for some:* SAT or ACT (for admission), ACT Compass.

**Costs (2017–18)** *Tuition:* state resident $4530 full-time, $3020 per credit hour part-time; nonresident $9060 full-time, $6040 per credit hour part-time. Full-time tuition and fees vary according to course load and reciprocity agreements. Part-time tuition and fees vary according to course load and reciprocity agreements. *Room and board:* $7286; room only: $4600. Room and board charges vary according to location. *Payment plan:* installment. *Waivers:* senior citizens and employees or children of employees.

**Financial Aid** Of all full-time matriculated undergraduates who enrolled in 2016, 377 Federal Work-Study jobs (averaging $1055).

**Applying** *Options:* electronic application, early admission, deferred entrance. *Required for some:* high school transcript, interview. *Application deadlines:* rolling (freshmen), rolling (transfers).

**Freshman Application Contact** Mr. Michael Lentsch, Director of Program Development, Des Moines Area Community College, 2006 South Ankeny Boulevard, Ankeny, IA 50021-8995. *Phone:* 515-965-7086. *Toll-free phone:* 800-362-2127. *E-mail:* mjleutsch@dmacc.edu. *Website:* http://www.dmacc.edu/.

# Ellsworth Community College
## Iowa Falls, Iowa

**Director of Admissions** Mrs. Nancy Walters, Registrar, Ellsworth Community College, 1100 College Avenue, Iowa Falls, IA 50126-1199. *Phone:* 641-648-4611. *Toll-free phone:* 800-ECC-9235. *Website:* http://ecc.iavalley.edu/.

# Hawkeye Community College
## Waterloo, Iowa

- **State and locally supported** 2-year, founded 1966
- **Rural** 320-acre campus
- **Endowment** $2.2 million
- **Coed,** 5,605 undergraduate students, 45% full-time, 54% women, 46% men

**Undergraduates** 2,525 full-time, 3,080 part-time. Students come from 14 states and territories; 9 other countries; 1% are from out of state; 9% Black or African American, non-Hispanic/Latino; 4% Hispanic/Latino; 2% Asian, non-Hispanic/Latino; 0.1% Native Hawaiian or other Pacific Islander, non-Hispanic/Latino; 0.2% American Indian or Alaska Native, non-Hispanic/Latino; 4% Two or more races, non-Hispanic/Latino; 0.5% international; 26% transferred in.

**Freshmen** *Admission:* 1,667 applied, 1,540 admitted, 1,041 enrolled. *Test scores:* ACT scores over 18: 47%; ACT scores over 24: 14%; ACT scores over 30: 2%.

**Faculty** *Total:* 326, 36% full-time, 12% with terminal degrees. *Student/faculty ratio:* 17:1.

**Majors** Accounting; agricultural/farm supplies retailing and wholesaling; agricultural power machinery operation; animal/livestock husbandry and production; autobody/collision and repair technology; automation engineer technology; automobile/automotive mechanics technology; carpentry; child-care provision; civil engineering technology; clinical/medical laboratory technology; commercial photography; computer/information technology services administration related; computer systems networking and telecommunications; criminal justice/police science; dental hygiene; desktop publishing and digital imaging design; diesel mechanics technology; digital communication and media/multimedia; electrical, electronic and communications engineering technology; electromechanical technology; emergency medical technology (EMT paramedic); energy management and systems technology; executive assistant/executive secretary; fire science/firefighting; golf course operation and grounds management; hospitality administration; human resources management; landscaping and groundskeeping; liberal arts and sciences/liberal studies; machine tool technology; medical administrative assistant and medical secretary; medical insurance coding; multi/interdisciplinary studies related; natural resources management and policy; occupational therapist assistant; physical therapy technology; registered nursing/registered nurse; respiratory care therapy; sales, distribution, and marketing operations; web page, digital/multimedia and information resources design; welding technology.

**Academics** *Calendar:* semesters. *Degree:* certificates, diplomas, and associate. *Special study options:* academic remediation for entering students, accelerated degree program, adult/continuing education programs, advanced placement credit, cooperative education, distance learning, English as a second language, external degree program, part-time degree program, services for LD students, study abroad, summer session for credit. *ROTC:* Army (c).

**Library** Hawkeye Community College Library. *Books:* 24,330 (physical), 165,000 (digital/electronic); *Serial titles:* 154 (physical), 42 (digital/electronic); *Databases:* 23. Weekly public service hours: 70; students can reserve study rooms.

**Student Life** *Housing:* college housing not available. *Activities and Organizations:* drama/theater group, choral group, Student Leadership, Phi Theta Kappa, Student Ambassadors, Student American Dental Hygienist Association, Photography. *Campus security:* 24-hour patrols. *Student services:* health clinic, personal/psychological counseling, women's center, veterans affairs office.

**Athletics** Member NJCAA. *Intercollegiate sports:* cross-country running M(s)/W(s), soccer M(s)/W(s), track and field M(s)/W(s). *Intramural sports:* badminton M/W, basketball M/W, bowling M/W, football M/W, golf M/W, softball M/W, table tennis M/W, volleyball M/W.

**Standardized Tests** *Required:* ACT ACCUPLACER or the equivalent from ACT or accredited college course(s) (for admission). *Required for some:* ACT (for admission).

**Costs (2017–18)** *Tuition:* state resident $4760 full-time, $170 per credit hour part-time; nonresident $5460 full-time, $195 per credit hour part-time. *Required fees:* $217 full-time, $8 per credit hour part-time. *Payment plan:* installment.

**Applying** *Options:* electronic application, deferred entrance. *Required:* high school transcript. *Application deadlines:* rolling (freshmen), rolling (transfers). *Notification:* continuous (freshmen), continuous (transfers).

**Freshman Application Contact** Ms. Holly Grimm-See, Associate Director, Admissions and Recruitment, Hawkeye Community College, PO Box 8015, Waterloo, IA 50704-8015. *Phone:* 319-296-4277. *Toll-free phone:* 800-670-4769. *Fax:* 319-296-2505. *E-mail:* holly.grimm-see@hawkeyecollege.edu. *Website:* http://www.hawkeyecollege.edu/.

# Indian Hills Community College
## Ottumwa, Iowa

**Freshman Application Contact** Mrs. Jane Sapp, Admissions Officer, Indian Hills Community College, 525 Grandview Avenue, Building #1, Ottumwa, IA 52501-1398. *Phone:* 641-683-5155. *Toll-free phone:* 800-726-2585. *Website:* http://www.ihcc.cc.ia.us/.

# Iowa Central Community College
## Fort Dodge, Iowa

- **State and locally supported** 2-year, founded 1966
- **Small-town** 110-acre campus
- **Coed,** 5,489 undergraduate students, 51% full-time, 50% women, 50% men

**Undergraduates** 2,774 full-time, 2,715 part-time. Students come from 40 states and territories; 34 other countries; 8% are from out of state; 9% Black or African American, non-Hispanic/Latino; 9% Hispanic/Latino; 2% Asian, non-Hispanic/Latino; 0.2% Native Hawaiian or other Pacific Islander, non-Hispanic/Latino; 1% American Indian or Alaska Native, non-Hispanic/Latino; 1% Two or more races, non-Hispanic/Latino; 6% Race/ethnicity unknown; 2% international; 18% live on campus.
**Freshmen** *Admission:* 1,186 applied.
**Faculty** *Total:* 427, 23% full-time. *Student/faculty ratio:* 18:1.
**Majors** Accounting; administrative assistant and secretarial science; airline pilot and flight crew; automobile/automotive mechanics technology; aviation/airway management; biological and physical sciences; broadcast journalism; business administration and management; business teacher education; carpentry; clinical/medical laboratory technology; community organization and advocacy; computer engineering technology; criminal justice/police science; data processing and data processing technology; drafting and design technology; education; electrical, electronic and communications engineering technology; hospitality and recreation marketing; industrial radiologic technology; journalism; liberal arts and sciences/liberal studies; licensed practical/vocational nurse training; machine tool technology; mass communication/media; medical/clinical assistant; occupational therapy; physical therapy; radio and television; registered nursing/registered nurse; science teacher education; social work; sociology; telecommunications technology; welding technology.
**Academics** *Calendar:* semesters. *Degree:* certificates, diplomas, and associate. *Special study options:* academic remediation for entering students, adult/continuing education programs, advanced placement credit, cooperative education, English as a second language, independent study, internships, part-time degree program, services for LD students, study abroad, summer session for credit.
**Library** Iowa Central Community College Library plus 1 other. Students can reserve study rooms.
**Student Life** *Housing Options:* men-only, women-only. Campus housing is university owned. *Activities and Organizations:* drama/theater group, student-run newspaper, radio station, choral group, marching band, Student Senate, BPA, Phi Beta Lambda. *Campus security:* 24-hour emergency response devices and patrols, student patrols, late-night transport/escort service, controlled dormitory access. *Student services:* health clinic, personal/psychological counseling, veterans affairs office.
**Athletics** Member NJCAA. *Intercollegiate sports:* baseball M(s), basketball M(s)/W(s), bowling M(s)/W(s), cheerleading M(s)/W(s), cross-country running M/W, football M(s), golf M(s)/W(s), rugby M(c), soccer M(s)/W(s), softball W(s), swimming and diving M/W, tennis M(s)/W(s), volleyball W(s), wrestling M(s). *Intramural sports:* basketball M/W, football M, golf M/W, softball W, table tennis M/W, tennis M/W, volleyball M/W, weight lifting M, wrestling M.
**Costs (2017–18)** *Tuition:* state resident $3936 full-time, $164 per credit part-time; nonresident $5796 full-time, $242 per credit part-time. Full-time tuition and fees vary according to course load and program. Part-time tuition and fees vary according to course load and program. *Required fees:* $336 full-time, $14 per credit hour part-time. *Room and board:* $6750. *Payment plan:* installment.
**Applying** *Options:* electronic application, early admission, deferred entrance. *Required for some:* high school transcript, letters of recommendation, interview. *Recommended:* high school transcript. *Application deadlines:* rolling (freshmen), rolling (transfers). *Notification:* continuous (freshmen), continuous (transfers).
**Freshman Application Contact** Mrs. Sue Flattery, Enrollment Management Secretary, Iowa Central Community College, One Triton Circle, Fort Dodge, IA 50501. *Phone:* 515-574-1010 Ext. 2402. *Toll-free phone:* 800-362-2793. *Fax:* 515-576-7207. *E-mail:* flattery@iowacentral.com. *Website:* http://www.iowacentral.edu/.

# Iowa Lakes Community College
## Estherville, Iowa

**Freshman Application Contact** Iowa Lakes Community College, IA. *Phone:* 712-362-7923 Ext. 7923. *Toll-free phone:* 800-521-5054. *E-mail:* info@iowalakes.edu. *Website:* http://www.iowalakes.edu/.

# Iowa Western Community College
## Council Bluffs, Iowa

**Freshman Application Contact** Ms. Tori Christie, Director of Admissions, Iowa Western Community College, 2700 College Road, Box 4-C, Council Bluffs, IA 51502. *Phone:* 712-325-3288. *Toll-free phone:* 800-432-5852. *E-mail:* admissions@iwcc.edu. *Website:* http://www.iwcc.edu/.

# Kaplan University, Cedar Falls
## Cedar Falls, Iowa

**Freshman Application Contact** Kaplan University, Cedar Falls, 7009 Nordic Drive, Cedar Falls, IA 50613. *Phone:* 319-277-0220. *Toll-free phone:* 800-987-7734. *Website:* http://www.kaplanuniversity.edu/.

# Kaplan University, Cedar Rapids
## Cedar Rapids, Iowa

**Freshman Application Contact** Kaplan University, Cedar Rapids, 3165 Edgewood Parkway, SW, Cedar Rapids, IA 52404. *Phone:* 319-363-0481. *Toll-free phone:* 800-987-7734. *Website:* http://www.kaplanuniversity.edu/.

# Kaplan University, Des Moines
## Urbandale, Iowa

**Freshman Application Contact** Kaplan University, Des Moines, 4655 121st Street, Urbandale, IA 50323. *Phone:* 515-727-2100. *Toll-free phone:* 800-987-7734. *Website:* http://www.kaplanuniversity.edu/.

# Kirkwood Community College
## Cedar Rapids, Iowa

**Freshman Application Contact** Kirkwood Community College, PO Box 2068, Cedar Rapids, IA 52406-2068. *Phone:* 319-398-5517. *Toll-free phone:* 800-332-2055. *Website:* http://www.kirkwood.edu/.

# Marshalltown Community College
## Marshalltown, Iowa

**Freshman Application Contact** Ms. Deana Inman, Director of Admissions, Marshalltown Community College, 3700 South Center Street, Marshalltown, IA 50158-4760. *Phone:* 641-752-7106. *Toll-free phone:* 866-622-4748. *Fax:* 641-752-8149. *Website:* http://mcc.iavalley.edu/.

# Muscatine Community College
## Muscatine, Iowa

**Freshman Application Contact** Gary Mohr, Executive Director of Enrollment Management and Marketing, Muscatine Community College, 152 Colorado Street, Muscatine, IA 52761-5396. *Phone:* 563-336-3322. *Toll-free phone:* 800-351-4669. *Fax:* 563-336-3350. *E-mail:* gmohr@eicc.edu. *Website:* http://www.eicc.edu/mcc/.

# Northeast Iowa Community College
## Calmar, Iowa

- **State and locally supported** 2-year, founded 1966, part of Iowa Area Community Colleges System
- **Rural** 210-acre campus
- **Coed,** 4,545 undergraduate students, 27% full-time, 57% women, 43% men

**Undergraduates** 1,221 full-time, 3,324 part-time. 12% are from out of state; 5% Black or African American, non-Hispanic/Latino; 3% Hispanic/Latino; 0.7% Asian, non-Hispanic/Latino; 0.4% Native Hawaiian or other Pacific Islander, non-Hispanic/Latino; 0.4% American Indian or Alaska Native, non-Hispanic/Latino; 0.8% Two or more races, non-Hispanic/Latino; 3% Race/ethnicity unknown; 0.8% international; 4% transferred in. *Retention:* 52% of full-time freshmen returned.
**Freshmen** *Admission:* 1,976 applied, 1,957 admitted, 583 enrolled.

**Faculty** *Total:* 293, 38% full-time, 3% with terminal degrees. *Student/faculty ratio:* 13:1.

**Majors** Accounting; administrative assistant and secretarial science; agribusiness; agricultural and food products processing; agricultural power machinery operation; agricultural production; automobile/automotive mechanics technology; business administration and management; business automation/technology/data entry; clinical/medical laboratory technology; computer programming (specific applications); construction trades; cosmetology; crop production; dairy husbandry and production; desktop publishing and digital imaging design; electrical, electronic and communications engineering technology; electrician; emergency medical technology (EMT paramedic); energy management and systems technology; fire science/firefighting; health information/medical records technology; liberal arts and sciences/liberal studies; plumbing technology; radiologic technology/science; registered nursing/registered nurse; respiratory care therapy; sales, distribution, and marketing operations; social work.

**Academics** *Calendar:* semesters. *Degree:* certificates, diplomas, and associate. *Special study options:* academic remediation for entering students, adult/continuing education programs, advanced placement credit, cooperative education, distance learning, double majors, external degree program, honors programs, internships, off-campus study, part-time degree program, services for LD students, summer session for credit.

**Library** Wilder Resource Center and Burton Payne Library plus 2 others.

**Student Life** *Housing:* college housing not available. *Activities and Organizations:* student-run newspaper, choral group, national fraternities, national sororities. *Campus security:* security personnel on weeknights. *Student services:* personal/psychological counseling.

**Athletics** *Intramural sports:* basketball M/W, bowling M/W, football M, golf M/W, skiing (downhill) M/W, softball M/W, volleyball M/W.

**Costs (2017–18)** *Tuition:* state resident $4890 full-time, $163 per credit hour part-time; nonresident $5190 full-time, $173 per credit hour part-time. Full-time tuition and fees vary according to course load and program. Part-time tuition and fees vary according to course load and program. *Required fees:* $660 full-time, $22 per credit hour part-time. *Payment plan:* installment. *Waivers:* employees or children of employees.

**Applying** *Options:* electronic application. *Recommended:* high school transcript.

**Freshman Application Contact** Ms. Brynn McConnell, Admissions Representative, Northeast Iowa Community College, Calmar, IA 52132. *Phone:* 563-562-3263 Ext. 307. *Toll-free phone:* 800-728-CALMAR. *Fax:* 563-562-4369. *E-mail:* mcconnellb@nicc.edu. *Website:* http://www.nicc.edu/.

# North Iowa Area Community College
## Mason City, Iowa

- **State and locally supported** 2-year, founded 1918, part of Iowa Community College System
- **Rural** 500-acre campus
- **Coed,** 2,947 undergraduate students, 46% full-time, 55% women, 45% men

**Undergraduates** 1,346 full-time, 1,601 part-time. 4% Black or African American, non-Hispanic/Latino; 5% Hispanic/Latino; 1% Asian, non-Hispanic/Latino; 0.2% American Indian or Alaska Native, non-Hispanic/Latino; 1% Two or more races, non-Hispanic/Latino; 0.1% Race/ethnicity unknown; 2% international; 12% live on campus.

**Freshmen** *Admission:* 599 enrolled.

**Faculty** *Total:* 127, 54% full-time, 9% with terminal degrees. *Student/faculty ratio:* 10:1.

**Majors** Accounting; accounting technology and bookkeeping; administrative assistant and secretarial science; agricultural economics; agricultural/farm supplies retailing and wholesaling; agricultural production; automobile/automotive mechanics technology; business administration and management; carpentry; clinical/medical laboratory technology; criminal justice/police science; desktop publishing and digital imaging design; electrical, electronic and communications engineering technology; emergency medical technology (EMT paramedic); entrepreneurship; heating, air conditioning, ventilation and refrigeration maintenance technology; legal administrative assistant/secretary; liberal arts and sciences/liberal studies; licensed practical/vocational nurse training; medical administrative assistant and medical secretary; medical/clinical assistant; nursing assistant/aide and patient care assistant/aide; registered nursing/registered nurse; sales, distribution, and marketing operations; sport and fitness administration/management; tool and die technology; welding technology.

**Academics** *Calendar:* semesters. *Degree:* certificates, diplomas, and associate. *Special study options:* academic remediation for entering students, advanced placement credit, cooperative education, distance learning, English as a second language, honors programs, internships, part-time degree program, services for LD students, student-designed majors, summer session for credit.

**Student Life** *Housing Options:* coed. Campus housing is university owned. *Activities and Organizations:* drama/theater group, student-run newspaper, choral group, Ski and Snowboard Club, intramurals, Student Senate, Education Club, Women in Learning and Leadership. *Campus security:* student patrols, late-night transport/escort service, controlled dormitory access. *Student services:* health clinic, personal/psychological counseling, veterans affairs office.

**Athletics** Member NJCAA. *Intercollegiate sports:* baseball M(s), basketball M(s)/W(s), cross-country running M(s)/W(s), golf M(s)/W(s), soccer M(s), softball W(s), track and field M(s)/W(s), volleyball W(s), wrestling M(s). *Intramural sports:* cheerleading W.

**Costs (2017–18)** *Tuition:* state resident $4433 full-time, $148 per semester hour part-time; nonresident $6649 full-time, $222 per semester hour part-time. Full-time tuition and fees vary according to course load. Part-time tuition and fees vary according to course load. *Required fees:* $780 full-time, $26 per semester hour part-time. *Room and board:* $6920. Room and board charges vary according to housing facility. *Payment plan:* installment. *Waivers:* senior citizens and employees or children of employees.

**Financial Aid** Of all full-time matriculated undergraduates who enrolled in 2016, 125 Federal Work-Study jobs (averaging $2000). 4 state and other part-time jobs (averaging $2000).

**Applying** *Options:* electronic application. *Required:* high school transcript. *Application deadlines:* rolling (freshmen), rolling (transfers). *Notification:* continuous (freshmen), continuous (transfers).

**Freshman Application Contact** Ms. Rachel McGuire, Director of Enrollment Services, North Iowa Area Community College, 500 College Drive, Mason City, IA 50401. *Phone:* 641-422-4104. *Toll-free phone:* 888-GO NIACC Ext. 4245. *Fax:* 641-422-4385. *E-mail:* request@niacc.edu. *Website:* http://www.niacc.edu/.

# Northwest Iowa Community College
## Sheldon, Iowa

**Director of Admissions** Ms. Lisa Story, Director of Enrollment Management, Northwest Iowa Community College, 603 West Park Street, Sheldon, IA 51201-1046. *Phone:* 712-324-5061 Ext. 115. *Toll-free phone:* 800-352-4907. *E-mail:* lstory@nwicc.edu. *Website:* http://www.nwicc.edu/.

# Ross College
## Bettendorf, Iowa

**Freshman Application Contact** Ross College, 2119 East Kimberly Road, Bettendorf, IA 52722. *Phone:* 563-344-1500. *Toll-free phone:* 866-815-5578. *Website:* http://www.rosseducation.edu/.

# St. Luke's College
## Sioux City, Iowa

- **Independent** primarily 2-year, founded 1967
- **Rural** 3-acre campus with easy access to Omaha
- **Endowment** $1.1 million
- **Coed,** 273 undergraduate students, 43% full-time, 89% women, 11% men

**Undergraduates** 118 full-time, 155 part-time. Students come from 14 states and territories; 1 other country; 36% are from out of state; 2% Black or African American, non-Hispanic/Latino; 9% Hispanic/Latino; 2% Asian, non-Hispanic/Latino; 0.4% Native Hawaiian or other Pacific Islander, non-Hispanic/Latino; 1% American Indian or Alaska Native, non-Hispanic/Latino; 2% Two or more races, non-Hispanic/Latino; 3% Race/ethnicity unknown; 8% transferred in. *Retention:* 100% of full-time freshmen returned.

**Freshmen** *Admission:* 15 applied, 4 admitted, 4 enrolled. *Average high school GPA:* 3.6. *Test scores:* ACT scores over 18: 75%; ACT scores over 24: 25%.

**Faculty** *Total:* 42, 62% full-time, 12% with terminal degrees. *Student/faculty ratio:* 6:1.

**Majors** Health services/allied health/health sciences; radiologic technology/science; registered nursing/registered nurse; respiratory care therapy.

**Academics** *Calendar:* semesters. *Degrees:* certificates, associate, and bachelor's. *Special study options:* advanced placement credit, distance learning, internships, services for LD students, summer session for credit.

**Library** *Books:* 2,531 (physical); *Serial titles:* 63 (physical); *Databases:* 7. Weekly public service hours: 65.

**Student Life** *Housing:* college housing not available. *Campus security:* 24-hour emergency response devices and patrols, late-night transport/escort service. *Student services:* health clinic, personal/psychological counseling.

**Standardized Tests** *Required:* SAT or ACT (for admission).

**Costs (2018–19)** *Tuition:* $18,900 full-time. Full-time tuition and fees vary according to course load, degree level, and program. Part-time tuition and fees vary according to course load, degree level, and program. *Required fees:*

$1560 full-time. *Payment plans:* installment, deferred payment. *Waivers:* employees or children of employees.

**Financial Aid** Of all full-time matriculated undergraduates who enrolled in 2016, 93 applied for aid, 93 were judged to have need. 7 Federal Work-Study jobs (averaging $1671). *Average percent of need met:* 80%. *Average financial aid package:* $12,430. *Average need-based loan:* $6512. *Average need-based gift aid:* $4756. *Average indebtedness upon graduation:* $14,158.

**Applying** *Options:* electronic application. *Required:* essay or personal statement, high school transcript, minimum 2.5 GPA, interview. *Application deadline:* 8/1 (freshmen). *Notification:* continuous (transfers).

**Freshman Application Contact** Ms. Sherry McCarthy, Admissions Coordinator, St. Luke's College, 2720 Stone Park Boulevard, Sioux City, IA 51104. *Phone:* 712-279-3149. *Toll-free phone:* 800-352-4660 Ext. 3149. *Fax:* 712-233-8017. *E-mail:* sherry.mccarthy@stlukescollege.edu. *Website:* http://stlukescollege.edu/.

## Scott Community College
### Bettendorf, Iowa

**Freshman Application Contact** Mr. Gary Mohr, Executive Director of Enrollment Management and Marketing, Scott Community College, 500 Belmont Road, Bettendorf, IA 52722-6804. *Phone:* 563-336-3322. *Toll-free phone:* 800-895-0811. *Fax:* 563-336-3350. *E-mail:* gmohr@eicc.edu. *Website:* http://www.eicc.edu/scc/.

## Southeastern Community College
### West Burlington, Iowa

- **State and locally supported** 2-year, founded 1968, part of Iowa Department of Education Division of Community Colleges
- **Small-town** 160-acre campus
- **Coed**

**Undergraduates** 1,312 full-time, 1,532 part-time. 12% are from out of state; 5% Black or African American, non-Hispanic/Latino; 5% Hispanic/Latino; 1% Asian, non-Hispanic/Latino; 0.1% Native Hawaiian or other Pacific Islander, non-Hispanic/Latino; 0.7% American Indian or Alaska Native, non-Hispanic/Latino; 4% Two or more races, non-Hispanic/Latino; 6% Race/ethnicity unknown; 0.9% international; 2% transferred in; 2% live on campus.

**Faculty** *Student/faculty ratio:* 17:1.

**Academics** *Calendar:* semesters. *Degree:* certificates, diplomas, and associate. *Special study options:* adult/continuing education programs, part-time degree program.

**Library** Yohe Memorial Library.

**Student Life** *Campus security:* controlled dormitory access, night patrols by trained security personnel.

**Athletics** Member NJCAA.

**Costs (2017–18)** *Tuition:* state resident $5280 full-time, $176 per credit hour part-time; nonresident $5430 full-time, $181 per credit hour part-time. *Required fees:* $120 full-time. *Room and board:* $7950.

**Financial Aid** Of all full-time matriculated undergraduates who enrolled in 2016, 1,073 applied for aid, 874 were judged to have need. In 2016, 26. *Average financial aid package:* $6384. *Average need-based loan:* $3233. *Average need-based gift aid:* $4335. *Average non-need-based aid:* $4278.

**Applying** *Options:* early admission, deferred entrance.

**Freshman Application Contact** Ms. Stacy White, Admissions, Southeastern Community College, 1500 West Agency Road, West Burlington, IA 52655-0180. *Phone:* 319-752-2731 Ext. 8137. *Toll-free phone:* 866-722-4692. *E-mail:* admoff@scciowa.edu. *Website:* http://www.scciowa.edu/.

## Southwestern Community College
### Creston, Iowa

- **State-supported** 2-year, founded 1966, part of Iowa Department of Education Division of Community Colleges
- **Rural** 406-acre campus
- **Coed,** 1,680 undergraduate students, 50% full-time, 64% women, 36% men

**Undergraduates** 839 full-time, 841 part-time. Students come from 21 states and territories; 2 other countries; 5% are from out of state; 6% transferred in; 6% live on campus. *Retention:* 57% of full-time freshmen returned.

**Freshmen** *Admission:* 219 enrolled. *Average high school GPA:* 3.0.

**Faculty** *Total:* 123, 35% full-time, 2% with terminal degrees. *Student/faculty ratio:* 16:1.

**Majors** Accounting technology and bookkeeping; agribusiness; autobody/collision and repair technology; automobile/automotive mechanics technology; business administration and management; carpentry; computer systems networking and telecommunications; electrician; industrial mechanics

and maintenance technology; liberal arts and sciences/liberal studies; library and information science; music; registered nursing/registered nurse; web page, digital/multimedia and information resources design; welding technology.

**Academics** *Calendar:* semesters. *Degree:* certificates, diplomas, and associate. *Special study options:* academic remediation for entering students, adult/continuing education programs, advanced placement credit, distance learning, double majors, independent study, part-time degree program, summer session for credit.

**Library** Learning Resources Center. *Books:* 15,796 (physical), 28,886 (digital/electronic); *Databases:* 60. Weekly public service hours: 58.

**Student Life** *Housing Options:* coed, men-only, women-only. Campus housing is university owned. *Activities and Organizations:* drama/theater group, choral group. *Campus security:* 24-hour emergency response devices, controlled dormitory access. *Student services:* personal/psychological counseling.

**Athletics** Member NCAA, NJCAA. All NCAA Division II. *Intercollegiate sports:* baseball M(s), basketball M(s)/W(s), cross-country running M/W, golf M/W, softball W, track and field M/W, volleyball W. *Intramural sports:* basketball M/W, football M, volleyball M/W.

**Standardized Tests** *Required for some:* SAT or ACT (for admission), ACT Compass/ACCUPLACER.

**Financial Aid** Of all full-time matriculated undergraduates who enrolled in 2016, 84 Federal Work-Study jobs (averaging $1075). 42 state and other part-time jobs (averaging $1080).

**Applying** *Options:* electronic application, early admission. *Required:* high school transcript. *Application deadlines:* 9/5 (freshmen), 9/5 (transfers). *Notification:* continuous (freshmen), continuous (transfers).

**Freshman Application Contact** Ms. Cait Maitlen, Director of Admissions, Southwestern Community College, 1501 West Townline Street, Creston, IA 50801. *Phone:* 641-782-7081 Ext. 453. *Toll-free phone:* 800-247-4023. *Fax:* 641-782-3312. *E-mail:* maitlen@swcciowa.edu. *Website:* http://www.swcciowa.edu/.

## Vatterott College
### Des Moines, Iowa

**Freshman Application Contact** Mr. Dana Smith, Co-Director, Vatterott College, 7000 Fleur Drive, Suite 290, Des Moines, IA 50321. *Phone:* 515-309-9000. *Toll-free phone:* 888-553-6627. *Fax:* 515-309-0366. *Website:* http://www.vatterott.edu/.

## Western Iowa Tech Community College
### Sioux City, Iowa

- **State-supported** 2-year, founded 1966, part of Iowa Department of Education Division of Community Colleges
- **Suburban** 143-acre campus
- **Endowment** $1.7 million
- **Coed,** 6,152 undergraduate students, 37% full-time, 57% women, 43% men

**Undergraduates** 2,292 full-time, 3,860 part-time. Students come from 30 states and territories; 8 other countries; 10% are from out of state; 3% Black or African American, non-Hispanic/Latino; 15% Hispanic/Latino; 2% Asian, non-Hispanic/Latino; 0.2% Native Hawaiian or other Pacific Islander, non-Hispanic/Latino; 2% American Indian or Alaska Native, non-Hispanic/Latino; 2% Two or more races, non-Hispanic/Latino; 11% Race/ethnicity unknown; 0.7% international; 4% transferred in; 5% live on campus. *Retention:* 52% of full-time freshmen returned.

**Freshmen** *Admission:* 689 enrolled. *Test scores:* ACT scores over 18: 74%; ACT scores over 24: 12%; ACT scores over 30: 1%.

**Faculty** *Total:* 518, 15% full-time, 7% with terminal degrees. *Student/faculty ratio:* 16:1.

**Majors** Accounting; accounting technology and bookkeeping; administrative assistant and secretarial science; agricultural/farm supplies retailing and wholesaling; animation, interactive technology, video graphics and special effects; architectural engineering technology; autobody/collision and repair technology; automobile/automotive mechanics technology; biomedical technology; business administration and management; business automation/technology/data entry; carpentry; child-care provision; cinematography and film/video production; commercial photography; computer/information technology services administration related; computer programming (specific applications); criminal justice/police science; crisis/emergency/disaster management; dental assisting; desktop publishing and digital imaging design; electrician; emergency medical technology (EMT paramedic); energy management and systems technology; finance; fire science/firefighting; game and interactive media design; heating, air conditioning, ventilation and refrigeration maintenance technology; human resources management; industrial mechanics and maintenance technology; interior design; legal assistant/paralegal; liberal arts and sciences/liberal studies; licensed practical/vocational nurse training; mechanical drafting and CAD/CADD; medical administrative assistant and medical secretary; medical/clinical assistant; medical office management; motorcycle maintenance and repair technology; multi/interdisciplinary studies related; musical instrument fabrication and repair; nursing assistant/aide and patient care assistant/aide; pharmacy technician; physical fitness technician; physical therapy technology; recording arts technology; registered nursing/registered nurse; retailing; sales, distribution, and marketing operations; securities services administration; surgical technology; teacher assistant/aide; telecommunications technology; veterinary/animal health technology; web page, digital/multimedia and information resources design; welding technology.

**Academics** *Calendar:* semesters. *Degree:* certificates, diplomas, and associate. *Special study options:* academic remediation for entering students, accelerated degree program, advanced placement credit, cooperative education, distance learning, double majors, English as a second language, honors programs, independent study, internships, off-campus study, part-time degree program, services for LD students, student-designed majors, study abroad, summer session for credit.

**Library** Western Iowa Tech Community College Library Services plus 1 other. *Books:* 17,232 (physical), 12,438 (digital/electronic). Weekly public service hours: 60.

**Student Life** *Housing Options:* coed. Campus housing is university owned. *Activities and Organizations:* drama/theater group, choral group, Shakespeare Overseas Traveling Club, Habitat for Humanity, Anime Club, Leadership Academy, Police Science Club. *Campus security:* 24-hour emergency response devices and patrols, controlled dormitory access. *Student services:* personal/psychological counseling.

**Athletics** *Intramural sports:* basketball M/W, bowling M/W, football M/W, rugby M/W, soccer M/W, softball M/W, volleyball M/W, wrestling M/W.

**Standardized Tests** *Recommended:* ACT (for admission), SAT or ACT (for admission).

**Financial Aid** Of all full-time matriculated undergraduates who enrolled in 2016, 148 Federal Work-Study jobs (averaging $1000). 2 state and other part-time jobs (averaging $2500).

**Applying** *Options:* electronic application, early admission, deferred entrance. *Recommended:* high school transcript. *Application deadlines:* rolling (freshmen), rolling (transfers). *Notification:* continuous (freshmen), continuous (transfers).

**Admissions Office Contact** Western Iowa Tech Community College, 4647 Stone Avenue, PO Box 5199, Sioux City, IA 51102-5199. *Toll-free phone:* 800-352-4649 Ext. 6403.

*Website:* http://www.witcc.edu/.

# KANSAS

## Allen Community College
### Iola, Kansas

- **State and locally supported** 2-year, founded 1923, part of Kansas State Board of Regents
- **Small-town** 88-acre campus
- **Coed**

**Faculty** *Student/faculty ratio:* 18:1.

**Academics** *Calendar:* semesters. *Degree:* certificates and associate. *Special study options:* academic remediation for entering students, adult/continuing education programs, cooperative education, distance learning, English as a second language, independent study, internships, part-time degree program, services for LD students, student-designed majors, summer session for credit.

**Library** Learning Resource Center plus 1 other.

**Athletics** Member NJCAA.

**Costs (2017–18)** *Tuition:* state resident $1920 full-time, $60 per credit hour part-time; nonresident $1920 full-time, $60 per credit hour part-time. *Required fees:* $1280 full-time, $40 per credit hour part-time. *Room and board:* $4950.

**Financial Aid** Of all full-time matriculated undergraduates who enrolled in 2008, 510 applied for aid, 411 were judged to have need, 384 had their need fully met. 40 Federal Work-Study jobs (averaging $2600). 112 state and other part-time jobs (averaging $2600). In 2008, 22. *Average percent of need met:* 80. *Average financial aid package:* $4738. *Average need-based loan:* $2482. *Average need-based gift aid:* $3257. *Average non-need-based aid:* $1241.

**Applying** *Options:* electronic application, early admission, deferred entrance. *Required:* high school transcript.

**Freshman Application Contact** Rebecca Bilderback, Director of Admissions, Allen Community College, 1801 North Cottonwood, Iola, KS 66749. *Phone:* 620-365-5116 Ext. 267. *Fax:* 620-365-7406. *E-mail:* bilderback@allencc.edu. *Website:* http://www.allencc.edu/.

## Barton County Community College
### Great Bend, Kansas

- **State and locally supported** 2-year, founded 1969, part of Kansas Board of Regents
- **Rural** 140-acre campus
- **Coed,** 4,131 undergraduate students, 21% full-time, 49% women, 51% men

**Undergraduates** 875 full-time, 3,256 part-time. 13% Black or African American, non-Hispanic/Latino; 12% Hispanic/Latino; 2% Asian, non-Hispanic/Latino; 0.7% Native Hawaiian or other Pacific Islander, non-Hispanic/Latino; 1% American Indian or Alaska Native, non-Hispanic/Latino; 3% Two or more races, non-Hispanic/Latino; 5% Race/ethnicity unknown; 0.3% international; 8% live on campus.

**Freshmen** *Admission:* 2,179 enrolled.

**Faculty** *Total:* 215, 33% full-time, 3% with terminal degrees. *Student/faculty ratio:* 20:1.

**Majors** Accounting; administrative assistant and secretarial science; agricultural business and management; agriculture; anthropology; architecture; art; athletic training; automobile/automotive mechanics technology; banking and financial support services; biology/biological sciences; business administration and management; chemistry; child-care and support services management; chiropractic assistant; clinical/medical laboratory technology; computer/information technology services administration related; computer programming (specific applications); computer science; computer systems networking and telecommunications; corrections; criminal justice/police science; crop production; cytotechnology; dance; dental hygiene; dietitian assistant; dramatic/theater arts; early childhood education; economics; elementary education; emergency care attendant (EMT ambulance); emergency medical technology (EMT paramedic); engineering technology; English; financial planning and services; fire science/firefighting; forestry; funeral service and mortuary science; general studies; geology/earth science; graphic design; hazardous materials management and waste technology; health aides/attendants/orderlies related; health and medical administrative services related; health information/medical records administration; history; home health aide/home attendant; homeland security, law enforcement, firefighting and protective services related; human resources management; human resources management and services related; industrial production technologies related; information science/studies; journalism; kinesiology and exercise science; liberal arts and sciences/liberal studies; licensed practical/vocational nurse training; livestock management; logistics, materials, and supply chain management; marketing/marketing management; mathematics; medical administrative assistant and medical secretary; medical/clinical assistant; medical insurance coding; medical office assistant; medical transcription; medication aide; military studies; modern languages; music; nursing assistant/aide and patient care assistant/aide; occupational therapy; optometric technician; pharmacy; pharmacy technician; philosophy; phlebotomy technology; physical education teaching and coaching; physical sciences; physical therapy; physical therapy technology; physician assistant; physics; political science and government; pre-dentistry studies; pre-engineering; pre-law studies; premedical studies; pre-veterinary studies; psychology; public administration; radiologic technology/science; registered nursing/registered nurse; religious studies; respiratory care therapy; secondary education; social work; sociology; speech communication and rhetoric; sport and fitness administration/management; wildlife, fish and wildlands science and management.

**Academics** *Calendar:* semesters. *Degree:* certificates and associate. *Special study options:* academic remediation for entering students, accelerated degree program, adult/continuing education programs, advanced placement credit, cooperative education, distance learning, double majors, English as a second language, external degree program, honors programs, independent study, internships, part-time degree program, services for LD students, summer session for credit. *ROTC:* Army (b).

**Library** Barton County Community College Library.

**Student Life** *Housing Options:* coed, special housing for students with disabilities. Campus housing is university owned. Freshman campus housing is guaranteed. *Activities and Organizations:* drama/theater group, student-run newspaper, choral group, Danceline, Business Professionals, Psychology Club, Agriculture Club, Cougarettes. *Campus security:* 24-hour emergency response devices and patrols. *Student services:* health clinic, personal/psychological counseling.

**Athletics** Member NJCAA. *Intercollegiate sports:* baseball M(s), basketball M(s)/W(s), cheerleading M(s)/W(s), cross-country running M(s)/W(s), golf M(s)/W(s), soccer M(s)/W(s), softball W(s), tennis M(s)/W(s), track and field M(s)/W(s), volleyball W(s), wrestling M(s). *Intramural sports:* basketball M/W, bowling M/W, football M/W, golf M/W, softball M/W, swimming and diving M/W, table tennis M/W, tennis M/W, track and field M/W, volleyball M/W.

**Costs (2017–18)** *Tuition:* state resident $2160 full-time, $72 per credit hour part-time; nonresident $2160 full-time, $72 per credit hour part-time. Full-time tuition and fees vary according to course load. Part-time tuition and fees vary according to course load. *Required fees:* $1080 full-time, $36 per credit hour part-time. *Room and board:* $8060. Room and board charges vary according to board plan. *Payment plans:* installment, deferred payment. *Waivers:* senior citizens and employees or children of employees.

**Applying** *Options:* electronic application, early admission. *Recommended:* high school transcript. *Application deadlines:* rolling (freshmen), rolling (transfers).

**Freshman Application Contact** Ms. Tana Cooper, Director of Admissions and Promotions, Barton County Community College, 245 Northeast 30th Road, Great Bend, KS 67530. *Phone:* 620-792-9241. *Toll-free phone:* 800-722-6842. *Fax:* 620-786-1160. *E-mail:* admissions@bartonccc.edu. *Website:* http://www.bartonccc.edu/.

## Bryan University
### Topeka, Kansas

**Admissions Office Contact** Bryan University, 1527 SW Fairlawn Road, Topeka, KS 66604. *Website:* http://www.bryanu.edu/.

## Butler Community College
### El Dorado, Kansas

**Freshman Application Contact** Mr. Glenn Lygrisse, Interim Director of Enrollment Management, Butler Community College, 901 South Haverhill Road, El Dorado, KS 67042. *Phone:* 316-321-2222. *Fax:* 316-322-3109. *E-mail:* admissions@butlercc.edu. *Website:* http://www.butlercc.edu/.

## Cloud County Community College
### Concordia, Kansas

- **State and locally supported** 2-year, founded 1965, part of Kansas Community College System
- **Rural** 35-acre campus
- **Coed,** 1,873 undergraduate students, 43% full-time, 56% women, 44% men

**Undergraduates** 814 full-time, 1,059 part-time. Students come from 26 states and territories; 33 other countries; 7% are from out of state; 6% Black or African American, non-Hispanic/Latino; 7% Hispanic/Latino; 1% Asian, non-Hispanic/Latino; 0.2% Native Hawaiian or other Pacific Islander, non-Hispanic/Latino; 0.8% American Indian or Alaska Native, non-Hispanic/Latino; 4% Two or more races, non-Hispanic/Latino; 5% Race/ethnicity unknown; 5% international; 7% transferred in. *Retention:* 64% of full-time freshmen returned.

**Freshmen** *Admission:* 346 enrolled.

**Faculty** *Total:* 237, 19% full-time. *Student/faculty ratio:* 11:1.

**Majors** Administrative assistant and secretarial science; agricultural business and management; agricultural/farm supplies retailing and wholesaling; agricultural production; air transportation related; biology/biotechnology laboratory technician; business administration and management; business, management, and marketing related; child-care and support services management; child development; criminal justice/police science; crop production; graphic design; journalism; legal assistant/paralegal; liberal arts and sciences/liberal studies; mechanic and repair technologies related; multi/interdisciplinary studies related; office occupations and clerical services; radio and television broadcasting technology; registered nursing/registered nurse; system, networking, and LAN/WAN management; teacher assistant/aide; web page, digital/multimedia and information resources design.

**Academics** *Calendar:* semesters. *Degree:* certificates, diplomas, and associate. *Special study options:* academic remediation for entering students, adult/continuing education programs, advanced placement credit, cooperative education, distance learning, English as a second language, freshman honors college, honors programs, internships, part-time degree program, services for LD students, summer session for credit.

**Library** Cloud County Community College Library. *Books:* 16,807 (physical), 9,784 (digital/electronic); *Databases:* 45. Weekly public service hours: 40.

**Student Life** *Housing Options:* Campus housing is university owned. *Activities and Organizations:* drama/theater group, student-run newspaper, radio and television station, choral group. *Campus security:* 24-hour emergency response devices. *Student services:* health clinic, veterans affairs office.

**Athletics** Member NJCAA. *Intercollegiate sports:* baseball M(s), basketball M(s)/W(s), cheerleading M(s)/W(s), cross-country running M(s)/W(s), soccer M(s)/W(s), softball W(s), tennis M(s)/W(s), track and field M(s)/W(s), volleyball W(s), wrestling M(s). *Intramural sports:* baseball M, basketball M/W, equestrian sports M/W, softball W, volleyball M/W.

**Costs (2017–18)** *Tuition:* area resident $2130 full-time, $71 per credit hour part-time; state resident $2280 full-time, $76 per credit hour part-time;

nonresident $2370 full-time, $79 per credit hour part-time. Full-time tuition and fees vary according to course level, course load, location, program, reciprocity agreements, and student level. Part-time tuition and fees vary according to course level, course load, location, program, reciprocity agreements, and student level. *Required fees:* $900 full-time, $25 per credit hour part-time. *Room and board:* $5800. Room and board charges vary according to board plan and housing facility. *Payment plan:* installment. *Waivers:* senior citizens and employees or children of employees.

**Financial Aid** Of all full-time matriculated undergraduates who enrolled in 2016, 122 Federal Work-Study jobs (averaging $800).

**Applying** *Options:* early admission, deferred entrance. *Required:* high school transcript. *Application deadlines:* 9/11 (freshmen), 9/11 (transfers). *Notification:* continuous (freshmen), continuous (transfers).

**Freshman Application Contact** Shane Olson, Director of Admissions, Cloud County Community College, 2221 Campus Drive, PO Box 1002, Concordia, KS 66901-1002. *Phone:* 785-243-1435 Ext. 213. *Toll-free phone:* 800-729-5101. *E-mail:* solson@cloud.edu. *Website:* http://www.cloud.edu/.

## Coffeyville Community College
### Coffeyville, Kansas

**Freshman Application Contact** Stacia Meek, Admissions Counselor/Marketing Event Coordinator, Coffeyville Community College, 400 West 11th Street, Coffeyville, KS 67337-5063. *Phone:* 620-252-7100. *Toll-free phone:* 877-51-RAVEN. *E-mail:* staciam@coffeyville.edu. *Website:* http://www.coffeyville.edu/.

## Colby Community College
### Colby, Kansas

**Freshman Application Contact** Ms. Nikol Nolan, Admissions Director, Colby Community College, Colby, KS 67701-4099. *Phone:* 785-462-3984 Ext. 5496. *Toll-free phone:* 888-634-9350. *Fax:* 785-460-4691. *E-mail:* admissions@colbycc.edu. *Website:* http://www.colbycc.edu/.

## Cowley County Community College and Area Vocational–Technical School
### Arkansas City, Kansas

**Freshman Application Contact** Ms. Lory West, Director of Admissions, Cowley County Community College and Area Vocational–Technical School, PO Box 1147, Arkansas City, KS 67005. *Phone:* 620-441-5594. *Toll-free phone:* 800-593-CCCC. *Fax:* 620-441-5350. *E-mail:* admissions@cowley.edu. *Website:* http://www.cowley.edu/.

## Dodge City Community College
### Dodge City, Kansas

- **State and locally supported** 2-year, founded 1935, part of Kansas State Board of Regents
- **Small-town** 143-acre campus
- **Coed**

**Undergraduates** 951 full-time, 853 part-time. 9% Black or African American, non-Hispanic/Latino; 40% Hispanic/Latino; 1% Asian, non-Hispanic/Latino; 0.2% Native Hawaiian or other Pacific Islander, non-Hispanic/Latino; 1% American Indian or Alaska Native, non-Hispanic/Latino; 2% Two or more races, non-Hispanic/Latino.

**Faculty** *Student/faculty ratio:* 12:1.

**Academics** *Calendar:* semesters. *Degree:* certificates and associate. *Special study options:* academic remediation for entering students, adult/continuing education programs, advanced placement credit, cooperative education, distance learning, English as a second language, external degree program, internships, off-campus study, part-time degree program, services for LD students, summer session for credit.

**Library** Learning Resource Center. Students can reserve study rooms.

**Student Life** *Campus security:* 24-hour emergency response devices and patrols, late-night transport/escort service, controlled dormitory access.

**Athletics** Member NJCAA.

**Costs (2017–18)** *One-time required fee:* $55. *Tuition:* area resident $930 full-time, $31 per credit hour part-time; state resident $1470 full-time, $49 per credit hour part-time; nonresident $1710 full-time, $57 per credit hour part-time. *Required fees:* $1800 full-time, $40 per credit hour part-time, $30 per term part-time. *Room and board:* $6590. Room and board charges vary according to board plan and housing facility. *Payment plans:* installment, deferred payment.

Applying *Options:* electronic application, early admission, deferred entrance. *Required:* high school transcript.

**Freshman Application Contact** Dodge City Community College, 2501 North 14th Avenue, Dodge City, KS 67801-2399. *Phone:* 620-225-1321. *Website:* http://www.dc3.edu/.

## Donnelly College
### Kansas City, Kansas

- **Independent Roman Catholic** primarily 2-year, founded 1949
- **Urban** 4-acre campus
- **Coed,** 294 undergraduate students, 61% full-time, 74% women, 26% men

**Undergraduates** 179 full-time, 115 part-time. Students come from 2 states and territories; 24 other countries; 31% are from out of state; 33% Black or African American, non-Hispanic/Latino; 39% Hispanic/Latino; 6% Asian, non-Hispanic/Latino; 0.7% Native Hawaiian or other Pacific Islander, non-Hispanic/Latino; 2% American Indian or Alaska Native, non-Hispanic/Latino; 4% Two or more races, non-Hispanic/Latino; 1% international; 16% transferred in. *Retention:* 55% of full-time freshmen returned.

**Freshmen** *Admission:* 349 applied, 349 admitted, 55 enrolled.

**Faculty** *Student/faculty ratio:* 11:1.

**Majors** Computer and information systems security; elementary education; liberal arts and sciences/liberal studies; nonprofit management.

**Academics** *Calendar:* semesters. *Degrees:* certificates, associate, and bachelor's. *Special study options:* academic remediation for entering students, advanced placement credit, distance learning, English as a second language, external degree program, honors programs, independent study, part-time degree program, services for LD students, summer session for credit.

**Library** Trant Memorial Library plus 1 other.

**Student Life** *Housing:* college housing not available. *Options:* men-only, women-only. Campus housing is university owned. *Activities and Organizations:* Organization of Student Leadership, Student Ambassadors, Healthy Student Task Force, Men's Soccer Club, Women's Soccer Club. *Campus security:* 24-hour emergency response devices. *Student services:* personal/psychological counseling.

**Athletics** *Intramural sports:* basketball M/W, soccer M/W, volleyball M/W.

**Costs (2017–18)** *Tuition:* $6960 full-time, $290 per credit hour part-time. Full-time tuition and fees vary according to degree level, location, and program. Part-time tuition and fees vary according to degree level and location. *Required fees:* $180 full-time, $5 per credit hour part-time, $30 per term part-time. *Payment plan:* installment. *Waivers:* senior citizens and employees or children of employees.

**Applying** *Options:* electronic application, early admission, deferred entrance. *Recommended:* high school transcript. *Application deadlines:* rolling (freshmen), rolling (transfers).

**Freshman Application Contact** Ms. Kimkisha Stevenson, Director of Admissions, Donnelly College, 608 North 18th Street, Kansas City, KS 66102. *Phone:* 913-621-8762. *Fax:* 913-621-8719. *E-mail:* admissions@donnelly.edu. *Website:* http://www.donnelly.edu/.

## Flint Hills Technical College
### Emporia, Kansas

**Freshman Application Contact** Admissions Office, Flint Hills Technical College, 3301 West 18th Avenue, Emporia, KS 66801. *Phone:* 620-341-1325. *Toll-free phone:* 800-711-6947. *Website:* http://www.fhtc.edu/.

## Fort Scott Community College
### Fort Scott, Kansas

**Director of Admissions** Mrs. Mert Barrows, Director of Admissions, Fort Scott Community College, 2108 South Horton, Fort Scott, KS 66701. *Phone:* 620-223-2700 Ext. 353. *Toll-free phone:* 800-874-3722. *Website:* http://www.fortscott.edu/.

## Garden City Community College
### Garden City, Kansas

**Freshman Application Contact** Office of Admissions, Garden City Community College, 801 Campus Drive, Garden City, KS 67846. *Phone:* 620-276-9531. *Toll-free phone:* 800-658-1696. *Fax:* 620-276-9650. *E-mail:* admissions@gcccks.edu. *Website:* http://www.gcccks.edu/.

## Hesston College
### Hesston, Kansas

- **Independent Mennonite** primarily 2-year, founded 1909
- **Small-town** 50-acre campus with easy access to Wichita
- **Endowment** $12.9 million
- **Coed,** 442 undergraduate students, 91% full-time, 60% women, 40% men

**Undergraduates** 403 full-time, 39 part-time. Students come from 29 states and territories; 15 other countries; 43% are from out of state; 5% Black or African American, non-Hispanic/Latino; 12% Hispanic/Latino; 2% Asian, non-Hispanic/Latino; 0.2% American Indian or Alaska Native, non-Hispanic/Latino; 3% Two or more races, non-Hispanic/Latino; 0.7% Race/ethnicity unknown; 13% international; 8% transferred in; 69% live on campus. *Retention:* 77% of full-time freshmen returned.

**Freshmen** *Admission:* 562 applied, 312 admitted, 166 enrolled. *Average high school GPA:* 3.3. *Test scores:* SAT evidence-based reading and writing scores over 500: 54%; SAT math scores over 500: 63%; ACT scores over 18: 86%; SAT evidence-based reading and writing scores over 600: 30%; SAT math scores over 600: 30%; ACT scores over 24: 23%; SAT evidence-based reading and writing scores over 700: 3%; SAT math scores over 700: 3%; ACT scores over 30: 1%.

**Faculty** *Total:* 53, 72% full-time, 25% with terminal degrees. *Student/faculty ratio:* 8:1.

**Majors** Aeronautics/aviation/aerospace science and technology; airline pilot and flight crew; air traffic control; biblical studies; business administration and management; computer/information technology services administration related; early childhood education; general studies; kindergarten/preschool education; liberal arts and sciences/liberal studies; pastoral studies/counseling; registered nursing/registered nurse; youth ministry.

**Academics** *Calendar:* semesters. *Degrees:* associate and bachelor's. *Special study options:* academic remediation for entering students, adult/continuing education programs, advanced placement credit, cooperative education, double majors, English as a second language, independent study, internships, part-time degree program, services for LD students, summer session for credit.

**Library** Mary Miller Library. Students can reserve study rooms.

**Student Life** *Housing:* on-campus residence required through sophomore year. *Options:* men-only, women-only. Campus housing is university owned. Freshman campus housing is guaranteed. *Activities and Organizations:* drama/theater group, student-run newspaper, choral group, Peace and Service Club, Intramural Sports, Ministry Assistants. *Campus security:* 24-hour emergency response devices, controlled dormitory access. *Student services:* personal/psychological counseling.

**Athletics** Member NJCAA. *Intercollegiate sports:* baseball M(s), basketball M(s)/W(s), cross-country running M(s)/W(s), golf M(s), soccer M(s)/W(s), softball W(s), tennis M(s)/W(s), track and field M(s)/W(s), volleyball W(s). *Intramural sports:* basketball M/W, golf M(c)/W(c), sand volleyball M/W, soccer M/W, ultimate Frisbee M/W, volleyball M/W.

**Standardized Tests** *Required:* SAT or ACT (for admission).

**Costs (2018–19)** *Comprehensive fee:* $35,700 includes full-time tuition ($26,460), mandatory fees ($440), and room and board ($8800). Full-time tuition and fees vary according to course load and program. Part-time tuition: $1102 per credit hour. Part-time tuition and fees vary according to course load. *Required fees:* $110 per term part-time. *Payment plans:* installment, deferred payment. *Waivers:* employees or children of employees.

**Financial Aid** Of all full-time matriculated undergraduates who enrolled in 2016, 120 Federal Work-Study jobs (averaging $800).

**Applying** *Options:* electronic application, early admission, deferred entrance. *Required:* high school transcript. *Required for some:* 2 letters of recommendation, interview. *Application deadlines:* rolling (freshmen), rolling (transfers).

**Freshman Application Contact** Rachel Swartzendruber-Miller, Vice President of Admissions, Hesston College, Hesston, KS 67062. *Phone:* 620-327-8206. *Toll-free phone:* 800-995-2757. *Fax:* 620-327-8300. *E-mail:* admissions@hesston.edu. *Website:* http://www.hesston.edu/.

## Highland Community College
### Highland, Kansas

**Director of Admissions** Ms. Cheryl Rasmussen, Vice President of Student Services, Highland Community College, 606 West Main Street, Highland, KS 66035. *Phone:* 785-442-6020. *Fax:* 785-442-6106. *Website:* http://www.highlandcc.edu/.

# Hutchinson Community College
## Hutchinson, Kansas

- **State and locally supported** 2-year, founded 1928, part of Kansas Board of Regents
- **Small-town** 47-acre campus with easy access to Wichita
- **Coed,** 5,854 undergraduate students, 38% full-time, 53% women, 47% men

**Undergraduates** 2,242 full-time, 3,612 part-time. Students come from 45 states and territories; 11 other countries; 7% are from out of state; 6% Black or African American, non-Hispanic/Latino; 11% Hispanic/Latino; 0.8% Asian, non-Hispanic/Latino; 0.9% American Indian or Alaska Native, non-Hispanic/Latino; 4% Two or more races, non-Hispanic/Latino; 7% Race/ethnicity unknown; 0.5% international; 6% transferred in; 8% live on campus.

**Freshmen** *Admission:* 2,877 applied, 2,877 admitted, 1,030 enrolled. *Average high school GPA:* 3.1.

**Faculty** *Total:* 361, 28% full-time, 10% with terminal degrees. *Student/faculty ratio:* 18:1.

**Majors** Administrative assistant and secretarial science; agricultural mechanics and equipment technology; agriculture; architectural drafting and CAD/CADD; autobody/collision and repair technology; automation engineer technology; automobile/automotive mechanics technology; biology/biological sciences; biology/biotechnology laboratory technician; business and personal/financial services marketing; business/commerce; carpentry; child-care and support services management; clinical/medical laboratory technology; communications technology; computer and information sciences; computer systems analysis; computer systems networking and telecommunications; cosmetology; criminal justice/police science; design and visual communications; drafting and design technology; drama and dance teacher education; education; electrical, electronic and communications engineering technology; electrical/electronics equipment installation and repair; emergency medical technology (EMT paramedic); engineering; English; family and consumer sciences/human sciences; farm and ranch management; fire science/firefighting; foreign languages and literatures; graphic communications; health information/medical records technology; legal assistant/paralegal; liberal arts and sciences/liberal studies; machine tool technology; manufacturing engineering technology; mathematics; mechanical drafting and CAD/CADD; medical radiologic technology; natural resources management and policy; pharmacy technician; physical sciences; physical therapy technology; psychology; radio and television broadcasting technology; radiologic technology/science; registered nursing/registered nurse; respiratory care therapy; respiratory therapy technician; retailing; social sciences; speech communication and rhetoric; sport and fitness administration/management; surgical technology; visual and performing arts; web page, digital/multimedia and information resources design; welding technology.

**Academics** *Calendar:* semesters. *Degree:* certificates and associate. *Special study options:* academic remediation for entering students, advanced placement credit, cooperative education, distance learning, double majors, English as a second language, honors programs, independent study, internships, part-time degree program, services for LD students, summer session for credit.

**Library** John F. Kennedy Library plus 1 other. *Books:* 41,383 (physical), 16,969 (digital/electronic); *Serial titles:* 109 (physical); *Databases:* 28. Weekly public service hours: 68.

**Student Life** *Housing Options:* men-only, women-only. Campus housing is university owned. *Activities and Organizations:* drama/theater group, student-run newspaper, choral group, CKI (Circle K), Social Dance Club, SPARK (non-denominational religious group), DragonLAN, Chess Club. *Campus security:* 24-hour emergency response devices and patrols, student patrols, late-night transport/escort service, controlled dormitory access. *Student services:* health clinic, personal/psychological counseling, veterans affairs office.

**Athletics** Member NJCAA. *Intercollegiate sports:* baseball M(s), basketball M(s)/W(s), cheerleading M(s)/W(s), cross-country running M(s)/W(s), football M(s), golf M(s), soccer W(s), softball W(s), track and field M(s)/W(s), volleyball W(s). *Intramural sports:* basketball M/W, football M/W, soccer M/W, table tennis M/W, tennis M/W, volleyball M/W.

**Costs (2018–19)** *Tuition:* area resident $2528 full-time, $79 per credit hour part-time; state resident $2848 full-time, $89 per credit hour part-time; nonresident $3840 full-time, $120 per credit hour part-time. *Required fees:* $672 full-time, $21 per credit hour part-time. *Room and board:* Room and board charges vary according to board plan and housing facility. *Payment plan:* installment. *Waivers:* employees or children of employees.

**Applying** *Options:* electronic application, early admission, deferred entrance. *Required:* high school transcript. *Required for some:* interview. *Application deadlines:* rolling (freshmen), rolling (transfers). *Notification:* continuous (freshmen), continuous (transfers).

**Freshman Application Contact** Mr. Corbin Strobel, Director of Admissions, Hutchinson Community College, 1300 North Plum, Hutchinson, KS 67501.

*Phone:* 620-665-3536. *Toll-free phone:* 888-GO-HUTCH. *Fax:* 620-665-3301. *E-mail:* strobelc@hutchcc.edu.
*Website:* http://www.hutchcc.edu/.

# Independence Community College
## Independence, Kansas

- **State-supported** 2-year, founded 1925, part of Kansas Board of Regents
- **Rural** 68-acre campus
- **Coed,** 897 undergraduate students, 57% full-time, 52% women, 48% men

**Undergraduates** 510 full-time, 387 part-time. Students come from 31 states and territories; 6 other countries; 44% are from out of state; 16% Black or African American, non-Hispanic/Latino; 5% Hispanic/Latino; 0.6% Asian, non-Hispanic/Latino; 0.6% Native Hawaiian or other Pacific Islander, non-Hispanic/Latino; 2% American Indian or Alaska Native, non-Hispanic/Latino; 6% Two or more races, non-Hispanic/Latino; 6% Race/ethnicity unknown; 2% international; 3% transferred in. *Retention:* 39% of full-time freshmen returned.

**Freshmen** *Admission:* 248 enrolled.

**Faculty** *Total:* 94, 38% full-time, 7% with terminal degrees. *Student/faculty ratio:* 12:1.

**Majors** Accounting; administrative assistant and secretarial science; architectural engineering technology; art; athletic training; biology/biological sciences; business administration and management; child-care and support services management; computer and information sciences; computer programming; computer science; computer systems networking and telecommunications; cosmetology; drafting and design technology; dramatic/theater arts; education; English; entrepreneurship; liberal arts and sciences/liberal studies; mathematics; music; physical sciences; small business administration; social sciences; veterinary/animal health technology; web page, digital/multimedia and information resources design.

**Academics** *Calendar:* semesters. *Degree:* certificates and associate. *Special study options:* academic remediation for entering students, advanced placement credit, cooperative education, distance learning, English as a second language, external degree program, independent study, part-time degree program, services for LD students, summer session for credit.

**Library** Independence Community College Library plus 1 other.

**Student Life** *Housing Options:* coed. Campus housing is university owned and is provided by a third party. Freshman campus housing is guaranteed. *Activities and Organizations:* drama/theater group, choral group, marching band, Phi Theta Kappa, Ambassadors, International Student Organization. *Campus security:* controlled dormitory access, night patrol.

**Athletics** Member NJCAA. *Intercollegiate sports:* baseball M(s), basketball M(s)/W(s), football M(s), softball W(s), volleyball W(s). *Intramural sports:* cheerleading M/W.

**Applying** *Required:* high school transcript. *Required for some:* essay or personal statement, minimum 2.5 GPA, 2 letters of recommendation, interview.

**Freshman Application Contact** Ms. Brittany Thornton, Admissions Coordinator, Independence Community College, PO Box 708, 1057 W. College Avenue, Independence, KS 67301. *Phone:* 620-332-5495. *Toll-free phone:* 800-842-6063. *Fax:* 620-331-0946. *E-mail:* bthornton@indycc.edu. *Website:* http://www.indycc.edu/.

# Johnson County Community College
## Overland Park, Kansas

- **State and locally supported** 2-year, founded 1967, part of Kansas State Board of Education
- **Suburban** 220-acre campus with easy access to Kansas City
- **Endowment** $20.0 million
- **Coed**

**Undergraduates** 6,059 full-time, 13,051 part-time. Students come from 40 states and territories; 88 other countries; 9% are from out of state; 6% Black or African American, non-Hispanic/Latino; 9% Hispanic/Latino; 4% Asian, non-Hispanic/Latino; 0.2% Native Hawaiian or other Pacific Islander, non-Hispanic/Latino; 0.6% American Indian or Alaska Native, non-Hispanic/Latino; 3% Two or more races, non-Hispanic/Latino; 5% Race/ethnicity unknown; 3% international; 5% transferred in. *Retention:* 64% of full-time freshmen returned.

**Faculty** *Student/faculty ratio:* 20:1.

**Academics** *Calendar:* semesters. *Degree:* certificates and associate. *Special study options:* academic remediation for entering students, adult/continuing education programs, advanced placement credit, cooperative education, distance learning, double majors, English as a second language, honors programs, independent study, internships, off-campus study, part-time degree program, services for LD students, student-designed majors, study abroad, summer session for credit.

**Library** Johnson County Community College Library. *Books:* 75,947 (physical); *Databases:* 137.

**Student Life** *Campus security:* 24-hour emergency response devices and patrols, late-night transport/escort service.

**Athletics** Member NJCAA.

**Costs (2017–18)** *Tuition:* area resident $2310 full-time, $77 per credit hour part-time; state resident $2820 full-time, $94 per credit hour part-time; nonresident $6120 full-time, $204 per credit hour part-time. Full-time tuition and fees vary according to course load and program. Part-time tuition and fees vary according to course load and program. *Required fees:* $480 full-time, $16 per credit hour part-time.

**Financial Aid** Of all full-time matriculated undergraduates who enrolled in 2016, 85 Federal Work-Study jobs (averaging $4000).

**Applying** *Options:* electronic application, early admission. *Required for some:* high school transcript.

**Freshman Application Contact** Johnson County Community College, 12345 College Boulevard, Overland Park, KS 66210-1299. *Phone:* 913-469-8500 Ext. 3865. *Website:* http://www.jccc.edu/.

## Kansas City Kansas Community College
### Kansas City, Kansas

**Freshman Application Contact** Dr. Denise McDowell, Dean of Enrollment Management/Registrar, Kansas City Kansas Community College, Admissions Office, 7250 State Avenue, Kansas City, KS 66112. *Phone:* 913-288-7694. *Fax:* 913-288-7648. *E-mail:* dmcdowell@kckcc.edu. *Website:* http://www.kckcc.edu/.

## Labette Community College
### Parsons, Kansas

**Freshman Application Contact** Ms. Tammy Fuentez, Director of Admission, Labette Community College, 200 South 14th Street, Parsons, KS 67357-4299. *Phone:* 620-421-6700. *Toll-free phone:* 888-522-3883. *Fax:* 620-421-0180. *Website:* http://www.labette.edu/.

## Manhattan Area Technical College
### Manhattan, Kansas

- **State and locally supported** 2-year, founded 1965
- **Rural** 18-acre campus
- **Coed**

**Undergraduates** 349 full-time, 476 part-time. Students come from 10 states and territories; 1% are from out of state; 6% Black or African American, non-Hispanic/Latino; 8% Hispanic/Latino; 2% Asian, non-Hispanic/Latino; 0.1% Native Hawaiian or other Pacific Islander, non-Hispanic/Latino; 0.6% American Indian or Alaska Native, non-Hispanic/Latino; 3% Two or more races, non-Hispanic/Latino; 1% Race/ethnicity unknown; 0.1% international; 16% transferred in. *Retention:* 26% of full-time freshmen returned.

**Faculty** *Student/faculty ratio:* 11:1.

**Academics** *Calendar:* semesters. *Degree:* certificates and associate. *Special study options:* academic remediation for entering students, adult/continuing education programs, advanced placement credit, cooperative education, distance learning, double majors, honors programs, internships, part-time degree program, services for LD students, student-designed majors, summer session for credit.

**Library** MATC Library. *Books:* 2,031 (physical), 3,665 (digital/electronic); *Databases:* 42. Weekly public service hours: 50.

**Student Life** *Campus security:* late-night transport/escort service, evening security guards.

**Costs (2017–18)** *Tuition:* state resident $4350 full-time, $175 per credit hour part-time; nonresident $4350 full-time, $175 per credit hour part-time. Full-time tuition and fees vary according to course load and program. Part-time tuition and fees vary according to course load and program. *Required fees:* $1500 full-time, $50 per credit hour part-time.

**Applying** *Options:* electronic application. *Application fee:* $40. *Required:* high school transcript. *Required for some:* essay or personal statement, 3 letters of recommendation, interview, specific admission criteria for pre-allied health programs, Class A CDL for electric power and distribution program.

**Freshman Application Contact** Mr. Neil Ross, Director of Admissions, Manhattan Area Technical College, 3136 Dickens Avenue, Manhattan, KS 66503. *Phone:* 785-320-4554. *Toll-free phone:* 800-352-7575. *Fax:* 785-587-2804. *E-mail:* neilross@manhattantech.edu. *Website:* http://www.manhattantech.edu/.

## Neosho County Community College
### Chanute, Kansas

**Freshman Application Contact** Ms. Lisa Last, Dean of Student Development, Neosho County Community College, 800 West 14th Street, Chanute, KS 66720. *Phone:* 620-431-2820 Ext. 213. *Toll-free phone:* 800-729-6222. *Fax:* 620-431-0082. *E-mail:* llast@neosho.edu. *Website:* http://www.neosho.edu/.

## North Central Kansas Technical College
### Beloit, Kansas

**Freshman Application Contact** Ms. Judy Heidrick, Director of Admissions, North Central Kansas Technical College, PO Box 507, 3033 US Highway 24, Beloit, KS 67420. *Toll-free phone:* 800-658-4655. *E-mail:* jheidrick@ncktc.tec.ks.us. *Website:* http://www.ncktc.edu/.

## Northwest Kansas Technical College
### Goodland, Kansas

**Admissions Office Contact** Northwest Kansas Technical College, PO Box 668, 1209 Harrison Street, Goodland, KS 67735. *Toll-free phone:* 800-316-4127. *Website:* http://www.nwktc.edu/.

## Pratt Community College
### Pratt, Kansas

**Freshman Application Contact** Ms. Theresa Ziehr, Office Assistant, Student Services, Pratt Community College, 348 Northeast State Road 61, Pratt, KS 67124. *Phone:* 620-450-2217. *Toll-free phone:* 800-794-3091. *Fax:* 620-672-5288. *E-mail:* theresaz@prattcc.edu. *Website:* http://www.prattcc.edu/.

## Salina Area Technical College
### Salina, Kansas

- **State and locally supported** 2-year, founded 1965
- **Small-town** campus
- **Coed**

**Undergraduates** 216 full-time, 366 part-time. 2% Black or African American, non-Hispanic/Latino; 7% Hispanic/Latino; 0.9% Asian, non-Hispanic/Latino; 0.2% Native Hawaiian or other Pacific Islander, non-Hispanic/Latino; 1% American Indian or Alaska Native, non-Hispanic/Latino; 4% Two or more races, non-Hispanic/Latino; 0.2% international.

**Academics** *Degree:* certificates and associate. *Special study options:* academic remediation for entering students, adult/continuing education programs, advanced placement credit, cooperative education, distance learning, independent study, internships, part-time degree program, services for LD students, student-designed majors, summer session for credit.

**Standardized Tests** *Required:* ACCUPLACER (for admission).

**Applying** *Options:* electronic application. *Required:* high school transcript. *Required for some:* essay or personal statement, 1 letter of recommendation.

**Freshman Application Contact** Mrs. Rebekah Ohlde, Director of Academic Advising, Salina Area Technical College, 2562 Centennial Road, Salina, KS 67401. *Phone:* 785-309-3119. *Fax:* 785-309-3101. *E-mail:* rebekah.ohlde@salinatech.edu. *Website:* http://www.salinatech.edu/.

## Seward County Community College and Area Technical School
### Liberal, Kansas

**Director of Admissions** Dr. Gerald Harris, Dean of Student Services, Seward County Community College and Area Technical School, PO Box 1137, Liberal, KS 67905-1137. *Phone:* 620-624-1951 Ext. 617. *Toll-free phone:* 800-373-9951. *Website:* http://www.sccc.edu/.

## Vatterott College
### Wichita, Kansas

**Admissions Office Contact** Vatterott College, 8853 37th Street North, Wichita, KS 67226. *Website:* http://www.vatterott.edu/.

## Wichita Area Technical College
### Wichita, Kansas

**Freshman Application Contact** Mr. Andy McFayden, Director, Admissions, Wichita Area Technical College, 4004 N. Webb Road, Suite 100, Wichita, KS

67226 . *Phone:* 316-677-9400. *Fax:* 316-677-9555. *E-mail:* info@watc.edu. *Website:* http://www.watc.edu/.

## Wichita Technical Institute
### Wichita, Kansas

**Admissions Office Contact** Wichita Technical Institute, 2051 S. Meridian Avenue, Wichita, KS 67213. *Website:* http://www.wti.edu/.

# KENTUCKY

## American National University
### Danville, Kentucky

**Director of Admissions** James McGuire, Campus Director, American National University, 115 East Lexington Avenue, Danville, KY 40422. *Phone:* 859-236-6991. *Toll-free phone:* 888-9-JOBREADY. *Website:* http://www.an.edu/.

## American National University
### Florence, Kentucky

**Director of Admissions** Mr. Terry Kovacs, Campus Director, American National University, 8095 Connector Drive, Florence, KY 41042. *Phone:* 859-525-6510. *Toll-free phone:* 888-9-JOBREADY. *Website:* http://www.an.edu/.

## American National University
### Lexington, Kentucky

**Director of Admissions** Kim Thomasson, Campus Director, American National University, 2376 Sir Barton Way, Lexington, KY 40509. *Phone:* 859-253-0621. *Toll-free phone:* 888-9-JOBREADY. *Website:* http://www.an.edu/.

## American National University
### Louisville, Kentucky

**Director of Admissions** Vincent C. Tinebra, Campus Director, American National University, 4205 Dixie Highway, Louisville, KY 40216. *Phone:* 502-447-7634. *Toll-free phone:* 888-9-JOBREADY. *Website:* http://www.an.edu/.

## American National University
### Pikeville, Kentucky

**Director of Admissions** Tammy Riley, Campus Director, American National University, 50 National College Boulevard, Pikeville, KY 41501. *Phone:* 606-478-7200. *Toll-free phone:* 888-9-JOBREADY. *Website:* http://www.an.edu/.

## American National University
### Richmond, Kentucky

**Director of Admissions** Ms. Keeley Gadd, Campus Director, American National University, 125 South Killarney Lane, Richmond, KY 40475. *Phone:* 859-623-8956. *Toll-free phone:* 888-9-JOBREADY. *Website:* http://www.an.edu/.

## Ashland Community and Technical College
### Ashland, Kentucky

**Freshman Application Contact** Ashland Community and Technical College, 1400 College Drive, Ashland, KY 41101-3683. *Phone:* 606-326-2008. *Toll-free phone:* 800-928-4256. *Website:* http://www.ashland.kctcs.edu/.

## ATA College
### Louisville, Kentucky

**Freshman Application Contact** Admissions Office, ATA College, 10180 Linn Station Road, Suite A200, Louisville, KY 40223. *Phone:* 502-371-8330. *Fax:* 502-371-8598. *Website:* http://www.ata.edu/.

## Beckfield College
### Florence, Kentucky

**Freshman Application Contact** Mrs. Leah Boerger, Director of Admissions, Beckfield College, 16 Spiral Drive, Florence, KY 41042. *Phone:* 859-371-9393. *E-mail:* lboerger@beckfield.edu. *Website:* http://www.beckfield.edu/.

## Big Sandy Community and Technical College
### Prestonsburg, Kentucky

**Director of Admissions** Jimmy Wright, Director of Admissions, Big Sandy Community and Technical College, One Bert T. Combs Drive, Prestonsburg, KY 41653-1815. *Phone:* 606-886-3863. *Toll-free phone:* 888-641-4132. *E-mail:* jimmy.wright@kctcs.edu. *Website:* http://www.bigsandy.kctcs.edu/.

## Bluegrass Community and Technical College
### Lexington, Kentucky

**Freshman Application Contact** Mrs. Shelbie Hugle, Director of Admission Services, Bluegrass Community and Technical College, 470 Cooper Drive, Lexington, KY 40506. *Phone:* 859-246-6216. *Toll-free phone:* 800-744-4872 (in-state); 866-744-4872 (out-of-state). *E-mail:* shelbie.hugle@kctcs.edu. *Website:* http://www.bluegrass.kctcs.edu/.

## Daymar College
### Bowling Green, Kentucky

**Freshman Application Contact** Mrs. Traci Henderson, Admissions Director, Daymar College, 2421 Fitzgerald Industrial Drive, Bowling Green, KY 42101. *Phone:* 270-843-6750. *Toll-free phone:* 877-258-7796. *E-mail:* thenderson@daymarcollege.edu. *Website:* http://www.daymarcollege.edu/.

## Elizabethtown Community and Technical College
### Elizabethtown, Kentucky

**Freshman Application Contact** Elizabethtown Community and Technical College, 620 College Street Road, Elizabethtown, KY 42701. *Phone:* 270-706-8800. *Toll-free phone:* 877-246-2322. *Website:* http://www.elizabethtown.kctcs.edu/.

## Galen College of Nursing
### Louisville, Kentucky

**Admissions Office Contact** Galen College of Nursing, 1031 Zorn Avenue, Suite 400, Louisville, KY 40207. *Toll-free phone:* 877-223-7040. *Website:* http://www.galencollege.edu/.

## Gateway Community and Technical College
### Florence, Kentucky

- **State-supported** 2-year, founded 1961, part of Kentucky Community and Technical College System
- **Suburban** campus with easy access to Cincinnati
- **Coed,** 4,215 undergraduate students

**Undergraduates** 5% are from out of state; 7% Black or African American, non-Hispanic/Latino; 4% Hispanic/Latino; 0.7% Asian, non-Hispanic/Latino; 0.2% American Indian or Alaska Native, non-Hispanic/Latino; 2% Two or more races, non-Hispanic/Latino; 2% Race/ethnicity unknown.
**Freshmen** *Admission:* 1,872 applied, 1,841 admitted. *Test scores:* ACT scores over 18: 59%; ACT scores over 24: 10%.
**Faculty** *Total:* 234, 36% full-time. *Student/faculty ratio:* 18:1.
**Majors** Allied health diagnostic, intervention, and treatment professions related; business administration and management; computer and information sciences; criminal justice/law enforcement administration; energy management and systems technology; engineering technology; fire science/firefighting; general studies; health professions related; industrial technology; liberal arts and sciences/liberal studies; registered nursing/registered nurse; teacher assistant/aide.
**Academics** *Calendar:* semesters. *Degree:* certificates, diplomas, and associate. *Special study options:* academic remediation for entering students,

cooperative education, distance learning, internships, part-time degree program, services for LD students, summer session for credit.
**Library** Main Library plus 3 others.
**Student Life** *Housing:* college housing not available. *Activities and Organizations:* National Technical Honor Society, Student Government Association, Speech Team, Phi Theta Kappa. *Campus security:* 24-hour emergency response devices, campus security during hours of operation. *Student services:* personal/psychological counseling, veterans affairs office.
**Standardized Tests** *Required:* ACT or SAT; KYOTE (Math); TABE-Advanced (Reading and Writing) (for admission).
**Costs (2017–18)** *Tuition:* state resident $3888 full-time, $162 per credit hour part-time; nonresident $13,608 full-time, $567 per credit hour part-time. Full-time tuition and fees vary according to course load. Part-time tuition and fees vary according to course load. *Required fees:* $8 per credit hour part-time, $40 per term part-time. *Payment plan:* installment. *Waivers:* senior citizens and employees or children of employees.
**Applying** *Options:* electronic application, early admission, deferred entrance. *Required:* high school transcript. *Application deadlines:* rolling (freshmen), rolling (transfers). *Notification:* continuous (freshmen), continuous (transfers).
**Freshman Application Contact** Gateway Community and Technical College, 500 Technology Way, Florence, KY 41042. *Phone:* 859-442-4176. *E-mail:* andre.washington@kctcs.edu.
*Website:* http://www.gateway.kctcs.edu/.

## Hazard Community and Technical College
### Hazard, Kentucky

**Freshman Application Contact** Director of Admissions, Hazard Community and Technical College, 1 Community College Drive, Hazard, KY 41701-2403. *Phone:* 606-487-3102. *Toll-free phone:* 800-246-7521. *Website:* http://www.hazard.kctcs.edu/.

## Henderson Community College
### Henderson, Kentucky

**Freshman Application Contact** Ms. Teresa Hamiton, Admissions Counselor, Henderson Community College, 2660 South Green Street, Henderson, KY 42420-4623. *Phone:* 270-827-1867 Ext. 354. *Toll-free phone:* 800-696-9958. *Website:* http://www.henderson.kctcs.edu/.

## Hopkinsville Community College
### Hopkinsville, Kentucky

- **State-supported** 2-year, founded 1965, part of Kentucky Community and Technical College System
- **Small-town** 69-acre campus with easy access to Nashville
- **Coed,** 3,120 undergraduate students, 40% full-time, 63% women, 37% men

**Undergraduates** 1,245 full-time, 1,875 part-time. 22% Black or African American, non-Hispanic/Latino; 9% Hispanic/Latino; 1% Asian, non-Hispanic/Latino; 0.8% Native Hawaiian or other Pacific Islander, non-Hispanic/Latino; 0.5% American Indian or Alaska Native, non-Hispanic/Latino; 4% Two or more races, non-Hispanic/Latino; 2% Race/ethnicity unknown; 0.2% international; 7% transferred in. *Retention:* 43% of full-time freshmen returned.
**Freshmen** *Admission:* 273 enrolled.
**Faculty** *Total:* 158, 36% full-time. *Student/faculty ratio:* 12:1.
**Majors** Administrative assistant and secretarial science; agricultural production; business administration and management; child-care provision; computer and information sciences; criminal justice/law enforcement administration; electrical, electronic and communications engineering technology; executive assistant/executive secretary; human services; industrial technology; liberal arts and sciences/liberal studies; multi/interdisciplinary studies related; registered nursing/registered nurse; social work.
**Academics** *Calendar:* semesters. *Degree:* certificates, diplomas, and associate. *Special study options:* academic remediation for entering students, advanced placement credit, cooperative education, distance learning, honors programs, independent study, part-time degree program, services for LD students, summer session for credit.
**Library** Learning Resource Center.
**Student Life** *Housing:* college housing not available. *Activities and Organizations:* student-run newspaper, Ag Tech, Amateur Radio, Ballroom Dance, Baptist Campus Ministries, Black Men United. *Campus security:* 24-hour emergency response devices, late-night transport/escort service, security provided by trained security personnel during hours of normal operation. *Student services:* veterans affairs office.

**Athletics** *Intramural sports:* basketball M, football M, golf M, table tennis M/W, volleyball M/W.
**Costs (2017–18)** *Tuition:* state resident $4860 full-time, $162 per credit hour part-time; nonresident $17,010 full-time, $567 per credit hour part-time. Full-time tuition and fees vary according to reciprocity agreements. Part-time tuition and fees vary according to reciprocity agreements. *Required fees:* $340 full-time, $8 per credit hour part-time. *Payment plan:* installment. *Waivers:* senior citizens and employees or children of employees.
**Financial Aid** Of all full-time matriculated undergraduates who enrolled in 2016, 30 Federal Work-Study jobs (averaging $1500). *Financial aid deadline:* 6/30.
**Applying** *Options:* electronic application, deferred entrance. *Recommended:* high school transcript. *Application deadlines:* rolling (freshmen), rolling (transfers). *Notification:* continuous (freshmen), continuous (transfers).
**Freshman Application Contact** Hopkinsville Community College, KY. *Phone:* 270-707-3811. *Toll-free phone:* 866-534-2224. *Website:* http://hopkinsville.kctcs.edu/.

## Interactive College of Technology
### Newport, Kentucky

**Freshman Application Contact** Diana Mamas, Interactive College of Technology, 76 Carothers Road, Newport, KY 41071. *Phone:* 859-282-8989. *Fax:* 859-282-8475. *E-mail:* dmamas@ict.edu. *Website:* http://ict.edu/.

## Jefferson Community and Technical College
### Louisville, Kentucky

**Freshman Application Contact** Ms. Melanie Vaughan-Cooke, Admissions Coordinator, Jefferson Community and Technical College, Louisville, KY 40202. *Phone:* 502-213-4000. *Fax:* 502-213-2540. *Website:* http://www.jefferson.kctcs.edu/.

## Madisonville Community College
### Madisonville, Kentucky

**Director of Admissions** Mr. Jay Parent, Registrar, Madisonville Community College, 2000 College Drive, Madisonville, KY 42431-9185. *Phone:* 270-821-2250. *Website:* http://www.madisonville.kctcs.edu/.

## Maysville Community and Technical College
### Maysville, Kentucky

- **State-supported** 2-year, founded 1967, part of Kentucky Community and Technical College System
- **Rural** 12-acre campus
- **Coed,** 3,495 undergraduate students, 40% full-time, 59% women, 41% men

**Undergraduates** 1,402 full-time, 2,093 part-time. 2% Black or African American, non-Hispanic/Latino; 2% Hispanic/Latino; 0.2% Asian, non-Hispanic/Latino; 0.1% Native Hawaiian or other Pacific Islander, non-Hispanic/Latino; 0.1% American Indian or Alaska Native, non-Hispanic/Latino; 2% Two or more races, non-Hispanic/Latino; 0.9% Race/ethnicity unknown.
**Majors** Business administration and management; child-care provision; clinical/medical laboratory technology; computer and information sciences; criminal justice/law enforcement administration; culinary arts; electromechanical technology; engineering technology; executive assistant/executive secretary; family systems; industrial mechanics and maintenance technology; interdisciplinary studies; liberal arts and sciences/liberal studies; machine shop technology; medical administrative assistant and medical secretary; registered nursing/registered nurse; respiratory care therapy; welding technology.
**Academics** *Calendar:* semesters. *Degree:* certificates, diplomas, and associate. *Special study options:* academic remediation for entering students, adult/continuing education programs, advanced placement credit, cooperative education, distance learning, English as a second language, external degree program, honors programs, independent study, internships, off-campus study, part-time degree program, services for LD students, summer session for credit.
**Library** Finch Library.
**Student Life** *Housing:* college housing not available. *Campus security:* 24-hour emergency response devices, student patrols, evening parking lot security. *Student services:* personal/psychological counseling, veterans affairs office.
**Financial Aid** Of all full-time matriculated undergraduates who enrolled in 2016, 30 Federal Work-Study jobs (averaging $1960).

**Applying** *Options:* electronic application, early admission. *Required:* high school transcript. *Application deadlines:* rolling (freshmen), rolling (transfers). *Notification:* continuous (freshmen), continuous (transfers).
**Freshman Application Contact** Maysville Community and Technical College, 1755 US 68, Maysville, KY 41056. *Phone:* 606-759-7141 Ext. 66271.
*Website:* http://www.maysville.kctcs.edu/.

# Maysville Community and Technical College
## Morehead, Kentucky

**Director of Admissions** Patee Massie, Registrar, Maysville Community and Technical College, 609 Viking Drive, Morehead, KY 40351. *Phone:* 606-759-7141 Ext. 66184. *Website:* http://www.maysville.kctcs.edu/.

# Owensboro Community and Technical College
## Owensboro, Kentucky

- **State-supported** 2-year, founded 1986, part of Kentucky Community and Technical College System
- **Suburban** 102-acre campus
- **Coed,** 3,789 undergraduate students, 40% full-time, 53% women, 47% men

**Undergraduates** 1,516 full-time, 2,273 part-time. Students come from 30 states and territories; 1 other country; 5% are from out of state; 4% Black or African American, non-Hispanic/Latino; 2% Hispanic/Latino; 0.7% Asian, non-Hispanic/Latino; 0.1% Native Hawaiian or other Pacific Islander, non-Hispanic/Latino; 3% Two or more races, non-Hispanic/Latino; 0.3% Race/ethnicity unknown; 4% transferred in. *Retention:* 51% of full-time freshmen returned.
**Freshmen** *Admission:* 496 enrolled.
**Faculty** *Total:* 137, 54% full-time, 12% with terminal degrees. *Student/faculty ratio:* 24:1.
**Majors** Agricultural production; automobile/automotive mechanics technology; business administration and management; child-care provision; computer and information sciences; criminal justice/law enforcement administration; diesel mechanics technology; dramatic/theater arts; electrical and electronic engineering technologies related; emergency medical technology (EMT paramedic); executive assistant/executive secretary; fine/studio arts; fire science/firefighting; health and medical administrative services related; heating, air conditioning, ventilation and refrigeration maintenance technology; human services; industrial mechanics and maintenance technology; liberal arts and sciences/liberal studies; machine shop technology; medical administrative assistant and medical secretary; medical/clinical assistant; multi/interdisciplinary studies related; radiologic technology/science; registered nursing/registered nurse; surgical technology; veterinary/animal health technology; welding technology.
**Academics** *Calendar:* semesters. *Degree:* certificates, diplomas, and associate. *Special study options:* academic remediation for entering students, adult/continuing education programs, advanced placement credit, cooperative education, distance learning, English as a second language, external degree program, honors programs, independent study, off-campus study, part-time degree program, services for LD students, student-designed majors, study abroad, summer session for credit. *ROTC:* Army (b).
**Library** Main Campus Library. *Books:* 24,913 (physical), 354,818 (digital/electronic); *Serial titles:* 19 (physical); *Databases:* 52. Weekly public service hours: 48.
**Student Life** *Housing:* college housing not available. *Activities and Organizations:* drama/theater group, choral group, Student Government Association. *Campus security:* 24-hour emergency response devices, late-night transport/escort service. *Student services:* veterans affairs office.
**Standardized Tests** *Recommended:* SAT or ACT (for admission).
**Costs (2017–18)** *Tuition:* state resident $4860 full-time, $162 per credit hour part-time; nonresident $17,010 full-time, $567 per credit hour part-time. Full-time tuition and fees vary according to course load and reciprocity agreements. Part-time tuition and fees vary according to course load and reciprocity agreements. *Required fees:* $240 full-time, $8 per credit hour part-time. *Payment plan:* installment. *Waivers:* senior citizens and employees or children of employees.
**Financial Aid** Of all full-time matriculated undergraduates who enrolled in 2016, 2,016 applied for aid, 1,803 were judged to have need, 263 had their need fully met. 31 Federal Work-Study jobs (averaging $4236). In 2016, 21 non-need-based awards were made. *Average financial aid package:* $5700. *Average need-based gift aid:* $3700. *Average non-need-based aid:* $1000. *Financial aid deadline:* 7/1.

**Applying** *Options:* electronic application. *Required:* high school transcript. *Application deadlines:* rolling (freshmen), rolling (transfers). *Notification:* continuous (freshmen), continuous (transfers).
**Freshman Application Contact** Ms. Barbara Tipmore, Director of Counseling Services, Owensboro Community and Technical College, 4800 New Hartford Road, Owensboro, KY 42303. *Phone:* 270-686-4530. *Toll-free phone:* 866-755-6282. *E-mail:* barb.tipmore@kctcs.edu.
*Website:* http://www.owensboro.kctcs.edu/.

# Ross College
## Hopkinsville, Kentucky

**Freshman Application Contact** Ross College, 4001 Fort Cambell Boulevard, Hopkinsville, KY 42240. *Phone:* 270-886-1302. *Toll-free phone:* 866-815-5578. *Website:* http://www.rosseducation.edu/.

# Somerset Community College
## Somerset, Kentucky

- **State-supported** 2-year, founded 1965, part of Kentucky Community and Technical College System
- **Small-town** 70-acre campus
- **Coed,** 5,900 undergraduate students

**Undergraduates** *Retention:* 58% of full-time freshmen returned.
**Faculty** *Total:* 222, 64% full-time. *Student/faculty ratio:* 24:1.
**Majors** Aircraft powerplant technology; business administration and management; child-care provision; clinical/medical laboratory assistant; computer and information sciences; criminal justice/law enforcement administration; culinary arts; electrical and electronic engineering technologies related; emergency medical technology (EMT paramedic); engineering technology; executive assistant/executive secretary; industrial mechanics and maintenance technology; liberal arts and sciences/liberal studies; medical administrative assistant and medical secretary; medical radiologic technology; multi/interdisciplinary studies related; physical therapy technology; radiologic technology/science; registered nursing/registered nurse; respiratory care therapy; surgical technology; teacher assistant/aide.
**Academics** *Calendar:* semesters. *Degree:* certificates, diplomas, and associate. *Special study options:* academic remediation for entering students, adult/continuing education programs, advanced placement credit, distance learning, part-time degree program, services for LD students, summer session for credit.
**Library** Somerset Community College Library.
**Student Life** *Housing:* college housing not available. *Activities and Organizations:* drama/theater group, student-run newspaper. *Student services:* veterans affairs office.
**Costs (2018–19)** *Tuition:* state resident $4860 full-time, $162 per credit hour part-time; nonresident $17,010 full-time, $567 per credit hour part-time. Full-time tuition and fees vary according to course load. Part-time tuition and fees vary according to course load. *Required fees:* $240 full-time, $8 per credit hour part-time. *Payment plan:* installment. *Waivers:* senior citizens and employees or children of employees.
**Applying** *Options:* electronic application, early admission. *Required:* high school transcript. *Application deadlines:* 8/14 (freshmen), 8/14 (transfers). *Notification:* continuous (freshmen), continuous (transfers).
**Freshman Application Contact** Director of Admission, Somerset Community College, 808 Monticello Street, Somerset, KY 42501-2973. *Phone:* 606-451-6630. *Toll-free phone:* 877-629-9722. *E-mail:* somerset-admissions@kctcs.edu.
*Website:* http://www.somerset.kctcs.edu/.

# Southcentral Kentucky Community and Technical College
## Bowling Green, Kentucky

- **State-supported** 2-year, founded 1938, part of Kentucky Community and Technical College System
- **Coed,** 4,953 undergraduate students

**Majors** Automobile/automotive mechanics technology; business administration and management; computer and information sciences; culinary arts; electrical and electronic engineering technologies related; electrician; electromechanical technology; engineering technology; fire science/firefighting; health information/medical records administration; heating, air conditioning, ventilation and refrigeration maintenance technology; industrial mechanics and maintenance technology; liberal arts and sciences/liberal studies; machine shop technology; medical radiologic technology; multi/interdisciplinary studies related; registered nursing/registered nurse; respiratory therapy technician; surgical technology; welding technology.

Academics *Calendar:* semesters. *Degree:* certificates, diplomas, and associate.

**Freshman Application Contact** Southcentral Kentucky Community and Technical College, 1845 Loop Drive, Bowling Green, KY 42101. *Phone:* 270-901-1114. *Toll-free phone:* 800-790-0990.

*Website:* http://southcentral.kctcs.edu/.

# Southeast Kentucky Community and Technical College
## Cumberland, Kentucky

- **State-supported** 2-year, founded 1960, part of Kentucky Community and Technical College System
- **Rural** 150-acre campus
- **Coed,** 3,125 undergraduate students, 47% full-time, 50% women, 50% men

**Undergraduates** 1,480 full-time, 1,645 part-time. Students come from 21 states and territories; 1 other country; 6% are from out of state; 2% Black or African American, non-Hispanic/Latino; 0.5% Hispanic/Latino; 0.2% Asian, non-Hispanic/Latino; 0.3% Native Hawaiian or other Pacific Islander, non-Hispanic/Latino; 0.6% American Indian or Alaska Native, non-Hispanic/Latino; 2% Two or more races, non-Hispanic/Latino; 5% Race/ethnicity unknown; 2% transferred in. *Retention:* 64% of full-time freshmen returned.

**Freshmen** *Admission:* 698 applied, 666 admitted, 420 enrolled. *Average high school GPA:* 3.0. *Test scores:* ACT scores over 18: 57%; ACT scores over 24: 12%; ACT scores over 30: 2%.

**Faculty** *Total:* 139, 65% full-time, 12% with terminal degrees. *Student/faculty ratio:* 20:1.

**Majors** Administrative assistant and secretarial science; business administration and management; clinical/medical laboratory technology; computer engineering technology; computer/information technology services administration related; criminal justice/police science; data processing and data processing technology; information technology; liberal arts and sciences/liberal studies; management information systems; medical radiologic technology; physical therapy technology; registered nursing/registered nurse; respiratory care therapy.

**Academics** *Calendar:* semesters. *Degree:* certificates, diplomas, and associate. *Special study options:* academic remediation for entering students, accelerated degree program, adult/continuing education programs, advanced placement credit, distance learning, independent study, part-time degree program, study abroad, summer session for credit.

**Library** Gertrude Dale Library plus 4 others.

**Student Life** *Housing:* college housing not available. *Activities and Organizations:* drama/theater group, student-run newspaper, choral group, Professional Business Leaders, Student Government Association, Phi Theta Kappa, Black Student Union, Nursing Club.

**Athletics** *Intramural sports:* basketball M/W, football M/W, golf M/W, table tennis M/W, volleyball M/W.

**Standardized Tests** *Recommended:* ACT (for admission).

**Costs (2018–19)** *Tuition:* state resident $162 per credit hour part-time; nonresident $567 per credit hour part-time. No tuition increase for student's term of enrollment. *Required fees:* $8 per credit hour part-time. *Payment plans:* tuition prepayment, installment.

**Financial Aid** Of all full-time matriculated undergraduates who enrolled in 2016, 90 Federal Work-Study jobs (averaging $635).

**Applying** *Required:* high school transcript. *Application deadline:* 8/20 (freshmen). *Notification:* continuous until 9/3 (freshmen), continuous until 9/3 (transfers).

**Freshman Application Contact** Southeast Kentucky Community and Technical College, 700 College Road, Cumberland, KY 40823-1099. *Phone:* 606-589-2145 Ext. 13018. *Toll-free phone:* 888-274-SECC.

*Website:* http://www.southeast.kctcs.edu/.

# Spencerian College
## Louisville, Kentucky

- **Proprietary** primarily 2-year, founded 1892
- **Urban** 4-acre campus
- **Coed,** 396 undergraduate students, 57% full-time, 86% women, 14% men

**Undergraduates** 226 full-time, 170 part-time. Students come from 5 states and territories; 17% are from out of state; 18% Black or African American,

non-Hispanic/Latino; 2% Hispanic/Latino; 1% Asian, non-Hispanic/Latino; 0.3% Native Hawaiian or other Pacific Islander, non-Hispanic/Latino; 0.3% American Indian or Alaska Native, non-Hispanic/Latino; 12% Two or more races, non-Hispanic/Latino; 10% Race/ethnicity unknown; 14% transferred in; 1% live on campus.

**Freshmen** *Admission:* 103 enrolled.

**Faculty** *Student/faculty ratio:* 6:1.

**Majors** Clinical laboratory science/medical technology; clinical/medical laboratory technology; massage therapy; medical administrative assistant and medical secretary; medical/clinical assistant; medical insurance coding; medical insurance/medical billing; nursing assistant/aide and patient care assistant/aide; nursing science; phlebotomy technology; radiologic technology/science; registered nursing/registered nurse; respiratory care therapy; surgical technology.

**Academics** *Calendar:* quarters. *Degrees:* certificates, diplomas, associate, and bachelor's. *Special study options:* distance learning, internships, summer session for credit.

**Library** Spencerian College Learning Resource Center.

**Student Life** *Housing Options:* coed. Campus housing is university owned. *Campus security:* security on campus during school hours.

**Costs (2017–18)** *Comprehensive fee:* $31,080 includes full-time tuition ($19,800), mandatory fees ($1725), and room and board ($9555). Full-time tuition and fees vary according to class time, degree level, and program. Part-time tuition: $395 per credit hour. Part-time tuition and fees vary according to class time, degree level, and program. *Required fees:* $60 per course part-time. *Room and board:* college room only: $6435. Room and board charges vary according to housing facility. *Waivers:* children of alumni and employees or children of employees.

**Applying** *Application fee:* $50. *Required:* high school transcript. *Required for some:* essay or personal statement, interview, specific selective admission criteria for some medical programs. *Notification:* continuous (freshmen), continuous (transfers).

**Freshman Application Contact** Spencerian College, 4000 Dupont Circle, Louisville, KY 40207. *Phone:* 502-447-1000 Ext. 7808. *Toll-free phone:* 800-264-1799.

*Website:* http://www.spencerian.edu/.

# Spencerian College–Lexington
## Lexington, Kentucky

- **Proprietary** 2-year, founded 1997, part of The Sullivan University System, Inc.
- **Urban** campus with easy access to Louisville
- **Coed**

**Undergraduates** 65 full-time, 9 part-time. Students come from 1 other state.

**Faculty** *Student/faculty ratio:* 3:1.

**Academics** *Calendar:* quarters. *Degree:* certificates, diplomas, and associate. *Special study options:* academic remediation for entering students, cooperative education, independent study, part-time degree program, services for LD students, summer session for credit.

**Library** Spencerian College Library.

**Student Life** *Campus security:* 24-hour emergency response devices.

**Standardized Tests** *Required for some:* ACT ASSET.

**Costs (2017–18)** *Tuition:* $19,800 full-time, $395 per credit hour part-time. Full-time tuition and fees vary according to class time, course load, program, and student level. Part-time tuition and fees vary according to class time, course load, program, and student level. *Payment plans:* tuition prepayment, installment, deferred payment.

**Applying** *Application fee:* $50. *Required:* high school transcript, interview.

**Freshman Application Contact** Spencerian College–Lexington, 2355 Harrodsburg Road, Lexington, KY 40504. *Phone:* 859-223-9608 Ext. 5430. *Toll-free phone:* 800-456-3253. *Website:* http://www.spencerian.edu/.

# Sullivan College of Technology and Design
## Louisville, Kentucky

**Freshman Application Contact** Ms. Heather Wilson, Director of Admissions, Sullivan College of Technology and Design, 3901 Atkinson Square Drive, Louisville, KY 40218. *Phone:* 502-456-6509 Ext. 8220. *Toll-free phone:* 800-884-6528. *Fax:* 502-456-2341. *E-mail:* hwilson@sctd.edu. *Website:* http://www.sctd.edu/.

## West Kentucky Community and Technical College

### Paducah, Kentucky

- **State-supported** 2-year, founded 1932, part of Kentucky Community and Technical College System
- **Small-town** 117-acre campus
- **Coed,** 6,088 undergraduate students, 35% full-time, 53% women, 47% men

**Undergraduates** 2,140 full-time, 3,948 part-time. Students come from 25 states and territories; 9% Black or African American, non-Hispanic/Latino; 5% Hispanic/Latino; 0.9% Asian, non-Hispanic/Latino; 0.1% Native Hawaiian or other Pacific Islander, non-Hispanic/Latino; 0.3% American Indian or Alaska Native, non-Hispanic/Latino; 4% Two or more races, non-Hispanic/Latino; 11% Race/ethnicity unknown. *Retention:* 59% of full-time freshmen returned. **Faculty** *Total:* 121. *Student/faculty ratio:* 18:1.

**Majors** Animation, interactive technology, video graphics and special effects; automobile/automotive mechanics technology; business administration and management; child-care provision; clinical/medical laboratory technology; computer and information sciences; criminal justice/law enforcement administration; culinary arts; diagnostic medical sonography and ultrasound technology; electrician; emergency medical technology (EMT paramedic); fine/studio arts; fire science/firefighting; health services/allied health/health sciences; homeland security, law enforcement, firefighting and protective services related; industrial mechanics and maintenance technology; liberal arts and sciences/liberal studies; logistics, materials, and supply chain management; machine shop technology; marine transportation related; mechanic and repair technologies related; medical administrative assistant and medical secretary; multi/interdisciplinary studies related; physical therapy technology; radiologic technology/science; registered nursing/registered nurse; surgical technology.

**Academics** *Calendar:* semesters. *Degree:* certificates, diplomas, and associate. *Special study options:* academic remediation for entering students, accelerated degree program, adult/continuing education programs, cooperative education, distance learning, English as a second language, external degree program, honors programs, independent study, part-time degree program, study abroad, summer session for credit.

**Library** WKCTC Matheson Library.

**Student Life** *Housing:* college housing not available. *Campus security:* 24-hour patrols. *Student services:* veterans affairs office.

**Athletics** *Intramural sports:* basketball M.

**Costs (2018–19)** *Tuition:* state resident $4860 full-time, $162 per credit hour part-time; nonresident $17,010 full-time, $567 per credit hour part-time. *Required fees:* $240 full-time, $8 per credit hour part-time. *Payment plan:* installment. *Waivers:* senior citizens and employees or children of employees.

**Financial Aid** Of all full-time matriculated undergraduates who enrolled in 2016, 50 Federal Work-Study jobs (averaging $1650).

**Applying** *Options:* electronic application, early admission. *Required:* high school transcript. *Application deadlines:* rolling (freshmen), rolling (transfers). *Notification:* continuous (freshmen), continuous (transfers).

**Freshman Application Contact** Mr. Trent Johnson, Director of Admission, West Kentucky Community and Technical College, 4810 Alben Barkley Drive, Paducah, KY 42001. *E-mail:* trent.johnson@kctcs.edu. *Website:* http://www.westkentucky.kctcs.edu/.

# LOUISIANA

## Baton Rouge Community College

### Baton Rouge, Louisiana

**Director of Admissions** Nancy Clay, Interim Executive Director for Enrollment Services, Baton Rouge Community College, 201 Community College Drive, Baton Rouge, LA 70806. *Phone:* 225-216-8700. *Toll-free phone:* 800-601-4558. *Website:* http://www.mybrcc.edu/.

## Baton Rouge School of Computers

### Baton Rouge, Louisiana

**Freshman Application Contact** Admissions Office, Baton Rouge School of Computers, 9352 Interline Avenue, Baton Rouge, LA 70809. *Phone:* 225-923-

2524. *Toll-free phone:* 888-920-2772. *Fax:* 225-923-2979. *E-mail:* admissions@brsc.net. *Website:* http://www.brsc.edu/.

## Bossier Parish Community College

### Bossier City, Louisiana

- **State-supported** 2-year, founded 1967, part of Louisiana Community and Technical College System
- **Urban** 64-acre campus with easy access to Shreveport
- **Coed,** 6,042 undergraduate students, 38% full-time, 66% women, 34% men

**Undergraduates** 2,310 full-time, 3,732 part-time. 3% are from out of state; 42% Black or African American, non-Hispanic/Latino; 1% Hispanic/Latino; 0.7% Asian, non-Hispanic/Latino; 0.2% Native Hawaiian or other Pacific Islander, non-Hispanic/Latino; 1% American Indian or Alaska Native, non-Hispanic/Latino; 3% Two or more races, non-Hispanic/Latino; 3% Race/ethnicity unknown; 0.1% international; 13% transferred in. *Retention:* 42% of full-time freshmen returned.

**Freshmen** *Admission:* 3,208 applied, 3,196 admitted, 1,950 enrolled. *Average high school GPA:* 2.7.

**Faculty** *Total:* 229, 51% full-time, 9% with terminal degrees. *Student/faculty ratio:* 22:1.

**Majors** Administrative assistant and secretarial science; audiovisual communications technologies related; business/commerce; child-care provision; computer/information technology services administration related; construction engineering; construction engineering technology; criminal justice/safety; culinary arts; drafting and design technology; dramatic/theater arts; education; educational/instructional technology; emergency medical technology (EMT paramedic); engineering; foods, nutrition, and wellness; general studies; hospital and health-care facilities administration; industrial mechanics and maintenance technology; industrial technology; information science/studies; liberal arts and sciences and humanities related; liberal arts and sciences/liberal studies; medical/clinical assistant; music; natural sciences; occupational therapist assistant; petroleum technology; pharmacy technician; physical therapy; physical therapy technology; recording arts technology; registered nursing/registered nurse; respiratory care therapy; visual and performing arts related.

**Academics** *Calendar:* semesters. *Degree:* certificates, diplomas, and associate. *Special study options:* academic remediation for entering students, adult/continuing education programs, advanced placement credit, distance learning, double majors, part-time degree program, services for LD students, summer session for credit.

**Library** Bossier Parish Community College Library.

**Student Life** *Housing:* college housing not available. *Activities and Organizations:* drama/theater group, student-run newspaper, choral group. *Campus security:* student patrols. *Student services:* personal/psychological counseling.

**Athletics** Member NJCAA. *Intercollegiate sports:* baseball M(s), basketball M(s), soccer W, softball W(s). *Intramural sports:* badminton M/W, bowling M/W, football M, racquetball M, softball M, table tennis M/W, volleyball M/W.

**Costs (2017–18)** *Tuition:* state resident $3335 full-time, $139 per credit hour part-time; nonresident $8012 full-time, $334 per credit hour part-time. Full-time tuition and fees vary according to course load, location, and program. Part-time tuition and fees vary according to course load, location, and program. *Required fees:* $948 full-time, $37 per credit hour part-time, $30 per term part-time. *Payment plan:* deferred payment. *Waivers:* employees or children of employees.

**Financial Aid** Of all full-time matriculated undergraduates who enrolled in 2016, 2,969 applied for aid, 2,718 were judged to have need, 71 had their need fully met. 142 Federal Work-Study jobs (averaging $771). In 2016, 1 non-need-based awards were made. *Average percent of need met:* 33%. *Average financial aid package:* $8324. *Average need-based loan:* $2121. *Average need-based gift aid:* $1728. *Average non-need-based aid:* $500.

**Applying** *Options:* early admission.

**Freshman Application Contact** Mr. Richard Cockerham, Registrar, Bossier Parish Community College, 6220 East Texas Street, Bossier City, LA 71111. *Phone:* 318-678-6093. *Fax:* 318-678-6390. *Website:* http://www.bpcc.edu/.

## Cameron College

### New Orleans, Louisiana

**Admissions Office Contact** Cameron College, 2740 Canal Street, New Orleans, LA 70119. *Website:* http://www.cameroncollege.com/.

# Central Louisiana Technical Community College
## Alexandria, Louisiana

- **State-supported** 2-year, part of Louisiana Technical Community College System
- **Small-town** campus
- **Endowment** $289,536
- **Coed,** 2,432 undergraduate students, 46% full-time, 45% women, 55% men

**Undergraduates** 1,107 full-time, 1,325 part-time. Students come from 3 states and territories; 2% are from out of state; 29% Black or African American, non-Hispanic/Latino; 0.4% Asian, non-Hispanic/Latino; 3% American Indian or Alaska Native, non-Hispanic/Latino; 2% Two or more races, non-Hispanic/Latino; 27% Race/ethnicity unknown; 9% transferred in. *Retention:* 69% of full-time freshmen returned.

**Freshmen** *Admission:* 1,687 applied, 1,687 admitted, 613 enrolled.

**Faculty** *Total:* 130, 65% full-time, 0.8% with terminal degrees. *Student/faculty ratio:* 24:1.

**Majors** Administrative assistant and secretarial science; criminal justice/police science; industrial technology.

**Academics** *Calendar:* semesters. *Degree:* certificates, diplomas, and associate. *Special study options:* academic remediation for entering students, advanced placement credit, distance learning, double majors, English as a second language, honors programs, independent study, internships, part-time degree program, services for LD students, summer session for credit.

**Library** *Books:* 1,484 (physical), 5,331 (digital/electronic); *Databases:* 86. Weekly public service hours: 40.

**Student Life** *Activities and Organizations:* Skills USA, Student Government Association. *Campus security:* 24-hour emergency response devices. *Student services:* personal/psychological counseling, veterans affairs office.

**Costs (2018–19)** *Tuition:* state resident $3335 full-time, $175 per credit hour part-time; nonresident $8053 full-time, $346 per credit hour part-time. Full-time tuition and fees vary according to course load, location, and program. Part-time tuition and fees vary according to course load, location, and program. *Required fees:* $754 full-time, $377 per term part-time. *Payment plan:* installment.

**Financial Aid** Of all full-time matriculated undergraduates who enrolled in 2016, 522 applied for aid, 522 were judged to have need, 43 had their need fully met. 29 Federal Work-Study jobs (averaging $2613). *Average percent of need met:* 78%. *Average financial aid package:* $9954. *Average need-based loan:* $11,388. *Average need-based gift aid:* $9846.

**Applying** *Options:* electronic application. *Application fee:* $5. *Required:* high school transcript. *Notification:* continuous (freshmen).

**Freshman Application Contact** Heather Renier, Director of Student Affairs and Services, Central Louisiana Technical Community College, 4311 South MacArthur Drive, Alexandria, LA 71302. *Phone:* -487-5443 Ext. 1129. *Fax:* 318-487-5970. *E-mail:* meredithclark@cltcc.edu.
*Website:* http://www.cltcc.edu/.

# Delgado Community College
## New Orleans, Louisiana

**Freshman Application Contact** Ms. Gwen Boute, Director of Admissions, Delgado Community College, 615 City Park Avenue, New Orleans, LA 70119. *Phone:* 504-671-5010. *Fax:* 504-483-1895. *E-mail:* enroll@dcc.edu. *Website:* http://www.dcc.edu/.

# Delta School of Business and Technology
## Lake Charles, Louisiana

**Freshman Application Contact** Jeffery Tibodeaux, Director of Admissions, Delta School of Business and Technology, 517 Broad Street, Lake Charles, LA 70601. *Phone:* 337-439-5765. *Website:* http://www.deltatech.edu/.

# Fletcher Technical Community College
## Schriever, Louisiana

**Director of Admissions** Admissions Office, Fletcher Technical Community College, 1407 Highway 311, Schriever, LA 70395. *Phone:* 985-857-3659. *Website:* http://www.fletcher.edu/.

# Fortis College
## Baton Rouge, Louisiana

**Director of Admissions** Ms. Sheri Kirley, Associate Director of Admissions, Fortis College, 9255 Interline Avenue, Baton Rouge, LA 70809. *Phone:* 225-248-1015. *Toll-free phone:* 855-4-FORTIS. *Website:* http://www.fortis.edu/.

# ITI Technical College
## Baton Rouge, Louisiana

- **Proprietary** 2-year, founded 1973
- **Suburban** 10-acre campus
- **Coed,** 622 undergraduate students, 100% full-time, 15% women, 85% men

**Undergraduates** 622 full-time. Students come from 2 states and territories; 45% Black or African American, non-Hispanic/Latino; 1% Hispanic/Latino; 0.3% Asian, non-Hispanic/Latino; 0.5% American Indian or Alaska Native, non-Hispanic/Latino; 2% Two or more races, non-Hispanic/Latino; 1% Race/ethnicity unknown.

**Freshmen** *Admission:* 165 enrolled.

**Majors** Computer technology/computer systems technology; construction management; drafting and design technology; electrical, electronic and communications engineering technology; information science/studies; information technology; instrumentation technology; manufacturing engineering technology; office occupations and clerical services.

**Academics** *Calendar:* quarters. *Degree:* certificates and associate. *Special study options:* internships.

**Library** ITI Technical College Library.

**Student Life** *Housing:* college housing not available. *Campus security:* electronic alarm devices during non-business hours, security cameras 24-hours.

**Applying** *Required:* high school transcript, interview.

**Freshman Application Contact** Mr. Shawn Norris, Admissions Director, ITI Technical College, 13944 Airline Highway, Baton Rouge, LA 70817. *Phone:* 225-752-4230 Ext. 261. *Toll-free phone:* 888-211-7165. *Fax:* 225-756-0903. *E-mail:* snorris@iticollege.edu.
*Website:* http://www.iticollege.edu/.

# Louisiana Culinary Institute
## Baton Rouge, Louisiana

**Admissions Office Contact** Louisiana Culinary Institute, 10550 Airline Highway, Baton Rouge, LA 70816. *Toll-free phone:* 877-533-3198. *Website:* http://www.lci.edu/.

# Louisiana Delta Community College
## Monroe, Louisiana

**Freshman Application Contact** Ms. Kathy Gardner, Interim Dean of Enrollment Services, Louisiana Delta Community College, 7500 Millhaven Drive, Monroe, LA 71203. *Phone:* 318-345-9261. *Toll-free phone:* 866-500-LDCC. *Website:* http://www.ladelta.edu/.

# Louisiana State University at Eunice
## Eunice, Louisiana

- **State-supported** 2-year, founded 1967, part of Louisiana State University System
- **Small-town** 199-acre campus
- **Endowment** $2.1 million
- **Coed,** 2,906 undergraduate students, 48% full-time, 70% women, 30% men

**Undergraduates** 1,388 full-time, 1,518 part-time. Students come from 16 states and territories; 6 other countries; 2% are from out of state; 25% Black or African American, non-Hispanic/Latino; 2% Hispanic/Latino; 0.7% Asian, non-Hispanic/Latino; 0.5% American Indian or Alaska Native, non-Hispanic/Latino; 2% Two or more races, non-Hispanic/Latino; 1% Race/ethnicity unknown; 0.3% international; 25% transferred in; 6% live on campus.

**Freshmen** *Admission:* 1,483 applied, 1,482 admitted, 869 enrolled.

**Faculty** *Total:* 140, 54% full-time, 16% with terminal degrees. *Student/faculty ratio:* 21:1.

**Majors** Business administration and management; child-care provision; computer programming; criminal justice/police science; data processing and data processing technology; fire science/firefighting; general studies; liberal arts and sciences and humanities related; radiologic technology/science; registered nursing/registered nurse; respiratory care therapy.

**Academics** *Calendar:* semesters. *Degree:* certificates and associate. *Special study options:* academic remediation for entering students, adult/continuing education programs, advanced placement credit, cooperative education, distance learning, honors programs, off-campus study, part-time degree program, services for LD students, summer session for credit.
**Library** Arnold LeDoux Library. *Books:* 65,807 (physical), 90 (digital/electronic). Weekly public service hours: 90.
**Student Life** *Housing Options:* men-only, women-only. Campus housing is university owned. *Activities and Organizations:* choral group, Student Government Association, Students in Free Enterprise (SIFE), Criminal Justice Society, Student Nurses Association, Phi Theta Kappa. *Campus security:* 24-hour emergency response devices and patrols, controlled dormitory access. *Student services:* personal/psychological counseling, veterans affairs office.
**Athletics** Member NJCAA. *Intercollegiate sports:* baseball M(s), basketball M/W(s), soccer M/W, softball W. *Intramural sports:* basketball M/W, tennis M/W, volleyball M/W.
**Costs (2018–19)** *Tuition:* state resident $2868 full-time, $177 per credit hour part-time; nonresident $8232 full-time, $401 per credit hour part-time. Full-time tuition and fees vary according to class time, course load, location, and program. Part-time tuition and fees vary according to class time, location, and program. *Required fees:* $1390 full-time, $30 per credit hour part-time. *Room and board:* Room and board charges vary according to housing facility. *Payment plan:* deferred payment. *Waivers:* senior citizens and employees or children of employees.
**Financial Aid** Of all full-time matriculated undergraduates who enrolled in 2016, 78 Federal Work-Study jobs (averaging $1525).
**Applying** *Options:* electronic application, early admission. *Application fee:* $25. *Required:* high school transcript. *Application deadlines:* 8/7 (freshmen), 8/7 (transfers).
**Freshman Application Contact** Ms. Tasha Naquin, Admissions Counselor, Louisiana State University at Eunice, PO Box 1129, Eunice, LA 70535. *Phone:* 337-550-1329. *Toll-free phone:* 888-367-5783. *E-mail:* admissions@lsue.edu.
*Website:* http://www.lsue.edu/.

## McCann School of Business & Technology
### Monroe, Louisiana

**Freshman Application Contact** Mrs. Susan Boudreaux, Admissions Office, McCann School of Business & Technology, 2319 Louisville Avenue, Monroe, LA 71201. *Phone:* 318-323-2889. *Toll-free phone:* 866-865-8065. *Fax:* 318-324-9883. *E-mail:* susan.boudreaux@careertc.edu. *Website:* http://www.mccann.edu/.

## Northshore Technical Community College
### Bogalusa, Louisiana

**Director of Admissions** Admissions Office, Northshore Technical Community College, 1710 Sullivan Drive, Bogalusa, LA 70427. *Phone:* 985-732-6640. *Website:* http://www.northshorecollege.edu/.

## Northwest Louisiana Technical College
### Minden, Louisiana

**Director of Admissions** Ms. Helen Deville, Admissions Office, Northwest Louisiana Technical College, 9500 Industrial Drive, Minden, LA 71055. *Phone:* 318-371-3035. *Toll-free phone:* 800-529-1387. *Fax:* 318-371-3155. *Website:* http://www.nwltc.edu/.

## Nunez Community College
### Chalmette, Louisiana

- **State-supported** 2-year, founded 1992, part of Louisiana Community and Technical College System
- **Suburban** 20-acre campus with easy access to New Orleans
- **Endowment** $1.2 million
- **Coed**, 2,599 undergraduate students, 38% full-time, 65% women, 35% men

**Undergraduates** 986 full-time, 1,613 part-time. Students come from 15 states and territories; 9 other countries; 1% are from out of state; 40% Black or African American, non-Hispanic/Latino; 7% Hispanic/Latino; 2% Asian, non-Hispanic/Latino; 0.2% Native Hawaiian or other Pacific Islander, non-Hispanic/Latino; 0.7% American Indian or Alaska Native, non-Hispanic/Latino; 3% Two or more races, non-Hispanic/Latino; 4% Race/ethnicity unknown; 0.6% international; 16% transferred in.
**Freshmen** *Admission:* 291 enrolled. *Average high school GPA:* 2.5.
**Faculty** *Total:* 106, 43% full-time. *Student/faculty ratio:* 23:1.
**Majors** Business/commerce; child-care provision; education; general studies; industrial technology; kindergarten/preschool education; legal assistant/paralegal; liberal arts and sciences and humanities related.
**Academics** *Calendar:* semesters. *Degree:* certificates, diplomas, and associate. *Special study options:* academic remediation for entering students, accelerated degree program, adult/continuing education programs, advanced placement credit, cooperative education, distance learning, double majors, independent study, internships, off-campus study, part-time degree program, services for LD students, student-designed majors, summer session for credit.
**Library** Nunez Community College Library.
**Student Life** *Housing:* college housing not available. *Campus security:* late-night transport/escort service, security cameras. *Student services:* health clinic, personal/psychological counseling, veterans affairs office.
**Athletics** Member NJCAA. *Intercollegiate sports:* baseball M.
**Costs (2017–18)** *Tuition:* state resident $6670 full-time; nonresident $13,668 full-time. Full-time tuition and fees vary according to course load and program. Part-time tuition and fees vary according to course load and program. *Required fees:* $1680 full-time. *Payment plan:* installment. *Waivers:* senior citizens and employees or children of employees.
**Financial Aid** Of all full-time matriculated undergraduates who enrolled in 2016, 2,599 applied for aid, 2,175 were judged to have need. 37 Federal Work-Study jobs (averaging $2567). *Average financial aid package:* $6229. *Average need-based loan:* $2703. *Average need-based gift aid:* $3526.
**Applying** *Options:* electronic application, early admission, deferred entrance. *Application fee:* $20. *Required for some:* high school transcript. *Application deadlines:* rolling (freshmen), rolling (transfers).
**Freshman Application Contact** Mrs. Becky Maillet, Nunez Community College, 3710 Paris Road, Chalmette, LA 70043. *Phone:* 504-278-6477. *E-mail:* bmaillet@nunez.edu.
*Website:* http://www.nunez.edu/.

## Remington College–Baton Rouge Campus
### Baton Rouge, Louisiana

**Director of Admissions** Monica Butler-Johnson, Director of Recruitment, Remington College–Baton Rouge Campus, 4520 South Sherwood Forrest Boulevard, Baton Rouge, LA 70816. *Phone:* 225-236-3200. *Toll-free phone:* 800-323-8122. *Fax:* 225-922-3250. *E-mail:* monica.johnson@remingtoncollege.edu. *Website:* http://www.remingtoncollege.edu/.

## Remington College–Lafayette Campus
### Lafayette, Louisiana

**Freshman Application Contact** Remington College–Lafayette Campus, 303 Rue Louis XIV, Lafayette, LA 70508. *Phone:* 337-981-4010. *Toll-free phone:* 800-323-8122. *Website:* http://www.remingtoncollege.edu/.

## Remington College–Shreveport
### Shreveport, Louisiana

**Freshman Application Contact** Mr. Marc Wright, Remington College–Shreveport, 2106 West Bert Kouns Industrial Loop, Shreveport, LA 71118. *Phone:* 318-671-4000. *Toll-free phone:* 800-323-8122. *Website:* http://www.remingtoncollege.edu/.

## River Parishes Community College
### Gonzales, Louisiana

**Director of Admissions** Ms. Allison Dauzat, Dean of Students and Enrollment Management, River Parishes Community College, 925 West Edenborne Parkway, Gonzales, LA 70737. *Phone:* 225-675-8270. *Fax:* 225-675-5478. *E-mail:* adauzat@rpcc.cc.la.us. *Website:* http://www.rpcc.edu/.

## South Central Louisiana Technical College
### Morgan City, Louisiana

**Director of Admissions** Ms. Melanie Henry, Admissions Office, South Central Louisiana Technical College, 900 Youngs Road, Morgan City, LA 70380. *Phone:* 504-380-2436. *Fax:* 504-380-2440. *Website:* http://www.scl.edu/.

# Southern University at Shreveport
## Shreveport, Louisiana

- **State-supported** 2-year, founded 1964, part of Southern University System
- **Urban** 103-acre campus
- **Endowment** $619,644
- **Coed,** 3,088 undergraduate students, 52% full-time, 67% women, 33% men
- 74% of applicants were admitted

**Undergraduates** 1,595 full-time, 1,493 part-time. Students come from 25 states and territories; 3 other countries; 3% are from out of state; 90% Black or African American, non-Hispanic/Latino; 0.3% Hispanic/Latino; 0.5% Asian, non-Hispanic/Latino; 0.1% American Indian or Alaska Native, non-Hispanic/Latino; 0.2% Two or more races, non-Hispanic/Latino; 3% international; 6% transferred in; 7% live on campus. *Retention:* 41% of full-time freshmen returned.

**Freshmen** *Admission:* 1 applied, 1,331 admitted, 625 enrolled. *Average high school GPA:* 2.0. *Test scores:* ACT scores over 18: 8%.

**Faculty** *Total:* 166, 45% full-time, 6% with terminal degrees. *Student/faculty ratio:* 21:1.

**Majors** Accounting; accounting technology and bookkeeping; avionics maintenance technology; biology/biological sciences; business/commerce; clinical/medical laboratory technology; computer science; criminal justice/law enforcement administration; dental hygiene; general studies; health information/medical records administration; health information/medical records technology; hospitality administration; human services; kindergarten/preschool education; liberal arts and sciences and humanities related; mathematics; medical radiologic technology; physical therapy technology; radiologic technology/science; registered nursing/registered nurse; respiratory care therapy; surgical technology; teacher assistant/aide.

**Academics** *Calendar:* semesters. *Degree:* certificates and associate. *Special study options:* academic remediation for entering students, adult/continuing education programs, advanced placement credit, cooperative education, distance learning, double majors, English as a second language, honors programs, internships, part-time degree program, services for LD students, student-designed majors, summer session for credit. *ROTC:* Army (c).

**Library** Library/Learning Resources Center plus 1 other. *Books:* 56,174 (physical), 11,097 (digital/electronic); *Serial titles:* 164 (physical); *Databases:* 76. Students can reserve study rooms.

**Student Life** *Housing Options:* coed. Campus housing is provided by a third party. *Activities and Organizations:* student-run newspaper, choral group, marching band, Afro-American Society, SUSLA Gospel Choir, Student Center Board, Allied Health, Engineering Club. *Campus security:* 24-hour emergency response devices and patrols, controlled dormitory access. *Student services:* personal/psychological counseling, veterans affairs office.

**Athletics** Member NJCAA. *Intercollegiate sports:* basketball M(s)/W(s). *Intramural sports:* basketball M/W, cheerleading M/W, soccer M.

**Standardized Tests** *Required for some:* SAT or ACT (for admission). *Recommended:* ACT (for admission).

**Costs (2018–19)** *One-time required fee:* $125. *Tuition:* area resident $2618 full-time; state resident $3733 full-time; nonresident $4814 full-time. Full-time tuition and fees vary according to program. Part-time tuition and fees vary according to program. *Required fees:* $1548 full-time. *Room and board:* $11,330; room only: $8460. Room and board charges vary according to board plan and housing facility. *Payment plan:* deferred payment. *Waivers:* employees or children of employees.

**Financial Aid** Of all full-time matriculated undergraduates who enrolled in 2016, 31 Federal Work-Study jobs (averaging $6688).

**Applying** *Application fee:* $25. *Recommended:* high school transcript. *Application deadlines:* rolling (freshmen), rolling (transfers).

**Freshman Application Contact** Ms. Danielle Anderson, Admissions Advisor, Southern University at Shreveport, 3050 Martin Luther King Jr. Drive, Shreveport, LA 71107. *Phone:* 318-670-9211. *Toll-free phone:* 800-458-1472. *Fax:* 318-670-6483. *E-mail:* danderson@susla.edu. *Website:* http://www.susla.edu/.

# South Louisiana Community College
## Lafayette, Louisiana

**Freshman Application Contact** Director of Admissions, South Louisiana Community College, 1101 Bertrand Drive, Lafayette, LA 70506. *Phone:* 337-521-8953. *E-mail:* admissions@solacc.edu. *Website:* http://www.solacc.edu/.

# Sowela Technical Community College
## Lake Charles, Louisiana

- **State-supported** 2-year, founded 1938, part of Louisiana Community and Technical College System
- **Urban** 84-acre campus
- **Endowment** $383,426
- **Coed,** 3,347 undergraduate students, 51% full-time, 47% women, 53% men
- 100% of applicants were admitted

**Undergraduates** 1,694 full-time, 1,653 part-time. Students come from 5 states and territories; 2 other countries; 1% are from out of state; 23% Black or African American, non-Hispanic/Latino; 4% Hispanic/Latino; 0.7% Asian, non-Hispanic/Latino; 0.2% Native Hawaiian or other Pacific Islander, non-Hispanic/Latino; 0.7% American Indian or Alaska Native, non-Hispanic/Latino; 3% Two or more races, non-Hispanic/Latino; 3% Race/ethnicity unknown; 0.5% international; 2% transferred in. *Retention:* 59% of full-time freshmen returned.

**Freshmen** *Admission:* 687 applied, 687 admitted, 681 enrolled. *Average high school GPA:* 2.9.

**Faculty** *Total:* 165, 56% full-time, 7% with terminal degrees. *Student/faculty ratio:* 24:1.

**Majors** Accounting technology and bookkeeping; administrative assistant and secretarial science; aircraft powerplant technology; business/commerce; chemical technology; commercial and advertising art; computer programming; computer systems networking and telecommunications; criminal justice/safety; culinary arts; drafting and design technology; general studies; industrial production technologies related; instrumentation technology; liberal arts and sciences and humanities related; registered nursing/registered nurse.

**Academics** *Calendar:* semesters. *Degree:* certificates, diplomas, and associate. *Special study options:* academic remediation for entering students, accelerated degree program, adult/continuing education programs, advanced placement credit, distance learning, double majors, external degree program, internships, off-campus study, part-time degree program, services for LD students, summer session for credit.

**Library** Library and Learning Resource Center plus 2 others. *Books:* 8,318 (physical), 11,838 (digital/electronic). Weekly public service hours: 50; students can reserve study rooms.

**Student Life** *Housing:* college housing not available. *Activities and Organizations:* student-run newspaper, choral group, SkillsUSA, Student Government Association (SGA), Phi Theta Kappa, Criminal Justice Club, Astronomy Club. *Campus security:* security guard on duty. *Student services:* personal/psychological counseling, veterans affairs office.

**Costs (2017–18)** *Tuition:* state resident $4169 full-time, $139 per credit hour part-time; nonresident $8543 full-time, $352 per credit hour part-time. Full-time tuition and fees vary according to class time, course load, program, and reciprocity agreements. Part-time tuition and fees vary according to class time, course load, program, and reciprocity agreements. *Required fees:* $1065 full-time, $35 per credit hour part-time, $5 per term part-time. *Payment plans:* installment, deferred payment. *Waivers:* employees or children of employees.

**Applying** *Options:* electronic application, early admission. *Required:* high school transcript, proof of immunization, proof of Selective Service status. *Application deadlines:* rolling (freshmen), rolling (transfers). *Notification:* continuous (freshmen), continuous (transfers).

**Freshman Application Contact** Office of Admissions, Sowela Technical Community College, 3820 Senator J. Bennett Johnston Avenue, Lake Charles, LA 70616. *Phone:* 337-421-6550. *Toll-free phone:* 800-256-0483. *Fax:* 337-491-2663. *Website:* http://www.sowela.edu/.

# Virginia College in Baton Rouge
## Baton Rouge, Louisiana

**Admissions Office Contact** Virginia College in Baton Rouge, 9501 Cortana Place, Baton Rouge, LA 70815. *Website:* http://www.vc.edu/.

# Virginia College in Shreveport/Bossier City
## Bossier City, Louisiana

**Admissions Office Contact** Virginia College in Shreveport/Bossier City, 2950 East Texas Street, Suite C, Bossier City, LA 71111. *Website:* http://www.vc.edu/.

# MAINE

## Beal College
### Bangor, Maine

- **Proprietary** 2-year, founded 1891
- **Small-town** 4-acre campus
- **Coed,** 464 undergraduate students, 78% full-time, 66% women, 34% men

**Undergraduates** 363 full-time, 101 part-time. Students come from 1 other state; 0.9% Black or African American, non-Hispanic/Latino; 1% Hispanic/Latino; 0.6% Asian, non-Hispanic/Latino; 0.2% Native Hawaiian or other Pacific Islander, non-Hispanic/Latino; 2% American Indian or Alaska Native, non-Hispanic/Latino; 4% Race/ethnicity unknown; 10% transferred in. *Retention:* 60% of full-time freshmen returned.
**Freshmen** *Admission:* 93 enrolled.
**Faculty** *Total:* 40, 20% full-time, 3% with terminal degrees. *Student/faculty ratio:* 30:1.
**Majors** Accounting; administrative assistant and secretarial science; criminal justice/law enforcement administration; health information/medical records technology; human resources management; information technology; medical/clinical assistant; medical office assistant; substance abuse/addiction counseling; welding technology.
**Academics** *Calendar:* modular. *Degree:* certificates, diplomas, and associate. *Special study options:* accelerated degree program, adult/continuing education programs, advanced placement credit, internships, part-time degree program, summer session for credit.
**Library** Beal College Library. *Books:* 4,256 (physical); *Serial titles:* 28 (physical). Weekly public service hours: 40.
**Student Life** *Housing:* college housing not available. *Activities and Organizations:* student-run newspaper.
**Standardized Tests** *Required:* entrance exam (for admission).
**Costs (2018–19)** *Tuition:* $10,440 full-time, $290 per credit hour part-time. Full-time tuition and fees vary according to course load and program. Part-time tuition and fees vary according to course load and program. *Required fees:* $1185 full-time, $25 per credit hour part-time. *Payment plan:* installment.
**Applying** *Options:* deferred entrance. *Application fee:* $30. *Required:* essay or personal statement, high school transcript, 1 letter of recommendation, interview, immunizations. *Application deadlines:* rolling (freshmen), rolling (transfers).
**Freshman Application Contact** Tasha Sullivan, Admissions Representative, Beal College, 99 Farm Road, Bangor, ME 04401. *Phone:* 207-947-4591. *Toll-free phone:* 800-660-7351. *Fax:* 207-947-0208. *E-mail:* admissions@bealcollege.edu.
*Website:* http://www.bealcollege.edu/.

## Central Maine Community College
### Auburn, Maine

- **State-supported** 2-year, founded 1964, part of Maine Community College System
- **Small-town** 135-acre campus
- **Endowment** $975,000
- **Coed,** 2,900 undergraduate students, 38% full-time, 53% women, 47% men

**Undergraduates** 1,095 full-time, 1,805 part-time. Students come from 12 states and territories; 3 other countries; 5% are from out of state; 8% Black or African American, non-Hispanic/Latino; 2% Hispanic/Latino; 0.7% Asian, non-Hispanic/Latino; 0.1% Native Hawaiian or other Pacific Islander, non-Hispanic/Latino; 0.5% American Indian or Alaska Native, non-Hispanic/Latino; 2% Two or more races, non-Hispanic/Latino; 21% Race/ethnicity unknown; 0.7% international; 7% transferred in; 8% live on campus.
**Freshmen** *Admission:* 569 enrolled.
**Faculty** *Total:* 203, 27% full-time, 1% with terminal degrees. *Student/faculty ratio:* 17:1.
**Majors** Accounting; administrative assistant and secretarial science; automobile/automotive mechanics technology; biology/biological sciences; building construction technology; business administration and management; civil engineering technology; construction trades related; criminal justice/law enforcement administration; criminal justice/safety; early childhood education; electromechanical technology; graphic and printing equipment operation/production; graphic communications; human services; liberal arts and sciences/liberal studies; licensed practical/vocational nurse training; machine tool technology; management information systems; medical/clinical assistant; multi/interdisciplinary studies related; physical fitness technician; registered nursing/registered nurse.
**Academics** *Calendar:* semesters. *Degree:* certificates and associate. *Special study options:* academic remediation for entering students, accelerated degree program, adult/continuing education programs, advanced placement credit, cooperative education, distance learning, English as a second language, honors programs, independent study, internships, part-time degree program, services for LD students, summer session for credit.
**Library** Central Maine Community College Library. *Books:* 7,810 (physical); *Serial titles:* 44 (physical); *Databases:* 92. Weekly public service hours: 53; students can reserve study rooms.
**Student Life** *Housing Options:* coed, men-only, women-only. Campus housing is university owned. Freshman applicants given priority for college housing. *Campus security:* 24-hour emergency response devices, student patrols, controlled dormitory access, night patrols by police. *Student services:* veterans affairs office.
**Athletics** Member USCAA. *Intercollegiate sports:* baseball M, basketball M/W, golf M/W, ice hockey M(c), soccer M/W, softball W. *Intramural sports:* volleyball M/W.
**Standardized Tests** *Recommended:* SAT and SAT Subject Tests or ACT (for admission).
**Costs (2018–19)** *Tuition:* state resident $2760 full-time, $1380 per year part-time; nonresident $5520 full-time, $2760 per year part-time. Full-time tuition and fees vary according to course load and program. Part-time tuition and fees vary according to course load and program. *Required fees:* $1080 full-time, $35 per credit hour part-time. *Room and board:* $9340. Room and board charges vary according to housing facility. *Payment plan:* installment. *Waivers:* employees or children of employees.
**Financial Aid** Of all full-time matriculated undergraduates who enrolled in 2016, 89 Federal Work-Study jobs (averaging $1200). *Financial aid deadline:* 8/1.
**Applying** *Options:* electronic application, deferred entrance. *Application fee:* $20. *Required:* high school transcript. *Recommended:* essay or personal statement. *Application deadlines:* rolling (freshmen), rolling (transfers). *Notification:* continuous (freshmen), continuous (transfers).
**Freshman Application Contact** Ms. Joan Nichols, Admissions Assistant, Central Maine Community College, 1250 Turner Street, Auburn, ME 04210. *Phone:* 207-755-5273. *Toll-free phone:* 800-891-2002. *Fax:* 207-755-5493. *E-mail:* enroll@cmcc.edu.
*Website:* http://www.cmcc.edu/.

## Eastern Maine Community College
### Bangor, Maine

**Freshman Application Contact** Mr. W. Gregory Swett, Director of Admissions, Eastern Maine Community College, 354 Hogan Road, Bangor, ME 04401. *Phone:* 207-974-4680. *Toll-free phone:* 800-286-9357. *Fax:* 207-974-4683. *E-mail:* admissions@emcc.edu. *Website:* http://www.emcc.edu/.

## Kaplan University, Lewiston
### Lewiston, Maine

**Freshman Application Contact** Kaplan University, Lewiston, 475 Lisbon Street, Lewiston, ME 04240. *Phone:* 207-333-3300. *Toll-free phone:* 800-987-7734. *Website:* http://www.kaplanuniversity.edu/.

## Kaplan University, South Portland
### South Portland, Maine

**Freshman Application Contact** Kaplan University, South Portland, 265 Western Avenue, South Portland, ME 04106. *Phone:* 207-774-6126. *Toll-free phone:* 800-987-7734. *Website:* http://www.kaplanuniversity.edu/.

## Kennebec Valley Community College
### Fairfield, Maine

- **State-supported** 2-year, founded 1970, part of Maine Community College System
- **Small-town** campus
- **Endowment** $3.1 million
- **Coed,** 2,554 undergraduate students, 22% full-time, 63% women, 37% men

**Undergraduates** 565 full-time, 1,989 part-time. Students come from 13 states and territories; 2% are from out of state; 1% Black or African American, non-Hispanic/Latino; 1% Hispanic/Latino; 0.7% Asian, non-Hispanic/Latino; 0.1% Native Hawaiian or other Pacific Islander, non-Hispanic/Latino; 0.7% American Indian or Alaska Native, non-Hispanic/Latino; 0.9% Two or more races, non-Hispanic/Latino; 9% Race/ethnicity unknown; 0.2% international; 8% transferred in.
**Freshmen** *Admission:* 330 enrolled.
**Faculty** *Total:* 163, 25% full-time.

**Majors** Accounting technology and bookkeeping; agroecology and sustainable agriculture; biology/biotechnology laboratory technician; building construction technology; child development; cooking and related culinary arts; drafting/design engineering technologies related; electrical, electronic and communications engineering technology; electrical/electronics maintenance and repair technology related; electrician; emergency medical technology (EMT paramedic); health information/medical records technology; heating, ventilation, air conditioning and refrigeration engineering technology; industrial mechanics and maintenance technology; liberal arts and sciences/liberal studies; lineworker; machine tool technology; management information systems; marketing/marketing management; medical administrative assistant and medical secretary; medical/clinical assistant; mental and social health services and allied professions related; multi/interdisciplinary studies related; occupational therapist assistant; physical therapy technology; radiologic technology/science; registered nursing/registered nurse; welding technology.

**Academics** *Calendar:* semesters. *Degree:* certificates, diplomas, and associate. *Special study options:* academic remediation for entering students, accelerated degree program, adult/continuing education programs, advanced placement credit, distance learning, external degree program, independent study, internships, part-time degree program, services for LD students, summer session for credit.

**Library** Lunder Library plus 2 others.

**Student Life** *Housing:* college housing not available. *Activities and Organizations:* choral group, Phi Theta Kappa, National Society for Leadership and Success, Student Senate, KV Federal Nurses Association. *Campus security:* evening security patrol. *Student services:* personal/psychological counseling.

**Athletics** *Intramural sports:* basketball M/W, bowling M/W, golf M/W, soccer M/W, softball M/W, volleyball M/W.

**Standardized Tests** *Required for some:* HESI nursing exam, HOBET for allied health programs, ACCUPLACER. *Recommended:* SAT or ACT (for admission).

**Costs (2017–18)** *Tuition:* state resident $2760 full-time, $92 per credit hour part-time; nonresident $5520 full-time, $184 per credit hour part-time. Full-time tuition and fees vary according to course load and program. Part-time tuition and fees vary according to course load and program. *Required fees:* $642 full-time. *Payment plan:* installment. *Waivers:* senior citizens and employees or children of employees.

**Financial Aid** Of all full-time matriculated undergraduates who enrolled in 2015, 1,875 applied for aid, 1,627 were judged to have need, 14 had their need fully met. 27 Federal Work-Study jobs (averaging $1338). In 2015, 12 non-need-based awards were made. *Average percent of need met:* 52%. *Average financial aid package:* $7483. *Average need-based loan:* $3217. *Average need-based gift aid:* $6087. *Average non-need-based aid:* $1214.

**Applying** *Options:* electronic application, deferred entrance. *Required:* essay or personal statement, high school transcript. *Required for some:* interview. *Application deadlines:* rolling (freshmen), rolling (transfers). *Notification:* continuous (freshmen), continuous (transfers).

**Freshman Application Contact** Mr. Crichton McKenna, Assistant Director of Admissions, Kennebec Valley Community College, 92 Western Avenue, Fairfield, ME 04937-1367. *Phone:* 207-453-5155. *Toll-free phone:* 800-528-5882. *Fax:* 207-453-5011. *E-mail:* admissions@kvcc.me.edu. *Website:* http://www.kvcc.me.edu/.

# The Landing School
## Arundel, Maine

**Freshman Application Contact** Kristin Potter, Admissions Representative, The Landing School, 286 River Road, Arundel, ME 04046. *Phone:* 207-985-7976. *E-mail:* info@landingschool.edu. *Website:* http://www.landingschool.edu/.

# Maine College of Health Professions
## Lewiston, Maine

- **Independent** primarily 2-year, founded 1891
- **Urban** campus
- **Coed,** 188 undergraduate students, 23% full-time, 88% women, 12% men

**Undergraduates** 44 full-time, 144 part-time. Students come from 1 other state; 2% Black or African American, non-Hispanic/Latino; 1% Hispanic/Latino; 2% Asian, non-Hispanic/Latino; 0.5% American Indian or Alaska Native, non-Hispanic/Latino; 2% Two or more races, non-Hispanic/Latino; 10% Race/ethnicity unknown; 50% transferred in; 4% live on campus.

**Freshmen** *Admission:* 13 applied, 9 enrolled. *Average high school GPA:* 3.6.

**Faculty** *Total:* 19, 89% full-time, 16% with terminal degrees. *Student/faculty ratio:* 5:1.

**Majors** Radiologic technology/science; registered nursing/registered nurse.

**Academics** *Calendar:* semesters. *Degrees:* certificates, associate, and bachelor's. *Special study options:* advanced placement credit, off-campus study, services for LD students, summer session for credit.

**Library** Gerrish True Health Sciences Library plus 1 other. *Books:* 2,816 (physical), 172 (digital/electronic); *Databases:* 17. Study areas open 24 hours, 5&-7 days a week.

**Student Life** *Housing Options:* coed. Campus housing is university owned. *Activities and Organizations:* Student Government. *Campus security:* 24-hour emergency response devices and patrols, late-night transport/escort service, controlled dormitory access. *Student services:* health clinic, personal/psychological counseling, veterans affairs office.

**Standardized Tests** *Required for some:* SAT or ACT (for admission), HESI Entrance Exam for nursing, ACCUPLACER.

**Costs (2018–19)** *Tuition:* $10,720 full-time, $5360 per year part-time. Full-time tuition and fees vary according to program. Part-time tuition and fees vary according to program. *Required fees:* $1525 full-time, $1525 per term part-time. *Room only:* $2350. *Payment plan:* installment. *Waivers:* employees or children of employees.

**Financial Aid** Of all full-time matriculated undergraduates who enrolled in 2017, 71 applied for aid, 70 were judged to have need.

**Applying** *Options:* electronic application. *Application fee:* $50. *Required:* essay or personal statement, high school transcript, high school or college-level algebra, second math, biology, chemistry. *Application deadline:* 4/14 (freshmen). *Notification:* 5/1 (freshmen).

**Freshman Application Contact** Ms. Erica Watson, Admissions Director, Maine College of Health Professions, 70 Middle Street, Lewiston, ME 04240. *Phone:* 207-795-2843. *Fax:* 207-795-2849. *E-mail:* watsoner@mchp.edu. *Website:* http://www.mchp.edu/.

# Northern Maine Community College
## Presque Isle, Maine

- **State-supported** 2-year, founded 1963, part of Maine Community College System
- **Small-town** 86-acre campus
- **Coed,** 955 undergraduate students

**Undergraduates** Students come from 4 states and territories; 4% are from out of state; 50% live on campus. *Retention:* 57% of full-time freshmen returned.

**Freshmen** *Admission:* 761 applied, 404 admitted.

**Faculty** *Total:* 77, 58% full-time. *Student/faculty ratio:* 15:1.

**Majors** Accounting; allied health and medical assisting services related; autobody/collision and repair technology; automobile/automotive mechanics technology; business administration and management; carpentry; computer systems networking and telecommunications; construction trades related; electrical, electronic and communications engineering technology; emergency medical technology (EMT paramedic); general studies; heating, air conditioning, ventilation and refrigeration maintenance technology; kindergarten/preschool education; liberal arts and sciences and humanities related; machine tool technology; registered nursing/registered nurse; water quality and wastewater treatment management and recycling technology.

**Academics** *Calendar:* semesters. *Degree:* certificates and associate. *Special study options:* academic remediation for entering students, adult/continuing education programs, advanced placement credit, cooperative education, double majors, independent study, internships, off-campus study, part-time degree program, services for LD students, summer session for credit.

**Library** Northern Maine Community College Library. Weekly public service hours: 40; students can reserve study rooms.

**Student Life** *Housing Options:* coed. Campus housing is university owned. *Activities and Organizations:* Student Senate, Alpha Beta Gamma, Phi Theta Kappa, Student Nurses Association. *Campus security:* 24-hour emergency response devices and patrols, controlled dormitory access. *Student services:* health clinic.

**Athletics** *Intramural sports:* basketball M(c)/W(c), volleyball M(c)/W(c).

**Costs (2018–19)** *One-time required fee:* $66. *Tuition:* state resident $2820 full-time, $94 per credit hour part-time; nonresident $5640 full-time, $188 per credit hour part-time. Full-time tuition and fees vary according to course load, program, and reciprocity agreements. Part-time tuition and fees vary according to course load, program, and reciprocity agreements. *Required fees:* $1000 full-time. *Room and board:* $7818. Room and board charges vary according to board plan and housing facility. *Payment plan:* installment. *Waivers:* senior citizens and employees or children of employees.

**Financial Aid** Of all full-time matriculated undergraduates who enrolled in 2012, 664 applied for aid, 612 were judged to have need, 17 had their need fully met. In 2012, 10 non-need-based awards were made. *Average percent of need met:* 48%. *Average financial aid package:* $6588. *Average need-based loan:* $3072. *Average need-based gift aid:* $4815. *Average non-need-based aid:* $890.

**Applying** *Options:* electronic application, early admission, deferred entrance. *Application fee:* $20. *Required:* high school transcript, interview.

*Recommended:* essay or personal statement, minimum 2.0 GPA. *Application deadline:* rolling (freshmen). *Notification:* continuous (freshmen).
**Freshman Application Contact** Ms. Nicole Poulin, Admissions Specialist, Northern Maine Community College, 33 Edgemont Drive, Presque Isle, ME 04769-2016. *Phone:* 207-768-2785. *Toll-free phone:* 800-535-6682. *Fax:* 207-768-2848. *E-mail:* nnpoulin@nmcc.edu.
*Website:* http://www.nmcc.edu/.

## Southern Maine Community College
### South Portland, Maine

**Freshman Application Contact** Amy Lee, Director of Enrollment Services, Southern Maine Community College, 2 Fort Road, South, Portland, ME 04106. *Phone:* 207-741-5800. *Toll-free phone:* 877-282-2182. *Fax:* 207-741-5760. *E-mail:* alee@smccme.edu. *Website:* http://www.smccme.edu/.

## Washington County Community College
### Calais, Maine

**Freshman Application Contact** Washington County Community College, One College Drive, Calais, ME 04619. *Phone:* 207-454-1000. *Toll-free phone:* 800-210-6932. *Website:* http://www.wccc.me.edu/.

## York County Community College
### Wells, Maine

- **State-supported** 2-year, founded 1994, part of Maine Community College System
- **Small-town** 84-acre campus with easy access to Boston
- **Coed,** 1,708 undergraduate students, 23% full-time, 62% women, 38% men

**Undergraduates** 399 full-time, 1,309 part-time. Students come from 8 states and territories; 3% are from out of state; 0.9% Black or African American, non-Hispanic/Latino; 2% Hispanic/Latino; 2% Asian, non-Hispanic/Latino; 0.3% American Indian or Alaska Native, non-Hispanic/Latino; 2% Two or more races, non-Hispanic/Latino; 24% Race/ethnicity unknown; 0.3% international; 14% transferred in. *Retention:* 64% of full-time freshmen returned.
**Freshmen** *Admission:* 488 applied, 486 admitted, 206 enrolled.
**Faculty** *Total:* 149, 15% full-time, 12% with terminal degrees. *Student/faculty ratio:* 13:1.
**Majors** Accounting; animation, interactive technology, video graphics and special effects; business administration and management; computer science; construction trades related; criminal justice/safety; culinary arts; drafting and design technology; early childhood education; education; gerontology; health information/medical records technology; health services/allied health/health sciences; hospitality administration; human services; liberal arts and sciences/liberal studies; machine tool technology; medical/clinical assistant; multi/interdisciplinary studies related; network and system administration; veterinary/animal health technology.
**Academics** *Calendar:* semesters. *Degree:* certificates and associate. *Special study options:* academic remediation for entering students, adult/continuing education programs, advanced placement credit, cooperative education, distance learning, internships, off-campus study, part-time degree program, services for LD students, summer session for credit.
**Library** Library and Learning Resource Center plus 1 other. *Books:* 12,399 (physical); *Serial titles:* 1,625 (physical); *Databases:* 28. Weekly public service hours: 57; students can reserve study rooms.
**Student Life** *Housing:* college housing not available. *Activities and Organizations:* Student Senate, Phi Theta Kappa, Criminal Justice Club. *Campus security:* full-time College Safety and Security Manager. *Student services:* personal/psychological counseling, veterans affairs office.
**Athletics** *Intramural sports:* basketball M/W, ice hockey M/W, soccer M/W, softball M/W, volleyball M/W.
**Standardized Tests** *Recommended:* SAT or ACT (for admission).
**Costs (2018–19)** *Tuition:* state resident $2760 full-time, $92 per credit part-time; nonresident $5520 full-time, $184 per credit part-time. Full-time tuition and fees vary according to course level, course load, and reciprocity agreements. Part-time tuition and fees vary according to course level, course load, and reciprocity agreements. *Required fees:* $810 full-time. *Payment plan:* installment. *Waivers:* senior citizens and employees or children of employees.
**Financial Aid** Of all full-time matriculated undergraduates who enrolled in 2016, 353 applied for aid, 289 were judged to have need, 16 had their need fully met. In 2016, 30 non-need-based awards were made. *Average percent of need met:* 51%. *Average financial aid package:* $6223. *Average need-based loan:* $2713. *Average need-based gift aid:* $5313. *Average non-need-based aid:* $866.

**Applying** *Options:* electronic application, deferred entrance. *Application fee:* $20. *Required:* high school transcript. *Recommended:* interview. *Application deadlines:* rolling (freshmen), rolling (transfers). *Notification:* continuous (freshmen), continuous (transfers).
**Freshman Application Contact** Fred Quistgard, Director of Admissions, York County Community College, 112 College Drive, Wells, ME 04090. *Phone:* 207-207-216-4406. *Toll-free phone:* 800-580-3820. *Fax:* 207-641-0837.
*Website:* http://www.yccc.edu/.

# MARYLAND

## Allegany College of Maryland
### Cumberland, Maryland

**Freshman Application Contact** Ms. Cathy Nolan, Director of Admissions and Registration, Allegany College of Maryland, Cumberland, MD 21502. *Phone:* 301-784-5000 Ext. 5202. *Fax:* 301-784-5220. *E-mail:* cnolan@allegany.edu. *Website:* http://www.allegany.edu/.

## Anne Arundel Community College
### Arnold, Maryland

- **State and locally supported** 2-year, founded 1961
- **Suburban** 230-acre campus with easy access to Baltimore and Washington, DC
- **Coed,** 13,354 undergraduate students, 29% full-time, 59% women, 41% men

**Undergraduates** 3,815 full-time, 9,539 part-time. Students come from 28 states and territories; 87 other countries; 1% are from out of state; 58% Black or African American, non-Hispanic/Latino; 8% Hispanic/Latino; 0.3% Asian, non-Hispanic/Latino; 0.2% Native Hawaiian or other Pacific Islander, non-Hispanic/Latino; 4% American Indian or Alaska Native, non-Hispanic/Latino; 4% Two or more races, non-Hispanic/Latino; 7% Race/ethnicity unknown; 2% international; 29% transferred in. *Retention:* 63% of full-time freshmen returned.
**Freshmen** *Admission:* 2,660 applied, 2,660 admitted, 2,134 enrolled.
**Faculty** *Total:* 1,226, 21% full-time, 9% with terminal degrees. *Student/faculty ratio:* 12:1.
**Majors** Accounting technology and bookkeeping; architectural drafting and CAD/CADD; business administration and management; business administration, management and operations related; business/commerce; chemistry teacher education; child-care and support services management; clinical/medical laboratory technology; communications technologies and support services related; computer and information sciences; computer and information systems security; computer systems networking and telecommunications; criminal justice/law enforcement administration; criminal justice/police science; early childhood education; electrical and electronics engineering; electrical, electronic and communications engineering technology; engineering; English/language arts teacher education; entrepreneurship; fire prevention and safety technology; gerontology; graphic design; health and physical education/fitness; health information/medical records technology; hotel/motel administration; legal assistant/paralegal; liberal arts and sciences and humanities related; liberal arts and sciences/liberal studies; management information systems; management information systems and services related; mathematics; mathematics teacher education; mechatronics, robotics, and automation engineering; medical administrative assistant and medical secretary; medical radiologic technology; multi/interdisciplinary studies related; occupational safety and health technology; physical therapy technology; physics teacher education; pre-law studies; psychiatric/mental health services technology; public health; registered nursing/registered nurse; Spanish language teacher education; substance abuse/addiction counseling; surgical technology.
**Academics** *Calendar:* semesters. *Degree:* certificates and associate. *Special study options:* academic remediation for entering students, advanced placement credit, cooperative education, distance learning, English as a second language, honors programs, independent study, internships, part-time degree program, services for LD students, summer session for credit. *ROTC:* Army (c), Air Force (c).
**Library** Andrew G. Truxal Library plus 1 other. *Books:* 152,186 (physical), 114,000 (digital/electronic); *Serial titles:* 135 (physical), 15,000 (digital/electronic); *Databases:* 60. Weekly public service hours: 77.
**Student Life** *Housing:* college housing not available. *Activities and Organizations:* drama/theater group, student-run newspaper, choral group, Adventure Society, Entrepreneurs Club, Christian Coalition Organization, Gay/Straight Alliance, History Club. *Campus security:* 24-hour emergency

response devices and patrols, student patrols, late-night transport/escort service. *Student services:* health clinic, personal/psychological counseling, veterans affairs office.

**Athletics** Member NJCAA. *Intercollegiate sports:* baseball M, basketball M/W, cross-country running W, golf M, lacrosse M/W, soccer M/W, softball W, volleyball W.

**Costs (2017–18)** *Tuition:* area resident $3300 full-time, $110 per credit hour part-time; state resident $6360 full-time, $212 per credit hour part-time; nonresident $11,220 full-time, $374 per credit hour part-time. Full-time tuition and fees vary according to program. Part-time tuition and fees vary according to program. *Required fees:* $800 full-time, $2 per credit hour part-time, $48 per term part-time. *Payment plans:* installment, deferred payment. *Waivers:* adult students, senior citizens, and employees or children of employees.

**Applying** *Options:* electronic application, early admission. *Required:* high school transcript. *Required for some:* letters of recommendation. *Application deadlines:* rolling (freshmen), rolling (transfers). *Notification:* continuous (freshmen), continuous (transfers).

**Freshman Application Contact** Mr. Thomas McGinn, Director of Enrollment Development and Admissions, Anne Arundel Community College, 101 College Parkway, Arnold, MD 21012-1895. *Phone:* 410-777-2240. *Fax:* 410-777-2246. *E-mail:* 4info@aacc.edu.
*Website:* http://www.aacc.edu/.

# Baltimore City Community College
## Baltimore, Maryland

**Freshman Application Contact** Baltimore City Community College, 2901 Liberty Heights Avenue, Baltimore, MD 21215-7893. *Phone:* 410-462-8311. *Toll-free phone:* 888-203-1261. *Website:* http://www.bccc.edu/.

# Brightwood College, Baltimore Campus
## Baltimore, Maryland

**Freshman Application Contact** Brightwood College, Baltimore Campus, 1520 South Caton Avenue, Baltimore, MD 21227. *Phone:* 410-644-6400. *Toll-free phone:* 866-543-0208. *Website:* http://www.brightwood.edu/.

# Brightwood College, Beltsville Campus
## Beltsville, Maryland

**Freshman Application Contact** Brightwood College, Beltsville Campus, 4600 Powder Mill Road, Beltsville, MD 20705. *Phone:* 301-937-8448. *Toll-free phone:* 866-543-0208. *Website:* http://www.brightwood.edu/.

# Brightwood College, Towson Campus
## Towson, Maryland

**Freshman Application Contact** Brightwood College, Towson Campus, 803 Glen Eagles Court, Towson, MD 21286. *Phone:* 410-296-5350. *Toll-free phone:* 866-543-0208. *Website:* http://www.brightwood.edu/.

# Carroll Community College
## Westminster, Maryland

- **State and locally supported** 2-year, founded 1993, part of Maryland Higher Education Commission
- **Suburban** 80-acre campus with easy access to Baltimore
- **Endowment** $7.7 million
- **Coed,** 3,020 undergraduate students, 33% full-time, 60% women, 40% men

**Undergraduates** 997 full-time, 2,023 part-time. Students come from 6 states and territories; 20 other countries; 2% are from out of state; 4% Black or African American, non-Hispanic/Latino; 5% Hispanic/Latino; 3% Asian, non-Hispanic/Latino; 0.1% Native Hawaiian or other Pacific Islander, non-Hispanic/Latino; 0.1% American Indian or Alaska Native, non-Hispanic/Latino; 2% Two or more races, non-Hispanic/Latino; 3% Race/ethnicity unknown; 0.2% international; 7% transferred in.

**Freshmen** *Admission:* 567 applied, 567 admitted, 561 enrolled.

**Faculty** *Total:* 225, 33% full-time, 7% with terminal degrees. *Student/faculty ratio:* 13:1.

**Majors** Accounting technology and bookkeeping; administrative assistant and secretarial science; architectural drafting and CAD/CADD; art; biology/biological sciences; business administration and management; chemistry teacher education; child-care and support services management; computer and information systems security; computer engineering; computer graphics; criminal justice/police science; early childhood education; education; electrical and electronics engineering; elementary education; emergency medical technology (EMT paramedic); English/language arts teacher

education; forensic science and technology; general studies; health information/medical records technology; health professions related; kinesiology and exercise science; legal studies; liberal arts and sciences/liberal studies; licensed practical/vocational nurse training; management information systems; mathematics teacher education; multi/interdisciplinary studies related; music; physical therapy technology; psychology; registered nursing/registered nurse; Spanish language teacher education; theater design and technology.

**Academics** *Calendar:* semesters plus winter and summer sessions. *Degree:* certificates and associate. *Special study options:* academic remediation for entering students, advanced placement credit, distance learning, English as a second language, honors programs, independent study, internships, part-time degree program, services for LD students, summer session for credit.

**Library** Carroll Community College Library. *Books:* 39,451 (physical), 150,490 (digital/electronic); *Serial titles:* 152 (physical), 18,508 (digital/electronic); *Databases:* 42.

**Student Life** *Housing:* college housing not available. *Activities and Organizations:* drama/theater group, Student Government Organization, S.T.E.M. Club, Campus Activities Board, Service Learning Club, Early Childhood Education Club. *Campus security:* 24-hour emergency response devices, late night security escort to vehicle in parking lot.

**Athletics** *Intramural sports:* basketball M/W, soccer M/W, volleyball M/W.

**Costs (2017–18)** *Tuition:* area resident $4884 full-time, $163 per credit hour part-time; state resident $7080 full-time, $236 per credit hour part-time; nonresident $9888 full-time, $330 per credit hour part-time. *Payment plan:* deferred payment. *Waivers:* senior citizens and employees or children of employees.

**Financial Aid** Of all full-time matriculated undergraduates who enrolled in 2016, 32 Federal Work-Study jobs (averaging $2658).

**Applying** *Options:* electronic application. *Required:* high school transcript. *Application deadlines:* rolling (freshmen), rolling (transfers). *Notification:* continuous (freshmen), continuous (transfers).

**Freshman Application Contact** Ms. Candace Edwards, Director of Admissions, Carroll Community College, 1601 Washington Road, Westminster, MD 21157. *Phone:* 410-386-8405. *Toll-free phone:* 888-221-9748. *Fax:* 410-386-8446. *E-mail:* cedwards@carrollcc.edu.
*Website:* http://www.carrollcc.edu/.

# Cecil College
## North East, Maryland

- **County-supported** primarily 2-year, founded 1968
- **Small-town** 159-acre campus with easy access to Baltimore
- **Coed,** 2,468 undergraduate students, 35% full-time, 64% women, 36% men

**Undergraduates** 867 full-time, 1,601 part-time. Students come from 9 states and territories; 21 other countries; 16% are from out of state; 10% Black or African American, non-Hispanic/Latino; 6% Hispanic/Latino; 1% Asian, non-Hispanic/Latino; 0.1% Native Hawaiian or other Pacific Islander, non-Hispanic/Latino; 0.3% American Indian or Alaska Native, non-Hispanic/Latino; 5% Two or more races, non-Hispanic/Latino; 1% Race/ethnicity unknown; 0.6% international; 4% transferred in. *Retention:* 56% of full-time freshmen returned.

**Freshmen** *Admission:* 409 enrolled.

**Faculty** *Total:* 295, 17% full-time, 5% with terminal degrees. *Student/faculty ratio:* 11:1.

**Majors** Administrative assistant and secretarial science; aeronautics/aviation/aerospace science and technology; air traffic control; animation, interactive technology, video graphics and special effects; applied horticulture/horticulture operations; biology/biological sciences; biotechnology; business administration and management; business/commerce; business/corporate communications; chemistry; child-care and support services management; commercial photography; criminal justice/police science; design and visual communications; drawing; education; electrical, electronic and communications engineering technology; elementary education; emergency medical technology (EMT paramedic); English/language arts teacher education; financial planning and services; fine/studio arts; fire science/firefighting; general studies; health services/allied health/health sciences; horse husbandry/equine science and management; human resources management; liberal arts and sciences/liberal studies; logistics, materials, and supply chain management; management information systems; marketing/marketing management; mathematics; office management; photography; physics; purchasing, procurement/acquisitions and contracts management; registered nursing/registered nurse; secondary education; transportation and materials moving related; transportation/mobility management; web page, digital/multimedia and information resources design.

**Academics** *Calendar:* semesters. *Degrees:* certificates, associate, and bachelor's. *Special study options:* academic remediation for entering students, accelerated degree program, adult/continuing education programs, advanced placement credit, cooperative education, distance learning, double majors,

English as a second language, independent study, internships, off-campus study, part-time degree program, services for LD students, summer session for credit.

**Library** Cecil County Veterans Memorial Library.

**Student Life** *Activities and Organizations:* drama/theater group, Student Government, Non-Traditional Student Organization, Student Nurses Association, national fraternities. *Campus security:* 24-hour emergency response devices, late-night transport/escort service, armed patrols from 6:30 am-7:00 pm. *Student services:* personal/psychological counseling, women's center.

**Athletics** Member NJCAA. *Intercollegiate sports:* baseball M(s), basketball M(s)/W(s), golf M, lacrosse M(c), soccer M(s)/W(s), softball W(s), tennis W(s), volleyball W(s).

**Costs (2018–19)** *Tuition:* area resident $3270 full-time, $109 per credit hour part-time; state resident $6090 full-time, $203 per credit hour part-time; nonresident $7530 full-time, $251 per credit hour part-time. *Required fees:* $420 full-time, $8 per credit hour part-time, $90 per term part-time. *Payment plan:* deferred payment. *Waivers:* senior citizens and employees or children of employees.

**Applying** *Options:* electronic application, early admission, deferred entrance. *Required:* high school transcript. *Application deadlines:* rolling (freshmen), rolling (transfers). *Notification:* continuous (freshmen), continuous (transfers).

**Freshman Application Contact** Dr. Christy Dryer, Cecil College, One Seahawk Drive, North East, MD 21901-1999. *Phone:* 410-287-6060. *Fax:* 410-287-1001. *E-mail:* cdryer@cecil.edu.

*Website:* http://www.cecil.edu/.

## Chesapeake College
### Wye Mills, Maryland

- **State and locally supported** 2-year, founded 1965
- **Rural** 170-acre campus with easy access to Baltimore and Washington, DC
- **Coed,** 2,189 undergraduate students, 26% full-time, 67% women, 33% men

**Undergraduates** 580 full-time, 1,609 part-time.

**Majors** Accounting technology and bookkeeping; agricultural production; biology/biological sciences; business administration and management; business/commerce; chemistry teacher education; child-care and support services management; computer and information sciences and support services related; computer and information systems security; computer science; corrections and criminal justice related; early childhood education; education; elementary education; emergency medical technology (EMT paramedic); engineering-related technologies; engineering technologies and engineering related; English/language arts teacher education; environmental science; general studies; health and physical education related; hospitality administration; hospitality administration related; landscape architecture; legal assistant/paralegal; liberal arts and sciences and humanities related; liberal arts and sciences/liberal studies; mathematics teacher education; medical radiologic technology; mental and social,health services and allied professions related; physical therapy; physical therapy technology; physics teacher education; registered nursing/registered nurse.

**Academics** *Calendar:* semesters. *Degree:* certificates and associate. *Special study options:* academic remediation for entering students, adult/continuing education programs, advanced placement credit, distance learning, English as a second language, honors programs, independent study, internships, part-time degree program, services for LD students, summer session for credit.

**Library** Learning Resource Center. *Books:* 44,000 (physical), 300,000 (digital/electronic); *Serial titles:* 38 (physical), 25,500 (digital/electronic); *Databases:* 56. Weekly public service hours: 56.

**Student Life** *Housing:* college housing not available. *Activities and Organizations:* drama/theater group, Student Senate, Geek club, Green Team, Phi Theta Kappa, UHURU. *Campus security:* 24-hour emergency response devices. *Student services:* veterans affairs office.

**Athletics** Member NJCAA. *Intercollegiate sports:* baseball M, basketball M/W, soccer M, softball W, volleyball W.

**Costs (2018–19)** *Tuition:* area resident $3660 full-time, $122 per credit hour part-time; state resident $5700 full-time, $190 per credit hour part-time; nonresident $8010 full-time, $267 per credit hour part-time. *Required fees:* $1100 full-time, $35 per credit hour part-time, $25 per term part-time. *Payment plan:* installment. *Waivers:* senior citizens and employees or children of employees.

**Financial Aid** Of all full-time matriculated undergraduates who enrolled in 2016, 32 Federal Work-Study jobs (averaging $1482).

**Applying** *Options:* electronic application. *Required:* high school transcript. *Application deadlines:* rolling (freshmen), rolling (transfers). *Notification:* continuous (freshmen), continuous (transfers).

**Freshman Application Contact** Ms. Angela Denherder, Director of Student Recruitment and Outreach, Chesapeake College, 1000 College Circle, Wye Mills, MD 21679. *Phone:* 410-827-5856. *E-mail:* adenherder@chesapeake.edu.

*Website:* http://www.chesapeake.edu/.

## College of Southern Maryland
### La Plata, Maryland

**Freshman Application Contact** Admissions Department, College of Southern Maryland, PO Box 910, La Plata, MD 20646-0910. *Phone:* 301-934-2251. *Toll-free phone:* 800-933-9177. *Fax:* 301-934-7698. *E-mail:* askme@csmd.edu. *Website:* http://www.csmd.edu/.

## Community College of Baltimore County
### Baltimore, Maryland

- **County-supported** 2-year, founded 1957
- **Suburban** 350-acre campus with easy access to Baltimore
- **Coed,** 19,349 undergraduate students, 28% full-time, 61% women, 39% men

**Undergraduates** 5,408 full-time, 13,941 part-time. 39% Black or African American, non-Hispanic/Latino; 5% Hispanic/Latino; 6% Asian, non-Hispanic/Latino; 0.3% Native Hawaiian or other Pacific Islander, non-Hispanic/Latino; 0.3% American Indian or Alaska Native, non-Hispanic/Latino; 4% Two or more races, non-Hispanic/Latino; 0.9% Race/ethnicity unknown; 6% international.

**Freshmen** *Admission:* 3,551 enrolled.

**Faculty** *Total:* 1,183, 36% full-time, 11% with terminal degrees.

**Majors** Accounting technology and bookkeeping; administrative assistant and secretarial science; aeronautics/aviation/aerospace science and technology; airline pilot and flight crew; air traffic control; applied horticulture/horticulture operations; architectural drafting and CAD/CADD; automobile/automotive mechanics technology; aviation/airway management; biological and physical sciences; building/construction finishing, management, and inspection related; building/construction site management; business administration and management; business/commerce; chemistry teacher education; child-care and support services management; clinical/medical laboratory technology; commercial and advertising art; communications technologies and support services related; computer and information sciences; computer and information systems security; computer engineering; computer systems networking and telecommunications; criminal justice/police science; cyber/computer forensics and counterterrorism; dental hygiene; early childhood education; education; electrical and electronics engineering; elementary education; emergency medical technology (EMT paramedic); engineering; engineering technologies and engineering related; English/language arts teacher education; funeral service and mortuary science; heating, ventilation, air conditioning and refrigeration engineering technology; hydraulics and fluid power technology; legal assistant/paralegal; liberal arts and sciences and humanities related; liberal arts and sciences/liberal studies; management information systems; manufacturing engineering technology; massage therapy; mathematics teacher education; medical administrative assistant and medical secretary; medical informatics; medical radiologic technology; occupational safety and health technology; occupational therapy; parks, recreation, leisure, and fitness studies related; physics teacher education; psychiatric/mental health services technology; registered nursing/registered nurse; respiratory care therapy; sign language interpretation and translation; Spanish language teacher education; substance abuse/addiction counseling; surveying technology; transportation/mobility management; veterinary/animal health technology; visual and performing arts.

**Academics** *Calendar:* semesters. *Degree:* certificates and associate. *Special study options:* academic remediation for entering students, advanced placement credit, cooperative education, distance learning, English as a second language, honors programs, independent study, internships, off-campus study, part-time degree program, services for LD students, study abroad, summer session for credit.

**Student Life** *Housing:* college housing not available. *Activities and Organizations:* drama/theater group, student-run newspaper, choral group. *Campus security:* 24-hour emergency response devices and patrols, late-night transport/escort service. *Student services:* veterans affairs office.

**Athletics** Member NJCAA. *Intercollegiate sports:* baseball M(s), basketball M(s)/W(s), cross-country running M(s)/W(s), lacrosse M(s)/W(s), soccer M(s)/W(s), softball W(s), volleyball W(s). *Intramural sports:* bowling M/W.

**Costs (2017–18)** *Tuition:* area resident $3600 full-time, $120 per credit hour part-time; state resident $6780 full-time, $226 per credit hour part-time; nonresident $10,290 full-time, $343 per credit hour part-time. Full-time tuition and fees vary according to course load. Part-time tuition and fees vary according to course load. *Required fees:* $1006 full-time. *Payment plan:* installment. *Waivers:* minority students, senior citizens, and employees or children of employees.

**Applying** *Options:* electronic application. *Required:* high school transcript. *Application deadlines:* rolling (freshmen), rolling (transfers).

**Freshman Application Contact** Ms. Diane Drake, Director of Admissions, Community College of Baltimore County, 7201 Rossville Boulevard, Baltimore, MD 21237-3899. *Phone:* 443-840-4392. *E-mail:* ddrake@ ccbcmd.edu.

*Website:* http://www.ccbcmd.edu/.

# Fortis College
## Landover, Maryland

**Admissions Office Contact** Fortis College, 4351 Garden City Drive, Landover, MD 20785. *Toll-free phone:* 855-4-FORTIS. *Website:* http://www.fortis.edu/.

# Frederick Community College
## Frederick, Maryland

- **State and locally supported** 2-year, founded 1957
- **Small-town** 100-acre campus with easy access to Baltimore and Washington, DC
- **Endowment** $13.8 million
- **Coed,** 6,220 undergraduate students, 33% full-time, 56% women, 44% men

**Undergraduates** 2,027 full-time, 4,193 part-time. 15% Black or African American, non-Hispanic/Latino; 13% Hispanic/Latino; 4% Asian, non-Hispanic/Latino; 0.1% Native Hawaiian or other Pacific Islander, non-Hispanic/Latino; 0.2% American Indian or Alaska Native, non-Hispanic/Latino; 5% Two or more races, non-Hispanic/Latino; 0.3% Race/ethnicity unknown; 1% international; 3% transferred in. *Retention:* 46% of full-time freshmen returned.

**Freshmen** *Admission:* 1,247 enrolled.

**Faculty** *Total:* 409, 25% full-time, 20% with terminal degrees. *Student/faculty ratio:* 15:1.

**Majors** Accounting; art; biology/biological sciences; building/construction finishing, management, and inspection related; business administration and management; chemistry; child development; computer science; criminal justice/law enforcement administration; drafting and design technology; early childhood education; education; elementary education; emergency medical technology (EMT paramedic); engineering; fire science/firefighting; general studies; hotel/motel administration; human services; information technology; legal assistant/paralegal; liberal arts and sciences and humanities related; liberal arts and sciences/liberal studies; mathematics; mathematics teacher education; medical administrative assistant and medical secretary; medical/clinical assistant; nuclear medical technology; political science and government; psychology; registered nursing/registered nurse; respiratory care therapy; science technologies related; social sciences; Spanish language teacher education; surgical technology.

**Academics** *Calendar:* semesters. *Degree:* certificates and associate. *Special study options:* academic remediation for entering students, adult/continuing education programs, advanced placement credit, cooperative education, distance learning, English as a second language, external degree program, freshman honors college, honors programs, independent study, internships, off-campus study, part-time degree program, services for LD students, study abroad, summer session for credit.

**Library** FCC Library. *Books:* 11,831 (physical), 52,846 (digital/electronic); *Serial titles:* 19 (physical); *Databases:* 25. Students can reserve study rooms.

**Student Life** *Housing:* college housing not available. *Activities and Organizations:* drama/theater group, student-run newspaper. *Campus security:* 24-hour emergency response devices and patrols, late-night transport/escort service. *Student services:* personal/psychological counseling, women's center, veterans affairs office.

**Athletics** Member NJCAA. *Intercollegiate sports:* baseball M, basketball M/W, golf M/W, lacrosse M/W, soccer M/W, softball W, volleyball W.

**Costs (2017–18)** *Tuition:* area resident $4385 full-time, $120 per credit hour part-time; state resident $8645 full-time, $262 per credit hour part-time; nonresident $11,435 full-time, $355 per credit hour part-time. Full-time tuition and fees vary according to course load. Part-time tuition and fees vary according to course load. *Required fees:* $785 full-time, $27 per credit hour part-time. *Payment plans:* installment, deferred payment. *Waivers:* senior citizens.

**Financial Aid** Of all full-time matriculated undergraduates who enrolled in 2016, 25 Federal Work-Study jobs (averaging $1368). 14 state and other part-time jobs (averaging $2715).

**Applying** *Options:* electronic application. *Recommended:* high school transcript. *Application deadlines:* rolling (freshmen), rolling (transfers). *Notification:* continuous (freshmen), continuous (transfers).

**Freshman Application Contact** Ms. Lisa A. Freel, Director of Admissions, Frederick Community College, 7932 Opossumtown Pike, Frederick, MD

21702. *Phone:* 301-846-2468. *Fax:* 301-624-2799. *E-mail:* admissions@ frederick.edu.

*Website:* http://www.frederick.edu/.

# Garrett College
## McHenry, Maryland

- **State and locally supported** 2-year, founded 1966
- **Rural** 62-acre campus
- **Coed**

**Undergraduates** 523 full-time, 231 part-time. Students come from 12 states and territories; 6 other countries; 19% are from out of state; 25% Black or African American, non-Hispanic/Latino; 1% Hispanic/Latino; 0.3% American Indian or Alaska Native, non-Hispanic/Latino; 3% Two or more races, non-Hispanic/Latino; 0.3% Race/ethnicity unknown; 1% international; 4% transferred in; 24% live on campus.

**Faculty** *Student/faculty ratio:* 19:1.

**Academics** *Calendar:* semesters. *Degree:* certificates and associate. *Special study options:* academic remediation for entering students, adult/continuing education programs, advanced placement credit, cooperative education, distance learning, double majors, external degree program, honors programs, independent study, internships, part-time degree program, services for LD students, summer session for credit.

**Library** Learning Resource Center. *Books:* 31,225 (physical), 35,243 (digital/electronic); *Serial titles:* 119 (physical); *Databases:* 21. Weekly public service hours: 64.

**Student Life** *Campus security:* 24-hour emergency response devices and patrols, controlled dormitory access.

**Athletics** Member NJCAA.

**Costs (2017–18)** *Tuition:* area resident $2940 full-time, $105 per credit hour part-time; state resident $6440 full-time, $230 per credit hour part-time; nonresident $7560 full-time, $270 per credit hour part-time. Full-time tuition and fees vary according to program and reciprocity agreements. Part-time tuition and fees vary according to program and reciprocity agreements. *Required fees:* $1008 full-time, $36 per credit hour part-time, $25 per term part-time. *Room and board:* $8162; room only: $5662. Room and board charges vary according to board plan and housing facility. *Payment plans:* installment, deferred payment.

**Financial Aid** Of all full-time matriculated undergraduates who enrolled in 2016, 890 applied for aid, 730 were judged to have need, 82 had their need fully met. 47 Federal Work-Study jobs (averaging $630). 10 state and other part-time jobs (averaging $1065). In 2016, 175. *Average percent of need met:* 53. *Average financial aid package:* $6444. *Average need-based loan:* $2980. *Average need-based gift aid:* $4520. *Average non-need-based aid:* $1943. *Average indebtedness upon graduation:* $8716.

**Applying** *Options:* electronic application, early admission, deferred entrance. *Required:* high school transcript.

**Freshman Application Contact** Mrs. Shauna McQuade, Director of Enrollment Management, Garrett College, 687 Mosser Road, McHenry, MD 21541. *Phone:* 301-387-3739. *Toll-free phone:* 866-55-GARRETT. *E-mail:* admissions@garrettcollege.edu. *Website:* http://www.garrettcollege.edu/.

# Hagerstown Community College
## Hagerstown, Maryland

- **State and locally supported** 2-year, founded 1946
- **Suburban** 319-acre campus with easy access to Baltimore and Washington, DC
- **Coed,** 4,069 undergraduate students, 25% full-time, 63% women, 37% men

**Undergraduates** 999 full-time, 3,070 part-time. 10% Black or African American, non-Hispanic/Latino; 6% Hispanic/Latino; 2% Asian, non-Hispanic/Latino; 0.1% Native Hawaiian or other Pacific Islander, non-Hispanic/Latino; 0.3% American Indian or Alaska Native, non-Hispanic/Latino; 4% Two or more races, non-Hispanic/Latino; 2% Race/ethnicity unknown; 1% international; 8% transferred in.

**Freshmen** *Admission:* 828 enrolled.

**Faculty** *Total:* 221, 35% full-time, 6% with terminal degrees. *Student/faculty ratio:* 17:1.

**Majors** Accounting technology and bookkeeping; animation, interactive technology, video graphics and special effects; biology/biotechnology laboratory technician; business administration and management; business/commerce; child-care and support services management; commercial and advertising art; computer and information sciences; computer and information systems security; criminal justice/police science; dental hygiene; early childhood education; education; elementary education; emergency medical technology (EMT paramedic); engineering; engineering technologies and engineering related; English/language arts teacher education; industrial technology; instrumentation technology; liberal arts and sciences and humanities related; liberal arts and sciences/liberal studies; management information systems; mechanical engineering/mechanical technology; medical radiologic technology; psychiatric/mental health services technology; registered nursing/registered nurse; transportation/mobility management; web page, digital/multimedia and information resources design.

**Academics** *Calendar:* semesters. *Degree:* certificates and associate. *Special study options:* academic remediation for entering students, accelerated degree program, adult/continuing education programs, advanced placement credit, cooperative education, distance learning, English as a second language, honors programs, independent study, internships, off-campus study, part-time degree program, services for LD students, summer session for credit.

**Library** William Brish Library.

**Student Life** *Housing:* college housing not available. *Activities and Organizations:* drama/theater group, student-run newspaper, choral group, Phi Theta Kappa, Robinwood Players Theater Club, Association of Nursing Students, Radiography Club, Art and Design Club. *Campus security:* 24-hour patrols, student patrols. *Student services:* personal/psychological counseling, veterans affairs office.

**Athletics** Member NJCAA. *Intercollegiate sports:* baseball M(s), basketball M(s)/W(s), cross-country running M(s)/W(s), golf M/W, soccer M(s)/W, softball W(s), track and field M(s)/W(s), volleyball W(s). *Intramural sports:* golf M/W, tennis W.

**Costs (2017–18)** *Tuition:* area resident $3094 full-time, $119 per credit hour part-time; state resident $4862 full-time, $187 per credit hour part-time; nonresident $6396 full-time, $246 per credit hour part-time. Full-time tuition and fees vary according to course load, program, and reciprocity agreements. Part-time tuition and fees vary according to course load, program, and reciprocity agreements. *Required fees:* $522 full-time, $12 per credit hour part-time, $30 per term part-time. *Payment plan:* installment. *Waivers:* senior citizens and employees or children of employees.

**Financial Aid** Of all full-time matriculated undergraduates who enrolled in 2016, 721 applied for aid, 587 were judged to have need, 31 had their need fully met. 43 Federal Work-Study jobs (averaging $2054). 170 state and other part-time jobs (averaging $2797). In 2016, 23 non-need-based awards were made. *Average percent of need met:* 44%. *Average financial aid package:* $5889. *Average need-based loan:* $2995. *Average need-based gift aid:* $4473. *Average non-need-based aid:* $964.

**Applying** *Options:* electronic application, deferred entrance. *Required for some:* high school transcript. *Application deadlines:* rolling (freshmen), rolling (transfers). *Notification:* continuous (freshmen), continuous (transfers).

**Admissions Office Contact** Hagerstown Community College, 11400 Robinwood Drive, Hagerstown, MD 21742.

*Website:* http://www.hagerstowncc.edu/.

# Harford Community College
## Bel Air, Maryland

- **State and locally supported** 2-year, founded 1957
- **Small-town** 352-acre campus with easy access to Baltimore
- **Coed,** 6,100 undergraduate students, 36% full-time, 57% women, 43% men

**Undergraduates** 2,183 full-time, 3,917 part-time. Students come from 23 states and territories; 51 other countries; 4% are from out of state; 16% Black or African American, non-Hispanic/Latino; 5% Hispanic/Latino; 2% Asian, non-Hispanic/Latino; 0.2% Native Hawaiian or other Pacific Islander, non-Hispanic/Latino; 0.3% American Indian or Alaska Native, non-Hispanic/Latino; 4% Two or more races, non-Hispanic/Latino; 0.8% Race/ethnicity unknown; 1% international.

**Freshmen** *Admission:* 1,191 applied, 1,191 admitted.

**Faculty** *Total:* 319, 31% full-time, 11% with terminal degrees. *Student/faculty ratio:* 21:1.

**Majors** Accounting; accounting technology and bookkeeping; agribusiness; agriculture; anthropology; biology/biological sciences; business administration and management; business/commerce; CAD/CADD drafting/design technology; chemistry; chemistry teacher education; communication and journalism related; communications technologies and support services related; computer and information sciences; computer and information systems security; computer science; criminal justice/police science; design and visual communications; digital arts; early childhood education; education; education (specific levels and methods) related; education (specific subject areas) related; electroneurodiagnostic/electroencephalographic technology; elementary education; engineering; engineering technologies and engineering related; English; English/language arts teacher education; entrepreneurship; environmental engineering technology; environmental studies; fine/studio arts; general studies; graphic design; history; human resources management; information science/studies; international relations and affairs; legal assistant/paralegal; legal studies; liberal arts and sciences and humanities related; liberal arts and sciences/liberal studies; management information systems; marketing/marketing management; mass communication/media; mathematics; mathematics teacher education; medical/clinical assistant;

medical office assistant; multi/interdisciplinary studies related; music; philosophy; photography; physics; physics teacher education; political science and government; psychiatric/mental health services technology; psychology; registered nursing, nursing administration, nursing research and clinical nursing related; registered nursing/registered nurse; social work; sociology; Spanish language teacher education; special education; special education–early childhood; special education–elementary school; teacher assistant/aide; theater design and technology; visual and performing arts.

**Academics** *Calendar:* semesters. *Degree:* certificates, diplomas, and associate. *Special study options:* academic remediation for entering students, adult/continuing education programs, advanced placement credit, cooperative education, distance learning, double majors, English as a second language, honors programs, independent study, internships, part-time degree program, services for LD students, student-designed majors, study abroad, summer session for credit.

**Library** Harford Community College Library. *Books:* 43,126 (physical), 324,718 (digital/electronic); *Serial titles:* 828 (physical), 75 (digital/electronic); *Databases:* 79.

**Student Life** *Housing:* college housing not available. *Activities and Organizations:* drama/theater group, student-run newspaper, radio station, choral group, Phi Theta Kappa, Student Nurses Association, Gamers Guild, Actor's Guild, Future Educators of America. *Campus security:* 24-hour patrols, late-night transport/escort service. *Student services:* personal/psychological counseling, veterans affairs office.

**Athletics** Member NJCAA. *Intercollegiate sports:* baseball M(s), basketball M(s)/W(s), cross-country running M(s)/W(s), golf M(s), lacrosse M(s)/W(s), soccer M(s)/W(s), softball W(s), tennis M(s)/W(s), volleyball W(s). *Intramural sports:* badminton M/W, basketball M/W, cheerleading M(c)/W(c), football M/W, soccer M/W, softball M/W, swimming and diving M/W, tennis M/W, volleyball M/W.

**Costs (2017–18)** *Tuition:* area resident $3794 full-time, $126 per credit hour part-time; state resident $6467 full-time, $215 per credit hour part-time; nonresident $9119 full-time, $304 per credit hour part-time. *Required fees:* $759 full-time, $25 per credit hour part-time. *Payment plan:* installment. *Waivers:* senior citizens and employees or children of employees.

**Financial Aid** Of all full-time matriculated undergraduates who enrolled in 2016, 1,286 applied for aid, 889 were judged to have need. 57 Federal Work-Study jobs (averaging $1984).

**Applying** *Options:* electronic application. *Application deadlines:* rolling (freshmen), rolling (transfers). *Notification:* continuous (freshmen), continuous (transfers).

**Admissions Office Contact** Harford Community College, 401 Thomas Run Road, Bel Air, MD 21015-1698.

*Website:* http://www.harford.edu/.

# Howard Community College
## Columbia, Maryland

- **State and locally supported** 2-year, founded 1966
- **Suburban** 122-acre campus with easy access to Baltimore and Washington, DC
- **Coed,** 9,726 undergraduate students

**Undergraduates** Students come from 13 states and territories; 110 other countries; 0.6% are from out of state; 31% Black or African American, non-Hispanic/Latino; 11% Hispanic/Latino; 13% Asian, non-Hispanic/Latino; 0.3% Native Hawaiian or other Pacific Islander, non-Hispanic/Latino; 0.3% American Indian or Alaska Native, non-Hispanic/Latino; 5% Two or more races, non-Hispanic/Latino; 4% Race/ethnicity unknown; 5% international.

**Freshmen** *Admission:* 2,661 applied, 2,661 admitted.

**Faculty** *Total:* 801, 25% full-time, 7% with terminal degrees. *Student/faculty ratio:* 14:1.

**Majors** Accounting; art; biological and physical sciences; biomedical technology; biotechnology; business administration and management; cardiovascular technology; child development; clinical laboratory science/medical technology; computer and information sciences related; computer graphics; computer/information technology services administration related; computer science; computer systems networking and telecommunications; criminal justice/law enforcement administration; design and applied arts related; diagnostic medical sonography and ultrasound technology; dramatic/theater arts; electrical, electronic and communications engineering technology; elementary education; emergency medical technology (EMT paramedic); engineering; environmental studies; financial planning and services; general studies; health teacher education; information science/studies; information technology; kindergarten/preschool education; legal administrative assistant/secretary; liberal arts and sciences/liberal studies; licensed practical/vocational nurse training; medical administrative assistant and medical secretary; music; nuclear medical technology; office management; photography; physical sciences; physical therapy technology; premedical studies; pre-pharmacy studies; registered nursing/registered nurse; secondary education; social sciences; sport and fitness administration/management;

substance abuse/addiction counseling; telecommunications technology; theater design and technology.

**Academics** *Calendar:* semesters. *Degree:* certificates and associate. *Special study options:* academic remediation for entering students, adult/continuing education programs, advanced placement credit, cooperative education, distance learning, double majors, English as a second language, external degree program, freshman honors college, honors programs, internships, off-campus study, part-time degree program, services for LD students, study abroad, summer session for credit.

**Library** Howard Community College Library. Students can reserve study rooms.

**Student Life** *Housing:* college housing not available. *Activities and Organizations:* drama/theater group, student-run newspaper, radio station, choral group, Phi Theta Kappa, Nursing Club, Black Leadership Organization, Student Newspaper, Student Government Association. *Campus security:* 24-hour emergency response devices and patrols, late-night transport/escort service. *Student services:* personal/psychological counseling, veterans affairs office.

**Athletics** Member NJCAA. *Intercollegiate sports:* basketball M/W, cross-country running M/W, lacrosse M/W, soccer M/W, track and field M/W, volleyball W. *Intramural sports:* basketball M/W.

**Standardized Tests** *Required for some:* SAT or ACT (for admission).

**Costs (2017–18)** *Tuition:* area resident $4080 full-time, $136 per semester hour part-time; state resident $6570 full-time, $219 per semester hour part-time; nonresident $7920 full-time, $264 per semester hour part-time. Full-time tuition and fees vary according to course load. Part-time tuition and fees vary according to course load. *Required fees:* $768 full-time, $26 per semester hour part-time. *Payment plan:* installment. *Waivers:* senior citizens and employees or children of employees.

**Financial Aid** Of all full-time matriculated undergraduates who enrolled in 2013, 571 applied for aid, 477 were judged to have need. In 2013, 31 non-need-based awards were made. *Average percent of need met:* 22%. *Average financial aid package:* $3871. *Average need-based loan:* $2525. *Average need-based gift aid:* $4032. *Average non-need-based aid:* $1288.

**Applying** *Options:* electronic application, early admission, deferred entrance. *Application fee:* $25. *Required for some:* essay or personal statement, high school transcript, minimum 3.2 GPA, 2 letters of recommendation. *Application deadlines:* rolling (freshmen), rolling (transfers). *Notification:* continuous (freshmen), continuous (transfers).

**Freshman Application Contact** Aaron Alder, Assistant Director of Admissions, Howard Community College, 10901 Little Patuxent Parkway, Columbia, MD 21044-3197. *Phone:* 443-518-4599. *Fax:* 443-518-4589. *E-mail:* admissions@howardcc.edu.
*Website:* http://www.howardcc.edu/.

# Kaplan University, Hagerstown
## Hagerstown, Maryland

**Freshman Application Contact** Kaplan University, Hagerstown, 18618 Crestwood Drive, Hagerstown, MD 21742. *Phone:* 301-739-2680 Ext. 217. *Toll-free phone:* 800-987-7734. *Website:* http://www.kaplanuniversity.edu/.

# Lincoln College of Technology
## Columbia, Maryland

**Admissions Office Contact** Lincoln College of Technology, 9325 Snowden River Parkway, Columbia, MD 21046. *Toll-free phone:* 844-215-1513. *Website:* http://www.lincolntech.edu/.

# Montgomery College
## Rockville, Maryland

- **State and locally supported** 2-year, founded 1946
- **Suburban** 333-acre campus with easy access to Washington, DC
- **Endowment** $26.1 million
- **Coed,** 22,875 undergraduate students, 35% full-time, 53% women, 47% men

**Undergraduates** 8,060 full-time, 14,815 part-time. Students come from 24 states and territories; 163 other countries; 3% are from out of state; 26% Black or African American, non-Hispanic/Latino; 25% Hispanic/Latino; 12% Asian, non-Hispanic/Latino; 0.2% Native Hawaiian or other Pacific Islander, non-Hispanic/Latino; 0.3% American Indian or Alaska Native, non-Hispanic/Latino; 3% Two or more races, non-Hispanic/Latino; 0.1% Race/ethnicity unknown; 10% international; 65% transferred in.

**Freshmen** *Admission:* 10,976 applied, 10,976 admitted, 3,566 enrolled.

**Faculty** *Total:* 1,331, 36% full-time, 33% with terminal degrees. *Student/faculty ratio:* 17:1.

**Majors** Accounting technology and bookkeeping; American Sign Language (ASL); animation, interactive technology, video graphics and special effects;

applied horticulture/horticulture operations; architectural drafting and CAD/CADD; art; automobile/automotive mechanics technology; biology/biotechnology laboratory technician; building/construction finishing, management, and inspection related; business/commerce; chemistry teacher education; child-care provision; commercial and advertising art; commercial photography; communications technologies and support services related; computer and information sciences; computer and information systems security; computer technology/computer systems technology; criminal justice/police science; crisis/emergency/disaster management; data entry/microcomputer applications; diagnostic medical sonography and ultrasound technology; early childhood education; elementary education; engineering; English/language arts teacher education; fire prevention and safety technology; geography; health information/medical records technology; hotel/motel administration; interior design; legal assistant/paralegal; liberal arts and sciences and humanities related; liberal arts and sciences/liberal studies; mathematics teacher education; medical radiologic technology; physical therapy technology; physics teacher education; psychiatric/mental health services technology; registered nursing/registered nurse; Spanish language teacher education; speech communication and rhetoric; surgical technology; web page, digital/multimedia and information resources design.

**Academics** *Calendar:* semesters. *Degree:* certificates, diplomas, and associate. *Special study options:* academic remediation for entering students, adult/continuing education programs, advanced placement credit, cooperative education, distance learning, double majors, English as a second language, external degree program, honors programs, independent study, internships, off-campus study, part-time degree program, services for LD students, study abroad, summer session for credit. *ROTC:* Air Force (c).

**Library** Montgomery College Library plus 3 others. *Books:* 211,641 (physical), 57,782 (digital/electronic); *Serial titles:* 9,356 (physical), 104,416 (digital/electronic); *Databases:* 176. Weekly public service hours: 73; students can reserve study rooms.

**Student Life** *Housing:* college housing not available. *Activities and Organizations:* drama/theater group, student-run newspaper, radio station, choral group, Math Club, Engineers without Borders (EWB), STEM Education Community Club, Cyber Security Club, Animation and Drone Club. *Campus security:* 24-hour emergency response devices and patrols.

**Athletics** Member NJCAA. *Intercollegiate sports:* baseball M, basketball M/W, cross-country running M/W, soccer M/W, softball W, swimming and diving M/W, tennis M/W, track and field M/W, volleyball W. *Intramural sports:* baseball M, basketball M/W, cheerleading W, cross-country running M/W, golf M, soccer M/W, softball W, swimming and diving M/W, tennis M/W, track and field M/W, volleyball W, wrestling M.

**Costs (2017–18)** *Tuition:* area resident $2976 full-time, $124 per credit hour part-time; state resident $6072 full-time, $253 per credit hour part-time; nonresident $8400 full-time, $350 per credit hour part-time. Full-time tuition and fees vary according to course load. Part-time tuition and fees vary according to course load. *Required fees:* $1003 full-time, $67 per credit hour part-time. *Room and board:* $13,938; room only: $5512. *Payment plan:* installment. *Waivers:* senior citizens and employees or children of employees.

**Applying** *Options:* electronic application, early admission, deferred entrance. *Application fee:* $25. *Recommended:* high school transcript, interview. *Application deadlines:* rolling (freshmen), rolling (transfers). *Notification:* continuous (freshmen), continuous (transfers).

**Freshman Application Contact** Montgomery College, 51 Mannakee Street, Rockville, MD 20850. *Phone:* 240-567-5036.
*Website:* http://www.montgomerycollege.edu/.

# Prince George's Community College
## Largo, Maryland

**Freshman Application Contact** Ms. Vera Bagley, Director of Admissions and Records, Prince George's Community College, 301 Largo Road, Largo, MD 20774-2199. *Phone:* 301-322-0801. *Fax:* 301-322-0119. *E-mail:* enrollmentservices@pgcc.edu. *Website:* http://www.pgcc.edu/.

# Wor-Wic Community College
## Salisbury, Maryland

- **State and locally supported** 2-year, founded 1976
- **Small-town** 202-acre campus
- **Endowment** $16.7 million
- **Coed,** 3,110 undergraduate students, 26% full-time, 64% women, 36% men

**Undergraduates** 798 full-time, 2,312 part-time. Students come from 12 states and territories; 9 other countries; 3% are from out of state; 28% Black or African American, non-Hispanic/Latino; 5% Hispanic/Latino; 2% Asian, non-Hispanic/Latino; 0.2% Native Hawaiian or other Pacific Islander, non-Hispanic/Latino; 0.2% American Indian or Alaska Native, non-

Hispanic/Latino; 4% Two or more races, non-Hispanic/Latino; 1% Race/ethnicity unknown; 0.7% international; 7% transferred in.

**Freshmen** *Admission:* 1,043 applied, 1,043 admitted, 614 enrolled.

**Faculty** *Total:* 158, 44% full-time, 24% with terminal degrees. *Student/faculty ratio:* 16:1.

**Majors** Administrative assistant and secretarial science; biological and physical sciences; business administration and management; business/commerce; child-care and support services management; computer and information sciences; computer systems analysis; criminal justice/police science; early childhood education; education; elementary education; emergency medical technology (EMT paramedic); hospitality administration; liberal arts and sciences and humanities related; liberal arts and sciences/liberal studies; medical radiologic technology; occupational therapist assistant; physical therapy technology; registered nursing/registered nurse; substance abuse/addiction counseling.

**Academics** *Calendar:* semesters. *Degree:* certificates and associate. *Special study options:* academic remediation for entering students, accelerated degree program, adult/continuing education programs, advanced placement credit, distance learning, double majors, English as a second language, honors programs, independent study, internships, part-time degree program, services for LD students, summer session for credit.

**Library** Patricia M. Hazel Resource Center plus 4 others. *Databases:* 75. Weekly public service hours: 70.

**Student Life** *Housing:* college housing not available. *Activities and Organizations:* Anime Club, Criminal Justice Club, Role Playing Game Association, Veterans and Military Association, Alpha Nu Omicron (PTK). *Campus security:* 24-hour emergency response devices, late-night transport/escort service, patrols by trained security personnel 6:30 am to 11:00 pm. *Student services:* personal/psychological counseling, veterans affairs office.

**Costs (2017–18)** *Tuition:* area resident $3240 full-time, $108 per credit part-time; state resident $7230 full-time, $241 per credit part-time; nonresident $8910 full-time, $297 per credit part-time. *Required fees:* $510 full-time, $17 per credit part-time. *Payment plan:* installment. *Waivers:* senior citizens and employees or children of employees.

**Applying** *Options:* electronic application, early admission. *Recommended:* high school transcript. *Application deadlines:* rolling (freshmen), rolling (transfers).

**Freshman Application Contact** Mr. Richard Webster, Director of Admissions, Wor-Wic Community College, 32000 Campus Drive, Salisbury, MD 21804. *Phone:* 410-334-2895. *Fax:* 410-334-2954. *E-mail:* admissions@worwic.edu.

*Website:* http://www.worwic.edu/.

# MASSACHUSETTS

## ★ Bay State College
### Boston, Massachusetts

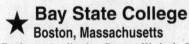

**Freshman Application Contact** Kimberly Odusami, Director of Admissions, Bay State College, 122 Commonwealth Avenue, Boston, MA 02116. *Phone:* 617-217-9186. *Toll-free phone:* 800-81-LEARN. *E-mail:* admissions@baystate.edu. *Website:* http://www.baystate.edu/.

## Benjamin Franklin Institute of Technology
### Boston, Massachusetts

**Freshman Application Contact** Ms. Brittainy Johnson, Associate Director of Admissions, Benjamin Franklin Institute of Technology, Boston, MA 02116. *Phone:* 617-423-4630 Ext. 122. *Toll-free phone:* 877-400-BFIT. *Fax:* 617-482-3706. *E-mail:* bjohnson@bfit.edu. *Website:* http://www.bfit.edu/.

## Berkshire Community College
### Pittsfield, Massachusetts

- **State-supported** 2-year, founded 1960, part of Massachusetts Public Higher Education System
- **Rural** 180-acre campus with easy access to Hartford, CT; Albany, NY
- **Coed**

**Undergraduates** 635 full-time, 1,324 part-time. 8% are from out of state; 7% Black or African American, non-Hispanic/Latino; 9% Hispanic/Latino; 2% Asian, non-Hispanic/Latino; 0.2% Native Hawaiian or other Pacific Islander, non-Hispanic/Latino; 0.6% American Indian or Alaska Native, non-Hispanic/Latino; 2% Two or more races, non-Hispanic/Latino; 4% Race/ethnicity unknown; 0.2% international; 4% transferred in.

**Faculty** *Student/faculty ratio:* 10:1.

**Academics** *Calendar:* semesters. *Degree:* certificates and associate. *Special study options:* academic remediation for entering students, accelerated degree program, adult/continuing education programs, advanced placement credit, cooperative education, distance learning, English as a second language, freshman honors college, honors programs, independent study, internships, off-campus study, part-time degree program, services for LD students, summer session for credit.

**Library** Jonathan Edwards Library. *Books:* 52,501 (physical), 45,753 (digital/electronic); *Serial titles:* 983 (physical), 88 (digital/electronic); *Databases:* 88. Weekly public service hours: 52; students can reserve study rooms.

**Student Life** *Campus security:* 24-hour emergency response devices and patrols, late-night transport/escort service.

**Costs (2017–18)** *Tuition:* state resident $1248 full-time; nonresident $12,480 full-time. Full-time tuition and fees vary according to class time, course load, and reciprocity agreements. Part-time tuition and fees vary according to class time, course load, and reciprocity agreements. *Required fees:* $9176 full-time.

**Financial Aid** Of all full-time matriculated undergraduates who enrolled in 2016, 1,331 applied for aid, 1,149 were judged to have need. 127 Federal Work-Study jobs (averaging $656). 127 state and other part-time jobs (averaging $636). In 2016, 4. *Average financial aid package:* $5314. *Average need-based loan:* $1274. *Average need-based gift aid:* $3441. *Average non-need-based aid:* $438. *Financial aid deadline:* 5/1.

**Applying** *Options:* electronic application, deferred entrance. *Required:* high school transcript.

**Freshman Application Contact** Ms. Tina Schettini, Senior Admissions Counselor, Berkshire Community College, 1350 West Street, Pittsfield, MA 01201-5786. *Phone:* 413-236-1635. *Toll-free phone:* 800-816-1233. *Fax:* 413-496-9511. *E-mail:* tschetti@berkshirecc.edu. *Website:* http://www.berkshirecc.edu/.

## Bristol Community College
### Fall River, Massachusetts

- **State-supported** 2-year, founded 1965, part of Massachusetts Community College System
- **Urban** 102-acre campus with easy access to Boston
- **Endowment** $9.5 million
- **Coed,** 7,637 undergraduate students

**Undergraduates** Students come from 7 other countries; 13% are from out of state; 8% Black or African American, non-Hispanic/Latino; 9% Hispanic/Latino; 2% Asian, non-Hispanic/Latino; 0.1% Native Hawaiian or other Pacific Islander, non-Hispanic/Latino; 0.2% American Indian or Alaska Native, non-Hispanic/Latino; 6% Two or more races, non-Hispanic/Latino; 5% Race/ethnicity unknown.

**Faculty** *Total:* 653, 20% full-time, 20% with terminal degrees. *Student/faculty ratio:* 16:1.

**Majors** Accounting; American Sign Language (ASL); baking and pastry arts; banking and financial support services; biology/biological sciences; business administration and management; business/commerce; business, management, and marketing related; business operations support and secretarial services related; civil engineering technology; clinical/medical laboratory technology; computer and information sciences; computer and information sciences related; computer programming; computer science; computer systems analysis; computer systems networking and telecommunications; criminal justice/safety; culinary arts related; data processing and data processing technology; dental hygiene; design and visual communications; dramatic/theater arts and stagecraft related; electromechanical technology; elementary education; engineering; engineering related; engineering science; engineering technologies and engineering related; entrepreneurship; environmental engineering technology; environmental studies; finance and financial management services related; fine/studio arts; fire science/firefighting; general studies; graphic design; health information/medical records technology; hospitality administration; humanities; information science/studies; intermedia/multimedia; kindergarten/preschool education; legal assistant/paralegal; legal professions and studies related; liberal arts and sciences/liberal studies; manufacturing engineering; marketing/marketing management; mathematics and statistics related; mechanical engineering; mechanical engineering/mechanical technology; medical administrative assistant and medical secretary; occupational therapist assistant; real estate; receptionist; registered nursing/registered nurse; small business administration; social sciences; social work; speech communication and rhetoric; structural engineering; veterinary/animal health technology.

**Academics** *Calendar:* semesters. *Degree:* certificates and associate. *Special study options:* academic remediation for entering students, accelerated degree program, adult/continuing education programs, advanced placement credit, cooperative education, distance learning, English as a second language, honors programs, independent study, internships, off-campus study, part-time degree program, services for LD students, student-designed majors, summer session for credit.

**Library** Learning Resources Center plus 3 others. *Books:* 53,650 (physical), 47,790 (digital/electronic); *Serial titles:* 98 (physical); *Databases:* 83. Weekly public service hours: 73; students can reserve study rooms.

**Student Life** *Housing:* college housing not available. *Activities and Organizations:* drama/theater group, student-run newspaper, International Club, STEM, Dental Hygiene, Medical Assisting, Seeds of Sustainability (SOS). *Campus security:* 24-hour emergency response devices and patrols, late-night transport/escort service. *Student services:* health clinic, personal/psychological counseling, women's center, veterans affairs office.

**Athletics** Member NJCAA. *Intramural sports:* basketball M/W, cross-country running M/W, golf M/W, soccer M/W, tennis M/W.

**Costs (2017–18)** *Tuition:* state resident $576 full-time, $24 per credit hour part-time; nonresident $5520 full-time, $230 per credit hour part-time. Full-time tuition and fees vary according to course load. Part-time tuition and fees vary according to course load. *Required fees:* $4080 full-time, $170 per credit hour part-time. *Payment plan:* installment. *Waivers:* senior citizens and employees or children of employees.

**Applying** *Options:* electronic application, deferred entrance. *Application fee:* $10. *Required:* high school transcript. *Notification:* continuous (freshmen), continuous (transfers).

**Freshman Application Contact** Dr. John McLaughlin, Dean of Admissions, Bristol Community College, 777 Elsbree Street, Fall River, MA 02720. *Phone:* 508-678-2811 Ext. 2947. *Fax:* 508-730-3265. *E-mail:* john.mclaughlin2@bristolcc.edu. *Website:* http://www.bristolcc.edu/.

# Bunker Hill Community College
## Boston, Massachusetts

- **State-supported** 2-year, founded 1973
- **Urban** 21-acre campus
- **Endowment** $4.6 million
- **Coed,** 12,996 undergraduate students, 35% full-time, 58% women, 42% men
- 81% of applicants were admitted

**Undergraduates** 4,520 full-time, 8,476 part-time. 25% Black or African American, non-Hispanic/Latino; 25% Hispanic/Latino; 11% Asian, non-Hispanic/Latino; 0.1% Native Hawaiian or other Pacific Islander, non-Hispanic/Latino; 0.4% American Indian or Alaska Native, non-Hispanic/Latino; 3% Two or more races, non-Hispanic/Latino; 10% Race/ethnicity unknown; 5% international.

**Freshmen** *Admission:* 7,370 applied, 5,992 admitted, 2,574 enrolled.

**Faculty** *Total:* 790, 19% full-time. *Student/faculty ratio:* 22:1.

**Majors** Accounting; art; bioengineering and biomedical engineering; biology/biological sciences; biotechnology; business administration and management; business administration, management and operations related; business operations support and secretarial services related; cardiovascular technology; chemistry; clinical/medical laboratory technology; computer and information sciences and support services related; computer and information systems security; computer/information technology services administration related; computer programming; computer programming (specific applications); computer science; computer systems networking and telecommunications; criminal justice/law enforcement administration; criminal justice/police science; culinary arts; data entry/microcomputer applications; design and visual communications; diagnostic medical sonography and ultrasound technology; dramatic/theater arts; early childhood education; education; electrical/electronics maintenance and repair technology related; emergency medical technology (EMT paramedic); engineering; English; entrepreneurship; finance; fine arts related; fire prevention and safety technology; foreign languages and literatures; general studies; health information/medical records administration; history; hospitality administration; hospitality administration related; human services; international business/trade/commerce; legal assistant/paralegal; mass communication/media; mathematics; medical administrative assistant and medical secretary; medical radiologic technology; music; operations management; physics; psychology; registered nursing/registered nurse; respiratory therapy technician; sociology; speech communication and rhetoric; sport and fitness administration/management; tourism and travel services management; web page, digital/multimedia and information resources design.

**Academics** *Calendar:* semesters. *Degree:* certificates and associate. *Special study options:* academic remediation for entering students, accelerated degree program, advanced placement credit, cooperative education, distance learning, English as a second language, external degree program, honors programs, independent study, internships, part-time degree program, services for LD students, study abroad, summer session for credit.

**Library** Bunker Hill Community College Library. *Books:* 45,625 (physical), 80,596 (digital/electronic); *Serial titles:* 92 (physical), 37 (digital/electronic); *Databases:* 105.

**Student Life** *Housing:* college housing not available. *Activities and Organizations:* drama/theater group, student-run radio station, choral group, Alpha Kappa Mu Honor Society, Asian-Pacific Students Association, Music Club, Latinos Unidos Club, Christian Fellowship. *Campus security:* 24-hour emergency response devices and patrols, late-night transport/escort service. *Student services:* health clinic, personal/psychological counseling, veterans affairs office.

**Athletics** Member NJCAA. *Intercollegiate sports:* baseball M, basketball M/W, soccer M/W, volleyball W.

**Costs (2017–18)** *Tuition:* state resident $576 full-time, $24 per credit hour part-time; nonresident $5520 full-time, $230 per credit hour part-time. Full-time tuition and fees vary according to course load, program, and reciprocity agreements. Part-time tuition and fees vary according to course load, program, and reciprocity agreements. *Required fees:* $3648 full-time, $152 per credit hour part-time. *Payment plan:* installment. *Waivers:* minority students, senior citizens, and employees or children of employees.

**Financial Aid** Of all full-time matriculated undergraduates who enrolled in 2016, 158 Federal Work-Study jobs (averaging $2858).

**Applying** *Options:* electronic application. *Required:* high school transcript. *Application deadlines:* rolling (freshmen), rolling (transfers). *Notification:* continuous (freshmen), continuous (transfers).

**Admissions Office Contact** Bunker Hill Community College, 250 New Rutherford Avenue, Boston, MA 02129. *Website:* http://www.bhcc.mass.edu/.

# Cape Cod Community College
## West Barnstable, Massachusetts

**Freshman Application Contact** Director of Admissions, Cape Cod Community College, 2240 Iyannough Road, West Barnstable, MA 02668-1599. *Phone:* 508-362-2131 Ext. 4311. *Toll-free phone:* 877-846-3672. *Fax:* 508-375-4089. *E-mail:* admiss@capecod.edu. *Website:* http://www.capecod.edu/.

# FINE Mortuary College, LLC
## Norwood, Massachusetts

- **Proprietary** 2-year, founded 1996
- **Suburban** campus with easy access to Boston
- **Coed,** 99 undergraduate students, 15% full-time, 67% women, 33% men

**Undergraduates** 15 full-time, 84 part-time. Students come from 6 states and territories; 23% are from out of state; 8% Black or African American, non-Hispanic/Latino; 4% Hispanic/Latino; 1% American Indian or Alaska Native, non-Hispanic/Latino; 1% Two or more races, non-Hispanic/Latino; 1% transferred in.

**Freshmen** *Admission:* 14 applied, 12 admitted, 12 enrolled.

**Faculty** *Total:* 17, 12% full-time, 53% with terminal degrees. *Student/faculty ratio:* 8:1.

**Majors** Funeral service and mortuary science.

**Academics** *Calendar:* continuous. *Degree:* associate. *Special study options:* academic remediation for entering students, adult/continuing education programs, cooperative education, distance learning, internships, off-campus study, part-time degree program, summer session for credit.

**Library** FINE Multimedia Center. *Books:* 550 (physical); *Serial titles:* 3 (physical).

**Student Life** *Housing:* college housing not available.

**Costs (2018–19)** *Tuition:* $20,520 full-time, $760 per credit hour part-time. *Payment plan:* installment. *Waivers:* employees or children of employees.

**Applying** *Application fee:* $75. *Required:* essay or personal statement, high school transcript, 1 letter of recommendation. *Recommended:* interview. *Application deadlines:* rolling (freshmen), rolling (transfers). *Notification:* continuous (freshmen), continuous (transfers), rolling (early decision).

**Freshman Application Contact** FINE Mortuary College, LLC, 150 Kerry Place, Norwood, MA 02062. *Phone:* 781-762-1211. *Website:* http://www.fmc.edu/.

# Greenfield Community College
## Greenfield, Massachusetts

**Freshman Application Contact** Ms. Colleen Kucinski, Assistant Director of Admission, Greenfield Community College, 1 College Drive, Greenfield, MA 01301-9739. *Phone:* 413-775-1000. *Fax:* 413-773-5129. *E-mail:* admission@gcc.mass.edu. *Website:* http://www.gcc.mass.edu/.

# Holyoke Community College
## Holyoke, Massachusetts

- **State-supported** 2-year, founded 1946, part of Massachusetts Public Higher Education System
- **Small-town** 135-acre campus
- **Endowment** $13.0 million
- **Coed,** 5,565 undergraduate students, 45% full-time, 62% women, 38% men

**Undergraduates** 2,506 full-time, 3,059 part-time. Students come from 18 states and territories; 1% are from out of state; 6% Black or African American, non-Hispanic/Latino; 27% Hispanic/Latino; 3% Asian, non-Hispanic/Latino; 0.4% American Indian or Alaska Native, non-Hispanic/Latino; 3% Two or more races, non-Hispanic/Latino; 2% Race/ethnicity unknown; 0.8% international; 7% transferred in.
**Freshmen** *Admission:* 3,380 applied, 2,954 admitted, 1,357 enrolled.
**Faculty** *Total:* 449, 29% full-time, 47% with terminal degrees. *Student/faculty ratio:* 15:1.
**Majors** Accounting technology and bookkeeping; administrative assistant and secretarial science; art; biology/biological sciences; biotechnology; business administration and management; chemistry; child-care and support services management; computer programming (specific applications); criminal justice/safety; engineering; environmental control technologies related; health and physical education/fitness; health services/allied health/health sciences; hospitality administration related; liberal arts and sciences and humanities related; liberal arts and sciences/liberal studies; mathematics; medical radiologic technology; music; physics; registered nursing/registered nurse; retailing; social work; sport and fitness administration/management; veterinary/animal health technology.
**Academics** *Calendar:* semesters. *Degree:* certificates and associate. *Special study options:* academic remediation for entering students, adult/continuing education programs, advanced placement credit, cooperative education, distance learning, double majors, English as a second language, honors programs, independent study, internships, off-campus study, part-time degree program, services for LD students, student-designed majors, study abroad, summer session for credit. *ROTC:* Army (c), Air Force (c).
**Library** Holyoke Community College Library plus 1 other. *Books:* 40,127 (physical), 62,355 (digital/electronic); *Serial titles:* 22 (physical), 32,539 (digital/electronic); *Databases:* 183. Weekly public service hours: 65; students can reserve study rooms.
**Student Life** *Housing:* college housing not available. *Activities and Organizations:* drama/theater group, student-run newspaper, radio station, Drama Club, Japanese Anime Club, Student Senate, LISA Club, STRIVE. *Campus security:* 24-hour emergency response devices and patrols, late-night transport/escort service. *Student services:* health clinic, personal/psychological counseling, women's center, veterans affairs office.
**Athletics** Member NJCAA. *Intercollegiate sports:* baseball M, basketball M/W, cross-country running M/W, golf M/W, soccer M/W, softball W, track and field M/W, volleyball W.
**Costs (2017–18)** *One-time required fee:* $65. *Tuition:* state resident $576 full-time, $183 per credit hour part-time; nonresident $5520 full-time, $389 per credit hour part-time. Full-time tuition and fees vary according to course load. Part-time tuition and fees vary according to course load. *Required fees:* $3990 full-time, $135 per term part-time. *Payment plan:* installment. *Waivers:* senior citizens and employees or children of employees.
**Applying** *Options:* electronic application, early admission, deferred entrance. *Required:* high school transcript. *Recommended:* interview. *Application deadlines:* rolling (freshmen), rolling (transfers). *Notification:* continuous (freshmen), continuous (transfers).
**Freshman Application Contact** Ms. Renee Tastad, Director of Admissions and Transfer Affairs, Holyoke Community College, Admission Office, Holyoke, MA 01040. *Phone:* 413-552-2321. *Fax:* 413-552-2045. *E-mail:* admissions@hcc.edu.
*Website:* http://www.hcc.edu/.

# Labouré College
## Milton, Massachusetts

**Director of Admissions** Ms. Gina M. Morrissette, Director of Admissions, Labouré College, 303 Adams Street, Milton, MA 02186. *Phone:* 617-296-8300. *Website:* http://www.laboure.edu/.

# Massachusetts Bay Community College
## Wellesley Hills, Massachusetts

- **State-supported** 2-year, founded 1961
- **Suburban** 84-acre campus with easy access to Boston
- **Coed,** 4,629 undergraduate students, 33% full-time, 52% women, 48% men

**Undergraduates** 1,539 full-time, 3,090 part-time. Students come from 16 states and territories; 89 other countries; 1% are from out of state; 14% Black or African American, non-Hispanic/Latino; 20% Hispanic/Latino; 5% Asian, non-Hispanic/Latino; 0.1% Native Hawaiian or other Pacific Islander, non-Hispanic/Latino; 0.3% American Indian or Alaska Native, non-Hispanic/Latino; 2% Two or more races, non-Hispanic/Latino; 6% Race/ethnicity unknown; 2% international; 6% transferred in. *Retention:* 56% of full-time freshmen returned.
**Freshmen** *Admission:* 2,448 applied, 2,358 admitted, 1,043 enrolled.
**Faculty** *Total:* 302, 25% full-time. *Student/faculty ratio:* 17:1.
**Majors** Accounting; animal physiology; automotive mechanics technology; bioinformatics; biological and biomedical sciences related; biology/biotechnology laboratory technician; business administration and management; business/commerce; community health and preventive medicine; computer and information sciences and support services related; computer and information systems security; computer/information technology services administration related; computer science; criminal justice/law enforcement administration; early childhood education; electrical and electronic engineering technologies related; electrical, electronic and communications engineering technology; elementary education; engineering technologies and engineering related; engineering technology; English; environmental control technologies related; general studies; hospitality administration; human services; international business/trade/commerce; international/global studies; legal assistant/paralegal; liberal arts and sciences/liberal studies; mathematics; mechanical engineering/mechanical technology; network and system administration; radiologic technology/science; registered nursing/registered nurse; social sciences.
**Academics** *Calendar:* semesters. *Degree:* certificates and associate. *Special study options:* academic remediation for entering students, adult/continuing education programs, advanced placement credit, cooperative education, distance learning, double majors, English as a second language, honors programs, independent study, internships, part-time degree program, services for LD students, study abroad, summer session for credit.
**Library** Perkins Library plus 1 other. *Books:* 44,482 (physical), 6,815 (digital/electronic); *Serial titles:* 46 (physical), 49,841 (digital/electronic); *Databases:* 113. Weekly public service hours: 66.
**Student Life** *Housing:* college housing not available. *Activities and Organizations:* drama/theater group, choral group, MassBay Veterans Club, Legal Studies and Criminal Justice Club, Nursing Club, Human Service Club, MassBay Gamer's Guild. *Campus security:* 24-hour emergency response devices and patrols. *Student services:* personal/psychological counseling, veterans affairs office.
**Athletics** Member NJCAA. *Intercollegiate sports:* baseball M, basketball M, cross-country running M/W, golf M, soccer M, volleyball W. *Intramural sports:* basketball M/W, soccer M/W, volleyball M/W.
**Costs (2017–18)** *Tuition:* state resident $576 full-time, $24 per credit part-time; nonresident $5520 full-time, $230 per credit part-time. Full-time tuition and fees vary according to class time, program, and reciprocity agreements. Part-time tuition and fees vary according to class time, program, and reciprocity agreements. *Required fees:* $4512 full-time, $188 per credit part-time. *Payment plan:* installment. *Waivers:* senior citizens and employees or children of employees.
**Applying** *Options:* electronic application, deferred entrance. *Required for some:* high school transcript. *Application deadlines:* rolling (freshmen), rolling (transfers). *Notification:* continuous (freshmen), continuous (transfers).
**Freshman Application Contact** Ms. Alison McCarty, Director of Admissions, Massachusetts Bay Community College, 50 Oakland Street, Wellesley Hills, MA 02481. *Phone:* 781-239-2506. *E-mail:* amccarty1@massbay.edu.
*Website:* http://www.massbay.edu/.

# Massasoit Community College
## Brockton, Massachusetts

**Freshman Application Contact** Michelle Hughes, Director of Admissions, Massasoit Community College, 1 Massasoit Boulevard, Brockton, MA 02302-3996. *Phone:* 508-588-9100. *Toll-free phone:* 800-CAREERS. *Website:* http://www.massasoit.mass.edu/.

# Middlesex Community College
## Bedford, Massachusetts

- **State-supported** 2-year, founded 1970, part of Massachusetts Public Higher Education System
- **Suburban** 200-acre campus with easy access to Boston
- **Coed**

**Undergraduates** 3,155 full-time, 5,590 part-time. 7% Black or African American, non-Hispanic/Latino; 19% Hispanic/Latino; 13% Asian, non-Hispanic/Latino; 0.2% American Indian or Alaska Native, non-Hispanic/Latino; 2% Two or more races, non-Hispanic/Latino; 0.4% Race/ethnicity unknown; 2% international.

**Academics** *Calendar:* semesters. *Degree:* certificates and associate. *Special study options:* academic remediation for entering students, accelerated degree program, adult/continuing education programs, advanced placement credit, cooperative education, distance learning, English as a second language, honors programs, independent study, internships, off-campus study, part-time degree program, services for LD students, study abroad, summer session for credit. *ROTC:* Air Force (c).

**Library** Main Library plus 1 other.

**Student Life** *Campus security:* 24-hour emergency response devices and patrols.

**Standardized Tests** *Required for some:* ACCUPLACER, TEAS.

**Costs (2017–18)** *One-time required fee:* $50. *Tuition:* state resident $4752 full-time; nonresident $9696 full-time. Full-time tuition and fees vary according to course load, program, and reciprocity agreements. Part-time tuition and fees vary according to course load, program, and reciprocity agreements.

**Financial Aid** Of all full-time matriculated undergraduates who enrolled in 2017, 65 Federal Work-Study jobs (averaging $2200).

**Applying** *Options:* electronic application, early admission. *Required for some:* high school transcript, 3 letters of recommendation, interview.

**Freshman Application Contact** Middlesex Community College, 591 Springs Road, Bedford, MA 01730-1655. *Phone:* 978-656-3211. *Toll-free phone:* 800-818-3434. *Website:* http://www.middlesex.mass.edu/.

# Mount Wachusett Community College
## Gardner, Massachusetts

- **State-supported** 2-year, founded 1963, part of Massachusetts Public Higher Education System
- **Small-town** 270-acre campus with easy access to Boston
- **Endowment** $399,545
- **Coed**, 3,854 undergraduate students, 35% full-time, 65% women, 35% men

**Undergraduates** 1,345 full-time, 2,509 part-time. Students come from 9 states and territories; 7 other countries; 7% Black or African American, non-Hispanic/Latino; 16% Hispanic/Latino; 2% Asian, non-Hispanic/Latino; 0.1% Native Hawaiian or other Pacific Islander, non-Hispanic/Latino; 0.4% American Indian or Alaska Native, non-Hispanic/Latino; 2% Two or more races, non-Hispanic/Latino; 4% Race/ethnicity unknown; 0.3% international; 7% transferred in.

**Freshmen** *Admission:* 1,627 applied, 1,599 admitted, 680 enrolled. *Average high school GPA:* 2.6.

**Faculty** *Total:* 419, 18% full-time, 14% with terminal degrees. *Student/faculty ratio:* 12:1.

**Majors** Allied health and medical assisting services related; alternative and complementary medical support services related; art; automobile/automotive mechanics technology; biology/biological sciences; biotechnology; business administration and management; business/commerce; chemistry; child-care and support services management; child development; clinical/medical laboratory technology; computer and information sciences; corrections; criminal justice/law enforcement administration; dental hygiene; dramatic/theater arts; elementary education; environmental studies; fire prevention and safety technology; general studies; health information/medical records administration; history; human services; kinesiology and exercise science; legal assistant/paralegal; liberal arts and sciences/liberal studies; mass communication/media; medical/clinical assistant; pharmacy; physical sciences; physical therapy technology; physics; plastics and polymer engineering technology; radio and television broadcasting technology; registered nursing/registered nurse; veterinary/animal health technology; web page, digital/multimedia and information resources design.

**Academics** *Calendar:* semesters. *Degree:* certificates, diplomas, and associate. *Special study options:* academic remediation for entering students, accelerated degree program, adult/continuing education programs, advanced placement credit, cooperative education, distance learning, double majors, English as a second language, honors programs, independent study, internships, part-time degree program, services for LD students, study abroad, summer session for credit. *ROTC:* Army (c).

**Library** LaChance Library. *Books:* 36,000 (physical), 43,164 (digital/electronic); *Serial titles:* 24 (physical); *Databases:* 67. Weekly public service hours: 57; students can reserve study rooms.

**Student Life** *Housing:* college housing not available. *Activities and Organizations:* drama/theater group, student-run newspaper, Otaku Anime Club, Dental Hygienist Club, Parent Support Group, Student Government Association, Student Nurses Association. *Campus security:* 24-hour emergency response devices and patrols, late-night transport/escort service, security cameras, access cards for laboratory access. *Student services:* health clinic, personal/psychological counseling, veterans affairs office.

**Athletics** *Intramural sports:* badminton M/W, basketball M/W, football M/W, soccer M/W, softball M/W, table tennis M/W, volleyball M/W, water polo M/W.

**Costs (2017–18)** *Tuition:* state resident $600 full-time, $25 per credit hour part-time; nonresident $5520 full-time, $230 per credit hour part-time. Full-time tuition and fees vary according to program and reciprocity agreements. Part-time tuition and fees vary according to program and reciprocity agreements. *Required fees:* $4728 full-time, $187 per credit hour part-time, $125 per credit hour part-time. *Payment plan:* installment. *Waivers:* senior citizens and employees or children of employees.

**Financial Aid** Of all full-time matriculated undergraduates who enrolled in 2016, 1,289 applied for aid, 994 were judged to have need, 40 had their need fully met. In 2016, 30 non-need-based awards were made. *Average percent of need met:* 97%. *Average financial aid package:* $5803. *Average need-based loan:* $1790. *Average need-based gift aid:* $5116. *Average non-need-based aid:* $683.

**Applying** *Options:* electronic application, early admission. *Required for some:* high school transcript. *Application deadlines:* 9/11 (freshmen), rolling (transfers). *Notification:* continuous (freshmen), continuous (transfers).

**Freshman Application Contact** Ms. Marcia Rosbury-Henne, Dean of Admissions and Enrollment, Mount Wachusett Community College, 444 Green Street, Gardner, MA 01440-1378. *Phone:* 978-632-6600 Ext. 337. *Fax:* 978-630-9558. *E-mail:* admissions@mwcc.mass.edu. *Website:* http://www.mwcc.edu/.

# Northern Essex Community College
## Haverhill, Massachusetts

- **State-supported** 2-year, founded 1960
- **Suburban** 106-acre campus with easy access to Boston
- **Endowment** $3.8 million
- **Coed**, 5,726 undergraduate students, 34% full-time, 61% women, 39% men

**Undergraduates** 1,943 full-time, 3,783 part-time. Students come from 9 states and territories; 1 other country; 13% are from out of state; 4% Black or African American, non-Hispanic/Latino; 42% Hispanic/Latino; 2% Asian, non-Hispanic/Latino; 0.3% Native Hawaiian or other Pacific Islander, non-Hispanic/Latino; 0.2% American Indian or Alaska Native, non-Hispanic/Latino; 1% Two or more races, non-Hispanic/Latino; 5% Race/ethnicity unknown; 0.6% international; 5% transferred in. *Retention:* 58% of full-time freshmen returned.

**Freshmen** *Admission:* 1,257 enrolled.

**Faculty** *Total:* 528, 21% full-time.

**Majors** Accounting; biology/biological sciences; business administration and management; business administration, management and operations related; business/commerce; business teacher education; civil engineering technology; commercial and advertising art; community health services counseling; computer and information sciences; computer programming; computer programming related; computer programming (specific applications); computer science; computer systems networking and telecommunications; computer technology/computer systems technology; criminal justice/police science; data processing and data processing technology; dental assisting; education; electrical, electronic and communications engineering technology; elementary education; emergency medical technology (EMT paramedic); engineering science; general studies; health and physical education/fitness; health information/medical records administration; hotel/motel administration; human services; industrial radiologic technology; journalism; kindergarten/preschool education; liberal arts and sciences/liberal studies; logistics, materials, and supply chain management; machine tool technology; marketing/marketing management; materials science; medical administrative assistant and medical secretary; medical radiologic technology; medical transcription; music; parks, recreation and leisure; physical education teaching and coaching; physical science technologies related; political science and government; psychiatric/mental health services technology; psychology; public health; radiologic technology/science; registered nursing/registered nurse; respiratory care therapy; respiratory therapy technician; science technologies; sign language interpretation and translation; telecommunications technology; web/multimedia management and webmaster; web page, digital/multimedia and information resources design.

**Academics** *Calendar:* semesters. *Degree:* certificates and associate. *Special study options:* academic remediation for entering students, adult/continuing education programs, advanced placement credit, cooperative education, distance learning, double majors, English as a second language, freshman honors college, honors programs, independent study, internships, off-campus study, part-time degree program, services for LD students, study abroad, summer session for credit. *ROTC:* Air Force (c).

**Library** Bentley Library. *Books:* 41,604 (physical), 11,287 (digital/electronic); *Serial titles:* 3,440 (physical), 27,741 (digital/electronic); *Databases:* 68.

**Student Life** *Housing:* college housing not available. *Activities and Organizations:* drama/theater group, student-run newspaper, choral group. *Campus security:* 24-hour emergency response devices and patrols. *Student services:* veterans affairs office.

**Athletics** Member NJCAA. *Intercollegiate sports:* baseball M, basketball M, cross-country running M/W, golf M/W, softball W, track and field M/W, volleyball W. *Intramural sports:* basketball M/W, cross-country running M/W, football M/W, soccer M/W, volleyball M/W, weight lifting M/W.

**Standardized Tests** *Required for some:* Psychological Corporation Aptitude Test for practical nursing.

**Costs (2017–18)** *Tuition:* state resident $600 full-time, $25 per credit hour part-time; nonresident $6384 full-time, $266 per credit hour part-time. Full-time tuition and fees vary according to program and reciprocity agreements. Part-time tuition and fees vary according to program and reciprocity agreements. *Required fees:* $4392 full-time, $183 per credit hour part-time. *Payment plan:* installment. *Waivers:* employees or children of employees.

**Financial Aid** Of all full-time matriculated undergraduates who enrolled in 2016, 74 Federal Work-Study jobs (averaging $1759).

**Applying** *Options:* early admission. *Required:* high school transcript. *Application deadlines:* rolling (freshmen), rolling (transfers). *Notification:* continuous (freshmen), continuous (transfers).

**Freshman Application Contact** Northern Essex Community College, 100 Elliott Street, Haverhill, MA 01830. *Phone:* 978-556-3616. *Website:* http://www.necc.mass.edu/.

# North Shore Community College
## Danvers, Massachusetts

- **State-supported** 2-year, founded 1965
- **Suburban** campus with easy access to Boston
- **Endowment** $7.4 million
- **Coed,** 6,087 undergraduate students

**Undergraduates** Students come from 14 states and territories; 7 other countries; 2% are from out of state; 10% Black or African American, non-Hispanic/Latino; 24% Hispanic/Latino; 4% Asian, non-Hispanic/Latino; 0.2% Native Hawaiian or other Pacific Islander, non-Hispanic/Latino; 0.1% American Indian or Alaska Native, non-Hispanic/Latino; 3% Two or more races, non-Hispanic/Latino; 1% Race/ethnicity unknown; 0.1% international.

**Freshmen** *Admission:* 3,870 applied, 3,570 admitted.

**Faculty** *Total:* 486, 28% full-time, 18% with terminal degrees. *Student/faculty ratio:* 17:1.

**Majors** Accounting; administrative assistant and secretarial science; airline pilot and flight crew; biology/biotechnology laboratory technician; business administration and management; child development; computer and information sciences related; computer engineering technology; computer graphics; computer programming; computer programming (specific applications); computer science; criminal justice/law enforcement administration; culinary arts; data entry/microcomputer applications; engineering science; fire science/firefighting; foods, nutrition, and wellness; gerontology; health professions related; hospitality administration; information science/studies; interdisciplinary studies; kindergarten/preschool education; legal administrative assistant/secretary; legal assistant/paralegal; liberal arts and sciences/liberal studies; marketing/marketing management; medical administrative assistant and medical secretary; medical radiologic technology; mental health counseling; occupational therapy; physical therapy technology; pre-engineering; registered nursing/registered nurse; respiratory care therapy; substance abuse/addiction counseling; tourism and travel services management; veterinary/animal health technology; web page, digital/multimedia and information resources design.

**Academics** *Calendar:* semesters. *Degree:* certificates and associate. *Special study options:* academic remediation for entering students, accelerated degree program, adult/continuing education programs, advanced placement credit, cooperative education, distance learning, English as a second language, honors programs, independent study, internships, part-time degree program, services for LD students, summer session for credit.

**Library** Learning Resource Center plus 2 others.

**Student Life** *Housing:* college housing not available. *Activities and Organizations:* drama/theater group, student-run newspaper, Program Council, Student Government, Performing Arts, Student Newspaper, Phi Theta Kappa, national fraternities. *Campus security:* 24-hour emergency response devices and patrols, late-night transport/escort service. *Student services:* health clinic, personal/psychological counseling, women's center.

**Athletics** *Intramural sports:* basketball M/W, soccer M/W.

**Costs (2017–18)** *One-time required fee:* $300. *Tuition:* state resident $600 full-time, $25 per credit part-time; nonresident $6168 full-time, $257 per credit part-time. Full-time tuition and fees vary according to program. Part-time tuition and fees vary according to program. *Required fees:* $4848 full-time, $177 per credit part-time. *Payment plan:* installment. *Waivers:* senior citizens and employees or children of employees.

**Financial Aid** Of all full-time matriculated undergraduates who enrolled in 2009, 1,658 applied for aid, 1,438 were judged to have need, 23 had their need fully met. 123 Federal Work-Study jobs (averaging $1359). In 2009, 11 non-need-based awards were made. *Average percent of need met:* 18%. *Average financial aid package:* $6856. *Average need-based loan:* $1639. *Average need-based gift aid:* $2522. *Average non-need-based aid:* $614.

**Applying** *Options:* electronic application, early admission, deferred entrance. *Required for some:* essay or personal statement, high school transcript, interview. *Application deadlines:* rolling (freshmen), rolling (transfers). *Notification:* continuous (freshmen), continuous (transfers).

**Freshman Application Contact** Mrs. Gissel Lopez, Academic Counselor, North Shore Community College, Danvers, MA 01923. *Phone:* 978-762-4000 Ext. 2108. *Fax:* 978-762-4015. *E-mail:* gilopez@northshore.edu. *Website:* http://www.northshore.edu/.

# Quincy College
## Quincy, Massachusetts

**Freshman Application Contact** Quincy College, 1250 Hancock Street, Quincy, MA 02169. *Phone:* 617-984-1710. *Toll-free phone:* 800-698-1700. *Website:* http://www.quincycollege.edu/.

# Quinsigamond Community College
## Worcester, Massachusetts

- **State-supported** 2-year, founded 1963, part of Massachusetts System of Higher Education
- **Urban** 57-acre campus with easy access to Boston
- **Endowment** $459,657
- **Coed,** 7,370 undergraduate students, 37% full-time, 58% women, 42% men

**Undergraduates** 2,706 full-time, 4,664 part-time. Students come from 25 states and territories; 43 other countries; 2% are from out of state; 13% Black or African American, non-Hispanic/Latino; 19% Hispanic/Latino; 5% Asian, non-Hispanic/Latino; 0.1% Native Hawaiian or other Pacific Islander, non-Hispanic/Latino; 0.4% American Indian or Alaska Native, non-Hispanic/Latino; 3% Two or more races, non-Hispanic/Latino; 5% Race/ethnicity unknown; 0.6% international; 7% transferred in.

**Freshmen** *Admission:* 3,829 applied, 2,254 admitted, 1,517 enrolled.

**Faculty** *Total:* 532, 27% full-time, 15% with terminal degrees. *Student/faculty ratio:* 16:1.

**Majors** Automobile/automotive mechanics technology; bioengineering and biomedical engineering; biology/biological sciences; biomedical technology; biotechnology; business administration and management; business/commerce; chemistry; community health and preventive medicine; computer and information sciences; computer and information systems security; computer engineering technology; computer graphics; computer programming; computer programming (specific applications); computer science; computer systems analysis; criminal justice/police science; data modeling/warehousing and database administration; deaf studies; dental hygiene; dental services and allied professions related; directing and theatrical production; early childhood education; electrical, electronic and communications engineering technology; electromechanical technology; elementary education; emergency medical technology (EMT paramedic); energy management and systems technology; English; environmental science; executive assistant/executive secretary; fire services administration; game and interactive media design; general studies; health information/medical records technology; health services/allied health/health sciences; history; hospitality administration; human services; kindergarten/preschool education; laser and optical technology; liberal arts and sciences/liberal studies; manufacturing engineering technology; medical administrative assistant and medical secretary; music; occupational therapist assistant; pre-engineering; pre-pharmacy studies; psychology; radiologic technology/science; registered nursing/registered nurse; respiratory care therapy; restaurant/food services management; telecommunications technology; trade and industrial teacher education; web page, digital/multimedia and information resources design.

**Academics** *Calendar:* semesters. *Degree:* certificates and associate. *Special study options:* academic remediation for entering students, accelerated degree program, advanced placement credit, cooperative education, distance learning, double majors, English as a second language, honors programs, independent study, internships, off-campus study, part-time degree program, services for LD students, summer session for credit. *ROTC:* Army (c).

**Library** Alden Library plus 1 other. *Books:* 43,098 (physical), 105,255 (digital/electronic); *Serial titles:* 20 (physical), 62,000 (digital/electronic); *Databases:* 61. Weekly public service hours: 67; students can reserve study rooms.

**Student Life** *Housing:* college housing not available. *Activities and Organizations:* drama/theater group, student-run newspaper, Academic-Related Clubs, Phi Theta Kappa, Student Senate, Anime Club, Psi Beta Club. *Campus security:* 24-hour emergency response devices and patrols, late-night transport/escort service. *Student services:* personal/psychological counseling, veterans affairs office.

**Athletics** Member NJCAA. *Intercollegiate sports:* baseball M, basketball M/W. *Intramural sports:* basketball M/W, cheerleading W(c), soccer M/W, table tennis M/W, ultimate Frisbee M/W, volleyball M/W.

**Costs (2018–19)** *Tuition:* state resident $720 full-time, $24 per credit part-time; nonresident $6900 full-time, $230 per credit part-time. Full-time tuition and fees vary according to course load and program. Part-time tuition and fees vary according to course load and program. *Required fees:* $6000 full-time, $173 per credit part-time, $310 per term part-time. *Payment plan:* installment. *Waivers:* senior citizens and employees or children of employees.

**Applying** *Options:* electronic application. *Application fee:* $20. *Required:* high school transcript. *Required for some:* interview. *Application deadlines:* rolling (freshmen), rolling (transfers). *Notification:* continuous (freshmen), continuous (transfers).

**Freshman Application Contact** Quinsigamond Community College, 670 West Boylston Street, Worcester, MA 01606-2092. *Phone:* 508-854-4576. *Website:* http://www.qcc.edu/.

# Roxbury Community College
## Roxbury Crossing, Massachusetts

**Director of Admissions** Nancy Santos, Director, Admissions, Roxbury Community College, 1234 Columbus Avenue, Roxbury Crossing, MA 02120-3400. *Phone:* 617-541-5310. *Website:* http://www.rcc.mass.edu/.

# Salter College
## Chicopee, Massachusetts

**Admissions Office Contact** Salter College, 645 Shawinigan Drive, Chicopee, MA 01020. *Website:* http://www.saltercollege.com/.

# Salter College
## West Boylston, Massachusetts

**Admissions Office Contact** Salter College, 184 West Boylston Street, West Boylston, MA 01583. *Website:* http://www.saltercollege.com/.

# Springfield Technical Community College
## Springfield, Massachusetts

- **State-supported** 2-year, founded 1967
- **Urban** 34-acre campus
- **Coed,** 5,343 undergraduate students, 43% full-time, 59% women, 41% men

**Undergraduates** 2,287 full-time, 3,056 part-time. Students come from 16 states and territories; 41 other countries; 2% are from out of state; 16% Black or African American, non-Hispanic/Latino; 29% Hispanic/Latino; 3% Asian, non-Hispanic/Latino; 0.1% Native Hawaiian or other Pacific Islander, non-Hispanic/Latino; 0.3% American Indian or Alaska Native, non-Hispanic/Latino; 3% Two or more races, non-Hispanic/Latino; 6% Race/ethnicity unknown; 6% transferred in. *Retention:* 55% of full-time freshmen returned.

**Freshmen** *Admission:* 3,295 applied, 2,634 admitted, 1,114 enrolled.

**Faculty** *Total:* 366, 40% full-time. *Student/faculty ratio:* 15:1.

**Majors** Accounting; administrative assistant and secretarial science; animation, interactive technology, video graphics and special effects; architectural and building sciences; automobile/automotive mechanics technology; biology/biological sciences; biotechnology; building/construction finishing, management, and inspection related; business administration and management; business/commerce; chemistry; civil engineering technology; clinical/medical laboratory technology; commercial and advertising art; commercial photography; computer and information systems security; computer engineering technology; computer programming (specific applications); computer science; criminal justice/police science; dental hygiene; diagnostic medical sonography and ultrasound technology; early childhood education; electrical, electronic and communications engineering technology; electromechanical technology; elementary education; engineering; fine/studio arts; fire prevention and safety technology; health information/medical records technology; heating, air conditioning, ventilation and refrigeration maintenance technology; landscaping and groundskeeping; laser and optical technology; liberal arts and sciences/liberal studies; marketing/marketing management; mathematics; mechanical engineering/mechanical technology; medical administrative assistant and medical secretary; medical/clinical assistant; medical insurance coding; occupational therapist assistant; physical therapy technology; physics; premedical studies; radio and television broadcasting technology; radiologic technology/science; recording arts technology; registered nursing/registered nurse; respiratory care therapy; secondary education; small business administration; surgical technology; telecommunications technology.

**Academics** *Calendar:* semesters. *Degree:* certificates and associate. *Special study options:* academic remediation for entering students, adult/continuing education programs, advanced placement credit, cooperative education, distance learning, English as a second language, honors programs, independent study, internships, off-campus study, part-time degree program, services for LD students, summer session for credit.

**Library** Springfield Technical Community College Library. *Books:* 45,975 (physical), 9,270 (digital/electronic); *Serial titles:* 159 (physical), 12 (digital/electronic); *Databases:* 93. Weekly public service hours: 61.

**Student Life** *Housing:* college housing not available. *Activities and Organizations:* drama/theater group, student-run newspaper, Gay Lesbian Bisexual Transgender Alliance (GLBTA), Respiratory Care Club, Cosmetology Club, Anime Club, Dental Hygiene Club. *Campus security:* 24-hour emergency response devices and patrols, late-night transport/escort service. *Student services:* health clinic, personal/psychological counseling, legal services, veterans affairs office.

**Athletics** Member NJCAA. *Intercollegiate sports:* basketball M/W, cross-country running M/W, golf M, soccer M/W, track and field M/W, wrestling M/W.

**Standardized Tests** *Required for some:* SAT (for admission).

**Costs (2017–18)** *Tuition:* state resident $750 full-time, $25 per credit part-time; nonresident $7260 full-time, $242 per credit part-time. Full-time tuition and fees vary according to course load and reciprocity agreements. Part-time tuition and fees vary according to course load and reciprocity agreements. No tuition increase for student's term of enrollment. *Required fees:* $5316 full-time, $159 per credit part-time, $108 per term part-time. *Payment plan:* installment. *Waivers:* senior citizens and employees or children of employees.

**Applying** *Options:* electronic application. *Required:* high school transcript. *Required for some:* interview. *Application deadlines:* rolling (freshmen), rolling (transfers). *Notification:* continuous (freshmen), continuous (transfers).

**Freshman Application Contact** Mr. LaRue Pierce, Dean of Students, Springfield Technical Community College, Springfield, MA 01105. *Phone:* 413-781-7822 Ext. 4078. *E-mail:* lapierce@stcc.edu. *Website:* http://www.stcc.edu/.

# Urban College of Boston
## Boston, Massachusetts

- **Independent** 2-year, founded 1993
- **Urban** campus with easy access to Boston
- **Coed, primarily women,** 812 undergraduate students, 7% full-time, 93% women, 7% men

**Undergraduates** 59 full-time, 753 part-time. 0.7% transferred in. *Retention:* 33% of full-time freshmen returned.

**Freshmen** *Admission:* 58 enrolled.

**Faculty** *Student/faculty ratio:* 12:1.

**Majors** Early childhood education; human services; liberal arts and sciences/liberal studies.

**Academics** *Calendar:* semesters. *Degree:* certificates and associate. *Special study options:* part-time degree program.

**Student Life** *Housing:* college housing not available. *Campus security:* 24-hour emergency response devices.

**Applying** *Application fee:* $10. *Required for some:* high school transcript.

**Admissions Office Contact** Urban College of Boston, 2 Boylston Street, 2nd Floor, Boston, MA 02116. *Website:* http://www.urbancollege.edu/.

# MICHIGAN

# Alpena Community College
## Alpena, Michigan

**Freshman Application Contact** Mr. Mike Kollien, Director of Admissions, Alpena Community College, 665 Johnson, Alpena, MI 49707. *Phone:* 989-

358-7339. *Toll-free phone:* 888-468-6222. *Fax:* 989-358-7540. *E-mail:* kollienm@alpenacc.edu. *Website:* http://www.alpenacc.edu/.

## Bay de Noc Community College
### Escanaba, Michigan

**Freshman Application Contact** Ms. Jessica LeMarch, Director of Admissions, Bay de Noc Community College, 2001 North Lincoln Road, Escanaba, MI 49829. *Phone:* 906-217-4010. *Toll-free phone:* 800-221-2001. *Fax:* 906-217-1714. *E-mail:* jessica.lamarch@baycollege.edu. *Website:* http://www.baycollege.edu/.

## Bay Mills Community College
### Brimley, Michigan

**Freshman Application Contact** Ms. Elaine Lehre, Admissions Officer, Bay Mills Community College, 12214 West Lakeshore Drive, Brimley, MI 49715. *Phone:* 906-248-3354. *Toll-free phone:* 800-844-BMCC. *Fax:* 906-248-3351. *Website:* http://www.bmcc.edu/.

## Career Quest Learning Center–Jackson
### Jackson, Michigan

**Admissions Office Contact** Career Quest Learning Center–Jackson, 209 East Washington Avenue, Suite 241, Jackson, MI 49201. *Website:* http://www.careerquest.edu/.

## Career Quest Learning Center–Lansing
### Lansing, Michigan

**Admissions Office Contact** Career Quest Learning Center–Lansing, 3215 South Pennsylvania Avenue, Lansing, MI 48910. *Website:* http://www.careerquest.edu/.

## Delta College
### University Center, Michigan

- **District-supported** 2-year, founded 1961
- **Rural** 640-acre campus
- **Endowment** $20.1 million
- **Coed**

**Undergraduates** 3,312 full-time, 5,820 part-time. Students come from 5 states and territories; 1 other country; 8% Black or African American, non-Hispanic/Latino; 6% Hispanic/Latino; 0.7% Asian, non-Hispanic/Latino; 0.5% American Indian or Alaska Native, non-Hispanic/Latino; 2% Two or more races, non-Hispanic/Latino; 2% Race/ethnicity unknown; 0.6% international; 3% transferred in.
**Faculty** *Student/faculty ratio:* 16:1.
**Academics** *Calendar:* semesters. *Degree:* certificates and associate. *Special study options:* academic remediation for entering students, adult/continuing education programs, advanced placement credit, cooperative education, distance learning, double majors, freshman honors college, honors programs, independent study, internships, off-campus study, part-time degree program, services for LD students, study abroad, summer session for credit.
**Library** Library Learning Information Center. *Books:* 55,653 (physical); *Serial titles:* 292 (physical); *Databases:* 35. Weekly public service hours: 71.
**Student Life** *Campus security:* 24-hour emergency response devices, student patrols, late-night transport/escort service.
**Athletics** Member NJCAA.
**Costs (2017–18)** *Tuition:* area resident $3210 full-time, $107 per credit hour part-time; state resident $5490 full-time, $183 per credit hour part-time; nonresident $10,320 full-time, $344 per credit hour part-time. Full-time tuition and fees vary according to course load. Part-time tuition and fees vary according to course load. *Required fees:* $590 full-time, $15 per credit hour part-time, $40 per term part-time.
**Financial Aid** Of all full-time matriculated undergraduates who enrolled in 2016, 115 Federal Work-Study jobs (averaging $2307). 67 state and other part-time jobs (averaging $2214).
**Applying** *Options:* electronic application, early admission, deferred entrance. *Required for some:* essay or personal statement. *Recommended:* high school transcript.
**Freshman Application Contact** Mr. Zachary Ward, Director of Admissions and Recruitment, Delta College, 1961 Delta Road, University Center, MI 48710. *Phone:* 989-686-9590. *Fax:* 989-667-2202. *E-mail:* admit@delta.edu. *Website:* http://www.delta.edu/.

## Glen Oaks Community College
### Centreville, Michigan

**Freshman Application Contact** Ms. Beverly M. Andrews, Director of Admissions/Registrar, Glen Oaks Community College, 62249 Shimmel Road, Centreville, MI 49032-9719. *Phone:* 269-294-4249. *Toll-free phone:* 888-994-7818. *Fax:* 269-467-4114. *E-mail:* thowden@glenoaks.edu. *Website:* http://www.glenoaks.edu/.

## Gogebic Community College
### Ironwood, Michigan

**Freshman Application Contact** Ms. Kim Zeckovich, Director of Admissions, Marketing, and Public Relations, Gogebic Community College, E. 4946 Jackson Road, Ironwood, MI 49938. *Phone:* 906-932-4231 Ext. 347. *Toll-free phone:* 800-682-5910. *Fax:* 906-932-2339. *E-mail:* jeanneg@gogebic.edu. *Website:* http://www.gogebic.edu/.

## Grand Rapids Community College
### Grand Rapids, Michigan

- **District-supported** 2-year, founded 1914, part of Michigan Department of Education
- **Urban** 35-acre campus
- **Endowment** $30.8 million
- **Coed,** 14,269 undergraduate students, 30% full-time, 52% women, 48% men

**Undergraduates** 4,252 full-time, 10,017 part-time. Students come from 10 states and territories; 23 other countries; 1% are from out of state; 9% Black or African American, non-Hispanic/Latino; 14% Hispanic/Latino; 4% Asian, non-Hispanic/Latino; 0.1% Native Hawaiian or other Pacific Islander, non-Hispanic/Latino; 0.4% American Indian or Alaska Native, non-Hispanic/Latino; 3% Two or more races, non-Hispanic/Latino; 3% Race/ethnicity unknown; 0.3% international. *Retention:* 53% of full-time freshmen returned.
**Freshmen** *Admission:* 5,018 applied, 2,922 enrolled. *Average high school GPA:* 2.9.
**Faculty** *Total:* 914, 27% full-time. *Student/faculty ratio:* 21:1.
**Majors** Architectural technology; architecture; art; automobile/automotive mechanics technology; business administration and management; chemistry; child-care and support services management; computer and information sciences; computer and information systems security; computer programming; computer programming (specific applications); computer support specialist; computer systems networking and telecommunications; corrections; criminal justice/law enforcement administration; criminal justice/police science; culinary arts; dental hygiene; electrical, electronic and communications engineering technology; elementary education; engineering; English; fashion merchandising; foreign languages and literatures; forestry; geology/earth science; heating, air conditioning, ventilation and refrigeration maintenance technology; industrial technology; journalism; landscaping and groundskeeping; liberal arts and sciences/liberal studies; library and information science; licensed practical/vocational nurse training; medical administrative assistant and medical secretary; music; music teacher education; physical education teaching and coaching; plastics and polymer engineering technology; quality control technology; recording arts technology; registered nursing/registered nurse; restaurant, culinary, and catering management; secondary education; welding technology.
**Academics** *Calendar:* semesters. *Degree:* certificates and associate. *Special study options:* academic remediation for entering students, adult/continuing education programs, advanced placement credit, cooperative education, distance learning, English as a second language, honors programs, independent study, internships, off-campus study, part-time degree program, services for LD students, study abroad, summer session for credit.
**Library** Arthur Andrews Memorial Library. *Books:* 68,321 (physical), 143,962 (digital/electronic); *Serial titles:* 347 (physical), 21,397 (digital/electronic); *Databases:* 107. Students can reserve study rooms.
**Student Life** *Housing:* college housing not available. *Activities and Organizations:* drama/theater group, student-run newspaper, choral group, Student Congress, Phi Theta Kappa, Hispanic Student Organization, Student Gamers Association, Foreign Affairs Club. *Campus security:* 24-hour emergency response devices, late-night transport/escort service. *Student services:* personal/psychological counseling, veterans affairs office.
**Athletics** Member NJCAA. *Intercollegiate sports:* baseball M(s), basketball M(s)/W(s), cross-country running M/W, golf M(s), softball W(s), volleyball W(s).
**Costs (2018–19)** *Tuition:* area resident $3420 full-time, $114 per contact hour part-time; state resident $7320 full-time, $244 per contact hour part-time; nonresident $10,860 full-time, $362 per contact hour part-time. Full-time tuition and fees vary according to course load and program. Part-time tuition

and fees vary according to course load and program. *Required fees:* $459 full-time, $15 per contact hour part-time, $90 per term part-time. *Payment plan:* installment. *Waivers:* employees or children of employees.

**Financial Aid** Of all full-time matriculated undergraduates who enrolled in 2008, 6,142 applied for aid, 4,896 were judged to have need, 1,012 had their need fully met. In 2008, 96 non-need-based awards were made. *Average financial aid package:* $4850. *Average need-based loan:* $2764. *Average need-based gift aid:* $3984. *Average non-need-based aid:* $1051.

**Applying** *Options:* electronic application, deferred entrance. *Required:* high school transcript. *Application deadline:* 8/30 (freshmen). *Notification:* continuous (freshmen), continuous (transfers).

**Freshman Application Contact** Ms. Diane Patrick, Director of Admissions, Grand Rapids Community College, Grand Rapids, MI 49503-3201. *Phone:* 616-234-4100. *Fax:* 616-234-4005. *E-mail:* dpatrick@grcc.edu. *Website:* http://www.grcc.edu/.

# Henry Ford College
## Dearborn, Michigan

**Freshman Application Contact** Admissions Office, Henry Ford College, 5101 Evergreen Road, Dearborn, MI 48128-1495. *Phone:* 313-845-6403. *Toll-free phone:* 800-585-HFCC. *Fax:* 313-845-6464. *E-mail:* enroll@hfcc.edu. *Website:* http://www.hfcc.edu/.

# Jackson College
## Jackson, Michigan

**Freshman Application Contact** Mr. Daniel Vainner, Registrar, Jackson College, 2111 Emmons Road, Jackson, MI 49201. *Phone:* 517-796-8425. *Toll-free phone:* 888-522-7344. *Fax:* 517-796-8446. *E-mail:* admissions@jccmi.edu. *Website:* http://www.jccmi.edu/.

# Kalamazoo Valley Community College
## Kalamazoo, Michigan

**Freshman Application Contact** Kalamazoo Valley Community College, PO Box 4070, Kalamazoo, MI 49003-4070. *Phone:* 269-488-4207. *Website:* http://www.kvcc.edu/.

# Kellogg Community College
## Battle Creek, Michigan

- **State and locally supported** 2-year, founded 1956, part of Michigan Department of Education
- **Urban** 120-acre campus
- **Coed,** 4,814 undergraduate students, 24% full-time, 67% women, 33% men

**Undergraduates** 1,160 full-time, 3,654 part-time. Students come from 3 other countries; 9% Black or African American, non-Hispanic/Latino; 5% Hispanic/Latino; 2% Asian, non-Hispanic/Latino; 0.1% Native Hawaiian or other Pacific Islander, non-Hispanic/Latino; 1% American Indian or Alaska Native, non-Hispanic/Latino; 4% Two or more races, non-Hispanic/Latino; 9% Race/ethnicity unknown; 0.4% international; 5% transferred in.

**Freshmen** *Admission:* 436 enrolled.

**Faculty** *Student/faculty ratio:* 17:1.

**Majors** Accounting technology and bookkeeping; administrative assistant and secretarial science; animation, interactive technology, video graphics and special effects; business administration and management; CAD/CADD drafting/design technology; child-care and support services management; community organization and advocacy; computer graphics; computer programming; computer programming (specific applications); computer technology/computer systems technology; corrections; criminal justice/safety; dental hygiene; drafting and design technology; electrician; elementary education; emergency medical technology (EMT paramedic); general studies; graphic design; heating, air conditioning, ventilation and refrigeration maintenance technology; industrial production technologies related; industrial technology; legal administrative assistant/secretary; liberal arts and sciences and humanities related; liberal arts and sciences/liberal studies; machine tool technology; medical administrative assistant and medical secretary; medical radiologic technology; physical therapy technology; pipefitting and sprinkler fitting; registered nursing/registered nurse; welding technology.

**Academics** *Calendar:* semesters. *Degree:* certificates and associate. *Special study options:* academic remediation for entering students, accelerated degree program, adult/continuing education programs, advanced placement credit, cooperative education, distance learning, double majors, English as a second language, freshman honors college, honors programs, independent study, internships, off-campus study, part-time degree program, services for LD students, summer session for credit.

**Library** Emory W. Morris Learning Resource Center. *Books:* 51,629 (physical), 20,975 (digital/electronic); *Serial titles:* 62 (physical), 74,000 (digital/electronic); *Databases:* 67. Weekly public service hours: 81; students can reserve study rooms.

**Student Life** *Housing:* college housing not available. *Activities and Organizations:* drama/theater group, student-run newspaper, choral group, Tech Club, Phi Theta Kappa, Student Nurses Association, Crude Arts Club, Art League. *Campus security:* 24-hour emergency response devices and patrols, late-night transport/escort service. *Student services:* veterans affairs office.

**Athletics** Member NJCAA. *Intercollegiate sports:* baseball M(s), basketball M(s)/W(s), bowling M/W, cross-country running W, soccer W, softball W(s), volleyball W(s).

**Costs (2018–19)** *Tuition:* area resident $3683 full-time; state resident $5693 full-time; nonresident $7950 full-time. *Payment plan:* installment. *Waivers:* senior citizens and employees or children of employees.

**Financial Aid** Of all full-time matriculated undergraduates who enrolled in 2016, 41 Federal Work-Study jobs (averaging $2251). 43 state and other part-time jobs (averaging $2058).

**Applying** *Options:* electronic application, early admission. *Required for some:* high school transcript, minimum 2.0 GPA. *Application deadlines:* rolling (freshmen), rolling (transfers). *Notification:* continuous (freshmen), continuous (transfers).

**Freshman Application Contact** Ms. Nicole Jewell, Director of Admissions, Kellogg Community College, 450 North Avenue, Battle Creek, MI 49017. *Phone:* 269-965-3931. *Fax:* 269-965-4133. *E-mail:* jewelln@kellogg.edu. *Website:* http://www.kellogg.edu/.

# Keweenaw Bay Ojibwa Community College
## Baraga, Michigan

**Freshman Application Contact** Ms. Megan Shanahan, Admissions Officer, Keweenaw Bay Ojibwa Community College, 111 Beartown Road, Baraga, MI 49908. *Phone:* 909-353-4600. *E-mail:* megan@kbocc.org. *Website:* http://www.kbocc.edu/.

# Kirtland Community College
## Roscommon, Michigan

- **District-supported** 2-year, founded 1966
- **Rural** 180-acre campus
- **Coed,** 1,528 undergraduate students, 33% full-time, 59% women, 41% men

**Undergraduates** 499 full-time, 1,029 part-time. Students come from 7 states and territories; 1% Black or African American, non-Hispanic/Latino; 2% Hispanic/Latino; 0.7% Asian, non-Hispanic/Latino; 1% American Indian or Alaska Native, non-Hispanic/Latino; 1% Two or more races, non-Hispanic/Latino; 1% Race/ethnicity unknown.

**Freshmen** *Admission:* 564 applied, 564 admitted, 201 enrolled. *Test scores:* ACT scores over 18: 55%; ACT scores over 24: 7%.

**Faculty** *Total:* 124, 27% full-time. *Student/faculty ratio:* 17:1.

**Majors** Accounting technology and bookkeeping; automobile/automotive mechanics technology; business administration and management; cardiovascular technology; cosmetology; criminal justice/law enforcement administration; criminal justice/police science; electrical, electronic and communications engineering technology; electromechanical technology; emergency medical technology (EMT paramedic); general studies; graphic design; health information/medical records technology; heating, air conditioning, ventilation and refrigeration maintenance technology; liberal arts and sciences/liberal studies; medical/clinical assistant; registered nursing/registered nurse; robotics technology; surgical technology; welding technology.

**Academics** *Calendar:* semesters. *Degree:* certificates and associate. *Special study options:* academic remediation for entering students, adult/continuing education programs, advanced placement credit, cooperative education, distance learning, honors programs, independent study, internships, part-time degree program, services for LD students, summer session for credit.

**Library** Kirtland Community College Library plus 1 other. *Books:* 27,089 (physical), 180,843 (digital/electronic); *Serial titles:* 105 (physical); *Databases:* 55. Weekly public service hours: 40; students can reserve study rooms.

**Student Life** *Housing:* college housing not available. *Campus security:* 24-hour emergency response devices, student patrols, late-night transport/escort service, campus warning siren, uniformed armed police officers, RAVE alert system (text, email, voice).

**Athletics** Member NJCAA. *Intercollegiate sports:* bowling M(s)/W(s), cross-country running M(s)/W(s), golf M(s)/W(s).

**Standardized Tests** *Recommended:* SAT or ACT (for admission).

**Costs (2017–18)** *Tuition:* area resident $3390 full-time, $113 per contact hour part-time; state resident $4980 full-time, $166 per contact hour part-time; nonresident $7500 full-time, $250 per contact hour part-time. *Required fees:* $630 full-time, $21 per contact hour part-time. *Payment plan:* installment. *Waivers:* senior citizens and employees or children of employees.

**Financial Aid** Of all full-time matriculated undergraduates who enrolled in 2016, 50 Federal Work-Study jobs (averaging $1253). 28 state and other part-time jobs (averaging $1647).

**Applying** *Options:* electronic application. *Required:* high school transcript. *Application deadlines:* rolling (freshmen), rolling (transfers). *Notification:* continuous until 8/15 (freshmen), continuous until 8/15 (transfers).

**Freshman Application Contact** Ms. Michelle Vyskocil, Dean of Student Services, Kirtland Community College, 10775 North Saint Helen Road, Roscommon, MI 48653. *Phone:* 989-275-5000 Ext. 248. *Fax:* 989-275-6789. *E-mail:* registrar@kirtland.edu. *Website:* http://www.kirtland.edu/.

# Lake Michigan College
## Benton Harbor, Michigan

**Freshman Application Contact** Mr. Louis Thomas, Lead Admissions Specialist, Lake Michigan College, 2755 East Napier Avenue, Benton Harbor, MI 49022-1899. *Phone:* 269-927-6584. *Toll-free phone:* 800-252-1LMC. *Fax:* 269-927-6718. *E-mail:* thomas@lakemichigancollege.edu. *Website:* http://www.lakemichigancollege.edu/.

# Lansing Community College
## Lansing, Michigan

- **State and locally supported** 2-year, founded 1957, part of Michigan Department of Education
- **Urban** 28-acre campus
- **Endowment** $7.3 million
- **Coed**

**Undergraduates** 5,088 full-time, 8,495 part-time. 10% Black or African American, non-Hispanic/Latino; 8% Hispanic/Latino; 3% Asian, non-Hispanic/Latino; 0.2% Native Hawaiian or other Pacific Islander, non-Hispanic/Latino; 0.5% American Indian or Alaska Native, non-Hispanic/Latino; 3% Two or more races, non-Hispanic/Latino; 5% Race/ethnicity unknown; 1% international.

**Academics** *Calendar:* semesters. *Degree:* certificates and associate. *Special study options:* academic remediation for entering students, adult/continuing education programs, advanced placement credit, cooperative education, distance learning, double majors, English as a second language, external degree program, honors programs, independent study, internships, part-time degree program, services for LD students, study abroad, summer session for credit. *ROTC:* Army (c), Air Force (c).

**Library** Lansing Community College Library.

**Student Life** *Campus security:* 24-hour emergency response devices and patrols, student patrols, late-night transport/escort service.

**Athletics** Member NJCAA.

**Costs (2017–18)** *Tuition:* area resident $2640 full-time; state resident $5280 full-time; nonresident $7920 full-time. *Required fees:* $380 full-time.

**Applying** *Options:* electronic application, early admission, deferred entrance. *Required for some:* essay or personal statement, high school transcript, 2 letters of recommendation, interview, specific additional requirements for health, aviation, music, police academy, and fire academy program admissions.

**Freshman Application Contact** Ms. Tammy Grossbauer, Director of Admissions/Registrar, Lansing Community College, 1121 Enrollment Services, PO BOX 40010, Lansing, MI 48901. *Phone:* 517-483-1200. *Toll-free phone:* 800-644-4LCC. *Fax:* 517-483-1170. *E-mail:* grossbt@lcc.edu. *Website:* http://www.lcc.edu/.

# Macomb Community College
## Warren, Michigan

- **District-supported** 2-year, founded 1954, part of Michigan Public Community College System
- **Suburban** 384-acre campus with easy access to Detroit
- **Endowment** $20.4 million
- **Coed,** 21,014 undergraduate students, 29% full-time, 53% women, 47% men

**Undergraduates** 6,116 full-time, 14,898 part-time. Students come from 4 states and territories; 11% Black or African American, non-Hispanic/Latino; 3% Hispanic/Latino; 5% Asian, non-Hispanic/Latino; 0.1% Native Hawaiian or other Pacific Islander, non-Hispanic/Latino; 0.5% American Indian or Alaska Native, non-Hispanic/Latino; 2% Two or more races, non-

Hispanic/Latino; 7% Race/ethnicity unknown; 2% international. *Retention:* 56% of full-time freshmen returned.

**Freshmen** *Admission:* 3,261 enrolled.

**Faculty** *Total:* 971, 21% full-time. *Student/faculty ratio:* 24:1.

**Majors** Accounting; administrative assistant and secretarial science; agriculture; architectural drafting and CAD/CADD; automobile/automotive mechanics technology; automotive engineering technology; biology/biological sciences; business administration and management; business automation/technology/data entry; business/commerce; cabinetmaking and millwork; chemistry; child-care and support services management; civil engineering technology; commercial and advertising art; computer programming; computer programming (specific applications); construction engineering technology; criminal justice/law enforcement administration; criminal justice/police science; culinary arts; drafting and design technology; drafting/design engineering technologies related; electrical, electronic and communications engineering technology; electrical/electronics equipment installation and repair; electromechanical technology; emergency medical technology (EMT paramedic); energy management and systems technology; engineering related; finance; fire prevention and safety technology; forensic science and technology; general studies; graphic and printing equipment operation/production; heating, air conditioning, ventilation and refrigeration maintenance technology; heating, ventilation, air conditioning and refrigeration engineering technology; industrial mechanics and maintenance technology; industrial technology; international/global studies; legal assistant/paralegal; legal studies; liberal arts and sciences/liberal studies; machine tool technology; manufacturing engineering technology; marketing/marketing management; mathematics; mechanical drafting and CAD/CADD; mechanical engineering/mechanical technology; mechanic and repair technologies related; medical/clinical assistant; mental health counseling; metallurgical technology; music performance; occupational therapist assistant; operations management; physical therapy technology; plastics and polymer engineering technology; plumbing technology; pre-engineering; quality control and safety technologies related; quality control technology; registered nursing/registered nurse; respiratory care therapy; robotics technology; sheet metal technology; social psychology; speech communication and rhetoric; surgical technology; surveying technology; tool and die technology; veterinary/animal health technology; welding technology.

**Academics** *Calendar:* semesters. *Degree:* certificates and associate. *Special study options:* academic remediation for entering students, adult/continuing education programs, advanced placement credit, cooperative education, English as a second language, honors programs, internships, off-campus study, part-time degree program, services for LD students, student-designed majors, summer session for credit.

**Library** Library of South Campus. *Books:* 181,121 (physical), 51,203 (digital/electronic); *Serial titles:* 51,079 (physical), 97,750 (digital/electronic). Students can reserve study rooms.

**Student Life** *Housing:* college housing not available. *Activities and Organizations:* drama/theater group, Phi Beta Kappa, Adventure Unlimited, Alpha Rho Rho, SADD. *Campus security:* 24-hour emergency response devices and patrols, late-night transport/escort service, security phones in parking lots, surveillance cameras. *Student services:* health clinic, personal/psychological counseling.

**Athletics** Member NJCAA. *Intercollegiate sports:* baseball M(s), basketball M(s), cross-country running M(s)/W(s), soccer M(s), softball W(s), track and field M(s)/W(s), volleyball W(s). *Intramural sports:* baseball M, basketball M, bowling M/W, cross-country running M/W, football M/W, skiing (cross-country) M/W, skiing (downhill) M/W, volleyball M/W.

**Costs (2017–18)** *Tuition:* area resident $3100 full-time, $100 per credit hour part-time; state resident $5766 full-time, $186 per credit hour part-time; nonresident $7347 full-time, $237 per credit hour part-time. Full-time tuition and fees vary according to course load. Part-time tuition and fees vary according to course load. *Required fees:* $275 full-time, $5 per credit hour part-time, $60 per term part-time. *Waivers:* employees or children of employees.

**Applying** *Options:* early admission, deferred entrance. *Application deadlines:* rolling (freshmen), rolling (transfers).

**Freshman Application Contact** Mr. Brian Bouwman, Coordinator of Admissions and Transfer Credit, Macomb Community College, 14500 East 12 Mile Road, Warren, MI 48088-3896. *Phone:* 586-445-7246. *Toll-free phone:* 866-MACOMB1. *Fax:* 586-445-7140. *E-mail:* stevensr@macomb.edu. *Website:* http://www.macomb.edu/.

# MIAT College of Technology
## Canton, Michigan

**Admissions Office Contact** MIAT College of Technology, 2955 South Haggerty Road, Canton, MI 48188. *Website:* http://www.miat.edu/.

# Mid Michigan Community College
## Harrison, Michigan

**Freshman Application Contact** Jennifer Casebeer, Admissions Specialist, Mid Michigan Community College, 1375 South Clare Avenue, Harrison, MI 48625-9447. *Phone:* 989-386-6661. *E-mail:* apply@midmich.edu. *Website:* http://www.midmich.edu/.

# Monroe County Community College
## Monroe, Michigan

- **County-supported** 2-year, founded 1964, part of Michigan Department of Education
- **Small-town** 150-acre campus with easy access to Detroit, Toledo
- **Coed,** 3,144 undergraduate students, 30% full-time, 57% women, 43% men

**Undergraduates** 954 full-time, 2,190 part-time. Students come from 2 other countries; 4% are from out of state; 3% Black or African American, non-Hispanic/Latino; 3% Hispanic/Latino; 0.8% Asian, non-Hispanic/Latino; 0.1% Native Hawaiian or other Pacific Islander, non-Hispanic/Latino; 0.3% American Indian or Alaska Native, non-Hispanic/Latino; 0.7% Two or more races, non-Hispanic/Latino; 8% Race/ethnicity unknown; 0.1% international.
**Freshmen** *Admission:* 2,500 applied, 2,500 admitted. *Average high school GPA:* 2.5.
**Faculty** *Total:* 170, 24% full-time.
**Majors** Accounting; administrative assistant and secretarial science; architectural engineering technology; art; biology/biological sciences; business administration and management; child development; clinical laboratory science/medical technology; computer and information sciences related; computer engineering technology; computer graphics; computer programming (specific applications); criminal justice/police science; criminal justice/safety; culinary arts; data processing and data processing technology; drafting and design technology; electrical, electronic and communications engineering technology; elementary education; English; finance; funeral service and mortuary science; industrial technology; information technology; journalism; legal administrative assistant/secretary; liberal arts and sciences/liberal studies; marketing/marketing management; mass communication/media; mathematics; medical administrative assistant and medical secretary; physical therapy; pre-engineering; psychology; registered nursing/registered nurse; respiratory care therapy; rhetoric and composition; social work; web/multimedia management and webmaster; web page, digital/multimedia and information resources design; welding technology; word processing.
**Academics** *Calendar:* semesters. *Degree:* certificates and associate. *Special study options:* academic remediation for entering students, advanced placement credit, distance learning, honors programs, independent study, part-time degree program, services for LD students, study abroad, summer session for credit.
**Library** Campbell Learning Resource Center.
**Student Life** *Housing:* college housing not available. *Activities and Organizations:* drama/theater group, student-run newspaper, choral group, Student Government, Society of Auto Engineers, Oasis, Nursing Students Organization, Respiratory Therapy. *Campus security:* police patrols during open hours.
**Standardized Tests** *Required:* ACT, ACT Compass, SAT, ACCUPLACER (for admission). *Recommended:* SAT (for admission), ACT (for admission).
**Costs (2018–19)** *Tuition:* area resident $3048 full-time; state resident $5040 full-time; nonresident $5556 full-time. Full-time tuition and fees vary according to reciprocity agreements. Part-time tuition and fees vary according to reciprocity agreements. *Required fees:* $80 full-time. *Payment plan:* installment. *Waivers:* senior citizens and employees or children of employees.
**Applying** *Options:* early admission, deferred entrance. *Required:* high school transcript. *Application deadline:* rolling (transfers). *Notification:* continuous (freshmen), continuous (transfers).
**Freshman Application Contact** Mr. Mark V. Hall, Director of Admissions and Guidance Services, Monroe County Community College, 1555 South Raisinville Road, Monroe, MI 48161. *Phone:* 734-384-4261. *Toll-free phone:* 877-YES-MCCC. *Fax:* 734-242-9711. *E-mail:* mhall@monroeccc.edu. *Website:* http://www.monroeccc.edu/.

# Montcalm Community College
## Sidney, Michigan

**Freshman Application Contact** Ms. Debra Alexander, Associate Dean of Student Services, Montcalm Community College, 2800 College Drive, SW,

Sidney, MI 48885. *Phone:* 989-328-1276. *Toll-free phone:* 877-328-2111. *E-mail:* admissions@montcalm.edu. *Website:* http://www.montcalm.edu/.

# Mott Community College
## Flint, Michigan

- **District-supported** 2-year, founded 1923
- **Urban** 32-acre campus with easy access to Detroit
- **Endowment** $40.1 million
- **Coed,** 7,689 undergraduate students, 26% full-time, 59% women, 41% men

**Undergraduates** 2,022 full-time, 5,667 part-time. 16% Black or African American, non-Hispanic/Latino; 5% Hispanic/Latino; 0.6% Asian, non-Hispanic/Latino; 0.1% Native Hawaiian or other Pacific Islander, non-Hispanic/Latino; 0.4% American Indian or Alaska Native, non-Hispanic/Latino; 4% Two or more races, non-Hispanic/Latino; 6% Race/ethnicity unknown; 0.3% international; 2% transferred in.
**Freshmen** *Admission:* 1,334 enrolled.
**Faculty** *Total:* 410, 38% full-time, 14% with terminal degrees. *Student/faculty ratio:* 16:1.
**Majors** Accounting technology and bookkeeping; architectural engineering technology; automation engineer technology; automobile/automotive mechanics technology; baking and pastry arts; biology/biological sciences; business administration and management; business/commerce; child-care provision; cinematography and film/video production; communications technology; community health services counseling; computer programming; computer programming (specific applications); computer systems networking and telecommunications; corrections; criminal justice/police science; culinary arts; dental assisting; dental hygiene; drafting and design technology; early childhood education; electrical, electronic and communications engineering technology; emergency medical technology (EMT paramedic); engineering technologies and engineering related; entrepreneurship; fire prevention and safety technology; food service systems administration; general studies; graphic design; heating, ventilation, air conditioning and refrigeration engineering technology; histologic technician; liberal arts and sciences/liberal studies; marketing/marketing management; mechanical engineering/mechanical technology; medical radiologic technology; music technology; occupational therapist assistant; photography; physical therapy technology; precision production related; registered nursing/registered nurse; respiratory care therapy; salon/beauty salon management; sign language interpretation and translation; visual and performing arts.
**Academics** *Calendar:* semesters. *Degree:* certificates and associate. *Special study options:* academic remediation for entering students, accelerated degree program, adult/continuing education programs, advanced placement credit, cooperative education, distance learning, double majors, English as a second language, honors programs, independent study, internships, part-time degree program, services for LD students, summer session for credit.
**Library** Charles Stewart Mott Library. Students can reserve study rooms.
**Student Life** *Housing:* college housing not available. *Activities and Organizations:* choral group, Otaku Club, Respiratory Care Student Society, Physical Therapist Assistants, Occupational Therapist Assistants, Transitions Cosmetology, national fraternities, national sororities. *Campus security:* 24-hour emergency response devices and patrols, student patrols, late-night transport/escort service, closed-circuit TV surveillance, whistle alert program, 3P Campaign: Prevent, Protect, and Prosecute Violence Against Women. *Student services:* health clinic, personal/psychological counseling, veterans affairs office.
**Athletics** Member NJCAA. *Intercollegiate sports:* baseball M(s), basketball M(s)/W(s), cross-country running M(s)/W(s), golf M(s), softball W(s), volleyball W(s). *Intramural sports:* cheerleading W(c).
**Costs (2018–19)** *Tuition:* area resident $4215 full-time, $140 per contact hour part-time; state resident $5502 full-time, $183 per contact hour part-time; nonresident $7842 full-time, $261 per contact hour part-time. Full-time tuition and fees vary according to course load. Part-time tuition and fees vary according to course load. *Required fees:* $18 per contact hour part-time, $140 per term part-time. *Payment plan:* installment. *Waivers:* senior citizens and employees or children of employees.
**Applying** *Options:* electronic application, early admission, deferred entrance. *Required:* high school transcript. *Application deadline:* 8/31 (freshmen). *Notification:* continuous (transfers).
**Freshman Application Contact** Ms. Regina Broomfield, Director, Admissions, Mott Community College, 1401 East Court Street, Flint, MI 48503. *Phone:* 810-762-0358. *Toll-free phone:* 800-852-8614. *Fax:* 810-232-9442. *E-mail:* regina.broomfield@mcc.edu. *Website:* http://www.mcc.edu/.

# Muskegon Community College
## Muskegon, Michigan

- **State and locally supported** 2-year, founded 1926, part of Michigan Department of Education
- **Small-town** 112-acre campus with easy access to Grand Rapids
- **Coed,** 4,506 undergraduate students, 33% full-time, 56% women, 44% men

**Undergraduates** 1,488 full-time, 3,018 part-time. Students come from 4 states and territories; 9% Black or African American, non-Hispanic/Latino; 3% Hispanic/Latino; 0.8% Asian, non-Hispanic/Latino; 0.1% Native Hawaiian or other Pacific Islander, non-Hispanic/Latino; 0.9% American Indian or Alaska Native, non-Hispanic/Latino; 4% Two or more races, non-Hispanic/Latino; 5% Race/ethnicity unknown; 0.4% international. *Retention:* 59% of full-time freshmen returned.
**Freshmen** *Admission:* 802 applied, 802 admitted, 802 enrolled.
**Faculty** *Total:* 324, 26% full-time. *Student/faculty ratio:* 19:1.
**Majors** Accounting; administrative assistant and secretarial science; advertising; anthropology; applied mathematics; art; art history, criticism and conservation; art teacher education; automobile/automotive mechanics technology; biology/biotechnology laboratory technician; biomedical technology; business administration and management; business machine repair; chemical engineering; child development; commercial and advertising art; criminal justice/law enforcement administration; data processing and data processing technology; design and applied arts related; developmental and child psychology; drafting and design technology; economics; education; electrical, electronic and communications engineering technology; electromechanical technology; elementary education; engineering technology; finance; hospitality administration; hospitality and recreation marketing; hotel/motel administration; industrial technology; information science/studies; legal administrative assistant/secretary; liberal arts and sciences/liberal studies; machine tool technology; marketing/marketing management; medical administrative assistant and medical secretary; parks, recreation and leisure; registered nursing/registered nurse; special products marketing; transportation and materials moving related; welding technology.
**Academics** *Calendar:* semesters. *Degree:* associate. *Special study options:* academic remediation for entering students, adult/continuing education programs, cooperative education, honors programs, part-time degree program, student-designed majors, summer session for credit.
**Library** Hendrik Meijer and Technology Center.
**Student Life** *Housing:* college housing not available. *Activities and Organizations:* drama/theater group, student-run newspaper, choral group, Respiratory Therapy, Hispanic Student Organization, Black Student Alliance, International Club, Rotaract. *Campus security:* 24-hour emergency response devices, on-campus security officer. *Student services:* personal/psychological counseling.
**Athletics** Member NJCAA. *Intercollegiate sports:* baseball M, basketball M(s)/W(s), golf M/W, softball W, tennis M/W, volleyball W(s), wrestling M. *Intramural sports:* basketball M/W, skiing (downhill) M(c)/W(c).
**Costs (2017–18)** *Tuition:* area resident $3150 full-time; state resident $5880 full-time; nonresident $8220 full-time. *Required fees:* $1080 full-time. *Payment plan:* deferred payment. *Waivers:* senior citizens.
**Financial Aid** Of all full-time matriculated undergraduates who enrolled in 2016, 250 Federal Work-Study jobs (averaging $2500). 50 state and other part-time jobs (averaging $2500).
**Applying** *Options:* electronic application, early admission, deferred entrance. *Required:* high school transcript. *Application deadlines:* rolling (freshmen), rolling (transfers). *Notification:* continuous (freshmen), continuous (transfers).
**Freshman Application Contact** Mr. Johnathon Skidmore, Senior Clerk 1 Admissions, Muskegon Community College, 221 South Quarterline Road, Muskegon, MI 49442-1493. *Phone:* 231-777-0366. *Toll-free phone:* 866-711-4622. *E-mail:* johnathon.skidmore@muskegoncc.edu. *Website:* http://www.muskegoncc.edu/.

# North Central Michigan College
## Petoskey, Michigan

**Director of Admissions** Ms. Julieanne Tobin, Director of Enrollment Management, North Central Michigan College, 1515 Howard Street, Petoskey, MI 49770-8717. *Phone:* 231-439-6511. *Toll-free phone:* 888-298-6605. *E-mail:* jtobin@ncmich.edu. *Website:* http://www.ncmich.edu/.

# Northwestern Michigan College
## Traverse City, Michigan

**Freshman Application Contact** Catheryn Claerhout, Director of Admissions, Northwestern Michigan College, 1701 E. Front Street, Traverse City, MI 49686. *Phone:* 231-995-1034. *Toll-free phone:* 800-748-0566. *E-mail:* c.claerhout@nmc.edu. *Website:* http://www.nmc.edu/.

# Oakland Community College
## Bloomfield Hills, Michigan

**Freshman Application Contact** Stephan M. Linden, Registrar, Oakland Community College, 2480 Opdyke Road, Bloomfield Hills, MI 48304-2266. *Phone:* 248-341-2192. *Fax:* 248-341-2099. *E-mail:* smlinden@oaklandcc.edu. *Website:* http://www.oaklandcc.edu/.

# Saginaw Chippewa Tribal College
## Mount Pleasant, Michigan

- **Independent** 2-year, founded 1998
- **Small-town** campus
- **Coed,** 140 undergraduate students, 26% full-time, 69% women, 31% men

**Undergraduates** 36 full-time, 104 part-time. 2% Black or African American, non-Hispanic/Latino; 6% Hispanic/Latino; 72% American Indian or Alaska Native, non-Hispanic/Latino; 2% Two or more races, non-Hispanic/Latino.
**Freshmen** *Admission:* 81 enrolled.
**Faculty** *Total:* 22, 36% full-time, 14% with terminal degrees. *Student/faculty ratio:* 6:1.
**Majors** American Indian/Native American studies; business/commerce; liberal arts and sciences/liberal studies.
**Academics** *Calendar:* semesters. *Degree:* associate. *Special study options:* part-time degree program, summer session for credit.
**Library** Saginaw Chippewa Tribal College Library. *Books:* 2,134 (physical), 12,155 (digital/electronic); *Serial titles:* 4 (physical). Students can reserve study rooms.
**Student Life** *Housing:* college housing not available.
**Costs (2018–19)** *One-time required fee:* $25. *Tuition:* $1560 full-time, $60 per credit hour part-time. Full-time tuition and fees vary according to class time, course level, course load, degree level, location, program, and student level. Part-time tuition and fees vary according to class time, course level, course load, degree level, location, program, and student level. *Required fees:* $25 per credit hour part-time. *Payment plans:* installment, deferred payment. *Waivers:* minority students.
**Applying** *Options:* electronic application. *Required:* high school transcript.
**Freshman Application Contact** Ms. Amanda Flaugher, Admissions Officer/Registrar/Financial Aid, Saginaw Chippewa Tribal College, 2274 Enterprise Drive, Mount Pleasant, MI 48858. *Phone:* 989-317-4760. *Fax:* 989-317-4781. *E-mail:* aflaugher@sagchip.edu. *Website:* http://www.sagchip.edu/.

# St. Clair County Community College
## Port Huron, Michigan

- **State and locally supported** 2-year, founded 1923, part of Michigan Department of Education
- **Small-town** 25-acre campus with easy access to Detroit
- **Coed**

**Undergraduates** 1,415 full-time, 2,210 part-time. *Retention:* 58% of full-time freshmen returned.
**Faculty** *Student/faculty ratio:* 19:1.
**Academics** *Calendar:* semesters. *Degree:* certificates and associate. *Special study options:* academic remediation for entering students, adult/continuing education programs, advanced placement credit, cooperative education, distance learning, honors programs, independent study, part-time degree program, services for LD students, summer session for credit.
**Library** Main Library plus 1 other.
**Student Life** *Campus security:* 24-hour emergency response devices, late-night transport/escort service, patrols by security until 10 pm.
**Athletics** Member NJCAA.
**Costs (2017–18)** *Tuition:* area resident $4154 full-time, $117 per contact hour part-time; state resident $7564 full-time, $227 per contact hour part-time; nonresident $10,757 full-time, $330 per contact hour part-time. Full-time tuition and fees vary according to course load and location. Part-time tuition and fees vary according to course load and location. *Required fees:* $174 full-time, $17 per contact hour part-time, $87 per term part-time.
**Applying** *Options:* electronic application, early admission. *Required:* high school transcript.
**Freshman Application Contact** St. Clair County Community College, 323 Erie Street, PO Box 5015, Port Huron, MI 48061-5015. *Phone:* 810-989-5501. *Toll-free phone:* 800-553-2427. *Website:* http://www.sc4.edu/.

# Schoolcraft College
## Livonia, Michigan

- **District-supported** primarily 2-year, founded 1961, part of Michigan Department of Education
- **Suburban** campus with easy access to Detroit
- **Coed,** 10,558 undergraduate students, 28% full-time, 53% women, 47% men

**Undergraduates** 2,955 full-time, 7,603 part-time. 14% Black or African American, non-Hispanic/Latino; 5% Hispanic/Latino; 4% Asian, non-Hispanic/Latino; 0.1% Native Hawaiian or other Pacific Islander, non-Hispanic/Latino; 0.6% American Indian or Alaska Native, non-Hispanic/Latino; 3% Two or more races, non-Hispanic/Latino; 7% Race/ethnicity unknown; 2% international; 23% transferred in. *Retention:* 62% of full-time freshmen returned.
**Freshmen** *Admission:* 1,906 enrolled. *Average high school GPA:* 2.8.
**Faculty** *Total:* 515, 20% full-time. *Student/faculty ratio:* 23:1.
**Majors** Accounting technology and bookkeeping; biomedical technology; business administration and management; business automation/technology/data entry; business/commerce; child development; computer graphics; computer programming; computer programming (specific applications); computer systems networking and telecommunications; criminal justice/police science; culinary arts; drafting and design technology; education; electrical, electronic and communications engineering technology; emergency medical technology (EMT paramedic); engineering; environmental engineering technology; fine arts related; fire science/firefighting; fire services administration; foods and nutrition related; general studies; health information/medical records technology; health services/allied health/health sciences; homeland security, law enforcement, firefighting and protective services related; manufacturing engineering technology; marketing/marketing management; massage therapy; mechatronics, robotics, and automation engineering; metallurgical technology; physical fitness technician; plastics and polymer engineering technology; pre-pharmacy studies; radio and television broadcasting technology; recording arts technology; registered nursing/registered nurse; salon/beauty salon management; small business administration; web page, digital/multimedia and information resources design; welding technology.
**Academics** *Calendar:* semesters. *Degrees:* certificates, associate, and bachelor's. *Special study options:* academic remediation for entering students, advanced placement credit, distance learning, English as a second language, honors programs, independent study, internships, part-time degree program, services for LD students, study abroad, summer session for credit.
**Library** Bradner Library plus 1 other. *Books:* 67,778 (physical), 74,201 (digital/electronic); *Databases:* 147. Students can reserve study rooms.
**Student Life** *Housing:* college housing not available. *Activities and Organizations:* drama/theater group, student-run newspaper, choral group, Phi Theta Kappa, The Schoolcraft Connection Newspaper, Student Activities Board, Project Playhem Gaming Club, Otaku Anime Japanese Animation Club. *Campus security:* 24-hour emergency response devices and patrols, late-night transport/escort service. *Student services:* health clinic, personal/psychological counseling, women's center, veterans affairs office.
**Athletics** Member NJCAA. *Intercollegiate sports:* baseball M, basketball M(s)/W(s), bowling M/W, cross-country running M/W, golf M, soccer M(s)/W(s), softball W, volleyball W(s).
**Costs (2017–18)** *Tuition:* area resident $3240 full-time, $108 per credit hour part-time; state resident $4710 full-time, $157 per credit hour part-time; nonresident $6930 full-time, $231 per credit hour part-time. *Required fees:* $952 full-time, $23 per credit hour part-time, $43 per term part-time. *Payment plans:* installment, deferred payment. *Waivers:* senior citizens and employees or children of employees.
**Financial Aid** Of all full-time matriculated undergraduates who enrolled in 2017, 124 Federal Work-Study jobs (averaging $4000).
**Applying** *Options:* electronic application, early admission, deferred entrance. *Required for some:* high school transcript. *Recommended:* high school transcript. *Application deadlines:* rolling (freshmen), rolling (transfers).
**Freshman Application Contact** Ms. Lisa Bushaw, Director of Admissions, Schoolcraft College, 18600 Haggerty Road, Livonia, MI 48152-2696. *Phone:* 734-462-4683. *E-mail:* admissions@schoolcraft.edu.
*Website:* http://www.schoolcraft.edu/.

# Southwestern Michigan College
## Dowagiac, Michigan

- **State and locally supported** 2-year, founded 1964
- **Rural** 240-acre campus
- **Coed,** 2,330 undergraduate students, 44% full-time, 57% women, 43% men

**Undergraduates** 1,035 full-time, 1,295 part-time. Students come from 11 states and territories; 15% are from out of state; 13% Black or African American, non-Hispanic/Latino; 5% Hispanic/Latino; 1% Asian, non-Hispanic/Latino; 0.1% Native Hawaiian or other Pacific Islander, non-Hispanic/Latino; 1% American Indian or Alaska Native, non-Hispanic/Latino; 5% Two or more races, non-Hispanic/Latino; 4% Race/ethnicity unknown; 7% transferred in; 23% live on campus. *Retention:* 54% of full-time freshmen returned.
**Freshmen** *Admission:* 2,175 applied, 2,175 admitted, 651 enrolled.
**Faculty** *Total:* 114, 49% full-time, 30% with terminal degrees. *Student/faculty ratio:* 20:1.
**Majors** Accounting technology and bookkeeping; agricultural production; automation engineer technology; automobile/automotive mechanics technology; business administration and management; carpentry; computer programming; computer systems networking and telecommunications; criminal justice/safety; early childhood education; engineering technology; fire science/firefighting; general studies; graphic design; health information/medical records technology; industrial mechanics and maintenance technology; liberal arts and sciences/liberal studies; medical/clinical assistant; registered nursing/registered nurse; social work; sport and fitness administration/management.
**Academics** *Calendar:* semesters. *Degree:* certificates and associate. *Special study options:* academic remediation for entering students, accelerated degree program, adult/continuing education programs, advanced placement credit, cooperative education, English as a second language, honors programs, independent study, internships, part-time degree program, services for LD students, summer session for credit.
**Library** Fred L. Mathews Library. *Books:* 22,764 (physical), 694 (digital/electronic); *Serial titles:* 6 (physical), 27,996 (digital/electronic); *Databases:* 24. Weekly public service hours: 61; students can reserve study rooms.
**Student Life** *Housing Options:* coed. Campus housing is university owned. *Activities and Organizations:* drama/theater group, choral group, Advocates for All, Business Club, Criminal Justice Club, Rock Climbing Club, STEM Club. *Campus security:* 24-hour emergency response devices and patrols, controlled dormitory access, Day and evening police patrols. *Student services:* personal/psychological counseling.
**Athletics** *Intramural sports:* basketball M/W, football M/W, racquetball M/W, rock climbing M/W, soccer M/W, softball M/W, ultimate Frisbee M/W, volleyball M/W.
**Costs (2017–18)** *Tuition:* area resident $3068 full-time, $118 per contact hour part-time; state resident $4004 full-time, $154 per contact hour part-time; nonresident $4368 full-time, $168 per contact hour part-time. *Required fees:* $1287 full-time, $50 per contact hour part-time. *Room and board:* $9950; room only: $6350. *Payment plan:* installment. *Waivers:* employees or children of employees.
**Financial Aid** Of all full-time matriculated undergraduates who enrolled in 2016, 125 Federal Work-Study jobs (averaging $1000). 75 state and other part-time jobs (averaging $1000).
**Applying** *Options:* electronic application, deferred entrance. *Required:* high school transcript. *Required for some:* interview. *Application deadlines:* rolling (freshmen), rolling (transfers). *Notification:* continuous (freshmen), continuous (transfers).
**Freshman Application Contact** Mr. Jason Smith, Director of Admissions, Southwestern Michigan College, Dowagiac, MI 49047. *Phone:* 269-782-1000 Ext. 1238. *Toll-free phone:* 800-456-8675. *Fax:* 269-782-1331. *E-mail:* jsmith07@swmich.edu.
*Website:* http://www.swmich.edu/.

# Washtenaw Community College
## Ann Arbor, Michigan

**Freshman Application Contact** Washtenaw Community College, 4800 East Huron River Drive, PO Box D-1, Ann Arbor, MI 48106. *Phone:* 734-973-3315. *Website:* http://www.wccnet.edu/.

# Wayne County Community College District
## Detroit, Michigan

- **State and locally supported** 2-year, founded 1967
- **Urban** campus
- **Coed,** 14,806 undergraduate students, 14% full-time, 64% women, 36% men

**Undergraduates** 2,062 full-time, 12,744 part-time. 67% Black or African American, non-Hispanic/Latino; 2% Hispanic/Latino; 0.8% Asian, non-Hispanic/Latino; 0.1% Native Hawaiian or other Pacific Islander, non-Hispanic/Latino; 0.2% American Indian or Alaska Native, non-Hispanic/Latino; 5% Two or more races, non-Hispanic/Latino; 7% Race/ethnicity unknown; 1% international; 10% transferred in.
**Freshmen** *Admission:* 2,332 enrolled.

**Faculty** *Student/faculty ratio:* 17:1.

**Majors** Accounting technology and bookkeeping; adult development and aging; aircraft powerplant technology; airframe mechanics and aircraft maintenance technology; American Sign Language (ASL); anesthesiologist assistant; autobody/collision and repair technology; automobile/automotive mechanics technology; biomedical technology; building/property maintenance; business administration and management; CAD/CADD drafting/design technology; child-care and support services management; computer numerically controlled (CNC) machinist technology; computer programming; corrections; criminal justice/police science; data modeling/warehousing and database administration; dental hygiene; digital communication and media/multimedia; e-commerce; electrical, electronic and communications engineering technology; elementary education; emergency medical technology (EMT paramedic); engineering-related technologies; fashion merchandising; fire prevention and safety technology; food service systems administration; game and interactive media design; heating, air conditioning, ventilation and refrigeration maintenance technology; legal assistant/paralegal; liberal arts and sciences/liberal studies; mortuary science and embalming; office management; pharmacy technician; physician assistant; pre-engineering; psychiatric/mental health services technology; registered nursing/registered nurse; social work; surgical technology; web/multimedia management and webmaster; welding technology.

**Academics** *Calendar:* semesters. *Degree:* certificates and associate. *Special study options:* academic remediation for entering students, adult/continuing education programs, advanced placement credit, cooperative education, distance learning, English as a second language, honors programs, internships, part-time degree program, services for LD students, study abroad, summer session for credit.

**Library** Learning Resource Center.

**Student Life** *Housing:* college housing not available. *Campus security:* 24-hour emergency response devices. *Student services:* veterans affairs office.

**Athletics** Member NJCAA. *Intercollegiate sports:* basketball M/W, bowling M/W, cross-country running M/W, golf M, volleyball W.

**Financial Aid** Of all full-time matriculated undergraduates who enrolled in 2016, 239 Federal Work-Study jobs (averaging $2360). 147 state and other part-time jobs (averaging $1200).

**Applying** *Options:* electronic application, early admission, deferred entrance. *Required:* high school transcript. *Application deadlines:* rolling (freshmen), rolling (transfers).

**Freshman Application Contact** Mr. Adrian Phillips, District Associate Vice Chancellor of Student Services, Wayne County Community College District, 801 West Fort Street, Detroit, MI 48226-9975. *Phone:* 313-496-2820. *Fax:* 313-962-1643. *E-mail:* aphilli1@wcccd.edu. *Website:* http://www.wcccd.edu/.

## West Shore Community College
### Scottville, Michigan

**Freshman Application Contact** Wendy Fought, Director of Admissions, West Shore Community College, PO Box 277, 3000 North Stiles Road, Scottville, MI 49454-0277. *Phone:* 231-843-5503. *Fax:* 231-845-3944. *E-mail:* admissions@westshore.edu. *Website:* http://www.westshore.edu/.

# MINNESOTA

## Alexandria Technical and Community College
### Alexandria, Minnesota

- **State-supported** 2-year, founded 1961, part of Minnesota State Colleges and Universities System
- **Small-town** 98-acre campus
- **Coed,** 2,647 undergraduate students

**Undergraduates** Students come from 25 states and territories; 3% are from out of state; 1% Black or African American, non-Hispanic/Latino; 2% Hispanic/Latino; 1% Asian, non-Hispanic/Latino; 0.1% Native Hawaiian or other Pacific Islander, non-Hispanic/Latino; 1% American Indian or Alaska Native, non-Hispanic/Latino; 7% Race/ethnicity unknown.

**Faculty** *Total:* 96, 67% full-time, 6% with terminal degrees. *Student/faculty ratio:* 20:1.

**Majors** Accounting; automation engineer technology; business administration and management; business/commerce; clinical/medical laboratory technology; commercial and advertising art; computer systems networking and telecommunications; criminal justice/police science; diesel mechanics technology; early childhood education; fashion merchandising; human services; information science/studies; interior design; legal administrative assistant/secretary; legal assistant/paralegal; liberal arts and sciences/liberal studies; mechanical drafting and CAD/CADD; medical administrative assistant and medical secretary; multi/interdisciplinary studies related; office management; physical fitness technician; pre-engineering; registered nursing/registered nurse; sales, distribution, and marketing operations; speech-language pathology assistant.

**Academics** *Calendar:* semesters. *Degree:* certificates, diplomas, and associate. *Special study options:* academic remediation for entering students, advanced placement credit, distance learning, double majors, independent study, internships, part-time degree program, services for LD students, student-designed majors, summer session for credit.

**Library** Learning Resource Center. *Books:* 7,582 (physical), 13,367 (digital/electronic); *Serial titles:* 24 (physical); *Databases:* 14. Weekly public service hours: 51; students can reserve study rooms.

**Student Life** *Housing:* college housing not available. *Activities and Organizations:* Student Senate, Intercultural Club, Trapshooting League, GAT (Gamers of Alex Tech), Book Club. *Campus security:* student patrols, late-night transport/escort service, security cameras inside and outside. *Student services:* personal/psychological counseling, veterans affairs office.

**Athletics** *Intramural sports:* basketball M/W, football M/W, softball M/W, volleyball M/W.

**Costs (2017–18)** *Tuition:* state resident $4816 full-time, $161 per credit part-time; nonresident $4816 full-time, $161 per credit part-time. *Required fees:* $594 full-time, $20 per credit part-time. *Payment plan:* deferred payment. *Waivers:* senior citizens and employees or children of employees.

**Financial Aid** Of all full-time matriculated undergraduates who enrolled in 2016, 94 Federal Work-Study jobs (averaging $1871).

**Applying** *Options:* electronic application, early admission, deferred entrance. *Application fee:* $20. *Required for some:* high school transcript, interview. *Recommended:* interview. *Application deadlines:* rolling (freshmen), rolling (transfers). *Notification:* continuous (freshmen), continuous (transfers).

**Freshman Application Contact** Vicki Sward, Information Center Manager, Alexandria Technical and Community College, 1601 Jefferson Street, Alexandria, MN 56308. *Phone:* 320-762-4600. *Toll-free phone:* 888-234-1222. *Fax:* 320-762-4501. *E-mail:* info@alextech.edu. *Website:* http://www.alextech.edu/.

## Anoka-Ramsey Community College
### Coon Rapids, Minnesota

- **State-supported** 2-year, founded 1965, part of Minnesota State Colleges and Universities System
- **Suburban** 230-acre campus with easy access to Minneapolis-St. Paul
- **Coed**

**Undergraduates** 3,386 full-time, 5,488 part-time. 9% Black or African American, non-Hispanic/Latino; 5% Hispanic/Latino; 4% Asian, non-Hispanic/Latino; 0.1% Native Hawaiian or other Pacific Islander, non-Hispanic/Latino; 0.5% American Indian or Alaska Native, non-Hispanic/Latino; 4% Two or more races, non-Hispanic/Latino; 0.8% Race/ethnicity unknown; 0.5% international; 25% transferred in. *Retention:* 54% of full-time freshmen returned.

**Faculty** *Student/faculty ratio:* 32:1.

**Academics** *Calendar:* semesters. *Degree:* certificates and associate. *Special study options:* academic remediation for entering students, accelerated degree program, advanced placement credit, cooperative education, distance learning, double majors, English as a second language, honors programs, independent study, internships, off-campus study, part-time degree program, services for LD students, study abroad, summer session for credit. *ROTC:* Air Force (c).

**Library** Coon Rapids Campus Library plus 1 other. *Books:* 56,573 (physical), 15,450 (digital/electronic); *Serial titles:* 176 (physical), 71 (digital/electronic); *Databases:* 30. Weekly public service hours: 63.

**Student Life** *Campus security:* 24-hour emergency response devices, late-night transport/escort service.

**Athletics** Member NJCAA.

**Costs (2017–18)** *Tuition:* state resident $4305 full-time, $144 per credit part-time; nonresident $4305 full-time, $144 per credit part-time. Full-time tuition and fees vary according to course load and program. Part-time tuition and fees vary according to course load and program. *Required fees:* $665 full-time, $22 per credit part-time. *Payment plans:* installment, deferred payment.

**Applying** *Options:* electronic application, early admission, deferred entrance. *Required for some:* high school transcript.

**Freshman Application Contact** Admissions Department, Anoka-Ramsey Community College, 11200 Mississippi Boulevard NW, Coon Rapids, MN 55433-3470. *Phone:* 763-433-1300. *Fax:* 763-433-1521. *E-mail:* admissions@anokaramsey.edu. *Website:* http://www.anokaramsey.edu/.

# Anoka Technical College
## Anoka, Minnesota

- **State-supported** 2-year, founded 1967, part of Minnesota State Colleges and Universities System
- **Small-town** 23-acre campus with easy access to Minneapolis-St. Paul
- **Coed**

**Undergraduates** 832 full-time, 977 part-time. 9% Black or African American, non-Hispanic/Latino; 4% Hispanic/Latino; 4% Asian, non-Hispanic/Latino; 0.1% Native Hawaiian or other Pacific Islander, non-Hispanic/Latino; 0.4% American Indian or Alaska Native, non-Hispanic/Latino; 4% Two or more races, non-Hispanic/Latino; 1% Race/ethnicity unknown; 0.1% international; 55% transferred in. *Retention:* 49% of full-time freshmen returned.
**Faculty** *Student/faculty ratio:* 18:1.
**Academics** *Calendar:* semesters. *Degree:* certificates, diplomas, and associate. *Special study options:* academic remediation for entering students, advanced placement credit, cooperative education, distance learning, double majors, English as a second language, internships, part-time degree program, services for LD students.
**Library** Anoka Technical College Library. *Books:* 7,402 (physical), 8,635 (digital/electronic); *Serial titles:* 17 (physical), 2 (digital/electronic); *Databases:* 41. Weekly public service hours: 59; students can reserve study rooms.
**Student Life** *Campus security:* 24-hour emergency response devices, late-night transport/escort service.
**Costs (2017–18)** *Tuition:* state resident $4960 full-time, $165 per credit part-time; nonresident $4960 full-time, $165 per credit part-time. Full-time tuition and fees vary according to course load, program, and reciprocity agreements. Part-time tuition and fees vary according to course load, program, and reciprocity agreements. *Required fees:* $575 full-time, $19 per credit part-time.
**Applying** *Options:* electronic application, deferred entrance. *Required:* high school transcript. *Required for some:* interview.
**Freshman Application Contact** Enrollment Services, Anoka Technical College, 1355 West Highway 10, Anoka, MN 55303. *Phone:* 763-576-7710. *E-mail:* enrollmentservices@anokatech.edu. *Website:* http://www.anokatech.edu/.

# Central Lakes College
## Brainerd, Minnesota

- **State-supported** 2-year, founded 1938, part of Minnesota State Colleges and Universities System
- **Small-town** campus
- **Endowment** $7.3 million
- **Coed,** 3,715 undergraduate students, 42% full-time, 56% women, 44% men

**Undergraduates** 1,559 full-time, 2,156 part-time. Students come from 26 states and territories; 2% are from out of state; 2% Black or African American, non-Hispanic/Latino; 2% Hispanic/Latino; 0.8% Asian, non-Hispanic/Latino; 0.1% Native Hawaiian or other Pacific Islander, non-Hispanic/Latino; 1% American Indian or Alaska Native, non-Hispanic/Latino; 4% Two or more races, non-Hispanic/Latino; 2% Race/ethnicity unknown; 0.2% international. *Retention:* 58% of full-time freshmen returned.
**Faculty** *Total:* 135, 69% full-time. *Student/faculty ratio:* 20:1.
**Majors** Accounting; administrative assistant and secretarial science; applied horticulture/horticulture operations; business administration and management; child-care and support services management; commercial and advertising art; computer systems networking and telecommunications; computer technology/computer systems technology; conservation biology; criminalistics and criminal science; criminal justice/police science; criminal justice/safety; developmental and child psychology; diesel mechanics technology; engineering; horticultural science; industrial electronics technology; industrial engineering; kindergarten/preschool education; legal administrative assistant/secretary; liberal arts and sciences/liberal studies; machine tool technology; marketing/marketing management; mechanical drafting and CAD/CADD; medical administrative assistant and medical secretary; natural resources/conservation; photographic and film/video technology; registered nursing/registered nurse; robotics technology; welding technology.
**Academics** *Calendar:* semesters. *Degree:* certificates, diplomas, and associate. *Special study options:* academic remediation for entering students, advanced placement credit, distance learning, English as a second language, external degree program, independent study, internships, off-campus study, part-time degree program, services for LD students, summer session for credit.
**Library** Learning Resource Center.
**Student Life** *Housing:* college housing not available. *Activities and Organizations:* drama/theater group, student-run newspaper, television station, choral group. *Campus security:* 24-hour emergency response devices and

patrols, student patrols, late-night transport/escort service. *Student services:* health clinic, personal/psychological counseling, veterans affairs office.
**Athletics** Member NJCAA. *Intercollegiate sports:* baseball M, basketball M/W, football M, softball W, volleyball W. *Intramural sports:* basketball M/W, bowling M/W, football M, softball M/W, tennis M/W, volleyball M/W.
**Costs (2017–18)** *Tuition:* state resident $4773 full-time, $159 per credit hour part-time; nonresident $4773 full-time, $159 per credit hour part-time. Full-time tuition and fees vary according to course load and program. Part-time tuition and fees vary according to course load and program. *Required fees:* $672 full-time, $22 per credit hour part-time. *Payment plan:* installment. *Waivers:* senior citizens and employees or children of employees.
**Applying** *Options:* electronic application, deferred entrance. *Application fee:* $20. *Required:* high school transcript. *Application deadlines:* rolling (freshmen), rolling (transfers).
**Freshman Application Contact** Ms. Rose Tretter, Central Lakes College, 501 West College Drive, Brainerd, MN 56401-3904. *Phone:* 218-855-8036. *Toll-free phone:* 800-933-0346. *Fax:* 218-855-8220. *E-mail:* rtretter@clcmn.edu. *Website:* http://www.clcmn.edu/.

# Century College
## White Bear Lake, Minnesota

- **State-supported** 2-year, founded 1970, part of Minnesota State Colleges and Universities System
- **Suburban** 170-acre campus with easy access to Minneapolis-St. Paul
- **Coed,** 8,442 undergraduate students, 43% full-time, 56% women, 44% men

**Undergraduates** 3,641 full-time, 4,801 part-time. Students come from 37 states and territories; 50 other countries; 6% are from out of state; 10% Black or African American, non-Hispanic/Latino; 8% Hispanic/Latino; 18% Asian, non-Hispanic/Latino; 0.1% Native Hawaiian or other Pacific Islander, non-Hispanic/Latino; 0.3% American Indian or Alaska Native, non-Hispanic/Latino; 5% Two or more races, non-Hispanic/Latino; 0.8% Race/ethnicity unknown; 2% international; 42% transferred in.
**Freshmen** *Admission:* 2,807 applied, 2,807 admitted, 1,126 enrolled.
**Faculty** *Total:* 362, 50% full-time, 16% with terminal degrees. *Student/faculty ratio:* 22:1.
**Majors** Accounting; administrative assistant and secretarial science; animation, interactive technology, video graphics and special effects; applied horticulture/horticulture operations; biology/biological sciences; building/property maintenance; business administration and management; business/commerce; CAD/CADD drafting/design technology; cinematography and film/video production; commercial photography; computer and information systems security; computer science; computer systems networking and telecommunications; computer technology/computer systems technology; cosmetology; criminal justice/police science; criminal justice/safety; cyber/computer forensics and counterterrorism; data processing and data processing technology; dental assisting; dental hygiene; e-commerce; education; emergency medical technology (EMT paramedic); energy management and systems technology; engineering technology; fine/studio arts; graphic design; health services/allied health/health sciences; heating, air conditioning, ventilation and refrigeration maintenance technology; homeland security, law enforcement, firefighting and protective services related; horticultural science; human services; information science/studies; interior design; language interpretation and translation; liberal arts and sciences/liberal studies; marketing/marketing management; medical administrative assistant and medical secretary; multi/interdisciplinary studies related; music; orthotics/prosthetics; pre-engineering; radiologic technology/science; registered nursing/registered nurse; substance abuse/addiction counseling; teacher assistant/aide; web page, digital/multimedia and information resources design.
**Academics** *Calendar:* semesters. *Degree:* certificates, diplomas, and associate. *Special study options:* academic remediation for entering students, advanced placement credit, distance learning, double majors, English as a second language, honors programs, independent study, internships, part-time degree program, services for LD students, student-designed majors, summer session for credit. *ROTC:* Air Force (c).
**Library** Century College Library. *Books:* 58,410 (physical), 180,870 (digital/electronic); *Serial titles:* 285 (physical), 39,784 (digital/electronic); *Databases:* 61. Weekly public service hours: 65; students can reserve study rooms.
**Student Life** *Housing:* college housing not available. *Activities and Organizations:* drama/theater group, student-run newspaper, choral group, Anime Club, Phi Theta Kappa, Planning Activities Committee, Spanish Club, Nursing. *Campus security:* late-night transport/escort service, day patrols. *Student services:* health clinic, personal/psychological counseling, veterans affairs office.
**Athletics** Member NJCAA. *Intercollegiate sports:* baseball M, soccer M/W, softball W. *Intramural sports:* badminton M/W, basketball M/W, bowling

M/W, football M/W, ice hockey M/W, skiing (downhill) M/W, soccer M/W, softball M/W, table tennis M/W, ultimate Frisbee M/W, volleyball M/W.

**Costs (2017–18)** *Tuition:* state resident $4817 full-time, $161 per semester hour part-time; nonresident $4817 full-time, $161 per semester hour part-time. Full-time tuition and fees vary according to class time, program, and reciprocity agreements. Part-time tuition and fees vary according to class time, program, and reciprocity agreements. *Required fees:* $600 full-time, $20 per semester hour part-time. *Payment plan:* installment. *Waivers:* senior citizens and employees or children of employees.

**Financial Aid** Of all full-time matriculated undergraduates who enrolled in 2016, 81 Federal Work-Study jobs (averaging $2763). 85 state and other part-time jobs (averaging $2646).

**Applying** *Options:* electronic application, deferred entrance. *Application fee:* $20. *Required:* high school transcript. *Application deadlines:* rolling (freshmen), rolling (transfers).

**Freshman Application Contact** Robert Beaver, Assistant Admissions Director, Century College, 3300 Century Avenue North, White Bear Lake, MN 55110. *Phone:* 651-779-5744. *Toll-free phone:* 800-228-1978. *Fax:* 651-773-1796. *E-mail:* admissions@century.edu. *Website:* http://www.century.edu/.

## Dakota County Technical College
### Rosemount, Minnesota

**Freshman Application Contact** Mr. Patrick Lair, Admissions Director, Dakota County Technical College, 1300 East 145th Street, Rosemount, MN 55068. *Phone:* 651-423-8399. *Toll-free phone:* 877-YES-DCTC. *Fax:* 651-423-8775. *E-mail:* admissions@dctc.mnscu.edu. *Website:* http://www.dctc.edu/.

## Dunwoody College of Technology
### Minneapolis, Minnesota

- **Independent** primarily 2-year, founded 1914
- **Urban** 12-acre campus with easy access to Minneapolis-St. Paul
- **Endowment** $22.3 million
- **Coed, primarily men,** 1,302 undergraduate students, 82% full-time, 17% women, 83% men

**Undergraduates** 1,073 full-time, 229 part-time. Students come from 3 other countries; 2% are from out of state; 4% Black or African American, non-Hispanic/Latino; 3% Hispanic/Latino; 7% Asian, non-Hispanic/Latino; 0.5% Native Hawaiian or other Pacific Islander, non-Hispanic/Latino; 0.5% American Indian or Alaska Native, non-Hispanic/Latino; 5% Two or more races, non-Hispanic/Latino; 6% Race/ethnicity unknown; 0.2% international; 21% transferred in. *Retention:* 89% of full-time freshmen returned.

**Freshmen** *Admission:* 1,171 applied, 791 admitted, 184 enrolled. *Average high school GPA:* 2.7.

**Faculty** *Total:* 165, 52% full-time, 15% with terminal degrees. *Student/faculty ratio:* 10:1.

**Majors** Architectural technology; architecture; autobody/collision and repair technology; automobile/automotive mechanics technology; building/construction site management; business administration and management; CAD/CADD drafting/design technology; civil engineering technology; computer numerically controlled (CNC) machinist technology; computer science; computer software engineering; computer systems networking and telecommunications; construction management; desktop publishing and digital imaging design; electrical, electronic and communications engineering technology; electrical/electronics drafting and CAD/CADD; electrician; graphic design; heating, air conditioning, ventilation and refrigeration maintenance technology; heating, ventilation, air conditioning and refrigeration engineering technology; interior design; manufacturing engineering; mechanical engineering; medical radiologic technology; robotics technology; web page, digital/multimedia and information resources design; welding technology.

**Academics** *Calendar:* semesters. *Degrees:* certificates, associate, and bachelor's. *Special study options:* academic remediation for entering students, adult/continuing education programs, cooperative education, distance learning, independent study, internships, study abroad, summer session for credit.

**Library** Learning Resource Center plus 1 other. *Books:* 5,500 (physical), 179,443 (digital/electronic); *Serial titles:* 133 (physical); *Databases:* 26. Weekly public service hours: 55.

**Student Life** *Housing:* college housing not available. *Activities and Organizations:* Phi Theta Kappa, Historic Green, Dunwoody Motorsports Club, Architectural Institute of America Student Chapter, Professional Association for Design. *Campus security:* 24-hour emergency response devices, late-night transport/escort service. *Student services:* women's center.

**Standardized Tests** *Required for some:* ACT (for admission).

**Costs (2017–18)** *Tuition:* $18,826 full-time, $654 per credit part-time. Full-time tuition and fees vary according to course load, degree level, and program. Part-time tuition and fees vary according to course load, degree level, and program. *Required fees:* $1652 full-time, $1458 per term part-time. *Payment plan:* installment. *Waivers:* employees or children of employees.

**Financial Aid** Of all full-time matriculated undergraduates who enrolled in 2016, 937 applied for aid, 829 were judged to have need, 32 had their need fully met. 24 Federal Work-Study jobs (averaging $3486). 29 state and other part-time jobs (averaging $3052). In 2016, 38 non-need-based awards were made. *Average percent of need met:* 36%. *Average financial aid package:* $8856. *Average need-based loan:* $3461. *Average need-based gift aid:* $6950. *Average non-need-based aid:* $3219. *Average indebtedness upon graduation:* $19,167.

**Applying** *Options:* electronic application. *Application fee:* $50. *Required:* essay or personal statement, high school transcript. *Required for some:* minimum 3.0 GPA, letters of recommendation, resume. *Recommended:* minimum 2.5 GPA, interview. *Application deadlines:* rolling (freshmen), rolling (transfers). *Notification:* continuous (freshmen), continuous (transfers).

**Freshman Application Contact** Kelly OBrien, Director of Admissions, Dunwoody College of Technology, 818 Dunwoody Boulevard, Minneapolis, MN 55403. *Phone:* 612-381-3302. *Toll-free phone:* 800-292-4625. *Fax:* 612-677-3131. *E-mail:* kobrien@dunwoody.edu. *Website:* http://www.dunwoody.edu/.

## Fond du Lac Tribal and Community College
### Cloquet, Minnesota

**Freshman Application Contact** Kathie Jubie, Admissions Representative, Fond du Lac Tribal and Community College, 2101 14th Street, Cloquet, MN 55720. *Phone:* 218-879-0808. *Toll-free phone:* 800-657-3712. *E-mail:* admissions@fdltcc.edu. *Website:* http://www.fdltcc.edu/.

## Hennepin Technical College
### Brooklyn Park, Minnesota

- **State-supported** 2-year, founded 1972, part of Minnesota State Colleges and Universities System
- **Suburban** 100-acre campus with easy access to Minneapolis-St. Paul
- **Endowment** $942,735
- **Coed**

**Undergraduates** 4% are from out of state; 23% Black or African American, non-Hispanic/Latino; 8% Hispanic/Latino; 10% Asian, non-Hispanic/Latino; 0.1% Native Hawaiian or other Pacific Islander, non-Hispanic/Latino; 0.5% American Indian or Alaska Native, non-Hispanic/Latino; 2% Two or more races, non-Hispanic/Latino; 2% Race/ethnicity unknown; 0.3% international.

**Faculty** *Student/faculty ratio:* 21:1.

**Academics** *Calendar:* semesters. *Degree:* certificates, diplomas, and associate. *Special study options:* academic remediation for entering students, adult/continuing education programs, advanced placement credit, cooperative education, distance learning, double majors, English as a second language, independent study, internships, part-time degree program, services for LD students, student-designed majors, summer session for credit.

**Library** Hennepin Technical College Library plus 1 other. *Books:* 10,784 (physical), 215,854 (digital/electronic); *Serial titles:* 30 (physical); *Databases:* 48. Weekly public service hours: 60.

**Student Life** *Campus security:* late-night transport/escort service, security service.

**Financial Aid** Of all full-time matriculated undergraduates who enrolled in 2016, 72 Federal Work-Study jobs (averaging $3000).

**Applying** *Options:* electronic application. *Recommended:* high school transcript.

**Freshman Application Contact** Admissions, Hennepin Technical College, 9000 Brooklyn Boulevard, Brooklyn Park, MN 55445. *Phone:* 763-488-2580. *Toll-free phone:* 800-345-4655 (in-state); 800-645-4655 (out-of-state). *Fax:* 763-550-2113. *E-mail:* info@hennepintech.edu. *Website:* http://www.hennepintech.edu/.

## Herzing University
### Minneapolis, Minnesota

**Freshman Application Contact** Ms. Shelly Larson, Director of Admissions, Herzing University, 5700 West Broadway, Minneapolis, MN 55428. *Phone:* 763-231-3155. *Toll-free phone:* 800-596-0724. *Fax:* 763-535-9205. *E-mail:* info@mpls.herzing.edu. *Website:* http://www.herzing.edu/minneapolis

# Hibbing Community College
## Hibbing, Minnesota

**Freshman Application Contact** Admissions, Hibbing Community College, 1515 East 25th Street, Hibbing, MN 55746. *Phone:* 218-262-7200. *Toll-free phone:* 800-224-4HCC. *Fax:* 218-262-6717. *E-mail:* admissions@hibbing.edu. *Website:* http://www.hcc.mnscu.edu/.

# The Institute of Production and Recording
## Minneapolis, Minnesota

**Freshman Application Contact** The Institute of Production and Recording, 300 North 1st Avenue, Suite 500, Minneapolis, MN 55401. *Website:* http://www.ipr.edu/.

# Inver Hills Community College
## Inver Grove Heights, Minnesota

**Freshman Application Contact** Mr. Casey Carmody, Admissions Representative, Inver Hills Community College, 2500 East 80th Street, Inver Grove Heights, MN 55076-3224. *Phone:* 651-450-3589. *Fax:* 651-450-3677. *E-mail:* admissions@inverhills.edu. *Website:* http://www.inverhills.edu/.

# Itasca Community College
## Grand Rapids, Minnesota

**Freshman Application Contact** Ms. Candace Perry, Director of Enrollment Services, Itasca Community College, Grand Rapids, MN 55744. *Phone:* 218-322-2340. *Toll-free phone:* 800-996-6422. *Fax:* 218-327-4350. *E-mail:* iccinfo@itascacc.edu. *Website:* http://www.itascacc.edu/.

# Lake Superior College
## Duluth, Minnesota

- **State-supported** 2-year, founded 1995, part of Minnesota State Colleges and Universities System
- **Urban** 105-acre campus
- **Coed,** 4,388 undergraduate students, 41% full-time, 56% women, 44% men

**Undergraduates** 1,789 full-time, 2,599 part-time. Students come from 33 states and territories; 13 other countries; 13% are from out of state; 3% Black or African American, non-Hispanic/Latino; 3% Hispanic/Latino; 1% Asian, non-Hispanic/Latino; 0.1% Native Hawaiian or other Pacific Islander, non-Hispanic/Latino; 2% American Indian or Alaska Native, non-Hispanic/Latino; 5% Two or more races, non-Hispanic/Latino; 0.8% Race/ethnicity unknown; 1% international; 40% transferred in.
**Freshmen** *Admission:* 1,111 applied, 1,111 admitted, 636 enrolled.
**Faculty** *Total:* 239, 43% full-time, 6% with terminal degrees. *Student/faculty ratio:* 18:1.
**Majors** Accounting; airframe mechanics and aircraft maintenance technology; airline pilot and flight crew; architectural drafting and CAD/CADD; automobile/automotive mechanics technology; aviation/airway management; building construction technology; business administration and management; business automation/technology/data entry; CAD/CADD drafting/design technology; carpentry; civil engineering technology; clinical/medical laboratory technology; computer numerically controlled (CNC) machinist technology; computer technology/computer systems technology; dental hygiene; electrical, electronic and communications engineering technology; electrician; fine/studio arts; fire prevention and safety technology; fire services administration; health services/allied health/health sciences; legal assistant/paralegal; liberal arts and sciences/liberal studies; management information systems; medical administrative assistant and medical secretary; multi/interdisciplinary studies related; network and system administration; office management; physical therapy technology; radiologic technology/science; registered nursing/registered nurse; respiratory care therapy; sheet metal technology; surgical technology; web page, digital/multimedia and information resources design; welding technology.
**Academics** *Calendar:* semesters. *Degree:* certificates, diplomas, and associate. *Special study options:* academic remediation for entering students, advanced placement credit, distance learning, double majors, independent study, internships, part-time degree program, services for LD students, study abroad, summer session for credit.
**Library** Harold P. Erickson Library. Students can reserve study rooms.
**Student Life** *Housing:* college housing not available. *Activities and Organizations:* choral group. *Campus security:* 24-hour emergency response

devices, late-night transport/escort service. *Student services:* personal/psychological counseling, veterans affairs office.
**Athletics** Member NJCAA. *Intercollegiate sports:* soccer M/W.
**Costs (2017–18)** *Tuition:* state resident $4417 full-time, $147 per credit part-time; nonresident $8747 full-time, $292 per credit part-time. Full-time tuition and fees vary according to program and reciprocity agreements. Part-time tuition and fees vary according to program and reciprocity agreements. *Required fees:* $749 full-time. *Payment plans:* installment, deferred payment. *Waivers:* senior citizens and employees or children of employees.
**Applying** *Options:* electronic application. *Application fee:* $20. *Required:* high school transcript. *Application deadlines:* rolling (freshmen), rolling (transfers). *Notification:* continuous (freshmen), continuous (transfers).
**Freshman Application Contact** Ms. Melissa Leno, Director of Admissions, Lake Superior College, 2101 Trinity Road, Duluth, MN 55811. *Phone:* 218-733-5903. *Toll-free phone:* 800-432-2884. *E-mail:* enroll@lsc.edu. *Website:* http://www.lsc.edu/.

# Leech Lake Tribal College
## Cass Lake, Minnesota

**Freshman Application Contact** Ms. Shelly Braford, Recruiter, Leech Lake Tribal College, PO Box 180, 6945 Littlewolf Road NW, Cass Lake, MN 56633. *Phone:* 218-335-4200 Ext. 4270. *Fax:* 218-335-4217. *E-mail:* shelly.braford@lltc.edu. *Website:* http://www.lltc.edu/.

# Mesabi Range College
## Virginia, Minnesota

- **State-supported** 2-year, founded 1918, part of Minnesota State Colleges and Universities System
- **Small-town** 30-acre campus
- **Coed**

**Undergraduates** 648 full-time, 502 part-time. Students come from 6 states and territories; 2 other countries; 4% are from out of state; 7% Black or African American, non-Hispanic/Latino; 1% Hispanic/Latino; 0.3% Asian, non-Hispanic/Latino; 3% American Indian or Alaska Native, non-Hispanic/Latino; 8% Race/ethnicity unknown; 10% live on campus.
**Faculty** *Student/faculty ratio:* 24:1.
**Academics** *Calendar:* semesters. *Degree:* certificates, diplomas, and associate. *Special study options:* academic remediation for entering students, adult/continuing education programs, advanced placement credit, cooperative education, distance learning, independent study, internships, off-campus study, part-time degree program, services for LD students, student-designed majors, study abroad, summer session for credit.
**Library** Mesabi Library.
**Athletics** Member NJCAA.
**Costs (2017–18)** *Tuition:* state resident $4680 full-time, $156 per credit hour part-time; nonresident $5850 full-time, $195 per credit hour part-time. *Required fees:* $582 full-time, $19 per credit hour part-time. *Room and board:* room only: $2100.
**Financial Aid** Of all full-time matriculated undergraduates who enrolled in 2011, 168 Federal Work-Study jobs (averaging $1227). 82 state and other part-time jobs (averaging $1380).
**Applying** *Options:* electronic application, early admission, deferred entrance. *Application fee:* $20. *Required:* high school transcript.
**Freshman Application Contact** Ms. Brenda Kochevar, Enrollment Services Director, Mesabi Range College, Virginia, MN 55792. *Phone:* 218-749-0314. *Toll-free phone:* 800-657-3860. *Fax:* 218-749-0318. *E-mail:* b.kochevar@mesabirange.edu. *Website:* http://www.mesabirange.edu/.

# Minneapolis Business College
## Roseville, Minnesota

**Freshman Application Contact** Admissions Office, Minneapolis Business College, 1711 West County Road B, Roseville, MN 55113. *Phone:* 651-636-7406. *Toll-free phone:* 800-279-5200. *Website:* http://www.minneapolisbusinesscollege.edu/.

# Minneapolis Community and Technical College
## Minneapolis, Minnesota

**Freshman Application Contact** Minneapolis Community and Technical College, 1501 Hennepin Avenue, Minneapolis, MN 55403. *Phone:* 612-659-6200. *Toll-free phone:* 800-247-0911. *E-mail:* admissions.office@minneapolis.edu. *Website:* http://www.minneapolis.edu/.

# Minnesota State College–Southeast Technical
## Winona, Minnesota

- **State-supported** 2-year, founded 1992, part of Minnesota State Colleges and Universities System
- **Small-town** 132-acre campus with easy access to Minneapolis-St. Paul
- **Coed**

**Undergraduates** 800 full-time, 1,161 part-time. 27% are from out of state; 5% Black or African American, non-Hispanic/Latino; 4% Hispanic/Latino; 2% Asian, non-Hispanic/Latino; 0.3% American Indian or Alaska Native, non-Hispanic/Latino; 2% Two or more races, non-Hispanic/Latino; 0.1% Race/ethnicity unknown; 0.5% international; 12% transferred in. *Retention:* 35% of full-time freshmen returned.
**Faculty** *Student/faculty ratio:* 15:1.
**Academics** *Calendar:* semesters. *Degree:* certificates, diplomas, and associate. *Special study options:* distance learning, double majors, internships.
**Library** Learning Resource Center.
**Student Life** *Campus security:* 24-hour emergency response devices, late-night transport/escort service.
**Costs (2017–18)** *Tuition:* state resident $4969 full-time, $166 per credit hour part-time; nonresident $4969 full-time, $166 per credit hour part-time. Full-time tuition and fees vary according to program. Part-time tuition and fees vary according to program. *Required fees:* $648 full-time, $22 per credit hour part-time.
**Financial Aid** Of all full-time matriculated undergraduates who enrolled in 2015, 728 applied for aid, 650 were judged to have need, 12 had their need fully met. 32 Federal Work-Study jobs (averaging $2381). In 2015, 31. *Average percent of need met:* 37. *Average financial aid package:* $6615. *Average need-based loan:* $3208. *Average need-based gift aid:* $4658. *Average non-need-based aid:* $2796. *Average indebtedness upon graduation:* $18,236.
**Applying** *Options:* electronic application. *Application fee:* $20. *Required:* high school transcript. *Recommended:* interview.
**Freshman Application Contact** Admissions, SE Technical, Minnesota State College–Southeast Technical, 1250 Homer Road, PO Box 409, Winona, MN 55987. *Phone:* 877-853-8324. *Toll-free phone:* 800-372-8164. *Fax:* 507-453-2715. *E-mail:* enrollmentservices@southeastmn.edu. *Website:* http://www.southeastmn.edu/.

# Minnesota State Community and Technical College
## Fergus Falls, Minnesota

- **State-supported** 2-year, founded 1960, part of Minnesota State Colleges and Universities System
- **Rural** campus
- **Coed,** 6,303 undergraduate students

**Undergraduates** 2% live on campus.
**Majors** Accounting; administrative assistant and secretarial science; agricultural and food products processing; architectural drafting and CAD/CADD; art; autobody/collision and repair technology; automobile/automotive mechanics technology; banking and financial support services; biochemistry and molecular biology; biology/biological sciences; building/construction site management; business administration and management; business automation/technology/data entry; business/commerce; cardiovascular technology; carpentry; chemistry; civil engineering technology; clinical/medical laboratory technology; computer and information systems security; computer engineering technology; computer programming; computer systems networking and telecommunications; computer technology/computer systems technology; construction management; cooking and related culinary arts; cosmetology; criminal justice/safety; dental assisting; dental hygiene; diesel mechanics technology; electrical and electronic engineering technologies related; electrical, electronic and communications engineering technology; environmental studies; equestrian studies; fashion merchandising; financial planning and services; fire services administration; graphic design; health information/medical records technology; heating, ventilation, air conditioning and refrigeration engineering technology; horse husbandry/equine science and management; human resources management; industrial mechanics and maintenance technology; information technology; legal administrative assistant/secretary; legal assistant/paralegal; liberal arts and sciences/liberal studies; licensed practical/vocational nurse training; lineworker; manufacturing engineering technology; marine maintenance and ship repair technology; marketing/marketing management; mechanical drafting and CAD/CADD; medical administrative assistant and medical secretary; merchandising, sales, and marketing operations related (general); multi/interdisciplinary studies related; music; office management; pharmacy technician; plumbing technology; pre-engineering; radiologic technology/science; registered nursing/registered nurse; sales, distribution, and marketing operations; sign language interpretation and translation; surgical technology; teacher assistant/aide; telecommunications technology; web page, digital/multimedia and information resources design.
**Academics** *Calendar:* semesters. *Degree:* certificates, diplomas, and associate. *Special study options:* academic remediation for entering students, accelerated degree program, advanced placement credit, cooperative education, distance learning, double majors, English as a second language, freshman honors college, honors programs, independent study, internships, off-campus study, part-time degree program, services for LD students, study abroad, summer session for credit.
**Library** Minnesota State Community and Technical College - Fergus Falls Library plus 4 others.
**Student Life** *Housing Options:* coed. Campus housing is university owned. *Activities and Organizations:* drama/theater group, choral group, Student Senate, Students In Free Enterprise (SIFE), Phi Theta Kappa, Business Professionals of America, SkillsUSA–VICA. *Campus security:* 24-hour emergency response devices, late-night transport/escort service, security for special events. *Student services:* personal/psychological counseling, women's center.
**Costs (2017–18)** *One-time required fee:* $20. *Tuition:* state resident $4774 full-time, $159 per credit part-time; nonresident $4774 full-time, $159 per credit part-time. Full-time tuition and fees vary according to location and program. Part-time tuition and fees vary according to location and program. *Required fees:* $514 full-time. *Room and board:* $6724. Room and board charges vary according to board plan and housing facility. *Waivers:* senior citizens and employees or children of employees.
**Financial Aid** *Financial aid deadline:* 7/1.
**Applying** *Options:* electronic application, early admission, deferred entrance. *Application fee:* $20.
**Admissions Office Contact** Minnesota State Community and Technical College, 1414 College Way, Fergus Falls, MN 56537-1009. *Toll-free phone:* 877-450-3322.
*Website:* http://www.minnesota.edu/.

# Minnesota State Community and Technical College–Detroit Lakes
## Detroit Lakes, Minnesota

- **State-supported** 2-year, founded 1966, part of Minnesota State Colleges and Universities System
- **Small-town** campus
- **Coed**

**Undergraduates** 2,658 full-time, 3,733 part-time. 18% Black or African American, non-Hispanic/Latino; 7% Hispanic/Latino; 4% Asian, non-Hispanic/Latino; 0.2% Native Hawaiian or other Pacific Islander, non-Hispanic/Latino; 1% American Indian or Alaska Native, non-Hispanic/Latino; 2% Two or more races, non-Hispanic/Latino; 0.3% international.
**Academics** *Calendar:* semesters. *Degree:* certificates and associate.
**Athletics** Member NJCAA.
**Costs (2017–18)** *Tuition:* state resident $4821 full-time, $161 per credit hour part-time; nonresident $4821 full-time, $161 per credit hour part-time. Full-time tuition and fees vary according to location and program. Part-time tuition and fees vary according to location and program. *Required fees:* $514 full-time.
**Applying** *Application fee:* $20. *Required:* high school transcript, immunization record.
**Freshman Application Contact** Minnesota State Community and Technical College–Detroit Lakes, 900 Highway 34, E, Detroit Lakes, MN 56501. *Phone:* 218-846-3777. *Toll-free phone:* 800-492-4836. *Website:* http://www.minnesota.edu/.

# Minnesota State Community and Technical College–Moorhead
## Moorhead, Minnesota

- **State-supported** 2-year, part of Minnesota State Colleges and Universities System
- **Rural** campus
- **Coed**

**Undergraduates** 2,581 full-time, 3,722 part-time.
**Academics** *Calendar:* semesters. *Degree:* certificates, diplomas, and associate.
**Costs (2017–18)** *Tuition:* state resident $4821 full-time, $161 per credit hour part-time; nonresident $4821 full-time, $161 per credit hour part-time. Full-time tuition and fees vary according to location and program. Part-time tuition and fees vary according to location and program. *Required fees:* $514 full-time.

**Applying** *Application fee:* $20. *Required:* high school transcript, immunization record.

**Freshman Application Contact** Minnesota State Community and Technical College–Moorhead, 1900 28th Avenue, South, Moorhead, MN 56560. *Phone:* 218-299-6824. *Toll-free phone:* 800-426-5603. *Website:* http://www.minnesota.edu/.

# Minnesota State Community and Technical College–Wadena

## Wadena, Minnesota

- **State-supported** 2-year
- **Small-town** campus
- **Coed**

**Undergraduates** 2,581 full-time, 3,722 part-time. 0.5% Black or African American, non-Hispanic/Latino; 3% Hispanic/Latino; 0.3% American Indian or Alaska Native, non-Hispanic/Latino; 3% Two or more races, non-Hispanic/Latino.

**Academics** *Calendar:* semesters. *Degree:* certificates and associate.

**Costs (2017–18)** *Tuition:* state resident $4821 full-time, $161 per credit hour part-time; nonresident $4821 full-time, $161 per credit hour part-time. Full-time tuition and fees vary according to location and program. Part-time tuition and fees vary according to location and program. *Required fees:* $514 full-time.

**Applying** *Application fee:* $20. *Required:* high school transcript, immunization record.

**Freshman Application Contact** Minnesota State Community and Technical College–Wadena, 405 Colfax Avenue, SW, PO Box 566, Wadena, MN 56482. *Phone:* 218-631-7818. *Toll-free phone:* 800-247-2007. *Website:* http://www.minnesota.edu/.

# Minnesota West Community and Technical College

## Pipestone, Minnesota

- **State-supported** 2-year, founded 1967, part of Minnesota State Colleges and Universities System
- **Rural** campus
- **Coed**, 3,182 undergraduate students, 36% full-time, 57% women, 43% men

**Undergraduates** 1,153 full-time, 2,029 part-time. 11% are from out of state; 5% Black or African American, non-Hispanic/Latino; 6% Hispanic/Latino; 3% Asian, non-Hispanic/Latino; 0.1% Native Hawaiian or other Pacific Islander, non-Hispanic/Latino; 0.9% American Indian or Alaska Native, non-Hispanic/Latino; 2% Two or more races, non-Hispanic/Latino; 5% Race/ethnicity unknown. *Retention:* 60% of full-time freshmen returned.

**Freshmen** *Admission:* 4,707 admitted. *Average high school GPA:* 2.6.

**Faculty** *Total:* 151, 46% full-time. *Student/faculty ratio:* 21:1.

**Majors** Accounting; administrative assistant and secretarial science; agribusiness; agricultural and food products processing; agricultural/farm supplies retailing and wholesaling; agricultural production; agriculture; agronomy and crop science; automobile/automotive mechanics technology; biology/biotechnology laboratory technician; business administration and management; business/commerce; child-care and support services management; clinical/medical laboratory technology; computer and information systems security; computer engineering technology; computer science; computer systems networking and telecommunications; computer technology/computer systems technology; criminal justice/police science; dental assisting; diesel mechanics technology; electrical and power transmission installation; electrical and power transmission installation related; electrician; energy management and systems technology; hospital and health-care facilities administration; human services; hydraulics and fluid power technology; information technology; liberal arts and sciences and humanities related; liberal arts and sciences/liberal studies; lineworker; manufacturing engineering technology; medical administrative assistant and medical secretary; medical/clinical assistant; medical insurance coding; plumbing technology; radiologic technology/science; registered nursing/registered nurse; robotics technology; surgical technology.

**Academics** *Calendar:* semesters. *Degrees:* certificates, diplomas, and associate (profile contains information from Canby, Granite Falls, Jackson, and Worthington campuses). *Special study options:* academic remediation for entering students, advanced placement credit, cooperative education, distance learning, double majors, external degree program, honors programs, independent study, internships, part-time degree program, services for LD students, summer session for credit.

**Library** Library and Academic Resource Center plus 4 others.

**Student Life** *Housing Options:* Campus housing is provided by a third party. *Activities and Organizations:* choral group. *Student services:* veterans affairs office.

**Athletics** Member NJCAA. *Intercollegiate sports:* baseball M, basketball M/W, cheerleading W, football M, softball W, volleyball W, wrestling M.

**Costs (2018–19)** *One-time required fee:* $20. *Tuition:* state resident $5146 full-time, $172 per credit part-time; nonresident $5146 full-time, $172 per credit part-time. Full-time tuition and fees vary according to program and reciprocity agreements. Part-time tuition and fees vary according to program and reciprocity agreements. *Required fees:* $546 full-time, $18 per credit part-time. *Payment plan:* installment. *Waivers:* senior citizens and employees or children of employees.

**Financial Aid** Of all full-time matriculated undergraduates who enrolled in 2016, 1,610 applied for aid, 1,610 were judged to have need. 118 Federal Work-Study jobs (averaging $2111). 92 state and other part-time jobs (averaging $1619).

**Applying** *Options:* electronic application. *Application fee:* $20. *Required:* high school transcript. *Application deadlines:* rolling (freshmen), rolling (transfers). *Notification:* continuous (freshmen), continuous (transfers).

**Freshman Application Contact** Ms. Crystal Strouth, College Registrar, Minnesota West Community and Technical College, 1450 Collegeway, Worthington, MN 56187. *Phone:* 507-372-3451. *Toll-free phone:* 800-658-2330. *Fax:* 507-372-5803. *E-mail:* crystal.strouth@mnwest.edu. *Website:* http://www.mnwest.edu/.

# Normandale Community College

## Bloomington, Minnesota

**Freshman Application Contact** Admissions Office, Normandale Community College, 9700 France Avenue South, Bloomington, MN 55431. *Phone:* 952-358-8201. *Toll-free phone:* 800-481-5412. *Fax:* 952-358-8230. *E-mail:* information@normandale.edu. *Website:* http://www.normandale.edu/.

# North Hennepin Community College

## Brooklyn Park, Minnesota

- **State-supported** 2-year, founded 1966, part of Minnesota State Colleges and Universities system
- **Suburban** 80-acre campus with easy access to Minneapolis-St. Paul
- **Endowment** $761,415
- **Coed**, 6,509 undergraduate students

**Faculty** *Total:* 222, 53% full-time.

**Majors** Accounting; accounting technology and bookkeeping; biology/biological sciences; business administration and management; chemistry; clinical/medical laboratory technology; computer science; construction management; creative writing; criminal justice/police science; criminal justice/safety; dramatic/theater arts; education; entrepreneurship; finance; fine/studio arts; graphic design; health and physical education/fitness; health services/allied health/health sciences; histologic technician; human services; legal assistant/paralegal; liberal arts and sciences/liberal studies; management information systems; marketing/marketing management; mathematics; multi/interdisciplinary studies related; music; physical education teaching and coaching; pre-engineering; registered nursing/registered nurse.

**Academics** *Calendar:* semesters. *Degree:* certificates and associate. *Special study options:* academic remediation for entering students, accelerated degree program, adult/continuing education programs, advanced placement credit, distance learning, double majors, English as a second language, external degree program, honors programs, independent study, internships, off-campus study, part-time degree program, services for LD students, student-designed majors, study abroad, summer session for credit. *ROTC:* Army (c), Navy (c), Air Force (c).

**Library** Learning Resource Center.

**Student Life** *Housing:* college housing not available. *Activities and Organizations:* drama/theater group, choral group, Hmong Student Club, Student Nurses Association, Student Senate, Badminton Club, Students Serving Our Community. *Campus security:* 24-hour emergency response devices, student patrols, late-night transport/escort service. *Student services:* health clinic, personal/psychological counseling, veterans affairs office.

**Athletics** *Intramural sports:* basketball M/W, bowling M/W, football M/W, ice hockey M(c)/W(c), lacrosse M/W, soccer M/W, softball M/W, table tennis M/W, volleyball M/W, weight lifting M/W.

**Costs (2017–18)** *Tuition:* state resident $3961 full-time, $165 per credit part-time; nonresident $3961 full-time, $165 per credit part-time. Full-time tuition and fees vary according to location and program. Part-time tuition and fees vary according to location and program. *Required fees:* $459 full-time, $19 per credit part-time. *Payment plan:* installment. *Waivers:* senior citizens and employees or children of employees.

**Applying** *Options:* electronic application, early admission, deferred entrance. *Application fee:* $20. *Recommended:* high school transcript. *Application*

*deadlines:* rolling (freshmen), rolling (transfers). *Notification:* continuous (freshmen), continuous (transfers).
**Freshman Application Contact** Mr. Sean Olson, Associate Director of Admissions and Outreach, North Hennepin Community College, 7411 85th Avenue North, Brooklyn Park, MN 55445. *Phone:* 763-424-0724. *Toll-free phone:* 800-818-0395. *Fax:* 763-493-0563. *E-mail:* solson2@nhcc.edu. *Website:* http://www.nhcc.edu/.

# Northland Community and Technical College
## Thief River Falls, Minnesota

- **State-supported** 2-year, founded 1949, part of Minnesota State Colleges and Universities System
- **Small-town** 239-acre campus
- **Coed,** 3,599 undergraduate students, 38% full-time, 56% women, 44% men

**Undergraduates** 1,375 full-time, 2,224 part-time. Students come from 24 states and territories; 1 other country; 7% are from out of state; 7% Black or African American, non-Hispanic/Latino; 4% Hispanic/Latino; 3% Asian, non-Hispanic/Latino; 0.1% Native Hawaiian or other Pacific Islander, non-Hispanic/Latino; 2% American Indian or Alaska Native, non-Hispanic/Latino; 4% Two or more races, non-Hispanic/Latino; 5% Race/ethnicity unknown; 0.5% international; 11% transferred in. *Retention:* 56% of full-time freshmen returned.
**Freshmen** *Admission:* 1,200 applied, 1,200 admitted, 527 enrolled.
**Faculty** *Total:* 150, 61% full-time, 7% with terminal degrees. *Student/faculty ratio:* 19:1.
**Majors** Accounting technology and bookkeeping; administrative assistant and secretarial science; agricultural mechanics and equipment technology; agriculture; airframe mechanics and aircraft maintenance technology; architectural drafting and CAD/CADD; autobody/collision and repair technology; automation engineer technology; automobile/automotive mechanics technology; business administration and management; computer support specialist; computer systems networking and telecommunications; criminal justice/police science; dietetic technology; emergency medical technology (EMT paramedic); fire prevention and safety technology; health services/allied health/health sciences; heating, air conditioning, ventilation and refrigeration maintenance technology; liberal arts and sciences/liberal studies; manufacturing engineering technology; medical administrative assistant and medical secretary; medical insurance coding; occupational therapist assistant; pharmacy technician; physical therapy technology; radiologic technology/science; registered nursing/registered nurse; respiratory care therapy; sales, distribution, and marketing operations; signal/geospatial intelligence; special products marketing; surgical technology; teacher assistant/aide.
**Academics** *Calendar:* semesters. *Degree:* certificates, diplomas, and associate. *Special study options:* academic remediation for entering students, adult/continuing education programs, advanced placement credit, cooperative education, distance learning, double majors, internships, off-campus study, part-time degree program, services for LD students, summer session for credit.
**Library** Northland Community and Technical College Library plus 1 other. *Books:* 24,000 (physical), 19,000 (digital/electronic); *Serial titles:* 55 (physical); *Databases:* 47. Weekly public service hours: 82; students can reserve study rooms.
**Student Life** *Housing:* college housing not available. *Activities and Organizations:* student-run radio station, choral group, Student Senate, PAMA, AD Nursing, PN Nursing, Fire Tech. *Campus security:* student patrols, late-night transport/escort service. *Student services:* personal/psychological counseling, women's center, veterans affairs office.
**Athletics** Member NJCAA. *Intercollegiate sports:* baseball M, basketball M/W, football M, softball W, volleyball W, wrestling M. *Intramural sports:* basketball M/W, bowling M/W, golf M/W, ice hockey M/W, racquetball M/W, rock climbing M/W, soccer M/W, softball M/W, volleyball M/W, weight lifting M/W.
**Costs (2017–18)** *Tuition:* state resident $4950 full-time, $165 per credit hour part-time; nonresident $4950 full-time, $165 per credit hour part-time. Full-time tuition and fees vary according to course load and program. Part-time tuition and fees vary according to course load and program. *Required fees:* $599 full-time, $299 per term part-time. *Waivers:* senior citizens and employees or children of employees.
**Financial Aid** Of all full-time matriculated undergraduates who enrolled in 2011, 98 Federal Work-Study jobs (averaging $2701). 68 state and other part-time jobs (averaging $2839).

**Applying** *Options:* electronic application, early admission, deferred entrance. *Application fee:* $20. *Required:* high school transcript. *Application deadlines:* 8/24 (freshmen), 8/24 (transfers). *Notification:* continuous (freshmen), continuous (transfers).
**Freshman Application Contact** Mrs. Nicki Carlson, Director of Enrollment Management, Northland Community and Technical College, 1101 Highway One East, Thief River Falls, MN 56701. *Phone:* 218-683-8546. *Toll-free phone:* 800-959-6282. *Fax:* 218-683-8980. *E-mail:* nicki.carlson@northlandcollege.edu.
*Website:* http://www.northlandcollege.edu/.

# Northwest Technical College
## Bemidji, Minnesota

**Freshman Application Contact** Ms. Kari Kantack-Miller, Diversity and Enrollment Representative, Northwest Technical College, 905 Grant Avenue, Southeast, Bemidji, MN 56601. *Phone:* 218-333-6645. *Toll-free phone:* 800-942-8324. *Fax:* 218-333-6694. *E-mail:* kari.kantack@ntcmn.edu. *Website:* http://www.ntcmn.edu/.

# Pine Technical and Community College
## Pine City, Minnesota

**Freshman Application Contact** Pine Technical and Community College, 900 4th Street SE, Pine City, MN 55063. *Phone:* 320-629-5100. *Toll-free phone:* 800-521-7463. *Website:* http://www.pine.edu/.

# Rainy River Community College
## International Falls, Minnesota

- **State-supported** 2-year, founded 1967, part of Minnesota State Colleges and Universities System
- **Small-town** 80-acre campus
- **Coed,** 241 undergraduate students, 84% full-time, 57% women, 43% men

**Undergraduates** 203 full-time, 38 part-time. Students come from 16 states and territories; 2 other countries; 19% Black or African American, non-Hispanic/Latino; 9% Hispanic/Latino; 1% Asian, non-Hispanic/Latino; 8% American Indian or Alaska Native, non-Hispanic/Latino; 7% international.
**Faculty** *Total:* 25, 40% full-time. *Student/faculty ratio:* 15:1.
**Majors** Administrative assistant and secretarial science; biological and physical sciences; business administration and management; health services/allied health/health sciences; liberal arts and sciences/liberal studies; pre-engineering.
**Academics** *Calendar:* semesters. *Degree:* certificates, diplomas, and associate. *Special study options:* academic remediation for entering students, adult/continuing education programs, advanced placement credit, cooperative education, honors programs, independent study, internships, part-time degree program, services for LD students, summer session for credit.
**Library** Rainy River Community College Library.
**Student Life** *Housing Options:* special housing for students with disabilities. Campus housing is university owned. *Activities and Organizations:* drama/theater group, Anishinaabe Student Coalition, Student Senate, Black Student Association. *Campus security:* 24-hour emergency response devices, late-night transport/escort service, controlled dormitory access. *Student services:* personal/psychological counseling, veterans affairs office.
**Athletics** Member NJCAA. *Intercollegiate sports:* baseball M, basketball M/W, ice hockey W, softball W, volleyball W. *Intramural sports:* archery M/W, badminton M/W, bowling M/W, ice hockey M, skiing (cross-country) M/W, skiing (downhill) M/W, swimming and diving M/W, table tennis M/W, tennis M/W, volleyball M/W, weight lifting M/W.
**Costs (2017–18)** *Tuition:* state resident $4728 full-time; nonresident $5910 full-time. Full-time tuition and fees vary according to course load and reciprocity agreements. Part-time tuition and fees vary according to course load and reciprocity agreements. *Required fees:* $595 full-time. *Room and board:* $4050; room only: $3250. *Waivers:* employees or children of employees.
**Applying** *Options:* electronic application, early admission, deferred entrance. *Application fee:* $20. *Recommended:* high school transcript. *Application deadlines:* rolling (freshmen), rolling (transfers). *Notification:* continuous (freshmen), continuous (transfers).
**Freshman Application Contact** Ms. Berta Wilcox, Registrar, Rainy River Community College, 1501 Highway 71, International Falls, MN 56649. *Phone:* 218-285-2207. *Toll-free phone:* 800-456-3996. *Fax:* 218-285-2314. *E-mail:* berta.wilcox@rainyriver.edu.
*Website:* http://www.rainyriver.edu/.

# Ridgewater College
## Willmar, Minnesota

- **State-supported** 2-year, founded 1961, part of Minnesota State Colleges and Universities System
- **Small-town** 83-acre campus
- **Coed,** 3,366 students

**Undergraduates** 1,942 full-time, 1,424 part-time.
**Faculty** *Total:* 173, 62% full-time.
**Majors** Accounting; administrative assistant and secretarial science; agribusiness; agricultural production; agriculture; agronomy and crop science; animal/livestock husbandry and production; autobody/collision and repair technology; automobile/automotive mechanics technology; biology/biological sciences; business administration and management; carpentry; chemistry; commercial photography; computer programming; computer science; computer systems networking and telecommunications; computer technology/computer systems technology; cosmetology; criminal justice/police science; crop production; dairy husbandry and production; desktop publishing and digital imaging design; digital communication and media/multimedia; early childhood education; electrical, electronic and communications engineering technology; electrician; electromechanical technology; health information/medical records technology; instrumentation technology; legal administrative assistant/secretary; liberal arts and sciences and humanities related; liberal arts and sciences/liberal studies; machine tool technology; marketing/marketing management; mechanical drafting and CAD/CADD; medical administrative assistant and medical secretary; medical/clinical assistant; network and system administration; radiologic technology/science; recording arts technology; registered nursing/registered nurse; sales, distribution, and marketing operations; selling skills and sales; teacher assistant/aide; telecommunications technology; therapeutic recreation; tool and die technology; veterinary/animal health technology; web page, digital/multimedia and information resources design; welding technology.
**Academics** *Calendar:* semesters. *Degree:* certificates, diplomas, and associate. *Special study options:* academic remediation for entering students, advanced placement credit, cooperative education, distance learning, internships, off-campus study, part-time degree program, services for LD students, student-designed majors, study abroad, summer session for credit.
**Student Life** *Housing:* college housing not available. *Campus security:* 24-hour emergency response devices. *Student services:* personal/psychological counseling, veterans affairs office.
**Athletics** Member NJCAA. *Intercollegiate sports:* baseball M, basketball M/W, football M, soccer M, softball W, volleyball W, wrestling M. *Intramural sports:* basketball M/W, football M, golf M/W, softball M/W, weight lifting M/W.
**Costs (2018–19)** *Tuition:* state resident $5760 full-time, $161 per credit hour part-time; nonresident $5760 full-time, $161 per credit hour part-time. Full-time tuition and fees vary according to course load and reciprocity agreements. Part-time tuition and fees vary according to course load and reciprocity agreements. *Required fees:* $579 full-time, $19 per credit hour part-time. *Waivers:* senior citizens.
**Financial Aid** Of all full-time matriculated undergraduates who enrolled in 2016, 350 Federal Work-Study jobs (averaging $3000). 133 state and other part-time jobs (averaging $2400).
**Applying** *Options:* electronic application. *Application fee:* $20. *Required:* high school transcript. *Required for some:* interview.
**Freshman Application Contact** Ms. Linda Duering, Admissions Assistant, Ridgewater College, 2101 15th Avenue NW, Willmar, MN 56201. *Phone:* 320-222-5976. *Toll-free phone:* 800-722-1151. *E-mail:* linda.duering@ridgewater.edu.
*Website:* http://www.ridgewater.edu/.

# Riverland Community College
## Austin, Minnesota

**Freshman Application Contact** Riverland Community College, 1900 8th Avenue, NW, Austin, MN 55912. *Phone:* 507-433-0600. *Toll-free phone:* 800-247-5039. *Website:* http://www.riverland.edu/.

# Rochester Community and Technical College
## Rochester, Minnesota

**Director of Admissions** Mr. Troy Tynsky, Director of Admissions, Rochester Community and Technical College, 851 30th Avenue, SE, Rochester, MN 55904-4999. *Phone:* 507-280-3509. *Website:* http://www.rctc.edu/.

# St. Cloud Technical & Community College
## St. Cloud, Minnesota

**Freshman Application Contact** Ms. Jodi Elness, Admissions Office, St. Cloud Technical & Community College, 1540 Northway Drive, St. Cloud, MN 56303. *Phone:* 320-308-5089. *Toll-free phone:* 800-222-1009. *Fax:* 320-308-5981. *E-mail:* jelness@sctcc.edu. *Website:* http://www.sctcc.edu/.

# Saint Paul College–A Community & Technical College
## St. Paul, Minnesota

**Freshman Application Contact** Ms. Sarah Carrico, Saint Paul College–A Community & Technical College, 235 Marshall Avenue, Saint Paul, MN 55102. *Phone:* 651-846-1424. *Toll-free phone:* 800-227-6029. *Fax:* 651-846-1703. *E-mail:* admissions@saintpaul.edu. *Website:* http://www.saintpaul.edu/.

# South Central College
## North Mankato, Minnesota

**Freshman Application Contact** Ms. Beverly Herda, Director of Admissions, South Central College, 1920 Lee Boulevard, North Mankato, MN 56003. *Phone:* 507-389-7334. *Fax:* 507-388-9951. *Website:* http://southcentral.edu/.

# Vermilion Community College
## Ely, Minnesota

**Freshman Application Contact** Mr. Todd Heiman, Director of Enrollment Services, Vermilion Community College, 1900 East Camp Street, Ely, MN 55731-1996. *Phone:* 218-365-7224. *Toll-free phone:* 800-657-3608. *Website:* http://www.vcc.edu/.

# White Earth Tribal and Community College
## Mahnomen, Minnesota

**Admissions Office Contact** White Earth Tribal and Community College, 102 3rd Street NE, Mahnomen, MN 56557. *Website:* http://www.wetcc.edu/.

# MISSISSIPPI

# Antonelli College
## Hattiesburg, Mississippi

**Freshman Application Contact** Mrs. Karen Gautreau, Director, Antonelli College, 1500 North 31st Avenue, Hattiesburg, MS 39401. *Phone:* 601-583-4100. *Fax:* 601-583-0839. *E-mail:* admissionsh@antonellicollege.edu. *Website:* http://www.antonellicollege.edu/.

# Antonelli College
## Jackson, Mississippi

**Freshman Application Contact** Antonelli College, 2323 Lakeland Drive, Jackson, MS 39232. *Phone:* 601-362-9991. *Website:* http://www.antonellicollege.edu/.

# Coahoma Community College
## Clarksdale, Mississippi

**Freshman Application Contact** Mrs. Wanda Holmes, Director of Admissions and Records, Coahoma Community College, Clarksdale, MS 38614-9799. *Phone:* 662-621-4205. *Toll-free phone:* 866-470-1CCC. *Website:* http://www.coahomacc.edu/.

# Concorde Career College
## Southaven, Mississippi

**Admissions Office Contact** Concorde Career College, 7900 Airways Boulevard, Suite 103, Southaven, MS 38671. *Website:* http://www.concorde.edu/.

# Copiah-Lincoln Community College
## Wesson, Mississippi

- **State and locally supported** 2-year, founded 1928, part of Mississippi Community College Board
- **Rural** 525-acre campus with easy access to Jackson
- **Endowment** $2.5 million
- **Coed**, 3,100 undergraduate students, 69% full-time, 62% women, 38% men

**Undergraduates** 2,128 full-time, 972 part-time. Students come from 8 states and territories; 1 other country; 1% are from out of state; 40% Black or African American, non-Hispanic/Latino; 0.9% Hispanic/Latino; 0.1% Asian, non-Hispanic/Latino; 0.5% Two or more races, non-Hispanic/Latino; 3% Race/ethnicity unknown; 5% transferred in; 30% live on campus.
**Freshmen** *Admission:* 789 enrolled.
**Faculty** *Total:* 197, 52% full-time.
**Majors** Accounting; accounting technology and bookkeeping; administrative assistant and secretarial science; agribusiness; agricultural business and management; agricultural business and management related; agricultural economics; agricultural/farm supplies retailing and wholesaling; agriculture; architecture; art teacher education; automobile/automotive mechanics technology; biological and physical sciences; biology/biological sciences; business administration and management; business automation/technology/data entry; chemistry; child-care provision; child development; civil engineering technology; clinical/medical laboratory technology; computer programming; computer systems networking and telecommunications; construction/heavy equipment/earthmoving equipment operation; cooking and related culinary arts; cosmetology; cosmetology, barber/styling, and nail instruction; criminal justice/police science; data processing and data processing technology; diesel mechanics technology; drafting and design technology; economics; education; electrical, electronic and communications engineering technology; elementary education; engineering; English; family and consumer sciences/home economics teacher education; farm and ranch management; food technology and processing; forestry; health and medical administrative services related; health teacher education; heating, air conditioning, ventilation and refrigeration maintenance technology; history; hospitality administration; industrial radiologic technology; journalism; liberal arts and sciences/liberal studies; library and information science; licensed practical/vocational nurse training; machine tool technology; manufacturing engineering technology; marketing/marketing management; military technologies and applied sciences related; music teacher education; physical education teaching and coaching; radiologic technology/science; registered nursing/registered nurse; respiratory care therapy; special products marketing; trade and industrial teacher education; truck and bus driver/commercial vehicle operation/instruction; welding technology.
**Academics** *Calendar:* semesters. *Degree:* certificates and associate. *Special study options:* academic remediation for entering students, accelerated degree program, adult/continuing education programs, advanced placement credit, distance learning, honors programs, part-time degree program, services for LD students, student-designed majors, study abroad, summer session for credit.
**Library** Oswalt Memorial Library.
**Student Life** *Housing Options:* men-only, women-only. Campus housing is university owned. *Activities and Organizations:* drama/theater group, student-run newspaper, radio station, choral group, marching band. *Campus security:* 24-hour patrols. *Student services:* health clinic, personal/psychological counseling, veterans affairs office.
**Athletics** Member NJCAA. *Intercollegiate sports:* baseball M(s), basketball M(s)/W(s), football M(s), golf M/W, softball W, tennis M/W, track and field M. *Intramural sports:* basketball M/W, football M, golf M/W, tennis M/W, volleyball M/W.
**Costs (2018–19)** *Tuition:* state resident $1400 full-time, $140 per credit hour part-time; nonresident $2400 full-time, $240 per credit hour part-time. *Required fees:* $190 full-time, $19 per credit hour part-time. *Room and board:* $1825; room only: $800. Room and board charges vary according to board plan and housing facility. *Payment plan:* installment. *Waivers:* employees or children of employees.
**Financial Aid** Of all full-time matriculated undergraduates who enrolled in 2016, 125 Federal Work-Study jobs (averaging $1000).
**Applying** *Options:* early admission. *Required:* high school transcript. *Application deadlines:* rolling (freshmen), rolling (transfers).
**Freshman Application Contact** Ms. Gay Langham, Student Records Manager, Copiah-Lincoln Community College, PO Box 649, Wesson, MS 39191-0457. *Phone:* 601-643-8307. *E-mail:* gay.langham@colin.edu. *Website:* http://www.colin.edu/.

# East Central Community College
## Decatur, Mississippi

**Director of Admissions** Ms. Donna Luke, Director of Admissions, Records, and Research, East Central Community College, PO Box 129, Decatur, MS 39327-0129. *Phone:* 601-635-2111 Ext. 206. *Toll-free phone:* 877-462-3222. *Website:* http://www.eccc.edu/.

# East Mississippi Community College
## Scooba, Mississippi

**Director of Admissions** Ms. Melinda Sciple, Admissions Officer, East Mississippi Community College, PO Box 158, Scooba, MS 39358-0158. *Phone:* 662-476-5041. *Website:* http://www.eastms.edu/.

# Hinds Community College
## Raymond, Mississippi

- **State and locally supported** 2-year, founded 1917, part of Mississippi Community College Board
- **Small-town** 671-acre campus with easy access to Jackson
- **Coed**, 12,061 undergraduate students, 60% full-time, 60% women, 40% men

**Undergraduates** 7,196 full-time, 4,865 part-time. Students come from 23 states and territories; 15 other countries; 3% are from out of state; 56% Black or African American, non-Hispanic/Latino; 2% Hispanic/Latino; 0.9% Asian, non-Hispanic/Latino; 0.2% American Indian or Alaska Native, non-Hispanic/Latino; 3% Two or more races, non-Hispanic/Latino; 2% Race/ethnicity unknown; 8% transferred in. *Retention:* 57% of full-time freshmen returned.
**Freshmen** *Admission:* 2,581 enrolled.
**Faculty** *Student/faculty ratio:* 17:1.
**Majors** Accounting technology and bookkeeping; administrative assistant and secretarial science; aeronautics/aviation/aerospace science and technology; agribusiness; agricultural mechanization related; airframe mechanics and aircraft maintenance technology; animal/livestock husbandry and production; applied horticulture/horticultural business services related; architectural engineering technology; arts, entertainment, and media management related; aviation/airway management; banking and financial support services; business administration and management; child-care provision; clinical/medical laboratory technology; computer and information systems security; computer installation and repair technology; computer programming; computer systems networking and telecommunications; cooking and related culinary arts; corrections and criminal justice related; court reporting; dental assisting; diagnostic medical sonography and ultrasound technology; diesel mechanics technology; drafting and design technology; electrical, electronic and communications engineering technology; electrical/electronics equipment installation and repair; electrician; electromechanical and instrumentation and maintenance technologies related; emergency medical technology (EMT paramedic); fashion merchandising; game and interactive media design; general studies; geographic information science and cartography; graphic design; health and medical administrative services related; health information/medical records technology; heating, air conditioning, ventilation and refrigeration maintenance technology; hospitality administration; landscaping and groundskeeping; legal assistant/paralegal; logistics, materials, and supply chain management; marketing/marketing management; medical/clinical assistant; multi/interdisciplinary studies related; photographic and film/video technology; physical therapy technology; plant protection and integrated pest management; plumbing technology; poultry science; radio and television broadcasting technology; radiologic technology/science; real estate; registered nursing/registered nurse; respiratory care therapy; sign language interpretation and translation; surgical technology; telecommunications technology; tourism and travel services management; veterinary/animal health technology.
**Academics** *Calendar:* semesters. *Degrees:* certificates and associate (profile includes Raymond, Jackson Academic and Technical Center, Jackson Nursing-Allied Health Center, Rankin, Utica, and Vicksburg campus locations). *Special study options:* academic remediation for entering students, accelerated degree program, adult/continuing education programs, advanced placement credit, cooperative education, distance learning, double majors, honors programs, independent study, internships, part-time degree program, services for LD students, study abroad, summer session for credit. *ROTC:* Army (b).
**Library** McLendon Library plus 5 others. Students can reserve study rooms.
**Student Life** *Housing Options:* coed, men-only, women-only, special housing for students with disabilities. Campus housing is university owned. *Activities and Organizations:* drama/theater group, student-run newspaper, choral group, marching band. *Campus security:* 24-hour emergency response devices and patrols, late-night transport/escort service, controlled dormitory access. *Student services:* personal/psychological counseling, veterans affairs office.

**Athletics** Member NJCAA. *Intercollegiate sports:* baseball M(s), basketball M(s)/W(s), cheerleading M(s)/W(s), cross-country running W(s), football M(s), golf M(s), soccer M(s)/W(s), softball W(s), tennis M(s)/W(s), track and field M(s)/W(s). *Intramural sports:* basketball M/W, bowling M/W, cross-country running M/W, football M/W, golf M/W, softball M/W, swimming and diving M/W, tennis M/W, ultimate Frisbee M/W, volleyball M/W.

**Costs (2017–18)** *Tuition:* state resident $2880 full-time, $120 per semester hour part-time; nonresident $5920 full-time, $340 per semester hour part-time. Part-time tuition and fees vary according to course load. *Required fees:* $200 full-time, $100 per term part-time. *Room and board:* $4500. Room and board charges vary according to housing facility. *Payment plan:* installment. *Waivers:* senior citizens and employees or children of employees.

**Financial Aid** Of all full-time matriculated undergraduates who enrolled in 2016, 300 Federal Work-Study jobs (averaging $1250). 200 state and other part-time jobs (averaging $1000).

**Applying** *Options:* electronic application.

**Freshman Application Contact** Hinds Community College, PO Box 1100, Raymond, MS 39154-1100. *Phone:* 601-857-3280. *Toll-free phone:* 800-HINDSCC.

*Website:* http://www.hindscc.edu/.

## Holmes Community College
### Goodman, Mississippi

**Director of Admissions** Dr. Lynn Wright, Dean of Admissions and Records, Holmes Community College, PO Box 369, Goodman, MS 39079-0369. *Phone:* 601-472-2312 Ext. 1023. *Toll-free phone:* 800-HOLMES-4. *Website:* http://www.holmescc.edu/.

## Itawamba Community College
### Fulton, Mississippi

**Freshman Application Contact** Mr. Larry Boggs, Director of Student Recruitment and Scholarships, Itawamba Community College, 602 West Hill Street, Fulton, MS 38843. *Phone:* 601-862-8252. *E-mail:* laboggs@iccms.edu. *Website:* http://www.iccms.edu/.

## Jones County Junior College
### Ellisville, Mississippi

**Director of Admissions** Mrs. Dianne Speed, Director of Admissions and Records, Jones County Junior College, 900 South Court Street, Ellisville, MS 39437-3901. *Phone:* 601-477-4025. *Website:* http://www.jcjc.edu/.

## Meridian Community College
### Meridian, Mississippi

- **State and locally supported** 2-year, founded 1937, part of Mississippi Community College Board
- **Small-town** 91-acre campus
- **Endowment** $12.7 million
- **Coed,** 3,555 undergraduate students, 68% full-time, 69% women, 31% men

**Undergraduates** 2,424 full-time, 1,131 part-time. 43% Black or African American, non-Hispanic/Latino; 1% Hispanic/Latino; 0.5% Asian, non-Hispanic/Latino; 2% American Indian or Alaska Native, non-Hispanic/Latino; 0.5% Two or more races, non-Hispanic/Latino; 5% Race/ethnicity unknown; 12% live on campus. *Retention:* 55% of full-time freshmen returned.

**Faculty** *Total:* 213, 62% full-time, 4% with terminal degrees. *Student/faculty ratio:* 18:1.

**Majors** Administrative assistant and secretarial science; child-care provision; clinical/medical laboratory technology; dental hygiene; drafting and design technology; electrical, electronic and communications engineering technology; emergency medical technology (EMT paramedic); fire science/firefighting; machine tool technology; marketing/marketing management; registered nursing/registered nurse; respiratory care therapy; telecommunications technology.

**Academics** *Calendar:* semesters. *Degree:* certificates and associate. *Special study options:* academic remediation for entering students, accelerated degree program, adult/continuing education programs, advanced placement credit, cooperative education, distance learning, double majors, English as a second language, freshman honors college, honors programs, independent study, internships, part-time degree program, services for LD students, summer session for credit.

**Library** L.O. Todd-Billy C. Beal Learning Resources Center. *Books:* 49,544 (physical), 174,022 (digital/electronic); *Serial titles:* 207 (physical), 11 (digital/electronic); *Databases:* 13.

**Student Life** *Housing Options:* coed, men-only, women-only. Campus housing is university owned. *Activities and Organizations:* drama/theater group, student-run radio station, choral group, Phi Theta Kappa, VICA (Vocational Industrial Clubs of America), Health Occupations Students of America, Organization of Student Nurses, Distributive Education Clubs of America. *Campus security:* 24-hour patrols by law enforcement officers. *Student services:* personal/psychological counseling, veterans affairs office.

**Athletics** Member NJCAA. *Intercollegiate sports:* baseball M(s), basketball M(s)/W(s), cross-country running M(s)/W(s), golf M(s), soccer M(s)/W(s), softball W(s), tennis M(s)/W(s), track and field M(s)/W(s). *Intramural sports:* basketball M/W, cross-country running M/W, swimming and diving M/W, tennis M/W, volleyball M/W.

**Costs (2017–18)** *Tuition:* state resident $2700 full-time, $150 per credit hour part-time; nonresident $3780 full-time, $177 per credit hour part-time. Full-time tuition and fees vary according to program. Part-time tuition and fees vary according to program. *Required fees:* $82 full-time, $6 per credit hour part-time, $16 per term part-time. *Room and board:* $4000. Room and board charges vary according to housing facility. *Waivers:* employees or children of employees.

**Applying** *Options:* early admission. *Required:* high school transcript, minimum 2.0 GPA. *Application deadlines:* rolling (freshmen), rolling (out-of-state freshmen), rolling (transfers). *Notification:* continuous (freshmen), continuous (out-of-state freshmen), continuous (transfers).

**Freshman Application Contact** Ms. Angela Payne, Director of Admissions, Meridian Community College, 910 Highway 19 North, Meridian, MS 39307. *Phone:* 601-484-8357. *Toll-free phone:* 800-MCC-THE-1. *E-mail:* apayne@meridiancc.edu.

*Website:* http://www.meridiancc.edu/.

## Mississippi Delta Community College
### Moorhead, Mississippi

**Freshman Application Contact** Mississippi Delta Community College, PO Box 668, Highway 3 and Cherry Street, Moorhead, MS 38761-0668. *Phone:* 662-246-6302. *Website:* http://www.msdelta.edu/.

## Mississippi Gulf Coast Community College
### Perkinston, Mississippi

**Freshman Application Contact** Mrs. Nichol Green, Director of Admissions, Mississippi Gulf Coast Community College, PO Box 548, Perkinston, MS 39573. *Phone:* 601-928-6264. *Fax:* 601-928-6345. *Website:* http://www.mgccc.edu/.

## Northeast Mississippi Community College
### Booneville, Mississippi

**Freshman Application Contact** Office of Enrollment Services, Northeast Mississippi Community College, 101 Cunningham Boulevard, Booneville, MS 38829. *Phone:* 662-720-7239. *Toll-free phone:* 800-555-2154. *E-mail:* admitme@nemcc.edu. *Website:* http://www.nemcc.edu/.

## Northwest Mississippi Community College
### Senatobia, Mississippi

- **State and locally supported** 2-year, founded 1927, part of Mississippi State Board for Community and Junior Colleges
- **Rural** 75-acre campus with easy access to Memphis
- **Coed,** 7,700 undergraduate students

**Undergraduates** *Retention:* 60% of full-time freshmen returned.

**Faculty** *Total:* 200. *Student/faculty ratio:* 20:1.

**Majors** Agricultural business and management; agricultural mechanization; animal sciences; civil engineering technology; commercial and advertising art; computer programming (specific applications); heating, air conditioning, ventilation and refrigeration maintenance technology; hotel/motel administration; legal assistant/paralegal; liberal arts and sciences/liberal studies; licensed practical/vocational nurse training; machine tool technology; office management; registered nursing/registered nurse.

**Academics** *Calendar:* semesters. *Degree:* associate. *Special study options:* academic remediation for entering students, adult/continuing education programs, distance learning, honors programs, part-time degree program, services for LD students, summer session for credit. *ROTC:* Air Force (b).

**Library** R. C. Pugh Library. Study areas open 24 hours, 5&-7 days a week.

**Student Life** *Housing Options:* men-only, women-only. Campus housing is university owned. *Activities and Organizations:* drama/theater group, student-run newspaper, choral group, marching band. *Campus security:* 24-hour emergency response devices and patrols, late-night transport/escort service, controlled dormitory access. *Student services:* personal/psychological counseling.

**Athletics** Member NJCAA. *Intercollegiate sports:* baseball M(s), basketball M(s)/W(s), equestrian sports M(s)/W(s), football M(s), soccer M(s)/W(s), softball W(s). *Intramural sports:* basketball M/W, football M.

**Applying** *Options:* electronic application, early admission, deferred entrance. *Required:* high school transcript. *Application deadlines:* 8/15 (freshmen), 9/7 (transfers). *Notification:* continuous (freshmen), continuous (transfers).

**Freshman Application Contact** Northwest Mississippi Community College, 4975 Highway 51 North, Senatobia, MS 38668-1701. *Phone:* 662-562-8217. *Website:* http://www.northwestms.edu/.

## Pearl River Community College
### Poplarville, Mississippi

**Freshman Application Contact** Mr. J. Dow Ford, Director of Admissions, Pearl River Community College, 101 Highway 11 North, Poplarville, MS 39470. *Phone:* 601-403-1000. *E-mail:* dford@prcc.edu. *Website:* http://www.prcc.edu/.

## Southwest Mississippi Community College
### Summit, Mississippi

**Freshman Application Contact** Mr. Matthew Calhoun, Vice President of Admissions and Records, Southwest Mississippi Community College, 1156 College Drive, Summit, MS 39666. *Phone:* 601-276-2001. *Fax:* 601-276-3888. *E-mail:* mattc@smcc.edu. *Website:* http://www.smcc.cc.ms.us/.

## Virginia College in Biloxi
### Biloxi, Mississippi

**Admissions Office Contact** Virginia College in Biloxi, 920 Cedar Lake Road, Biloxi, MS 39532. *Website:* http://www.vc.edu/.

## Virginia College in Jackson
### Jackson, Mississippi

**Director of Admissions** Director of Admissions, Virginia College in Jackson, 5841 Ridgewood Road, Jackson, MS 39211. *Phone:* 601-977-0960. *Website:* http://www.vc.edu/.

# MISSOURI

## American Trade School
### Saint Ann, Missouri

**Admissions Office Contact** American Trade School, 3925 Industrial Drive, Saint Ann, MO 63074. *Website:* http://www.americantradeschool.edu/.

## Bryan University
### Columbia, Missouri

**Admissions Office Contact** Bryan University, 3215 LeMone Industrial Boulevard, Columbia, MO 65201. *Toll-free phone:* 855-566-0650. *Website:* http://www.bryanu.edu/.

## Concorde Career College
### Kansas City, Missouri

**Freshman Application Contact** Deborah Crow, Director, Concorde Career College, 3239 Broadway Street, Kansas City, MO 64111. *Phone:* 816-531-5223. *Fax:* 816-756-3231. *E-mail:* dcrow@concorde.edu. *Website:* http://www.concorde.edu/.

## Cottey College
### Nevada, Missouri

- **Independent** primarily 2-year, founded 1884
- **Small-town** 51-acre campus
- **Endowment** $108.8 million
- **Women only,** 265 undergraduate students, 98% full-time

**Undergraduates** 260 full-time, 5 part-time. Students come from 32 states and territories; 18 other countries; 85% are from out of state; 5% Black or African American, non-Hispanic/Latino; 8% Hispanic/Latino; 0.4% Asian, non-Hispanic/Latino; 0.4% Native Hawaiian or other Pacific Islander, non-Hispanic/Latino; 2% American Indian or Alaska Native, non-Hispanic/Latino; 5% Two or more races, non-Hispanic/Latino; 15% international; 4% transferred in; 90% live on campus. *Retention:* 70% of full-time freshmen returned.

**Freshmen** *Admission:* 525 applied, 338 admitted, 82 enrolled. *Average high school GPA:* 3.4. *Test scores:* SAT evidence-based reading and writing scores over 500: 73%; SAT math scores over 500: 52%; SAT evidence-based reading and writing scores over 600: 18%; SAT math scores over 600: 9%; SAT math scores over 700: 3%.

**Faculty** *Total:* 52, 79% full-time, 75% with terminal degrees. *Student/faculty ratio:* 7:1.

**Majors** Biological and physical sciences; business administration and management; criminology; English; environmental studies; ethnic, cultural minority, gender, and group studies related; fine/studio arts; international business/trade/commerce; international relations and affairs; organizational leadership; physical sciences; psychology; secondary education.

**Academics** *Calendar:* semesters. *Degrees:* associate and bachelor's. *Special study options:* advanced placement credit, distance learning, independent study, internships, part-time degree program, services for LD students, study abroad.

**Library** Blanche Skiff Ross Memorial Library plus 1 other. Weekly public service hours: 88.

**Student Life** *Housing Options:* women-only. Campus housing is university owned. *Activities and Organizations:* drama/theater group, choral group, Inter-Society, Golden Key, French Club, Student Government, Global Citizens. *Campus security:* 24-hour emergency response devices and patrols, late-night transport/escort service, controlled dormitory access. *Student services:* health clinic, personal/psychological counseling.

**Athletics** Member NJCAA. *Intercollegiate sports:* basketball W(s), cross-country running W(s), golf W(s), softball W(s), track and field W, volleyball W(s).

**Standardized Tests** *Required:* SAT or ACT (for admission). *Required for some:* TOEFL, IELTS.

**Costs (2018–19)** *Comprehensive fee:* $28,850 includes full-time tuition ($19,900), mandatory fees ($1250), and room and board ($7700). Part-time tuition: $125 per credit hour. Part-time tuition and fees vary according to course load. *Required fees:* $22 per credit hour part-time, $88 per term part-time. *Room and board:* college room only: $4200. Room and board charges vary according to housing facility. *Payment plan:* installment. *Waivers:* employees or children of employees.

**Financial Aid** Of all full-time matriculated undergraduates who enrolled in 2017, 208 applied for aid, 190 were judged to have need, 64 had their need fully met. 20 Federal Work-Study jobs (averaging $2071). In 2017, 69 non-need-based awards were made. *Average percent of need met:* 84%. *Average financial aid package:* $20,620. *Average need-based loan:* $3241. *Average need-based gift aid:* $16,929. *Average non-need-based aid:* $14,729. *Average indebtedness upon graduation:* $26,427.

**Applying** *Options:* electronic application, early admission, deferred entrance. *Application fee:* $20. *Required:* essay or personal statement, high school transcript, 1 letter of recommendation. *Recommended:* minimum 2.6 GPA, interview. *Application deadlines:* rolling (freshmen), rolling (transfers). *Notification:* continuous (freshmen), continuous (transfers).

**Freshman Application Contact** Mrs. Angela Moore, Enrollment Office, Cottey College, 1000 West Austin Boulevard, Nevada, MO 64772. *Phone:* 417-667-8181. *Toll-free phone:* 888-526-8839. *Fax:* 417-667-8103. *E-mail:* amoore@cottey.edu. *Website:* http://www.cottey.edu/.

## Crowder College
### Neosho, Missouri

- **State and locally supported** 2-year, founded 1963, part of Missouri Coordinating Board for Higher Education
- **Rural** 608-acre campus
- **Coed,** 4,960 undergraduate students

**Undergraduates** Students come from 12 states and territories; 6% are from out of state; 1% Black or African American, non-Hispanic/Latino; 9% Hispanic/Latino; 2% Asian, non-Hispanic/Latino; 0.4% Native Hawaiian or

other Pacific Islander, non-Hispanic/Latino; 2% American Indian or Alaska Native, non-Hispanic/Latino; 5% Two or more races, non-Hispanic/Latino; 2% Race/ethnicity unknown; 1% international; 10% live on campus. *Retention:* 64% of full-time freshmen returned.
**Faculty** *Total:* 454, 23% full-time, 7% with terminal degrees. *Student/faculty ratio:* 11:1.
**Majors** Administrative assistant and secretarial science; agribusiness; agricultural mechanization; agriculture; art; autobody/collision and repair technology; automobile/automotive mechanics technology; biology/biological sciences; business administration and management; business automation/technology/data entry; computer systems analysis; computer systems networking and telecommunications; construction engineering technology; construction trades; drafting and design technology; dramatic/theater arts; education; electrical, electronic and communications engineering technology; elementary education; emergency medical technology (EMT paramedic); energy management and systems technology; environmental engineering technology; executive assistant/executive secretary; farm and ranch management; fire science/firefighting; general studies; health information/medical records technology; industrial technology; legal administrative assistant/secretary; liberal arts and sciences/liberal studies; manufacturing engineering technology; mass communication/media; mathematics; mathematics and computer science; medical administrative assistant and medical secretary; music; occupational therapist assistant; physical education teaching and coaching; physical sciences; pre-engineering; psychology; public relations/image management; registered nursing/registered nurse; solar energy technology; veterinary/animal health technology; welding technology.
**Academics** *Calendar:* semesters. *Degree:* certificates and associate. *Special study options:* academic remediation for entering students, adult/continuing education programs, advanced placement credit, cooperative education, English as a second language, freshman honors college, honors programs, independent study, part-time degree program, student-designed majors, study abroad, summer session for credit.
**Library** Bill & Margot Lee Library.
**Student Life** *Housing Options:* men-only, women-only. Campus housing is university owned. *Activities and Organizations:* drama/theater group, student-run newspaper, choral group, Phi Theta Kappa, Students in Free Enterprise (SIFE), Baptist Student Union, Student Senate, Student Ambassadors. *Campus security:* 24-hour patrols.
**Athletics** Member NJCAA. *Intercollegiate sports:* baseball M(s), basketball W(s), soccer M(s).
**Costs (2017–18)** *Tuition:* area resident $2640 full-time, $88 per credit hour part-time; state resident $4110 full-time, $137 per credit hour part-time; nonresident $4110 full-time, $137 per credit hour part-time. Full-time tuition and fees vary according to program. Part-time tuition and fees vary according to program. *Required fees:* $690 full-time, $23 per credit hour part-time. *Room and board:* $3300; room only: $2300. Room and board charges vary according to board plan and housing facility. *Payment plan:* installment. *Waivers:* senior citizens and employees or children of employees.
**Financial Aid** Of all full-time matriculated undergraduates who enrolled in 2016, 150 Federal Work-Study jobs (averaging $1000).
**Applying** *Application fee:* $25. *Required:* high school transcript. *Application deadlines:* rolling (freshmen), rolling (transfers). *Notification:* continuous (freshmen).
**Freshman Application Contact** Mr. James P. Dickey, Admissions Coordinator, Crowder College, Neosho, MO 64850. *Phone:* 417-451-3223 Ext. 5466. *Toll-free phone:* 866-238-7788. *Fax:* 417-455-5731. *E-mail:* jamesdickey@crowder.edu.
*Website:* http://www.crowder.edu/.

## East Central College
### Union, Missouri

- **District-supported** 2-year, founded 1959
- **Rural** 207-acre campus with easy access to St. Louis
- **Endowment** $3.1 million
- **Coed,** 2,897 undergraduate students, 45% full-time, 60% women, 40% men

**Undergraduates** 1,292 full-time, 1,605 part-time. Students come from 1 other state; 1% Black or African American, non-Hispanic/Latino; 2% Hispanic/Latino; 0.9% Asian, non-Hispanic/Latino; 0.1% Native Hawaiian or other Pacific Islander, non-Hispanic/Latino; 0.5% American Indian or Alaska Native, non-Hispanic/Latino; 1% Two or more races, non-Hispanic/Latino; 0.9% Race/ethnicity unknown; 4% transferred in.
**Freshmen** *Admission:* 605 admitted, 605 enrolled.
**Faculty** *Total:* 222, 32% full-time, 5% with terminal degrees.
**Majors** Accounting technology and bookkeeping; automobile/automotive mechanics technology; biology/biotechnology laboratory technician; business/commerce; child-care and support services management; commercial and advertising art; computer systems networking and telecommunications;

construction trades; culinary arts; education; emergency medical technology (EMT paramedic); engineering; fine/studio arts; fire science/firefighting; general studies; health information/medical records technology; heating, air conditioning, ventilation and refrigeration maintenance technology; heavy/industrial equipment maintenance technologies related; machine tool technology; medical/clinical assistant; medical radiologic technology; music; occupational therapist assistant; precision production related; registered nursing/registered nurse; technical teacher education; welding technology.
**Academics** *Calendar:* semesters. *Degree:* certificates and associate. *Special study options:* academic remediation for entering students, adult/continuing education programs, advanced placement credit, distance learning, English as a second language, honors programs, independent study, internships, off-campus study, part-time degree program, services for LD students, study abroad, summer session for credit.
**Library** East Central College Library. *Books:* 23,718 (physical), 196,243 (digital/electronic); *Serial titles:* 50 (physical), 9 (digital/electronic); *Databases:* 40. Weekly public service hours: 55; students can reserve study rooms.
**Student Life** *Housing:* college housing not available. *Activities and Organizations:* drama/theater group, student-run newspaper, choral group, Student Nurse Association - Union Campus, Rolla Student Nurse Organization, R&R Club, Art Club, Engineering Club. *Campus security:* 24-hour emergency response devices, late-night transport/escort service. *Student services:* personal/psychological counseling.
**Athletics** Member NJCAA. *Intercollegiate sports:* soccer M(s), softball W(s), volleyball W(s).
**Costs (2018–19)** *Tuition:* area resident $2040 full-time, $85 per credit hour part-time; state resident $2928 full-time, $122 per credit hour part-time; nonresident $4344 full-time, $181 per credit hour part-time. Full-time tuition and fees vary according to course load and program. Part-time tuition and fees vary according to course load and program. *Required fees:* $552 full-time, $23 per credit hour part-time. *Payment plan:* installment. *Waivers:* senior citizens and employees or children of employees.
**Applying** *Options:* electronic application, early admission, deferred entrance. *Required:* high school transcript. *Application deadlines:* rolling (freshmen), rolling (transfers).
**Freshman Application Contact** Mr. Nathaniel Mitchell, Director, Admissions, East Central College, 1964 Prairie Dell Road, Union, MO 63084. *Phone:* 636-584-6552. *E-mail:* nathaniel.mitchell@eastcentral.edu. *Website:* http://www.eastcentral.edu/.

## Jefferson College
### Hillsboro, Missouri

**Freshman Application Contact** Dr. Kimberly Harvey, Director of Student Records and Admissions Services, Jefferson College, 1000 Viking Drive, Hillsboro, MO 63050-2441. *Phone:* 636-481-3205 Ext. 3205. *Fax:* 636-789-5103. *E-mail:* admissions@jeffco.edu. *Website:* http://www.jeffco.edu/.

## L'Ecole Culinaire–Kansas City
### Kansas City, Missouri

**Admissions Office Contact** L'Ecole Culinaire–Kansas City, 310 Ward Parkway, Kansas City, MO 64112. *Toll-free phone:* 855-549-7577. *Website:* http://www.lecole.edu/kansas-city/kansas-city-culinary-school.asp.

## L'Ecole Culinaire–St. Louis
### St. Louis, Missouri

**Admissions Office Contact** L'Ecole Culinaire–St. Louis, 9811 South Forty Drive, St. Louis, MO 63124. *Toll-free phone:* 855-764-0043. *Website:* http://www.lecole.edu/st-louis/st-louis-culinary-school.asp.

## Metro Business College
### Cape Girardeau, Missouri

**Director of Admissions** Ms. Kyla Evans, Admissions Director, Metro Business College, 1732 North Kingshighway, Cape Girardeau, MO 63701. *Phone:* 573-334-9181. *Toll-free phone:* 888-206-4545. *Fax:* 573-334-0617. *Website:* http://www.metrobusinesscollege.edu/.

## Metro Business College
### Jefferson City, Missouri

**Freshman Application Contact** Ms. Cheri Chockley, Campus Director, Metro Business College, 210 El Mercado Plaza, Jefferson City, MO 65109. *Phone:* 573-635-6600. *Toll-free phone:* 888-206-4545. *Fax:* 573-635-6999.

*E-mail:* cheri@metrobusinesscollege.edu. *Website:* http://www.metrobusinesscollege.edu/.

# Metro Business College
## Rolla, Missouri

**Freshman Application Contact** Admissions Office, Metro Business College, 1202 East Highway 72, Rolla, MO 65401. *Phone:* 573-364-8464. *Toll-free phone:* 888-206-4545. *Fax:* 573-364-8077. *E-mail:* inforolla@ metrobusinesscollege.edu. *Website:* http://www.metrobusinesscollege.edu/.

# Metropolitan Community College–Kansas City
## Kansas City, Missouri

**Freshman Application Contact** Dr. Tuesday Stanley, Vice Chancellor of Student Development and Enrollment Services, Metropolitan Community College–Kansas City, 3200 Broadway, Kansas City, MO 64111-2429. *Phone:* 816-604-1253. *E-mail:* tuesday.stanley@mcckc.edu. *Website:* http://www.mcckc.edu/.

# Midwest Institute
## Fenton, Missouri

**Freshman Application Contact** Admissions Office, Midwest Institute, 964 South Highway Drive, Fenton, MO 63026. *Toll-free phone:* 800-695-5550. *Website:* http://www.midwestinstitute.com/.

# Midwest Institute
## St. Louis, Missouri

**Freshman Application Contact** Admissions Office, Midwest Institute, 4260 Shoreline Drive, St. Louis, MO 63045. *Phone:* 314-344-4440. *Toll-free phone:* 800-695-5550. *Fax:* 314-344-0495. *Website:* http://www.midwestinstitute.com/.

# Mineral Area College
## Park Hills, Missouri

**Freshman Application Contact** Pam Reeder, Registrar, Mineral Area College, PO Box 1000, Park Hills, MO 63601-1000. *Phone:* 573-518-2204. *Fax:* 573-518-2166. *E-mail:* preeder@mineralarea.edu. *Website:* http://www.mineralarea.edu/.

# Missouri State University–West Plains
## West Plains, Missouri

- **State-supported** 2-year, founded 1963, part of Missouri State University
- **Small-town** 20-acre campus
- **Endowment** $7.4 million
- **Coed,** 1,918 undergraduate students, 49% full-time, 64% women, 36% men

**Undergraduates** 949 full-time, 969 part-time. Students come from 15 states and territories; 12 other countries; 3% are from out of state; 0.9% Black or African American, non-Hispanic/Latino; 2% Hispanic/Latino; 0.2% Asian, non-Hispanic/Latino; 83% Native Hawaiian or other Pacific Islander, non-Hispanic/Latino; 6% American Indian or Alaska Native, non-Hispanic/Latino; 3% Two or more races, non-Hispanic/Latino; 3% Race/ethnicity unknown; 0.7% international; 3% transferred in; 9% live on campus.
**Freshmen** *Admission:* 990 applied, 418 enrolled. *Average high school GPA:* 3.2.
**Faculty** *Total:* 115, 34% full-time, 14% with terminal degrees. *Student/faculty ratio:* 20:1.
**Majors** Agriculture; animation, interactive technology, video graphics and special effects; business/commerce; criminal justice/police science; elementary education; engineering; food science; general studies; health/medical preparatory programs related; health services/allied health/health sciences; human development and family studies; industrial production technologies related; registered nursing/registered nurse; respiratory care therapy; restaurant, culinary, and catering management; viticulture and enology.
**Academics** *Calendar:* semesters. *Degree:* certificates and associate. *Special study options:* academic remediation for entering students, adult/continuing education programs, advanced placement credit, cooperative education, distance learning, honors programs, internships, off-campus study, part-time

degree program, services for LD students, study abroad, summer session for credit.
**Library** Garnett Library. *Books:* 43,711 (physical), 261,723 (digital/electronic); *Serial titles:* 121 (physical), 2,889 (digital/electronic). Weekly public service hours: 78.
**Student Life** *Housing:* on-campus residence required for freshman year. *Options:* coed, special housing for students with disabilities. Campus housing is university owned and is provided by a third party. *Activities and Organizations:* Student Government Association, Grizzly Madness, Student Ambassadors, CCH, Phi Beta Lambda. *Campus security:* 24-hour patrols, student patrols, late-night transport/escort service, access only with key, agreement with city police for patrols. *Student services:* personal/psychological counseling, legal services, veterans affairs office.
**Athletics** Member NJCAA. *Intercollegiate sports:* basketball M(s), volleyball W(s).
**Costs (2018–19)** *Tuition:* state resident $3900 full-time, $130 per credit hour part-time; nonresident $7800 full-time, $260 per credit hour part-time. Full-time tuition and fees vary according to program and reciprocity agreements. Part-time tuition and fees vary according to program and reciprocity agreements. *Required fees:* $555 full-time, $555 per year part-time. *Room and board:* $6118. Room and board charges vary according to housing facility. *Payment plan:* deferred payment. *Waivers:* senior citizens and employees or children of employees.
**Financial Aid** Of all full-time matriculated undergraduates who enrolled in 2016, 63 Federal Work-Study jobs (averaging $2000).
**Applying** *Options:* electronic application. *Required for some:* high school transcript. *Application deadlines:* rolling (freshmen), rolling (transfers). *Notification:* continuous (freshmen), continuous (transfers).
**Freshman Application Contact** Ms. Melissa Jett, Coordinator of Admissions, Missouri State University–West Plains, 128 Garfield, West Plains, MO 65775. *Phone:* 417-255-7955. *Toll-free phone:* 888-466-7897. *Fax:* 417-255-7959. *E-mail:* melissajett@missouristate.edu. *Website:* http://wp.missouristate.edu/.

# Moberly Area Community College
## Moberly, Missouri

**Freshman Application Contact** Dr. James Grant, Dean of Student Services, Moberly Area Community College, Moberly, MO 65270-1304. *Phone:* 660-263-4110 Ext. 235. *Toll-free phone:* 800-622-2070. *Fax:* 660-263-2406. *E-mail:* info@macc.edu. *Website:* http://www.macc.edu/.

# North Central Missouri College
## Trenton, Missouri

- **District-supported** 2-year, founded 1925
- **Small-town** 2-acre campus
- **Coed**

**Undergraduates** 796 full-time, 709 part-time. Students come from 10 states and territories; 1% are from out of state; 6% transferred in. *Retention:* 69% of full-time freshmen returned.
**Faculty** *Student/faculty ratio:* 16:1.
**Academics** *Calendar:* semesters. *Degree:* certificates and associate. *Special study options:* academic remediation for entering students, accelerated degree program, adult/continuing education programs, advanced placement credit, cooperative education, distance learning, internships, part-time degree program, services for LD students, summer session for credit.
**Library** North Central Missouri College Library.
**Student Life** *Campus security:* controlled dormitory access.
**Athletics** Member NJCAA.
**Standardized Tests** *Recommended:* SAT or ACT (for admission).
**Costs (2017–18)** *Tuition:* area resident $2550 full-time, $85 per credit hour part-time; state resident $4350 full-time, $145 per credit hour part-time; nonresident $5250 full-time, $175 per credit hour part-time. Full-time tuition and fees vary according to location and program. Part-time tuition and fees vary according to location and program. *Required fees:* $960 full-time, $32 per credit hour part-time. *Room and board:* $5936. Room and board charges vary according to board plan.
**Financial Aid** Of all full-time matriculated undergraduates who enrolled in 2016, 40 Federal Work-Study jobs (averaging $1500). 25 state and other part-time jobs (averaging $1200).
**Applying** *Application fee:* $15. *Required:* high school transcript.
**Freshman Application Contact** Jamie Cunningham, Admissions Recruiter, North Central Missouri College, Trenton, MO 64683. *Phone:* 660-359-3948 Ext. 1414. *E-mail:* jcunningham@mail.ncmissouri.edu. *Website:* http://www.ncmissouri.edu/.

# Ozarks Technical Community College
## Springfield, Missouri

- **District-supported** 2-year, founded 1990, part of Missouri Coordinating Board for Higher Education
- **Urban** campus
- **Endowment** $2.8 million
- **Coed,** 13,260 undergraduate students, 44% full-time, 59% women, 41% men

**Undergraduates** 5,826 full-time, 7,434 part-time. Students come from 31 states and territories; 2% are from out of state; 3% Black or African American, non-Hispanic/Latino; 5% Hispanic/Latino; 1% Asian, non-Hispanic/Latino; 0.2% Native Hawaiian or other Pacific Islander, non-Hispanic/Latino; 0.5% American Indian or Alaska Native, non-Hispanic/Latino; 5% Two or more races, non-Hispanic/Latino; 2% Race/ethnicity unknown.
**Faculty** *Total:* 994, 21% full-time. *Student/faculty ratio:* 21:1.
**Majors** Accounting technology and bookkeeping; autobody/collision and repair technology; automobile/automotive mechanics technology; biology/biological sciences; biomedical technology; chemical technology; chemistry; child-care provision; communications technology; computer programming; computer systems networking and telecommunications; construction trades; culinary arts; dental assisting; dental hygiene; drafting and design technology; education (specific subject areas) related; electrical and electronic engineering technologies related; emergency medical technology (EMT paramedic); engineering; environmental science; fire science/firefighting; graphic communications; health information/medical records technology; health professions related; hearing instrument specialist; heating, ventilation, air conditioning and refrigeration engineering technology; heavy equipment maintenance technology; heavy/industrial equipment maintenance technologies related; liberal arts and sciences and humanities related; licensed practical/vocational nurse training; machine tool technology; manufacturing engineering technology; marketing/marketing management; medical insurance coding; occupational therapist assistant; physical therapy technology; precision production related; pre-pharmacy studies; registered nursing/registered nurse; respiratory care therapy; restaurant, culinary, and catering management; surgical technology; turf and turfgrass management; welding technology.
**Academics** *Calendar:* semesters. *Degree:* certificates, diplomas, and associate. *Special study options:* academic remediation for entering students, adult/continuing education programs, cooperative education, distance learning, double majors, English as a second language, honors programs, internships, off-campus study, part-time degree program, services for LD students, summer session for credit.
**Library** Main Library plus 1 other.
**Student Life** *Housing:* college housing not available. *Activities and Organizations:* student-run newspaper, choral group, Phi Theta Kappa. *Campus security:* 24-hour emergency response devices. *Student services:* personal/psychological counseling, veterans affairs office.
**Costs (2018–19)** *Tuition:* area resident $2592 full-time, $108 per credit hour part-time; state resident $3564 full-time, $149 per credit hour part-time; nonresident $4752 full-time, $198 per credit hour part-time. Full-time tuition and fees vary according to program. Part-time tuition and fees vary according to program. *Required fees:* $500 full-time, $22 per credit hour part-time, $50 per term part-time. *Payment plans:* installment, deferred payment. *Waivers:* employees or children of employees.
**Financial Aid** Of all full-time matriculated undergraduates who enrolled in 2016, 180 Federal Work-Study jobs (averaging $1533).
**Applying** *Options:* electronic application. *Required:* high school transcript. *Application deadlines:* rolling (freshmen), rolling (transfers). *Notification:* continuous (freshmen), continuous (transfers).
**Freshman Application Contact** Ozarks Technical Community College, 1001 E. Chestnut Expressway, Springfield, MO 65802.
*Website:* http://www.otc.edu/.

# Pinnacle Career Institute
## Kansas City, Missouri

**Director of Admissions** Ms. Ruth Matous, Director of Admissions, Pinnacle Career Institute, 10301 Hickman Mills Drive, Kansas City, MO 64137. *Phone:* 816-331-5700 Ext. 212. *Toll-free phone:* 877-241-3097. *Website:* http://www.pcitraining.edu/.

# Pinnacle Career Institute
## Kansas City, Missouri

**Freshman Application Contact** Pinnacle Career Institute, 11500 NW Ambassador Drive, Suite 221, Kansas City, MO 64153. *Phone:* 816-331-5700. *Toll-free phone:* 877-241-3097. *Website:* http://www.pcitraining.edu/.

# Ranken Technical College
## St. Louis, Missouri

**Freshman Application Contact** Ranken Technical College, 4431 Finney Avenue, St. Louis, MO 63113. *Phone:* 314-371-0233 Ext. 4811. *Toll-free phone:* 866-4-RANKEN. *Website:* http://www.ranken.edu/.

# St. Charles Community College
## Cottleville, Missouri

- **State-supported** 2-year, founded 1986, part of Missouri Coordinating Board for Higher Education
- **Suburban** 228-acre campus with easy access to St. Louis
- **Endowment** $80,985
- **Coed,** 6,563 undergraduate students, 50% full-time, 56% women, 44% men

**Undergraduates** 3,252 full-time, 3,311 part-time. Students come from 23 states and territories; 34 other countries; 7% Black or African American, non-Hispanic/Latino; 5% Hispanic/Latino; 2% Asian, non-Hispanic/Latino; 0.1% Native Hawaiian or other Pacific Islander, non-Hispanic/Latino; 0.3% American Indian or Alaska Native, non-Hispanic/Latino; 3% Two or more races, non-Hispanic/Latino; 4% Race/ethnicity unknown; 1% international; 8% transferred in.
**Freshmen** *Admission:* 1,376 enrolled.
**Faculty** *Total:* 369, 29% full-time, 23% with terminal degrees. *Student/faculty ratio:* 20:1.
**Majors** Accounting technology and bookkeeping; biology/biological sciences; chemistry; child-care and support services management; commercial and advertising art; computer programming; criminal justice/police science; drafting and design technology; education (specific subject areas) related; emergency medical technology (EMT paramedic); environmental health; general studies; health information/medical records technology; human services; industrial technology; liberal arts and sciences/liberal studies; manufacturing engineering technology; marketing/marketing management; music; occupational therapist assistant; office management; precision production related; pre-engineering; pre-pharmacy studies; registered nursing/registered nurse; teacher assistant/aide; welding technology.
**Academics** *Calendar:* semesters. *Degree:* certificates and associate. *Special study options:* academic remediation for entering students, adult/continuing education programs, advanced placement credit, cooperative education, distance learning, double majors, English as a second language, honors programs, independent study, internships, part-time degree program, services for LD students, study abroad, summer session for credit.
**Library** Paul and Helen Schnare Library. *Books:* 68,529 (physical), 30,188 (digital/electronic); *Serial titles:* 349 (physical), 318,195 (digital/electronic); *Databases:* 43. Weekly public service hours: 72.
**Student Life** *Activities and Organizations:* drama/theater group, student-run newspaper, choral group, Phi Theta Kappa, GAMES Club, Genders & Sexualities Alliance, Cougar Activities Crew, Student Ambassadors. *Campus security:* 24-hour emergency response devices and patrols, late-night transport/escort service, campus police officers on duty during normal operating hours. *Student services:* personal/psychological counseling, veterans affairs office.
**Athletics** Member NJCAA. *Intercollegiate sports:* baseball M(s), soccer M(s)/W(s), softball W(s).
**Costs (2017–18)** *Tuition:* area resident $2472 full-time, $103 per credit hour part-time; state resident $3696 full-time, $154 per credit hour part-time; nonresident $5184 full-time, $216 per credit hour part-time. Full-time tuition and fees vary according to course load, location, and program. Part-time tuition and fees vary according to course load, location, and program. *Required fees:* $192 full-time, $8 per credit hour part-time. *Payment plan:* installment. *Waivers:* senior citizens and employees or children of employees.
**Financial Aid** Of all full-time matriculated undergraduates who enrolled in 2016, 27 Federal Work-Study jobs (averaging $2630).
**Applying** *Options:* electronic application, early admission, deferred entrance. *Application fee:* $10. *Required for some:* high school transcript, minimum 2.5 GPA. *Recommended:* high school transcript. *Application deadlines:* rolling (freshmen), rolling (transfers). *Notification:* continuous (freshmen), continuous (transfers).
**Freshman Application Contact** Ms. Cassie Akins, Director of Enrollment Services/Registrar, St. Charles Community College, 4601 Mid Rivers Mall Drive, Cottleville, MO 63376-0975. *Phone:* 636-922-8436. *Fax:* 636-922-8236. *E-mail:* cakins@stchas.edu.
*Website:* http://www.stchas.edu/.

# St. Louis College of Health Careers
## Fenton, Missouri

**Admissions Office Contact** St. Louis College of Health Careers, 1297 North Highway Drive, Fenton, MO 63026. *Toll-free phone:* 866-529-2070. *Website:* http://www.slchc.com/.

# St. Louis College of Health Careers
## St. Louis, Missouri

**Freshman Application Contact** Admissions Office, St. Louis College of Health Careers, 909 South Taylor Avenue, St. Louis, MO 63110. *Phone:* 314-652-0300. *Toll-free phone:* 866-529-2070. *Fax:* 314-652-4825. *Website:* http://www.slchc.com/.

# St. Louis Community College
## St. Louis, Missouri

- **Public** 2-year, founded 1962, part of St. Louis Community College
- **Suburban** campus with easy access to St. Louis
- **Coed,** 18,835 undergraduate students, 38% full-time, 60% women, 40% men

**Undergraduates** 7,089 full-time, 11,746 part-time. Students come from 28 states and territories; 109 other countries; 2% are from out of state; 34% Black or African American, non-Hispanic/Latino; 3% Hispanic/Latino; 3% Asian, non-Hispanic/Latino; 0.1% Native Hawaiian or other Pacific Islander, non-Hispanic/Latino; 0.3% American Indian or Alaska Native, non-Hispanic/Latino; 5% Two or more races, non-Hispanic/Latino; 2% Race/ethnicity unknown; 1% international; 6% transferred in. *Retention:* 61% of full-time freshmen returned.
**Freshmen** *Admission:* 3,494 enrolled.
**Faculty** *Total:* 1,422, 28% full-time. *Student/faculty ratio:* 17:1.
**Majors** Accounting; automobile/automotive mechanics technology; baking and pastry arts; behavioral sciences; biotechnology; business administration and management; child development; clinical laboratory science/medical technology; computer and information systems security; computer software engineering; criminal justice/police science; culinary arts; dental hygiene; diesel mechanics technology; education; electrical and electronics engineering; emergency medical technology (EMT paramedic); engineering science; fire protection related; funeral service and mortuary science; general studies; graphic communications; health information/medical records technology; horticultural science; hospitality administration; human services; interior design; legal assistant/paralegal; management information systems; manufacturing engineering; network and system administration; nursing science; occupational therapist assistant; photography; physical therapy; radiologic technology/science; respiratory care therapy; sign language interpretation and translation; surgical technology.
**Academics** *Calendar:* semesters. *Degree:* certificates and associate. *Special study options:* academic remediation for entering students, accelerated degree program, adult/continuing education programs, advanced placement credit, distance learning, English as a second language, honors programs, independent study, internships, part-time degree program, services for LD students, study abroad, summer session for credit.
**Student Life** *Housing:* college housing not available. *Activities and Organizations:* drama/theater group, student-run newspaper. *Campus security:* 24-hour emergency response devices, late-night transport/escort service. *Student services:* personal/psychological counseling, veterans affairs office.
**Athletics** Member NJCAA. *Intercollegiate sports:* baseball M(s), basketball M(s)/W(s), soccer M(s)/W(s), softball W(s), volleyball W(s).
**Costs (2018–19)** *Tuition:* area resident $2790 full-time, $93 per credit hour part-time; state resident $4200 full-time, $140 per credit hour part-time; nonresident $5940 full-time, $198 per credit hour part-time. Full-time tuition and fees vary according to course load. Part-time tuition and fees vary according to course load. *Required fees:* $495 full-time, $17 per credit hour part-time. *Payment plan:* installment. *Waivers:* senior citizens and employees or children of employees.
**Applying** *Options:* electronic application. *Required for some:* high school transcript, interview. *Application deadlines:* rolling (freshmen), rolling (transfers). *Notification:* continuous (freshmen), continuous (transfers).
**Freshman Application Contact** St. Louis Community College, 300 South Broadway, St. Louis, MO 63102.
*Website:* http://www.stlcc.edu/.

# Southeast Missouri Hospital College of Nursing and Health Sciences
## Cape Girardeau, Missouri

**Freshman Application Contact** Southeast Missouri Hospital College of Nursing and Health Sciences, 2001 William Street, Cape Girardeau, MO 63701. *Phone:* 573-334-6825 Ext. 12. *Website:* http://www.sehcollege.edu/.

# State Fair Community College
## Sedalia, Missouri

**Freshman Application Contact** State Fair Community College, 3201 West 16th Street, Sedalia, MO 65301-2199. *Phone:* 660-596-7379. *Toll-free phone:* 877-311-7322. *Website:* http://www.sfccmo.edu/.

# State Technical College of Missouri
## Linn, Missouri

- **State-supported** 2-year, founded 1961
- **Rural** 350-acre campus
- **Coed, primarily men,** 1,256 undergraduate students, 83% full-time, 18% women, 82% men

**Undergraduates** 1,041 full-time, 215 part-time. Students come from 7 states and territories; 3% are from out of state; 1% Black or African American, non-Hispanic/Latino; 2% Hispanic/Latino; 0.2% Asian, non-Hispanic/Latino; 0.3% American Indian or Alaska Native, non-Hispanic/Latino; 0.1% Two or more races, non-Hispanic/Latino; 2% Race/ethnicity unknown; 10% transferred in; 11% live on campus. *Retention:* 86% of full-time freshmen returned.
**Freshmen** *Admission:* 521 enrolled.
**Faculty** *Total:* 111, 79% full-time, 2% with terminal degrees. *Student/faculty ratio:* 11:1.
**Majors** Aircraft powerplant technology; airframe mechanics and aircraft maintenance technology; autobody/collision and repair technology; automobile/automotive mechanics technology; civil engineering technology; computer programming; computer systems networking and telecommunications; drafting and design technology; electrical, electronic and communications engineering technology; electrical/electronics equipment installation and repair; electrician; heating, air conditioning, ventilation and refrigeration maintenance technology; heavy equipment maintenance technology; lineworker; machine tool technology; management information systems; manufacturing engineering technology; motorcycle maintenance and repair technology; nuclear/nuclear power technology; physical therapy technology; turf and turfgrass management; welding technology.
**Academics** *Calendar:* semesters. *Degree:* certificates and associate. *Special study options:* academic remediation for entering students, adult/continuing education programs, advanced placement credit, cooperative education, distance learning, double majors, external degree program, independent study, internships, off-campus study, part-time degree program, services for LD students, summer session for credit.
**Library** State Technical College of Missouri Library plus 1 other. Weekly public service hours: 64; students can reserve study rooms.
**Student Life** *Housing Options:* coed, men-only, women-only, special housing for students with disabilities. Campus housing is university owned. *Activities and Organizations:* SkillsUSA, Phi Theta Kappa, Student Government Association, Aviation Club, Electricity Club. *Campus security:* 24-hour emergency response devices, student patrols, controlled dormitory access, indoor and outdoor surveillance cameras. *Student services:* health clinic, personal/psychological counseling.
**Athletics** *Intramural sports:* archery M/W, basketball M/W, riflery M/W, softball M/W, volleyball M/W.
**Standardized Tests** *Required:* ACCUPLACER (for admission). *Required for some:* ACT (for admission).
**Financial Aid** Of all full-time matriculated undergraduates who enrolled in 2016, 70 Federal Work-Study jobs (averaging $769).
**Applying** *Options:* electronic application, early admission, early decision, early action. *Required:* high school transcript. *Required for some:* essay or personal statement, 1 letter of recommendation, interview. *Application deadlines:* rolling (freshmen), rolling (transfers). *Notification:* continuous (freshmen), continuous (transfers).
**Freshman Application Contact** State Technical College of Missouri, One Technology Drive, Linn, MO 65051-9606. *Phone:* 573-897-5196. *Toll-free phone:* 800-743-TECH.
*Website:* http://www.statetechmo.edu/.

# Texas County Technical College
## Houston, Missouri

**Admissions Office Contact** Texas County Technical College, 6915 S. Hwy 63, Houston, MO 65483. *Website:* http://www.texascountytech.edu/.

# Three Rivers College
## Poplar Bluff, Missouri

- **State and locally supported** 2-year, founded 1966, part of Missouri Coordinating Board for Higher Education
- **Rural** 80-acre campus
- **Coed,** 3,226 undergraduate students, 55% full-time, 66% women, 34% men

**Undergraduates** 1,789 full-time, 1,437 part-time. Students come from 14 states and territories; 1 other country; 3% are from out of state; 10% Black or African American, non-Hispanic/Latino; 2% Hispanic/Latino; 0.5% Asian, non-Hispanic/Latino; 0.1% Native Hawaiian or other Pacific Islander, non-Hispanic/Latino; 0.5% American Indian or Alaska Native, non-Hispanic/Latino; 7% Race/ethnicity unknown; 0.2% international; 2% transferred in; 5% live on campus.
**Freshmen** *Admission:* 818 applied, 818 admitted, 818 enrolled.
**Faculty** *Total:* 306, 22% full-time, 7% with terminal degrees.
**Majors** Accounting technology and bookkeeping; administrative assistant and secretarial science; agricultural mechanization; child-care and support services management; clinical/medical laboratory technology; computer systems networking and telecommunications; construction engineering technology; criminal justice/police science; education (multiple levels); education (specific subject areas) related; emergency medical technology (EMT paramedic); environmental health; fire science/firefighting; forest/forest resources management; forest technology; health/medical preparatory programs related; liberal arts and sciences/liberal studies; manufacturing engineering technology; marketing/marketing management; mechanic and repair technologies related; occupational safety and health technology; occupational therapist assistant; pre-engineering; prenursing studies; pre-optometry; pre-pharmacy studies; registered nursing/registered nurse; welding technology.
**Academics** *Calendar:* semesters. *Degree:* certificates and associate. *Special study options:* academic remediation for entering students, adult/continuing education programs, advanced placement credit, cooperative education, distance learning, double majors, English as a second language, external degree program, honors programs, independent study, off-campus study, part-time degree program, services for LD students, summer session for credit.
**Library** Rutland Library. *Books:* 15,286 (physical), 200,299 (digital/electronic); *Serial titles:* 40 (physical); *Databases:* 53. Weekly public service hours: 57; students can reserve study rooms.
**Student Life** *Housing Options:* coed. Campus housing is university owned. *Activities and Organizations:* drama/theater group, choral group, Marketing Management Association, Phi Theta Kappa, Phi Beta Lambda, GO FAR, TRCC Aggies. *Campus security:* 24-hour emergency response devices, 24-hour Mass Notification and Storm Warning System. *Student services:* personal/psychological counseling, veterans affairs office.
**Athletics** Member NJCAA. *Intercollegiate sports:* baseball M(s), basketball M(s)/W(s), softball W(s).
**Costs (2018–19)** *Tuition:* area resident $2760 full-time, $92 per credit hour part-time; state resident $4200 full-time, $140 per credit hour part-time; nonresident $5340 full-time, $178 per credit hour part-time. *Required fees:* $1200 full-time, $40 per credit hour part-time. *Room and board:* room only: $3440. *Payment plan:* installment. *Waivers:* senior citizens and employees or children of employees.
**Applying** *Options:* electronic application, early admission. *Required for some:* high school transcript. *Recommended:* high school transcript. *Application deadlines:* rolling (freshmen), rolling (transfers). *Notification:* continuous (freshmen), continuous (transfers).
**Freshman Application Contact** Three Rivers College, 2080 Three Rivers Boulevard, Poplar Bluff, MO 63901-2393. *Toll-free phone:* 877-TRY-TRCC. *Website:* http://www.trcc.edu/.

# Vatterott College
## Berkeley, Missouri

**Director of Admissions** Ann Farajallah, Director of Admissions, Vatterott College, 8580 Evans Avenue, Berkeley, MO 63134. *Phone:* 314-264-1020. *Toll-free phone:* 888-553-6627. *Website:* http://www.vatterott.edu/.

# Vatterott College
## Joplin, Missouri

**Admissions Office Contact** Vatterott College, 809 Illinois Avenue, Joplin, MO 64801. *Toll-free phone:* 800-934-6975. *Website:* http://www.vatterott.edu/.

# Vatterott College
## Kansas City, Missouri

**Admissions Office Contact** Vatterott College, 4131 N. Corrington Avenue, Kansas City, MO 64117. *Toll-free phone:* 888-553-6627. *Website:* http://www.vatterott.edu/.

# Vatterott College
## St. Charles, Missouri

**Director of Admissions** Gertrude Bogan-Jones, Director of Admissions, Vatterott College, 3550 West Clay Street, St. Charles, MO 63301. *Phone:* 636-978-7488. *Toll-free phone:* 888-553-6627. *Fax:* 636-978-5121. *E-mail:* ofallon@vatterott-college.edu. *Website:* http://www.vatterott.edu/.

# Vatterott College
## St. Joseph, Missouri

**Director of Admissions** Director of Admissions, Vatterott College, 3709 Belt Highway, St. Joseph, MO 64506. *Phone:* 816-364-5399. *Toll-free phone:* 888-553-6627. *Fax:* 816-364-1593. *Website:* http://www.vatterott.edu/.

# Vatterott College
## Springfield, Missouri

**Freshman Application Contact** Mr. Scott Lester, Director of Admissions, Vatterott College, 3850 South Campbell Avenue, Springfield, MO 65807. *Phone:* 417-831-8116. *Toll-free phone:* 888-553-6627. *Fax:* 417-831-5099. *E-mail:* springfield@vatterott-college.edu. *Website:* http://www.vatterott.edu/.

# Vatterott College
## Sunset Hills, Missouri

**Director of Admissions** Director of Admission, Vatterott College, 12900 Maurer Industrial Drive, Sunset Hills, MO 63127. *Phone:* 314-843-4200. *Toll-free phone:* 888-553-6627. *Fax:* 314-843-1709. *Website:* http://www.vatterott.edu/.

# WellSpring School of Allied Health
## Kansas City, Missouri

**Admissions Office Contact** WellSpring School of Allied Health, 9140 Ward Parkway, Suite 100, Kansas City, MO 64114. *Website:* http://www.wellspring.edu/.

# MONTANA

# Aaniiih Nakoda College
## Harlem, Montana

- **Federally supported** 2-year, founded 1984
- **Rural** 3-acre campus
- **Coed**

**Faculty** *Student/faculty ratio:* 11:1.
**Academics** *Calendar:* quarters. *Degree:* certificates and associate. *Special study options:* academic remediation for entering students, cooperative education, part-time degree program.
**Library** Fort Belknap College Library.
**Student Life** *Campus security:* 24-hour patrols.
**Applying** *Options:* early admission, deferred entrance. *Application fee:* $10. *Required:* high school transcript.
**Freshman Application Contact** Aaniiih Nakoda College, PO Box 159, Harlem, MT 59526-0159. *Phone:* 406-353-2607 Ext. 233. *Website:* http://www.ancollege.edu/.

# Blackfeet Community College
## Browning, Montana

**Freshman Application Contact** Ms. Deana M. McNabb, Registrar and Admissions Officer, Blackfeet Community College, PO Box 819, Browning, MT 59417-0819. *Phone:* 406-338-5421. *Toll-free phone:* 800-549-7457. *Fax:* 406-338-3272. *Website:* http://www.bfcc.edu/.

# Chief Dull Knife College
## Lame Deer, Montana

**Freshman Application Contact** Director of Admissions, Chief Dull Knife College, PO Box 98, 1 College Drive, Lame Deer, MT 59043-0098. *Phone:* 406-477-6215. *Website:* http://www.cdkc.edu/.

# Dawson Community College
## Glendive, Montana

- **State and locally supported** 2-year, founded 1940, part of Montana University System
- **Rural** 300-acre campus
- **Endowment** $3.5 million
- **Coed,** 329 undergraduate students, 62% full-time, 50% women, 50% men

**Undergraduates** 205 full-time, 124 part-time. Students come from 19 states and territories; 2 other countries; 80% are from out of state; 5% Black or African American, non-Hispanic/Latino; 3% Hispanic/Latino; 0.9% Asian, non-Hispanic/Latino; 0.3% Native Hawaiian or other Pacific Islander, non-Hispanic/Latino; 3% American Indian or Alaska Native, non-Hispanic/Latino; 4% Two or more races, non-Hispanic/Latino; 2% Race/ethnicity unknown; 2% international; 11% transferred in.

**Freshmen** *Admission:* 326 applied, 326 admitted, 112 enrolled.

**Faculty** *Total:* 32, 41% full-time, 16% with terminal degrees. *Student/faculty ratio:* 17:1.

**Majors** Agricultural business and management; business/commerce; child-care provision; clinical/medical social work; community psychology; computer and information sciences; computer and information sciences related; criminal justice/police science; industrial production technologies related; liberal arts and sciences/liberal studies; music; substance abuse/addiction counseling; welding technology.

**Academics** *Calendar:* semesters. *Degree:* certificates and associate. *Special study options:* academic remediation for entering students, adult/continuing education programs, distance learning, independent study, internships, part-time degree program, services for LD students, summer session for credit.

**Library** Jane Carey Memorial Library plus 1 other. *Books:* 33,477 (physical), 13,359 (digital/electronic); *Serial titles:* 81 (physical); *Databases:* 118. Weekly public service hours: 40; students can reserve study rooms.

**Student Life** *Housing Options:* coed. Campus housing is university owned. *Activities and Organizations:* drama/theater group, choral group, Phi Theta Kappa, Associated Student Body, Rodeo Club, Intervarsity, FFA. *Campus security:* 24-hour emergency response devices.

**Athletics** Member NJCAA. *Intercollegiate sports:* baseball M, basketball M(s)/W(s), equestrian sports M(s)/W(s), softball W, volleyball W(s). *Intramural sports:* basketball M/W, bowling M/W, golf M/W, racquetball M/W, softball M/W, table tennis M/W, tennis M/W, volleyball M/W.

**Costs (2018–19)** *Tuition:* area resident $2100 full-time, $70 per credit hour part-time; state resident $3630 full-time, $121 per credit hour part-time; nonresident $6150 full-time, $205 per credit hour part-time. *Required fees:* $1620 full-time, $54 per credit hour part-time. *Room and board:* $7574. Room and board charges vary according to board plan. *Payment plan:* deferred payment. *Waivers:* senior citizens and employees or children of employees.

**Financial Aid** Of all full-time matriculated undergraduates who enrolled in 2016, 158 applied for aid, 158 were judged to have need. 35 Federal Work-Study jobs (averaging $2200). 8 state and other part-time jobs (averaging $2200).

**Applying** *Options:* electronic application, deferred entrance. *Application fee:* $30. *Required:* high school transcript. *Application deadlines:* rolling (freshmen), rolling (transfers). *Notification:* continuous (freshmen), continuous (transfers).

**Freshman Application Contact** Ms. Julie Brandt, Admissions Specialist, Dawson Community College, 300 College Drive, Glendive, MT 59330. *Phone:* 406-377-9411. *Toll-free phone:* 800-821-8320. *Fax:* 406-377-8132. *E-mail:* jbrandt@dawson.edu. *Website:* http://www.dawson.edu/.

# Flathead Valley Community College
## Kalispell, Montana

**Freshman Application Contact** Ms. Marlene C. Stoltz, Admissions/Graduation Coordinator, Flathead Valley Community College, 777 Grandview Drive, Kalispell, MT 59901-2622. *Phone:* 406-756-3846. *Toll-free phone:* 800-313-3822. *E-mail:* mstoltz@fvcc.cc.mt.us. *Website:* http://www.fvcc.edu/.

# Fort Peck Community College
## Poplar, Montana

**Director of Admissions** Mr. Robert McAnally, Vice President for Student Services, Fort Peck Community College, PO Box 398, Poplar, MT 59255-0398. *Phone:* 406-768-6329. *Website:* http://www.fpcc.edu/.

# Great Falls College Montana State University
## Great Falls, Montana

- **State-supported** 2-year, founded 1969, part of Montana University System
- **Small-town** 40-acre campus
- **Endowment** $11,300
- **Coed,** 1,690 undergraduate students, 38% full-time, 71% women, 29% men

**Undergraduates** 646 full-time, 1,044 part-time. Students come from 28 states and territories; 2 other countries; 4% are from out of state; 2% Black or African American, non-Hispanic/Latino; 5% Hispanic/Latino; 0.9% Asian, non-Hispanic/Latino; 0.1% Native Hawaiian or other Pacific Islander, non-Hispanic/Latino; 5% American Indian or Alaska Native, non-Hispanic/Latino; 5% Two or more races, non-Hispanic/Latino; 2% Race/ethnicity unknown; 0.1% international; 7% transferred in.

**Freshmen** *Admission:* 412 applied, 353 admitted, 201 enrolled.

**Faculty** *Total:* 114, 39% full-time, 16% with terminal degrees. *Student/faculty ratio:* 15:1.

**Majors** Accounting; computer programming; computer systems networking and telecommunications; dental hygiene; emergency medical technology (EMT paramedic); health information/medical records technology; information technology; liberal arts and sciences and humanities related; licensed practical/vocational nurse training; medical/clinical assistant; physical therapy technology; registered nursing/registered nurse; respiratory care therapy; surgical technology; welding technology.

**Academics** *Calendar:* semesters. *Degree:* certificates and associate. *Special study options:* academic remediation for entering students, advanced placement credit, distance learning, double majors, independent study, internships, off-campus study, part-time degree program, services for LD students, summer session for credit.

**Library** Weaver Library plus 1 other. *Books:* 9,239 (physical), 266,102 (digital/electronic); *Serial titles:* 60 (physical), 121,995 (digital/electronic); *Databases:* 55. Students can reserve study rooms.

**Student Life** *Housing:* college housing not available. *Activities and Organizations:* choral group, The Associated Students of Great Falls College Montana State University, Phi Theta Kappa, Medical Assistant Club, Dental Hygiene Club, Nursing Club. *Campus security:* 24-hour emergency response devices, patrol by security personnel. *Student services:* veterans affairs office.

**Costs (2017–18)** *Tuition:* state resident $2621 full-time, $109 per credit hour part-time; nonresident $9819 full-time, $471 per credit hour part-time. Full-time tuition and fees vary according to course load, location, and program. Part-time tuition and fees vary according to course load, location, and program. *Required fees:* $634 full-time, $59 per credit hour part-time, $30 per term part-time. *Payment plan:* deferred payment. *Waivers:* minority students, senior citizens, and employees or children of employees.

**Financial Aid** Of all full-time matriculated undergraduates who enrolled in 2015, 658 applied for aid, 656 were judged to have need, 170 had their need fully met. In 2015, 12 non-need-based awards were made. *Average percent of need met:* 75%. *Average financial aid package:* $8997. *Average need-based loan:* $5841. *Average need-based gift aid:* $4807. *Average non-need-based aid:* $684.

**Applying** *Options:* electronic application, early admission. *Application fee:* $30. *Required:* high school transcript, proof of immunization. *Application deadlines:* rolling (freshmen), rolling (transfers). *Notification:* continuous (freshmen), continuous (transfers).

**Freshman Application Contact** Mr. Joe Simonsen, Admissions, Great Falls College Montana State University, 2100 16th Avenue South, Great Falls, MT 59405. *Phone:* 406-771-4309. *Toll-free phone:* 800-446-2698. *Fax:* 406-771-2267. *E-mail:* joe.simonsen@gfcmsu.edu. *Website:* http://www.gfcmsu.edu/.

## Helena College University of Montana
Helena, Montana

Freshman Application Contact Mr. Ryan Loomis, Admissions Representative/Recruiter, Helena College University of Montana, 1115 North Roberts Street, Helena, MT 59601. *Phone:* 406-447-6904. *Toll-free phone:* 800-241-4882. *Website:* http://www.umhelena.edu/.

## Highlands College of Montana Tech
Butte, Montana

Admissions Office Contact Highlands College of Montana Tech, 25 Basin Creek Road, Butte, MT 59701. *Website:* http://www.mtech.edu/academics/highlands/.

## Little Big Horn College
Crow Agency, Montana

Freshman Application Contact Ms. Ann Bullis, Dean of Student Services, Little Big Horn College, Box 370, 1 Forest Lane, Crow Agency, MT 59022-0370. *Phone:* 406-638-2228 Ext. 50. *Website:* http://www.lbhc.edu/.

## Miles Community College
Miles City, Montana

Freshman Application Contact Mr. Haley Anderson, Admissions Representative, Miles Community College, 2715 Dickinson Street, Miles City, MT 59301. *Phone:* 406-874-6178. *Toll-free phone:* 800-541-9281. *E-mail:* andersonh@milescc.edu. *Website:* http://www.milescc.edu/.

## Pima Medical Institute
Dillon, Montana

Admissions Office Contact Pima Medical Institute, 434 East Poindexter Street, Dillon, MT 59725. *Website:* http://www.pmi.edu/.

## Salish Kootenai College
Pablo, Montana

Freshman Application Contact Ms. Jackie Moran, Admissions Officer, Salish Kootenai College, PO Box 70, Pablo, MT 59855-0117. *Phone:* 406-275-4866. *Fax:* 406-275-4810. *E-mail:* jackie_moran@skc.edu. *Website:* http://www.skc.edu/.

## Stone Child College
Box Elder, Montana

Director of Admissions Mr. Ted Whitford, Director of Admissions/Registrar, Stone Child College, 8294 Upper Box Elder Road, Box Elder, MT 59521. *Phone:* 406-395-4313 Ext. 110. *E-mail:* uanet337@quest.ocsc.montana.edu. *Website:* http://www.stonechild.edu/.

# NEBRASKA

## Central Community College–Columbus Campus
Columbus, Nebraska

Freshman Application Contact Ms. Erica Leffler, Admissions/Recruiting Coordinator, Central Community College–Columbus Campus, PO Box 1027, Columbus, NE 68602-1027. *Phone:* 402-562-1296. *Toll-free phone:* 877-CCC-0780. *Fax:* 402-562-1201. *E-mail:* eleffler@cccneb.edu. *Website:* http://www.cccneb.edu/.

## Central Community College–Grand Island Campus
Grand Island, Nebraska

Freshman Application Contact Michelle Lubken, Admissions Director, Central Community College–Grand Island Campus, PO Box 4903, Grand Island, NE 68802-4903. *Phone:* 308-398-7406 Ext. 406. *Toll-free phone:* 877-CCC-0780. *Fax:* 308-398-7398. *E-mail:* mlubken@cccneb.edu. *Website:* http://www.cccneb.edu/.

## Central Community College–Hastings Campus
Hastings, Nebraska

Freshman Application Contact Mr. Robert Glenn, Admissions and Recruiting Director, Central Community College–Hastings Campus, PO Box 1024, East Highway 6, Hastings, NE 68902-1024. *Phone:* 402-461-2428. *Toll-free phone:* 877-CCC-0780. *E-mail:* rglenn@ccneb.edu. *Website:* http://www.cccneb.edu/.

## CHI Health School of Radiologic Technology
Omaha, Nebraska

- **Independent** 2-year
- **Urban** 1-acre campus with easy access to Omaha, NE
- **Coed,** 15 undergraduate students, 100% full-time, 87% women, 13% men

Undergraduates 15 full-time. Students come from 4 states and territories; 20% are from out of state; 7% Black or African American, non-Hispanic/Latino. *Retention:* 9% of full-time freshmen returned.
Faculty *Total:* 3. *Student/faculty ratio:* 7:1.
Majors Radiologic technology/science.
Academics *Degree:* associate. *Special study options:* academic remediation for entering students, services for LD students.
Student Life *Housing:* college housing not available. *Campus security:* 24-hour emergency response devices and patrols. *Student services:* health clinic, personal/psychological counseling, legal services.
Standardized Tests *Required:* entrance exam (for admission).
Costs (2018–19) *One-time required fee:* $25. *Tuition:* $6250 full-time. No tuition increase for student's term of enrollment. *Payment plan:* installment.
Applying *Application fee:* $25. *Required:* essay or personal statement, high school transcript, minimum 2.0 GPA, 3 letters of recommendation, interview. *Required for some:* interview. *Application deadline:* 2/1 (freshmen).
Freshman Application Contact CHI Health School of Radiologic Technology, 6911 North 68th Plaza, Omaha, NE 68122. *Phone:* 402-572-3650.
*Website:* http://www.chihealth.com/school-of-radiologic-technology.

## Kaplan University, Lincoln
Lincoln, Nebraska

Freshman Application Contact Kaplan University, Lincoln, 1821 K Street, Lincoln, NE 68508. *Phone:* 402-474-5315. *Toll-free phone:* 800-987-7734. *Website:* http://www.kaplanuniversity.edu/.

## Kaplan University, Omaha
Omaha, Nebraska

Freshman Application Contact Kaplan University, Omaha, 5425 North 103rd Street, Omaha, NE 68134. *Phone:* 402-572-8500. *Toll-free phone:* 800-987-7734. *Website:* http://www.kaplanuniversity.edu/.

## Little Priest Tribal College
Winnebago, Nebraska

Freshman Application Contact Little Priest Tribal College, PO Box 270, Winnebago, NE 68071. *Phone:* 402-878-2380 Ext. 112. *Website:* http://www.littlepriest.edu/.

## Metropolitan Community College
Omaha, Nebraska

- **State and locally supported** 2-year, founded 1974, part of Nebraska Coordinating Commission for Postsecondary Education
- **Urban** 172-acre campus
- **Endowment** $1.4 million
- **Coed**

Undergraduates 7,095 full-time, 9,908 part-time. 3% are from out of state; 17% transferred in. *Retention:* 50% of full-time freshmen returned.
Faculty *Student/faculty ratio:* 16:1.
Academics *Calendar:* quarters. *Degree:* certificates, diplomas, and associate. *Special study options:* academic remediation for entering students, adult/continuing education programs, advanced placement credit, cooperative education, distance learning, English as a second language, independent study, internships, part-time degree program, services for LD students, summer session for credit. *ROTC:* Army (c).

**Library** Metropolitan Community College plus 2 others.
**Student Life** *Campus security:* 24-hour emergency response devices and patrols, late-night transport/escort service, controlled dormitory access, security on duty 9 pm to 6 am.
**Costs (2017–18)** *Tuition:* state resident $3015 full-time, $61 per credit hour part-time; nonresident $4342 full-time, $92 per credit hour part-time. Full-time tuition and fees vary according to course load and program. Part-time tuition and fees vary according to course load and program. *Required fees:* $225 full-time, $5 per credit hour part-time. *Room and board:* $2850. *Payment plans:* installment, deferred payment.
**Applying** *Options:* early admission. *Recommended:* high school transcript.
**Freshman Application Contact** Ms. Maria Vazquez, Associate Vice President for Student Affairs, Metropolitan Community College, PO Box 3777, Omaha, NE 69103-0777. *Phone:* 402-457-2430. *Toll-free phone:* 800-228-9553. *Fax:* 402-457-2238. *E-mail:* mvazquez@mccneb.edu. *Website:* http://www.mccneb.edu/.

# Mid-Plains Community College
## North Platte, Nebraska

- **District-supported** 2-year, founded 1973
- **Small-town** campus
- **Endowment** $6.6 million
- **Coed,** 2,222 undergraduate students, 36% full-time, 59% women, 41% men

**Undergraduates** 800 full-time, 1,422 part-time. Students come from 30 states and territories; 13 other countries; 9% are from out of state; 2% Black or African American, non-Hispanic/Latino; 8% Hispanic/Latino; 0.6% Asian, non-Hispanic/Latino; 0.1% Native Hawaiian or other Pacific Islander, non-Hispanic/Latino; 0.5% American Indian or Alaska Native, non-Hispanic/Latino; 2% Two or more races, non-Hispanic/Latino; 2% Race/ethnicity unknown; 2% international; 20% live on campus.
**Freshmen** *Admission:* 321 admitted.
**Faculty** *Total:* 384, 16% full-time, 2% with terminal degrees. *Student/faculty ratio:* 8:1.
**Majors** Administrative assistant and secretarial science; autobody/collision and repair technology; automobile/automotive mechanics technology; building/construction finishing, management, and inspection related; business administration and management; clinical/medical laboratory technology; commercial and advertising art; computer and information sciences; construction engineering technology; dental assisting; diesel mechanics technology; fine arts related; fire science/firefighting; heating, air conditioning, ventilation and refrigeration maintenance technology; liberal arts and sciences/liberal studies; licensed practical/vocational nurse training; registered nursing/registered nurse; transportation and materials moving related; welding technology.
**Academics** *Calendar:* semesters. *Degree:* certificates, diplomas, and associate. *Special study options:* academic remediation for entering students, accelerated degree program, adult/continuing education programs, advanced placement credit, cooperative education, distance learning, double majors, English as a second language, external degree program, independent study, internships, part-time degree program, services for LD students, summer session for credit.
**Library** von Riesen Library plus 1 other. *Books:* 17,993 (physical), 51,889 (digital/electronic); *Serial titles:* 50 (physical); *Databases:* 37. Weekly public service hours: 70; students can reserve study rooms.
**Student Life** *Housing Options:* coed, special housing for students with disabilities. Campus housing is university owned. *Activities and Organizations:* drama/theater group, student-run newspaper, choral group, Student Senate, Phi Theta Kappa, Phi Beta Lambda, Intercollegiate Athletics, MPCC Student Nurses Association, national fraternities, national sororities. *Campus security:* controlled dormitory access. *Student services:* personal/psychological counseling.
**Athletics** Member NJCAA. *Intercollegiate sports:* baseball M(s), basketball M(s)/W(s), golf M(s), softball W(s), volleyball W(s). *Intramural sports:* baseball M, basketball M/W, softball W, volleyball W.
**Standardized Tests** *Required for some:* ACCUPLACER. *Recommended:* ACT (for admission).
**Costs (2018–19)** *Tuition:* state resident $2760 full-time, $92 per credit hour part-time; nonresident $4050 full-time, $120 per credit hour part-time. Full-time tuition and fees vary according to course load, program, and reciprocity agreements. Part-time tuition and fees vary according to course load, program, and reciprocity agreements. *Required fees:* $450 full-time, $15 per credit hour part-time. *Room and board:* $6500; room only: $3000. Room and board charges vary according to board plan, housing facility, and location. *Payment*

*plan:* installment. *Waivers:* senior citizens and employees or children of employees.
**Financial Aid** Of all full-time matriculated undergraduates who enrolled in 2016, 591 applied for aid, 481 were judged to have need, 83 had their need fully met. 36 Federal Work-Study jobs (averaging $1017). In 2016, 118 non-need-based awards were made. *Average percent of need met:* 68%. *Average financial aid package:* $6851. *Average need-based loan:* $2556. *Average need-based gift aid:* $5644. *Average non-need-based aid:* $1881.
**Applying** *Options:* electronic application, deferred entrance. *Required:* high school transcript. *Required for some:* 2 letters of recommendation, interview. *Application deadlines:* rolling (freshmen), rolling (transfers). *Notification:* continuous (freshmen), continuous (transfers).
**Freshman Application Contact** Ms. Sandy Ablard, Admissions Specialist, Mid-Plains Community College, 1101 Halligan Drive, North Platte, NE 69101. *Phone:* 308-535-3609. *Toll-free phone:* 800-658-4308 (in-state); 800-658-4348 (out-of-state). *Fax:* 308-534-5767. *E-mail:* ablards@mpcc.edu. *Website:* http://www.mpcc.edu/.

# Myotherapy Institute
## Lincoln, Nebraska

**Freshman Application Contact** Admissions Office, Myotherapy Institute, 4001 Pioneers Woods Drive, Lincoln, NE 68506. *Phone:* 402-421-7410. *Website:* http://www.myotherapy.edu/.

# Nebraska College of Technical Agriculture
## Curtis, Nebraska

**Freshman Application Contact** Kevin Martin, Assistant Admissions Coordinator, Nebraska College of Technical Agriculture, 404 East 7th Street, Curtis, NE 69025. *Phone:* 308-367-4124. *Toll-free phone:* 800-3CURTIS. *Website:* http://www.ncta.unl.edu/.

# Nebraska Indian Community College
## Macy, Nebraska

- **Federally supported** 2-year, founded 1979
- **Rural** 22-acre campus with easy access to Omaha
- **Coed,** 180 undergraduate students, 26% full-time, 69% women, 31% men
- **100%** of applicants were admitted

**Undergraduates** 47 full-time, 133 part-time. Students come from 3 states and territories; 13% are from out of state; 2% transferred in.
**Freshmen** *Admission:* 57 applied, 57 admitted, 54 enrolled.
**Faculty** *Total:* 22, 36% full-time, 5% with terminal degrees. *Student/faculty ratio:* 5:1.
**Majors** American Indian/Native American studies; building/construction finishing, management, and inspection related; business administration and management; child-care and support services management; clinical/medical social work; liberal arts and sciences/liberal studies; teacher assistant/aide.
**Academics** *Calendar:* semesters. *Degree:* certificates and associate. *Special study options:* academic remediation for entering students, adult/continuing education programs, distance learning, double majors, independent study, internships, part-time degree program, services for LD students, study abroad, summer session for credit.
**Library** Macy Library plus 1 other. *Books:* 17,555 (physical), 370 (digital/electronic). Weekly public service hours: 40.
**Student Life** *Housing:* college housing not available. *Activities and Organizations:* Student Senate, AIHEC.
**Costs (2018–19)** *One-time required fee:* $25. *Tuition:* state resident $4080 full-time, $170 per credit hour part-time; nonresident $4080 full-time, $170 per credit hour part-time. Full-time tuition and fees vary according to course load. Part-time tuition and fees vary according to course load. *Payment plan:* installment. *Waivers:* children of alumni, senior citizens, and employees or children of employees.
**Applying** *Options:* electronic application, early admission. *Required:* high school transcript. *Required for some:* certificate of tribal enrollment. *Application deadlines:* rolling (freshmen), rolling (out-of-state freshmen), rolling (transfers).
**Freshman Application Contact** Troy Munhofen, Registrar, Nebraska Indian Community College, PO Box 428, Macy, NE 68039. *Phone:* 402-241-5922. *Toll-free phone:* 844-440-NICC. *Fax:* 402-837-4183. *E-mail:* tmunhofen@thenicc.edu. *Website:* http://www.thenicc.edu/.

# Northeast Community College
## Norfolk, Nebraska

- **State and locally supported** 2-year, founded 1973, part of Nebraska Coordinating Commission for Postsecondary Education
- **Small-town** 202-acre campus
- **Coed,** 5,075 undergraduate students, 42% full-time, 46% women, 54% men

**Undergraduates** 2,121 full-time, 2,954 part-time. Students come from 12 states and territories; 5% are from out of state; 1% Black or African American, non-Hispanic/Latino; 10% Hispanic/Latino; 0.4% Asian, non-Hispanic/Latino; 1% American Indian or Alaska Native, non-Hispanic/Latino; 2% Two or more races, non-Hispanic/Latino; 4% Race/ethnicity unknown; 1% international; 5% transferred in; 20% live on campus. *Retention:* 70% of full-time freshmen returned.

**Freshmen** *Admission:* 951 enrolled.

**Faculty** *Total:* 300, 42% full-time. *Student/faculty ratio:* 17:1.

**Majors** Accounting; administrative assistant and secretarial science; agribusiness; agriculture; agronomy and crop science; animal sciences; applied horticulture/horticultural business services related; architectural drafting and CAD/CADD; art; athletic training; audiovisual communications technologies related; autobody/collision and repair technology; automobile/automotive mechanics technology; biology/biological sciences; building/construction finishing, management, and inspection related; business administration and management; business/commerce; chemistry; computer and information sciences; computer science; corrections; criminal justice/police science; diesel mechanics technology; dietetics; dramatic/theater arts; early childhood education; education; electrician; electromechanical technology; elementary education; emergency medical technology (EMT paramedic); energy management and systems technology; engineering; English; farm and ranch management; finance; funeral service and mortuary science; general studies; graphic design; health and physical education/fitness; health information/medical records technology; health/medical preparatory programs related; heating, air conditioning, ventilation and refrigeration maintenance technology; human services; kinesiology and exercise science; liberal arts and sciences/liberal studies; library and archives assisting; library and information science; lineworker; mass communication/media; mathematics; medical administrative assistant and medical secretary; medical radiologic technology; music management; music performance; music teacher education; office occupations and clerical services; physical therapy technology; physics; predentistry studies; pre-law studies; premedical studies; prenursing studies; prepharmacy studies; pre-veterinary studies; psychology; registered nursing/registered nurse; respiratory care therapy; secondary education; social sciences; speech communication and rhetoric; surgical technology; veterinary/animal health technology.

**Academics** *Calendar:* semesters. *Degree:* certificates, diplomas, and associate. *Special study options:* academic remediation for entering students, adult/continuing education programs, advanced placement credit, cooperative education, distance learning, double majors, English as a second language, independent study, internships, off-campus study, part-time degree program, services for LD students, study abroad, summer session for credit.

**Library** Library Resource Center. *Books:* 20,648 (physical); *Serial titles:* 411 (physical); *Databases:* 70. Weekly public service hours: 78.

**Student Life** *Housing Options:* coed, special housing for students with disabilities. Campus housing is university owned. *Activities and Organizations:* drama/theater group, student-run newspaper, radio and television station, choral group, Phi Theta Kappa, Farm Bureau Club, Enactus, Christian Student Fellowship, Love Your Melon. *Campus security:* 24-hour emergency response devices and patrols, controlled dormitory access, building walk-throughs and parking lot patrols, door and dorm checks, armed security. *Student services:* health clinic, personal/psychological counseling.

**Athletics** Member NJCAA. *Intercollegiate sports:* baseball M(s), basketball M(s)/W(s), golf M(s), soccer M(s)/W(s), softball W(s), volleyball W(s). *Intramural sports:* basketball M/W, bowling M/W, football M/W, sand volleyball M/W, softball M/W, table tennis M/W, volleyball M/W.

**Costs (2018–19)** *Tuition:* state resident $2880 full-time, $96 per credit hour part-time; nonresident $4035 full-time, $135 per credit hour part-time. *Required fees:* $600 full-time, $20 per credit hour part-time. *Room and board:* $8605; room only: $5420. Room and board charges vary according to board plan and housing facility. *Payment plan:* installment. *Waivers:* employees or children of employees.

**Financial Aid** Of all full-time matriculated undergraduates who enrolled in 2016, 1,671 applied for aid, 1,347 were judged to have need, 190 had their need fully met. 53 Federal Work-Study jobs (averaging $1194). In 2016, 13 non-need-based awards were made. *Average percent of need met:* 66%. *Average financial aid package:* $6488. *Average need-based loan:* $3034. *Average need-based gift aid:* $5155. *Average non-need-based aid:* $971. *Average indebtedness upon graduation:* $11,311.

**Applying** *Options:* electronic application, early admission. *Required for some:* essay or personal statement, high school transcript, 3 letters of recommendation, interview. *Recommended:* high school transcript. *Application deadlines:* rolling (freshmen), rolling (transfers). *Notification:* continuous (freshmen), continuous (transfers).

**Freshman Application Contact** Tiffany Hopper, Admissions Specialist, Northeast Community College, 801 East Benjamin Avenue, PO Box 469, Norfolk, NE 68702-0469. *Phone:* 402-844-7260. *Toll-free phone:* 800-348-9033 Ext. 7260. *E-mail:* admission@northeast.edu. *Website:* http://www.northeast.edu/.

# Omaha School of Massage and Healthcare of Herzing University
## Omaha, Nebraska

**Admissions Office Contact** Omaha School of Massage and Healthcare of Herzing University, 9748 Park Drive, Omaha, NE 68127. *Website:* http://www.osmhc.com/.

# Southeast Community College, Beatrice Campus
## Beatrice, Nebraska

**Freshman Application Contact** Admissions Office, Southeast Community College, Beatrice Campus, 4771 West Scott Road, Beatrice, NE 68310. *Phone:* 402-228-3468. *Toll-free phone:* 800-233-5027. *Fax:* 402-228-2218. *Website:* http://www.southeast.edu/.

# Southeast Community College, Lincoln Campus
## Lincoln, Nebraska

- **District-supported** 2-year, founded 1973, part of Southeast Community College Area
- **Suburban** 115-acre campus with easy access to Omaha
- **Coed**

**Undergraduates** 3,942 full-time, 5,320 part-time. 7% are from out of state; 6% Black or African American, non-Hispanic/Latino; 8% Hispanic/Latino; 3% Asian, non-Hispanic/Latino; 0.1% Native Hawaiian or other Pacific Islander, non-Hispanic/Latino; 0.7% American Indian or Alaska Native, non-Hispanic/Latino; 4% Two or more races, non-Hispanic/Latino; 0.5% Race/ethnicity unknown.

**Faculty** *Student/faculty ratio:* 12:1.

**Academics** *Calendar:* quarters. *Degree:* certificates, diplomas, and associate. *Special study options:* academic remediation for entering students, advanced placement credit, cooperative education, distance learning, English as a second language, independent study, internships, off-campus study, part-time degree program, services for LD students, summer session for credit.

**Library** Lincoln Campus Learning Resource Center. *Books:* 26,473 (physical), 37,630 (digital/electronic); *Serial titles:* 338 (physical), 97 (digital/electronic); *Databases:* 67. Weekly public service hours: 68.

**Student Life** *Campus security:* late-night transport/escort service.

**Standardized Tests** *Recommended:* ACT (for admission).

**Costs (2017–18)** *Tuition:* state resident $2948 full-time, $66 per quarter hour part-time; nonresident $3578 full-time, $80 per quarter hour part-time. Full-time tuition and fees vary according to course load. Part-time tuition and fees vary according to course load. *Required fees:* $90 full-time, $2 per quarter hour part-time.

**Applying** *Options:* electronic application, early admission, deferred entrance. *Required:* high school transcript.

**Freshman Application Contact** Admissions Office, Southeast Community College, Lincoln Campus, 8800 O Street, Lincoln, NE 68520. *Phone:* 402-471-3333. *Toll-free phone:* 800-642-4075. *Fax:* 402-437-2404. *E-mail:* admissions@southeast.edu. *Website:* http://www.southeast.edu/.

# Southeast Community College, Milford Campus
## Milford, Nebraska

- **District-supported** 2-year, founded 1941, part of Southeast Community College System
- **Small-town** 50-acre campus with easy access to Omaha
- **Coed, primarily men**

**Undergraduates** 3,942 full-time, 5,320 part-time. 7% are from out of state; 6% Black or African American, non-Hispanic/Latino; 8% Hispanic/Latino; 3% Asian, non-Hispanic/Latino; 0.1% Native Hawaiian or other Pacific Islander, non-Hispanic/Latino; 0.7% American Indian or Alaska Native, non-

Hispanic/Latino; 4% Two or more races, non-Hispanic/Latino; 0.5% Race/ethnicity unknown.

**Faculty** *Student/faculty ratio:* 12:1.

**Academics** *Calendar:* quarters. *Degree:* diplomas and associate. *Special study options:* academic remediation for entering students, advanced placement credit, cooperative education, distance learning, internships, part-time degree program, services for LD students, summer session for credit.

**Library** Milford Campus Learning Resource Center. *Books:* 26,473 (physical), 37,630 (digital/electronic); *Serial titles:* 338 (physical), 97 (digital/electronic); *Databases:* 67. Weekly public service hours: 51; students can reserve study rooms.

**Student Life** *Campus security:* late-night transport/escort service, controlled dormitory access.

**Athletics** Member NJCAA.

**Standardized Tests** *Recommended:* ACT (for admission).

**Costs (2017–18)** *Tuition:* state resident $2948 full-time, $66 per quarter hour part-time; nonresident $3578 full-time, $80 per quarter hour part-time. Full-time tuition and fees vary according to course load. Part-time tuition and fees vary according to course load. *Required fees:* $90 full-time, $2 per quarter hour part-time. *Room and board:* $6150. Room and board charges vary according to board plan, gender, housing facility, location, and student level.

**Applying** *Options:* electronic application, early admission, deferred entrance. *Required:* high school transcript.

**Freshman Application Contact** Admissions Office, Southeast Community College, Milford Campus, 600 State Street, Milford, NE 68405. *Phone:* 402-761-2131. *Toll-free phone:* 800-933-7223. *Fax:* 402-761-2324. *E-mail:* admissions@southeast.edu. *Website:* http://www.southeast.edu/.

## Universal College of Healing Arts
### Omaha, Nebraska

**Admissions Office Contact** Universal College of Healing Arts, 8702 North 30th Street, Omaha, NE 68112-1810. *Website:* http://www.ucha.edu/.

## Western Nebraska Community College
### Sidney, Nebraska

**Director of Admissions** Mr. Troy Archuleta, Admissions and Recruitment Director, Western Nebraska Community College, 371 College Drive, Sidney, NE 69162. *Phone:* 308-635-6015. *Toll-free phone:* 800-222-9682. *E-mail:* rhovey@wncc.net. *Website:* http://www.wncc.net/.

# NEVADA

## Brightwood College, Las Vegas Campus
### Las Vegas, Nevada

**Freshman Application Contact** Admissions Office, Brightwood College, Las Vegas Campus, 3535 West Sahara Avenue, Las Vegas, NV 89102. *Phone:* 702-368-2338. *Toll-free phone:* 866-543-0208. *Website:* http://www.brightwood.edu/.

## Career College of Northern Nevada
### Sparks, Nevada

- **Proprietary** 2-year, founded 1984
- **Urban** 2-acre campus with easy access to Reno, NV
- **Coed,** 342 undergraduate students, 100% full-time, 43% women, 57% men

**Undergraduates** 342 full-time. Students come from 1 other country; 3% are from out of state.

**Freshmen** *Admission:* 270 applied, 270 admitted.

**Faculty** *Total:* 23, 48% full-time, 17% with terminal degrees. *Student/faculty ratio:* 20:1.

**Majors** Electrical, electronic and communications engineering technology; health information/medical records administration; industrial electronics technology; industrial mechanics and maintenance technology; medical/clinical assistant; network and system administration.

**Academics** *Calendar:* quarters 6-week terms. *Degree:* diplomas and associate. *Special study options:* academic remediation for entering students, accelerated degree program, cooperative education, double majors, internships, summer session for credit.

**Library** Library. *Books:* 1,200 (physical), 110,000 (digital/electronic). Weekly public service hours: 50.

**Student Life** *Housing:* college housing not available. *Campus security:* 24-hour emergency response devices.

**Standardized Tests** *Required:* Wonderlic aptitude test (for admission).

**Financial Aid** Of all full-time matriculated undergraduates who enrolled in 2016, 6 Federal Work-Study jobs (averaging $3000).

**Applying** *Application fee:* $25. *Required:* high school transcript, interview. *Application deadlines:* rolling (freshmen), rolling (transfers). *Notification:* continuous (freshmen), continuous (transfers).

**Freshman Application Contact** Ms. Maria Clark, Director of Admissions, Career College of Northern Nevada, 1421 Pullman Dr, Sparks, NV 89434. *Phone:* 775-856-2266. *Fax:* 775-856-0935. *E-mail:* mclark@ccnn4u.com. *Website:* http://www.ccnn.edu/.

## Carrington College–Las Vegas
### Las Vegas, Nevada

- **Proprietary** 2-year, part of Carrington Colleges Group, Inc.
- **Coed**

**Undergraduates** 299 full-time, 53 part-time. 2% are from out of state; 15% Black or African American, non-Hispanic/Latino; 32% Hispanic/Latino; 18% Asian, non-Hispanic/Latino; 6% Native Hawaiian or other Pacific Islander, non-Hispanic/Latino; 0.3% American Indian or Alaska Native, non-Hispanic/Latino; 2% Two or more races, non-Hispanic/Latino; 5% Race/ethnicity unknown; 23% transferred in.

**Faculty** *Student/faculty ratio:* 21:1.

**Academics** *Degree:* certificates and associate.

**Costs (2017–18)** *Tuition:* $42,232 per degree program part-time. Full-time tuition and fees vary according to program. Part-time tuition and fees vary according to program.

**Applying** *Required:* essay or personal statement, interview. *Required for some:* high school transcript.

**Freshman Application Contact** Carrington College–Las Vegas, 5740 South Eastern Avenue, Suite 140, Las Vegas, NV 89119. *Website:* http://www.carrington.edu/.

## Carrington College–Reno
### Reno, Nevada

- **Proprietary** 2-year, part of Carrington Colleges Group, Inc.
- **Coed**

**Undergraduates** 292 full-time, 68 part-time. 12% are from out of state; 1% Black or African American, non-Hispanic/Latino; 20% Hispanic/Latino; 6% Asian, non-Hispanic/Latino; 0.6% Native Hawaiian or other Pacific Islander, non-Hispanic/Latino; 0.3% American Indian or Alaska Native, non-Hispanic/Latino; 2% Two or more races, non-Hispanic/Latino; 0.8% Race/ethnicity unknown; 17% transferred in.

**Faculty** *Student/faculty ratio:* 15:1.

**Academics** *Degree:* certificates and associate.

**Standardized Tests** *Required:* institutional entrance exam (for admission).

**Costs (2017–18)** *Tuition:* $49,730 per degree program part-time. Full-time tuition and fees vary according to program. Part-time tuition and fees vary according to program.

**Applying** *Required:* essay or personal statement, high school transcript, interview.

**Freshman Application Contact** Carrington College–Reno, 5580 Kietzke Lane, Reno, NV 89511. *Phone:* 775-335-2900. *Website:* http://www.carrington.edu/.

## College of Southern Nevada
### Las Vegas, Nevada

**Freshman Application Contact** Admissions and Records, College of Southern Nevada, 6375 West Charleston Boulevard, Las Vegas, NV 89146. *Phone:* 702-651-4060. *Website:* http://www.csn.edu/.

## Great Basin College
### Elko, Nevada

- **State-supported** primarily 2-year, founded 1967, part of Nevada System of Higher Education
- **Small-town** 45-acre campus
- **Endowment** $6.7 million
- **Coed**

**Undergraduates** 903 full-time, 2,459 part-time. Students come from 28 states and territories; 26 other countries; 6% are from out of state; 2% Black or African American, non-Hispanic/Latino; 19% Hispanic/Latino; 2% Asian, non-Hispanic/Latino; 0.6% Native Hawaiian or other Pacific Islander, non-Hispanic/Latino; 3% American Indian or Alaska Native, non-Hispanic/Latino; 3% Two or more races, non-Hispanic/Latino; 6% Race/ethnicity unknown; 7%

transferred in; 4% live on campus. *Retention:* 65% of full-time freshmen returned.

**Academics** *Calendar:* semesters. *Degrees:* certificates, associate, bachelor's, and postbachelor's certificates. *Special study options:* academic remediation for entering students, accelerated degree program, adult/continuing education programs, cooperative education, distance learning, double majors, English as a second language, external degree program, independent study, off-campus study, part-time degree program, services for LD students, summer session for credit.

**Library** Learning Resource Center. *Books:* 94,193 (physical), 250,157 (digital/electronic); *Serial titles:* 2,946 (physical), 230,872 (digital/electronic); *Databases:* 80. Weekly public service hours: 46; students can reserve study rooms.

**Student Life** *Campus security:* late-night transport/escort service, evening patrols by trained security personnel.

**Costs (2017–18)** *Tuition:* state resident $2850 full-time, $1330 per year part-time; nonresident $9628 full-time, $2383 per year part-time. *Required fees:* $165 full-time, $6 per unit part-time. *Room and board:* room only: $3150. Room and board charges vary according to housing facility.

**Financial Aid** Of all full-time matriculated undergraduates who enrolled in 2017, 395 applied for aid, 349 were judged to have need, 32 had their need fully met. In 2017, 91. *Average financial aid package:* $2590. *Average need-based loan:* $3134. *Average need-based gift aid:* $2866. *Average non-need-based aid:* $1027.

**Applying** *Options:* electronic application, early admission, deferred entrance. *Application fee:* $10.

**Freshman Application Contact** Ms. Jan King, Director of Admissions and Registrar, Great Basin College, 1500 College Parkway, Elko, NV 89801. *Phone:* 775-753-2102. *E-mail:* jan.king@gbcnv.edu. *Website:* http://www.gbcnv.edu/.

# Northwest Career College
## Las Vegas, Nevada

**Admissions Office Contact** Northwest Career College, 7398 Smoke Ranch Road, Suite 100, Las Vegas, NV 89128. *Website:* http://www.northwestcareercollege.edu/.

# Pima Medical Institute
## Las Vegas, Nevada

**Freshman Application Contact** Admissions Office, Pima Medical Institute, 3333 East Flamingo Road, Las Vegas, NV 89121. *Phone:* 702-458-9650 Ext. 202. *Toll-free phone:* 800-477-PIMA. *Website:* http://www.pmi.edu/.

# Truckee Meadows Community College
## Reno, Nevada

- **State-supported** primarily 2-year, founded 1971, part of Nevada System of Higher Education
- **Suburban** 63-acre campus
- **Endowment** $9.4 million
- **Coed**, 10,720 undergraduate students, 26% full-time, 54% women, 46% men

**Undergraduates** 2,816 full-time, 7,904 part-time. Students come from 24 states and territories; 19 other countries; 7% are from out of state; 2% Black or African American, non-Hispanic/Latino; 29% Hispanic/Latino; 6% Asian, non-Hispanic/Latino; 0.1% Native Hawaiian or other Pacific Islander, non-Hispanic/Latino; 1% American Indian or Alaska Native, non-Hispanic/Latino; 4% Two or more races, non-Hispanic/Latino; 2% Race/ethnicity unknown; 0.4% international; 5% transferred in. *Retention:* 63% of full-time freshmen returned.

**Freshmen** *Admission:* 1,888 applied, 1,888 admitted, 1,459 enrolled.

**Faculty** *Total:* 530, 29% full-time. *Student/faculty ratio:* 21:1.

**Majors** Anthropology; architectural drafting and CAD/CADD; architecture; automobile/automotive mechanics technology; biology/biological sciences; business/commerce; chemistry; civil engineering; commercial and advertising art; computer programming (specific applications); computer systems networking and telecommunications; cooking and related culinary arts; criminal justice/police science; criminal justice/safety; crisis/emergency/disaster management; dental assisting; dental hygiene; diesel mechanics technology; dietetics; drafting and design technology; elementary education; energy management and systems technology; engineering; engineering technologies and engineering related; English; entrepreneurial and small business related; environmental science; fine arts related; fire prevention and safety technology; foods, nutrition, and wellness; general studies; geology/earth science; heating, air conditioning, ventilation and refrigeration maintenance technology; history; kindergarten/preschool education; landscape architecture; legal assistant/paralegal; liberal arts and sciences/liberal studies;

logistics, materials, and supply chain management; management information systems and services related; manufacturing engineering technology; mathematics; medical radiologic technology; mental health counseling; music; music performance; natural resources/conservation; philosophy; physics; psychology; registered nursing/registered nurse; science, technology and society; veterinary/animal health technology; welding technology.

**Academics** *Calendar:* semesters. *Degrees:* certificates, associate, and bachelor's. *Special study options:* academic remediation for entering students, accelerated degree program, adult/continuing education programs, advanced placement credit, cooperative education, distance learning, double majors, English as a second language, independent study, internships, part-time degree program, services for LD students, summer session for credit. *ROTC:* Army (c).

**Library** Elizabeth Sturm Library.

**Student Life** *Housing:* college housing not available. *Activities and Organizations:* drama/theater group, student-run newspaper, Entrepreneurship Club, International Club, Phi Theta Kappa, Student Government Association, Student Media and Broadcasting Club. *Campus security:* 24-hour emergency response devices and patrols, late-night transport/escort service. *Student services:* personal/psychological counseling, veterans affairs office.

**Costs (2017–18)** *Tuition:* state resident $95 per credit hour part-time; nonresident $200 per credit hour part-time. Full-time tuition and fees vary according to course level, course load, degree level, and program. Part-time tuition and fees vary according to course level, course load, degree level, and program. *Required fees:* $8 per credit hour part-time. *Payment plan:* installment. *Waivers:* employees or children of employees.

**Financial Aid** Of all full-time matriculated undergraduates who enrolled in 2016, 126 Federal Work-Study jobs (averaging $5000). 368 state and other part-time jobs (averaging $5000).

**Applying** *Options:* electronic application, early admission. *Application fee:* $10. *Application deadlines:* rolling (freshmen), rolling (transfers). *Notification:* continuous (freshmen), continuous (transfers).

**Freshman Application Contact** Truckee Meadows Community College, 7000 Dandini Boulevard, Reno, NV 89512-3901. *Phone:* 775-673-7240. *Website:* http://www.tmcc.edu/.

# Western Nevada College
## Carson City, Nevada

- **State-supported** primarily 2-year, founded 1971, part of Nevada System of Higher Education
- **Small-town** 200-acre campus
- **Endowment** $250,000
- **Coed**

**Undergraduates** 1,231 full-time, 2,336 part-time. Students come from 6 states and territories; 21 other countries; 3% are from out of state; 2% Black or African American, non-Hispanic/Latino; 22% Hispanic/Latino; 2% Asian, non-Hispanic/Latino; 0.8% Native Hawaiian or other Pacific Islander, non-Hispanic/Latino; 2% American Indian or Alaska Native, non-Hispanic/Latino; 3% Two or more races, non-Hispanic/Latino; 4% Race/ethnicity unknown; 0.3% international; 6% transferred in. *Retention:* 55% of full-time freshmen returned.

**Faculty** *Student/faculty ratio:* 18:1.

**Academics** *Calendar:* semesters. *Degrees:* certificates, associate, and bachelor's. *Special study options:* academic remediation for entering students, adult/continuing education programs, advanced placement credit, cooperative education, distance learning, double majors, English as a second language, honors programs, independent study, internships, part-time degree program, services for LD students, summer session for credit.

**Library** Western Nevada College Library and Media Services plus 1 other. *Books:* 35,923 (physical), 4,544 (digital/electronic); *Serial titles:* 2,725 (physical); *Databases:* 33. Weekly public service hours: 61; students can reserve study rooms.

**Student Life** *Campus security:* late-night transport/escort service.

**Costs (2017–18)** *Tuition:* state resident $3015 full-time; nonresident $9793 full-time. Full-time tuition and fees vary according to degree level. Part-time tuition and fees vary according to degree level. *Payment plans:* tuition prepayment, installment.

**Financial Aid** Of all full-time matriculated undergraduates who enrolled in 2017, 412 applied for aid, 386 were judged to have need, 21 had their need fully met. In 2017, 41. *Average financial aid package:* $2460. *Average need-based loan:* $3302. *Average need-based gift aid:* $2681.

**Applying** *Options:* electronic application, early admission. *Application fee:* $15. *Required for some:* high school transcript. *Recommended:* high school transcript.

**Freshman Application Contact** Admissions and Records, Western Nevada College, 2201 West College Parkway, Carson City, NV 89703. *Phone:* 775-445-2377. *Fax:* 775-445-3147. *E-mail:* wncc_aro@wncc.edu. *Website:* http://www.wnc.edu/.

# NEW HAMPSHIRE

## Great Bay Community College
### Portsmouth, New Hampshire

**Freshman Application Contact** Mr. Matt Thornton, Admissions Coordinator, Great Bay Community College, 320 Corporate Drive, Portsmouth, NH 03801. *Phone:* 603-427-7605. *Toll-free phone:* 800-522-1194. *E-mail:* askgreatbay@ ccsnh.edu. *Website:* http://www.greatbay.edu/.

## Lakes Region Community College
### Laconia, New Hampshire

- **State-supported** 2-year, part of Community College System of New Hampshire
- **Small-town** campus
- **Coed,** 1,179 undergraduate students, 42% full-time, 54% women, 46% men

**Undergraduates** 490 full-time, 689 part-time. Students come from 5 states and territories; 2 other countries; 3% are from out of state; 0.5% Black or African American, non-Hispanic/Latino; 1% Hispanic/Latino; 0.5% Asian, non-Hispanic/Latino; 0.1% Native Hawaiian or other Pacific Islander, non-Hispanic/Latino; 0.5% American Indian or Alaska Native, non-Hispanic/Latino; 0.9% Two or more races, non-Hispanic/Latino; 22% Race/ethnicity unknown.
**Freshmen** *Admission:* 311 enrolled.
**Faculty** *Student/faculty ratio:* 9:1.
**Majors** Accounting; animation, interactive technology, video graphics and special effects; automobile/automotive mechanics technology; business automation/technology/data entry; business/commerce; computer and information sciences; culinary arts; early childhood education; electrical/electronics equipment installation and repair; fine/studio arts; fire prevention and safety technology; fire science/firefighting; general studies; gerontology; graphic and printing equipment operation/production; hospitality administration; human services; liberal arts and sciences/liberal studies; marine maintenance and ship repair technology; registered nursing/registered nurse; restaurant/food services management.
**Academics** *Calendar:* semesters accelerated terms also offered. *Degree:* certificates and associate. *Special study options:* academic remediation for entering students, accelerated degree program, adult/continuing education programs, cooperative education, distance learning, double majors, external degree program, independent study, internships, part-time degree program, services for LD students, student-designed majors, summer session for credit.
**Library** Hugh Bennett Library plus 1 other. Students can reserve study rooms.
**Student Life** *Housing Options:* coed, special housing for students with disabilities. Campus housing is leased by the school. *Campus security:* 24-hour emergency response devices, late-night transport/escort service, controlled dormitory access, Evening patrols by trained security personnel. *Student services:* personal/psychological counseling, veterans affairs office.
**Costs (2018–19)** *Tuition:* state resident $5040 full-time, $210 per credit part-time; nonresident $11,472 full-time, $478 per credit part-time. *Required fees:* $6 per credit part-time. *Room and board:* Room and board charges vary according to housing facility. *Payment plan:* installment. *Waivers:* senior citizens.
**Applying** *Options:* electronic application, deferred entrance. *Required:* high school transcript. *Notification:* continuous (freshmen), continuous (transfers).
**Admissions Office Contact** Lakes Region Community College, 379 Belmont Road, Laconia, NH 03246. *Toll-free phone:* 800-357-2992. *Website:* http://www.lrcc.edu/.

## Manchester Community College
### Manchester, New Hampshire

**Freshman Application Contact** Ms. Jacquie Poirier, Coordinator of Admissions, Manchester Community College, 1066 Front Street, Manchester, NH 03102-8518. *Phone:* 603-668-6706 Ext. 283. *Toll-free phone:* 800-924-3445. *E-mail:* jpoirier@nhctc.edu. *Website:* http://www.mccnh.edu/.

## Nashua Community College
### Nashua, New Hampshire

**Freshman Application Contact** Ms. Patricia Goodman, Vice President of Student Services, Nashua Community College, Nashua, NH 03063. *Phone:* 603-882-6923 Ext. 1529. *Fax:* 603-882-8690. *E-mail:* pgoodman@ ccsnh.edu. *Website:* http://www.nashuacc.edu/.

## NHTI, Concord's Community College
### Concord, New Hampshire

- **State-supported** 2-year, founded 1964, part of Community College System of New Hampshire
- **Small-town** 225-acre campus with easy access to Boston
- **Coed**

**Undergraduates** 23% live on campus.
**Faculty** *Student/faculty ratio:* 15:1.
**Academics** *Calendar:* semesters. *Degree:* certificates, diplomas, and associate. *Special study options:* academic remediation for entering students, adult/continuing education programs, advanced placement credit, distance learning, double majors, English as a second language, external degree program, part-time degree program, services for LD students, summer session for credit.
**Library** Main Library plus 1 other.
**Student Life** *Campus security:* 24-hour emergency response devices and patrols, late-night transport/escort service, controlled dormitory access, cameras in vital locations.
**Standardized Tests** *Required for some:* National League of Nursing Exam. *Recommended:* SAT or ACT (for admission).
**Applying** *Options:* electronic application. *Application fee:* $20. *Required:* high school transcript. *Required for some:* essay or personal statement, interview. *Recommended:* minimum 2.0 GPA.
**Freshman Application Contact** NHTI, Concord's Community College, 31 College Drive, Concord, NH 03301-7412. *Toll-free phone:* 800-247-0179. *Website:* http://www.nhti.edu/.

## River Valley Community College
### Claremont, New Hampshire

**Freshman Application Contact** River Valley Community College, 1 College Place, Claremont, NH 03743. *Phone:* 603-542-7744 Ext. 5323. *Toll-free phone:* 800-837-0658. *Website:* http://www.rivervalley.edu/.

## St. Joseph School of Nursing
### Nashua, New Hampshire

- **Independent** 2-year, founded 1964, affiliated with Roman Catholic Church
- **Urban** campus with easy access to Boston, Portland
- **Coed,** 144 undergraduate students, 44% full-time, 90% women, 10% men

**Undergraduates** 63 full-time, 81 part-time. Students come from 3 states and territories; 9 other countries; 27% are from out of state; 24% transferred in.
**Freshmen** *Admission:* 5 applied, 2 admitted, 2 enrolled. *Average high school GPA:* 3.3.
**Faculty** *Total:* 20, 55% full-time, 100% with terminal degrees.
**Majors** Registered nursing, nursing administration, nursing research and clinical nursing related.
**Academics** *Calendar:* semesters. *Degree:* associate. *Special study options:* academic remediation for entering students, advanced placement credit, services for LD students, summer session for credit.
**Student Life** *Housing:* college housing not available. *Campus security:* 24-hour emergency response devices and patrols, late-night transport/escort service.
**Applying** *Options:* electronic application. *Application fee:* $50. *Required:* essay or personal statement, high school transcript, minimum 2.5 GPA, 3 letters of recommendation, interview. *Application deadline:* 7/10 (freshmen).
**Freshman Application Contact** Mrs. L. Nadeau, Admissions, St. Joseph School of Nursing, 5 Woodward Avenue, Nashua, NH 03060. *Toll-free phone:* 800-370-3169. *Website:* http://www.sjson.edu/.

## White Mountains Community College
### Berlin, New Hampshire

- **State-supported** 2-year, founded 1966, part of Community College System of New Hampshire
- **Rural** 325-acre campus
- **Coed,** 802 undergraduate students, 37% full-time, 66% women, 34% men

**Undergraduates** 299 full-time, 503 part-time. Students come from 6 states and territories; 13% are from out of state; 0.2% Black or African American, non-Hispanic/Latino; 1% Hispanic/Latino; 0.4% Asian, non-Hispanic/Latino; 0.1% American Indian or Alaska Native, non-Hispanic/Latino; 9% Race/ethnicity unknown; 4% transferred in.
**Freshmen** *Admission:* 320 applied, 318 admitted, 207 enrolled.
**Faculty** *Total:* 133, 18% full-time, 8% with terminal degrees. *Student/faculty ratio:* 8:1.

**Majors** Accounting; automobile/automotive mechanics technology; baking and pastry arts; business administration and management; computer and information sciences; criminal justice/safety; culinary arts; diesel mechanics technology; early childhood education; education; environmental studies; general studies; health services/allied health/health sciences; human services; international business/trade/commerce; liberal arts and sciences/liberal studies; medical/clinical assistant; medical office assistant; office management; registered nursing/registered nurse; resort management.

**Academics** *Calendar:* semesters. *Degree:* certificates and associate. *Special study options:* academic remediation for entering students, adult/continuing education programs, advanced placement credit, cooperative education, distance learning, double majors, external degree program, independent study, internships, part-time degree program, services for LD students, student-designed majors, summer session for credit.

**Library** Fortier Library. *Books:* 17,808 (physical); *Serial titles:* 35 (physical); *Databases:* 48. Weekly public service hours: 55; students can reserve study rooms.

**Student Life** *Housing:* college housing not available. *Activities and Organizations:* Student Senate. *Campus security:* 24-hour emergency response devices, late-night transport/escort service. *Student services:* personal/psychological counseling.

**Standardized Tests** *Required for some:* TEAS for associate's degree nursing program.

**Costs (2018–19)** *One-time required fee:* $65. *Tuition:* state resident $6400 full-time, $210 per credit hour part-time; nonresident $14,960 full-time, $478 per credit hour part-time. Full-time tuition and fees vary according to class time, location, and program. Part-time tuition and fees vary according to class time, location, and program. *Required fees:* $944 full-time, $17 per credit hour part-time. *Payment plans:* installment, deferred payment. *Waivers:* senior citizens and employees or children of employees.

**Applying** *Options:* electronic application, deferred entrance. *Application fee:* $20. *Required:* high school transcript. *Required for some:* letters of recommendation. *Application deadlines:* rolling (freshmen), rolling (out-of-state freshmen), rolling (transfers). *Notification:* continuous (freshmen), continuous (out-of-state freshmen), continuous (transfers).

**Freshman Application Contact** Ms. Amanda Gaeb, Admissions Counselor, White Mountains Community College, 2020 Riverside Drive, Berlin, NH 03570. *Phone:* 603-342-3006. *Toll-free phone:* 800-445-4525. *Fax:* 603-752-6335. *E-mail:* agaeb@ccsnh.edu.
*Website:* http://www.wmcc.edu/.

# NEW JERSEY

## Assumption College for Sisters
### Denville, New Jersey

**Freshman Application Contact** Sr. Gerardine Tantsits, Academic Dean/Registrar, Assumption College for Sisters, 350 Bernardsville Road, Mendham, NJ 07945-2923. *Phone:* 973-543-6528 Ext. 228. *Fax:* 973-543-1738. *E-mail:* deanregistrar@acs350.org. *Website:* http://www.acs350.org/.

## Atlantic Cape Community College
### Mays Landing, New Jersey

**Freshman Application Contact** Mrs. Linda McLeod, Assistant Director, Admissions and College Recruitment, Atlantic Cape Community College, 5100 Black Horse Pike, Mays Landing, NJ 08330-2699. *Phone:* 609-343-5009. *Fax:* 609-343-4921. *E-mail:* accadmit@atlantic.edu. *Website:* http://www.atlantic.edu/.

## Bergen Community College
### Paramus, New Jersey

**Freshman Application Contact** Admissions Office, Bergen Community College, 400 Paramus Road, Paramus, NJ 07652-1595. *Phone:* 201-447-7195. *E-mail:* admsoffice@bergen.edu. *Website:* http://www.bergen.edu/.

## Brookdale Community College
### Lincroft, New Jersey

**Director of Admissions** Ms. Kim Toomey, Registrar, Brookdale Community College, 765 Newman Springs Road, Lincroft, NJ 07738-1597. *Phone:* 732-224-2268. *Website:* http://www.brookdalecc.edu/.

## Camden County College
### Blackwood, New Jersey

- **State and locally supported** 2-year, founded 1967, part of New Jersey Office of the Secretary of Higher Education
- **Suburban** 320-acre campus with easy access to Philadelphia
- **Coed**, 10,492 undergraduate students, 48% full-time, 57% women, 43% men

**Undergraduates** 5,041 full-time, 5,451 part-time. Students come from 21 states and territories; 2% are from out of state; 20% Black or African American, non-Hispanic/Latino; 17% Hispanic/Latino; 6% Asian, non-Hispanic/Latino; 0.3% Native Hawaiian or other Pacific Islander, non-Hispanic/Latino; 1% American Indian or Alaska Native, non-Hispanic/Latino; 0.6% Two or more races, non-Hispanic/Latino; 6% Race/ethnicity unknown; 3% international; 8% transferred in.

**Freshmen** *Admission:* 6,383 applied, 1,859 enrolled.

**Faculty** *Total:* 678, 19% full-time.

**Majors** Accounting technology and bookkeeping; administrative assistant and secretarial science; automotive engineering technology; biology/biotechnology laboratory technician; business administration and management; cinematography and film/video production; clinical/medical laboratory technology; computer and information sciences; criminal justice/police science; dental assisting; dental hygiene; desktop publishing and digital imaging design; dietetic technology; drafting and design technology; early childhood education; education (multiple levels); electrical, electronic and communications engineering technology; electromechanical technology; emergency medical technology (EMT paramedic); engineering science; engineering technologies and engineering related; fine/studio arts; fire prevention and safety technology; fire services administration; health information/medical records administration; health services/allied health/health sciences; hospitality administration; industrial production technologies related; legal assistant/paralegal; liberal arts and sciences/liberal studies; management information systems; marketing/marketing management; massage therapy; mechanical engineering/mechanical technology; mechanical engineering technologies related; occupational therapist assistant; opticianry; radio and television broadcasting technology; registered nursing/registered nurse; rehabilitation and therapeutic professions related; sign language interpretation and translation; social work; sport and fitness administration/management; substance abuse/addiction counseling; veterinary/animal health technology; web page, digital/multimedia and information resources design.

**Academics** *Calendar:* semesters. *Degree:* certificates and associate. *Special study options:* academic remediation for entering students, adult/continuing education programs, advanced placement credit, cooperative education, distance learning, double majors, English as a second language, external degree program, freshman honors college, honors programs, independent study, internships, off-campus study, part-time degree program, services for LD students, study abroad, summer session for credit.

**Library** Wolverton Center Library.

**Student Life** *Housing:* college housing not available. *Activities and Organizations:* drama/theater group, student-run newspaper, radio station, choral group. *Campus security:* 24-hour emergency response devices and patrols, late-night transport/escort service. *Student services:* health clinic, veterans affairs office.

**Athletics** Member NJCAA. *Intercollegiate sports:* baseball M, basketball M/W, cross-country running M/W, golf M/W, soccer M/W, softball W, tennis W, wrestling M.

**Costs (2018–19)** *Tuition:* area resident $3210 full-time, $107 per credit hour part-time; state resident $3330 full-time, $111 per credit hour part-time; nonresident $3330 full-time, $111 per credit hour part-time. Full-time tuition and fees vary according to course load and program. Part-time tuition and fees vary according to course load and program. *Required fees:* $1110 full-time, $37 per credit hour part-time. *Payment plans:* installment, deferred payment. *Waivers:* senior citizens and employees or children of employees.

**Financial Aid** Of all full-time matriculated undergraduates who enrolled in 2016, 117 Federal Work-Study jobs (averaging $1126).

**Applying** *Options:* electronic application, early admission. *Required for some:* high school transcript. *Application deadlines:* rolling (freshmen), rolling (transfers).

**Freshman Application Contact** Mr. Donald Delaney, Director of Program Outreach, Camden County College, PO Box 200, Blackwood, NJ 08012-0200. *Phone:* 856-227-7200 Ext. 4660. *Fax:* 856-374-4916. *E-mail:* ddelaney@camdencc.edu.
*Website:* http://www.camdencc.edu/.

## County College of Morris
### Randolph, New Jersey

- **County-supported** 2-year, founded 1966
- **Suburban** 218-acre campus with easy access to New York City
- **Endowment** $5.4 million
- **Coed,** 7,949 undergraduate students, 48% full-time, 48% women, 52% men

**Undergraduates** 3,819 full-time, 4,130 part-time. Students come from 6 states and territories; 0.4% are from out of state; 5% Black or African American, non-Hispanic/Latino; 21% Hispanic/Latino; 6% Asian, non-Hispanic/Latino; 0.2% Native Hawaiian or other Pacific Islander, non-Hispanic/Latino; 0.4% American Indian or Alaska Native, non-Hispanic/Latino; 2% Two or more races, non-Hispanic/Latino; 6% Race/ethnicity unknown; 2% international; 5% transferred in. *Retention:* 72% of full-time freshmen returned.
**Freshmen** *Admission:* 4,036 applied, 2,524 admitted, 1,624 enrolled.
**Majors** Agricultural business and management; airline pilot and flight crew; biology/biotechnology laboratory technician; business administration and management; business, management, and marketing related; chemical technology; communication and media related; computer science; criminal justice/police science; culinary arts; design and applied arts related; electrical, electronic and communications engineering technology; engineering science; engineering technologies and engineering related; fine arts related; fire prevention and safety technology; graphic design; hospitality administration; information technology; kindergarten/preschool education; kinesiology and exercise science; liberal arts and sciences/liberal studies; management information systems; mechanical engineering/mechanical technology; multi/interdisciplinary studies related; music related; occupational therapist assistant; photography; public administration; public health; radiologic technology/science; registered nursing/registered nurse; respiratory care therapy; telecommunications technology; web page, digital/multimedia and information resources design.
**Academics** *Calendar:* semesters. *Degree:* certificates and associate. *Special study options:* academic remediation for entering students, accelerated degree program, advanced placement credit, cooperative education, distance learning, double majors, English as a second language, independent study, internships, services for LD students, study abroad, summer session for credit.
**Library** Learning Resource Center plus 1 other. *Books:* 38,594 (physical), 3,508 (digital/electronic); *Serial titles:* 26 (physical), 5 (digital/electronic); *Databases:* 123. Weekly public service hours: 68.
**Student Life** *Housing:* college housing not available. *Activities and Organizations:* drama/theater group, student-run newspaper, choral group, Phi Theta Kappa Honor Society, EOF Student Alliance, Student Nurses Association, New Social Engine, Cyber Security Club. *Campus security:* 24-hour emergency response devices and patrols, late-night transport/escort service. *Student services:* health clinic, personal/psychological counseling, women's center, veterans affairs office.
**Athletics** Member NJCAA. *Intercollegiate sports:* baseball M(s), basketball M(s)/W(s), golf M, lacrosse M, soccer M/W(s), softball W(s), volleyball W. *Intramural sports:* badminton M/W, basketball M/W, bowling M/W, soccer M/W, table tennis M/W, tennis M/W, volleyball M/W.
**Costs (2017–18)** *Tuition:* area resident $3750 full-time, $125 per credit hour part-time; state resident $7500 full-time, $250 per credit hour part-time; nonresident $10,710 full-time, $357 per credit hour part-time. Full-time tuition and fees vary according to course load, location, and program. Part-time tuition and fees vary according to course load, location, and program. *Required fees:* $1080 full-time, $29 per credit hour part-time, $21 per course part-time. *Waivers:* senior citizens and employees or children of employees.
**Financial Aid** Of all full-time matriculated undergraduates who enrolled in 2016, 588 Federal Work-Study jobs (averaging $1947).
**Applying** *Options:* electronic application. *Application fee:* $30. *Required:* high school transcript. *Application deadlines:* rolling (freshmen), rolling (transfers). *Notification:* continuous (freshmen), continuous (transfers).
**Freshman Application Contact** County College of Morris, 214 Center Grove Road, Randolph, NJ 07869-2086. *Phone:* 973-328-5096.
*Website:* http://www.ccm.edu/.

## Cumberland County College
### Vineland, New Jersey

**Freshman Application Contact** Ms. Anne Daly-Eimer, Director of Admissions and Registration, Cumberland County College, 3322 College Drive, Vineland, NJ 08360. *Phone:* 856-691-8600. *Website:* http://www.cccnj.edu/.

## Eastern International College
### Belleville, New Jersey

- **Proprietary** primarily 2-year
- **Urban** campus with easy access to Manhattan, New York
- **Coed**

**Academics** *Degrees:* associate and bachelor's.
**Freshman Application Contact** Eastern International College, 251 Washington Avenue, Belleville, NJ 07109.
*Website:* http://www.eicollege.edu/.

## Eastern International College
### Jersey City, New Jersey

**Admissions Office Contact** Eastern International College, 684 Newark Avenue, Jersey City, NJ 07306. *Website:* http://www.eicollege.edu/.

## Eastwick College
### Hackensack, New Jersey

**Admissions Office Contact** Eastwick College, 250 Moore Street, Hackensack, NJ 07601. *Website:* http://www.eastwickcollege.edu/.

## Eastwick College
### Nutley, New Jersey

**Admissions Office Contact** Eastwick College, 103 Park Avenue, Nutley, NJ 07110. *Website:* http://www.eastwickcollege.edu/.

## Eastwick College
### Ramsey, New Jersey

**Admissions Office Contact** Eastwick College, 10 South Franklin Turnpike, Ramsey, NJ 07446. *Website:* http://www.eastwickcollege.edu/.

## Essex County College
### Newark, New Jersey

**Freshman Application Contact** Ms. Marva Mack, Director of Admissions, Essex County College, 303 University Avenue, Newark, NJ 07102. *Phone:* 973-877-3119. *Fax:* 973-623-6449. *Website:* http://www.essex.edu/.

## Hudson County Community College
### Jersey City, New Jersey

- **State and locally supported** 2-year, founded 1974
- **Urban** campus with easy access to New York City
- **Coed,** 8,864 undergraduate students, 58% full-time, 59% women, 41% men

**Undergraduates** 5,136 full-time, 3,728 part-time. 14% Black or African American, non-Hispanic/Latino; 55% Hispanic/Latino; 8% Asian, non-Hispanic/Latino; 0.5% Native Hawaiian or other Pacific Islander, non-Hispanic/Latino; 0.3% American Indian or Alaska Native, non-Hispanic/Latino; 2% Two or more races, non-Hispanic/Latino; 8% Race/ethnicity unknown; 0.5% international; 4% transferred in. *Retention:* 58% of full-time freshmen returned.
**Freshmen** *Admission:* 2,115 enrolled.
**Faculty** *Total:* 661, 13% full-time. *Student/faculty ratio:* 35:1.
**Majors** Accounting; accounting technology and bookkeeping; baking and pastry arts; biological and physical sciences; building/construction finishing, management, and inspection related; business administration and management; child-care provision; computer and information sciences; computer and information systems security; computer engineering technology; computer graphics; criminal justice/police science; culinary arts; data processing and data processing technology; electrical, electronic and communications engineering technology; emergency care attendant (EMT ambulance); emergency medical technology (EMT paramedic); engineering science; environmental studies; fine/studio arts; health and physical education/fitness; health information/medical records technology; health services/allied health/health sciences; hospitality administration; kinesiology and exercise science; liberal arts and sciences/liberal studies; licensed practical/vocational nurse training; logistics, materials, and supply chain management; medical/clinical assistant; medical transcription; radiologic technology/science; registered nursing/registered nurse; social work.
**Academics** *Calendar:* semesters. *Degree:* certificates and associate. *Special study options:* academic remediation for entering students, advanced placement credit, distance learning, English as a second language, honors

programs, independent study, internships, part-time degree program, services for LD students, summer session for credit.
**Library** Hudson County Community College Library plus 1 other. *Books:* 49,853 (physical), 2,881 (digital/electronic); *Serial titles:* 1,269 (physical), 750 (digital/electronic); *Databases:* 74. Students can reserve study rooms.
**Student Life** *Housing:* college housing not available. *Activities and Organizations:* drama/theater group, student-run newspaper. *Campus security:* 24-hour emergency response devices, late-night transport/escort service. *Student services:* personal/psychological counseling.
**Costs (2018–19)** *Tuition:* area resident $4050 full-time, $135 per credit hour part-time; state resident $8100 full-time, $270 per credit hour part-time; nonresident $11,970 full-time, $399 per credit hour part-time. Full-time tuition and fees vary according to course load and program. Part-time tuition and fees vary according to course load and program. *Required fees:* $1483 full-time, $48 per credit hour part-time, $25 per term part-time. *Payment plan:* installment. *Waivers:* senior citizens and employees or children of employees.
**Financial Aid** Of all full-time matriculated undergraduates who enrolled in 2016, 102 Federal Work-Study jobs (averaging $3000).
**Applying** *Options:* electronic application. *Application fee:* $20. *Application deadlines:* 9/1 (freshmen), 9/1 (transfers). *Notification:* continuous until 9/1 (freshmen), continuous until 9/1 (transfers).
**Freshman Application Contact** Hudson County Community College, 70 Sip Avenue, Jersey City, NJ 07306. *Phone:* 201-360-4111.
*Website:* http://www.hccc.edu/.

# Jersey College
## Teterboro, New Jersey

- **Proprietary** 2-year, founded 2003
- **Urban** 1-acre campus with easy access to New York City
- **Coed, primarily women**
- 71% of applicants were admitted

**Undergraduates** 2,743 full-time. Students come from 14 states and territories; 28% are from out of state; 63% Black or African American, non-Hispanic/Latino; 10% Hispanic/Latino; 4% Asian, non-Hispanic/Latino; 0.5% Native Hawaiian or other Pacific Islander, non-Hispanic/Latino; 0.3% American Indian or Alaska Native, non-Hispanic/Latino; 1% Two or more races, non-Hispanic/Latino; 7% Race/ethnicity unknown; 15% transferred in.
**Faculty** *Student/faculty ratio:* 16:1.
**Academics** *Degree:* diplomas and associate. *Special study options:* academic remediation for entering students, accelerated degree program, adult/continuing education programs.
**Library** Main Library. *Books:* 14,981 (physical), 145,557 (digital/electronic); *Serial titles:* 555 (physical); *Databases:* 3. Students can reserve study rooms.
**Standardized Tests** *Required for some:* math and reading entrance exams. *Recommended:* SAT or ACT (for admission).
**Applying** *Required:* essay or personal statement, high school transcript, 2 letters of recommendation, interview, proof of U.S. citizenship or Permanent Resident Card.
**Freshman Application Contact** Jersey College, 546 US Highway 46, Teterboro, NJ 07608. *Website:* http://www.jerseycollege.edu/.

# Mercer County Community College
## Trenton, New Jersey

- **State and locally supported** 2-year, founded 1966
- **Suburban** 292-acre campus with easy access to New York City, Philadelphia
- **Coed**

**Undergraduates** 3,077 full-time, 4,902 part-time. Students come from 7 states and territories; 89 other countries; 1% are from out of state; 22% Black or African American, non-Hispanic/Latino; 18% Hispanic/Latino; 6% Asian, non-Hispanic/Latino; 0.2% Native Hawaiian or other Pacific Islander, non-Hispanic/Latino; 0.2% American Indian or Alaska Native, non-Hispanic/Latino; 2% Two or more races, non-Hispanic/Latino; 9% Race/ethnicity unknown; 4% international; 3% transferred in. *Retention:* 71% of full-time freshmen returned.
**Faculty** *Student/faculty ratio:* 18:1.
**Academics** *Calendar:* semesters. *Degree:* certificates and associate. *Special study options:* academic remediation for entering students, accelerated degree program, adult/continuing education programs, advanced placement credit, cooperative education, distance learning, double majors, English as a second language, external degree program, independent study, internships, part-time degree program, services for LD students, student-designed majors, summer session for credit. *ROTC:* Army (c), Air Force (c).
**Library** Mercer County Community College Library plus 1 other.
**Student Life** *Campus security:* 24-hour emergency response devices and patrols.
**Athletics** Member NJCAA.

**Costs (2017–18)** *Tuition:* area resident $2988 full-time, $125 per credit hour part-time; state resident $4176 full-time, $174 per credit hour part-time; nonresident $6336 full-time, $264 per credit hour part-time. Full-time tuition and fees vary according to program and reciprocity agreements. Part-time tuition and fees vary according to program and reciprocity agreements. *Required fees:* $912 full-time, $38 per credit hour part-time.
**Financial Aid** Of all full-time matriculated undergraduates who enrolled in 2016, 76 Federal Work-Study jobs (averaging $2348). 10 state and other part-time jobs (averaging $1952).
**Applying** *Options:* electronic application, deferred entrance. *Required:* high school transcript. *Recommended:* interview.
**Freshman Application Contact** Dr. L. Campbell, Dean for Student and Academic Services, Mercer County Community College, 1200 Old Trenton Road, PO Box B, Trenton, NJ 08690-1004. *Phone:* 609-586-4800 Ext. 3222. *Toll-free phone:* 800-392-MCCC. *Fax:* 609-586-6944. *E-mail:* admiss@ mccc.edu. *Website:* http://www.mccc.edu/.

# Middlesex County College
## Edison, New Jersey

- **County-supported** 2-year, founded 1964
- **Suburban** 200-acre campus with easy access to New York City
- **Coed**

**Undergraduates** 11% Black or African American, non-Hispanic/Latino; 30% Hispanic/Latino; 14% Asian, non-Hispanic/Latino; 0.5% Native Hawaiian or other Pacific Islander, non-Hispanic/Latino; 0.4% American Indian or Alaska Native, non-Hispanic/Latino; 3% Two or more races, non-Hispanic/Latino; 7% Race/ethnicity unknown; 2% international. *Retention:* 62% of full-time freshmen returned.
**Faculty** *Student/faculty ratio:* 24:1.
**Academics** *Calendar:* semesters. *Degree:* certificates and associate. *Special study options:* academic remediation for entering students, adult/continuing education programs, advanced placement credit, cooperative education, distance learning, English as a second language, independent study, internships, off-campus study, part-time degree program, services for LD students, study abroad, summer session for credit. *ROTC:* Army (c).
**Library** Middlesex County College Library plus 1 other.
**Student Life** *Campus security:* 24-hour emergency response devices and patrols.
**Athletics** Member NJCAA.
**Costs (2017–18)** *One-time required fee:* $86. *Tuition:* $110 per credit part-time; state resident $220 per credit part-time; nonresident $220 per credit part-time. *Required fees:* $35 per credit part-time.
**Applying** *Options:* early admission, deferred entrance. *Application fee:* $25. *Required:* high school transcript.
**Freshman Application Contact** Middlesex County College, 2600 Woodbridge Avenue, PO Box 3050, Edison, NJ 08818-3050. *Website:* http://www.middlesexcc.edu/.

# Ocean County College
## Toms River, New Jersey

**Freshman Application Contact** Ms. Sheenah Hartigan, CRM Communications Administrator, Ocean County College, College Drive, PO Box 2001, Toms River, NJ 08754-2001. *Phone:* 732-255-0400 Ext. 2189. *E-mail:* shartigan@ocean.edu. *Website:* http://www.ocean.edu/.

# Passaic County Community College
## Paterson, New Jersey

**Freshman Application Contact** Mr. Patrick Noonan, Director of Admissions, Passaic County Community College, One College Boulevard, Paterson, NJ 07505-1179. *Phone:* 973-684-6304. *Website:* http://www.pccc.cc.nj.us/.

# Raritan Valley Community College
## Branchburg, New Jersey

- **State and locally supported** 2-year, founded 1965
- **Suburban** 240-acre campus with easy access to New York City, Philadelphia
- **Endowment** $956,851
- **Coed**, 8,079 undergraduate students, 42% full-time, 50% women, 50% men
- 100% of applicants were admitted

**Undergraduates** 3,371 full-time, 4,708 part-time. Students come from 11 states and territories; 1% are from out of state; 11% Black or African American, non-Hispanic/Latino; 23% Hispanic/Latino; 6% Asian, non-Hispanic/Latino; 0.4% Native Hawaiian or other Pacific Islander, non-

Hispanic/Latino; 0.3% American Indian or Alaska Native, non-Hispanic/Latino; 2% Two or more races, non-Hispanic/Latino; 7% Race/ethnicity unknown; 2% international; 5% transferred in. *Retention:* 73% of full-time freshmen returned.

**Freshmen** *Admission:* 2,441 applied, 2,441 admitted, 1,676 enrolled.

**Faculty** *Total:* 492, 26% full-time. *Student/faculty ratio:* 20:1.

**Majors** Accounting related; accounting technology and bookkeeping; administrative assistant and secretarial science; allied health and medical assisting services related; animation, interactive technology, video graphics and special effects; automotive engineering technology; business administration and management; business/commerce; child-care provision; communication and media related; computer and information sciences; computer programming; construction engineering technology; criminal justice/law enforcement administration; crisis/emergency/disaster management; dance; dental hygiene; engineering science; engineering technologies and engineering related; English; fine/studio arts; health information/medical records technology; health services/allied health/health sciences; heating, ventilation, air conditioning and refrigeration engineering technology; human services; information technology; interior design; kindergarten/preschool education; kinesiology and exercise science; legal assistant/paralegal; liberal arts and sciences/liberal studies; lineworker; management information systems; manufacturing engineering technology; medical/clinical assistant; meeting and event planning; modeling, virtual environments and simulation; multi/interdisciplinary studies related; music; occupational therapist assistant; opticianry; optometric technician; registered nursing/registered nurse; rehabilitation and therapeutic professions related; respiratory care therapy; restaurant, culinary, and catering management; small business administration.

**Academics** *Calendar:* semesters. *Degree:* certificates and associate. *Special study options:* academic remediation for entering students, adult/continuing education programs, advanced placement credit, cooperative education, distance learning, double majors, English as a second language, freshman honors college, honors programs, independent study, internships, off-campus study, part-time degree program, services for LD students, summer session for credit. *ROTC:* Army (c), Air Force (c).

**Library** Evelyn S. Field Library. *Books:* 63,518 (physical), 105,637 (digital/electronic); *Serial titles:* 115 (physical), 240,256 (digital/electronic); *Databases:* 71.

**Student Life** *Housing:* college housing not available. *Activities and Organizations:* drama/theater group, student-run newspaper, radio station, choral group, Phi Theta Kappa, Rotaract, Enactus, Health Oriented Peer Educators (HOPE), Orgullo Latino (OLC). *Campus security:* 24-hour emergency response devices and patrols, late-night transport/escort service, 24-hour outdoor and indoor surveillance cameras, 24-hour communication center. *Student services:* personal/psychological counseling.

**Athletics** Member NJCAA. *Intercollegiate sports:* baseball M(s), basketball M(s)/W(s), cross-country running M/W, golf M/W, soccer M/W, volleyball W. *Intramural sports:* basketball M/W, soccer M/W, softball W, volleyball M/W.

**Costs (2017–18)** *Tuition:* area resident $4410 full-time, $147 per credit hour part-time; state resident $5610 full-time, $187 per credit hour part-time; nonresident $5610 full-time, $187 per credit hour part-time. *Required fees:* $1044 full-time, $26 per credit hour part-time, $112 per term part-time. *Payment plan:* installment. *Waivers:* employees or children of employees.

**Financial Aid** Of all full-time matriculated undergraduates who enrolled in 2016, 12 Federal Work-Study jobs (averaging $2500).

**Applying** *Options:* electronic application. *Application fee:* $25. *Required:* high school transcript. *Application deadlines:* rolling (freshmen), rolling (transfers). *Notification:* continuous (freshmen), continuous (out-of-state freshmen), continuous (transfers).

**Freshman Application Contact** Mr. Daniel Palubniak, Registrar, Enrollment Services, Raritan Valley Community College, 118 Lamington Road, Branchburg, NJ 08876. *Phone:* 908-526-1200 Ext. 8206. *Fax:* 908-704-3442. *E-mail:* dpalubni@raritanval.edu. *Website:* http://www.raritanval.edu/.

# Rowan College at Burlington County
## Pemberton, New Jersey

**Freshman Application Contact** Rowan College at Burlington County, 601 Pemberton Browns Mills Road, Pemberton, NJ 08068. *Phone:* 609-894-9311 Ext. 1200. *Website:* http://www.rcbc.edu/.

# Rowan College at Gloucester County
## Sewell, New Jersey

**Freshman Application Contact** Ms. Judy Atkinson, Registrar/Admissions, Rowan College at Gloucester County, 1400 Tanyard Road, Sewell, NJ 08080. *Phone:* 856-415-2209. *E-mail:* jatkinso@gccnj.edu. *Website:* http://www.rcgc.edu/.

# Salem Community College
## Carneys Point, New Jersey

**Freshman Application Contact** Kelly McShay, Director of Retention and Admissions, Salem Community College, 460 Hollywood Avenue, Carneys Point, NJ 08069. *Phone:* 856-351-2919. *E-mail:* kmcshay@salemcc.edu. *Website:* http://www.salemcc.edu/.

# Sussex County Community College
## Newton, New Jersey

- **State and locally supported** 2-year, founded 1981, part of New Jersey Commission on Higher Education
- **Small-town** 160-acre campus with easy access to New York City
- **Coed**

**Undergraduates** 1,412 full-time, 1,127 part-time. Students come from 3 states and territories; 2% Black or African American, non-Hispanic/Latino; 4% Hispanic/Latino; 1% Asian, non-Hispanic/Latino; 0.1% Native Hawaiian or other Pacific Islander, non-Hispanic/Latino; 0.4% American Indian or Alaska Native, non-Hispanic/Latino; 7% Two or more races, non-Hispanic/Latino; 0.7% Race/ethnicity unknown.

**Academics** *Calendar:* semesters. *Degree:* certificates and associate. *Special study options:* academic remediation for entering students, advanced placement credit, distance learning, double majors, English as a second language, internships, part-time degree program, services for LD students, summer session for credit.

**Library** Sussex County Community College Library. Students can reserve study rooms.

**Student Life** *Campus security:* late-night transport/escort service, trained security personnel.

**Athletics** Member NJCAA.

**Financial Aid** Of all full-time matriculated undergraduates who enrolled in 2016, 29 Federal Work-Study jobs (averaging $1500).

**Applying** *Options:* electronic application.

**Freshman Application Contact** Mr. Todd Poltersdorf, Director of Admissions, Sussex County Community College, 1 College Hill Road, Newton, NJ 07860. *Phone:* 973-300-2253. *E-mail:* tpoltersdorf@sussex.edu. *Website:* http://www.sussex.edu/.

# Union County College
## Cranford, New Jersey

- **State and locally supported** 2-year, founded 1933
- **Urban** 47-acre campus with easy access to New York City
- **Coed,** 9,711 undergraduate students, 44% full-time, 61% women, 39% men
- **100% of applicants were admitted**

**Undergraduates** 4,297 full-time, 5,414 part-time. 27% Black or African American, non-Hispanic/Latino; 35% Hispanic/Latino; 4% Asian, non-Hispanic/Latino; 0.4% Native Hawaiian or other Pacific Islander, non-Hispanic/Latino; 0.4% American Indian or Alaska Native, non-Hispanic/Latino; 1% Two or more races, non-Hispanic/Latino; 12% Race/ethnicity unknown; 3% international; 7% transferred in. *Retention:* 68% of full-time freshmen returned.

**Freshmen** *Admission:* 4,464 applied, 4,464 admitted, 1,823 enrolled.

**Majors** Accounting technology and bookkeeping; automobile/automotive mechanics technology; biology/biological sciences; business administration and management; business/commerce; chemistry; computer and information sciences and support services related; computer science; criminal justice/law enforcement administration; dental hygiene; diagnostic medical sonography and ultrasound technology; electromechanical technology; emergency medical technology (EMT paramedic); engineering; engineering technologies and engineering related; English; fire prevention and safety technology; health services/allied health/health sciences; history; hospitality administration; human services; information technology; legal assistant/paralegal; liberal arts and sciences/liberal studies; logistics, materials, and supply chain management; marketing/marketing management; mass communication/media; mathematics; physical therapy technology; radiologic technology/science; registered nursing/registered nurse; rehabilitation and therapeutic professions related; respiratory care therapy; sport and fitness administration/management.

**Academics** *Calendar:* semesters. *Degree:* certificates and associate. *Special study options:* academic remediation for entering students, adult/continuing education programs, advanced placement credit, distance learning, English as a second language, honors programs, independent study, internships, off-campus study, part-time degree program, services for LD students, summer session for credit. *ROTC:* Air Force (c).

**Library** MacKay Library plus 2 others. *Books:* 88,357 (physical), 211,505 (digital/electronic); *Serial titles:* 241 (physical), 316,369 (digital/electronic); *Databases:* 96.

**Student Life** *Housing:* college housing not available. *Activities and Organizations:* drama/theater group, student-run newspaper, radio station. *Campus security:* 24-hour emergency response devices and patrols. *Student services:* personal/psychological counseling, veterans affairs office.

**Athletics** Member NJCAA. *Intercollegiate sports:* baseball M, basketball M/W(s), bowling W, cross-country running M/W, golf M/W, lacrosse M(s), soccer M/W, track and field M/W, volleyball W.

**Costs (2017–18)** *Tuition:* area resident $4804 full-time, $191 per credit hour part-time; state resident $9608 full-time, $382 per credit hour part-time; nonresident $9608 full-time, $382 per credit hour part-time. Full-time tuition and fees vary according to course load. Part-time tuition and fees vary according to course load. *Payment plan:* installment. *Waivers:* senior citizens and employees or children of employees.

**Applying** *Options:* electronic application. *Required:* high school transcript, Immunization records. *Required for some:* essay or personal statement, interview. *Application deadlines:* rolling (freshmen), rolling (transfers). *Notification:* continuous (freshmen), continuous (transfers).

**Freshman Application Contact** Ms. Beatriz Rodriguez, Director of Enrollment Services, Union County College, Cranford, NJ 07016. *Phone:* 908-709-7448. *E-mail:* rodriguez@ucc.edu. *Website:* http://www.ucc.edu/.

## Warren County Community College
### Washington, New Jersey

**Freshman Application Contact** Shannon Horwath, Associate Director of Admissions, Warren County Community College, 475 Route 57 West, Washington, NJ 07882-9605. *Phone:* 908-835-2300. *E-mail:* shorwath@warren.edu. *Website:* http://www.warren.edu/.

# NEW MEXICO

## Carrington College–Albuquerque
### Albuquerque, New Mexico

- **Proprietary** 2-year, part of Carrington Colleges Group, Inc.
- **Coed**

**Undergraduates** 400 full-time, 34 part-time. 2% are from out of state; 2% Black or African American, non-Hispanic/Latino; 48% Hispanic/Latino; 1% Asian, non-Hispanic/Latino; 31% American Indian or Alaska Native, non-Hispanic/Latino; 1% Two or more races, non-Hispanic/Latino; 0.7% Race/ethnicity unknown; 25% transferred in.

**Faculty** *Student/faculty ratio:* 28:1.

**Academics** *Degree:* certificates and associate.

**Standardized Tests** *Required:* institutional entrance exam (for admission).

**Costs (2017–18)** *Tuition:* $14,178 per degree program part-time. Full-time tuition and fees vary according to program. Part-time tuition and fees vary according to program.

**Applying** *Required:* essay or personal statement, high school transcript, interview.

**Freshman Application Contact** Carrington College–Albuquerque, 1001 Menaul Boulevard NE, Albuquerque, NM 87107. *Website:* http://www.carrington.edu/.

## Central New Mexico Community College
### Albuquerque, New Mexico

- **State-supported** 2-year, founded 1965
- **Urban** 304-acre campus
- **Endowment** $1.8 million
- **Coed**, 24,442 undergraduate students, 27% full-time, 57% women, 43% men

**Undergraduates** 6,684 full-time, 17,758 part-time. Students come from 1 other country; 0.6% are from out of state; 3% Black or African American, non-Hispanic/Latino; 51% Hispanic/Latino; 2% Asian, non-Hispanic/Latino; 0.2% Native Hawaiian or other Pacific Islander, non-Hispanic/Latino; 7% American Indian or Alaska Native, non-Hispanic/Latino; 2% Two or more races, non-Hispanic/Latino; 7% Race/ethnicity unknown; 4% transferred in.

**Freshmen** *Admission:* 4,984 applied, 4,984 admitted, 3,715 enrolled.

**Faculty** *Total:* 981, 33% full-time. *Student/faculty ratio:* 23:1.

**Majors** Accounting; administrative assistant and secretarial science; airframe mechanics and aircraft maintenance technology; anthropology; architectural drafting and CAD/CADD; art; biology/biological sciences; biotechnology; building construction technology; business administration and management; chemistry; cinematography and film/video production; clinical/medical laboratory technology; communication; computer and information sciences; computer science; construction management; cosmetology; criminal justice/law enforcement administration; criminology; culinary arts; diagnostic medical sonography and ultrasound technology; early childhood education; education (multiple levels); electrician; emergency medical technology (EMT paramedic); English; environmental design/architecture; fire science/firefighting; general studies; geographic information science and cartography; geography; health and physical education/fitness; health information/medical records administration; health information/medical records technology; health services/allied health/health sciences; heating, air conditioning, ventilation and refrigeration maintenance technology; history; hospitality administration; human development and family studies; Latin American studies; liberal arts and sciences/liberal studies; machine tool technology; mathematics; nursing assistant/aide and patient care assistant/aide; physical therapy technology; physics; pre-engineering; pre-law studies; psychology; radiologic technology/science; registered nursing/registered nurse; respiratory care therapy; sociology; surgical technology; surveying engineering; technology/industrial arts teacher education; vehicle maintenance and repair technologies related; veterinary/animal health technology; welding technology.

**Academics** *Calendar:* trimesters. *Degree:* certificates and associate. *Special study options:* academic remediation for entering students, accelerated degree program, adult/continuing education programs, advanced placement credit, cooperative education, distance learning, English as a second language, honors programs, independent study, internships, off-campus study, part-time degree program, services for LD students, summer session for credit. *ROTC:* Army (c), Navy (c), Air Force (c).

**Library** Main Campus Library plus 5 others.

**Student Life** *Housing:* college housing not available. *Activities and Organizations:* student-run newspaper. *Campus security:* 24-hour emergency response devices and patrols, late-night transport/escort service. *Student services:* veterans affairs office.

**Costs (2017–18)** *Tuition:* state resident $1296 full-time, $54 per credit hour part-time; nonresident $6888 full-time, $287 per credit hour part-time. *Required fees:* $282 full-time, $8 per credit hour part-time, $45 per term part-time. *Payment plan:* installment. *Waivers:* senior citizens and employees or children of employees.

**Applying** *Options:* electronic application. *Application deadlines:* rolling (freshmen), rolling (transfers). *Notification:* continuous (freshmen), continuous (transfers).

**Freshman Application Contact** Glenn Damiani, Senior Director, Enrollment Services, Central New Mexico Community College, Albuquerque, NM 87106. *Phone:* 505-224-3223. *E-mail:* gdamiani@cnm.edu. *Website:* http://www.cnm.edu/.

## Clovis Community College
### Clovis, New Mexico

**Freshman Application Contact** Ms. Rosie Corrie, Director of Admissions and Records/Registrar, Clovis Community College, Clovis, NM 88101-8381. *Phone:* 575-769-4962. *Toll-free phone:* 800-769-1409. *Fax:* 575-769-4190. *E-mail:* admissions@clovis.edu. *Website:* http://www.clovis.edu/.

## Doña Ana Community College
### Las Cruces, New Mexico

**Freshman Application Contact** Mrs. Ricci Montes, Admissions Advisor, Doña Ana Community College, MSC-3DA, Box 30001, 3400 South Espina Street, Las Cruces, NM 88003-8001. *Phone:* 575-527-7683. *Toll-free phone:* 800-903-7503. *Fax:* 575-527-7515. *Website:* http://dacc.nmsu.edu/.

## Eastern New Mexico University–Roswell
### Roswell, New Mexico

**Freshman Application Contact** Eastern New Mexico University–Roswell, PO Box 6000, Roswell, NM 88202-6000. *Phone:* 505-624-7142. *Toll-free phone:* 800-243-6687 (in-state); 800-624-7000 (out-of-state). *Website:* http://www.roswell.enmu.edu/.

## IntelliTec College
### Albuquerque, New Mexico

**Admissions Office Contact** IntelliTec College, 5001 Montgomery Boulevard NE, Suite A24, Albuquerque, NM 87109. *Website:* http://www.intelliteccollege.edu/.

# Luna Community College
Las Vegas, New Mexico

**Freshman Application Contact** Ms. Henrietta Griego, Director of Admissions, Recruitment, and Retention, Luna Community College, PO Box 1510, Las Vegas, NM 87701. *Phone:* 505-454-2020. *Toll-free phone:* 800-588-7232. *Fax:* 505-454-2588. *E-mail:* hgriego@luna.cc.nm.us. *Website:* http://www.luna.edu/.

# Mesalands Community College
Tucumcari, New Mexico

- **State-supported** 2-year, founded 1979
- **Small-town** campus
- **Coed,** 1,005 undergraduate students

**Faculty** *Total:* 50, 30% full-time. *Student/faculty ratio:* 18:1.
**Majors** Accounting related; agricultural and domestic animal services related; agricultural business and management; automobile/automotive mechanics technology; business administration and management; child-care provision; computer and information sciences; criminal justice/police science; criminal justice/safety; diesel mechanics technology; education; engineering technologies and engineering related; liberal arts and sciences/liberal studies; office occupations and clerical services; paleontology; premedical studies; public administration; sculpture; social work.
**Academics** *Calendar:* semesters. *Degree:* certificates and associate.
**Student Life** *Campus security:* 24-hour emergency response devices.
**Costs (2017–18)** *Tuition:* state resident $1392 full-time, $58 per credit hour part-time; nonresident $2496 full-time, $104 per credit hour part-time. Full-time tuition and fees vary according to course load. Part-time tuition and fees vary according to course load. *Required fees:* $420 full-time, $15 per credit hour part-time, $420 per year part-time. *Room and board:* $2956. *Payment plan:* deferred payment. *Waivers:* senior citizens.
**Applying** *Required:* high school transcript. *Application deadlines:* rolling (freshmen), rolling (transfers).
**Freshman Application Contact** Mesalands Community College, 911 South Tenth Street, Tucumcari, NM 88401. *Phone:* 575-461-4413. *Website:* http://www.mesalands.edu/.

# New Mexico Junior College
Hobbs, New Mexico

- **State and locally supported** 2-year, founded 1965, part of New Mexico Commission on Higher Education
- **Small-town** 185-acre campus
- **Coed**

**Undergraduates** Students come from 17 states and territories; 7 other countries; 10% are from out of state; 15% live on campus.
**Faculty** *Student/faculty ratio:* 19:1.
**Academics** *Calendar:* semesters. *Degree:* certificates and associate. *Special study options:* academic remediation for entering students, advanced placement credit, cooperative education, distance learning, internships, part-time degree program, services for LD students, summer session for credit.
**Library** Pannell Library.
**Student Life** *Campus security:* 24-hour emergency response devices and patrols, late-night transport/escort service, controlled dormitory access.
**Athletics** Member NJCAA.
**Costs (2017–18)** *Tuition:* area resident $1050 full-time, $37 per credit hour part-time; state resident $1620 full-time, $57 per credit hour part-time; nonresident $1860 full-time, $64 per credit hour part-time. Full-time tuition and fees vary according to course load. Part-time tuition and fees vary according to course load. *Required fees:* $510 full-time, $19 per credit hour part-time. *Room and board:* $4800; room only: $3400. Room and board charges vary according to board plan and housing facility. *Payment plans:* installment, deferred payment.
**Applying** *Options:* electronic application, early admission, deferred entrance.
**Freshman Application Contact** New Mexico Junior College, 5317 Lovington Highway, Hobbs, NM 88240-9123. *Phone:* 575-492-2587. *Toll-free phone:* 800-657-6260. *Website:* http://www.nmjc.edu/.

# New Mexico Military Institute
Roswell, New Mexico

**Freshman Application Contact** New Mexico Military Institute, Roswell, NM 88201-5173. *Phone:* 505-624-8050. *Toll-free phone:* 800-421-5376. *Fax:* 505-624-8058. *E-mail:* admissions@nmmi.edu. *Website:* http://www.nmmi.edu/.

# New Mexico State University–Alamogordo
Alamogordo, New Mexico

- **State-supported** 2-year, founded 1958, part of New Mexico State University System
- **Small-town** 540-acre campus
- **Endowment** $147,086
- **Coed,** 1,710 undergraduate students, 25% full-time, 62% women, 38% men

**Undergraduates** 425 full-time, 1,285 part-time. Students come from 9 states and territories; 3 other countries; 4% Black or African American, non-Hispanic/Latino; 45% Hispanic/Latino; 1% Asian, non-Hispanic/Latino; 0.4% Native Hawaiian or other Pacific Islander, non-Hispanic/Latino; 4% American Indian or Alaska Native, non-Hispanic/Latino; 3% Two or more races, non-Hispanic/Latino; 2% Race/ethnicity unknown; 2% international; 4% transferred in. *Retention:* 46% of full-time freshmen returned.
**Freshmen** *Admission:* 153 enrolled.
**Faculty** *Total:* 89, 38% full-time. *Student/faculty ratio:* 16:1.
**Majors** Administrative assistant and secretarial science; animation, interactive technology, video graphics and special effects; automobile/automotive mechanics technology; biomedical technology; business/commerce; computer programming; criminal justice/safety; early childhood education; education; electrical, electronic and communications engineering technology; emergency medical technology (EMT paramedic); ethnic, cultural minority, gender, and group studies related; fine/studio arts; graphic design; health services/allied health/health sciences; human services; information technology; legal assistant/paralegal; office occupations and clerical services; pre-engineering.
**Academics** *Calendar:* semesters. *Degree:* certificates and associate. *Special study options:* academic remediation for entering students, adult/continuing education programs, advanced placement credit, distance learning, double majors, independent study, internships, off-campus study, part-time degree program, services for LD students, study abroad, summer session for credit.
**Library** David H. Townsend Library.
**Student Life** *Housing:* college housing not available. *Activities and Organizations:* national fraternities. *Campus security:* late-night transport/escort service. *Student services:* veterans affairs office.
**Costs (2018–19)** *Tuition:* area resident $1872 full-time, $78 per credit hour part-time; state resident $2232 full-time, $93 per credit hour part-time; nonresident $5184 full-time, $216 per credit hour part-time. Full-time tuition and fees vary according to course load and reciprocity agreements. Part-time tuition and fees vary according to reciprocity agreements. *Required fees:* $192 full-time, $8 per credit hour part-time. *Payment plans:* installment, deferred payment. *Waivers:* senior citizens and employees or children of employees.
**Financial Aid** Of all full-time matriculated undergraduates who enrolled in 2016, 10 Federal Work-Study jobs (averaging $3300). 60 state and other part-time jobs (averaging $3300). *Financial aid deadline:* 5/1.
**Applying** *Options:* electronic application, early admission, deferred entrance. *Application fee:* $20. *Required:* high school transcript, minimum 2.0 GPA. *Application deadlines:* rolling (freshmen), rolling (out-of-state freshmen), rolling (transfers). *Notification:* continuous (freshmen), continuous (out-of-state freshmen), continuous (transfers).
**Freshman Application Contact** Ms. Elma Hernandez, Coordinator of Admissions and Records, New Mexico State University–Alamogordo, 2400 North Scenic Drive, Alamogordo, NM 88311-0477. *Phone:* 575-439-3700. *E-mail:* advisor@nmsu.edu. *Website:* http://nmsua.edu/.

# New Mexico State University–Carlsbad
Carlsbad, New Mexico

**Freshman Application Contact** Ms. Everal Shannon, Records Specialist, New Mexico State University–Carlsbad, 1500 University Drive, Carlsbad, NM 88220. *Phone:* 575-234-9222. *Fax:* 575-885-4951. *E-mail:* eshannon@nmsu.edu. *Website:* http://www.cavern.nmsu.edu/.

# New Mexico State University–Grants
Grants, New Mexico

**Director of Admissions** Ms. Irene Lutz, Campus Student Services Officer, New Mexico State University–Grants, 1500 3rd Street, Grants, NM 87020-2025. *Phone:* 505-287-7981. *Website:* http://grants.nmsu.edu/.

# Pima Medical Institute
Albuquerque, New Mexico

**Freshman Application Contact** Admissions Office, Pima Medical Institute, 4400 Cutler Avenue NE, Albuquerque, NM 87110. *Phone:* 505-881-1234.

*Toll-free phone:* 800-477-PIMA. *Fax:* 505-881-5329. *Website:* http://www.pmi.edu/.

# San Juan College
## Farmington, New Mexico

- **State-supported** 2-year, founded 1958, part of New Mexico Higher Education Department
- **Small-town** 698-acre campus
- **Endowment** $15.0 million
- **Coed,** 5,172 undergraduate students, 46% full-time, 67% women, 33% men

**Undergraduates** 2,364 full-time, 2,808 part-time. Students come from 53 states and territories; 32 other countries; 28% are from out of state; 1% Black or African American, non-Hispanic/Latino; 17% Hispanic/Latino; 0.9% Asian, non-Hispanic/Latino; 0.1% Native Hawaiian or other Pacific Islander, non-Hispanic/Latino; 34% American Indian or Alaska Native, non-Hispanic/Latino; 2% Two or more races, non-Hispanic/Latino; 4% Race/ethnicity unknown; 1% international; 10% transferred in.
**Freshmen** *Admission:* 1,035 applied, 1,035 admitted, 707 enrolled.
**Faculty** *Total:* 312, 49% full-time. *Student/faculty ratio:* 20:1.
**Majors** Accounting technology and bookkeeping; American Indian/Native American studies; autobody/collision and repair technology; automobile/automotive mechanics technology; biology/biological sciences; business administration and management; carpentry; chemistry; child-care provision; clinical/medical laboratory technology; commercial and advertising art; cosmetology; criminal justice/police science; data processing and data processing technology; dental hygiene; diesel mechanics technology; drafting and design technology; electrical, electronic and communications engineering technology; elementary education; emergency medical technology (EMT paramedic); engineering; engineering technology; fire science/firefighting; general studies; geology/earth science; health and physical education/fitness; health information/medical records technology; industrial mechanics and maintenance technology; industrial technology; instrumentation technology; landscaping and groundskeeping; legal assistant/paralegal; liberal arts and sciences/liberal studies; mathematics; occupational safety and health technology; occupational therapist assistant; parks, recreation and leisure; physical sciences; physical therapy technology; physics; premedical studies; psychology; registered nursing/registered nurse; respiratory care therapy; secondary education; social work; special education; surgical technology; theater design and technology; veterinary/animal health technology; welding technology.
**Academics** *Calendar:* semesters. *Degree:* certificates, diplomas, and associate. *Special study options:* academic remediation for entering students, adult/continuing education programs, advanced placement credit, cooperative education, distance learning, double majors, English as a second language, freshman honors college, honors programs, independent study, internships, part-time degree program, services for LD students, summer session for credit.
**Library** San Juan College Library. *Books:* 78,053 (physical), 191,277 (digital/electronic); *Serial titles:* 251 (physical), 35,953 (digital/electronic); *Databases:* 102. Weekly public service hours: 69.
**Student Life** *Housing:* college housing not available. *Activities and Organizations:* drama/theater group, choral group, National Society of Leadership and Success (NSLS), Student American Dental Hygienists'; Association, Student Nurses Association, Parent and Educator's Club, All Nations Leadership Association, national fraternities, national sororities. *Campus security:* 24-hour emergency response devices and patrols, late-night transport/escort service. *Student services:* personal/psychological counseling, veterans affairs office.
**Athletics** *Intramural sports:* basketball M/W, soccer M/W, ultimate Frisbee M/W, volleyball M/W.
**Costs (2018–19)** *Tuition:* state resident $1104 full-time, $46 per credit hour part-time; nonresident $3504 full-time, $146 per credit hour part-time. Full-time tuition and fees vary according to reciprocity agreements. Part-time tuition and fees vary according to course load and reciprocity agreements. *Required fees:* $406 full-time, $78 per term part-time. *Payment plan:* installment. *Waivers:* senior citizens and employees or children of employees.
**Financial Aid** Of all full-time matriculated undergraduates who enrolled in 2016, 150 Federal Work-Study jobs (averaging $2500). 175 state and other part-time jobs (averaging $2500).
**Applying** *Options:* electronic application, early admission, deferred entrance. *Application fee:* $10. *Required:* high school transcript. *Application deadlines:* rolling (freshmen), rolling (transfers). *Notification:* continuous (freshmen), continuous (transfers).
**Freshman Application Contact** Mrs. Abby Calcote, Coordinator of Enrollment Services, San Juan College, 4601 College Boulevard, Farmington, NM 87402. *Phone:* 505-566-3572. *Fax:* 505-566-3500. *E-mail:* calcotea@sanjuancollege.edu.
*Website:* http://www.sanjuancollege.edu/.

# Santa Fe Community College
## Santa Fe, New Mexico

- **State and locally supported** 2-year, founded 1983
- **Rural** 366-acre campus with easy access to Albuquerque
- **Coed**

**Undergraduates** 2,243 full-time, 7,376 part-time. Students come from 42 states and territories; 2% Black or African American, non-Hispanic/Latino; 44% Hispanic/Latino; 2% Asian, non-Hispanic/Latino; 0.1% Native Hawaiian or other Pacific Islander, non-Hispanic/Latino; 5% American Indian or Alaska Native, non-Hispanic/Latino; 1% Two or more races, non-Hispanic/Latino; 3% Race/ethnicity unknown; 0.1% international. *Retention:* 51% of full-time freshmen returned.
**Faculty** *Student/faculty ratio:* 13:1.
**Academics** *Calendar:* semesters. *Degrees:* certificates, associate, and postbachelor's certificates. *Special study options:* academic remediation for entering students, adult/continuing education programs, advanced placement credit, cooperative education, distance learning, double majors, English as a second language, external degree program, honors programs, independent study, internships, part-time degree program, services for LD students, summer session for credit.
**Library** Learning Resource Center.
**Student Life** *Campus security:* 24-hour emergency response devices and patrols, late-night transport/escort service.
**Applying** *Options:* electronic application, early admission, deferred entrance. *Recommended:* high school transcript.
**Freshman Application Contact** Marcos Maez, Student Recruitment and Outreach Administrator, Santa Fe Community College, 6401 Richards Ave, Santa Fe, NM 87508. *Phone:* 505-428-1779. *E-mail:* marcos.maez@sfcc.edu. *Website:* http://www.sfcc.edu/.

# Southwestern Indian Polytechnic Institute
## Albuquerque, New Mexico

- **Federally supported** 2-year, founded 1971
- **Suburban** 144-acre campus with easy access to Albuquerque
- **Coed,** 402 undergraduate students, 86% full-time, 55% women, 45% men

**Undergraduates** 346 full-time, 56 part-time. Students come from 18 states and territories; 60% live on campus.
**Freshmen** *Admission:* 183 applied, 157 admitted, 103 enrolled. *Average high school GPA:* 2.1.
**Faculty** *Total:* 41, 56% full-time, 12% with terminal degrees. *Student/faculty ratio:* 16:1.
**Majors** Accounting technology and bookkeeping; business administration and management; business/commerce; early childhood education; engineering; geographic information science and cartography; institutional food workers; liberal arts and sciences/liberal studies; natural resources and conservation related; opticianry; system, networking, and LAN/WAN management.
**Academics** *Calendar:* trimesters. *Degree:* certificates and associate. *Special study options:* academic remediation for entering students, advanced placement credit, cooperative education, distance learning, double majors, internships, part-time degree program, services for LD students, summer session for credit.
**Library** Southwestern Indian Polytechnic Institute Library.
**Student Life** *Housing Options:* men-only, women-only. Campus housing is university owned. *Activities and Organizations:* Dance Club, Student Senate, Culinary Arts, Natural Resources, Pow-Wow Club. *Campus security:* 24-hour emergency response devices and patrols, late-night transport/escort service. *Student services:* personal/psychological counseling.
**Athletics** *Intramural sports:* basketball M/W, softball M/W, volleyball M/W.
**Costs (2018–19)** *Tuition:* area resident $0 full-time. The Bureau of Indian Education (BIE) provides tuition, room board, and books to students at minimal charge. *Required fees:* $1095 full-time, $290 per term part-time. *Room and board:* $675. *Payment plan:* deferred payment.
**Financial Aid** Of all full-time matriculated undergraduates who enrolled in 2016, 202 applied for aid, 202 were judged to have need. 14 Federal Work-Study jobs (averaging $700). 15 state and other part-time jobs (averaging $800). *Average percent of need met:* 43%. *Average financial aid package:* $4592. *Average need-based gift aid:* $3550.
**Applying** *Required:* high school transcript, Certificate of Indian Blood, physical, immunization records. *Application deadlines:* 7/30 (freshmen), 7/30 (transfers). *Notification:* continuous (freshmen).
**Freshman Application Contact** Tawna Harrison, First Year Counselor, Southwestern Indian Polytechnic Institute, PO Box 10146, 9169 Coors Rd NW, Albuquerque, NM 87184. *Phone:* 505-922-6516. *Toll-free phone:* 800-586-7474. *E-mail:* tawna.harrison@bie.edu.
*Website:* http://www.sipi.edu/.

# University of New Mexico–Gallup
## Gallup, New Mexico

**Freshman Application Contact** University of New Mexico–Gallup, 705 Gurley Avenue, Gallup, NM 87301. *Phone:* 505-863-7576. *Website:* http://www.gallup.unm.edu/.

# University of New Mexico–Los Alamos Branch
## Los Alamos, New Mexico

**Freshman Application Contact** Mrs. Irene K. Martinez, Enrollment Representative, University of New Mexico–Los Alamos Branch, 4000 University Drive, Los Alamos, NM 87544-2233. *Phone:* 505-662-0332. *E-mail:* l65130@unm.edu. *Website:* http://losalamos.unm.edu/.

# University of New Mexico–Taos
## Taos, New Mexico

**Director of Admissions** Vickie Alvarez, Student Enrollment Associate, University of New Mexico–Taos, 115 Civic Plaza Drive, Taos, NM 87571. *Phone:* 575-737-6425. *E-mail:* valvarez@unm.edu. *Website:* http://taos.unm.edu/.

# University of New Mexico–Valencia Campus
## Los Lunas, New Mexico

**Director of Admissions** Richard M. Hulett, Director of Admissions and Recruitment, University of New Mexico–Valencia Campus, 280 La Entrada, Los Lunas, NM 87031-7633. *Phone:* 505-277-2446. *E-mail:* mhulett@unm.edu. *Website:* http://valencia.unm.edu/.

# NEW YORK

# Adirondack Community College
## Queensbury, New York

- **State and locally supported** 2-year, founded 1960, part of State University of New York System
- **Small-town** 141-acre campus
- **Endowment** $3.9 million
- **Coed,** 3,973 undergraduate students, 55% full-time, 56% women, 44% men

**Undergraduates** 2,189 full-time, 1,784 part-time. Students come from 10 states and territories; 19 other countries; 0.9% are from out of state; 3% Black or African American, non-Hispanic/Latino; 3% Hispanic/Latino; 0.9% Asian, non-Hispanic/Latino; 0.5% American Indian or Alaska Native, non-Hispanic/Latino; 2% Two or more races, non-Hispanic/Latino; 13% Race/ethnicity unknown; 0.2% international; 5% transferred in. *Retention:* 63% of full-time freshmen returned.
**Freshmen** *Admission:* 2,006 applied, 1,947 admitted, 944 enrolled.
**Faculty** *Total:* 256, 35% full-time. *Student/faculty ratio:* 17:1.
**Majors** Accounting; accounting technology and bookkeeping; business administration and management; computer science; computer systems networking and telecommunications; cooking and related culinary arts; creative writing; criminal justice/police science; design and visual communications; electrical, electronic and communications engineering technology; electrician; engineering; food technology and processing; hospitality administration; information technology; liberal arts and sciences/liberal studies; marketing/marketing management; music; music performance; parks, recreation and leisure facilities management; radio and television broadcasting technology; registered nursing/registered nurse; sport and fitness administration/management; substance abuse/addiction counseling; tourism and travel services management.
**Academics** *Calendar:* semesters. *Degree:* certificates and associate. *Special study options:* academic remediation for entering students, accelerated degree program, adult/continuing education programs, advanced placement credit, cooperative education, distance learning, double majors, English as a second language, independent study, internships, part-time degree program, services for LD students, study abroad, summer session for credit.
**Library** SUNY Adirondack Library.
**Student Life** *Housing Options:* coed. *Activities and Organizations:* drama/theater group, student-run radio and television station, choral group.

*Campus security:* late-night transport/escort service, patrols by trained security personnel 8 am to 10 pm. *Student services:* personal/psychological counseling, veterans affairs office.
**Athletics** Member NJCAA. *Intercollegiate sports:* baseball M, basketball M/W, bowling M/W, cross-country running M/W, golf M/W, soccer M/W, softball W, tennis M/W, volleyball W. *Intramural sports:* badminton M/W, basketball M/W, volleyball M/W.
**Costs (2017–18)** *One-time required fee:* $40. *Tuition:* state resident $4392 full-time, $183 per credit hour part-time; nonresident $8784 full-time, $366 per credit hour part-time. Full-time tuition and fees vary according to course load and program. Part-time tuition and fees vary according to course load and program. *Required fees:* $583 full-time, $2 per term part-time. *Room and board:* $11,270; room only: $7680. Room and board charges vary according to board plan. *Payment plan:* installment. *Waivers:* senior citizens and employees or children of employees.
**Financial Aid** Of all full-time matriculated undergraduates who enrolled in 2016, 98 Federal Work-Study jobs (averaging $462).
**Applying** *Options:* electronic application. *Application fee:* $35.
**Freshman Application Contact** Office of Admissions, Adirondack Community College, 640 Bay Road, Queensbury, NY 12804. *Phone:* 518-743-2264. *Toll-free phone:* 888-SUNY-ADK. *Fax:* 518-743-2200. *Website:* http://www.sunyacc.edu/.

# American Academy McAllister Institute of Funeral Service
## New York, New York

**Freshman Application Contact** Mr. Norman Provost, Registrar, American Academy McAllister Institute of Funeral Service, 450 West 56th Street, New York, NY 10019-3602. *Phone:* 212-757-1190. *Toll-free phone:* 866-932-2264. *Website:* http://www.funeraleducation.org/.

# ★ American Academy of Dramatic Arts–New York
## New York, New York

- **Independent** 2-year, founded 1884
- **Urban** campus
- **Coed,** 310 undergraduate students, 100% full-time, 68% women, 32% men

**Undergraduates** 310 full-time. Students come from 28 states and territories; 25 other countries; 84% are from out of state; 8% Black or African American, non-Hispanic/Latino; 5% Hispanic/Latino; 0.6% Asian, non-Hispanic/Latino; 0.3% American Indian or Alaska Native, non-Hispanic/Latino; 6% Two or more races, non-Hispanic/Latino; 0.3% Race/ethnicity unknown; 28% international; 53% live on campus. *Retention:* 75% of full-time freshmen returned.
**Freshmen** *Admission:* 524 applied, 418 admitted, 113 enrolled.
**Faculty** *Total:* 39, 21% full-time, 41% with terminal degrees. *Student/faculty ratio:* 8:1.
**Majors** Dramatic/theater arts.
**Academics** *Calendar:* semesters. *Degree:* certificates and associate. *Special study options:* academic remediation for entering students, honors programs.
**Library** Academy/CBS Library.
**Student Life** *Housing Options:* coed. Campus housing is leased by the school. Freshman applicants given priority for college housing. *Campus security:* 24-hour emergency response devices and patrols, controlled dormitory access, trained security guard during hours of operation and for campus housing. *Student services:* personal/psychological counseling.
**Costs (2018–19)** *Comprehensive fee:* $53,155 includes full-time tuition ($34,410), mandatory fees ($750), and room and board ($17,995). *Room and board:* Room and board charges vary according to housing facility. *Payment plan:* installment. *Waivers:* employees or children of employees.
**Financial Aid** Of all full-time matriculated undergraduates who enrolled in 2012, 240 applied for aid, 231 were judged to have need. 50 Federal Work-Study jobs (averaging $900). 50 state and other part-time jobs (averaging $2000). In 2012, 59 non-need-based awards were made. *Average percent of need met:* 67%. *Average financial aid package:* $18,150. *Average need-based loan:* $4500. *Average need-based gift aid:* $7000. *Average non-need-based aid:* $7000. *Average indebtedness upon graduation:* $15,000. *Financial aid deadline:* 5/15.
**Applying** *Options:* electronic application, deferred entrance. *Application fee:* $50. *Required:* essay or personal statement, high school transcript, minimum 2.0 GPA, 2 letters of recommendation, interview, audition. *Application deadlines:* rolling (freshmen), rolling (transfers). *Notification:* continuous (freshmen), continuous (transfers).
**Freshman Application Contact** Kerin Reilly, Director of Admissions, American Academy of Dramatic Arts–New York, 120 Madison Avenue, New

York, NY 10016. *Phone:* 212-686-9244 Ext. 333. *Toll-free phone:* 800-463-8990. *E-mail:* kreilly@aada.edu.
*Website:* http://www.aada.edu/.

## ASA College
### Brooklyn, New York

**Freshman Application Contact** Admissions Office, ASA College, 81 Willoughby Street, Brooklyn, NY 11201. *Phone:* 718-522-9073. *Toll-free phone:* 877-679-8772. *Website:* http://www.asa.edu/.

## The Belanger School of Nursing
### Schenectady, New York

- **Independent** 2-year, founded 1906
- **Urban** campus
- **Coed,** 114 undergraduate students, 32% full-time, 82% women, 18% men

**Undergraduates** 37 full-time, 77 part-time. Students come from 1 other state; 8% Black or African American, non-Hispanic/Latino; 5% Hispanic/Latino; 15% Asian, non-Hispanic/Latino; 0.9% American Indian or Alaska Native, non-Hispanic/Latino; 0.9% Two or more races, non-Hispanic/Latino; 3% Race/ethnicity unknown.
**Freshmen** *Admission:* 5 applied.
**Faculty** *Student/faculty ratio:* 4:1.
**Majors** Registered nursing/registered nurse.
**Academics** *Degree:* associate. *Special study options:* honors programs, part-time degree program, summer session for credit.
**Library** Ellis Medicine's Health Services Library. *Books:* 2,000 (physical). Weekly public service hours: 40.
**Student Life** *Housing:* college housing not available. *Activities and Organizations:* Student Government. *Campus security:* on-campus security department 24/7.
**Standardized Tests** *Required:* Kaplan Admission Test (for admission).
**Costs (2017–18)** *Tuition:* $10,094 full-time, $6650 per year part-time. Full-time tuition and fees vary according to course load. Part-time tuition and fees vary according to course load. *Required fees:* $1700 full-time, $52 per credit hour part-time, $980 per year part-time. *Payment plan:* installment.
**Applying** *Options:* electronic application. *Application fee:* $70. *Required:* essay or personal statement, high school transcript, minimum 3.0 GPA, 2 letters of recommendation. *Application deadline:* 1/15 (freshmen). *Notification:* 3/15 (freshmen).
**Freshman Application Contact** Carolyn Lansing, Student Services Manager, The Belanger School of Nursing, 650 McClellan Street, Schenectady, NY 12304. *Phone:* 518-831-8810. *Fax:* 518-243-4470. *E-mail:* lansingc@ellismedicine.org.
*Website:* http://www.ellismedicine.org/school-of-nursing/.

## Bill and Sandra Pomeroy College of Nursing at Crouse Hospital
### Syracuse, New York

**Freshman Application Contact** Ms. Amy Graham, Enrollment Management Supervisor, Bill and Sandra Pomeroy College of Nursing at Crouse Hospital, 765 Irving Avenue, Syracuse, NY 13210. *Phone:* 315-470-7481. *Fax:* 315-470-7925. *E-mail:* amygraham@crouse.org. *Website:* http://www.crouse.org/nursing/.

## Borough of Manhattan Community College of the City University of New York
### New York, New York

- **State and locally supported** 2-year, founded 1963, part of City University of New York System
- **Urban** 5-acre campus
- **Coed**

**Undergraduates** 18,189 full-time, 8,559 part-time. 3% are from out of state; 30% Black or African American, non-Hispanic/Latino; 40% Hispanic/Latino; 13% Asian, non-Hispanic/Latino; 0.4% American Indian or Alaska Native, non-Hispanic/Latino; 6% international; 6% transferred in.
**Faculty** *Student/faculty ratio:* 24:1.
**Academics** *Calendar:* semesters. *Degree:* certificates and associate. *Special study options:* academic remediation for entering students, accelerated degree program, adult/continuing education programs, advanced placement credit, cooperative education, distance learning, English as a second language, honors programs, independent study, internships, off-campus study, part-time degree program, services for LD students, study abroad, summer session for credit.
**Library** A. Philip Randolph Library plus 1 other. *Books:* 124,572 (physical), 488,639 (digital/electronic); *Serial titles:* 1,292 (physical), 94,735 (digital/electronic); *Databases:* 33,624. Weekly public service hours: 80; students can reserve study rooms.
**Student Life** *Campus security:* 24-hour patrols.
**Athletics** Member NJCAA.
**Standardized Tests** *Recommended:* SAT or ACT (for admission).
**Costs (2017–18)** *Tuition:* state resident $4800 full-time, $210 per credit part-time; nonresident $7680 full-time, $320 per credit part-time. Part-time tuition and fees vary according to course load. *Required fees:* $369 full-time, $100 per term part-time. *Payment plans:* installment, deferred payment.
**Financial Aid** Of all full-time matriculated undergraduates who enrolled in 2016, 15,563 applied for aid, 14,511 were judged to have need.
**Applying** *Options:* electronic application, deferred entrance. *Application fee:* $65. *Required:* high school transcript.
**Freshman Application Contact** Dr. Eugenio Barrios, Director of Enrollment Management, Borough of Manhattan Community College of the City University of New York, 199 Chambers Street, Room S-310, New York, NY 10007. *Phone:* 212-220-1265. *Toll-free phone:* 866-583-5729. *Fax:* 212-220-2366. *E-mail:* admissions@bmcc.cuny.edu. *Website:* http://www.bmcc.cuny.edu/.

## Bronx Community College of the City University of New York
### Bronx, New York

**Freshman Application Contact** Ms. Patricia A. Ramos, Admissions Officer, Bronx Community College of the City University of New York, 2155 University Avenue, Bronx, NY 10453. *Phone:* 718-289-5888. *E-mail:* admission@bcc.cuny.edu. *Website:* http://www.bcc.cuny.edu/.

## Bryant & Stratton College–Albany Campus
### Albany, New York

**Freshman Application Contact** Mr. Robert Ferrell, Director of Admissions, Bryant & Stratton College–Albany Campus, 1259 Central Avenue, Albany, NY 12205. *Phone:* 518-437-1802 Ext. 205. *Fax:* 518-437-1048. *Website:* http://www.bryantstratton.edu/.

## Bryant & Stratton College–Amherst Campus
### Clarence, New York

**Freshman Application Contact** Mr. Brian K. Dioguardi, Director of Admissions, Bryant & Stratton College–Amherst Campus, Audubon Business Center, 40 Hazelwood Drive, Amherst, NY 14228. *Phone:* 716-691-0012. *Fax:* 716-691-0012. *E-mail:* bkdioguardi@bryantstratton.edu. *Website:* http://www.bryantstratton.edu/.

## Bryant & Stratton College–Buffalo Campus
### Buffalo, New York

**Freshman Application Contact** Mr. Philip J. Struebel, Director of Admissions, Bryant & Stratton College–Buffalo Campus, 465 Main Street, Suite 400, Buffalo, NY 14203. *Phone:* 716-884-9120. *Fax:* 716-884-0091. *E-mail:* pjstruebel@bryantstratton.edu. *Website:* http://www.bryantstratton.edu/.

## Bryant & Stratton College–Greece Campus
### Rochester, New York

**Freshman Application Contact** Bryant & Stratton College–Greece Campus, 854 Long Pond Road, Rochester, NY 14612. *Phone:* 585-720-0660. *Website:* http://www.bryantstratton.edu/.

# Bryant & Stratton College–Henrietta Campus
## Rochester, New York

**Freshman Application Contact** Bryant & Stratton College–Henrietta Campus, 1225 Jefferson Road, Rochester, NY 14623. *Phone:* 585-292-5627 Ext. 101. *Website:* http://www.bryantstratton.edu/.

# Bryant & Stratton College–Orchard Park Campus
## Orchard Park, New York

**Freshman Application Contact** Bryant & Stratton College–Orchard Park Campus, 200 Redtail Road, Orchard Park, NY 14127. *Phone:* 716-677-9500. *Website:* http://www.bryantstratton.edu/.

# Bryant & Stratton College–Syracuse Campus
## Syracuse, New York

**Freshman Application Contact** Ms. Dawn Rajkowski, Director of High School Enrollments, Bryant & Stratton College–Syracuse Campus, 953 James Street, Syracuse, NY 13203-2502. *Phone:* 315-472-6603 Ext. 248. *Fax:* 315-474-4383. *Website:* http://www.bryantstratton.edu/.

# Bryant & Stratton College–Syracuse North Campus
## Liverpool, New York

**Freshman Application Contact** Ms. Heather Macnik, Director of Admissions, Bryant & Stratton College–Syracuse North Campus, 8687 Carling Road, Liverpool, NY 13090. *Phone:* 315-652-6500. *Website:* http://www.bryantstratton.edu/.

# Cayuga County Community College
## Auburn, New York

- **State and locally supported** 2-year, founded 1953, part of State University of New York System
- **Small-town** 50-acre campus with easy access to Rochester, Syracuse
- **Endowment** $14.1 million
- **Coed,** 4,921 undergraduate students, 32% full-time, 60% women, 40% men

**Undergraduates** 1,585 full-time, 3,336 part-time. Students come from 11 states and territories; 10 other countries; 1% are from out of state; 6% Black or African American, non-Hispanic/Latino; 4% Hispanic/Latino; 1% Asian, non-Hispanic/Latino; 0.5% American Indian or Alaska Native, non-Hispanic/Latino; 1% Two or more races, non-Hispanic/Latino; 6% Race/ethnicity unknown; 0.5% international; 4% transferred in. *Retention:* 55% of full-time freshmen returned.
**Freshmen** *Admission:* 670 applied, 576 enrolled. *Average high school GPA:* 2.6.
**Faculty** *Total:* 222, 20% full-time. *Student/faculty ratio:* 26:1.
**Majors** Accounting technology and bookkeeping; art; business administration and management; child-care and support services management; communication and journalism related; communications systems installation and repair technology; computer and information sciences; computer and information sciences and support services related; corrections; criminal justice/police science; drafting and design technology; education (multiple levels); electrical, electronic and communications engineering technology; entrepreneurship; fine/studio arts; game and interactive media design; general studies; geography; graphic design; health services/allied health/health sciences; humanities; information science/studies; liberal arts and sciences/liberal studies; literature related; mathematics related; mechanical engineering; mechanical engineering/mechanical technology; music related; occupational therapist assistant; psychology related; radio, television, and digital communication related; registered nursing/registered nurse; science technologies related; sport and fitness administration/management; telecommunications technology; wine steward/sommelier; writing.
**Academics** *Calendar:* semesters. *Degree:* certificates and associate. *Special study options:* academic remediation for entering students, advanced placement credit, cooperative education, distance learning, honors programs,

internships, off-campus study, part-time degree program, services for LD students, study abroad, summer session for credit.
**Library** Norman F. Bourke Memorial Library plus 2 others. *Books:* 71,419 (physical), 151,020 (digital/electronic); *Serial titles:* 287 (physical), 61,585 (digital/electronic); *Databases:* 118. Weekly public service hours: 61; students can reserve study rooms.
**Student Life** *Housing:* college housing not available. *Activities and Organizations:* drama/theater group, student-run newspaper, radio and television station, choral group, Student Activity Board, Student Government, Criminal Justice Club, Tutor Club, Early Childhood Club. *Campus security:* security from 8 am to 9 pm. *Student services:* health clinic, personal/psychological counseling, veterans affairs office.
**Athletics** Member NJCAA. *Intercollegiate sports:* baseball M, basketball M/W, bowling M/W, cross-country running M/W, golf M/W, soccer M/W, softball W, volleyball W. *Intramural sports:* basketball M/W.
**Costs (2017–18)** *Tuition:* state resident $4544 full-time, $189 per credit hour part-time; nonresident $9088 full-time, $378 per credit hour part-time. Full-time tuition and fees vary according to course load, location, and program. Part-time tuition and fees vary according to course load, location, and program. *Required fees:* $351 full-time. *Payment plan:* installment. *Waivers:* employees or children of employees.
**Financial Aid** Of all full-time matriculated undergraduates who enrolled in 2016, 150 Federal Work-Study jobs (averaging $2000). 200 state and other part-time jobs (averaging $1000).
**Applying** *Options:* electronic application. *Required:* high school transcript. *Required for some:* specific additional requirements for nursing and occupational therapy programs. *Application deadlines:* rolling (freshmen), rolling (transfers). *Notification:* continuous (freshmen), continuous (transfers).
**Freshman Application Contact** Cayuga County Community College, 197 Franklin Street, Auburn, NY 13021-3099. *Phone:* 315-255-1743 Ext. 2244. *Toll-free phone:* 866-598-8883.
*Website:* http://www.cayuga-cc.edu/.

# Clinton Community College
## Plattsburgh, New York

- **State and locally supported** 2-year, founded 1969, part of State University of New York System
- **Small-town** 100-acre campus
- **Coed**

**Undergraduates** 960 full-time, 953 part-time. Students come from 12 states and territories; 22 other countries; 3% are from out of state; 5% Black or African American, non-Hispanic/Latino; 2% Hispanic/Latino; 2% Asian, non-Hispanic/Latino; 0.3% Native Hawaiian or other Pacific Islander, non-Hispanic/Latino; 0.5% American Indian or Alaska Native, non-Hispanic/Latino; 3% Two or more races, non-Hispanic/Latino; 10% Race/ethnicity unknown; 2% international; 17% transferred in; 10% live on campus. *Retention:* 58% of full-time freshmen returned.
**Faculty** *Student/faculty ratio:* 11:1.
**Academics** *Calendar:* semesters. *Degree:* certificates and associate. *Special study options:* academic remediation for entering students, adult/continuing education programs, advanced placement credit, cooperative education, distance learning, English as a second language, external degree program, honors programs, independent study, internships, off-campus study, part-time degree program, services for LD students, student-designed majors, summer session for credit.
**Library** Clinton Community College Learning Resource Center plus 1 other. *Books:* 10,000 (physical); *Databases:* 100. Study areas open 24 hours, 5&-7 days a week; students can reserve study rooms.
**Student Life** *Campus security:* 24-hour emergency response devices and patrols, late-night transport/escort service, controlled dormitory access.
**Athletics** Member NJCAA.
**Costs (2017–18)** *Tuition:* state resident $4300 full-time, $179 per credit hour part-time; nonresident $9300 full-time, $383 per credit hour part-time. Full-time tuition and fees vary according to course load and program. Part-time tuition and fees vary according to course load and program. *Required fees:* $1047 full-time, $33 per credit hour part-time. *Room and board:* $9692; room only: $5170. Room and board charges vary according to board plan.
**Financial Aid** Of all full-time matriculated undergraduates who enrolled in 2016, 25 Federal Work-Study jobs (averaging $1386).
**Applying** *Options:* electronic application, deferred entrance. *Required:* high school transcript. *Required for some:* essay or personal statement, 3 letters of recommendation, interview.
**Freshman Application Contact** Clinton Community College, 136 Clinton Point Drive, Plattsburgh, NY 12901-9573. *Phone:* 518-562-4171. *Toll-free phone:* 800-552-1160. *Website:* http://www.clinton.edu/.

## Cochran School of Nursing
### Yonkers, New York

- **Independent** 2-year, founded 1894
- **Urban** campus with easy access to New York City
- **Coed, primarily women,** 120 undergraduate students, 23% full-time, 87% women, 13% men

**Undergraduates** 27 full-time, 93 part-time. 6% are from out of state; 11% Black or African American, non-Hispanic/Latino; 38% Hispanic/Latino; 2% Asian, non-Hispanic/Latino; 0.8% Two or more races, non-Hispanic/Latino; 42% Race/ethnicity unknown; 0.8% international; 32% transferred in.
**Faculty** Total: 9, 89% full-time, 11% with terminal degrees. *Student/faculty ratio:* 13:1.
**Majors** Registered nursing/registered nurse.
**Academics** *Calendar:* semesters. *Degree:* associate. *Special study options:* advanced placement credit, part-time degree program.
**Library** Cochran School of Nursing Library. *Books:* 2,340 (physical), 559 (digital/electronic); *Serial titles:* 29 (physical), 7 (digital/electronic); *Databases:* 13. Weekly public service hours: 24; study areas open 24 hours, 5&-7 days a week.
**Student Life** *Housing:* college housing not available. *Campus security:* 24-hour emergency response devices and patrols, late-night transport/escort service. *Student services:* health clinic, personal/psychological counseling.
**Costs (2017–18)** *Tuition:* $9571 full-time, $563 per credit part-time. Full-time tuition and fees vary according to course load and student level. Part-time tuition and fees vary according to course load and student level. *Required fees:* $1571 full-time, $734 per term part-time. *Payment plan:* installment.
**Applying** *Options:* deferred entrance. *Application fee:* $50. *Required:* high school transcript. *Application deadline:* 5/15 (freshmen). *Notification:* 5/15 (freshmen), continuous (transfers).
**Freshman Application Contact** Brandy Haughton, Admissions Counselor, Cochran School of Nursing, 967 North Broadway, Yonkers, NY 10701. *Phone:* 914-964-4606. *Fax:* 914-964-4796. *E-mail:* bhaughton@ riversidehealth.org.
*Website:* http://www.cochranschoolofnursing.us/.

## The College of Westchester
### White Plains, New York

- **Proprietary** primarily 2-year, founded 1915
- **Suburban** campus with easy access to New York City
- **Coed,** 915 undergraduate students, 79% full-time, 64% women, 36% men

**Undergraduates** 721 full-time, 194 part-time. Students come from 5 states and territories; 4% are from out of state; 38% Black or African American, non-Hispanic/Latino; 47% Hispanic/Latino; 2% Asian, non-Hispanic/Latino; 0.2% Native Hawaiian or other Pacific Islander, non-Hispanic/Latino; 0.1% American Indian or Alaska Native, non-Hispanic/Latino; 1% Two or more races, non-Hispanic/Latino; 3% Race/ethnicity unknown; 10% transferred in. *Retention:* 65% of full-time freshmen returned.
**Freshmen** *Admission:* 1,002 applied, 984 admitted, 161 enrolled.
**Faculty** Total: 69, 46% full-time. *Student/faculty ratio:* 20:1.
**Majors** Accounting; business administration and management; commercial and advertising art; computer software and media applications related; health/health-care administration; health information/medical records administration; information technology; medical/clinical assistant; network and system administration; web page, digital/multimedia and information resources design.
**Academics** *Calendar:* semesters. *Degrees:* certificates, associate, and bachelor's. *Special study options:* academic remediation for entering students, accelerated degree program, adult/continuing education programs, cooperative education, distance learning, double majors, honors programs, internships, part-time degree program, summer session for credit.
**Library** Dr. William R. Papallo Library.
**Student Life** *Housing:* college housing not available. *Activities and Organizations:* student-run newspaper. *Student services:* personal/psychological counseling, veterans affairs office.
**Standardized Tests** *Recommended:* SAT (for admission).
**Costs (2017–18)** *Tuition:* $20,115 full-time, $745 per credit part-time. *Required fees:* $900 full-time, $100 per course part-time. *Payment plan:* installment. *Waivers:* employees or children of employees.
**Applying** *Options:* electronic application, deferred entrance. *Application fee:* $40. *Required:* high school transcript, interview. *Required for some:* essay or personal statement. *Application deadlines:* rolling (freshmen), rolling (transfers).
**Freshman Application Contact** Mr. Matt Curtis, Vice President, Enrollment Management, The College of Westchester, 325 Central Avenue, PO Box 710, White Plains, NY 10602. *Phone:* 914-948-4442 Ext. 313. *Toll-free phone:* 855-403-7722. *Fax:* 914-948-5441. *E-mail:* admissions@cw.edu.
*Website:* http://www.cw.edu/.

## Columbia-Greene Community College
### Hudson, New York

- **State and locally supported** 2-year, founded 1966, part of State University of New York System
- **Rural** 143-acre campus
- **Coed,** 1,624 undergraduate students, 37% full-time, 63% women, 37% men
- 100% of applicants were admitted

**Undergraduates** 596 full-time, 1,028 part-time. Students come from 3 states and territories; 1 other country; 9% Black or African American, non-Hispanic/Latino; 9% Hispanic/Latino; 3% Asian, non-Hispanic/Latino; 0.1% Native Hawaiian or other Pacific Islander, non-Hispanic/Latino; 0.2% American Indian or Alaska Native, non-Hispanic/Latino; 3% Two or more races, non-Hispanic/Latino; 0.7% Race/ethnicity unknown; 0.1% international; 5% transferred in. *Retention:* 61% of full-time freshmen returned.
**Freshmen** *Admission:* 318 applied, 317 admitted, 279 enrolled.
**Faculty** Total: 84, 52% full-time. *Student/faculty ratio:* 15:1.
**Majors** Accounting technology and bookkeeping; art; automobile/automotive mechanics technology; business administration and management; business/commerce; computer and information sciences; criminal justice/law enforcement administration; environmental studies; general studies; humanities; human services; information technology; liberal arts and sciences/liberal studies; medical/clinical assistant; registered nursing/registered nurse.
**Academics** *Calendar:* semesters. *Degree:* certificates and associate. *Special study options:* academic remediation for entering students, advanced placement credit, cooperative education, distance learning, English as a second language, honors programs, independent study, internships, part-time degree program, services for LD students, summer session for credit.
**Student Life** *Housing:* college housing not available. *Activities and Organizations:* student-run radio station, Criminal Justice Club, Human Services Club, Psychology Club, Student Senate, Animal Advocates. *Campus security:* 24-hour emergency response devices and patrols, student patrols, late-night transport/escort service. *Student services:* personal/psychological counseling, veterans affairs office.
**Athletics** Member NCAA, NJCAA. All NCAA Division III. *Intercollegiate sports:* baseball M, basketball M, cross-country running M/W, softball W. *Intramural sports:* badminton M/W, basketball M/W, table tennis M/W, volleyball M/W.
**Costs (2017–18)** *Tuition:* state resident $4536 full-time, $189 per semester hour part-time; nonresident $9072 full-time, $378 per semester hour part-time. Full-time tuition and fees vary according to course load and program. Part-time tuition and fees vary according to course load and program. *Required fees:* $352 full-time, $15 per semester hour part-time, $5 per term part-time. *Payment plan:* installment. *Waivers:* senior citizens and employees or children of employees.
**Applying** *Options:* electronic application, deferred entrance. *Required:* high school transcript. *Required for some:* interview. *Application deadlines:* rolling (freshmen), rolling (out-of-state freshmen), rolling (transfers).
**Freshman Application Contact** Ms. Rachel Kappel, Director of Admissions, Columbia-Greene Community College, 4400 Route 23, Hudson, NY 12534. *Phone:* 518-828-4181 Ext. 3370. *Fax:* 518-822-2015. *E-mail:* rachel.kappel@sunycgcc.edu.
*Website:* http://www.sunycgcc.edu/.

## Corning Community College
### Corning, New York

**Freshman Application Contact** Corning Community College, One Academic Drive, Corning, NY 14830-3297. *Phone:* 607-962-9540. *Toll-free phone:* 800-358-7171. *Website:* http://www.corning-cc.edu/.

## Dutchess Community College
### Poughkeepsie, New York

- **State and locally supported** 2-year, founded 1957, part of State University of New York System
- **Suburban** 130-acre campus with easy access to New York City
- **Coed,** 9,061 undergraduate students, 42% full-time, 55% women, 45% men

**Undergraduates** 3,839 full-time, 5,222 part-time. 1% are from out of state; 11% Black or African American, non-Hispanic/Latino; 19% Hispanic/Latino; 3% Asian, non-Hispanic/Latino; 0.1% Native Hawaiian or other Pacific Islander, non-Hispanic/Latino; 0.1% American Indian or Alaska Native, non-Hispanic/Latino; 4% Two or more races, non-Hispanic/Latino; 2% Race/ethnicity unknown; 0.9% international; 3% transferred in; 5% live on campus.

**Applying** *Options:* electronic application. *Application fee:* $50. *Required:* essay or personal statement, high school transcript. *Required for some:* portfolio for art and design programs. *Application deadlines:* 1/1 (freshmen), 1/1 (transfers). *Notification:* 4/1 (freshmen), 4/1 (transfers).

**Freshman Application Contact** Ms. Magda Francois, Director of Admissions and Strategic Recruitment, Fashion Institute of Technology, Seventh Avenue at 27th Street, New York, NY 10001-5992. *E-mail:* fitinfo@fitnyc.edu. *Website:* http://www.fitnyc.edu/.

See below for display ad and page 322 for the College Close-Up.

## Finger Lakes Community College
### Canandaigua, New York

- **State and locally supported** 2-year, founded 1965, part of State University of New York System
- **Small-town** 300-acre campus with easy access to Rochester
- **Coed**

**Undergraduates** 2,587 full-time, 3,934 part-time. Students come from 15 states and territories; 2 other countries; 0.3% are from out of state; 5% Black or African American, non-Hispanic/Latino; 5% Hispanic/Latino; 1% Asian, non-Hispanic/Latino; 0.3% American Indian or Alaska Native, non-Hispanic/Latino; 3% Two or more races, non-Hispanic/Latino; 13% Race/ethnicity unknown; 3% transferred in.

**Faculty** *Student/faculty ratio:* 22:1.

**Academics** *Calendar:* semesters. *Degree:* certificates and associate. *Special study options:* academic remediation for entering students, accelerated degree program, advanced placement credit, distance learning, double majors, honors programs, independent study, internships, off-campus study, part-time degree program, services for LD students, study abroad, summer session for credit. *ROTC:* Air Force (c).

**Library** Charles Meder Library. Students can reserve study rooms.

**Student Life** *Campus security:* 24-hour emergency response devices and patrols, late-night transport/escort service.

**Athletics** Member NJCAA.

**Costs (2017–18)** *Tuition:* state resident $4522 full-time, $189 per credit hour part-time; nonresident $9044 full-time, $378 per credit hour part-time. Full-time tuition and fees vary according to course load. Part-time tuition and fees vary according to course load. *Required fees:* $600 full-time.

**Financial Aid** Of all full-time matriculated undergraduates who enrolled in 2016, 2,180 applied for aid, 2,109 were judged to have need. In 2016, 7. *Average non-need-based aid:* $1837.

**Applying** *Options:* electronic application, early admission, deferred entrance. *Application fee:* $20. *Required:* high school transcript.

**Freshman Application Contact** Ms. Bonnie B. Ritts, Director of Admissions, Finger Lakes Community College, 3325 Marvin Sands Drive, Canandaigua, NY 14424-8395. *Phone:* 585-785-1279. *Fax:* 585-785-1734. *E-mail:* admissions@flcc.edu. *Website:* http://www.flcc.edu/.

## Finger Lakes Health College of Nursing
### Geneva, New York

**Admissions Office Contact** Finger Lakes Health College of Nursing, 196 North Street, Geneva, NY 14456. *Website:* http://www.flhcon.edu/.

## Fiorello H. LaGuardia Community College of the City University of New York
### Long Island City, New York

- **State and locally supported** 2-year, founded 1970, part of City University of New York System
- **Urban** 25-acre campus with easy access to New York City
- **Coed,** 19,356 undergraduate students, 56% full-time, 57% women, 43% men

**Undergraduates** 10,838 full-time, 8,518 part-time. Students come from 17 states and territories; 148 other countries; 0.4% are from out of state; 17% Black or African American, non-Hispanic/Latino; 48% Hispanic/Latino; 20% Asian, non-Hispanic/Latino; 0.4% Native Hawaiian or other Pacific Islander, non-Hispanic/Latino; 0.6% American Indian or Alaska Native, non-Hispanic/Latino; 4% international; 9% transferred in. *Retention:* 37% of full-time freshmen returned.

**Freshmen** *Admission:* 20,331 applied, 20,331 admitted, 2,959 enrolled.

**Faculty** *Total:* 1,088, 38% full-time, 31% with terminal degrees. *Student/faculty ratio:* 21:1.

**Majors** Accounting technology and bookkeeping; administrative assistant and secretarial science; adult development and aging; biology/biological sciences; business administration and management; civil engineering; commercial photography; computer and information sciences and support services related; computer installation and repair technology; computer programming; computer science; computer systems networking and telecommunications; criminal justice/safety; dietetic technology; digital arts; dramatic/theater arts;

electrical and electronics engineering; emergency medical technology (EMT paramedic); energy management and systems technology; English; environmental science; fine/studio arts; industrial and product design; Japanese; legal assistant/paralegal; liberal arts and sciences/liberal studies; licensed practical/vocational nurse training; mechanical engineering; medical radiologic technology; occupational therapist assistant; philosophy; physical therapy technology; psychiatric/mental health services technology; psychology; recording arts technology; registered nursing/registered nurse; restaurant/food services management; Spanish; speech communication and rhetoric; teacher assistant/aide; tourism and travel services management; veterinary/animal health technology; visual and performing arts.

**Academics** *Calendar:* enhanced semester. *Degree:* certificates and associate. *Special study options:* academic remediation for entering students, accelerated degree program, adult/continuing education programs, advanced placement credit, cooperative education, distance learning, double majors, English as a second language, honors programs, independent study, internships, off-campus study, part-time degree program, services for LD students, student-designed majors, study abroad, summer session for credit.

**Library** Fiorello H. LaGuardia Community College Library Media Resources Center plus 1 other. *Books:* 89,478 (physical), 545,512 (digital/electronic); *Serial titles:* 491 (physical), 105,706 (digital/electronic); *Databases:* 211,328. Weekly public service hours: 82; students can reserve study rooms.

**Student Life** *Housing:* college housing not available. *Activities and Organizations:* drama/theater group, student-run newspaper, radio station, Bangladesh Student Association, Christian Club, Chinese Club, Web Radio, Black Student Union. *Campus security:* 24-hour emergency response devices and patrols, late-night transport/escort service. *Student services:* health clinic, personal/psychological counseling, women's center, legal services.

**Athletics** *Intercollegiate sports:* basketball M/W. *Intramural sports:* basketball M/W, bowling M/W, cheerleading M/W, soccer M/W, swimming and diving M/W, table tennis M/W, volleyball M/W.

**Costs (2017–18)** *Tuition:* state resident $4800 full-time, $210 per credit part-time; nonresident $7680 full-time, $320 per credit part-time. *Required fees:* $417 full-time, $105 per term part-time. *Payment plan:* installment. *Waivers:* senior citizens and employees or children of employees.

**Financial Aid** Of all full-time matriculated undergraduates who enrolled in 2016, 8,560 applied for aid, 8,413 were judged to have need, 3 had their need fully met. *Average percent of need met:* 32%. *Average financial aid package:* $5631. *Average need-based loan:* $4255. *Average need-based gift aid:* $5341.

**Applying** *Options:* electronic application, early admission, deferred entrance. *Application fee:* $65. *Required:* high school transcript. *Application deadlines:* rolling (freshmen), rolling (transfers). *Notification:* continuous (freshmen), continuous (transfers).

**Freshman Application Contact** Ms. LaVora Desvigne, Director of Admissions, Fiorello H. LaGuardia Community College of the City University of New York, RM-147, 31-10 Thomson Avenue, Long Island City, NY 11101. *Phone:* 718-482-5114. *Fax:* 718-482-5112. *E-mail:* admissions@lagcc.cuny.edu. *Website:* http://www.lagcc.cuny.edu/.

# Fulton-Montgomery Community College
## Johnstown, New York

**Freshman Application Contact** Fulton-Montgomery Community College, 2805 State Highway 67, Johnstown, NY 12095-3790. *Phone:* 518-762-4651 Ext. 8301. *Website:* http://www.fmcc.suny.edu/.

# Genesee Community College
## Batavia, New York

- **State and locally supported** 2-year, founded 1966, part of State University of New York System
- **Small-town** 256-acre campus with easy access to Buffalo, Rochester
- **Endowment** $5.0 million
- **Coed,** 5,906 undergraduate students, 40% full-time, 62% women, 38% men

**Undergraduates** 2,353 full-time, 3,553 part-time. Students come from 25 states and territories; 20 other countries; 2% are from out of state; 6% Black or African American, non-Hispanic/Latino; 4% Hispanic/Latino; 1% Asian, non-Hispanic/Latino; 0.7% American Indian or Alaska Native, non-Hispanic/Latino; 3% Two or more races, non-Hispanic/Latino; 9% Race/ethnicity unknown; 3% international.

**Freshmen** *Admission:* 2,885 applied, 2,885 admitted.

**Faculty** *Total:* 347, 26% full-time, 10% with terminal degrees. *Student/faculty ratio:* 15:1.

**Majors** Accounting; biology/biological sciences; biology/biotechnology laboratory technician; biotechnology; business administration and management; business administration, management and operations related; business, management, and marketing related; business operations support and

secretarial services related; chemistry; civil drafting and CAD/CADD; clinical/medical laboratory technology; computer and information sciences related; computer graphics; computer installation and repair technology; computer programming related; computer science; computer software and media applications related; computer support specialist; computer systems networking and telecommunications; corrections and criminal justice related; criminal justice/law enforcement administration; criminal justice/police science; criminal justice/safety; criminology; digital arts; drafting and design technology; drafting/design engineering technologies related; dramatic/theater arts; dramatic/theater arts and stagecraft related; e-commerce; education; education (multiple levels); education related; elementary education; engineering; engineering science; entrepreneurship; fashion/apparel design; fashion merchandising; fine/studio arts; food technology and processing; foreign languages related; general studies; gerontology; graphic design; health and physical education/fitness; health and physical education related; health professions related; hospitality administration; hotel/motel administration; humanities; human services; information science/studies; kindergarten/preschool education; legal assistant/paralegal; liberal arts and sciences and humanities related; liberal arts and sciences/liberal studies; marketing/marketing management; mass communication/media; mathematics; mathematics related; medical administrative assistant and medical secretary; nanotechnology; network and system administration; nursing practice; parks, recreation, leisure, and fitness studies related; physical education teaching and coaching; physical therapy; physical therapy technology; polysomnography; psychology; psychology related; radio and television; radio and television broadcasting technology; radio, television, and digital communication related; registered nursing, nursing administration, nursing research and clinical nursing related; registered nursing/registered nurse; respiratory care therapy; social sciences; social sciences related; social work; social work related; sports studies; substance abuse/addiction counseling; teacher assistant/aide; theater design and technology; theater/theater arts management; tourism and travel services management; tourism promotion; veterinary/animal health technology; web page, digital/multimedia and information resources design.

**Academics** *Calendar:* semesters. *Degree:* certificates and associate. *Special study options:* academic remediation for entering students, adult/continuing education programs, advanced placement credit, cooperative education, distance learning, double majors, English as a second language, honors programs, independent study, internships, part-time degree program, services for LD students, study abroad, summer session for credit. *ROTC:* Army (c).

**Library** Alfred C. OConnell Library. *Books:* 79,535 (physical), 17,645 (digital/electronic); *Serial titles:* 164 (physical), 67,604 (digital/electronic); *Databases:* 89. Weekly public service hours: 76.

**Student Life** *Housing Options:* special housing for students with disabilities. Campus housing is provided by a third party. *Activities and Organizations:* drama/theater group, student-run newspaper, radio station, choral group, DECA (Distributive Education Clubs of America), PTK Honor Society, Multi Cultural Communications Club, Education Club, FORUM Theater Group. *Campus security:* 24-hour emergency response devices and patrols, student patrols, late-night transport/escort service, controlled dormitory access. *Student services:* health clinic, personal/psychological counseling, veterans affairs office.

**Athletics** Member NJCAA. *Intercollegiate sports:* baseball M, basketball M/W, golf M/W, lacrosse M/W, soccer M/W, softball W, swimming and diving M/W, volleyball W. *Intramural sports:* badminton M/W, basketball M/W, softball M/W, volleyball M/W.

**Costs (2018–19)** *Tuition:* state resident $4150 full-time, $160 per credit hour part-time; nonresident $4750 full-time, $185 per credit hour part-time. *Required fees:* $510 full-time. *Room and board:* $8720; room only: $6200.

**Financial Aid** Of all full-time matriculated undergraduates who enrolled in 2016, 2,444 applied for aid, 2,060 were judged to have need, 1,078 had their need fully met. 117 Federal Work-Study jobs (averaging $1189). 91 state and other part-time jobs (averaging $2071). *Average percent of need met:* 84%. *Average financial aid package:* $5061. *Average need-based loan:* $3642. *Average need-based gift aid:* $3325.

**Applying** *Options:* electronic application. *Required:* high school transcript. *Required for some:* 1 letter of recommendation. *Application deadlines:* rolling (freshmen), rolling (transfers). *Notification:* continuous (freshmen), continuous (transfers).

**Freshman Application Contact** Mrs. Tanya Lane-Martin, Director of Admissions, Genesee Community College, Batavia, NY 14020. *Phone:* 585-343-0055 Ext. 6413. *Toll-free phone:* 866-CALL GCC. *Fax:* 585-345-6892. *E-mail:* tmlanemartin@genesee.edu. *Website:* http://www.genesee.edu/.

# Helene Fuld College of Nursing
## New York, New York

**Freshman Application Contact** Helene Fuld College of Nursing, 24 East 120th Street, New York, NY 10035. *Phone:* 212-616-7271. *Website:* http://www.helenefuld.edu/.

# Herkimer County Community College
## Herkimer, New York

**Freshman Application Contact** Herkimer County Community College, 100 Reservoir Road, Herkimer, NY 13350. *Phone:* 315-866-0300 Ext. 8278. *Toll-free phone:* 888-464-4222 Ext. 8278. *Website:* http://www.herkimer.edu/.

# Hudson Valley Community College
## Troy, New York

**Freshman Application Contact** Ms. Marie Claire Bauer, Director of Admissions, Hudson Valley Community College, 80 Vandenburgh Avenue, Troy, NY 12180-6096. *Phone:* 518-629-7309. *Toll-free phone:* 877-325-HVCC. *Website:* http://www.hvcc.edu/.

# Island Drafting and Technical Institute
## Amityville, New York

**Freshman Application Contact** Larry Basile, Island Drafting and Technical Institute, 128 Broadway, Amityville, NY 11701. *Phone:* 631-691-8733 Ext. 114. *Fax:* 631-691-8738. *E-mail:* info@idti.edu. *Website:* http://www.idti.edu/.

# Jamestown Business College
## Jamestown, New York

- **Proprietary** primarily 2-year, founded 1886
- **Small-town** 1-acre campus
- **Coed**

**Undergraduates** 305 full-time, 6 part-time. Students come from 2 states and territories; 10% are from out of state; 2% Black or African American, non-Hispanic/Latino; 20% Hispanic/Latino; 0.3% Asian, non-Hispanic/Latino; 5% American Indian or Alaska Native, non-Hispanic/Latino; 4% Two or more races, non-Hispanic/Latino; 1% Race/ethnicity unknown; 14% transferred in.
**Faculty** *Student/faculty ratio:* 23:1.
**Academics** *Calendar:* quarters. *Degrees:* certificates, associate, and bachelor's. *Special study options:* advanced placement credit, double majors, part-time degree program, summer session for credit.
**Library** James Prendergast Library. *Books:* 173,745 (physical), 12,508 (digital/electronic); *Serial titles:* 103 (physical), 70 (digital/electronic); *Databases:* 55. Weekly public service hours: 55; study areas open 24 hours, 5&-7 days a week.
**Student Life** *Campus security:* 24-hour emergency response devices, student key card for building entrance.
**Applying** *Application fee:* $25. *Required:* essay or personal statement, high school transcript, interview.
**Freshman Application Contact** Mrs. Brenda Salemme, Director of Admissions, Jamestown Business College, 7 Fairmount Avenue, Box 429, Jamestown, NY 14702-0429. *Phone:* 716-664-5100. *Fax:* 716-664-3144. *E-mail:* brendasalemme@jbc.edu. *Website:* http://www.jbc.edu/.

# Jamestown Community College
## Jamestown, New York

- **State and locally supported** 2-year, founded 1950, part of State University of New York System
- **Small-town** 107-acre campus
- **Coed,** 4,463 undergraduate students, 46% full-time, 58% women, 42% men

**Undergraduates** 2,060 full-time, 2,403 part-time. Students come from 10 states and territories; 18 other countries; 10% are from out of state; 5% Black or African American, non-Hispanic/Latino; 6% Hispanic/Latino; 0.8% Asian, non-Hispanic/Latino; 0.1% Native Hawaiian or other Pacific Islander, non-Hispanic/Latino; 1% American Indian or Alaska Native, non-Hispanic/Latino; 3% Two or more races, non-Hispanic/Latino; 1% Race/ethnicity unknown; 0.9% international; 5% transferred in; 11% live on campus.
**Freshmen** *Admission:* 1,719 applied, 1,710 admitted, 794 enrolled. *Average high school GPA:* 3.3.
**Faculty** *Total:* 306, 24% full-time. *Student/faculty ratio:* 16:1.
**Majors** Accounting technology and bookkeeping; administrative assistant and secretarial science; biology/biotechnology laboratory technician; business administration and management; computer and information sciences; criminal justice/law enforcement administration; criminal justice/police science; engineering; environmental science; fine/studio arts; general studies; health and physical education/fitness; health information/medical records technology; humanities; human services; information science/studies; information technology; international/global studies; liberal arts and sciences and humanities related; liberal arts and sciences/liberal studies; mechanical

engineering/mechanical technology; music; occupational therapist assistant; registered nursing/registered nurse; speech communication and rhetoric; substance abuse/addiction counseling; teacher assistant/aide; welding technology.
**Academics** *Calendar:* semesters. *Degree:* certificates and associate. *Special study options:* academic remediation for entering students, adult/continuing education programs, advanced placement credit, distance learning, honors programs, independent study, internships, off-campus study, part-time degree program, services for LD students, study abroad, summer session for credit.
**Library** Hultquist Library plus 1 other. *Books:* 90,813 (physical), 2,360 (digital/electronic); *Serial titles:* 687 (physical), 14 (digital/electronic); *Databases:* 89. Weekly public service hours: 63.
**Student Life** *Housing Options:* coed. Campus housing is university owned. *Activities and Organizations:* drama/theater group, choral group, Nursing Club, SOTA (occupational therapy), Earth Awareness Club, JCC Pride, Impact (Interfaith Christian Club). *Campus security:* 24-hour emergency response devices, controlled dormitory access. *Student services:* health clinic, personal/psychological counseling.
**Athletics** Member NJCAA. *Intercollegiate sports:* baseball M, basketball M/W, golf M/W, soccer M/W, swimming and diving M/W, volleyball W, wrestling M. *Intramural sports:* basketball M/W, bowling M/W, cross-country running M/W, softball M/W, volleyball M/W.
**Costs (2017–18)** *One-time required fee:* $85. *Tuition:* state resident $4750 full-time, $198 per credit hour part-time; nonresident $9500 full-time, $396 per credit hour part-time. Full-time tuition and fees vary according to course load and program. Part-time tuition and fees vary according to course load and program. *Required fees:* $870 full-time, $26 per credit hour part-time. *Room and board:* $10,750; room only: $7500. Room and board charges vary according to board plan. *Payment plan:* installment. *Waivers:* employees or children of employees.
**Financial Aid** Of all full-time matriculated undergraduates who enrolled in 2016, 85 Federal Work-Study jobs (averaging $1500). 85 state and other part-time jobs (averaging $1300).
**Applying** *Options:* electronic application, deferred entrance. *Required:* high school transcript. *Application deadlines:* rolling (freshmen), rolling (transfers). *Notification:* continuous (freshmen), continuous (transfers).
**Freshman Application Contact** Ms. Wendy Present, Director of Admissions, Jamestown Community College, 525 Falconer Street, PO Box 20, Jamestown, NY 14702-0020. *Phone:* 716-338-1001. *Toll-free phone:* 800-388-8557. *Fax:* 716-338-1450. *E-mail:* admissions@mail.sunyjcc.edu. *Website:* http://www.sunyjcc.edu/.

# Jefferson Community College
## Watertown, New York

- **State and locally supported** 2-year, founded 1961, part of State University of New York System
- **Small-town** 90-acre campus with easy access to Syracuse
- **Coed,** 3,632 undergraduate students, 57% full-time, 56% women, 44% men

**Undergraduates** 2,082 full-time, 1,550 part-time. 7% Black or African American, non-Hispanic/Latino; 10% Hispanic/Latino; 1% Asian, non-Hispanic/Latino; 0.2% Native Hawaiian or other Pacific Islander, non-Hispanic/Latino; 0.6% American Indian or Alaska Native, non-Hispanic/Latino; 3% Two or more races, non-Hispanic/Latino; 3% Race/ethnicity unknown; 0.9% international; 6% transferred in.
**Freshmen** *Admission:* 853 enrolled.
**Faculty** *Total:* 239, 31% full-time.
**Majors** Accounting; accounting technology and bookkeeping; administrative assistant and secretarial science; animal/livestock husbandry and production; business administration and management; child-care and support services management; child development; community organization and advocacy; computer and information sciences; computer and information sciences and support services related; computer/information technology services administration related; computer science; computer technology/computer systems technology; criminal justice/law enforcement administration; early childhood education; emergency medical technology (EMT paramedic); engineering; engineering science; fire prevention and safety technology; fire services administration; hospitality administration; humanities; human services; information science/studies; legal assistant/paralegal; liberal arts and sciences/liberal studies; mathematics; mechanical engineering technologies related; medical administrative assistant and medical secretary; office management; office occupations and clerical services; registered nursing/registered nurse; sport and fitness administration/management; teacher assistant/aide; tourism promotion.
**Academics** *Calendar:* semesters. *Degree:* certificates and associate. *Special study options:* academic remediation for entering students, advanced placement credit, cooperative education, distance learning, double majors, honors programs, independent study, internships, part-time degree program, services for LD students, student-designed majors, summer session for credit.

**Library** Melvil Dewey Library plus 1 other. Students can reserve study rooms.
**Student Life** *Activities and Organizations:* student-run newspaper. *Campus security:* 24-hour emergency response devices and patrols, late-night transport/escort service, controlled dormitory access. *Student services:* health clinic, personal/psychological counseling, veterans affairs office.
**Athletics** Member NJCAA. *Intercollegiate sports:* baseball M, basketball M/W, lacrosse M/W, soccer M/W, softball W, volleyball W.
**Standardized Tests** *Recommended:* SAT or ACT (for admission).
**Financial Aid** Of all full-time matriculated undergraduates who enrolled in 2009, 1,748 applied for aid. 98 Federal Work-Study jobs (averaging $1093).
**Applying** *Options:* electronic application, early admission, deferred entrance. *Required:* high school transcript. *Required for some:* interview. *Application deadlines:* 9/6 (freshmen), rolling (transfers). *Notification:* continuous (freshmen), continuous (transfers).
**Freshman Application Contact** Sandra L. Spadoni, Dean for Enrollment, Jefferson Community College, 1220 Coffeen Street, Watertown, NY 13601. *Phone:* 315-786-2437. *Toll-free phone:* 888-435-6522. *Fax:* 315-786-2349. *E-mail:* admissions@sunyjefferson.edu.
*Website:* http://www.sunyjefferson.edu/.

## Kingsborough Community College of the City University of New York
### Brooklyn, New York

- **State and locally supported** 2-year, founded 1963, part of City University of New York System
- **Urban** 72-acre campus with easy access to New York City
- **Coed,** 15,280 undergraduate students, 54% full-time, 55% women, 45% men

**Undergraduates** 8,298 full-time, 6,982 part-time. Students come from 13 states and territories; 136 other countries; 1% are from out of state; 29% Black or African American, non-Hispanic/Latino; 17% Hispanic/Latino; 15% Asian, non-Hispanic/Latino; 0.2% American Indian or Alaska Native, non-Hispanic/Latino; 3% international; 4% transferred in. *Retention:* 71% of full-time freshmen returned.
**Freshmen** *Admission:* 1,979 enrolled. *Average high school GPA:* 2.7.
**Faculty** *Total:* 333.
**Majors** Accounting; administrative assistant and secretarial science; art; biology/biological sciences; broadcast journalism; business administration and management; chemistry; commercial and advertising art; community health services counseling; computer and information sciences; computer science; cooking and related culinary arts; criminal justice/law enforcement administration; data processing and data processing technology; design and applied arts related; dramatic/theater arts; early childhood education; education; elementary education; emergency medical technology (EMT paramedic); engineering science; fashion merchandising; health and physical education related; human services; journalism; labor and industrial relations; liberal arts and sciences/liberal studies; marine maintenance and ship repair technology; marketing/marketing management; mathematics; mental health counseling; music; parks, recreation and leisure; physical therapy; physical therapy technology; physics; polysomnography; psychiatric/mental health services technology; registered nursing/registered nurse; sport and fitness administration/management; surgical technology; teacher assistant/aide; tourism and travel services management.
**Academics** *Calendar:* semesters. *Degree:* certificates and associate. *Special study options:* academic remediation for entering students, accelerated degree program, adult/continuing education programs, advanced placement credit, cooperative education, distance learning, English as a second language, honors programs, independent study, internships, off-campus study, part-time degree program, services for LD students, summer session for credit.
**Library** Robert J. Kibbee Library. *Books:* 224,727 (physical), 481,635 (digital/electronic); *Serial titles:* 230 (physical), 77,212 (digital/electronic); *Databases:* 140. Weekly public service hours: 79.
**Student Life** *Housing:* college housing not available. *Activities and Organizations:* drama/theater group, student-run newspaper, radio station, choral group, Peer Advisors, Caribbean Club, DECA. *Campus security:* 24-hour emergency response devices and patrols. *Student services:* health clinic, personal/psychological counseling, women's center, legal services, veterans affairs office.
**Athletics** Member NJCAA. *Intercollegiate sports:* baseball M, basketball M/W, soccer M, softball W, tennis M/W, track and field M/W, volleyball W. *Intramural sports:* baseball M, basketball M/W, soccer M, softball W, tennis M/W, track and field M/W, volleyball W.

**Costs (2018–19)** *Tuition:* state resident $4800 full-time, $210 per credit hour part-time; nonresident $7680 full-time, $320 per credit hour part-time. *Required fees:* $453 full-time, $121 per term part-time. *Payment plan:* installment. *Waivers:* senior citizens.
**Applying** *Options:* electronic application. *Application fee:* $65. *Required:* high school transcript. *Application deadlines:* 8/15 (freshmen), rolling (transfers).
**Freshman Application Contact** Mr. Javier Morgades, Director of Admissions Information Center, Kingsborough Community College of the City University of New York, 2001 Oriental Boulevard, Brooklyn, NY 11235. *Phone:* 718-368-4600. *E-mail:* info@kbcc.cuny.edu.
*Website:* http://www.kbcc.cuny.edu/.

## Long Island Business Institute
### Flushing, New York

- **Proprietary** 2-year, founded 1968
- **Urban** campus with easy access to New York City
- **Coed**

**Undergraduates** 985 full-time, 133 part-time. Students come from 2 states and territories; 19 other countries; 12% Black or African American, non-Hispanic/Latino; 21% Hispanic/Latino; 52% Asian, non-Hispanic/Latino; 0.1% American Indian or Alaska Native, non-Hispanic/Latino; 0.1% Two or more races, non-Hispanic/Latino; 0.2% Race/ethnicity unknown; 7% international.
**Faculty** *Student/faculty ratio:* 19:1.
**Academics** *Calendar:* semesters. *Degrees:* certificates and associate (information provided for Commack and Flushing campuses). *Special study options:* academic remediation for entering students, adult/continuing education programs, advanced placement credit, cooperative education, English as a second language, honors programs, independent study, part-time degree program, summer session for credit.
**Library** Flushing Main Campus Library plus 2 others. *Books:* 2,000 (physical), 250 (digital/electronic); *Serial titles:* 10 (physical), 3 (digital/electronic); *Databases:* 5.
**Student Life** *Campus security:* 24-hour emergency response devices.
**Costs (2017–18)** *Tuition:* $13,299 full-time, $375 per credit hour part-time. *Required fees:* $1650 full-time, $490 per term part-time. *Payment plans:* installment, deferred payment.
**Applying** *Options:* electronic application. *Required:* high school transcript, interview.
**Freshman Application Contact** Mr. Keith Robertson, Director of Admissions, Long Island Business Institute, 408 Broadway, 2nd Floor, New York, NY 10013. *Phone:* 212-226-7300. *E-mail:* krobertson@libi.edu. *Website:* http://www.libi.edu/.

## Mandl School
### New York, New York

**Admissions Office Contact** Mandl School, 254 West 54th Street, 9th Floor, New York, NY 10019. *Website:* http://www.mandl.edu/.

## Memorial College of Nursing
### Albany, New York

**Freshman Application Contact** Admissions Office, Memorial College of Nursing, 600 Northern Boulevard, Albany, NY 12204. *Website:* http://www.nehealth.com/son/.

## Mildred Elley–New York City
### New York, New York

**Admissions Office Contact** Mildred Elley–New York City, 25 Broadway, 16th Floor, New York, NY 10004-1010. *Website:* http://www.mildred-elley.edu/.

## Mildred Elley School
### Albany, New York

**Director of Admissions** Mr. Michael Cahalan, Enrollment Manager, Mildred Elley School, 855 Central Avenue, Albany, NY 12206. *Phone:* 518-786-3171 Ext. 227. *Toll-free phone:* 800-622-6327. *Website:* http://www.mildred-elley.edu/.

# Mohawk Valley Community College
## Utica, New York

- **State and locally supported** 2-year, founded 1946, part of State University of New York System
- **Suburban** 80-acre campus
- **Endowment** $4.9 million
- **Coed,** 6,506 undergraduate students, 51% full-time, 54% women, 46% men

**Undergraduates** 3,324 full-time, 3,182 part-time. Students come from 16 states and territories; 22 other countries; 41% are from out of state; 11% Black or African American, non-Hispanic/Latino; 8% Hispanic/Latino; 6% Asian, non-Hispanic/Latino; 0.2% Native Hawaiian or other Pacific Islander, non-Hispanic/Latino; 0.3% American Indian or Alaska Native, non-Hispanic/Latino; 3% Two or more races, non-Hispanic/Latino; 0.1% Race/ethnicity unknown; 1% international; 3% transferred in; 7% live on campus.
**Freshmen** *Admission:* 2,726 applied, 2,720 admitted, 1,286 enrolled. *Average high school GPA:* 2.6.
**Faculty** *Total:* 448, 30% full-time, 14% with terminal degrees. *Student/faculty ratio:* 18:1.
**Majors** Accounting technology and bookkeeping; administrative assistant and secretarial science; advertising; aeronautical/aerospace engineering technology; airframe mechanics and aircraft maintenance technology; art; banking and financial support services; business administration and management; CAD/CADD drafting/design technology; carpentry; chemical technology; civil engineering technology; commercial and advertising art; commercial photography; computer and information sciences; computer and information sciences and support services related; computer and information systems security; computer programming; criminal justice/law enforcement administration; criminal justice/police science; culinary arts; dietetic technology; digital arts; electrical and power transmission installation; electrical, electronic and communications engineering technology; electrical/electronics maintenance and repair technology related; emergency care attendant (EMT ambulance); engineering; fire services administration; general studies; health information/medical records technology; heating, air conditioning, ventilation and refrigeration maintenance technology; hotel/motel administration; humanities; human services; law enforcement investigation and interviewing; liberal arts and sciences and humanities related; liberal arts and sciences/liberal studies; mechanical engineering/mechanical technology; mechanical engineering technologies related; medical/clinical assistant; medical radiologic technology; operations management; parks, recreation and leisure facilities management; photographic and film/video technology; physical education teaching and coaching; registered nursing/registered nurse; respiratory care therapy; restaurant, culinary, and catering management; semiconductor manufacturing technology; sign language interpretation and translation; substance abuse/addiction counseling; web page, digital/multimedia and information resources design; welding technology.
**Academics** *Calendar:* semesters. *Degree:* certificates and associate. *Special study options:* academic remediation for entering students, accelerated degree program, advanced placement credit, distance learning, double majors, English as a second language, honors programs, independent study, internships, off-campus study, part-time degree program, services for LD students, student-designed majors, summer session for credit.
**Library** Mohawk Valley Community College Library plus 1 other. *Books:* 98,450 (physical), 278,863 (digital/electronic); *Serial titles:* 461 (physical), 105,147 (digital/electronic); *Databases:* 103. Weekly public service hours: 126.
**Student Life** *Housing Options:* coed, men-only, women-only, special housing for students with disabilities. Campus housing is provided by a third party. Freshman applicants given priority for college housing. *Activities and Organizations:* drama/theater group, student-run newspaper, Program Board, Student Congress, Gender Sexuality Alliance, Black Student Union, Drama Club. *Campus security:* 24-hour emergency response devices and patrols, late-night transport/escort service, controlled dormitory access. *Student services:* health clinic, personal/psychological counseling, veterans affairs office.
**Athletics** Member NJCAA. *Intercollegiate sports:* baseball M, basketball M/W, bowling M/W, cross-country running M/W, golf M/W, lacrosse M/W, soccer M/W, softball W, tennis M/W, track and field M/W, volleyball W. *Intramural sports:* badminton M/W, basketball M/W, soccer M/W, volleyball M/W.
**Costs (2017–18)** *Tuition:* state resident $4284 full-time, $170 per credit hour part-time; nonresident $8568 full-time, $340 per credit hour part-time. *Required fees:* $776 full-time, $29 per credit hour part-time, $26 per term part-time. *Room and board:* Room and board charges vary according to board plan. *Payment plans:* installment, deferred payment. *Waivers:* senior citizens and employees or children of employees.
**Financial Aid** Of all full-time matriculated undergraduates who enrolled in 2016, 229 Federal Work-Study jobs (averaging $1750).

**Applying** *Options:* electronic application, deferred entrance. *Required for some:* high school transcript. *Recommended:* interview. *Application deadlines:* rolling (freshmen), rolling (transfers). *Notification:* continuous (freshmen), continuous (transfers).
**Freshman Application Contact** Kirsten Edwards, Technical Assistant, Admissions, Mohawk Valley Community College, 1101 Sherman Drive, Utica, NY 13501. *Phone:* 315-792-5640. *Toll-free phone:* 800-SEE-MVCC. *Fax:* 315-792-5527. *E-mail:* kedwards@mvcc.edu. *Website:* http://www.mvcc.edu/.

# Monroe Community College
## Rochester, New York

- **State and locally supported** 2-year, founded 1961, part of State University of New York System
- **Suburban** 314-acre campus with easy access to Buffalo
- **Coed,** 12,907 undergraduate students, 61% full-time, 52% women, 48% men

**Undergraduates** 7,866 full-time, 5,041 part-time. Students come from 40 states and territories; 46 other countries; 1% are from out of state; 20% Black or African American, non-Hispanic/Latino; 10% Hispanic/Latino; 5% Asian, non-Hispanic/Latino; 0.1% Native Hawaiian or other Pacific Islander, non-Hispanic/Latino; 0.5% American Indian or Alaska Native, non-Hispanic/Latino; 4% Two or more races, non-Hispanic/Latino; 0.7% Race/ethnicity unknown; 1% international. *Retention:* 51% of full-time freshmen returned.
**Freshmen** *Admission:* 16,328 applied, 11,928 admitted, 2,821 enrolled.
**Faculty** *Total:* 740, 40% full-time, 13% with terminal degrees. *Student/faculty ratio:* 22:1.
**Majors** Accounting; administrative assistant and secretarial science; art; automobile/automotive mechanics technology; behavioral sciences; biological and physical sciences; biology/biological sciences; biology/biotechnology laboratory technician; business administration and management; chemical engineering; chemistry; civil engineering technology; commercial and advertising art; computer and information sciences and support services related; computer and information sciences related; computer engineering related; computer engineering technology; computer science; construction engineering technology; consumer merchandising/retailing management; corrections; criminal justice/law enforcement administration; criminal justice/police science; data processing and data processing technology; dental hygiene; electrical, electronic and communications engineering technology; engineering science; environmental studies; family and consumer sciences/human sciences; fashion/apparel design; fashion merchandising; fire science/firefighting; food technology and processing; forestry; graphic and printing equipment operation/production; health information/medical records administration; heating, air conditioning, ventilation and refrigeration maintenance technology; history; hotel/motel administration; human services; industrial radiologic technology; industrial technology; information science/studies; information technology; instrumentation technology; interior design; international business/trade/commerce; landscape architecture; laser and optical technology; legal administrative assistant/secretary; liberal arts and sciences/liberal studies; marketing/marketing management; mass communication/media; mathematics; mechanical engineering/mechanical technology; music; parks, recreation and leisure; physical education teaching and coaching; physics; political science and government; pre-pharmacy studies; quality control technology; registered nursing/registered nurse; social sciences; special products marketing; telecommunications technology; tourism and travel services management.
**Academics** *Calendar:* semesters. *Degree:* certificates and associate. *Special study options:* academic remediation for entering students, accelerated degree program, adult/continuing education programs, advanced placement credit, cooperative education, English as a second language, honors programs, internships, off-campus study, part-time degree program, services for LD students, summer session for credit. *ROTC:* Army (c), Navy (c), Air Force (c).
**Library** LeRoy V. Good Library. Weekly public service hours: 58; students can reserve study rooms.
**Student Life** *Housing Options:* coed, men-only, women-only. Campus housing is university owned. *Activities and Organizations:* drama/theater group, student-run newspaper, radio station, choral group, Student Newspaper, Phi Theta Kappa, Student Government. *Campus security:* 24-hour emergency response devices and patrols, late-night transport/escort service, controlled dormitory access. *Student services:* health clinic, personal/psychological counseling, veterans affairs office.
**Athletics** Member NCAA, NJCAA. All NCAA Division III. *Intercollegiate sports:* baseball M(s), basketball M(s)/W(s), golf M, ice hockey M(s), lacrosse M(s), soccer M(s)/W(s), softball W, swimming and diving M(s)/W(s), tennis M/W, volleyball W. *Intramural sports:* archery M/W, basketball M/W, bowling M/W, cheerleading W, cross-country running M/W, football M, lacrosse W, racquetball M/W, rugby M, skiing (cross-country) M/W, soccer M/W, softball M/W, swimming and diving M/W, tennis M/W, volleyball M/W.

**Costs (2017–18)** *Tuition:* state resident $4280 full-time, $179 per credit hour part-time; nonresident $8560 full-time, $358 per credit hour part-time. Full-time tuition and fees vary according to program. Part-time tuition and fees vary according to course load and program. *Required fees:* $712 full-time, $76 per credit hour part-time. *Room and board:* room only: $6350. Room and board charges vary according to housing facility. *Payment plan:* installment. *Waivers:* senior citizens and employees or children of employees.
**Applying** *Options:* electronic application, early admission. *Required:* high school transcript. *Application deadlines:* rolling (freshmen), rolling (transfers). *Notification:* continuous (freshmen), continuous (transfers).
**Freshman Application Contact** Ms. Sarah Hagreen, Interim Director of Admissions, Monroe Community College, 1000 East Henrietta Road, Rochester, NY 14623. *Phone:* 585-292-2222. *Fax:* 585-292-3860. *E-mail:* admissions@monroecc.edu.
*Website:* http://www.monroecc.edu/.

## Montefiore School of Nursing
### Mount Vernon, New York

**Director of Admissions** Sandra Farrior, Coordinator of Student Services, Montefiore School of Nursing, 53 Valentine Street, Mount Vernon, NY 10550. *Phone:* 914-361-6472. *E-mail:* hopferadmissions@sshsw.org. *Website:* http://www.montefiorehealthsystem.org/landing.cfm?id=19.

## Nassau Community College
### Garden City, New York

- **State and locally supported** 2-year, founded 1959, part of State University of New York System
- **Suburban** 225-acre campus with easy access to New York City
- **Coed,** 20,267 undergraduate students, 57% full-time, 51% women, 49% men

**Undergraduates** 11,558 full-time, 8,709 part-time. Students come from 19 states and territories; 69 other countries; 0.3% are from out of state; 22% Black or African American, non-Hispanic/Latino; 26% Hispanic/Latino; 7% Asian, non-Hispanic/Latino; 0.3% Native Hawaiian or other Pacific Islander, non-Hispanic/Latino; 0.3% American Indian or Alaska Native, non-Hispanic/Latino; 0.9% Two or more races, non-Hispanic/Latino; 5% Race/ethnicity unknown; 0.9% international; 7% transferred in. *Retention:* 32% of full-time freshmen returned.
**Freshmen** *Admission:* 4,080 enrolled. *Average high school GPA:* 2.5.
**Faculty** *Total:* 1,368, 35% full-time, 30% with terminal degrees. *Student/faculty ratio:* 21:1.
**Majors** Accounting; accounting technology and bookkeeping; administrative assistant and secretarial science; African American/Black studies; art; business administration and management; civil engineering technology; clinical/medical laboratory technology; commercial and advertising art; computer and information sciences; computer and information sciences related; computer graphics; computer science; computer systems networking and telecommunications; criminal justice/law enforcement administration; criminal justice/safety; dance; data processing and data processing technology; design and visual communications; dramatic/theater arts; engineering; entrepreneurship; fashion/apparel design; fashion merchandising; funeral service and mortuary science; general studies; hotel/motel administration; instrumentation technology; insurance; interior design; kindergarten/preschool education; legal administrative assistant/secretary; legal assistant/paralegal; liberal arts and sciences/liberal studies; management information systems; marketing/marketing management; mass communication/media; mathematics; medical administrative assistant and medical secretary; medical radiologic technology; music performance; photography; physical therapy technology; real estate; registered nursing/registered nurse; rehabilitation and therapeutic professions related; respiratory care therapy; retailing; speech communication and rhetoric; surgical technology; theater design and technology; transportation and materials moving related; visual and performing arts.
**Academics** *Calendar:* semesters. *Degree:* certificates and associate. *Special study options:* academic remediation for entering students, adult/continuing education programs, advanced placement credit, cooperative education, distance learning, English as a second language, honors programs, internships, off-campus study, part-time degree program, services for LD students, summer session for credit.
**Library** A. Holly Patterson Library.
**Student Life** *Housing:* college housing not available. *Activities and Organizations:* drama/theater group, student-run newspaper, radio station, choral group, Muslim Student Association, Make a Difference Club, Interact Club, Political Science Club, Investment Club. *Campus security:* 24-hour emergency response devices and patrols, late-night transport/escort service. *Student services:* personal/psychological counseling, women's center.
**Athletics** Member NJCAA. *Intercollegiate sports:* baseball M, basketball M/W, bowling M/W, cheerleading M/W, cross-country running M/W, football

M, golf M/W, lacrosse M/W, soccer M/W, softball W, tennis M/W, track and field M/W, volleyball W, wrestling M. *Intramural sports:* badminton M/W, baseball M, basketball M/W, racquetball M/W, soccer M/W, softball M/W, swimming and diving M/W, table tennis M/W, tennis M/W, volleyball M/W.
**Costs (2017–18)** *Tuition:* state resident $5102 full-time, $213 per credit part-time; nonresident $10,204 full-time, $426 per credit part-time. Full-time tuition and fees vary according to program. Part-time tuition and fees vary according to program. *Required fees:* $220 full-time.
**Financial Aid** Of all full-time matriculated undergraduates who enrolled in 2016, 400 Federal Work-Study jobs (averaging $3000).
**Applying** *Options:* electronic application, deferred entrance. *Application fee:* $40. *Required:* high school transcript. *Required for some:* minimum 3.0 GPA, interview. *Recommended:* minimum 2.0 GPA. *Application deadlines:* 8/7 (freshmen), 8/7 (transfers). *Notification:* continuous (freshmen), continuous (transfers).
**Freshman Application Contact** Nassau Community College, 1 Education Drive, Garden City, NY 11530-6793. *Phone:* 516-572-7345.
*Website:* http://www.ncc.edu/.

## Niagara County Community College
### Sanborn, New York

- **State and locally supported** 2-year, founded 1962, part of State University of New York System
- **Rural** 287-acre campus with easy access to Buffalo
- **Endowment** $10.0 million
- **Coed,** 5,466 undergraduate students, 59% full-time, 57% women, 43% men

**Undergraduates** 3,228 full-time, 2,238 part-time. Students come from 17 states and territories; 3 other countries; 1% are from out of state; 11% Black or African American, non-Hispanic/Latino; 4% Hispanic/Latino; 2% Asian, non-Hispanic/Latino; 1% American Indian or Alaska Native, non-Hispanic/Latino; 5% Race/ethnicity unknown; 8% transferred in; 4% live on campus.
**Freshmen** *Admission:* 2,859 applied, 2,191 admitted, 1,119 enrolled. *Average high school GPA:* 2.5.
**Faculty** *Total:* 316, 32% full-time, 11% with terminal degrees. *Student/faculty ratio:* 17:1.
**Majors** Accounting; administrative assistant and secretarial science; animal sciences; baking and pastry arts; biological and physical sciences; business administration and management; business, management, and marketing related; chemical technology; computer science; consumer merchandising/retailing management; criminal justice/law enforcement administration; culinary arts; design and applied arts related; drafting and design technology; drafting/design engineering technologies related; dramatic/theater arts; elementary education; fine/studio arts; general studies; hospitality administration; humanities; human services; information science/studies; liberal arts and sciences/liberal studies; massage therapy; mass communication/media; mathematics; medical/clinical assistant; medical radiologic technology; music; natural resources/conservation; occupational health and industrial hygiene; parks, recreation and leisure; physical education teaching and coaching; physical therapy technology; registered nursing/registered nurse; social sciences; sport and fitness administration/management; surgical technology; tourism and travel services management; web page, digital/multimedia and information resources design; wine steward/sommelier.
**Academics** *Calendar:* semesters. *Degree:* certificates and associate. *Special study options:* academic remediation for entering students, adult/continuing education programs, advanced placement credit, cooperative education, distance learning, double majors, honors programs, independent study, internships, off-campus study, part-time degree program, services for LD students, student-designed majors, study abroad, summer session for credit. *ROTC:* Army (c).
**Library** Henrietta G. Lewis Library. *Books:* 77,511 (physical); *Serial titles:* 290 (physical); *Databases:* 95. Weekly public service hours: 64; students can reserve study rooms.
**Student Life** *Housing Options:* coed. Campus housing is provided by a third party. *Activities and Organizations:* drama/theater group, student-run newspaper, radio station, choral group, Student Radio Station, Student Nurses Association, Phi Theta Kappa, Alpha Beta Gamma, Physical Education Club. *Campus security:* 24-hour emergency response devices and patrols, student patrols, late-night transport/escort service. *Student services:* health clinic, personal/psychological counseling, veterans affairs office.
**Athletics** Member NJCAA. *Intercollegiate sports:* baseball M, basketball M(s)/W(s), golf M/W, soccer M/W, softball W, volleyball W, wrestling M(s). *Intramural sports:* basketball M/W, ice hockey M, racquetball M/W, soccer M/W, tennis M/W.
**Costs (2017–18)** *Tuition:* state resident $4224 full-time, $176 per credit hour part-time; nonresident $10,560 full-time, $440 per credit hour part-time. Full-time tuition and fees vary according to course load and program. Part-time tuition and fees vary according to course load and program. *Required fees:*

$474 full-time, $119 per term part-time. *Room and board:* $11,189; room only: $8698. Room and board charges vary according to housing facility. *Payment plan:* installment. *Waivers:* senior citizens and employees or children of employees.

**Financial Aid** Of all full-time matriculated undergraduates who enrolled in 2016, 5,526 applied for aid, 5,526 were judged to have need. 68 Federal Work-Study jobs (averaging $1266). *Average percent of need met:* 85%. *Average financial aid package:* $5150. *Average need-based loan:* $3010. *Average need-based gift aid:* $759.

**Applying** *Options:* electronic application, early admission. *Required:* high school transcript. *Required for some:* minimum 2.0 GPA. *Notification:* continuous until 8/31 (freshmen), continuous until 8/31 (transfers).

**Freshman Application Contact** Robert McKeown, Assistant Vice President of Enrollment Management, Niagara County Community College, 3111 Saunders Settlement Road, Sanborn, NY 14132. *Phone:* 716-614-6200. *Fax:* 716-614-6820. *E-mail:* admissions@niagaracc.suny.edu. *Website:* http://www.niagaracc.suny.edu/.

## North Country Community College
### Saranac Lake, New York

**Freshman Application Contact** Enrollment Management Assistant, North Country Community College, 23 Santanoni Avenue, PO Box 89, Saranac Lake, NY 12983-0089. *Phone:* 518-891-2915 Ext. 686. *Toll-free phone:* 800-TRY-NCCC (in-state); 888-TRY-NCCC (out-of-state). *Fax:* 518-891-0898. *E-mail:* info@nccc.edu. *Website:* http://www.nccc.edu/.

## Onondaga Community College
### Syracuse, New York

**Freshman Application Contact** Mr. Denny Nicholson, Onondaga Community College, 4585 West Seneca Turnpike, Syracuse, NY 13215. *Phone:* 315-488-2912. *Fax:* 315-488-2107. *E-mail:* admissions@sunyocc.edu. *Website:* http://www.sunyocc.edu/.

## Orange County Community College
### Middletown, New York

**Freshman Application Contact** Michael Roe, Director of Admissions and Recruitment, Orange County Community College, 115 South Street, Middletown, NY 10940. *Phone:* 845-341-4205. *Fax:* 845-343-1228. *E-mail:* apply@sunyorange.edu. *Website:* http://www.sunyorange.edu/.

## Phillips Beth Israel School of Nursing
### New York, New York

**Freshman Application Contact** Mrs. Bernice Pass-Stern, Assistant Dean, Phillips Beth Israel School of Nursing, 776 Sixth Avenue, 4th Floor, New York, NY 10010-6354. *Phone:* 212-614-6176. *Fax:* 212-614-6109. *E-mail:* bstern@chpnet.org. *Website:* http://www.mountsinai.org/locations/beth-israel/pson.

## Plaza College
### Forest Hills, New York

**Freshman Application Contact** Dean Vanessa Lopez, Dean of Admissions, Plaza College, 118-33 Queens Boulevard, Forest Hills, NY 11375. *Phone:* 718-779-1430. *E-mail:* info@plazacollege.edu. *Website:* http://www.plazacollege.edu/.

## Queensborough Community College of the City University of New York
### Bayside, New York

- **State and locally supported** 2-year, founded 1958, part of City University of New York
- **Urban** 37-acre campus with easy access to New York City
- **Coed,** 15,400 undergraduate students, 60% full-time, 53% women, 47% men

**Undergraduates** 9,208 full-time, 6,192 part-time. Students come from 128 other countries; 2% are from out of state; 22% Black or African American, non-Hispanic/Latino; 32% Hispanic/Latino; 25% Asian, non-Hispanic/Latino; 0.7% Native Hawaiian or other Pacific Islander, non-Hispanic/Latino; 0.9% American Indian or Alaska Native, non-Hispanic/Latino; 1% Two or more races, non-Hispanic/Latino; 5% international; 7% transferred in. *Retention:* 62% of full-time freshmen returned.

**Freshmen** *Admission:* 12,479 applied, 12,043 admitted, 3,146 enrolled.

**Faculty** *Total:* 848, 48% full-time. *Student/faculty ratio:* 20:1.

**Majors** Accounting; accounting technology and bookkeeping; administrative assistant and secretarial science; art; biotechnology; business administration and management; business, management, and marketing related; chemistry; clinical/medical laboratory technology; communication and journalism related; computer and information sciences; computer engineering technology; computer installation and repair technology; criminal justice/law enforcement administration; dance; data processing and data processing technology; digital arts; dramatic/theater arts; electrical, electronic and communications engineering technology; engineering; engineering science; environmental design/architecture; environmental engineering technology; environmental health; fine/studio arts; forensic science and technology; general studies; health professions related; health services/allied health/health sciences; information science/studies; information technology; liberal arts and sciences/liberal studies; massage therapy; mechanical drafting and CAD/CADD; mechanical engineering/mechanical technology; medical/clinical assistant; medical office management; museum studies; musical instrument fabrication and repair; music history, literature, and theory; physical sciences; public health; recording arts technology; registered nursing/registered nurse; telecommunications technology; visual and performing arts.

**Academics** *Calendar:* semesters. *Degree:* certificates and associate. *Special study options:* academic remediation for entering students, accelerated degree program, advanced placement credit, cooperative education, distance learning, double majors, English as a second language, honors programs, independent study, internships, off-campus study, part-time degree program, services for LD students, student-designed majors, study abroad, summer session for credit. *ROTC:* Army (c).

**Library** The Kurt R. Schmeller Library. *Books:* 109,962 (physical), 581,791 (digital/electronic); *Serial titles:* 1,195 (physical), 103,782 (digital/electronic); *Databases:* 145. Weekly public service hours: 78.

**Student Life** *Housing:* college housing not available. *Activities and Organizations:* drama/theater group, student-run newspaper, choral group, Phi Theta kappa, Student Organization for Disability Awareness (SODA), ASAP Club, CSTEP Club, Chemistry Club. *Campus security:* 24-hour emergency response devices and patrols, late-night transport/escort service. *Student services:* health clinic, personal/psychological counseling, legal services, veterans affairs office.

**Athletics** Member NJCAA. *Intercollegiate sports:* baseball M, basketball M/W, cross-country running M/W, soccer M, softball W, swimming and diving M/W, track and field M/W, volleyball W. *Intramural sports:* badminton M/W, basketball M/W, football M/W, swimming and diving M/W, table tennis M/W, volleyball M/W.

**Costs (2018–19)** *Tuition:* state resident $4800 full-time, $210 per credit part-time; nonresident $9600 full-time, $320 per credit part-time. Full-time tuition and fees vary according to course load. Part-time tuition and fees vary according to course load. *Required fees:* $409 full-time, $106 per term part-time. *Payment plan:* installment. *Waivers:* senior citizens and employees or children of employees.

**Applying** *Options:* electronic application, deferred entrance. *Application fee:* $65. *Required:* high school transcript. *Application deadlines:* 2/1 (freshmen), 2/1 (transfers). *Notification:* continuous (freshmen), continuous (transfers).

**Freshman Application Contact** Mr. Anthony Davis, Director of Admissions and Recruitment, Queensborough Community College of the City University of New York, 222-05 56th Avenue, Bayside, NY 11364. *Phone:* 718-281-5000 Ext. 1. *Fax:* 718-281-5189. *Website:* http://www.qcc.cuny.edu/.

## Rockland Community College
### Suffern, New York

**Freshman Application Contact** Rockland Community College, 145 College Road, Suffern, NY 10901-3699. *Phone:* 845-574-4484. *Toll-free phone:* 800-722-7666. *Website:* http://www.sunyrockland.edu/.

## St. Elizabeth College of Nursing
### Utica, New York

**Freshman Application Contact** Donna Ernst, Director of Recruitment, St. Elizabeth College of Nursing, 2215 Genesee Street, Utica, NY 13501. *Phone:* 315-798-8189. *E-mail:* dernst@secon.edu. *Website:* http://www.secon.edu/.

## St. Joseph's College of Nursing
### Syracuse, New York

**Freshman Application Contact** Ms. Felicia Corp, Recruiter, St. Joseph's College of Nursing, 206 Prospect Avenue, Syracuse, NY 13203. *Phone:* 315-448-5040. *Fax:* 315-448-5745. *E-mail:* collegeofnursing@sjhsyr.org. *Website:* http://www.sjhcon.edu/.

## St. Paul's School of Nursing

### Queens, New York

**Director of Admissions** Nancy Wolinski, Chairperson of Admissions, St. Paul's School of Nursing, 97-77 Queens Boulevard, Queens, NY 11374. *Phone:* 718-357-0500 Ext. 131. *E-mail:* nwolinski@svcmcny.org. *Website:* http://www.stpaulsschoolofnursing.edu/.

## St. Paul's School of Nursing

### Staten Island, New York

**Admissions Office Contact** St. Paul's School of Nursing, Corporate Commons Two, 2 Teleport Drive, Suite 203, Staten Island, NY 10311. *Website:* http://www.stpaulsschoolofnursing.edu/.

## Samaritan Hospital School of Nursing

### Troy, New York

**Director of Admissions** Ms. Diane Dyer, Student Services Coordinator, Samaritan Hospital School of Nursing, 1300 Massachusetts Avenue, Troy, NY 12180. *Phone:* 518-271-3734. *Fax:* 518-271-3303. *E-mail:* marronej@nehealth.com. *Website:* http://www.nehealth.com/.

## Schenectady County Community College

### Schenectady, New York

- **State and locally supported** 2-year, founded 1969, part of State University of New York System
- **Urban** 50-acre campus
- **Coed,** 6,634 undergraduate students, 33% full-time, 55% women, 45% men

**Undergraduates** 2,184 full-time, 4,450 part-time. 14% Black or African American, non-Hispanic/Latino; 7% Hispanic/Latino; 7% Asian, non-Hispanic/Latino; 0.4% Native Hawaiian or other Pacific Islander, non-Hispanic/Latino; 0.8% American Indian or Alaska Native, non-Hispanic/Latino; 1% Two or more races, non-Hispanic/Latino; 3% Race/ethnicity unknown; 5% transferred in.
**Freshmen** *Admission:* 5,769 applied, 3,985 admitted, 787 enrolled.
**Faculty** *Total:* 133, 43% full-time, 24% with terminal degrees. *Student/faculty ratio:* 21:1.
**Majors** Accounting technology and bookkeeping; avionics maintenance technology; business administration and management; business, management, and marketing related; community organization and advocacy; computer/information technology services administration related; computer programming; criminal justice/law enforcement administration; data processing and data processing technology; education; electrical, electronic and communications engineering technology; fire science/firefighting; hotel/motel administration; interdisciplinary studies; liberal arts and sciences/liberal studies; public administration and social service professions related; restaurant/food services management; science technologies related; teacher assistant/aide; transportation and materials moving related; visual and performing arts.
**Academics** *Calendar:* semesters. *Degree:* certificates and associate. *Special study options:* academic remediation for entering students, adult/continuing education programs, advanced placement credit, distance learning, double majors, English as a second language, honors programs, internships, off-campus study, part-time degree program, services for LD students, summer session for credit.
**Library** Begley Library.
**Student Life** *Housing:* college housing not available. *Activities and Organizations:* drama/theater group, choral group. *Campus security:* 24-hour emergency response devices and patrols, late-night transport/escort service. *Student services:* personal/psychological counseling.
**Athletics** Member NJCAA. *Intercollegiate sports:* baseball M, basketball M/W, bowling M/W, softball W. *Intramural sports:* soccer M/W, volleyball M/W.
**Costs (2017–18)** *Tuition:* state resident $3936 full-time, $164 per credit hour part-time; nonresident $7872 full-time, $328 per credit hour part-time. Full-time tuition and fees vary according to course load and program. Part-time tuition and fees vary according to course load and program. *Required fees:* $698 full-time, $10 per course part-time, $30 per term part-time. *Payment plan:* installment. *Waivers:* senior citizens and employees or children of employees.
**Financial Aid** Of all full-time matriculated undergraduates who enrolled in 2016, 50 Federal Work-Study jobs (averaging $2400).

**Applying** *Options:* electronic application, early admission, deferred entrance. *Required:* high school transcript. *Application deadlines:* rolling (freshmen), rolling (transfers). *Notification:* continuous (freshmen), continuous (transfers).
**Freshman Application Contact** Mr. David Sampson, Director of Admissions, Schenectady County Community College, 78 Washington Avenue, Schenectady, NY 12305-2294. *Phone:* 518-381-1370 Ext. 1370. *E-mail:* sampsodg@gw.sunysccc.edu.
*Website:* http://www.sunysccc.edu/.

## State University of New York Broome Community College

### Binghamton, New York

**Freshman Application Contact** Ms. Jenae Norris, Director of Admissions, State University of New York Broome Community College, PO Box 1017, Upper Front Street, Binghamton, NY 13902. *Phone:* 607-778-5001. *Fax:* 607-778-5394. *E-mail:* admissions@sunybroome.edu. *Website:* http://www.sunybroome.edu/.

## State University of New York College of Technology at Alfred

### Alfred, New York

- **State-supported** primarily 2-year, founded 1908, part of State University of New York System
- **Rural** 1084-acre campus with easy access to Rochester, Buffalo
- **Endowment** $4.5 million
- **Coed,** 3,686 undergraduate students, 92% full-time, 36% women, 64% men

**Undergraduates** 3,396 full-time, 290 part-time. Students come from 27 states and territories; 14 other countries; 4% are from out of state; 13% Black or African American, non-Hispanic/Latino; 9% Hispanic/Latino; 1% Asian, non-Hispanic/Latino; 0.1% Native Hawaiian or other Pacific Islander, non-Hispanic/Latino; 0.3% American Indian or Alaska Native, non-Hispanic/Latino; 3% Two or more races, non-Hispanic/Latino; 0.8% Race/ethnicity unknown; 1% international; 8% transferred in; 65% live on campus. *Retention:* 65% of full-time freshmen returned.
**Freshmen** *Admission:* 5,395 applied, 3,650 admitted, 1,120 enrolled. *Average high school GPA:* 3.0. *Test scores:* SAT evidence-based reading and writing scores over 500: 57%; SAT math scores over 500: 61%; ACT scores over 18: 85%; SAT evidence-based reading and writing scores over 600: 16%; SAT math scores over 600: 15%; ACT scores over 24: 43%; SAT evidence-based reading and writing scores over 700: 2%; SAT math scores over 700: 2%; ACT scores over 30: 6%.
**Faculty** *Total:* 249, 67% full-time, 33% with terminal degrees. *Student/faculty ratio:* 18:1.
**Majors** Accounting technology and bookkeeping; agribusiness; agriculture; animation, interactive technology, video graphics and special effects; architectural engineering technology; architecture; autobody/collision and repair technology; automobile/automotive mechanics technology; biology/biological sciences; business administration and management; business, management, and marketing related; computer and information sciences; computer and information systems security; computer engineering technology; computer programming (specific applications); construction engineering technology; construction management; construction trades related; court reporting; criminology; culinary arts; diagnostic medical sonography and ultrasound technology; diesel mechanics technology; drafting and design technology; electrical and power transmission installation; electrical, electronic and communications engineering technology; engineering; environmental engineering technology; financial planning and services; forensic science and technology; general studies; graphic design; health/health-care administration; health information/medical records technology; health services/allied health/health sciences; heating, air conditioning, ventilation and refrigeration maintenance technology; heavy/industrial equipment maintenance technologies related; humanities; human resources management; human services; information science/studies; interior design; intermedia/multimedia; liberal arts and sciences and humanities related; liberal arts and sciences/liberal studies; machine shop technology; masonry; mechanical engineering/mechanical technology; motorcycle maintenance and repair technology; radiologic technology/science; registered nursing/registered nurse; sales, distribution, and marketing operations; sport and fitness administration/management; surveying technology; system, networking, and LAN/WAN management; vehicle maintenance and repair technologies related; veterinary/animal health technology; web/multimedia management and webmaster; welding technology.
**Academics** *Calendar:* semesters. *Degrees:* certificates, associate, and bachelor's. *Special study options:* academic remediation for entering students,

accelerated degree program, adult/continuing education programs, advanced placement credit, cooperative education, distance learning, double majors, English as a second language, honors programs, independent study, internships, off-campus study, part-time degree program, services for LD students, student-designed majors, study abroad, summer session for credit. *ROTC:* Army (c).

**Library** Walter C. Hinkle Memorial Library plus 1 other. *Books:* 54,671 (physical), 49,782 (digital/electronic); *Serial titles:* 253 (physical), 164,768 (digital/electronic); *Databases:* 193. Weekly public service hours: 88.

**Student Life** *Housing Options:* coed, men-only, women-only, special housing for students with disabilities. Campus housing is university owned. Freshman campus housing is guaranteed. *Activities and Organizations:* drama/theater group, student-run newspaper, radio station, choral group, Outdoor Recreation Club, Caribbean Student Association, Alfred Programming Board, Pioneer Woodsmen, Disaster Relief Team. *Campus security:* 24-hour emergency response devices and patrols, late-night transport/escort service, controlled dormitory access, residence hall entrance guards. *Student services:* health clinic, personal/psychological counseling, veterans affairs office.

**Athletics** Member NCAA, USCAA. All Division III. *Intercollegiate sports:* baseball M, basketball M/W, cross-country running M/W, equestrian sports M/W, football M, lacrosse M, soccer M/W, softball W, swimming and diving M/W, track and field M/W, volleyball W, wrestling M. *Intramural sports:* basketball M/W, equestrian sports M(c)/W(c), football M, golf M/W, ice hockey M(c), rock climbing M/W, soccer M/W, softball M/W, swimming and diving M/W, tennis M/W, ultimate Frisbee M/W, volleyball M/W.

**Standardized Tests** *Required for some:* SAT or ACT (for admission). *Recommended:* SAT or ACT (for admission).

**Costs (2018–19)** *One-time required fee:* $110. *Tuition:* state resident $6670 full-time, $278 per credit hour part-time; nonresident $9740 full-time, $406 per credit hour part-time. Full-time tuition and fees vary according to course load and degree level. Part-time tuition and fees vary according to course load and degree level. *Required fees:* $1657 full-time, $66 per credit hour part-time, $10 per credit hour part-time. *Room and board:* $12,250; room only: $7500. Room and board charges vary according to board plan and housing facility. *Payment plan:* installment. *Waivers:* employees or children of employees.

**Financial Aid** Of all full-time matriculated undergraduates who enrolled in 2016, 3,170 applied for aid, 2,762 were judged to have need, 219 had their need fully met. In 2016, 162 non-need-based awards were made. *Average percent of need met:* 58%. *Average financial aid package:* $10,778. *Average need-based loan:* $3916. *Average need-based gift aid:* $6709. *Average non-need-based aid:* $5675. *Average indebtedness upon graduation:* $32,017.

**Applying** *Options:* electronic application. *Application fee:* $50. *Required:* high school transcript, minimum 2.0 GPA, Common Application with essay on supplemental application. *Recommended:* essay or personal statement, interview. *Application deadlines:* rolling (freshmen), rolling (transfers). *Notification:* continuous (freshmen), continuous (transfers).

**Freshman Application Contact** Mrs. Deborah Goodrich, Associate Vice President for Enrollment Management, State University of New York College of Technology at Alfred, Huntington Administration Building, 10 Upper College Drive, Alfred, NY 14802. *Phone:* 607-587-3945. *Toll-free phone:* 800-4-ALFRED. *Fax:* 607-587-4299. *E-mail:* admissions@alfredstate.edu. *Website:* http://www.alfredstate.edu/.

# Stella and Charles Guttman Community College
## New York, New York

**Admissions Office Contact** Stella and Charles Guttman Community College, 50 West 40th Street, New York, NY 10018. *Website:* http://guttman.cuny.edu/.

# Suffolk County Community College
## Selden, New York

**Freshman Application Contact** Suffolk County Community College, 533 College Road, Selden, NY 11784-2899. *Phone:* 631-451-4000. *Website:* http://www.sunysuffolk.edu/.

# Sullivan County Community College
## Loch Sheldrake, New York

- **State and locally supported** 2-year, founded 1962, part of State University of New York System
- **Rural** 405-acre campus
- **Endowment** $921,102
- **Coed,** 1,610 undergraduate students, 51% full-time, 52% women, 48% men

**Undergraduates** 820 full-time, 790 part-time. Students come from 4 states and territories; 3 other countries; 3% are from out of state; 18% Black or African American, non-Hispanic/Latino; 22% Hispanic/Latino; 2% Asian, non-Hispanic/Latino; 0.2% Native Hawaiian or other Pacific Islander, non-Hispanic/Latino; 0.1% American Indian or Alaska Native, non-Hispanic/Latino; 3% Two or more races, non-Hispanic/Latino; 4% Race/ethnicity unknown; 0.6% international; 6% transferred in; 22% live on campus.

**Freshmen** *Admission:* 1,433 applied, 1,371 admitted, 343 enrolled. *Average high school GPA:* 2.9.

**Faculty** *Total:* 101, 41% full-time, 16% with terminal degrees. *Student/faculty ratio:* 21:1.

**Majors** Accounting; administrative assistant and secretarial science; baking and pastry arts; business administration and management; commercial and advertising art; computer graphics; computer programming (specific applications); construction engineering technology; consumer merchandising/retailing management; criminal justice/police science; crisis/emergency/disaster management; culinary arts; data entry/microcomputer applications; electrical, electronic and communications engineering technology; elementary education; environmental studies; fire prevention and safety technology; forensic science and technology; hospitality administration; human services; information science/studies; kindergarten/preschool education; legal assistant/paralegal; liberal arts and sciences/liberal studies; marketing/marketing management; mathematics; medical/clinical assistant; parks, recreation and leisure; photography; psychology; radio and television; radio, television, and digital communication related; registered nursing/registered nurse; respiratory care therapy; science technologies related; sport and fitness administration/management; tourism and travel services management.

**Academics** *Calendar:* semesters. *Degree:* certificates and associate. *Special study options:* academic remediation for entering students, adult/continuing education programs, advanced placement credit, cooperative education, distance learning, double majors, honors programs, independent study, internships, off-campus study, part-time degree program, services for LD students, summer session for credit.

**Library** Hermann Memorial Library plus 1 other. *Books:* 55,406 (physical), 145,000 (digital/electronic); *Serial titles:* 109 (physical), 52,671 (digital/electronic); *Databases:* 118. Weekly public service hours: 62.

**Student Life** *Housing Options:* coed. Campus housing is provided by a third party. Freshman applicants given priority for college housing. *Activities and Organizations:* drama/theater group, Science Alliance, Black Student Union, Gay-Straight Alliance, Dance Club, Honor Society. *Campus security:* 24-hour emergency response devices and patrols, student patrols, controlled dormitory access. *Student services:* health clinic, personal/psychological counseling, legal services.

**Athletics** Member NJCAA. *Intercollegiate sports:* baseball M, basketball M/W, cross-country running M/W, softball W, volleyball W, wrestling M. *Intramural sports:* baseball M, basketball M/W, bowling M/W, cross-country running M/W, golf M/W, racquetball M/W, soccer M/W, softball M/W, table tennis M/W, tennis M/W, volleyball M/W, weight lifting M/W.

**Costs (2017–18)** *Tuition:* state resident $4814 full-time, $199 per credit hour part-time; nonresident $9628 full-time, $322 per credit hour part-time. Full-time tuition and fees vary according to program. Part-time tuition and fees vary according to program. *Required fees:* $876 full-time, $37 per credit hour part-time. *Room and board:* $9450; room only: $6050. Room and board charges vary according to board plan and housing facility. *Payment plans:* installment, deferred payment. *Waivers:* senior citizens and employees or children of employees.

**Financial Aid** Of all full-time matriculated undergraduates who enrolled in 2016, 739 applied for aid, 692 were judged to have need, 692 had their need fully met. 39 Federal Work-Study jobs (averaging $1272). 23 state and other part-time jobs (averaging $831). *Average percent of need met:* 100%. *Average financial aid package:* $3756. *Average need-based loan:* $1658. *Average need-based gift aid:* $3756.

**Applying** *Options:* electronic application, early admission, deferred entrance. *Required:* high school transcript. *Application deadlines:* rolling (freshmen), rolling (transfers). *Notification:* continuous (freshmen), continuous (transfers).

**Freshman Application Contact** Mr. Steven Alhona, Director of Admissions, Sullivan County Community College, 112 College Road, Loch Sheldrake, NY

12759.  *Phone:* 845-434-5750 Ext. 4356.  *Toll-free phone:* 800-577-5243.  *Fax:* 845-434-4806.  *E-mail:* salhona@sunysullivan.edu.  *Website:* http://www.sullivan.suny.edu/.

# Tompkins Cortland Community College
## Dryden, New York

- **State and locally supported** 2-year, founded 1968, part of State University of New York System
- **Rural** 300-acre campus
- **Coed,** 2,632 undergraduate students, 70% full-time, 56% women, 44% men

**Undergraduates** 1,830 full-time, 802 part-time. Students come from 17 states and territories; 23 other countries; 3% are from out of state; 14% Black or African American, non-Hispanic/Latino; 10% Hispanic/Latino; 2% Asian, non-Hispanic/Latino; 0.2% American Indian or Alaska Native, non-Hispanic/Latino; 4% Two or more races, non-Hispanic/Latino; 7% Race/ethnicity unknown; 3% international; 8% transferred in.
**Freshmen** *Admission:* 652 enrolled.
**Faculty** *Total:* 250, 25% full-time, 22% with terminal degrees. *Student/faculty ratio:* 18:1.
**Majors** Accounting technology and bookkeeping; agroecology and sustainable agriculture; biology/biotechnology laboratory technician; business administration and management; child-care and support services management; commercial and advertising art; computer and information sciences; computer support specialist; construction engineering technology; creative writing; criminal justice/law enforcement administration; criminal justice/police science; culinary arts; digital communication and media/multimedia; engineering; entrepreneurship; environmental studies; hotel, motel, and restaurant management; humanities; human services; information science/studies; international business/trade/commerce; international/global studies; legal assistant/paralegal; liberal arts and sciences and humanities related; liberal arts and sciences/liberal studies; parks, recreation and leisure; parks, recreation and leisure facilities management; photographic and film/video technology; radio and television broadcasting technology; registered nursing/registered nurse; special products marketing; speech communication and rhetoric; sport and fitness administration/management; substance abuse/addiction counseling.
**Academics** *Calendar:* semesters. *Degree:* certificates and associate. *Special study options:* academic remediation for entering students, adult/continuing education programs, advanced placement credit, cooperative education, distance learning, double majors, English as a second language, freshman honors college, honors programs, independent study, internships, off-campus study, part-time degree program, services for LD students, study abroad, summer session for credit.
**Library** Gerald A. Barry Memorial Library plus 1 other.
**Student Life** *Housing Options:* coed. Campus housing is provided by a third party. *Activities and Organizations:* drama/theater group, Sport Management Club, Nursing Club, Student Government Association, Writer's Guild. *Campus security:* 24-hour patrols, late-night transport/escort service, controlled dormitory access, armed peace officers. *Student services:* health clinic, personal/psychological counseling.
**Athletics** Member NJCAA. *Intercollegiate sports:* baseball M, basketball M/W, golf M/W, lacrosse M, soccer M/W, softball W, volleyball W. *Intramural sports:* archery M/W, badminton M/W, basketball M/W, bowling M/W, football M/W, golf M/W, lacrosse M/W, racquetball M/W, skiing (cross-country) M/W, skiing (downhill) M/W, soccer M/W, softball M/W, squash M/W, swimming and diving M/W, table tennis M/W, tennis M/W, ultimate Frisbee M/W, volleyball M/W, water polo M/W, weight lifting M/W, wrestling M/W.
**Costs (2017–18)** *Tuition:* state resident $4950 full-time, $181 per credit hour part-time; nonresident $10,200 full-time, $372 per credit hour part-time. Part-time tuition and fees vary according to course load. *Required fees:* $1064 full-time, $37 per credit hour part-time, $18 per term part-time. *Room and board:* $11,350. Room and board charges vary according to board plan and housing facility. *Payment plans:* installment, deferred payment. *Waivers:* employees or children of employees.
**Financial Aid** Of all full-time matriculated undergraduates who enrolled in 2016, 150 Federal Work-Study jobs (averaging $1000). 150 state and other part-time jobs (averaging $1000).
**Applying** *Options:* electronic application, early admission, deferred entrance. *Required:* high school transcript. *Required for some:* essay or personal statement, interview. *Application deadlines:* rolling (freshmen), rolling (transfers). *Notification:* continuous (freshmen), continuous (transfers).
**Admissions Office Contact** Tompkins Cortland Community College, 170 North Street, PO Box 139, Dryden, NY 13053-0139. *Toll-free phone:* 888-567-8211.
*Website:* http://www.TC3.edu/.

# Trocaire College
## Buffalo, New York

**Freshman Application Contact** Trocaire College, 360 Choate Avenue, Buffalo, NY 14220-2094. *Phone:* 716-826-2558. *Website:* http://www.trocaire.edu/.

# Ulster County Community College
## Stone Ridge, New York

- **State and locally supported** 2-year, founded 1961, part of State University of New York System
- **Rural** 165-acre campus
- **Endowment** $8.0 million
- **Coed**

**Undergraduates** 1,380 full-time, 2,036 part-time. Students come from 8 states and territories; 2 other countries; 0.2% are from out of state; 7% Black or African American, non-Hispanic/Latino; 12% Hispanic/Latino; 1% Asian, non-Hispanic/Latino; 0.2% Native Hawaiian or other Pacific Islander, non-Hispanic/Latino; 0.2% American Indian or Alaska Native, non-Hispanic/Latino; 4% Two or more races, non-Hispanic/Latino; 4% Race/ethnicity unknown; 0.5% international; 5% transferred in.
**Faculty** *Student/faculty ratio:* 20:1.
**Academics** *Calendar:* semesters. *Degree:* certificates, diplomas, and associate. *Special study options:* academic remediation for entering students, adult/continuing education programs, advanced placement credit, cooperative education, distance learning, double majors, English as a second language, honors programs, independent study, internships, off-campus study, part-time degree program, services for LD students, student-designed majors, study abroad, summer session for credit.
**Library** McDonald Dewitt Library. *Books:* 77,078 (physical), 164,597 (digital/electronic); *Serial titles:* 139 (physical), 135,595 (digital/electronic); *Databases:* 77. Weekly public service hours: 44.
**Student Life** *Campus security:* 24-hour emergency response devices.
**Athletics** Member NJCAA.
**Costs (2017–18)** *Tuition:* state resident $4480 full-time, $170 per credit hour part-time; nonresident $8960 full-time, $340 per credit hour part-time. *Required fees:* $874 full-time, $65 per course part-time, $38 per term part-time. *Payment plans:* installment, deferred payment.
**Financial Aid** Of all full-time matriculated undergraduates who enrolled in 2016, 45 Federal Work-Study jobs (averaging $1000).
**Applying** *Options:* electronic application, early admission, deferred entrance. *Required:* high school transcript.
**Freshman Application Contact** Admissions Office, Ulster County Community College, 491 Cottekill Road, Stone Ridge, NY 12484. *Phone:* 845-687-5022. *Toll-free phone:* 800-724-0833. *E-mail:* admissionsoffice@sunyulster.edu. *Website:* http://www.sunyulster.edu/.

# Westchester Community College
## Valhalla, New York

- **State and locally supported** 2-year, founded 1946, part of State University of New York System
- **Suburban** 218-acre campus with easy access to New York City
- **Coed,** 12,571 undergraduate students, 54% full-time, 53% women, 47% men

**Undergraduates** 6,748 full-time, 5,823 part-time. 6% transferred in.
**Freshmen** *Admission:* 4,754 applied, 4,754 admitted, 2,573 enrolled.
**Faculty** *Total:* 824, 21% full-time.
**Majors** Accounting; accounting technology and bookkeeping; administrative assistant and secretarial science; animal sciences; art; athletic training; business administration and management; child-care and support services management; civil engineering technology; commercial and advertising art; community organization and advocacy; computer and information sciences; computer and information sciences and support services related; computer and information systems security; consumer merchandising/retailing management; corrections; design and applied arts related; dietitian assistant; digital arts; digital communication and media/multimedia; drafting and design technology; education (multiple levels); electrical, electronic and communications engineering technology; emergency medical technology (EMT paramedic); engineering; environmental control technologies related; environmental science; environmental studies; food service systems administration; humanities; information science/studies; international business/trade/commerce; journalism; legal assistant/paralegal; liberal arts and sciences/liberal studies; marketing related; mechanical engineering/mechanical technology; medical administrative assistant and medical secretary; medical radiologic technology; practical nursing, vocational nursing and nursing assistants related; registered nursing/registered nurse; respiratory care therapy; restaurant, culinary, and catering management;

retailing; small business administration; speech communication and rhetoric; substance abuse/addiction counseling; teacher assistant/aide; visual and performing arts.

**Academics** *Calendar:* semesters. *Degree:* certificates and associate. *Special study options:* academic remediation for entering students, adult/continuing education programs, advanced placement credit, cooperative education, distance learning, double majors, English as a second language, honors programs, independent study, internships, off-campus study, part-time degree program, services for LD students, study abroad, summer session for credit.

**Library** Harold L. Drimmer Library.

**Student Life** *Housing:* college housing not available. *Activities and Organizations:* student-run newspaper, radio station, choral group, Deca Fashion Retail, Future Educators, Respiratory Club, Black Student Union, Diversity Action. *Campus security:* 24-hour emergency response devices and patrols, late-night transport/escort service. *Student services:* health clinic, personal/psychological counseling, women's center, veterans affairs office.

**Athletics** Member NJCAA. *Intercollegiate sports:* baseball M, basketball M/W, bowling M/W, golf M, soccer M, softball W, volleyball W. *Intramural sports:* badminton M/W, basketball M/W, softball M/W, swimming and diving M/W, tennis M/W, volleyball M/W, weight lifting M/W.

**Costs (2017–18)** *Tuition:* state resident $4280 full-time, $179 per credit hour part-time; nonresident $11,770 full-time, $493 per credit hour part-time. Full-time tuition and fees vary according to location. Part-time tuition and fees vary according to location. *Required fees:* $463 full-time, $106 per term part-time. *Payment plan:* installment.

**Financial Aid** Of all full-time matriculated undergraduates who enrolled in 2016, 4,844 applied for aid, 4,162 were judged to have need. In 2016, 266 non-need-based awards were made. *Average percent of need met:* 60%. *Average financial aid package:* $3648. *Average need-based loan:* $1727. *Average need-based gift aid:* $3451. *Average non-need-based aid:* $1720.

**Applying** *Options:* electronic application, early action. *Application fee:* $35. *Required:* high school transcript. *Required for some:* interview. *Application deadline:* rolling (freshmen).

**Freshman Application Contact** Ms. Gloria Leon, Director of Admissions, Westchester Community College, 75 Grasslands Road, Administration Building, Valhalla, NY 10595-1698. *Phone:* 914-606-6735. *Fax:* 914-606-6540. *E-mail:* admissions@sunywcc.edu.

*Website:* http://www.sunywcc.edu/.

## Wood Tobe–Coburn School
### New York, New York

**Freshman Application Contact** Admissions Office, Wood Tobe–Coburn School, 8 East 40th Street, New York, NY 10016. *Phone:* 212-686-9040. *Toll-free phone:* 800-394-9663. *Website:* http://www.woodtobecoburn.edu/.

# NORTH CAROLINA

## Alamance Community College
### Graham, North Carolina

- **State-supported** 2-year, founded 1958, part of North Carolina Community College System
- **Small-town** 48-acre campus
- **Endowment** $2.9 million
- **Coed,** 4,259 undergraduate students, 61% full-time, 60% women, 40% men

**Undergraduates** 2,578 full-time, 1,681 part-time. Students come from 7 states and territories; 6 other countries; 1% are from out of state; 21% Black or African American, non-Hispanic/Latino; 9% Hispanic/Latino; 2% Asian, non-Hispanic/Latino; 0.4% American Indian or Alaska Native, non-Hispanic/Latino; 3% Two or more races, non-Hispanic/Latino; 0.7% international; 28% transferred in.

**Freshmen** *Admission:* 458 enrolled.

**Faculty** *Total:* 435, 26% full-time, 3% with terminal degrees. *Student/faculty ratio:* 20:1.

**Majors** Accounting technology and bookkeeping; animal sciences; applied horticulture/horticulture operations; automobile/automotive mechanics technology; banking and financial support services; biotechnology; business administration and management; carpentry; clinical/medical laboratory technology; commercial and advertising art; criminal justice/safety; culinary arts; electrical, electronic and communications engineering technology; executive assistant/executive secretary; heating, ventilation, air conditioning and refrigeration engineering technology; information science/studies; kindergarten/preschool education; legal administrative assistant/secretary; liberal arts and sciences/liberal studies; machine tool technology; mechanical

engineering/mechanical technology; medical administrative assistant and medical secretary; medical/clinical assistant; office occupations and clerical services; registered nursing/registered nurse; retailing; teacher assistant/aide; welding technology.

**Academics** *Calendar:* semesters. *Degree:* certificates, diplomas, and associate. *Special study options:* academic remediation for entering students, adult/continuing education programs, cooperative education, distance learning, double majors, English as a second language, independent study, off-campus study, part-time degree program, services for LD students, summer session for credit.

**Library** Learning Resources Center. Weekly public service hours: 64; students can reserve study rooms.

**Student Life** *Housing:* college housing not available. *Campus security:* 24-hour emergency response devices and patrols, student patrols, late-night transport/escort service. *Student services:* personal/psychological counseling, veterans affairs office.

**Costs (2018–19)** *Tuition:* state resident $2432 full-time, $76 per credit hour part-time; nonresident $8576 full-time, $268 per credit hour part-time. Full-time tuition and fees vary according to course load. Part-time tuition and fees vary according to course load. *Required fees:* $30 full-time, $5 per credit hour part-time. *Payment plan:* installment.

**Financial Aid** Of all full-time matriculated undergraduates who enrolled in 2010, 4,000 applied for aid, 3,000 were judged to have need. 200 Federal Work-Study jobs (averaging $1250). *Average percent of need met:* 30%. *Average financial aid package:* $4500. *Average need-based gift aid:* $4500. *Average indebtedness upon graduation:* $2500.

**Applying** *Options:* electronic application. *Required:* high school transcript. *Application deadlines:* rolling (freshmen), rolling (transfers). *Notification:* continuous (freshmen), continuous (transfers).

**Freshman Application Contact** Ms. Elizabeth Brehler, Director for Enrollment Management, Alamance Community College, Graham, NC 27253-8000. *Phone:* 336-506-4120. *Fax:* 336-506-4264. *E-mail:* brehlere@alamancecc.edu.

*Website:* http://www.alamancecc.edu/.

## Asheville-Buncombe Technical Community College
### Asheville, North Carolina

- **State-supported** 2-year, founded 1959, part of North Carolina Community College System
- **Urban** 126-acre campus
- **Coed,** 7,542 undergraduate students

**Undergraduates** 1% are from out of state.

**Faculty** *Student/faculty ratio:* 15:1.

**Majors** Accounting; automobile/automotive mechanics technology; baking and pastry arts; biology/biotechnology laboratory technician; building/property maintenance; business administration and management; CAD/CADD drafting/design technology; civil engineering technology; clinical/medical laboratory technology; clinical/medical social work; computer and information systems security; computer engineering technology; computer software and media applications related; computer systems networking and telecommunications; criminal justice/safety; culinary arts; dental hygiene; diagnostic medical sonography and ultrasound technology; diesel mechanics technology; drafting/design engineering technologies related; early childhood education; electrical, electronic and communications engineering technology; electrician; electromechanical and instrumentation and maintenance technologies related; elementary education; emergency medical technology (EMT paramedic); fire prevention and safety technology; general studies; heating, air conditioning, ventilation and refrigeration maintenance technology; hotel/motel administration; human resources management; information science/studies; information technology; liberal arts and sciences/liberal studies; machine shop technology; marketing/marketing management; mechanical engineering technologies related; office management; radiologic technology/science; registered nursing/registered nurse; surgical technology; surveying technology; veterinary/animal health technology; welding technology.

**Academics** *Calendar:* semesters. *Degree:* certificates, diplomas, and associate. *Special study options:* academic remediation for entering students, adult/continuing education programs, advanced placement credit, cooperative education, distance learning, double majors, independent study, internships, part-time degree program, services for LD students, summer session for credit.

**Library** Locke Learning Resources Center. Students can reserve study rooms.

**Student Life** *Housing:* college housing not available. *Activities and Organizations:* drama/theater group, student-run newspaper, choral group. *Campus security:* 24-hour emergency response devices and patrols. *Student services:* health clinic, personal/psychological counseling, veterans affairs office.

**Financial Aid** Of all full-time matriculated undergraduates who enrolled in 2016, 55 Federal Work-Study jobs (averaging $2000).

**Applying** *Options:* deferred entrance. *Required:* high school transcript. *Required for some:* interview. *Application deadlines:* rolling (freshmen), rolling (transfers). *Notification:* continuous (freshmen), continuous (transfers).

**Freshman Application Contact** Asheville-Buncombe Technical Community College, 340 Victoria Road, Asheville, NC 28801-4897. *Phone:* 828-398-7900 Ext. 7887.

*Website:* http://www.abtech.edu/.

## Beaufort County Community College
### Washington, North Carolina

**Freshman Application Contact** Mr. Gary Burbage, Director of Admissions, Beaufort County Community College, PO Box 1069, 5337 US Highway 264 East, Washington, NC 27889-1069. *Phone:* 252-940-6233. *Fax:* 252-940-6393. *E-mail:* garyb@beaufortccc.edu. *Website:* http://www.beaufortccc.edu/.

## Bladen Community College
### Dublin, North Carolina

**Freshman Application Contact** Ms. Andrea Fisher, Enrollment Specialist, Bladen Community College, PO Box 266, Dublin, NC 28332. *Phone:* 910-879-5593. *Fax:* 910-879-5564. *E-mail:* acarterfisher@bladencc.edu. *Website:* http://www.bladencc.edu/.

## Blue Ridge Community College
### Flat Rock, North Carolina

**Freshman Application Contact** Blue Ridge Community College, 180 West Campus Drive, Flat Rock, NC 28731. *Phone:* 828-694-1810. *Website:* http://www.blueridge.edu/.

## Brightwood College, Charlotte Campus
### Charlotte, North Carolina

**Freshman Application Contact** Director of Admissions, Brightwood College, Charlotte Campus, 6070 East Independence Boulevard, Charlotte, NC 28212. *Phone:* 704-567-3700. *Toll-free phone:* 866-543-0208. *Website:* http://www.brightwood.edu/.

## Brunswick Community College
### Supply, North Carolina

**Freshman Application Contact** Admissions Counselor, Brunswick Community College, 50 College Road, PO Box 30, Supply, NC 28462-0030. *Phone:* 910-755-7300. *Toll-free phone:* 800-754-1050. *Fax:* 910-754-9609. *E-mail:* admissions@brunswickcc.edu. *Website:* http://www.brunswickcc.edu/.

## Caldwell Community College and Technical Institute
### Hudson, North Carolina

- **State-supported** 2-year, founded 1964, part of North Carolina Community College System
- **Small-town** 50-acre campus
- **Coed,** 3,514 undergraduate students, 35% full-time, 57% women, 43% men

**Undergraduates** 1,240 full-time, 2,274 part-time.

**Freshmen** *Admission:* 1,439 applied, 1,439 admitted, 434 enrolled.

**Faculty** *Total:* 420, 31% full-time, 9% with terminal degrees. *Student/faculty ratio:* 18:1.

**Majors** Accounting; automobile/automotive mechanics technology; biological and physical sciences; biomedical technology; business administration and management; computer programming; cosmetology; culinary arts; diagnostic medical sonography and ultrasound technology; early childhood education; education; electrical and electronics engineering; emergency medical technology (EMT paramedic); fine/studio arts; hotel, motel, and restaurant management; information technology; landscape architecture; legal assistant/paralegal; liberal arts and sciences/liberal studies; mechanical engineering/mechanical technology; medical/clinical assistant; medical office management; nuclear medical technology; office occupations and clerical services; physical therapy technology; radiologic technology/science; registered nursing/registered nurse; speech-language pathology assistant.

**Academics** *Calendar:* semesters. *Degree:* certificates, diplomas, and associate. *Special study options:* academic remediation for entering students,

adult/continuing education programs, advanced placement credit, cooperative education, distance learning, double majors, independent study, part-time degree program, services for LD students, summer session for credit.

**Library** Broyhill Center for Learning Resources. Students can reserve study rooms.

**Student Life** *Housing:* college housing not available. *Activities and Organizations:* drama/theater group, choral group. *Campus security:* trained security personnel during hours of operation. *Student services:* personal/psychological counseling.

**Athletics** Member NJCAA. *Intercollegiate sports:* basketball M/W. *Intramural sports:* basketball M/W.

**Costs (2018–19)** *Tuition:* state resident $1872 full-time; nonresident $6864 full-time. Full-time tuition and fees vary according to course load and program. Part-time tuition and fees vary according to course load and program. *Required fees:* $38 full-time. *Payment plan:* installment.

**Financial Aid** Of all full-time matriculated undergraduates who enrolled in 2016, 69 Federal Work-Study jobs (averaging $960).

**Applying** *Options:* early admission. *Required:* high school transcript. *Application deadlines:* rolling (freshmen), rolling (transfers). *Notification:* continuous (freshmen), continuous (transfers).

**Freshman Application Contact** Patricia Brinkley, Admissions Representative, Caldwell Community College and Technical Institute, 2855 Hickory Boulevard, Hudson, NC 28638. *Phone:* 828-726-2700. *Fax:* 828-726-2709. *E-mail:* pbrinkley@cccti.edu. *Website:* http://www.cccti.edu/.

## Cape Fear Community College
### Wilmington, North Carolina

- **State-supported** 2-year, founded 1959, part of North Carolina Community College System
- **Urban** 150-acre campus
- **Endowment** $8.8 million
- **Coed**

**Undergraduates** 3,898 full-time, 5,169 part-time. Students come from 48 states and territories; 52 other countries; 6% are from out of state; 12% Black or African American, non-Hispanic/Latino; 8% Hispanic/Latino; 1% Asian, non-Hispanic/Latino; 0.2% Native Hawaiian or other Pacific Islander, non-Hispanic/Latino; 0.7% American Indian or Alaska Native, non-Hispanic/Latino; 3% Two or more races, non-Hispanic/Latino; 1% Race/ethnicity unknown; 0.1% international; 8% transferred in.

**Faculty** *Student/faculty ratio:* 12:1.

**Academics** *Calendar:* semesters. *Degree:* certificates, diplomas, and associate. *Special study options:* academic remediation for entering students, adult/continuing education programs, advanced placement credit, cooperative education, distance learning, double majors, English as a second language, independent study, off-campus study, part-time degree program, services for LD students, summer session for credit.

**Library** Cape Fear Community College Library.

**Student Life** *Campus security:* 24-hour emergency response devices and patrols, late-night transport/escort service, armed police officers.

**Athletics** Member NJCAA.

**Applying** *Options:* electronic application, early admission. *Required for some:* high school transcript, interview.

**Freshman Application Contact** Ms. Linda Kasyan, Director of Admissions, Cape Fear Community College, 411 North Front Street, Wilmington, NC 28401-3993. *Phone:* 910-362-7054. *Toll-free phone:* 877-799-2322. *Fax:* 910-362-7080. *E-mail:* admissions@cfcc.edu. *Website:* http://www.cfcc.edu/.

## Carolinas College of Health Sciences
### Charlotte, North Carolina

- **Public** 2-year, founded 1990
- **Urban** 3-acre campus with easy access to Charlotte
- **Endowment** $2.4 million
- **Coed**

**Undergraduates** 49 full-time, 384 part-time. Students come from 12 states and territories; 10% are from out of state; 10% Black or African American, non-Hispanic/Latino; 6% Hispanic/Latino; 3% Asian, non-Hispanic/Latino; 0.5% Native Hawaiian or other Pacific Islander, non-Hispanic/Latino; 0.2% American Indian or Alaska Native, non-Hispanic/Latino; 3% Two or more races, non-Hispanic/Latino; 4% Race/ethnicity unknown.

**Faculty** *Student/faculty ratio:* 9:1.

**Academics** *Calendar:* semesters. *Degree:* certificates, diplomas, and associate. *Special study options:* advanced placement credit, distance learning, independent study, off-campus study, part-time degree program, services for LD students, study abroad, summer session for credit.

**Library** AHEC Library. Study areas open 24 hours, 5&-7 days a week; students can reserve study rooms.

**Student Life** *Campus security:* 24-hour emergency response devices and patrols, late-night transport/escort service.
**Standardized Tests** *Required for some:* SAT or ACT (for admission).
**Costs (2017–18)** *Tuition:* state resident $14,335 full-time, $333 per credit hour part-time; nonresident $14,335 full-time, $333 per credit hour part-time. Full-time tuition and fees vary according to course load and program. Part-time tuition and fees vary according to course load and program. *Required fees:* $1480 full-time, $175 per term part-time.
**Financial Aid** Of all full-time matriculated undergraduates who enrolled in 2014, 7 Federal Work-Study jobs (averaging $3569).
**Applying** *Options:* electronic application. *Application fee:* $50. *Required:* minimum 2.5 GPA. *Required for some:* high school transcript, 3 letters of recommendation, interview.
**Freshman Application Contact** Ms. Merritt Newman, Admissions Representative, Carolinas College of Health Sciences, 1200 Blythe Boulevard, Charlotte, NC 28203. *Phone:* 704-355-5583. *Fax:* 704-355-9336. *E-mail:* merritt.newman@carolinascollege.edu. *Website:* http://www.carolinascollege.edu/.

## Carteret Community College
### Morehead City, North Carolina

- **State-supported** 2-year, founded 1963, part of North Carolina Community College System
- **Small-town** 41-acre campus
- **Endowment** $4.8 million
- **Coed,** 1,363 undergraduate students, 42% full-time, 69% women, 31% men

**Undergraduates** 571 full-time, 792 part-time. Students come from 8 states and territories; 1% are from out of state; 9% Black or African American, non-Hispanic/Latino; 4% Hispanic/Latino; 1% Asian, non-Hispanic/Latino; 0.2% Native Hawaiian or other Pacific Islander, non-Hispanic/Latino; 0.7% American Indian or Alaska Native, non-Hispanic/Latino; 3% Two or more races, non-Hispanic/Latino; 2% Race/ethnicity unknown; 11% transferred in.
**Freshmen** *Admission:* 1,593 applied, 1,532 admitted, 207 enrolled.
**Faculty** *Total:* 158, 36% full-time, 5% with terminal degrees. *Student/faculty ratio:* 10:1.
**Majors** Aquaculture; baking and pastry arts; business administration and management; computer engineering technology; computer software and media applications related; computer systems networking and telecommunications; criminal justice/law enforcement administration; culinary arts; early childhood education; emergency medical technology (EMT paramedic); hotel, motel, and restaurant management; information technology; legal assistant/paralegal; liberal arts and sciences/liberal studies; massage therapy; medical administrative assistant and medical secretary; medical/clinical assistant; medical office computer specialist; mental and social health services and allied professions related; office management; photographic and film/video technology; radiologic technology/science; registered nursing/registered nurse; respiratory care therapy.
**Academics** *Calendar:* semesters. *Degrees:* certificates, diplomas, associate, and postbachelor's certificates. *Special study options:* academic remediation for entering students, adult/continuing education programs, cooperative education, distance learning, double majors, internships, part-time degree program, services for LD students, summer session for credit.
**Library** Michael J. Smith Learning Resource Center. *Books:* 18,182 (physical), 173,614 (digital/electronic); *Databases:* 74. Weekly public service hours: 63.
**Student Life** *Housing:* college housing not available. *Activities and Organizations:* Student Government Association, Medical Assisting Club, Respiratory Therapy Club, Radiography Club, National Society of Leadership and Success. *Campus security:* late-night transport/escort service, security service from 7 am until 11:30 pm. *Student services:* veterans affairs office.
**Athletics** Member NCAA. All Division I. *Intramural sports:* basketball M/W, football M/W, tennis M/W.
**Costs (2017–18)** *Tuition:* state resident $1800 full-time, $76 per credit hour part-time; nonresident $6522 full-time, $268 per credit hour part-time. *Required fees:* $90 full-time, $24 per term part-time.
**Applying** *Options:* electronic application. *Required for some:* high school transcript. *Application deadlines:* rolling (freshmen), rolling (transfers). *Notification:* continuous (freshmen), continuous (transfers).
**Admissions Office Contact** Carteret Community College, 3505 Arendell Street, Morehead City, NC 28557-2989. *Website:* http://www.carteret.edu/.

## Catawba Valley Community College
### Hickory, North Carolina

**Freshman Application Contact** Catawba Valley Community College, 2550 Highway 70 SE, Hickory, NC 28602-9699. *Phone:* 828-327-7000 Ext. 4618. *Website:* http://www.cvcc.edu/.

## Central Carolina Community College
### Sanford, North Carolina

**Freshman Application Contact** Mrs. Jamie Tyson Childress, Dean of Enrollment/Registrar, Central Carolina Community College, 1105 Kelly Drive, Sanford, NC 27330-9000. *Phone:* 919-718-7239. *Toll-free phone:* 800-682-8353. *Fax:* 919-718-7380. *Website:* http://www.cccc.edu/.

## Central Piedmont Community College
### Charlotte, North Carolina

**Freshman Application Contact** Ms. Linda McComb, Associate Dean, Central Piedmont Community College, PO Box 35009, Charlotte, NC 28235-5009. *Phone:* 704-330-6784. *Fax:* 704-330-6136. *Website:* http://www.cpcc.edu/.

## Cleveland Community College
### Shelby, North Carolina

- **State-supported** 2-year, founded 1965, part of North Carolina Community College System
- **Small-town** 43-acre campus with easy access to Charlotte
- **Coed,** 2,700 undergraduate students, 37% full-time, 63% women, 37% men

**Undergraduates** 990 full-time, 1,710 part-time. 18% Black or African American, non-Hispanic/Latino; 4% Hispanic/Latino; 0.9% Asian, non-Hispanic/Latino; 0.1% Native Hawaiian or other Pacific Islander, non-Hispanic/Latino; 0.5% American Indian or Alaska Native, non-Hispanic/Latino; 3% Two or more races, non-Hispanic/Latino; 2% Race/ethnicity unknown; 0.7% international.
**Freshmen** *Admission:* 347 enrolled.
**Faculty** *Student/faculty ratio:* 11:1.
**Majors** Accounting; automation engineer technology; banking and financial support services; biotechnology; business administration and management; criminal justice/safety; early childhood education; electrical, electronic and communications engineering technology; electrician; elementary education; emergency medical technology (EMT paramedic); entrepreneurship; fire prevention and safety technology; general studies; information technology; language interpretation and translation; legal administrative assistant/secretary; liberal arts and sciences and humanities related; liberal arts and sciences/liberal studies; marketing/marketing management; mechanical drafting and CAD/CADD; medical/clinical assistant; medical office management; office management; operations management; radio and television broadcasting technology; radiologic technology/science; registered nursing/registered nurse.
**Academics** *Calendar:* semesters. *Degree:* certificates, diplomas, and associate. *Special study options:* academic remediation for entering students, adult/continuing education programs, advanced placement credit, cooperative education, distance learning, double majors, English as a second language, independent study, off-campus study, part-time degree program, summer session for credit.
**Library** Jim & Patsy Rose Library.
**Student Life** *Housing:* college housing not available. *Activities and Organizations:* drama/theater group, student-run television station. *Campus security:* security personnel during hours of operation. *Student services:* personal/psychological counseling, veterans affairs office.
**Costs (2017–18)** *Tuition:* state resident $2432 full-time, $76 per credit hour part-time; nonresident $8576 full-time, $268 per credit hour part-time. Full-time tuition and fees vary according to course load. Part-time tuition and fees vary according to course load. *Required fees:* $94 full-time.
**Financial Aid** Of all full-time matriculated undergraduates who enrolled in 2016, 20 Federal Work-Study jobs.
**Applying** *Options:* electronic application, deferred entrance. *Required:* high school transcript. *Application deadlines:* rolling (freshmen), rolling (transfers). *Notification:* continuous (freshmen), continuous (transfers).
**Freshman Application Contact** Cleveland Community College, 137 South Post Road, Shelby, NC 28152. *Phone:* 704-669-4321. *Website:* http://www.clevelandcc.edu/.

# Coastal Carolina Community College
## Jacksonville, North Carolina

**Freshman Application Contact** Ms. Heather Calihan, Counseling Coordinator, Coastal Carolina Community College, Jacksonville, NC 28546. *Phone:* 910-938-6241. *Fax:* 910-455-2767. *E-mail:* calihanh@coastal.cc.nc.us. *Website:* http://www.coastalcarolina.edu/.

# College of The Albemarle
## Elizabeth City, North Carolina

- **State-supported** 2-year, founded 1960, part of North Carolina Community College System
- **Small-town** 40-acre campus
- **Coed,** 1,947 undergraduate students, 50% full-time, 65% women, 35% men

**Undergraduates** 966 full-time, 981 part-time. Students come from 9 states and territories; 2 other countries; 14% Black or African American, non-Hispanic/Latino; 4% Hispanic/Latino; 1% Asian, non-Hispanic/Latino; 0.2% Native Hawaiian or other Pacific Islander, non-Hispanic/Latino; 0.6% American Indian or Alaska Native, non-Hispanic/Latino; 3% Two or more races, non-Hispanic/Latino; 4% Race/ethnicity unknown; 4% international.
**Freshmen** *Admission:* 375 enrolled.
**Majors** Administrative assistant and secretarial science; architectural engineering technology; art; biotechnology; business administration and management; computer engineering technology; computer programming; computer programming (specific applications); construction trades; crafts, folk art and artisanry; criminal justice/law enforcement administration; culinary arts; data entry/microcomputer applications; drafting/design engineering technologies related; dramatic/theater arts; education; information science/studies; information technology; liberal arts and sciences/liberal studies; licensed practical/vocational nurse training; marine maintenance and ship repair technology; medical administrative assistant and medical secretary; metal and jewelry arts; music; registered nursing/registered nurse; teacher assistant/aide.
**Academics** *Calendar:* semesters. *Degree:* certificates, diplomas, and associate. *Special study options:* academic remediation for entering students, adult/continuing education programs, advanced placement credit, cooperative education, English as a second language, part-time degree program, services for LD students, summer session for credit.
**Library** Learning Resources Center.
**Student Life** *Housing:* college housing not available. *Activities and Organizations:* drama/theater group, choral group, Phi Beta Lambda, Phi Theta Kappa. *Campus security:* 24-hour patrols. *Student services:* personal/psychological counseling.
**Athletics** *Intramural sports:* archery M/W, baseball M/W, basketball M/W, football M/W, golf M/W, gymnastics M/W, sailing M/W, soccer M(c), softball M/W, swimming and diving M/W, table tennis M/W, tennis M/W, volleyball M/W.
**Costs (2017–18)** *One-time required fee:* $147. *Tuition:* state resident $2076 full-time, $76 per credit hour part-time; nonresident $7290 full-time, $268 per credit hour part-time. Full-time tuition and fees vary according to course load, location, and program. *Payment plans:* installment, deferred payment.
**Applying** *Options:* electronic application, early admission, deferred entrance. *Required:* high school transcript. *Application deadlines:* rolling (freshmen), rolling (transfers). *Notification:* continuous (freshmen), continuous (transfers).
**Freshman Application Contact** Angie Godfrey-Dawson, Director of Admissions/Financial Aid, College of The Albemarle, PO Box 2327, Elizabeth City, NC 27906-2327. *Phone:* 252-335-0821 Ext. 2360. *Fax:* 252-335-2011. *Website:* http://www.albemarle.edu/.

# Craven Community College
## New Bern, North Carolina

- **State-supported** 2-year, founded 1965, part of North Carolina Community College System
- **Suburban** 100-acre campus
- **Coed,** 3,021 undergraduate students, 37% full-time, 58% women, 42% men

**Undergraduates** 1,126 full-time, 1,895 part-time. 16% Black or African American, non-Hispanic/Latino; 8% Hispanic/Latino; 3% Asian, non-Hispanic/Latino; 0.5% Native Hawaiian or other Pacific Islander, non-Hispanic/Latino; 0.7% American Indian or Alaska Native, non-Hispanic/Latino; 4% Two or more races, non-Hispanic/Latino; 4% Race/ethnicity unknown; 1% international; 13% transferred in.
**Freshmen** *Admission:* 277 enrolled.
**Faculty** *Student/faculty ratio:* 19:1.
**Majors** Accounting; airframe mechanics and aircraft maintenance technology; automobile/automotive mechanics technology; banking and financial support

services; business administration and management; computer and information systems security; computer programming (specific applications); computer systems networking and telecommunications; criminal justice/law enforcement administration; criminal justice/safety; early childhood education; electrical, electronic and communications engineering technology; electromechanical technology; elementary education; entrepreneurship; general studies; health information/medical records technology; heating, air conditioning, ventilation and refrigeration maintenance technology; hotel, motel, and restaurant management; information technology; legal administrative assistant/secretary; liberal arts and sciences and humanities related; liberal arts and sciences/liberal studies; machine shop technology; mechanical engineering/mechanical technology; medical administrative assistant and medical secretary; medical/clinical assistant; medical office management; office management; physical therapy technology; pre-engineering; registered nursing/registered nurse; special education; system, networking, and LAN/WAN management; tool and die technology; welding technology.
**Academics** *Calendar:* semesters. *Degree:* certificates, diplomas, and associate. *Special study options:* academic remediation for entering students, adult/continuing education programs, advanced placement credit, cooperative education, distance learning, double majors, English as a second language, honors programs, independent study, internships, part-time degree program, services for LD students, study abroad, summer session for credit.
**Library** R. C. Godwin Memorial Library. *Books:* 17,065 (physical), 240,000 (digital/electronic); *Serial titles:* 27 (physical), 18,759 (digital/electronic); *Databases:* 86. Students can reserve study rooms.
**Student Life** *Housing:* college housing not available. *Activities and Organizations:* choral group. *Campus security:* 24-hour emergency response devices and patrols. *Student services:* personal/psychological counseling, legal services, veterans affairs office.
**Costs (2018–19)** *Tuition:* state resident $1824 full-time, $76 per credit hour part-time; nonresident $6432 full-time, $268 per credit hour part-time. Full-time tuition and fees vary according to course load. Part-time tuition and fees vary according to course load. *Required fees:* $229 full-time, $114 per term part-time. *Payment plan:* installment. *Waivers:* senior citizens.
**Applying** *Options:* electronic application. *Required:* high school transcript. *Application deadlines:* rolling (freshmen), rolling (transfers).
**Freshman Application Contact** Craven Community College, 800 College Court, New Bern, NC 28562. *Phone:* 252-638-4597. *Website:* http://www.cravencc.edu/.

# Davidson County Community College
## Lexington, North Carolina

**Freshman Application Contact** Davidson County Community College, PO Box 1287, Lexington, NC 27293-1287. *Phone:* 336-249-8186 Ext. 6715. *Fax:* 336-224-0240. *E-mail:* admissions@davidsonccc.edu. *Website:* http://www.davidsonccc.edu/.

# Durham Technical Community College
## Durham, North Carolina

**Director of Admissions** Ms. Penny Augustine, Director of Admissions and Testing, Durham Technical Community College, 1637 Lawson Street, Durham, NC 27703-5023. *Phone:* 919-686-3619. *Website:* http://www.durhamtech.edu/.

# Edgecombe Community College
## Tarboro, North Carolina

**Freshman Application Contact** Ms. Jackie Heath, Admissions Officer, Edgecombe Community College, 2009 West Wilson Street, Tarboro, NC 27886-9399. *Phone:* 252-823-5166 Ext. 254. *Website:* http://www.edgecombe.edu/.

# Fayetteville Technical Community College
## Fayetteville, North Carolina

- **State-supported** 2-year, founded 1961, part of North Carolina Community College System
- **Suburban** 204-acre campus with easy access to Raleigh
- **Endowment** $39,050
- **Coed,** 11,640 undergraduate students, 39% full-time, 58% women, 42% men

**Undergraduates** 4,533 full-time, 7,107 part-time. Students come from 49 states and territories; 30 other countries; 24% are from out of state; 38% Black or African American, non-Hispanic/Latino; 12% Hispanic/Latino; 2% Asian, non-Hispanic/Latino; 0.5% Native Hawaiian or other Pacific Islander, non-Hispanic/Latino; 2% American Indian or Alaska Native, non-Hispanic/Latino; 5% Two or more races, non-Hispanic/Latino; 4% Race/ethnicity unknown; 0.5% international; 7% transferred in.

**Freshmen** *Admission:* 4,782 applied, 4,782 admitted, 2,063 enrolled. *Average high school GPA:* 2.7.

**Faculty** *Total:* 560, 49% full-time, 5% with terminal degrees. *Student/faculty ratio:* 19:1.

**Majors** Accounting; applied horticulture/horticulture operations; architectural engineering technology; autobody/collision and repair technology; automobile/automotive mechanics technology; building/construction finishing, management, and inspection related; business administration and management; civil engineering technology; commercial and advertising art; cosmetology; criminal justice/safety; crisis/emergency/disaster management; culinary arts; dental hygiene; early childhood education; electrical, electronic and communications engineering technology; electrician; electromechanical and instrumentation and maintenance technologies related; elementary education; emergency medical technology (EMT paramedic); fire prevention and safety technology; forensic science and technology; funeral service and mortuary science; game and interactive media design; general studies; gunsmithing; health and physical education related; heating, air conditioning, ventilation and refrigeration maintenance technology; hotel, motel, and restaurant management; information technology; legal assistant/paralegal; liberal arts and sciences and humanities related; liberal arts and sciences/liberal studies; logistics, materials, and supply chain management; machine shop technology; medical office management; office management; pharmacy technician; physical therapy technology; pre-engineering; radiologic technology/science; registered nursing/registered nurse; respiratory care therapy; speech-language pathology assistant; surgical technology; surveying technology.

**Academics** *Calendar:* semesters. *Degree:* certificates, diplomas, and associate. *Special study options:* academic remediation for entering students, accelerated degree program, adult/continuing education programs, advanced placement credit, cooperative education, distance learning, double majors, English as a second language, freshman honors college, honors programs, independent study, internships, off-campus study, part-time degree program, services for LD students, summer session for credit. *ROTC:* Air Force (c).

**Library** Paul H. Thompson Library plus 1 other. *Books:* 55,830 (physical), 250,000 (digital/electronic); *Serial titles:* 53 (physical), 2 (digital/electronic); *Databases:* 200.

**Student Life** *Housing:* college housing not available. *Activities and Organizations:* choral group, Parents for Higher Education, Phi Theta Kappa, Phi Beta Lambda, Surgical Technology Club, Student Veterans of America. *Campus security:* 24-hour emergency response devices and patrols, late-night transport/escort service, campus-wide emergency notification system. *Student services:* personal/psychological counseling, veterans affairs office.

**Athletics** Member NJCAA. *Intercollegiate sports:* basketball M(s)/W(s), golf M(s)/W(s). *Intramural sports:* basketball M/W.

**Costs (2017–18)** *One-time required fee:* $25. *Tuition:* state resident $2432 full-time, $76 per credit hour part-time; nonresident $8576 full-time, $268 per credit hour part-time. Full-time tuition and fees vary according to course load. Part-time tuition and fees vary according to course load. *Required fees:* $96 full-time, $48 per term part-time. *Payment plan:* installment. *Waivers:* employees or children of employees.

**Financial Aid** Of all full-time matriculated undergraduates who enrolled in 2016, 75 Federal Work-Study jobs (averaging $2000). *Financial aid deadline:* 6/1.

**Applying** *Options:* electronic application, deferred entrance. *Required:* high school transcript. *Required for some:* essay or personal statement, interview. *Application deadlines:* rolling (freshmen), rolling (transfers). *Notification:* continuous (freshmen), continuous (transfers).

**Freshman Application Contact** Dr. Louanna Castleman, Director of Admissions, Fayetteville Technical Community College, 2201 Hull Road, PO Box 35236, Fayetteville, NC 28303. *Phone:* 910-678-0141. *Fax:* 910-678-0085. *E-mail:* castleml@faytechcc.edu. *Website:* http://www.faytechcc.edu/.

# Forsyth Technical Community College
## Winston-Salem, North Carolina

**Freshman Application Contact** Admissions Office, Forsyth Technical Community College, 2100 Silas Creek Parkway, Winston-Salem, NC 27103-5197. *Phone:* 336-734-7556. *E-mail:* admissions@forsythtech.edu. *Website:* http://www.forsythtech.edu/.

# Gaston College
## Dallas, North Carolina

**Freshman Application Contact** Terry Basier, Director of Enrollment Management and Admissions, Gaston College, 201 Highway 321 South,

Dallas, NC 28034. *Phone:* 704-922-6214. *Fax:* 704-922-6443. *Website:* http://www.gaston.edu/.

# Guilford Technical Community College
## Jamestown, North Carolina

**Freshman Application Contact** Guilford Technical Community College, PO Box 309, Jamestown, NC 27282-0309. *Phone:* 336-334-4822 Ext. 50125. *Website:* http://www.gtcc.edu/.

# Halifax Community College
## Weldon, North Carolina

- **State and locally supported** 2-year, founded 1967, part of North Carolina Community College System
- **Rural** 109-acre campus
- **Endowment** $1.3 million
- **Coed,** 1,113 undergraduate students, 43% full-time, 61% women, 39% men
- **100% of applicants were admitted**

**Undergraduates** 483 full-time, 630 part-time. Students come from 2 states and territories; 5 other countries; 52% Black or African American, non-Hispanic/Latino; 3% Hispanic/Latino; 0.6% Asian, non-Hispanic/Latino; 0.1% Native Hawaiian or other Pacific Islander, non-Hispanic/Latino; 2% American Indian or Alaska Native, non-Hispanic/Latino; 6% Two or more races, non-Hispanic/Latino; 2% Race/ethnicity unknown; 0.4% international; 4% transferred in. *Retention:* 59% of full-time freshmen returned.

**Freshmen** *Admission:* 640 applied, 640 admitted, 184 enrolled. *Average high school GPA:* 2.5.

**Faculty** *Total:* 105, 51% full-time, 5% with terminal degrees. *Student/faculty ratio:* 11:1.

**Majors** Business administration and management; clinical/medical laboratory technology; commercial and advertising art; criminal justice/safety; dental hygiene; early childhood education; electromechanical and instrumentation and maintenance technologies related; information technology; legal assistant/paralegal; liberal arts and sciences and humanities related; liberal arts and sciences/liberal studies; medical administrative assistant and medical secretary; medical office management; mental and social health services and allied professions related; office management; registered nursing/registered nurse; welding technology.

**Academics** *Calendar:* semesters. *Degree:* certificates, diplomas, and associate. *Special study options:* academic remediation for entering students, cooperative education, distance learning, double majors, English as a second language, independent study, internships, part-time degree program, services for LD students, summer session for credit.

**Library** Learning Resources Center. *Books:* 28,668 (physical), 197,546 (digital/electronic); *Serial titles:* 91 (physical), 1,478 (digital/electronic); *Databases:* 88. Weekly public service hours: 52.

**Student Life** *Housing:* college housing not available. *Activities and Organizations:* Phi Theta Kappa, PRIDE, Women of Excellence. *Campus security:* 24-hour emergency response devices, 12-hour patrols by trained security personnel. *Student services:* health clinic, veterans affairs office.

**Costs (2018–19)** *Tuition:* state resident $2432 full-time, $76 per credit hour part-time; nonresident $8576 full-time, $268 per credit hour part-time. Full-time tuition and fees vary according to course load. Part-time tuition and fees vary according to course load. *Required fees:* $66 full-time, $56 per term part-time. *Payment plan:* installment.

**Applying** *Required:* high school transcript. *Application deadlines:* rolling (freshmen), rolling (out-of-state freshmen), rolling (transfers). *Notification:* continuous (freshmen), continuous (out-of-state freshmen), continuous (transfers).

**Freshman Application Contact** Mrs. Chalisa Harrell, Director of Admissions, Halifax Community College, PO Drawer 809, Weldon, NC 27890-0809. *Phone:* 252-536-7220. *E-mail:* charrell821@halifaxcc.edu. *Website:* http://www.halifaxcc.edu/.

# Harrison College
## Morrisville, North Carolina

**Freshman Application Contact** Mr. Jason Howanec, Vice President of Enrollment, Harrison College, 500 N. Meridian Street, Indianapolis, IN 46204. *Phone:* 800-919-2500. *E-mail:* admissions@harrison.edu. *Website:* http://www.harrison.edu/.

# Haywood Community College

## Clyde, North Carolina

- **State and locally supported** 2-year, founded 1965, part of North Carolina Community College System
- **Rural** 85-acre campus
- **Endowment** $8.5 million
- **Coed**

**Undergraduates** Students come from 4 states and territories; 8% Black or African American, non-Hispanic/Latino; 3% Hispanic/Latino; 0.5% Asian, non-Hispanic/Latino; 0.1% Native Hawaiian or other Pacific Islander, non-Hispanic/Latino; 2% American Indian or Alaska Native, non-Hispanic/Latino; 0.6% Two or more races, non-Hispanic/Latino; 1% Race/ethnicity unknown; 0.1% international.

**Majors** Accounting; accounting technology and bookkeeping; applied horticulture/horticulture operations; autobody/collision and repair technology; automobile/automotive mechanics technology; building/construction finishing, management, and inspection related; business administration and management; child-care and support services management; computer systems networking and telecommunications; cosmetology; crafts, folk art and artisanry; criminal justice/law enforcement administration; criminal justice/safety; early childhood education; electrical, electronic and communications engineering technology; electrician; electromechanical and instrumentation and maintenance technologies related; elementary education; entrepreneurship; fiber, textile and weaving arts; forest technology; information technology; liberal arts and sciences and humanities related; liberal arts and sciences/liberal studies; machine shop technology; medical/clinical assistant; medical office management; metal and jewelry arts; pre-engineering; registered nursing/registered nurse; welding technology; wildlife, fish and wildlands science and management.

**Academics** *Calendar:* semesters. *Degree:* certificates, diplomas, and associate. *Special study options:* academic remediation for entering students, adult/continuing education programs, advanced placement credit, cooperative education, distance learning, double majors, English as a second language, honors programs, independent study, internships, part-time degree program, services for LD students, study abroad, summer session for credit.

**Library** Freedlander Learning Resource Center. *Books:* 35,901 (physical), 367,546 (digital/electronic); *Serial titles:* 123 (physical), 24,280 (digital/electronic); *Databases:* 90. Weekly public service hours: 57; students can reserve study rooms.

**Student Life** *Housing:* college housing not available. *Campus security:* 24-hour emergency response devices and patrols. *Student services:* veterans affairs office.

**Athletics** *Intramural sports:* archery M(c)/W(c).

**Costs (2018–19)** *Tuition:* state resident $1216 full-time, $76 per credit hour part-time; nonresident $4288 full-time, $268 per credit hour part-time. Full-time tuition and fees vary according to course load and reciprocity agreements. Part-time tuition and fees vary according to course load and reciprocity agreements. *Required fees:* $142 full-time, $62 per term part-time. *Payment plans:* installment, deferred payment. *Waivers:* senior citizens.

**Financial Aid** Of all full-time matriculated undergraduates who enrolled in 2016, 41 Federal Work-Study jobs (averaging $857).

**Applying** *Options:* electronic application. *Required:* high school transcript. *Required for some:* interview. *Application deadlines:* rolling (freshmen), rolling (transfers).

**Freshman Application Contact** Enrollment Technician, Haywood Community College, 185 Freedlander Drive, Clyde, NC 28721-9453. *Phone:* 828-627-4669. *Toll-free phone:* 866-GOTOHCC. *E-mail:* enrollment@haywood.edu. *Website:* http://www.haywood.edu/.

# Isothermal Community College

## Spindale, North Carolina

**Freshman Application Contact** Ms. Vickie Searcy, Enrollment Management Office, Isothermal Community College, PO Box 804, Spindale, NC 28160-0804. *Phone:* 828-286-3636 Ext. 251. *Fax:* 828-286-8109. *E-mail:* vsearcy@isothermal.edu. *Website:* http://www.isothermal.edu/.

# James Sprunt Community College

## Kenansville, North Carolina

- **State-supported** 2-year, founded 1964, part of North Carolina Community College System
- **Rural** 51-acre campus with easy access to Raleigh, Wilmington
- **Endowment** $1.3 million
- **Coed,** 1,219 undergraduate students, 35% full-time, 67% women, 33% men

**Undergraduates** 424 full-time, 795 part-time. Students come from 3 states and territories; 1% are from out of state; 28% Black or African American, non-Hispanic/Latino; 21% Hispanic/Latino; 0.3% Asian, non-Hispanic/Latino; 0.1% Native Hawaiian or other Pacific Islander, non-Hispanic/Latino; 0.4% American Indian or Alaska Native, non-Hispanic/Latino; 2% Two or more races, non-Hispanic/Latino; 2% Race/ethnicity unknown; 0.3% international; 6% transferred in.

**Freshmen** *Admission:* 1,043 applied, 1,043 admitted, 202 enrolled.

**Faculty** *Total:* 72, 47% full-time. *Student/faculty ratio:* 10:1.

**Majors** Accounting; agribusiness; animal/livestock husbandry and production; animal sciences; business administration and management; child development; commercial and advertising art; cosmetology; criminal justice/safety; early childhood education; elementary education; general studies; information technology; institutional food workers; liberal arts and sciences and humanities related; liberal arts and sciences/liberal studies; livestock management; medium/heavy vehicle and truck technology; office management; registered nursing/registered nurse; viticulture and enology.

**Academics** *Calendar:* semesters. *Degree:* certificates, diplomas, and associate. *Special study options:* academic remediation for entering students, accelerated degree program, advanced placement credit, cooperative education, distance learning, double majors, English as a second language, independent study, internships, part-time degree program, services for LD students, summer session for credit.

**Library** James Sprunt Community College Library. *Books:* 24,762 (physical), 197,656 (digital/electronic); *Serial titles:* 58 (physical), 24,281 (digital/electronic); *Databases:* 92. Weekly public service hours: 46.

**Student Life** *Housing:* college housing not available. *Activities and Organizations:* student-run newspaper, Student Government Association, Phi Theta Kappa, Scholarly Men of Success, Scholarly Women of Tomorrow, national sororities. *Campus security:* day, evening, and Saturday trained security personnel. *Student services:* personal/psychological counseling, veterans affairs office.

**Athletics** *Intramural sports:* basketball M/W, soccer M/W.

**Costs (2018–19)** *Tuition:* state resident $2542 full-time, $76 per semester hour part-time; nonresident $8686 full-time, $268 per semester hour part-time. Full-time tuition and fees vary according to course load. Part-time tuition and fees vary according to course load. *Required fees:* $76 full-time, $35 per term part-time.

**Financial Aid** Of all full-time matriculated undergraduates who enrolled in 2016, 35 Federal Work-Study jobs (averaging $1057).

**Applying** *Options:* electronic application. *Required:* high school transcript. *Application deadlines:* rolling (freshmen), rolling (transfers). *Notification:* continuous (freshmen), continuous (transfers).

**Freshman Application Contact** Ms. Wanda Edwards, Admissions Specialist, James Sprunt Community College, PO Box 398, 133 James Sprunt Drive, Kenansville, NC 28349. *Phone:* 910-275-6364. *Fax:* 910-296-1222. *E-mail:* wedwards@jamessprunt.edu. *Website:* http://www.jamessprunt.edu/.

# Johnston Community College

## Smithfield, North Carolina

- **State-supported** 2-year, founded 1969, part of North Carolina Community College System
- **Rural** 100-acre campus
- **Endowment** $5.1 million
- **Coed,** 4,152 undergraduate students, 37% full-time, 64% women, 36% men

**Undergraduates** 1,546 full-time, 2,606 part-time. 13% Black or African American, non-Hispanic/Latino; 14% Hispanic/Latino; 0.7% Asian, non-Hispanic/Latino; 0.1% Native Hawaiian or other Pacific Islander, non-Hispanic/Latino; 0.6% American Indian or Alaska Native, non-Hispanic/Latino; 2% Two or more races, non-Hispanic/Latino; 7% Race/ethnicity unknown; 1% international. *Retention:* 66% of full-time freshmen returned.

**Freshmen** *Admission:* 589 enrolled.

**Majors** Accounting; administrative assistant and secretarial science; business administration and management; criminal justice/police science; diesel mechanics technology; early childhood education; heating, air conditioning, ventilation and refrigeration maintenance technology; legal assistant/paralegal;

liberal arts and sciences/liberal studies; medical/clinical assistant; medical office management; office management; registered nursing/registered nurse.
**Academics** *Calendar:* semesters. *Degree:* certificates, diplomas, and associate. *Special study options:* academic remediation for entering students, adult/continuing education programs, advanced placement credit, cooperative education, distance learning, double majors, honors programs, independent study, part-time degree program, services for LD students, summer session for credit.
**Library** Johnston Community College Library plus 1 other. Weekly public service hours: 57; students can reserve study rooms.
**Student Life** *Housing:* college housing not available. *Campus security:* 24-hour patrols. *Student services:* personal/psychological counseling.
**Athletics** Member NJCAA. *Intercollegiate sports:* basketball M/W, golf M/W.
**Standardized Tests** *Required:* NC DAP (for admission). *Recommended:* SAT or ACT (for admission).
**Costs (2017–18)** *Tuition:* state resident $2432 full-time, $76 per credit part-time; nonresident $8576 full-time, $268 per credit part-time. *Required fees:* $225 full-time. *Payment plan:* installment.
**Financial Aid** Of all full-time matriculated undergraduates who enrolled in 2016, 35 Federal Work-Study jobs (averaging $1853).
**Applying** *Options:* electronic application. *Required:* high school transcript, interview. *Application deadlines:* rolling (freshmen), rolling (transfers). *Notification:* continuous (freshmen), continuous (transfers).
**Admissions Office Contact** Johnston Community College, PO Box 2350, Smithfield, NC 27577-2350.
*Website:* http://www.johnstoncc.edu/.

# King's College
## Charlotte, North Carolina

**Freshman Application Contact** Admissions Office, King's College, 322 Lamar Avenue, Charlotte, NC 28204-2436. *Phone:* 704-372-0266. *Toll-free phone:* 800-768-2255. *Website:* http://www.kingscollegecharlotte.edu/.

# Lenoir Community College
## Kinston, North Carolina

- **State-supported** 2-year, founded 1960, part of North Carolina Community College System
- **Small-town** 86-acre campus
- **Coed,** 2,664 undergraduate students, 38% full-time, 61% women, 39% men

**Undergraduates** 1,013 full-time, 1,651 part-time. Students come from 27 states and territories; 1 other country; 3% are from out of state; 34% Black or African American, non-Hispanic/Latino; 8% Hispanic/Latino; 0.6% Asian, non-Hispanic/Latino; 0.1% Native Hawaiian or other Pacific Islander, non-Hispanic/Latino; 0.6% American Indian or Alaska Native, non-Hispanic/Latino; 1% Two or more races, non-Hispanic/Latino; 0.1% international; 7% transferred in.
**Freshmen** *Admission:* 1,750 applied, 1,559 admitted, 322 enrolled.
**Faculty** *Total:* 130, 64% full-time, 6% with terminal degrees. *Student/faculty ratio:* 15:1.
**Majors** Accounting; aeronautical/aerospace engineering technology; agroecology and sustainable agriculture; airline pilot and flight crew; applied horticulture/horticulture operations; autobody/collision and repair technology; automobile/automotive mechanics technology; business administration and management; computer engineering technology; cosmetology; criminal justice/safety; crisis/emergency/disaster management; culinary arts; dental hygiene; dietitian assistant; electromechanical and instrumentation and maintenance technologies related; emergency medical technology (EMT paramedic); energy management and systems technology; general studies; graphic design; gunsmithing; industrial electronics technology; industrial technology; information technology; liberal arts and sciences and humanities related; liberal arts and sciences/liberal studies; logistics, materials, and supply chain management; machine shop technology; marketing/marketing management; massage therapy; mechanical engineering/mechanical technology; medical/clinical assistant; medical office management; mental and social health services and allied professions related; office management; operations management; polysomnography; pre-engineering; prenursing studies; radiologic technology/science; registered nursing/registered nurse; trade and industrial teacher education; welding technology.
**Academics** *Calendar:* semesters. *Degree:* certificates, diplomas, and associate. *Special study options:* academic remediation for entering students, adult/continuing education programs, advanced placement credit, cooperative education, distance learning, double majors, English as a second language, independent study, part-time degree program, summer session for credit.
**Library** Learning Resources Center plus 1 other. *Books:* 26,338 (physical), 370,363 (digital/electronic); *Serial titles:* 22 (physical), 135,249 (digital/electronic); *Databases:* 139. Students can reserve study rooms.

**Student Life** *Housing:* college housing not available. *Activities and Organizations:* choral group, Student Government Association, Surgical Technology, Computer Engineering, Nightingals, Transitional and Career Studies. *Campus security:* 24-hour emergency response devices and patrols, student patrols. *Student services:* personal/psychological counseling, veterans affairs office.
**Athletics** Member NJCAA. *Intercollegiate sports:* baseball M, basketball M/W, volleyball W.
**Standardized Tests** *Recommended:* SAT or ACT (for admission).
**Costs (2018–19)** *Tuition:* state resident $2280 full-time, $76 per credit part-time; nonresident $8040 full-time, $268 per credit part-time. Full-time tuition and fees vary according to course load. Part-time tuition and fees vary according to course load. *Required fees:* $119 full-time. *Waivers:* employees or children of employees.
**Applying** *Options:* electronic application, early admission. *Required:* high school transcript. *Application deadlines:* rolling (freshmen), rolling (transfers). *Notification:* continuous (freshmen), continuous (transfers).
**Freshman Application Contact** Mrs. Kim Hill, Director of Admissions, Lenoir Community College, 231 Hwy 58 South, Kinston, NC 28502-0188. *Phone:* 252-527-6223 Ext. 301. *Fax:* 252-233-6895. *E-mail:* krhill01@lenoircc.edu.
*Website:* http://www.lenoircc.edu/.

# Louisburg College
## Louisburg, North Carolina

**Freshman Application Contact** Ms. Stephanie Tolbert, Vice President for Enrollment Management, Louisburg College, 501 North Main Street, Louisburg, NC 27549-2399. *Phone:* 919-497-3233. *Toll-free phone:* 800-775-0208. *Fax:* 919-496-1788. *E-mail:* admissions@louisburg.edu. *Website:* http://www.louisburg.edu/.

# Martin Community College
## Williamston, North Carolina

**Freshman Application Contact** Martin Community College, 1161 Kehukee Park Road, Williamston, NC 27892. *Phone:* 252-792-1521 Ext. 244. *Website:* http://www.martincc.edu/.

# Mayland Community College
## Spruce Pine, North Carolina

**Director of Admissions** Ms. Cathy Morrison, Director of Admissions, Mayland Community College, PO Box 547, Spruce Pine, NC 28777-0547. *Phone:* 828-765-7351 Ext. 224. *Toll-free phone:* 800-462-9526. *Website:* http://www.mayland.edu/.

# McDowell Technical Community College
## Marion, North Carolina

**Freshman Application Contact** Mr. Rick L. Wilson, Director of Admissions, McDowell Technical Community College, 54 College Drive, Marion, NC 28752. *Phone:* 828-652-0632. *Fax:* 828-652-1014. *E-mail:* rickw@mcdowelltech.edu. *Website:* http://www.mcdowelltech.edu/.

# Miller-Motte College
## Cary, North Carolina

**Admissions Office Contact** Miller-Motte College, 2205 Walnut Street, Cary, NC 27518. *Toll-free phone:* 800-705-9182. *Website:* http://www.miller-motte.edu/.

# Miller-Motte College
## Fayetteville, North Carolina

**Admissions Office Contact** Miller-Motte College, 3725 Ramsey Street, Fayetteville, NC 28311. *Toll-free phone:* 800-705-9182. *Website:* http://www.miller-motte.edu/.

# Miller-Motte College
## Jacksonville, North Carolina

**Admissions Office Contact** Miller-Motte College, 1291 Hargett Street, Jacksonville, NC 28540. *Toll-free phone:* 800-705-9182. *Website:* http://www.miller-motte.edu/.

# Miller-Motte College
## Raleigh, North Carolina

**Admissions Office Contact** Miller-Motte College, 3901 Capital Boulevard, Suite 151, Raleigh, NC 27604. *Toll-free phone:* 800-705-9182. *Website:* http://www.miller-motte.edu/.

# Miller-Motte College
## Wilmington, North Carolina

**Freshman Application Contact** Admissions Office, Miller-Motte College, 5000 Market Street, Wilmington, NC 28405. *Toll-free phone:* 800-705-9182. *Website:* http://www.miller-motte.edu/.

# Mitchell Community College
## Statesville, North Carolina

- **State-supported** 2-year, founded 1852, part of North Carolina Community College System
- **Small-town** 14-acre campus with easy access to Charlotte
- **Endowment** $3.7 million
- **Coed,** 3,204 undergraduate students, 35% full-time, 61% women, 39% men

**Undergraduates** 1,118 full-time, 2,086 part-time. 13% Black or African American, non-Hispanic/Latino; 11% Hispanic/Latino; 2% Asian, non-Hispanic/Latino; 0.1% Native Hawaiian or other Pacific Islander, non-Hispanic/Latino; 0.6% American Indian or Alaska Native, non-Hispanic/Latino; 3% Two or more races, non-Hispanic/Latino; 0.9% Race/ethnicity unknown; 1% international; 4% transferred in. *Retention:* 57% of full-time freshmen returned.
**Freshmen** *Admission:* 2,646 applied, 2,646 admitted, 388 enrolled.
**Faculty** *Total:* 158, 46% full-time. *Student/faculty ratio:* 18:1.
**Majors** Accounting; agribusiness; business administration and management; child-care and support services management; computer programming; computer programming (specific applications); computer systems analysis; cooking and related culinary arts; criminal justice/law enforcement administration; early childhood education; electrical, electronic and communications engineering technology; electrician; electromechanical and instrumentation and maintenance technologies related; elementary education; engineering/industrial management; executive assistant/executive secretary; general studies; health professions related; information science/studies; information technology; kindergarten/preschool education; liberal arts and sciences and humanities related; liberal arts and sciences/liberal studies; machine shop technology; manufacturing engineering; manufacturing engineering technology; mechanical drafting and CAD/CADD; mechanical engineering/mechanical technology; mechatronics, robotics, and automation engineering; medical/clinical assistant; office management; operations management; registered nursing/registered nurse; special education–early childhood; teacher assistant/aide.
**Academics** *Calendar:* semesters. *Degree:* certificates, diplomas, and associate. *Special study options:* academic remediation for entering students, adult/continuing education programs, advanced placement credit, cooperative education, distance learning, English as a second language, part-time degree program, services for LD students, summer session for credit.
**Library** Huskins Library. *Books:* 14,909 (physical), 203,358 (digital/electronic); *Serial titles:* 2 (digital/electronic); *Databases:* 96. Students can reserve study rooms.
**Student Life** *Housing:* college housing not available. *Activities and Organizations:* choral group, Cosmetology Club, Early Childhood Association, Student Nurses Association, Phi Theta Kappa, Student Government Association. *Campus security:* late-night transport/escort service, day and evening security guards. *Student services:* personal/psychological counseling, veterans affairs office.
**Costs (2018–19)** *Tuition:* state resident $2280 full-time, $76 per credit hour part-time; nonresident $8040 full-time, $268 per credit hour part-time. Full-time tuition and fees vary according to course load. Part-time tuition and fees vary according to course load. *Required fees:* $171 full-time, $6 per credit hour part-time, $26 per term part-time. *Payment plan:* installment.
**Financial Aid** Of all full-time matriculated undergraduates who enrolled in 2016, 30 Federal Work-Study jobs.
**Applying** *Options:* electronic application. *Required:* high school transcript. *Application deadlines:* rolling (freshmen), rolling (transfers). *Notification:* continuous (freshmen), continuous (transfers).
**Freshman Application Contact** Mitchell Community College, 500 West Broad Street, Statesville, NC 28677. *Phone:* 704-878-3281. *Website:* http://www.mitchellcc.edu/.

# Montgomery Community College
## Troy, North Carolina

- **State-supported** 2-year, founded 1967, part of North Carolina Community College System
- **Rural** 159-acre campus
- **Coed,** 925 undergraduate students, 34% full-time, 65% women, 35% men

**Undergraduates** 314 full-time, 611 part-time. Students come from 11 states and territories; 1% are from out of state; 18% Black or African American, non-Hispanic/Latino; 17% Hispanic/Latino; 2% Asian, non-Hispanic/Latino; 0.1% Native Hawaiian or other Pacific Islander, non-Hispanic/Latino; 1% American Indian or Alaska Native, non-Hispanic/Latino; 2% Two or more races, non-Hispanic/Latino; 0.2% Race/ethnicity unknown; 0.3% international. *Retention:* 70% of full-time freshmen returned.
**Faculty** *Total:* 186, 18% full-time. *Student/faculty ratio:* 8:1.
**Majors** Business administration and management; criminal justice/safety; early childhood education; electrician; electromechanical and instrumentation and maintenance technologies related; forest technology; gunsmithing; heating, air conditioning, ventilation and refrigeration maintenance technology; information technology; liberal arts and sciences/liberal studies; medical/clinical assistant; medical office management; mental and social health services and allied professions related; office management; pre-engineering.
**Academics** *Calendar:* semesters. *Degree:* certificates, diplomas, and associate. *Special study options:* academic remediation for entering students, advanced placement credit, distance learning, English as a second language, part-time degree program, services for LD students, summer session for credit.
**Library** Montgomery Community College Learning Resource Center. *Books:* 17,572 (physical), 197,546 (digital/electronic); *Serial titles:* 55 (physical), 24,280 (digital/electronic); *Databases:* 104. Weekly public service hours: 55; students can reserve study rooms.
**Student Life** *Housing:* college housing not available. *Activities and Organizations:* Student Government Association, Nursing Club, Gunsmithing Society, Medical Assisting Club, Forestry Club. *Campus security:* 24-hour emergency response devices. *Student services:* personal/psychological counseling, veterans affairs office.
**Costs (2017–18)** *Tuition:* state resident $2432 full-time, $76 per credit hour part-time; nonresident $8576 full-time, $268 per credit hour part-time. Full-time tuition and fees vary according to course load. Part-time tuition and fees vary according to course load. *Required fees:* $105 full-time, $53 per term part-time. *Payment plan:* installment.
**Financial Aid** Of all full-time matriculated undergraduates who enrolled in 2016, 24 Federal Work-Study jobs (averaging $500).
**Applying** *Options:* electronic application, early admission, deferred entrance. *Required:* high school transcript. *Application deadlines:* rolling (freshmen), rolling (transfers). *Notification:* continuous (freshmen), continuous (transfers).
**Admissions Office Contact** Montgomery Community College, 1011 Page Street, Troy, NC 27371. *Toll-free phone:* 877-572-6222. *Website:* http://www.montgomery.edu/.

# Nash Community College
## Rocky Mount, North Carolina

**Freshman Application Contact** Ms. Dorothy Gardner, Admissions Officer, Nash Community College, PO Box 7488, Rocky Mount, NC 27804. *Phone:* 252-451-8300. *E-mail:* dgardner@nashcc.edu. *Website:* http://www.nashcc.edu/.

# Pamlico Community College
## Grantsboro, North Carolina

**Director of Admissions** Mr. Floyd H. Hardison, Admissions Counselor, Pamlico Community College, PO Box 185, Grantsboro, NC 28529-0185. *Phone:* 252-249-1851 Ext. 28. *Website:* http://www.pamlicocc.edu/.

# Piedmont Community College
## Roxboro, North Carolina

- **State-supported** 2-year, founded 1970, part of North Carolina Community College System
- **Small-town** 178-acre campus
- **Coed,** 1,311 undergraduate students, 31% full-time, 60% women, 40% men

**Undergraduates** 403 full-time, 908 part-time.
**Faculty** *Student/faculty ratio:* 12:1.
**Majors** Accounting; business administration and management; child-care and support services management; cinematography and film/video production; criminal justice/safety; early childhood education; electrical and power

transmission installation; electrician; electromechanical and instrumentation and maintenance technologies related; general studies; graphic communications; health professions related; historic preservation and conservation; industrial technology; information technology; liberal arts and sciences and humanities related; liberal arts and sciences/liberal studies; medical administrative assistant and medical secretary; medical/clinical assistant; medical office management; mental and social health services and allied professions related; office management; registered nursing/registered nurse.

**Academics** *Calendar:* semesters. *Degree:* certificates, diplomas, and associate. *Special study options:* academic remediation for entering students, adult/continuing education programs, advanced placement credit, cooperative education, distance learning, double majors, English as a second language, off-campus study, part-time degree program, summer session for credit.

**Library** Learning Resource Center.

**Student Life** *Housing:* college housing not available. *Activities and Organizations:* drama/theater group. *Campus security:* routine patrols by the local sheriff department. *Student services:* veterans affairs office.

**Costs (2017–18)** *Tuition:* state resident $1824 full-time, $76 per credit hour part-time; nonresident $6432 full-time, $268 per credit hour part-time. Full-time tuition and fees vary according to course load. Part-time tuition and fees vary according to course load. *Required fees:* $115 full-time, $57 per term part-time. *Payment plan:* installment.

**Applying** *Options:* electronic application, early admission, deferred entrance. *Required for some:* high school transcript. *Application deadlines:* rolling (freshmen), rolling (transfers). *Notification:* continuous (freshmen), continuous (transfers).

**Freshman Application Contact** Piedmont Community College, PO Box 1197, Roxboro, NC 27573-1197. *Phone:* 336-599-1181. *Website:* http://www.piedmontcc.edu/.

# Pitt Community College
## Winterville, North Carolina

**Freshman Application Contact** Dr. Kimberly Williamson, Interim Coordinator of Counseling, Pitt Community College, PO Drawer 7007, Greenville, NC 27835-7007. *Phone:* 252-493-7217. *Fax:* 252-321-4612. *E-mail:* pittadm@pcc.pitt.cc.nc.us. *Website:* http://www.pittcc.edu/.

# Randolph Community College
## Asheboro, North Carolina

- **State-supported** 2-year, founded 1962, part of North Carolina Community College System
- **Small-town** 44-acre campus with easy access to Greensboro, Winston-Salem, High Point
- **Endowment** $11.6 million
- **Coed,** 2,647 undergraduate students, 35% full-time, 61% women, 39% men

**Undergraduates** 914 full-time, 1,733 part-time. Students come from 2 states and territories; 5% Black or African American, non-Hispanic/Latino; 10% Hispanic/Latino; 0.8% Asian, non-Hispanic/Latino; 0.1% Native Hawaiian or other Pacific Islander, non-Hispanic/Latino; 0.5% American Indian or Alaska Native, non-Hispanic/Latino; 0.8% Two or more races, non-Hispanic/Latino; 23% Race/ethnicity unknown; 2% international; 2% transferred in.

**Freshmen** *Admission:* 1,283 applied, 1,283 admitted, 472 enrolled.

**Faculty** *Total:* 286, 29% full-time. *Student/faculty ratio:* 10:1.

**Majors** Accounting; autobody/collision and repair technology; automobile/automotive mechanics technology; business administration and management; commercial and advertising art; commercial photography; computer systems networking and telecommunications; cosmetology; criminal justice/safety; early childhood education; electrician; electromechanical technology; human services; information technology; interior design; liberal arts and sciences and humanities related; liberal arts and sciences/liberal studies; machine shop technology; mechatronics, robotics, and automation engineering; medical/clinical assistant; medical office management; photographic and film/video technology; photojournalism; radiologic technology/science; registered nursing/registered nurse.

**Academics** *Calendar:* semesters. *Degree:* certificates, diplomas, and associate. *Special study options:* academic remediation for entering students, adult/continuing education programs, advanced placement credit, cooperative education, distance learning, double majors, English as a second language, independent study, internships, off-campus study, part-time degree program, services for LD students, summer session for credit. *ROTC:* Air Force (c).

**Library** R. Alton Cox Learning Resources Center. *Books:* 25,000 (physical).

**Student Life** *Housing:* college housing not available. *Activities and Organizations:* Student Government Association, Phi Theta Kappa, Student Nurse Association, Phi Beta Lambda, Veterans Club. *Campus security:* 24-hour emergency response devices, security officer during hours of operation. *Student services:* veterans affairs office.

**Costs (2018–19)** *Tuition:* state resident $2432 full-time, $76 per credit hour part-time; nonresident $8576 full-time, $268 per credit hour part-time. *Required fees:* $108 full-time, $3 per credit hour part-time, $10 per term part-time. *Payment plan:* installment.

**Applying** *Options:* electronic application, deferred entrance. *Application deadlines:* rolling (freshmen), rolling (transfers). *Notification:* continuous (freshmen), continuous (transfers).

**Freshman Application Contact** Ms. Hillary D Pritchard, Director of Admissions, Records and Registration, Randolph Community College, 629 Industrial Park Avenue, Asheboro, NC 27205-7333. *Phone:* 336-633-0122. *Fax:* 336-629-9547. *E-mail:* hdpritchard@randolph.edu. *Website:* http://www.randolph.edu/.

# Richmond Community College
## Hamlet, North Carolina

- **State-supported** 2-year, founded 1964, part of North Carolina Community College System
- **Rural** 163-acre campus
- **Coed,** 2,528 undergraduate students, 41% full-time, 65% women, 35% men

**Undergraduates** 1,039 full-time, 1,489 part-time. 0.4% are from out of state; 22% Black or African American, non-Hispanic/Latino; 4% Hispanic/Latino; 1% Asian, non-Hispanic/Latino; 8% American Indian or Alaska Native, non-Hispanic/Latino; 3% Two or more races, non-Hispanic/Latino; 26% Race/ethnicity unknown; 0.2% international; 6% transferred in.

**Freshmen** *Admission:* 329 enrolled.

**Faculty** *Student/faculty ratio:* 15:1.

**Majors** Accounting; business administration and management; computer engineering technology; criminal justice/safety; early childhood education; electrical and power transmission installation; electrical, electronic and communications engineering technology; electromechanical and instrumentation and maintenance technologies related; electromechanical technology; elementary education; entrepreneurship; health information/medical records technology; health professions related; heating, air conditioning, ventilation and refrigeration maintenance technology; information technology; liberal arts and sciences/liberal studies; mechanical engineering/mechanical technology; medical/clinical assistant; medical office computer specialist; medical office management; mental and social health services and allied professions related; office management; registered nursing/registered nurse.

**Academics** *Calendar:* semesters. *Degree:* certificates, diplomas, and associate. *Special study options:* academic remediation for entering students, adult/continuing education programs, advanced placement credit, cooperative education, distance learning, double majors, English as a second language, independent study, internships, part-time degree program, student-designed majors, summer session for credit.

**Library** Richmond Community College Library.

**Student Life** *Housing:* college housing not available. *Activities and Organizations:* choral group. *Campus security:* 24-hour emergency response devices, security guard during hours of operation. *Student services:* personal/psychological counseling.

**Costs (2017–18)** *Tuition:* state resident $2432 full-time, $76 per credit hour part-time; nonresident $8576 full-time, $268 per credit hour part-time. Full-time tuition and fees vary according to course load. Part-time tuition and fees vary according to course load. *Required fees:* $84 full-time, $35 per term part-time. *Payment plan:* installment. *Waivers:* employees or children of employees.

**Financial Aid** Of all full-time matriculated undergraduates who enrolled in 2016, 35 Federal Work-Study jobs (averaging $2000).

**Applying** *Options:* electronic application, deferred entrance. *Required:* high school transcript. *Application deadlines:* rolling (freshmen), rolling (transfers). *Notification:* continuous (freshmen), continuous (transfers).

**Freshman Application Contact** Cayce Holmes, Registrar, Richmond Community College, PO Box 1189, 1042 W. Hamlet Avenue, Hamlet, NC 28345. *Phone:* 910-410-1737. *Fax:* 910-582-7102. *E-mail:* ccholmes@richmondcc.edu. *Website:* http://www.richmondcc.edu/.

# Roanoke-Chowan Community College
## Ahoskie, North Carolina

**Director of Admissions** Miss Sandra Copeland, Director, Counseling Services, Roanoke-Chowan Community College, 109 Community College Road, Ahoskie, NC 27910. *Phone:* 252-862-1225. *Website:* http://www.roanokechowan.edu/.

# Robeson Community College
## Lumberton, North Carolina

**Freshman Application Contact** Ms. Patricia Locklear, College Recruiter, Robeson Community College, PO Box 1420, Lumberton, NC 28359. *Phone:* 910-272-3356 Ext. 251. *Fax:* 910-618-5686. *E-mail:* plocklear@robeson.edu. *Website:* http://www.robeson.edu/.

# Rockingham Community College
## Wentworth, North Carolina

- **State-supported** 2-year, founded 1964, part of North Carolina Community College System
- **Rural** 257-acre campus
- **Coed**

**Undergraduates** 668 full-time, 1,111 part-time. Students come from 2 states and territories.
**Faculty** *Student/faculty ratio:* 18:1.
**Academics** *Calendar:* semesters. *Degree:* certificates, diplomas, and associate. *Special study options:* academic remediation for entering students, adult/continuing education programs, advanced placement credit, cooperative education, part-time degree program, student-designed majors, summer session for credit.
**Library** Gerald B. James Library.
**Student Life** *Campus security:* 24-hour emergency response devices and patrols.
**Athletics** Member NJCAA.
**Costs (2017–18)** *Tuition:* state resident $1716 full-time, $76 per credit hour part-time; nonresident $6324 full-time, $268 per credit hour part-time. *Required fees:* $116 full-time, $44 per term part-time.
**Financial Aid** Of all full-time matriculated undergraduates who enrolled in 2016, 37 Federal Work-Study jobs (averaging $2300).
**Applying** *Options:* electronic application, early admission, deferred entrance.
**Freshman Application Contact** Mr. Derrick Satterfield, Director of Enrollment Services, Rockingham Community College, PO Box 38, Wentworth, NC 27375-0038. *Phone:* 336-342-4261 Ext. 2114. *Fax:* 336-342-1809. *E-mail:* admissions@rockinghamcc.edu. *Website:* http://www.rockinghamcc.edu/.

# Rowan-Cabarrus Community College
## Salisbury, North Carolina

- **State-supported** 2-year, founded 1963, part of North Carolina Community College System
- **Small-town** 100-acre campus with easy access to Charlotte
- **Coed,** 7,579 undergraduate students

**Undergraduates** Students come from 11 states and territories; 1% are from out of state; 19% Black or African American, non-Hispanic/Latino; 10% Hispanic/Latino; 2% Asian, non-Hispanic/Latino; 0.1% Native Hawaiian or other Pacific Islander, non-Hispanic/Latino; 0.5% American Indian or Alaska Native, non-Hispanic/Latino; 3% Two or more races, non-Hispanic/Latino; 1% Race/ethnicity unknown; 1% international.
**Faculty** *Total:* 430, 35% full-time. *Student/faculty ratio:* 15:1.
**Majors** Accounting; automobile/automotive mechanics technology; building/property maintenance; business administration and management; business administration, management and operations related; computer and information systems security; computer programming; cosmetology; criminal justice/law enforcement administration; early childhood education; electrical, electronic and communications engineering technology; electrician; elementary education; general studies; industrial technology; information science/studies; information technology; liberal arts and sciences/liberal studies; marketing/marketing management; medical office management; occupational therapist assistant; office management; radiologic technology/science; registered nursing/registered nurse; system, networking, and LAN/WAN management.
**Academics** *Calendar:* semesters. *Degree:* certificates, diplomas, and associate. *Special study options:* academic remediation for entering students, adult/continuing education programs, advanced placement credit, cooperative education, distance learning, English as a second language, internships, part-time degree program, services for LD students, summer session for credit.
**Library** Learning Resource Center. Students can reserve study rooms.
**Student Life** *Housing:* college housing not available. *Campus security:* on-campus security during hours of operation. *Student services:* personal/psychological counseling.
**Costs (2018–19)** *Tuition:* state resident $2432 full-time, $76 per credit hour part-time; nonresident $8576 full-time, $268 per credit hour part-time. Full-time tuition and fees vary according to course load. Part-time tuition and fees vary according to course load. *Required fees:* $194 full-time, $79 per term

part-time. *Payment plan:* installment. *Waivers:* employees or children of employees.
**Applying** *Required:* high school transcript. *Application deadlines:* rolling (freshmen), rolling (transfers).
**Freshman Application Contact** Rowan-Cabarrus Community College, 1333 Jake Alexander Boulevard South, Salisbury, NC 28146. *Website:* http://www.rccc.edu/.

# Sampson Community College
## Clinton, North Carolina

**Director of Admissions** Mr. William R. Jordan, Director of Admissions, Sampson Community College, PO Box 318, 1801 Sunset Avenue, Highway 24 West, Clinton, NC 28329-0318. *Phone:* 910-592-8084 Ext. 2022. *Website:* http://www.sampsoncc.edu/.

# Sandhills Community College
## Pinehurst, North Carolina

**Freshman Application Contact** Mr. Isai Robledo, Recruiter, Sandhills Community College, 3395 Airport Road, Pinehurst, NC 28374-8299. *Phone:* 910-246-5365. *Toll-free phone:* 800-338-3944. *Fax:* 910-695-3981. *E-mail:* robledoi@sandhills.edu. *Website:* http://www.sandhills.edu/.

# Southeastern Community College
## Whiteville, North Carolina

**Freshman Application Contact** Ms. Sylvia McQueen, Registrar, Southeastern Community College, PO Box 151, Whiteville, NC 28472. *Phone:* 910-642-7141 Ext. 249. *Fax:* 910-642-5658. *Website:* http://www.sccnc.edu/.

# South Piedmont Community College
## Polkton, North Carolina

**Freshman Application Contact** Ms. Amanda Secrest, Assistant Director Admissions and Testing, South Piedmont Community College, PO Box 126, Polkton, NC 28135. *Phone:* 704-290-5847. *Toll-free phone:* 800-766-0319. *E-mail:* asecrest@spcc.edu. *Website:* http://www.spcc.edu/.

# Southwestern Community College
## Sylva, North Carolina

- **State-supported** 2-year, founded 1964, part of North Carolina Community College System
- **Small-town** 77-acre campus
- **Coed,** 2,574 undergraduate students, 35% full-time, 60% women, 40% men

**Undergraduates** 910 full-time, 1,664 part-time. 1% Black or African American, non-Hispanic/Latino; 7% Hispanic/Latino; 1% Asian, non-Hispanic/Latino; 0.1% Native Hawaiian or other Pacific Islander, non-Hispanic/Latino; 7% American Indian or Alaska Native, non-Hispanic/Latino; 2% Two or more races, non-Hispanic/Latino; 0.9% Race/ethnicity unknown; 1% international.
**Freshmen** *Admission:* 299 enrolled.
**Faculty** *Student/faculty ratio:* 16:1.
**Majors** Accounting; automobile/automotive mechanics technology; business administration and management; child development; clinical/medical laboratory technology; commercial and advertising art; computer engineering technology; cosmetology; criminal justice/police science; culinary arts; electrical, electronic and communications engineering technology; emergency medical technology (EMT paramedic); environmental studies; health information/medical records administration; health information/medical records technology; information science/studies; legal assistant/paralegal; liberal arts and sciences/liberal studies; massage therapy; medical radiologic technology; mental health counseling; parks, recreation, leisure, and fitness studies related; physical therapy technology; registered nursing/registered nurse; respiratory care therapy; substance abuse/addiction counseling; system, networking, and LAN/WAN management; trade and industrial teacher education.
**Academics** *Calendar:* semesters. *Degree:* certificates, diplomas, and associate. *Special study options:* academic remediation for entering students, adult/continuing education programs, advanced placement credit, cooperative education, distance learning, double majors, English as a second language, honors programs, independent study, off-campus study, part-time degree program, services for LD students, summer session for credit.
**Library** Holt Library.

**Student Life** *Housing:* college housing not available. *Campus security:* security during hours of operation. *Student services:* personal/psychological counseling, veterans affairs office.

**Costs (2017–18)** *Tuition:* state resident $2128 full-time, $76 per credit hour part-time; nonresident $7504 full-time, $268 per credit hour part-time. Full-time tuition and fees vary according to course load and program. Part-time tuition and fees vary according to course load and program. *Required fees:* $85 full-time, $3 per credit hour part-time, $1 per year part-time. *Payment plan:* installment.

**Applying** *Required:* high school transcript. *Required for some:* minimum 2.5 GPA, interview.

**Freshman Application Contact** Martin Aucoin, Director of Enrollment Management, Southwestern Community College, 447 College Drive, Sylva, NC 28779. *Phone:* 828-339-4217. *Toll-free phone:* 800-447-4091 (in-state); 800-447-7091 (out-of-state). *E-mail:* m_aucoin@southwesterncc.edu. *Website:* http://www.southwesterncc.edu/.

## Stanly Community College
### Albemarle, North Carolina

**Freshman Application Contact** Mrs. Denise B. Ross, Associate Dean, Admissions, Stanly Community College, 141 College Drive, Albemarle, NC 28001. *Phone:* 704-982-0121 Ext. 264. *Fax:* 704-982-0255. *E-mail:* dross7926@stanly.edu. *Website:* http://www.stanly.edu/.

## Surry Community College
### Dobson, North Carolina

**Freshman Application Contact** Renita Hazelwood, Director of Admissions, Surry Community College, 630 South Main Street, Dobson, NC 27017. *Phone:* 336-386-3392. *Fax:* 336-386-3690. *E-mail:* hazelwoodr@surry.edu. *Website:* http://www.surry.edu/.

## Tri-County Community College
### Murphy, North Carolina

- **State-supported** 2-year, founded 1964, part of North Carolina Community College System
- **Rural** 40-acre campus
- **Coed,** 1,160 undergraduate students

**Faculty** *Total:* 80, 58% full-time, 5% with terminal degrees. *Student/faculty ratio:* 21:1.

**Majors** Accounting; automobile/automotive mechanics technology; business administration and management; early childhood education; electrical, electronic and communications engineering technology; engine machinist; information technology; liberal arts and sciences/liberal studies; medical/clinical assistant; registered nursing/registered nurse; welding technology.

**Academics** *Calendar:* semesters. *Degree:* certificates, diplomas, and associate. *Special study options:* academic remediation for entering students, adult/continuing education programs, distance learning, double majors, internships, part-time degree program, study abroad, summer session for credit.

**Student Life** *Housing:* college housing not available. *Student services:* personal/psychological counseling, veterans affairs office.

**Standardized Tests** *Recommended:* SAT and SAT Subject Tests or ACT (for admission).

**Financial Aid** Of all full-time matriculated undergraduates who enrolled in 2016, 11 Federal Work-Study jobs.

**Applying** *Options:* electronic application. *Required:* high school transcript. *Application deadlines:* rolling (freshmen), rolling (transfers). *Notification:* continuous (freshmen), continuous (transfers).

**Freshman Application Contact** Mrs. Samantha Jones, First Year Success Coach and Retention Specialist, Tri-County Community College, 21 Campus Circle, Murphy, NC 28906-7919. *Phone:* 828-837-6810. *Fax:* 828-837-3266. *E-mail:* sjones@tricountycc.edu. *Website:* http://www.tricountycc.edu/.

## Vance-Granville Community College
### Henderson, North Carolina

**Freshman Application Contact** Ms. Kathy Kutl, Admissions Officer, Vance-Granville Community College, PO Box 917, State Road 1126, Henderson, NC 27536. *Phone:* 252-492-2061 Ext. 3265. *Fax:* 252-430-0460. *Website:* http://www.vgcc.edu/.

## Virginia College in Greensboro
### Greensboro, North Carolina

**Admissions Office Contact** Virginia College in Greensboro, 3740 South Holden Road, Greensboro, NC 27406. *Website:* http://www.vc.edu/.

## Wake Technical Community College
### Raleigh, North Carolina

**Director of Admissions** Ms. Susan Bloomfield, Director of Admissions, Wake Technical Community College, 9101 Fayetteville Road, Raleigh, NC 27603-5696. *Phone:* 919-866-5452. *E-mail:* srbloomfield@waketech.edu. *Website:* http://www.waketech.edu/.

## Wayne Community College
### Goldsboro, North Carolina

- **State and locally supported** 2-year, founded 1957, part of North Carolina Community College System
- **Small-town** 175-acre campus with easy access to Raleigh
- **Endowment** $92,408
- **Coed,** 3,837 undergraduate students, 47% full-time, 60% women, 40% men

**Undergraduates** 1,813 full-time, 2,024 part-time. 4% are from out of state; 27% Black or African American, non-Hispanic/Latino; 8% Hispanic/Latino; 2% Asian, non-Hispanic/Latino; 0.3% Native Hawaiian or other Pacific Islander, non-Hispanic/Latino; 0.6% American Indian or Alaska Native, non-Hispanic/Latino; 0.8% Two or more races, non-Hispanic/Latino; 2% Race/ethnicity unknown; 0.3% international; 26% transferred in.

**Freshmen** *Admission:* 2,328 applied, 1,335 admitted, 655 enrolled.

**Faculty** *Total:* 333, 42% full-time, 1% with terminal degrees. *Student/faculty ratio:* 20:1.

**Majors** Accounting; agribusiness; agroecology and sustainable agriculture; airframe mechanics and aircraft maintenance technology; animal/livestock husbandry and production; autobody/collision and repair technology; automobile/automotive mechanics technology; biology/biotechnology laboratory technician; business administration and management; criminal justice/police science; criminal justice/safety; crisis/emergency/disaster management; dental hygiene; early childhood education; electrical, electronic and communications engineering technology; electromechanical and instrumentation and maintenance technologies related; elementary education; energy management and systems technology; forensic science and technology; forest technology; game and interactive media design; information technology; liberal arts and sciences and humanities related; liberal arts and sciences/liberal studies; machine shop technology; mechanical engineering/mechanical technology; medical/clinical assistant; medical office management; mental and social health services and allied professions related; office management; operations management; registered nursing/registered nurse; turf and turfgrass management.

**Academics** *Calendar:* semesters. *Degree:* certificates, diplomas, and associate. *Special study options:* academic remediation for entering students, adult/continuing education programs, advanced placement credit, cooperative education, distance learning, double majors, English as a second language, external degree program, honors programs, part-time degree program, services for LD students, summer session for credit.

**Library** Dr. Clyde A. Erwin, Jr. Library.

**Student Life** *Housing:* college housing not available. *Activities and Organizations:* choral group, Student Government Association, Phi Beta Lambda, Phi Theta Kappa, Criminal Justice Club, International Club. *Campus security:* 24-hour emergency response devices and patrols. *Student services:* personal/psychological counseling.

**Standardized Tests** *Required for some:* SAT or ACT (for admission).

**Costs (2018–19)** *Tuition:* state resident $2432 full-time, $76 per credit hour part-time; nonresident $8576 full-time, $268 per credit hour part-time. *Required fees:* $92 full-time, $46 per term part-time.

**Financial Aid** Of all full-time matriculated undergraduates who enrolled in 2016, 100 Federal Work-Study jobs (averaging $2000).

**Applying** *Options:* electronic application. *Required:* high school transcript, interview. *Application deadlines:* rolling (freshmen), rolling (transfers). *Notification:* continuous (freshmen), continuous (transfers).

**Freshman Application Contact** Mrs. Lea Matthews, Associate Director of Admissions and Records, Wayne Community College, PO Box 8002, Goldsboro, NC 27533. *Phone:* 919-735-5151 Ext. 6717. *Fax:* 919-736-9425. *E-mail:* rlmatthews@waynecc.edu. *Website:* http://www.waynecc.edu/.

## Western Piedmont Community College
### Morganton, North Carolina

**Freshman Application Contact** Susan Williams, Director of Admissions, Western Piedmont Community College, 1001 Burkemont Avenue, Morganton, NC 28655-4511. *Phone:* 828-438-6051. *Fax:* 828-438-6065. *E-mail:* swilliams@wpcc.edu. *Website:* http://www.wpcc.edu/.

## Wilkes Community College
### Wilkesboro, North Carolina

**Freshman Application Contact** Mr. Mac Warren, Director of Admissions, Wilkes Community College, PO Box 120, Wilkesboro, NC 28697. *Phone:* 336-838-6141. *Fax:* 336-838-6547. *E-mail:* mac.warren@wilkescc.edu. *Website:* http://www.wilkescc.edu/.

## Wilson Community College
### Wilson, North Carolina

**Freshman Application Contact** Mrs. Maegan Williams, Admissions Technician, Wilson Community College, Wilson, NC 27893-0305. *Phone:* 252-246-1275. *Fax:* 252-243-7148. *E-mail:* mwilliams@wilsoncc.edu. *Website:* http://www.wilsoncc.edu/.

# NORTH DAKOTA

## Bismarck State College
### Bismarck, North Dakota

- **State-supported** primarily 2-year, founded 1939, part of North Dakota University System
- **Urban** 120-acre campus
- **Endowment** $16.3 million
- **Coed**

**Undergraduates** 2,241 full-time, 1,735 part-time. Students come from 49 states and territories; 8 other countries; 22% are from out of state; 3% Black or African American, non-Hispanic/Latino; 3% Hispanic/Latino; 0.6% Asian, non-Hispanic/Latino; 0.2% Native Hawaiian or other Pacific Islander, non-Hispanic/Latino; 2% American Indian or Alaska Native, non-Hispanic/Latino; 3% Two or more races, non-Hispanic/Latino; 2% Race/ethnicity unknown; 0.3% international; 7% transferred in; 14% live on campus. *Retention:* 74% of full-time freshmen returned.
**Faculty** *Student/faculty ratio:* 14:1.
**Academics** *Calendar:* semesters. *Degrees:* certificates, diplomas, associate, and bachelor's. *Special study options:* academic remediation for entering students, adult/continuing education programs, advanced placement credit, cooperative education, distance learning, double majors, independent study, internships, part-time degree program, services for LD students, study abroad, summer session for credit.
**Library** Bismarck State College Library. *Books:* 61,059 (physical), 16,804 (digital/electronic); *Serial titles:* 121 (physical), 114 (digital/electronic); *Databases:* 88. Weekly public service hours: 67; students can reserve study rooms.
**Student Life** *Campus security:* late-night transport/escort service, controlled dormitory access.
**Athletics** Member NJCAA.
**Standardized Tests** *Recommended:* ACT (for admission).
**Costs (2017–18)** *Tuition:* state resident $3791 full-time, $126 per credit hour part-time; nonresident $10,121 full-time, $337 per credit hour part-time. Full-time tuition and fees vary according to course level, course load, degree level, location, program, and reciprocity agreements. Part-time tuition and fees vary according to course level, course load, degree level, location, program, and reciprocity agreements. *Required fees:* $800 full-time, $33 per credit hour part-time. *Room and board:* $6992; room only: $2892. Room and board charges vary according to board plan and housing facility.
**Financial Aid** Of all full-time matriculated undergraduates who enrolled in 2015, 1,507 applied for aid, 906 were judged to have need, 341 had their need fully met. In 2015, 230. *Average percent of need met:* 67. *Average financial aid package:* $8283. *Average need-based loan:* $4493. *Average need-based gift aid:* $4696. *Average non-need-based aid:* $1388.
**Applying** *Options:* electronic application, early admission, deferred entrance. *Application fee:* $35. *Required:* high school transcript. *Required for some:* interview.
**Freshman Application Contact** Karen Erickson, Director of Admissions and Enrollment Services, Bismarck State College, PO Box 5587, Bismarck, ND 58506. *Phone:* 701-224-5424. *Toll-free phone:* 800-445-5073. *Fax:* 701-224-

5643. *E-mail:* karen.erickson@bismarckstate.edu. *Website:* http://www.bismarckstate.edu/.

## Cankdeska Cikana Community College
### Fort Totten, North Dakota

**Director of Admissions** DeShawn Lawrence, Registrar, Cankdeska Cikana Community College, PO Box 269, Fort Totten, ND 58335-0269. *Phone:* 701-766-1342. *Toll-free phone:* 888-783-1463. *Website:* http://www.littlehoop.edu/.

## Dakota College at Bottineau
### Bottineau, North Dakota

- **State-supported** 2-year, founded 1906, part of North Dakota University System
- **Small-town** 35-acre campus
- **Coed**

**Faculty** *Student/faculty ratio:* 8:1.
**Academics** *Calendar:* semesters. *Degree:* certificates, diplomas, and associate. *Special study options:* academic remediation for entering students, advanced placement credit, cooperative education, distance learning, double majors, off-campus study, part-time degree program, services for LD students, summer session for credit.
**Library** Dakota College at Bottineau Library plus 1 other.
**Student Life** *Campus security:* controlled dormitory access, security cameras.
**Athletics** Member NJCAA.
**Financial Aid** Of all full-time matriculated undergraduates who enrolled in 2015, 296 applied for aid, 246 were judged to have need, 62 had their need fully met. 65 Federal Work-Study jobs (averaging $668). In 2015, 26. *Average percent of need met:* 70. *Average financial aid package:* $10,004. *Average need-based loan:* $5400. *Average need-based gift aid:* $5196. *Average non-need-based aid:* $2012. *Average indebtedness upon graduation:* $12,305.
**Applying** *Options:* electronic application, early admission, deferred entrance. *Application fee:* $35. *Required:* high school transcript, immunization records, previous college official transcripts.
**Freshman Application Contact** Mrs. Robyn Poitra, Admissions Clerk, Dakota College at Bottineau, 105 Simrall Boulevard, Bottineau, ND 58318. *Phone:* 701-228-5487. *Toll-free phone:* 800-542-6866. *Fax:* 701-228-5499. *E-mail:* robyn.poitra@dakotacollege.edu. *Website:* http://www.dakotacollege.edu/.

## Lake Region State College
### Devils Lake, North Dakota

- **State-supported** 2-year, founded 1941, part of North Dakota University System
- **Small-town** 120-acre campus
- **Coed,** 1,972 undergraduate students, 27% full-time, 55% women, 45% men

**Undergraduates** 527 full-time, 1,445 part-time. Students come from 37 states and territories; 15 other countries; 15% are from out of state; 4% Black or African American, non-Hispanic/Latino; 6% Hispanic/Latino; 0.4% Asian, non-Hispanic/Latino; 0.1% Native Hawaiian or other Pacific Islander, non-Hispanic/Latino; 4% American Indian or Alaska Native, non-Hispanic/Latino; 5% Two or more races, non-Hispanic/Latino; 1% Race/ethnicity unknown; 5% international; 12% live on campus. *Retention:* 58% of full-time freshmen returned.
**Freshmen** *Admission:* 214 enrolled.
**Faculty** *Total:* 108, 39% full-time.
**Majors** Agricultural business and management; automobile/automotive mechanics technology; business administration and management; child-care provision; computer installation and repair technology; criminal justice/police science; electrical and electronic engineering technologies related; language interpretation and translation; liberal arts and sciences/liberal studies; management information systems; merchandising, sales, and marketing operations related (general); physical fitness technician; registered nursing/registered nurse; speech-language pathology.
**Academics** *Calendar:* semesters. *Degree:* certificates, diplomas, and associate. *Special study options:* academic remediation for entering students, cooperative education, distance learning, double majors, English as a second language, honors programs, internships, off-campus study, part-time degree program, services for LD students, summer session for credit.
**Library** Paul Hoghaug Library. *Books:* 21,465 (physical), 17,762 (digital/electronic); *Databases:* 71. Students can reserve study rooms.
**Student Life** *Housing Options:* coed, men-only, women-only. Campus housing is university owned. *Activities and Organizations:* drama/theater

group, Student Senate, Phi Theta Kappa, Delta Epsilon Chi, Phi Theta Lambda, Student Nurse Organization. *Campus security:* 24-hour emergency response devices, controlled dormitory access. *Student services:* personal/psychological counseling.

**Athletics** Member NJCAA. *Intercollegiate sports:* baseball M(s), basketball M(s)/W(s), softball W(s), volleyball W(s). *Intramural sports:* basketball M/W, riflery M/W, soccer M/W, volleyball M/W, weight lifting M/W.

**Standardized Tests** *Required for some:* SAT or ACT (for admission).

**Costs (2017–18)** *Tuition:* state resident $3459 full-time, $144 per credit part-time; nonresident $3459 full-time, $144 per credit part-time. *Required fees:* $877 full-time, $29 per credit part-time. *Room and board:* $6525. Room and board charges vary according to board plan and housing facility. *Payment plan:* installment. *Waivers:* minority students, senior citizens, and employees or children of employees.

**Financial Aid** Of all full-time matriculated undergraduates who enrolled in 2017, 371 applied for aid, 294 were judged to have need, 109 had their need fully met. In 2017, 105 non-need-based awards were made. *Average percent of need met:* 77%. *Average financial aid package:* $9828. *Average need-based loan:* $5912. *Average need-based gift aid:* $5599. *Average non-need-based aid:* $1062. *Average indebtedness upon graduation:* $15,163.

**Applying** *Options:* electronic application. *Application fee:* $35. *Required for some:* high school transcript, immunization records, college transcripts. *Application deadlines:* rolling (freshmen), rolling (transfers). *Notification:* continuous (freshmen), continuous (transfers).

**Freshman Application Contact** Lisa Howard, Admissions Associate, Lake Region State College, 1801 College Drive North, Devils Lake, ND 58301. *Phone:* 701-662-1519. *Toll-free phone:* 800-443-1313. *Fax:* 701-662-1581. *E-mail:* lisa.howard@lrsc.edu. *Website:* http://www.lrsc.edu/.

# North Dakota State College of Science
## Wahpeton, North Dakota

- **State-supported** 2-year, founded 1903, part of North Dakota University System
- **Rural** 128-acre campus
- **Endowment** $18.4 million
- **Coed,** 2,985 undergraduate students, 57% full-time, 43% women, 57% men

**Undergraduates** 1,707 full-time, 1,278 part-time. Students come from 35 states and territories; 7 other countries; 42% are from out of state; 7% Black or African American, non-Hispanic/Latino; 2% Hispanic/Latino; 1% Asian, non-Hispanic/Latino; 0.8% American Indian or Alaska Native, non-Hispanic/Latino; 4% Two or more races, non-Hispanic/Latino; 1% Race/ethnicity unknown; 1% international; 7% transferred in; 58% live on campus.

**Freshmen** *Admission:* 1,216 applied, 856 admitted, 737 enrolled.

**Faculty** *Total:* 283, 37% full-time, 7% with terminal degrees. *Student/faculty ratio:* 13:1.

**Majors** Agricultural business and management; agricultural business technology; agricultural mechanics and equipment technology; animal sciences; architectural engineering technology; autobody/collision and repair technology; automobile/automotive mechanics technology; building construction technology; business administration and management; civil engineering technology; computer and information sciences; computer systems networking and telecommunications; construction engineering technology; culinary arts; dental assisting; dental hygiene; diesel mechanics technology; electrical and electronic engineering technologies related; emergency medical technology (EMT paramedic); entrepreneurship; health information/medical records technology; heating, air conditioning, ventilation and refrigeration maintenance technology; heating, ventilation, air conditioning and refrigeration engineering technology; industrial production technologies related; liberal arts and sciences/liberal studies; licensed practical/vocational nurse training; livestock management; machine tool technology; manufacturing engineering technology; marketing/marketing management; occupational therapist assistant; pharmacy technician; registered nursing/registered nurse; restaurant/food services management; small engine mechanics and repair technology; vehicle maintenance and repair technologies related; web page, digital/multimedia and information resources design; welding technology.

**Academics** *Calendar:* semesters. *Degree:* certificates, diplomas, and associate. *Special study options:* academic remediation for entering students, cooperative education, distance learning, double majors, English as a second language, independent study, internships, part-time degree program, services for LD students, student-designed majors, summer session for credit.

**Library** Mildred Johnson Library. *Books:* 57,489 (physical), 15,859 (digital/electronic); *Serial titles:* 204 (physical), 23,940 (digital/electronic); *Databases:* 80.

**Student Life** *Housing:* on-campus residence required for freshman year. *Options:* coed, men-only, women-only, special housing for students with

disabilities. Campus housing is university owned. Freshman campus housing is guaranteed. *Activities and Organizations:* drama/theater group, choral group, marching band, SkillsUSA, Welding Club, Dental Club, Diesel Club, HVAC. *Campus security:* 24-hour patrols, late-night transport/escort service, controlled dormitory access. *Student services:* health clinic, personal/psychological counseling, veterans affairs office.

**Athletics** Member NJCAA. *Intercollegiate sports:* basketball M(s)/W(s), football M(s), softball W, volleyball W(s). *Intramural sports:* basketball M/W, football M, racquetball M/W, softball M/W, ultimate Frisbee M/W, volleyball M/W.

**Costs (2018–19)** *Tuition:* state resident $131 per credit part-time; nonresident $350 per credit part-time. *Room and board:* Room and board charges vary according to board plan and housing facility. *Waivers:* employees or children of employees.

**Financial Aid** Of all full-time matriculated undergraduates who enrolled in 2015, 1,431 applied for aid, 1,046 were judged to have need, 411 had their need fully met. 134 Federal Work-Study jobs (averaging $1535). In 2015, 80 non-need-based awards were made. *Average percent of need met:* 62%. *Average financial aid package:* $10,781. *Average need-based loan:* $5470. *Average need-based gift aid:* $4941. *Average non-need-based aid:* $856. *Average indebtedness upon graduation:* $16,885.

**Applying** *Options:* electronic application, early admission. *Application fee:* $35. *Required:* high school transcript. *Application deadlines:* rolling (freshmen), rolling (transfers). *Notification:* continuous (freshmen), continuous (transfers).

**Freshman Application Contact** Mr. Justin Grams, Director of Admissions, North Dakota State College of Science, 800 North 6th Street, Wahpeton, ND 58076. *Phone:* 701-671-2189. *Toll-free phone:* 800-342-4325. *E-mail:* justin.grams@ndscs.edu. *Website:* http://www.ndscs.edu/.

# Nueta Hidatsa Sahnish College
## New Town, North Dakota

**Freshman Application Contact** Office of Admissions, Nueta Hidatsa Sahnish College, PO Box 490, 220 8th Avenue North, New Town, ND 58763-0490. *Phone:* 701-627-4738 Ext. 295. *Website:* http://www.nhsc.edu/.

# Turtle Mountain Community College
## Belcourt, North Dakota

**Director of Admissions** Ms. Joni LaFontaine, Admissions/Records Officer, Turtle Mountain Community College, Box 340, Belcourt, ND 58316-0340. *Phone:* 701-477-5605 Ext. 217. *E-mail:* jlafontaine@tm.edu. *Website:* http://my.tm.edu/.

# United Tribes Technical College
## Bismarck, North Dakota

**Freshman Application Contact** Ms. Vivian Gillette, Director of Admissions, United Tribes Technical College, Bismarck, ND 58504. *Phone:* 701-255-3285 Ext. 1334. *Fax:* 701-530-0640. *E-mail:* vgillette@uttc.edu. *Website:* http://www.uttc.edu/.

# Williston State College
## Williston, North Dakota

- **State-supported** 2-year, founded 1957, part of North Dakota University System
- **Small-town** 80-acre campus
- **Endowment** $52,232
- **Coed,** 1,098 undergraduate students, 56% full-time, 60% women, 40% men

**Undergraduates** 615 full-time, 483 part-time. Students come from 29 states and territories; 7 other countries; 18% are from out of state; 4% Black or African American, non-Hispanic/Latino; 7% Hispanic/Latino; 0.7% Asian, non-Hispanic/Latino; 0.1% Native Hawaiian or other Pacific Islander, non-Hispanic/Latino; 2% American Indian or Alaska Native, non-Hispanic/Latino; 5% Two or more races, non-Hispanic/Latino; 3% Race/ethnicity unknown; 3% international; 15% transferred in. *Retention:* 57% of full-time freshmen returned.

**Freshmen** *Admission:* 564 applied, 465 admitted, 306 enrolled.

**Faculty** *Total:* 34, 94% full-time, 3% with terminal degrees. *Student/faculty ratio:* 30:1.

**Majors** Accounting technology and bookkeeping; agriculture; business administration, management and operations related; diesel mechanics technology; liberal arts and sciences/liberal studies; licensed practical/vocational nurse training; massage therapy; medium/heavy vehicle and truck technology; multi/interdisciplinary studies related; petroleum technology; psychiatric/mental health services technology; registered nursing/registered nurse; speech-language pathology; system, networking, and LAN/WAN management; welding technology.

**Academics** *Calendar:* semesters. *Degree:* certificates and associate. *Special study options:* academic remediation for entering students, advanced placement credit, cooperative education, distance learning, double majors, English as a second language, independent study, part-time degree program, services for LD students, student-designed majors, study abroad, summer session for credit.

**Library** Williston State College Learning Commons. *Books:* 8,865 (physical), 6,889 (digital/electronic); *Databases:* 45. Students can reserve study rooms.

**Student Life** *Housing Options:* coed, special housing for students with disabilities. Campus housing is university owned. *Activities and Organizations:* student-run newspaper, choral group, Phi Theta Kappa, Student Senate, Teton Activity Board, Biz-Tech, Student Nurses Organization. *Campus security:* controlled dormitory access. *Student services:* personal/psychological counseling.

**Athletics** Member NJCAA. *Intercollegiate sports:* baseball M(s), basketball M(s)/W(s), ice hockey M(c), softball W(s), volleyball W(s).

**Costs (2017–18)** *One-time required fee:* $35. *Tuition:* state resident $3064 full-time, $118 per credit hour part-time; nonresident $3064 full-time, $118 per credit hour part-time. Full-time tuition and fees vary according to course load, location, program, and reciprocity agreements. Part-time tuition and fees vary according to course load, location, program, and reciprocity agreements. *Required fees:* $1465 full-time, $56 per credit hour part-time. *Room and board:* $9066; room only: $5200. Room and board charges vary according to board plan and housing facility. *Payment plan:* installment. *Waivers:* minority students, senior citizens, and employees or children of employees.

**Financial Aid** Of all full-time matriculated undergraduates who enrolled in 2017, 530 applied for aid, 337 were judged to have need, 67 had their need fully met. In 2017, 176 non-need-based awards were made. *Average percent of need met:* 53%. *Average financial aid package:* $8504. *Average need-based loan:* $4888. *Average need-based gift aid:* $5676. *Average non-need-based aid:* $4633. *Average indebtedness upon graduation:* $7902.

**Applying** *Options:* electronic application, deferred entrance. *Application fee:* $35. *Required:* high school transcript. *Application deadlines:* rolling (freshmen), rolling (transfers). *Notification:* continuous (freshmen), continuous (transfers).

**Freshman Application Contact** Ms. Jamee Robbins, Enrollment Services Associate, Williston State College, 1410 University Avenue, Williston, ND 58801. *Phone:* 701-774-4278. *Toll-free phone:* 888-863-9455. *E-mail:* wsc.admission@willistonstate.edu.

*Website:* http://www.willistonstate.edu/.

# NORTHERN MARIANA ISLANDS

## Northern Marianas College
### Saipan, Northern Mariana Islands

**Freshman Application Contact** Ms. Leilani M. Basa-Alam, Admission Specialist, Northern Marianas College, PO Box 501250, Saipan, MP 96950-1250. *Phone:* 670-234-3690 Ext. 1539. *Fax:* 670-235-4967. *E-mail:* leilanib@nmcnet.edu. *Website:* http://www.marianas.edu/.

# OHIO

## AIC College of Design
### Cincinnati, Ohio

- **Independent** primarily 2-year, founded 1976
- **Urban** 3-acre campus with easy access to Cincinnati
- **Coed,** 34 undergraduate students, 88% full-time, 65% women, 35% men

**Undergraduates** 30 full-time, 4 part-time. Students come from 3 states and territories; 27% are from out of state; 18% Black or African American, non-Hispanic/Latino. *Retention:* 90% of full-time freshmen returned.

**Freshmen** *Admission:* 36 applied, 24 admitted, 6 enrolled. *Average high school GPA:* 3.3.

**Faculty** *Total:* 11, 36% full-time, 18% with terminal degrees. *Student/faculty ratio:* 5:1.

**Majors** Computer graphics.

**Academics** *Degrees:* associate and bachelor's. *Special study options:* academic remediation for entering students, accelerated degree program,

adult/continuing education programs, advanced placement credit, cooperative education, part-time degree program, services for LD students.

**Library** AIC College of Design Library plus 1 other.

**Student Life** *Housing:* college housing not available. *Activities and Organizations:* AIGA Student Chapter. *Campus security:* 24-hour emergency response devices, SMS. *Student services:* personal/psychological counseling.

**Standardized Tests** *Recommended:* SAT or ACT (for admission).

**Costs (2017–18)** *Tuition:* $511 per credit hour part-time. Full-time tuition and fees vary according to course load. Part-time tuition and fees vary according to course load. No tuition increase for student's term of enrollment. *Payment plan:* installment. *Waivers:* employees or children of employees.

**Applying** *Options:* early admission, early decision, deferred entrance. *Application fee:* $100. *Required:* essay or personal statement, high school transcript, interview. *Recommended:* minimum 2.0 GPA, letters of recommendation. *Application deadlines:* rolling (freshmen), rolling (transfers). *Notification:* continuous (freshmen), continuous (transfers).

**Freshman Application Contact** Megan Orsburn, Admissions Assistant, AIC College of Design, 1171 E. Kemper Road, Cincinnati, OH 45246. *Phone:* 513-751-1206.

*Website:* http://www.aic-arts.edu/.

## American Institute of Alternative Medicine
### Columbus, Ohio

**Admissions Office Contact** American Institute of Alternative Medicine, 6685 Doubletree Avenue, Columbus, OH 43229. *Website:* http://www.aiam.edu/.

## American National University
### Kettering, Ohio

**Director of Admissions** Gregory J. Shields, Director, American National University, 1837 Woodman Center Drive, Kettering, OH 45420. *Phone:* 937-299-9450. *Website:* http://www.an.edu/.

## American National University
### Youngstown, Ohio

**Admissions Office Contact** American National University, 3487 Belmont Avenue, Youngstown, OH 44505. *Website:* http://www.an.edu/.

## Antonelli College
### Cincinnati, Ohio

**Freshman Application Contact** Antonelli College, 124 East Seventh Street, Cincinnati, OH 45202. *Phone:* 513-241-4338. *Toll-free phone:* 877-500-4304. *Website:* http://www.antonellicollege.edu/.

## Beckfield College
### Cincinnati, Ohio

**Freshman Application Contact** Beckfield College, 225 Pictoria Drive, Suite 200, Cincinnati, OH 45246. *Website:* http://www.beckfield.edu/.

## Belmont College
### St. Clairsville, Ohio

**Director of Admissions** Michael Sterling, Director of Recruitment, Belmont College, 120 Fox Shannon Place, St. Clairsville, OH 43950-9735. *Phone:* 740-695-9500 Ext. 1563. *Toll-free phone:* 800-423-1188. *E-mail:* msterling@btc.edu. *Website:* http://www.belmontcollege.edu/.

## Bowling Green State University–Firelands College
### Huron, Ohio

- **State-supported** primarily 2-year, founded 1968, part of Bowling Green State University System
- **Rural** 216-acre campus with easy access to Cleveland, Toledo
- **Coed,** 1,970 undergraduate students, 48% full-time, 64% women, 36% men

**Undergraduates** 936 full-time, 1,034 part-time. Students come from 6 states and territories; 1 other country; 1% are from out of state; 6% Black or African American, non-Hispanic/Latino; 5% Hispanic/Latino; 0.8% Asian, non-Hispanic/Latino; 0.2% American Indian or Alaska Native, non-Hispanic/Latino; 4% Two or more races, non-Hispanic/Latino; 5%

Race/ethnicity unknown; 0.1% international. *Retention:* 53% of full-time freshmen returned.
**Freshmen** *Admission:* 419 enrolled. *Average high school GPA:* 2.8.
**Faculty** *Total:* 102, 43% full-time. *Student/faculty ratio:* 20:1.
**Majors** Allied health and medical assisting services related; business administration and management; communications technologies and support services related; computer and information sciences and support services related; computer systems networking and telecommunications; criminal justice/safety; design and visual communications; diagnostic medical sonography and ultrasound technology; education; health professions related; human services; industrial technology; interdisciplinary studies; liberal arts and sciences/liberal studies; management information systems and services related; mechanical engineering/mechanical technology; medical radiologic technology; registered nursing/registered nurse; respiratory care therapy; social work.
**Academics** *Calendar:* semesters. *Degrees:* certificates, associate, and bachelor's (also offers some upper-level and graduate courses). *Special study options:* academic remediation for entering students, adult/continuing education programs, advanced placement credit, cooperative education, distance learning, double majors, honors programs, independent study, internships, part-time degree program, services for LD students, student-designed majors, study abroad, summer session for credit. *ROTC:* Army (c), Air Force (c).
**Library** BGSU Firelands College Library.
**Student Life** *Housing:* college housing not available. *Activities and Organizations:* drama/theater group, choral group, Society of Fandom and Gaming, Student Government, Student Theater Guild, Safe Space, Society of Leadership and Success. *Campus security:* 24-hour emergency response devices, late-night transport/escort service, patrols by trained security personnel.
**Athletics** *Intramural sports:* basketball M/W, bowling M/W, football M, table tennis M/W, volleyball M/W.
**Costs (2018–19)** *Tuition:* state resident $4706 full-time, $196 per credit hour part-time; nonresident $12,014 full-time, $510 per credit hour part-time. Full-time tuition and fees vary according to location and reciprocity agreements. Part-time tuition and fees vary according to location and reciprocity agreements. *Required fees:* $240 full-time, $9 per credit hour part-time, $120 per term part-time. *Payment plan:* installment. *Waivers:* children of alumni, senior citizens, and employees or children of employees.
**Applying** *Options:* electronic application, early admission, deferred entrance. *Application fee:* $45. *Required:* high school transcript. *Application deadlines:* 8/6 (freshmen), 8/6 (transfers). *Notification:* continuous (freshmen), continuous (transfers).
**Freshman Application Contact** Dr. Megan Zahler, Assistant Dean for Strategic Enrollment Planning, Bowling Green State University–Firelands College, One University Drive, Huron, OH 44839-9791. *Phone:* 419-433-5560. *Toll-free phone:* 800-322-4787. *Fax:* 419-372-0604. *E-mail:* mzahler@bgsu.edu.
*Website:* http://www.firelands.bgsu.edu/.

# Bradford School
## Columbus, Ohio

**Freshman Application Contact** Admissions Office, Bradford School, 2469 Stelzer Road, Columbus, OH 43219. *Phone:* 614-416-6200. *Toll-free phone:* 800-678-7981. *Website:* http://www.bradfordschoolcolumbus.edu/.

# Brightwood College, Dayton Campus
## Dayton, Ohio

**Freshman Application Contact** Brightwood College, Dayton Campus, 2800 East River Road, Dayton, OH 45439. *Phone:* 937-294-6155. *Toll-free phone:* 866-543-0208. *Website:* http://www.brightwood.edu/.

# Bryant & Stratton College–Eastlake Campus
## Eastlake, Ohio

**Freshman Application Contact** Ms. Melanie Pettit, Director of Admissions, Bryant & Stratton College–Eastlake Campus, 35350 Curtis Boulevard, Eastlake, OH 44095. *Phone:* 440-510-1112. *Website:* http://www.bryantstratton.edu/.

# Bryant & Stratton College–Parma Campus
## Parma, Ohio

**Freshman Application Contact** Bryant & Stratton College–Parma Campus, 12955 Snow Road, Parma, OH 44130-1005. *Phone:* 216-265-3151. *Toll-free phone:* 866-948-0571. *Website:* http://www.bryantstratton.edu/.

# Central Ohio Technical College
## Newark, Ohio

- **State-supported** 2-year, founded 1971, part of Ohio Department of Higher Education
- **Small-town** 177-acre campus with easy access to Columbus
- **Endowment** $3.0 million
- **Coed,** 3,479 undergraduate students, 20% full-time, 67% women, 33% men

**Undergraduates** 692 full-time, 2,787 part-time. 1% are from out of state; 11% Black or African American, non-Hispanic/Latino; 2% Hispanic/Latino; 2% Asian, non-Hispanic/Latino; 0.1% Native Hawaiian or other Pacific Islander, non-Hispanic/Latino; 0.3% American Indian or Alaska Native, non-Hispanic/Latino; 3% Two or more races, non-Hispanic/Latino; 12% Race/ethnicity unknown; 0.1% international; 10% transferred in. *Retention:* 53% of full-time freshmen returned.
**Freshmen** *Admission:* 400 enrolled.
**Faculty** *Total:* 312, 18% full-time. *Student/faculty ratio:* 11:1.
**Majors** Accounting; advertising; architectural drafting and CAD/CADD; business administration and management; CAD/CADD drafting/design technology; civil drafting and CAD/CADD; civil engineering technology; computer graphics; computer programming; computer support specialist; criminal justice/law enforcement administration; criminal justice/police science; culinary arts; diagnostic medical sonography and ultrasound technology; early childhood education; electrical, electronic and communications engineering technology; emergency medical technology (EMT paramedic); fire science/firefighting; forensic science and technology; health services/allied health/health sciences; human services; liberal arts and sciences/liberal studies; licensed practical/vocational nurse training; manufacturing engineering technology; mechanical engineering/mechanical technology; radiologic technology/science; registered nursing/registered nurse; surgical technology; web page, digital/multimedia and information resources design.
**Academics** *Calendar:* semesters. *Degree:* certificates and associate. *Special study options:* academic remediation for entering students, accelerated degree program, adult/continuing education programs, advanced placement credit, cooperative education, distance learning, double majors, internships, off-campus study, part-time degree program, services for LD students, student-designed majors, summer session for credit.
**Library** Newark Campus Library. *Books:* 45,000 (physical); *Serial titles:* 170 (physical). Students can reserve study rooms.
**Student Life** *Housing:* college housing not available. *Activities and Organizations:* drama/theater group, choral group, Radiologic Technology Student Organization, Phi Theta Kappa, Society of Engineering Technology, The Human Services Committee, Digital Media Design Coshocton. *Campus security:* 24-hour emergency response devices and patrols, student patrols, late-night transport/escort service. *Student services:* personal/psychological counseling, veterans affairs office.
**Athletics** *Intramural sports:* badminton M/W, basketball M/W, sand volleyball M/W, soccer M/W, softball M/W, table tennis M/W, ultimate Frisbee M/W, volleyball M/W.
**Costs (2017–18)** *One-time required fee:* $80. *Tuition:* state resident $4296 full-time, $179 per semester hour part-time; nonresident $7056 full-time, $294 per semester hour part-time. Full-time tuition and fees vary according to course load. Part-time tuition and fees vary according to course load. *Payment plan:* installment. *Waivers:* senior citizens and employees or children of employees.
**Financial Aid** Of all full-time matriculated undergraduates who enrolled in 2016, 43 Federal Work-Study jobs (averaging $4000).
**Applying** *Options:* electronic application, early admission, deferred entrance. *Required for some:* high school transcript. *Application deadlines:* rolling (freshmen), rolling (transfers).
**Admissions Office Contact** Central Ohio Technical College, 1179 University Drive, Newark, OH 43055-1767. *Toll-free phone:* 800-9NEWARK. *Website:* http://www.cotc.edu/.

# Chatfield College
## St. Martin, Ohio

**Freshman Application Contact** Chatfield College, 20918 State Route 251, St. Martin, OH 45118-9705. *Phone:* 513-875-3344 Ext. 138. *Website:* http://www.chatfield.edu/.

# The Christ College of Nursing and Health Sciences
## Cincinnati, Ohio

**Freshman Application Contact** Mr. Bradley Jackson, Admissions, The Christ College of Nursing and Health Sciences, 2139 Auburn Avenue, Cincinnati, OH 45219. *Phone:* 513-585-0016. *E-mail:* bradley.jackson@thechristcollege.edu. *Website:* http://www.thechristcollege.edu/.

# Cincinnati State Technical and Community College
## Cincinnati, Ohio

**Freshman Application Contact** Ms. Gabriele Boeckermann, Director of Admission, Cincinnati State Technical and Community College, Office of Admissions, 3520 Central Parkway, Cincinnati, OH 45223-2690. *Phone:* 513-569-1550. *Toll-free phone:* 877-569-0115. *Fax:* 513-569-1562. *E-mail:* adm@cincinnatistate.edu. *Website:* http://www.cincinnatistate.edu/.

# Clark State Community College
## Springfield, Ohio

**Freshman Application Contact** Admissions Office, Clark State Community College, PO Box 570, Springfield, OH 45501-0570. *Phone:* 937-328-3858. *Fax:* 937-328-6133. *E-mail:* admissions@clarkstate.edu. *Website:* http://www.clarkstate.edu/.

# Columbus Culinary Institute at Bradford School
## Columbus, Ohio

**Freshman Application Contact** Admissions Office, Columbus Culinary Institute at Bradford School, 2435 Stelzer Road, Columbus, OH 43219. *Phone:* 614-944-4200. *Toll-free phone:* 877-506-5006. *Website:* http://www.columbusculinary.com/.

# Columbus State Community College
## Columbus, Ohio

- **State-supported** 2-year, founded 1963, part of Ohio Department of Higher Education
- **Urban** 188-acre campus with easy access to Columbus
- **Coed**

**Undergraduates** 7,025 full-time, 20,084 part-time. Students come from 49 states and territories; 81 other countries; 2% are from out of state; 18% Black or African American, non-Hispanic/Latino; 5% Hispanic/Latino; 3% Asian, non-Hispanic/Latino; 0.1% Native Hawaiian or other Pacific Islander, non-Hispanic/Latino; 0.4% American Indian or Alaska Native, non-Hispanic/Latino; 3% Two or more races, non-Hispanic/Latino; 6% Race/ethnicity unknown; 1% international; 14% transferred in. *Retention:* 61% of full-time freshmen returned.
**Faculty** *Student/faculty ratio:* 19:1.
**Academics** *Calendar:* semesters. *Degree:* certificates and associate. *Special study options:* academic remediation for entering students, adult/continuing education programs, advanced placement credit, cooperative education, distance learning, double majors, English as a second language, honors programs, independent study, internships, off-campus study, part-time degree program, services for LD students, student-designed majors, study abroad, summer session for credit. *ROTC:* Army (c).
**Library** Columbus State Library plus 1 other. *Books:* 32,991 (physical), 52,921 (digital/electronic); *Databases:* 185. Weekly public service hours: 76.
**Student Life** *Campus security:* 24-hour emergency response devices and patrols, late-night transport/escort service, Vehicle Assistance with lockouts and jump starts.
**Athletics** Member NCAA, NJCAA. All NCAA Division III.
**Costs (2017–18)** *One-time required fee:* $50. *Tuition:* state resident $3808 full-time, $136 per credit hour part-time; nonresident $8430 full-time, $301 per credit hour part-time. *Required fees:* $60 per term part-time. *Payment plans:* installment, deferred payment.

**Financial Aid** Of all full-time matriculated undergraduates who enrolled in 2016, 133 Federal Work-Study jobs (averaging $1500).
**Applying** *Options:* electronic application, early admission, deferred entrance. *Application fee:* $50. *Required for some:* essay or personal statement, high school transcript, minimum 3.0 GPA, 1 letter of recommendation, interview. *Recommended:* high school transcript.
**Freshman Application Contact** Director of Admissions, Columbus State Community College, 550 E. Spring Street, Columbus, OH 43215. *Phone:* 614-287-2669. *Toll-free phone:* 800-621-6407 Ext. 2669. *Fax:* 614-287-6019. *Website:* http://www.cscc.edu/.

# Cuyahoga Community College
## Cleveland, Ohio

**Freshman Application Contact** Mr. Kevin McDaniel, Director of Admissions and Records, Cuyahoga Community College, Cleveland, OH 44115. *Phone:* 216-987-4030. *Toll-free phone:* 800-954-8742. *Fax:* 216-696-2567. *Website:* http://www.tri-c.edu/.

# Davis College
## Toledo, Ohio

**Freshman Application Contact** Mr. Timothy Brunner, Davis College, 4747 Monroe Street, Toledo, OH 43623-4307. *Phone:* 419-473-2700. *Toll-free phone:* 800-477-7021. *Fax:* 419-473-2472. *E-mail:* tbrunner@daviscollege.edu. *Website:* http://www.daviscollege.edu/.

# Daymar College
## Columbus, Ohio

**Freshman Application Contact** Holly Hankinson, Admissions Office, Daymar College, 2745 Winchester Pike, Columbus, OH 43232. *Phone:* 740-687-6126. *Toll-free phone:* 877-258-7796. *E-mail:* hhankinson@daymarcollege.edu. *Website:* http://www.daymarcollege.edu/.

# Eastern Gateway Community College
## Steubenville, Ohio

- **State and locally supported** 2-year, founded 1966, part of Ohio Board of Regents
- **Small-town** 83-acre campus with easy access to Pittsburgh
- **Endowment** $448,293
- **Coed,** 8,546 undergraduate students, 21% full-time, 66% women, 34% men

**Undergraduates** 1,770 full-time, 6,776 part-time. Students come from 50 states and territories; 1 other country; 53% are from out of state; 19% Black or African American, non-Hispanic/Latino; 9% Hispanic/Latino; 1% Asian, non-Hispanic/Latino; 0.5% Native Hawaiian or other Pacific Islander, non-Hispanic/Latino; 0.5% American Indian or Alaska Native, non-Hispanic/Latino; 4% Two or more races, non-Hispanic/Latino; 1% Race/ethnicity unknown; 0.8% transferred in.
**Freshmen** *Admission:* 1,594 enrolled.
**Faculty** *Total:* 237, 18% full-time. *Student/faculty ratio:* 23:1.
**Majors** Accounting; administrative assistant and secretarial science; business administration and management; child-care and support services management; computer engineering related; corrections; criminal justice/police science; data processing and data processing technology; dental assisting; drafting and design technology; electrical, electronic and communications engineering technology; emergency medical technology (EMT paramedic); industrial radiologic technology; industrial technology; legal administrative assistant/secretary; licensed practical/vocational nurse training; mechanical engineering/mechanical technology; medical administrative assistant and medical secretary; medical/clinical assistant; real estate; respiratory care therapy.
**Academics** *Calendar:* semesters. *Degree:* certificates and associate. *Special study options:* academic remediation for entering students, accelerated degree program, adult/continuing education programs, cooperative education, distance learning, double majors, off-campus study, part-time degree program, services for LD students, summer session for credit.
**Library** Eastern Gateway Community College Library. *Books:* 15,948 (physical); *Serial titles:* 6 (physical), 29,684 (digital/electronic); *Databases:* 142.
**Student Life** *Housing:* college housing not available. *Activities and Organizations:* Student Senate, Phi Theta Kappa. *Campus security:* 24-hour emergency response devices, day and evening security. *Student services:* veterans affairs office.
**Athletics** Member NJCAA. *Intramural sports:* softball M/W.
**Standardized Tests** *Required for some:* SAT or ACT (for admission).

**Financial Aid** Of all full-time matriculated undergraduates who enrolled in 2016, 30 Federal Work-Study jobs (averaging $1500).
**Applying** *Options:* electronic application, early admission, deferred entrance. *Application fee:* $20. *Required for some:* high school transcript. *Notification:* continuous (freshmen), continuous (transfers).
**Freshman Application Contact** Ms. Marlise Barker, Registrar, Eastern Gateway Community College, 4000 Sunset Boulevard, Steubenville, OH 43952. *Phone:* 740-264-5591 Ext. 1611. *Toll-free phone:* 800-68-COLLEGE. *E-mail:* mbarker@egcc.edu.
*Website:* http://www.egcc.edu/.

## Edison State Community College
### Piqua, Ohio

- **State-supported** 2-year, founded 1973, part of Ohio Board of Regents
- **Small-town** 131-acre campus with easy access to Dayton, Columbus, Cincinnati
- **Coed,** 3,248 undergraduate students, 23% full-time, 60% women, 40% men

**Undergraduates** 753 full-time, 2,495 part-time. Students come from 8 states and territories; 12% are from out of state; 5% Black or African American, non-Hispanic/Latino; 2% Hispanic/Latino; 0.9% Asian, non-Hispanic/Latino; 0.3% Native Hawaiian or other Pacific Islander, non-Hispanic/Latino; 0.2% American Indian or Alaska Native, non-Hispanic/Latino; 2% Two or more races, non-Hispanic/Latino; 2% Race/ethnicity unknown; 0.4% transferred in. *Retention:* 83% of full-time freshmen returned.
**Freshmen** *Admission:* 462 enrolled. *Average high school GPA:* 2.9.
**Faculty** *Total:* 178, 28% full-time, 9% with terminal degrees. *Student/faculty ratio:* 17:1.
**Majors** Accounting; art; biology/biological sciences; business administration and management; child development; clinical/medical laboratory technology; computer and information sciences; computer and information systems security; computer programming; computer systems networking and telecommunications; criminal justice/police science; dramatic/theater arts; economics; education; electrical, electronic and communications engineering technology; electromechanical technology; English; executive assistant/executive secretary; geology/earth science; health/medical preparatory programs related; history; human resources management; industrial technology; legal assistant/paralegal; liberal arts and sciences/liberal studies; logistics, materials, and supply chain management; manufacturing engineering technology; marketing/marketing management; mathematics; mechanical drafting and CAD/CADD; medical administrative assistant and medical secretary; medical/clinical assistant; medium/heavy vehicle and truck technology; philosophy and religious studies related; physical therapy technology; prenursing studies; psychology; registered nursing/registered nurse; social work; speech communication and rhetoric.
**Academics** *Calendar:* semesters. *Degrees:* certificates, associate, and postbachelor's certificates. *Special study options:* academic remediation for entering students, accelerated degree program, adult/continuing education programs, advanced placement credit, distance learning, double majors, English as a second language, honors programs, independent study, internships, off-campus study, part-time degree program, services for LD students, student-designed majors, summer session for credit.
**Library** Edison Community College Library. *Books:* 18,825 (physical), 112,623 (digital/electronic); *Serial titles:* 61 (physical), 11,044 (digital/electronic); *Databases:* 149. Weekly public service hours: 50; students can reserve study rooms.
**Student Life** *Housing:* college housing not available. *Activities and Organizations:* drama/theater group, student-run newspaper. *Campus security:* late-night transport/escort service, 18-hour patrols by trained security personnel. *Student services:* health clinic, veterans affairs office.
**Athletics** Member NJCAA. *Intercollegiate sports:* baseball M(s), basketball M(s)/W(s), softball W, volleyball W(s).
**Costs (2018–19)** *Tuition:* state resident $4399 full-time, $147 per credit hour part-time; nonresident $8008 full-time, $267 per credit hour part-time. *Payment plan:* installment. *Waivers:* senior citizens and employees or children of employees.
**Financial Aid** Of all full-time matriculated undergraduates who enrolled in 2016, 42 Federal Work-Study jobs (averaging $3000).
**Applying** *Options:* electronic application. *Required:* high school transcript. *Application deadlines:* rolling (freshmen), rolling (transfers).
**Freshman Application Contact** Dr. Loleta Collins, Director of Student Services, Edison State Community College, 1973 Edison Drive, Piqua, OH 45356. *Phone:* 937-778-7983. *E-mail:* lcollins@edisonohio.edu.
*Website:* http://www.edisonohio.edu/.

## ETI Technical College of Niles
### Niles, Ohio

**Freshman Application Contact** Ms. Diane Marsteller, Director of Admissions, ETI Technical College of Niles, 2076 Youngstown-Warren Road, Niles, OH 44446-4398. *Phone:* 330-652-9919 Ext. 16. *Fax:* 330-652-4399. *E-mail:* dianemarsteller@eticollege.edu. *Website:* http://eticollege.edu/.

## Fortis College
### Centerville, Ohio

**Freshman Application Contact** Fortis College, 555 East Alex Bell Road, Centerville, OH 45459. *Phone:* 937-433-3410. *Toll-free phone:* 855-4-FORTIS. *Website:* http://www.fortis.edu/.

## Fortis College
### Cincinnati, Ohio

**Admissions Office Contact** Fortis College, 11499 Chester Road, Suite 200, Cincinnati, OH 45246. *Toll-free phone:* 855-4-FORTIS. *Website:* http://www.fortis.edu/.

## Fortis College
### Cuyahoga Falls, Ohio

**Freshman Application Contact** Admissions Office, Fortis College, 2545 Bailey Road, Cuyahoga Falls, OH 44221. *Phone:* 330-923-9959. *Toll-free phone:* 855-4-FORTIS. *Fax:* 330-923-0886. *Website:* http://www.fortis.edu/.

## Fortis College
### Ravenna, Ohio

**Freshman Application Contact** Admissions Office, Fortis College, 653 Enterprise Parkway, Ravenna, OH 44266. *Toll-free phone:* 855-4-FORTIS. *Website:* http://www.fortis.edu/.

## Fortis College
### Westerville, Ohio

**Admissions Office Contact** Fortis College, 4151 Executive Parkway, Suite 120, Westerville, OH 43081. *Toll-free phone:* 855-4-FORTIS. *Website:* http://www.fortis.edu/.

## Good Samaritan College of Nursing and Health Science
### Cincinnati, Ohio

**Freshman Application Contact** Admissions Office, Good Samaritan College of Nursing and Health Science, 375 Dixmyth Avenue, Cincinnati, OH 45220. *Phone:* 513-862-2743. *Fax:* 513-862-3572. *Website:* http://www.gscollege.edu/.

## Herzing University
### Akron, Ohio

**Admissions Office Contact** Herzing University, 1600 South Arlington Street, Suite 100, Akron, OH 44306. *Toll-free phone:* 800-596-0724. *Website:* http://www.herzing.edu/akron.

## Herzing University
### Toledo, Ohio

**Admissions Office Contact** Herzing University, 5212 Hill Avenue, Toledo, OH 43615. *Toll-free phone:* 800-596-0724. *Website:* http://www.herzing.edu/toledo.

## Hocking College
### Nelsonville, Ohio

**Freshman Application Contact** Hocking College, 3301 Hocking Parkway, Nelsonville, OH 45764-9588. *Phone:* 740-753-3591 Ext. 7080. *Website:* http://www.hocking.edu/.

# Hondros College
## Westerville, Ohio

**Director of Admissions** Ms. Carol Thomas, Operations Manager, Hondros College, 4140 Executive Parkway, Westerville, OH 43081-3855. *Phone:* 614-508-7244. *Toll-free phone:* 888-HONDROS. *Website:* http://www.hondros.edu/.

# International College of Broadcasting
## Dayton, Ohio

- **Proprietary** 2-year, founded 1968
- **Urban** campus with easy access to Dayton
- **Coed**

**Academics** *Calendar:* semesters. *Degree:* diplomas and associate. *Special study options:* academic remediation for entering students, internships, services for LD students.

**Applying** *Options:* early admission. *Required:* high school transcript, interview.

**Freshman Application Contact** International College of Broadcasting, 6 South Smithville Road, Dayton, OH 45431-1833. *Phone:* 937-258-8251. *Toll-free phone:* 800-517-7284. *Website:* http://www.icb.edu/.

# James A. Rhodes State College
## Lima, Ohio

**Freshman Application Contact** Traci Cox, Director, Office of Admissions, James A. Rhodes State College, Lima, OH 45804-3597. *Phone:* 419-995-8040. *E-mail:* cox.t@rhodesstate.edu. *Website:* http://www.rhodesstate.edu/.

# Kent State University at Ashtabula
## Ashtabula, Ohio

- **State-supported** primarily 2-year, founded 1958, part of Kent State University System
- **Small-town** 83-acre campus with easy access to Cleveland
- **Coed,** 1,971 undergraduate students, 52% full-time, 64% women, 36% men

**Undergraduates** 1,027 full-time, 944 part-time. Students come from 25 states and territories; 3 other countries; 5% are from out of state; 5% Black or African American, non-Hispanic/Latino; 5% Hispanic/Latino; 1% Asian, non-Hispanic/Latino; 0.2% Native Hawaiian or other Pacific Islander, non-Hispanic/Latino; 0.2% American Indian or Alaska Native, non-Hispanic/Latino; 3% Two or more races, non-Hispanic/Latino; 2% Race/ethnicity unknown; 0.4% international; 4% transferred in. *Retention:* 51% of full-time freshmen returned.

**Freshmen** *Admission:* 375 applied, 370 admitted, 232 enrolled. *Average high school GPA:* 2.8. *Test scores:* SAT evidence-based reading and writing scores over 500: 83%; SAT math scores over 500: 50%; ACT scores over 18: 64%; SAT evidence-based reading and writing scores over 600: 33%; ACT scores over 24: 10%; SAT evidence-based reading and writing scores over 700: 17%; ACT scores over 30: 1%.

**Faculty** *Total:* 99, 51% full-time. *Student/faculty ratio:* 20:1.

**Majors** Accounting technology and bookkeeping; administrative assistant and secretarial science; aerospace, aeronautical and astronautical/space engineering; business administration and management; business/commerce; computer programming (specific applications); computer technology/computer systems technology; criminal justice/safety; English; general studies; health and medical administrative services related; health/medical preparatory programs related; hospitality administration; liberal arts and sciences and humanities related; medical radiologic technology; occupational therapist assistant; physical therapy technology; psychology; registered nursing/registered nurse; respiratory care therapy; speech communication and rhetoric; viticulture and enology.

**Academics** *Calendar:* semesters. *Degrees:* certificates, associate, and bachelor's (also offers some upper-level and graduate courses). *Special study options:* academic remediation for entering students, advanced placement credit, distance learning, double majors, independent study, internships, part-time degree program, services for LD students, student-designed majors, study abroad, summer session for credit. *ROTC:* Army (c), Air Force (c).

**Library** Kent State at Ashtabula Library. Weekly public service hours: 56.

**Student Life** *Housing:* college housing not available. *Activities and Organizations:* Student Government, Student Veterans Association, Student Nurses Association, Student Occupational Therapy Association, Media Club. *Campus security:* 24-hour emergency response devices. *Student services:* veterans affairs office.

**Athletics** *Intramural sports:* volleyball M(c)/W(c).

**Standardized Tests** *Required for some:* SAT or ACT (for admission). *Recommended:* SAT or ACT (for admission).

**Costs (2018–19)** *One-time required fee:* $150. *Tuition:* state resident $5664 full-time, $258 per credit hour part-time; nonresident $14,196 full-time, $620 per credit hour part-time. Full-time tuition and fees vary according to course level and course load. Part-time tuition and fees vary according to course level and course load. *Payment plan:* installment. *Waivers:* senior citizens and employees or children of employees.

**Financial Aid** Of all full-time matriculated undergraduates who enrolled in 2017, 453 applied for aid, 401 were judged to have need, 21 had their need fully met. 13 Federal Work-Study jobs (averaging $3234). In 2017, 19 non-need-based awards were made. *Average percent of need met:* 57%. *Average financial aid package:* $7604. *Average need-based loan:* $3887. *Average need-based gift aid:* $5044. *Average non-need-based aid:* $1544.

**Applying** *Options:* electronic application, deferred entrance. *Application fee:* $40. *Required:* high school transcript. *Application deadlines:* 8/1 (freshmen), rolling (transfers). *Notification:* continuous (freshmen), continuous (transfers).

**Freshman Application Contact** Megan Krippel, Admissions Coordinator, Kent State University at Ashtabula, 3300 Lake Road West, Ashtabula, OH 44004. *Phone:* 440-964-4277. *Fax:* 440-964-4269. *E-mail:* ashtabula_admissions@kent.edu. *Website:* http://www.ashtabula.kent.edu/.

# Kent State University at East Liverpool
## East Liverpool, Ohio

- **State-supported** primarily 2-year, founded 1967, part of Kent State University System
- **Small-town** 3-acre campus with easy access to Pittsburgh, Youngstown
- **Coed,** 1,174 undergraduate students, 54% full-time, 68% women, 32% men

**Undergraduates** 635 full-time, 539 part-time. Students come from 13 states and territories; 10 other countries; 6% are from out of state; 5% Black or African American, non-Hispanic/Latino; 2% Hispanic/Latino; 0.6% Asian, non-Hispanic/Latino; 0.2% American Indian or Alaska Native, non-Hispanic/Latino; 4% Two or more races, non-Hispanic/Latino; 2% Race/ethnicity unknown; 0.6% international; 4% transferred in. *Retention:* 65% of full-time freshmen returned.

**Freshmen** *Admission:* 83 applied, 82 admitted, 66 enrolled. *Average high school GPA:* 2.8. *Test scores:* ACT scores over 18: 83%; ACT scores over 24: 7%.

**Faculty** *Total:* 55, 38% full-time. *Student/faculty ratio:* 25:1.

**Majors** Accounting technology and bookkeeping; business/commerce; computer programming (specific applications); criminal justice/safety; English; general studies; legal assistant/paralegal; liberal arts and sciences and humanities related; occupational therapist assistant; physical therapy technology; psychology; registered nursing/registered nurse; speech communication and rhetoric.

**Academics** *Calendar:* semesters. *Degrees:* certificates, associate, and bachelor's. *Special study options:* academic remediation for entering students, accelerated degree program, adult/continuing education programs, advanced placement credit, distance learning, double majors, freshman honors college, honors programs, independent study, internships, part-time degree program, services for LD students, student-designed majors, study abroad, summer session for credit. *ROTC:* Army (c), Air Force (c).

**Library** Paul Blair Memorial Library. Weekly public service hours: 46.

**Student Life** *Housing:* college housing not available. *Activities and Organizations:* Undergraduate Student Government, Student Nurses Association, Environmental Club, Student Occupational Therapist Assistants, Physical Therapist Assistant Club. *Campus security:* 24-hour emergency response devices, student patrols, late-night transport/escort service. *Student services:* personal/psychological counseling, veterans affairs office.

**Standardized Tests** *Required for some:* SAT or ACT (for admission). *Recommended:* SAT or ACT (for admission).

**Costs (2018–19)** *One-time required fee:* $150. *Tuition:* state resident $5664 full-time, $258 per credit hour part-time; nonresident $14,196 full-time, $620 per credit hour part-time. Full-time tuition and fees vary according to course level and course load. Part-time tuition and fees vary according to course level and course load. *Payment plan:* installment. *Waivers:* senior citizens and employees or children of employees.

**Financial Aid** Of all full-time matriculated undergraduates who enrolled in 2017, 172 applied for aid, 152 were judged to have need, 8 had their need fully met. 4 Federal Work-Study jobs (averaging $2941). In 2017, 10 non-need-based awards were made. *Average percent of need met:* 56%. *Average financial aid package:* $7507. *Average need-based loan:* $3723. *Average need-based gift aid:* $4569. *Average non-need-based aid:* $2755.

**Applying** *Options:* electronic application, deferred entrance. *Application fee:* $40. *Required:* high school transcript. *Application deadlines:* 8/1 (freshmen), rolling (transfers). *Notification:* continuous (freshmen), continuous (transfers).
**Freshman Application Contact** Office of Admissions, Kent State University at East Liverpool, 400 East 4th Street, East Liverpool, OH 43920-3497. *Phone:* 330-385-3805.
*Website:* http://www.eliv.kent.edu/.

## Kent State University at Salem
### Salem, Ohio

- **State-supported** primarily 2-year, founded 1966, part of Kent State University System
- **Rural** 100-acre campus with easy access to Youngstown
- **Coed,** 1,694 undergraduate students, 63% full-time, 70% women, 30% men

**Undergraduates** 1,062 full-time, 632 part-time. Students come from 7 states and territories; 2% are from out of state; 4% Black or African American, non-Hispanic/Latino; 2% Hispanic/Latino; 0.9% Asian, non-Hispanic/Latino; 0.1% American Indian or Alaska Native, non-Hispanic/Latino; 2% Two or more races, non-Hispanic/Latino; 3% Race/ethnicity unknown; 0.1% international; 6% transferred in. *Retention:* 53% of full-time freshmen returned.
**Freshmen** *Admission:* 264 applied, 264 admitted, 175 enrolled. *Average high school GPA:* 2.9. *Test scores:* ACT scores over 18: 69%; ACT scores over 24: 13%.
**Faculty** *Total:* 115, 36% full-time. *Student/faculty ratio:* 19:1.
**Majors** Accounting technology and bookkeeping; administrative assistant and secretarial science; applied horticulture/horticulture operations; business administration and management; business/commerce; computer programming (specific applications); criminal justice/safety; early childhood education; education related; English; general studies; health and medical administrative services related; human development and family studies; liberal arts and sciences and humanities related; medical radiologic technology; psychology; registered nursing/registered nurse; speech communication and rhetoric.
**Academics** *Calendar:* semesters. *Degrees:* certificates, associate, and bachelor's (also offers some upper-level and graduate courses). *Special study options:* academic remediation for entering students, accelerated degree program, adult/continuing education programs, advanced placement credit, cooperative education, distance learning, double majors, freshman honors college, honors programs, independent study, part-time degree program, services for LD students, student-designed majors, study abroad, summer session for credit. *ROTC:* Army (c), Air Force (c).
**Library** Kent State Salem Library. *Books:* 23,500 (physical); *Serial titles:* 4,500 (physical).
**Student Life** *Housing:* college housing not available. *Campus security:* 24-hour emergency response devices, late-night transport/escort service. *Student services:* personal/psychological counseling.
**Standardized Tests** *Required for some:* SAT or ACT (for admission). *Recommended:* SAT or ACT (for admission).
**Costs (2017–18)** *One-time required fee:* $150. *Tuition:* state resident $5664 full-time, $258 per credit hour part-time; nonresident $14,028 full-time, $620 per credit hour part-time. Full-time tuition and fees vary according to course level and course load. Part-time tuition and fees vary according to course level and course load. *Payment plan:* installment. *Waivers:* senior citizens and employees or children of employees.
**Financial Aid** Of all full-time matriculated undergraduates who enrolled in 2017, 539 applied for aid, 447 were judged to have need, 37 had their need fully met. 18 Federal Work-Study jobs (averaging $1756). In 2017, 28 non-need-based awards were made. *Average percent of need met:* 59%. *Average financial aid package:* $7407. *Average need-based loan:* $3954. *Average need-based gift aid:* $4835. *Average non-need-based aid:* $1257.
**Applying** *Options:* electronic application, deferred entrance. *Application fee:* $40. *Required:* high school transcript. *Required for some:* essay or personal statement. *Application deadlines:* 12/15 (freshmen), 12/15 (transfers). *Notification:* continuous (freshmen), continuous (transfers).
**Freshman Application Contact** Office of Admissions, Kent State University at Salem, 2491 State Route 45 South, Salem, OH 44460-9412. *Phone:* 330-332-0361.
*Website:* http://www.salem.kent.edu/.

## Kent State University at Trumbull
### Warren, Ohio

- **State-supported** primarily 2-year, founded 1954, part of Kent State University System
- **Suburban** 438-acre campus with easy access to Akron, Youngstown
- **Coed,** 2,277 undergraduate students, 65% full-time, 62% women, 38% men

**Undergraduates** 1,476 full-time, 801 part-time. Students come from 6 states and territories; 3% are from out of state; 8% Black or African American, non-Hispanic/Latino; 3% Hispanic/Latino; 0.9% Asian, non-Hispanic/Latino; 0.1% Native Hawaiian or other Pacific Islander, non-Hispanic/Latino; 0.2% American Indian or Alaska Native, non-Hispanic/Latino; 3% Two or more races, non-Hispanic/Latino; 3% Race/ethnicity unknown; 0.4% international. *Retention:* 60% of full-time freshmen returned.
**Freshmen** *Admission:* 388 applied, 388 admitted. *Average high school GPA:* 2.7. *Test scores:* SAT evidence-based reading and writing scores over 500: 50%; SAT math scores over 500: 50%; ACT scores over 18: 68%; ACT scores over 24: 9%.
**Faculty** *Total:* 106, 48% full-time. *Student/faculty ratio:* 25:1.
**Majors** Accounting technology and bookkeeping; administrative assistant and secretarial science; business administration and management; business/commerce; computer programming (specific applications); criminal justice/safety; electrical and electronic engineering technologies related; emergency medical technology (EMT paramedic); English; environmental engineering technology; general studies; health/health-care administration; industrial production technologies related; industrial technology; legal assistant/paralegal; liberal arts and sciences and humanities related; mechanical engineering/mechanical technology; psychology; public health; registered nursing/registered nurse; speech communication and rhetoric; urban forestry.
**Academics** *Calendar:* semesters. *Degrees:* associate and bachelor's (also offers some upper-level and graduate courses). *Special study options:* academic remediation for entering students, adult/continuing education programs, advanced placement credit, distance learning, double majors, freshman honors college, honors programs, independent study, internships, part-time degree program, services for LD students, student-designed majors, summer session for credit. *ROTC:* Army (c), Air Force (c).
**Library** Gelbke Library at Kent State Trumbull. *Books:* 40,000 (physical), 100,000 (digital/electronic); *Serial titles:* 40 (physical); *Databases:* 459. Weekly public service hours: 56.
**Student Life** *Housing:* college housing not available. *Activities and Organizations:* drama/theater group, The National Society for Leadership and Success, Sigma Alpha Pi, Jurisprudence Organization, Student Nurses Association, Pride Alliance, S.E.E.D.S.. *Campus security:* 24-hour emergency response devices, late-night transport/escort service, patrols by trained security personnel during hours of operation. *Student services:* personal/psychological counseling.
**Athletics** *Intramural sports:* cross-country running M(c)/W(c).
**Standardized Tests** *Recommended:* SAT or ACT (for admission).
**Costs (2017–18)** *One-time required fee:* $150. *Tuition:* state resident $5664 full-time, $258 per credit hour part-time; nonresident $14,028 full-time, $620 per credit hour part-time. Full-time tuition and fees vary according to course level and course load. Part-time tuition and fees vary according to course level and course load. *Payment plan:* installment. *Waivers:* senior citizens and employees or children of employees.
**Financial Aid** Of all full-time matriculated undergraduates who enrolled in 2017, 725 applied for aid, 638 were judged to have need, 36 had their need fully met. 20 Federal Work-Study jobs (averaging $2713). In 2017, 27 non-need-based awards were made. *Average percent of need met:* 59%. *Average financial aid package:* $7668. *Average need-based loan:* $3896. *Average need-based gift aid:* $4965. *Average non-need-based aid:* $2303.
**Applying** *Options:* electronic application, deferred entrance. *Application fee:* $40. *Required:* high school transcript. *Application deadlines:* 8/15 (freshmen), 8/15 (transfers).
**Freshman Application Contact** Office of Enrollment Management, Kent State University at Trumbull, 4314 Mahoning Avenue, NW, Warren, OH 44483-1998. *Phone:* 330-675-8860. *E-mail:* trumbullinfo@kent.edu.
*Website:* http://www.trumbull.kent.edu/.

# Kent State University at Tuscarawas
## New Philadelphia, Ohio

- **State-supported** primarily 2-year, founded 1962, part of Kent State University System
- **Small-town** 180-acre campus with easy access to Akron, Canton
- **Coed,** 2,131 undergraduate students, 61% full-time, 57% women, 43% men

**Undergraduates** 1,299 full-time, 832 part-time. Students come from 8 states and territories; 3 other countries; 2% are from out of state; 4% Black or African American, non-Hispanic/Latino; 2% Hispanic/Latino; 0.7% Asian, non-Hispanic/Latino; 0.4% American Indian or Alaska Native, non-Hispanic/Latino; 2% Two or more races, non-Hispanic/Latino; 2% Race/ethnicity unknown; 0.5% international; 6% transferred in. *Retention:* 62% of full-time freshmen returned.

**Freshmen** *Admission:* 415 applied, 414 admitted, 288 enrolled. *Average high school GPA:* 3.0. *Test scores:* ACT scores over 18: 76%; ACT scores over 24: 16%; ACT scores over 30: 2%.

**Faculty** *Total:* 122, 39% full-time. *Student/faculty ratio:* 22:1.

**Majors** Accounting technology and bookkeeping; administrative assistant and secretarial science; agribusiness; business administration and management; business/commerce; CAD/CADD drafting/design technology; computer programming (specific applications); criminal justice/safety; early childhood education; education related; electrical and electronic engineering technologies related; engineering technology; English; general studies; industrial technology; liberal arts and sciences and humanities related; mechanical engineering/mechanical technology; psychology; registered nursing/registered nurse; speech communication and rhetoric; veterinary/animal health technology.

**Academics** *Calendar:* semesters. *Degrees:* certificates, diplomas, associate, and bachelor's (also offers some upper-level and graduate courses). *Special study options:* academic remediation for entering students, accelerated degree program, adult/continuing education programs, advanced placement credit, distance learning, double majors, freshman honors college, honors programs, independent study, internships, part-time degree program, services for LD students, student-designed majors, study abroad, summer session for credit. *ROTC:* Army (c), Air Force (c).

**Library** Kent State Tuscarawas Library. *Books:* 52,500 (physical), 12 (digital/electronic); *Serial titles:* 540 (physical).

**Student Life** *Housing:* college housing not available. *Activities and Organizations:* choral group, Student Nurses Association, Technology Club, Vet Tech Student Chapter, Realms of Roleplay, Vision. *Campus security:* 24-hour emergency response devices.

**Athletics** Member USCAA. *Intercollegiate sports:* baseball M, basketball M/W, cross-country running M/W, golf M/W, softball W, track and field M/W, volleyball W, wrestling M.

**Standardized Tests** *Recommended:* SAT or ACT (for admission).

**Costs (2017–18)** *One-time required fee:* $150. *Tuition:* state resident $5664 full-time, $258 per credit hour part-time; nonresident $14,028 full-time, $620 per credit hour part-time. Full-time tuition and fees vary according to course level and course load. Part-time tuition and fees vary according to course level and course load. *Payment plan:* installment. *Waivers:* senior citizens and employees or children of employees.

**Financial Aid** Of all full-time matriculated undergraduates who enrolled in 2017, 643 applied for aid, 542 were judged to have need, 65 had their need fully met. 21 Federal Work-Study jobs (averaging $2495). In 2017, 43 non-need-based awards were made. *Average percent of need met:* 63%. *Average financial aid package:* $6767. *Average need-based loan:* $3651. *Average need-based gift aid:* $4391. *Average non-need-based aid:* $2398.

**Applying** *Options:* electronic application, deferred entrance. *Application fee:* $40. *Required:* high school transcript. *Application deadlines:* 8/15 (freshmen), 8/15 (transfers). *Notification:* continuous (freshmen), continuous (transfers).

**Freshman Application Contact** Office of Admissions, Kent State University at Tuscarawas, 330 University Drive NE, New Philadelphia, OH 44663-9403. *Phone:* 330-339-3391. *E-mail:* infotusc@kent.edu. *Website:* http://www.tusc.kent.edu/.

# Lakeland Community College
## Kirtland, Ohio

- **State and locally supported** 2-year, founded 1967, part of Ohio Department of Higher Education
- **Suburban** 380-acre campus with easy access to Cleveland
- **Endowment** $35,367
- **Coed,** 7,581 undergraduate students, 29% full-time, 58% women, 42% men

**Undergraduates** 2,198 full-time, 5,383 part-time. Students come from 5 states and territories; 1 other country; 13% Black or African American, non-

Hispanic/Latino; 3% Hispanic/Latino; 1% Asian, non-Hispanic/Latino; 0.2% Native Hawaiian or other Pacific Islander, non-Hispanic/Latino; 0.3% American Indian or Alaska Native, non-Hispanic/Latino; 2% Two or more races, non-Hispanic/Latino; 2% Race/ethnicity unknown; 0.1% international; 5% transferred in.

**Freshmen** *Admission:* 805 enrolled.

**Faculty** *Total:* 405, 25% full-time. *Student/faculty ratio:* 17:1.

**Majors** Accounting; administrative assistant and secretarial science; biotechnology; business administration and management; child-care provision; civil engineering technology; clinical/medical laboratory technology; commercial and advertising art; computer engineering technology; computer programming (specific applications); computer systems analysis; computer systems networking and telecommunications; computer technology/computer systems technology; corrections; criminal justice/police science; dental hygiene; electrical, electronic and communications engineering technology; energy management and systems technology; fire prevention and safety technology; health professions related; homeland security, law enforcement, firefighting and protective services related; hospitality administration; instrumentation technology; legal assistant/paralegal; liberal arts and sciences/liberal studies; management information systems; marketing/marketing management; mechanical engineering/mechanical technology; medical radiologic technology; nuclear medical technology; ophthalmic technology; quality control technology; registered nursing/registered nurse; respiratory care therapy; restaurant, culinary, and catering management; sign language interpretation and translation; social work; surgical technology; tourism and travel services management.

**Academics** *Calendar:* semesters. *Degree:* certificates and associate. *Special study options:* academic remediation for entering students, adult/continuing education programs, advanced placement credit, cooperative education, distance learning, English as a second language, external degree program, independent study, internships, off-campus study, part-time degree program, services for LD students, study abroad, summer session for credit.

**Library** Lakeland Community College Library.

**Student Life** *Housing:* college housing not available. *Activities and Organizations:* drama/theater group, student-run newspaper, radio station, choral group, Campus Activities Board, Lakeland Student Government, Lakeland Signers, Gamer's Guild. *Campus security:* 24-hour emergency response devices and patrols, student patrols, late-night transport/escort service. *Student services:* health clinic, personal/psychological counseling, women's center, veterans affairs office.

**Athletics** Member NJCAA. *Intercollegiate sports:* baseball M(s), basketball M(s)/W(s), golf M(s), soccer M(s), softball W(s), volleyball W(s).

**Standardized Tests** *Required:* ACT Compass (for admission).

**Costs (2017–18)** *Tuition:* area resident $3287 full-time, $110 per credit hour part-time; state resident $4136 full-time, $138 per credit hour part-time; nonresident $9176 full-time, $306 per credit hour part-time. Full-time tuition and fees vary according to course load. Part-time tuition and fees vary according to course load. *Required fees:* $29 full-time, $14 per term part-time. *Payment plan:* installment. *Waivers:* senior citizens and employees or children of employees.

**Financial Aid** Of all full-time matriculated undergraduates who enrolled in 2015, 3,430 applied for aid, 2,959 were judged to have need, 469 had their need fully met. 63 Federal Work-Study jobs (averaging $3489). *Average percent of need met:* 56%. *Average financial aid package:* $7024. *Average need-based loan:* $3232. *Average need-based gift aid:* $5250.

**Applying** *Options:* electronic application, early admission, deferred entrance. *Application fee:* $15. *Required:* high school transcript. *Application deadlines:* 9/1 (freshmen), 9/1 (transfers). *Notification:* continuous until 9/1 (freshmen), continuous until 9/1 (transfers).

**Freshman Application Contact** Lakeland Community College, 7700 Clocktower Drive, Kirtland, OH 44094-5198. *Phone:* 440-525-7230. *Toll-free phone:* 800-589-8520. *Website:* http://www.lakelandcc.edu/.

# Lorain County Community College
## Elyria, Ohio

- **State and locally supported** 2-year, founded 1963, part of University System of Ohio
- **Suburban** 280-acre campus with easy access to Cleveland
- **Coed,** 11,042 undergraduate students, 27% full-time, 61% women, 39% men

**Undergraduates** 2,956 full-time, 8,086 part-time. Students come from 28 states and territories; 29 other countries; 0.6% are from out of state; 9% Black or African American, non-Hispanic/Latino; 10% Hispanic/Latino; 1% Asian, non-Hispanic/Latino; 0.1% Native Hawaiian or other Pacific Islander, non-Hispanic/Latino; 0.4% American Indian or Alaska Native, non-Hispanic/Latino; 4% Two or more races, non-Hispanic/Latino; 1% Race/ethnicity unknown; 0.6% international; 5% transferred in. *Retention:* 63% of full-time freshmen returned.

**Freshmen** *Admission:* 1,478 enrolled.

**Faculty** *Total:* 316, 20% full-time.

**Majors** Accounting; agroecology and sustainable agriculture; building/construction site management; business administration and management; clinical/medical laboratory technology; computer engineering technologies related; computer engineering technology; computer programming related; computer systems networking and telecommunications; computer technology/computer systems technology; construction engineering technology; corrections; criminal justice/police science; culinary arts; cyber/electronic operations and warfare; dental hygiene; diagnostic medical sonography and ultrasound technology; early childhood education; education (multiple levels); electrical, electronic and communications engineering technology; energy management and systems technology; entrepreneurship; fire science/firefighting; human resources management; liberal arts and sciences/liberal studies; manufacturing engineering technology; mechatronics, robotics, and automation engineering; medical/clinical assistant; medical radiologic technology; occupational therapist assistant; physical therapy technology; public administration; real estate; registered nursing/registered nurse; social work; solar energy technology; sport and fitness administration/management; surgical technology; tourism and travel services management; web page, digital/multimedia and information resources design; welding technology.

**Academics** *Calendar:* semesters. *Degree:* certificates and associate. *Special study options:* academic remediation for entering students, adult/continuing education programs, advanced placement credit, distance learning, double majors, English as a second language, independent study, internships, off-campus study, part-time degree program, services for LD students, student-designed majors, study abroad, summer session for credit.

**Library** Barbara and Mike Bass Library & Community Resource Center plus 1 other. *Books:* 88,354 (physical), 192,532 (digital/electronic); *Serial titles:* 919 (physical), 132,353 (digital/electronic); *Databases:* 178. Weekly public service hours: 54; students can reserve study rooms.

**Student Life** *Housing:* college housing not available. *Activities and Organizations:* drama/theater group, student-run newspaper, radio and television station, choral group, Phi Theta Kappa, Black Progressives, Los Unidos, Student Nurses Association, Student Dental Hygienist Club. *Campus security:* 24-hour emergency response devices and patrols, late-night transport/escort service. *Student services:* health clinic, personal/psychological counseling, women's center, legal services, veterans affairs office.

**Athletics** Member NJCAA. *Intercollegiate sports:* baseball M, basketball M/W, cross-country running M/W, soccer M(c)/W(c), softball W, tennis M(c)/W(c), volleyball W. *Intramural sports:* bowling M/W, football M/W, golf M/W, table tennis M/W, weight lifting M/W.

**Costs (2017–18)** *Tuition:* area resident $2796 full-time, $108 per credit hour part-time; state resident $3398 full-time, $131 per credit hour part-time; nonresident $7021 full-time, $270 per credit hour part-time. *Required fees:* $429 full-time, $16 per credit hour part-time. *Payment plans:* installment, deferred payment. *Waivers:* senior citizens and employees or children of employees.

**Financial Aid** Of all full-time matriculated undergraduates who enrolled in 2016, 2,391 applied for aid, 1,879 were judged to have need, 112 had their need fully met. 87 Federal Work-Study jobs (averaging $2065). In 2016, 262 non-need-based awards were made. *Average percent of need met:* 60%. *Average financial aid package:* $5399. *Average need-based loan:* $2146. *Average need-based gift aid:* $4652. *Average non-need-based aid:* $3061.

**Applying** *Options:* electronic application. *Required for some:* high school transcript. *Application deadlines:* rolling (freshmen), rolling (transfers). *Notification:* continuous (freshmen), continuous (transfers).

**Freshman Application Contact** Lorain County Community College, 1005 Abbe Road, North, Elyria, OH 44035. *Phone:* 440-366-7622. *Toll-free phone:* 800-995-5222 Ext. 4032.

*Website:* http://www.lorainccc.edu/.

## Marion Technical College
### Marion, Ohio

**Freshman Application Contact** Mr. Joel Liles, Dean of Enrollment Services, Marion Technical College, 1467 Mount Vernon Avenue, Marion, OH 43302. *Phone:* 740-389-4636 Ext. 249. *Fax:* 740-389-6136. *E-mail:* enroll@mtc.edu. *Website:* http://www.mtc.edu/.

## North Central State College
### Mansfield, Ohio

**Freshman Application Contact** Ms. Nikia L. Fletcher, Director of Admissions, North Central State College, 2441 Kenwood Circle, PO Box 698, Mansfield, OH 44901-0698. *Phone:* 419-755-4813. *Toll-free phone:* 888-755-4899. *E-mail:* nfletcher@ncstatecollege.edu. *Website:* http://www.ncstatecollege.edu/.

## Northwest State Community College
### Archbold, Ohio

**Freshman Application Contact** Mrs. Amanda Potts, Director of Admissions, Northwest State Community College, 22600 State Route 34, Archbold, OH 43502. *Phone:* 419-267-1364. *Toll-free phone:* 855-267-5511. *Fax:* 419-267-3688. *E-mail:* apotts@northweststate.edu. *Website:* http://www.northweststate.edu/.

## Ohio Business College
### Sandusky, Ohio

**Freshman Application Contact** Ohio Business College, 5202 Timber Commons Drive, Sandusky, OH 44870. *Phone:* 419-627-8345. *Toll-free phone:* 888-627-8345. *Website:* http://www.ohiobusinesscollege.edu/.

## Ohio Business College
### Sheffield Village, Ohio

**Freshman Application Contact** Ohio Business College, 5095 Waterford Drive, Sheffield Village, OH 44035. *Toll-free phone:* 888-514-3126. *Website:* http://www.ohiobusinesscollege.edu/.

## The Ohio State University Agricultural Technical Institute
### Wooster, Ohio

- **State-supported** 2-year, founded 1971, part of The Ohio State University
- **Small-town** 1942-acre campus with easy access to Cleveland, Columbus, Akron, Canton
- **Coed,** 757 undergraduate students, 93% full-time, 50% women, 50% men

**Undergraduates** 707 full-time, 50 part-time. Students come from 9 states and territories; 2% are from out of state; 4% transferred in. *Retention:* 67% of full-time freshmen returned.

**Freshmen** *Admission:* 630 applied, 584 admitted, 332 enrolled. *Test scores:* ACT scores over 18: 57%; ACT scores over 24: 11%.

**Faculty** *Total:* 70, 47% full-time, 33% with terminal degrees. *Student/faculty ratio:* 21:1.

**Majors** Agribusiness; agricultural business and management; agricultural business technology; agricultural communication/journalism; agricultural economics; agricultural mechanization; agricultural power machinery operation; agricultural teacher education; agronomy and crop science; animal/livestock husbandry and production; animal sciences; biology/biotechnology laboratory technician; building/construction site management; construction engineering technology; construction management; crop production; dairy husbandry and production; dairy science; environmental science; equestrian studies; floriculture/floristry management; greenhouse management; heavy equipment maintenance technology; horse husbandry/equine science and management; horticultural science; hydraulics and fluid power technology; industrial technology; landscaping and groundskeeping; livestock management; natural resources management and policy; natural resources management and policy related; plant nursery management; soil science and agronomy; turf and turfgrass management.

**Academics** *Calendar:* semesters. *Degree:* certificates, diplomas, and associate. *Special study options:* academic remediation for entering students, accelerated degree program, adult/continuing education programs, advanced placement credit, cooperative education, distance learning, double majors, independent study, internships, off-campus study, part-time degree program, services for LD students, student-designed majors, study abroad. *ROTC:* Army (c), Navy (c), Air Force (c).

**Library** Agricultural Technical Institute Library plus 1 other.

**Student Life** *Housing:* on-campus residence required for freshman year. *Options:* coed, special housing for students with disabilities. Campus housing is university owned. *Activities and Organizations:* Hoof-n-Hide Club, Collegiate FFA, Campus Crusade for Christ, Phi Theta Kappa, Community Council. *Campus security:* 24-hour emergency response devices and patrols, controlled dormitory access. *Student services:* personal/psychological counseling, veterans affairs office.

**Athletics** *Intramural sports:* archery M/W, badminton M/W, basketball M/W, bowling M/W, football M/W, racquetball M/W, soccer M/W, softball M/W, volleyball M/W, weight lifting M/W.

**Standardized Tests** *Required for some:* SAT or ACT (for admission).

**Costs (2017–18)** *Tuition:* state resident $7516 full-time, $305 per credit hour part-time; nonresident $26,620 full-time, $1111 per credit hour part-time. Full-time tuition and fees vary according to course load, location, and program.

Part-time tuition and fees vary according to course load, location, and program. *Room and board:* $8520; room only: $6920. Room and board charges vary according to board plan and location. *Payment plan:* installment. *Waivers:* senior citizens and employees or children of employees.

**Financial Aid** Of all full-time matriculated undergraduates who enrolled in 2010, 540 applied for aid, 474 were judged to have need, 25 had their need fully met. 64 Federal Work-Study jobs (averaging $2000). In 2010, 24 non-need-based awards were made. *Average percent of need met:* 44%. *Average financial aid package:* $6859. *Average need-based loan:* $3826. *Average need-based gift aid:* $4241. *Average non-need-based aid:* $2107.

**Applying** *Options:* electronic application. *Application fee:* $60. *Required:* high school transcript. *Application deadlines:* 6/1 (freshmen), 6/1 (transfers). *Notification:* continuous (freshmen).

**Freshman Application Contact** Ms. Julia Morris, Admissions Counselor, The Ohio State University Agricultural Technical Institute, 1328 Dover Road, Wooster, OH 44691. *Phone:* 330-287-1327. *Toll-free phone:* 800-647-8283 Ext. 1327. *Fax:* 330-287-1333. *E-mail:* morris.878@osu.edu. *Website:* http://www.ati.osu.edu/.

## Ohio Technical College
### Cleveland, Ohio

- **Proprietary** 2-year, founded 1969
- **Urban** 18-acre campus
- **Coed,** 883 undergraduate students, 100% full-time, 6% women, 94% men
- 100% of applicants were admitted

**Undergraduates** 883 full-time. Students come from 32 states and territories; 3 other countries; 41% are from out of state; 19% Black or African American, non-Hispanic/Latino; 8% Hispanic/Latino; 0.5% Asian, non-Hispanic/Latino; 0.2% Native Hawaiian or other Pacific Islander, non-Hispanic/Latino; 0.6% American Indian or Alaska Native, non-Hispanic/Latino; 2% Two or more races, non-Hispanic/Latino; 0.3% Race/ethnicity unknown; 3% transferred in. *Retention:* 69% of full-time freshmen returned.

**Freshmen** *Admission:* 251 applied, 251 admitted, 251 enrolled.

**Faculty** *Total:* 64, 80% full-time. *Student/faculty ratio:* 16:1.

**Majors** Autobody/collision and repair technology; automobile/automotive mechanics technology; diesel mechanics technology; high performance and custom engine technology; mechanic and repair technologies related; vehicle maintenance and repair technologies; welding technology.

**Academics** *Degree:* certificates, diplomas, and associate.

**Library** Ohio Technical College Library Resource Center. *Books:* 3,859 (physical), 21 (digital/electronic); *Databases:* 6. Weekly public service hours: 40.

**Student Life** *Housing Options:* Campus housing is provided by a third party. *Campus security:* late-night transport/escort service. *Student services:* personal/psychological counseling.

**Costs (2017–18)** *Comprehensive fee:* $28,856 includes full-time tuition ($27,660) and room and board ($1196). Full-time tuition and fees vary according to degree level and program. No tuition increase for student's term of enrollment. *Room and board:* college room only: $848. *Payment plan:* installment.

**Applying** *Required:* high school transcript, interview. *Application deadlines:* rolling (freshmen), rolling (out-of-state freshmen).

**Freshman Application Contact** Ohio Technical College, 1374 East 51st Street, Cleveland, OH 44103. *Phone:* 216-881-1700. *Toll-free phone:* 800-322-7000. *Website:* http://www.ohiotech.edu/.

## Ohio Valley College of Technology
### East Liverpool, Ohio

**Freshman Application Contact** Mr. Scott S. Rogers, Director, Ohio Valley College of Technology, 15258 State Route 170, East Liverpool, OH 43920. *Phone:* 330-385-1070. *Website:* http://www.ovct.edu/.

## Owens Community College
### Toledo, Ohio

**Freshman Application Contact** Ms. Meghan L. Schmidbauer, Director, Admissions, Owens Community College, PO Box 10000, Toledo, OH 43699. *Phone:* 567-661-2155. *Toll-free phone:* 800-GO-OWENS. *Fax:* 567-661-7734. *E-mail:* meghan_schmidbauer@owens.edu. *Website:* http://www.owens.edu/.

## Professional Skills Institute
### Maumee, Ohio

**Director of Admissions** Ms. Hope Finch, Director of Marketing, Professional Skills Institute, 1505 Holland Road, Maumee, OH 43537. *Phone:* 419-531-9610. *Website:* http://www.proskills.edu/.

## Remington College–Cleveland Campus
### Cleveland, Ohio

**Director of Admissions** Director of Recruitment, Remington College–Cleveland Campus, 14445 Broadway Avenue, Cleveland, OH 44125. *Phone:* 216-475-7520. *Toll-free phone:* 800-323-8122. *Fax:* 216-475-6055. *Website:* http://www.remingtoncollege.edu/.

## Rosedale Bible College
### Irwin, Ohio

- **Independent Mennonite** 2-year, founded 1952
- **Rural** campus with easy access to Columbus
- **Coed**

**Faculty** *Student/faculty ratio:* 14:1.

**Academics** *Calendar:* 4-1-4. *Degree:* associate. *Special study options:* adult/continuing education programs, cooperative education, independent study, internships, off-campus study, part-time degree program, services for LD students, study abroad. *ROTC:* Army (c), Navy (c), Air Force (c).

**Costs (2017–18)** *One-time required fee:* $50. *Comprehensive fee:* $14,381 includes full-time tuition ($8400), mandatory fees ($331), and room and board ($5650). Full-time tuition and fees vary according to course load. Part-time tuition: $280 per credit hour. *Required fees:* $70 per year part-time. *Room and board:* Room and board charges vary according to housing facility.

**Applying** *Options:* electronic application, early admission. *Application fee:* $50. *Required:* essay or personal statement, high school transcript, 2 letters of recommendation.

**Freshman Application Contact** Rosedale Bible College, 2270 Rosedale Road, Irwin, OH 43029-9501. *Phone:* 740-857-1311. *Website:* http://www.rosedale.edu/.

## Ross College
### Canton, Ohio

**Freshman Application Contact** Ross College, 4300 Munson Street NW, Canton, OH 44718. *Phone:* 330-494-1214. *Toll-free phone:* 866-815-5578. *Website:* http://www.rosseducation.edu/.

## Ross College
### Sylvania, Ohio

**Admissions Office Contact** Ross College, 5834 Monroe Street, Suite F-J, Sylvania, OH 43560. *Toll-free phone:* 866-815-5578. *Website:* http://www.rosseducation.edu/.

## School of Advertising Art
### Kettering, Ohio

- **Proprietary** 2-year, founded 1983
- **Suburban** 5-acre campus with easy access to Columbus
- **Coed,** 194 undergraduate students, 98% full-time, 70% women, 30% men

**Undergraduates** 191 full-time, 3 part-time. Students come from 3 states and territories; 9% are from out of state; 6% Black or African American, non-Hispanic/Latino; 4% Hispanic/Latino; 2% Asian, non-Hispanic/Latino; 1% American Indian or Alaska Native, non-Hispanic/Latino; 0.5% Two or more races, non-Hispanic/Latino; 0.5% Race/ethnicity unknown; 5% transferred in. *Retention:* 79% of full-time freshmen returned.

**Freshmen** *Admission:* 547 applied, 270 admitted, 96 enrolled. *Average high school GPA:* 3.1.

**Faculty** *Total:* 21, 57% full-time, 5% with terminal degrees. *Student/faculty ratio:* 14:1.

**Majors** Commercial and advertising art.

**Academics** *Calendar:* semesters. *Degree:* associate.

**Library** SAA Library. *Books:* 881 (physical), 45,000 (digital/electronic); *Serial titles:* 32 (physical); *Databases:* 2. Weekly public service hours: 60.

**Student Life** *Housing:* college housing not available. *Activities and Organizations:* Fine Art Club, Photography Club, Student Senate. *Student services:* personal/psychological counseling.

**Costs (2018–19)** *Tuition:* $27,778 full-time. Full-time tuition and fees vary according to class time, course level, course load, degree level, location, program, reciprocity agreements, and student level. *Required fees:* $1070 full-

time. *Payment plan:* installment. *Waivers:* employees or children of employees.
**Applying** *Options:* electronic application. *Required:* high school transcript, minimum 2.0 GPA, interview. *Required for some:* essay or personal statement, 2 letters of recommendation.
**Freshman Application Contact** Mrs. Mariesa Brewster, Director of Admissions, School of Advertising Art, 1725 E. David Rd., Kettering, OH 45440. *Phone:* 937-294-0592. *Toll-free phone:* 877-300-9866. *Fax:* 937-294-5869. *E-mail:* mariesa@saa.edu.
*Website:* http://www.saa.edu/.

## Sinclair Community College
### Dayton, Ohio

**Freshman Application Contact** Ms. Sara Smith, Director and Systems Manager, Outreach Services, Sinclair Community College, 444 West Third Street, Dayton, OH 45402-1460. *Phone:* 937-512-3060. *Toll-free phone:* 800-315-3000. *Fax:* 937-512-2393. *E-mail:* ssmith@sinclair.edu. *Website:* http://www.sinclair.edu/.

## Southern State Community College
### Hillsboro, Ohio

**Freshman Application Contact** Ms. Wendy Johnson, Director of Admissions, Southern State Community College, Hillsboro, OH 45133. *Phone:* 937-393-3431 Ext. 2720. *Toll-free phone:* 800-628-7722. *Fax:* 937-393-6682. *E-mail:* wjohnson@sscc.edu. *Website:* http://www.sscc.edu/.

## Stark State College
### North Canton, Ohio

- **State-related** 2-year, founded 1960, part of University System of Ohio
- **Suburban** 100-acre campus with easy access to Cleveland
- **Endowment** $6.2 million
- **Coed,** 11,028 undergraduate students, 28% full-time, 59% women, 41% men

**Undergraduates** 3,090 full-time, 7,938 part-time. Students come from 10 states and territories; 1 other country; 1% are from out of state; 13% Black or African American, non-Hispanic/Latino; 2% Hispanic/Latino; 2% Asian, non-Hispanic/Latino; 0.1% Native Hawaiian or other Pacific Islander, non-Hispanic/Latino; 0.4% American Indian or Alaska Native, non-Hispanic/Latino; 4% Two or more races, non-Hispanic/Latino; 7% Race/ethnicity unknown; 0.1% international; 8% transferred in.
**Freshmen** *Admission:* 1,422 enrolled. *Average high school GPA:* 2.7.
**Faculty** *Total:* 480, 39% full-time. *Student/faculty ratio:* 21:1.
**Majors** Accounting; accounting and finance; administrative assistant and secretarial science; biomedical technology; business administration and management; civil engineering technology; clinical/medical laboratory technology; computer and information sciences; computer programming (specific applications); computer systems networking and telecommunications; court reporting; dental hygiene; finance; health information/medical records administration; human services; industrial technology; legal administrative assistant/secretary; marketing/marketing management; mechanical engineering/mechanical technology; medical/clinical assistant; occupational therapy; operations management; physical therapy; registered nursing/registered nurse; respiratory care therapy; substance abuse/addiction counseling; surgical technology; web page, digital/multimedia and information resources design.
**Academics** *Calendar:* semesters. *Degree:* certificates and associate. *Special study options:* academic remediation for entering students, adult/continuing education programs, cooperative education, distance learning, double majors, external degree program, independent study, internships, off-campus study, part-time degree program, services for LD students, student-designed majors, summer session for credit.
**Library** Learning Resource Center plus 1 other.
**Student Life** *Activities and Organizations:* student-run newspaper, Phi Theta Kappa, Business Student Club, Institute of Management Accountants, Stark State College Association of Medical Assistants, Student Health Information Management Association. *Campus security:* 24-hour emergency response devices and patrols, student patrols, late-night transport/escort service, patrols by trained security personnel during hours of operation. *Student services:* personal/psychological counseling, veterans affairs office.
**Costs (2017–18)** *One-time required fee:* $95. *Tuition:* state resident $2796 full-time, $117 per credit hour part-time; nonresident $4980 full-time, $208 per credit hour part-time. Full-time tuition and fees vary according to course load and program. Part-time tuition and fees vary according to program. *Required fees:* $890 full-time, $37 per credit hour part-time, $30 per term part-time. *Payment plan:* installment. *Waivers:* senior citizens and employees or children of employees.

**Financial Aid** Of all full-time matriculated undergraduates who enrolled in 2014, 1,939 applied for aid, 1,697 were judged to have need, 6 had their need fully met. 74 Federal Work-Study jobs (averaging $2306). *Average need-based loan:* $2537. *Average need-based gift aid:* $4317.
**Applying** *Options:* electronic application. *Required:* high school transcript. *Application deadlines:* rolling (freshmen), rolling (out-of-state freshmen), rolling (transfers). *Notification:* continuous (freshmen), continuous (out-of-state freshmen), continuous (transfers).
**Freshman Application Contact** J. P. Cooney, Executive Director to Recruitment, Admissions and Marketing, Stark State College, 6200 Frank Road NE, Canton, OH 44720. *Phone:* 330-494-6170 Ext. 4401. *Toll-free phone:* 800-797-8275. *E-mail:* info@starkstate.edu. *Website:* http://www.starkstate.edu/.

## Stautzenberger College
### Brecksville, Ohio

**Admissions Office Contact** Stautzenberger College, 8001 Katherine Boulevard, Brecksville, OH 44141. *Toll-free phone:* 800-437-2997. *Website:* http://www.sctoday.edu/.

## Stautzenberger College
### Maumee, Ohio

**Director of Admissions** Ms. Karen Fitzgerald, Director of Admissions and Marketing, Stautzenberger College, 1796 Indian Wood Circle, Maumee, OH 43537. *Phone:* 419-866-0261. *Toll-free phone:* 800-552-5099. *Fax:* 419-867-9821. *E-mail:* klfitzgerald@stautzenberger.com. *Website:* http://www.sctoday.edu/maumee/.

## Terra State Community College
### Fremont, Ohio

**Freshman Application Contact** Mr. Heath Martin, Director of Admissions and Enrollment Services, Terra State Community College, 2830 Napoleon Road, Fremont, OH 43420. *Phone:* 419-559-2154. *Toll-free phone:* 866-AT-TERRA. *Fax:* 419-559-2352. *Website:* http://www.terra.edu/.

## The University of Akron Wayne College
### Orrville, Ohio

**Freshman Application Contact** Ms. Alicia Broadus, Student Services Counselor, The University of Akron Wayne College, Orrville, OH 44667. *Phone:* 800-221-8308 Ext. 8901. *Toll-free phone:* 800-221-8308. *Fax:* 330-684-8989. *E-mail:* wayneadmissions@uakron.edu. *Website:* http://www.wayne.uakron.edu/.

## University of Cincinnati Blue Ash College
### Cincinnati, Ohio

- **State-supported** primarily 2-year, founded 1967, part of Ohio Department of Higher Education
- **Suburban** 120-acre campus with easy access to Cincinnati
- **Endowment** $457,000
- **Coed**

**Undergraduates** 3,241 full-time, 1,824 part-time. Students come from 9 states and territories; 12 other countries; 3% are from out of state; 21% Black or African American, non-Hispanic/Latino; 3% Hispanic/Latino; 3% Asian, non-Hispanic/Latino; 0.1% Native Hawaiian or other Pacific Islander, non-Hispanic/Latino; 0.3% American Indian or Alaska Native, non-Hispanic/Latino; 3% Two or more races, non-Hispanic/Latino; 7% Race/ethnicity unknown; 2% international; 11% transferred in. *Retention:* 64% of full-time freshmen returned.
**Faculty** *Student/faculty ratio:* 16:1.
**Academics** *Calendar:* semesters. *Degrees:* certificates, associate, bachelor's, and postbachelor's certificates. *Special study options:* academic remediation for entering students, adult/continuing education programs, advanced placement credit, distance learning, double majors, off-campus study, part-time degree program, services for LD students, study abroad, summer session for credit. *ROTC:* Army (c), Air Force (c).
**Library** UC Blue Ash College Library. *Books:* 19,690 (physical). Weekly public service hours: 50; students can reserve study rooms.
**Student Life** *Campus security:* 24-hour emergency response devices and patrols, student patrols, late-night transport/escort service.
**Costs (2017–18)** *Tuition:* state resident $6010 full-time, $251 per credit hour part-time; nonresident $14,808 full-time, $617 per credit hour part-time. Full-

time tuition and fees vary according to course load, degree level, location, program, and reciprocity agreements. Part-time tuition and fees vary according to course load, degree level, location, and reciprocity agreements. *Required fees:* $736 full-time.

**Financial Aid** Of all full-time matriculated undergraduates who enrolled in 2016, 285 Federal Work-Study jobs (averaging $2903).

**Applying** *Options:* electronic application, deferred entrance. *Application fee:* $50. *Required:* high school transcript.

**Freshman Application Contact** University of Cincinnati Blue Ash College, 9555 Plainfield Road, Cincinnati, OH 45236-1007. *Phone:* 513-745-5700. *Website:* http://www.ucblueash.edu/.

## University of Cincinnati Clermont College
### Batavia, Ohio

- **State-supported** primarily 2-year, founded 1972, part of University of Cincinnati System
- **Rural** 91-acre campus with easy access to Cincinnati
- **Coed**

**Undergraduates** 1,595 full-time, 1,288 part-time. 4% are from out of state; 2% Black or African American, non-Hispanic/Latino; 3% Hispanic/Latino; 1% Asian, non-Hispanic/Latino; 0.1% Native Hawaiian or other Pacific Islander, non-Hispanic/Latino; 0.2% American Indian or Alaska Native, non-Hispanic/Latino; 2% Two or more races, non-Hispanic/Latino; 9% Race/ethnicity unknown; 0.3% international. *Retention:* 61% of full-time freshmen returned.

**Faculty** *Student/faculty ratio:* 13:1.

**Academics** *Calendar:* semesters. *Degrees:* certificates, associate, bachelor's, and postbachelor's certificates. *Special study options:* academic remediation for entering students, adult/continuing education programs, advanced placement credit, cooperative education, distance learning, double majors, independent study, internships, off-campus study, part-time degree program, services for LD students, student-designed majors, study abroad, summer session for credit. *ROTC:* Army (c).

**Library** UC Clermont College Library. Students can reserve study rooms.

**Student Life** *Campus security:* 24-hour emergency response devices and patrols.

**Athletics** Member USCAA.

**Costs (2017–18)** *Tuition:* state resident $5316 full-time, $222 per credit part-time; nonresident $12,548 full-time, $523 per credit part-time. Full-time tuition and fees vary according to course level, degree level, program, and reciprocity agreements. Part-time tuition and fees vary according to course level, degree level, program, and reciprocity agreements.

**Financial Aid** Of all full-time matriculated undergraduates who enrolled in 2017, 1,129 applied for aid, 941 were judged to have need, 18 had their need fully met. 64 Federal Work-Study jobs (averaging $3002). In 2017, 93. *Average percent of need met:* 35. *Average financial aid package:* $6273. *Average need-based loan:* $3498. *Average need-based gift aid:* $4834. *Average non-need-based aid:* $1611.

**Applying** *Options:* electronic application, deferred entrance. *Application fee:* $50. *Required:* high school transcript.

**Freshman Application Contact** Mrs. Jamie Adkins, University Services Associate, University of Cincinnati Clermont College, 4200 Clermont College Drive, Batavia, OH 45103. *Phone:* 513-732-5294. *Toll-free phone:* 866-446-2822. *Fax:* 513-732-5303. *E-mail:* jamie.adkins@uc.edu. *Website:* http://www.ucclermont.edu/.

## Valor Christian College
### Canal Winchester, Ohio

**Admissions Office Contact** Valor Christian College, 4595 Gender Road, PO Box 800, Canal Winchester, OH 43110. *Website:* http://www.valorcollege.edu/.

## Vatterott College
### Broadview Heights, Ohio

**Director of Admissions** Mr. Jack Chalk, Director of Admissions, Vatterott College, 5025 East Royalton Road, Broadview Heights, OH 44147. *Phone:* 440-526-1660. *Toll-free phone:* 888-553-6627. *Website:* http://www.vatterott.edu/.

## Vet Tech Institute at Bradford School
### Columbus, Ohio

**Freshman Application Contact** Admissions Office, Vet Tech Institute at Bradford School, 2469 Stelzer Road, Columbus, OH 43219. *Phone:* 800-678-7981. *Toll-free phone:* 800-678-7981. *Website:* http://columbus.vettechinstitute.edu/.

## Washington State Community College
### Marietta, Ohio

**Freshman Application Contact** Ms. Rebecca Peroni, Director of Admissions, Washington State Community College, 110 Colegate Drive, Marietta, OH 45750. *Phone:* 740-374-8716. *Fax:* 740-376-0257. *E-mail:* rperoni@wscc.edu. *Website:* http://www.wscc.edu/.

## Zane State College
### Zanesville, Ohio

**Director of Admissions** Mr. Paul Young, Director of Admissions, Zane State College, 1555 Newark Road, Zanesville, OH 43701-2626. *Phone:* 740-454-2501 Ext. 1225. *Toll-free phone:* 800-686-8324. *E-mail:* pyoung@zanestate.edu. *Website:* http://www.zanestate.edu/.

# OKLAHOMA

## Carl Albert State College
### Poteau, Oklahoma

- **State-supported** 2-year, founded 1934, part of Oklahoma State Regents for Higher Education
- **Small-town** 78-acre campus
- **Coed,** 2,194 undergraduate students, 60% full-time, 63% women, 37% men

**Undergraduates** 1,320 full-time, 874 part-time. Students come from 9 states and territories; 3% Black or African American, non-Hispanic/Latino; 7% Hispanic/Latino; 0.3% Asian, non-Hispanic/Latino; 25% American Indian or Alaska Native, non-Hispanic/Latino; 6% Two or more races, non-Hispanic/Latino; 1% Race/ethnicity unknown; 1% international; 12% live on campus.

**Freshmen** *Admission:* 586 enrolled.

**Faculty** *Student/faculty ratio:* 16:1.

**Majors** Biology/biological sciences; business administration and management; business/commerce; child development; computer and information sciences; elementary education; engineering; engineering technologies and engineering related; English; foods, nutrition, and wellness; health professions related; health services/allied health/health sciences; hotel/motel administration; management information systems; mathematics; physical education teaching and coaching; physical sciences; physical therapy technology; pre-law studies; registered nursing/registered nurse; rhetoric and composition; secondary education; social sciences; telecommunications technology.

**Academics** *Calendar:* semesters. *Degree:* certificates and associate. *Special study options:* academic remediation for entering students, adult/continuing education programs, cooperative education, part-time degree program.

**Library** Joe E. White Library.

**Student Life** *Housing Options:* men-only, women-only. Campus housing is university owned. *Activities and Organizations:* drama/theater group, student-run newspaper, radio station, choral group, Student Government Association, Phi Theta Kappa, Baptist Student Union, BACCHUS, Student Physical Therapist Assistant Association. *Campus security:* security guards. *Student services:* health clinic, personal/psychological counseling.

**Athletics** Member NJCAA. *Intercollegiate sports:* baseball M, basketball M(s)/W(s), softball M. *Intramural sports:* tennis M/W, volleyball M/W, weight lifting M.

**Standardized Tests** *Recommended:* SAT or ACT (for admission).

**Costs (2017–18)** *Tuition:* state resident $2414 full-time, $80 per credit hour part-time; nonresident $5782 full-time, $80 per credit hour part-time. Full-time tuition and fees vary according to course load. Part-time tuition and fees vary according to course load. *Required fees:* $1858 full-time, $500 per term part-time. *Room and board:* $3650. Room and board charges vary according to board plan. *Payment plan:* installment. *Waivers:* employees or children of employees.

**Financial Aid** Of all full-time matriculated undergraduates who enrolled in 2016, 112 Federal Work-Study jobs (averaging $2100).

**Applying** *Required:* high school transcript. *Notification:* continuous (freshmen), continuous (transfers).

**Admissions Office Contact** Carl Albert State College, 1507 South McKenna, Poteau, OK 74953-5208. *Website:* http://www.carlalbert.edu/.

# Clary Sage College
## Tulsa, Oklahoma

- **Proprietary** 2-year, founded 2006
- **Urban** 6-acre campus with easy access to Tulsa
- **Coed, primarily women**

**Undergraduates** 406 full-time. Students come from 9 states and territories; 3% are from out of state; 20% Black or African American, non-Hispanic/Latino; 5% Hispanic/Latino; 3% Asian, non-Hispanic/Latino; 0.5% Native Hawaiian or other Pacific Islander, non-Hispanic/Latino; 17% American Indian or Alaska Native, non-Hispanic/Latino; 4% Two or more races, non-Hispanic/Latino; 4% Race/ethnicity unknown; 58% transferred in.
**Faculty** *Student/faculty ratio:* 15:1.
**Academics** *Calendar:* continuous. *Degree:* diplomas and associate. *Special study options:* adult/continuing education programs, distance learning, internships.
**Student Life** *Campus security:* security guard during hours of operation.
**Costs (2017–18)** *Tuition:* $12,987 full-time. Full-time tuition and fees vary according to class time, course level, course load, degree level, location, program, reciprocity agreements, and student level. Part-time tuition and fees vary according to class time, course level, location, reciprocity agreements, and student level. *Required fees:* $1233 full-time. *Payment plans:* tuition prepayment, installment.
**Applying** *Options:* electronic application. *Application fee:* $100. *Required:* essay or personal statement, high school transcript, interview.
**Freshman Application Contact** Dr. Raye Mahlberg, Campus Director, Clary Sage College, 3131 South Sheridan, Tulsa, OK 74145. *Phone:* 918-298-8200 Ext. 1025. *E-mail:* rmahlberg@clarysagecollege.com. *Website:* http://www.clarysagecollege.com/.

# College of the Muscogee Nation
## Okmulgee, Oklahoma

**Admissions Office Contact** College of the Muscogee Nation, 2170 Raven Circle, Okmulgee, OK 74447-0917. *Website:* http://www.cmn.edu/.

# Community Care College
## Tulsa, Oklahoma

- **Independent** 2-year, founded 1995
- **Urban** 6-acre campus with easy access to Tulsa
- **Coed, primarily women**

**Undergraduates** 623 full-time. Students come from 18 states and territories; 4% are from out of state; 17% Black or African American, non-Hispanic/Latino; 7% Hispanic/Latino; 2% Asian, non-Hispanic/Latino; 0.2% Native Hawaiian or other Pacific Islander, non-Hispanic/Latino; 19% American Indian or Alaska Native, non-Hispanic/Latino; 3% Two or more races, non-Hispanic/Latino; 2% Race/ethnicity unknown.
**Faculty** *Student/faculty ratio:* 25:1.
**Academics** *Calendar:* continuous. *Degree:* diplomas and associate. *Special study options:* adult/continuing education programs, distance learning, independent study, internships, services for LD students.
**Student Life** *Campus security:* campus security personnel during school hours.
**Costs (2017–18)** *Tuition:* $13,175 full-time. Full-time tuition and fees vary according to class time, course level, course load, degree level, location, program, and reciprocity agreements. Part-time tuition and fees vary according to class time, course level, location, and reciprocity agreements. *Required fees:* $1062 full-time. *Payment plans:* tuition prepayment, installment.
**Applying** *Options:* electronic application. *Required:* essay or personal statement, high school transcript, interview. *Required for some:* 1 letter of recommendation.
**Freshman Application Contact** Dr. Kevin Kirk, President, Community Care College, 4242 South Sheridan, Tulsa, OK 74145. *Phone:* 918-610-0027 Ext. 2003. *Fax:* 918-610-0029. *E-mail:* kkirk@communitycarecollege.edu. *Website:* http://www.communitycarecollege.edu/.

# Connors State College
## Warner, Oklahoma

**Freshman Application Contact** Ms. Sonya Baker, Registrar, Connors State College, Route 1 Box 1000, Warner, OK 74469-9700. *Phone:* 918-463-6233. *Website:* http://www.connorsstate.edu/.

# Eastern Oklahoma State College
## Wilburton, Oklahoma

**Freshman Application Contact** Ms. Leah McLaughlin, Director of Admissions, Eastern Oklahoma State College, 1301 West Main, Wilburton, OK 74578-4999. *Phone:* 918-465-1811. *Toll-free phone:* 855-534-3672. *Fax:* 918-465-2431. *E-mail:* lmiller@eosc.edu. *Website:* http://www.eosc.edu/.

# Murray State College
## Tishomingo, Oklahoma

- **State-supported** 2-year, founded 1908, part of Oklahoma State Regents for Higher Education
- **Rural** 120-acre campus
- **Coed**

**Undergraduates** 1,317 full-time, 1,357 part-time. Students come from 19 states and territories; 9 other countries; 4% are from out of state; 5% Black or African American, non-Hispanic/Latino; 6% Hispanic/Latino; 0.3% Asian, non-Hispanic/Latino; 0.1% Native Hawaiian or other Pacific Islander, non-Hispanic/Latino; 13% American Indian or Alaska Native, non-Hispanic/Latino; 9% Two or more races, non-Hispanic/Latino; 2% Race/ethnicity unknown; 0.1% international; 11% live on campus. *Retention:* 49% of full-time freshmen returned.
**Faculty** *Student/faculty ratio:* 20:1.
**Academics** *Calendar:* semesters. *Degree:* associate. *Special study options:* academic remediation for entering students, advanced placement credit, distance learning, honors programs, internships, part-time degree program, services for LD students, summer session for credit.
**Library** Murray State College Library plus 1 other.
**Student Life** *Campus security:* 24-hour patrols.
**Athletics** Member NJCAA.
**Standardized Tests** *Required:* SAT or ACT (for admission).
**Financial Aid** Of all full-time matriculated undergraduates who enrolled in 2016, 68 Federal Work-Study jobs (averaging $3354). 20 state and other part-time jobs (averaging $2516).
**Applying** *Options:* electronic application, early admission. *Required:* high school transcript.
**Freshman Application Contact** Murray State College, One Murray Campus, Tishomingo, OK 73460. *Phone:* 580-371-2371 Ext. 171. *Website:* http://www.mscok.edu/.

# Northeastern Oklahoma Agricultural and Mechanical College
## Miami, Oklahoma

**Freshman Application Contact** Amy Ishmael, Vice President for Enrollment Management, Northeastern Oklahoma Agricultural and Mechanical College, 200 I Street, NE, Miami, OK 74354-6434. *Phone:* 918-540-6212. *Toll-free phone:* 800-464-6636. *Fax:* 918-540-6946. *E-mail:* neoadmission@neo.edu. *Website:* http://www.neo.edu/.

# Northern Oklahoma College
## Tonkawa, Oklahoma

**Freshman Application Contact** Ms. Sheri Snyder, Director of College Relations, Northern Oklahoma College, 1220 East Grand Avenue, PO Box 310, Tonkawa, OK 74653-0310. *Phone:* 580-628-6290. *Website:* http://www.noc.edu/.

# Oklahoma City Community College
## Oklahoma City, Oklahoma

- **State-supported** 2-year, founded 1969, part of Oklahoma State Regents for Higher Education
- **Urban** 143-acre campus with easy access to Oklahoma City
- **Endowment** $310,298
- **Coed,** 12,314 undergraduate students, 35% full-time, 59% women, 41% men

**Undergraduates** 4,359 full-time, 7,955 part-time. Students come from 22 states and territories; 94 other countries; 5% are from out of state; 10% Black or African American, non-Hispanic/Latino; 17% Hispanic/Latino; 5% Asian, non-Hispanic/Latino; 0.2% Native Hawaiian or other Pacific Islander, non-Hispanic/Latino; 5% American Indian or Alaska Native, non-Hispanic/Latino; 8% Two or more races, non-Hispanic/Latino; 4% Race/ethnicity unknown; 3% international; 29% transferred in.
**Freshmen** *Admission:* 3,983 applied, 2,913 admitted, 2,439 enrolled.

**Faculty** *Total:* 554, 24% full-time, 12% with terminal degrees. *Student/faculty ratio:* 23:1.

**Majors** Accounting and finance; allied health and medical assisting services related; anesthesiologist assistant; architectural drafting and CAD/CADD; art; automobile/automotive mechanics technology; biology/biological sciences; broadcast journalism; business/commerce; CAD/CADD drafting/design technology; chemistry; child development; cinematography and film/video production; clinical research coordinator; computer and information systems security; computer programming; computer science; computer software engineering; computer support specialist; computer systems analysis; diesel mechanics technology; digital communication and media/multimedia; dramatic/theater arts; education; emergency medical technology (EMT paramedic); engineering; engineering technology; French; general studies; geographic information science and cartography; graphic design; history; humanities; journalism; liberal arts and sciences/liberal studies; mathematics; medical/clinical assistant; modern languages; music; occupational therapist assistant; photography; physical therapy; physics; political science and government; pre-dentistry studies; premedical studies; prenursing studies; pre-pharmacy studies; psychology; public health; public relations, advertising, and applied communication; registered nursing/registered nurse; respiratory care therapy; sociology; Spanish; speech communication and rhetoric; speech-language pathology assistant; surgical technology; web page, digital/multimedia and information resources design.

**Academics** *Calendar:* semesters. *Degree:* certificates and associate. *Special study options:* academic remediation for entering students, accelerated degree program, advanced placement credit, cooperative education, distance learning, double majors, honors programs, independent study, internships, part-time degree program, services for LD students, student-designed majors, summer session for credit.

**Library** Keith Leftwich Memorial Library. *Books:* 85,305 (physical), 19,895 (digital/electronic); *Serial titles:* 101 (physical), 11,707 (digital/electronic); *Databases:* 44. Weekly public service hours: 70.

**Student Life** *Housing:* college housing not available. *Activities and Organizations:* drama/theater group, student-run newspaper, choral group, Phi Theta Kappa, Hispanic Organization to Promote Education, Baptist Collegiate Ministry, Engineering Club, Black Student Association. *Campus security:* 24-hour emergency response devices and patrols, late-night transport/escort service. *Student services:* personal/psychological counseling, veterans affairs office.

**Costs (2017–18)** *One-time required fee:* $30. *Tuition:* state resident $2935 full-time, $98 per credit hour part-time; nonresident $8468 full-time, $282 per credit hour part-time. Full-time tuition and fees vary according to course level. Part-time tuition and fees vary according to course level. *Required fees:* $974 full-time, $32 per credit hour part-time. *Payment plan:* installment. *Waivers:* children of alumni, senior citizens, and employees or children of employees.

**Financial Aid** Of all full-time matriculated undergraduates who enrolled in 2016, 108 Federal Work-Study jobs (averaging $2643). 440 state and other part-time jobs (averaging $3211).

**Applying** *Options:* electronic application. *Application fee:* $30. *Required for some:* high school transcript, college and university transcripts. *Application deadlines:* rolling (freshmen), rolling (transfers). *Notification:* continuous (freshmen), continuous (transfers).

**Freshman Application Contact** Ms. Jillian C. Hibblen, Acting Director of Recruitment and Admissions, Oklahoma City Community College, 7777 South May Avenue, Oklahoma City, OK 73159. *Phone:* 405-682-7743. *Fax:* 405-682-7817. *E-mail:* jhibblen@occc.edu. *Website:* http://www.occc.edu/.

# Oklahoma State University Institute of Technology

## Okmulgee, Oklahoma

- **State-supported** primarily 2-year, founded 1946, part of Oklahoma State University
- **Small-town** 160-acre campus with easy access to Tulsa
- **Endowment** $7.6 million
- **Coed,** 2,502 undergraduate students, 70% full-time, 36% women, 64% men

**Undergraduates** 1,744 full-time, 758 part-time. Students come from 23 states and territories; 10 other countries; 7% are from out of state; 5% Black or African American, non-Hispanic/Latino; 6% Hispanic/Latino; 1% Asian, non-Hispanic/Latino; 12% American Indian or Alaska Native, non-Hispanic/Latino; 11% Two or more races, non-Hispanic/Latino; 12% Race/ethnicity unknown; 0.6% international; 9% transferred in; 25% live on campus. *Retention:* 64% of full-time freshmen returned.

**Freshmen** *Admission:* 2,925 applied, 856 admitted, 697 enrolled. *Average high school GPA:* 3.1. *Test scores:* ACT scores over 18: 55%; ACT scores over 24: 9%.

**Faculty** *Total:* 155, 75% full-time, 6% with terminal degrees. *Student/faculty ratio:* 15:1.

**Majors** Autobody/collision and repair technology; automobile/automotive mechanics technology; business/commerce; civil engineering technology; computer and information systems security; construction trades; culinary arts related; diesel mechanics technology; education (multiple levels); electrical and power transmission installation; engineering technology; graphic design; health services/allied health/health sciences; heating, air conditioning, ventilation and refrigeration maintenance technology; industrial mechanics and maintenance technology; information technology; instrumentation technology; interdisciplinary studies; intermedia/multimedia; mechanical engineering/mechanical technology; multi/interdisciplinary studies related; orthotics/prosthetics; petroleum technology; photography; registered nursing/registered nurse; watchmaking and jewelrymaking.

**Academics** *Calendar:* trimesters. *Degrees:* associate and bachelor's. *Special study options:* academic remediation for entering students, adult/continuing education programs, advanced placement credit, distance learning, double majors, independent study, internships, part-time degree program, services for LD students, summer session for credit.

**Library** Oklahoma State University Institute of Technology Library. *Books:* 9,520 (physical), 147,054 (digital/electronic); *Serial titles:* 149 (physical), 70,987 (digital/electronic); *Databases:* 106. Weekly public service hours: 73; students can reserve study rooms.

**Student Life** *Housing:* on-campus residence required for freshman year. *Options:* coed, men-only. Campus housing is university owned. Freshman applicants given priority for college housing. *Activities and Organizations:* Phi Theta Kappa, Visual Communications Collective, Air Conditioning and Refrigeration Club, Future Chefs Association, Association of Information Technology Professionals. *Campus security:* 24-hour emergency response devices and patrols, late-night transport/escort service, controlled dormitory access. *Student services:* health clinic, personal/psychological counseling, veterans affairs office.

**Athletics** *Intramural sports:* basketball M/W, football M/W, racquetball M/W, soccer M/W, softball M/W, table tennis M/W, volleyball M/W.

**Standardized Tests** *Required for some:* SAT or ACT (for admission). *Recommended:* ACT (for admission).

**Costs (2018–19)** *Tuition:* state resident $4050 full-time, $135 per credit hour part-time; nonresident $9660 full-time, $322 per credit hour part-time. Full-time tuition and fees vary according to course level, course load, degree level, location, program, and student level. Part-time tuition and fees vary according to course level, course load, degree level, location, program, and student level. *Required fees:* $1200 full-time, $40 per credit hour part-time. *Room and board:* $6724. Room and board charges vary according to board plan and housing facility. *Payment plan:* installment. *Waivers:* senior citizens and employees or children of employees.

**Financial Aid** Of all full-time matriculated undergraduates who enrolled in 2017, 1,479 applied for aid, 1,316 were judged to have need, 234 had their need fully met. In 2017, 32 non-need-based awards were made. *Average percent of need met:* 45%. *Average financial aid package:* $8193. *Average need-based loan:* $3582. *Average need-based gift aid:* $5104. *Average non-need-based aid:* $1849. *Financial aid deadline:* 6/30.

**Applying** *Options:* deferred entrance. *Required:* high school transcript. *Application deadlines:* rolling (freshmen), rolling (transfers).

**Freshman Application Contact** Kyle Gregorio, Assistant Registrar, Oklahoma State University Institute of Technology, 1801 E. 4th Street, Okmulgee, OK 74447. *Phone:* 918-293-5274. *Toll-free phone:* 800-722-4471. *Fax:* 918-293-4643. *E-mail:* kyleg@okstate.edu. *Website:* http://www.osuit.edu/.

# Oklahoma State University–Oklahoma City

## Oklahoma City, Oklahoma

- **State-supported** primarily 2-year, founded 1961, part of Oklahoma State University
- **Urban** 110-acre campus with easy access to Oklahoma City
- **Coed,** 5,839 undergraduate students, 30% full-time, 62% women, 38% men

**Undergraduates** 1,728 full-time, 4,111 part-time. Students come from 28 states and territories; 12 other countries; 4% are from out of state; 11% Black or African American, non-Hispanic/Latino; 16% Hispanic/Latino; 3% Asian, non-Hispanic/Latino; 0.2% Native Hawaiian or other Pacific Islander, non-Hispanic/Latino; 4% American Indian or Alaska Native, non-Hispanic/Latino; 7% Two or more races, non-Hispanic/Latino; 4% Race/ethnicity unknown; 2% international; 13% transferred in. *Retention:* 51% of full-time freshmen returned.

**Freshmen** *Admission:* 3,765 applied, 1,267 admitted, 1,007 enrolled. *Average high school GPA:* 2.8.

**Faculty** *Total:* 355, 24% full-time. *Student/faculty ratio:* 16:1.

**Majors** Accounting; American Sign Language (ASL); architectural drafting and CAD/CADD; architectural engineering technology; building/home/construction inspection; business administration and management; cardiovascular technology; construction engineering technology; construction management; construction trades; criminal justice/police science; dietetics and clinical nutrition services related; early childhood education; electrical and power transmission installation; electrical and power transmission installation related; electrical, electronic and communications engineering technology; electrocardiograph technology; emergency medical technology (EMT paramedic); energy management and systems technology; engineering technology; fire science/firefighting; general studies; health/health-care administration; homeland security, law enforcement, firefighting and protective services related; horticultural science; information science/studies; information technology; language interpretation and translation; management science; public administration and social service professions related; radiologic technology/science; registered nursing/registered nurse; sign language interpretation and translation; substance abuse/addiction counseling; surveying technology; veterinary/animal health technology.

**Academics** *Calendar:* semesters. *Degrees:* certificates, associate, and bachelor's. *Special study options:* academic remediation for entering students, advanced placement credit, distance learning, double majors, honors programs, independent study, internships, part-time degree program, services for LD students, study abroad, summer session for credit.

**Library** Oklahoma State University, Oklahoma City Library. *Books:* 34,772 (physical), 198,662 (digital/electronic); *Serial titles:* 229 (physical); *Databases:* 72. Weekly public service hours: 75.

**Student Life** *Housing:* college housing not available. *Activities and Organizations:* OSU-OKC Chapter of the OK Student Nurse Association, Veterinary Technician Association, Hispanic Student Association, Phi Theta Kappa, Student Government Association. *Campus security:* 24-hour patrols, late-night transport/escort service. *Student services:* veterans affairs office.

**Costs (2017–18)** *Tuition:* state resident $2938 full-time, $122 per credit hour part-time; nonresident $8171 full-time, $340 per credit hour part-time. Full-time tuition and fees vary according to class time, course level, and degree level. Part-time tuition and fees vary according to class time, course level, and degree level. No tuition increase for student's term of enrollment. *Required fees:* $70 full-time, $35 per term part-time. *Payment plans:* tuition prepayment, installment. *Waivers:* senior citizens and employees or children of employees.

**Financial Aid** Of all full-time matriculated undergraduates who enrolled in 2017, 1,116 applied for aid, 1,116 were judged to have need, 856 had their need fully met. 192 Federal Work-Study jobs (averaging $275). In 2017, 611 non-need-based awards were made. *Average percent of need met:* 81%. *Average financial aid package:* $1757. *Average need-based gift aid:* $2293. *Average non-need-based aid:* $1025. *Average indebtedness upon graduation:* $3119.

**Applying** *Options:* electronic application. *Required for some:* high school transcript. *Application deadlines:* rolling (freshmen), rolling (transfers). *Notification:* continuous (freshmen), continuous (transfers).

**Freshman Application Contact** Mr. Kyle Williams, Senior Director of Enrollment Management, Oklahoma State University–Oklahoma City, 900 North Portland Avenue, AD202, Oklahoma City, OK 73107. *Phone:* 405-945-9152. *Toll-free phone:* 800-560-4099. *E-mail:* wilkylw@osuokc.edu. *Website:* http://www.osuokc.edu/.

## Oklahoma Technical College
### Tulsa, Oklahoma

- **Independent** 2-year, founded 2009
- **Urban** 9-acre campus with easy access to Tulsa
- **Coed**

**Undergraduates** 186 full-time. Students come from 6 states and territories; 5% are from out of state; 11% Black or African American, non-Hispanic/Latino; 8% Hispanic/Latino; 1% Asian, non-Hispanic/Latino; 0.5% Native Hawaiian or other Pacific Islander, non-Hispanic/Latino; 18% American Indian or Alaska Native, non-Hispanic/Latino; 1% Two or more races, non-Hispanic/Latino; 6% Race/ethnicity unknown.

**Faculty** *Student/faculty ratio:* 10:1.

**Academics** *Calendar:* continuous. *Degree:* diplomas and associate. *Special study options:* adult/continuing education programs, internships, services for LD students.

**Student Life** *Campus security:* campus security during school hours.

**Costs (2017–18)** *Tuition:* $17,325 full-time. Full-time tuition and fees vary according to class time, course level, course load, location, program, and student level. Part-time tuition and fees vary according to class time. *Required fees:* $1858 full-time. *Payment plans:* tuition prepayment, installment.

**Applying** *Options:* electronic application. *Application fee:* $100. *Required:* essay or personal statement, high school transcript, interview.

**Freshman Application Contact** Mr. Jeremy Cooper, Campus Director, Oklahoma Technical College, 4444 South Sheridan Road, Tulsa, OK 74145. *Phone:* 918-895-7500 Ext. 3007. *Fax:* 918-895-7885. *E-mail:* jcooper@oklahomatechnicalcollege.com. *Website:* http://www.oklahomatechnicaicollege.com/.

## Platt College
### Moore, Oklahoma

**Admissions Office Contact** Platt College, 201 North Eastern Avenue, Moore, OK 73160. *Toll-free phone:* 877-392-6616. *Website:* http://www.plattcolleges.edu/.

## Platt College
### Oklahoma City, Oklahoma

**Admissions Office Contact** Platt College, 2727 West Memorial Road, Oklahoma City, OK 73134. *Toll-free phone:* 877-392-6616. *Website:* http://www.plattcolleges.edu/.

## Platt College
### Oklahoma City, Oklahoma

**Freshman Application Contact** Ms. Kim Lamb, Director of Admissions, Platt College, 309 South Ann Arbor, Oklahoma City, OK 73128. *Phone:* 405-946-7799. *Toll-free phone:* 877-392-6616. *Fax:* 405-943-2150. *E-mail:* klamb@plattcollege.org. *Website:* http://www.plattcolleges.edu/.

## Platt College
### Tulsa, Oklahoma

**Director of Admissions** Mrs. Susan Rone, Director, Platt College, 3801 South Sheridan Road, Tulsa, OK 74145. *Phone:* 918-663-9000. *Toll-free phone:* 877-392-6616. *Fax:* 918-622-1240. *E-mail:* susanr@plattcollege.org. *Website:* http://www.plattcolleges.edu/.

## Redlands Community College
### El Reno, Oklahoma

**Freshman Application Contact** Redlands Community College, 1300 South Country Club Road, El Reno, OK 73036-5304. *Phone:* 405-262-2552 Ext. 1263. *Toll-free phone:* 866-415-6367. *Website:* http://www.redlandscc.edu/.

## Rose State College
### Midwest City, Oklahoma

**Freshman Application Contact** Ms. Mechelle Aitson-Roessler, Registrar and Director of Admissions, Rose State College, 6420 Southeast 15th Street, Midwest City, OK 73110-2799. *Phone:* 405-733-7308. *Toll-free phone:* 866-621-0987. *Fax:* 405-736-0203. *E-mail:* maitson@ms.rose.cc.ok.us. *Website:* http://www.rose.edu/.

## Seminole State College
### Seminole, Oklahoma

- **State-supported** 2-year, founded 1931, part of Oklahoma State Regents for Higher Education
- **Small-town** 40-acre campus with easy access to Oklahoma City
- **Endowment** $3.1 million
- **Coed,** 1,633 undergraduate students, 59% full-time, 65% women, 35% men

**Undergraduates** 967 full-time, 666 part-time. Students come from 9 states and territories; 9 other countries; 1% are from out of state; 6% Black or African American, non-Hispanic/Latino; 2% Hispanic/Latino; 0.6% Asian, non-Hispanic/Latino; 0.2% Native Hawaiian or other Pacific Islander, non-Hispanic/Latino; 26% American Indian or Alaska Native, non-Hispanic/Latino; 1% Two or more races, non-Hispanic/Latino; 3% Race/ethnicity unknown; 1% international; 5% transferred in; 10% live on campus.

**Freshmen** *Admission:* 404 applied, 404 admitted, 337 enrolled.

**Faculty** *Total:* 87, 46% full-time, 3% with terminal degrees. *Student/faculty ratio:* 19:1.

**Majors** Accounting; art; behavioral sciences; biological and biomedical sciences related; biology/biological sciences; business administration and management; business/commerce; child development; clinical/medical laboratory technology; computer science; criminal justice/law enforcement administration; criminal justice/police science; elementary education; engineering; English; fine arts related; general studies; humanities; liberal arts and sciences/liberal studies; management information systems and services related; mathematics; physical education teaching and coaching; physical sciences; pre-engineering; psychology related; registered nursing/registered nurse; social sciences.

**Academics** *Calendar:* semesters. *Degree:* certificates, diplomas, and associate. *Special study options:* academic remediation for entering students, adult/continuing education programs, advanced placement credit, cooperative education, distance learning, double majors, English as a second language, independent study, off-campus study, part-time degree program, services for LD students, study abroad, summer session for credit.

**Library** Boren Library plus 1 other. *Books:* 29,131 (physical); *Serial titles:* 35 (physical), 11 (digital/electronic); *Databases:* 8. Weekly public service hours: 48.

**Student Life** *Housing:* on-campus residence required through sophomore year. *Options:* coed, special housing for students with disabilities. Campus housing is university owned. *Activities and Organizations:* Student Government Association, Native American Student Association, Psi Beta Honor Society, Student Nurses Association, Phi Theta Kappa. *Campus security:* 24-hour emergency response devices and patrols, student patrols, late-night transport/escort service, controlled dormitory access, police department staffed with state certified officers. *Student services:* veterans affairs office.

**Athletics** Member NJCAA. *Intercollegiate sports:* baseball M(s), basketball M(s)/W(s), golf M(s)/W(s), soccer W, softball W(s), tennis M(s)/W(s), volleyball W(s).

**Costs (2018–19)** *One-time required fee:* $25. *Tuition:* state resident $2880 full-time, $96 per credit hour part-time; nonresident $8820 full-time, $294 per credit hour part-time. Full-time tuition and fees vary according to course load, location, and program. Part-time tuition and fees vary according to course load, location, and program. *Required fees:* $1560 full-time, $52 per credit hour part-time. *Room and board:* $7070. *Payment plan:* installment. *Waivers:* senior citizens and employees or children of employees.

**Financial Aid** Of all full-time matriculated undergraduates who enrolled in 2016, 17 Federal Work-Study jobs (averaging $5600).

**Applying** *Options:* early admission, deferred entrance. *Application fee:* $15. *Recommended:* high school transcript. *Application deadlines:* rolling (freshmen), rolling (transfers). *Notification:* continuous (freshmen), continuous (transfers).

**Admissions Office Contact** Seminole State College, 2701 Boren Boulevard, PO Box 351, Seminole, OK 74818-0351.
*Website:* http://www.sscok.edu/.

# Spartan College of Aeronautics and Technology
## Tulsa, Oklahoma

**Freshman Application Contact** Mr. Mark Fowler, Vice President of Student Records and Finance, Spartan College of Aeronautics and Technology, 8820 East Pine Street, Tulsa, OK 74115. *Phone:* 918-836-6886. *Toll-free phone:* 800-331-1204. *Website:* http://www.spartan.edu/.

# Tulsa Community College
## Tulsa, Oklahoma

- **State-supported** 2-year, founded 1968, part of Oklahoma State Regents for Higher Education
- **Urban** 160-acre campus
- **Coed**, 16,787 undergraduate students, 30% full-time, 61% women, 39% men

**Undergraduates** 4,960 full-time, 11,827 part-time. 9% Black or African American, non-Hispanic/Latino; 8% Hispanic/Latino; 4% Asian, non-Hispanic/Latino; 0.1% Native Hawaiian or other Pacific Islander, non-Hispanic/Latino; 7% American Indian or Alaska Native, non-Hispanic/Latino; 10% Two or more races, non-Hispanic/Latino; 4% Race/ethnicity unknown; 3% international; 4% transferred in.

**Freshmen** *Admission:* 7,198 applied, 7,195 admitted, 3,826 enrolled. *Average high school GPA:* 3.0. *Test scores:* ACT scores over 18: 76%; ACT scores over 24: 20%; ACT scores over 30: 2%.

**Faculty** *Total:* 823, 34% full-time. *Student/faculty ratio:* 19:1.

**Majors** Accounting technology and bookkeeping; aeronautical/aerospace engineering technology; air traffic control; applied horticulture/horticulture operations; biotechnology; business administration and management; business/commerce; business, management, and marketing related; child development; clinical/medical laboratory technology; communication; computer and information sciences and support services related; computer and information sciences related; computer installation and repair technology; computer science; criminal justice/police science; dental hygiene; diagnostic

medical sonography and ultrasound technology; digital communication and media/multimedia; dramatic/theater arts; education; electrical, electronic and communications engineering technology; engineering-related technologies; environmental science; fine/studio arts; fire services administration; foreign languages related; general studies; graphic and printing equipment operation/production; health information/medical records technology; health/medical preparatory programs related; human resources management; interior design; international business/trade/commerce; legal assistant/paralegal; marketing/marketing management; mathematics; medical radiologic technology; multi/interdisciplinary studies related; music; nutrition sciences; occupational therapy; physical sciences; physical therapy technology; pre-engineering; prenursing studies; pre-pharmacy studies; registered nursing/registered nurse; respiratory care therapy; sign language interpretation and translation; social sciences; social work; sport and fitness administration/management; surgical technology; veterinary/animal health technology.

**Academics** *Calendar:* semesters. *Degree:* certificates and associate. *Special study options:* academic remediation for entering students, accelerated degree program, adult/continuing education programs, advanced placement credit, cooperative education, distance learning, English as a second language, freshman honors college, honors programs, independent study, internships, off-campus study, part-time degree program, services for LD students, student-designed majors, study abroad, summer session for credit.

**Student Life** *Housing:* college housing not available. *Activities and Organizations:* drama/theater group, student-run newspaper, radio station, choral group. *Campus security:* 24-hour emergency response devices and patrols, student patrols, late-night transport/escort service. *Student services:* health clinic, personal/psychological counseling, women's center.

**Athletics** *Intramural sports:* basketball M/W, football M/W, soccer M/W, softball M/W, volleyball M/W.

**Costs (2017–18)** *Tuition:* state resident $4026 full-time, $103 per credit hour part-time; nonresident $10,296 full-time, $313 per credit hour part-time. *Required fees:* $930 full-time, $29 per credit hour part-time, $5 per term part-time. *Payment plan:* installment. *Waivers:* senior citizens and employees or children of employees.

**Financial Aid** Of all full-time matriculated undergraduates who enrolled in 2017, 4,030 applied for aid, 2,957 were judged to have need, 300 had their need fully met. In 2017, 520 non-need-based awards were made. *Average percent of need met:* 71%. *Average financial aid package:* $3328. *Average need-based loan:* $1800. *Average need-based gift aid:* $2939. *Average non-need-based aid:* $1747.

**Applying** *Options:* electronic application, early admission. *Required:* high school transcript. *Application deadlines:* rolling (freshmen), rolling (transfers).

**Freshman Application Contact** Ms. Traci Heck, Dean of Enrollment Management, Tulsa Community College, 6111 East Skelly Drive, Tulsa, OK 74135. *Phone:* 918-595-3411. *E-mail:* traci.heck@tulsacc.edu. *Website:* http://www.tulsacc.edu/.

# Tulsa Welding School
## Tulsa, Oklahoma

**Freshman Application Contact** Mrs. Debbie Renee Burke, Vice President/Executive Director, Tulsa Welding School, 2545 East 11th Street, Tulsa, OK 74104. *Phone:* 918-587-6789 Ext. 2258. *Toll-free phone:* 888-765-5555. *Fax:* 918-295-6812. *E-mail:* dburke@twsweld.com. *Website:* http://www.tulsaweldingschool.com/.

# Vatterott College
## Tulsa, Oklahoma

**Freshman Application Contact** Mr. Terry Queeno, Campus Director, Vatterott College, 4343 South 118th East Avenue, Suite A, Tulsa, OK 74146. *Phone:* 918-836-6656. *Toll-free phone:* 888-553-6627. *Fax:* 918-836-9698. *E-mail:* tulsa@vatterott-college.edu. *Website:* http://www.vatterott.edu/.

# Vatterott College
## Warr Acres, Oklahoma

**Freshman Application Contact** Mr. Mark Hybers, Director of Admissions, Vatterott College, Oklahoma City, OK 73127. *Phone:* 405-945-0088 Ext. 4416. *Toll-free phone:* 888-553-6627. *Fax:* 405-945-0788. *E-mail:* mark.hybers@vatterott-college.edu. *Website:* http://www.vatterott.edu/.

# Virginia College in Tulsa
## Tulsa, Oklahoma

**Admissions Office Contact** Virginia College in Tulsa, 5124 South Peoria Avenue, Tulsa, OK 74105. *Website:* http://www.vc.edu/.

## Western Oklahoma State College
### Altus, Oklahoma

**Freshman Application Contact** Dean Chad E. Wiginton, Dean of Student Support Services, Western Oklahoma State College, 2801 North Main, Altus, OK 73521. *Phone:* 580-477-7918. *Fax:* 580-477-7716. *E-mail:* chad.wiginton@wosc.edu. *Website:* http://www.wosc.edu/.

# OREGON

## Blue Mountain Community College
### Pendleton, Oregon

**Director of Admissions** Ms. Theresa Bosworth, Director of Admissions, Blue Mountain Community College, 2411 Northwest Carden Avenue, PO Box 100, Pendleton, OR 97801-1000. *Phone:* 541-278-5774. *E-mail:* tbosworth@bluecc.edu. *Website:* http://www.bluecc.edu/.

## Central Oregon Community College
### Bend, Oregon

- **District-supported** 2-year, founded 1949, part of Oregon Community College Association
- **Small-town** 193-acre campus
- **Coed,** 5,205 undergraduate students, 46% full-time, 54% women, 46% men

**Undergraduates** 2,377 full-time, 2,828 part-time. 0.5% Black or African American, non-Hispanic/Latino; 12% Hispanic/Latino; 1% Asian, non-Hispanic/Latino; 0.4% Native Hawaiian or other Pacific Islander, non-Hispanic/Latino; 2% American Indian or Alaska Native, non-Hispanic/Latino; 4% Two or more races, non-Hispanic/Latino; 7% Race/ethnicity unknown; 8% transferred in. *Retention:* 55% of full-time freshmen returned.
**Freshmen** *Admission:* 2,061 applied, 2,061 admitted, 1,132 enrolled.
**Faculty** *Total:* 338, 39% full-time. *Student/faculty ratio:* 19:1.
**Majors** Accounting; airline pilot and flight crew; art; automobile/automotive mechanics technology; biological and physical sciences; biology/biological sciences; business administration and management; CAD/CADD drafting/design technology; child-care and support services management; computer and information sciences related; computer science; computer systems networking and telecommunications; cooking and related culinary arts; customer service management; dental assisting; dietetics; drafting and design technology; early childhood education; education; electrical, electronic and communications engineering technology; emergency medical technology (EMT paramedic); engineering; entrepreneurship; fire science/firefighting; fishing and fisheries sciences and management; foreign languages and literatures; forestry; forest technology; health and physical education/fitness; health information/medical records technology; hotel/motel administration; humanities; industrial technology; kinesiology and exercise science; liberal arts and sciences/liberal studies; licensed practical/vocational nurse training; management information systems; manufacturing engineering technology; marketing/marketing management; massage therapy; mathematics; medical/clinical assistant; natural resources/conservation; physical sciences; physical therapy; polymer/plastics engineering; pre-law studies; premedical studies; pre-pharmacy studies; radiologic technology/science; registered nursing/registered nurse; retailing; social sciences; speech communication and rhetoric; sport and fitness administration/management; substance abuse/addiction counseling.
**Academics** *Calendar:* quarters. *Degree:* certificates, diplomas, and associate. *Special study options:* academic remediation for entering students, cooperative education, distance learning, double majors, English as a second language, independent study, internships, part-time degree program, services for LD students, student-designed majors, study abroad, summer session for credit. *ROTC:* Army (c).
**Library** COCC Library plus 1 other.
**Student Life** *Housing Options:* coed, special housing for students with disabilities. Campus housing is university owned. *Activities and Organizations:* drama/theater group, student-run newspaper, choral group, Club Sports, Student Newspaper, Criminal Justice Club, Aviation Club. *Campus security:* 24-hour emergency response devices and patrols, late-night transport/escort service, controlled dormitory access. *Student services:* personal/psychological counseling, veterans affairs office.
**Athletics** *Intercollegiate sports:* golf M/W. *Intramural sports:* baseball M, basketball M/W, cross-country running M/W, football M, rugby M, skiing (cross-country) M/W, skiing (downhill) M/W, soccer M/W, track and field M/W, volleyball M/W, weight lifting M/W.

**Costs (2017–18)** *Tuition:* area resident $3699 full-time, $95 per credit hour part-time; state resident $4959 full-time, $130 per credit hour part-time; nonresident $9855 full-time, $266 per credit hour part-time. *Required fees:* $349 full-time, $8 per credit hour part-time. *Room and board:* $10,701. Room and board charges vary according to board plan. *Payment plan:* installment. *Waivers:* employees or children of employees.
**Financial Aid** Of all full-time matriculated undergraduates who enrolled in 2017, 1,799 applied for aid, 1,521 were judged to have need, 137 had their need fully met. In 2017, 25 non-need-based awards were made. *Average percent of need met:* 71%. *Average financial aid package:* $11,530. *Average need-based loan:* $3438. *Average need-based gift aid:* $6543. *Average non-need-based aid:* $1389.
**Applying** *Options:* electronic application. *Application fee:* $25. *Application deadlines:* rolling (freshmen), rolling (transfers). *Notification:* continuous (freshmen), continuous (transfers).
**Freshman Application Contact** Central Oregon Community College, 2600 Northwest College Way, Bend, OR 97703. *Phone:* 541-383-7500. *Website:* http://www.cocc.edu/.

## Chemeketa Community College
### Salem, Oregon

**Freshman Application Contact** Admissions Office, Chemeketa Community College, PO Box 14009, Salem, OR 97309. *Phone:* 503-399-5001. *E-mail:* admissions@chemeketa.edu. *Website:* http://www.chemeketa.edu/.

## Clackamas Community College
### Oregon City, Oregon

**Freshman Application Contact** Ms. Tara Sprehe, Registrar, Clackamas Community College, 19600 South Molalla Avenue, Oregon City, OR 97045. *Phone:* 503-657-6958 Ext. 2742. *Fax:* 503-650-6654. *E-mail:* pattyw@clackamas.edu. *Website:* http://www.clackamas.edu/.

## Clatsop Community College
### Astoria, Oregon

**Freshman Application Contact** Ms. Monica Van Steenberg, Recruiting Coordinator, Clatsop Community College, 1651 Lexington Avenue, Astoria, OR 97103. *Phone:* 503-338-2417. *Toll-free phone:* 855-252-8767. *Fax:* 503-325-5738. *E-mail:* admissions@clatsopcc.edu. *Website:* http://www.clatsopcc.edu/.

## Columbia Gorge Community College
### The Dalles, Oregon

**Freshman Application Contact** Columbia Gorge Community College, 400 East Scenic Drive, The Dalles, OR 97058. *Phone:* 541-506-6025. *Website:* http://www.cgcc.edu/.

## Concorde Career College
### Portland, Oregon

**Admissions Office Contact** Concorde Career College, 1425 NE Irving Street, Portland, OR 97232. *Website:* http://www.concorde.edu/.

## Klamath Community College
### Klamath Falls, Oregon

**Freshman Application Contact** Tammi Garlock, Retention Coordinator, Klamath Community College, 7390 South 6th Street, Klamath Falls, OR 97603. *Phone:* 541-882-3521. *Fax:* 541-885-7758. *E-mail:* garlock@klamathcc.edu. *Website:* http://www.klamathcc.edu/.

## Lane Community College
### Eugene, Oregon

**Freshman Application Contact** Lane Community College, 4000 East 30th Avenue, Eugene, OR 97405-0640. *Phone:* 541-747-4501 Ext. 2686. *Website:* http://www.lanecc.edu/.

## Linn-Benton Community College
### Albany, Oregon

**Freshman Application Contact** Ms. Kim Sullivan, Outreach Coordinator, Linn-Benton Community College, 6500 Pacific Boulevard, SW, Albany, OR

97321. *Phone:* 541-917-4847. *Fax:* 541-917-4838. *E-mail:* admissions@linnbenton.edu. *Website:* http://www.linnbenton.edu/.

## Mt. Hood Community College
### Gresham, Oregon

**Director of Admissions** Dr. Craig Kolins, Associate Vice President of Enrollment Services, Mt. Hood Community College, 26000 Southeast Stark Street, Gresham, OR 97030-3300. *Phone:* 503-491-7265. *Website:* http://www.mhcc.edu/.

## Oregon Coast Community College
### Newport, Oregon

- **Public** 2-year, founded 1987
- **Small-town** 24-acre campus
- **Coed**

**Undergraduates** 227 full-time, 259 part-time. Students come from 4 states and territories; 1% are from out of state; 0.2% Black or African American, non-Hispanic/Latino; 13% Hispanic/Latino; 1% Asian, non-Hispanic/Latino; 0.7% Native Hawaiian or other Pacific Islander, non-Hispanic/Latino; 2% American Indian or Alaska Native, non-Hispanic/Latino; 7% Two or more races, non-Hispanic/Latino; 3% Race/ethnicity unknown; 6% transferred in. *Retention:* 65% of full-time freshmen returned.
**Faculty** *Student/faculty ratio:* 17:1.
**Academics** *Calendar:* quarters. *Degree:* certificates and associate. *Special study options:* academic remediation for entering students, cooperative education, distance learning, English as a second language, honors programs, internships, part-time degree program, services for LD students, summer session for credit.
**Library** Oregon Coast Community College Library. *Books:* 13,033 (physical), 110,699 (digital/electronic); *Serial titles:* 2,771 (physical); *Databases:* 53. Students can reserve study rooms.
**Student Life** *Campus security:* 24-hour emergency response devices.
**Costs (2017–18)** *Tuition:* state resident $3564 full-time, $99 per credit part-time; nonresident $7704 full-time, $214 per credit part-time. Full-time tuition and fees vary according to course load and program. Part-time tuition and fees vary according to course load and program. *Required fees:* $576 full-time, $16 per credit part-time.
**Applying** *Options:* electronic application. *Required for some:* essay or personal statement, 2 letters of recommendation, interview.
**Freshman Application Contact** Student Services, Oregon Coast Community College, 400 SE College Way, Newport, OR 97366. *Phone:* 541-265-2283. *Fax:* 541-265-3820. *E-mail:* webinfo@occc.cc.or.us. *Website:* http://www.oregoncoastcc.org/.

## Pioneer Pacific College
### Wilsonville, Oregon

**Freshman Application Contact** Ms. Juli Lau, Vice President of Admissions, Pioneer Pacific College, 27375 Southwest Parkway Avenue, Wilsonville, OR 97070. *Phone:* 503-682-1862. *Toll-free phone:* 866-PPC-INFO. *Fax:* 503-682-1514. *E-mail:* info@pioneerpacific.edu. *Website:* http://www.pioneerpacific.edu/.

## Portland Community College
### Portland, Oregon

**Freshman Application Contact** Admissions and Registration Office, Portland Community College, PO Box 19000, Portland, OR 97280. *Phone:* 503-977-8888. *Toll-free phone:* 866-922-1010. *Website:* http://www.pcc.edu/.

## Rogue Community College
### Grants Pass, Oregon

- **State and locally supported** 2-year, founded 1970
- **Rural** 84-acre campus
- **Endowment** $9.3 million
- **Coed**

**Undergraduates** 1,896 full-time, 3,005 part-time. Students come from 26 states and territories; 4 other countries; 3% are from out of state; 0.9% Black or African American, non-Hispanic/Latino; 17% Hispanic/Latino; 2% Asian, non-Hispanic/Latino; 0.5% Native Hawaiian or other Pacific Islander, non-Hispanic/Latino; 1% American Indian or Alaska Native, non-Hispanic/Latino; 4% Two or more races, non-Hispanic/Latino; 4% Race/ethnicity unknown; 0.1% international; 5% transferred in.
**Faculty** *Student/faculty ratio:* 18:1.

**Academics** *Calendar:* quarters. *Degree:* certificates and associate. *Special study options:* academic remediation for entering students, adult/continuing education programs, advanced placement credit, cooperative education, distance learning, double majors, English as a second language, independent study, internships, part-time degree program, services for LD students, study abroad, summer session for credit.
**Library** Rogue Community College Library. *Books:* 26,630 (physical).
**Student Life** *Campus security:* 24-hour emergency response devices and patrols, late-night transport/escort service.
**Financial Aid** Of all full-time matriculated undergraduates who enrolled in 2016, 1,490 applied for aid, 1,252 were judged to have need, 78 had their need fully met. 68 Federal Work-Study jobs (averaging $3011). In 2016, 41. *Average percent of need met:* 78. *Average financial aid package:* $8375. *Average need-based loan:* $3194. *Average need-based gift aid:* $5840. *Average non-need-based aid:* $1710.
**Applying** *Options:* electronic application, early admission.
**Freshman Application Contact** Mr. John Duarte, Director of Enrollment Services, Rogue Community College, 3345 Redwood Highway, Grants Pass, OR 97527-9291. *Phone:* 541-956-7176. *Fax:* 541-471-3585. *E-mail:* jduarte@roguecc.edu. *Website:* http://www.roguecc.edu/.

## Southwestern Oregon Community College
### Coos Bay, Oregon

**Freshman Application Contact** Miss Barb Shreckengost, Admissions, Southwestern Oregon Community College, 1988 Newmark Avenue, Coos Bay, OR 97420. *Phone:* 541-888-7636. *Toll-free phone:* 800-962-2838. *E-mail:* lwells@socc.edu. *Website:* http://www.socc.edu/.

## Sumner College
### Portland, Oregon

**Freshman Application Contact** Sumner College, 15115 SW Sequoia Parkway, Suite 200, Portland, OR 97224. *Website:* http://www.sumnercollege.edu/.

## Tillamook Bay Community College
### Tillamook, Oregon

- **District-supported** 2-year, founded 1984
- **Rural** 7-acre campus
- **Endowment** $475,359
- **Coed,** 261 undergraduate students, 49% full-time, 56% women, 44% men

**Undergraduates** 127 full-time, 134 part-time. Students come from 1 other state; 18% Hispanic/Latino; 2% Asian, non-Hispanic/Latino; 0.4% Native Hawaiian or other Pacific Islander, non-Hispanic/Latino; 2% American Indian or Alaska Native, non-Hispanic/Latino; 3% Race/ethnicity unknown; 4% international; 3% transferred in. *Retention:* 14% of full-time freshmen returned.
**Freshmen** *Admission:* 108 enrolled.
**Faculty** *Total:* 53, 15% full-time, 23% with terminal degrees. *Student/faculty ratio:* 15:1.
**Majors** Agriculture; criminal justice/law enforcement administration; general studies; industrial mechanics and maintenance technology; liberal arts and sciences/liberal studies.
**Academics** *Calendar:* quarters. *Degree:* certificates and associate. *Special study options:* academic remediation for entering students, advanced placement credit, distance learning, English as a second language, independent study, part-time degree program, services for LD students, summer session for credit.
**Library** Tillamook Bay Community College Library. *Books:* 3,696 (physical), 172,327 (digital/electronic); *Serial titles:* 27 (physical), 44,286 (digital/electronic). Weekly public service hours: 48; students can reserve study rooms.
**Student Life** *Campus security:* alarmed exterior doors, classroom door locks.
**Costs (2018–19)** *Tuition:* state resident $4320 full-time, $96 per credit hour part-time; nonresident $5220 full-time, $116 per credit hour part-time. *Required fees:* $270 full-time, $6 per credit hour part-time. *Payment plans:* installment, deferred payment. *Waivers:* senior citizens and employees or children of employees.
**Applying** *Options:* electronic application. *Recommended:* high school transcript. *Application deadlines:* rolling (freshmen), rolling (transfers).
**Freshman Application Contact** Rhoda Hanson, Director of Student Services, Tillamook Bay Community College, 4301 Third St, Tillamook, OR 97224. *Phone:* 503-842-8222 Ext. 1110. *Fax:* 503-842-8334. *E-mail:* rhodahanson@tillamookbaycc.edu.
*Website:* http://www.tillamookbaycc.edu/.

# Treasure Valley Community College

## Ontario, Oregon

- **State and locally supported** 2-year, founded 1962
- **Rural** 90-acre campus with easy access to Boise
- **Endowment** $5.3 million
- **Coed,** 2,170 undergraduate students, 44% full-time, 57% women, 43% men

**Undergraduates** 958 full-time, 1,212 part-time. Students come from 15 states and territories; 2 other countries; 67% are from out of state; 2% Black or African American, non-Hispanic/Latino; 25% Hispanic/Latino; 0.7% Asian, non-Hispanic/Latino; 0.3% Native Hawaiian or other Pacific Islander, non-Hispanic/Latino; 1% American Indian or Alaska Native, non-Hispanic/Latino; 3% Two or more races, non-Hispanic/Latino; 4% Race/ethnicity unknown; 0.4% international; 5% transferred in; 6% live on campus. *Retention:* 40% of full-time freshmen returned.

**Freshmen** *Admission:* 2,447 applied, 2,447 admitted, 455 enrolled.

**Faculty** *Total:* 86, 55% full-time, 79% with terminal degrees. *Student/faculty ratio:* 21:1.

**Majors** Agricultural business and management; agricultural economics; agriculture; agronomy and crop science; airline pilot and flight crew; animal sciences; business administration and management; carpentry; computer and information sciences; computer science; criminal justice/police science; drafting and design technology; elementary education; farm and ranch management; fire prevention and safety technology; general studies; horse husbandry/equine science and management; horticultural science; industrial technology; liberal arts and sciences/liberal studies; management information systems; medical administrative assistant and medical secretary; medical/clinical assistant; medical transcription; natural resources/conservation; office management; range science and management; registered nursing/registered nurse; soil science and agronomy; solar energy technology; substance abuse/addiction counseling; welding technology; wildlife, fish and wildlands science and management.

**Academics** *Calendar:* quarters. *Degree:* certificates and associate. *Special study options:* academic remediation for entering students, accelerated degree program, adult/continuing education programs, advanced placement credit, cooperative education, distance learning, English as a second language, honors programs, independent study, internships, off-campus study, part-time degree program, services for LD students, summer session for credit.

**Library** Treasure Valley Community College Library. *Books:* 28,887 (physical), 28,887 (digital/electronic); *Serial titles:* 57 (physical), 15 (digital/electronic); *Databases:* 11. Weekly public service hours: 72; students can reserve study rooms.

**Student Life** *Housing Options:* coed, special housing for students with disabilities. Campus housing is university owned. *Activities and Organizations:* choral group, Phi Theta Kappa, Natural Resources, International Business Club, Circle K International (service organization), Ag Ambassadors. *Campus security:* 24-hour emergency response devices, late-night transport/escort service, controlled dormitory access, emergency response phone and computer notifications.

**Athletics** *Intercollegiate sports:* baseball M(s), basketball M(s)/W(s), cross-country running M(s)/W(s), soccer M(s)/W(s), softball W(s), tennis M(s)/W(s), track and field M(s)/W(s), volleyball W(s). *Intramural sports:* basketball M/W, soccer M/W, softball M/W, table tennis M/W, volleyball M/W.

**Costs (2018–19)** *Tuition:* state resident $3564 full-time, $99 per credit part-time; nonresident $3924 full-time, $109 per credit part-time. Full-time tuition and fees vary according to location and program. Part-time tuition and fees vary according to location and program. *Required fees:* $990 full-time, $22 per credit part-time. *Room and board:* $7187; room only: $3926. *Payment plan:* installment. *Waivers:* employees or children of employees.

**Financial Aid** Of all full-time matriculated undergraduates who enrolled in 2016, 90 Federal Work-Study jobs (averaging $1500).

**Applying** *Options:* electronic application, early admission, deferred entrance. *Application deadlines:* rolling (freshmen), rolling (transfers). *Notification:* continuous (freshmen), continuous (transfers).

**Freshman Application Contact** Mr. Sage Mwiinga, Executive Director of Enrollment Management, Treasure Valley Community College, 650 College Boulevard, Ontario, OR 97914. *Phone:* 541-881-5813. *E-mail:* smwiinga@tvcc.cc. *Website:* http://www.tvcc.cc/.

# Umpqua Community College

## Roseburg, Oregon

**Freshman Application Contact** Admissions Office, Umpqua Community College, PO Box 967, Roseburg, OR 97470-0226. *Phone:* 541-440-7743. *Fax:* 541-440-4612. *Website:* http://www.umpqua.edu/.

# PENNSYLVANIA

# All-State Career School–Essington Campus

## Essington, Pennsylvania

**Admissions Office Contact** All-State Career School–Essington Campus, 50 West Powhattan Ave, Essington, PA 19029. *Website:* http://www.allstatecareer.edu/.

# Antonelli Institute

## Erdenheim, Pennsylvania

**Freshman Application Contact** Admissions Office, Antonelli Institute, 300 Montgomery Avenue, Erdenheim, PA 19038. *Phone:* 800-722-7871. *Toll-free phone:* 800-722-7871. *Website:* http://www.antonelli.edu/.

# Berks Technical Institute

## Wyomissing, Pennsylvania

**Freshman Application Contact** Mr. Allan Brussolo, Academic Dean, Berks Technical Institute, 2205 Ridgewood Road, Wyomissing, PA 19610-1168. *Phone:* 610-372-1722. *Toll-free phone:* 866-591-8384. *Fax:* 610-376-4684. *E-mail:* abrussolo@berks.edu. *Website:* http://www.berks.edu/.

# Bidwell Training Center

## Pittsburgh, Pennsylvania

**Freshman Application Contact** Admissions Office, Bidwell Training Center, 1815 Metropolitan Street, Pittsburgh, PA 15233. *Phone:* 412-322-1773. *Toll-free phone:* 800-516-1800. *E-mail:* admissions@mcg-btc.org. *Website:* http://www.bidwelltraining.edu/.

# Bradford School

## Pittsburgh, Pennsylvania

**Freshman Application Contact** Admissions Office, Bradford School, 125 West Station Square Drive, Pittsburgh, PA 15219. *Phone:* 412-391-6710. *Toll-free phone:* 800-391-6810. *Website:* http://www.bradfordpittsburgh.edu/.

# Brightwood Career Institute, Broomall Campus

## Broomall, Pennsylvania

**Freshman Application Contact** Brightwood Career Institute, Broomall Campus, 1991 Sproul Road, Suite 42, Broomall, PA 19008. *Phone:* 610-353-3300. *Toll-free phone:* 866-536-2023. *Website:* http://www.brightwoodcareer.edu/.

# Brightwood Career Institute, Harrisburg Campus

## Harrisburg, Pennsylvania

**Freshman Application Contact** Brightwood Career Institute, Harrisburg Campus, 5650 Derry Street, Harrisburg, PA 17111. *Phone:* 717-558-1300. *Toll-free phone:* 866-536-2023. *Website:* http://www.brightwoodcareer.edu/.

# Brightwood Career Institute, Philadelphia Campus

## Philadelphia, Pennsylvania

**Freshman Application Contact** Admissions Director, Brightwood Career Institute, Philadelphia Campus, 3010 Market Street, Philadelphia, PA 19104. *Toll-free phone:* 866-536-2023. *Website:* http://www.brightwoodcareer.edu/.

# Brightwood Career Institute, Philadelphia Mills Campus

## Philadelphia, Pennsylvania

**Freshman Application Contact** Brightwood Career Institute, Philadelphia Mills Campus, 177 Franklin Mills Boulevard, Philadelphia, PA 19154. *Phone:*

215-612-6600. *Toll-free phone:* 866-536-2023. *Website:* http://www.brightwoodcareer.edu/.

# Brightwood Career Institute, Pittsburgh Campus
## Pittsburgh, Pennsylvania

**Freshman Application Contact** Brightwood Career Institute, Pittsburgh Campus, 933 Penn Avenue, Pittsburgh, PA 15222. *Phone:* 412-261-2647. *Toll-free phone:* 866-536-2023. *Website:* http://www.brightwoodcareer.edu/.

# Bucks County Community College
## Newtown, Pennsylvania

- **County-supported** 2-year, founded 1964
- **Suburban** 200-acre campus with easy access to Philadelphia
- **Endowment** $6.3 million
- **Coed,** 7,783 undergraduate students, 34% full-time, 55% women, 45% men

**Undergraduates** 2,641 full-time, 5,142 part-time. Students come from 19 states and territories; 1% are from out of state; 5% Black or African American, non-Hispanic/Latino; 7% Hispanic/Latino; 4% Asian, non-Hispanic/Latino; 0.2% Native Hawaiian or other Pacific Islander, non-Hispanic/Latino; 0.5% American Indian or Alaska Native, non-Hispanic/Latino; 2% Two or more races, non-Hispanic/Latino; 11% Race/ethnicity unknown; 75% transferred in. *Retention:* 70% of full-time freshmen returned.
**Freshmen** *Admission:* 2,704 applied, 2,634 admitted, 1,838 enrolled.
**Faculty** *Total:* 655, 22% full-time, 24% with terminal degrees. *Student/faculty ratio:* 15:1.
**Majors** Accounting technology and bookkeeping; art history, criticism and conservation; baking and pastry arts; biology/biotechnology laboratory technician; biology teacher education; business administration and management; business/commerce; cabinetmaking and millwork; chemical technology; child-care provision; cinematography and film/video production; commercial and advertising art; commercial photography; computer and information sciences; computer systems networking and telecommunications; criminal justice/safety; critical infrastructure protection; culinary arts; early childhood education; engineering; engineering technology; English; environmental science; fire services administration; food service systems administration; health professions related; health services/allied health/health sciences; history; history teacher education; hospitality administration; information science/studies; journalism; kinesiology and exercise science; legal professions and studies related; liberal arts and sciences and humanities related; liberal arts and sciences/liberal studies; mathematics; mathematics teacher education; medical/clinical assistant; medical insurance coding; meeting and event planning; multi/interdisciplinary studies related; music; network and system administration; neuroscience; physical education teaching and coaching; psychology; radiologic technology/science; registered nursing/registered nurse; small business administration; social sciences; social work; speech communication and rhetoric; sport and fitness administration/management; visual and performing arts; web page, digital/multimedia and information resources design.
**Academics** *Calendar:* semesters. *Degree:* certificates and associate. *Special study options:* academic remediation for entering students, adult/continuing education programs, advanced placement credit, cooperative education, distance learning, English as a second language, external degree program, independent study, internships, part-time degree program, services for LD students, student-designed majors, summer session for credit.
**Library** Bucks County Community College Library. *Books:* 112,367 (physical), 8,465 (digital/electronic); *Serial titles:* 205 (physical), 66 (digital/electronic); *Databases:* 56. Weekly public service hours: 72; students can reserve study rooms.
**Student Life** *Housing:* college housing not available. *Activities and Organizations:* drama/theater group, student-run newspaper, radio and television station, choral group, National Society of Leadership and Success, Phi Theta Kappa, Muslim Students Association, Habitat for Humanity, Bucks Business Association. *Campus security:* 24-hour emergency response devices and patrols, late-night transport/escort service. *Student services:* personal/psychological counseling, women's center, veterans affairs office.
**Athletics** Member NJCAA. *Intercollegiate sports:* baseball M, basketball M/W, golf M, soccer M/W, softball W, tennis M/W, volleyball W. *Intramural sports:* baseball M, basketball M/W, equestrian sports W(c), football M, skiing (downhill) M(c)/W(c), soccer M/W, table tennis M, tennis M/W, ultimate Frisbee M/W, volleyball W.
**Costs (2017–18)** *Tuition:* area resident $4350 full-time, $145 per credit hour part-time; state resident $8700 full-time, $290 per credit hour part-time; nonresident $13,050 full-time, $435 per credit hour part-time. *Required fees:* $1160 full-time, $62 per credit hour part-time, $247 per term part-time.

*Payment plans:* installment, deferred payment. *Waivers:* senior citizens and employees or children of employees.
**Financial Aid** Of all full-time matriculated undergraduates who enrolled in 2016, 147 Federal Work-Study jobs (averaging $1708).
**Applying** *Options:* electronic application, early admission. *Required:* high school transcript. *Required for some:* essay or personal statement, interview.
**Admissions Office Contact** Bucks County Community College, 275 Swamp Road, Newtown, PA 18940-1525.
*Website:* http://www.bucks.edu/.

# Butler County Community College
## Butler, Pennsylvania

**Freshman Application Contact** Mr. Robert Morris, Director of Admissions, Butler County Community College, College Drive, PO Box 1205, Butler, PA 16003-1203. *Phone:* 724-287-8711 Ext. 344. *Toll-free phone:* 888-826-2829. *Fax:* 724-287-4961. *E-mail:* robert.morris@bc3.edu. *Website:* http://www.bc3.edu/.

# Career Training Academy
## Lower Burrell, Pennsylvania

**Director of Admissions** Ms. Tyna Pitignano, Career Training Academy, 179 Hillcrest Shopping Center, Lower Burrell, PA 15068. *Phone:* 724-337-1000. *Toll-free phone:* 866-673-7773. *E-mail:* admissions@careeta.edu. *Website:* http://www.careerta.edu/.

# Career Training Academy
## Pittsburgh, Pennsylvania

**Freshman Application Contact** Jaimie Vignone, Career Training Academy, 1014 West View Park Drive, Pittsburgh, PA 15229. *Phone:* 412-367-4000. *Toll-free phone:* 866-673-7773. *Fax:* 412-369-7223. *E-mail:* admission3@careerta.edu. *Website:* http://www.careerta.edu/.

# Commonwealth Technical Institute
## Johnstown, Pennsylvania

**Freshman Application Contact** Mr. Jason Gies, Admissions Supervisor, Commonwealth Technical Institute, Hiram G. Andrews Center, 727 Goucher Street, Johnstown, PA 15905. *Phone:* 814-255-8200 Ext. 0564. *Toll-free phone:* 800-762-4211. *Fax:* 814-255-8283. *E-mail:* jgies@pa.gov. *Website:* http://www.dli.pa.gov/Individuals/Disability-Services/hgac/Pages/default.aspx.

# Community College of Allegheny County
## Pittsburgh, Pennsylvania

- **County-supported** 2-year, founded 1966
- **Urban** 242-acre campus
- **Coed,** 16,147 undergraduate students, 35% full-time, 55% women, 45% men

**Undergraduates** 5,669 full-time, 10,478 part-time. 18% Black or African American, non-Hispanic/Latino; 3% Hispanic/Latino; 3% Asian, non-Hispanic/Latino; 0.1% Native Hawaiian or other Pacific Islander, non-Hispanic/Latino; 0.4% American Indian or Alaska Native, non-Hispanic/Latino; 2% Two or more races, non-Hispanic/Latino; 13% Race/ethnicity unknown.
**Freshmen** *Admission:* 4,039 enrolled.
**Faculty** *Student/faculty ratio:* 18:1.
**Majors** Accounting technology and bookkeeping; administrative assistant and secretarial science; airline pilot and flight crew; applied horticulture/horticulture operations; architectural drafting and CAD/CADD; art; athletic training; automobile/automotive mechanics technology; automotive engineering technology; aviation/airway management; banking and financial support services; biology/biological sciences; biotechnology; building construction technology; building/property maintenance; business administration and management; business automation/technology/data entry; business machine repair; CAD/CADD drafting/design technology; carpentry; chemical technology; chemistry; child-care provision; child development; civil drafting and CAD/CADD; civil engineering technology; clinical/medical laboratory technology; commercial and advertising art; communications technologies and support services related; community health services counseling; computer engineering technology; computer systems networking and telecommunications; computer technology/computer systems technology; construction engineering technology; construction trades; construction trades related; corrections; cosmetology and personal grooming arts related; court reporting; criminal justice/police science; critical infrastructure protection;

culinary arts; diagnostic medical sonography and ultrasound technology; dietitian assistant; drafting and design technology; drafting/design engineering technologies related; dramatic/theater arts; education (specific levels and methods) related; education (specific subject areas) related; electrical, electronic and communications engineering technology; electroneurodiagnostic/electroencephalographic technology; elementary education; emergency medical technology (EMT paramedic); energy management and systems technology; engineering science; engineering technologies and engineering related; English; entrepreneurship; environmental engineering technology; fire prevention and safety technology; food service systems administration; foreign languages and literatures; game and interactive media design; general studies; graphic design; greenhouse management; health and physical education/fitness; health information/medical records technology; health professions related; health unit coordinator/ward clerk; heating, air conditioning, ventilation and refrigeration maintenance technology; hotel/motel administration; housing and human environments related; human development and family studies related; humanities; human resources management; hydraulics and fluid power technology; industrial and product design; industrial technology; insurance; journalism; landscaping and groundskeeping; legal administrative assistant/secretary; legal assistant/paralegal; liberal arts and sciences/liberal studies; licensed practical/vocational nurse training; machine shop technology; management information systems; manufacturing engineering technology; marketing/marketing management; mathematics; mechanical drafting and CAD/CADD; mechatronics, robotics, and automation engineering; medical administrative assistant and medical secretary; medical/clinical assistant; medical radiologic technology; middle school education; music; nanotechnology; nuclear medical technology; nursing assistant/aide and patient care assistant/aide; occupational therapist assistant; office management; ornamental horticulture; painting and wall covering; perioperative/operating room and surgical nursing; pharmacy technician; physical therapy technology; physics; plant nursery management; psychiatric/mental health services technology; psychology; quality control technology; radiologic technology/science; real estate; registered nursing/registered nurse; respiratory care therapy; restaurant, culinary, and catering management; retailing; robotics technology; science technologies related; sheet metal technology; sign language interpretation and translation; social sciences; social work; sociology; solar energy technology; substance abuse/addiction counseling; surgical technology; teacher assistant/aide; therapeutic recreation; tourism promotion; turf and turfgrass management; visual and performing arts related; welding technology.

**Academics** *Calendar:* semesters. *Degree:* certificates, diplomas, and associate. *Special study options:* academic remediation for entering students, accelerated degree program, distance learning, English as a second language, honors programs, off-campus study, part-time degree program, services for LD students, study abroad, summer session for credit.

**Library** Community College of Allegheny County Library.

**Student Life** *Housing:* college housing not available. *Activities and Organizations:* drama/theater group, student-run radio and television station, choral group. *Campus security:* 24-hour emergency response devices and patrols, late-night transport/escort service. *Student services:* health clinic, personal/psychological counseling, veterans affairs office.

**Athletics** Member NJCAA. *Intercollegiate sports:* baseball M, basketball M/W, bowling M/W, golf M/W, ice hockey M, softball W, table tennis M/W, tennis M/W, volleyball W. *Intramural sports:* badminton M/W, basketball M/W, bowling M/W, cross-country running M/W, football M, golf M/W, lacrosse M, racquetball M/W, softball M/W, table tennis M/W, tennis M/W, volleyball M/W, weight lifting M/W.

**Costs (2017–18)** *Tuition:* area resident $3300 full-time, $110 per credit hour part-time; state resident $6600 full-time, $220 per credit hour part-time; nonresident $9900 full-time, $330 per credit hour part-time. Full-time tuition and fees vary according to course load and program. Part-time tuition and fees vary according to course load and program. *Payment plan:* installment. *Waivers:* senior citizens and employees or children of employees.

**Applying** *Options:* early decision, early action. *Recommended:* high school transcript.

**Freshman Application Contact** Admissions Office, Community College of Allegheny County, 808 Ridge Avenue, Pittsburgh, PA 15212. *Phone:* 412-237-2511. *Website:* http://www.ccac.edu/.

## Community College of Beaver County
### Monaca, Pennsylvania

**Freshman Application Contact** Enrollment Management, Community College of Beaver County, One Campus Drive, Monaca, PA 15061-2588. *Phone:* 724-480-3500. *Toll-free phone:* 800-335-0222. *E-mail:* admissions@ccbc.edu. *Website:* http://www.ccbc.edu/.

## Community College of Philadelphia
### Philadelphia, Pennsylvania

- **State and locally supported** 2-year, founded 1964
- **Urban** 14-acre campus with easy access to Philadelphia
- **Coed,** 30,194 undergraduate students

**Undergraduates** Students come from 50 other countries.
**Faculty** *Total:* 1,038, 42% full-time.
**Majors** Accounting; art; automobile/automotive mechanics technology; biology/biological sciences; business administration and management; chemistry; clinical/medical laboratory technology; computer science; construction engineering technology; criminal justice/law enforcement administration; culinary arts; dental hygiene; drafting and design technology; education; engineering; engineering technology; English; fire science/firefighting; health professions related; hotel/motel administration; human services; kindergarten/preschool education; liberal arts and sciences/liberal studies; medical radiologic technology; music; photography; psychology; recording arts technology; respiratory care therapy; sign language interpretation and translation.
**Academics** *Calendar:* semesters. *Degree:* certificates, diplomas, and associate. *Special study options:* academic remediation for entering students, accelerated degree program, adult/continuing education programs, advanced placement credit, cooperative education, distance learning, English as a second language, external degree program, honors programs, independent study, internships, off-campus study, part-time degree program, services for LD students, student-designed majors, study abroad, summer session for credit. *ROTC:* Army (c).
**Library** Main Campus Library plus 2 others. *Books:* 84,000 (physical); *Databases:* 40. Weekly public service hours: 30; students can reserve study rooms.
**Student Life** *Housing:* college housing not available. *Activities and Organizations:* drama/theater group, student-run newspaper, choral group, Philadelphia L.E.A.D.S, Phi Theta Kappa, Student Government Association, Vanguard Student Newspaper, Fundraising Club. *Campus security:* 24-hour emergency response devices and patrols, late-night transport/escort service, phone/alert systems in classrooms/buildings, electronic messages/alerts, ID required to enter buildings. *Student services:* personal/psychological counseling, women's center, legal services, veterans affairs office.
**Athletics** Member NJCAA. *Intercollegiate sports:* basketball M/W, cross-country running M/W, track and field M/W, volleyball W. *Intramural sports:* soccer M/W, ultimate Frisbee M/W, volleyball M/W.
**Costs (2018–19)** *Tuition:* area resident $5264 full-time, $159 per credit hour part-time; state resident $9320 full-time, $318 per credit hour part-time; nonresident $13,376 full-time, $477 per credit hour part-time. Full-time tuition and fees vary according to course load and program. Part-time tuition and fees vary according to course load and program. *Payment plan:* installment. *Waivers:* senior citizens and employees or children of employees.
**Applying** *Options:* electronic application, early admission, deferred entrance. *Required for some:* high school transcript, specific entry requirements for allied health and nursing programs. *Application deadlines:* rolling (freshmen), rolling (transfers). *Notification:* continuous (freshmen), continuous (transfers).
**Freshman Application Contact** Community College of Philadelphia, 1700 Spring Garden Street, Philadelphia, PA 19130-3991. *Phone:* 215-751-8010. *Website:* http://www.ccp.edu/.

## Consolidated School of Business
### York, Pennsylvania

**Freshman Application Contact** Ms. Sandra Swanger, Admissions Representative, Consolidated School of Business, 1605 Clugston Road, York, PA 17404. *Phone:* 717-764-9550. *Toll-free phone:* 800-520-0691. *Fax:* 717-764-9469. *E-mail:* sswanger@csb.edu. *Website:* http://www.csb.edu/.

## Dean Institute of Technology
### Pittsburgh, Pennsylvania

**Director of Admissions** Mr. Nicholas Ali, Admissions Director, Dean Institute of Technology, 1501 West Liberty Avenue, Pittsburgh, PA 15226-1103. *Phone:* 412-531-4433. *Website:* http://www.deantech.edu/.

## Delaware County Community College
### Media, Pennsylvania

**Freshman Application Contact** Ms. Hope Diehl, Director of Admissions and Enrollment Services, Delaware County Community College, 901 South Media Line Road, Media, PA 19063-1094. *Phone:* 610-359-5050. *Fax:* 610-723-1530. *E-mail:* admiss@dccc.edu. *Website:* http://www.dccc.edu/.

# Douglas Education Center
## Monessen, Pennsylvania

**Freshman Application Contact** Ms. Sherry Lee Walters, Director of Enrollment Services, Douglas Education Center, 130 Seventh Street, Monessen, PA 15062. *Phone:* 724-684-3684 Ext. 2181. *Toll-free phone:* 800-413-6013. *Website:* http://www.dec.edu/.

# Erie Institute of Technology
## Erie, Pennsylvania

**Freshman Application Contact** Erie Institute of Technology, 940 Millcreek Mall, Erie, PA 16565. *Phone:* 814-868-9900. *Toll-free phone:* 866-868-3743. *Website:* http://www.erieit.edu/.

# Fortis Institute
## Erie, Pennsylvania

**Director of Admissions** Guy M. Euliano, President, Fortis Institute, 5757 West 26th Street, Erie, PA 16506. *Phone:* 814-838-7673. *Toll-free phone:* 855-4-FORTIS. *Fax:* 814-838-8642. *E-mail:* geuliano@tsbi.org. *Website:* http://www.fortis.edu/.

# Fortis Institute
## Forty Fort, Pennsylvania

**Freshman Application Contact** Admissions Office, Fortis Institute, 166 Slocum Street, Forty Fort, PA 18704. *Phone:* 570-288-8400. *Toll-free phone:* 855-4-FORTIS. *Website:* http://www.fortis.edu/.

# Fortis Institute
## Scranton, Pennsylvania

**Director of Admissions** Ms. Heather Contardi, Director of Admissions, Fortis Institute, 517 Ash Street, Scranton, PA 18509. *Phone:* 570-558-1818. *Toll-free phone:* 855-4-FORTIS. *Fax:* 570-342-4537. *E-mail:* heatherp@markogroup.com. *Website:* http://www.fortis.edu/.

# Great Lakes Institute of Technology
## Erie, Pennsylvania

**Admissions Office Contact** Great Lakes Institute of Technology, 5100 Peach Street, Erie, PA 16509. *Website:* http://www.glit.edu/.

# Harcum College
## Bryn Mawr, Pennsylvania

**Freshman Application Contact** Office of Enrollment Management, Harcum College, 750 Montgomery Avenue, Bryn Mawr, PA 19010-3476. *Phone:* 610-526-6050. *E-mail:* enroll@harcum.edu. *Website:* http://www.harcum.edu/.

# Harrisburg Area Community College
## Harrisburg, Pennsylvania

- **State and locally supported** 2-year, founded 1964
- **Urban** 212-acre campus
- **Coed,** 18,681 undergraduate students, 30% full-time, 64% women, 36% men

**Undergraduates** 5,516 full-time, 13,165 part-time. 3% are from out of state; 39% Black or African American, non-Hispanic/Latino; 40% Hispanic/Latino; 11% Asian, non-Hispanic/Latino; 0.5% Native Hawaiian or other Pacific Islander, non-Hispanic/Latino; 0.9% American Indian or Alaska Native, non-Hispanic/Latino; 0.6% Two or more races, non-Hispanic/Latino; 0.3% Race/ethnicity unknown; 7% international; 8% transferred in.
**Freshmen** *Admission:* 12,739 applied, 12,737 admitted, 2,437 enrolled.
**Faculty** *Total:* 1,113, 29% full-time, 37% with terminal degrees. *Student/faculty ratio:* 17:1.
**Majors** Accounting technology and bookkeeping; administrative assistant and secretarial science; architectural engineering technology; architecture; automobile/automotive mechanics technology; biology/biological sciences; business administration and management; business/commerce; cardiovascular technology; chemistry; civil engineering technology; clinical/medical laboratory technology; communication and journalism related; computer and information sciences; computer and information systems security; computer science; computer systems networking and telecommunications; construction engineering technology; construction trades; criminal justice/law enforcement administration; criminal justice/police science; culinary arts; dental hygiene;

design and visual communications; diagnostic medical sonography and ultrasound technology; dietetics; dramatic/theater arts; early childhood education; electrical, electronic and communications engineering technology; electrician; emergency medical technology (EMT paramedic); engineering; engineering technologies and engineering related; environmental science; fire science/firefighting; general studies; geographic information science and cartography; graphic design; health and physical education/fitness; health/health-care administration; health professions related; health services administration; heating, air conditioning, ventilation and refrigeration maintenance technology; human services; international relations and affairs; legal assistant/paralegal; mathematics; mechanical engineering/mechanical technology; mechatronics, robotics, and automation engineering; medical/clinical assistant; medical informatics; music management; nuclear medical technology; philosophy; photography; physical sciences; psychology; radiologic technology/science; registered nursing/registered nurse; respiratory care therapy; sales, distribution, and marketing operations; secondary education; social sciences; social work; structural engineering; surgical technology; visual and performing arts; viticulture and enology; web page, digital/multimedia and information resources design.
**Academics** *Calendar:* semesters. *Degree:* certificates, diplomas, and associate. *Special study options:* academic remediation for entering students, adult/continuing education programs, advanced placement credit, distance learning, double majors, English as a second language, honors programs, independent study, internships, part-time degree program, services for LD students, summer session for credit. *ROTC:* Army (b).
**Library** McCormick Library.
**Student Life** *Housing:* college housing not available. *Activities and Organizations:* drama/theater group, student-run newspaper, Student Government Association, Phi Theta Kappa, African-American Student Association, Mosiaco Club, Fourth Estate. *Campus security:* 24-hour emergency response devices and patrols, late-night transport/escort service. *Student services:* veterans affairs office.
**Athletics** *Intercollegiate sports:* basketball M/W, golf M/W, soccer M, volleyball M/W.
**Costs (2017–18)** *Tuition:* area resident $5228 full-time, $174 per credit hour part-time; state resident $6330 full-time, $211 per credit hour part-time; nonresident $7680 full-time, $256 per credit hour part-time. Full-time tuition and fees vary according to location and program. Part-time tuition and fees vary according to location and program. *Required fees:* $1245 full-time, $42 per credit hour part-time. *Payment plan:* installment. *Waivers:* employees or children of employees.
**Financial Aid** Of all full-time matriculated undergraduates who enrolled in 2017, 3,838 applied for aid, 3,035 were judged to have need.
**Applying** *Options:* electronic application, early admission, deferred entrance. *Required for some:* high school transcript, 1 letter of recommendation, interview.
**Freshman Application Contact** Harrisburg Area Community College, Harrisburg, PA 17110. *Toll-free phone:* 800-ABC-HACC. *E-mail:* admit@hacc.edu.
*Website:* http://www.hacc.edu/.

# JNA Institute of Culinary Arts
## Philadelphia, Pennsylvania

- **Proprietary** 2-year, founded 1988
- **Urban** campus with easy access to Philadelphia
- **Coed**

**Undergraduates** 59 full-time. Students come from 7 states and territories; 10% are from out of state; 57% Black or African American, non-Hispanic/Latino; 11% Hispanic/Latino; 3% Asian, non-Hispanic/Latino. *Retention:* 60% of full-time freshmen returned.
**Academics** *Calendar:* continuous. *Degree:* associate.
**Costs (2017–18)** *Tuition:* $12,650 full-time, $600 per credit hour part-time. Full-time tuition and fees vary according to program. No tuition increase for student's term of enrollment. *Required fees:* $75 full-time.
**Freshman Application Contact** Admissions Office, JNA Institute of Culinary Arts, 1212 South Broad Street, Philadelphia, PA 19146. *Website:* http://www.culinaryarts.com/.

# Johnson College
## Scranton, Pennsylvania

- **Independent** 2-year, founded 1912
- **Urban** 65-acre campus
- **Coed,** 376 undergraduate students, 97% full-time, 28% women, 72% men

**Undergraduates** 363 full-time, 13 part-time. *Retention:* 69% of full-time freshmen returned.
**Freshmen** *Admission:* 156 enrolled. *Average high school GPA:* 3.0.

**Faculty** *Total:* 23, 91% full-time, 22% with terminal degrees. *Student/faculty ratio:* 17:1.

**Majors** Architectural drafting and CAD/CADD; automobile/automotive mechanics technology; biomedical technology; building/home/construction inspection; cabinetmaking and millwork; carpentry; diesel mechanics technology; electrical, electronic and communications engineering technology; electrician; heating, air conditioning, ventilation and refrigeration maintenance technology; industrial electronics technology; industrial mechanics and maintenance technology; information technology; machine shop technology; machine tool technology; medical radiologic technology; precision production trades; sales, distribution, and marketing operations; veterinary/animal health technology.

**Academics** *Calendar:* semesters. *Degree:* certificates and associate. *Special study options:* academic remediation for entering students, adult/continuing education programs, internships, part-time degree program, services for LD students, summer session for credit.

**Library** Johnson College Library.

**Student Life** *Housing Options:* coed. Campus housing is provided by a third party. *Activities and Organizations:* Student Government, Social Force Club, trade/technical/clinical clubs. *Campus security:* 24-hour emergency response devices. *Student services:* personal/psychological counseling.

**Athletics** *Intercollegiate sports:* basketball M/W, bowling M/W, cross-country running M/W, golf M/W. *Intramural sports:* softball M/W, table tennis M/W, volleyball M/W.

**Standardized Tests** *Required for some:* SAT (for admission). *Recommended:* SAT (for admission).

**Financial Aid** Of all full-time matriculated undergraduates who enrolled in 2016, 40 Federal Work-Study jobs (averaging $800).

**Applying** *Options:* electronic application, deferred entrance. *Application fee:* $30. *Required:* essay or personal statement, high school transcript. *Required for some:* interview. *Application deadlines:* 5/1 (freshmen), rolling (transfers). *Notification:* 8/15 (transfers).

**Freshman Application Contact** Johnson College, 3427 North Main Avenue, Scranton, PA 18508-1495. *Phone:* 570-702-8911. *Toll-free phone:* 800-2WE-WORK.

*Website:* http://www.johnson.edu/.

# Lackawanna College
## Scranton, Pennsylvania

- **Independent** primarily 2-year, founded 1894
- **Urban** 4-acre campus
- **Endowment** $5.7 million
- **Coed,** 1,604 undergraduate students, 73% full-time, 49% women, 51% men

**Undergraduates** 1,169 full-time, 435 part-time. Students come from 16 states and territories; 16% Black or African American, non-Hispanic/Latino; 11% Hispanic/Latino; 1% Asian, non-Hispanic/Latino; 0.1% Native Hawaiian or other Pacific Islander, non-Hispanic/Latino; 0.4% American Indian or Alaska Native, non-Hispanic/Latino; 2% Two or more races, non-Hispanic/Latino; 8% Race/ethnicity unknown; 0.4% international; 10% transferred in. *Retention:* 55% of full-time freshmen returned.

**Freshmen** *Admission:* 434 enrolled.

**Faculty** *Total:* 172, 17% full-time. *Student/faculty ratio:* 16:1.

**Majors** Accounting; administrative assistant and secretarial science; banking and financial support services; biology/biological sciences; biology/biotechnology laboratory technician; business administration and management; business administration, management and operations related; business/commerce; cardiovascular science; child-care provision; communication and media related; criminal justice/law enforcement administration; criminal justice/police science; criminal justice/safety; culinary arts; diagnostic medical sonography and ultrasound technology; dramatic/theater arts and stagecraft related; e-commerce; education; emergency medical technology (EMT paramedic); environmental science; financial planning and services; health information/medical records technology; health professions related; hospitality administration; hotel/motel administration; human services; industrial mechanics and maintenance technology; industrial technology; legal assistant/paralegal; liberal arts and sciences and humanities related; liberal arts and sciences/liberal studies; management information systems; medical administrative assistant and medical secretary; mental and social health services and allied professions related; multi/interdisciplinary studies related; organizational behavior; petroleum technology; physical therapy technology; psychology; psychology related; surgical technology.

**Academics** *Calendar:* semesters. *Degrees:* certificates, diplomas, associate, and bachelor's. *Special study options:* academic remediation for entering students, adult/continuing education programs, cooperative education, double majors, English as a second language, internships, part-time degree program, services for LD students, summer session for credit. *ROTC:* Army (c), Air Force (c).

**Library** Albright Memorial Library plus 1 other. Students can reserve study rooms.

**Student Life** *Housing:* on-campus residence required through sophomore year. *Options:* coed, men-only. Campus housing is university owned. *Activities and Organizations:* Student Government Association, V.O.L.C. (Volunteers of Lackawanna College), Falcon Ambassador Board (FAB), COMMunity Club, Pineapple Club (Hospitality & Culinary Club). *Campus security:* 24-hour emergency response devices and patrols, late-night transport/escort service, controlled dormitory access, patrols by college liaison staff. *Student services:* personal/psychological counseling, veterans affairs office.

**Athletics** Member NJCAA. *Intercollegiate sports:* baseball M(s), basketball M(s)/W(s), cross-country running M(s)/W(s), football M(s), golf M(s), soccer M(s)/W(s), softball W(s), tennis W(s), volleyball W(s), wrestling M(s). *Intramural sports:* cheerleading W.

**Standardized Tests** *Recommended:* SAT or ACT (for admission).

**Costs (2018–19)** *Comprehensive fee:* $25,960 includes full-time tuition ($14,850), mandatory fees ($810), and room and board ($10,300). Full-time tuition and fees vary according to course load. Part-time tuition: $520 per credit. *Required fees:* $75 per course part-time, $405 per term part-time. *Room and board:* college room only: $6500. Room and board charges vary according to board plan. *Payment plans:* installment, deferred payment. *Waivers:* employees or children of employees.

**Financial Aid** Of all full-time matriculated undergraduates who enrolled in 2016, 1,049 applied for aid, 953 were judged to have need, 38 had their need fully met. 80 Federal Work-Study jobs (averaging $779). 21 state and other part-time jobs (averaging $619). In 2016, 18 non-need-based awards were made. *Average percent of need met:* 47%. *Average financial aid package:* $9537. *Average need-based loan:* $3247. *Average need-based gift aid:* $7272. *Average non-need-based aid:* $4882. *Average indebtedness upon graduation:* $7347.

**Applying** *Options:* electronic application, early admission, deferred entrance. *Application fee:* $35. *Required:* high school transcript, interview. *Application deadlines:* rolling (freshmen), rolling (transfers).

**Freshman Application Contact** Mr. Eddie Perry, Admissions Advisor, Lackawanna College, 501 Vine Street, Scranton, PA 18509. *Phone:* 570-961-7889. *Toll-free phone:* 877-346-3552. *E-mail:* perrye@lackawanna.edu. *Website:* http://www.lackawanna.edu/.

# Lancaster County Career and Technology Center
## Willow Street, Pennsylvania

**Admissions Office Contact** Lancaster County Career and Technology Center, 1730 Hans Herr Drive, Willow Street, PA 17584. *Website:* http://www.lancasterctc.edu/.

# Lansdale School of Business
## North Wales, Pennsylvania

- **Proprietary** 2-year, founded 1918
- **Suburban** campus with easy access to Philadelphia
- **Coed**

**Academics** *Calendar:* semesters. *Degree:* certificates, diplomas, and associate. *Special study options:* accelerated degree program, adult/continuing education programs, double majors, honors programs, independent study, internships, off-campus study, part-time degree program, summer session for credit.

**Library** Lansdale School of Business Library.

**Applying** *Application fee:* $30. *Required:* high school transcript, interview.

**Freshman Application Contact** Lansdale School of Business, 290 Wissahickon Avenue, North Wales, PA 19454. *Phone:* 215-699-5700 Ext. 112. *Toll-free phone:* 800-219-0486. *Website:* http://www.lsb.edu/.

# Laurel Business Institute
## Uniontown, Pennsylvania

**Freshman Application Contact** Mrs. Lisa Dolan, Laurel Business Institute, 11 East Penn Street, PO Box 877, Uniontown, PA 15401. *Phone:* 724-439-4900 Ext. 158. *Fax:* 724-439-3607. *E-mail:* ldolan@laurel.edu. *Website:* http://www.laurel.edu/locations/uniontown.

# Laurel Technical Institute
## Sharon, Pennsylvania

**Freshman Application Contact** Irene Lewis, Laurel Technical Institute, 200 Sterling Avenue, Sharon, PA 16146. *Phone:* 724-983-0700. *Fax:* 724-983-8355. *E-mail:* info@biop.edu. *Website:* http://www.laurel.edu/locations/sharon.

# Lehigh Carbon Community College
## Schnecksville, Pennsylvania

- **State and locally supported** 2-year, founded 1966
- **Suburban** 254-acre campus with easy access to Philadelphia
- **Endowment** $5.7 million
- **Coed,** 6,953 undergraduate students, 36% full-time, 61% women, 39% men

**Undergraduates** 2,476 full-time, 4,477 part-time. Students come from 11 states and territories; 18 other countries; 0.4% are from out of state; 7% Black or African American, non-Hispanic/Latino; 22% Hispanic/Latino; 2% Asian, non-Hispanic/Latino; 0.1% American Indian or Alaska Native, non-Hispanic/Latino; 4% Two or more races, non-Hispanic/Latino; 3% Race/ethnicity unknown; 0.4% international; 53% transferred in.
**Freshmen** *Admission:* 4,125 applied, 4,125 admitted, 1,410 enrolled.
**Faculty** *Total:* 460, 18% full-time, 3% with terminal degrees. *Student/faculty ratio:* 18:1.
**Majors** Accounting technology and bookkeeping; administrative assistant and secretarial science; aeronautics/aviation/aerospace science and technology; airline pilot and flight crew; animation, interactive technology, video graphics and special effects; art; biology/biological sciences; biotechnology; building/construction site management; business administration and management; business/commerce; chemical technology; chemistry; computer and information sciences; computer and information systems security; computer programming; computer programming (specific applications); computer systems analysis; computer systems networking and telecommunications; construction trades; criminal justice/law enforcement administration; criminal justice/safety; drafting and design technology; early childhood education; education; electrical, electronic and communications engineering technology; engineering; environmental science; fashion/apparel design; game and interactive media design; general studies; geographic information science and cartography; graphic design; health information/medical records technology; health services/allied health/health sciences; heating, air conditioning, ventilation and refrigeration maintenance technology; human resources management; human services; industrial electronics technology; interior design; kinesiology and exercise science; legal assistant/paralegal; liberal arts and sciences/liberal studies; manufacturing engineering technology; mathematics; mechanical engineering/mechanical technology; medical/clinical assistant; nanotechnology; occupational therapist assistant; physical sciences; physical therapy technology; psychology; public administration; radio and television broadcasting technology; recording arts technology; registered nursing/registered nurse; resort management; social work; special education; speech communication and rhetoric; sport and fitness administration/management; teacher assistant/aide; veterinary/animal health technology; web page, digital/multimedia and information resources design.
**Academics** *Calendar:* semesters. *Degree:* certificates, diplomas, and associate. *Special study options:* academic remediation for entering students, advanced placement credit, cooperative education, distance learning, English as a second language, external degree program, honors programs, independent study, internships, off-campus study, part-time degree program, services for LD students, summer session for credit. *ROTC:* Army (c).
**Library** Rothrock Library. *Books:* 48,142 (physical), 68,508 (digital/electronic); *Serial titles:* 220 (physical), 182 (digital/electronic); *Databases:* 46. Weekly public service hours: 71.
**Student Life** *Housing:* college housing not available. *Activities and Organizations:* drama/theater group, student-run newspaper, choral group, Phi Theta Kappa, Justice Society, PSI BETA (psychology club), Student Government Association, Teacher Education Student Association (TESA). *Campus security:* 24-hour emergency response devices. *Student services:* personal/psychological counseling, veterans affairs office.
**Athletics** Member NJCAA. *Intercollegiate sports:* baseball M, basketball M, golf M/W, soccer M/W, softball W, volleyball W. *Intramural sports:* basketball M/W, golf M/W, table tennis M/W, volleyball M/W.
**Costs (2018–19)** *Tuition:* area resident $3000 full-time, $100 per credit hour part-time; state resident $6270 full-time, $209 per credit hour part-time; nonresident $9540 full-time, $318 per credit hour part-time. Full-time tuition and fees vary according to course load. *Required fees:* $1080 full-time, $40 per credit hour part-time. *Payment plan:* installment. *Waivers:* senior citizens and employees or children of employees.
**Applying** *Options:* electronic application. *Required for some:* essay or personal statement, high school transcript, interview. *Application deadlines:* rolling (freshmen), rolling (transfers). *Notification:* continuous (freshmen), continuous (transfers).
**Freshman Application Contact** Ms. Nancy Kelley, Admission Representative, Lehigh Carbon Community College, 4525 Education Park Drive, Schnecksville, PA 18078. *Phone:* 610-799-1558. *Fax:* 610-799-1527. *E-mail:* admissions@lccc.edu.
*Website:* http://www.lccc.edu/.

# Lincoln Technical Institute
## Allentown, Pennsylvania

**Freshman Application Contact** Admissions Office, Lincoln Technical Institute, 5151 Tilghman Street, Allentown, PA 18104. *Phone:* 610-398-5301. *Toll-free phone:* 844-215-1513. *Website:* http://www.lincolntech.edu/.

# Lincoln Technical Institute
## Philadelphia, Pennsylvania

**Director of Admissions** Mr. James Kuntz, Executive Director, Lincoln Technical Institute, 9191 Torresdale Avenue, Philadelphia, PA 19136. *Phone:* 215-335-0800. *Toll-free phone:* 844-215-1513. *Fax:* 215-335-1443. *E-mail:* jkuntz@lincolntech.com. *Website:* http://www.lincolntech.edu/.

# Luzerne County Community College
## Nanticoke, Pennsylvania

- **County-supported** 2-year, founded 1966
- **Suburban** 122-acre campus with easy access to Philadelphia
- **Coed**

**Undergraduates** 2,526 full-time, 3,143 part-time. 4% Black or African American, non-Hispanic/Latino; 12% Hispanic/Latino; 1% Asian, non-Hispanic/Latino; 0.2% Native Hawaiian or other Pacific Islander, non-Hispanic/Latino; 0.4% American Indian or Alaska Native, non-Hispanic/Latino; 1% Two or more races, non-Hispanic/Latino; 10% Race/ethnicity unknown. *Retention:* 55% of full-time freshmen returned.
**Faculty** *Student/faculty ratio:* 15:1.
**Academics** *Calendar:* semesters. *Degree:* certificates, diplomas, and associate. *Special study options:* academic remediation for entering students, accelerated degree program, advanced placement credit, distance learning, external degree program, internships, part-time degree program, services for LD students, summer session for credit. *ROTC:* Army (c).
**Library** Learning Resources Center plus 1 other. Students can reserve study rooms.
**Student Life** *Campus security:* 24-hour patrols.
**Athletics** Member NJCAA.
**Applying** *Options:* electronic application. *Recommended:* high school transcript.
**Freshman Application Contact** Mr. James Domzalski, Director of Enrollment Management, Luzerne County Community College, 1333 South Prospect Street, Nanticoke, PA 18634. *Phone:* 570-740-0342. *Toll-free phone:* 800-377-5222 Ext. 7337. *Fax:* 570-740-0238. *E-mail:* admissions@luzerne.edu. *Website:* http://www.luzerne.edu/.

# Manor College
## Jenkintown, Pennsylvania

- **Independent Byzantine Catholic** 2-year, founded 1947
- **Suburban** 35-acre campus with easy access to Philadelphia
- **Endowment** $2.8 million
- **Coed,** 632 undergraduate students, 68% full-time, 72% women, 28% men

**Undergraduates** 428 full-time, 204 part-time. Students come from 5 states and territories; 2 other countries; 3% are from out of state; 36% Black or African American, non-Hispanic/Latino; 14% Hispanic/Latino; 3% Asian, non-Hispanic/Latino; 0.2% Native Hawaiian or other Pacific Islander, non-Hispanic/Latino; 0.8% American Indian or Alaska Native, non-Hispanic/Latino; 2% Two or more races, non-Hispanic/Latino; 0.6% Race/ethnicity unknown; 0.8% international; 16% transferred in; 11% live on campus. *Retention:* 59% of full-time freshmen returned.
**Freshmen** *Admission:* 658 applied, 609 admitted, 184 enrolled. *Average high school GPA:* 2.7. *Test scores:* SAT math scores over 500: 21%; ACT scores over 18: 20%; SAT math scores over 600: 7%; ACT scores over 24: 10%; SAT math scores over 700: 5%.
**Faculty** *Total:* 104, 21% full-time, 34% with terminal degrees. *Student/faculty ratio:* 10:1.
**Majors** Accounting; business, management, and marketing related; communication and media related; computer programming (specific applications); criminal justice/law enforcement administration; dental assisting; dental hygiene; education (specific levels and methods) related; elementary education; health/health-care administration; health/medical preparatory programs related; health professions related; legal assistant/paralegal; liberal arts and sciences/liberal studies; marketing/marketing management; prenursing studies; pre-occupational therapy; pre-pharmacy studies; pre-physical therapy; psychology; sport and fitness administration/management; veterinary/animal health technology.
**Academics** *Calendar:* semesters. *Degrees:* certificates, associate, and postbachelor's certificates. *Special study options:* academic remediation for entering students, accelerated degree program, advanced placement credit,

distance learning, double majors, honors programs, independent study, internships, part-time degree program, services for LD students, summer session for credit.

**Library** Basileiad Library. *Books:* 28,400 (physical), 5,047 (digital/electronic); *Serial titles:* 8 (physical); *Databases:* 12. Weekly public service hours: 65.

**Student Life** *Housing Options:* coed. Campus housing is university owned. *Activities and Organizations:* choral group, Rotoract (student service organization), Vet Tech Club, Campus Activities Board, Macrinian Yearbook, Phi Theta Kappa (honor society). *Campus security:* 24-hour emergency response devices and patrols, late-night transport/escort service. *Student services:* personal/psychological counseling, veterans affairs office.

**Athletics** Member NJCAA. *Intercollegiate sports:* baseball M, basketball M/W, soccer M/W, volleyball W.

**Standardized Tests** *Required for some:* SAT or ACT (for admission). *Recommended:* SAT or ACT (for admission).

**Costs (2018–19)** *Comprehensive fee:* $24,754 includes full-time tuition ($16,428), mandatory fees ($600), and room and board ($7726). Full-time tuition and fees vary according to course load and program. Part-time tuition: $669 per credit hour. Part-time tuition and fees vary according to course load and program. *Required fees:* $100 per term part-time. *Room and board:* Room and board charges vary according to housing facility. *Payment plan:* installment. *Waivers:* adult students, senior citizens, and employees or children of employees.

**Financial Aid** Of all full-time matriculated undergraduates who enrolled in 2009, 35 Federal Work-Study jobs (averaging $3000). 10 state and other part-time jobs (averaging $3600).

**Applying** *Options:* electronic application, deferred entrance. *Required:* high school transcript, . *Application deadlines:* rolling (freshmen), rolling (transfers). *Notification:* continuous (freshmen), continuous (transfers).

**Freshman Application Contact** Stephanie Walker, Director of Admissions, Manor College, 700 Fox Chase Road, Jenkintown, PA 19046. *Phone:* 215-885-2216 Ext. 205. *Fax:* 215-576-6564. *E-mail:* swalker@manor.edu. *Website:* http://www.manor.edu/.

# McCann School of Business & Technology
## Allentown, Pennsylvania

**Admissions Office Contact** McCann School of Business & Technology, 2200 North Irving Street, Allentown, PA 18109. *Website:* http://www.mccann.edu/.

# McCann School of Business & Technology
## Lewisburg, Pennsylvania

**Admissions Office Contact** McCann School of Business & Technology, 7495 Westbranch Highway, Lewisburg, PA 17837. *Toll-free phone:* 866-865-8065. *Website:* http://www.mccann.edu/.

# McCann School of Business & Technology
## Pottsville, Pennsylvania

**Freshman Application Contact** Mrs. Amelia Hopkins, Director, Pottsville Campus, McCann School of Business & Technology, 2650 Woodglen Road, Pottsville, PA 17901. *Phone:* 570-622-7622. *Toll-free phone:* 866-865-8065. *Fax:* 570-622-7770. *Website:* http://www.mccann.edu/.

# Mercyhurst North East
## North East, Pennsylvania

**Director of Admissions** Travis Lindahl, Director of Admissions, Mercyhurst North East, 16 West Division Street, North East, PA 16428. *Phone:* 814-725-6217. *Toll-free phone:* 866-846-6042. *Fax:* 814-725-6251. *E-mail:* neadmiss@mercyhurst.edu. *Website:* http://northeast.mercyhurst.edu/.

# Montgomery County Community College
## Blue Bell, Pennsylvania

- **County-supported** 2-year, founded 1964
- **Suburban** 186-acre campus with easy access to Philadelphia
- **Coed,** 10,392 undergraduate students, 34% full-time, 56% women, 44% men

**Undergraduates** 3,518 full-time, 6,874 part-time. Students come from 7 states and territories; 96 other countries; 1% are from out of state; 15% Black or African American, non-Hispanic/Latino; 8% Hispanic/Latino; 6% Asian, non-Hispanic/Latino; 0.2% Native Hawaiian or other Pacific Islander, non-Hispanic/Latino; 0.3% American Indian or Alaska Native, non-Hispanic/Latino; 3% Two or more races, non-Hispanic/Latino; 7% Race/ethnicity unknown; 2% international. *Retention:* 60% of full-time freshmen returned.

**Freshmen** *Admission:* 7,608 applied, 7,608 admitted, 156 enrolled.
**Faculty** *Total:* 766, 24% full-time. *Student/faculty ratio:* 18:1.
**Majors** Accounting technology and bookkeeping; acting; administrative assistant and secretarial science; applied behavior analysis; art; automobile/automotive mechanics technology; baking and pastry arts; biology/biotechnology laboratory technician; biotechnology; business administration and management; business/commerce; child-care and support services management; clinical/medical laboratory technology; computer programming; computer science; computer technology/computer systems technology; criminal justice/police science; culinary arts; dance; dental hygiene; drafting and design technology; electrical and electronics engineering; electrical, electronic and communications engineering technology; elementary education; engineering science; engineering technologies and engineering related; environmental studies; fire prevention and safety technology; food service and dining room management; game and interactive media design; graphic design; health and physical education/fitness; hospitality and recreation marketing; information technology; liberal arts and sciences/liberal studies; mathematics; mechanical engineering; mechanical engineering/mechanical technology; medical office management; middle school education; music teacher education; nanotechnology; network and system administration; physical education teaching and coaching; physical sciences; psychiatric/mental health services technology; public health; radiologic technology/science; radio, television, and digital communication related; real estate; recording arts technology; registered nursing/registered nurse; sales, distribution, and marketing operations; science technologies related; secondary education; securities services administration; social sciences; speech communication and rhetoric; substance abuse/addiction counseling; surgical technology; teacher assistant/aide; tourism and travel services marketing; web/multimedia management and webmaster; web page, digital/multimedia and information resources design.

**Academics** *Calendar:* semesters plus winter term. *Degree:* certificates and associate. *Special study options:* academic remediation for entering students, accelerated degree program, adult/continuing education programs, advanced placement credit, cooperative education, distance learning, English as a second language, honors programs, independent study, internships, part-time degree program, services for LD students, student-designed majors, study abroad, summer session for credit.

**Library** The Brendlinger Library. *Books:* 73,691 (physical), 98,911 (digital/electronic); *Serial titles:* 237 (physical), 19,750 (digital/electronic); *Databases:* 37. Weekly public service hours: 76; students can reserve study rooms.

**Student Life** *Housing Options:* Campus housing is provided by a third party. *Activities and Organizations:* drama/theater group, student-run newspaper, radio and television station, choral group, West End Student Theater (drama club), Phi Theta Kappa, Writers Club, Japanese Culture Club, Student Government. *Campus security:* 24-hour emergency response devices and patrols, late-night transport/escort service, bicycle patrol. *Student services:* health clinic, personal/psychological counseling, veterans affairs office.

**Athletics** Member NJCAA. *Intercollegiate sports:* baseball M, basketball M/W, soccer M/W, softball W, volleyball W. *Intramural sports:* badminton M/W, basketball M/W, bowling M/W, cross-country running M/W, football M, racquetball M/W, soccer M/W, table tennis M/W, tennis M/W, volleyball M/W, weight lifting M/W.

**Costs (2017–18)** *Tuition:* area resident $4320 full-time, $144 per credit part-time; state resident $8940 full-time, $288 per credit part-time; nonresident $13,560 full-time, $432 per credit part-time. Full-time tuition and fees vary according to program. Part-time tuition and fees vary according to program. *Required fees:* $1410 full-time, $47 per credit part-time. *Room and board:* Room and board charges vary according to board plan. *Payment plans:* installment, deferred payment. *Waivers:* senior citizens and employees or children of employees.

**Financial Aid** Of all full-time matriculated undergraduates who enrolled in 2016, 60 Federal Work-Study jobs (averaging $2500).

**Applying** *Options:* electronic application, early admission, deferred entrance. *Required:* high school transcript. *Required for some:* interview. *Application deadline:* rolling (transfers). *Notification:* continuous (freshmen), continuous (transfers).

**Freshman Application Contact** Montgomery County Community College, Blue Bell, PA 19422. *Phone:* 215-641-6551. *Fax:* 215-619-7188. *E-mail:* admrec@admin.mc3.edu.

*Website:* http://www.mc3.edu/.

## New Castle School of Trades
### New Castle, Pennsylvania

- **Independent** 2-year, founded 1945
- **Rural** 20-acre campus with easy access to Pittsburgh
- **Coed, primarily men,** 503 undergraduate students, 100% full-time, 5% women, 95% men

**Undergraduates** 503 full-time. Students come from 3 states and territories; 1 other country; 14% Black or African American, non-Hispanic/Latino; 3% Hispanic/Latino; 2% Asian, non-Hispanic/Latino; 0.2% international.

**Freshmen** *Admission:* 103 enrolled.

**Faculty** *Total:* 46, 67% full-time, 2% with terminal degrees. *Student/faculty ratio:* 10:1.

**Majors** Automotive engineering technology; construction engineering technology; diesel mechanics technology; electrical, electronic and communications engineering technology; heating, ventilation, air conditioning and refrigeration engineering technology; industrial mechanics and maintenance technology; machine tool technology.

**Academics** *Calendar:* quarters. *Degree:* diplomas and associate. *Special study options:* part-time degree program.

**Library** New Castle School of Trades plus 1 other. *Books:* 600 (physical). Weekly public service hours: 60.

**Student Life** *Housing:* college housing not available. *Campus security:* 24-hour emergency response devices. *Student services:* personal/psychological counseling.

**Standardized Tests** *Required:* Wonderlic aptitude test (for admission).

**Costs (2017–18)** *Tuition:* $23,220 per degree program part-time. Full-time tuition and fees vary according to location and program. Part-time tuition and fees vary according to location and program. No tuition increase for student's term of enrollment. *Payment plans:* installment, deferred payment. *Waivers:* employees or children of employees.

**Applying** *Application fee:* $25. *Required:* high school transcript, interview. *Required for some:* essay or personal statement.

**Freshman Application Contact** Mr. Joe Blazak, Admissions Director, New Castle School of Trades, 4117 Pulaski Road, New Castle, PA 16101. *Phone:* 724-964-8811. *Toll-free phone:* 800-837-8299. *Fax:* 724-964-8177.

*Website:* http://www.ncstrades.edu/.

## Northampton Community College
### Bethlehem, Pennsylvania

- **State and locally supported** 2-year, founded 1967
- **Suburban** 165-acre campus with easy access to Philadelphia
- **Coed,** 9,921 undergraduate students, 45% full-time, 60% women, 40% men

**Undergraduates** 4,415 full-time, 5,506 part-time. 2% are from out of state; 14% Black or African American, non-Hispanic/Latino; 22% Hispanic/Latino; 2% Asian, non-Hispanic/Latino; 0.2% Native Hawaiian or other Pacific Islander, non-Hispanic/Latino; 0.2% American Indian or Alaska Native, non-Hispanic/Latino; 3% Two or more races, non-Hispanic/Latino; 1% Race/ethnicity unknown; 1% international; 9% transferred in; 6% live on campus.

**Freshmen** *Admission:* 5,285 applied, 5,285 admitted, 2,008 enrolled.

**Faculty** *Total:* 728, 16% full-time, 17% with terminal degrees. *Student/faculty ratio:* 19:1.

**Majors** Accounting technology and bookkeeping; acting; administrative assistant and secretarial science; applied psychology; architectural engineering technology; athletic training; automobile/automotive mechanics technology; biology/biological sciences; biotechnology; business administration and management; business/commerce; CAD/CADD drafting/design technology; chemistry; computer and information systems security; computer programming; computer science; computer support specialist; computer systems networking and telecommunications; construction management; criminal justice/safety; culinary arts; dental hygiene; diagnostic medical sonography and ultrasound technology; early childhood education; electrical, electronic and communications engineering technology; electrician; electromechanical technology; engineering; environmental science; fine/studio arts; fire science/firefighting; fire services administration; funeral service and mortuary science; general studies; graphic design; heating, air conditioning, ventilation and refrigeration maintenance technology; hotel/motel administration; industrial electronics technology; interior design; international/global studies; journalism; legal assistant/paralegal; liberal arts and sciences and humanities related; liberal arts and sciences/liberal studies; marketing/marketing management; mathematics; medical administrative assistant and medical secretary; meeting and event planning; middle school education; physics; public health education and promotion; quality control technology; radio and television broadcasting technology; radiologic technology/science; registered nursing/registered nurse; restaurant/food services management; secondary education; social work; speech communication and rhetoric; sport and fitness administration/management; teacher assistant/aide; veterinary/animal health technology; web page, digital/multimedia and information resources design; welding technology.

**Academics** *Calendar:* semesters. *Degree:* certificates, diplomas, and associate. *Special study options:* academic remediation for entering students, adult/continuing education programs, advanced placement credit, distance learning, English as a second language, honors programs, independent study, internships, off-campus study, part-time degree program, services for LD students, student-designed majors, study abroad, summer session for credit.

**Library** Paul & Harriett Mack Library. Weekly public service hours: 83; students can reserve study rooms.

**Student Life** *Housing Options:* coed. Campus housing is university owned. *Activities and Organizations:* student-run newspaper, radio station, choral group, Phi Theta Kappa, Student Senate, Nursing Student Organization, American Dental Hygiene Association (ADHA), International Student Organization. *Campus security:* 24-hour emergency response devices and patrols, controlled dormitory access. *Student services:* health clinic, personal/psychological counseling, veterans affairs office.

**Athletics** Member NJCAA. *Intercollegiate sports:* baseball M, basketball M/W, cross-country running M/W, golf M, lacrosse M, soccer M/W, softball W, tennis W, volleyball W. *Intramural sports:* basketball M/W, cheerleading M(c)/W(c), soccer M/W, volleyball M/W.

**Costs (2017–18)** *Tuition:* area resident $3000 full-time, $100 per credit hour part-time; state resident $6000 full-time, $200 per credit hour part-time; nonresident $9000 full-time, $300 per credit hour part-time. Full-time tuition and fees vary according to course load. Part-time tuition and fees vary according to course load. *Required fees:* $1230 full-time, $41 per credit hour part-time. *Room and board:* $8824; room only: $5304. Room and board charges vary according to board plan and housing facility. *Payment plan:* installment. *Waivers:* senior citizens and employees or children of employees.

**Financial Aid** Of all full-time matriculated undergraduates who enrolled in 2017, 202 Federal Work-Study jobs (averaging $2400). 124 state and other part-time jobs (averaging $2000).

**Applying** *Options:* electronic application, deferred entrance. *Application fee:* $25. *Required for some:* high school transcript, minimum 2.5 GPA, interview, interview for radiography and veterinary programs. *Recommended:* high school transcript. *Application deadlines:* rolling (freshmen), rolling (transfers). *Notification:* continuous (freshmen), continuous (transfers).

**Freshman Application Contact** Mr. James McCarthy, Director of Admissions, Northampton Community College, 3835 Green Pond Road, Bethlehem, PA 18020-7599. *Phone:* 610-861-5506. *Fax:* 610-861-5551. *E-mail:* jrmccarthy@northampton.edu.

*Website:* http://www.northampton.edu/.

## Penn Commercial Business and Technical School
### Washington, Pennsylvania

**Director of Admissions** Mr. Michael John Joyce, Director of Admissions, Penn Commercial Business and Technical School, 242 Oak Spring Road, Washington, PA 15301. *Phone:* 724-222-5330 Ext. 1. *Toll-free phone:* 888-309-7484. *E-mail:* mjoyce@penn-commercial.com. *Website:* http://www.penncommercial.edu/.

## Pennco Tech
### Bristol, Pennsylvania

**Freshman Application Contact** Pennco Tech, 3815 Otter Street, Bristol, PA 19007-3696. *Phone:* 215-785-0111. *Toll-free phone:* 800-575-9399. *Website:* http://www.penncotech.edu/.

# Penn State DuBois
## DuBois, Pennsylvania

- **State-related** primarily 2-year, founded 1935, part of Pennsylvania State University
- **Small-town** campus
- **Coed,** 585 undergraduate students, 79% full-time, 39% women, 61% men

**Undergraduates** 464 full-time, 121 part-time. 3% are from out of state; 2% Black or African American, non-Hispanic/Latino; 2% Hispanic/Latino; 2% Asian, non-Hispanic/Latino; 1% Two or more races, non-Hispanic/Latino; 0.6% Race/ethnicity unknown; 1% international; 4% transferred in. *Retention:* 80% of full-time freshmen returned.

**Freshmen** *Admission:* 465 applied, 390 admitted, 132 enrolled. *Average high school GPA:* 3.2. *Test scores:* SAT evidence-based reading and writing scores over 500: 70%; SAT math scores over 500: 76%; ACT scores over 18: 100%; SAT evidence-based reading and writing scores over 600: 21%; SAT math scores over 600: 29%; ACT scores over 24: 50%; SAT math scores over 700: 3%; ACT scores over 30: 50%.

**Faculty** *Total:* 54, 70% full-time, 50% with terminal degrees. *Student/faculty ratio:* 12:1.

**Majors** Accounting; acting; actuarial science; adult and continuing education administration; advertising; aerospace, aeronautical and astronautical/space engineering; African American/Black studies; agribusiness; agricultural and extension education; agricultural business and management related; agricultural engineering; agricultural mechanization; agriculture; agronomy and crop science; animal sciences; animal sciences related; anthropology; applied economics; archeology; architectural engineering; art; art history, criticism and conservation; art teacher education; Asian studies (East); astronomy; atmospheric sciences and meteorology; biochemistry; bioengineering and biomedical engineering; biological and biomedical sciences related; biological and physical sciences; biology/biological sciences; biology/biotechnology laboratory technician; biomedical technology; business administration and management; business/commerce; business/managerial economics; chemical engineering; chemistry; civil engineering; classics and classical languages; clinical/medical laboratory technology; communication and journalism related; communication sciences and disorders; comparative literature; computer and information sciences; computer engineering; criminal justice/law enforcement administration; economics; electrical and electronics engineering; electrical, electronic and communications engineering technology; elementary education; engineering science; English; environmental/environmental health engineering; film/cinema/video studies; finance; food science; foreign language teacher education; forest sciences and biology; forest technology; French; geography; geological and earth sciences/geosciences related; geology/earth science; German; graphic design; health/health-care administration; history; horticultural science; hospitality administration related; human development and family studies; human nutrition; industrial engineering; information science/studies; international business/trade/commerce; international relations and affairs; Italian; Japanese; Jewish/Judaic studies; journalism; kinesiology and exercise science; labor and industrial relations; landscaping and groundskeeping; Latin American studies; liberal arts and sciences/liberal studies; management information systems; marketing/marketing management; materials science; mathematics; mechanical engineering; mechanical engineering/mechanical technology; medical microbiology and bacteriology; medieval and Renaissance studies; metallurgical technology; mining and mineral engineering; music; natural resources and conservation related; natural resources/conservation; nuclear engineering; occupational therapist assistant; organizational behavior; parks, recreation and leisure facilities management; petroleum engineering; philosophy; physical therapy technology; physics; political science and government; premedical studies; psychology; registered nursing/registered nurse; rehabilitation and therapeutic professions related; religious studies; Russian; secondary education; sociology; soil science and agronomy; Spanish; special education; speech communication and rhetoric; statistics; telecommunications technology; theater design and technology; toxicology; turf and turfgrass management; visual and performing arts; wildlife, fish and wildlands science and management; women's studies.

**Academics** *Calendar:* semesters. *Degrees:* certificates, associate, and bachelor's. *Special study options:* adult/continuing education programs, external degree program.

**Student Life** *Housing:* college housing not available.

**Athletics** Member NJCAA. *Intercollegiate sports:* basketball M, cross-country running M/W, golf M/W, volleyball W. *Intramural sports:* basketball M/W, football M, soccer M/W, table tennis M/W, volleyball M/W.

**Standardized Tests** *Required:* SAT or ACT (for admission).

**Costs (2017–18)** *Tuition:* state resident $12,718 full-time, $524 per credit hour part-time; nonresident $20,352 full-time, $848 per credit hour part-time. Full-time tuition and fees vary according to course level, degree level, location, program, and student level. Part-time tuition and fees vary according to course level, course load, degree level, location, program, and student level. *Required*

*fees:* $914 full-time. *Payment plans:* installment, deferred payment. *Waivers:* senior citizens and employees or children of employees.

**Financial Aid** Of all full-time matriculated undergraduates who enrolled in 2016, 429 applied for aid, 378 were judged to have need, 71 had their need fully met. In 2016, 21 non-need-based awards were made. *Average percent of need met:* 60%. *Average financial aid package:* $9917. *Average need-based loan:* $3892. *Average need-based gift aid:* $4702. *Average non-need-based aid:* $3244. *Average indebtedness upon graduation:* $34,309.

**Applying** *Options:* electronic application, early admission, deferred entrance. *Application fee:* $65. *Required:* high school transcript. *Required for some:* interview. *Recommended:* essay or personal statement. *Application deadlines:* rolling (freshmen), rolling (transfers). *Notification:* continuous (freshmen), continuous (transfers).

**Freshman Application Contact** Admissions Office, Penn State DuBois, 1 College Place, DuBois, PA 15801. *Phone:* 814-375-4720. *Toll-free phone:* 800-346-7627. *Fax:* 814-375-4784. *E-mail:* duboisinfo@psi.edu. *Website:* http://www.ds.psu.edu/.

# Penn State Fayette, The Eberly Campus
## Lemont Furnace, Pennsylvania

- **State-related** primarily 2-year, founded 1934, part of Pennsylvania State University
- **Small-town** campus
- **Coed,** 652 undergraduate students, 90% full-time, 57% women, 43% men

**Undergraduates** 589 full-time, 63 part-time. 5% are from out of state; 4% Black or African American, non-Hispanic/Latino; 3% Hispanic/Latino; 0.8% Asian, non-Hispanic/Latino; 0.2% Native Hawaiian or other Pacific Islander, non-Hispanic/Latino; 0.3% American Indian or Alaska Native, non-Hispanic/Latino; 4% Two or more races, non-Hispanic/Latino; 0.9% Race/ethnicity unknown; 1% international; 5% transferred in. *Retention:* 78% of full-time freshmen returned.

**Freshmen** *Admission:* 728 applied, 598 admitted, 182 enrolled. *Average high school GPA:* 3.2. *Test scores:* SAT evidence-based reading and writing scores over 500: 66%; SAT math scores over 500: 58%; ACT scores over 18: 50%; SAT evidence-based reading and writing scores over 600: 18%; SAT math scores over 600: 13%; ACT scores over 24: 17%; SAT evidence-based reading and writing scores over 700: 1%; SAT math scores over 700: 1%; ACT scores over 30: 17%.

**Faculty** *Total:* 69, 57% full-time, 38% with terminal degrees. *Student/faculty ratio:* 12:1.

**Majors** Accounting; acting; actuarial science; adult and continuing education administration; advertising; aerospace, aeronautical and astronautical/space engineering; African American/Black studies; agribusiness; agricultural and extension education; agricultural business and management related; agricultural engineering; agricultural mechanization; agriculture; agronomy and crop science; animal sciences; animal sciences related; anthropology; applied economics; archeology; architectural engineering; architectural engineering technology; art; art history, criticism and conservation; art teacher education; Asian studies (East); astronomy; atmospheric sciences and meteorology; biochemistry; bioengineering and biomedical engineering; biological and biomedical sciences related; biological and physical sciences; biology/biological sciences; biology/biotechnology laboratory technician; biomedical technology; business administration and management; business/commerce; business/managerial economics; chemical engineering; chemistry; civil engineering; classics and classical languages; communication and journalism related; communication sciences and disorders; comparative literature; computer and information sciences; computer engineering; criminal justice/law enforcement administration; criminal justice/safety; economics; electrical and electronics engineering; electrical, electronic and communications engineering technology; elementary education; engineering science; English; environmental/environmental health engineering; film/cinema/video studies; finance; food science; foreign language teacher education; forest sciences and biology; forest technology; French; geography; geological and earth sciences/geosciences related; geology/earth science; German; graphic design; health/health-care administration; history; horticultural science; hospitality administration related; human development and family studies; human nutrition; industrial engineering; information science/studies; international relations and affairs; Italian; Japanese; Jewish/Judaic studies; journalism; kinesiology and exercise science; labor and industrial relations; landscaping and groundskeeping; Latin American studies; liberal arts and sciences/liberal studies; logistics, materials, and supply chain management; management information systems; manufacturing engineering; marketing/marketing management; materials science; mathematics; mechanical engineering; medical microbiology and bacteriology; medieval and Renaissance studies; metallurgical technology; mining and mineral engineering; natural resources and conservation related; natural resources/conservation; nuclear engineering; organizational behavior; parks, recreation and leisure facilities management; petroleum engineering; philosophy; physics; political science and government; premedical studies;

psychology; registered nursing/registered nurse; rehabilitation and therapeutic professions related; religious studies; Russian; secondary education; sociology; soil science and agronomy; Spanish; special education; speech communication and rhetoric; statistics; telecommunications technology; theater design and technology; toxicology; turf and turfgrass management; visual and performing arts; women's studies.

**Academics** *Calendar:* semesters. *Degrees:* certificates, associate, and bachelor's. *Special study options:* adult/continuing education programs, external degree program.

**Student Life** *Housing:* college housing not available. *Campus security:* student patrols, 8-hour patrols by trained security personnel.

**Athletics** Member NJCAA. *Intercollegiate sports:* baseball M, basketball M, softball W, volleyball W. *Intramural sports:* badminton M/W, basketball M/W, cheerleading M(c)/W(c), equestrian sports M(c)/W(c), football M/W, golf M(c)/W(c), softball M/W, tennis M/W, volleyball M/W, weight lifting M/W.

**Standardized Tests** *Required:* SAT or ACT (for admission).

**Costs (2017–18)** *Tuition:* state resident $12,718 full-time, $524 per credit hour part-time; nonresident $20,352 full-time, $848 per credit hour part-time. Full-time tuition and fees vary according to course level, degree level, location, program, and student level. Part-time tuition and fees vary according to course level, course load, degree level, location, program, and student level. *Required fees:* $914 full-time. *Payment plans:* installment, deferred payment. *Waivers:* senior citizens and employees or children of employees.

**Financial Aid** Of all full-time matriculated undergraduates who enrolled in 2016, 503 applied for aid, 436 were judged to have need, 101 had their need fully met. In 2016, 51 non-need-based awards were made. *Average percent of need met:* 63%. *Average financial aid package:* $10,993. *Average need-based loan:* $3877. *Average need-based gift aid:* $5349. *Average non-need-based aid:* $3248. *Average indebtedness upon graduation:* $37,496.

**Applying** *Options:* electronic application, early admission, deferred entrance. *Application fee:* $65. *Required:* high school transcript. *Required for some:* interview. *Recommended:* essay or personal statement. *Application deadlines:* rolling (freshmen), rolling (transfers). *Notification:* continuous (freshmen), continuous (transfers).

**Freshman Application Contact** Admissions Office, Penn State Fayette, The Eberly Campus, 2201 University Drive, Lemont Furnace, PA 15456. *Phone:* 724-430-4130. *Toll-free phone:* 877-568-4130. *Fax:* 724-430-4175. *E-mail:* feadm@psu.edu.

*Website:* http://www.fe.psu.edu/.

# Penn State Mont Alto

## Mont Alto, Pennsylvania

- **State-related** primarily 2-year, founded 1929, part of Pennsylvania State University
- **Small-town** campus
- **Coed,** 917 undergraduate students, 71% full-time, 54% women, 46% men

**Undergraduates** 653 full-time, 264 part-time. 15% are from out of state; 5% Black or African American, non-Hispanic/Latino; 8% Hispanic/Latino; 3% Asian, non-Hispanic/Latino; 4% Two or more races, non-Hispanic/Latino; 0.8% Race/ethnicity unknown; 0.5% international; 3% transferred in; 24% live on campus. *Retention:* 83% of full-time freshmen returned.

**Freshmen** *Admission:* 711 applied, 552 admitted, 203 enrolled. *Average high school GPA:* 3.2. *Test scores:* ACT scores over 18: 96%; ACT scores over 24: 46%; ACT scores over 30: 17%.

**Faculty** *Total:* 95, 60% full-time, 34% with terminal degrees. *Student/faculty ratio:* 11:1.

**Majors** Accounting; acting; actuarial science; adult and continuing education administration; advertising; aerospace, aeronautical and astronautical/space engineering; African American/Black studies; agribusiness; agricultural and extension education; agricultural business and management related; agricultural engineering; agricultural mechanization; agriculture; agronomy and crop science; animal sciences; animal sciences related; anthropology; applied economics; archeology; architectural engineering; art; art history, criticism and conservation; art teacher education; Asian studies (East); astronomy; atmospheric sciences and meteorology; biochemistry; bioengineering and biomedical engineering; biological and biomedical sciences related; biological and physical sciences; biology/biological sciences; biology/biotechnology laboratory technician; business administration and management; business/commerce; business/managerial economics; chemical engineering; chemistry; civil engineering; classics and classical languages; communication and journalism related; communication sciences and disorders; comparative literature; computer and information sciences; computer engineering; criminal justice/law enforcement administration; economics; electrical and electronics engineering; elementary education; engineering science; English; environmental/environmental health engineering; film/cinema/video studies; finance; food science; foreign language teacher education; forest sciences and biology; forest technology; French; geography; geological and earth sciences/geosciences related; geology/earth science;

German; graphic design; health/health-care administration; history; horticultural science; hospitality administration related; human development and family studies; human nutrition; industrial engineering; information science/studies; international relations and affairs; Italian; Japanese; Jewish/Judaic studies; journalism; kinesiology and exercise science; labor and industrial relations; landscaping and groundskeeping; Latin American studies; liberal arts and sciences/liberal studies; management information systems; marketing/marketing management; materials science; mathematics; mechanical engineering; medical microbiology and bacteriology; medieval and Renaissance studies; mining and mineral engineering; music; natural resources and conservation related; natural resources/conservation; nuclear engineering; occupational therapist assistant; occupational therapy; organizational behavior; parks, recreation and leisure facilities management; petroleum engineering; philosophy; physical therapy technology; physics; political science and government; premedical studies; psychology; registered nursing/registered nurse; rehabilitation and therapeutic professions related; religious studies; Russian; secondary education; sociology; soil science and agronomy; Spanish; special education; speech communication and rhetoric; statistics; theater design and technology; toxicology; turf and turfgrass management; visual and performing arts; women's studies.

**Academics** *Calendar:* semesters. *Degrees:* certificates, associate, and bachelor's. *Special study options:* adult/continuing education programs, external degree program. *ROTC:* Army (c).

**Student Life** *Housing Options:* coed, special housing for students with disabilities. Campus housing is university owned. Freshman campus housing is guaranteed. *Campus security:* 24-hour patrols, controlled dormitory access.

**Athletics** Member NJCAA. *Intercollegiate sports:* basketball M/W, cheerleading M/W, cross-country running M/W, golf M/W, soccer M/W, softball W, tennis M/W, volleyball W. *Intramural sports:* badminton M/W, basketball M/W, cheerleading M(c)/W(c), racquetball M/W, soccer M/W, softball W, volleyball M/W.

**Standardized Tests** *Required:* SAT or ACT (for admission).

**Costs (2017–18)** *Tuition:* state resident $12,718 full-time, $524 per credit hour part-time; nonresident $20,352 full-time, $848 per credit hour part-time. Full-time tuition and fees vary according to course level, degree level, location, program, and student level. Part-time tuition and fees vary according to course level, course load, degree level, location, program, and student level. *Required fees:* $976 full-time. *Room and board:* $11,280; room only: $6180. Room and board charges vary according to board plan, housing facility, and location. *Payment plans:* installment, deferred payment. *Waivers:* senior citizens and employees or children of employees.

**Financial Aid** Of all full-time matriculated undergraduates who enrolled in 2016, 616 applied for aid, 536 were judged to have need, 139 had their need fully met. In 2016, 38 non-need-based awards were made. *Average percent of need met:* 66%. *Average financial aid package:* $10,905. *Average need-based loan:* $3980. *Average need-based gift aid:* $4930. *Average non-need-based aid:* $5036. *Average indebtedness upon graduation:* $43,874.

**Applying** *Options:* electronic application, early admission, deferred entrance. *Application fee:* $65. *Required:* high school transcript. *Required for some:* interview. *Recommended:* essay or personal statement. *Application deadlines:* rolling (freshmen), rolling (transfers). *Notification:* continuous (freshmen), continuous (transfers).

**Freshman Application Contact** Admissions Office, Penn State Mont Alto, 1 Campus Drive, Mont Alto, PA 17237. *Phone:* 717-749-6130. *Toll-free phone:* 800-392-6173. *Fax:* 717-749-6132. *E-mail:* psuma@psu.edu.

*Website:* http://www.ma.psu.edu/.

# Pennsylvania Highlands Community College

## Johnstown, Pennsylvania

- **State and locally supported** 2-year, founded 1994
- **Small-town** campus
- **Coed,** 2,784 undergraduate students, 28% full-time, 59% women, 41% men

**Undergraduates** 782 full-time, 2,002 part-time. Students come from 3 states and territories; 1% are from out of state; 5% Black or African American, non-Hispanic/Latino; 2% Hispanic/Latino; 0.7% Asian, non-Hispanic/Latino; 0.1% American Indian or Alaska Native, non-Hispanic/Latino; 3% Two or more races, non-Hispanic/Latino; 4% Race/ethnicity unknown. *Retention:* 48% of full-time freshmen returned.

**Freshmen** *Admission:* 579 applied, 579 admitted.

**Faculty** *Total:* 108, 25% full-time. *Student/faculty ratio:* 18:1.

**Majors** Accounting; airline pilot and flight crew; architectural drafting and CAD/CADD; business/commerce; child-care and support services management; computer and information sciences; computer science; corrections; criminal justice/law enforcement administration; early childhood education; education; emergency medical technology (EMT paramedic); engineering technologies and engineering related; general studies; health information/medical records technology; health professions related; histologic technician; human services; lineworker; medical/clinical assistant; operations management; psychology; radiologic technology/science; radio, television, and digital communication related; welding technology.

**Academics** *Calendar:* semesters. *Degree:* certificates, diplomas, and associate. *Special study options:* academic remediation for entering students, adult/continuing education programs, advanced placement credit, cooperative education, distance learning, independent study, internships, part-time degree program, services for LD students, summer session for credit.

**Library** Mangarella Library. *Books:* 1,274 (physical), 2,192 (digital/electronic); *Databases:* 35.

**Student Life** *Housing:* college housing not available. *Activities and Organizations:* Student Senate Organization, Phi Theta Kappa Honor Society (PTK), National Society of Leadership and Success Organization (Sigma Alpha Pi), Black Bear Bowling Club, Anime Art Style Club. *Student services:* personal/psychological counseling, veterans affairs office.

**Athletics** Member NJCAA. *Intercollegiate sports:* basketball M, bowling M/W, cross-country running M/W, volleyball W. *Intramural sports:* basketball M/W, bowling M/W, cheerleading M/W, soccer M/W, table tennis M/W, volleyball M/W.

**Costs (2018–19)** *Tuition:* area resident $3990 full-time, $133 per credit hour part-time; state resident $6300 full-time, $210 per credit hour part-time; nonresident $9630 full-time, $321 per credit hour part-time. Full-time tuition and fees vary according to program. Part-time tuition and fees vary according to course load and program. *Required fees:* $1860 full-time, $62 per credit hour part-time. *Payment plan:* installment. *Waivers:* employees or children of employees.

**Financial Aid** Of all full-time matriculated undergraduates who enrolled in 2016, 25 Federal Work-Study jobs (averaging $2500).

**Applying** *Options:* electronic application. *Application deadlines:* rolling (freshmen), rolling (transfers). *Notification:* continuous (freshmen), continuous (transfers).

**Freshman Application Contact** Mr. Jeff Maul, Admissions Officer, Pennsylvania Highlands Community College, 101 Community College Way, Johnstown, PA 15904. *Phone:* 814-262-6431. *Toll-free phone:* 888-385-7325. *Fax:* 814-269-9743. *E-mail:* jmaul@pennhighlands.edu. *Website:* http://www.pennhighlands.edu/.

## Pennsylvania Institute of Health and Technology

### Mount Braddock, Pennsylvania

**Admissions Office Contact** Pennsylvania Institute of Health and Technology, 1015 Mount Braddock Road, Mount Braddock, PA 15465. *Website:* http://www.piht.edu/.

## Pennsylvania Institute of Technology

### Media, Pennsylvania

- **Independent** 2-year, founded 1953
- **Small-town** 12-acre campus with easy access to Philadelphia
- **Coed,** 447 undergraduate students, 58% full-time, 79% women, 21% men

**Undergraduates** 261 full-time, 186 part-time.

**Faculty** *Total:* 62, 23% full-time. *Student/faculty ratio:* 11:1.

**Majors** Allied health and medical assisting services related; biomedical technology; business administration and management; communication; computer science; corrections and criminal justice related; early childhood education; electrical, electronic and communications engineering technology; engineering technology; general studies; health/health-care administration; health information/medical records technology; health services/allied health/health sciences; medical office management; pharmacy technician; physical therapy technology; practical nursing, vocational nursing and nursing assistants related; psychiatric/mental health services technology.

**Academics** *Calendar:* 4 terms. *Degree:* certificates and associate. *Special study options:* academic remediation for entering students, adult/continuing education programs, advanced placement credit, cooperative education, distance learning, part-time degree program, summer session for credit.

**Library** Pennsylvania Institute of Technology Library/Learning Resource Center plus 1 other.

**Student Life** *Housing:* college housing not available. *Campus security:* 24-hour emergency response devices. *Student services:* personal/psychological counseling.

**Costs (2018–19)** *Tuition:* $10,260 full-time, $380 per credit hour part-time. Full-time tuition and fees vary according to course load and program. Part-time tuition and fees vary according to course load and program. *Required fees:* $3105 full-time, $115 per credit hour part-time. *Payment plan:* installment. *Waivers:* employees or children of employees.

**Financial Aid** Of all full-time matriculated undergraduates who enrolled in 2016, 15 Federal Work-Study jobs (averaging $1025). *Financial aid deadline:* 8/1.

**Applying** *Options:* electronic application, deferred entrance. *Application fee:* $25. *Required:* high school transcript, interview. *Recommended:* essay or personal statement. *Application deadlines:* 10/8 (freshmen), 10/8 (transfers). *Notification:* continuous until 10/8 (freshmen), continuous until 10/8 (transfers).

**Freshman Application Contact** Mr. Matthew Meyers, Director of Admissions, Pennsylvania Institute of Technology, 800 Manchester Avenue, Media, PA 19063-4036. *Phone:* 610-892-1543. *Toll-free phone:* 800-422-0025. *Fax:* 610-892-1510. *E-mail:* info@pit.edu. *Website:* http://www.pit.edu/.

## Pittsburgh Career Institute

### Pittsburgh, Pennsylvania

- **Proprietary** 2-year, founded 1980
- **Urban** campus
- **Coed**

**Academics** *Calendar:* continuous. *Degree:* associate. *Special study options:* academic remediation for entering students, accelerated degree program, adult/continuing education programs, advanced placement credit, cooperative education, English as a second language, internships, services for LD students.

**Library** Campus Library.

**Student Life** *Campus security:* 24-hour emergency response devices, 14-hour security patrols Monday through Friday.

**Standardized Tests** *Recommended:* SAT or ACT (for admission), SAT Subject Tests (for admission).

**Financial Aid** Of all full-time matriculated undergraduates who enrolled in 2016, 25 Federal Work-Study jobs (averaging $1200).

**Applying** *Options:* electronic application, early admission, deferred entrance. *Application fee:* $25. *Required:* high school transcript, interview.

**Freshman Application Contact** Pittsburgh Career Institute, 421 Seventh Avenue, Pittsburgh, PA 15219-1907. *Phone:* 412-281-2600. *Toll-free phone:* 800-333-6607. *Website:* http://www.pci.edu/.

## Pittsburgh Institute of Aeronautics

### Pittsburgh, Pennsylvania

- **Independent** 2-year, founded 1929
- **Suburban** campus
- **Coed, primarily men**

**Undergraduates** 368 full-time. Students come from 19 states and territories; 26% are from out of state; 6% Black or African American, non-Hispanic/Latino; 3% Hispanic/Latino; 2% Asian, non-Hispanic/Latino; 0.5% Native Hawaiian or other Pacific Islander, non-Hispanic/Latino; 0.8% American Indian or Alaska Native, non-Hispanic/Latino; 4% Two or more races, non-Hispanic/Latino; 0.3% Race/ethnicity unknown; 8% transferred in.

**Faculty** *Student/faculty ratio:* 10:1.

**Academics** *Calendar:* quarters. *Degree:* certificates and associate. *Special study options:* academic remediation for entering students.

**Library** Technical Library.

**Costs (2017–18)** *One-time required fee:* $150. *Tuition:* $15,990 full-time.

**Applying** *Options:* electronic application, deferred entrance. *Required:* high school transcript, PIA Math Skills Assessment. *Recommended:* interview.

**Freshman Application Contact** Steven D. Sabold, Director of Admissions, Pittsburgh Institute of Aeronautics, PO Box 10897, Pittsburgh, PA 15236-0897. *Phone:* 412-346-2100. *Toll-free phone:* 800-444-1440. *Fax:* 412-466-5013. *E-mail:* admissions@pia.edu. *Website:* http://www.pia.edu/.

## Pittsburgh Institute of Mortuary Science, Incorporated

### Pittsburgh, Pennsylvania

- **Independent** 2-year, founded 1939
- **Urban** campus
- **Coed**

**Undergraduates** 85 full-time, 108 part-time. Students come from 12 states and territories; 1 other country; 37% are from out of state.

**Faculty** *Student/faculty ratio:* 13:1.

**Academics** *Calendar:* trimesters. *Degree:* diplomas and associate. *Special study options:* academic remediation for entering students, adult/continuing education programs, distance learning, part-time degree program, services for LD students.

**Library** William J. Musmanno Memorial Library. Weekly public service hours: 12.

**Student Life** *Campus security:* 24-hour emergency response devices.

**Costs (2017–18)** *One-time required fee:* $500. *Tuition:* $12,400 full-time, $360 per credit hour part-time. Full-time tuition and fees vary according to program. Part-time tuition and fees vary according to program. *Required fees:* $2005 full-time, $2005 per year part-time.

**Applying** *Options:* electronic application. *Application fee:* $50. *Required:* essay or personal statement, high school transcript, minimum 2.0 GPA, 2 letters of recommendation, interview, immunizations.

**Freshman Application Contact** Ms. Karen Rocco, Registrar, Pittsburgh Institute of Mortuary Science, Incorporated, 5808 Baum Boulevard, Pittsburgh, PA 15206-3706. *Phone:* 412-362-8500 Ext. 105. *Fax:* 412-362-1684. *E-mail:* pims5808@aol.com. *Website:* http://www.pims.edu/.

## Pittsburgh Technical College
### Oakdale, Pennsylvania

- **Proprietary** primarily 2-year, founded 1946
- **Suburban** 180-acre campus with easy access to Pittsburgh
- **Coed,** 1,835 undergraduate students, 100% full-time, 42% women, 58% men
- 87% of applicants were admitted

**Undergraduates** 1,835 full-time. Students come from 17 states and territories; 2 other countries; 17% are from out of state; 7% Black or African American, non-Hispanic/Latino; 0.4% Hispanic/Latino; 0.7% Asian, non-Hispanic/Latino; 0.1% Native Hawaiian or other Pacific Islander, non-Hispanic/Latino; 0.3% American Indian or Alaska Native, non-Hispanic/Latino; 4% Two or more races, non-Hispanic/Latino; 21% Race/ethnicity unknown; 11% transferred in; 44% live on campus. *Retention:* 55% of full-time freshmen returned.

**Freshmen** *Admission:* 1,608 applied, 1,402 admitted, 516 enrolled. *Average high school GPA:* 2.6.

**Faculty** *Total:* 153, 51% full-time, 6% with terminal degrees. *Student/faculty ratio:* 12:1.

**Majors** Business administration and management; computer and information systems security; computer graphics; computer programming; cooking and related culinary arts; drafting and design technology; electrical, electronic and communications engineering technology; electrical/electronics equipment installation and repair; heating, air conditioning, ventilation and refrigeration maintenance technology; homeland security, law enforcement, firefighting and protective services related; hotel/motel administration; medical/health management and clinical assistant; medical office assistant; network and system administration; registered nursing/registered nurse; surgical technology; web page, digital/multimedia and information resources design; welding technology.

**Academics** *Calendar:* quarters. *Degrees:* certificates, associate, and bachelor's. *Special study options:* academic remediation for entering students, adult/continuing education programs, advanced placement credit, cooperative education, distance learning, double majors, internships, services for LD students.

**Library** Library Resource Center. *Books:* 7,378 (physical), 46,000 (digital/electronic); *Serial titles:* 116 (physical), 6 (digital/electronic); *Databases:* 12. Weekly public service hours: 58.

**Student Life** *Housing Options:* coed. Campus housing is university owned and leased by the school. *Activities and Organizations:* drama/theater group, Software Development Club, Drama Club, DECA, Gay-Straight Alliance, Magic Club. *Campus security:* 24-hour emergency response devices and patrols, student patrols, late-night transport/escort service, controlled dormitory access. *Student services:* personal/psychological counseling.

**Athletics** *Intramural sports:* basketball M/W, sand volleyball M/W, soccer M/W, softball M/W, ultimate Frisbee M/W, volleyball M/W.

**Standardized Tests** *Required:* entrance exams for practical nursing certificate and nursing and surgical technology Associate degrees (for admission). *Required for some:* SAT or ACT (for admission).

**Costs (2018–19)** *Comprehensive fee:* $26,847 includes full-time tuition ($16,920) and room and board ($9927). Full-time tuition and fees vary according to degree level and program. No tuition increase for student's term of enrollment. *Room and board:* college room only: $7344. Room and board charges vary according to housing facility. *Payment plans:* installment, deferred payment. *Waivers:* children of alumni and employees or children of employees.

**Applying** *Options:* electronic application, deferred entrance. *Required:* high school transcript. *Required for some:* essay or personal statement, criminal background check, minimum rank in top 80% of class. *Recommended:* interview. *Application deadlines:* rolling (freshmen), rolling (transfers). *Notification:* continuous (freshmen), continuous (transfers).

**Freshman Application Contact** Ms. Nancy Goodlin, Admissions Office Assistant, Pittsburgh Technical College, 1111 McKee Road, Oakdale, PA 15071. *Phone:* 412-809-5100. *Toll-free phone:* 800-784-9675. *Fax:* 412-809-5351. *E-mail:* goodlin.nancy@ptcollege.edu. *Website:* http://www.ptcollege.edu/.

## Reading Area Community College
### Reading, Pennsylvania

**Freshman Application Contact** Ms. Debbie Hettinger, Enrollment Services Coordinator/Communications Specialist, Reading Area Community College, PO Box 1706, Reading, PA 19603-1706. *Phone:* 610-372-4721 Ext. 5130. *E-mail:* dhettinger@racc.edu. *Website:* http://www.racc.edu/.

## The Restaurant School at Walnut Hill College
### Philadelphia, Pennsylvania

**Freshman Application Contact** Mr. John English, Director of Admissions, The Restaurant School at Walnut Hill College, 4207 Walnut Street, Philadelphia, PA 19104-3518. *Phone:* 267-295-2353. *Fax:* 215-222-4219. *E-mail:* jenglish@walnuthillcollege.edu. *Website:* http://www.walnuthillcollege.edu/.

## Rosedale Technical Institute
### Pittsburgh, Pennsylvania

**Freshman Application Contact** Ms. Debbie Bier, Director of Admissions, Rosedale Technical Institute, 215 Beecham Drive, Suite 2, Pittsburgh, PA 15205-9791. *Phone:* 412-521-6200. *Toll-free phone:* 800-521-6262. *Fax:* 412-521-2520. *E-mail:* admissions@rosedaletech.org. *Website:* http://www.rosedaletech.org/.

## South Hills School of Business & Technology
### State College, Pennsylvania

**Freshman Application Contact** Mr. Troy R. Otradovec, Regional Director of Admissions, South Hills School of Business & Technology, 480 Waupelani Drive, State College, PA 16801-4516. *Phone:* 814-234-7755 Ext. 2020. *Toll-free phone:* 888-282-7427. *Fax:* 814-234-0926. *E-mail:* admissions@southhills.edu. *Website:* http://www.southhills.edu/.

## Thaddeus Stevens College of Technology
### Lancaster, Pennsylvania

- **State-supported** 2-year, founded 1905
- **Urban** 33-acre campus with easy access to Philadelphia
- **Endowment** $696,058
- **Coed,** 1,142 undergraduate students, 99% full-time, 9% women, 91% men

**Undergraduates** 1,135 full-time, 7 part-time. Students come from 1 other state; 10% Black or African American, non-Hispanic/Latino; 14% Hispanic/Latino; 1% Asian, non-Hispanic/Latino; 0.6% American Indian or Alaska Native, non-Hispanic/Latino; 4% Two or more races, non-Hispanic/Latino; 0.4% Race/ethnicity unknown; 7% transferred in; 45% live on campus. *Retention:* 69% of full-time freshmen returned.

**Freshmen** *Admission:* 2,673 applied, 817 admitted, 562 enrolled.

**Faculty** *Total:* 80, 73% full-time. *Student/faculty ratio:* 12:1.

**Majors** Architectural technology; autobody/collision and repair technology; automotive engineering technology; cabinetmaking and millwork; CAD/CADD drafting/design technology; carpentry; computer and information sciences and support services related; electrical and electronic engineering technologies related; electrical, electronic and communications engineering technology; engineering-related technologies; executive assistant/executive secretary; graphic communications related; heating, air conditioning, ventilation and refrigeration maintenance technology; machine shop technology; masonry; plumbing technology; respiratory care therapy; sheet metal technology; water quality and wastewater treatment management and recycling technology; welding technology.

**Academics** *Calendar:* semesters. *Degree:* certificates and associate. *Special study options:* academic remediation for entering students, advanced placement credit, internships, services for LD students.

**Library** K. W. Schuler Learning Resources Center plus 1 other. *Books:* 59,073 (physical), 1,187 (digital/electronic); *Serial titles:* 21 (physical), 2,823 (digital/electronic); *Databases:* 21. Weekly public service hours: 78; students can reserve study rooms.

**Student Life** *Housing Options:* men-only, women-only. Campus housing is university owned. Freshman applicants given priority for college housing. *Activities and Organizations:* Phi Theta Kappa, Student Congress, Residence Hall Council, American Institute of Architectural Students (AIAS), Society of

Manufacturing Engineers (SME). *Campus security:* 24-hour emergency response devices and patrols, controlled dormitory access. *Student services:* personal/psychological counseling, women's center.
**Athletics** Member NJCAA. *Intercollegiate sports:* basketball M, cross-country running M, football M, track and field M, wrestling M.
**Standardized Tests** *Required:* ACT, SAT, or ACT Compass (for admission).
**Costs (2017–18)** *Tuition:* state resident $7800 full-time, $308 per credit hour part-time; nonresident $7800 full-time, $308 per credit hour part-time. *Required fees:* $45 full-time, $30 per year part-time. *Room and board:* $9040; room only: $4700. Room and board charges vary according to board plan and housing facility. *Payment plan:* installment. *Waivers:* employees or children of employees.
**Applying** *Options:* electronic application, deferred entrance. *Application fee:* $45. *Required:* essay or personal statement, high school transcript, minimum 2.0 GPA. *Required for some:* interview. *Application deadlines:* 6/30 (freshmen), 6/30 (transfers). *Notification:* continuous until 7/15 (freshmen), continuous until 7/15 (transfers).
**Freshman Application Contact** Ms. Amy Kwiatkowski, Thaddeus Stevens College of Technology, 750 East King Street, Lancaster, PA 17055. *Phone:* 717-391-3540. *Toll-free phone:* 800-842-3832. *E-mail:* kwiatkowski@stevenscollege.edu.
*Website:* http://www.stevenscollege.edu/.

# Triangle Tech, Bethlehem
## Bethlehem, Pennsylvania

**Freshman Application Contact** Triangle Tech, Bethlehem, 3184 Airport Road, Bethlehem, PA 18017. *Website:* http://www.triangle-tech.edu/.

# Triangle Tech, DuBois
## Falls Creek, Pennsylvania

**Freshman Application Contact** Terry Kucic, Director of Admissions, Triangle Tech, DuBois, PO Box 551, DuBois, PA 15801. *Phone:* 814-371-2090. *Toll-free phone:* 800-874-8324. *Fax:* 814-371-9227. *E-mail:* tkucic@triangle-tech.com. *Website:* http://www.triangle-tech.edu/.

# Triangle Tech, Erie
## Erie, Pennsylvania

**Freshman Application Contact** Admissions Representative, Triangle Tech, Erie, 2000 Liberty Street, Erie, PA 16502-2594. *Phone:* 814-453-6016. *Toll-free phone:* 800-874-8324 (in-state); 800-TRI-TECH (out-of-state). *Website:* http://www.triangle-tech.edu/.

# Triangle Tech, Greensburg
## Greensburg, Pennsylvania

**Freshman Application Contact** Mr. John Mazzarese, Vice President of Admissions, Triangle Tech, Greensburg, 222 East Pittsburgh Street, Greensburg, PA 15601. *Phone:* 412-359-1000. *Toll-free phone:* 800-874-8324. *Website:* http://www.triangle-tech.edu/.

# Triangle Tech, Pittsburgh
## Pittsburgh, Pennsylvania

**Freshman Application Contact** Director of Admissions, Triangle Tech, Pittsburgh, 1940 Perrysville Avenue, Pittsburgh, PA 15214-3897. *Phone:* 412-359-1000. *Toll-free phone:* 800-874-8324. *Fax:* 412-359-1012. *E-mail:* info@triangle-tech.edu. *Website:* http://www.triangle-tech.edu/.

# Triangle Tech, Sunbury
## Sunbury, Pennsylvania

**Freshman Application Contact** Triangle Tech, Sunbury, 191 Performance Road, Sunbury, PA 17801. *Phone:* 412-359-1000. *Website:* http://www.triangle-tech.edu/.

# University of Pittsburgh at Titusville
## Titusville, Pennsylvania

- **State-related** 2-year, founded 1963, part of University of Pittsburgh System
- **Small-town** 10-acre campus
- **Endowment** $850,000
- **Coed**

**Undergraduates** 313 full-time, 75 part-time. Students come from 15 states and territories; 8% are from out of state; 14% Black or African American, non-Hispanic/Latino; 4% Hispanic/Latino; 2% Asian, non-Hispanic/Latino; 2% Two or more races, non-Hispanic/Latino; 2% Race/ethnicity unknown; 4% transferred in; 57% live on campus.
**Faculty** *Student/faculty ratio:* 15:1.
**Academics** *Calendar:* semesters. *Degree:* associate. *Special study options:* academic remediation for entering students, advanced placement credit, distance learning, internships, part-time degree program, summer session for credit.
**Library** Haskell Memorial Library.
**Student Life** *Campus security:* 24-hour emergency response devices and patrols, late-night transport/escort service, controlled dormitory access.
**Athletics** Member NJCAA.
**Standardized Tests** *Required:* SAT or ACT (for admission).
**Costs (2017–18)** *One-time required fee:* $60. *Tuition:* state resident $10,958 full-time, $456 per credit part-time; nonresident $20,702 full-time, $862 per credit part-time. Full-time tuition and fees vary according to program. Part-time tuition and fees vary according to program. *Required fees:* $830 full-time, $135 per term part-time. *Room and board:* $10,678; room only: $5504. Room and board charges vary according to board plan.
**Financial Aid** Of all full-time matriculated undergraduates who enrolled in 2016, 264 applied for aid, 253 were judged to have need, 12 had their need fully met. In 2016, 5. *Average percent of need met:* 54. *Average financial aid package:* $11,531. *Average need-based loan:* $3958. *Average need-based gift aid:* $8195. *Average non-need-based aid:* $1899.
**Applying** *Required:* high school transcript, minimum 2.0 GPA. *Required for some:* essay or personal statement. *Recommended:* interview.
**Freshman Application Contact** Ms. Colleen R. Motter, Admissions Counselor, University of Pittsburgh at Titusville, 504 East Main Street, Titusville, PA 16354. *Phone:* 814-827-4408. *Toll-free phone:* 888-878-0462. *Fax:* 814-827-4519. *E-mail:* motter@pitt.edu. *Website:* http://www.upt.pitt.edu/.

# Valley Forge Military College
## Wayne, Pennsylvania

**Freshman Application Contact** Maj. Greg Potts, Dean of Enrollment Management, Valley Forge Military College, 1001 Eagle Road, Wayne, PA 19087-3695. *Phone:* 610-989-1300. *Toll-free phone:* 800-234-8362. *Fax:* 610-688-1545. *E-mail:* admissions@vfmac.edu. *Website:* http://www.vfmac.edu/.

# Vet Tech Institute
## Pittsburgh, Pennsylvania

**Freshman Application Contact** Admissions Office, Vet Tech Institute, 125 7th Street, Pittsburgh, PA 15222-3400. *Phone:* 412-391-7021. *Toll-free phone:* 800-570-0693. *Website:* http://pittsburgh.vettechinstitute.edu/.

# Westmoreland County Community College
## Youngwood, Pennsylvania

- **County-supported** 2-year, founded 1970
- **Rural** 85-acre campus with easy access to Pittsburgh
- **Endowment** $1.2 million
- **Coed**

**Undergraduates** 2,340 full-time, 3,214 part-time. Students come from 12 states and territories; 0.3% are from out of state; 3% Black or African American, non-Hispanic/Latino; 2% Hispanic/Latino; 0.6% Asian, non-Hispanic/Latino; 0.1% Native Hawaiian or other Pacific Islander, non-Hispanic/Latino; 0.1% American Indian or Alaska Native, non-Hispanic/Latino; 3% Two or more races, non-Hispanic/Latino; 20% transferred in. *Retention:* 62% of full-time freshmen returned.
**Faculty** *Student/faculty ratio:* 17:1.
**Academics** *Calendar:* semesters. *Degree:* certificates, diplomas, and associate. *Special study options:* academic remediation for entering students, accelerated degree program, adult/continuing education programs, advanced placement credit, cooperative education, distance learning, double majors,

English as a second language, honors programs, independent study, internships, off-campus study, part-time degree program, services for LD students, summer session for credit.

**Library** Westmoreland County Community College Learning Resources Center. *Books:* 41,368 (physical), 168,542 (digital/electronic); *Serial titles:* 71 (physical); *Databases:* 24. Weekly public service hours: 60.

**Student Life** *Campus security:* 24-hour emergency response devices and patrols, late-night transport/escort service, county police office on campus.

**Athletics** Member NJCAA.

**Costs (2017–18)** *Tuition:* area resident $3720 full-time, $124 per credit part-time; state resident $7440 full-time, $248 per credit part-time; nonresident $11,160 full-time, $372 per credit part-time. Full-time tuition and fees vary according to course load. Part-time tuition and fees vary according to course load. *Required fees:* $1470 full-time, $55 per credit part-time. *Payment plans:* installment, deferred payment.

**Applying** *Options:* electronic application, early admission.

**Freshman Application Contact** Ms. Shawna Little, Admissions Coordinator, Westmoreland County Community College, 145 Pavillon Lane, Youngwood, PA 15697. *Phone:* 724-925-4064. *Toll-free phone:* 800-262-2103. *Fax:* 724-925-4292. *E-mail:* littles@wccc.edu. *Website:* http://www.westmoreland.edu/.

## Williamson College of the Trades
### Media, Pennsylvania

**Freshman Application Contact** Mr. Jay Merillat, Dean of Admissions, Williamson College of the Trades, 106 South New Middletown Road, Media, PA 19063. *Phone:* 610-566-1776 Ext. 235. *E-mail:* jmerillat@williamson.edu. *Website:* http://www.williamson.edu/.

## The Workforce Institute's City College
### Philadelphia, Pennsylvania

**Freshman Application Contact** Admissions Office, The Workforce Institute's City College, 1231 North Broad Street, Philadelphia, PA 19122. *Phone:* 215-568-7861. *Website:* http://www.theworkforce-institute.org/.

## WyoTech Blairsville
### Blairsville, Pennsylvania

**Freshman Application Contact** Mr. Tim Smyers, WyoTech Blairsville, 500 Innovation Drive, Blairsville, PA 15717. *Phone:* 724-459-2311. *Toll-free phone:* 888-577-7559. *Fax:* 724-459-6499. *E-mail:* tsmyers@wyotech.edu. *Website:* http://www.wyotech.edu/.

## YTI Career Institute–Altoona
### Altoona, Pennsylvania

**Admissions Office Contact** YTI Career Institute–Altoona, 2900 Fairway Drive, Altoona, PA 16602. *Website:* http://www.yti.edu/.

## YTI Career Institute–York
### York, Pennsylvania

**Freshman Application Contact** YTI Career Institute–York, 1405 Williams Road, York, PA 17402-9017. *Phone:* 717-757-1100 Ext. 318. *Toll-free phone:* 800-557-6335. *Website:* http://www.yti.edu/.

# PUERTO RICO

## The Center of Cinematography, Arts and Television
### Bayamon, Puerto Rico

**Admissions Office Contact** The Center of Cinematography, Arts and Television, 51 Dr. Veve Street, Degetau Street Corner, Bayamon, PR 00960. *Website:* http://ccatmiami.com/.

## Centro de Estudios Multidisciplinarios
### Mayaguez, Puerto Rico

**Admissions Office Contact** Centro de Estudios Multidisciplinarios, Calle Cristy #56, Mayaguez, PR 00680. *Website:* http://www.cempr.edu/.

## Centro de Estudios Multidisciplinarios
### Rio Piedras, Puerto Rico

**Director of Admissions** Admissions Department, Centro de Estudios Multidisciplinarios, Calle 13 #1206, Ext. San Agustin, Rio Piedras, PR 00926. *Phone:* 787-765-4210 Ext. 115. *Toll-free phone:* 877-779-CDEM. *Website:* http://www.cempr.edu/.

## Dewey University–Bayamón
### Bayamón, Puerto Rico

**Admissions Office Contact** Dewey University–Bayamón, Carr. #2, Km. 15.9, Parque Industrial Corujo, Hato Tejas, Bayamón, PR 00959. *Website:* http://www.dewey.edu/.

## Dewey University–Carolina
### Carolina, Puerto Rico

**Admissions Office Contact** Dewey University–Carolina, Carr. #3, Km. 11, Parque Industrial de Carolina, Lote 7, Carolina, PR 00986. *Website:* http://www.dewey.edu/.

## Dewey University–Fajardo
### Fajardo, Puerto Rico

**Admissions Office Contact** Dewey University–Fajardo, 267 Calle General Valero, Fajardo, PR 00910. *Website:* http://www.dewey.edu/.

## Dewey University–Hato Rey
### Hato Rey, Puerto Rico

**Admissions Office Contact** Dewey University–Hato Rey, 427 Avenida Barbosa, Hato Rey, PR 00923. *Website:* http://www.dewey.edu/.

## Dewey University–Juana Diaz
### Juana Diaz, Puerto Rico

**Admissions Office Contact** Dewey University–Juana Diaz, Carr. 149, Km. 55.9, Parque Industrial Lomas, Juana Diaz, PR 00910. *Website:* http://www.dewey.edu/.

## Dewey University–Manati
### Manati, Puerto Rico

**Admissions Office Contact** Dewey University–Manati, Carr. 604, Km. 49.1 Barrio Tierras Nuevas, Salientes, Manati, PR 00674. *Toll-free phone:* 866-773-3939. *Website:* http://www.dewey.edu/.

## Dewey University–Mayaguez
### Mayaguez, Puerto Rico

**Admissions Office Contact** Dewey University–Mayaguez, Carr. #64 Km 6.6 Barrio Algarrobo, Mayaguez, PR 00682. *Website:* http://www.dewey.edu/.

## EDIC College
### Caguas, Puerto Rico

**Admissions Office Contact** EDIC College, Ave. Rafael Cordero Calle GÃ©nova Urb. Caguas Norte, Caguas, PR 00726. *Website:* http://www.ediccollege.edu/.

## Huertas College
### Caguas, Puerto Rico

**Director of Admissions** Mrs. Barbara Hassim López, Director of Admissions, Huertas College, PO Box 8429, Caguas, PR 00726. *Phone:* 787-743-1242. *Fax:* 787-743-0203. *E-mail:* huertas@huertas.org. *Website:* http://www.huertas.edu/.

## Humacao Community College
Humacao, Puerto Rico

- **Independent** primarily 2-year, part of N/A
- **Urban** campus
- **Endowment** $1.3 million
- **Coed,** 467 undergraduate students, 77% full-time, 63% women, 37% men

**Undergraduates** 359 full-time, 108 part-time. Students come from 1 other state; 100% Hispanic/Latino; 32% transferred in. *Retention:* 54% of full-time freshmen returned.

**Freshmen** *Admission:* 140 applied, 124 admitted, 71 enrolled. *Average high school GPA:* 2.9.

**Faculty** *Total:* 33, 36% full-time, 100% with terminal degrees. *Student/faculty ratio:* 30:1.

**Majors** Biotechnology; business/commerce; chemical technology; computer programming (specific applications); dental assisting; electrical and electronics engineering; environmental science; executive assistant/executive secretary; health information/medical records administration; heating, ventilation, air conditioning and refrigeration engineering technology; medical administrative assistant and medical secretary; microbiology; pharmacy technician; registered nursing/registered nurse.

**Academics** *Calendar:* trimesters. *Degrees:* certificates, diplomas, associate, and bachelor's. *Special study options:* academic remediation for entering students, adult/continuing education programs, cooperative education, internships, part-time degree program, services for LD students.

**Library** Santiago N. Manuez Educational Resources Center plus 1 other. *Books:* 5,320 (physical); *Serial titles:* 43 (physical), 2 (digital/electronic); *Databases:* 5. Weekly public service hours: 56.

**Student Life** *Housing:* college housing not available. *Activities and Organizations:* Enactus Humacao Community College, Students Council. *Campus security:* 24-hour emergency response devices and patrols. *Student services:* personal/psychological counseling.

**Costs (2018–19)** *One-time required fee:* $140. *Tuition:* $4932 full-time, $2466 per year part-time. Full-time tuition and fees vary according to course load and degree level. Part-time tuition and fees vary according to course load and degree level. *Required fees:* $450 full-time, $450 per year part-time. *Payment plan:* installment. *Waivers:* employees or children of employees.

**Financial Aid** Of all full-time matriculated undergraduates who enrolled in 2016, 64 Federal Work-Study jobs (averaging $546).

**Applying** *Application fee:* $15. *Required:* high school transcript, interview. *Required for some:* certificate of Immunization for students under 21 years. *Notification:* continuous (freshmen).

**Freshman Application Contact** Mrs. Arlene Osorio, Recruitment and Promotion Official, Humacao Community College, PO Box 9139, Humacao, PR 00792, Puerto Rico. *Phone:* 787-852-1430 Ext. 225. *Fax:* 787-850-1577. *E-mail:* arlene.osorio@hccpr.edu. *Website:* http://www.hccpr.edu/.

## ICPR Junior College–Hato Rey Campus
Hato Rey, Puerto Rico

**Freshman Application Contact** Admissions Office, ICPR Junior College–Hato Rey Campus, 558 Munoz Rivera Avenue, PO Box 190304, Hato Rey, PR 00919-0304. *Phone:* 787-753-6335. *Website:* http://www.icprjc.edu/.

## Ponce Paramedical College
Ponce, Puerto Rico

**Admissions Office Contact** Ponce Paramedical College, L-15 Acacia Street Villa Flores Urbanizacion, Ponce, PR 00731. *Website:* http://www.popac.edu/.

# RHODE ISLAND

## Community College of Rhode Island
Warwick, Rhode Island

- **State-supported** 2-year, founded 1964
- **Urban** 205-acre campus with easy access to Boston
- **Coed**

**Undergraduates** 4,441 full-time, 10,660 part-time. Students come from 9 states and territories; 4% are from out of state; 9% Black or African American, non-Hispanic/Latino; 20% Hispanic/Latino; 3% Asian, non-Hispanic/Latino; 0.5% American Indian or Alaska Native, non-Hispanic/Latino; 5% Two or more races, non-Hispanic/Latino; 4% Race/ethnicity unknown; 0.1% international; 3% transferred in.

**Faculty** *Student/faculty ratio:* 18:1.

**Academics** *Calendar:* semesters. *Degree:* certificates, diplomas, and associate. *Special study options:* academic remediation for entering students, adult/continuing education programs, advanced placement credit, cooperative education, distance learning, double majors, English as a second language, external degree program, honors programs, independent study, internships, off-campus study, part-time degree program, services for LD students, study abroad, summer session for credit. *ROTC:* Army (c).

**Library** Community College of Rhode Island Learning Resources Center plus 3 others.

**Student Life** *Campus security:* 24-hour emergency response devices and patrols.

**Athletics** Member NJCAA.

**Costs (2017–18)** *Tuition:* state resident $4148 full-time, $189 per credit hour part-time; nonresident $11,740 full-time, $561 per credit hour part-time. Full-time tuition and fees vary according to program. Part-time tuition and fees vary according to course load and program. *Required fees:* $416 full-time, $12 per credit hour part-time. *Payment plans:* installment, deferred payment.

**Financial Aid** Of all full-time matriculated undergraduates who enrolled in 2016, 500 Federal Work-Study jobs (averaging $2500).

**Applying** *Options:* deferred entrance. *Application fee:* $20.

**Freshman Application Contact** Community College of Rhode Island, Flanagan Campus, 1762 Louisquisset Pike, Lincoln, RI 02865-4585. *Phone:* 401-333-7490. *Fax:* 401-333-7122. *E-mail:* webadmission@ccri.edu. *Website:* http://www.ccri.edu/.

# SOUTH CAROLINA

## Aiken Technical College
Graniteville, South Carolina

**Freshman Application Contact** Jessica Moon, Director of Enrollment Services, Aiken Technical College, 2276 J. Davis Highway, Graniteville, SC 29829. *Phone:* 803-508-7262 Ext. 156. *E-mail:* moonj@atc.edu. *Website:* http://www.atc.edu/.

## Central Carolina Technical College
Sumter, South Carolina

**Freshman Application Contact** Ms. Barbara Wright, Director of Admissions and Counseling, Central Carolina Technical College, 506 North Guignard Drive, Sumter, SC 29150. *Phone:* 803-778-6695. *Toll-free phone:* 800-221-8711. *Fax:* 803-778-6696. *E-mail:* wrightb@cctech.edu. *Website:* http://www.cctech.edu/.

## Centura College
Columbia, South Carolina

**Admissions Office Contact** Centura College, 7500 Two Notch Road, Columbia, SC 29223. *Website:* http://www.centuracollege.edu/.

## Clinton College
Rock Hill, South Carolina

**Director of Admissions** Robert M. Copeland, Vice President for Student Affairs, Clinton College, 1029 Crawford Road, Rock Hill, SC 29730. *Phone:* 803-327-7402. *Toll-free phone:* 877-837-9645. *Fax:* 803-327-3261. *E-mail:* rcopeland@clintonjrcollege.org. *Website:* http://www.clintoncollege.edu/.

## Denmark Technical College
Denmark, South Carolina

**Freshman Application Contact** Ms. Kara Troy, Administrative Specialist II, Denmark Technical College, PO Box 327, 1126 Solomon Blatt Boulevard, Denmark, SC 29042. *Phone:* 803-793-5180. *Fax:* 803-793-5942. *E-mail:* troyk@denmarktech.edu. *Website:* http://www.denmarktech.edu/.

## Florence-Darlington Technical College
Florence, South Carolina

**Director of Admissions** Shelley Fortin, Vice President for Enrollment Management and Student Services, Florence-Darlington Technical College, 2715 West Lucas Street, PO Box 100548, Florence, SC 29501-0548. *Phone:* 843-661-8111 Ext. 117. *Toll-free phone:* 800-228-5745. *E-mail:* shelley.fortin@fdtc.edu. *Website:* http://www.fdtc.edu/.

# Forrest College
## Anderson, South Carolina

**Freshman Application Contact** Ms. Janie Turmon, Admissions and Placement Coordinator/Representative, Forrest College, 601 East River Street, Anderson, SC 29624. *Phone:* 864-225-7653. *Fax:* 864-261-7471. *E-mail:* janieturmon@forrestcollege.edu. *Website:* http://www.forrestcollege.edu/.

# Fortis College
## Columbia, South Carolina

**Admissions Office Contact** Fortis College, 246 Stoneridge Drive, Suite 101, Columbia, SC 29210. *Toll-free phone:* 855-4-FORTIS. *Website:* http://www.fortis.edu/.

# Golf Academy of America
## Myrtle Beach, South Carolina

**Admissions Office Contact** Golf Academy of America, 1900 Mr. Joe White Avenue, Myrtle Beach, SC 29577. *Website:* http://www.golfacademy.edu/.

# Greenville Technical College
## Greenville, South Carolina

- **State-supported** 2-year, founded 1962, part of South Carolina State Board for Technical and Comprehensive Education
- **Urban** 604-acre campus
- **Coed,** 11,745 undergraduate students, 41% full-time, 60% women, 40% men

**Undergraduates** 4,809 full-time, 6,936 part-time. 1% are from out of state; 22% Black or African American, non-Hispanic/Latino; 10% Hispanic/Latino; 2% Asian, non-Hispanic/Latino; 0.1% Native Hawaiian or other Pacific Islander, non-Hispanic/Latino; 0.3% American Indian or Alaska Native, non-Hispanic/Latino; 3% Two or more races, non-Hispanic/Latino; 2% Race/ethnicity unknown; 0.6% international.
**Freshmen** *Admission:* 4,922 applied, 4,911 admitted, 2,240 enrolled.
**Faculty** *Total:* 819, 41% full-time, 10% with terminal degrees. *Student/faculty ratio:* 14:1.
**Majors** Accounting; administrative assistant and secretarial science; architectural engineering technology; autobody/collision and repair technology; automobile/automotive mechanics technology; business administration and management; child-care and support services management; clinical/medical laboratory technology; computer numerically controlled (CNC) machinist technology; construction engineering technology; criminal justice/safety; culinary arts; data processing and data processing technology; dental hygiene; diagnostic medical sonography and ultrasound technology; drafting and design technology; electrical, electronic and communications engineering technology; electromechanical and instrumentation and maintenance technologies related; emergency medical technology (EMT paramedic); fire science/firefighting; health information/medical records technology; human services; legal assistant/paralegal; liberal arts and sciences/liberal studies; machine tool technology; mechanical drafting and CAD/CADD; mechanical engineering/mechanical technology; mechanic and repair technologies related; medical radiologic technology; multi/interdisciplinary studies related; occupational therapist assistant; physical therapy technology; purchasing, procurement/acquisitions and contracts management; registered nursing/registered nurse; respiratory care therapy; sales, distribution, and marketing operations.
**Academics** *Calendar:* semesters. *Degree:* certificates, diplomas, and associate. *Special study options:* academic remediation for entering students, advanced placement credit, cooperative education, distance learning, double majors, English as a second language, honors programs, independent study, internships, part-time degree program, services for LD students, summer session for credit.
**Library** J. Verne Smith Library plus 3 others. *Books:* 35,076 (physical), 430,325 (digital/electronic); *Serial titles:* 132 (physical), 9 (digital/electronic); *Databases:* 30. Weekly public service hours: 59.
**Student Life** *Housing Options:* coed. Campus housing is university owned and is provided by a third party. *Activities and Organizations:* Phi Theta Kappa, AAMLI, Cosmetology Club, Engineering Club, SGA/SAT Club. *Campus security:* 24-hour emergency response devices and patrols, late-night transport/escort service. *Student services:* veterans affairs office.
**Athletics** *Intramural sports:* badminton M(c)/W(c), basketball M(c)/W(c), bowling M(c)/W(c), football M(c)/W(c), softball M(c)/W(c), table tennis M(c)/W(c), tennis M(c)/W(c), volleyball M(c)/W(c).

**Costs (2017–18)** *Tuition:* area resident $4422 full-time, $173 per credit hour part-time; state resident $4806 full-time, $189 per credit hour part-time; nonresident $8776 full-time, $354 per credit hour part-time. Full-time tuition and fees vary according to course load and program. Part-time tuition and fees vary according to course load and program. *Required fees:* $270 full-time, $5 per credit hour part-time, $75 per term part-time. *Payment plans:* installment, deferred payment. *Waivers:* senior citizens.
**Applying** *Options:* electronic application, early admission, deferred entrance. *Required:* high school transcript. *Application deadlines:* rolling (freshmen), rolling (transfers). *Notification:* continuous until 8/18 (freshmen), continuous until 8/18 (transfers).
**Freshman Application Contact** Greenville Technical College, PO Box 5616, Greenville, SC 29606-5616. *Phone:* 864-250-8107. *Toll-free phone:* 800-992-1183 (in-state); 800-723-0673 (out-of-state). *Website:* http://www.gvltec.edu/.

# Horry-Georgetown Technical College
## Conway, South Carolina

- **State and locally supported** 2-year, founded 1966, part of South Carolina State Board for Technical and Comprehensive Education
- **Small-town** 150-acre campus
- **Endowment** $2.7 million
- **Coed**

**Undergraduates** 3,039 full-time, 3,979 part-time. Students come from 26 states and territories; 38 other countries; 15% are from out of state; 21% Black or African American, non-Hispanic/Latino; 4% Hispanic/Latino; 1% Asian, non-Hispanic/Latino; 0.1% Native Hawaiian or other Pacific Islander, non-Hispanic/Latino; 0.6% American Indian or Alaska Native, non-Hispanic/Latino; 3% Two or more races, non-Hispanic/Latino; 0.9% Race/ethnicity unknown; 0.1% international; 7% transferred in. *Retention:* 57% of full-time freshmen returned.
**Faculty** *Student/faculty ratio:* 21:1.
**Academics** *Calendar:* semesters. *Degree:* certificates, diplomas, and associate. *Special study options:* academic remediation for entering students, adult/continuing education programs, advanced placement credit, cooperative education, distance learning, double majors, independent study, internships, part-time degree program, services for LD students, summer session for credit.
**Library** Conway Campus Library plus 2 others.
**Student Life** *Campus security:* 24-hour emergency response devices and patrols.
**Costs (2017–18)** *Tuition:* area resident $4800 full-time, $160 per credit hour part-time; state resident $5970 full-time, $199 per credit hour part-time; nonresident $9780 full-time, $326 per credit hour part-time. *Required fees:* $268 full-time, $268 per year part-time.
**Applying** *Options:* early admission. *Application fee:* $25. *Required for some:* high school transcript.
**Freshman Application Contact** Cynthia Johnston, Assistant Vice President for Enrollment Services, Horry-Georgetown Technical College, 2050 Highway 501 East, PO Box 261966, Conway, SC 29528-6066. *Phone:* 843-349-7835. *Fax:* 843-349-7588. *E-mail:* cynthia.johnston@hgtc.edu. *Website:* http://www.hgtc.edu/.

# Midlands Technical College
## Columbia, South Carolina

**Freshman Application Contact** Ms. Sylvia Littlejohn, Director of Admissions, Midlands Technical College, PO Box 2408, Columbia, SC 29202. *Phone:* 803-738-8324. *Toll-free phone:* 800-922-8038. *Fax:* 803-790-7524. *E-mail:* admissions@midlandstech.edu. *Website:* http://www.midlandstech.edu/.

# Miller-Motte Technical College
## Conway, South Carolina

**Admissions Office Contact** Miller-Motte Technical College, 2451 Highway 501 East, Conway, SC 29526. *Toll-free phone:* 800-705-9182. *Website:* http://www.miller-motte.edu/.

# Miller-Motte Technical College
## North Charleston, South Carolina

**Freshman Application Contact** Ms. Elaine Cue, Campus President, Miller-Motte Technical College, 8085 Rivers Avenue, North Charleston, SC 29406. *Phone:* 843-574-0101. *Toll-free phone:* 800-705-9182. *Fax:* 843-266-3424. *E-mail:* juliasc@miller-mott.net. *Website:* http://www.miller-motte.edu/.

# Northeastern Technical College
## Cheraw, South Carolina

- **State and locally supported** 2-year, founded 1967, part of South Carolina State Board for Technical and Comprehensive Education
- **Rural** 59-acre campus
- **Endowment** $31,355
- **Coed,** 976 undergraduate students, 46% full-time, 72% women, 28% men

**Undergraduates** 446 full-time, 530 part-time. Students come from 3 states and territories; 1% are from out of state; 3% transferred in.
**Freshmen** *Admission:* 468 applied, 468 admitted, 249 enrolled.
**Faculty** *Student/faculty ratio:* 25:1.
**Majors** Accounting; administrative assistant and secretarial science; business administration and management; computer programming; computer science; data processing and data processing technology; drafting/design engineering technologies related; electrical, electronic and communications engineering technology; liberal arts and sciences/liberal studies; machine tool technology; marketing/marketing management; registered nursing/registered nurse.
**Academics** *Calendar:* semesters. *Degree:* certificates, diplomas, and associate. *Special study options:* academic remediation for entering students, adult/continuing education programs, advanced placement credit, distance learning, independent study, part-time degree program, study abroad.
**Library** Northeastern Technical College Library.
**Student Life** *Housing:* college housing not available. *Activities and Organizations:* Student Government Association, Alpha Beta Delta. *Campus security:* 24-hour emergency response devices. *Student services:* personal/psychological counseling.
**Standardized Tests** *Required:* ACT Compass (for admission). *Required for some:* SAT (for admission).
**Costs (2017–18)** *Tuition:* area resident $2460 full-time, $164 per credit hour part-time; state resident $2595 full-time, $173 per credit hour part-time; nonresident $4185 full-time, $279 per credit hour part-time. Full-time tuition and fees vary according to class time, course level, course load, degree level, program, reciprocity agreements, and student level. Part-time tuition and fees vary according to class time, course level, course load, degree level, program, reciprocity agreements, and student level. *Required fees:* $195 full-time, $72 per credit hour part-time, $15 per term part-time. *Payment plan:* installment. *Waivers:* senior citizens.
**Financial Aid** Of all full-time matriculated undergraduates who enrolled in 2016, 26 Federal Work-Study jobs (averaging $2800).
**Applying** *Options:* electronic application, early admission. *Application fee:* $25. *Required:* high school transcript, interview. *Application deadlines:* 8/4 (freshmen), rolling (transfers). *Notification:* continuous (freshmen).
**Freshman Application Contact** Mrs. Joy L. Hicks, Admissions Administrative Specialist, Northeastern Technical College, 1201 Chesterfield Highway, Cheraw, SC 29520-1007. *Phone:* 843-921-1461. *Toll-free phone:* 800-921-7399. *Fax:* 843-921-1476. *E-mail:* jhicks@netc.edu. *Website:* http://www.netc.edu/.

# Orangeburg-Calhoun Technical College
## Orangeburg, South Carolina

**Freshman Application Contact** Mr. Dana Rickards, Director of Recruitment, Orangeburg-Calhoun Technical College, 3250 St Matthews Road, NE, Orangeburg, SC 29118-8299. *Phone:* 803-535-1219. *Toll-free phone:* 800-813-6519. *Website:* http://www.octech.edu/.

# Piedmont Technical College
## Greenwood, South Carolina

**Director of Admissions** Mr. Steve Coleman, Director of Admissions, Piedmont Technical College, 620 North Emerald Road, PO Box 1467, Greenwood, SC 29648-1467. *Phone:* 864-941-8603. *Toll-free phone:* 800-868-5528. *Website:* http://www.ptc.edu/.

# Spartanburg Community College
## Spartanburg, South Carolina

- **State-supported** 2-year, founded 1961, part of South Carolina State Board for Technical and Comprehensive Education
- **Suburban** 104-acre campus with easy access to Charlotte
- **Coed**

**Undergraduates** 2,179 full-time, 2,536 part-time. Students come from 7 states and territories; 2 other countries; 2% are from out of state; 21% Black or African American, non-Hispanic/Latino; 7% Hispanic/Latino; 4% Asian, non-Hispanic/Latino; 0.1% Native Hawaiian or other Pacific Islander, non-Hispanic/Latino; 0.4% American Indian or Alaska Native, non-Hispanic/Latino; 3% Two or more races, non-Hispanic/Latino; 2%

Race/ethnicity unknown; 8% transferred in. *Retention:* 63% of full-time freshmen returned.
**Faculty** *Student/faculty ratio:* 15:1.
**Academics** *Calendar:* semesters condensed semesters plus summer sessions. *Degree:* certificates, diplomas, and associate. *Special study options:* academic remediation for entering students, adult/continuing education programs, advanced placement credit, cooperative education, distance learning, English as a second language, part-time degree program, services for LD students, summer session for credit.
**Library** Spartanburg Community College Library.
**Student Life** *Campus security:* 24-hour emergency response devices and patrols.
**Standardized Tests** *Required for some:* SAT or ACT (for admission).
**Financial Aid** Of all full-time matriculated undergraduates who enrolled in 2014, 41 Federal Work-Study jobs (averaging $3020).
**Applying** *Options:* electronic application, early admission. *Application fee:* $25. *Required:* high school transcript. *Recommended:* interview.
**Freshman Application Contact** Ms. Sabrina Sims, Admissions Counselor, Spartanburg Community College, PO Box 4386, Spartanburg, SC 29305. *Phone:* 864-592-4816. *Toll-free phone:* 866-591-3700. *Fax:* 864-592-4564. *E-mail:* admissions@sccsc.edu. *Website:* http://www.sccsc.edu/.

# Spartanburg Methodist College
## Spartanburg, South Carolina

- **Independent Methodist** 2-year, founded 1911
- **Suburban** 110-acre campus with easy access to Charlotte
- **Endowment** $22.0 million
- **Coed,** 790 undergraduate students, 99% full-time, 49% women, 51% men

**Undergraduates** 784 full-time, 6 part-time. Students come from 16 states and territories; 3 other countries; 9% are from out of state; 38% Black or African American, non-Hispanic/Latino; 8% Hispanic/Latino; 0.9% Asian, non-Hispanic/Latino; 0.3% American Indian or Alaska Native, non-Hispanic/Latino; 3% Two or more races, non-Hispanic/Latino; 0.4% international; 5% transferred in; 67% live on campus.
**Freshmen** *Admission:* 1,748 applied, 1,068 admitted, 493 enrolled. *Average high school GPA:* 3.5. *Test scores:* ACT scores over 18: 45%; ACT scores over 24: 7%.
**Faculty** *Total:* 65, 42% full-time, 48% with terminal degrees. *Student/faculty ratio:* 20:1.
**Majors** Business/commerce; criminal justice/law enforcement administration; liberal arts and sciences/liberal studies; religious studies related; visual and performing arts.
**Academics** *Calendar:* semesters. *Degree:* associate. *Special study options:* academic remediation for entering students, advanced placement credit, English as a second language, honors programs, independent study, part-time degree program, services for LD students, summer session for credit.
**Library** Marie Blair Burgess Library. *Books:* 46,541 (physical), 155,060 (digital/electronic); *Databases:* 80. Weekly public service hours: 72; students can reserve study rooms.
**Student Life** *Housing Options:* coed, men-only, women-only. Campus housing is university owned. Freshman campus housing is guaranteed. *Activities and Organizations:* drama/theater group, student-run newspaper, choral group, College Christian Movement, Alpha Phi Omega, Campus Union, Fellowship of Christian Athletes, Kappa Sigma Alpha. *Campus security:* 24-hour emergency response devices and patrols, student patrols, late-night transport/escort service, controlled dormitory access. *Student services:* health clinic, personal/psychological counseling.
**Athletics** Member NJCAA. *Intercollegiate sports:* baseball M(s), basketball M(s)/W(s), cross-country running M(s)/W(s), golf M(s)/W(s), soccer M(s)/W(s), softball W(s), tennis M(s)/W(s), volleyball W(s), wrestling M(s). *Intramural sports:* basketball M/W, cheerleading M/W, football M/W, softball M/W, table tennis M/W, volleyball M/W.
**Standardized Tests** *Required:* SAT or ACT (for admission).
**Costs (2017–18)** *One-time required fee:* $200. *Comprehensive fee:* $26,020 includes full-time tuition ($15,750), mandatory fees ($1170), and room and board ($9100). Full-time tuition and fees vary according to course load. Part-time tuition: $425 per credit hour. Part-time tuition and fees vary according to course load. *Payment plan:* installment. *Waivers:* senior citizens and employees or children of employees.
**Financial Aid** Of all full-time matriculated undergraduates who enrolled in 2016, 80 Federal Work-Study jobs (averaging $1600). 90 state and other part-time jobs (averaging $1600). *Financial aid deadline:* 8/30.
**Applying** *Options:* electronic application, deferred entrance. *Application fee:* $25. *Required:* essay or personal statement, high school transcript, minimum 2.0 GPA. *Required for some:* interview. *Recommended:* interview. *Application deadlines:* rolling (freshmen), rolling (transfers). *Notification:* continuous (freshmen), continuous (transfers).
**Freshman Application Contact** Mr. Wells Shepard, Vice President for Enrollment, Spartanburg Methodist College, 1000 Powell Mill Road,

Spartanburg, SC 29301-5899. *Phone:* 864-587-4254. *Toll-free phone:* 800-772-7286. *Fax:* 864-587-4355. *E-mail:* admiss@smcsc.edu. *Website:* http://www.smcsc.edu/.

## Technical College of the Lowcountry
### Beaufort, South Carolina

**Freshman Application Contact** Rhonda Cole, Admissions Services Manager, Technical College of the Lowcountry, 921 Ribaut Road, PO Box 1288, Beaufort, SC 29901-1288. *Phone:* 843-525-8229. *Fax:* 843-525-8285. *E-mail:* rcole@tcl.edu. *Website:* http://www.tcl.edu/.

## Tri-County Technical College
### Pendleton, South Carolina

**Freshman Application Contact** Tri-County Technical College, PO Box 587, 7900 Highway 76, Pendleton, SC 29670-0587. *Phone:* 864-646-1550. *Website:* http://www.tctc.edu/.

## Trident Technical College
### Charleston, South Carolina

- **State and locally supported** 2-year, founded 1964, part of South Carolina State Board for Technical and Comprehensive Education
- **Urban** campus
- **Coed,** 13,271 undergraduate students, 42% full-time, 60% women, 40% men

**Undergraduates** 5,517 full-time, 7,754 part-time. Students come from 85 other countries; 2% are from out of state; 28% Black or African American, non-Hispanic/Latino; 6% Hispanic/Latino; 2% Asian, non-Hispanic/Latino; 0.3% Native Hawaiian or other Pacific Islander, non-Hispanic/Latino; 0.4% American Indian or Alaska Native, non-Hispanic/Latino; 3% Two or more races, non-Hispanic/Latino; 2% Race/ethnicity unknown; 8% transferred in.
**Freshmen** *Admission:* 2,233 enrolled.
**Faculty** *Total:* 627, 52% full-time, 8% with terminal degrees. *Student/faculty ratio:* 21:1.
**Majors** Accounting; administrative assistant and secretarial science; airframe mechanics and aircraft maintenance technology; automobile/automotive mechanics technology; biological and physical sciences; business administration and management; child-care provision; civil engineering technology; clinical/medical laboratory technology; commercial and advertising art; computer engineering technology; computer graphics; computer/information technology services administration related; computer programming (specific applications); computer systems networking and telecommunications; criminal justice/law enforcement administration; culinary arts; dental hygiene; electrical, electronic and communications engineering technology; engineering technology; horticultural science; hotel/motel administration; human services; industrial technology; legal assistant/paralegal; legal studies; liberal arts and sciences/liberal studies; machine tool technology; marketing/marketing management; mechanical engineering/mechanical technology; medical administrative assistant and medical secretary; occupational therapy; physical therapy; registered nursing/registered nurse; respiratory care therapy; telecommunications technology; veterinary/animal health technology; web/multimedia management and webmaster; web page, digital/multimedia and information resources design.
**Academics** *Calendar:* semesters. *Degree:* certificates, diplomas, and associate. *Special study options:* academic remediation for entering students, advanced placement credit, cooperative education, distance learning, double majors, English as a second language, internships, off-campus study, part-time degree program, services for LD students, study abroad, summer session for credit.
**Library** Learning Resource Center plus 2 others. Students can reserve study rooms.
**Student Life** *Housing:* college housing not available. *Activities and Organizations:* drama/theater group, student-run newspaper, radio station, Phi Theta Kappa, Lex Artis Paralegal Society, Hospitality and Culinary Student Association, Partnership for Change in Communities and Families. *Campus security:* 24-hour emergency response devices and patrols, late-night transport/escort service. *Student services:* personal/psychological counseling.
**Costs (2017–18)** *One-time required fee:* $32. *Tuition:* area resident $4248 full-time, $177 per credit hour part-time; state resident $4714 full-time, $196 per credit hour part-time; nonresident $8042 full-time, $335 per credit hour part-time. *Required fees:* $146 full-time. *Payment plan:* installment. *Waivers:* senior citizens.
**Applying** *Options:* electronic application, early admission. *Application fee:* $30. *Required for some:* high school transcript. *Application deadlines:* 8/6

(freshmen), 8/6 (transfers). *Notification:* continuous (freshmen), continuous (transfers).
**Freshman Application Contact** Ms. Clara Martin, Admissions Director, Trident Technical College, Charleston, SC 29423-8067. *Phone:* 843-574-6326. *Fax:* 843-574-6109. *E-mail:* clara.martin@tridenttech.edu. *Website:* http://www.tridenttech.edu/.

## University of South Carolina Lancaster
### Lancaster, South Carolina

- **State-supported** 2-year, founded 1959, part of University of South Carolina System
- **Small-town** 17-acre campus with easy access to Charlotte
- **Coed,** 1,593 undergraduate students, 50% full-time, 60% women, 40% men

**Undergraduates** 794 full-time, 799 part-time. Students come from 10 states and territories; 2 other countries; 1% are from out of state.
**Freshmen** *Admission:* 557 applied, 555 admitted.
**Faculty** *Total:* 105, 60% full-time, 44% with terminal degrees. *Student/faculty ratio:* 14:1.
**Majors** Business administration and management; criminal justice/law enforcement administration; liberal arts and sciences/liberal studies; registered nursing/registered nurse.
**Academics** *Calendar:* semesters. *Degree:* associate. *Special study options:* academic remediation for entering students, advanced placement credit, distance learning, honors programs, independent study, internships, part-time degree program, services for LD students.
**Library** Medford Library.
**Student Life** *Housing:* college housing not available. *Activities and Organizations:* drama/theater group, student-run newspaper. *Student services:* personal/psychological counseling.
**Athletics** Member NJCAA. *Intercollegiate sports:* baseball M, golf M, soccer W, tennis M/W.
**Standardized Tests** *Required:* SAT or ACT (for admission).
**Applying** *Options:* electronic application, early admission. *Application fee:* $40. *Required:* high school transcript. *Application deadlines:* rolling (freshmen), rolling (transfers). *Notification:* continuous (freshmen), continuous (transfers).
**Freshman Application Contact** Jennifer Blackmon, Admissions Processor, University of South Carolina Lancaster, PO Box 889, Lancaster, SC 29721. *Phone:* 803-313-7073. *Fax:* 803-313-7116. *E-mail:* jblackmo@mailbox.sc.edu.
*Website:* http://usclancaster.sc.edu/.

## University of South Carolina Salkehatchie
### Allendale, South Carolina

- **State-supported** 2-year, founded 1965, part of University of South Carolina System
- **Rural** 95-acre campus
- **Coed**

**Undergraduates** 5% are from out of state. *Retention:* 45% of full-time freshmen returned.
**Faculty** *Student/faculty ratio:* 17:1.
**Academics** *Calendar:* semesters. *Degree:* associate. *Special study options:* academic remediation for entering students, adult/continuing education programs, advanced placement credit, cooperative education, distance learning, independent study, internships, part-time degree program, services for LD students, study abroad, summer session for credit.
**Library** Salkehatchie Learning Resource Center.
**Student Life** *Campus security:* 24-hour emergency response devices, late-night transport/escort service.
**Athletics** Member NJCAA.
**Standardized Tests** *Required:* SAT or ACT (for admission).
**Applying** *Options:* electronic application. *Application fee:* $40. *Required:* high school transcript, minimum 2.0 GPA.
**Freshman Application Contact** Ms. Carmen Brown, Admissions Coordinator, University of South Carolina Salkehatchie, PO Box 617, Allendale, SC 29810. *Phone:* 803-584-3446. *Toll-free phone:* 800-922-5500. *Fax:* 803-584-3884. *E-mail:* cdbrown@mailbox.sc.edu. *Website:* http://uscsalkehatchie.sc.edu/.

## University of South Carolina Sumter
### Sumter, South Carolina

**Freshman Application Contact** Mr. Keith Britton, Director of Admissions, University of South Carolina Sumter, 200 Miller Road, Sumter, SC 29150-

2498. *Phone:* 803-938-3882. *Fax:* 803-938-3901. *E-mail:* kbritton@usc.sumter.edu. *Website:* http://www.uscsumter.edu/.

## University of South Carolina Union
### Union, South Carolina

- **State-supported** primarily 2-year, founded 1965, part of University of South Carolina System
- **Small-town** 7-acre campus with easy access to Charlotte, North Carolina
- **Endowment** $1.2 million
- **Coed,** 905 undergraduate students, 54% full-time, 53% women, 47% men

**Undergraduates** 487 full-time, 418 part-time. Students come from 3 states and territories; 1 other country; 2% are from out of state; 43% Black or African American, non-Hispanic/Latino; 3% Hispanic/Latino.
**Freshmen** *Admission:* 1,378 applied, 930 admitted. *Average high school GPA:* 3.3. *Test scores:* ACT scores over 18: 75%; ACT scores over 24: 5%.
**Faculty** *Total:* 42, 29% full-time. *Student/faculty ratio:* 18:1.
**Majors** Biological and physical sciences; liberal arts and sciences/liberal studies.
**Academics** *Calendar:* semesters. *Degrees:* associate and bachelor's. *Special study options:* advanced placement credit, cooperative education, distance learning, double majors, independent study, internships, part-time degree program, study abroad, summer session for credit.
**Library** USC Union Campus Library plus 1 other. Study areas open 24 hours, 5&-7 days a week.
**Student Life** *Housing:* college housing not available. *Activities and Organizations:* drama/theater group, choral group. *Campus security:* 24-hour emergency response devices. *Student services:* personal/psychological counseling, veterans affairs office.
**Athletics** Member NJCAA. *Intramural sports:* baseball M, soccer M/W, softball W.
**Standardized Tests** *Required:* SAT or ACT (for admission).
**Costs (2018–19)** *Tuition:* state resident $285 per credit hour part-time; nonresident $721 per credit hour part-time. Full-time tuition and fees vary according to class time, course load, degree level, location, program, and student level. Part-time tuition and fees vary according to class time, location, program, and student level. *Payment plan:* deferred payment. *Waivers:* senior citizens.
**Financial Aid** Of all full-time matriculated undergraduates who enrolled in 2016, 16 Federal Work-Study jobs (averaging $3400).
**Applying** *Options:* electronic application. *Application fee:* $40. *Required:* high school transcript. *Application deadlines:* rolling (freshmen), rolling (transfers). *Notification:* continuous (freshmen), continuous (transfers).
**Freshman Application Contact** Mr. Michael B. Greer, Director of Enrollment Services, University of South Carolina Union, PO Drawer 729, Union, SC 29379-0729. *Phone:* 864-424-8039. *E-mail:* greerm@mailbox.sc.edu. *Website:* http://uscunion.sc.edu/.

## Virginia College in Charleston
### North Charleston, South Carolina

**Admissions Office Contact** Virginia College in Charleston, 6185 Rivers Avenue, North Charleston, SC 29406. *Website:* http://www.vc.edu/.

## Virginia College in Columbia
### Columbia, South Carolina

**Admissions Office Contact** Virginia College in Columbia, 7201 Two Notch Road, Suite 1000, Columbia, SC 29223. *Website:* http://www.vc.edu/.

## Virginia College in Florence
### Florence, South Carolina

**Admissions Office Contact** Virginia College in Florence, 2400 David H. McLeod Boulevard, Florence, SC 29501. *Website:* http://www.vc.edu/.

## Virginia College in Greenville
### Greenville, South Carolina

**Admissions Office Contact** Virginia College in Greenville, 78 Global Drive, Suite 200, Greenville, SC 29607. *Website:* http://www.vc.edu/.

## Virginia College in Spartanburg
### Spartanburg, South Carolina

**Admissions Office Contact** Virginia College in Spartanburg, 8150 Warren H. Abernathy Highway, Spartanburg, SC 29301. *Website:* http://www.vc.edu/.

## Williamsburg Technical College
### Kingstree, South Carolina

- **State-supported** 2-year, founded 1969, part of South Carolina State Board for Technical and Comprehensive Education
- **Rural** 41-acre campus
- **Coed,** 732 undergraduate students, 27% full-time, 61% women, 39% men

**Undergraduates** 194 full-time, 538 part-time. Students come from 1 other state; 76% Black or African American, non-Hispanic/Latino; 0.3% Asian, non-Hispanic/Latino; 0.1% American Indian or Alaska Native, non-Hispanic/Latino; 0.4% Race/ethnicity unknown; 4% transferred in. *Retention:* 45% of full-time freshmen returned.
**Freshmen** *Admission:* 103 enrolled.
**Faculty** *Total:* 49, 37% full-time. *Student/faculty ratio:* 12:1.
**Majors** Administrative assistant and secretarial science; business/commerce; child-care and support services management; interdisciplinary studies; liberal arts and sciences/liberal studies.
**Academics** *Calendar:* semesters. *Degree:* certificates, diplomas, and associate. *Special study options:* academic remediation for entering students, advanced placement credit, distance learning, double majors, independent study, part-time degree program, services for LD students, summer session for credit.
**Library** Learning Resource Center. *Books:* 18,002 (physical), 391,203 (digital/electronic); *Serial titles:* 91 (physical); *Databases:* 44. Students can reserve study rooms.
**Student Life** *Housing:* college housing not available. *Activities and Organizations:* Phi Theta Kappa, Student Government Association. *Student services:* personal/psychological counseling, veterans affairs office.
**Costs (2017–18)** *Tuition:* area resident $4032 full-time, $168 per credit hour part-time; state resident $4152 full-time, $173 per credit hour part-time; nonresident $7824 full-time, $326 per credit hour part-time. *Required fees:* $192 full-time, $8 per credit hour part-time. *Payment plans:* installment, deferred payment. *Waivers:* senior citizens and employees or children of employees.
**Applying** *Options:* electronic application, early admission, deferred entrance. *Required:* high school transcript. *Application deadlines:* rolling (freshmen), rolling (transfers). *Notification:* continuous (freshmen), continuous (transfers).
**Freshman Application Contact** Ms. Cheryl DuBose, Director of Admissions, Williamsburg Technical College, 601 MLK Jr. Avenue, Kingstree, SC 29556-4197. *Phone:* 843-355-4165. *Toll-free phone:* 800-768-2021. *Fax:* 843-35-54289. *E-mail:* dubosec@wiltech.edu. *Website:* http://www.wiltech.edu/.

## York Technical College
### Rock Hill, South Carolina

**Freshman Application Contact** Mr. Kenny Aldridge, Admissions Department Manager, York Technical College, Rock Hill, SC 29730. *Phone:* 803-327-8008. *Toll-free phone:* 800-922-8324. *Fax:* 803-981-7237. *E-mail:* kaldridge@yorktech.com. *Website:* http://www.yorktech.edu/.

# SOUTH DAKOTA

## Lake Area Technical Institute
### Watertown, South Dakota

- **State-supported** 2-year, founded 1965, part of South Dakota Department of Education
- **Small-town** 40-acre campus
- **Endowment** $2.8 million
- **Coed,** 2,055 undergraduate students, 74% full-time, 46% women, 54% men

**Undergraduates** 1,517 full-time, 538 part-time. Students come from 17 states and territories; 4 other countries; 19% are from out of state; 0.7% Black or African American, non-Hispanic/Latino; 2% Hispanic/Latino; 1% Asian, non-Hispanic/Latino; 0.3% Native Hawaiian or other Pacific Islander, non-Hispanic/Latino; 2% American Indian or Alaska Native, non-Hispanic/Latino; 3% Race/ethnicity unknown; 0.3% international; 8% transferred in.
**Freshmen** *Admission:* 676 enrolled. *Test scores:* ACT scores over 18: 70%; ACT scores over 24: 15%; ACT scores over 30: 1%.
**Faculty** *Total:* 157, 69% full-time. *Student/faculty ratio:* 17:1.
**Majors** Agricultural business and management; aircraft powerplant technology; autobody/collision and repair technology; automobile/automotive mechanics technology; banking and financial support services; building construction technology; clinical/medical laboratory technology; community health services counseling; computer science; construction engineering

technology; construction/heavy equipment/earthmoving equipment operation; criminal justice/police science; dental assisting; diesel mechanics technology; electrical, electronic and communications engineering technology; emergency medical technology (EMT paramedic); engine machinist; environmental science; human services; machine tool technology; manufacturing engineering technology; marketing/marketing management; medical/clinical assistant; occupational therapist assistant; physical therapy technology; registered nursing/registered nurse; robotics technology; welding technology.

**Academics** *Calendar:* semesters. *Degree:* certificates, diplomas, and associate. *Special study options:* academic remediation for entering students, advanced placement credit, cooperative education, distance learning, double majors, English as a second language, independent study, internships, off-campus study, part-time degree program, services for LD students, summer session for credit.

**Library** Leonard H. Timmerman Library plus 1 other. *Books:* 2,500 (physical), 250,000 (digital/electronic); *Serial titles:* 25 (physical); *Databases:* 40. Weekly public service hours: 58.

**Student Life** *Housing:* college housing not available. *Activities and Organizations:* Campus Crusades, Campus Activities Board, Student Voice, Student Ambassador, SkillsUSA. *Campus security:* 24-hour emergency response devices, partnership with local police department. *Student services:* personal/psychological counseling, veterans affairs office.

**Athletics** *Intramural sports:* basketball M/W, bowling M/W, equestrian sports M/W, football M, softball M/W, volleyball M/W.

**Standardized Tests** *Required for some:* ACCUPLACER, TEAS. *Recommended:* ACT (for admission).

**Costs (2018–19)** *Tuition:* state resident $3480 full-time, $116 per credit part-time; nonresident $3480 full-time, $116 per credit part-time. Full-time tuition and fees vary according to course load and program. Part-time tuition and fees vary according to course load and program. *Required fees:* $2884 full-time, $105 per credit part-time. *Payment plan:* installment. *Waivers:* employees or children of employees.

**Financial Aid** Of all full-time matriculated undergraduates who enrolled in 2016, 1,291 applied for aid, 1,056 were judged to have need, 108 had their need fully met. 118 Federal Work-Study jobs (averaging $2009). In 2016, 92 non-need-based awards were made. *Average percent of need met:* 54%. *Average financial aid package:* $7919. *Average need-based loan:* $3844. *Average need-based gift aid:* $4948. *Average non-need-based aid:* $976.

**Applying** *Options:* electronic application. *Application fee:* $25. *Required:* high school transcript. *Required for some:* essay or personal statement, interview. *Application deadlines:* rolling (freshmen), rolling (transfers). *Notification:* continuous (freshmen), continuous (transfers).

**Freshman Application Contact** Ms. LuAnn Strait, Director of Student Services, Lake Area Technical Institute, 1201 Arrow Avenue, PO Box 730, Watertown, SD 57201. *Phone:* 605-882-5284 Ext. 241. *Toll-free phone:* 800-657-4344. *Fax:* 605-882-6299. *E-mail:* straitl@lakeareatech.edu. *Website:* http://www.lakeareatech.edu/.

# Mitchell Technical Institute
## Mitchell, South Dakota

- **State-supported** 2-year, founded 1968, part of South Dakota Board of Technical Education
- **Small-town** 90-acre campus
- **Coed,** 1,253 undergraduate students, 67% full-time, 31% women, 69% men

**Undergraduates** 843 full-time, 410 part-time. Students come from 22 states and territories; 1 other country; 10% are from out of state; 0.6% Black or African American, non-Hispanic/Latino; 2% Hispanic/Latino; 1% Asian, non-Hispanic/Latino; 0.1% Native Hawaiian or other Pacific Islander, non-Hispanic/Latino; 3% American Indian or Alaska Native, non-Hispanic/Latino; 1% Two or more races, non-Hispanic/Latino; 2% Race/ethnicity unknown; 0.2% international; 11% transferred in. *Retention:* 82% of full-time freshmen returned.

**Freshmen** *Admission:* 916 applied, 527 admitted, 358 enrolled. *Average high school GPA:* 2.9. *Test scores:* ACT scores over 18: 67%; ACT scores over 24: 13%.

**Faculty** *Total:* 82, 88% full-time, 1% with terminal degrees. *Student/faculty ratio:* 13:1.

**Majors** Accounting and business/management; agricultural mechanics and equipment technology; agricultural production; automation engineer technology; building construction technology; business automation/technology/data entry; clinical/medical laboratory technology; computer support specialist; construction trades related; culinary arts; electrician; energy management and systems technology; geographic information science and cartography; heating, air conditioning, ventilation and refrigeration maintenance technology; human services; licensed practical/vocational nurse training; lineworker; magnetic resonance imaging (MRI) technology; medical/clinical assistant; medical office assistant; medical radiologic technology; network and system administration; radiologic

technology/science; small engine mechanics and repair technology; speech-language pathology assistant; telecommunications technology; truck and bus driver/commercial vehicle operation/instruction; welding engineering technology.

**Academics** *Calendar:* semesters. *Degree:* certificates, diplomas, and associate. *Special study options:* academic remediation for entering students, advanced placement credit, cooperative education, distance learning, double majors, internships, part-time degree program, services for LD students, summer session for credit.

**Library** Center for Student Success. *Books:* 1,657 (physical), 929 (digital/electronic); *Databases:* 17. Weekly public service hours: 45.

**Student Life** *Housing:* college housing not available. *Activities and Organizations:* Student Representative Board, SkillsUSA, Post-Secondary Agricultural Students, Rodeo Club, Diversity Club. *Campus security:* 24-hour emergency response devices. *Student services:* personal/psychological counseling.

**Athletics** *Intercollegiate sports:* equestrian sports M/W. *Intramural sports:* basketball M/W, bowling M/W, riflery M/W, softball M/W, volleyball M/W.

**Standardized Tests** *Required:* ACT (for admission), ACCUPLACER (for admission).

**Costs (2017–18)** *Tuition:* state resident $3648 full-time, $114 per credit hour part-time; nonresident $3648 full-time, $114 per credit hour part-time. Full-time tuition and fees vary according to course load and program. Part-time tuition and fees vary according to course load and program. *Required fees:* $2944 full-time, $92 per credit hour part-time. *Payment plan:* installment. *Waivers:* employees or children of employees.

**Applying** *Options:* electronic application. *Required:* high school transcript. *Required for some:* essay or personal statement, interview. *Recommended:* minimum 2.0 GPA. *Application deadlines:* rolling (freshmen), rolling (transfers). *Notification:* continuous (freshmen), continuous (transfers).

**Freshman Application Contact** Mr. Clayton Deuter, Director of Admissions, Mitchell Technical Institute, 1800 East Spruce Street, Mitchell, SD 57301. *Phone:* 605-995-3025. *Toll-free phone:* 800-684-1969. *Fax:* 605-995-3067. *E-mail:* clayton.deuter@mitchelltech.edu. *Website:* http://www.mitchelltech.edu/.

# Sisseton-Wahpeton College
## Sisseton, South Dakota

- **Federally supported** 2-year, founded 1979
- **Rural** 2-acre campus
- **Coed,** 175 undergraduate students, 73% full-time, 61% women, 39% men

**Undergraduates** 127 full-time, 48 part-time. 14% are from out of state; 5% Black or African American, non-Hispanic/Latino; 3% Hispanic/Latino; 85% American Indian or Alaska Native, non-Hispanic/Latino; 2% transferred in.

**Freshmen** *Admission:* 79 enrolled.

**Faculty** *Total:* 30, 33% full-time, 33% with terminal degrees. *Student/faculty ratio:* 10:1.

**Majors** Accounting; American Indian/Native American studies; business administration and management; electrical, electronic and communications engineering technology; hospitality administration; information science/studies; kindergarten/preschool education; liberal arts and sciences/liberal studies; natural sciences; nutrition sciences; registered nursing/registered nurse; substance abuse/addiction counseling.

**Academics** *Calendar:* semesters. *Degree:* certificates and associate. *Special study options:* academic remediation for entering students, adult/continuing education programs, cooperative education, double majors, internships, off-campus study, part-time degree program, summer session for credit.

**Library** Sisseton-Wahpeton Community College Library.

**Student Life** *Activities and Organizations:* AIHEC, AISES, Student Senate, Student Nurses Association, AIBL. *Campus security:* 24-hour emergency response devices. *Student services:* personal/psychological counseling.

**Athletics** *Intramural sports:* basketball M/W.

**Standardized Tests** *Required:* ACT Compass (for admission).

**Costs (2017–18)** *One-time required fee:* $540. *Tuition:* state resident $3250 full-time, $125 per credit hour part-time; nonresident $3250 full-time, $125 per credit hour part-time. Full-time tuition and fees vary according to class time, course level, course load, location, program, and student level. Part-time tuition and fees vary according to class time, course level, course load, location, program, and student level. No tuition increase for student's term of enrollment. *Required fees:* $590 full-time, $125 per credit hour part-time, $245 per term part-time. *Room and board:* $6500; room only: $6500. Room and board charges vary according to student level. *Payment plan:* installment. *Waivers:* minority students, adult students, senior citizens, and employees or children of employees.

**Financial Aid** Of all full-time matriculated undergraduates who enrolled in 2017, 157 applied for aid, 140 were judged to have need, 8 had their need fully met. In 2017, 11 non-need-based awards were made. *Average percent of need met:* 56%. *Average financial aid package:* $5934. *Average need-based gift aid:* $5934. *Average non-need-based aid:* $2385.

**Applying** *Required:* high school transcript. *Required for some:* Certificate of Indian Blood for enrolled tribal members. *Recommended:* minimum 2.0 GPA, interview. *Application deadlines:* rolling (freshmen), 7/8 (out-of-state freshmen), rolling (transfers).
**Freshman Application Contact** Sisseton-Wahpeton College, Old Agency Box 689, Sisseton, SD 57262. *Phone:* 605-698-3966 Ext. 1180.
*Website:* http://www.swc.tc/.

## Southeast Technical Institute
### Sioux Falls, South Dakota

- **State-supported** 2-year, founded 1968
- **Urban** 138-acre campus
- **Coed,** 2,244 undergraduate students, 64% full-time, 52% women, 48% men

**Undergraduates** 1,426 full-time, 818 part-time. Students come from 11 states and territories; 10% are from out of state; 2% Black or African American, non-Hispanic/Latino; 4% Hispanic/Latino; 3% Asian, non-Hispanic/Latino; 0.4% American Indian or Alaska Native, non-Hispanic/Latino; 0.8% Two or more races, non-Hispanic/Latino; 5% Race/ethnicity unknown; 17% transferred in; 2% live on campus. *Retention:* 72% of full-time freshmen returned.
**Freshmen** *Admission:* 3,272 applied, 1,669 admitted, 538 enrolled. *Average high school GPA:* 2.4.
**Faculty** *Total:* 208, 49% full-time. *Student/faculty ratio:* 15:1.
**Majors** Accounting; accounting technology and bookkeeping; administrative assistant and secretarial science; animation, interactive technology, video graphics and special effects; applied horticulture/horticulture operations; architectural engineering technology; autobody/collision and repair technology; automobile/automotive mechanics technology; banking and financial support services; business administration and management; business/commerce; cardiovascular technology; child-care and support services management; child-care provision; civil engineering technology; clinical/medical laboratory science and allied professions related; clinical/medical laboratory technology; computer and information sciences and support services related; computer and information systems security; computer programming; computer systems networking and telecommunications; computer technology/computer systems technology; construction engineering technology; criminal justice/police science; desktop publishing and digital imaging design; diagnostic medical sonography and ultrasound technology; diesel mechanics technology; electrical, electronic and communications engineering technology; electrical/electronics equipment installation and repair; electrician; electromechanical technology; electroneurodiagnostic/electroencephalographic technology; health services/allied health/health sciences; health unit coordinator/ward clerk; heating, air conditioning, ventilation and refrigeration maintenance technology; horticultural science; insurance; landscaping and groundskeeping; licensed practical/vocational nurse training; marketing/marketing management; mechanical engineering/mechanical technology; medical insurance coding; network and system administration; office occupations and clerical services; pharmacy technician; plumbing technology; registered nursing/registered nurse; small business administration; surgical technology; surveying technology; turf and turfgrass management; welding technology.
**Academics** *Calendar:* semesters. *Degree:* certificates, diplomas, and associate. *Special study options:* academic remediation for entering students, advanced placement credit, distance learning, double majors, English as a second language, independent study, internships, part-time degree program, services for LD students, summer session for credit.
**Library** Southeast Library.
**Student Life** *Housing Options:* coed. Campus housing is provided by a third party. *Activities and Organizations:* Student Government Association, SkillsUSA. *Campus security:* 24-hour patrols, late-night transport/escort service, controlled dormitory access. *Student services:* personal/psychological counseling, veterans affairs office.
**Athletics** *Intramural sports:* basketball M/W, bowling M/W, volleyball M/W.
**Standardized Tests** *Required for some:* ACT (for admission). *Recommended:* ACT (for admission).
**Financial Aid** Of all full-time matriculated undergraduates who enrolled in 2016, 35 Federal Work-Study jobs (averaging $2550).
**Applying** *Options:* electronic application. *Required:* high school transcript, minimum 2.0 GPA. *Required for some:* interview, background check, drug screening. *Application deadlines:* rolling (freshmen), rolling (transfers). *Notification:* continuous (freshmen), continuous (transfers).
**Freshman Application Contact** Mr. Scott Dorman, Recruiter, Southeast Technical Institute, Sioux Falls, SD 57107. *Phone:* 605-367-4458. *Toll-free phone:* 800-247-0789. *Fax:* 605-367-8305. *E-mail:* scott.dorman@southeasttech.edu.
*Website:* http://www.southeasttech.edu/.

## Western Dakota Technical Institute
### Rapid City, South Dakota

- **State-supported** 2-year, founded 1968
- **Small-town** 5-acre campus
- **Endowment** $187,302
- **Coed,** 1,049 undergraduate students, 58% full-time, 52% women, 48% men

**Undergraduates** 613 full-time, 436 part-time. Students come from 13 states and territories; 5% are from out of state; 2% Black or African American, non-Hispanic/Latino; 5% Hispanic/Latino; 0.8% Asian, non-Hispanic/Latino; 0.2% Native Hawaiian or other Pacific Islander, non-Hispanic/Latino; 13% American Indian or Alaska Native, non-Hispanic/Latino; 3% Two or more races, non-Hispanic/Latino; 1% Race/ethnicity unknown; 11% transferred in.
**Freshmen** *Admission:* 634 applied, 331 admitted, 201 enrolled. *Average high school GPA:* 2.4.
**Faculty** *Total:* 86, 52% full-time, 2% with terminal degrees. *Student/faculty ratio:* 13:1.
**Majors** Accounting; business administration and management; clinical/medical laboratory technology; computer systems networking and telecommunications; criminal justice/police science; criminal justice/safety; drafting and design technology; electrician; emergency medical technology (EMT paramedic); environmental control technologies related; fire science/firefighting; health services/allied health/health sciences; heating, air conditioning, ventilation and refrigeration maintenance technology; interdisciplinary studies; library and archives assisting; licensed practical/vocational nurse training; machine tool technology; medical/clinical assistant; medical transcription; pharmacy technician; surgical technology; vehicle maintenance and repair technologies related; welding technology.
**Academics** *Calendar:* semesters. *Degree:* certificates, diplomas, and associate. *Special study options:* academic remediation for entering students, advanced placement credit, distance learning, independent study, internships, part-time degree program, services for LD students, summer session for credit.
**Library** Western Dakota Technical Institute Library plus 1 other. *Books:* 3,500 (physical), 158,080 (digital/electronic); *Databases:* 12. Weekly public service hours: 48.
**Student Life** *Housing:* college housing not available. *Campus security:* 24-hour video surveillance.
**Standardized Tests** *Recommended:* SAT or ACT (for admission).
**Costs (2018–19)** *One-time required fee:* $155. *Tuition:* state resident $3591 full-time, $120 per credit hour part-time; nonresident $3591 full-time, $120 per credit hour part-time. Full-time tuition and fees vary according to course load and program. Part-time tuition and fees vary according to course load and program. *Required fees:* $159 per credit hour part-time, $131 per term part-time. *Payment plans:* installment, deferred payment. *Waivers:* employees or children of employees.
**Financial Aid** Of all full-time matriculated undergraduates who enrolled in 2017, 526 applied for aid, 494 were judged to have need, 27 had their need fully met. 19 Federal Work-Study jobs (averaging $1800). In 2017, 5 non-need-based awards were made. *Average percent of need met:* 71%. *Average financial aid package:* $12,298. *Average need-based loan:* $3574. *Average need-based gift aid:* $6753. *Average non-need-based aid:* $1800.
**Applying** *Options:* electronic application. *Required:* high school transcript. *Required for some:* essay or personal statement, 3 letters of recommendation, interview. *Recommended:* minimum 2.0 GPA. *Application deadlines:* 8/1 (freshmen), 8/1 (transfers). *Notification:* continuous until 8/15 (freshmen), continuous until 8/15 (transfers).
**Freshman Application Contact** Ms. Jill Elder, Admissions Coordinator, Western Dakota Technical Institute, 800 Mickelson Drive, Rapid City, SD 57703. *Phone:* 605-718-2411. *Toll-free phone:* 800-544-8765. *Fax:* 605-394-2204. *E-mail:* jill.elder@wdt.edu.
*Website:* http://www.wdt.edu/.

# TENNESSEE

## Brightwood College, Nashville Campus
### Nashville, Tennessee

**Freshman Application Contact** Brightwood College, Nashville Campus, 750 Envious Lane, Nashville, TN 37217. *Phone:* 615-269-9900. *Toll-free phone:* 866-543-0208. *Website:* http://www.brightwood.edu/.

# Chattanooga College–Medical, Dental and Technical Careers
## Chattanooga, Tennessee

**Freshman Application Contact** Chattanooga College–Medical, Dental and Technical Careers, 248 Northgate Mall Drive, Suite 130, Chattanooga, TN 37415. *Phone:* 423-305-7781. *Toll-free phone:* 877-313-2373. *Website:* http://www.chattanoogacollege.edu/.

# Chattanooga State Community College
## Chattanooga, Tennessee

**Freshman Application Contact** Brad McCormick, Director of Admissions and Records, Chattanooga State Community College, 4501 Amnicola Highway, Chattanooga, TN 37406. *Phone:* 423-697-4401 Ext. 3264. *Toll-free phone:* 866-547-3733. *Fax:* 423-697-4709. *E-mail:* brad.mccormick@chattanoogastate.edu. *Website:* http://www.chattanoogastate.edu/.

# Cleveland State Community College
## Cleveland, Tennessee

- **State-supported** 2-year, founded 1967, part of Tennessee Board of Regents
- **Suburban** 83-acre campus
- **Endowment** $8.8 million
- **Coed,** 3,005 undergraduate students, 54% full-time, 58% women, 42% men

**Undergraduates** 1,613 full-time, 1,392 part-time. Students come from 9 states and territories; 1 other country; 1% are from out of state; 5% Black or African American, non-Hispanic/Latino; 5% Hispanic/Latino; 1% Asian, non-Hispanic/Latino; 0.1% Native Hawaiian or other Pacific Islander, non-Hispanic/Latino; 0.1% American Indian or Alaska Native, non-Hispanic/Latino; 1% Two or more races, non-Hispanic/Latino; 4% Race/ethnicity unknown; 0.2% international; 5% transferred in.
**Freshmen** *Admission:* 1,693 applied, 718 enrolled. *Average high school GPA:* 3.1.
**Faculty** *Total:* 195, 36% full-time, 16% with terminal degrees. *Student/faculty ratio:* 19:1.
**Majors** Administrative assistant and secretarial science; business administration and management; child development; computer and information sciences; criminal justice/police science; electrical, electronic and communications engineering technology; electromechanical technology; emergency medical technology (EMT paramedic); engineering technology; general studies; industrial technology; liberal arts and sciences/liberal studies; medical informatics; music performance; public administration and social service professions related; registered nursing/registered nurse; science technologies related.
**Academics** *Calendar:* semesters. *Degree:* certificates and associate. *Special study options:* academic remediation for entering students, adult/continuing education programs, advanced placement credit, cooperative education, distance learning, double majors, external degree program, honors programs, independent study, internships, off-campus study, part-time degree program, services for LD students, summer session for credit.
**Library** Cleveland State Community College Library. *Books:* 185,889 (physical), 225,457 (digital/electronic); *Serial titles:* 329 (physical); *Databases:* 76.
**Student Life** *Housing:* college housing not available. *Activities and Organizations:* choral group, Human Services/Social Work, Computer-Aided Design, Phi Theta Kappa, Student Nursing Association, Early Childhood Education. *Campus security:* 24-hour emergency response devices and patrols. *Student services:* personal/psychological counseling.
**Athletics** Member NJCAA. *Intercollegiate sports:* baseball M(s), basketball M(s)/W(s), cross-country running M(s)/W(s), golf M(s)/W(s), softball W(s), volleyball W(s). *Intramural sports:* archery M/W, basketball M/W, bowling M/W, cheerleading M(c)/W(c), softball W, table tennis M/W, volleyball M/W.
**Costs (2017–18)** *Tuition:* state resident $4032 full-time, $160 per credit hour part-time; nonresident $16,608 full-time, $659 per credit hour part-time. Full-time tuition and fees vary according to course load. Part-time tuition and fees vary according to course load. *Required fees:* $299 full-time, $14 per credit hour part-time, $37 per term part-time. *Payment plan:* deferred payment. *Waivers:* senior citizens and employees or children of employees.
**Financial Aid** Of all full-time matriculated undergraduates who enrolled in 2016, 52 Federal Work-Study jobs (averaging $1025).
**Applying** *Options:* electronic application, early admission, deferred entrance. *Required:* high school transcript. *Application deadlines:* rolling (freshmen), rolling (transfers). *Notification:* continuous (freshmen), continuous (transfers).
**Freshman Application Contact** Mrs. Suzanne Bayne, Director of Admissions, Recruiting, and High School Relations, Cleveland State Community College, PO Box 3570, Cleveland, TN 37320-3570. *Phone:* 423-472-7141 Ext. 280. *Toll-free phone:* 800-604-2722. *Fax:* 423-614-8711. *E-mail:* sbayne@clevelandstatecc.edu. *Website:* http://www.clevelandstatecc.edu/.

# Columbia State Community College
## Columbia, Tennessee

**Freshman Application Contact** Mr. Joey Scruggs, Coordinator of Recruitment, Columbia State Community College, 1665 Hampshire Pike, Columbia, TN 38401. *Phone:* 931-540-2540. *E-mail:* scruggs@coscc.cc.tn.us. *Website:* http://www.columbiastate.edu/.

# Concorde Career College
## Memphis, Tennessee

**Freshman Application Contact** Dee Vickers, Director, Concorde Career College, 5100 Poplar Avenue, Suite 132, Memphis, TN 38137. *Phone:* 901-761-9494. *Fax:* 901-761-3293. *E-mail:* dvickers@concorde.edu. *Website:* http://www.concorde.edu/.

# Daymar College
## Clarksville, Tennessee

**Freshman Application Contact** Daymar College, 2691 Trenton Road, Clarksville, TN 37040. *Phone:* 931-552-7600 Ext. 204. *Website:* http://www.daymarcollege.edu/.

# Daymar College
## Murfreesboro, Tennessee

**Admissions Office Contact** Daymar College, 415 Golden Bear Court, Murfreesboro, TN 37128. *Website:* http://www.daymarcollege.edu/.

# Daymar College
## Nashville, Tennessee

**Director of Admissions** Admissions Office, Daymar College, 560 Royal Parkway, Nashville, TN 37214. *Phone:* 615-361-7555. *Fax:* 615-367-2736. *Website:* http://www.daymarcollege.edu/.

# Dyersburg State Community College
## Dyersburg, Tennessee

- **State-supported** 2-year, founded 1969, part of Tennessee Board of Regents
- **Small-town** 115-acre campus with easy access to Memphis
- **Endowment** $4.0 million
- **Coed,** 2,816 undergraduate students, 44% full-time, 65% women, 35% men

**Undergraduates** 1,253 full-time, 1,563 part-time. Students come from 4 states and territories; 1 other country; 19% Black or African American, non-Hispanic/Latino; 3% Hispanic/Latino; 1% Asian, non-Hispanic/Latino; 0.4% American Indian or Alaska Native, non-Hispanic/Latino; 2% Two or more races, non-Hispanic/Latino; 1% Race/ethnicity unknown; 0.2% international; 5% transferred in. *Retention:* 50% of full-time freshmen returned.
**Freshmen** *Admission:* 609 enrolled. *Average high school GPA:* 3.0. *Test scores:* ACT scores over 18: 68%; ACT scores over 24: 15%; ACT scores over 30: 1%.
**Faculty** *Total:* 130, 41% full-time, 9% with terminal degrees. *Student/faculty ratio:* 21:1.
**Majors** Agriculture; automation engineer technology; business administration and management; child development; computer and information sciences; computer and information systems security; criminal justice/police science; criminal justice/safety; education; emergency medical technology (EMT paramedic); general studies; health information/medical records technology; health services/allied health/health sciences; industrial electronics technology; industrial mechanics and maintenance technology; information science/studies; information technology; liberal arts and sciences/liberal studies; registered nursing/registered nurse.
**Academics** *Calendar:* semesters. *Degree:* certificates and associate. *Special study options:* academic remediation for entering students, accelerated degree program, adult/continuing education programs, advanced placement credit, cooperative education, distance learning, double majors, honors programs, independent study, internships, off-campus study, part-time degree program, services for LD students, study abroad, summer session for credit.

**Library** Learning Resource Center plus 2 others. *Books:* 17,817 (physical), 225,400 (digital/electronic); *Serial titles:* 29 (digital/electronic); *Databases:* 121. Weekly public service hours: 66; students can reserve study rooms.

**Student Life** *Activities and Organizations:* drama/theater group, choral group, Psychology Club, Phi Theta Kappa, Student Government, Student Nurses Association, Criminal Justice Association. *Campus security:* 24-hour emergency response devices and patrols. *Student services:* personal/psychological counseling.

**Athletics** Member NJCAA. *Intercollegiate sports:* baseball M(s), basketball M(s)/W(s), cheerleading M(s)/W(s), softball W(s). *Intramural sports:* soccer M/W, table tennis M/W, ultimate Frisbee M/W, volleyball M/W.

**Standardized Tests** *Required:* SAT or ACT (for admission). *Required for some:* ACT Compass for students who are over 21.

**Costs (2017–18)** *Tuition:* state resident $4032 full-time, $160 per credit hour part-time; nonresident $16,608 full-time, $684 per credit hour part-time. Full-time tuition and fees vary according to course load. Part-time tuition and fees vary according to course load. *Required fees:* $299 full-time, $150 per term part-time. *Payment plan:* deferred payment. *Waivers:* senior citizens and employees or children of employees.

**Financial Aid** Of all full-time matriculated undergraduates who enrolled in 2016, 34 Federal Work-Study jobs (averaging $1342). 75 state and other part-time jobs (averaging $1360).

**Applying** *Options:* electronic application. *Required:* high school transcript. *Application deadlines:* rolling (freshmen), rolling (out-of-state freshmen), rolling (transfers).

**Freshman Application Contact** Mrs. Heather Page, Director of Admissions and Records, Dyersburg State Community College, Dyersburg, TN 38024. *Phone:* 731-286-3331. *Fax:* 731-286-3325. *E-mail:* page@dscc.edu. *Website:* http://www.dscc.edu/.

# Fortis Institute
## Cookeville, Tennessee

**Director of Admissions** Ms. Sharon Mellott, Director of Admissions, Fortis Institute, 1025 Highway 111, Cookeville, TN 38501. *Phone:* 931-526-3660. *Toll-free phone:* 855-4-FORTIS. *Website:* http://www.fortis.edu/.

# Fortis Institute
## Nashville, Tennessee

**Admissions Office Contact** Fortis Institute, 3354 Perimeter Hill Drive, Suite 105, Nashville, TN 37211. *Toll-free phone:* 855-4-FORTIS. *Website:* http://www.fortis.edu/.

# Fountainhead College of Technology
## Knoxville, Tennessee

**Freshman Application Contact** Mr. Joel B. Southern, Director of Admissions, Fountainhead College of Technology, 10208 Technology Drive, Knoxville, TN 37932. *Phone:* 865-688-9422. *Toll-free phone:* 888-218-7335. *Fax:* 865-688-2419. *E-mail:* joel.southern@fountainheadcollege.edu. *Website:* http://www.fountainheadcollege.edu/.

# Hiwassee College
## Madisonville, Tennessee

**Director of Admissions** Jamie Williamson, Director of Admission, Hiwassee College, 225 Hiwassee College Drive, Madisonville, TN 37354. *Phone:* 423-420-1891. *Toll-free phone:* 800-356-2187. *Website:* http://www.hiwassee.edu/.

# Jackson State Community College
## Jackson, Tennessee

**Freshman Application Contact** Ms. Andrea Winchester, Director of High School Initiatives, Jackson State Community College, 2046 North Parkway, Jackson, TN 38301-3797. *Phone:* 731-424-3520 Ext. 50484. *Toll-free phone:* 800-355-5722. *Fax:* 731-425-9559. *E-mail:* awinchester@jscc.edu. *Website:* http://www.jscc.edu/.

# John A. Gupton College
## Nashville, Tennessee

**Freshman Application Contact** John A. Gupton College, 1616 Church Street, Nashville, TN 37203-2920. *Phone:* 615-327-3927. *Website:* http://www.guptoncollege.edu/.

# L'Ecole Culinaire–Memphis
## Cordova, Tennessee

**Admissions Office Contact** L'Ecole Culinaire–Memphis, 1245 North Germantown Parkway, Cordova, TN 38016. *Toll-free phone:* 888-238-2077. *Website:* http://www.lecole.edu/memphis/.

# Lincoln College of Technology
## Nashville, Tennessee

**Freshman Application Contact** Ms. Tanya Smith, Director of Admissions, Lincoln College of Technology, 1524 Gallatin Road, Nashville, TN 37206. *Phone:* 615-226-3990 Ext. 71703. *Toll-free phone:* 844-215-1513. *Fax:* 615-262-8466. *E-mail:* tlegg-smith@lincolntech.com. *Website:* http://www.lincolntech.edu/.

# Miller-Motte Technical College
## Chattanooga, Tennessee

**Admissions Office Contact** Miller-Motte Technical College, 6397 Lee Highway, Suite 100, Chattanooga, TN 37421. *Toll-free phone:* 800-705-9182. *Website:* http://www.miller-motte.edu/.

# Motlow State Community College
## Tullahoma, Tennessee

- **State-supported** 2-year, founded 1969, part of Tennessee Board of Regents
- **Rural** 187-acre campus with easy access to Nashville
- **Endowment** $6.1 million
- **Coed,** 5,838 undergraduate students, 57% full-time, 58% women, 42% men

**Undergraduates** 3,334 full-time, 2,504 part-time. Students come from 9 states and territories; 4 other countries; 1% are from out of state; 9% Black or African American, non-Hispanic/Latino; 6% Hispanic/Latino; 3% Asian, non-Hispanic/Latino; 0.1% Native Hawaiian or other Pacific Islander, non-Hispanic/Latino; 0.3% American Indian or Alaska Native, non-Hispanic/Latino; 3% Two or more races, non-Hispanic/Latino; 0.9% Race/ethnicity unknown; 0.3% international.

**Faculty** *Total:* 374, 29% full-time, 5% with terminal degrees. *Student/faculty ratio:* 18:1.

**Majors** Business administration and management; education; general studies; liberal arts and sciences/liberal studies; registered nursing/registered nurse; special education–early childhood; web page, digital/multimedia and information resources design.

**Academics** *Calendar:* semesters. *Degree:* certificates and associate. *Special study options:* academic remediation for entering students, accelerated degree program, adult/continuing education programs, advanced placement credit, cooperative education, distance learning, double majors, honors programs, independent study, part-time degree program, services for LD students, study abroad, summer session for credit.

**Library** Clayton-Glass Library. *Books:* 67,588 (physical), 400,000 (digital/electronic); *Serial titles:* 83 (digital/electronic); *Databases:* 80. Students can reserve study rooms.

**Student Life** *Housing:* college housing not available. *Activities and Organizations:* drama/theater group, student-run newspaper, choral group, Phi Theta Kappa, Communication Club, Student Government Association, Art Club, Baptist Student Union. *Campus security:* 24-hour patrols, late-night transport/escort service. *Student services:* personal/psychological counseling, veterans affairs office.

**Athletics** Member NJCAA. *Intercollegiate sports:* baseball M(s), basketball M(s)/W(s), soccer W(s), softball W(s). *Intramural sports:* badminton M/W, basketball M/W, bowling M/W, golf M/W, tennis M/W, volleyball M/W.

**Costs (2017–18)** *Tuition:* state resident $3840 full-time, $160 per credit hour part-time; nonresident $11,976 full-time, $499 per credit hour part-time. Full-time tuition and fees vary according to course load and program. Part-time tuition and fees vary according to program. *Required fees:* $307 full-time, $38 per credit hour part-time, $90 per term part-time. *Payment plans:* installment, deferred payment. *Waivers:* senior citizens and employees or children of employees.

**Financial Aid** Of all full-time matriculated undergraduates who enrolled in 2016, 2,830 applied for aid, 2,119 were judged to have need, 264 had their need fully met. In 2016, 663 non-need-based awards were made. *Average percent of need met:* 56%. *Average financial aid package:* $5878. *Average need-based gift aid:* $4960. *Average non-need-based aid:* $3911.

Applying *Options:* electronic application, early admission, deferred entrance. *Required:* high school transcript. *Application deadlines:* 8/27 (freshmen), 8/13 (transfers). *Notification:* continuous (freshmen), continuous (transfers).
**Freshman Application Contact** Motlow State Community College, PO Box 8500, Lynchburg, TN 37352-8500. *Phone:* 931-393-1530. *Toll-free phone:* 800-654-4877.
*Website:* http://www.mscc.edu/.

# Nashville State Community College
## Nashville, Tennessee

- **State-supported** 2-year, founded 1970, part of Tennessee Board of Regents
- **Urban** 85-acre campus
- **Coed**

**Undergraduates** Students come from 55 other countries; 2% are from out of state; 27% Black or African American, non-Hispanic/Latino; 6% Hispanic/Latino; 4% Asian, non-Hispanic/Latino; 0.2% Native Hawaiian or other Pacific Islander, non-Hispanic/Latino; 0.3% American Indian or Alaska Native, non-Hispanic/Latino; 4% Two or more races, non-Hispanic/Latino; 0.8% Race/ethnicity unknown.
**Faculty** *Student/faculty ratio:* 19:1.
**Academics** *Calendar:* semesters. *Degree:* certificates and associate. *Special study options:* academic remediation for entering students, adult/continuing education programs, advanced placement credit, cooperative education, distance learning, double majors, English as a second language, off-campus study, part-time degree program, services for LD students, study abroad, summer session for credit.
**Library** Jane G. Kisber Memorial Library. Students can reserve study rooms.
**Student Life** *Campus security:* 24-hour emergency response devices and patrols, late-night transport/escort service.
**Standardized Tests** *Required:* SAT or ACT (for admission).
**Financial Aid** Of all full-time matriculated undergraduates who enrolled in 2015, 3,942 applied for aid, 3,514 were judged to have need, 917 had their need fully met. 188 Federal Work-Study jobs (averaging $5400). 64 state and other part-time jobs (averaging $3600). In 2015, 3. *Average percent of need met:* 33. *Average financial aid package:* $6616. *Average need-based loan:* $2970. *Average need-based gift aid:* $3331. *Average non-need-based aid:* $950.
**Applying** *Options:* electronic application. *Application fee:* $20. *Required:* high school transcript.
**Freshman Application Contact** Mr. Tyler White, Coordinator of Recruitment, Nashville State Community College, 120 White Bridge Road, Nashville, TN 37209-4515. *Phone:* 615-353-3265. *Toll-free phone:* 800-272-7363. *E-mail:* recruiting@nscc.edu. *Website:* http://www.nscc.edu/.

# National College
## Bristol, Tennessee

**Freshman Application Contact** National College, 1328 Highway 11 West, Bristol, TN 37620. *Phone:* 423-878-4440. *Toll-free phone:* 888-9-JOBREADY. *Website:* http://www.national-college.edu/.

# National College
## Nashville, Tennessee

**Director of Admissions** Jerry Lafferty, Campus Director, National College, 1638 Bell Road, Nashville, TN 37211. *Phone:* 615-333-3344. *Toll-free phone:* 888-9-JOBREADY. *Website:* http://www.national-college.edu/.

# North Central Institute
## Clarksville, Tennessee

- **Proprietary** 2-year, founded 1988
- **Suburban** 14-acre campus
- **Coed, primarily men,** 88 undergraduate students

**Undergraduates** 29% are from out of state.
**Faculty** *Total:* 7. *Student/faculty ratio:* 10:1.
**Majors** Avionics maintenance technology.
**Academics** *Calendar:* continuous. *Degree:* associate. *Special study options:* advanced placement credit, external degree program, independent study, part-time degree program, summer session for credit.
**Library** Media Resource Center.
**Student Life** *Housing:* college housing not available. *Campus security:* 24-hour emergency response devices.
**Costs (2018–19)** *Tuition:* $292 per course part-time. Full-time tuition and fees vary according to course load and program. *Waivers:* employees or children of employees.

Applying *Options:* electronic application, early admission. *Application fee:* $35. *Recommended:* high school transcript. *Application deadline:* rolling (freshmen). *Notification:* continuous (freshmen).
**Freshman Application Contact** Dale Wood, Director of Admissions, North Central Institute, 168 Jack Miller Boulevard, Clarksville, TN 37042. *Phone:* 931-431-9700. *Toll-free phone:* 800-603-4116. *Fax:* 931-431-9771. *E-mail:* admissions@nci.edu.
*Website:* http://www.nci.edu/.

# Northeast State Community College
## Blountville, Tennessee

- **State-supported** 2-year, founded 1966, part of Tennessee Board of Regents
- **Small-town** 95-acre campus
- **Endowment** $9.9 million
- **Coed,** 6,088 undergraduate students, 56% full-time, 52% women, 48% men

**Undergraduates** 3,421 full-time, 2,667 part-time. Students come from 4 states and territories; 5 other countries; 2% are from out of state; 2% Black or African American, non-Hispanic/Latino; 3% Hispanic/Latino; 0.7% Asian, non-Hispanic/Latino; 0.1% Native Hawaiian or other Pacific Islander, non-Hispanic/Latino; 0.3% American Indian or Alaska Native, non-Hispanic/Latino; 3% Two or more races, non-Hispanic/Latino; 1% Race/ethnicity unknown; 0.2% international; 4% transferred in. *Retention:* 61% of full-time freshmen returned.
**Freshmen** *Admission:* 2,657 applied, 1,923 admitted, 1,565 enrolled. *Average high school GPA:* 3.1. *Test scores:* ACT scores over 18: 57%; ACT scores over 24: 8%; ACT scores over 30: 1%.
**Faculty** *Total:* 279, 44% full-time, 18% with terminal degrees. *Student/faculty ratio:* 24:1.
**Majors** Administrative assistant and secretarial science; aircraft powerplant technology; business administration and management; cardiovascular technology; child development; criminal justice/safety; education; electrical, electronic and communications engineering technology; emergency medical technology (EMT paramedic); general studies; health professions related; industrial technology; information technology; interdisciplinary studies; liberal arts and sciences/liberal studies; recording arts technology; registered nursing/registered nurse; surgical technology.
**Academics** *Calendar:* semesters. *Degree:* certificates and associate. *Special study options:* academic remediation for entering students, advanced placement credit, cooperative education, distance learning, double majors, honors programs, part-time degree program, services for LD students, study abroad, summer session for credit.
**Library** Wayne G. Basler Library plus 1 other. *Books:* 63,647 (physical), 316,562 (digital/electronic); *Serial titles:* 132 (physical), 48,455 (digital/electronic); *Databases:* 93.
**Student Life** *Housing:* college housing not available. *Activities and Organizations:* drama/theater group, Phi Theta Kappa, G.R.E.E.N.S., Argumentation and Debate Society, Skills, USA, Sci-Fi Fantasy Guild. *Campus security:* 24-hour emergency response devices and patrols, late-night transport/escort service, Safe Northeast Program. *Student services:* personal/psychological counseling, veterans affairs office.
**Costs (2017–18)** *Tuition:* state resident $3840 full-time, $160 per credit hour part-time; nonresident $15,816 full-time, $659 per credit hour part-time. Full-time tuition and fees vary according to course load. Part-time tuition and fees vary according to course load. *Required fees:* $311 full-time, $13 per credit hour part-time, $31 per term part-time. *Payment plan:* installment. *Waivers:* senior citizens and employees or children of employees.
**Financial Aid** Of all full-time matriculated undergraduates who enrolled in 2016, 109 Federal Work-Study jobs (averaging $1318). 35 state and other part-time jobs.
**Applying** *Options:* electronic application. *Required:* high school transcript.
**Freshman Application Contact** Mrs. Jennifer G. Starling, Dean of Enrollment Management, Northeast State Community College, PO Box 246, Blountville, TN 37617. *Phone:* 423-279-7635. *Toll-free phone:* 800-836-7822. *Fax:* 423-323-0240. *E-mail:* jgstarling@northeaststate.edu.
*Website:* http://www.northeaststate.edu/.

# Pellissippi State Community College
## Knoxville, Tennessee

**Freshman Application Contact** Director of Admissions and Records, Pellissippi State Community College, PO Box 22990, Knoxville, TN 37933-0990. *Phone:* 865-694-6400. *Fax:* 865-539-7217. *Website:* http://www.pstcc.edu/.

## Remington College–Memphis Campus
### Memphis, Tennessee

**Director of Admissions** Randal Hayes, Director of Recruitment, Remington College–Memphis Campus, 2710 Nonconnah Boulevard, Memphis, TN 38132. *Phone:* 901-345-1000. *Toll-free phone:* 800-323-8122. *Fax:* 901-396-8310. *E-mail:* randal.hayes@remingtoncollege.edu. *Website:* http://www.remingtoncollege.edu/.

## Remington College–Nashville Campus
### Nashville, Tennessee

**Director of Admissions** Mr. Frank Vivelo, Campus President, Remington College–Nashville Campus, 441 Donelson Pike, Suite 150, Nashville, TN 37214. *Phone:* 615-889-5520. *Toll-free phone:* 800-323-8122. *Fax:* 615-889-5528. *E-mail:* frank.vivelo@remingtoncollege.edu. *Website:* http://www.remingtoncollege.edu/.

## Roane State Community College
### Harriman, Tennessee

**Freshman Application Contact** Admissions Office, Roane State Community College, 276 Patton Lane, Harriman, TN 37748. *Phone:* 865-882-4523. *Toll-free phone:* 866-462-7722 Ext. 4554. *E-mail:* admissionsrecords@roanestate.edu. *Website:* http://www.roanestate.edu/.

## SAE Institute Nashville
### Nashville, Tennessee

**Admissions Office Contact** SAE Institute Nashville, 7 Music Circle N, Nashville, TN 37203. *Website:* http://www.sae.edu/.

## Southwest Tennessee Community College
### Memphis, Tennessee

**Freshman Application Contact** Mrs. Vanessa Dowdy, Southwest Tennessee Community College, 5983 Macon Cove, Memphis, TN 38134. *Phone:* 901-333-4275. *Toll-free phone:* 877-717-STCC. *E-mail:* vdowdy@southwest.tn.edu. *Website:* http://www.southwest.tn.edu/.

## Vatterott College
### Memphis, Tennessee

**Admissions Office Contact** Vatterott College, 2655 Dividend Drive, Memphis, TN 38132. *Toll-free phone:* 888-553-6627. *Website:* http://www.vatterott.edu/.

## Vatterott College
### Memphis, Tennessee

**Admissions Office Contact** Vatterott College, 6991 Appling Farms Parkway, Memphis, TN 38133. *Website:* http://www.vatterott.edu/.

## Virginia College in Chattanooga
### Chattanooga, Tennessee

**Admissions Office Contact** Virginia College in Chattanooga, 721 Eastgate Loop Road, Chattanooga, TN 37411. *Website:* http://www.vc.edu/.

## Virginia College in Knoxville
### Knoxville, Tennessee

**Admissions Office Contact** Virginia College in Knoxville, 5003 North Broadway Street, Knoxville, TN 37918. *Website:* http://www.vc.edu/.

## Volunteer State Community College
### Gallatin, Tennessee

- **State-supported** 2-year, founded 1970, part of Tennessee Board of Regents
- **Suburban** 110-acre campus with easy access to Nashville
- **Endowment** $4.4 million
- **Coed,** 8,838 undergraduate students, 56% full-time, 61% women, 39% men

**Undergraduates** 4,974 full-time, 3,864 part-time. Students come from 14 states and territories; 15 other countries; 1% are from out of state; 10% Black or African American, non-Hispanic/Latino; 6% Hispanic/Latino; 2% Asian, non-Hispanic/Latino; 0.1% Native Hawaiian or other Pacific Islander, non-Hispanic/Latino; 0.4% American Indian or Alaska Native, non-Hispanic/Latino; 3% Two or more races, non-Hispanic/Latino; 2% Race/ethnicity unknown; 0.4% international; 5% transferred in.

**Freshmen** *Admission:* 2,850 applied, 2,850 admitted, 2,397 enrolled. *Average high school GPA:* 3.0. *Test scores:* ACT scores over 18: 66%; ACT scores over 24: 13%; ACT scores over 30: 1%.

**Faculty** *Total:* 434, 41% full-time, 14% with terminal degrees. *Student/faculty ratio:* 23:1.

**Majors** Business administration and management; child development; clinical/medical laboratory technology; computer and information sciences; criminal justice/police science; criminal justice/safety; digital arts; education; electromechanical technology; fire science/firefighting; general studies; health information/medical records technology; health professions related; information technology; legal assistant/paralegal; liberal arts and sciences/liberal studies; medical informatics; medical radiologic technology; music performance; ophthalmic technology; physical therapy technology; respiratory care therapy; veterinary/animal health technology.

**Academics** *Calendar:* semesters. *Degree:* certificates and associate. *Special study options:* academic remediation for entering students, accelerated degree program, adult/continuing education programs, advanced placement credit, cooperative education, distance learning, double majors, English as a second language, honors programs, independent study, internships, part-time degree program, services for LD students, study abroad, summer session for credit.

**Library** Thigpen Library.

**Student Life** *Housing:* college housing not available. *Activities and Organizations:* drama/theater group, student-run newspaper, radio station, choral group, Gamma Beta Phi, Returning Woman's Organization, Phi Theta Kappa, Student Government Association, The Settler. *Campus security:* 24-hour emergency response devices and patrols, late-night transport/escort service. *Student services:* personal/psychological counseling, veterans affairs office.

**Athletics** Member NJCAA. *Intercollegiate sports:* baseball M, basketball M/W, softball W.

**Standardized Tests** *Required for some:* SAT or ACT (for admission).

**Costs (2017–18)** *Tuition:* state resident $3840 full-time, $160 per credit hour part-time; nonresident $15,816 full-time, $659 per credit hour part-time. Full-time tuition and fees vary according to course load. Part-time tuition and fees vary according to course load. *Required fees:* $293 full-time, $9 per hour part-time, $34 per term part-time. *Payment plan:* deferred payment. *Waivers:* senior citizens and employees or children of employees.

**Financial Aid** Of all full-time matriculated undergraduates who enrolled in 2016, 4,298 applied for aid, 2,888 were judged to have need, 177 had their need fully met. 42 Federal Work-Study jobs (averaging $2202). In 2016, 51 non-need-based awards were made. *Average percent of need met:* 52%. *Average financial aid package:* $5879. *Average need-based loan:* $2891. *Average need-based gift aid:* $4899. *Average non-need-based aid:* $1858.

**Applying** *Options:* electronic application, early admission, deferred entrance. *Required:* high school transcript. *Required for some:* minimum 2.0 GPA, interview. *Application deadlines:* 8/25 (freshmen), 8/25 (transfers). *Notification:* continuous (freshmen), continuous (transfers).

**Freshman Application Contact** Mr. Tim Amyx, Director of Admissions, Volunteer State Community College, 1480 Nashville Pike, Gallatin, TN 37066-3188. *Phone:* 615-452-8600 Ext. 3614. *Toll-free phone:* 888-335-8722. *Fax:* 615-230-4875. *E-mail:* admissions@volstate.edu. *Website:* http://www.volstate.edu/.

## Walters State Community College
### Morristown, Tennessee

- **State-supported** 2-year, founded 1970, part of Tennessee Board of Regents
- **Small-town** 100-acre campus
- **Coed,** 6,075 undergraduate students, 54% full-time, 62% women, 38% men

**Undergraduates** 3,294 full-time, 2,781 part-time. 1% are from out of state; 3% Black or African American, non-Hispanic/Latino; 4% Hispanic/Latino;

0.7% Asian, non-Hispanic/Latino; 0.1% Native Hawaiian or other Pacific Islander, non-Hispanic/Latino; 0.3% American Indian or Alaska Native, non-Hispanic/Latino; 3% Two or more races, non-Hispanic/Latino; 0.6% international; 4% transferred in.

**Freshmen** *Admission:* 3,987 applied, 3,984 admitted, 1,691 enrolled. *Average high school GPA:* 3.2.

**Faculty** *Total:* 358, 47% full-time, 26% with terminal degrees. *Student/faculty ratio:* 18:1.

**Majors** Business administration and management; child development; computer and information sciences; criminal justice/police science; criminal justice/safety; data processing and data processing technology; education; energy management and systems technology; general studies; health information/medical records technology; industrial technology; liberal arts and sciences/liberal studies; music performance; occupational therapist assistant; ornamental horticulture; physical therapy technology; registered nursing/registered nurse; respiratory care therapy; surgical technology; web page, digital/multimedia and information resources design.

**Academics** *Calendar:* semesters. *Degree:* certificates and associate. *Special study options:* academic remediation for entering students, accelerated degree program, advanced placement credit, cooperative education, distance learning, English as a second language, freshman honors college, honors programs, independent study, internships, off-campus study, part-time degree program, services for LD students, student-designed majors, study abroad, summer session for credit. *ROTC:* Army (c).

**Library** Walters State Library.

**Student Life** *Housing:* college housing not available. *Activities and Organizations:* drama/theater group, choral group, Baptist Collegiate Ministry, Phi Theta Kappa, Debate Club, Student Government Association, Service Learners Club. *Campus security:* 24-hour emergency response devices and patrols, late-night transport/escort service, security cameras. *Student services:* health clinic, personal/psychological counseling.

**Athletics** Member NJCAA. *Intercollegiate sports:* baseball M(s), basketball M(s)/W(s), golf M(s), softball W(s), volleyball W(s). *Intramural sports:* baseball M, basketball M/W.

**Costs (2017–18)** *Tuition:* state resident $4128 full-time, $160 per credit hour part-time; nonresident $16,104 full-time, $659 per credit hour part-time. Full-time tuition and fees vary according to course load and program. Part-time tuition and fees vary according to course load and program. *Required fees:* $288 full-time, $16 per credit hour part-time, $20 per term part-time. *Payment plan:* installment. *Waivers:* senior citizens and employees or children of employees.

**Financial Aid** Of all full-time matriculated undergraduates who enrolled in 2016, 2,690 applied for aid, 2,195 were judged to have need, 239 had their need fully met. In 2016, 468 non-need-based awards were made. *Average percent of need met:* 59%. *Average financial aid package:* $6061. *Average need-based gift aid:* $4830. *Average non-need-based aid:* $4404.

**Applying** *Options:* electronic application, early admission. *Required:* high school transcript. *Application deadlines:* rolling (freshmen), rolling (transfers). *Notification:* continuous (freshmen), continuous (transfers).

**Freshman Application Contact** Mr. Michael Campbell, Assistant Vice President for Student Affairs, Walters State Community College, 500 South Davy Crockett Parkway, Morristown, TN 37813-6899. *Phone:* 423-585-2682. *Toll-free phone:* 800-225-4770. *Fax:* 423-585-6876. *E-mail:* mike.campbell@ws.edu.

*Website:* http://www.ws.edu/.

## West Tennessee Business College
### Jackson, Tennessee

**Admissions Office Contact** West Tennessee Business College, 1186 Highway 45 Bypass, Jackson, TN 38343. *Website:* http://www.wtbc.edu/.

# TEXAS

## Alvin Community College
### Alvin, Texas

- **State and locally supported** 2-year, founded 1949
- **Suburban** 114-acre campus with easy access to Houston
- **Coed,** 5,785 undergraduate students, 24% full-time, 57% women, 43% men

**Undergraduates** 1,411 full-time, 4,374 part-time. Students come from 2 other countries; 15% Black or African American, non-Hispanic/Latino; 40% Hispanic/Latino; 5% Asian, non-Hispanic/Latino; 0.3% Native Hawaiian or other Pacific Islander, non-Hispanic/Latino; 1% American Indian or Alaska Native, non-Hispanic/Latino; 2% Race/ethnicity unknown; 1% international. *Retention:* 62% of full-time freshmen returned.

**Freshmen** *Admission:* 1,022 enrolled.

**Faculty** *Total:* 361, 29% full-time, 10% with terminal degrees. *Student/faculty ratio:* 14:1.

**Majors** Accounting; administrative assistant and secretarial science; aeronautics/aviation/aerospace science and technology; art; automobile/automotive mechanics technology; biology/biological sciences; business administration and management; business/commerce; chemical technology; child development; computer engineering technology; computer programming; corrections; court reporting; criminalistics and criminal science; criminal justice/police science; criminal justice/safety; culinary arts; desktop publishing and digital imaging design; diagnostic medical sonography and ultrasound technology; drafting and design technology; dramatic/theater arts; early childhood education; electrical, electronic and communications engineering technology; electroneurodiagnostic/electroencephalographic technology; emergency medical technology (EMT paramedic); executive assistant/executive secretary; general studies; health and physical education/fitness; health services/allied health/health sciences; history; legal administrative assistant/secretary; legal assistant/paralegal; legal studies; liberal arts and sciences/liberal studies; licensed practical/vocational nurse training; marketing/marketing management; mathematics; medical administrative assistant and medical secretary; mental health counseling; middle school education; music; office occupations and clerical services; pharmacy technician; physical education teaching and coaching; physical sciences; psychiatric/mental health services technology; psychology; radio and television; registered nursing/registered nurse; respiratory care therapy; secondary education; sociology; substance abuse/addiction counseling; voice and opera.

**Academics** *Calendar:* semesters. *Degree:* certificates, diplomas, and associate. *Special study options:* academic remediation for entering students, accelerated degree program, adult/continuing education programs, advanced placement credit, cooperative education, distance learning, double majors, English as a second language, honors programs, independent study, internships, part-time degree program, services for LD students, student-designed majors, study abroad, summer session for credit.

**Library** Alvin Community College Library. *Books:* 11,000 (physical), 30,000 (digital/electronic); *Databases:* 80. Weekly public service hours: 67; students can reserve study rooms.

**Student Life** *Housing:* college housing not available. *Activities and Organizations:* drama/theater group, student-run radio and television station, choral group. *Campus security:* 24-hour patrols, late-night transport/escort service, Vehicle Assist, emergency messages. *Student services:* personal/psychological counseling, veterans affairs office.

**Athletics** Member NJCAA. *Intercollegiate sports:* baseball M(s), softball W(s).

**Costs (2018–19)** *Tuition:* area resident $1104 full-time, $46 per credit hour part-time; state resident $2208 full-time, $92 per credit hour part-time; nonresident $3360 full-time, $140 per credit hour part-time. Full-time tuition and fees vary according to course load and program. Part-time tuition and fees vary according to course load and program. *Required fees:* $528 full-time, $7 per credit hour part-time, $204 per term part-time. *Payment plan:* installment.

**Applying** *Required for some:* high school transcript.

**Freshman Application Contact** Alvin Community College, 3110 Mustang Road, Alvin, TX 77511-4898. *Phone:* 281-756-3527.

*Website:* http://www.alvincollege.edu/.

## Amarillo College
### Amarillo, Texas

- **State and locally supported** 2-year, founded 1929
- **Urban** 1542-acre campus
- **Endowment** $40.0 million
- **Coed**

**Undergraduates** 5% Black or African American, non-Hispanic/Latino; 39% Hispanic/Latino; 3% Asian, non-Hispanic/Latino; 0.1% Native Hawaiian or other Pacific Islander, non-Hispanic/Latino; 0.5% American Indian or Alaska Native, non-Hispanic/Latino; 2% Two or more races, non-Hispanic/Latino; 1% Race/ethnicity unknown. *Retention:* 52% of full-time freshmen returned.

**Faculty** *Total:* 775, 25% full-time, 4% with terminal degrees.

**Majors** Accounting; administrative assistant and secretarial science; airframe mechanics and aircraft maintenance technology; architectural engineering technology; art; automobile/automotive mechanics technology; behavioral sciences; biblical studies; biology/biological sciences; broadcast journalism; business administration and management; business teacher education; chemical technology; chemistry; child development; clinical laboratory science/medical technology; commercial and advertising art; computer engineering technology; computer programming; computer science; computer systems analysis; corrections; criminal justice/law enforcement administration; criminal justice/police science; dental hygiene; drafting and design technology; dramatic/theater arts; electrical, electronic and communications engineering technology; elementary education; emergency medical technology

(EMT paramedic); engineering; English; environmental health; fine/studio arts; fire science/firefighting; funeral service and mortuary science; general studies; geology/earth science; health information/medical records administration; heating, air conditioning, ventilation and refrigeration maintenance technology; heavy equipment maintenance technology; history; industrial radiologic technology; information science/studies; instrumentation technology; interior design; journalism; laser and optical technology; legal administrative assistant/secretary; liberal arts and sciences/liberal studies; licensed practical/vocational nurse training; machine tool technology; mass communication/media; mathematics; medical administrative assistant and medical secretary; modern languages; music; music teacher education; natural sciences; nuclear medical technology; occupational therapy; photography; physical education teaching and coaching; physical sciences; physical therapy; physics; pre-engineering; pre-pharmacy studies; psychology; public relations/image management; radio and television; radiologic technology/science; real estate; registered nursing/registered nurse; religious studies; respiratory care therapy; rhetoric and composition; social sciences; social work; substance abuse/addiction counseling; telecommunications technology; tourism and travel services management; visual and performing arts.

**Academics** *Calendar:* semesters. *Degree:* certificates and associate. *Special study options:* academic remediation for entering students, adult/continuing education programs, advanced placement credit, cooperative education, distance learning, English as a second language, freshman honors college, honors programs, part-time degree program, services for LD students, summer session for credit.

**Library** Lynn Library Learning Center plus 2 others.

**Student Life** *Housing:* college housing not available. *Activities and Organizations:* drama/theater group, student-run newspaper, radio station, choral group. *Campus security:* 24-hour emergency response devices, late-night transport/escort service, campus police patrol Monday through Saturday 7 am-11 pm. *Student services:* personal/psychological counseling, veterans affairs office.

**Athletics** *Intramural sports:* basketball M/W, soccer M/W, softball M/W, tennis M/W, volleyball M/W.

**Costs (2017–18)** *Tuition:* area resident $2136 full-time, $89 per semester hour part-time; state resident $3168 full-time, $132 per semester hour part-time; nonresident $4704 full-time, $196 per semester hour part-time. Full-time tuition and fees vary according to course load. Part-time tuition and fees vary according to course load. *Payment plan:* installment. *Waivers:* senior citizens and employees or children of employees.

**Financial Aid** Of all full-time matriculated undergraduates who enrolled in 2016, 100 Federal Work-Study jobs (averaging $3000).

**Applying** *Options:* early admission, deferred entrance. *Required:* high school transcript. *Notification:* continuous (freshmen), continuous (transfers).

**Freshman Application Contact** Amarillo College, PO Box 447, Amarillo, TX 79178-0001. *Phone:* 806-371-5000. *Toll-free phone:* 800-227-8784. *Fax:* 806-371-5497. *E-mail:* askac@actx.edu.

*Website:* http://www.actx.edu/.

# Angelina College
## Lufkin, Texas

**Freshman Application Contact** Angelina College, PO Box 1768, Lufkin, TX 75902-1768. *Phone:* 936-633-5213. *Website:* http://www.angelina.edu/.

# Auguste Escoffier School of Culinary Arts
## Austin, Texas

**Admissions Office Contact** Auguste Escoffier School of Culinary Arts, 6020-B Dillard, Austin, TX 78752. *Website:* http://www.escoffier.edu/.

# Austin Community College District
## Austin, Texas

- **State and locally supported** 2-year, founded 1972
- **Urban** campus with easy access to Austin
- **Endowment** $5.9 million
- **Coed**, 40,803 undergraduate students, 22% full-time, 55% women, 45% men

**Undergraduates** 9,130 full-time, 31,673 part-time.

**Faculty** *Total:* 1,823, 31% full-time, 23% with terminal degrees. *Student/faculty ratio:* 20:1.

**Majors** Accounting; accounting technology and bookkeeping; administrative assistant and secretarial science; animation, interactive technology, video graphics and special effects; anthropology; Arabic; archeology; art; autobody/collision and repair technology; automobile/automotive mechanics technology; biology/biological sciences; biology/biotechnology laboratory technician; biomedical technology; business administration and management; business/commerce; carpentry; chemistry; child development; Chinese; clinical/medical laboratory technology; commercial photography; computer and information sciences; computer programming; computer systems networking and telecommunications; corrections; creative writing; criminal justice/police science; culinary arts; dance; dental hygiene; design and visual communications; diagnostic medical sonography and ultrasound technology; drafting and design technology; dramatic/theater arts; early childhood education; economics; electrical, electronic and communications engineering technology; emergency medical technology (EMT paramedic); engineering; English; environmental engineering technology; environmental science; fire prevention and safety technology; French; general studies; geographic information science and cartography; geography; geology/earth science; German; health and physical education/fitness; health information/medical records technology; heating, ventilation, air conditioning and refrigeration engineering technology; history; hospitality administration; hotel/motel administration; international business/trade/commerce; Italian; Japanese; journalism; kinesiology and exercise science; Latin; legal assistant/paralegal; logistics, materials, and supply chain management; marketing/marketing management; mathematics; mental health counseling; middle school education; multi/interdisciplinary studies related; music; music management; occupational therapist assistant; pharmacy technician; philosophy; photographic and film/video technology; physical therapy technology; physics; political science and government; premedical studies; professional, technical, business, and scientific writing; psychology; radio and television; radiologic technology/science; real estate; registered nursing/registered nurse; rhetoric and composition; Russian; secondary education; sign language interpretation and translation; social work; sociology; Spanish; substance abuse/addiction counseling; surgical technology; surveying technology; therapeutic recreation; tourism and travel services management; veterinary/animal health technology; watchmaking and jewelrymaking; welding technology.

**Academics** *Calendar:* semesters. *Degrees:* certificates, associate, and postbachelor's certificates. *Special study options:* academic remediation for entering students, accelerated degree program, adult/continuing education programs, advanced placement credit, cooperative education, distance learning, English as a second language, honors programs, independent study, internships, part-time degree program, services for LD students, summer session for credit. *ROTC:* Army (c), Air Force (c).

**Library** Main Library plus 11 others. *Books:* 149,084 (physical), 37,268 (digital/electronic); *Serial titles:* 394 (physical), 82,407 (digital/electronic); *Databases:* 104. Weekly public service hours: 83; students can reserve study rooms.

**Student Life** *Housing:* college housing not available. *Activities and Organizations:* Intramurals, Students for Environmental Outreach, Phi Theta Kappa (PTK), National Society of Collegiate Scholars, Students for Community Involvement. *Campus security:* 24-hour emergency response devices, late-night transport/escort service, 24-hour patrols by police officers. *Student services:* personal/psychological counseling, veterans affairs office.

**Athletics** *Intramural sports:* basketball M/W, soccer M/W, volleyball W.

**Costs (2017–18)** *Tuition:* area resident $2010 full-time, $67 per credit hour part-time; state resident $10,350 full-time, $345 per credit hour part-time; nonresident $12,540 full-time, $418 per credit hour part-time. Full-time tuition and fees vary according to course load. Part-time tuition and fees vary according to course load. *Required fees:* $540 full-time, $18 per semester hour part-time. *Payment plan:* installment. *Waivers:* senior citizens and employees or children of employees.

**Financial Aid** Of all full-time matriculated undergraduates who enrolled in 2017, 4,815 applied for aid, 4,289 were judged to have need. 196 Federal Work-Study jobs (averaging $2125). 22 state and other part-time jobs (averaging $2329). *Average need-based loan:* $3263. *Average need-based gift aid:* $4012.

**Applying** *Options:* electronic application. *Required:* high school transcript. *Application deadlines:* rolling (freshmen), rolling (transfers).

**Freshman Application Contact** Ms. Linda Kluck, Executive Director, Admissions and Records, Austin Community College District, 5930 Middle Fiskville Road, Austin, TX 78752. *Phone:* 512-223-7503, *Fax:* 512-223-7963. *E-mail:* admission@austincc.edu.

*Website:* http://www.austincc.edu/.

# Blinn College
## Brenham, Texas

- **State and locally supported** 2-year, founded 1883
- **Small-town** 100-acre campus with easy access to Houston
- **Endowment** $10.3 million
- **Coed**

**Undergraduates** 10,473 full-time, 8,274 part-time. Students come from 42 other countries; 1% are from out of state; 10% Black or African American, non-Hispanic/Latino; 21% Hispanic/Latino; 2% Asian, non-Hispanic/Latino; 0.1% Native Hawaiian or other Pacific Islander, non-Hispanic/Latino; 0.4% American Indian or Alaska Native, non-Hispanic/Latino; 3% Two or more races, non-Hispanic/Latino; 2% Race/ethnicity unknown; 0.7% international; 10% transferred in; 9% live on campus.

**Academics** *Calendar:* semesters. *Degree:* certificates, diplomas, and associate. *Special study options:* academic remediation for entering students, adult/continuing education programs, advanced placement credit, distance learning, double majors, English as a second language, freshman honors college, part-time degree program, services for LD students, summer session for credit.

**Library** W. L. Moody, Jr. Library plus 1 other.

**Student Life** *Campus security:* 24-hour emergency response devices and patrols, controlled dormitory access.

**Athletics** Member NJCAA.

**Costs (2017–18)** *Tuition:* area resident $1248 full-time, $52 per credit hour part-time; state resident $2616 full-time, $109 per credit hour part-time; nonresident $6408 full-time, $267 per credit hour part-time. Full-time tuition and fees vary according to course load. Part-time tuition and fees vary according to course load. *Required fees:* $1680 full-time, $52 per credit hour part-time. *Room and board:* $7667; room only: $4467. Room and board charges vary according to board plan and housing facility.

**Financial Aid** Of all full-time matriculated undergraduates who enrolled in 2016, 130 Federal Work-Study jobs (averaging $1702).

**Applying** *Options:* electronic application, early admission, deferred entrance. *Required:* high school transcript.

**Freshman Application Contact** Ms. Jennifer Bynum, Director Prospective Student Relations/Community Outreach, Blinn College, PO Box 6030, Bryan, TX 77805-6030. *Phone:* 979-209-7640. *E-mail:* jennifer.bynum@blinn.edu. *Website:* http://www.blinn.edu/.

# Brazosport College
## Lake Jackson, Texas

**Freshman Application Contact** Brazosport College, 500 College Drive, Lake Jackson, TX 77566-3199. *Phone:* 979-230-3020. *Website:* http://www.brazosport.edu/.

# Brightwood College, Arlington Campus
## Arlington, Texas

**Freshman Application Contact** Brightwood College, Arlington Campus, 2241 South Watson Road, Suite 181, Arlington, TX 76010. *Phone:* 866-249-2074. *Toll-free phone:* 866-543-0208. *Website:* http://www.brightwood.edu/.

# Brightwood College, Beaumont Campus
## Beaumont, Texas

**Freshman Application Contact** Admissions Office, Brightwood College, Beaumont Campus, 6115 Eastex Freeway, Beaumont, TX 77706. *Phone:* 409-833-2722. *Toll-free phone:* 866-543-0208. *Website:* http://www.brightwood.edu/.

# Brightwood College, Brownsville Campus
## Brownsville, Texas

**Freshman Application Contact** Director of Admissions, Brightwood College, Brownsville Campus, 1900 North Expressway, Suite O, Brownsville, TX 78521. *Phone:* 956-547-8200. *Toll-free phone:* 866-543-0208. *Website:* http://www.brightwood.edu/.

# Brightwood College, Corpus Christi Campus
## Corpus Christi, Texas

**Freshman Application Contact** Admissions Director, Brightwood College, Corpus Christi Campus, 1620 South Padre Island Drive, Suite 600, Corpus Christi, TX 78416. *Phone:* 361-852-2900. *Toll-free phone:* 866-543-0208. *Website:* http://www.brightwood.edu/.

# Brightwood College, Dallas Campus
## Dallas, Texas

**Freshman Application Contact** Brightwood College, Dallas Campus, 12005 Ford Road, Suite 100, Dallas, TX 75234. *Phone:* 972-385-1446. *Toll-free phone:* 866-543-0208. *Website:* http://www.brightwood.edu/.

# Brightwood College, El Paso Campus
## El Paso, Texas

**Freshman Application Contact** Director of Admissions, Brightwood College, El Paso Campus, 8360 Burnham Road, Suite 100, El Paso, TX 79907. *Toll-free phone:* 866-543-0208. *Website:* http://www.brightwood.edu/.

# Brightwood College, Fort Worth Campus
## Fort Worth, Texas

**Freshman Application Contact** Director of Admissions, Brightwood College, Fort Worth Campus, 2001 Beach Street, Suite 201, Fort Worth, TX 76103. *Phone:* 817-413-2000. *Toll-free phone:* 866-543-0208. *Website:* http://www.brightwood.edu/.

# Brightwood College, Friendswood Campus
## Friendswood, Texas

**Freshman Application Contact** Admissions Office, Brightwood College, Friendswood Campus, 3208 Farm to Market Road 528, Friendswood, TX 77546. *Toll-free phone:* 866-543-0208. *Website:* http://www.brightwood.edu/.

# Brightwood College, Houston Campus
## Houston, Texas

**Freshman Application Contact** Admissions Office, Brightwood College, Houston Campus, 711 East Airtex Drive, Houston, TX 77073. *Phone:* 281-443-8900. *Toll-free phone:* 866-543-0208. *Website:* http://www.brightwood.edu/.

# Brightwood College, Laredo Campus
## Laredo, Texas

**Freshman Application Contact** Admissions Office, Brightwood College, Laredo Campus, 6410 McPherson Road, Laredo, TX 78041. *Phone:* 956-717-5909. *Toll-free phone:* 866-543-0208. *Website:* http://www.brightwood.edu/.

# Brightwood College, McAllen Campus
## McAllen, Texas

**Admissions Office Contact** Brightwood College, McAllen Campus, 1500 South Jackson Road, McAllen, TX 78503. *Toll-free phone:* 866-543-0208. *Website:* http://www.brightwood.edu/.

# Brightwood College, San Antonio Ingram Campus
## San Antonio, Texas

**Freshman Application Contact** Admissions Office, Brightwood College, San Antonio Ingram Campus, 6441 NW Loop 410, San Antonio, TX 78238. *Phone:* 210-308-8584. *Toll-free phone:* 866-543-0208. *Website:* http://www.brightwood.edu/.

# Brightwood College, San Antonio San Pedro Campus
## San Antonio, Texas

**Freshman Application Contact** Director of Admissions, Brightwood College, San Antonio San Pedro Campus, 7142 San Pedro Avenue, Suite 100, San Antonio, TX 78216. *Toll-free phone:* 866-543-0208. *Website:* http://www.brightwood.edu/.

# Brookhaven College
## Farmers Branch, Texas

- **County-supported** 2-year, founded 1978, part of Dallas County Community College District System
- **Suburban** 200-acre campus with easy access to Dallas-Fort Worth
- **Coed,** 13,284 undergraduate students, 17% full-time, 58% women, 42% men

**Undergraduates** 2,257 full-time, 11,027 part-time. Students come from 35 states and territories; 88 other countries; 3% are from out of state; 14% Black or African American, non-Hispanic/Latino; 31% Hispanic/Latino; 12% Asian, non-Hispanic/Latino; 0.2% Native Hawaiian or other Pacific Islander, non-Hispanic/Latino; 2% American Indian or Alaska Native, non-Hispanic/Latino; 4% Two or more races, non-Hispanic/Latino; 5% Race/ethnicity unknown; 2% international; 9% transferred in.

**Freshmen** *Admission:* 5,469 enrolled.

**Faculty** *Total:* 588, 22% full-time. *Student/faculty ratio:* 21:1.

**Majors** Accounting; automobile/automotive mechanics technology; business administration and management; business/commerce; child development; computer engineering technology; computer programming; computer technology/computer systems technology; criminal justice/law enforcement administration; design and visual communications; e-commerce; education (multiple levels); emergency medical technology (EMT paramedic); executive assistant/executive secretary; general studies; geographic information science and cartography; graphic design; humanities; information science/studies; liberal arts and sciences/liberal studies; marketing/marketing management; music; office management; radiologic technology/science; registered nursing/registered nurse; secondary education; speech communication and rhetoric.

**Academics** *Calendar:* semesters. *Degree:* certificates and associate. *Special study options:* academic remediation for entering students, adult/continuing education programs, advanced placement credit, cooperative education, distance learning, English as a second language, honors programs, independent study, internships, off-campus study, part-time degree program, services for LD students, student-designed majors, study abroad, summer session for credit.

**Library** Brookhaven College Learning Resources Center plus 1 other. *Books:* 55,595 (physical); *Serial titles:* 80 (physical).

**Student Life** *Housing:* college housing not available. *Activities and Organizations:* drama/theater group, student-run newspaper, choral group. *Campus security:* 24-hour emergency response devices and patrols, late-night transport/escort service. *Student services:* health clinic, personal/psychological counseling, veterans affairs office.

**Athletics** Member NJCAA. *Intercollegiate sports:* baseball M, basketball M, soccer W, volleyball W.

**Costs (2018–19)** *Tuition:* area resident $1770 full-time, $59 per credit hour part-time; state resident $3330 full-time, $111 per credit hour part-time; nonresident $5220 full-time, $174 per credit hour part-time. *Payment plan:* installment. *Waivers:* senior citizens and employees or children of employees.

**Applying** *Options:* electronic application, early admission, deferred entrance. *Required:* high school transcript. *Required for some:* HESI score, minimum GPA in prerequisite courses, completion of support courses for nursing program. *Application deadlines:* rolling (freshmen), rolling (transfers).

**Freshman Application Contact** Admissions Office, Brookhaven College, 3939 Valley View Lane, Farmers Branch, TX 75244-4997. *Phone:* 972-860-4883. *Fax:* 972-860-4886. *E-mail:* bhcadmissions@dcccd.edu. *Website:* http://www.brookhavencollege.edu/.

# Carrington College–Mesquite
## Mesquite, Texas

**Admissions Office Contact** Carrington College–Mesquite, 3733 West Emporium Circle, Mesquite, TX 75150-6509. *Website:* http://www.carrington.edu/.

# Cedar Valley College
## Lancaster, Texas

- **State-supported** 2-year, founded 1977, part of Dallas County Community College District System
- **Suburban** 353-acre campus with easy access to Dallas-Fort Worth
- **Coed,** 7,249 undergraduate students
- 100% of applicants were admitted

**Undergraduates** Students come from 49 states and territories; 6 other countries; 15% are from out of state; 44% Black or African American, non-Hispanic/Latino; 29% Hispanic/Latino; 3% Asian, non-Hispanic/Latino; 0.1% Native Hawaiian or other Pacific Islander, non-Hispanic/Latino; 0.4% American Indian or Alaska Native, non-Hispanic/Latino; 3% Race/ethnicity unknown; 0.2% international. *Retention:* 17% of full-time freshmen returned.

**Freshmen** *Admission:* 1,138 applied, 1,138 admitted.

**Faculty** *Total:* 296, 25% full-time, 100% with terminal degrees. *Student/faculty ratio:* 24:1.

**Majors** Accounting; automobile/automotive mechanics technology; business administration and management; business/commerce; computer programming; computer systems networking and telecommunications; criminal justice/safety; data processing and data processing technology; education; executive assistant/executive secretary; general studies; graphic design; heating, air conditioning, ventilation and refrigeration maintenance technology; marketing/marketing management; multi/interdisciplinary studies related; music management; music performance; music theory and composition; radio and television broadcasting technology; real estate; veterinary/animal health technology.

**Academics** *Calendar:* semesters. *Degree:* certificates and associate. *Special study options:* academic remediation for entering students, advanced placement credit, cooperative education, distance learning, double majors, English as a second language, internships, off-campus study, part-time degree program, services for LD students, summer session for credit.

**Library** Cedar Valley College Library plus 1 other.

**Student Life** *Housing:* college housing not available. *Activities and Organizations:* choral group, Phi Theta Kappa (PTK), Brother 2 Brother, Sustainability, Commercial Music Association, Family Music Club. *Campus security:* 24-hour emergency response devices and patrols, late-night transport/escort service. *Student services:* health clinic, personal/psychological counseling, veterans affairs office.

**Athletics** Member NJCAA. *Intercollegiate sports:* baseball M, basketball M, soccer W, volleyball W.

**Standardized Tests** *Required:* SAT or ACT (for admission), TSI (for admission). *Required for some:* SAT and SAT Subject Tests or ACT (for admission).

**Applying** *Options:* electronic application. *Required:* high school transcript, minimum 2.0 GPA.

**Freshman Application Contact** Admissions Office, Cedar Valley College, Lancaster, TX 75134-3799. *Phone:* 972-860-8206. *Fax:* 972-860-8207. *Website:* http://www.cedarvalleycollege.edu/.

# Center for Advanced Legal Studies
## Houston, Texas

**Freshman Application Contact** Mr. James Scheffer, Center for Advanced Legal Studies, 3910 Kirby, Suite 200, Houston, TX 77098. *Phone:* 713-529-2778. *Toll-free phone:* 800-446-6931. *Fax:* 713-523-2715. *E-mail:* james.scheffer@paralegal.edu. *Website:* http://www.paralegal.edu/.

# Central Texas College
## Killeen, Texas

- **State and locally supported** 2-year, founded 1967
- **Suburban** 500-acre campus with easy access to Austin
- **Endowment** $7.6 million
- **Coed,** 15,672 undergraduate students, 23% full-time, 50% women, 50% men

**Undergraduates** 3,671 full-time, 12,001 part-time. Students come from 48 states and territories; 28% Black or African American, non-Hispanic/Latino; 24% Hispanic/Latino; 3% Asian, non-Hispanic/Latino; 2% Native Hawaiian or other Pacific Islander, non-Hispanic/Latino; 0.7% American Indian or Alaska Native, non-Hispanic/Latino; 4% Two or more races, non-Hispanic/Latino; 3% Race/ethnicity unknown; 0.7% international; 1% live on campus. *Retention:* 47% of full-time freshmen returned.

**Freshmen** *Admission:* 2,169 enrolled.

**Faculty** *Total:* 1,248, 16% full-time. *Student/faculty ratio:* 17:1.

**Majors** Administrative assistant and secretarial science; agriculture; airline pilot and flight crew; autobody/collision and repair technology; automobile/automotive mechanics technology; biology/biological sciences; building/property maintenance; business administration and management; business/commerce; chemistry; clinical/medical laboratory technology; clinical/medical social work; commercial and advertising art; computer and information systems security; computer programming; computer technology/computer systems technology; criminal justice/safety; diesel mechanics technology; drafting and design technology; dramatic/theater arts; early childhood education; emergency medical technology (EMT paramedic); engineering; environmental science; farm and ranch management; fine/studio arts; fire services administration; foreign languages and literatures; general studies; geology/earth science; graphic and printing equipment operation/production; heating, air conditioning, ventilation and refrigeration maintenance technology; hospitality administration; journalism; kinesiology and exercise science; legal assistant/paralegal; liberal arts and sciences/liberal studies; licensed practical/vocational nurse training; mathematics; medical administrative assistant and medical secretary; medical insurance coding;

music; public administration; radio and television; registered nursing/registered nurse; restaurant/food services management; social sciences; welding technology.

**Academics** *Calendar:* semesters. *Degree:* certificates and associate. *Special study options:* academic remediation for entering students, accelerated degree program, adult/continuing education programs, advanced placement credit, cooperative education, distance learning, English as a second language, external degree program, internships, part-time degree program, services for LD students, student-designed majors, summer session for credit. *ROTC:* Army (b).

**Library** Oveta Culp Hobby Memorial Library. *Books:* 46,095 (physical), 34,502 (digital/electronic); *Serial titles:* 128 (physical); *Databases:* 82. Weekly public service hours: 85; students can reserve study rooms.

**Student Life** *Housing Options:* coed. Campus housing is university owned. *Activities and Organizations:* drama/theater group, International Student Association, Phi Theta Kappa, Net Impact, Student Nurses Association, Student Veterans Organization. *Campus security:* 24-hour emergency response devices and patrols. *Student services:* veterans affairs office.

**Athletics** *Intramural sports:* basketball M/W, football M/W, soccer M/W, softball M/W, volleyball M/W.

**Standardized Tests** *Required for some:* TSI Assessment required for those that are not TSI exempt or waived.

**Costs (2018–19)** *Tuition:* area resident $2700 full-time, $90 per credit hour part-time; state resident $3390 full-time, $113 per credit hour part-time; nonresident $7050 full-time, $235 per credit hour part-time. Full-time tuition and fees vary according to location and program. Part-time tuition and fees vary according to location and program. *Room and board:* $5600. *Payment plan:* installment. *Waivers:* senior citizens and employees or children of employees.

**Financial Aid** Of all full-time matriculated undergraduates who enrolled in 2016, 68 Federal Work-Study jobs (averaging $3658).

**Applying** *Options:* electronic application, early admission, deferred entrance. *Required:* high school transcript. *Application deadlines:* rolling (freshmen), rolling (transfers).

**Freshman Application Contact** Admissions Office, Central Texas College, PO Box 1800, Killeen, TX 76540-1800. *Phone:* 254-526-1696. *Toll-free phone:* 800-223-4760 (in-state); 800-792-3348 (out-of-state). *E-mail:* admissions@ctcd.edu. *Website:* http://www.ctcd.edu/.

## Cisco College
### Cisco, Texas

**Freshman Application Contact** Mr. Olin O. Odom III, Dean of Admission/Registrar, Cisco College, 101 College Heights, Cisco, TX 76437-9321. *Phone:* 254-442-2567 Ext. 5130. *E-mail:* oodom@cjc.edu. *Website:* http://www.cisco.edu/.

## Clarendon College
### Clarendon, Texas

**Freshman Application Contact** Ms. Martha Smith, Admissions Director, Clarendon College, PO Box 968, Clarendon, TX 79226. *Phone:* 806-874-3571 Ext. 106. *Toll-free phone:* 800-687-9737. *Fax:* 806-874-3201. *E-mail:* martha.smith@clarendoncollege.edu. *Website:* http://www.clarendoncollege.edu/.

## Coastal Bend College
### Beeville, Texas

**Freshman Application Contact** Mrs. Tammy Adams, Director of Admissions/Registrar, Coastal Bend College, Beeville, TX 78102-2197. *Phone:* 361-354-2245. *Toll-free phone:* 866-722-2838 (in-state); 866-262-2838 (out-of-state). *Fax:* 361-354-2254. *E-mail:* tadams@coastalbend.edu. *Website:* http://www.coastalbend.edu/.

## The College of Health Care Professions
### Austin, Texas

**Admissions Office Contact** The College of Health Care Professions, 6505 Airport Boulevard, Austin, TX 78752. *Website:* http://www.chcp.edu/.

## The College of Health Care Professions
### Fort Worth, Texas

**Admissions Office Contact** The College of Health Care Professions, 4248 North Freeway, Fort Worth, TX 76137-5021. *Website:* http://www.chcp.edu/.

## The College of Health Care Professions
### Houston, Texas

**Freshman Application Contact** Admissions Office, The College of Health Care Professions, 240 Northwest Mall Boulevard, Houston, TX 77092. *Phone:* 713-425-3100. *Toll-free phone:* 800-487-6728. *Fax:* 713-425-3193. *Website:* http://www.chcp.edu/.

## The College of Health Care Professions
### McAllen, Texas

**Admissions Office Contact** The College of Health Care Professions, 1917 Nolana Avenue, Suite 100, McAllen, TX 78504. *Website:* http://www.chcp.edu/.

## The College of Health Care Professions
### San Antonio, Texas

**Admissions Office Contact** The College of Health Care Professions, 4738 NW Loop 410, San Antonio, TX 78229. *Website:* http://www.chcp.edu/.

## College of the Mainland
### Texas City, Texas

**Freshman Application Contact** Mr. Martin Perez, Director of Admissions/International Affairs, College of the Mainland, 1200 Amburn Road, Texas City, TX 77591. *Phone:* 409-933-8653. *Toll-free phone:* 888-258-8859 Ext. 8264. *E-mail:* mperez@com.edu. *Website:* http://www.com.edu/.

## Collin County Community College District
### McKinney, Texas

- **State and locally supported** 2-year, founded 1985
- **Suburban** 277-acre campus with easy access to Dallas-Fort Worth
- **Endowment** $9.5 million
- **Coed,** 31,619 undergraduate students, 32% full-time, 55% women, 45% men

**Undergraduates** 10,231 full-time, 21,388 part-time. Students come from 51 states and territories; 99 other countries; 5% are from out of state; 12% Black or African American, non-Hispanic/Latino; 20% Hispanic/Latino; 10% Asian, non-Hispanic/Latino; 0.2% Native Hawaiian or other Pacific Islander, non-Hispanic/Latino; 0.4% American Indian or Alaska Native, non-Hispanic/Latino; 4% Two or more races, non-Hispanic/Latino; 1% Race/ethnicity unknown; 3% international; 6% transferred in. *Retention:* 66% of full-time freshmen returned.

**Freshmen** *Admission:* 5,763 applied, 5,763 admitted, 5,763 enrolled.

**Faculty** *Total:* 1,195, 34% full-time, 27% with terminal degrees. *Student/faculty ratio:* 24:1.

**Majors** Administrative assistant and secretarial science; baking and pastry arts; business administration and management; business/commerce; child-care provision; child development; commercial and advertising art; commercial photography; computer and information sciences; computer and information systems security; computer systems networking and telecommunications; criminal justice/law enforcement administration; culinary arts; dental hygiene; diagnostic medical sonography and ultrasound technology; drafting and design technology; early childhood education; electrical, electronic and communications engineering technology; electroneurodiagnostic/electroencephalographic technology; emergency medical technology (EMT paramedic); engineering; fire prevention and safety technology; fire science/firefighting; game and interactive media design; geographic information science and cartography; graphic design; health information/medical records technology; health services/allied health/health sciences; heating, ventilation, air conditioning and refrigeration engineering technology; hospitality administration; illustration; interior design; legal assistant/paralegal; liberal arts and sciences/liberal studies; logistics, materials, and supply chain management; medical insurance coding; middle school education; music; music management; network and system administration; real estate; registered nursing/registered nurse; respiratory care therapy; retail management; secondary education; sign language interpretation and translation; speech communication and rhetoric; surgical technology; system, networking, and LAN/WAN management; telecommunications technology; web page, digital/multimedia and information resources design; welding technology.

**Academics** *Calendar:* semesters. *Degree:* certificates and associate. *Special study options:* academic remediation for entering students, adult/continuing education programs, advanced placement credit, cooperative education,

distance learning, English as a second language, honors programs, internships, part-time degree program, services for LD students, summer session for credit. *ROTC:* Air Force (c).
**Library** Collin College Library. *Books:* 229,978 (physical), 36,785 (digital/electronic); *Serial titles:* 841 (physical), 94 (digital/electronic); *Databases:* 120. Students can reserve study rooms.
**Student Life** *Housing:* college housing not available. *Activities and Organizations:* drama/theater group, choral group, Phi Theta Kappa, National Society of Collegiate Scholars, Student Government Association, Fellowship of Christian University Students, Collin Organized Greek Society. *Campus security:* 24-hour emergency response devices and patrols, late-night transport/escort service. *Student services:* personal/psychological counseling, veterans affairs office.
**Athletics** Member NJCAA. *Intercollegiate sports:* basketball M(s)/W(s), tennis M(s)/W(s).
**Costs (2018–19)** *Tuition:* area resident $1440 full-time, $48 per credit hour part-time; state resident $2820 full-time, $94 per credit hour part-time; nonresident $4800 full-time, $160 per credit hour part-time. *Required fees:* $64 full-time, $2 per credit hour part-time, $2 per term part-time. *Payment plan:* installment. *Waivers:* senior citizens.
**Applying** *Options:* electronic application. *Required for some:* high school transcript. *Application deadlines:* rolling (freshmen), rolling (transfers). *Notification:* continuous (freshmen), continuous (transfers).
**Freshman Application Contact** Mr. Todd E. Fields, Director of Admissions/Registrar, Collin County Community College District, 2800 E. Spring Creek Parkway, Plano, TX 75074. *Phone:* 972-881-5174. *Fax:* 972-881-5175. *E-mail:* tfields@collin.edu.
*Website:* http://www.collin.edu/.

## Commonwealth Institute of Funeral Service
### Houston, Texas

**Freshman Application Contact** Ms. Patricia Moreno, Registrar, Commonwealth Institute of Funeral Service, 415 Barren Springs Drive, Houston, TX 77090. *Phone:* 281-873-0262. *Toll-free phone:* 800-628-1580. *Fax:* 281-873-5232. *E-mail:* p.moreno@commonwealth.edu. *Website:* http://www.commonwealth.edu/.

## Concorde Career College
### Dallas, Texas

**Admissions Office Contact** Concorde Career College, 12606 Greenville Avenue, Suite 130, Dallas, TX 75243. *Website:* http://www.concorde.edu/.

## Concorde Career College
### Grand Prairie, Texas

**Admissions Office Contact** Concorde Career College, 3015 West Interstate 20, Grand Prairie, TX 75052. *Toll-free phone:* 800-693-7010. *Website:* http://www.concorde.edu/.

## Concorde Career College
### San Antonio, Texas

**Admissions Office Contact** Concorde Career College, 4803 NW Loop 410, Suite 200, San Antonio, TX 78229. *Website:* http://www.concorde.edu/.

## Culinary Institute LeNotre
### Houston, Texas

- **Proprietary** 2-year, founded 1998
- **Urban** campus with easy access to Houston
- **Coed,** 320 undergraduate students

**Undergraduates** Students come from 6 other countries.
**Faculty** *Student/faculty ratio:* 12:1.
**Majors** Baking and pastry arts; culinary arts; restaurant, culinary, and catering management.
**Academics** *Degree:* certificates, diplomas, and associate. *Special study options:* academic remediation for entering students, adult/continuing education programs, cooperative education, internships, part-time degree program.
**Library** Learning Resource Center.
**Student Life** *Housing:* college housing not available. *Campus security:* late-night transport/escort service, security personnel patrol during class hours.
**Standardized Tests** *Required:* ACCUPLACER (for admission).

**Costs (2017–18)** *Tuition:* $47,329 per degree program part-time. Full-time tuition and fees vary according to program. Part-time tuition and fees vary according to program. *Payment plan:* installment.
**Applying** *Options:* electronic application. *Application fee:* $50. *Required:* high school transcript, interview.
**Freshman Application Contact** Ellen Hogaboom, Admissions Manager, Culinary Institute LeNotre, 7070 Allensby Street, Houston, TX 77022. *Phone:* 713-692-0077. *Toll-free phone:* 888-LENOTRE. *Fax:* 713-692-7399. *E-mail:* ehogaboom@ciaml.com.
*Website:* http://www.culinaryinstitute.edu/.

## Dallas Institute of Funeral Service
### Dallas, Texas

- **Independent** 2-year, founded 1945, part of Pierce Mortuary Colleges, Inc.
- **Urban** 4-acre campus with easy access to Dallas-Fort Worth
- **Coed,** 95 undergraduate students, 100% full-time, 51% women, 49% men

**Undergraduates** 95 full-time. Students come from 6 states and territories; 12% are from out of state; 35% Black or African American, non-Hispanic/Latino; 23% Hispanic/Latino; 3% Asian, non-Hispanic/Latino; 42% transferred in.
**Freshmen** *Admission:* 24 enrolled.
**Faculty** *Total:* 10, 10% with terminal degrees. *Student/faculty ratio:* 15:1.
**Majors** Funeral service and mortuary science.
**Academics** *Calendar:* quarters. *Degree:* certificates and associate. *Special study options:* advanced placement credit, cooperative education, distance learning, services for LD students.
**Library** J. Frank Pierce Library. *Books:* 2,223 (physical).
**Student Life** *Housing:* college housing not available. *Activities and Organizations:* Lions Club International, Women in Black, Epsilon Chapter of Pi Sigma Eta National Mortician's Honors Fraternity. *Campus security:* 24-hour emergency response devices, electronically locked doors.
**Costs (2017–18)** *Tuition:* $260 per quarter hour part-time. Full-time tuition and fees vary according to course load and program. Part-time tuition and fees vary according to course load and program. No tuition increase for student's term of enrollment. *Required fees:* $260 per quarter hour part-time. *Payment plan:* installment.
**Applying** *Options:* electronic application. *Application fee:* $50. *Required:* high school transcript. *Application deadlines:* rolling (freshmen), rolling (transfers).
**Freshman Application Contact** Olga Retana, Admissions Representative, Dallas Institute of Funeral Service, 3909 South Buckner Boulevard, Dallas, TX 75227. *Phone:* 214-388-5466 Ext. 817. *Toll-free phone:* 800-235-5444. *Fax:* 214-388-0316. *E-mail:* oretana@dallasinstitute.edu.
*Website:* http://www.dallasinstitute.edu/.

## Dallas Nursing Institute
### Dallas, Texas

**Admissions Office Contact** Dallas Nursing Institute, 12170 N. Abrams Road, Suite 200, Dallas, TX 75243. *Website:* http://www.dni.edu/.

## Del Mar College
### Corpus Christi, Texas

- **State and locally supported** 2-year, founded 1935
- **Urban** 159-acre campus
- **Coed,** 11,833 undergraduate students, 23% full-time, 57% women, 43% men

**Undergraduates** 2,671 full-time, 9,162 part-time. Students come from 41 states and territories; 30 other countries; 2% are from out of state; 3% Black or African American, non-Hispanic/Latino; 67% Hispanic/Latino; 2% Asian, non-Hispanic/Latino; 0.2% Native Hawaiian or other Pacific Islander, non-Hispanic/Latino; 0.2% American Indian or Alaska Native, non-Hispanic/Latino; 3% Two or more races, non-Hispanic/Latino; 0.4% Race/ethnicity unknown; 0.2% international; 6% transferred in. *Retention:* 56% of full-time freshmen returned.
**Freshmen** *Admission:* 952 enrolled.
**Faculty** *Total:* 560, 48% full-time. *Student/faculty ratio:* 18:1.
**Majors** Accounting; accounting technology and bookkeeping; administrative assistant and secretarial science; architectural engineering technology; art; art teacher education; automobile/automotive mechanics technology; biology/biological sciences; building/property maintenance; business administration and management; business/commerce; business machine repair; chemical technology; chemistry; child development; clinical laboratory science/medical technology; clinical/medical laboratory technology; community organization and advocacy; computer and information sciences and support services related; computer and information sciences related;

computer programming; computer programming related; computer programming (specific applications); computer programming (vendor/product certification); computer science; computer systems networking and telecommunications; computer typography and composition equipment operation; consumer merchandising/retailing management; cosmetology; court reporting; criminal justice/law enforcement administration; criminal justice/police science; culinary arts; data entry/microcomputer applications; dental hygiene; design and applied arts related; diagnostic medical sonography and ultrasound technology; drafting and design technology; dramatic/theater arts; e-commerce; education; electrical, electronic and communications engineering technology; elementary education; emergency medical technology (EMT paramedic); English; finance; fine/studio arts; fire prevention and safety technology; fire science/firefighting; geography; geology/earth science; health information/medical records technology; health teacher education; heavy equipment maintenance technology; history; hotel/motel administration; industrial radiologic technology; information science/studies; information technology; interdisciplinary studies; journalism; kindergarten/preschool education; legal administrative assistant/secretary; legal studies; liberal arts and sciences/liberal studies; machine tool technology; management information systems; mathematics; medical administrative assistant and medical secretary; medical radiologic technology; mental health counseling; music; music teacher education; network and system administration; nuclear medical technology; occupational safety and health technology; occupational therapist assistant; office occupations and clerical services; parks, recreation and leisure; physical education teaching and coaching; physics; political science and government; pre-engineering; psychology; public administration; public policy analysis; radio and television; real estate; registered nursing/registered nurse; respiratory care therapy; rhetoric and composition; sign language interpretation and translation; social work; sociology; special products marketing; trade and industrial teacher education; transportation/mobility management; voice and opera; web/multimedia management and webmaster; web page, digital/multimedia and information resources design; welding technology; word processing.

**Academics** *Calendar:* semesters. *Degree:* certificates and associate. *Special study options:* academic remediation for entering students, accelerated degree program, adult/continuing education programs, advanced placement credit, cooperative education, distance learning, double majors, English as a second language, freshman honors college, honors programs, internships, off-campus study, part-time degree program, services for LD students, summer session for credit. *ROTC:* Army (b).

**Library** White Library plus 1 other. *Books:* 145,107 (physical), 192,073 (digital/electronic); *Serial titles:* 1,635 (physical), 74,730 (digital/electronic); *Databases:* 172.

**Student Life** *Housing:* college housing not available. *Activities and Organizations:* drama/theater group, student-run newspaper, radio station, choral group, Phi Theta Kappa, Alpha Beta Gamma, Student Government Association. *Campus security:* 24-hour emergency response devices and patrols. *Student services:* personal/psychological counseling.

**Athletics** *Intramural sports:* badminton M/W, basketball M/W, bowling M/W, football M/W, golf M/W, racquetball M/W, tennis M/W, track and field M/W, volleyball M/W, weight lifting M/W.

**Financial Aid** Of all full-time matriculated undergraduates who enrolled in 2016, 259 Federal Work-Study jobs (averaging $960). 449 state and other part-time jobs (averaging $1082).

**Applying** *Options:* electronic application, early admission, deferred entrance. *Required:* high school transcript. *Application deadlines:* rolling (freshmen), rolling (transfers).

**Freshman Application Contact** Del Mar College, 101 Baldwin Boulevard, Corpus Christi, TX 78404-3897. *Phone:* 361-698-1248. *Toll-free phone:* 800-652-3357.
*Website:* http://www.delmar.edu/.

# Eastfield College
## Mesquite, Texas

**Freshman Application Contact** Ms. Glynis Miller, Director of Admissions/Registrar, Eastfield College, 3737 Motley Drive, Mesquite, TX 75150-2099. *Phone:* 972-860-7010. *Fax:* 972-860-8306. *E-mail:* efc@dcccd.edu. *Website:* http://www.eastfieldcollege.edu/.

# El Centro College
## Dallas, Texas

**Freshman Application Contact** Ms. Rebecca Garza, Director of Admissions and Registrar, El Centro College, Dallas, TX 75202. *Phone:* 214-860-2618. *Fax:* 214-860-2233. *E-mail:* rgarza@dcccd.edu. *Website:* http://www.elcentrocollege.edu/.

# El Paso Community College
## El Paso, Texas

- **County-supported** 2-year, founded 1969
- **Urban** campus
- **Endowment** $742,942
- **Coed,** 28,750 undergraduate students, 30% full-time, 57% women, 43% men

**Undergraduates** 8,710 full-time, 20,040 part-time. Students come from 49 states and territories; 34 other countries; 3% are from out of state; 2% Black or African American, non-Hispanic/Latino; 85% Hispanic/Latino; 0.7% Asian, non-Hispanic/Latino; 0.1% Native Hawaiian or other Pacific Islander, non-Hispanic/Latino; 0.2% American Indian or Alaska Native, non-Hispanic/Latino; 0.2% Two or more races, non-Hispanic/Latino; 2% Race/ethnicity unknown; 2% international; 4% transferred in.

**Freshmen** *Admission:* 4,554 enrolled.

**Faculty** *Total:* 1,231, 12% with terminal degrees. *Student/faculty ratio:* 13:1.

**Majors** Accounting; administrative assistant and secretarial science; adult development and aging; automobile/automotive mechanics technology; business administration and management; business automation/technology/data entry; business/commerce; child-care and support services management; child development; cinematography and film/video production; clinical/medical laboratory technology; commercial and advertising art; computer and information sciences; computer programming; corrections; corrections and criminal justice related; court reporting; criminal justice/police science; criminal justice/safety; culinary arts; dental assisting; dental hygiene; diagnostic medical sonography and ultrasound technology; dietetics; drafting and design technology; electrical, electronic and communications engineering technology; emergency medical technology (EMT paramedic); engineering; environmental engineering technology; fashion/apparel design; fire prevention and safety technology; general studies; health information/medical records administration; heating, air conditioning, ventilation and refrigeration maintenance technology; homeland security, law enforcement, firefighting and protective services related; hotel/motel administration; institutional food workers; interior design; international business/trade/commerce; kindergarten/preschool education; legal assistant/paralegal; liberal arts and sciences/liberal studies; machine tool technology; medical/clinical assistant; medical radiologic technology; middle school education; multi/interdisciplinary studies related; music; opticianry; optometric technician; pharmacy technician; physical therapy technology; plastics and polymer engineering technology; psychiatric/mental health services technology; radiologic technology/science; real estate; registered nursing/registered nurse; respiratory care therapy; sign language interpretation and translation; social work; speech communication and rhetoric; substance abuse/addiction counseling; surgical technology; system, networking, and LAN/WAN management; tourism and travel services management.

**Academics** *Calendar:* semesters. *Degree:* certificates and associate. *Special study options:* academic remediation for entering students, adult/continuing education programs, advanced placement credit, cooperative education, distance learning, English as a second language, external degree program, honors programs, independent study, internships, off-campus study, part-time degree program, services for LD students, summer session for credit. *ROTC:* Army (c).

**Library** El Paso Community College Learning Resource Center plus 4 others. *Books:* 140,571 (physical), 149,708 (digital/electronic); *Serial titles:* 231 (physical), 56 (digital/electronic); *Databases:* 90. Weekly public service hours: 80.

**Student Life** *Housing:* college housing not available. *Activities and Organizations:* drama/theater group, student-run newspaper, radio and television station, choral group. *Campus security:* 24-hour patrols, late-night transport/escort service. *Student services:* health clinic, personal/psychological counseling, veterans affairs office.

**Athletics** Member NJCAA. *Intercollegiate sports:* baseball M(s), cross-country running M(s)/W(s), softball W(s). *Intramural sports:* baseball M, cross-country running M/W, softball W.

**Costs (2017–18)** *Tuition:* state resident $2256 full-time, $564 per term part-time; nonresident $4126 full-time, $1055 per term part-time. Full-time tuition and fees vary according to course level, course load, program, and student level. Part-time tuition and fees vary according to course level, course load, program, and student level. *Required fees:* $480 full-time, $20 per credit hour part-time. *Payment plan:* installment. *Waivers:* senior citizens and employees or children of employees.

**Applying** *Options:* electronic application, early admission, deferred entrance. *Application fee:* $10.

**Freshman Application Contact** Cassandra Lachica-Chavez, Executive Director Admission and Registrar, El Paso Community College, PO Box 20500, El Paso, TX 79998. *Phone:* 915-831-2580. *E-mail:* clachica@epcc.edu.
*Website:* http://www.epcc.edu/.

# Florida Career College
## Houston, Texas

**Admissions Office Contact** Florida Career College, 70-A Farm to Market Road 1960 West, Houston, TX 77090. *Website:* http://www.floridacareercollege.edu/.

# Fortis College
## Grand Prairie, Texas

**Admissions Office Contact** Fortis College, 401 East Palace Parkway, Suite 100, Grand Prairie, TX 75050. *Toll-free phone:* 855-4-FORTIS. *Website:* http://www.fortis.edu/.

# Fortis College
## Houston, Texas

**Admissions Office Contact** Fortis College, 1201 West Oaks Mall, Houston, TX 77082. *Toll-free phone:* 855-4-FORTIS. *Website:* http://www.fortis.edu/.

# Frank Phillips College
## Borger, Texas

**Freshman Application Contact** Ms. Michele Stevens, Director of Enrollment Management, Frank Phillips College, PO Box 5118, Borger, TX 79008-5118. *Phone:* 806-457-4200 Ext. 707. *Fax:* 806-457-4225. *E-mail:* mstevens@fpctx.edu. *Website:* http://www.fpctx.edu/.

# Galen College of Nursing
## San Antonio, Texas

**Admissions Office Contact** Galen College of Nursing, 7411 John Smith Drive, Suite 1400, San Antonio, TX 78229. *Toll-free phone:* 877-223-7040. *Website:* http://www.galencollege.edu/.

# Galveston College
## Galveston, Texas

- **State and locally supported** 2-year, founded 1967
- **Urban** 11-acre campus with easy access to Houston
- **Coed,** 2,208 undergraduate students, 26% full-time, 61% women, 39% men

**Undergraduates** 584 full-time, 1,624 part-time. 16% Black or African American, non-Hispanic/Latino; 38% Hispanic/Latino; 3% Asian, non-Hispanic/Latino; 0.2% Native Hawaiian or other Pacific Islander, non-Hispanic/Latino; 0.3% American Indian or Alaska Native, non-Hispanic/Latino; 1% Two or more races, non-Hispanic/Latino; 2% Race/ethnicity unknown; 1% international; 12% transferred in. *Retention:* 53% of full-time freshmen returned.
**Freshmen** *Admission:* 251 enrolled.
**Faculty** *Total:* 97, 55% full-time, 19% with terminal degrees. *Student/faculty ratio:* 16:1.
**Majors** Behavioral sciences; biological and physical sciences; business administration and management; computer science; criminal justice/safety; culinary arts; dramatic/theater arts; education; electromechanical technology; emergency medical technology (EMT paramedic); English; general studies; heating, air conditioning, ventilation and refrigeration maintenance technology; history; humanities; liberal arts and sciences/liberal studies; mathematics; medical administrative assistant and medical secretary; medical radiologic technology; music; natural sciences; nuclear medical technology; physical education teaching and coaching; radiologic technology/science; registered nursing/registered nurse; social sciences; social work; welding technology.
**Academics** *Calendar:* semesters. *Degree:* certificates and associate. *Special study options:* adult/continuing education programs, advanced placement credit, cooperative education, distance learning, internships, off-campus study, part-time degree program, services for LD students, summer session for credit.
**Library** David Glenn Hunt Memorial Library. *Books:* 48,028 (physical), 91,209 (digital/electronic); *Serial titles:* 73 (physical); *Databases:* 68. Students can reserve study rooms.
**Student Life** *Housing Options:* Campus housing is university owned. *Activities and Organizations:* drama/theater group, choral group, Student Government, Phi Theta Kappa, Student Nurses Association, ATTC, Hispanic Student Organization. *Campus security:* 24-hour emergency response devices and patrols, late-night transport/escort service. *Student services:* personal/psychological counseling.

**Athletics** Member NJCAA. *Intercollegiate sports:* baseball M(s), softball W(s). *Intramural sports:* badminton M/W, basketball M/W, soccer M/W, tennis M/W, volleyball M/W.
**Standardized Tests** *Required:* TSI or exemption test scores and documentation (for admission).
**Costs (2017–18)** *Tuition:* area resident $1200 full-time, $40 per credit hour part-time; state resident $1800 full-time, $60 per credit hour part-time; nonresident $3750 full-time, $125 per credit hour part-time. Full-time tuition and fees vary according to course level, course load, and program. Part-time tuition and fees vary according to course level, course load, and program. *Required fees:* $850 full-time, $22 per credit hour part-time, $95 per term part-time. *Payment plan:* installment. *Waivers:* senior citizens.
**Financial Aid** Of all full-time matriculated undergraduates who enrolled in 2016, 27 Federal Work-Study jobs (averaging $3000). 3 state and other part-time jobs (averaging $3000).
**Applying** *Options:* electronic application. *Required for some:* high school transcript. *Application deadlines:* rolling (freshmen), rolling (transfers). *Notification:* continuous (freshmen), continuous (transfers).
**Freshman Application Contact** Galveston College, 4015 Avenue Q, Galveston, TX 77550. *Phone:* 409-944-1216. *Website:* http://www.gc.edu/.

# Golf Academy of America
## Farmers Branch, Texas

**Admissions Office Contact** Golf Academy of America, 1861 Valley View Lane, Suite 100, Farmers Branch, TX 75234. *Toll-free phone:* 800-342-7342. *Website:* http://www.golfacademy.edu/.

# Grayson College
## Denison, Texas

**Freshman Application Contact** Charles Leslie, Enrollment Advisor, Grayson College, 6101Grayson Drive, Denison, TX 75020. *Phone:* 903-415-2532. *Fax:* 903-463-5284. *E-mail:* lesliec@grayson.edu. *Website:* http://www.grayson.edu/.

# Hill College
## Hillsboro, Texas

- **District-supported** 2-year, founded 1923
- **Small-town** 80-acre campus with easy access to Dallas-Fort Worth
- **Coed,** 4,075 undergraduate students

**Undergraduates** 5% Black or African American, non-Hispanic/Latino; 23% Hispanic/Latino; 0.7% Asian, non-Hispanic/Latino; 0.3% Native Hawaiian or other Pacific Islander, non-Hispanic/Latino; 0.6% American Indian or Alaska Native, non-Hispanic/Latino; 3% Two or more races, non-Hispanic/Latino; 0.9% Race/ethnicity unknown; 1% international. *Retention:* 53% of full-time freshmen returned.
**Faculty** *Total:* 209. *Student/faculty ratio:* 17:1.
**Majors** Accounting; administrative assistant and/ secretarial science; agricultural business and management; agriculture; art; autobody/collision and repair technology; automobile/automotive mechanics technology; behavioral sciences; biology/biological sciences; business administration and management; business/commerce; chemistry; child-care provision; commercial and advertising art; computer and information sciences; computer programming; corrections; corrections and criminal justice related; cosmetology; cosmetology, barber/styling, and nail instruction; criminal justice/law enforcement administration; drafting and design technology; dramatic/theater arts; economics; elementary education; emergency medical technology (EMT paramedic); engineering; English; family and consumer sciences/human sciences; fire science/firefighting; foreign languages and literatures; general studies; geology/earth science; health and physical education/fitness; heating, air conditioning, ventilation and refrigeration maintenance technology; history; industrial electronics technology; industrial mechanics and maintenance technology; mathematics; music; philosophy; physical therapy; physics; political science and government; pre-dentistry studies; pre-law studies; premedical studies; prenursing studies; pre-pharmacy studies; pre-veterinary studies; psychology; registered nursing/registered nurse; religious studies; rhetoric and composition; secondary education; security and loss prevention; sociology; special education; speech communication and rhetoric; system, networking, and LAN/WAN management; teacher assistant/aide; welding technology.
**Academics** *Calendar:* semesters. *Degree:* certificates and associate. *Special study options:* academic remediation for entering students, advanced placement credit, cooperative education, distance learning, services for LD students, summer session for credit.

**Library** Hill College Library plus 1 other. *Books:* 55,000 (physical), 203 (digital/electronic); *Serial titles:* 75 (physical); *Databases:* 105. Weekly public service hours: 65.

**Student Life** *Housing Options:* men-only, women-only. Campus housing is university owned. *Activities and Organizations:* drama/theater group, choral group, Student Government, Phi Theta Kappa. *Campus security:* 24-hour emergency response devices, late-night transport/escort service, security officers. *Student services:* veterans affairs office.

**Athletics** Member NJCAA. *Intercollegiate sports:* baseball M(s), basketball M(s)/W(s), soccer M/W(s), softball W(s), volleyball W(s). *Intramural sports:* basketball M/W, volleyball W.

**Costs (2017–18)** *Tuition:* area resident $924 full-time, $462 per term part-time; state resident $1224 full-time, $612 per term part-time; nonresident $1424 full-time, $812 per term part-time. Full-time tuition and fees vary according to course load. Part-time tuition and fees vary according to course load. *Required fees:* $147 full-time, $81 per term part-time. *Room and board:* $1925; room only: $400. *Payment plan:* installment. *Waivers:* senior citizens and employees or children of employees.

**Financial Aid** Of all full-time matriculated undergraduates who enrolled in 2016, 51 Federal Work-Study jobs (averaging $858). 20 state and other part-time jobs (averaging $230).

**Applying** *Options:* electronic application, early admission. *Required:* high school transcript. *Application deadlines:* rolling (freshmen), rolling (transfers).

**Freshman Application Contact** Enrollment Management, Hill College, 112 Lamar Drive, Hillsboro, TX 76645. *Phone:* 254-659-7600. *Fax:* 254-582-7591. *E-mail:* enrollmentinfo@hillcollege.edu. *Website:* http://www.hillcollege.edu/.

# Houston Community College
## Houston, Texas

- **State and locally supported** 2-year, founded 1971
- **Urban** campus with easy access to Houston
- **Coed,** 57,120 undergraduate students, 30% full-time, 58% women, 42% men

**Undergraduates** 17,226 full-time, 39,894 part-time. Students come from 30 states and territories; 145 other countries; 28% Black or African American, non-Hispanic/Latino; 34% Hispanic/Latino; 10% Asian, non-Hispanic/Latino; 0.2% Native Hawaiian or other Pacific Islander, non-Hispanic/Latino; 0.2% American Indian or Alaska Native, non-Hispanic/Latino; 2% Two or more races, non-Hispanic/Latino; 2% Race/ethnicity unknown; 12% international; 7% transferred in.

**Freshmen** *Admission:* 8,246 enrolled.

**Faculty** *Total:* 2,375, 35% full-time. *Student/faculty ratio:* 24:1.

**Majors** Accounting; animation, interactive technology, video graphics and special effects; anthropology; applied horticulture/horticulture operations; automobile/automotive mechanics technology; banking and financial support services; biology/biological sciences; biology/biotechnology laboratory technician; business administration and management; business automation/technology/data entry; business/corporate communications; cardiovascular technology; chemical technology; chemistry; child development; cinematography and film/video production; clinical/medical laboratory science and allied professions related; clinical/medical laboratory technology; commercial photography; computer engineering technology; computer programming; computer programming (specific applications); computer science; computer systems networking and telecommunications; construction engineering technology; cosmetology; court reporting; criminal justice/police science; culinary arts; desktop publishing and digital imaging design; drafting and design technology; early childhood education; education (multiple levels); emergency medical technology (EMT paramedic); energy management and systems technology; engineering science; English; fashion/apparel design; fashion merchandising; fine/studio arts; fire prevention and safety technology; general studies; health and physical education/fitness; health information/medical records technology; health services/allied health/health sciences; histologic technician; hotel/motel administration; instrumentation technology; interior design; international business/trade/commerce; legal assistant/paralegal; logistics, materials, and supply chain management; manufacturing engineering technology; marketing/marketing management; mathematics; music management; music performance; music theory and composition; network and system administration; nuclear medical technology; occupational safety and health technology; occupational therapist assistant; petroleum technology; physical therapy technology; physics; psychiatric/mental health services technology; public administration; radio and television broadcasting technology; radiologic technology/science; real estate; registered nursing/registered nurse; respiratory care therapy; secondary education; sign language interpretation and translation; speech communication and rhetoric; tourism and travel services management; turf and turfgrass management.

**Academics** *Calendar:* semesters. *Degree:* certificates and associate. *Special study options:* academic remediation for entering students, advanced placement credit, cooperative education, distance learning, English as a second language, honors programs, internships, part-time degree program, services for LD students, study abroad, summer session for credit. *ROTC:* Army (c), Air Force (c).

**Library** Houston Community College Libraries. Students can reserve study rooms.

**Student Life** *Housing:* college housing not available. *Activities and Organizations:* student-run newspaper. *Campus security:* 24-hour emergency response devices and patrols, late-night transport/escort service, crime prevention services. *Student services:* veterans affairs office.

**Costs (2017–18)** *Tuition:* area resident $1632 full-time, $411 per term part-time; state resident $3360 full-time, $843 per term part-time; nonresident $3756 full-time, $942 per term part-time. Full-time tuition and fees vary according to course load. Part-time tuition and fees vary according to course load. *Payment plan:* installment. *Waivers:* senior citizens and employees or children of employees.

**Financial Aid** Of all full-time matriculated undergraduates who enrolled in 2016, 281 Federal Work-Study jobs (averaging $3593). 257 state and other part-time jobs (averaging $4018).

**Applying** *Options:* electronic application. *Required for some:* high school transcript, interview. *Application deadlines:* rolling (freshmen), rolling (transfers).

**Freshman Application Contact** Ms. Mary Lemburg, Registrar, Houston Community College, 3100 Main Street, PO Box 667517, Houston, TX 77266-7517. *Phone:* 713-718-2000. *Toll-free phone:* 877-422-6111. *Fax:* 713-718-2111. *E-mail:* student.info@hccs.edu. *Website:* http://www.hccs.edu/.

# Howard College
## Big Spring, Texas

**Freshman Application Contact** Ms. TaNeal Richardson, Assistant Registrar, Howard College, 1001 Birdwell Lane, Big Spring, TX 79720-3702. *Phone:* 432-264-5105. *Toll-free phone:* 866-HC-HAWKS. *Fax:* 432-264-5604. *E-mail:* trichardson@howardcollege.edu. *Website:* http://www.howardcollege.edu/.

# Interactive College of Technology
## Houston, Texas

**Freshman Application Contact** Interactive College of Technology, 4473 I-45 N. Freeway, Airline Plaza, Houston, TX 77022. *Website:* http://ict.edu/.

# Interactive College of Technology
## Houston, Texas

**Freshman Application Contact** Interactive College of Technology, 6200 Hillcroft Avenue, Suite 200, Houston, TX 77081. *Website:* http://ict.edu/.

# Interactive College of Technology
## Pasadena, Texas

**Freshman Application Contact** Interactive College of Technology, 213 West Southmore Street, Suite 101, Pasadena, TX 77502. *Website:* http://ict.edu/.

# International Business College
## El Paso, Texas

**Admissions Office Contact** International Business College, 1155 North Zaragosa Road, El Paso, TX 79907. *Website:* http://www.ibcelpaso.edu/.

# International Business College
## El Paso, Texas

**Admissions Office Contact** International Business College, 5700 Cromo Drive, El Paso, TX 79912. *Website:* http://www.ibcelpaso.edu/.

# Jacksonville College
## Jacksonville, Texas

**Freshman Application Contact** Danny Morris, Director of Admissions, Jacksonville College, 105 B.J. Albritton Drive, Jacksonville, TX 75766. *Phone:* 903-589-7110. *Toll-free phone:* 800-256-8522. *E-mail:* admissions@jacksonville-college.org. *Website:* http://www.jacksonville-college.edu/.

# KD Conservatory College of Film and Dramatic Arts
## Dallas, Texas

- **Proprietary** 2-year, founded 1979
- **Urban** campus
- **Coed,** 236 undergraduate students, 100% full-time, 46% women, 54% men

**Undergraduates** 236 full-time. Students come from 11 states and territories; 1 other country; 5% are from out of state. *Retention:* 69% of full-time freshmen returned.
**Freshmen** *Admission:* 70 applied, 24 admitted, 24 enrolled.
**Faculty** *Total:* 28, 100% full-time, 4% with terminal degrees. *Student/faculty ratio:* 12:1.
**Majors** Acting; dramatic/theater arts; film/cinema/video studies; musical theater; visual and performing arts.
**Academics** *Calendar:* semesters. *Degree:* associate.
**Library** KD Studio Library.
**Student Life** *Housing:* college housing not available. *Activities and Organizations:* drama/theater group, Student Council. *Campus security:* 24-hour emergency response devices and patrols.
**Costs (2018–19)** *Tuition:* $15,300 full-time. Full-time tuition and fees vary according to program. No tuition increase for student's term of enrollment. *Required fees:* $450 full-time. *Payment plans:* tuition prepayment, installment.
**Applying** *Options:* electronic application, deferred entrance. *Required:* essay or personal statement, high school transcript, interview, audition and/or interview with Program Chair or Director of School. *Application deadlines:* rolling (freshmen), rolling (transfers).
**Freshman Application Contact** Mr. Michael Schraeder, Director of Education and Acting Program Chair, KD Conservatory College of Film and Dramatic Arts, 2600 Stemmons Freeway, Suite 117, Dallas, TX 75207. *Phone:* 214-638-0484. *Toll-free phone:* 877-278-2283. *Fax:* 214-630-5140. *E-mail:* mschraeder@kdstudio.com.
*Website:* http://www.kdstudio.com/.

# Kilgore College
## Kilgore, Texas

**Freshman Application Contact** Kilgore College, 1100 Broadway Boulevard, Kilgore, TX 75662-3299. *Phone:* 903-983-8200. *E-mail:* register@kilgore.cc.tx.us. *Website:* http://www.kilgore.edu/.

# Lamar Institute of Technology
## Beaumont, Texas

**Freshman Application Contact** Admissions Office, Lamar Institute of Technology, 855 East Lavaca, Beaumont, TX 77705. *Phone:* 409-880-8354. *Toll-free phone:* 800-950-6989. *Website:* http://www.lit.edu/.

# Lamar State College–Orange
## Orange, Texas

**Freshman Application Contact** Kerry Olson, Director of Admissions and Financial Aid, Lamar State College–Orange, 410 Front Street, Orange, TX 77632. *Phone:* 409-882-3362. *Fax:* 409-882-3374. *Website:* http://www.lsco.edu/.

# Lamar State College–Port Arthur
## Port Arthur, Texas

**Freshman Application Contact** Ms. Connie Nicholas, Registrar, Lamar State College–Port Arthur, PO Box 310, Port Arthur, TX 77641-0310. *Phone:* 409-984-6165. *Toll-free phone:* 800-477-5872. *Fax:* 409-984-6025. *E-mail:* nichoca@lamarpa.edu. *Website:* http://www.lamarpa.edu/.

# Laredo Community College
## Laredo, Texas

**Freshman Application Contact** Ms. Josie Soliz, Admissions Records Supervisor, Laredo Community College, Laredo, TX 78040-4395. *Phone:* 956-721-5177. *Fax:* 956-721-5493. *Website:* http://www.laredo.edu/.

# Lee College
## Baytown, Texas

**Director of Admissions** Ms. Becki Griffith, Registrar, Lee College, PO Box 818, Baytown, TX 77522-0818. *Phone:* 281-425-6399. *E-mail:* bgriffit@lee.edu. *Website:* http://www.lee.edu/.

# Lincoln College of Technology
## Grand Prairie, Texas

**Admissions Office Contact** Lincoln College of Technology, 2915 Alouette Drive, Grand Prairie, TX 75052. *Toll-free phone:* 844-215-1513. *Website:* http://www.lincolntech.edu/.

# Lone Star College–CyFair
## Cypress, Texas

- **State and locally supported** 2-year, founded 2002, part of Lone Star College
- **Suburban** campus with easy access to Houston
- **Coed**

**Undergraduates** 6,757 full-time, 14,879 part-time. Students come from 67 other countries; 13% Black or African American, non-Hispanic/Latino; 43% Hispanic/Latino; 11% Asian, non-Hispanic/Latino; 0.2% American Indian or Alaska Native, non-Hispanic/Latino; 3% Two or more races, non-Hispanic/Latino; 3% Race/ethnicity unknown; 25% transferred in.
**Faculty** *Student/faculty ratio:* 37:1.
**Academics** *Calendar:* semesters. *Degree:* certificates, diplomas, and associate. *Special study options:* academic remediation for entering students, accelerated degree program, adult/continuing education programs, advanced placement credit, cooperative education, distance learning, double majors, English as a second language, honors programs, independent study, internships, part-time degree program, services for LD students, study abroad, summer session for credit.
**Library** LSC–CyFair Library.
**Student Life** *Campus security:* 24-hour emergency response devices and patrols, late-night transport/escort service.
**Costs (2017–18)** *Tuition:* area resident $1088 full-time, $44 per credit hour part-time; state resident $2888 full-time, $119 per credit hour part-time; nonresident $3248 full-time, $134 per credit hour part-time. Full-time tuition and fees vary according to course load and program. Part-time tuition and fees vary according to course load and program. *Required fees:* $544 full-time, $20 per credit hour part-time, $32 per term part-time. *Payment plans:* installment, deferred payment.
**Applying** *Options:* electronic application, early admission. *Recommended:* high school transcript.
**Freshman Application Contact** Admissions Office, Lone Star College–CyFair, 9191 Barker Cypress Road, Cypress, TX 77433-1383. *Phone:* 281-290-3200. *E-mail:* cfc.info@lonestar.edu. *Website:* http://www.lonestar.edu/cyfair.

# Lone Star College–Kingwood
## Kingwood, Texas

- **State and locally supported** 2-year, founded 1984, part of Lone Star College
- **Suburban** 264-acre campus with easy access to Houston
- **Coed**

**Undergraduates** 3,785 full-time, 8,502 part-time. Students come from 48 other countries; 14% Black or African American, non-Hispanic/Latino; 35% Hispanic/Latino; 4% Asian, non-Hispanic/Latino; 0.3% American Indian or Alaska Native, non-Hispanic/Latino; 3% Two or more races, non-Hispanic/Latino; 4% Race/ethnicity unknown; 28% transferred in.
**Faculty** *Student/faculty ratio:* 21:1.
**Academics** *Calendar:* semesters. *Degree:* certificates and associate. *Special study options:* academic remediation for entering students, accelerated degree program, adult/continuing education programs, advanced placement credit, cooperative education, distance learning, double majors, English as a second language, honors programs, independent study, internships, part-time degree program, services for LD students, study abroad, summer session for credit.
**Library** LSC–Kingwood Library.
**Student Life** *Campus security:* 24-hour emergency response devices and patrols, late-night transport/escort service.
**Costs (2017–18)** *Tuition:* area resident $1088 full-time, $44 per credit hour part-time; state resident $2888 full-time, $119 per credit hour part-time; nonresident $3248 full-time, $134 per credit hour part-time. Full-time tuition and fees vary according to course load and program. Part-time tuition and fees vary according to course load and program. *Required fees:* $544 full-time, $20

per credit hour part-time, $32 per term part-time. *Payment plans:* installment, deferred payment.

**Financial Aid** Of all full-time matriculated undergraduates who enrolled in 2009, 28 Federal Work-Study jobs (averaging $3394). 6 state and other part-time jobs (averaging $2606). *Financial aid deadline:* 4/1.

**Applying** *Options:* electronic application, early admission. *Recommended:* high school transcript.

**Freshman Application Contact** Admissions Office, Lone Star College–Kingwood, 20000 Kingwood Drive, Kingwood, TX 77339. *Phone:* 281-312-1525. *Fax:* 281-312-1477. *E-mail:* kingwoodadvising@lonestar.edu. *Website:* http://www.lonestar.edu/kingwood.htm.

## Lone Star College–Montgomery
### Conroe, Texas

- **State and locally supported** 2-year, founded 1995, part of Lone Star College
- **Suburban** campus with easy access to Houston
- **Coed**

**Undergraduates** 4,466 full-time, 9,945 part-time. Students come from 63 other countries; 10% Black or African American, non-Hispanic/Latino; 30% Hispanic/Latino; 4% Asian, non-Hispanic/Latino; 0.3% American Indian or Alaska Native, non-Hispanic/Latino; 3% Two or more races, non-Hispanic/Latino; 4% Race/ethnicity unknown; 26% transferred in.

**Faculty** *Student/faculty ratio:* 25:1.

**Academics** *Calendar:* semesters. *Degree:* certificates and associate. *Special study options:* academic remediation for entering students, adult/continuing education programs, advanced placement credit, cooperative education, distance learning, double majors, English as a second language, honors programs, independent study, internships, part-time degree program, services for LD students, study abroad, summer session for credit.

**Library** LSC–Montgomery Library.

**Student Life** *Campus security:* 24-hour emergency response devices and patrols, late-night transport/escort service.

**Costs (2017–18)** *Tuition:* area resident $1088 full-time, $44 per credit hour part-time; state resident $2888 full-time, $119 per credit hour part-time; nonresident $3248 full-time, $134 per credit hour part-time. Full-time tuition and fees vary according to course load and program. Part-time tuition and fees vary according to course load and program. *Required fees:* $544 full-time, $20 per credit hour part-time, $32 per term part-time. *Payment plans:* installment, deferred payment.

**Financial Aid** Of all full-time matriculated undergraduates who enrolled in 2016, 25 Federal Work-Study jobs (averaging $2500). 4 state and other part-time jobs.

**Applying** *Options:* electronic application, early admission. *Recommended:* high school transcript.

**Freshman Application Contact** Lone Star College–Montgomery, 3200 College Park Drive, Conroe, TX 77384. *Phone:* 281-290-2721. *Website:* http://www.lonestar.edu/montgomery.

## Lone Star College–North Harris
### Houston, Texas

- **State and locally supported** 2-year, founded 1972, part of Lone Star College
- **Suburban** campus with easy access to Houston
- **Coed**

**Undergraduates** 4,797 full-time, 11,493 part-time. Students come from 49 other countries; 26% Black or African American, non-Hispanic/Latino; 46% Hispanic/Latino; 5% Asian, non-Hispanic/Latino; 0.2% American Indian or Alaska Native, non-Hispanic/Latino; 3% Two or more races, non-Hispanic/Latino; 5% Race/ethnicity unknown; 27% transferred in.

**Faculty** *Student/faculty ratio:* 20:1.

**Academics** *Calendar:* semesters. *Degree:* certificates and associate. *Special study options:* academic remediation for entering students, adult/continuing education programs, advanced placement credit, cooperative education, distance learning, double majors, English as a second language, honors programs, independent study, internships, part-time degree program, services for LD students, study abroad, summer session for credit.

**Library** LSC–North Harris Library.

**Student Life** *Campus security:* 24-hour emergency response devices and patrols, late-night transport/escort service.

**Costs (2017–18)** *Tuition:* area resident $1088 full-time, $44 per credit hour part-time; state resident $2888 full-time, $119 per credit hour part-time; nonresident $3248 full-time, $134 per credit hour part-time. Full-time tuition and fees vary according to course load and program. Part-time tuition and fees vary according to course load and program. *Required fees:* $544 full-time, $20

per credit hour part-time, $32 per term part-time. *Payment plans:* installment, deferred payment.

**Applying** *Options:* electronic application, early admission.

**Freshman Application Contact** Admissions Office, Lone Star College–North Harris, 2700 W. W. Thorne Drive, Houston, TX 77073-3499. *Phone:* 281-618-5410. *E-mail:* nhcounselor@lonestar.edu. *Website:* http://www.lonestar.edu/northharris.

## Lone Star College–Tomball
### Tomball, Texas

- **State and locally supported** 2-year, founded 1988, part of Lone Star College
- **Suburban** campus with easy access to Houston
- **Coed**

**Undergraduates** 2,705 full-time, 6,308 part-time. Students come from 44 other countries; 13% Black or African American, non-Hispanic/Latino; 29% Hispanic/Latino; 5% Asian, non-Hispanic/Latino; 0.3% American Indian or Alaska Native, non-Hispanic/Latino; 3% Two or more races, non-Hispanic/Latino; 5% Race/ethnicity unknown; 31% transferred in.

**Faculty** *Student/faculty ratio:* 24:1.

**Academics** *Calendar:* semesters. *Degree:* certificates and associate. *Special study options:* academic remediation for entering students, adult/continuing education programs, advanced placement credit, cooperative education, distance learning, double majors, English as a second language, honors programs, independent study, internships, part-time degree program, services for LD students, study abroad, summer session for credit.

**Library** LSC–Tomball Community Library.

**Student Life** *Campus security:* 24-hour emergency response devices and patrols, late-night transport/escort service, trained security personnel during hours of operation.

**Costs (2017–18)** *Tuition:* area resident $1088 full-time, $44 per credit hour part-time; state resident $2888 full-time, $119 per credit hour part-time; nonresident $3248 full-time, $134 per credit hour part-time. Full-time tuition and fees vary according to course load and program. Part-time tuition and fees vary according to course load and program. *Required fees:* $544 full-time, $20 per credit hour part-time, $32 per term part-time. *Payment plans:* installment, deferred payment.

**Financial Aid** Of all full-time matriculated undergraduates who enrolled in 2016, 34 Federal Work-Study jobs (averaging $3000).

**Applying** *Options:* electronic application, early admission. *Recommended:* high school transcript.

**Freshman Application Contact** Admissions Office, Lone Star College–Tomball, 30555 Tomball Parkway, Tomball, TX 77375-4036. *Phone:* 281-351-3310. *E-mail:* tcinfo@lonestar.edu. *Website:* http://www.lonestar.edu/tomball.

## Lone Star College–University Park
### Houston, Texas

- **State and locally supported** 2-year, founded 2010, part of Lone Star College
- **Suburban** campus with easy access to Houston
- **Coed**

**Undergraduates** 3,645 full-time, 8,379 part-time. Students come from 57 other countries; 13% Black or African American, non-Hispanic/Latino; 38% Hispanic/Latino; 12% Asian, non-Hispanic/Latino; 0.2% American Indian or Alaska Native, non-Hispanic/Latino; 4% Two or more races, non-Hispanic/Latino; 6% Race/ethnicity unknown; 25% transferred in.

**Faculty** *Student/faculty ratio:* 29:1.

**Academics** *Degree:* certificates and associate. *Special study options:* academic remediation for entering students, advanced placement credit, cooperative education, distance learning, English as a second language, honors programs, independent study, internships, off-campus study, part-time degree program, services for LD students, study abroad, summer session for credit.

**Student Life** *Campus security:* 24-hour emergency response devices and patrols, late-night transport/escort service.

**Costs (2017–18)** *Tuition:* area resident $1088 full-time, $44 per credit hour part-time; state resident $2888 full-time, $119 per credit hour part-time; nonresident $3248 full-time, $134 per credit hour part-time. Full-time tuition and fees vary according to course load and program. Part-time tuition and fees vary according to course load and program. *Required fees:* $544 full-time, $20 per credit hour part-time, $32 per term part-time. *Payment plans:* installment, deferred payment.

**Applying** *Recommended:* high school transcript.

**Freshman Application Contact** Lone Star College–University Park, 20515 SH 249, Houston, TX 77070. *Phone:* 281-290-2721. *Website:* http://www.lonestar.edu/universitypark.

# McLennan Community College
## Waco, Texas

- **County-supported** 2-year, founded 1965
- **Urban** 200-acre campus
- **Endowment** $15.3 million
- **Coed**, 8,799 undergraduate students

**Undergraduates** Students come from 17 states and territories; 2% are from out of state; 12% Black or African American, non-Hispanic/Latino; 30% Hispanic/Latino; 1% Asian, non-Hispanic/Latino; 0.4% American Indian or Alaska Native, non-Hispanic/Latino; 3% Two or more races, non-Hispanic/Latino; 1% Race/ethnicity unknown.

**Freshmen** *Admission:* 2,362 applied, 2,362 admitted.

**Faculty** *Total:* 389, 14% with terminal degrees. *Student/faculty ratio:* 17:1.

**Majors** Accounting; administrative assistant and secretarial science; art teacher education; business administration and management; clinical/medical laboratory technology; computer engineering technology; criminal justice/law enforcement administration; criminal justice/police science; developmental and child psychology; finance; health information/medical records administration; industrial radiologic technology; information science/studies; kindergarten/preschool education; legal administrative assistant/secretary; legal assistant/paralegal; liberal arts and sciences/liberal studies; medical administrative assistant and medical secretary; mental health counseling; music; physical education teaching and coaching; physical therapy; real estate; registered nursing/registered nurse; respiratory care therapy; sign language interpretation and translation.

**Academics** *Calendar:* semesters. *Degree:* certificates and associate. *Special study options:* academic remediation for entering students, adult/continuing education programs, advanced placement credit, cooperative education, distance learning, honors programs, internships, off-campus study, part-time degree program, services for LD students, study abroad, summer session for credit. *ROTC:* Air Force (c).

**Library** McLennan Community College Library. *Books:* 69,255 (physical), 237,879 (digital/electronic); *Serial titles:* 290 (physical), 61 (digital/electronic); *Databases:* 134. Students can reserve study rooms.

**Student Life** *Housing:* college housing not available. *Activities and Organizations:* drama/theater group, student-run newspaper, choral group. *Campus security:* 24-hour emergency response devices and patrols. *Student services:* personal/psychological counseling.

**Athletics** Member NCAA, NJCAA. All NCAA Division I. *Intercollegiate sports:* baseball M(s), basketball M(s)/W(s), golf M(s)/W(s), softball W(s). *Intramural sports:* basketball M/W, volleyball M/W.

**Costs (2018–19)** *Tuition:* area resident $3180 full-time, $106 per semester hour part-time; state resident $3720 full-time, $124 per semester hour part-time; nonresident $5430 full-time, $181 per semester hour part-time. *Required fees:* $270 full-time, $9 per semester hour part-time. *Payment plan:* installment. *Waivers:* employees or children of employees.

**Financial Aid** Of all full-time matriculated undergraduates who enrolled in 2016, 265 Federal Work-Study jobs (averaging $850). 35 state and other part-time jobs (averaging $1000).

**Applying** *Options:* electronic application, early admission. *Required:* high school transcript. *Application deadlines:* rolling (freshmen), rolling (transfers). *Notification:* continuous until 9/2 (freshmen), continuous until 9/2 (transfers).

**Freshman Application Contact** Amanda Straten, Coordinator of Student Admissions, McLennan Community College, 1400 College Drive, Waco, TX 76708. *Phone:* 254-299-8657. *Fax:* 254-299-8694. *E-mail:* astraten@mclennan.edu.

*Website:* http://www.mclennan.edu/.

# MediaTech Institute
## Dallas, Texas

**Admissions Office Contact** MediaTech Institute, 13300 Branch View Lane, Dallas, TX 75234. *Toll-free phone:* 866-498-1122. *Website:* http://www.mediatech.edu/.

# Mountain View College
## Dallas, Texas

- **State and locally supported** 2-year, founded 1970, part of Dallas County Community College District System
- **Urban** 200-acre campus
- **Coed**

**Undergraduates** 2,066 full-time, 7,002 part-time. Students come from 12 states and territories; 26% Black or African American, non-Hispanic/Latino; 53% Hispanic/Latino; 4% Asian, non-Hispanic/Latino; 0.3% American Indian or Alaska Native, non-Hispanic/Latino; 0.5% Two or more races, non-Hispanic/Latino; 3% Race/ethnicity unknown; 0.3% international; 18% transferred in. *Retention:* 57% of full-time freshmen returned.

**Faculty** *Student/faculty ratio:* 28:1.

**Academics** *Calendar:* semesters. *Degree:* certificates and associate. *Special study options:* academic remediation for entering students, adult/continuing education programs, advanced placement credit, cooperative education, distance learning, double majors, English as a second language, external degree program, freshman honors college, honors programs, independent study, internships, part-time degree program, services for LD students, summer session for credit.

**Student Life** *Campus security:* 24-hour patrols, late-night transport/escort service.

**Athletics** Member NJCAA.

**Costs (2017–18)** *Tuition:* $52 per credit hour part-time; state resident $97 per credit hour part-time; nonresident $153 per credit hour part-time.

**Financial Aid** Of all full-time matriculated undergraduates who enrolled in 2016, 145 Federal Work-Study jobs (averaging $2700).

**Applying** *Options:* electronic application, early admission, deferred entrance. *Required:* high school transcript.

**Freshman Application Contact** Ms. Glenda Hall, Director of Admissions, Mountain View College, 4849 West Illinois Avenue, Dallas, TX 75211-6599. *Phone:* 214-860-8666. *Fax:* 214-860-8570. *E-mail:* ghall@dcccd.edu. *Website:* http://www.mountainviewcollege.edu/.

# Navarro College
## Corsicana, Texas

- **State and locally supported** 2-year, founded 1946
- **Small-town** 275-acre campus with easy access to Dallas-Fort Worth
- **Coed**, 8,968 undergraduate students, 34% full-time, 59% women, 41% men

**Undergraduates** 3,057 full-time, 5,911 part-time. Students come from 39 other countries; 2% are from out of state; 18% Black or African American, non-Hispanic/Latino; 22% Hispanic/Latino; 1% Asian, non-Hispanic/Latino; 0.3% Native Hawaiian or other Pacific Islander, non-Hispanic/Latino; 0.6% American Indian or Alaska Native, non-Hispanic/Latino; 2% Two or more races, non-Hispanic/Latino; 0.7% Race/ethnicity unknown; 1% international; 25% live on campus.

**Freshmen** *Admission:* 1,506 enrolled.

**Faculty** *Total:* 497, 27% full-time, 8% with terminal degrees. *Student/faculty ratio:* 16:1.

**Majors** Accounting; administrative assistant and secretarial science; agricultural mechanization; art; biological and physical sciences; biology/biological sciences; business administration and management; chemistry; clinical/medical laboratory technology; commercial and advertising art; computer graphics; computer programming; computer science; consumer merchandising/retailing management; corrections; criminal justice/law enforcement administration; criminal justice/police science; data processing and data processing technology; developmental and child psychology; drafting and design technology; dramatic/theater arts; education; elementary education; engineering; English; fire science/firefighting; industrial technology; legal administrative assistant/secretary; legal assistant/paralegal; legal studies; licensed practical/vocational nurse training; marketing/marketing management; mathematics; music; occupational therapy; pharmacy; physical education teaching and coaching; physical sciences; physics; pre-engineering; psychology; registered nursing/registered nurse; rhetoric and composition; social sciences; sociology; voice and opera.

**Academics** *Calendar:* semesters. *Degree:* certificates, diplomas, and associate. *Special study options:* academic remediation for entering students, adult/continuing education programs, advanced placement credit, cooperative education, distance learning, freshman honors college, honors programs, part-time degree program, services for LD students, student-designed majors, summer session for credit.

**Library** Richard M. Sanchez Library.

**Student Life** *Housing Options:* men-only, women-only. Campus housing is university owned. *Activities and Organizations:* drama/theater group, choral group, marching band, Student Government Association, Phi Theta Kappa, Ebony Club, Que Pasa. *Campus security:* 24-hour emergency response devices. *Student services:* personal/psychological counseling, veterans affairs office.

**Athletics** Member NJCAA. *Intercollegiate sports:* baseball M(s), basketball M(s), football M(s), soccer W, softball W, volleyball W(s). *Intramural sports:* basketball M/W, bowling M/W, football M, soccer M, softball M/W, volleyball M/W.

**Costs (2017–18)** *Tuition:* area resident $1260 full-time, $126 per credit hour part-time; state resident $1440 full-time, $144 per credit hour part-time; nonresident $2970 full-time, $297 per credit hour part-time. Full-time tuition and fees vary according to course load. Part-time tuition and fees vary according to course load. *Required fees:* $1140 full-time, $109 per credit hour part-time. *Room and board:* $6621. Room and board charges vary according to board plan. *Payment plan:* installment. *Waivers:* employees or children of employees.

**Applying** *Options:* electronic application, early admission. *Required:* high school transcript.

**Freshman Application Contact** Tammy Adams, Registrar, Navarro College, 3200 West 7th Avenue, Corsicana, TX 75110-4899. *Phone:* 903-875-7348. *Toll-free phone:* 800-NAVARRO (in-state); 800-628-2776 (out-of-state). *Fax:* 903-875-7353. *E-mail:* tammy.adams@navarrocollege.edu. *Website:* http://www.navarrocollege.edu/.

## North Central Texas College
### Gainesville, Texas

- **State and locally supported** 2-year, founded 1924
- **Suburban** 132-acre campus with easy access to Dallas-Fort Worth
- **Endowment** $4.3 million
- **Coed,** 10,327 undergraduate students, 26% full-time, 56% women, 44% men

**Undergraduates** 2,693 full-time, 7,634 part-time. Students come from 28 states and territories; 15 other countries; 0.9% are from out of state; 9% Black or African American, non-Hispanic/Latino; 23% Hispanic/Latino; 3% Asian, non-Hispanic/Latino; 0.1% Native Hawaiian or other Pacific Islander, non-Hispanic/Latino; 0.7% American Indian or Alaska Native, non-Hispanic/Latino; 3% Two or more races, non-Hispanic/Latino; 1% Race/ethnicity unknown; 2% international; 8% transferred in; 1% live on campus. *Retention:* 99% of full-time freshmen returned.

**Freshmen** *Admission:* 2,929 enrolled.

**Faculty** *Total:* 403, 38% full-time, 9% with terminal degrees. *Student/faculty ratio:* 16:1.

**Majors** Administrative assistant and secretarial science; agricultural mechanization; animal/livestock husbandry and production; automobile/automotive mechanics technology; biological and physical sciences; business administration and management; business and personal/financial services marketing; computer and information sciences and support services related; computer engineering technology; computer graphics; computer/information technology services administration related; computer programming; computer programming related; computer programming (specific applications); computer programming (vendor/product certification); computer science; criminal justice/law enforcement administration; criminal justice/police science; data processing and data processing technology; drafting and design technology; electrical, electronic and communications engineering technology; emergency medical technology (EMT paramedic); engineering technology; equestrian studies; farm and ranch management; health information/medical records administration; industrial mechanics and maintenance technology; information science/studies; legal administrative assistant/secretary; legal assistant/paralegal; liberal arts and sciences/liberal studies; machine shop technology; machine tool technology; merchandising; occupational therapy; pre-engineering; real estate; registered nursing/registered nurse; retailing; sales, distribution, and marketing operations; welding technology; word processing.

**Academics** *Calendar:* semesters. *Degree:* certificates, diplomas, and associate. *Special study options:* academic remediation for entering students, adult/continuing education programs, advanced placement credit, cooperative education, distance learning, internships, part-time degree program, services for LD students, summer session for credit. *ROTC:* Army (c).

**Library** North Central Texas College Library plus 1 other.

**Student Life** *Housing Options:* coed. Campus housing is university owned. *Activities and Organizations:* drama/theater group, choral group, Student Nursing Association, Residence Hall Association, Cosmetology Student Association, Student Government Association, Gainesville Program Council. *Campus security:* late-night transport/escort service, controlled dormitory access, security cameras. *Student services:* personal/psychological counseling.

**Athletics** Member NJCAA. *Intercollegiate sports:* baseball M(s), equestrian sports M(s)/W(s), softball W(s), tennis W(s), volleyball W(s). *Intramural sports:* archery M/W, basketball M/W, bowling M/W, field hockey M/W, football M/W, golf M/W, soccer M/W, softball M/W, swimming and diving M/W, table tennis M/W, tennis M/W, ultimate Frisbee M/W, volleyball M/W.

**Costs (2017–18)** *Tuition:* area resident $1824 full-time, $76 per credit hour part-time; state resident $3120 full-time, $130 per credit hour part-time; nonresident $5232 full-time, $218 per credit hour part-time. Full-time tuition and fees vary according to location. Part-time tuition and fees vary according to location. *Room and board:* $1985; room only: $760. Room and board charges vary according to housing facility. *Payment plans:* installment, deferred payment. *Waivers:* employees or children of employees.

**Financial Aid** Of all full-time matriculated undergraduates who enrolled in 2016, 108 Federal Work-Study jobs (averaging $1253). 29 state and other part-time jobs (averaging $392).

**Applying** *Options:* electronic application, early admission. *Required:* high school transcript. *Application deadlines:* rolling (freshmen), rolling (transfers).

**Freshman Application Contact** Melinda Carroll, Director of Admissions/Registrar, North Central Texas College, 1525 West California, Gainesville, TX 76240-4699. *Phone:* 940-668-7731. *Fax:* 940-668-7075. *E-mail:* mcarroll@nctc.edu. *Website:* http://www.nctc.edu/.

## Northeast Texas Community College
### Mount Pleasant, Texas

**Freshman Application Contact** Linda Bond, Admissions Specialist, Northeast Texas Community College, PO Box 1307, Mount Pleasant, TX 75456-1307. *Phone:* 903-434-8140. *Toll-free phone:* 800-870-0142. *E-mail:* lbond@ntcc.edu. *Website:* http://www.ntcc.edu/.

## North Lake College
### Irving, Texas

**Freshman Application Contact** Admissions/Registration Office, North Lake College, 5001 North MacArthur Boulevard, Irving, TX 75038. *Phone:* 972-273-3183. *Website:* http://www.northlakecollege.edu/.

## Northwest Vista College
### San Antonio, Texas

- **State and locally supported** 2-year, founded 1995, part of Alamo Community College District System
- **Urban** 137-acre campus with easy access to San Antonio
- **Coed,** 13,115 undergraduate students, 31% full-time, 54% women, 46% men

**Undergraduates** 4,043 full-time, 9,072 part-time. 6% Black or African American, non-Hispanic/Latino; 65% Hispanic/Latino; 3% Asian, non-Hispanic/Latino; 0.2% Native Hawaiian or other Pacific Islander, non-Hispanic/Latino; 0.2% American Indian or Alaska Native, non-Hispanic/Latino; 4% Two or more races, non-Hispanic/Latino; 0.5% Race/ethnicity unknown; 0.3% international; 7% transferred in.

**Freshmen** *Admission:* 2,611 enrolled.

**Faculty** *Total:* 564, 31% full-time. *Student/faculty ratio:* 25:1.

**Majors** Accounting; accounting technology and bookkeeping; administrative assistant and secretarial science; biology/biotechnology laboratory technician; business administration, management and operations related; community health and preventive medicine; computer and information sciences; computer and information sciences and support services related; computer and information systems security; computer/information technology services administration related; computer programming; computer science; criminal justice/safety; international/global studies; liberal arts and sciences/liberal studies; pre-engineering; recording arts technology; water quality and wastewater treatment management and recycling technology; web page, digital/multimedia and information resources design.

**Academics** *Calendar:* semesters. *Degree:* certificates and associate. *Special study options:* academic remediation for entering students, advanced placement credit, cooperative education, distance learning, double majors, English as a second language, independent study, internships, off-campus study, part-time degree program, services for LD students, study abroad, summer session for credit. *ROTC:* Army (c).

**Library** Redbud Learning Center. *Books:* 19,338 (physical), 233,202 (digital/electronic); *Serial titles:* 48 (physical), 33,000 (digital/electronic); *Databases:* 133. Weekly public service hours: 67.

**Student Life** *Housing:* college housing not available. *Activities and Organizations:* drama/theater group, Business Student Organization, Psychology Club, Neko Anime Club. *Campus security:* 24-hour emergency response devices, student patrols, late-night transport/escort service. *Student services:* personal/psychological counseling, veterans affairs office.

**Athletics** *Intramural sports:* basketball M/W, cross-country running M/W, soccer M/W, volleyball M/W.

**Applying** *Options:* electronic application, early admission. *Required:* high school transcript. *Application deadline:* rolling (transfers). *Notification:* continuous (transfers).

**Freshman Application Contact** Ms. Robin Sandberg, Director of Enrollment Management, Northwest Vista College, 3535 North Ellison Drive, San Antonio, TX 78251. *Phone:* 210-486-4134. *Fax:* 210-486-9091. *E-mail:* rsandberg@alamo.edu. *Website:* http://www.alamo.edu/nvc/.

# Odessa College
## Odessa, Texas

- **State and locally supported** 2-year, founded 1946
- **Urban** 87-acre campus
- **Coed,** 6,308 undergraduate students, 36% full-time, 62% women, 38% men

**Undergraduates** 2,243 full-time, 4,065 part-time. Students come from 24 states and territories; 4 other countries; 6% are from out of state; 5% Black or African American, non-Hispanic/Latino; 63% Hispanic/Latino; 1% Asian, non-Hispanic/Latino; 0.1% Native Hawaiian or other Pacific Islander, non-Hispanic/Latino; 0.5% American Indian or Alaska Native, non-Hispanic/Latino; 0.7% Race/ethnicity unknown; 1% international.

**Freshmen** *Admission:* 883 enrolled.

**Faculty** *Total:* 190, 68% full-time, 11% with terminal degrees.

**Majors** Accounting; administrative assistant and secretarial science; agriculture; art; athletic training; automobile/automotive mechanics technology; biology/biological sciences; business administration and management; chemistry; child development; clinical/medical laboratory technology; computer and information sciences; computer science; computer systems networking and telecommunications; construction engineering technology; cosmetology; criminal justice/law enforcement administration; criminal justice/police science; culinary arts; data processing and data processing technology; design and applied arts related; drafting and design technology; education; electrical, electronic and communications engineering technology; emergency medical technology (EMT paramedic); English; fire science/firefighting; geology/earth science; hazardous materials management and waste technology; heating, air conditioning, ventilation and refrigeration maintenance technology; history; human services; industrial radiologic technology; information science/studies; kindergarten/preschool education; legal administrative assistant/secretary; liberal arts and sciences/liberal studies; machine tool technology; mathematics; modern languages; music; photography; physical education teaching and coaching; physical therapy; physics; political science and government; pre-engineering; psychology; registered nursing/registered nurse; rhetoric and composition; social sciences; sociology; substance abuse/addiction counseling; teacher assistant/aide; welding technology.

**Academics** *Calendar:* semesters. *Degree:* certificates and associate. *Special study options:* academic remediation for entering students, adult/continuing education programs, advanced placement credit, cooperative education, distance learning, independent study, internships, part-time degree program, services for LD students, summer session for credit.

**Library** Murry H. Fly Learning Resources Center plus 1 other.

**Student Life** *Housing Options:* coed. Campus housing is provided by a third party. *Activities and Organizations:* choral group, Baptist Student Union, Student Government Association, Rodeo Club, Physical Therapy Assistant Club, American Chemical Society. *Campus security:* 24-hour emergency response devices and patrols, late-night transport/escort service, controlled dormitory access. *Student services:* personal/psychological counseling.

**Athletics** Member NJCAA. *Intercollegiate sports:* baseball M(s), basketball M(s)/W(s), cross-country running M(s)/W(s), golf M(s), softball W(s). *Intramural sports:* basketball M/W, bowling M/W, football M, racquetball M/W, softball M/W, table tennis M/W, volleyball M/W, weight lifting M/W.

**Financial Aid** Of all full-time matriculated undergraduates who enrolled in 2016, 59 Federal Work-Study jobs (averaging $1527). 8 state and other part-time jobs (averaging $1904).

**Applying** *Options:* electronic application, early admission, deferred entrance. *Application deadlines:* rolling (freshmen), rolling (transfers). *Notification:* continuous (freshmen), continuous (transfers).

**Freshman Application Contact** Ms. Tracy Avery, Director of Recruitment, Odessa College, 201 West University Avenue, Odessa, TX 79764. *Phone:* 432-335-6765. *Fax:* 432-335-6303. *E-mail:* tavery@odessa.edu. *Website:* http://www.odessa.edu/.

# Palo Alto College
## San Antonio, Texas

**Freshman Application Contact** Ms. Elizabeth Aguilar-Villarreal, Director of Enrollment Management, Palo Alto College, 1400 West Villaret Boulevard, San Antonio, TX 78224. *Phone:* 210-486-3713. *E-mail:* eaguilar-villarr@alamo.edu. *Website:* http://www.alamo.edu/pac/.

# Panola College
## Carthage, Texas

- **State and locally supported** 2-year, founded 1947
- **Small-town** 35-acre campus
- **Coed,** 2,646 undergraduate students, 50% full-time, 69% women, 31% men

**Undergraduates** 1,334 full-time, 1,312 part-time. Students come from 10 states and territories; 10 other countries; 8% are from out of state; 23% Black or African American, non-Hispanic/Latino; 11% Hispanic/Latino; 0.6% Asian, non-Hispanic/Latino; 0.4% American Indian or Alaska Native, non-Hispanic/Latino; 1% Two or more races, non-Hispanic/Latino; 2% international; 11% transferred in.

**Freshmen** *Admission:* 441 enrolled.

**Faculty** *Total:* 152, 46% full-time, 6% with terminal degrees. *Student/faculty ratio:* 18:1.

**Majors** Administrative assistant and secretarial science; agriculture; architecture; art; biology/biological sciences; business administration and management; business automation/technology/data entry; chemistry; clinical/medical laboratory technology; computer/information technology services administration related; computer science; construction engineering technology; criminology; dramatic/theater arts; education; electrician; English; farm and ranch management; foreign languages and literatures; forestry; general studies; geology/earth science; health information/medical records technology; health professions related; history; industrial technology; information science/studies; information technology; journalism; liberal arts and sciences and humanities related; management information systems; mathematics; medical/clinical assistant; middle school education; music; occupational therapist assistant; petroleum technology; physical education teaching and coaching; physics; pre-dentistry studies; pre-law studies; pre-pharmacy studies; pre-veterinary studies; psychology; registered nursing/registered nurse; sociology; speech communication and rhetoric; welding technology.

**Academics** *Calendar:* semesters. *Degree:* certificates and associate. *Special study options:* academic remediation for entering students, advanced placement credit, cooperative education, distance learning, English as a second language, part-time degree program, services for LD students, summer session for credit.

**Library** M. P. Baker Library. *Books:* 27,616 (physical), 651,787 (digital/electronic); *Serial titles:* 42 (physical), 15 (digital/electronic); *Databases:* 72. Weekly public service hours: 64; students can reserve study rooms.

**Student Life** *Housing Options:* coed, men-only, special housing for students with disabilities. Campus housing is university owned. *Activities and Organizations:* drama/theater group, student-run newspaper, choral group, History Club, SOTA (Student Occupational Therapy Assistant), NSLS (National Society of Leadership and Success, PTK (Phi Theta Kappa), BSM (Baptist Student Ministry). *Campus security:* controlled dormitory access, 24-hour campus police department. *Student services:* personal/psychological counseling, veterans affairs office.

**Athletics** Member NJCAA. *Intercollegiate sports:* baseball M(s), basketball M(s)/W(s), equestrian sports M(s)/W(s), volleyball W(s). *Intramural sports:* basketball M/W, table tennis M/W, volleyball M/W, weight lifting M/W.

**Financial Aid** Of all full-time matriculated undergraduates who enrolled in 2016, 960 applied for aid, 729 were judged to have need. 26 Federal Work-Study jobs (averaging $1354). 16 state and other part-time jobs (averaging $990). *Average percent of need met:* 50%. *Average financial aid package:* $7588. *Average need-based loan:* $10,743. *Average need-based gift aid:* $7692.

**Applying** *Options:* electronic application. *Required for some:* high school transcript. *Recommended:* high school transcript.

**Freshman Application Contact** Mr. Jeremy Dorman, Registrar/Director of Admissions, Panola College, 1109 West Panola Street, Carthage, TX 75633-2397. *Phone:* 903-693-2009. *Fax:* 903-693-2031. *E-mail:* bsimpson@panola.edu. *Website:* http://www.panola.edu/.

# Paris Junior College
## Paris, Texas

- **State and locally supported** 2-year, founded 1924
- **Rural** 54-acre campus with easy access to Dallas-Fort Worth
- **Endowment** $22.0 million
- **Coed,** 4,835 undergraduate students, 38% full-time, 59% women, 41% men

**Undergraduates** 1,829 full-time, 3,006 part-time. Students come from 21 states and territories; 5 other countries; 3% are from out of state; 11% Black or African American, non-Hispanic/Latino; 17% Hispanic/Latino; 1% Asian, non-Hispanic/Latino; 0.2% Native Hawaiian or other Pacific Islander, non-

Hispanic/Latino; 1% American Indian or Alaska Native, non-Hispanic/Latino; 2% Two or more races, non-Hispanic/Latino; 0.2% Race/ethnicity unknown; 0.2% international; 3% transferred in; 6% live on campus.
**Freshmen** *Admission:* 993 enrolled.
**Faculty** *Total:* 203, 40% full-time.
**Majors** Accounting; agricultural mechanization; agriculture; art; biological and physical sciences; biology/biological sciences; business administration and management; business automation/technology/data entry; business/commerce; business teacher education; chemistry; computer and information sciences; computer engineering technology; computer typography and composition equipment operation; cosmetology; criminal justice/safety; criminology; drafting and design technology; dramatic/theater arts; early childhood education; education; education (multiple levels); electrical, electronic and communications engineering technology; electromechanical technology; elementary education; emergency medical technology (EMT paramedic); engineering; English; foreign languages and literatures; general studies; health and physical education/fitness; health information/medical records technology; health services/allied health/health sciences; heating, air conditioning, ventilation and refrigeration maintenance technology; history; information science/studies; journalism; liberal arts and sciences/liberal studies; mathematics; medical insurance coding; metal and jewelry arts; music; nursing administration; physical sciences; physics; political science and government; pre-law studies; premedical studies; prenursing studies; pre-pharmacy studies; psychology; radiologic technology/science; registered nursing/registered nurse; rhetoric and composition; secondary education; social sciences; social work; sociology; surgical technology; system, networking, and LAN/WAN management; watchmaking and jewelrymaking; welding technology.
**Academics** *Calendar:* semesters. *Degree:* certificates, diplomas, and associate. *Special study options:* academic remediation for entering students, adult/continuing education programs, advanced placement credit, cooperative education, distance learning, double majors, part-time degree program, services for LD students, summer session for credit.
**Library** Mike Rheudasil Learning Center.
**Student Life** *Housing Options:* men-only, women-only. Campus housing is university owned. *Activities and Organizations:* drama/theater group, student-run newspaper, choral group, Student Government Organization, Blends Club (for all ethic groups). *Campus security:* 24-hour emergency response devices and patrols, late-night transport/escort service, controlled dormitory access.
**Athletics** Member NJCAA. *Intercollegiate sports:* baseball M(s), basketball M(s)/W(s), soccer M(s)/W(s), softball W(s). *Intramural sports:* basketball M, football M, table tennis M/W, tennis M/W.
**Costs (2018–19)** *Tuition:* area resident $1650 full-time, $55 per credit hour part-time; state resident $3150 full-time, $105 per credit hour part-time; nonresident $4650 full-time, $155 per credit hour part-time. Full-time tuition and fees vary according to class time, course level, course load, degree level, location, program, and student level. Part-time tuition and fees vary according to class time, course level, course load, degree level, location, program, and student level. *Required fees:* $750 full-time. *Room and board:* $5000. Room and board charges vary according to board plan and housing facility. *Payment plan:* installment. *Waivers:* senior citizens and employees or children of employees.
**Financial Aid** Of all full-time matriculated undergraduates who enrolled in 2015, 57 Federal Work-Study jobs (averaging $3600). 8 state and other part-time jobs (averaging $3600).
**Applying** *Options:* electronic application, early admission. *Required:* high school transcript. *Application deadlines:* rolling (freshmen), rolling (out-of-state freshmen), rolling (transfers). *Notification:* continuous (freshmen), continuous (out-of-state freshmen), continuous (transfers).
**Freshman Application Contact** Paris Junior College, 2400 Clarksville Street, Paris, TX 75460-6298. *Phone:* 903-782-0211. *Toll-free phone:* 800-232-5804.
*Website:* http://www.parisjc.edu/.

# Pima Medical Institute
## El Paso, Texas

**Admissions Office Contact** Pima Medical Institute, 6926 Gateway Boulevard East, El Paso, TX 79915. *Website:* http://www.pmi.edu/.

# Pima Medical Institute
## Houston, Texas

**Freshman Application Contact** Mr. Christopher Luebke, Corporate Director of Admissions, Pima Medical Institute, 2160 South Power Road, Mesa, AZ 85209. *Phone:* 480-610-6063. *Toll-free phone:* 800-477-PIMA. *E-mail:* cluebke@pmi.edu. *Website:* http://www.pmi.edu/.

# Quest College
## San Antonio, Texas

**Admissions Office Contact** Quest College, 5430 Fredericksburg Road, Suite 310, San Antonio, TX 78229. *Website:* http://www.questcollege.edu/.

# Ranger College
## Ranger, Texas

**Freshman Application Contact** Dr. Jim Davis, Dean of Students, Ranger College, 1100 College Circle, Ranger, TX 76470. *Phone:* 254-647-3234 Ext. 110. *Website:* http://www.rangercollege.edu/.

# Remington College–Dallas Campus
## Garland, Texas

**Director of Admissions** Ms. Shonda Wisenhunt, Remington College–Dallas Campus, 1800 Eastgate Drive, Garland, TX 75041. *Phone:* 972-686-7878. *Toll-free phone:* 800-323-8122. *Fax:* 972-686-5116. *E-mail:* shonda.wisenhunt@remingtoncollege.edu. *Website:* http://www.remingtoncollege.edu/.

# Remington College–Fort Worth Campus
## Fort Worth, Texas

**Director of Admissions** Marcia Kline, Director of Recruitment, Remington College–Fort Worth Campus, 300 East Loop 820, Fort Worth, TX 76112. *Phone:* 817-451-0017. *Toll-free phone:* 800-323-8122. *Fax:* 817-496-1257. *E-mail:* marcia.kline@remingtoncollege.edu. *Website:* http://www.remingtoncollege.edu/.

# Remington College–Houston Southeast Campus
## Webster, Texas

**Director of Admissions** Lori Minor, Director of Recruitment, Remington College–Houston Southeast Campus, 20985 Gulf Freeway, Webster, TX 77598. *Phone:* 281-554-1700. *Toll-free phone:* 800-323-8122. *Fax:* 281-554-1765. *E-mail:* lori.minor@remingtoncollege.edu. *Website:* http://www.remingtoncollege.edu/.

# Remington College–North Houston Campus
## Houston, Texas

**Director of Admissions** Edmund Flores, Director of Recruitment, Remington College–North Houston Campus, 11310 Greens Crossing Boulevard, Suite 300, Houston, TX 77067. *Phone:* 281-885-4450. *Toll-free phone:* 800-323-8122. *Fax:* 281-875-9964. *E-mail:* edmund.flores@remingtoncollege.edu. *Website:* http://www.remingtoncollege.edu/.

# Richland College
## Dallas, Texas

- **State and locally supported** 2-year, founded 1972, part of Dallas County Community College District System
- **Suburban** 250-acre campus
- **Coed**, 19,736 undergraduate students

**Undergraduates** Students come from 24 states and territories; 21 other countries; 19% Black or African American, non-Hispanic/Latino; 34% Hispanic/Latino; 16% Asian, non-Hispanic/Latino; 0.7% Two or more races, non-Hispanic/Latino; 6% Race/ethnicity unknown.
**Faculty** *Total:* 665, 25% full-time.
**Majors** Accounting; administrative assistant and secretarial science; artificial intelligence; business administration and management; computer programming; data processing and data processing technology; drafting/design engineering technologies related; electrical, electronic and communications engineering technology; engineering; industrial technology; international business/trade/commerce; liberal arts and sciences/liberal studies; mechanical engineering/mechanical technology; ornamental horticulture; real estate.
**Academics** *Calendar:* semesters. *Degree:* certificates and associate. *Special study options:* academic remediation for entering students, adult/continuing education programs, advanced placement credit, cooperative education, distance learning, English as a second language, freshman honors college, honors programs, off-campus study, part-time degree program, services for LD students, study abroad, summer session for credit.

**Library** Richland College Library.
**Student Life** *Housing:* college housing not available. *Activities and Organizations:* drama/theater group, student-run newspaper, radio station, choral group. *Campus security:* 24-hour emergency response devices and patrols, late-night transport/escort service, emergency call boxes. *Student services:* health clinic, personal/psychological counseling, women's center, veterans affairs office.
**Athletics** Member NJCAA. *Intercollegiate sports:* baseball M, basketball M, soccer M/W, volleyball W, wrestling M. *Intramural sports:* badminton M/W, basketball M/W, bowling M/W, cross-country running M/W, football M/W, golf M/W, soccer M/W, softball M/W, tennis M/W, track and field M/W, volleyball M/W, weight lifting M/W, wrestling M.
**Costs (2017–18)** *Tuition:* area resident $1770 full-time, $59 per credit hour part-time; state resident $3330 full-time, $111 per credit hour part-time; nonresident $5220 full-time, $174 per credit hour part-time. *Payment plan:* installment. *Waivers:* senior citizens and employees or children of employees.
**Financial Aid** Of all full-time matriculated undergraduates who enrolled in 2016, 123 Federal Work-Study jobs (averaging $2000).
**Applying** *Options:* electronic application. *Required for some:* high school transcript. *Application deadlines:* rolling (freshmen), rolling (out-of-state freshmen), rolling (transfers). *Notification:* continuous (freshmen), continuous (out-of-state freshmen), continuous (transfers).
**Freshman Application Contact** Richland College, 12800 Abrams Road, Dallas, TX 75243. *Phone:* 972-328-6948. *E-mail:* rlcadmissions@dcccd.edu. *Website:* http://www.richlandcollege.edu/.

## St. Philip's College
### San Antonio, Texas

- **District-supported** 2-year, founded 1898, part of Alamo Community College District System
- **Urban** 68-acre campus with easy access to San Antonio
- **Coed,** 12,050 undergraduate students, 13% full-time, 57% women, 43% men

**Undergraduates** 1,601 full-time, 10,449 part-time. 1% are from out of state; 9% Black or African American, non-Hispanic/Latino; 57% Hispanic/Latino; 2% Asian, non-Hispanic/Latino; 0.1% Native Hawaiian or other Pacific Islander, non-Hispanic/Latino; 0.4% American Indian or Alaska Native, non-Hispanic/Latino; 4% Two or more races, non-Hispanic/Latino; 2% Race/ethnicity unknown; 0.2% international; 5% transferred in.
**Freshmen** *Admission:* 1,022 enrolled.
**Faculty** *Total:* 398, 53% full-time, 7% with terminal degrees. *Student/faculty ratio:* 19:1.
**Majors** Accounting technology and bookkeeping; administrative assistant and secretarial science; aircraft powerplant technology; airframe mechanics and aircraft maintenance technology; American government and politics; art; autobody/collision and repair technology; automobile/automotive mechanics technology; baking and pastry arts; biology/biological sciences; biomedical technology; biotechnology; business administration and management; cardiovascular technology; chemistry; child development; clinical/medical laboratory technology; computer and information systems security; computer programming; computer science; computer technology/computer systems technology; construction engineering technology; criminal justice/safety; culinary arts; data entry/microcomputer applications; design and visual communications; diagnostic medical sonography and ultrasound technology; diesel mechanics technology; dramatic/theater arts; economics; education (multiple levels); electrician; engineering; English; fine/studio arts; foreign languages and literatures; health information/medical records technology; health services/allied health/health sciences; heating, ventilation, air conditioning and refrigeration engineering technology; history; hotel/motel administration; instrumentation technology; kinesiology and exercise science; liberal arts and sciences/liberal studies; machine tool technology; mathematics; mechanical engineering; music; occupational therapist assistant; physical therapy technology; pre-dentistry studies; premedical studies; prenursing studies; pre-pharmacy studies; psychology; radiologic technology/science; registered nursing/registered nurse; respiratory care therapy; restaurant, culinary, and catering management; rhetoric and composition; social work; sociology; surgical technology; system, networking, and LAN/WAN management; tourism and travel services management; welding technology.
**Academics** *Calendar:* semesters. *Degree:* certificates, diplomas, and associate. *Special study options:* academic remediation for entering students, adult/continuing education programs, advanced placement credit, cooperative education, distance learning, double majors, English as a second language, honors programs, independent study, internships, off-campus study, part-time degree program, services for LD students, study abroad, summer session for credit. *ROTC:* Army (c).
**Library** St. Philip's College Library. *Books:* 63,136 (physical), 56,724 (digital/electronic); *Serial titles:* 53 (physical), 72,126 (digital/electronic); *Databases:* 118. Weekly public service hours: 68.

**Student Life** *Housing:* college housing not available. *Activities and Organizations:* drama/theater group, choral group, Student Government, Future United Latino Leaders of Change, Collegiate 100. *Campus security:* 24-hour emergency response devices and patrols, late-night transport/escort service. *Student services:* health clinic, veterans affairs office.
**Athletics** *Intramural sports:* basketball M/W, cheerleading M/W, table tennis M/W, volleyball M/W, weight lifting M/W.
**Costs (2017–18)** *Tuition:* area resident $2580 full-time, $86 per credit hour part-time; state resident $6990 full-time, $202 per credit hour part-time; nonresident $13,590 full-time, $453 per credit hour part-time. Full-time tuition and fees vary according to course load and program. Part-time tuition and fees vary according to course load and program. *Required fees:* $80 full-time, $1 per credit hour part-time, $25 per term part-time. *Payment plan:* installment. *Waivers:* senior citizens and employees or children of employees.
**Applying** *Options:* electronic application, early admission. *Required:* high school transcript. *Application deadlines:* rolling (freshmen), rolling (transfers). *Notification:* continuous (freshmen), continuous (transfers).
**Freshman Application Contact** Ms. Angela Molina, Coordinator, Student Success, St. Philip's College, 1801 Martin Luther King Drive, San Antonio, TX 78203-2098. *Phone:* 210-486-2403. *Fax:* 210-486-2103. *E-mail:* amolina@alamo.edu. *Website:* http://www.alamo.edu/spc/.

## San Antonio College
### San Antonio, Texas

**Director of Admissions** Mr. J. Martin Ortega, Director of Admissions and Records, San Antonio College, 1819 North Main Avenue, San Antonio, TX 78212-3941. *Phone:* 210-733-2582. *Toll-free phone:* 844-202-5266. *Website:* http://www.alamo.edu/sac/.

## San Jacinto College District
### Pasadena, Texas

- **State and locally supported** 2-year, founded 1961
- **Suburban** 445-acre campus with easy access to Houston
- **Endowment** $6.9 million
- **Coed,** 30,509 undergraduate students, 23% full-time, 57% women, 43% men

**Undergraduates** 7,081 full-time, 23,428 part-time. Students come from 40 states and territories; 84 other countries; 1% are from out of state; 9% Black or African American, non-Hispanic/Latino; 57% Hispanic/Latino; 5% Asian, non-Hispanic/Latino; 0.1% Native Hawaiian or other Pacific Islander, non-Hispanic/Latino; 0.2% American Indian or Alaska Native, non-Hispanic/Latino; 2% Two or more races, non-Hispanic/Latino; 1% Race/ethnicity unknown; 2% international; 5% transferred in. *Retention:* 61% of full-time freshmen returned.
**Freshmen** *Admission:* 12,201 applied, 7,096 admitted, 5,531 enrolled.
**Faculty** *Total:* 1,174, 41% full-time, 15% with terminal degrees. *Student/faculty ratio:* 21:1.
**Majors** Accounting; administrative assistant and secretarial science; agribusiness; agriculture; airline pilot and flight crew; art; autobody/collision and repair technology; automobile/automotive mechanics technology; baking and pastry arts; behavioral sciences; biology/biological sciences; business administration and management; business/commerce; cardiovascular technology; chemical technology; chemistry; child development; clinical/medical laboratory technology; commercial and advertising art; computer and information sciences; construction engineering technology; cosmetology; cosmetology, barber/styling, and nail instruction; criminal justice/police science; culinary arts; dance; diagnostic medical sonography and ultrasound technology; diesel mechanics technology; digital communication and media/multimedia; drafting and design technology; dramatic/theater arts; electrical and power transmission installation; electrical, electronic and communications engineering technology; emergency medical technology (EMT paramedic); engineering; English; environmental science; fire science/firefighting; foreign languages and literatures; general studies; geology/earth science; health and physical education/fitness; health information/medical records technology; heating, air conditioning, ventilation and refrigeration maintenance technology; Hispanic-American, Puerto Rican, and Mexican-American/Chicano studies; history; instrumentation technology; interior design; international business/trade/commerce; journalism; kinesiology and exercise science; legal assistant/paralegal; management information systems; marine science/merchant marine officer; mathematics; medical/clinical assistant; music; occupational safety and health technology; occupational therapy; optometric technician; pharmacy technician; philosophy; physical sciences; physical therapy technology; physics; political science and government; psychiatric/mental health services technology; psychology; radio and television broadcasting technology; radiologic technology/science; real estate; registered nursing/registered nurse; respiratory

care therapy; restaurant, culinary, and catering management; rhetoric and composition; science teacher education; secondary education; social sciences; sociology; surgical technology; welding technology.

**Academics** *Calendar:* semesters. *Degree:* certificates, diplomas, and associate. *Special study options:* academic remediation for entering students, accelerated degree program, adult/continuing education programs, advanced placement credit, cooperative education, distance learning, double majors, English as a second language, honors programs, part-time degree program, services for LD students, student-designed majors, study abroad, summer session for credit. *ROTC:* Army (c), Air Force (c).

**Library** Lee Davis Library(Central),Edwin E. Lehr(North),Parker Williams(South). *Books:* 177,560 (physical), 15,541 (digital/electronic); *Serial titles:* 1,308 (physical). Weekly public service hours: 68; students can reserve study rooms.

**Student Life** *Housing:* college housing not available. *Activities and Organizations:* drama/theater group, student-run newspaper, choral group, Phi Theta Kappa honor society, Phi Beta Lambda, Student Government Association, Nurses Association, Men of Honor. *Campus security:* 24-hour emergency response devices and patrols, late-night transport/escort service. *Student services:* personal/psychological counseling, veterans affairs office.

**Athletics** Member NJCAA. *Intercollegiate sports:* baseball M(s), basketball M(s)/W(s), soccer M(s), softball W(s), volleyball W(s). *Intramural sports:* basketball M/W, football M/W, soccer M/W, tennis M/W, volleyball M/W, weight lifting M/W.

**Costs (2017–18)** *Tuition:* area resident $1500 full-time, $50 per credit hour part-time; state resident $2850 full-time, $95 per credit hour part-time; nonresident $4800 full-time, $160 per credit hour part-time. Full-time tuition and fees vary according to course load. Part-time tuition and fees vary according to course load. *Required fees:* $300 full-time. *Payment plan:* installment. *Waivers:* senior citizens.

**Applying** *Options:* electronic application, early admission. *Required:* high school transcript. *Required for some:* interview. *Recommended:* interview for nursing and EMT programs. *Application deadlines:* rolling (freshmen), rolling (transfers). *Notification:* continuous (freshmen), continuous (transfers).

**Freshman Application Contact** San Jacinto College District, 4624 Fairmont Parkway, Pasadena, TX 77504-3323. *Phone:* 281-998-6150. *Website:* http://www.sanjac.edu/.

# School of Automotive Machinists & Technology
## Houston, Texas

**Admissions Office Contact** School of Automotive Machinists & Technology, 1911 Antoine Drive, Houston, TX 77055. *Website:* http://www.samtech.edu/.

# South Plains College
## Levelland, Texas

- **State and locally supported** 2-year, founded 1958
- **Small-town** 177-acre campus
- **Endowment** $3.0 million
- **Coed**

**Undergraduates** 4,605 full-time, 4,448 part-time. Students come from 31 states and territories; 28 other countries; 2% are from out of state; 6% Black or African American, non-Hispanic/Latino; 45% Hispanic/Latino; 1% Asian, non-Hispanic/Latino; 0.1% Native Hawaiian or other Pacific Islander, non-Hispanic/Latino; 0.4% American Indian or Alaska Native, non-Hispanic/Latino; 0.9% international; 29% transferred in; 10% live on campus. *Retention:* 8% of full-time freshmen returned.

**Faculty** *Student/faculty ratio:* 20:1.

**Academics** *Calendar:* semesters. *Degree:* certificates and associate. *Special study options:* academic remediation for entering students, accelerated degree program, adult/continuing education programs, advanced placement credit, distance learning, double majors, internships, off-campus study, part-time degree program, services for LD students, study abroad, summer session for credit. *ROTC:* Army (c), Air Force (c).

**Library** South Plains College Library plus 1 other. Weekly public service hours: 57; students can reserve study rooms.

**Student Life** *Campus security:* 24-hour emergency response devices and patrols, controlled dormitory access.

**Athletics** Member NJCAA.

**Standardized Tests** *Recommended:* SAT or ACT (for admission).

**Costs (2017–18)** *Tuition:* area resident $696 full-time, $29 per semester hour part-time; state resident $1920 full-time, $80 per semester hour part-time; nonresident $2304 full-time, $96 per semester hour part-time. Full-time tuition and fees vary according to course load and location. Part-time tuition and fees vary according to course load and location. *Required fees:* $1544 full-time.

*Room and board:* $4108. Room and board charges vary according to housing facility.

**Financial Aid** Of all full-time matriculated undergraduates who enrolled in 2016, 80 Federal Work-Study jobs (averaging $2000). 22 state and other part-time jobs (averaging $2000).

**Applying** *Options:* electronic application, early admission. *Required:* high school transcript, proof of meningitis vaccination.

**Freshman Application Contact** Mrs. Andrea Rangel, Dean of Admissions and Records, South Plains College, 1401 College Avenue, Levelland, TX 78336. *Phone:* 806-894-9611 Ext. 2370. *Fax:* 806-897-3167. *E-mail:* arangel@southplainscollege.edu. *Website:* http://www.southplainscollege.edu/.

# South Texas College
## McAllen, Texas

**Freshman Application Contact** Mr. Matthew Hebbard, Director of Enrollment Services and Registrar, South Texas College, 3201 West Pecan, McAllen, TX 78501. *Phone:* 956-872-2147. *Toll-free phone:* 800-742-7822. *E-mail:* mshebbar@southtexascollege.edu. *Website:* http://www.southtexascollege.edu/.

# Southwest Texas Junior College
## Uvalde, Texas

- **State and locally supported** 2-year, founded 1946
- **Small-town** 97-acre campus with easy access to San Antonio
- **Coed**

**Undergraduates** Students come from 8 states and territories; 3 other countries; 1% Black or African American, non-Hispanic/Latino; 85% Hispanic/Latino; 0.2% Asian, non-Hispanic/Latino; 0.8% American Indian or Alaska Native, non-Hispanic/Latino; 0.4% Two or more races, non-Hispanic/Latino; 0.8% Race/ethnicity unknown; 9% live on campus.

**Majors** Agricultural mechanization; autobody/collision and repair technology; automobile/automotive mechanics technology; biological and physical sciences; business administration and management; business automation/technology/data entry; child development; computer and information sciences; computer engineering technology; construction trades; cosmetology; criminal justice/law enforcement administration; criminal justice/police science; criminal justice/safety; data processing and data processing technology; diesel mechanics technology; education; engineering; farm and ranch management; general studies; heating, air conditioning, ventilation and refrigeration maintenance technology; liberal arts and sciences/liberal studies; radiologic technology/science; registered nursing/registered nurse; teacher assistant/aide; wildlife, fish and wildlands science and management.

**Academics** *Calendar:* semesters. *Degree:* certificates and associate. *Special study options:* academic remediation for entering students, adult/continuing education programs, advanced placement credit, distance learning, English as a second language, external degree program, part-time degree program, summer session for credit.

**Library** Will C. Miller Memorial Library.

**Student Life** *Housing Options:* coed, women-only. Campus housing is university owned. *Activities and Organizations:* drama/theater group, student-run newspaper, Catholic Students Club, Business Administration Club. *Campus security:* 24-hour patrols, controlled dormitory access. *Student services:* health clinic, personal/psychological counseling, veterans affairs office.

**Athletics** *Intercollegiate sports:* basketball M/W, cross-country running M/W, equestrian sports M/W. *Intramural sports:* basketball M/W, equestrian sports M/W, football M, golf M/W, racquetball M/W, swimming and diving M/W, tennis M/W, volleyball M/W.

**Costs (2017–18)** *Tuition:* area resident $1464 full-time; state resident $3024 full-time, $61 per semester hour part-time; nonresident $5252 full-time, $61 per semester hour part-time. *Required fees:* $844 full-time, $42 per semester hour part-time. *Room and board:* $5060; room only: $2600. Room and board charges vary according to board plan. *Payment plan:* installment. *Waivers:* employees or children of employees.

**Financial Aid** Of all full-time matriculated undergraduates who enrolled in 2016, 150 Federal Work-Study jobs (averaging $1250). 75 state and other part-time jobs (averaging $1250).

**Applying** *Options:* electronic application, early admission, deferred entrance. *Required:* high school transcript. *Application deadlines:* rolling (freshmen), rolling (transfers). *Notification:* continuous (freshmen), continuous (transfers).

**Freshman Application Contact** Southwest Texas Junior College, 2401 Garner Field Road, Uvalde, TX 78801-6297. *Phone:* 830-278-4401 Ext. 7280. *Website:* http://www.swtjc.edu/.

# Tarrant County College District
## Fort Worth, Texas

- **County-supported** 2-year, founded 1967
- **Urban** 667-acre campus with easy access to Dallas-Fort Worth
- **Endowment** $5.8 million
- **Coed,** 51,350 undergraduate students, 29% full-time, 58% women, 42% men

**Undergraduates** 14,922 full-time, 36,428 part-time. Students come from 40 states and territories; 64 other countries; 17% Black or African American, non-Hispanic/Latino; 32% Hispanic/Latino; 6% Asian, non-Hispanic/Latino; 0.2% Native Hawaiian or other Pacific Islander, non-Hispanic/Latino; 0.4% American Indian or Alaska Native, non-Hispanic/Latino; 3% Two or more races, non-Hispanic/Latino; 1% Race/ethnicity unknown; 0.9% international; 4% transferred in.

**Freshmen** *Admission:* 8,053 applied, 8,053 admitted, 8,053 enrolled.

**Faculty** *Total:* 2,062, 34% full-time. *Student/faculty ratio:* 25:1.

**Majors** Accounting; administrative assistant and secretarial science; architectural engineering technology; automobile/automotive mechanics technology; avionics maintenance technology; business administration and management; clinical laboratory science/medical technology; clinical/medical laboratory technology; computer programming; computer science; construction engineering technology; consumer merchandising/retailing management; criminal justice/law enforcement administration; dental hygiene; developmental and child psychology; dietetics; drafting and design technology; educational/instructional technology; electrical, electronic and communications engineering technology; electromechanical technology; emergency medical technology (EMT paramedic); fashion merchandising; fire science/firefighting; food technology and processing; graphic and printing equipment operation/production; health information/medical records administration; heating, air conditioning, ventilation and refrigeration maintenance technology; horticultural science; industrial radiologic technology; legal assistant/paralegal; liberal arts and sciences/liberal studies; machine tool technology; marketing/marketing management; mechanical engineering/mechanical technology; mental health counseling; physical therapy; quality control technology; registered nursing/registered nurse; respiratory care therapy; sign language interpretation and translation; surgical technology; welding technology.

**Academics** *Calendar:* semesters. *Degree:* certificates and associate. *Special study options:* academic remediation for entering students, adult/continuing education programs, advanced placement credit, distance learning, English as a second language, honors programs, part-time degree program, services for LD students, summer session for credit. *ROTC:* Army (c), Air Force (c).

**Library** Main Library plus 5 others. *Books:* 200,377 (physical), 197,576 (digital/electronic); *Serial titles:* 496 (physical), 63,698 (digital/electronic); *Databases:* 155.

**Student Life** *Housing:* college housing not available. *Activities and Organizations:* drama/theater group, student-run newspaper, choral group. *Campus security:* 24-hour emergency response devices and patrols, late-night transport/escort service. *Student services:* health clinic, personal/psychological counseling, veterans affairs office.

**Athletics** *Intramural sports:* basketball M/W, football M/W, golf M, sailing M/W, table tennis M, tennis M/W, volleyball M/W.

**Costs (2018–19)** *Tuition:* area resident $1593 full-time, $59 per credit hour part-time; state resident $2862 full-time, $106 per credit hour part-time; nonresident $6885 full-time, $255 per credit hour part-time. Full-time tuition and fees vary according to course load and program. Part-time tuition and fees vary according to course load and program. *Payment plans:* installment, deferred payment. *Waivers:* senior citizens and employees or children of employees.

**Financial Aid** Of all full-time matriculated undergraduates who enrolled in 2016, 7,182 applied for aid, 6,589 were judged to have need. 296 Federal Work-Study jobs (averaging $1624). 75 state and other part-time jobs (averaging $2677). In 2016, 56 non-need-based awards were made. *Average need-based loan:* $985. *Average need-based gift aid:* $5032. *Average non-need-based aid:* $1413.

**Applying** *Options:* electronic application. *Application deadlines:* rolling (freshmen), rolling (transfers).

**Freshman Application Contact** Ms. Nichole Mancone, District Director of Admissions and Records, Tarrant County College District, 300 Trinity Campus Circle, Fort Worth, TX 76102-6599. *Phone:* 817-515-1581. *E-mail:* nichole.mancone@tccd.edu.

*Website:* http://www.tccd.edu/.

# Temple College
## Temple, Texas

**Freshman Application Contact** Ms. Toni Cuellar, Director of Admissions and Records, Temple College, 2600 South First Street, Temple, TX 76504. *Phone:* 254-298-8303. *Toll-free phone:* 800-460-4636. *E-mail:* carey.rose@templejc.edu. *Website:* http://www.templejc.edu/.

# Texarkana College
## Texarkana, Texas

- **State and locally supported** 2-year, founded 1927
- **Urban** 105-acre campus
- **Coed,** 4,251 undergraduate students

**Undergraduates** Students come from 2 other countries; 12% are from out of state; 21% Black or African American, non-Hispanic/Latino; 8% Hispanic/Latino; 1% Asian, non-Hispanic/Latino; 0.1% Native Hawaiian or other Pacific Islander, non-Hispanic/Latino; 0.7% American Indian or Alaska Native, non-Hispanic/Latino; 4% Two or more races, non-Hispanic/Latino; 1% Race/ethnicity unknown; 0.7% international; 1% live on campus.

**Faculty** *Total:* 215, 43% full-time. *Student/faculty ratio:* 22:1.

**Majors** Administrative assistant and secretarial science; agriculture; art; automobile/automotive mechanics technology; biology/biological sciences; business administration and management; business/commerce; chemistry; child-care and support services management; child development; computer and information sciences; cosmetology; criminal justice/law enforcement administration; criminal justice/safety; culinary arts; diesel mechanics technology; drafting and design technology; dramatic/theater arts; electrical, electronic and communications engineering technology; emergency medical technology (EMT paramedic); engineering; foreign languages and literatures; health aide; heating, air conditioning, ventilation and refrigeration maintenance technology; history; humanities; industrial mechanics and maintenance technology; journalism; liberal arts and sciences/liberal studies; licensed practical/vocational nurse training; marketing/marketing management; mathematics; music; pharmacy technician; physics; political science and government; registered nursing/registered nurse; social sciences; substance abuse/addiction counseling; welding technology.

**Academics** *Calendar:* semesters. *Degree:* certificates and associate. *Special study options:* academic remediation for entering students, adult/continuing education programs, advanced placement credit, cooperative education, distance learning, freshman honors college, honors programs, independent study, internships, part-time degree program, services for LD students, study abroad, summer session for credit.

**Library** Palmer Memorial Library.

**Student Life** *Housing Options:* coed. Campus housing is university owned. *Activities and Organizations:* drama/theater group, student-run newspaper, choral group, Black Student Association, Earth Club, Culinary Arts Club, Cultural Awareness Student Association, Cosmetology Club. *Campus security:* 24-hour patrols. *Student services:* personal/psychological counseling, veterans affairs office.

**Athletics** *Intramural sports:* basketball M/W, racquetball M/W, soccer M/W, tennis M/W, volleyball M/W.

**Costs (2018–19)** *Tuition:* area resident $1176 full-time, $52 per credit hour part-time; state resident $2448 full-time, $106 per credit hour part-time; nonresident $3648 full-time, $156 per credit hour part-time. Full-time tuition and fees vary according to program. Part-time tuition and fees vary according to program. *Required fees:* $940 full-time, $35 per credit hour part-time, $50 per term part-time. *Payment plan:* installment. *Waivers:* employees or children of employees.

**Financial Aid** Of all full-time matriculated undergraduates who enrolled in 2016, 30 Federal Work-Study jobs (averaging $3090).

**Applying** *Options:* electronic application, early admission, deferred entrance. *Required:* high school transcript. *Recommended:* interview for nursing program, meningitis vaccine. *Application deadlines:* rolling (freshmen), rolling (transfers).

**Freshman Application Contact** Mr. Lee Williams, Director of Admissions, Texarkana College, 2500 North Robison Road, Texarkana, TX 75599-0001. *Phone:* 903-823-3016. *Fax:* 903-823-3451. *E-mail:* lee.williams@texarkanacollege.edu.

*Website:* http://www.texarkanacollege.edu/.

# Texas Southmost College
## Brownsville, Texas

**Freshman Application Contact** New Student Relations, Texas Southmost College, 80 Fort Brown, Brownsville, TX 78520-4991. *Phone:* 956-882-8860. *Toll-free phone:* 877-882-8721. *Fax:* 956-882-8959. *Website:* http://www.utb.edu/.

# Texas State Technical College
## Waco, Texas

- **State-supported** 2-year, founded 1965
- **Suburban** 200-acre campus
- **Coed**, 12,717 undergraduate students, 39% full-time, 33% women, 67% men

**Undergraduates** 4,931 full-time, 7,786 part-time. Students come from 35 states and territories; 6% Black or African American, non-Hispanic/Latino; 55% Hispanic/Latino; 0.6% Asian, non-Hispanic/Latino; 0.1% Native Hawaiian or other Pacific Islander, non-Hispanic/Latino; 0.3% American Indian or Alaska Native, non-Hispanic/Latino; 0.9% Two or more races, non-Hispanic/Latino; 5% Race/ethnicity unknown; 8% transferred in.
**Freshmen** *Admission:* 2,088 enrolled.
**Faculty** *Total:* 645, 82% full-time, 3% with terminal degrees. *Student/faculty ratio:* 13:1.
**Majors** Aircraft powerplant technology; airframe mechanics and aircraft maintenance technology; airline pilot and flight crew; air traffic control; autobody/collision and repair technology; automobile/automotive mechanics technology; avionics maintenance technology; biomedical technology; chemical technology; computer and information systems security; computer programming; computer technology/computer systems technology; construction trades; culinary arts; diesel mechanics technology; drafting and design technology; educational/instructional technology; electrical, electronic and communications engineering technology; electromechanical technology; environmental engineering technology; game and interactive media design; graphic design; heating, ventilation, air conditioning and refrigeration engineering technology; instrumentation technology; laser and optical technology; manufacturing engineering technology; mechanical engineering/mechanical technology; network and system administration; nuclear/nuclear power technology; occupational safety and health technology; robotics technology; solar energy technology; surveying technology; system, networking, and LAN/WAN management; telecommunications technology; turf and turfgrass management; viticulture and enology; web page, digital/multimedia and information resources design.
**Academics** *Calendar:* trimesters. *Degree:* certificates and associate. *Special study options:* academic remediation for entering students, adult/continuing education programs, cooperative education, distance learning, internships, part-time degree program, services for LD students, summer session for credit.
**Library** Texas State Technical College-Waco Campus Library.
**Student Life** *Housing:* on-campus residence required for freshman year. *Options:* coed, men-only, women-only, special housing for students with disabilities. Campus housing is university owned. *Activities and Organizations:* Student Ambassador Association, SkillsUSA, Student Leadership Council, Phi Theta Kappa, Hispanic Student Association. *Campus security:* 24-hour emergency response devices and patrols, late-night transport/escort service, controlled dormitory access. *Student services:* health clinic, personal/psychological counseling, women's center, veterans affairs office.
**Athletics** *Intramural sports:* basketball M/W, football M, golf M/W, racquetball M/W, softball M/W, volleyball M/W, weight lifting M.
**Standardized Tests** *Required:* Texas Success Initiative assessment (for admission).
**Costs (2018–19)** *Tuition:* state resident $5123 full-time, $2561 per term part-time; nonresident $10,080 full-time, $5040 per term part-time. Full-time tuition and fees vary according to course load and program. Part-time tuition and fees vary according to course load and program. *Room and board:* $6742; room only: $4117. Room and board charges vary according to board plan and housing facility. *Payment plan:* installment. *Waivers:* senior citizens and employees or children of employees.
**Financial Aid** Of all full-time matriculated undergraduates who enrolled in 2016, 4,274 applied for aid, 4,247 were judged to have need, 320 had their need fully met. 129 Federal Work-Study jobs (averaging $1480). 27 state and other part-time jobs (averaging $955). In 2016, 5 non-need-based awards were made. *Average percent of need met:* 32%. *Average financial aid package:* $2787. *Average need-based loan:* $1246. *Average need-based gift aid:* $2787. *Average non-need-based aid:* $250.
**Applying** *Options:* electronic application, early admission. *Required:* high school transcript. *Required for some:* interview. *Application deadlines:* rolling (freshmen), rolling (transfers). *Notification:* continuous (freshmen), continuous (transfers).
**Freshman Application Contact** Mrs. Paula Arredondo, Registrar/Director of Admission and Records, Texas State Technical College, 3801 Campus Drive,

Waco, TX 76705. *Phone:* 254-867-3363. *Toll-free phone:* 800-792-8784 Ext. 2362. *E-mail:* mary.daniel@tstc.edu.
*Website:* http://www.tstc.edu/.

# Trinity Valley Community College
## Athens, Texas

- **State and locally supported** 2-year, founded 1946
- **Rural** 65-acre campus with easy access to Dallas-Fort Worth
- **Coed**, 6,726 undergraduate students, 31% full-time, 56% women, 44% men

**Undergraduates** 2,112 full-time, 4,614 part-time. Students come from 33 states and territories; 17 other countries; 1% are from out of state; 13% Black or African American, non-Hispanic/Latino; 19% Hispanic/Latino; 0.7% Asian, non-Hispanic/Latino; 0.1% Native Hawaiian or other Pacific Islander, non-Hispanic/Latino; 0.4% American Indian or Alaska Native, non-Hispanic/Latino; 3% Two or more races, non-Hispanic/Latino; 3% Race/ethnicity unknown; 0.8% international; 6% live on campus.
**Faculty** *Total:* 252, 65% full-time. *Student/faculty ratio:* 19:1.
**Majors** Accounting; agricultural teacher education; animal sciences; art; automobile/automotive mechanics technology; biology/biological sciences; business administration and management; business teacher education; chemistry; child development; commercial photography; computer science; corrections; cosmetology; criminal justice/law enforcement administration; criminal justice/police science; dance; data processing and data processing technology; developmental and child psychology; drafting and design technology; dramatic/theater arts; education; elementary education; emergency medical technology (EMT paramedic); English; farm and ranch management; fashion merchandising; finance; geology/earth science; heating, air conditioning, ventilation and refrigeration maintenance technology; history; horticultural science; insurance; journalism; kindergarten/preschool education; legal administrative assistant/secretary; liberal arts and sciences/liberal studies; licensed practical/vocational nurse training; marketing/marketing management; mathematics; music; physical education teaching and coaching; physical sciences; political science and government; pre-engineering; psychology; range science and management; real estate; registered nursing/registered nurse; religious studies; rhetoric and composition; sociology; Spanish; surgical technology; welding technology.
**Academics** *Calendar:* semesters. *Degree:* certificates, diplomas, and associate. *Special study options:* academic remediation for entering students, adult/continuing education programs, advanced placement credit, cooperative education, distance learning, double majors, English as a second language, honors programs, independent study, internships, part-time degree program, services for LD students, summer session for credit.
**Library** Ginger Murchison Learning Resource Center plus 3 others. *Books:* 47,948 (physical), 49,908 (digital/electronic); *Serial titles:* 124 (physical), 3 (digital/electronic); *Databases:* 68.
**Student Life** *Housing Options:* coed, men-only, women-only. Campus housing is university owned. *Activities and Organizations:* drama/theater group, student-run newspaper, choral group, marching band, Student Senate, Phi Theta Kappa, Delta Epsilon Chi. *Campus security:* 24-hour emergency response devices and patrols, controlled dormitory access. *Student services:* personal/psychological counseling.
**Athletics** Member NJCAA. *Intercollegiate sports:* basketball M(s)/W(s), cheerleading M(s)/W(s), football M(s), softball W(s), volleyball W(s). *Intramural sports:* baseball M/W, basketball M/W, football M, table tennis M/W, volleyball M/W.
**Costs (2018–19)** *Tuition:* area resident $1170 full-time, $39 per credit hour part-time; state resident $3450 full-time, $115 per credit hour part-time; nonresident $4500 full-time, $150 per credit hour part-time. Full-time tuition and fees vary according to course load. Part-time tuition and fees vary according to course load. *Required fees:* $1470 full-time, $49 per credit hour part-time. *Room and board:* Room and board charges vary according to board plan. *Payment plan:* installment. *Waivers:* employees or children of employees.
**Financial Aid** Of all full-time matriculated undergraduates who enrolled in 2014, 90 Federal Work-Study jobs (averaging $1176). 56 state and other part-time jobs (averaging $660).
**Applying** *Options:* electronic application, early admission. *Required:* high school transcript. *Application deadlines:* rolling (freshmen), rolling (transfers). *Notification:* continuous (freshmen), continuous (transfers).
**Freshman Application Contact** Ms. Tammy Denney, Registrar, Trinity Valley Community College, 100 Cardinal Drive, Athens, TX 75751. *Phone:* 903-675-6209 Ext. 209.
*Website:* http://www.tvcc.edu/.

# Tyler Junior College
## Tyler, Texas

- **State and locally supported** primarily 2-year, founded 1926
- **Suburban** 137-acre campus
- **Endowment** $42.2 million
- **Coed,** 11,478 undergraduate students, 51% full-time, 58% women, 42% men

**Undergraduates** 5,904 full-time, 5,574 part-time. Students come from 27 states and territories; 31 other countries; 3% are from out of state; 20% Black or African American, non-Hispanic/Latino; 20% Hispanic/Latino; 1% Asian, non-Hispanic/Latino; 0.2% Native Hawaiian or other Pacific Islander, non-Hispanic/Latino; 0.5% American Indian or Alaska Native, non-Hispanic/Latino; 3% Two or more races, non-Hispanic/Latino; 1% Race/ethnicity unknown; 0.8% international; 5% transferred in; 11% live on campus. *Retention:* 54% of full-time freshmen returned.
**Freshmen** *Admission:* 10,778 applied, 10,778 admitted, 2,995 enrolled.
**Faculty** *Total:* 559, 56% full-time, 9% with terminal degrees. *Student/faculty ratio:* 20:1.
**Majors** Animation, interactive technology, video graphics and special effects; art; athletic training; automobile/automotive mechanics technology; biology/biological sciences; business administration and management; business/commerce; chemistry; child development; clinical/medical laboratory technology; computer science; computer systems networking and telecommunications; criminalistics and criminal science; criminal justice/safety; dance; dental hygiene; diagnostic medical sonography and ultrasound technology; drafting and design technology; dramatic/theater arts; economics; education (multiple levels); electromechanical technology; emergency medical technology (EMT paramedic); engineering; family and consumer sciences/human sciences; fire prevention and safety technology; foreign languages and literatures; forest/forest resources management; general studies; geology/earth science; graphic design; health and physical education/fitness; health information/medical records technology; heating, air conditioning, ventilation and refrigeration maintenance technology; history; industrial electronics technology; journalism; legal assistant/paralegal; literature; mathematics; medical administrative assistant and medical secretary; middle school education; music; natural sciences; occupational therapist assistant; physical education teaching and coaching; physical therapy technology; physics; political science and government; psychology; public administration; radio and television; radiologic technology/science; registered nursing/registered nurse; respiratory care therapy; secondary education; sign language interpretation and translation; social work; sociology; speech communication and rhetoric; substance abuse/addiction counseling; surgical technology; surveying technology; system, networking, and LAN/WAN management; veterinary/animal health technology; welding technology.
**Academics** *Calendar:* semesters. *Degrees:* certificates, diplomas, associate, and bachelor's. *Special study options:* academic remediation for entering students, accelerated degree program, adult/continuing education programs, advanced placement credit, distance learning, freshman honors college, honors programs, part-time degree program, services for LD students, study abroad, summer session for credit.
**Library** Vaughn Library and Learning Resource Center. *Books:* 85,418 (physical), 135,816 (digital/electronic); *Databases:* 100. Weekly public service hours: 74.
**Student Life** *Housing Options:* coed, men-only, women-only. Campus housing is university owned and is provided by a third party. *Activities and Organizations:* drama/theater group, student-run newspaper, choral group, marching band, Student Government, Religious Affiliation Clubs, Phi Theta Kappa, national sororities. *Campus security:* 24-hour emergency response devices and patrols, controlled dormitory access. *Student services:* health clinic, personal/psychological counseling, veterans affairs office.
**Athletics** Member NJCAA. *Intercollegiate sports:* baseball M, basketball M(s)/W(s), cheerleading W(s), football M(s), golf M/W, soccer M(s)/W(s), softball W(s), tennis M(s)/W(s), volleyball W(s). *Intramural sports:* basketball M/W, cheerleading W, racquetball M/W, volleyball M/W, weight lifting M/W.
**Costs (2017–18)** *Tuition:* area resident $960 full-time, $32 per credit hour part-time; state resident $2700 full-time, $92 per credit hour part-time; nonresident $3420 full-time, $116 per credit hour part-time. *Required fees:* $10 per credit hour part-time, $132 per term part-time. *Room and board:* $8538; room only: $5940. Room and board charges vary according to housing facility. *Payment plan:* installment. *Waivers:* senior citizens and employees or children of employees.
**Financial Aid** Of all full-time matriculated undergraduates who enrolled in 2016, 74 Federal Work-Study jobs (averaging $2027). 17 state and other part-time jobs (averaging $2214). *Average need-based loan:* $5177. *Average need-*

based gift aid: $4911. *Average indebtedness upon graduation:* $14,743. *Financial aid deadline:* 6/1.
**Applying** *Options:* electronic application, early admission. *Required:* high school transcript. *Application deadlines:* rolling (freshmen), rolling (transfers). *Notification:* continuous (freshmen), continuous (transfers).
**Freshman Application Contact** Ms. Janna Chancey, Director of Enrollment Management, Tyler Junior College, PO Box 9020, Tyler, TX 75711-9020. *Phone:* 903-510-3325. *Toll-free phone:* 800-687-5680. *E-mail:* jcha@tjc.edu. *Website:* http://www.tjc.edu/.

# Vernon College
## Vernon, Texas

**Director of Admissions** Mr. Joe Hite, Dean of Admissions/Registrar, Vernon College, 4400 College Drive, Vernon, TX 76384-4092. *Phone:* 940-552-6291 Ext. 2204. *Website:* http://www.vernoncollege.edu/.

# Vet Tech Institute of Houston
## Houston, Texas

**Freshman Application Contact** Admissions Office, Vet Tech Institute of Houston, 4669 Southwest Freeway, Suite 100, Houston, TX 77027. *Phone:* 800-275-2736. *Toll-free phone:* 800-275-2736. *Website:* http://houston.vettechinstitute.edu/.

# Victoria College
## Victoria, Texas

- **County-supported** 2-year, founded 1925
- **Rural** 80-acre campus
- **Coed,** 4,000 undergraduate students, 26% full-time, 66% women, 34% men

**Undergraduates** 1,053 full-time, 2,947 part-time. Students come from 5 states and territories; 0.1% are from out of state; 6% Black or African American, non-Hispanic/Latino; 48% Hispanic/Latino; 2% Asian, non-Hispanic/Latino; 0.1% Native Hawaiian or other Pacific Islander, non-Hispanic/Latino; 0.2% American Indian or Alaska Native, non-Hispanic/Latino; 1% Two or more races, non-Hispanic/Latino; 0.5% Race/ethnicity unknown; 6% transferred in.
**Freshmen** *Admission:* 866 applied, 866 admitted, 765 enrolled.
**Faculty** *Total:* 211, 42% full-time, 9% with terminal degrees. *Student/faculty ratio:* 17:1.
**Majors** Business administration and management; chemical technology; criminal justice/police science; electrical, electronic and communications engineering technology; emergency medical technology (EMT paramedic); industrial technology; interdisciplinary studies; physical therapy technology; registered nursing/registered nurse; respiratory care therapy.
**Academics** *Calendar:* semesters. *Degree:* certificates and associate. *Special study options:* academic remediation for entering students, advanced placement credit, distance learning, English as a second language, off-campus study, part-time degree program, services for LD students, summer session for credit.
**Library** Victoria College/University of Houston-Victoria Library. *Books:* 118,781 (physical), 119,216 (digital/electronic); *Serial titles:* 133 (physical), 81,953 (digital/electronic); *Databases:* 137. Weekly public service hours: 76; students can reserve study rooms.
**Student Life** *Housing:* college housing not available. *Activities and Organizations:* choral group, Student Government Association. *Campus security:* 24-hour emergency response devices. *Student services:* personal/psychological counseling, veterans affairs office.
**Athletics** *Intercollegiate sports:* basketball M/W, volleyball W. *Intramural sports:* basketball M/W, sand volleyball M/W, soccer M/W, volleyball M/W.
**Costs (2018–19)** *Tuition:* area resident $1440 full-time, $48 per credit hour part-time; state resident $2910 full-time, $97 per credit hour part-time; nonresident $3690 full-time, $123 per credit hour part-time. Full-time tuition and fees vary according to program. Part-time tuition and fees vary according to program. *Required fees:* $1350 full-time, $45 per credit hour part-time. *Payment plan:* installment. *Waivers:* employees or children of employees.
**Applying** *Options:* electronic application, early admission. *Required:* high school transcript. *Application deadlines:* rolling (freshmen), rolling (transfers).
**Freshman Application Contact** Madelyne Tolliver, Registrar, Victoria College, 2200 E. Red River, Victoria, TX 77901. *Phone:* 361-572-6400. *Toll-free phone:* 877-843-4369. *Fax:* 361-582-2525. *E-mail:* registrar@victoriacollege.edu.
*Website:* http://www.victoriacollege.edu/.

# Virginia College in Austin
## Austin, Texas

Admissions Office Contact Virginia College in Austin, 14200 North Interstate Highway 35, Austin, TX 78728. *Website:* http://www.vc.edu/.

# Virginia College in Lubbock
## Lubbock, Texas

Admissions Office Contact Virginia College in Lubbock, 5005 50th Street, Lubbock, TX 79414. *Website:* http://www.vc.edu/.

# Vista College
## El Paso, Texas

Director of Admissions Ms. Sarah Hernandez, Registrar, Vista College, 6101 Montana Avenue, El Paso, TX 79925. *Phone:* 915-779-8031. *Toll-free phone:* 866-442-4197. *Website:* http://www.vistacollege.edu/.

# Vista College–Online Campus
## Richardson, Texas

Admissions Office Contact Vista College–Online Campus, 300 North Coit Road, Suite 300, Richardson, TX 75080. *Website:* http://www.vistacollege.edu/.

# Wade College
## Dallas, Texas

- **Proprietary** primarily 2-year, founded 1965
- **Urban** 175-acre campus with easy access to Dallas Fort Worth
- **Coed**, 238 undergraduate students

**Undergraduates** Students come from 4 other countries; 10% are from out of state. *Retention:* 60% of full-time freshmen returned.
**Faculty** *Total:* 18, 50% full-time, 33% with terminal degrees. *Student/faculty ratio:* 12:1.
**Majors** Fashion/apparel design; information technology; interior design; merchandising, sales, and marketing operations related (specialized).
**Academics** *Calendar:* trimesters. *Degrees:* associate and bachelor's. *Special study options:* academic remediation for entering students, advanced placement credit, internships, part-time degree program, services for LD students, summer session for credit.
**Library** College Library. *Books:* 8,500 (physical), 45,000 (digital/electronic); *Databases:* 10.
**Student Life** *Activities and Organizations:* student-run newspaper, Wade College Student Association. *Campus security:* 24-hour emergency response devices and patrols, late-night transport/escort service, controlled dormitory access. *Student services:* veterans affairs office.
**Applying** *Options:* electronic application. *Required:* high school transcript, interview. *Application deadlines:* 9/26 (freshmen), 9/26 (transfers). *Notification:* continuous (freshmen), continuous (transfers).
**Freshman Application Contact** Wade College, INFOMart, 1950 Stemmons Freeway, Suite 4080, LB 562, Dallas, TX 75207. *Phone:* 214-637-3530. *Toll-free phone:* 800-624-4850.
*Website:* http://www.wadecollege.edu/.

# Weatherford College
## Weatherford, Texas

- **State and locally supported** 2-year, founded 1869
- **Small-town** 94-acre campus with easy access to Dallas-Fort Worth
- **Coed**

**Undergraduates** 7% live on campus.
**Faculty** *Student/faculty ratio:* 22:1.
**Academics** *Calendar:* semesters. *Degree:* certificates, diplomas, and associate. *Special study options:* academic remediation for entering students, adult/continuing education programs, cooperative education, distance learning, freshman honors college, honors programs, internships, part-time degree program, services for LD students, student-designed majors, summer session for credit. *ROTC:* Army (c), Air Force (c).
**Library** Weatherford College Library. *Books:* 50,220 (physical). Students can reserve study rooms.
**Student Life** *Campus security:* 24-hour emergency response devices and patrols, late-night transport/escort service.
**Athletics** Member NJCAA.
**Costs (2017–18)** *Tuition:* area resident $1920 full-time, $80 per semester hour part-time; state resident $2976 full-time, $124 per semester hour part-time; nonresident $4224 full-time, $176 per semester hour part-time. Full-time

tuition and fees vary according to course load and program. Part-time tuition and fees vary according to course load and program. *Room and board:* $7430; room only: $4530. Room and board charges vary according to board plan.
**Applying** *Options:* electronic application, early admission. *Recommended:* high school transcript.
**Freshman Application Contact** Mr. Ralph Willingham, Director of Admissions, Weatherford College, 225 College Park Drive, Weatherford, TX 76086-5699. *Phone:* 817-598-6248. *Toll-free phone:* 800-287-5471. *Fax:* 817-598-6205. *E-mail:* rwillingham@wc.edu. *Website:* http://www.wc.edu/.

# Western Technical College
## El Paso, Texas

**Freshman Application Contact** Ms. Laura Pena, Director of Admissions, Western Technical College, 9451 Diana Drive, El Paso, TX 79930-2610. *Phone:* 915-566-9621. *Toll-free phone:* 800-201-9232. *E-mail:* lpena@westerntech.edu. *Website:* http://www.westerntech.edu/.

# Western Technical College
## El Paso, Texas

**Freshman Application Contact** Mr. Bill Terrell, Chief Admissions Officer, Western Technical College, 9624 Plaza Circle, El Paso, TX 79927. *Phone:* 915-532-3737 Ext. 117. *Fax:* 915-532-6946. *E-mail:* bterrell@wtc-ep.edu. *Website:* http://www.westerntech.edu/.

# Western Texas College
## Snyder, Texas

- **State and locally supported** 2-year, founded 1969
- **Small-town** 165-acre campus
- **Coed**, 2,250 undergraduate students, 26% full-time, 49% women, 51% men

**Undergraduates** 579 full-time, 1,671 part-time. Students come from 30 states and territories; 17 other countries; 4% are from out of state; 9% Black or African American, non-Hispanic/Latino; 42% Hispanic/Latino; 1% Asian, non-Hispanic/Latino; 0.1% Native Hawaiian or other Pacific Islander, non-Hispanic/Latino; 0.8% American Indian or Alaska Native, non-Hispanic/Latino; 2% Two or more races, non-Hispanic/Latino; 6% international; 3% transferred in; 50% live on campus.
**Freshmen** *Admission:* 668 applied, 599 admitted, 348 enrolled.
**Faculty** *Total:* 88, 39% full-time, 8% with terminal degrees. *Student/faculty ratio:* 22:1.
**Majors** Accounting; administrative assistant and secretarial science; agricultural teacher education; agriculture; applied horticulture/horticulture operations; art; art teacher education; biology/biological sciences; business administration and management; child-care provision; computer and information sciences; computer engineering technology; computer science; corrections; criminal justice/law enforcement administration; criminal justice/police science; dramatic/theater arts; early childhood education; engineering; health and physical education/fitness; landscape architecture; liberal arts and sciences/liberal studies; marketing/marketing management; mass communication/media; mathematics; parks, recreation and leisure facilities management; petroleum technology; pre-law studies; premedical studies; radio and television; secondary education; social sciences; turf and turfgrass management; welding technology.
**Academics** *Calendar:* semesters. *Degree:* certificates and associate. *Special study options:* academic remediation for entering students, adult/continuing education programs, advanced placement credit, distance learning, honors programs, independent study, internships, part-time degree program, services for LD students, student-designed majors, summer session for credit.
**Library** Western Texas College Resource Center. *Books:* 31,884 (physical), 29,077 (digital/electronic); *Serial titles:* 97 (physical); *Databases:* 25. Weekly public service hours: 56.
**Student Life** *Housing:* on-campus residence required through sophomore year. *Options:* coed, men-only. Campus housing is university owned. *Activities and Organizations:* drama/theater group, student-run radio station, Student Government Association, Phi Theta Kappa, Agriculture Club, Art Club, Fellowship of Christian Athletes. *Campus security:* 24-hour emergency response devices and patrols, late-night transport/escort service. *Student services:* health clinic, personal/psychological counseling, veterans affairs office.
**Athletics** Member NCAA, NJCAA. All NCAA Division I. *Intercollegiate sports:* baseball M(s), basketball M(s)/W(s), cross-country running M(s)/W(s), golf M(s)/W(s), soccer M(s)/W(s), softball W(s), track and field M(s)/W(s), volleyball W(s). *Intramural sports:* basketball M/W, football M, golf M/W, racquetball M/W, soccer M/W, softball M/W, table tennis M/W, volleyball M/W, weight lifting M/W.

Costs (2018–19) *Tuition:* area resident $1740 full-time, $58 per credit hour part-time; state resident $2850 full-time, $95 per credit hour part-time; nonresident $3960 full-time, $132 per credit hour part-time. Full-time tuition and fees vary according to course load, location, and program. Part-time tuition and fees vary according to course load, location, and program. *Required fees:* $990 full-time, $33 per credit hour part-time. *Room and board:* $5275. Room and board charges vary according to housing facility. *Payment plan:* installment.
**Applying** *Options:* electronic application, early admission, deferred entrance. *Required:* high school transcript. *Application deadlines:* rolling (freshmen), rolling (transfers). *Notification:* continuous (freshmen), continuous (transfers).
**Freshman Application Contact** Donna Morris, Registrar, Western Texas College, 6200 S College Ave, Snyder, TX 79549. *Phone:* 325-573-8511. *Toll-free phone:* 888-GO-TO-WTC. *Fax:* 325-573-9321. *E-mail:* dmorris@wtc.edu.
*Website:* http://www.wtc.edu/.

# Wharton County Junior College
## Wharton, Texas

**Freshman Application Contact** Mr. Albert Barnes, Dean of Admissions and Registration, Wharton County Junior College, 911 Boling Highway, Wharton, TX 77488-3298. *Phone:* 979-532-6381. *E-mail:* albertb@wcjc.edu. *Website:* http://www.wcjc.edu/.

# UTAH

# Ameritech College of Healthcare
## Draper, Utah

**Admissions Office Contact** Ameritech College of Healthcare, 12257 South Business Park Drive, Suite 108, Draper, UT 84020-6545. *Website:* http://www.ameritech.edu/.

# Fortis College
## Salt Lake City, Utah

**Admissions Office Contact** Fortis College, 3949 South 700 East, Suite 150, Salt Lake City, UT 84107. *Toll-free phone:* 855-4-FORTIS. *Website:* http://www.fortis.edu/.

# LDS Business College
## Salt Lake City, Utah

- **Independent** 2-year, founded 1886, affiliated with The Church of Jesus Christ of Latter-day Saints, part of The Church Educational System (CES) of The Church of Jesus Christ of Latter-day Saints
- **Urban** 2-acre campus with easy access to Salt Lake City
- **Coed**

**Undergraduates** 2% Black or African American, non-Hispanic/Latino; 14% Hispanic/Latino; 1% Asian, non-Hispanic/Latino; 2% Native Hawaiian or other Pacific Islander, non-Hispanic/Latino; 0.4% American Indian or Alaska Native, non-Hispanic/Latino; 3% Two or more races, non-Hispanic/Latino; 1% Race/ethnicity unknown; 22% international.
**Faculty** *Student/faculty ratio:* 25:1.
**Majors** Accounting; accounting and business/management; accounting technology and bookkeeping; administrative assistant and secretarial science; architecture related; business administration and management; business administration, management and operations related; business, management, and marketing related; computer and information sciences; computer and information sciences and support services related; computer and information sciences related; computer and information systems security; computer/information technology services administration related; computer programming; computer programming related; computer programming (specific applications); computer science; computer software engineering; computer support specialist; computer systems networking and telecommunications; cosmetology and personal grooming arts related; data modeling/warehousing and database administration; design and applied arts related; engineering/industrial management; entrepreneurial and small business related; entrepreneurship; food service and dining room management; general studies; health information/medical records administration; health professions related; information technology; interior design; management science; marketing/marketing management; medical administrative assistant and medical secretary; multi/interdisciplinary studies related; network and system administration; operations management; photography; project

management; sales, distribution, and marketing operations; small business administration.
**Academics** *Calendar:* semesters. *Degree:* certificates and associate. *Special study options:* academic remediation for entering students, adult/continuing education programs, advanced placement credit, distance learning, double majors, English as a second language, internships, part-time degree program, services for LD students, summer session for credit. *ROTC:* Army (c), Air Force (c).
**Library** LDS Business College Library. Weekly public service hours: 74; students can reserve study rooms.
**Student Life** *Housing:* college housing not available. *Activities and Organizations:* choral group, DECA, Baseball Club, Soccer Club, Mentor, Service. *Campus security:* 24-hour emergency response devices and patrols. *Student services:* personal/psychological counseling.
**Standardized Tests** *Recommended:* SAT or ACT (for admission).
**Costs (2018–19)** *Tuition:* $1670 full-time. *Payment plan:* installment. *Waivers:* employees or children of employees.
**Applying** *Options:* electronic application, deferred entrance. *Application fee:* $35. *Application deadlines:* rolling (freshmen), rolling (transfers). *Notification:* continuous (freshmen), continuous (transfers).
**Freshman Application Contact** Kristen Whittaker, Director of Enrollment Management, LDS Business College, 95 North 300 West, Salt Lake City, UT 84101-3500. *Phone:* 801-524-8145. *Toll-free phone:* 800-999-5767. *E-mail:* admissions@ldsbc.edu.
*Website:* http://www.ldsbc.edu/.

# Nightingale College
## Ogden, Utah

**Freshman Application Contact** Nightingale College, 4155 Harrison Boulevard #100, Ogden, UT 84403. *Website:* http://www.nightingale.edu/.

# Provo College
## Provo, Utah

**Director of Admissions** Mr. Gordon Peters, College Director, Provo College, 1450 West 820 North, Provo, UT 84601. *Phone:* 801-375-1861. *Toll-free phone:* 877-777-5886. *Fax:* 801-375-9728. *E-mail:* gordonp@provocollege.org. *Website:* http://www.provocollege.edu/.

# Salt Lake Community College
## Salt Lake City, Utah

- **State-supported** 2-year, founded 1948, part of Utah System of Higher Education
- **Urban** 114-acre campus with easy access to Salt Lake City
- **Endowment** $837,612
- **Coed,** 29,620 undergraduate students, 26% full-time, 52% women, 48% men

**Undergraduates** 7,811 full-time, 21,809 part-time. 2% Black or African American, non-Hispanic/Latino; 18% Hispanic/Latino; 4% Asian, non-Hispanic/Latino; 1% Native Hawaiian or other Pacific Islander, non-Hispanic/Latino; 0.8% American Indian or Alaska Native, non-Hispanic/Latino; 3% Two or more races, non-Hispanic/Latino; 2% Race/ethnicity unknown; 1% international; 7% transferred in.
**Freshmen** *Admission:* 4,397 applied, 4,397 admitted, 4,397 enrolled.
**Faculty** *Total:* 1,514, 22% full-time. *Student/faculty ratio:* 17:1.
**Majors** Accounting technology and bookkeeping; airline pilot and flight crew; architectural engineering technology; autobody/collision and repair technology; avionics maintenance technology; biology/biological sciences; biology/biotechnology laboratory technician; building/construction finishing, management, and inspection related; business administration and management; chemistry; clinical/medical laboratory technology; computer and information sciences; computer science; criminal justice/law enforcement administration; culinary arts; dental hygiene; design and visual communications; diesel mechanics technology; drafting and design technology; economics; electrical, electronic and communications engineering technology; engineering; engineering technology; English; entrepreneurship; environmental engineering technology; finance; general studies; geology/earth science; graphic design; health professions related; heating, air conditioning, ventilation and refrigeration maintenance technology; history; human development and family studies; humanities; industrial radiologic technology; information science/studies; information technology; instrumentation technology; international/global studies; international relations and affairs; kinesiology and exercise science; legal assistant/paralegal; marketing/marketing management; mass communication/media; medical/clinical assistant; medical radiologic technology; music; occupational therapist assistant; photographic and film/video technology; physical sciences; physical therapy technology; physics; political science and government; psychology; public health related;

quality control technology; radio and television broadcasting technology; registered nursing/registered nurse; sign language interpretation and translation; social work; sociology; speech communication and rhetoric; sport and fitness administration/management; surveying technology; teacher assistant/aide; telecommunications technology; welding technology.

**Academics** *Calendar:* semesters. *Degree:* certificates, diplomas, and associate. *Special study options:* academic remediation for entering students, advanced placement credit, cooperative education, distance learning, double majors, English as a second language, internships, part-time degree program, services for LD students, student-designed majors, study abroad, summer session for credit. *ROTC:* Army (c), Air Force (c).

**Library** Markosian Library plus 2 others.

**Student Life** *Housing:* college housing not available. *Activities and Organizations:* drama/theater group, student-run newspaper, radio and television station, choral group, marching band. *Campus security:* 24-hour emergency response devices and patrols, late-night transport/escort service. *Student services:* health clinic, personal/psychological counseling.

**Athletics** Member NJCAA. *Intercollegiate sports:* baseball M(s), basketball M(s)/W(s), cheerleading M(s)/W(s), soccer M(c)/W(c), softball W(s), volleyball W(s).

**Costs (2017–18)** *Tuition:* state resident $3319 full-time, $138 per credit hour part-time; nonresident $11,558 full-time, $481 per credit hour part-time. *Required fees:* $462 full-time. *Payment plan:* installment. *Waivers:* senior citizens and employees or children of employees.

**Applying** *Options:* electronic application, early admission. *Application fee:* $40. *Application deadlines:* rolling (freshmen), rolling (transfers).

**Admissions Office Contact** Salt Lake Community College, PO Box 30808, Salt Lake City, UT 84130-0808.
*Website:* http://www.slcc.edu/.

## Snow College
### Ephraim, Utah

**Freshman Application Contact** Ms. Lorie Parry, Admissions Advisor, Snow College, 150 East College Avenue, Ephraim, UT 84627. *Phone:* 435-283-7144. *Fax:* 435-283-7157. *E-mail:* snowcollege@snow.edu. *Website:* http://www.snow.edu/.

# VERMONT

## Community College of Vermont
### Montpelier, Vermont

- **State-supported** 2-year, founded 1973, part of Vermont State Colleges System
- **Rural** campus
- **Coed**

**Undergraduates** 862 full-time, 5,489 part-time. Students come from 25 states and territories; 4% are from out of state. *Retention:* 57% of full-time freshmen returned.

**Faculty** *Student/faculty ratio:* 13:1.

**Academics** *Calendar:* semesters. *Degree:* certificates and associate. *Special study options:* academic remediation for entering students, accelerated degree program, adult/continuing education programs, advanced placement credit, cooperative education, distance learning, double majors, English as a second language, external degree program, independent study, internships, part-time degree program, services for LD students, student-designed majors, study abroad, summer session for credit.

**Library** Hartness Library plus 1 other.

**Standardized Tests** *Required for some:* ACCUPLACER or SAT/ACT. *Recommended:* SAT or ACT (for admission).

**Costs (2017–18)** *Tuition:* state resident $7830 full-time, $261 per credit hour part-time; nonresident $15,660 full-time, $522 per credit hour part-time. Full-time tuition and fees vary according to reciprocity agreements. Part-time tuition and fees vary according to reciprocity agreements. *Required fees:* $150 full-time, $75 per term part-time.

**Financial Aid** Of all full-time matriculated undergraduates who enrolled in 2016, 111 Federal Work-Study jobs (averaging $1214).

**Applying** *Options:* electronic application.

**Freshman Application Contact** Community College of Vermont, 660 Elm Street, Montpelier, VT 05602. *Phone:* 802-654-0505. *Toll-free phone:* 800-CCV-6686. *Website:* http://www.ccv.edu/.

## Landmark College
### Putney, Vermont

**Freshman Application Contact** Admissions Main Desk, Landmark College, Admissions Office, River Road South, Putney, VT 05346. *Phone:* 802-387-6718. *Fax:* 802-387-6868. *E-mail:* admissions@landmark.edu. *Website:* http://www.landmark.edu/.

## New England Culinary Institute
### Montpelier, Vermont

- **Proprietary** primarily 2-year, founded 1980
- **Small-town** campus
- **Coed**

**Undergraduates** 257 full-time, 43 part-time. Students come from 39 states and territories; 6 other countries; 80% are from out of state; 8% Black or African American, non-Hispanic/Latino; 5% Hispanic/Latino; 4% Asian, non-Hispanic/Latino; 1% American Indian or Alaska Native, non-Hispanic/Latino; 1% Two or more races, non-Hispanic/Latino; 13% Race/ethnicity unknown; 6% transferred in. *Retention:* 86% of full-time freshmen returned.

**Faculty** *Student/faculty ratio:* 15:1.

**Academics** *Calendar:* quarters. *Degrees:* certificates, associate, and bachelor's. *Special study options:* academic remediation for entering students, accelerated degree program, advanced placement credit, cooperative education, distance learning, honors programs, internships, services for LD students.

**Library** New England Culinary Institute Library.

**Student Life** *Campus security:* 24-hour emergency response devices, student patrols.

**Standardized Tests** *Recommended:* SAT or ACT (for admission).

**Costs (2017–18)** *Comprehensive fee:* $33,419 includes full-time tuition ($16,800), mandatory fees ($2420), and room and board ($14,199). Full-time tuition and fees vary according to course load. Part-time tuition: $700 per credit hour. Part-time tuition and fees vary according to course load.

**Financial Aid** Of all full-time matriculated undergraduates who enrolled in 2016, 320 Federal Work-Study jobs (averaging $1000).

**Applying** *Options:* electronic application, early admission, deferred entrance. *Application fee:* $35. *Required:* essay or personal statement, high school transcript, 1 letter of recommendation, interview. *Recommended:* culinary experience.

**Freshman Application Contact** Adonica Williams, New England Culinary Institute, 7 School Street, Montpelier, VT 05602-3115. *Phone:* 802-225-3210. *Toll-free phone:* 877-223-6324. *Fax:* 802-225-3280. *E-mail:* admissions@neci.edu. *Website:* http://www.neci.edu/.

# VIRGINIA

## Advanced Technology Institute
### Virginia Beach, Virginia

**Freshman Application Contact** Admissions Office, Advanced Technology Institute, 5700 Southern Boulevard, Suite 100, Virginia Beach, VA 23462. *Phone:* 757-490-1241. *Toll-free phone:* 888-468-1093. *Website:* http://www.auto.edu/.

## American National University
### Charlottesville, Virginia

**Director of Admissions** Kimberly Moore, Campus Director, American National University, 3926 Seminole Trail, Charlottesville, VA 22911. *Phone:* 434-295-0136. *Toll-free phone:* 888-9-JOBREADY. *Fax:* 434-979-8061. *Website:* http://www.an.edu/.

## American National University
### Danville, Virginia

**Freshman Application Contact** Admissions Office, American National University, 336 Old Riverside Drive, Danville, VA 24541. *Phone:* 434-793-6822. *Toll-free phone:* 888-9-JOBREADY. *Website:* http://www.an.edu/.

## American National University
### Harrisonburg, Virginia

**Director of Admissions** Jack Evey, Campus Director, American National University, 1515 Country Club Road, Harrisonburg, VA 22802. *Phone:* 540-432-0943. *Toll-free phone:* 888-9-JOBREADY. *Website:* http://www.an.edu/.

## American National University
### Lynchburg, Virginia

**Freshman Application Contact** Admissions Representative, American National University, 104 Candlewood Court, Lynchburg, VA 24502. *Phone:* 804-239-3500. *Toll-free phone:* 888-9-JOBREADY. *Website:* http://www.an.edu/.

## Blue Ridge Community College
### Weyers Cave, Virginia

**Freshman Application Contact** Blue Ridge Community College, PO Box 80, Weyers Cave, VA 24486-0080. *Phone:* 540-453-2217. *Toll-free phone:* 888-750-2722. *Website:* http://www.brcc.edu/.

## Bryant & Stratton College–Richmond Campus
### Richmond, Virginia

**Freshman Application Contact** Mr. David K. Mayle, Director of Admissions, Bryant & Stratton College–Richmond Campus, 8141 Hull Street Road, Richmond, VA 23235-6411. *Phone:* 804-745-2444. *Fax:* 804-745-6884. *E-mail:* tlawson@bryanstratton.edu. *Website:* http://www.bryantstratton.edu/.

## Bryant & Stratton College–Virginia Beach Campus
### Virginia Beach, Virginia

**Freshman Application Contact** Bryant & Stratton College–Virginia Beach Campus, 301 Centre Pointe Drive, Virginia Beach, VA 23462. *Phone:* 757-499-7900 Ext. 173. *Website:* http://www.bryantstratton.edu/.

## Centra College of Nursing
### Lynchburg, Virginia

**Admissions Office Contact** Centra College of Nursing, 905 Lakeside Drive, Suite A, Lynchburg, VA 24501. *Website:* http://www.centrahealth.com/facilities/centra-college-nursing/.

## Central Virginia Community College
### Lynchburg, Virginia

- **State-supported** 2-year, founded 1966, part of Virginia Community College System
- **Suburban** 104-acre campus
- **Coed,** 4,128 undergraduate students, 31% full-time, 55% women, 45% men

**Undergraduates** 1,269 full-time, 2,859 part-time. Students come from 12 states and territories; 1% are from out of state; 18% Black or African American, non-Hispanic/Latino; 3% Hispanic/Latino; 3% Asian, non-Hispanic/Latino; 0.1% Native Hawaiian or other Pacific Islander, non-Hispanic/Latino; 0.4% American Indian or Alaska Native, non-Hispanic/Latino; 5% Two or more races, non-Hispanic/Latino; 0.7% Race/ethnicity unknown.
**Freshmen** *Admission:* 705 applied, 704 admitted.
**Faculty** *Total:* 333, 17% full-time. *Student/faculty ratio:* 18:1.
**Majors** Business administration and management; business/commerce; business operations support and secretarial services related; computer and information sciences; criminal justice/law enforcement administration; culinary arts; design and visual communications; education; emergency medical technology (EMT paramedic); engineering; engineering technology; industrial technology; liberal arts and sciences/liberal studies; management science; medical/clinical assistant; radiologic technology/science; respiratory care therapy; science technologies.

**Academics** *Calendar:* semesters. *Degree:* certificates, diplomas, and associate. *Special study options:* academic remediation for entering students, advanced placement credit, cooperative education, distance learning, independent study, internships, part-time degree program, services for LD students, summer session for credit.
**Library** Bedford Learning Resources Center.
**Student Life** *Housing:* college housing not available. *Campus security:* 24-hour emergency response devices. *Student services:* veterans affairs office.
**Costs (2017–18)** *Tuition:* state resident $4725 full-time, $158 per credit hour part-time; nonresident $10,653 full-time, $355 per credit hour part-time. *Payment plan:* installment. *Waivers:* senior citizens.
**Financial Aid** Of all full-time matriculated undergraduates who enrolled in 2016, 65 Federal Work-Study jobs (averaging $2700).
**Applying** *Options:* electronic application, early admission, deferred entrance. *Application deadlines:* rolling (freshmen), rolling (transfers). *Notification:* continuous (freshmen), continuous (transfers).
**Freshman Application Contact** Admissions Office, Central Virginia Community College, 3506 Wards Road, Lynchburg, VA 24502. *Phone:* 434-832-7633. *Toll-free phone:* 800-562-3060. *Fax:* 434-832-7793. *Website:* http://www.centralvirginia.edu/.

## Centura College
### Chesapeake, Virginia

**Director of Admissions** Director of Admissions, Centura College, 932 Ventures Way, Chesapeake, VA 23320. *Phone:* 757-549-2121. *Toll-free phone:* 877-575-5627. *Fax:* 575-549-1196. *Website:* http://www.centuracollege.edu/.

## Centura College
### Newport News, Virginia

**Director of Admissions** Victoria Whitehead, Director of Admissions, Centura College, 616 Denbigh Boulevard, Newport News, VA 23608. *Phone:* 757-874-2121. *Toll-free phone:* 877-575-5627. *Fax:* 757-874-3857. *E-mail:* admdircpen@centura.edu. *Website:* http://www.centuracollege.edu/.

## Centura College
### Norfolk, Virginia

**Director of Admissions** Director of Admissions, Centura College, 7020 North Military Highway, Norfolk, VA 23518. *Phone:* 757-853-2121. *Toll-free phone:* 877-575-5627. *Fax:* 757-852-9017. *Website:* http://www.centuracollege.edu/.

## Centura College
### North Chesterfield, Virginia

**Freshman Application Contact** Admissions Office, Centura College, 7914 Midlothian Turnpike, North Chesterfield, VA 23235-5230. *Phone:* 804-330-0111. *Toll-free phone:* 877-575-5627. *Fax:* 804-330-3809. *Website:* http://www.centuracollege.edu/.

## Centura College
### Virginia Beach, Virginia

**Freshman Application Contact** Admissions Office, Centura College, 2697 Dean Drive, Suite 100, Virginia Beach, VA 23452. *Phone:* 757-340-2121. *Toll-free phone:* 877-575-5627. *Fax:* 757-340-9704. *Website:* http://www.centuracollege.edu/.

## Chester Career College
### Chester, Virginia

**Admissions Office Contact** Chester Career College, 751 West Hundred Road, Chester, VA 23836. *Website:* http://www.chestercareercollege.edu/.

## Columbia College
### Vienna, Virginia

**Admissions Office Contact** Columbia College, 8620 Westwood Center Drive, Vienna, VA 22182. *Website:* http://www.ccdc.edu/.

# Dabney S. Lancaster Community College
## Clifton Forge, Virginia

- **State-supported** 2-year, founded 1964, part of Virginia Community College System
- **Rural** 117-acre campus
- **Endowment** $6.6 million
- **Coed,** 1,186 undergraduate students, 36% full-time, 61% women, 39% men

**Undergraduates** 428 full-time, 758 part-time. Students come from 3 states and territories; 4% are from out of state; 4% Black or African American, non-Hispanic/Latino; 2% Hispanic/Latino; 0.6% Asian, non-Hispanic/Latino; 0.7% American Indian or Alaska Native, non-Hispanic/Latino; 4% Two or more races, non-Hispanic/Latino; 0.6% Race/ethnicity unknown; 0.1% international; 29% transferred in.

**Freshmen** *Admission:* 1,010 applied, 1,010 admitted, 183 enrolled.

**Faculty** *Total:* 116, 16% full-time, 9% with terminal degrees. *Student/faculty ratio:* 10:1.

**Majors** Administrative assistant and secretarial science; biological and physical sciences; business administration and management; computer programming; criminal justice/law enforcement administration; data processing and data processing technology; drafting and design technology; drafting/design engineering technologies related; education; electrical, electronic and communications engineering technology; forest technology; information science/studies; legal administrative assistant/secretary; liberal arts and sciences/liberal studies; medical administrative assistant and medical secretary; registered nursing/registered nurse; wood science and wood products/pulp and paper technology.

**Academics** *Calendar:* semesters. *Degree:* certificates and associate. *Special study options:* academic remediation for entering students, adult/continuing education programs, advanced placement credit, cooperative education, distance learning, double majors, independent study, internships, off-campus study, part-time degree program, services for LD students, summer session for credit.

**Library** DSLCC Library. *Books:* 35,154 (physical), 74,281 (digital/electronic); *Serial titles:* 5 (physical), 95,157 (digital/electronic); *Databases:* 117. Weekly public service hours: 60; students can reserve study rooms.

**Student Life** *Housing:* college housing not available. *Activities and Organizations:* Nursing Student Association, Phi Theta Kappa, National Student Leadership Society, LGBT+, Forestry Club. *Campus security:* 24-hour emergency response devices, Security Cameras at Rockbridge Regional Center. *Student services:* personal/psychological counseling, veterans affairs office.

**Athletics** *Intramural sports:* basketball M/W, softball M/W, volleyball M/W.

**Standardized Tests** *Required for some:* SAT and SAT Subject Tests or ACT (for admission), SAT Subject Tests (for admission).

**Applying** *Options:* electronic application. *Recommended:* high school transcript. *Notification:* continuous (freshmen), continuous (out-of-state freshmen), continuous (transfers), rolling (early decision plan 1), rolling (early decision plan 2), rolling (early action).

**Freshman Application Contact** Ms. Suzanne Ostling, Admissions Officer, Dabney S. Lancaster Community College, 1000 Dabney Drive, Clifton Forge, VA 24422. *Phone:* 540-863-2826. *Toll-free phone:* 877-73-DSLCC. *Fax:* 540-863-2915. *E-mail:* sostling@dslcc.edu. *Website:* http://www.dslcc.edu/.

# Danville Community College
## Danville, Virginia

**Freshman Application Contact** Cathy Pulliam, Coordinator of Student Recruitment and Enrollment, Danville Community College, 1008 South Main Street, Danville, VA 24541-4088. *Phone:* 434-797-8538. *Toll-free phone:* 800-560-4291. *E-mail:* cpulliam@dcc.vccs.edu. *Website:* http://www.dcc.vccs.edu/.

# Eastern Shore Community College
## Melfa, Virginia

- **State-supported** 2-year, founded 1971, part of Virginia Community College System
- **Rural** 117-acre campus with easy access to Hampton Roads/Virginia Beach, Norfolk
- **Coed,** 857 undergraduate students, 31% full-time, 67% women, 33% men

**Undergraduates** 264 full-time, 593 part-time. 1% are from out of state; 39% Black or African American, non-Hispanic/Latino; 6% Hispanic/Latino; 1% Asian, non-Hispanic/Latino; 0.2% American Indian or Alaska Native, non-Hispanic/Latino; 0.8% Race/ethnicity unknown.

**Faculty** *Total:* 87, 20% full-time. *Student/faculty ratio:* 13:1.

**Majors** Biological and physical sciences; business administration and management; computer and information sciences and support services related; computer/information technology services administration related; education; electrical, electronic and communications engineering technology; liberal arts and sciences/liberal studies; registered nursing/registered nurse.

**Academics** *Calendar:* semesters. *Degree:* certificates and associate. *Special study options:* academic remediation for entering students, adult/continuing education programs, distance learning, internships, off-campus study, part-time degree program, services for LD students, summer session for credit.

**Library** Learning Resources Center plus 1 other.

**Student Life** *Housing:* college housing not available. *Activities and Organizations:* All Christians Together in Service (ACTS), Phi Theta Kappa, Phi Beta Lambda, The Electronics Club, Chess Club. *Campus security:* security guards, day and night during classes when the college is in session. *Student services:* veterans affairs office.

**Costs (2017–18)** *Tuition:* state resident $4374 full-time, $156 per credit hour part-time; nonresident $9906 full-time, $318 per credit hour part-time. Full-time tuition and fees vary according to course load. Part-time tuition and fees vary according to course load. *Required fees:* $406 full-time. *Payment plan:* installment. *Waivers:* senior citizens.

**Financial Aid** Of all full-time matriculated undergraduates who enrolled in 2016, 11 Federal Work-Study jobs.

**Applying** *Options:* electronic application. *Required:* high school transcript. *Application deadlines:* rolling (freshmen), rolling (transfers). *Notification:* continuous (freshmen), continuous (transfers).

**Freshman Application Contact** Ms. Cheryll Mills, Coordinator of Student Services, Eastern Shore Community College, 29300 Lankford Highway, Melfa, VA 23410. *Phone:* 757-789-1730. *Toll-free phone:* 877-871-8455. *Fax:* 757-789-1737. *E-mail:* cmills@es.vccs.edu. *Website:* http://www.es.vccs.edu/.

# Eastern Virginia Career College
## Fredericksburg, Virginia

**Admissions Office Contact** Eastern Virginia Career College, 10304 Spotsylvania Avenue, Suite 400, Fredericksburg, VA 22408. *Website:* http://www.evcc.edu/.

# Fortis College
## Norfolk, Virginia

**Admissions Office Contact** Fortis College, 6300 Center Drive, Suite 100, Norfolk, VA 23502. *Toll-free phone:* 855-4-FORTIS. *Website:* http://www.fortis.edu/.

# Fortis College
## Richmond, Virginia

**Admissions Office Contact** Fortis College, 2000 Westmoreland Street, Suite A, Richmond, VA 23230. *Toll-free phone:* 855-4-FORTIS. *Website:* http://www.fortis.edu/.

# Germanna Community College
## Locust Grove, Virginia

**Freshman Application Contact** Ms. Rita Dunston, Registrar, Germanna Community College, 10000 Germanna Point Drive, Fredericksburg, VA 22408. *Phone:* 540-891-3020. *Fax:* 540-891-3092. *Website:* http://www.germanna.edu/.

# John Tyler Community College
## Chester, Virginia

- **State-supported** 2-year, founded 1967, part of Virginia Community College System
- **Suburban** 160-acre campus with easy access to Richmond
- **Coed,** 10,380 undergraduate students, 24% full-time, 57% women, 43% men

**Undergraduates** 2,536 full-time, 7,844 part-time. 3% are from out of state; 23% Black or African American, non-Hispanic/Latino; 8% Hispanic/Latino; 3% Asian, non-Hispanic/Latino; 0.1% Native Hawaiian or other Pacific Islander, non-Hispanic/Latino; 0.5% American Indian or Alaska Native, non-Hispanic/Latino; 5% Two or more races, non-Hispanic/Latino; 1% Race/ethnicity unknown.

**Freshmen** *Admission:* 1,531 enrolled.

**Faculty** *Total:* 521, 23% full-time. *Student/faculty ratio:* 20:1.

**Majors** Accounting related; architectural technology; business administration and management; business administration, management and operations related; child-care provision; computer and information sciences; criminal justice/law enforcement administration; electrician; emergency medical technology (EMT paramedic); engineering; funeral service and mortuary science; general studies; humanities; industrial technology; information technology; manufacturing engineering technology; mechanical engineering technologies related; mental and social health services and allied professions related; registered nursing/registered nurse; visual and performing arts related.

**Academics** *Calendar:* semesters. *Degree:* certificates and associate. *Special study options:* academic remediation for entering students, adult/continuing education programs, advanced placement credit, distance learning, external degree program, honors programs, off-campus study, part-time degree program, services for LD students, study abroad, summer session for credit. *ROTC:* Army (c).

**Library** John Tyler Community College Learning Resource and Technology Center.

**Student Life** *Housing:* college housing not available. *Activities and Organizations:* drama/theater group, choral group, Phi Theta Kappa, Human Services Club, Future Teachers Club, Student Nurses'; Association, Student Veteran's Organization. *Campus security:* 24-hour emergency response devices and patrols. *Student services:* veterans affairs office.

**Athletics** *Intramural sports:* basketball M(c)/W(c), soccer M(c)/W(c).

**Costs (2017–18)** *Tuition:* state resident $4283 full-time, $151 per credit hour part-time; nonresident $9581 full-time, $349 per credit hour part-time. Full-time tuition and fees vary according to course load. Part-time tuition and fees vary according to course load. *Required fees:* $325 full-time, $35 per term part-time. *Payment plan:* installment. *Waivers:* senior citizens.

**Financial Aid** Of all full-time matriculated undergraduates who enrolled in 2016, 45 Federal Work-Study jobs (averaging $2574).

**Applying** *Options:* electronic application, early admission, deferred entrance. *Recommended:* high school transcript. *Application deadline:* rolling (freshmen). *Notification:* continuous (freshmen).

**Freshman Application Contact** Mr. Leigh Baxter, Director Admissions and Records and Registrar, John Tyler Community College, Office of Admissions and Records, 800 Charter Colony Parkway, Midlothian, VA 23831. *Phone:* 804-594-1549. *Toll-free phone:* 800-552-3490. *Fax:* 804-594-1543. *E-mail:* lbaxter@jtcc.edu.
*Website:* http://www.jtcc.edu/.

## J. Sargeant Reynolds Community College
### Richmond, Virginia

- **State-supported** 2-year, founded 1972, part of Virginia Community College System
- **Suburban** 207-acre campus with easy access to Richmond
- **Endowment** $10.0 million
- **Coed,** 9,334 undergraduate students, 28% full-time, 59% women, 41% men

**Undergraduates** 2,567 full-time, 6,767 part-time. Students come from 21 states and territories; 16 other countries; 1% are from out of state; 33% Black or African American, non-Hispanic/Latino; 3% Hispanic/Latino; 6% Asian, non-Hispanic/Latino; 0.2% Native Hawaiian or other Pacific Islander, non-Hispanic/Latino; 0.4% American Indian or Alaska Native, non-Hispanic/Latino; 8% Two or more races, non-Hispanic/Latino; 1% Race/ethnicity unknown; 5% transferred in. *Retention:* 51% of full-time freshmen returned.

**Freshmen** *Admission:* 1,339 enrolled.
**Faculty** *Total:* 585, 22% full-time, 6% with terminal degrees. *Student/faculty ratio:* 17:1.
**Majors** Accounting related; applied horticulture/horticulture operations; architectural and building sciences; automobile/automotive mechanics technology; baking and pastry arts; biological and physical sciences; building/construction site management; business administration and management; child-care provision; clinical/medical laboratory technology; computer and information sciences; computer programming; computer systems networking and telecommunications; consumer merchandising/retailing management; cooking and related culinary arts; criminal justice/law enforcement administration; dental laboratory technology; educational leadership and administration; emergency medical technology (EMT paramedic); engineering; fire science/firefighting; floriculture/floristry management; hospitality administration; hospitality administration related; hotel/motel administration; legal assistant/paralegal; liberal arts and sciences and humanities related; licensed practical/vocational nurse training; mathematics; mental and social health services and allied professions related; opticianry; pharmacy technician; respiratory care therapy; restaurant/food services management; sign language interpretation and translation; small business administration; social sciences; substance abuse/addiction counseling; web page, digital/multimedia and information resources design.

**Academics** *Calendar:* semesters. *Degree:* certificates and associate. *Special study options:* academic remediation for entering students, adult/continuing education programs, advanced placement credit, distance learning, double majors, English as a second language, honors programs, independent study, internships, off-campus study, part-time degree program, services for LD students, summer session for credit.

**Library** J. Sargeant Reynolds Community College Library plus 2 others. *Books:* 85,000 (physical), 62,000 (digital/electronic); *Serial titles:* 225 (physical), 52,000 (digital/electronic); *Databases:* 145. Weekly public service hours: 66.

**Student Life** *Housing:* college housing not available. *Campus security:* 24-hour emergency response devices and patrols, late-night transport/escort service, security during hours of operation. *Student services:* personal/psychological counseling, veterans affairs office.

**Costs (2018–19)** *Tuition:* state resident $4846 full-time, $146 per credit hour part-time; nonresident $10,814 full-time, $322 per credit hour part-time. Full-time tuition and fees vary according to course load and program. Part-time tuition and fees vary according to course load and program. *Required fees:* $510 full-time, $17 per credit hour part-time. *Payment plan:* installment. *Waivers:* senior citizens.

**Financial Aid** Of all full-time matriculated undergraduates who enrolled in 2017, 3,045 applied for aid, 1,710 were judged to have need. 40 Federal Work-Study jobs (averaging $1707). *Average financial aid package:* $3503. *Average need-based gift aid:* $2665.

**Applying** *Options:* electronic application. *Required:* high school transcript. *Required for some:* interview, interview, criminal background check and/or drug screening, physical standard minimum. *Application deadlines:* rolling (freshmen), rolling (transfers). *Notification:* continuous (freshmen), continuous (transfers).

**Admissions Office Contact** J. Sargeant Reynolds Community College, PO Box 85622, Richmond, VA 23285-5622.
*Website:* http://www.reynolds.edu/.

## Lord Fairfax Community College
### Middletown, Virginia

**Freshman Application Contact** Karen Bucher, Director of Enrollment Management, Lord Fairfax Community College, 173 Skirmisher Lane, Middletown, VA 22645. *Phone:* 540-868-7132. *Toll-free phone:* 800-906-LFCC. *Fax:* 540-868-7005. *E-mail:* kbucher@lfcc.edu. *Website:* http://www.lfcc.edu/.

## Mountain Empire Community College
### Big Stone Gap, Virginia

**Freshman Application Contact** Mountain Empire Community College, 3441 Mountain Empire Road, Big Stone Gap, VA 24219. *Phone:* 276-523-2400 Ext. 219. *Website:* http://www.mecc.edu/.

## New River Community College
### Dublin, Virginia

- **State-supported** 2-year, founded 1969, part of Virginia Community College System
- **Rural** 100-acre campus
- **Coed,** 4,400 undergraduate students

**Majors** Accounting; administrative assistant and secretarial science; architectural engineering technology; automobile/automotive mechanics technology; biological and physical sciences; business administration and management; child development; community organization and advocacy; computer engineering technology; computer graphics; criminal justice/law enforcement administration; criminal justice/police science; drafting and design technology; education; electrical, electronic and communications engineering technology; engineering; forensic science and technology; general studies; information science/studies; instrumentation technology; liberal arts and sciences/liberal studies; licensed practical/vocational nurse training; machine tool technology; marketing/marketing management; mental and social health services and allied professions related; registered nursing/registered nurse; welding technology.

**Academics** *Calendar:* semesters. *Degree:* certificates, diplomas, and associate. *Special study options:* academic remediation for entering students, adult/continuing education programs, advanced placement credit, cooperative education, distance learning, double majors, independent study, internships, part-time degree program, services for LD students, summer session for credit.

**Library** New River Community College Library plus 1 other.

**Student Life** *Housing:* college housing not available. *Activities and Organizations:* Phi Theta Kappa, Phi Beta Lambda, NRCC Computer Club. *Campus security:* 24-hour patrols. *Student services:* veterans affairs office.

**Athletics** *Intramural sports:* baseball M, basketball M/W, soccer M/W, softball W.

**Costs (2017–18)** *Tuition:* state resident $153 per credit hour part-time; nonresident $350 per credit hour part-time. Full-time tuition and fees vary according to course load and program. Part-time tuition and fees vary according to course load and program. *Payment plans:* installment, deferred payment. *Waivers:* senior citizens.

**Applying** *Options:* electronic application, early admission. *Required for some:* high school transcript. *Recommended:* high school transcript. *Application deadlines:* rolling (freshmen), rolling (transfers). *Notification:* continuous (freshmen), continuous (transfers).

**Freshman Application Contact** Mrs. Tammy L. Smith, Coordinator, Admissions and Records, New River Community College, 5251 College Drive, Dublin, VA 24084. *Phone:* 540-674-3600 Ext. 4203. *Toll-free phone:* 866-462-6722. *Fax:* 540-674-3644. *E-mail:* tsmith@nr.edu. *Website:* http://www.nr.edu/.

# Northern Virginia Community College
## Annandale, Virginia

**Freshman Application Contact** Northern Virginia Community College, 8333 Little River Turnpike, Annandale, VA 22003. *Phone:* 703-323-3195. *Website:* http://www.nvcc.edu/.

# Patrick Henry Community College
## Martinsville, Virginia

- **State-supported** 2-year, founded 1962, part of Virginia Community College System
- **Rural** 137-acre campus with easy access to Greensboro
- **Endowment** $10.6 million
- **Coed**

**Undergraduates** 1,214 full-time, 1,191 part-time. Students come from 6 states and territories; 1% are from out of state; 19% Black or African American, non-Hispanic/Latino; 7% Hispanic/Latino; 0.8% Asian, non-Hispanic/Latino; 0.1% American Indian or Alaska Native, non-Hispanic/Latino; 3% Two or more races, non-Hispanic/Latino; 0.3% Race/ethnicity unknown; 0.4% international. *Retention:* 65% of full-time freshmen returned.

**Faculty** *Student/faculty ratio:* 20:1.

**Academics** *Calendar:* semesters. *Degree:* certificates and associate. *Special study options:* academic remediation for entering students, adult/continuing education programs, advanced placement credit, cooperative education, distance learning, independent study, internships, part-time degree program, services for LD students, summer session for credit.

**Library** Lester Library. *Books:* 25,464 (physical), 197,427 (digital/electronic); *Serial titles:* 174 (physical), 73,546 (digital/electronic); *Databases:* 190.

**Student Life** *Campus security:* 24-hour emergency response devices and patrols, late-night transport/escort service.

**Athletics** Member NJCAA.

**Costs (2017–18)** *Tuition:* state resident $4608 full-time, $142 per credit hour part-time; nonresident $10,536 full-time, $318 per credit hour part-time. Full-time tuition and fees vary according to course load. Part-time tuition and fees vary according to course load. *Required fees:* $355 full-time. *Payment plans:* installment, deferred payment.

**Applying** *Options:* electronic application, early admission. *Required:* high school transcript.

**Freshman Application Contact** Mr. Travis Tisdale, Coordinator, Admissions and Records, Patrick Henry Community College, 645 Patriot Avenue, Martinsville, VA 24112. *Phone:* 276-656-0311. *Toll-free phone:* 800-232-7997. *Fax:* 276-656-0352. *Website:* http://www.patrickhenry.edu/.

# Paul D. Camp Community College
## Franklin, Virginia

**Freshman Application Contact** Mrs. Trina Jones, Dean Student Services, Paul D. Camp Community College, PO Box 737, 100 N. College Drive, Franklin, VA 23851. *Phone:* 757-569-6720. *E-mail:* tjones@pdc.edu. *Website:* http://www.pdc.edu/.

# Piedmont Virginia Community College
## Charlottesville, Virginia

- **State-supported** 2-year, founded 1972, part of Virginia Community College System
- **Suburban** 114-acre campus with easy access to Richmond
- **Endowment** $6.8 million
- **Coed,** 5,608 undergraduate students, 22% full-time, 58% women, 42% men

**Undergraduates** 1,257 full-time, 4,351 part-time. 13% Black or African American, non-Hispanic/Latino; 7% Hispanic/Latino; 5% Asian, non-Hispanic/Latino; 0.2% Native Hawaiian or other Pacific Islander, non-Hispanic/Latino; 0.3% American Indian or Alaska Native, non-Hispanic/Latino; 5% Two or more races, non-Hispanic/Latino; 1% Race/ethnicity unknown.

**Majors** Accounting; art; biotechnology; business administration and management; computer and information sciences; computer and information systems security; computer technology/computer systems technology; criminal justice/police science; culinary arts; diagnostic medical sonography and ultrasound technology; education; emergency medical technology (EMT paramedic); engineering; general studies; information technology; liberal arts and sciences and humanities related; management science; music; nursing science; radiologic technology/science; theater literature, history and criticism.

**Academics** *Calendar:* semesters. *Degree:* certificates and associate. *Special study options:* academic remediation for entering students, adult/continuing education programs, advanced placement credit, cooperative education, distance learning, English as a second language, honors programs, independent study, internships, part-time degree program, services for LD students, summer session for credit. *ROTC:* Army (c), Air Force (c).

**Library** Jessup Library.

**Student Life** *Housing:* college housing not available. *Activities and Organizations:* drama/theater group, student-run newspaper, choral group. *Campus security:* 24-hour emergency response devices and patrols, late-night transport/escort service, establishment of Campus Police. *Student services:* veterans affairs office.

**Athletics** *Intramural sports:* basketball M/W, golf M/W, soccer M/W, table tennis M/W, tennis M/W, ultimate Frisbee M/W, volleyball M/W, weight lifting M/W.

**Costs (2017–18)** *Tuition:* state resident $4163 full-time; nonresident $9461 full-time. Full-time tuition and fees vary according to course load. Part-time tuition and fees vary according to course load. *Required fees:* $395 full-time. *Payment plan:* installment. *Waivers:* senior citizens and employees or children of employees.

**Financial Aid** *Average indebtedness upon graduation:* $4127.

**Applying** *Options:* electronic application, early admission, deferred entrance. *Required for some:* high school transcript, prerequisite courses for nursing, practical nursing, radiography, sonography, surgical technology, emergency medical services, health information management, and patient admissions coordination. *Application deadlines:* rolling (freshmen), rolling (transfers). *Notification:* continuous (freshmen), continuous (transfers).

**Freshman Application Contact** Ms. Mary Lee Walsh, Dean of Student Services, Piedmont Virginia Community College, 501 College Drive, Charlottesville, VA 22902-7589. *Phone:* 434-961-6540. *Fax:* 434-961-5425. *E-mail:* mwalsh@pvcc.edu. *Website:* http://www.pvcc.edu/.

# Rappahannock Community College
## Glenns, Virginia

- **State and locally supported** 2-year, founded 1970, part of Virginia Community College System
- **Rural** campus
- **Coed,** 3,463 undergraduate students, 23% full-time, 62% women, 38% men

**Undergraduates** 793 full-time, 2,670 part-time.

**Majors** Accounting; administrative assistant and secretarial science; biological and physical sciences; business administration and management; business administration, management and operations related; criminal justice/law enforcement administration; criminal justice/police science; engineering technology; information science/studies; liberal arts and sciences/liberal studies; registered nursing/registered nurse.

**Academics** *Calendar:* semesters. *Degree:* certificates and associate. *Special study options:* academic remediation for entering students, adult/continuing education programs, distance learning, honors programs, internships, off-campus study, part-time degree program, services for LD students, summer session for credit.

**Student Life** *Student services:* personal/psychological counseling, veterans affairs office.

**Athletics** *Intercollegiate sports:* softball W.

Costs (2017–18) *Tuition:* state resident $4253 full-time, $142 per credit hour part-time; nonresident $9551 full-time, $318 per credit hour part-time. Full-time tuition and fees vary according to course load. Part-time tuition and fees vary according to course load. *Required fees:* $455 full-time, $15 per credit hour part-time. *Payment plan:* deferred payment. *Waivers:* senior citizens.

**Financial Aid** Of all full-time matriculated undergraduates who enrolled in 2016, 40 Federal Work-Study jobs (averaging $1015).

**Applying** *Options:* electronic application, early admission. *Application deadlines:* rolling (freshmen), rolling (transfers). *Notification:* continuous (freshmen), continuous (transfers).

**Freshman Application Contact** Ms. Felicia Packett, Admissions and Records Officer, Rappahannock Community College, 12745 College Drive, Glenns, VA 23149-0287. *Phone:* 804-758-6740. *Toll-free phone:* 800-836-9381. *Website:* http://www.rappahannock.edu/.

## Richard Bland College of The College of William and Mary

**Petersburg, Virginia**

**Freshman Application Contact** Office of Admissions, Richard Bland College of The College of William and Mary, 8311 Halifax Road, Petersburg, VA 23805. *Phone:* 804-862-6100 Ext. 6249. *E-mail:* apply@rbc.edu. *Website:* http://www.rbc.edu/.

## Riverside College of Health Careers

**Newport News, Virginia**

**Admissions Office Contact** Riverside College of Health Careers, 316 Main Street, Newport News, VA 23601. *Website:* http://www.riverside.edu/.

## Saint Michael College of Allied Health

**Alexandria, Virginia**

**Admissions Office Contact** Saint Michael College of Allied Health, 8305 Richmond Highway, Alexandria, VA 22309. *Website:* http://www.stmichaelcollegeva.edu/.

## Southside Regional Medical Center Professional Schools

**Colonial Heights, Virginia**

**Admissions Office Contact** Southside Regional Medical Center Professional Schools, 430 Clairmont Court, Suite 200, Colonial Heights, VA 23834. *Website:* http://www.srmconline.com/Southside-Regional-Medical-Center/nursingeducation.aspx.

## Southside Virginia Community College

**Alberta, Virginia**

**Freshman Application Contact** Mr. Brent Richey, Dean of Enrollment Management, Southside Virginia Community College, 109 Campus Drive, Alberta, VA 23821. *Phone:* 434-949-1012. *Fax:* 434-949-7863. *E-mail:* rhina.jones@sv.vccs.edu. *Website:* http://www.southside.edu/.

## Southwest Virginia Community College

**Richlands, Virginia**

- **State-supported** 2-year, founded 1968, part of Virginia Community College System
- **Rural** 100-acre campus
- **Endowment** $20.0 million
- **Coed,** 2,304 undergraduate students

**Undergraduates** Students come from 7 states and territories; 1 other country; 3% are from out of state; 3% Black or African American, non-Hispanic/Latino; 0.7% Hispanic/Latino; 0.4% Asian, non-Hispanic/Latino; 0.4% American Indian or Alaska Native, non-Hispanic/Latino; 1% Two or more races, non-Hispanic/Latino; 0.3% Race/ethnicity unknown. *Retention:* 55% of full-time freshmen returned.

**Faculty** *Total:* 110, 36% full-time. *Student/faculty ratio:* 24:1.

**Majors** Accounting related; business administration, management and operations related; business operations support and secretarial services related; child-care provision; computer and information sciences; criminal justice/law enforcement administration; electrical, electronic and communications engineering technology; emergency medical technology (EMT paramedic); liberal arts and sciences/liberal studies; mental and social health services and

allied professions related; radiologic technology/science; registered nursing/registered nurse.

**Academics** *Calendar:* semesters. *Degree:* certificates, diplomas, and associate. *Special study options:* academic remediation for entering students, accelerated degree program, adult/continuing education programs, advanced placement credit, distance learning, double majors, honors programs, internships, off-campus study, part-time degree program, summer session for credit.

**Library** Southwest Virginia Community College Library. *Books:* 42,207 (physical), 62,566 (digital/electronic); *Serial titles:* 275 (physical), 118,007 (digital/electronic); *Databases:* 118. Students can reserve study rooms.

**Student Life** *Housing:* college housing not available. *Activities and Organizations:* choral group, Phi Theta Kappa, Phi Beta Lambda, Intervoice, Helping Minds Club, Project ACHEIVE. *Campus security:* 24-hour emergency response devices and patrols, student patrols, extensive security camera system. *Student services:* personal/psychological counseling, veterans affairs office.

**Standardized Tests** *Required:* VCCS Math and English Assessments (for admission).

**Costs (2017–18)** *Tuition:* state resident $4253 full-time, $142 per credit hour part-time; nonresident $9551 full-time, $318 per credit hour part-time. Full-time tuition and fees vary according to reciprocity agreements. Part-time tuition and fees vary according to reciprocity agreements. *Required fees:* $338 full-time, $11 per credit hour part-time. *Payment plan:* installment. *Waivers:* senior citizens.

**Financial Aid** Of all full-time matriculated undergraduates who enrolled in 2016, 150 Federal Work-Study jobs (averaging $1140).

**Applying** *Options:* electronic application, early admission, deferred entrance. *Required:* high school transcript, interview. *Application deadlines:* rolling (freshmen), rolling (transfers).

**Freshman Application Contact** Ms. Dionne Cook, Admissions Counselor, Southwest Virginia Community College, Box SVCC, Richlands, VA 24641. *Phone:* 276-964-7301. *Toll-free phone:* 800-822-7822. *Fax:* 276-964-7716. *E-mail:* dionne.cook@sw.edu. *Website:* http://www.sw.edu/.

## Standard Healthcare Services, College of Nursing

**Falls Church, Virginia**

**Admissions Office Contact** Standard Healthcare Services, College of Nursing, 7704 Leesburg Pike, Suite 1000, Falls Church, VA 22043. *Website:* http://www.standardcollege.edu/.

## Thomas Nelson Community College

**Hampton, Virginia**

**Freshman Application Contact** Ms. Geraldine Newson, Senior Admission Specialist, Thomas Nelson Community College, PO Box 9407, Hampton, VA 23670-0407. *Phone:* 757-825-2800. *Fax:* 757-825-2763. *E-mail:* admissions@tncc.edu. *Website:* http://www.tncc.edu/.

## Tidewater Community College

**Norfolk, Virginia**

- **State-supported** 2-year, founded 1968, part of Virginia Community College System
- **Suburban** 520-acre campus
- **Endowment** $7.1 million
- **Coed,** 22,776 undergraduate students, 36% full-time, 59% women, 41% men

**Undergraduates** 8,198 full-time, 14,578 part-time. 16% are from out of state; 31% Black or African American, non-Hispanic/Latino; 9% Hispanic/Latino; 5% Asian, non-Hispanic/Latino; 0.7% Native Hawaiian or other Pacific Islander, non-Hispanic/Latino; 0.5% American Indian or Alaska Native, non-Hispanic/Latino; 6% Two or more races, non-Hispanic/Latino; 0.8% Race/ethnicity unknown; 0.6% international. *Retention:* 59% of full-time freshmen returned.

**Faculty** *Total:* 1,241, 27% full-time. *Student/faculty ratio:* 20:1.

**Majors** Accounting; administrative assistant and secretarial science; advertising; automobile/automotive mechanics technology; biological and physical sciences; business administration and management; civil engineering; commercial and advertising art; computer programming; drafting and design technology; education; electrical, electronic and communications engineering technology; engineering; finance; fine/studio arts; graphic design; horticultural science; information technology; interior design; kindergarten/preschool education; legal assistant/paralegal; liberal arts and sciences/liberal studies;

marketing/marketing management; music; real estate; registered nursing/registered nurse.

**Academics** *Calendar:* semesters. *Degree:* certificates and associate. *Special study options:* academic remediation for entering students, accelerated degree program, adult/continuing education programs, advanced placement credit, cooperative education, distance learning, English as a second language, honors programs, independent study, internships, off-campus study, part-time degree program, services for LD students, summer session for credit.

**Library** Main Library plus 5 others.

**Student Life** *Housing:* college housing not available. *Activities and Organizations:* drama/theater group, student-run newspaper. *Campus security:* 24-hour patrols. *Student services:* personal/psychological counseling, women's center.

**Athletics** *Intramural sports:* basketball M/W, soccer M, softball W, tennis M/W, volleyball W.

**Costs (2017–18)** *Tuition:* state resident $3450 full-time, $144 per credit hour part-time; nonresident $7688 full-time, $320 per credit hour part-time. *Required fees:* $896 full-time, $37 per credit hour part-time. *Payment plan:* installment. *Waivers:* senior citizens.

**Financial Aid** Of all full-time matriculated undergraduates who enrolled in 2016, 64 Federal Work-Study jobs (averaging $2000).

**Applying** *Options:* electronic application, early admission, deferred entrance. *Application deadlines:* rolling (freshmen), rolling (transfers). *Notification:* continuous (freshmen), continuous (transfers).

**Freshman Application Contact** Registrar, Tidewater Community College, Norfolk, VA 23510. *Phone:* 757-822-1900. *E-mail:* centralrecords@tcc.edu. *Website:* http://www.tcc.edu/.

## Virginia College in Richmond
### Richmond, Virginia

**Admissions Office Contact** Virginia College in Richmond, 7200 Midlothian Turnpike, Richmond, VA 23225. *Website:* http://www.vc.edu/.

## Virginia Highlands Community College
### Abingdon, Virginia

**Freshman Application Contact** Karen Cheers, Acting Director of Admissions, Records, and Financial Aid, Virginia Highlands Community College, PO Box 828, 100 VHCC Drive Abingdon, Abingdon, VA 24212. *Phone:* 276-739-2490. *Toll-free phone:* 877-207-6115. *E-mail:* kcheers@vhcc.edu. *Website:* http://www.vhcc.edu/.

## Virginia Western Community College
### Roanoke, Virginia

- **State-supported** 2-year, founded 1966, part of Virginia Community College System
- **Suburban** 70-acre campus
- **Coed**

**Undergraduates** 2,527 full-time, 6,105 part-time. Students come from 34 states and territories; 62 other countries; 2% are from out of state; 15% Black or African American, non-Hispanic/Latino; 3% Hispanic/Latino; 3% Asian, non-Hispanic/Latino; 0.1% Native Hawaiian or other Pacific Islander, non-Hispanic/Latino; 0.3% American Indian or Alaska Native, non-Hispanic/Latino; 3% Two or more races, non-Hispanic/Latino; 0.6% Race/ethnicity unknown; 0.3% international; 3% transferred in. *Retention:* 53% of full-time freshmen returned.

**Faculty** *Student/faculty ratio:* 34:1.

**Academics** *Calendar:* semesters. *Degree:* certificates and associate. *Special study options:* academic remediation for entering students, advanced placement credit, cooperative education, distance learning, double majors, English as a second language, honors programs, independent study, internships, part-time degree program, services for LD students, summer session for credit.

**Library** Brown Library.

**Student Life** *Campus security:* 24-hour emergency response devices and patrols, late-night transport/escort service.

**Costs (2017–18)** *Tuition:* state resident $4313 full-time, $144 per credit hour part-time; nonresident $9611 full-time, $320 per credit hour part-time. *Required fees:* $915 full-time, $30 per credit hour part-time.

**Applying** *Options:* electronic application, early admission, deferred entrance. *Required for some:* high school transcript. *Recommended:* high school transcript.

**Freshman Application Contact** Admissions Office, Virginia Western Community College, PO Box 14007, Roanoke, VA 24038. *Phone:* 540-857-7231. *Website:* http://www.virginiawestern.edu/.

## Wytheville Community College
### Wytheville, Virginia

- **State-supported** 2-year, founded 1963, part of Virginia Community College System
- **Rural** 141-acre campus
- **Coed,** 2,745 undergraduate students, 34% full-time, 61% women, 39% men

**Undergraduates** 940 full-time, 1,805 part-time. Students come from 9 states and territories; 2% are from out of state; 4% Black or African American, non-Hispanic/Latino; 2% Hispanic/Latino; 0.8% Asian, non-Hispanic/Latino; 0.1% Native Hawaiian or other Pacific Islander, non-Hispanic/Latino; 0.4% American Indian or Alaska Native, non-Hispanic/Latino; 4% Two or more races, non-Hispanic/Latino; 0.2% Race/ethnicity unknown. *Retention:* 62% of full-time freshmen returned.

**Faculty** *Total:* 137, 29% full-time. *Student/faculty ratio:* 23:1.

**Majors** Accounting; administrative assistant and secretarial science; biological and physical sciences; business administration and management; civil engineering technology; clinical/medical laboratory technology; corrections; criminal justice/law enforcement administration; criminal justice/police science; dental hygiene; drafting and design technology; education; electrical, electronic and communications engineering technology; information science/studies; liberal arts and sciences/liberal studies; machine tool technology; mass communication/media; mechanical engineering/mechanical technology; medical administrative assistant and medical secretary; physical therapy; registered nursing/registered nurse.

**Academics** *Calendar:* semesters. *Degree:* certificates, diplomas, and associate. *Special study options:* academic remediation for entering students, adult/continuing education programs, advanced placement credit, distance learning, external degree program, independent study, part-time degree program, services for LD students, summer session for credit.

**Library** Wytheville Community College Library. *Books:* 33,041 (physical), 51,770 (digital/electronic); *Serial titles:* 3,319 (physical), 3,418 (digital/electronic); *Databases:* 101. Students can reserve study rooms.

**Student Life** *Housing:* college housing not available. *Activities and Organizations:* drama/theater group. *Campus security:* 24-hour emergency response devices and patrols.

**Costs (2017–18)** *Tuition:* state resident $4253 full-time, $142 per credit hour part-time; nonresident $9551 full-time, $318 per credit hour part-time. *Required fees:* $360 full-time, $12 per credit hour part-time. *Waivers:* senior citizens.

**Financial Aid** Of all full-time matriculated undergraduates who enrolled in 2016, 125 Federal Work-Study jobs (averaging $2592).

**Applying** *Options:* electronic application, early admission. *Required:* high school transcript. *Required for some:* interview. *Application deadlines:* rolling (freshmen), rolling (transfers). *Notification:* continuous (freshmen), continuous (transfers).

**Freshman Application Contact** Wytheville Community College, 1000 East Main Street, Wytheville, VA 24382-3308. *Phone:* 276-223-4701. *Toll-free phone:* 800-468-1195. *Website:* http://www.wcc.vccs.edu/.

# WASHINGTON

## Bates Technical College
### Tacoma, Washington

**Director of Admissions** Director of Admissions, Bates Technical College, 1101 South Yakima Avenue, Tacoma, WA 98405-4895. *Phone:* 253-680-7000. *E-mail:* registration@bates.ctc.edu. *Website:* http://www.bates.ctc.edu/.

## Bellevue College
### Bellevue, Washington

**Freshman Application Contact** Morenika Jacobs, Associate Dean of Enrollment Services, Bellevue College, 3000 Landerholm Circle, SE, Bellevue, WA 98007-6484. *Phone:* 425-564-2205. *Fax:* 425-564-4065. *Website:* http://www.bcc.ctc.edu/.

## Bellingham Technical College
### Bellingham, Washington

**Freshman Application Contact** Bellingham Technical College, 3028 Lindbergh Avenue, Bellingham, WA 98225. *Phone:* 360-752-8324. *Website:* http://www.btc.edu/.

# Big Bend Community College
## Moses Lake, Washington

**Freshman Application Contact** Candis Lacher, Associate Vice President of Student Services, Big Bend Community College, 7662 Chanute Street NE, Moses Lake, WA 98837. *Phone:* 509-793-2061. *Toll-free phone:* 877-745-1212. *Fax:* 509-793-6243. *E-mail:* admissions@bigbend.edu. *Website:* http://www.bigbend.edu/.

# Carrington College–Spokane
## Spokane, Washington

- **Proprietary** 2-year, founded 1976, part of Carrington Colleges Group, Inc.
- **Coed**

**Undergraduates** 407 full-time. 18% are from out of state; 2% Black or African American, non-Hispanic/Latino; 12% Hispanic/Latino; 2% Asian, non-Hispanic/Latino; .5% Native Hawaiian or other Pacific Islander, non-Hispanic/Latino; 3% American Indian or Alaska Native, non-Hispanic/Latino; 4% Two or more races, non-Hispanic/Latino; .7% Race/ethnicity unknown; 19% transferred in.
**Faculty** *Student/faculty ratio:* 35:1.
**Academics** *Degree:* certificates and associate.
**Standardized Tests** *Required:* institutional entrance exam (for admission).
**Applying** *Required:* essay or personal statement, high school transcript, interview.
**Freshman Application Contact** Carrington College–Spokane, 10102 East Knox Avenue, Suite 200, Spokane, WA 99206. *Website:* http://www.carrington.edu/.

# Cascadia College
## Bothell, Washington

**Freshman Application Contact** Ms. Erin Blakeney, Dean for Student Success, Cascadia College, 18345 Campus Way, NE, Bothell, WA 98011. *Phone:* 425-352-8000. *Fax:* 425-352-8137. *E-mail:* admissions@cascadia.edu. *Website:* http://www.cascadia.edu/.

# Centralia College
## Centralia, Washington

**Freshman Application Contact** Admissions Office, Centralia College, Centralia, WA 98531. *Phone:* 360-736-9391 Ext. 221. *Fax:* 360-330-7503. *E-mail:* admissions@centralia.edu. *Website:* http://www.centralia.edu/.

# Clark College
## Vancouver, Washington

- **State-supported** primarily 2-year, founded 1933, part of Washington State Board for Community and Technical Colleges
- **Urban** 101-acre campus with easy access to Portland
- **Endowment** $61.0 million
- **Coed,** 10,477 undergraduate students, 48% full-time, 57% women, 43% men

**Undergraduates** 5,035 full-time, 5,442 part-time. 4% are from out of state; 2% Black or African American, non-Hispanic/Latino; 9% Hispanic/Latino; 4% Asian, non-Hispanic/Latino; 0.1% Native Hawaiian or other Pacific Islander, non-Hispanic/Latino; 0.6% American Indian or Alaska Native, non-Hispanic/Latino; 8% Two or more races, non-Hispanic/Latino; 6% Race/ethnicity unknown; 1% international; 3% transferred in.
**Freshmen** *Admission:* 1,349 applied; 1,349 admitted; 1,215 enrolled.
**Faculty** *Student/faculty ratio:* 24:1.
**Majors** Accounting technology and bookkeeping; automobile/automotive mechanics technology; baking and pastry arts; business administration and management; business automation/technology/data entry; computer programming; computer systems networking and telecommunications; culinary arts; data entry/microcomputer applications; dental hygiene; diesel mechanics technology; early childhood education; electrical, electronic and communications engineering technology; emergency medical technology (EMT paramedic); executive assistant/executive secretary; graphic communications; human resources management; liberal arts and sciences/liberal studies; machine tool technology; manufacturing engineering technology; medical administrative assistant and medical secretary; medical/clinical assistant; registered nursing/registered nurse; retailing; selling skills and sales; substance abuse/addiction counseling; surveying technology; telecommunications technology; web/multimedia management and webmaster; welding technology.

**Academics** *Calendar:* quarters. *Degrees:* certificates, diplomas, associate, and bachelor's. *Special study options:* academic remediation for entering students, adult/continuing education programs, cooperative education, distance learning, English as a second language, honors programs, internships, part-time degree program, services for LD students, summer session for credit. *ROTC:* Army (c), Air Force (c).
**Library** Lewis D. Cannell Library. Students can reserve study rooms.
**Student Life** *Housing:* college housing not available. *Activities and Organizations:* drama/theater group, student-run newspaper, choral group. *Campus security:* 24-hour patrols, late-night transport/escort service, security staff during hours of operation. *Student services:* health clinic, personal/psychological counseling, legal services, veterans affairs office.
**Athletics** *Intercollegiate sports:* baseball M, basketball M(s)/W(s), cross-country running M(s)/W(s), fencing M(c)/W(c), soccer M(s)/W(s), softball W, track and field M(s)/W(s), volleyball W(s). *Intramural sports:* basketball M/W, fencing M/W, soccer M/W, softball M/W, volleyball M/W.
**Costs (2017–18)** *Tuition:* area resident $4121 full-time, $109 per credit hour part-time; state resident $5543 full-time, $155 per credit hour part-time; nonresident $9539 full-time, $286 per credit hour part-time. Full-time tuition and fees vary according to course level, course load, degree level, program, and reciprocity agreements. Part-time tuition and fees vary according to course level, course load, degree level, program, and reciprocity agreements. *Payment plan:* installment. *Waivers:* senior citizens and employees or children of employees.
**Applying** *Options:* electronic application, early admission, deferred entrance. *Application fee:* $25.
**Freshman Application Contact** Ms. Vanessa Watkins, Associate Director of Entry Services, Clark College, Vancouver, WA 98663. *Phone:* 360-992-2308. *Fax:* 360-992-2867. *E-mail:* admissions@clark.edu. *Website:* http://www.clark.edu/.

# Clover Park Technical College
## Lakewood, Washington

**Director of Admissions** Ms. Judy Richardson, Registrar, Clover Park Technical College, 4500 Steilacoom Boulevard, SW, Lakewood, WA 98499. *Phone:* 253-589-5570. *Website:* http://www.cptc.edu/.

# Columbia Basin College
## Pasco, Washington

**Freshman Application Contact** Admissions Department, Columbia Basin College, 2600 North 20th Avenue, Pasco, WA 99301-3397. *Phone:* 509-542-4524. *Fax:* 509-544-2023. *E-mail:* admissions@columbiabasin.edu. *Website:* http://www.columbiabasin.edu/.

# Edmonds Community College
## Lynnwood, Washington

**Freshman Application Contact** Ms. Nancy Froemming, Enrollment Services Office Manager, Edmonds Community College, 20000 68th Avenue West, Lynnwood, WA 98036-5999. *Phone:* 425-640-1853. *Fax:* 425-640-1159. *E-mail:* nanci.froemming@edcc.edu. *Website:* http://www.edcc.edu/.

# Everett Community College
## Everett, Washington

**Freshman Application Contact** Ms. Linda Baca, Entry Services Manager, Everett Community College, 2000 Tower Street, Everett, WA 98201-1327. *Phone:* 425-388-9219. *Fax:* 425-388-9173. *E-mail:* admissions@everettcc.edu. *Website:* http://www.everettcc.edu/.

# Grays Harbor College
## Aberdeen, Washington

**Freshman Application Contact** Ms. Brenda Dell, Admissions Officer, Grays Harbor College, 1620 Edward P. Smith Drive, Aberdeen, WA 98520. *Phone:* 360-532-4216. *Toll-free phone:* 800-562-4830. *Website:* http://www.ghc.edu/.

# Green River College
## Auburn, Washington

**Freshman Application Contact** Ms. Peggy Morgan, Program Support Supervisor, Green River College, 12401 Southeast 320th Street, Auburn, WA 98092-3699. *Phone:* 253-833-9111. *Fax:* 253-288-3454. *Website:* http://www.greenriver.edu/.

# Highline College
## Des Moines, Washington

Freshman Application Contact Ms. Michelle Kuwasaki, Director of Admissions, Highline College, 2400 South 240th Street, Des Moines, WA 98198-9800. *Phone:* 206-878-3710 Ext. 9800. *Website:* http://www.highline.edu/.

# Lake Washington Institute of Technology
## Kirkland, Washington

Freshman Application Contact Shawn Miller, Registrar, Enrollment Services, Lake Washington Institute of Technology, 11605 132nd Avenue NE, Kirkland, WA 98034-8506. *Phone:* 425-739-8104. *E-mail:* info@lwtc.edu. *Website:* http://www.lwtech.edu/.

# Lower Columbia College
## Longview, Washington

Freshman Application Contact Ms. Nichole Seroshek, Director of Registration, Lower Columbia College, 1600 Maple Street, Longview, WA 98632. *Phone:* 360-442-2372. *Toll-free phone:* 866-900-2311. *Fax:* 360-442-2379. *E-mail:* registration@lowercolumbia.edu. *Website:* http://www.lowercolumbia.edu/.

# North Seattle College
## Seattle, Washington

Freshman Application Contact Ms. Betsy Abts, Registrar, North Seattle College, Seattle, WA 98103-3599. *Phone:* 206-934-3663. *Fax:* 206-934-3671. *E-mail:* arrc@seattlecolleges.edu. *Website:* http://www.northseattle.edu/.

# Northwest Indian College
## Bellingham, Washington

Freshman Application Contact Office of Admissions, Northwest Indian College, 2522 Kwina Road, Bellingham, WA 98226. *Phone:* 360-676-2772. *Toll-free phone:* 866-676-2772. *Fax:* 360-392-4333. *E-mail:* admissions@nwic.edu. *Website:* http://www.nwic.edu/.

# Northwest School of Wooden Boatbuilding
## Port Hadlock, Washington

- **Independent** 2-year, founded 1980
- **Small-town** 6-acre campus
- **Coed**

**Undergraduates** Students come from 20 states and territories; 3 other countries; 59% are from out of state.
**Faculty** *Student/faculty ratio:* 12:1.
**Academics** *Calendar:* quarters. *Degree:* diplomas and associate.
**Library** School Library.
**Costs (2017–18)** *Tuition:* $19,400 full-time. No tuition increase for student's term of enrollment. *Required fees:* $100 full-time.
**Applying** *Options:* electronic application. *Required:* essay or personal statement, high school transcript.
**Freshman Application Contact** Northwest School of Wooden Boatbuilding, 42 North Water Street, Port Hadlock, WA 98339. *Phone:* 360-385-4948 Ext. 305. *Website:* http://www.nwswb.edu/.

# Olympic College
## Bremerton, Washington

- **State-supported** primarily 2-year, founded 1946, part of Washington State Board for Community and Technical Colleges
- **Suburban** 33-acre campus with easy access to Seattle, Tacoma
- **Coed**

**Undergraduates** 5% Black or African American, non-Hispanic/Latino; 8% Hispanic/Latino; 10% Asian, non-Hispanic/Latino; 2% American Indian or Alaska Native, non-Hispanic/Latino; 2% international; 1% live on campus.
**Academics** *Calendar:* quarters. *Degrees:* certificates, diplomas, associate, and bachelor's. *Special study options:* academic remediation for entering students, adult/continuing education programs, advanced placement credit, cooperative education, distance learning, English as a second language, independent study, internships, off-campus study, part-time degree program, services for LD students, study abroad, summer session for credit.
**Library** Haselwood Library plus 1 other. Students can reserve study rooms.
**Student Life** *Campus security:* 24-hour emergency response devices and patrols, student patrols, late-night transport/escort service.
**Financial Aid** Of all full-time matriculated undergraduates who enrolled in 2016, 105 Federal Work-Study jobs (averaging $2380). 31 state and other part-time jobs (averaging $2880).
**Applying** *Options:* electronic application. *Required for some:* essay or personal statement, high school transcript, 2 letters of recommendation.
**Freshman Application Contact** Ms. Nora Downard, Program Manager, Olympic College, 1600 Chester Avenue, Bremerton, WA 98337-1699. *Phone:* 360-475-7445. *Toll-free phone:* 800-259-6718. *Fax:* 360-475-7202. *E-mail:* ndownard@olympic.edu. *Website:* http://www.olympic.edu/.

# Peninsula College
## Port Angeles, Washington

Freshman Application Contact Ms. Pauline Marvin, Peninsula College, 1502 East Lauridsen Boulevard, Port Angeles, WA 98362. *Phone:* 360-417-6596. *Toll-free phone:* 877-452-9277. *Fax:* 360-457-8100. *E-mail:* admissions@pencol.edu. *Website:* http://www.pc.ctc.edu/.

# Pierce College Fort Steilacoom
## Lakewood, Washington

Freshman Application Contact Admissions Office, Pierce College Fort Steilacoom, 9401 Farwest Drive SW, Lakewood, WA 98498. *Phone:* 253-964-6501. *E-mail:* admiss1@pierce.ctc.edu. *Website:* http://www.pierce.ctc.edu/.

# Pierce College Puyallup
## Puyallup, Washington

Freshman Application Contact Pierce College Puyallup, 1601 39th Avenue Southeast, Puyallup, WA 98374. *Phone:* 253-840-8400. *Website:* http://www.pierce.ctc.edu/.

# Pima Medical Institute
## Renton, Washington

Freshman Application Contact Pima Medical Institute, 555 South Renton Village Place, Renton, WA 98057. *Phone:* 425-228-9600. *Toll-free phone:* 800-477-PIMA. *Website:* http://www.pmi.edu/.

# Pima Medical Institute
## Seattle, Washington

Freshman Application Contact Admissions Office, Pima Medical Institute, 9709 Third Avenue NE, Suite 400, Seattle, WA 98115. *Phone:* 206-322-6100. *Toll-free phone:* 800-477-PIMA. *Website:* http://www.pmi.edu/.

# Renton Technical College
## Renton, Washington

- **State-supported** primarily 2-year, founded 1942, part of Washington State Board for Community and Technical Colleges
- **Suburban** 30-acre campus with easy access to Seattle
- **Endowment** $837,103
- **Coed,** 3,763 undergraduate students, 38% full-time, 31% women, 69% men

**Undergraduates** 1,420 full-time, 2,343 part-time. Students come from 22 states and territories; 0.1% are from out of state; 14% Black or African American, non-Hispanic/Latino; 12% Hispanic/Latino; 21% Asian, non-Hispanic/Latino; 0.9% Native Hawaiian or other Pacific Islander, non-Hispanic/Latino; 0.3% American Indian or Alaska Native, non-Hispanic/Latino; 6% Two or more races, non-Hispanic/Latino; 7% Race/ethnicity unknown; 0.5% international; 16% transferred in.
**Freshmen** *Admission:* 174 enrolled.
**Faculty** *Total:* 242, 29% full-time. *Student/faculty ratio:* 16:1.
**Majors** Accounting and business/management; anesthesiologist assistant; appliance installation and repair technology; autobody/collision and repair technology; automobile/automotive mechanics technology; building/property maintenance; business automation/technology/data entry; civil drafting and CAD/CADD; computer science; computer systems networking and telecommunications; construction management; culinary arts; dental assisting; drafting and design technology; early childhood education; heating, air conditioning, ventilation and refrigeration maintenance technology; industrial

mechanics and maintenance technology; legal administrative assistant/secretary; machine tool technology; massage therapy; medical administrative assistant and medical secretary; medical/clinical assistant; medical insurance coding; musical instrument fabrication and repair; office management; ophthalmic technology; pharmacy technician; registered nursing/registered nurse; surgical technology; surveying technology; welding technology.

**Academics** *Calendar:* quarters. *Degrees:* certificates, diplomas, associate, and bachelor's. *Special study options:* academic remediation for entering students, adult/continuing education programs, advanced placement credit, cooperative education, distance learning, English as a second language, internships, off-campus study, part-time degree program, services for LD students, summer session for credit.

**Library** Renton Technical College Library.

**Student Life** *Housing:* college housing not available. *Campus security:* patrols by security, security system. *Student services:* personal/psychological counseling, veterans affairs office.

**Standardized Tests** *Required for some:* ACT ASSET, CLEP, ACCUPLACER, DSP.

**Costs (2018–19)** *Tuition:* state resident $4836 full-time. Full-time tuition and fees vary according to course load, degree level, and program. Part-time tuition and fees vary according to course load, degree level, and program. *Payment plan:* installment. *Waivers:* employees or children of employees.

**Applying** *Options:* electronic application, early admission. *Application fee:* $30. *Required for some:* essay or personal statement, high school transcript, interview. *Application deadlines:* rolling (freshmen), rolling (transfers). *Notification:* continuous (freshmen), continuous (transfers).

**Admissions Office Contact** Renton Technical College, 3000 NE Fourth Street, Renton, WA 98056. *Website:* http://www.rtc.edu/.

## Seattle Central College
### Seattle, Washington

**Freshman Application Contact** Admissions Office, Seattle Central College, 1701 Broadway, Seattle, WA 98122-2400. *Phone:* 206-587-5450. *Website:* http://www.seattlecentral.edu/.

## Shoreline Community College
### Shoreline, Washington

**Freshman Application Contact** Shoreline Community College, 16101 Greenwood Avenue North, Shoreline, WA 98133-5696. *Phone:* 206-546-4613. *Website:* http://www.shoreline.edu/.

## Skagit Valley College
### Mount Vernon, Washington

**Freshman Application Contact** Ms. Karen Marie Bade, Admissions and Recruitment Coordinator, Skagit Valley College, 2405 College Way, Mount Vernon, WA 98273-5899. *Phone:* 360-416-7620. *E-mail:* karenmarie.bade@skagit.edu. *Website:* http://www.skagit.edu/.

## South Puget Sound Community College
### Olympia, Washington

**Freshman Application Contact** Ms. Heidi Dearborn, South Puget Sound Community College, 2011 Mottman Road, SW, Olympia, WA 98512-6292. *Phone:* 360-754-7711 Ext. 5358. *E-mail:* hdearborn@spcc.edu. *Website:* http://www.spscc.edu/.

## South Seattle College
### Seattle, Washington

**Director of Admissions** Ms. Kim Manderbach, Dean of Student Services/Registration, South Seattle College, 6000 16th Avenue, SW, Seattle, WA 98106-1499. *Phone:* 206-764-5378. *Fax:* 206-764-7947. *E-mail:* kimmanderb@sccd.ctc.edu. *Website:* http://southseattle.edu/.

## Spokane Community College
### Spokane, Washington

**Freshman Application Contact** Ann Hightower-Chavez, Researcher, District Institutional Research, Spokane Community College, Spokane, WA 99217-5399. *Phone:* 509-434-5242. *Toll-free phone:* 800-248-5644. *Fax:* 509-434-5249. *E-mail:* mlee@ccs.spokane.edu. *Website:* http://www.scc.spokane.edu/.

## Spokane Falls Community College
### Spokane, Washington

**Freshman Application Contact** Admissions Office, Spokane Falls Community College, Admissions MS 3011, 3410 West Fort George Wright Drive, Spokane, WA 99224. *Phone:* 509-533-3401. *Toll-free phone:* 888-509-7944. *Fax:* 509-533-3852. *Website:* http://www.spokanefalls.edu/.

## Tacoma Community College
### Tacoma, Washington

**Freshman Application Contact** Enrollment Services, Tacoma Community College, 6501 South 19th Street, Tacoma, WA 98466. *Phone:* 253-566-5325. *Fax:* 253-566-6034. *Website:* http://www.tacomacc.edu/.

## Walla Walla Community College
### Walla Walla, Washington

**Freshman Application Contact** Walla Walla Community College, 500 Tausick Way, Walla Walla, WA 99362-9267. *Phone:* 509-522-2500. *Toll-free phone:* 877-992-9922. *Website:* http://www.wwcc.edu/.

## Wenatchee Valley College
### Wenatchee, Washington

**Freshman Application Contact** Wenatchee Valley College, 1300 Fifth Street, Wenatchee, WA 98801-1799. *Phone:* 509-682-6835. *Toll-free phone:* 877-982-4968. *Website:* http://www.wvc.edu/.

## Whatcom Community College
### Bellingham, Washington

**Freshman Application Contact** Entry and Advising Center, Whatcom Community College, 237 West Kellogg Road, Bellingham, WA 98226-8003. *Phone:* 360-676-2170. *Fax:* 360-676-2171. *E-mail:* admit@whatcom.ctc.edu. *Website:* http://www.whatcom.ctc.edu/.

## Yakima Valley Community College
### Yakima, Washington

**Freshman Application Contact** Ms. Denise Anderson, Registrar and Director for Enrollment Services, Yakima Valley Community College, PO Box 1647, Yakima, WA 98907-1647. *Phone:* 509-574-4702. *Fax:* 509-574-6879. *E-mail:* admis@yvcc.edu. *Website:* http://www.yvcc.edu/.

# WEST VIRGINIA

## Blue Ridge Community and Technical College
### Martinsburg, West Virginia

- **State-supported** 2-year, founded 1974, part of Community and Technical College System of West Virginia
- **Small-town** 46-acre campus
- **Coed,** 5,708 undergraduate students, 17% full-time, 64% women, 36% men

**Undergraduates** 996 full-time, 4,712 part-time. 11% are from out of state; 6% Black or African American, non-Hispanic/Latino; 3% Hispanic/Latino; 2% Asian, non-Hispanic/Latino; 0.3% Native Hawaiian or other Pacific Islander, non-Hispanic/Latino; 0.4% American Indian or Alaska Native, non-Hispanic/Latino; 2% Two or more races, non-Hispanic/Latino; 0.2% Race/ethnicity unknown; 4% transferred in. *Retention:* 51% of full-time freshmen returned.

**Freshmen** *Admission:* 350 enrolled.

**Faculty** *Total:* 205, 37% full-time, 12% with terminal degrees. *Student/faculty ratio:* 22:1.

**Majors** Accounting; allied health and medical assisting services related; automation engineer technology; baking and pastry arts; business administration and management; business administration, management and operations related; clinical/medical laboratory technology; computer and information systems security; criminal justice/safety; culinary arts; data entry/microcomputer applications related; electrical and electronic engineering technologies related; emergency medical technology (EMT paramedic); general studies; information technology; legal assistant/paralegal; liberal arts and sciences/liberal studies; medical/clinical assistant; multi/interdisciplinary studies related; operations management; physical therapy technology; registered nursing/registered nurse; restaurant, culinary, and catering management; science technologies related; system, networking, and LAN/WAN management.

**Academics** *Calendar:* semesters. *Degree:* certificates and associate. *Special study options:* academic remediation for entering students, accelerated degree program, adult/continuing education programs, advanced placement credit, double majors, English as a second language, independent study, internships, part-time degree program, services for LD students.

**Student Life** *Housing:* college housing not available. *Activities and Organizations:* drama/theater group, Student Leadership Academy, Drama Club, Phi Theta Kappa, Phi Beta Lambda, Student Nurses Association. *Campus security:* late-night transport/escort service. *Student services:* personal/psychological counseling.

**Standardized Tests** *Recommended:* SAT and SAT Subject Tests or ACT (for admission).

**Costs (2017–18)** *Tuition:* state resident $4032 full-time, $168 per credit hour part-time; nonresident $7296 full-time, $304 per credit hour part-time. Full-time tuition and fees vary according to class time and course load. Part-time tuition and fees vary according to class time and course load. *Payment plan:* installment. *Waivers:* employees or children of employees.

**Applying** *Options:* electronic application, deferred entrance. *Application fee:* $25. *Required:* high school transcript. *Required for some:* interview.

**Freshman Application Contact** Brenda K. Neal, Dean of Students, Blue Ridge Community and Technical College, 13650 Apple Harvest Drive, Martinsburg, WV 25403. *Phone:* 304-260-4380 Ext. 2109. *Fax:* 304-260-4376. *E-mail:* bneal@blueridgectc.edu. *Website:* http://www.blueridgectc.edu/.

## BridgeValley Community and Technical College
### Montgomery, West Virginia

**Director of Admissions** Ms. Lisa Graham, Director of Admissions, BridgeValley Community and Technical College, 619 2nd Avenue, Montgomery, WV 25136. *Phone:* 304-442-3167. *Website:* http://www.bridgevalley.edu/.

## BridgeValley Community and Technical College
### South Charleston, West Virginia

**Freshman Application Contact** Mr. Bryce Casto, Vice President, Student Affairs, BridgeValley Community and Technical College, 2001 Union Carbide Drive, South Charleston, WV 25303. *Phone:* 304-766-3140. *Fax:* 304-766-4158. *E-mail:* castosb@wvstateu.edu. *Website:* http://www.bridgevalley.edu/.

## Eastern West Virginia Community and Technical College
### Moorefield, West Virginia

**Freshman Application Contact** Learner Support Services, Eastern West Virginia Community and Technical College, HC 65 Box 402, Moorefield, WV 26836. *Phone:* 304-434-8000. *Toll-free phone:* 877-982-2322. *Fax:* 304-434-7000. *E-mail:* askeast@eastern.wvnet.edu. *Website:* http://www.eastern.wvnet.edu/.

## Huntington Junior College
### Huntington, West Virginia

**Director of Admissions** Mr. James Garrett, Educational Services Director, Huntington Junior College, 900 Fifth Avenue, Huntington, WV 25701-2004. *Phone:* 304-697-7550. *Toll-free phone:* 800-344-4522. *Website:* http://www.huntingtonjuniorcollege.com/.

## Martinsburg College
### Martinsburg, West Virginia

**Admissions Office Contact** Martinsburg College, 341 Aikens Center, Martinsburg, WV 25404. *Website:* http://www.martinsburgcollege.edu/.

## Mountain State College
### Parkersburg, West Virginia

**Freshman Application Contact** Ms. Judith Sutton, President, Mountain State College, 1508 Spring Street, Parkersburg, WV 26101-3993. *Phone:* 304-485-5487. *Toll-free phone:* 800-841-0201. *Fax:* 304-485-3524. *E-mail:* jsutton@msc.edu. *Website:* http://www.msc.edu/.

## Mountwest Community & Technical College
### Huntington, West Virginia

**Freshman Application Contact** Dr. Tammy Johnson, Admissions Director, Mountwest Community & Technical College, 1 John Marshall Drive, Huntington, WV 25755. *Phone:* 304-696-3160. *Toll-free phone:* 866-676-5533. *Fax:* 304-696-3135. *E-mail:* admissions@marshall.edu. *Website:* http://www.mctc.edu/.

## New River Community and Technical College
### Beaver, West Virginia

**Director of Admissions** Dr. Allen B. Withers, Vice President, Student Services, New River Community and Technical College, 280 University Drive, Beaver, WV 25813. *Phone:* 304-929-5011. *Toll-free phone:* 866-349-3739. *E-mail:* awithers@newriver.edu. *Website:* http://www.newriver.edu/.

## Pierpont Community & Technical College
### Fairmont, West Virginia

**Freshman Application Contact** Mr. Steve Leadman, Director of Admissions and Recruiting, Pierpont Community & Technical College, 1201 Locust Avenue, Fairmont, WV 26554. *Phone:* 304-367-4892. *Toll-free phone:* 800-641-5678. *Fax:* 304-367-4789. *Website:* http://www.pierpont.edu/.

## Potomac State College of West Virginia University
### Keyser, West Virginia

- **State-supported** primarily 2-year, founded 1901, part of West Virginia Higher Education Policy Commission
- **Small-town** 18-acre campus
- **Coed,** 1,475 undergraduate students, 78% full-time, 54% women, 46% men

**Undergraduates** 1,156 full-time, 319 part-time. Students come from 24 states and territories; 2 other countries; 37% are from out of state; 21% Black or African American, non-Hispanic/Latino; 3% Hispanic/Latino; 0.2% Asian, non-Hispanic/Latino; 0.2% Native Hawaiian or other Pacific Islander, non-Hispanic/Latino; 0.5% American Indian or Alaska Native, non-Hispanic/Latino; 4% Two or more races, non-Hispanic/Latino; 1% Race/ethnicity unknown; 0.6% international; 3% transferred in; 52% live on campus. *Retention:* 44% of full-time freshmen returned.

**Freshmen** *Admission:* 2,582 applied, 1,241 admitted, 588 enrolled. *Average high school GPA:* 2.9. *Test scores:* ACT scores over 18: 60%; ACT scores over 24: 19%; ACT scores over 30: 1%.

**Faculty** *Total:* 85, 53% full-time, 16% with terminal degrees. *Student/faculty ratio:* 22:1.

**Majors** Administrative assistant and secretarial science; agricultural and extension education; agricultural business and management; agriculture; agriculture and agriculture operations related; agronomy and crop science; animal sciences; biology/biological sciences; business administration and management; business automation/technology/data entry; chemistry; civil engineering; communication; computer and information sciences; criminal justice/safety; criminology; data entry/microcomputer applications related; early childhood education; economics; electrical and electronics engineering; elementary education; English; forensic science and technology; forest resources production and management; geological and earth sciences/geosciences related; geology/earth science; history; horse husbandry/equine science and management; horticultural science; hospitality administration; journalism; liberal arts and sciences/liberal studies; mathematics; mechanical engineering; medical/clinical assistant; modern languages; parks, recreation and leisure facilities management; physical education teaching and coaching; physics; political science and government; pre-dentistry studies; pre-law studies; premedical studies; prenursing studies; pre-occupational therapy; pre-pharmacy studies; pre-physical therapy; pre-

veterinary studies; psychology; secondary education; social work; sociology; wildlife, fish and wildlands science and management; wood science and wood products/pulp and paper technology.
**Academics** *Calendar:* semesters. *Degrees:* associate and bachelor's. *Special study options:* academic remediation for entering students, adult/continuing education programs, advanced placement credit, cooperative education, distance learning, double majors, honors programs, independent study, internships, part-time degree program, services for LD students, study abroad, summer session for credit.
**Library** Mary F. Shipper Library.
**Student Life** *Housing:* on-campus residence required through sophomore year. *Options:* coed. Campus housing is university owned. Freshman applicants given priority for college housing. *Activities and Organizations:* drama/theater group, student-run newspaper, choral group, Agriculture and Forestry Club, Black Student Alliance, Gamers and Geeks Club, Campus and Community Ministries. *Campus security:* 24-hour patrols, late-night transport/escort service, controlled dormitory access. *Student services:* health clinic, personal/psychological counseling, veterans affairs office.
**Athletics** Member NJCAA. *Intercollegiate sports:* baseball M(s), basketball M(s)/W(s), cross-country running M(s)/W(s), lacrosse M(s)/W(s), soccer M/W, softball W(s), volleyball W(s). *Intramural sports:* basketball M/W, football M/W, soccer M/W, softball M/W, table tennis M/W, ultimate Frisbee M/W, volleyball M/W.
**Standardized Tests** *Recommended:* SAT or ACT (for admission).
**Financial Aid** Of all full-time matriculated undergraduates who enrolled in 2016, 949 applied for aid, 779 were judged to have need, 76 had their need fully met. In 2016, 49 non-need-based awards were made. *Average financial aid package:* $7048. *Average need-based loan:* $4663. *Average need-based gift aid:* $5295. *Average non-need-based aid:* $1456. *Average indebtedness upon graduation:* $19,002.
**Applying** *Options:* electronic application. *Required:* high school transcript. *Application deadlines:* rolling (freshmen), rolling (transfers).
**Freshman Application Contact** Ms. Beth Little, Director of Enrollment Services, Potomac State College of West Virginia University, 75 Arnold Street, Keyser, WV 26726. *Phone:* 304-788-6820. *Toll-free phone:* 800-262-7332 Ext. 6820. *Fax:* 304-788-6939. *E-mail:* go2psc@mail.wvu.edu. *Website:* http://www.potomacstatecollege.edu/.

## Southern West Virginia Community and Technical College
### Mount Gay, West Virginia

**Freshman Application Contact** Mr. Roy Simmons, Registrar, Southern West Virginia Community and Technical College, PO Box 2900, Mt. Gay, WV 25637. *Phone:* 304-792-7160 Ext. 120. *Fax:* 304-792-7096. *E-mail:* admissions@southern.wvnet.edu. *Website:* http://southernwv.edu/.

## West Virginia Junior College–Bridgeport
### Bridgeport, West Virginia

- **Proprietary** 2-year, founded 1922
- **Small-town** 3-acre campus
- **Coed**

**Undergraduates** 150 full-time. Students come from 4 states and territories; 7% transferred in. *Retention:* 80% of full-time freshmen returned.
**Faculty** *Student/faculty ratio:* 15:1.
**Academics** *Calendar:* quarters. *Degree:* diplomas and associate. *Special study options:* academic remediation for entering students, cooperative education, distance learning, independent study, internships, services for LD students, summer session for credit.
**Library** WVJC Library plus 1 other. *Books:* 350 (physical), 15 (digital/electronic); *Serial titles:* 12 (physical); *Databases:* 5. Weekly public service hours: 50.
**Student Life** *Campus security:* 24-hour emergency response devices.
**Financial Aid** Of all full-time matriculated undergraduates who enrolled in 2016, 10 Federal Work-Study jobs.
**Applying** *Options:* electronic application. *Application fee:* $25. *Required:* minimum 2.5 GPA, interview, meeting with an Admissions Representative. *Required for some:* essay or personal statement, 1 letter of recommendation. *Recommended:* high school transcript.
**Freshman Application Contact** Ms. Kristen Kirk, High School Admissions Representative, West Virginia Junior College–Bridgeport, 176 Thompson Drive, Bridgeport, WV 26330. *Phone:* 304-842-4007. *Toll-free phone:* 800-470-5627. *Fax:* 304-842-8191. *E-mail:* kkirk@wvjc.edu. *Website:* http://www.wvjc.edu/.

## West Virginia Junior College–Charleston
### Charleston, West Virginia

**Freshman Application Contact** West Virginia Junior College–Charleston, 1000 Virginia Street East, Charleston, WV 25301-2817. *Phone:* 304-345-2820. *Toll-free phone:* 800-924-5208. *Website:* http://www.wvjc.edu/.

## West Virginia Junior College–Morgantown
### Morgantown, West Virginia

**Freshman Application Contact** Admissions Office, West Virginia Junior College–Morgantown, 148 Willey Street, Morgantown, WV 26505-5521. *Phone:* 304-296-8282. *Website:* http://www.wvjcmorgantown.edu/.

## West Virginia Northern Community College
### Wheeling, West Virginia

**Freshman Application Contact** Mrs. Janet Fike, Vice President of Student Services, West Virginia Northern Community College, 1704 Market Street, Wheeling, WV 26003. *Phone:* 304-214-8837. *E-mail:* jfike@northern.wvnet.edu. *Website:* http://www.wvncc.edu/.

## West Virginia University at Parkersburg
### Parkersburg, West Virginia

**Freshman Application Contact** Christine Post, Associate Dean of Enrollment Management, West Virginia University at Parkersburg, 300 Campus Drive, Parkersburg, WV 26104. *Phone:* 304-424-8223 Ext. 223. *Toll-free phone:* 800-WVA-WVUP. *Fax:* 304-424-8332. *E-mail:* christine.post@mail.wvu.edu. *Website:* http://www.wvup.edu/.

# WISCONSIN

## Blackhawk Technical College
### Janesville, Wisconsin

- **District-supported** 2-year, founded 1968, part of Wisconsin Technical College System
- **Small-town** 84-acre campus
- **Coed**

**Undergraduates** 822 full-time, 1,212 part-time. Students come from 3 states and territories; 1% are from out of state; 6% Black or African American, non-Hispanic/Latino; 10% Hispanic/Latino; 1% Asian, non-Hispanic/Latino; 0.6% American Indian or Alaska Native, non-Hispanic/Latino; 2% Two or more races, non-Hispanic/Latino; 2% Race/ethnicity unknown. *Retention:* 54% of full-time freshmen returned.
**Faculty** *Student/faculty ratio:* 8:1.
**Academics** *Calendar:* semesters. *Degree:* certificates, diplomas, and associate. *Special study options:* academic remediation for entering students, accelerated degree program, adult/continuing education programs, advanced placement credit, cooperative education, distance learning, English as a second language, independent study, internships, part-time degree program, services for LD students, student-designed majors, summer session for credit.
**Library** Blackhawk Technical College Library. *Books:* 12,369 (physical), 89,551 (digital/electronic); *Serial titles:* 109 (physical), 13 (digital/electronic); *Databases:* 68. Weekly public service hours: 57.
**Student Life** *Campus security:* student patrols.
**Costs (2017–18)** *Tuition:* state resident $4329 full-time, $132 per credit hour part-time; nonresident $6312 full-time, $198 per credit hour part-time. Full-time tuition and fees vary according to course load. Part-time tuition and fees vary according to course load. *Required fees:* $412 full-time. *Payment plans:* installment, deferred payment.
**Financial Aid** Of all full-time matriculated undergraduates who enrolled in 2016, 33 Federal Work-Study jobs (averaging $1150).
**Applying** *Options:* electronic application. *Required:* high school transcript.
**Freshman Application Contact** Blackhawk Technical College, 6004 South County Road G, Janesville, WI 53546-9458. *Phone:* 608-757-7713. *Website:* http://www.blackhawk.edu/.

# Broadview University–Madison
## Madison, Wisconsin

**Freshman Application Contact** Broadview University–Madison, 4901 Eastpark Boulevard, Madison, WI 53718. *Website:* http://www.broadviewuniversity.edu/.

# Bryant & Stratton College–Bayshore Campus
## Glendale, Wisconsin

**Admissions Office Contact** Bryant & Stratton College–Bayshore Campus, 500 West Silver Spring Drive, Bayshore Town Center, Suite K340, Glendale, WI 53217. *Website:* http://www.bryantstratton.edu/.

# Bryant & Stratton College–Milwaukee Campus
## Milwaukee, Wisconsin

**Freshman Application Contact** Mr. Dan Basile, Director of Admissions, Bryant & Stratton College–Milwaukee Campus, 310 West Wisconsin Avenue, Suite 500 East, Milwaukee, WI 53203-2214. *Phone:* 414-276-5200. *Website:* http://www.bryantstratton.edu/.

# Chippewa Valley Technical College
## Eau Claire, Wisconsin

- **District-supported** 2-year, founded 1912, part of Wisconsin Technical College System
- **Suburban** 255-acre campus
- **Coed,** 7,134 undergraduate students, 30% full-time, 52% women, 48% men

**Undergraduates** 2,129 full-time, 5,005 part-time. 1% Black or African American, non-Hispanic/Latino; 2% Hispanic/Latino; 4% Asian, non-Hispanic/Latino; 0.2% Native Hawaiian or other Pacific Islander, non-Hispanic/Latino; 0.7% American Indian or Alaska Native, non-Hispanic/Latino; 2% Two or more races, non-Hispanic/Latino; 5% Race/ethnicity unknown; 5% transferred in. *Retention:* 60% of full-time freshmen returned.

**Freshmen** *Admission:* 934 enrolled.

**Faculty** *Total:* 411, 54% full-time. *Student/faculty ratio:* 13:1.

**Majors** Accounting; administrative assistant and secretarial science; agronomy and crop science; animal/livestock husbandry and production; applied horticulture/horticultural business services related; business administration and management; civil engineering technology; clinical/medical laboratory technology; computer programming; computer systems networking and telecommunications; criminal justice/police science; dental hygiene; diagnostic medical sonography and ultrasound technology; digital communication and media/multimedia; early childhood education; electromechanical technology; emergency medical technology (EMT paramedic); health information/medical records technology; heating, ventilation, air conditioning and refrigeration engineering technology; human resources management; industrial mechanics and maintenance technology; legal assistant/paralegal; liberal arts and sciences/liberal studies; library and information science; manufacturing engineering technology; marketing/marketing management; mechanical drafting and CAD/CADD; medical radiologic technology; multi/interdisciplinary studies related; operations management; physical therapy technology; public relations, advertising, and applied communication; registered nursing/registered nurse; respiratory care therapy; substance abuse/addiction counseling.

**Academics** *Calendar:* semesters. *Degree:* certificates, diplomas, and associate. *Special study options:* academic remediation for entering students, accelerated degree program, adult/continuing education programs, advanced placement credit, cooperative education, distance learning, double majors, English as a second language, honors programs, independent study, internships, part-time degree program, services for LD students, student-designed majors, summer session for credit.

**Library** The Learning Center. *Books:* 10,758 (physical), 158,463 (digital/electronic); *Serial titles:* 110 (physical), 3,589 (digital/electronic); *Databases:* 116. Weekly public service hours: 66; students can reserve study rooms.

**Student Life** *Housing:* college housing not available. *Activities and Organizations:* Chippewa Valley Nurses, Radiography (IMAGERS), Criminal Justice, Physical Therapy, Structural Drafting. *Campus security:* 24-hour emergency response devices, late-night transport/escort service, security cameras. *Student services:* health clinic, personal/psychological counseling, veterans affairs office.

**Costs (2017–18)** *Tuition:* state resident $3966 full-time, $132 per credit part-time; nonresident $5949 full-time, $198 per credit part-time. Full-time tuition and fees vary according to course load and reciprocity agreements. Part-time tuition and fees vary according to course load and reciprocity agreements. *Required fees:* $338 full-time, $338 per year part-time. *Payment plans:* installment, deferred payment. *Waivers:* senior citizens.

**Financial Aid** Of all full-time matriculated undergraduates who enrolled in 2016, 218 Federal Work-Study jobs (averaging $875).

**Applying** *Options:* electronic application, early admission, deferred entrance. *Application fee:* $30. *Application deadlines:* rolling (freshmen), rolling (transfers). *Notification:* continuous (freshmen), continuous (transfers).

**Freshman Application Contact** Admissions Office, Chippewa Valley Technical College, 620 W. Clairemont Avenue, Eau Claire, WI 54701. *Phone:* 715-833-6200. *Toll-free phone:* 800-547-2882. *Fax:* 715-833-6470. *E-mail:* infocenter@cvtc.edu.

*Website:* http://www.cvtc.edu/.

# College of Menominee Nation
## Keshena, Wisconsin

**Director of Admissions** Tessa James, Admissions Coordinator, College of Menominee Nation, PO Box 1179, Keshena, WI 54135. *Phone:* 715-799-5600 Ext. 3053. *Toll-free phone:* 800-567-2344. *E-mail:* tjames@menominee.edu. *Website:* http://www.menominee.edu/.

# Fox Valley Technical College
## Appleton, Wisconsin

- **State and locally supported** 2-year, founded 1967, part of Wisconsin Technical College System
- **Suburban** 100-acre campus
- **Endowment** $3.8 million
- **Coed,** 11,658 undergraduate students, 19% full-time, 44% women, 56% men
- **69% of applicants were admitted**

**Undergraduates** 2,186 full-time, 9,472 part-time. Students come from 13 states and territories; 5 other countries; 0.7% are from out of state; 2% Black or African American, non-Hispanic/Latino; 4% Hispanic/Latino; 4% Asian, non-Hispanic/Latino; 0.2% Native Hawaiian or other Pacific Islander, non-Hispanic/Latino; 0.9% American Indian or Alaska Native, non-Hispanic/Latino; 1% Two or more races, non-Hispanic/Latino; 12% Race/ethnicity unknown; 0.6% international.

**Freshmen** *Admission:* 2,358 applied, 1,627 admitted, 836 enrolled.

**Faculty** *Total:* 813, 39% full-time. *Student/faculty ratio:* 11:1.

**Majors** Accounting; administrative assistant and secretarial science; agricultural/farm supplies retailing and wholesaling; agricultural mechanization; airline pilot and flight crew; autobody/collision and repair technology; automation engineer technology; automobile/automotive mechanics technology; avionics maintenance technology; banking and financial support services; biology/biotechnology laboratory technician; building/construction site management; business administration and management; clinical/medical laboratory technology; computer and information systems security; computer programming; computer support specialist; computer systems networking and telecommunications; court reporting; criminal justice/police science; culinary arts; dental hygiene; diesel mechanics technology; early childhood education; electrical and electronic engineering technologies related; electrical, electronic and communications engineering technology; electromechanical technology; electroneurodiagnostic/electroencephalographic technology; fire science/firefighting; forensic science and technology; health information/medical records technology; homeland security related; hospitality administration; human resources management; industrial safety technology; interior design; legal assistant/paralegal; logistics, materials, and supply chain management; manufacturing engineering technology; marketing/marketing management; mechanical drafting and CAD/CADD; medical office management; meeting and event planning; multi/interdisciplinary studies related; natural resources/conservation; occupational therapist assistant; office management; professional, technical, business, and scientific writing; radio, television, and digital communication related; registered nursing/registered nurse; substance abuse/addiction counseling; web/multimedia management and webmaster; welding technology; wildland/forest firefighting and investigation.

**Academics** *Calendar:* semesters. *Degree:* certificates, diplomas, and associate. *Special study options:* academic remediation for entering students, accelerated degree program, advanced placement credit, cooperative education, distance learning, double majors, English as a second language, independent study, internships, off-campus study, part-time degree program, services for LD students, student-designed majors, study abroad, summer session for credit.

**Library** Student Success Center Library. *Books:* 9,016 (physical), 354,485 (digital/electronic); *Serial titles:* 35 (physical), 31,678 (digital/electronic); *Databases:* 111. Weekly public service hours: 65; students can reserve study rooms.

**Student Life** *Housing:* college housing not available. *Activities and Organizations:* student-run newspaper, Student Government Association, Phi Theta Kappa, Culinary Arts Club, Machine Tool Club, Post Secondary Agribusiness Club. *Campus security:* 24-hour emergency response devices, late-night transport/escort service, trained security personnel patrol during hours of operation. *Student services:* health clinic, personal/psychological counseling, veterans affairs office.

**Standardized Tests** *Required for some:* ACT or ACCUPLACER, TEAS, Bennett Mechanical Comprehension Test.

**Costs (2017–18)** *Tuition:* state resident $3966 full-time, $132 per credit part-time; nonresident $5949 full-time, $198 per credit part-time. *Required fees:* $531 full-time, $18 per credit part-time. *Payment plan:* installment.

**Financial Aid** Of all full-time matriculated undergraduates who enrolled in 2016, 118 Federal Work-Study jobs (averaging $2166).

**Applying** *Options:* electronic application. *Application fee:* $30. *Required for some:* high school transcript, interview. *Application deadlines:* rolling (freshmen), rolling (transfers).

**Freshman Application Contact** Admissions Center, Fox Valley Technical College, 1825 North Bluemound Drive, PO Box 2277, Appleton, WI 54912-2277. *Phone:* 920-735-5643. *Toll-free phone:* 800-735-3882. *Fax:* 920-735-2582.

*Website:* http://www.fvtc.edu/.

## Gateway Technical College
### Kenosha, Wisconsin

- **State and locally supported** 2-year, founded 1911, part of Wisconsin Technical College System
- **Urban** 10-acre campus with easy access to Chicago, Milwaukee
- **Endowment** $5.7 million
- **Coed,** 8,722 undergraduate students, 16% full-time, 56% women, 44% men

**Undergraduates** 1,379 full-time, 7,343 part-time. Students come from 5 states and territories; 2% are from out of state; 10% Black or African American, non-Hispanic/Latino; 15% Hispanic/Latino; 1% Asian, non-Hispanic/Latino; 0.1% Native Hawaiian or other Pacific Islander, non-Hispanic/Latino; 0.5% American Indian or Alaska Native, non-Hispanic/Latino; 3% Two or more races, non-Hispanic/Latino; 7% Race/ethnicity unknown; 10% transferred in. *Retention:* 57% of full-time freshmen returned.

**Freshmen** *Admission:* 2,804 applied, 1,859 admitted, 1,202 enrolled.

**Faculty** *Total:* 699, 35% full-time, 3% with terminal degrees. *Student/faculty ratio:* 10:1.

**Majors** Accounting; administrative assistant and secretarial science; airline pilot and flight crew; applied horticulture/horticulture operations; architectural engineering technology; automation engineer technology; automobile/automotive mechanics technology; business administration and management; computer programming; computer support specialist; computer systems networking and telecommunications; criminal justice/police science; culinary arts; diesel mechanics technology; early childhood education; electrical, electronic and communications engineering technology; electromechanical technology; emergency medical technology (EMT paramedic); graphic design; health information/medical records technology; heating, air conditioning, ventilation and refrigeration maintenance technology; hospitality administration; interdisciplinary studies; interior design; marketing/marketing management; mechanical drafting and CAD/CADD; office management; physical therapy technology; professional, technical, business, and scientific writing; psychiatric/mental health services technology; registered nursing/registered nurse; surgical technology; surveying technology; teacher assistant/aide; transportation and highway engineering; urban forestry; veterinary/animal health technology; water resources engineering; web/multimedia management and webmaster.

**Academics** *Calendar:* semesters. *Degree:* certificates, diplomas, and associate. *Special study options:* academic remediation for entering students, advanced placement credit, cooperative education, distance learning, double majors, English as a second language, independent study, internships, off-campus study, part-time degree program, services for LD students, student-designed majors, summer session for credit.

**Library** Library/Learning Resources Center plus 2 others. *Books:* 23,575 (physical), 4,369 (digital/electronic); *Serial titles:* 131 (physical); *Databases:* 41. Weekly public service hours: 59; students can reserve study rooms.

**Student Life** *Activities and Organizations:* student-run newspaper, International Club, United Student Government, Outdoor Adventure Club,

Team EXCEED, Collegiate DECA. *Campus security:* 24-hour emergency response devices, late-night transport/escort service, patrols by trained security when open, locked/alarmed when closed. *Student services:* personal/psychological counseling, veterans affairs office.

**Costs (2018–19)** *Tuition:* state resident $4242 full-time, $132 per credit part-time; nonresident $5806 full-time, $198 per credit part-time. Full-time tuition and fees vary according to course level, course load, program, and reciprocity agreements. Part-time tuition and fees vary according to course level, course load, program, and reciprocity agreements. *Required fees:* $480 full-time. *Payment plans:* installment, deferred payment. *Waivers:* senior citizens and employees or children of employees.

**Applying** *Options:* electronic application, early admission, deferred entrance. *Application fee:* $30. *Required:* high school transcript. *Required for some:* interview. *Application deadlines:* rolling (freshmen), rolling (transfers). *Notification:* continuous (freshmen), continuous (transfers).

**Freshman Application Contact** Admissions, Gateway Technical College, 3520 30th Avenue, Kenosha, WI 53144-1690. *Phone:* 262-564-2300. *Fax:* 262-564-2301. *E-mail:* admissions@gtc.edu.

*Website:* http://www.gtc.edu/.

## Lac Courte Oreilles Ojibwa Community College
### Hayward, Wisconsin

**Freshman Application Contact** Ms. Annette Wiggins, Registrar, Lac Courte Oreilles Ojibwa Community College, 13466 West Trepania Road, Hayward, WI 54843-2181. *Phone:* 715-634-4790 Ext. 104. *Toll-free phone:* 888-526-6221. *Website:* http://www.lco.edu/.

## Lakeshore Technical College
### Cleveland, Wisconsin

- **State and locally supported** 2-year, founded 1967, part of Wisconsin Technical College System
- **Rural** 160-acre campus with easy access to Milwaukee
- **Coed**

**Undergraduates** Students come from 5 states and territories; 1% are from out of state.

**Freshmen** *Admission:* 1,982 applied, 1,010 admitted.

**Faculty** *Total:* 229, 43% full-time. *Student/faculty ratio:* 14:1.

**Majors** Accounting; administrative assistant and secretarial science; computer and information sciences related; computer programming; computer programming related; computer systems analysis; court reporting; criminal justice/police science; dental hygiene; drafting/design engineering technologies related; electrical, electronic and communications engineering technology; electromechanical technology; finance; legal assistant/paralegal; management science; marketing/marketing management; medical administrative assistant and medical secretary; quality control technology; radiologic technology/science; registered nursing/registered nurse.

**Academics** *Calendar:* semesters. *Degree:* certificates, diplomas, and associate. *Special study options:* academic remediation for entering students, accelerated degree program, adult/continuing education programs, advanced placement credit, cooperative education, distance learning, double majors, English as a second language, external degree program, independent study, internships, part-time degree program, services for LD students, student-designed majors, summer session for credit.

**Student Life** *Housing:* college housing not available. *Activities and Organizations:* Student Government, Business Professionals of America, Police Science Club, Lakeshore Student Nurse Association, Dairy Herd Club. *Campus security:* 24-hour patrols, student patrols, late-night transport/escort service. *Student services:* health clinic, personal/psychological counseling.

**Standardized Tests** *Recommended:* SAT or ACT (for admission), ACCUPLACER/ACT ASSET.

**Financial Aid** Of all full-time matriculated undergraduates who enrolled in 2016, 37 Federal Work-Study jobs.

**Applying** *Options:* electronic application, early admission, deferred entrance. *Application fee:* $30. *Required for some:* high school transcript, interview. *Application deadlines:* rolling (freshmen), rolling (transfers). *Notification:* continuous (freshmen), continuous (transfers).

**Freshman Application Contact** Lakeshore Technical College, 1290 North Avenue, Cleveland, WI 53015. *Phone:* 920-693-1339. *Toll-free phone:* 888-GO TO LTC. *Fax:* 920-693-3561.

*Website:* http://www.gotoltc.edu/.

# Madison Area Technical College
## Madison, Wisconsin

- **District-supported** 2-year, founded 1911, part of Wisconsin Technical College System
- **Urban** 150-acre campus
- **Coed**

**Undergraduates** 5,037 full-time, 11,500 part-time. Students come from 10 states and territories; 5 other countries; 3% are from out of state; 6% Black or African American, non-Hispanic/Latino; 9% Hispanic/Latino; 4% Asian, non-Hispanic/Latino; 0.1% Native Hawaiian or other Pacific Islander, non-Hispanic/Latino; 0.5% American Indian or Alaska Native, non-Hispanic/Latino; 4% Two or more races, non-Hispanic/Latino; 1% Race/ethnicity unknown; 1% international; 5% transferred in.
**Faculty** *Student/faculty ratio:* 13:1.
**Academics** *Calendar:* semesters. *Degree:* certificates, diplomas, and associate. *Special study options:* academic remediation for entering students, accelerated degree program, adult/continuing education programs, cooperative education, distance learning, English as a second language, internships, off-campus study, part-time degree program, services for LD students, summer session for credit.
**Library** Truax-Information Resource Center.
**Student Life** *Campus security:* 24-hour emergency response devices and patrols, late-night transport/escort service.
**Athletics** Member NJCAA.
**Financial Aid** Of all full-time matriculated undergraduates who enrolled in 2016, 200 Federal Work-Study jobs (averaging $2000). 300 state and other part-time jobs (averaging $2000).
**Applying** *Options:* electronic application, early admission. *Application fee:* $25. *Required for some:* high school transcript.
**Freshman Application Contact** Ms. Lori Sebranek, Dean, Enrollment Services, Madison Area Technical College, 1701 Wright Street, Madison, WI 53704. *Phone:* 608-243-4185. *Toll-free phone:* 800-322-6282. *Fax:* 608-243-4353. *E-mail:* enrollmentservices@madisoncollege.edu. *Website:* http://madisoncollege.edu/.

# Madison Media Institute
## Madison, Wisconsin

**Freshman Application Contact** Mr. Chris K. Hutchings, President/Director, Madison Media Institute, 2702 Agriculture Drive, Madison, WI 53718. *Phone:* 608-237-8301. *Toll-free phone:* 800-236-4997. *Website:* http://www.mediainstitute.edu/.

# Mid-State Technical College
## Wisconsin Rapids, Wisconsin

- **State and locally supported** 2-year, founded 1917, part of Wisconsin Technical College System
- **Small-town** 155-acre campus
- **Endowment** $1.2 million
- **Coed,** 2,636 undergraduate students, 36% full-time, 60% women, 40% men

**Undergraduates** 950 full-time, 1,686 part-time. 1% Black or African American, non-Hispanic/Latino; 1% Hispanic/Latino; 3% Asian, non-Hispanic/Latino; 0.1% Native Hawaiian or other Pacific Islander, non-Hispanic/Latino; 1% American Indian or Alaska Native, non-Hispanic/Latino; 2% Two or more races, non-Hispanic/Latino; 2% Race/ethnicity unknown; 3% transferred in.
**Freshmen** *Admission:* 1,100 applied, 1,045 admitted, 363 enrolled.
**Faculty** *Total:* 178, 46% full-time. *Student/faculty ratio:* 12:1.
**Majors** Accounting; administrative assistant and secretarial science; business administration and management; civil engineering technology; computer and information sciences related; computer engineering technology; computer programming related; computer programming (specific applications); corrections; criminal justice/police science; data entry/microcomputer applications; drafting/design engineering technologies related; electrical, electronic and communications engineering technology; hotel/motel administration; industrial technology; information science/studies; instrumentation technology; marketing/marketing management; quality control technology; registered nursing/registered nurse; respiratory care therapy.
**Academics** *Calendar:* semesters. *Degree:* certificates, diplomas, and associate. *Special study options:* academic remediation for entering students, adult/continuing education programs, cooperative education, distance learning, double majors, English as a second language, independent study, internships, part-time degree program, services for LD students, summer session for credit.
**Library** Mid-State Technical College Library.

**Student Life** *Housing:* college housing not available. *Activities and Organizations:* student-run newspaper, Business Professionals of America, Civil Tech Club, Barber and Cosmetology Club, Society of Hosteurs, UICA. *Student services:* health clinic, personal/psychological counseling, women's center.
**Athletics** Member NJCAA. *Intercollegiate sports:* basketball M/W, bowling M/W, golf M, volleyball W. *Intramural sports:* basketball M, bowling M/W, football M, golf M/W, volleyball M/W.
**Costs (2018–19)** *Tuition:* state resident $3911 full-time; nonresident $5866 full-time.
**Financial Aid** Of all full-time matriculated undergraduates who enrolled in 2009, 1,426 applied for aid, 1,426 were judged to have need. 352 Federal Work-Study jobs (averaging $1000).
**Applying** *Options:* electronic application, early admission, deferred entrance. *Application fee:* $30. *Required:* high school transcript. *Application deadlines:* rolling (freshmen), rolling (transfers). *Notification:* continuous (freshmen), continuous (transfers).
**Freshman Application Contact** Ms. Carole Prochnow, Admissions Assistant, Mid-State Technical College, 500 32nd Street North, Wisconsin Rapids, WI 54494-5599. *Phone:* 715-422-5444. *Website:* http://www.mstc.edu/.

# Milwaukee Area Technical College
## Milwaukee, Wisconsin

**Freshman Application Contact** Sarah Adams, Director, Enrollment Services, Milwaukee Area Technical College, 700 West State Street, Milwaukee, WI 53233-1443. *Phone:* 414-297-6595. *Fax:* 414-297-7800. *E-mail:* adamss4@matc.edu. *Website:* http://www.matc.edu/.

# Milwaukee Career College
## Milwaukee, Wisconsin

**Admissions Office Contact** Milwaukee Career College, 3077 N. Mayfair Road, Suite 300, Milwaukee, WI 53222. *Website:* http://www.mkecc.edu/.

# Moraine Park Technical College
## Fond du Lac, Wisconsin

**Freshman Application Contact** Karen Jarvis, Student Services, Moraine Park Technical College, 235 North National Avenue, Fond du Lac, WI 54935. *Phone:* 920-924-3200. *Toll-free phone:* 800-472-4554. *Fax:* 920-924-3421. *E-mail:* kjarvis@morainepark.edu. *Website:* http://www.morainepark.edu/.

# Nicolet Area Technical College
## Rhinelander, Wisconsin

**Freshman Application Contact** Ms. Susan Kordula, Director of Admissions, Nicolet Area Technical College, PO Box 518, Rhinelander, WI 54501. *Phone:* 715-365-4451. *Toll-free phone:* 800-544-3039. *E-mail:* inquire@nicoletcollege.edu. *Website:* http://www.nicoletcollege.edu/.

# Northcentral Technical College
## Wausau, Wisconsin

- **District-supported** 2-year, founded 1912, part of Wisconsin Technical College System
- **Rural** 96-acre campus
- **Coed,** 5,167 undergraduate students, 26% full-time, 58% women, 42% men

**Undergraduates** 1,361 full-time, 3,806 part-time. Students come from 24 states and territories; 0.9% Black or African American, non-Hispanic/Latino; 2% Hispanic/Latino; 5% Asian, non-Hispanic/Latino; 0.1% Native Hawaiian or other Pacific Islander, non-Hispanic/Latino; 0.8% American Indian or Alaska Native, non-Hispanic/Latino; 0.9% Two or more races, non-Hispanic/Latino; 25% Race/ethnicity unknown.
**Freshmen** *Admission:* 708 enrolled.
**Faculty** *Student/faculty ratio:* 23:1.
**Majors** Accounting; administrative assistant and secretarial science; agribusiness; agronomy and crop science; architectural engineering technology; automobile/automotive mechanics technology; business administration and management; cinematography and film/video production; clinical/medical laboratory technology; computer and information sciences and support services related; computer systems analysis; computer systems networking and telecommunications; criminal justice/police science; culinary arts; dental hygiene; diesel mechanics technology; early childhood education; electromechanical technology; emergency medical technology (EMT paramedic); entrepreneurship; furniture design and manufacturing; general

studies; graphic communications; logistics, materials, and supply chain management; manufacturing engineering technology; marketing/marketing management; mechanical drafting and CAD/CADD; medical insurance/medical billing; medical radiologic technology; mental and social health services and allied professions related; merchandising, sales, and marketing operations related (general); multi/interdisciplinary studies related; operations management; registered nursing/registered nurse; sign language interpretation and translation; substance abuse/addiction counseling; teacher assistant/aide.

**Academics** *Calendar:* semesters. *Degree:* certificates, diplomas, and associate. *Special study options:* academic remediation for entering students, accelerated degree program, adult/continuing education programs, advanced placement credit, cooperative education, distance learning, double majors, English as a second language, independent study, internships, off-campus study, part-time degree program, services for LD students, student-designed majors, summer session for credit.

**Library** Northcentral Technical College, Wausau Campus Library.

**Student Life** *Housing Options:* coed. Campus housing is provided by a third party. *Campus security:* 24-hour emergency response devices, student patrols, late-night transport/escort service. *Student services:* personal/psychological counseling, women's center, veterans affairs office.

**Athletics** *Intramural sports:* basketball M/W, football M/W, soccer M/W, ultimate Frisbee M/W, volleyball M/W.

**Costs (2017–18)** *Tuition:* state resident $3497 full-time; nonresident $5083 full-time. Full-time tuition and fees vary according to course level, course load, and program. Part-time tuition and fees vary according to course level, course load, and program. *Room and board:* $6265; room only: $4365. Room and board charges vary according to board plan and housing facility. *Payment plans:* installment, deferred payment. *Waivers:* senior citizens.

**Financial Aid** Of all full-time matriculated undergraduates who enrolled in 2016, 1,037 applied for aid, 910 were judged to have need, 910 had their need fully met. 142 state and other part-time jobs (averaging $1500). In 2016, 109 non-need-based awards were made. *Average financial aid package:* $5561. *Average need-based loan:* $2978. *Average need-based gift aid:* $4506. *Average non-need-based aid:* $679.

**Applying** *Options:* electronic application, early admission, deferred entrance. *Application fee:* $30. *Required for some:* high school transcript, interview. *Application deadlines:* rolling (freshmen), rolling (transfers). *Notification:* continuous (freshmen), continuous (transfers).

**Freshman Application Contact** Northcentral Technical College, 1000 West Campus Drive, Wausau, WI 54401-1899. *Phone:* 715-675-3331. *Website:* http://www.ntc.edu/.

## Northeast Wisconsin Technical College
### Green Bay, Wisconsin

**Freshman Application Contact** Christine Lemerande, Program Enrollment Supervisor, Northeast Wisconsin Technical College, 2740 W Mason Street, PO Box 19042, Green Bay, WI 54307-9042. *Phone:* 920-498-5444. *Toll-free phone:* 888-385-6982. *Fax:* 920-498-6882. *Website:* http://www.nwtc.edu/.

## Southwest Wisconsin Technical College
### Fennimore, Wisconsin

**Freshman Application Contact** Student Services, Southwest Wisconsin Technical College, 1800 Bronson Boulevard, Fennimore, WI 53809-9778. *Phone:* 608-822-2354. *Toll-free phone:* 800-362-3322. *Fax:* 608-822-6019. *E-mail:* student-services@swtc.edu. *Website:* http://www.swtc.edu/.

## University of Wisconsin–Baraboo/Sauk County
### Baraboo, Wisconsin

- **State-supported** primarily 2-year, founded 1968, part of University of Wisconsin System
- **Small-town** 68-acre campus with easy access to Madison
- **Coed,** 512 undergraduate students

**Faculty** *Student/faculty ratio:* 16:1.

**Majors** Agriculture; biology/biological sciences; business/commerce; chemistry; communication; computer and information sciences; economics; education; engineering; English; geography; health services/allied health/health sciences; history; interdisciplinary studies; liberal arts and sciences/liberal studies; mathematics; natural resources/conservation; philosophy; physical education teaching and coaching; political science and government; psychology; sociology; visual and performing arts; zoology/animal biology.

**Academics** *Calendar:* semesters. *Degrees:* certificates, associate, and bachelor's. *Special study options:* academic remediation for entering students, advanced placement credit, distance learning, external degree program, honors programs, independent study, internships, off-campus study, part-time degree program, services for LD students, student-designed majors, study abroad, summer session for credit.

**Library** T. N. Savides Library plus 1 other.

**Student Life** *Housing:* college housing not available. *Activities and Organizations:* drama/theater group, student-run newspaper, choral group. *Student services:* personal/psychological counseling.

**Athletics** Member NJCAA. *Intercollegiate sports:* basketball M(s), soccer M/W, tennis M/W, volleyball W. *Intramural sports:* softball M/W.

**Standardized Tests** *Required:* ACT (for admission).

**Costs (2017–18)** *One-time required fee:* $180. *Tuition:* state resident $4750 full-time, $198 per credit hour part-time; nonresident $12,321 full-time, $513 per credit hour part-time. Full-time tuition and fees vary according to reciprocity agreements. Part-time tuition and fees vary according to course load. *Required fees:* $487 full-time, $41 per year part-time. *Room and board:* Room and board charges vary according to location. *Payment plan:* installment.

**Applying** *Options:* electronic application. *Application fee:* $50. *Required:* high school transcript. *Application deadlines:* 8/30 (freshmen), rolling (out-of-state freshmen), 8/30 (transfers).

**Freshman Application Contact** University of Wisconsin–Baraboo/Sauk County, 1006 Connie Road, Baraboo, WI 53913. *Website:* http://www.baraboo.uwc.edu/.

## University of Wisconsin–Barron County
### Rice Lake, Wisconsin

- **State-supported** primarily 2-year, founded 1968, part of University of Wisconsin System
- **Small-town** 110-acre campus
- **Coed,** 505 undergraduate students

**Faculty** *Student/faculty ratio:* 12:1.

**Majors** Agriculture; biology/biological sciences; business/commerce; chemistry; communication; computer and information sciences; economics; education; engineering; English; geography; health services/allied health/health sciences; history; interdisciplinary studies; liberal arts and sciences/liberal studies; mathematics; natural resources/conservation; philosophy; physical education teaching and coaching; political science and government; psychology; sociology; visual and performing arts; zoology/animal biology.

**Academics** *Calendar:* semesters. *Degrees:* associate and bachelor's. *Special study options:* academic remediation for entering students, adult/continuing education programs, advanced placement credit, distance learning, independent study, internships, off-campus study, part-time degree program, services for LD students, study abroad, summer session for credit.

**Library** UW Barron County Library plus 1 other.

**Student Life** *Housing:* college housing not available.

**Athletics** *Intercollegiate sports:* baseball M(c), basketball M, cross-country running M(c)/W(c), golf M(c)/W(c), volleyball W.

**Standardized Tests** *Required:* ACT (for admission).

**Costs (2017–18)** *One-time required fee:* $180. *Tuition:* state resident $4750 full-time, $198 per credit hour part-time; nonresident $12,321 full-time, $513 per credit hour part-time. Full-time tuition and fees vary according to reciprocity agreements. Part-time tuition and fees vary according to course load. *Required fees:* $472 full-time, $39 per year part-time. *Room and board:* Room and board charges vary according to location. *Payment plan:* installment.

**Applying** *Options:* electronic application, deferred entrance. *Application fee:* $50. *Required:* high school transcript. *Application deadlines:* 8/30 (freshmen), 8/30 (transfers).

**Freshman Application Contact** University of Wisconsin–Barron County, 1800 College Drive, Rice Lake, WI 54868. *Website:* http://www.barron.uwc.edu/.

## University of Wisconsin Colleges Online
### Madison, Wisconsin

**Admissions Office Contact** University of Wisconsin Colleges Online, 34 Schroeder Court, Suite 200, Madison, WI 53711. *Toll-free phone:* 877-449-1877. *Website:* http://www.online.uwc.edu/.

# University of Wisconsin–Fond du Lac
## Fond du Lac, Wisconsin

- **State-supported** 2-year, founded 1972, part of University of Wisconsin System
- **Small-town** 183-acre campus with easy access to Milwaukee
- **Coed,** 519 undergraduate students

**Undergraduates** 1% are from out of state.
**Faculty** *Student/faculty ratio:* 15:1.
**Majors** Agriculture; biology/biological sciences; business/commerce; chemistry; communication; computer and information sciences; economics; education; engineering; English; geography; health services/allied health/health sciences; history; interdisciplinary studies; liberal arts and sciences/liberal studies; mathematics; natural resources/conservation; philosophy; physical education teaching and coaching; political science and government; psychology; sociology; visual and performing arts; zoology/animal biology.
**Academics** *Calendar:* semesters. *Degree:* certificates and associate. *Special study options:* academic remediation for entering students, accelerated degree program, advanced placement credit, cooperative education, distance learning, external degree program, independent study, off-campus study, part-time degree program, services for LD students, study abroad, summer session for credit.
**Library** UW-Fond du Lac Library plus 1 other.
**Student Life** *Housing:* college housing not available. *Activities and Organizations:* drama/theater group, student-run newspaper, choral group. *Campus security:* 24-hour emergency response devices. *Student services:* personal/psychological counseling.
**Athletics** Member NJCAA. *Intercollegiate sports:* baseball M(c), basketball M/W, volleyball M(c)/W.
**Standardized Tests** *Required:* ACT (for admission).
**Costs (2017–18)** *One-time required fee:* $180. *Tuition:* state resident $4750 full-time, $198 per credit hour part-time; nonresident $12,321 full-time, $513 per credit hour part-time. Full-time tuition and fees vary according to reciprocity agreements. Part-time tuition and fees vary according to course load. *Required fees:* $484 full-time, $40 per year part-time. *Room and board:* Room and board charges vary according to location. *Payment plan:* installment.
**Applying** *Options:* electronic application. *Application fee:* $50. *Required:* high school transcript. *Application deadlines:* 8/30 (freshmen), 8/30 (transfers).
**Freshman Application Contact** University of Wisconsin–Fond du Lac, 400 University Drive, Fond du Lac, WI 54935.
*Website:* http://www.fdl.uwc.edu/.

# University of Wisconsin–Fox Valley
## Menasha, Wisconsin

- **State-supported** 2-year, founded 1960, part of University of Wisconsin System
- **Small-town** 45-acre campus
- **Coed,** 1,364 undergraduate students

**Faculty** *Student/faculty ratio:* 17:1.
**Majors** Agriculture; biology/biological sciences; business/commerce; chemistry; communication; computer and information sciences; economics; education; engineering; English; geography; health services/allied health/health sciences; history; interdisciplinary studies; liberal arts and sciences/liberal studies; mathematics; natural resources/conservation; philosophy; physical education teaching and coaching; political science and government; psychology; sociology; visual and performing arts; zoology/animal biology.
**Academics** *Calendar:* semesters. *Degree:* certificates and associate. *Special study options:* academic remediation for entering students, accelerated degree program, advanced placement credit, cooperative education, distance learning, external degree program, honors programs, independent study, internships, off-campus study, part-time degree program, services for LD students, study abroad, summer session for credit.
**Library** UW-Fox Valley Library plus 1 other. Students can reserve study rooms.
**Student Life** *Housing:* college housing not available. *Activities and Organizations:* drama/theater group, student-run newspaper, radio and television station, choral group. *Campus security:* 24-hour emergency response devices, late-night transport/escort service. *Student services:* personal/psychological counseling.
**Athletics** Member NJCAA. *Intercollegiate sports:* baseball M(c), basketball M/W, soccer M/W, volleyball W.
**Standardized Tests** *Required:* ACT (for admission).
**Costs (2017–18)** *One-time required fee:* $180. *Tuition:* state resident $4750 full-time, $198 per credit hour part-time; nonresident $12,321 full-time, $513

per credit hour part-time. Full-time tuition and fees vary according to reciprocity agreements. Part-time tuition and fees vary according to course load. *Required fees:* $310 full-time, $26 per year part-time. *Room and board:* Room and board charges vary according to location. *Payment plan:* installment.
**Applying** *Options:* electronic application. *Application fee:* $50. *Required:* high school transcript. *Application deadlines:* 8/30 (freshmen), 8/30 (transfers).
**Freshman Application Contact** University of Wisconsin–Fox Valley, 1478 Midway Road, Menasha, WI 54952.
*Website:* http://www.uwfox.uwc.edu/.

# University of Wisconsin–Manitowoc
## Manitowoc, Wisconsin

- **State-supported** 2-year, founded 1962, part of University of Wisconsin System
- **Small-town** 40-acre campus with easy access to Milwaukee
- **Coed,** 354 undergraduate students
- 100% of applicants were admitted

**Freshmen** *Admission:* 458 applied, 458 admitted.
**Faculty** *Student/faculty ratio:* 14:1.
**Majors** Agriculture; biology/biological sciences; business/commerce; chemistry; communication; computer and information sciences; economics; education; engineering; English; geography; health services/allied health/health sciences; history; interdisciplinary studies; liberal arts and sciences/liberal studies; mathematics; natural resources/conservation; philosophy; physical education teaching and coaching; political science and government; psychology; sociology; visual and performing arts; zoology/animal biology.
**Academics** *Calendar:* semesters. *Degree:* certificates and associate. *Special study options:* academic remediation for entering students, advanced placement credit, cooperative education, distance learning, external degree program, internships, off-campus study, part-time degree program, services for LD students, student-designed majors, study abroad.
**Library** UW-Manitowoc Library plus 1 other.
**Student Life** *Housing:* college housing not available. *Activities and Organizations:* drama/theater group, student-run newspaper, choral group. *Student services:* personal/psychological counseling.
**Athletics** *Intercollegiate sports:* basketball M/W, tennis M/W, volleyball W.
**Standardized Tests** *Required:* SAT or ACT (for admission).
**Costs (2017–18)** *One-time required fee:* $180. *Tuition:* state resident $4750 full-time, $198 per credit hour part-time; nonresident $12,321 full-time, $513 per credit hour part-time. Full-time tuition and fees vary according to reciprocity agreements. Part-time tuition and fees vary according to course load. *Required fees:* $406 full-time, $34 per year part-time. *Room and board:* Room and board charges vary according to location. *Payment plan:* installment.
**Applying** *Options:* electronic application, early admission, deferred entrance. *Application fee:* $50. *Required:* high school transcript. *Application deadlines:* 8/30 (freshmen), 8/30 (transfers).
**Freshman Application Contact** University of Wisconsin–Manitowoc, 705 Viebahn Street, Manitowoc, WI 54220.
*Website:* http://www.manitowoc.uwc.edu/.

# University of Wisconsin–Marathon County
## Wausau, Wisconsin

- **State-supported** 2-year, founded 1997, part of University of Wisconsin System
- **Small-town** 7-acre campus
- **Coed,** 838 undergraduate students

**Faculty** *Student/faculty ratio:* 17:1.
**Majors** Agriculture; biology/biological sciences; business/commerce; chemistry; communication; computer and information sciences; economics; education; engineering; English; geography; health services/allied health/health sciences; history; interdisciplinary studies; liberal arts and sciences/liberal studies; mathematics; natural resources/conservation; philosophy; physical education teaching and coaching; political science and government; psychology; sociology; visual and performing arts; zoology/animal biology.
**Academics** *Calendar:* semesters. *Degree:* certificates and associate. *Special study options:* academic remediation for entering students, advanced placement credit, external degree program, honors programs, off-campus study, part-time degree program, student-designed majors, study abroad, summer session for credit. *ROTC:* Army (c).
**Library** UW-Marathon County Library plus 1 other.

**Student Life** *Housing Options:* coed. Campus housing is university owned. *Campus security:* 24-hour emergency response devices, controlled dormitory access.

**Athletics** *Intercollegiate sports:* basketball M/W, volleyball W.

**Standardized Tests** *Required:* ACT (for admission).

**Costs (2017–18)** *One-time required fee:* $180. *Tuition:* state resident $4750 full-time, $198 per credit hour part-time; nonresident $12,321 full-time, $513 per credit hour part-time. Full-time tuition and fees vary according to reciprocity agreements. Part-time tuition and fees vary according to course load. *Required fees:* $424 full-time, $35 per year part-time. *Room and board:* Room and board charges vary according to location. *Payment plan:* installment.

**Applying** *Options:* electronic application, early admission, deferred entrance. *Application fee:* $50. *Required:* high school transcript. *Application deadlines:* 8/29 (freshmen), 8/30 (transfers).

**Freshman Application Contact** University of Wisconsin–Marathon County, 518 South 7th Avenue, Wausau, WI 54401. *Toll-free phone:* 888-367-8962. *Website:* http://www.uwmc.uwc.edu/.

# University of Wisconsin–Marinette
## Marinette, Wisconsin

- **State-supported** 2-year, founded 1972, part of University of Wisconsin System
- **Small-town** 36-acre campus
- **Coed,** 286 undergraduate students

**Faculty** *Student/faculty ratio:* 10:1.

**Majors** Agriculture; biology/biological sciences; business/commerce; chemistry; communication; computer and information sciences; economics; education; engineering; English; geography; health services/allied health/health sciences; history; interdisciplinary studies; liberal arts and sciences/liberal studies; mathematics; natural resources/conservation; philosophy; physical education teaching and coaching; political science and government; psychology; sociology; visual and performing arts; zoology/animal biology.

**Academics** *Calendar:* semesters. *Degree:* certificates and associate. *Special study options:* academic remediation for entering students, advanced placement credit, cooperative education, distance learning, English as a second language, external degree program, independent study, internships, off-campus study, part-time degree program, services for LD students, summer session for credit.

**Library** UW-Marinette Library plus 1 other.

**Student Life** *Housing:* college housing not available. *Activities and Organizations:* drama/theater group, student-run newspaper, choral group, Student Senate, Writers Club/Literature Club, Phi Theta Kappa, Student Ambassadors. *Student services:* personal/psychological counseling.

**Athletics** *Intercollegiate sports:* basketball M/W, volleyball W.

**Standardized Tests** *Required:* ACT (for admission).

**Costs (2017–18)** *One-time required fee:* $180. *Tuition:* state resident $4750 full-time, $198 per credit hour part-time; nonresident $12,321 full-time, $513 per credit hour part-time. Full-time tuition and fees vary according to reciprocity agreements. Part-time tuition and fees vary according to course load. *Required fees:* $386 full-time, $32 per credit hour part-time. *Room and board:* Room and board charges vary according to location. *Payment plan:* installment.

**Applying** *Options:* electronic application. *Application fee:* $50. *Required:* high school transcript. *Application deadlines:* 8/30 (freshmen), 8/30 (transfers).

**Freshman Application Contact** University of Wisconsin–Marinette, 750 West Bay Shore, Marinette, WI 54143. *Website:* http://www.marinette.uwc.edu/.

# University of Wisconsin–Marshfield/Wood County
## Marshfield, Wisconsin

- **State-supported** primarily 2-year, founded 1963, part of University of Wisconsin System
- **Small-town** 114-acre campus
- **Coed,** 535 undergraduate students

**Faculty** *Student/faculty ratio:* 15:1.

**Majors** Agriculture; biology/biological sciences; business/commerce; chemistry; communication; computer and information sciences; economics; education; engineering; English; geography; health services/allied health/health sciences; history; interdisciplinary studies; liberal arts and sciences/liberal studies; mathematics; natural resources/conservation; philosophy; physical education teaching and coaching; political science and government; psychology; sociology; visual and performing arts; zoology/animal biology.

**Academics** *Calendar:* semesters. *Degrees:* certificates, associate, and bachelor's. *Special study options:* academic remediation for entering students, accelerated degree program, advanced placement credit, distance learning, external degree program, independent study, off-campus study, part-time degree program, services for LD students, study abroad, summer session for credit. *ROTC:* Army (c).

**Library** Hamilton Roddis Memorial Library plus 1 other.

**Student Life** *Activities and Organizations:* drama/theater group, student-run newspaper, choral group. *Campus security:* 24-hour patrols, patrols by city police.

**Athletics** *Intercollegiate sports:* basketball M/W, golf M, tennis M/W, volleyball W.

**Standardized Tests** *Required:* ACT (for admission).

**Costs (2017–18)** *One-time required fee:* $180. *Tuition:* state resident $4750 full-time, $198 per credit hour part-time; nonresident $12,321 full-time, $513 per credit hour part-time. Full-time tuition and fees vary according to reciprocity agreements. Part-time tuition and fees vary according to course load. *Required fees:* $386 full-time, $32 per year part-time. *Room and board:* Room and board charges vary according to location. *Payment plan:* installment.

**Applying** *Options:* electronic application, early admission, deferred entrance. *Application fee:* $50. *Required:* high school transcript. *Application deadlines:* 8/30 (freshmen), 8/30 (transfers).

**Freshman Application Contact** University of Wisconsin–Marshfield/Wood County, 2000 West 5th Street, Marshfield, WI 54449. *Website:* http://marshfield.uwc.edu/.

# University of Wisconsin–Richland
## Richland Center, Wisconsin

- **State-supported** primarily 2-year, founded 1967, part of University of Wisconsin System
- **Small-town** 135-acre campus
- **Coed,** 259 undergraduate students

**Faculty** *Student/faculty ratio:* 8:1.

**Majors** Agriculture; biology/biological sciences; business/commerce; chemistry; communication; computer and information sciences; economics; education; engineering; English; geography; health services/allied health/health sciences; history; interdisciplinary studies; liberal arts and sciences/liberal studies; mathematics; natural resources/conservation; philosophy; physical education teaching and coaching; political science and government; psychology; sociology; visual and performing arts; zoology/animal biology.

**Academics** *Calendar:* semesters. *Degrees:* certificates, associate, and bachelor's. *Special study options:* academic remediation for entering students, advanced placement credit, distance learning, external degree program, independent study, off-campus study, part-time degree program, services for LD students, study abroad, summer session for credit.

**Library** Miller Memorial Library plus 1 other.

**Student Life** *Housing Options:* coed. Campus housing is provided by a third party. *Activities and Organizations:* drama/theater group, choral group. *Student services:* personal/psychological counseling.

**Athletics** *Intercollegiate sports:* basketball M/W. *Intramural sports:* softball M/W, volleyball M/W.

**Standardized Tests** *Required:* ACT (for admission).

**Costs (2017–18)** *One-time required fee:* $180. *Tuition:* state resident $4750 full-time, $198 per credit hour part-time; nonresident $12,321 full-time, $513 per credit hour part-time. Full-time tuition and fees vary according to reciprocity agreements. Part-time tuition and fees vary according to course load. *Required fees:* $597 full-time, $50 per year part-time. *Room and board:* room only: $3600. Room and board charges vary according to location. *Payment plan:* installment.

**Applying** *Options:* electronic application. *Application fee:* $50. *Required:* high school transcript. *Application deadlines:* 8/30 (freshmen), 8/30 (transfers).

**Freshman Application Contact** University of Wisconsin–Richland, 1200 Highway 14 West, Richland Center, WI 53581. *Website:* http://richland.uwc.edu/.

# University of Wisconsin–Rock County
## Janesville, Wisconsin

- **State-supported** primarily 2-year, founded 1966, part of University of Wisconsin System
- **Small-town** 50-acre campus with easy access to Milwaukee
- **Coed,** 970 undergraduate students

**Faculty** *Student/faculty ratio:* 16:1.

**Majors** Agriculture; biology/biological sciences; business/commerce; chemistry; communication; computer and information sciences; education; engineering; English; geography; health services/allied health/health sciences; history; interdisciplinary studies; liberal arts and sciences/liberal studies; mathematics; natural resources/conservation; philosophy; physical education teaching and coaching; political science and government; psychology; sociology; visual and performing arts; zoology/animal biology.

**Academics** *Calendar:* semesters. *Degrees:* certificates, associate, and bachelor's. *Special study options:* academic remediation for entering students, advanced placement credit, distance learning, external degree program, off-campus study, part-time degree program, services for LD students, summer session for credit.

**Library** Gary J. Lenox Library plus 1 other.

**Student Life** *Housing:* college housing not available.

**Athletics** *Intercollegiate sports:* basketball M/W, tennis M/W, volleyball W.

**Standardized Tests** *Required:* ACT (for admission).

**Costs (2017–18)** *One-time required fee:* $180. *Tuition:* state resident $4750 full-time, $198 per credit hour part-time; nonresident $12,321 full-time, $513 per credit hour part-time. Full-time tuition and fees vary according to reciprocity agreements. Part-time tuition and fees vary according to course load. *Required fees:* $382 full-time, $32 per year part-time. *Room and board:* Room and board charges vary according to location. *Payment plan:* installment.

**Applying** *Options:* electronic application, deferred entrance. *Application fee:* $50. *Required:* high school transcript. *Application deadlines:* 8/30 (freshmen), 8/30 (transfers).

**Freshman Application Contact** University of Wisconsin–Rock County, 2909 Kellogg Avenue, Janesville, WI 53546. *Toll-free phone:* 888-INFO-UWC. *Website:* http://rock.uwc.edu/.

## University of Wisconsin–Sheboygan
### Sheboygan, Wisconsin

- **State-supported** 2-year, founded 1933, part of University of Wisconsin System
- **Small-town** 70-acre campus with easy access to Milwaukee
- **Coed,** 602 undergraduate students

**Faculty** *Student/faculty ratio:* 14:1.

**Majors** Agriculture; biology/biological sciences; business/commerce; chemistry; communication; computer and information sciences; economics; education; engineering; English; geography; health services/allied health/health sciences; history; interdisciplinary studies; liberal arts and sciences/liberal studies; mathematics; natural resources/conservation; philosophy; physical education teaching and coaching; political science and government; psychology; sociology; visual and performing arts; zoology/animal biology.

**Academics** *Calendar:* semesters. *Degree:* certificates and associate. *Special study options:* academic remediation for entering students, advanced placement credit, cooperative education, distance learning, English as a second language, external degree program, independent study, off-campus study, part-time degree program, services for LD students, summer session for credit.

**Library** University Library plus 1 other.

**Student Life** *Housing:* college housing not available. *Activities and Organizations:* drama/theater group, student-run newspaper, choral group. *Campus security:* 24-hour patrols by city police. *Student services:* personal/psychological counseling.

**Athletics** *Intercollegiate sports:* basketball M, tennis M/W, volleyball W.

**Standardized Tests** *Required:* ACT (for admission).

**Costs (2017–18)** *One-time required fee:* $180. *Tuition:* state resident $4750 full-time, $198 per credit hour part-time; nonresident $12,321 full-time, $513 per credit hour part-time. Full-time tuition and fees vary according to reciprocity agreements. Part-time tuition and fees vary according to course load. *Required fees:* $382 full-time. *Room and board:* Room and board charges vary according to location. *Payment plan:* installment.

**Applying** *Options:* electronic application. *Application fee:* $50. *Required:* high school transcript. *Application deadlines:* 8/30 (freshmen), 8/30 (transfers).

**Freshman Application Contact** University of Wisconsin–Sheboygan, One University Drive, Sheboygan, WI 53081. *Website:* http://www.sheboygan.uwc.edu/.

## University of Wisconsin–Washington County
### West Bend, Wisconsin

- **State-supported** 2-year, founded 1968, part of University of Wisconsin System
- **Small-town** 87-acre campus with easy access to Milwaukee
- **Coed,** 544 undergraduate students

**Faculty** *Student/faculty ratio:* 17:1.

**Majors** Agriculture; biology/biological sciences; business/commerce; chemistry; communication; computer and information sciences; economics; education; engineering; English; geography; health services/allied health/health sciences; history; interdisciplinary studies; liberal arts and sciences/liberal studies; mathematics; natural resources/conservation; philosophy; physical education teaching and coaching; political science and government; psychology; sociology; visual and performing arts; zoology/animal biology.

**Academics** *Calendar:* semesters. *Degree:* certificates and associate. *Special study options:* academic remediation for entering students, advanced placement credit, distance learning, double majors, external degree program, honors programs, independent study, off-campus study, part-time degree program, services for LD students, summer session for credit.

**Library** UW-Washington County Library plus 1 other.

**Student Life** *Housing:* college housing not available. *Activities and Organizations:* drama/theater group, student-run newspaper, choral group. *Student services:* personal/psychological counseling.

**Athletics** Member NAIA. *Intercollegiate sports:* basketball M/W, golf M/W, tennis M/W, volleyball W.

**Standardized Tests** *Required:* ACT (for admission).

**Costs (2017–18)** *One-time required fee:* $180. *Tuition:* state resident $4750 full-time, $198 per credit hour part-time; nonresident $12,321 full-time, $513 per credit hour part-time. Full-time tuition and fees vary according to reciprocity agreements. Part-time tuition and fees vary according to course load. *Required fees:* $368 full-time, $31 per year part-time. *Room and board:* Room and board charges vary according to location. *Payment plan:* installment.

**Applying** *Options:* electronic application, deferred entrance. *Application fee:* $50. *Required:* high school transcript. *Application deadlines:* 8/30 (freshmen), 8/30 (transfers).

**Freshman Application Contact** University of Wisconsin–Washington County, 400 University Drive, West Bend, WI 53095. *Website:* http://www.washington.uwc.edu/.

## University of Wisconsin–Waukesha
### Waukesha, Wisconsin

- **State-supported** primarily 2-year, founded 1966, part of University of Wisconsin System
- **Small-town** 86-acre campus with easy access to Milwaukee
- **Coed,** 1,782 undergraduate students

**Faculty** *Student/faculty ratio:* 17:1.

**Majors** Agriculture; biology/biological sciences; business/commerce; chemistry; communication; computer and information sciences; economics; education; engineering; English; geography; health services/allied health/health sciences; history; interdisciplinary studies; liberal arts and sciences/liberal studies; mathematics; natural resources/conservation; philosophy; physical education teaching and coaching; political science and government; psychology; sociology; visual and performing arts; zoology/animal biology.

**Academics** *Calendar:* semesters. *Degrees:* associate and bachelor's. *Special study options:* academic remediation for entering students, accelerated degree program, advanced placement credit, distance learning, external degree program, honors programs, internships, off-campus study, part-time degree program, services for LD students, study abroad, summer session for credit.

**Library** University of Wisconsin-Waukesha Library plus 1 other.

**Student Life** *Housing:* college housing not available. *Activities and Organizations:* drama/theater group, student-run newspaper, choral group. *Campus security:* late-night transport/escort service, part-time patrols by trained security personnel. *Student services:* personal/psychological counseling.

**Athletics** Member NJCAA. *Intercollegiate sports:* basketball M/W, golf M/W, soccer M/W, tennis M/W, volleyball W.

**Standardized Tests** *Required:* ACT (for admission).

**Costs (2017–18)** *One-time required fee:* $230. *Tuition:* state resident $4750 full-time, $198 per credit hour part-time; nonresident $12,321 full-time, $513 per credit hour part-time. Full-time tuition and fees vary according to reciprocity agreements. Part-time tuition and fees vary according to course load. *Required fees:* $398 full-time, $33 per year part-time. *Room and board:*

Room and board charges vary according to location. *Payment plan:* installment.

**Applying** *Options:* electronic application, early admission, deferred entrance. *Application fee:* $50. *Required:* high school transcript. *Application deadlines:* 8/30 (freshmen), 8/30 (transfers).

**Freshman Application Contact** University of Wisconsin–Waukesha, 1500 North University Drive, Waukesha, WI 53188. *Website:* http://www.waukesha.uwc.edu/.

# Waukesha County Technical College
## Pewaukee, Wisconsin

- **State and locally supported** 2-year, founded 1923, part of Wisconsin Technical College System
- **Suburban** 137-acre campus with easy access to Milwaukee
- **Coed,** 7,696 undergraduate students, 20% full-time, 49% women, 51% men

**Undergraduates** 1,565 full-time, 6,131 part-time. 6% Black or African American, non-Hispanic/Latino; 8% Hispanic/Latino; 3% Asian, non-Hispanic/Latino; 0.2% Native Hawaiian or other Pacific Islander, non-Hispanic/Latino; 0.3% American Indian or Alaska Native, non-Hispanic/Latino; 2% Two or more races, non-Hispanic/Latino; 3% Race/ethnicity unknown; 0.1% international.

**Freshmen** *Admission:* 459 enrolled.

**Faculty** *Total:* 749, 26% full-time. *Student/faculty ratio:* 17:1.

**Majors** Accounting; administrative assistant and secretarial science; architectural drafting and CAD/CADD; automation engineer technology; automobile/automotive mechanics technology; baking and pastry arts; business administration and management; business administration, management and operations related; computer and information systems security; computer programming; computer support specialist; computer systems networking and telecommunications; criminal justice/police science; data modeling/warehousing and database administration; dental hygiene; diesel mechanics technology; early childhood education; electrical, electronic and communications engineering technology; emergency medical technology (EMT paramedic); fire science/firefighting; graphic design; health information/medical records technology; hospitality administration; human resources management; interior design; international business/trade/commerce; manufacturing engineering technology; marketing/marketing management; mechanical drafting and CAD/CADD; metal fabricator; multi/interdisciplinary studies related; office management; psychiatric/mental health services technology; real estate; registered nursing/registered nurse; restaurant, culinary, and catering management; surgical technology; teacher assistant/aide; web/multimedia management and webmaster.

**Academics** *Calendar:* semesters. *Degree:* certificates, diplomas, and associate. *Special study options:* academic remediation for entering students, accelerated degree program, adult/continuing education programs, advanced placement credit, cooperative education, distance learning, double majors, English as a second language, independent study, internships, part-time degree program, services for LD students, student-designed majors, study abroad, summer session for credit.

**Student Life** *Housing:* college housing not available. *Campus security:* patrols by police officers 8 am to 10 pm. *Student services:* veterans affairs office.

**Costs (2017–18)** *Tuition:* state resident $3966 full-time, $132 per credit hour part-time; nonresident $5949 full-time, $198 per credit hour part-time. Full-time tuition and fees vary according to program. Part-time tuition and fees vary according to program. *Required fees:* $239 full-time, $8 per credit hour part-time. *Payment plans:* installment, deferred payment. *Waivers:* senior citizens.

**Financial Aid** Of all full-time matriculated undergraduates who enrolled in 2016, 180 Federal Work-Study jobs (averaging $2709).

**Applying** *Options:* electronic application. *Application fee:* $30. *Required:* high school transcript. *Required for some:* interview. *Application deadlines:* rolling (freshmen), rolling (transfers).

**Freshman Application Contact** Waukesha County Technical College, 800 Main Street, Pewaukee, WI 53072-4601. *Phone:* 262-691-5464. *Website:* http://www.wctc.edu/.

# Western Technical College
## La Crosse, Wisconsin

**Freshman Application Contact** Ms. Jane Wells, Manager of Admissions, Registration, and Records, Western Technical College, PO Box 908, La Crosse, WI 54602-0908. *Phone:* 608-785-9158. *Toll-free phone:* 800-322-9982. *Fax:* 608-785-9094. *E-mail:* mildes@wwtc.edu. *Website:* http://www.westerntc.edu/.

# Wisconsin Indianhead Technical College
## Shell Lake, Wisconsin

- **District-supported** 2-year, founded 1912, part of Wisconsin Technical College System
- **Suburban** 118-acre campus with easy access to Minneapolis-St Paul Metro Area
- **Endowment** $4.7 million
- **Coed,** 3,021 undergraduate students, 36% full-time, 62% women, 38% men

**Undergraduates** 1,086 full-time, 1,935 part-time. Students come from 6 states and territories; 9% are from out of state; 0.6% Black or African American, non-Hispanic/Latino; 0.5% Hispanic/Latino; 1% Asian, non-Hispanic/Latino; 0.1% Native Hawaiian or other Pacific Islander, non-Hispanic/Latino; 2% American Indian or Alaska Native, non-Hispanic/Latino; 2% Two or more races, non-Hispanic/Latino; 1% Race/ethnicity unknown.

**Freshmen** *Admission:* 500 enrolled.

**Faculty** *Total:* 289, 55% full-time. *Student/faculty ratio:* 9:1.

**Majors** Accounting; administrative assistant and secretarial science; architectural engineering technology; automation engineer technology; business administration and management; child-care and support services management; computer programming; computer support specialist; computer systems networking and telecommunications; criminal justice/safety; emergency medical technology (EMT paramedic); finance; gerontology; health information/medical records technology; human resources management; interdisciplinary studies; liberal arts and sciences/liberal studies; medical administrative assistant and medical secretary; multi/interdisciplinary studies related; occupational therapist assistant; office management; psychiatric/mental health services technology; registered nursing/registered nurse.

**Academics** *Calendar:* semesters. *Degree:* certificates, diplomas, and associate. *Special study options:* academic remediation for entering students, adult/continuing education programs, advanced placement credit, distance learning, double majors, English as a second language, external degree program, independent study, internships, off-campus study, part-time degree program, services for LD students, summer session for credit.

**Library Books:** 5,569 (physical), 50,557 (digital/electronic); *Serial titles:* 89 (physical), 35,291 (digital/electronic); *Databases:* 85. Students can reserve study rooms.

**Student Life** *Housing:* college housing not available. *Campus security:* 24-hour emergency response devices. *Student services:* health clinic, veterans affairs office.

**Costs (2017–18)** *Tuition:* state resident $4672 full-time, $146 per credit hour part-time; nonresident $6784 full-time, $212 per credit hour part-time. Full-time tuition and fees vary according to course load, program, and reciprocity agreements. Part-time tuition and fees vary according to course load, program, and reciprocity agreements. *Required fees:* $432 full-time, $132 per credit hour part-time. *Payment plans:* installment, deferred payment.

**Applying** *Options:* electronic application, early admission, deferred entrance. *Application fee:* $30. *Required:* interview. *Required for some:* high school transcript. *Application deadline:* rolling (freshmen).

**Freshman Application Contact** Mr. Steve Bitzer, Vice President, Student Affairs and Campus Administrator, Wisconsin Indianhead Technical College, 2100 Beaser Avenue, Ashland, WI 54806. *Phone:* 715-468-2815 Ext. 3149. *Toll-free phone:* 800-243-9482. *Fax:* 715-468-2819. *E-mail:* steve.bitzer@witc.edu. *Website:* http://www.witc.edu/.

# WYOMING

# Casper College
## Casper, Wyoming

- **State and locally supported** 2-year, founded 1945
- **Small-town** 200-acre campus
- **Coed**

**Undergraduates** 1,733 full-time, 1,893 part-time. Students come from 37 states and territories; 17 other countries; 10% are from out of state; 1% Black or African American, non-Hispanic/Latino; 7% Hispanic/Latino; 0.8% Asian, non-Hispanic/Latino; 0.2% Native Hawaiian or other Pacific Islander, non-Hispanic/Latino; 0.6% American Indian or Alaska Native, non-Hispanic/Latino; 3% Two or more races, non-Hispanic/Latino; 2% Race/ethnicity unknown; 0.9% international; 2% transferred in; 16% live on campus.

**Faculty** *Student/faculty ratio:* 14:1.

**Academics** *Calendar:* semesters. *Degree:* certificates and associate. *Special study options:* academic remediation for entering students, accelerated degree program, advanced placement credit, cooperative education, distance learning, English as a second language, honors programs, independent study, internships, off-campus study, part-time degree program, services for LD students, summer session for credit.

**Library** Goodstein Foundation Library. *Books:* 66,488 (physical), 184,000 (digital/electronic); *Serial titles:* 4,300 (physical); *Databases:* 415. Weekly public service hours: 82; students can reserve study rooms.

**Student Life** *Campus security:* 24-hour emergency response devices and patrols, late-night transport/escort service.

**Athletics** Member NJCAA.

**Financial Aid** Of all full-time matriculated undergraduates who enrolled in 2016, 80 Federal Work-Study jobs (averaging $2000).

**Applying** *Options:* electronic application, early admission. *Required:* high school transcript.

**Freshman Application Contact** Ms. Kyla Foltz, Director of Admissions Services, Casper College, 125 College Drive, Casper, WY 82601. *Phone:* 307-268-2111. *Toll-free phone:* 800-442-2963. *Fax:* 307-268-2611. *E-mail:* kfoltz@caspercollege.edu. *Website:* http://www.caspercollege.edu/.

# Central Wyoming College
## Riverton, Wyoming

- **State and locally supported** 2-year, founded 1966, part of Wyoming Community College Commission
- **Small-town** 200-acre campus
- **Endowment** $20.0 million
- **Coed**

**Undergraduates** 688 full-time, 1,328 part-time. Students come from 41 states and territories; 6 other countries; 13% are from out of state; 0.8% Black or African American, non-Hispanic/Latino; 9% Hispanic/Latino; 0.8% Asian, non-Hispanic/Latino; 0.0% Native Hawaiian or other Pacific Islander, non-Hispanic/Latino; 10% American Indian or Alaska Native, non-Hispanic/Latino; 3% Two or more races, non-Hispanic/Latino; 2% Race/ethnicity unknown; 0.3% international; 5% transferred in; 18% live on campus. *Retention:* 54% of full-time freshmen returned.

**Faculty** *Student/faculty ratio:* 13:1.

**Academics** *Calendar:* semesters. *Degree:* certificates, diplomas, and associate. *Special study options:* academic remediation for entering students, adult/continuing education programs, advanced placement credit, cooperative education, distance learning, double majors, English as a second language, honors programs, independent study, internships, off-campus study, part-time degree program, services for LD students, summer session for credit.

**Library** Central Wyoming College Library. *Books:* 53,204 (physical), 5 (digital/electronic); *Serial titles:* 152 (physical), 8 (digital/electronic); *Databases:* 141. Weekly public service hours: 82.

**Student Life** *Campus security:* 24-hour emergency response devices, late-night transport/escort service, controlled dormitory access.

**Athletics** Member NJCAA.

**Costs (2017–18)** *Tuition:* state resident $2256 full-time, $94 per credit part-time; nonresident $6768 full-time, $282 per credit part-time. Full-time tuition and fees vary according to course load, program, and reciprocity agreements. Part-time tuition and fees vary according to course load, program, and reciprocity agreements. *Required fees:* $768 full-time, $32 per credit part-time. *Room and board:* $6681; room only: $2644. Room and board charges vary according to board plan and housing facility. *Payment plans:* installment, deferred payment.

**Financial Aid** Of all full-time matriculated undergraduates who enrolled in 2015, 410 applied for aid, 336 were judged to have need. 89 Federal Work-Study jobs (averaging $1673). *Financial aid deadline:* 6/30.

**Applying** *Options:* electronic application, early admission, deferred entrance. *Recommended:* high school transcript.

**Freshman Application Contact** Ms. Tawnie DeJong, Student Recruiter, Central Wyoming College, 2660 Peck Avenue, Riverton, WY 82501-2273. *Phone:* 307-855-2231. *Toll-free phone:* 800-735-8418. *Fax:* 307-855-2065. *E-mail:* tdejong@cwc.edu. *Website:* http://www.cwc.edu/.

# Eastern Wyoming College
## Torrington, Wyoming

- **State and locally supported** 2-year, founded 1948, part of Wyoming Community College Commission
- **Rural** 40-acre campus
- **Endowment** $4.6 million
- **Coed**

**Undergraduates** 602 full-time, 1,002 part-time. Students come from 20 states and territories; 9 other countries; 26% are from out of state; 1% Black or African American, non-Hispanic/Latino; 6% Hispanic/Latino; 0.3% Asian, non-Hispanic/Latino; 0.8% Native Hawaiian or other Pacific Islander, non-Hispanic/Latino; 2% American Indian or Alaska Native, non-Hispanic/Latino;

0.2% Two or more races, non-Hispanic/Latino; 3% international; 8% transferred in; 21% live on campus.

**Faculty** *Student/faculty ratio:* 20:1.

**Academics** *Calendar:* semesters. *Degree:* certificates, diplomas, and associate. *Special study options:* academic remediation for entering students, accelerated degree program, advanced placement credit, distance learning, double majors, English as a second language, independent study, internships, part-time degree program, services for LD students, student-designed majors, summer session for credit.

**Library** Eastern Wyoming College Library. *Books:* 30,339 (physical), 681,514 (digital/electronic); *Serial titles:* 86 (physical); *Databases:* 268. Weekly public service hours: 61.

**Student Life** *Campus security:* 24-hour emergency response devices, controlled dormitory access.

**Athletics** Member NJCAA.

**Costs (2017–18)** *Tuition:* state resident $2256 full-time, $94 per credit hour part-time; nonresident $6768 full-time, $282 per credit hour part-time. Full-time tuition and fees vary according to course load, location, and program. Part-time tuition and fees vary according to course load, location, and program. *Required fees:* $672 full-time, $28 per credit hour part-time. *Room and board:* $6136; room only: $3292. Room and board charges vary according to board plan and housing facility.

**Applying** *Recommended:* high school transcript.

**Freshman Application Contact** Dr. Rex Cogdill, Vice President for Students Services, Eastern Wyoming College, 3200 West C Street, Torrington, WY 82240. *Phone:* 307-532-8257. *Toll-free phone:* 866-327-8996. *Fax:* 307-532-8222. *E-mail:* rex.cogdill@ewc.wy.edu. *Website:* http://www.ewc.wy.edu/.

# Laramie County Community College
## Cheyenne, Wyoming

- **District-supported** 2-year, founded 1968, part of Wyoming Community College Commission
- **Small-town** 271-acre campus
- **Coed,** 4,226 undergraduate students, 39% full-time, 58% women, 42% men

**Undergraduates** 1,634 full-time, 2,592 part-time. 14% are from out of state; 2% Black or African American, non-Hispanic/Latino; 15% Hispanic/Latino; 0.9% Asian, non-Hispanic/Latino; 0.5% Native Hawaiian or other Pacific Islander, non-Hispanic/Latino; 0.9% American Indian or Alaska Native, non-Hispanic/Latino; 3% Two or more races, non-Hispanic/Latino; 7% Race/ethnicity unknown; 1% international; 4% transferred in; 13% live on campus.

**Freshmen** *Admission:* 1,720 applied, 1,720 admitted, 521 enrolled. *Average high school GPA:* 3.0.

**Faculty** *Total:* 282, 40% full-time, 10% with terminal degrees. *Student/faculty ratio:* 15:1.

**Majors** Accounting; agribusiness; agricultural business technology; agricultural production; agriculture; anthropology; art; autobody/collision and repair technology; automobile/automotive mechanics technology; biological and physical sciences; biology/biological sciences; business administration and management; business/commerce; chemistry; computer programming; computer science; corrections; criminal justice/law enforcement administration; dental hygiene; diagnostic medical sonography and ultrasound technology; diesel mechanics technology; digital communication and media/multimedia; drafting and design technology; early childhood education; economics; education; emergency medical technology (EMT paramedic); energy management and systems technology; engineering; English; entrepreneurship; equestrian studies; fire science/firefighting; general studies; heating, air conditioning, ventilation and refrigeration maintenance technology; history; homeland security, law enforcement, firefighting and protective services related; humanities; human services; kinesiology and exercise science; legal assistant/paralegal; mass communication/media; mathematics; mechanic and repair technologies related; medical insurance coding; music; physical education teaching and coaching; physical therapy technology; political science and government; pre-law studies; pre-pharmacy studies; psychology; public administration; radiologic technology/science; registered nursing/registered nurse; religious studies; social sciences; sociology; Spanish; speech communication and rhetoric; surgical technology; wildlife, fish and wildlands science and management.

**Academics** *Calendar:* semesters. *Degree:* certificates, diplomas, and associate. *Special study options:* academic remediation for entering students, adult/continuing education programs, advanced placement credit, cooperative education, distance learning, double majors, English as a second language, honors programs, independent study, internships, off-campus study, part-time degree program, services for LD students, summer session for credit. *ROTC:* Army (c), Air Force (c).

**Library** Ludden Library.

**Student Life** *Housing Options:* coed. Campus housing is university owned. *Activities and Organizations:* drama/theater group, student-run newspaper, choral group, Student Government Association, Phi Theta Kappa, Block and Bridle, Student Nursing Club, SkillsUSA. *Campus security:* 24-hour emergency response devices and patrols, late-night transport/escort service, controlled dormitory access. *Student services:* health clinic, personal/psychological counseling.

**Athletics** Member NJCAA. *Intercollegiate sports:* basketball M(s), cheerleading M(s)/W(s), equestrian sports M(s)/W(s), soccer M(s)/W(s), volleyball W(s). *Intramural sports:* basketball M/W, equestrian sports M/W, racquetball M/W, rock climbing M/W, skiing (cross-country) M/W, soccer M/W, softball M/W, table tennis M/W, ultimate Frisbee M/W, volleyball M/W.

**Costs (2018–19)** *Tuition:* state resident $2256 full-time, $94 per credit hour part-time; nonresident $6768 full-time, $282 per credit hour part-time. Full-time tuition and fees vary according to course load. Part-time tuition and fees vary according to course load. *Required fees:* $1170 full-time, $49 per credit hour part-time. *Room and board:* $8140. Room and board charges vary according to board plan and housing facility. *Payment plan:* installment. *Waivers:* senior citizens and employees or children of employees.

**Financial Aid** Of all full-time matriculated undergraduates who enrolled in 2016, 1,287 applied for aid, 938 were judged to have need, 146 had their need fully met. In 2016, 510 non-need-based awards were made. *Average percent of need met:* 70%. *Average financial aid package:* $6631. *Average need-based loan:* $3150. *Average need-based gift aid:* $1851. *Average non-need-based aid:* $1417.

**Applying** *Options:* electronic application, deferred entrance. *Required for some:* high school transcript, interview.

**Admissions Office Contact** Laramie County Community College, 1400 East College Drive, Cheyenne, WY 82007-3299. *Toll-free phone:* 800-522-2993 Ext. 1357.
*Website:* http://www.lccc.wy.edu/.

# Northwest College
## Powell, Wyoming

- **State and locally supported** 2-year, founded 1946, part of Wyoming Community College System
- **Rural** 132-acre campus
- **Endowment** $35.0 million
- **Coed,** 1,654 undergraduate students, 58% full-time, 58% women, 42% men

**Undergraduates** 953 full-time, 701 part-time. Students come from 34 states and territories; 28 other countries; 24% are from out of state; 1% Black or African American, non-Hispanic/Latino; 7% Hispanic/Latino; 0.4% Asian, non-Hispanic/Latino; 0.3% Native Hawaiian or other Pacific Islander, non-Hispanic/Latino; 0.3% American Indian or Alaska Native, non-Hispanic/Latino; 4% Two or more races, non-Hispanic/Latino; 5% international; 46% live on campus. *Retention:* 61% of full-time freshmen returned.

**Freshmen** *Admission:* 373 enrolled.
**Faculty** *Total:* 145, 50% full-time. *Student/faculty ratio:* 12:1.
**Majors** Accounting; agribusiness; agricultural communication/journalism; agricultural production; agricultural teacher education; airline pilot and flight crew; allied health and medical assisting services related; animal sciences; anthropology; archeology; art; athletic training; biology/biological sciences; business administration and management; business/commerce; CAD/CADD drafting/design technology; chemistry; commercial and advertising art; commercial photography; computer and information sciences; criminal justice/safety; crop production; early childhood education; electrician; elementary education; engineering; English; equestrian studies; farm and ranch management; general studies; health and physical education/fitness; health/medical preparatory programs related; history; international relations and affairs; mathematics; music; music technology; natural resources management and policy; parks, recreation and leisure; physics; political science and government; pre-optometry; pre-pharmacy studies; psychology; range science and management; registered nursing/registered nurse; secondary education; social sciences; sociology; Spanish; speech communication and rhetoric; veterinary/animal health technology; welding technology.
**Academics** *Calendar:* semesters. *Degree:* certificates and associate. *Special study options:* academic remediation for entering students, adult/continuing education programs, advanced placement credit, cooperative education, distance learning, double majors, English as a second language, external degree program, independent study, internships, off-campus study, part-time degree program, services for LD students, study abroad, summer session for credit.
**Library** John Taggart Hinckley Library.
**Student Life** *Housing:* on-campus residence required for freshman year. *Options:* coed, women-only, special housing for students with disabilities. Campus housing is university owned. Freshman campus housing is guaranteed. *Activities and Organizations:* drama/theater group, choral group. *Campus security:* 24-hour emergency response devices and patrols, late-night

transport/escort service, controlled dormitory access. *Student services:* health clinic, personal/psychological counseling, veterans affairs office.

**Athletics** Member NJCAA. *Intercollegiate sports:* basketball M(s)/W(s), equestrian sports M(s)/W(s), soccer M(s)/W(s), volleyball W(s), wrestling M(s). *Intramural sports:* basketball M/W, football M/W, golf M/W, softball M/W, ultimate Frisbee M/W, volleyball M/W.

**Costs (2017–18)** *Tuition:* state resident $2256 full-time, $94 per credit hour part-time; nonresident $6768 full-time, $282 per credit hour part-time. Full-time tuition and fees vary according to course load, location, and program. Part-time tuition and fees vary according to course load, location, and program. *Required fees:* $1130 full-time, $32 per credit hour part-time, $73 per term part-time. *Room and board:* $5840. Room and board charges vary according to board plan and housing facility. *Payment plan:* installment. *Waivers:* children of alumni, senior citizens, and employees or children of employees.

**Financial Aid** Of all full-time matriculated undergraduates who enrolled in 2016, 115 Federal Work-Study jobs (averaging $2700). 215 state and other part-time jobs (averaging $2700).

**Applying** *Options:* electronic application. *Required:* high school transcript. *Required for some:* minimum 2.0 GPA. *Recommended:* minimum 2.0 GPA. *Application deadlines:* rolling (freshmen), rolling (transfers). *Notification:* continuous (freshmen), continuous (transfers).

**Freshman Application Contact** Mr. West Hernandez, Admissions Manager, Northwest College, 231 W 6th St, Orendorff Building 1, Powell, WY 82435-1898. *Phone:* 307-754-6103. *Toll-free phone:* 800-560-4692. *Fax:* 307-754-6249. *E-mail:* west.hernandez@nwc.edu.
*Website:* http://www.nwc.edu/.

# Sheridan College
## Sheridan, Wyoming

**Freshman Application Contact** Mr. Matt Adams, Admissions Coordinator, Sheridan College, PO Box 1500, Sheridan, WY 82801-1500. *Phone:* 307-674-6446 Ext. 2005. *Toll-free phone:* 800-913-9139 Ext. 2002. *Fax:* 307-674-3373. *E-mail:* madams@sheridan.edu. *Website:* http://www.sheridan.edu/.

# Western Wyoming Community College
## Rock Springs, Wyoming

- **State and locally supported** 2-year, founded 1959
- **Small-town** 342-acre campus
- **Endowment** $23.4 million
- **Coed,** 3,390 undergraduate students, 32% full-time, 52% women, 48% men

**Undergraduates** 1,073 full-time, 2,317 part-time. Students come from 26 states and territories; 8% are from out of state; 1% Black or African American, non-Hispanic/Latino; 11% Hispanic/Latino; 0.5% Asian, non-Hispanic/Latino; 0.3% Native Hawaiian or other Pacific Islander, non-Hispanic/Latino; 1% American Indian or Alaska Native, non-Hispanic/Latino; 3% Two or more races, non-Hispanic/Latino; 0.1% Race/ethnicity unknown; 3% international; 11% live on campus.

**Freshmen** *Admission:* 2,347 applied, 1,160 admitted, 613 enrolled.
**Faculty** *Total:* 320, 26% full-time, 6% with terminal degrees. *Student/faculty ratio:* 11:1.
**Majors** Accounting; administrative assistant and secretarial science; anthropology; archeology; art; automobile/automotive mechanics technology; biological and physical sciences; biology/biological sciences; business administration and management; chemistry; computer and information sciences; computer programming (specific applications); computer science; criminal justice/law enforcement administration; criminology; dance; data entry/microcomputer applications; data processing and data processing technology; diesel mechanics technology; dramatic/theater arts; early childhood education; economics; education; education (multiple levels); electrical, electronic and communications engineering technology; electrical/electronics equipment installation and repair; electrician; elementary education; engineering technology; English; environmental science; forestry; general studies; geology/earth science; health/medical preparatory programs related; health services/allied health/health sciences; heavy equipment maintenance technology; history; humanities; human services; industrial electronics technology; industrial mechanics and maintenance technology; information science/studies; information technology; instrumentation technology; journalism; kinesiology and exercise science; legal administrative assistant/secretary; liberal arts and sciences/liberal studies; licensed practical/vocational nurse training; marketing/marketing management; mathematics; mechanics and repair; medical administrative assistant and medical secretary; medical/clinical assistant; medical office assistant; medical office computer specialist; mining technology; music; nursing assistant/aide and patient care assistant/aide; photography; political science and government; pre-dentistry studies; pre-engineering; pre-law studies; premedical studies; prenursing studies; pre-pharmacy studies; pre-veterinary studies; psychology;

secondary education; social sciences; social work; sociology; Spanish; speech communication and rhetoric; theater design and technology; visual and performing arts; web/multimedia management and webmaster; web page, digital/multimedia and information resources design; welding technology; wildlife, fish and wildlands science and management; word processing.

**Academics** *Calendar:* semesters. *Degree:* certificates, diplomas, and associate. *Special study options:* academic remediation for entering students, advanced placement credit, cooperative education, distance learning, English as a second language, honors programs, independent study, internships, part-time degree program, services for LD students, summer session for credit.

**Library** Hay Library. *Books:* 53,688 (physical), 747,995 (digital/electronic); *Serial titles:* 136 (physical), 63,272 (digital/electronic); *Databases:* 416. Weekly public service hours: 81; students can reserve study rooms.

**Student Life** *Housing Options:* coed, special housing for students with disabilities. Campus housing is university owned. *Activities and Organizations:* drama/theater group, student-run newspaper, radio station, choral group, Association of Non-Traditional Students (ANTS), Spanish Club, Residence Hall Association, International Club, Latter Day Saints Student Association. *Campus security:* 24-hour emergency response devices and patrols, late-night transport/escort service, controlled dormitory access, patrols by trained security personnel from 4 pm to 8 am, 24-hour patrols on weekends and holidays. *Student services:* personal/psychological counseling, veterans affairs office.

**Athletics** Member NJCAA. *Intercollegiate sports:* basketball M(s)/W(s), cheerleading M(s)/W(s), soccer M(s)/W(s), volleyball W(s), wrestling M(s).

**Costs (2017–18)** *Tuition:* $94 per credit hour part-time; state resident $2953 full-time, $89 per credit hour part-time; nonresident $7345 full-time, $267 per credit hour part-time. *Required fees:* $697 full-time, $31 per credit hour part-time, $348 per credit hour part-time. *Room and board:* $5654; room only: $2610. Room and board charges vary according to board plan and housing facility. *Waivers:* senior citizens and employees or children of employees.

**Financial Aid** Of all full-time matriculated undergraduates who enrolled in 2016, 20 Federal Work-Study jobs (averaging $1500).

**Applying** *Options:* electronic application, early admission, deferred entrance. *Recommended:* high school transcript. *Application deadlines:* rolling (freshmen), rolling (transfers).

**Freshman Application Contact** Ms. Erin M. Grey, Director of Admissions, Western Wyoming Community College, 2500 College Drive, Rock Springs, WY 82901. *Phone:* 307-382-1647. *Toll-free phone:* 800-226-1181. *Fax:* 307-382-1636. *E-mail:* admissions@westernwyoming.edu. *Website:* http://www.westernwyoming.edu/.

## WyoTech Laramie
### Laramie, Wyoming

**Director of Admissions** Director of Admissions, WyoTech Laramie, 1889 Venture Drive, Laramie, WY 82070. *Phone:* 307-742-3776. *Toll-free phone:* 888-577-7559. *Fax:* 307-721-4854. *Website:* http://www.wyotech.edu/.

# CANADA

## CANADA

## Southern Alberta Institute of Technology
### Calgary, Alberta, Canada

**Freshman Application Contact** Southern Alberta Institute of Technology, 1301 16th Avenue NW, Calgary, AB T2M 0L4, Canada. *Phone:* 403-284-8857. *Toll-free phone:* 877-284-SAIT. *Website:* http://www.sait.ca/.

# INTERNATIONAL

## BERMUDA

## Bermuda College
### Paget, Bermuda

**Admissions Office Contact** Bermuda College, 21 Stonington Avenue, South Road, Paget PG 04, Bermuda. *Website:* http://www.college.bm/.

## MARSHALL ISLANDS

## College of the Marshall Islands
### Majuro, Marshall Islands

- **State-supported** 2-year
- **Rural** campus
- **Endowment** $1.2 million
- **Coed**

**Undergraduates** 693 full-time, 302 part-time. 100% Native Hawaiian or other Pacific Islander, non-Hispanic/Latino; 0.3% American Indian or Alaska Native, non-Hispanic/Latino; 0.4% international; 0.3% transferred in.

**Faculty** *Student/faculty ratio:* 14:1.

**Academics** *Degree:* associate.

**Costs (2017–18)** *Tuition:* state resident $3500 full-time, $130 per credit hour part-time; nonresident $3720 full-time, $200 per credit hour part-time. Full-time tuition and fees vary according to class time, course level, course load, degree level, location, program, and student level. Part-time tuition and fees vary according to class time, course level, course load, degree level, location, program, and student level. *Required fees:* $790 full-time, $711 per credit hour part-time. *Room and board:* $1320; room only: $740. Room and board charges vary according to housing facility and location.

**Financial Aid** Of all full-time matriculated undergraduates who enrolled in 2015, 984 applied for aid, 984 were judged to have need. *Average financial aid package:* $4372. *Average need-based gift aid:* $4372. *Financial aid deadline:* 7/15.

**Applying** *Application fee:* $5. *Required:* high school transcript, minimum 2.0 GPA, health examination form.

**Freshman Application Contact** Ms. Jomi Monica Capelle, Director of Admissions and Records, College of the Marshall Islands, PO Box 1258, Majuro, MH 96960, Marshall Islands. *Phone:* 692-625-6823. *Fax:* 692-625-7203. *E-mail:* cmiadmissions@cmi.edu. *Website:* http://www.cmi.edu/.

# MICRONESIA

## College of Micronesia–FSM
### Kolonia Pohnpei, Micronesia

**Freshman Application Contact** Rita Hinga, Student Services Specialist, College of Micronesia–FSM, PO Box 159, Kolonia Pohnpei, FM 96941, Micronesia. *Phone:* 691-320-3795 Ext. 15. *E-mail:* rhinga@comfsm.fm. *Website:* http://www.comfsm.fm/.

# PALAU

## Palau Community College
### Koror, Palau

**Freshman Application Contact** Ms. Dahlia Katosang, Director of Admissions and Financial Aid, Palau Community College, PO Box 9, Koror, PW 96940-0009. *Phone:* 680-488-2471 Ext. 233. *Fax:* 680-488-4468. *E-mail:* dahliapcc@palaunet.com. *Website:* http://www.palau.edu/.

# Institutional Changes Since *Peterson's® Two-Year Colleges 2018*

The following is an alphabetical listing of institutions that have closed, merged with other institutions, or changed their names or status since the release of *Peterson's® Two-Year Colleges 2018*.

Advance Science Institute (Hialeah, FL): *name changed to Advance Science College.*

American College of Healthcare Sciences (Portland, OR): *now classified as a 4-year college.*

American National University (Martinsville, VA): *closed.*

AmeriTech College (Draper, UT): *name changed to Ameritech College of Healthcare.*

Arizona Automotive Institute (Glendale, AZ): *no longer degree granting.*

ATS Institute of Technology (Highland Heights, OH): *name changed to MDT College of Health Sciences and no longer degree granting.*

Bainbridge State College (Bainbridge, GA): *merged into a single entry for Abraham Baldwin Agricultural College (Tifton, GA).*

Blue Cliff College–Gulfport (Gulfport, MS): *no longer degree granting.*

Brightwood College, North Hollywood Campus (North Hollywood, CA): *name changed to Brightwood College, Los Angeles (Van Nuys) Campus.*

Broome Community College (Binghamton, NY): *name changed to State University of New York Broome Community College.*

Career Training Academy (Monroeville, PA): *closed.*

Colorado School of Healing Arts (Lakewood, CO): *no longer degree granting.*

Consolidated School of Business (Lancaster, PA): *closed.*

Court Reporting Institute of St. Louis (Clayton, MO): *closed.*

Crowley's Ridge College (Paragould, AR): *now classified as a 4-year college.*

Culinary Institute of St. Louis at Hickey College (St. Louis, MO): *closed.*

Daymar College (Bellevue, KY): *closed.*

Delaware Technical & Community College, Stanton/Wilmington Campus (Newark, DE): *name changed to Delaware Technical & Community College, Stanton/George Campus.*

Duluth Business University (Duluth, MN): *closed.*

Eastern Idaho Technical College (Idaho Falls, ID): *name changed to College of Eastern Idaho.*

Emory University, Oxford College (Oxford, GA): *merged into a single entry for Emory University (Atlanta, GA) by request from the institution.*

Everest College (Colorado Springs, CO): *name changed to Altierus Career College and closed.*

Everest College (Thornton, CO): *name changed to Altierus Career College and closed.*

Everest College (Henderson, NV): *name changed to Altierus Career College and closed.*

Everest College (Arlington, TX): *name changed to Altierus Career College and closed.*

Everest College (Fort Worth, TX): *name changed to Altierus Career College and closed.*

Everest College (Chesapeake, VA): *name changed to Altierus Career College and closed.*

Everest College (Tacoma, WA): *name changed to Altierus Career College and closed.*

Everest University (Orange Park, FL): *name changed to Altierus Career College and closed.*

Florida College of Natural Health (Maitland, FL): *name changed to Cortiva Institute–Orlando and no longer degree granting.*

Florida College of Natural Health (Miami, FL): *name changed to Cortiva Institute–Miami and no longer degree granting.*

Florida College of Natural Health (Pompano Beach, FL): *name changed to Cortiva Institute–Fort Lauderdale/Pompano and no longer degree granting.*

Gallipolis Career College (Gallipolis, OH): *closed.*

Global Health College (Alexandria, VA): *no longer offers associate's degrees.*

Horry Georgetown Technical College (Conway, SC): *name changed to Horry-Georgetown Technical College.*

Huertas Junior College (Caguas, PR): *name changed to Huertas College.*

Keystone Technical Institute (Harrisburg, PA): *closed.*

Lincoln College (Lincoln, IL): *now classified as a 4-year college.*

Living Arts College (Raleigh, NC): *now classified as a 4-year college.*

McCann School of Business & Technology (Shreveport, LA): *closed.*

McCann School of Business & Technology (Hazelton, PA): *closed.*

Medtech College (Marietta, GA): *name changed to Gwinnett College.*

Miami University Middletown (Middletown, OH): *now classified as a 4-year college.*

Miller-Motte College (Greenville, NC): *closed.*

Miller-Motte Technical College (Gulfport, MS): *closed.*

Miller-Motte Technical College (Clarksville, TN): *closed.*

Miller-Motte Technical College (Madison, TN): *closed.*

Miller-Motte Technical College (Lynchburg, VA): *closed.*

Miller-Motte Technical College (Roanoke, VA): *closed.*

National College (Knoxville, TN): *closed.*

Ohio Business College (Hilliard, OH): *closed.*

Penn State Shenango (Sharon, PA): *now classified as a 4-year college.*

Pierce College at Fort Steilacoom (Lakewood, WA): *name changed to Pierce College Fort Steilacoom.*

Pierce College at Puyallup (Puyallup, WA): *name changed to Pierce College Puyallup.*

Pinnacle Career Institute (Lawrence, KS): *closed.*

Pulaski Technical College (North Little Rock, AR): *name changed to University of Arkansas–Pulaski Technical College.*

Rich Mountain Community College (Mena, AR): *name changed to University of Arkansas Rich Mountain.*

Sage College (Moreno Valley, CA): *closed.*

South Hills School of Business & Technology (Altoona, PA): *merged into a single entry for South Hills School of Business & Technology (State College, PA).*

TCI–College of Technology (New York, NY): *closed.*

Three Rivers Community College (Poplar Bluff, MO): *name changed to Three Rivers College.*

Trumbull Business College (Warren, OH): *closed.*

Valley College (Beckley, WV): *no longer degree granting.*

Vet Tech Institute at Hickey College (St. Louis, MO): *closed.*

Virginia Marti College of Art and Design (Lakewood, OH): *now classified as a 4-year college.*

Wentworth Military Academy and College (Lexington, MO): *closed.*

West Hills Community College (Coalinga, CA): *name changed to West Hills College Coalinga.*

West Hills Community College–Lemoore (Lemoore, CA): *name changed to West Hills College Lemoore.*

West Virginia Business College (Wheeling, WV): *closed.*

# Featured Two-Year Colleges

# FASHION INSTITUTE OF TECHNOLOGY
## State University of New York
NEW YORK, NEW YORK

★ To read more about this school, visit http://petersons.to/fit

## The College and Its Mission

The Fashion Institute of Technology, FIT, a college of the State University of New York, has been a leader in career education in art, design, business, and technology for nearly 75 years. The college infuses its nearly 36 majors with a comprehensive liberal arts education, providing a singular blend of practical experience and a pioneering curriculum that prepares students for success and leadership in the competitive global marketplace. FIT offers a range of innovative programs that are affordable and relevant to today's rapidly changing industries. Internationally renowned, FIT draws on its New York City location to provide a vibrant, creative community in which to learn. The schools of Art and Design, Business and Technology, and Liberal Arts offer Associate in Applied Science (A.A.S.), Bachelor of Fine Arts (B.F.A.), and Bachelor of Science (B.S.) degrees. The School of Graduate Studies offers Master of Arts (M.A.), Master of Fine Arts (M.F.A.), and Master of Professional Studies (M.P.S.) degrees. The college is accredited by the Middle States Commission on Higher Education, the National Association of Schools of Art and Design, and the Council for Interior Design Accreditation. FIT serves approximately 9,000 students from the greater metropolitan area, New York State, across the country, and around the world, providing full- and part-time study, evening/weekend degree programs, noncredit, certificate, and online courses.

FIT's faculty members bring high-level industry experience to the classroom, working as corporate executives, entrepreneurs, consultants, designers, artists, filmmakers, and authors. Both practitioners and scholars, they connect students with real-world practice, fostering collaboration, innovation, and a global perspective. Academic departments consult with industry leaders to ensure that curricula and classroom technology remain current with evolving professional practice.

FIT offers a complete college experience, with a vibrant campus life that includes over 60 clubs and organizations, athletic teams, and an active student government. Four residence halls house 2,300 undergraduate students in traditional and apartment-style rooms. Professional staff and residence assistants live in each hall to ensure that students are fully enjoying their residential experience.

## Academic Programs

Each undergraduate program includes a core of liberal arts courses, providing students with a global perspective, critical-thinking skills, and the ability to communicate effectively. All degree programs are designed to prepare students for careers in the creative industries and to provide them with the prerequisite studies to go on to baccalaureate, master's, or doctoral degrees.

Typically, undergraduate students apply to and enroll in the two-year A.A.S. degree program. For those who have already earned a degree or have taken the requisite general education courses at other institutions, FIT also offers one-year A.A.S. degree programs. Upon earning the A.A.S. degree (either at FIT or another institution), students apply to FIT's bachelor's programs to earn the B.F.A. or B.S. degree.

**Associate's Degree Programs:** For the A.A.S. degree, FIT offers ten majors through the School of Art and Design, four through the Jay and Patty Baker School of Business and Technology, and one through the School of Liberal Arts. The A.A.S. programs are accessories design*, advertising and marketing communications*, communication design foundation*, fashion design*, fashion business management* (with an online option), film and media, fine arts, illustration, interior design, jewelry design, menswear, photography and related media, production management: fashion and related industries, textile development and marketing*, and textile/surface design*. Programs with an asterisk (*) also offer a one-year A.A.S. degree for eligible transfer applicants.

**Bachelor's Degree Programs:** The majority of FIT's A.A.S. graduates choose to pursue a related baccalaureate program at the college. FIT offers twenty-six baccalaureate programs—fourteen B.F.A. programs through the School of Art and Design, ten B.S. programs through the Baker School of Business and Technology, and two B.S. programs through the School of Liberal Arts. The B.F.A. programs are accessories

design; advertising design; animation, interactive media, and game design; fabric styling; fashion design (with specializations in children's wear, intimate apparel, knitwear, special occasion, and sportswear); fine arts; graphic design; illustration; interior design; packaging design; photography and related media; textile/surface design; toy design; and visual presentation and exhibition design. The B.S. programs are advertising and marketing communications, art history and museum professions, cosmetics and fragrance marketing, direct and interactive marketing, entrepreneurship for the fashion and design industries, fashion business management, film and media, home products development, international trade and marketing for the fashion industries, production management: fashion and related industries, technical design, and textile development and marketing.

**Minors:** FIT's curriculum offers a range of subject-based and interdisciplinary minors that let students expand and deepen their major studies or explore additional interests. Liberal Arts minors include communication studies, dance, film and media, economics, international politics, Latin American studies, Mandarin Chinese, and women and gender studies; Art and Design minors are creative technology and design thinking; the Business and Technology minor is international trade and marketing; and the ethics and sustainability minor is offered jointly through all three schools.

**Evening/Weekend Programs:** FIT provides evening and weekend credit and noncredit classes to students and working professionals interested in pursuing a degree or furthering their knowledge of a particular industry, while balancing the demands of career or family.

**Certificate Programs:** FIT's Center for Continuing and Professional Studies offers credit and noncredit certificates through its two divisions: Enterprise Studies and Digital Design and Professional Studies. Certificate programs include leather apparel, millinery, retail management, fashion styling, pet product design and marketing, and sustainable design entrepreneurship. The center also provides career and personal development courses designed for adults with busy schedules.

**Honors Program:** The Presidential Scholars honors program, available to academically exceptional students in all majors, offers special courses, projects, colloquia, and off-campus activities that broaden horizons and stimulate discourse. Presidential Scholars receive priority course registration and an annual merit stipend.

**Internships:** Internships are a required element of most programs and are available to all matriculated students. Nearly one third of FIT student interns are offered employment on completion of their internships; past sponsors include American Eagle Outfitters, Bloomingdale's, Calvin Klein, Estée Lauder, Hearst Magazines, MTV, and Saatchi & Saatchi.

**Precollege Programs:** Precollege programs are available to middle and high school students during the fall, spring, and summer. More than 100 courses provide the chance to learn in an innovative environment, develop art and design portfolios, explore the business and technological sides of many creative careers, and discover natural talents and abilities.

## Off-Campus Programs

The study-abroad experience lets students immerse themselves in diverse cultures and prepares them to live and work in a global community. FIT has two campuses in Italy—one in Milan, one in Florence—and one near Seoul, South Korea, where students study fashion design or fashion business management and gain firsthand experience in the dynamics of global fashion. FIT also offers study-abroad opportunities on six continents. Students can study abroad during the winter or summer sessions, for a semester, or for a full academic year.

## Costs

As a SUNY college, FIT offers affordable tuition for both New York State residents and nonresidents. The 2017–18 associate-level tuition per semester for in-state residents was $2,345; for nonresidents, $7,035. Baccalaureate-level tuition per semester was $3,335 for in-state residents and $10,096 for nonresidents. Per-semester housing costs were $5,888–$7,075 for traditional residence hall accommodations with mandatory meal plan and $6,299–$10,495 for apartment-style accommodations. Meal plans ranged from $1,915 to $2,451 per semester. Textbook costs and other nominal fees, such as locker rental or laboratory use, vary per program. All costs are subject to change.

## Financial Aid

FIT offers scholarships, grants, loans, and federal work-study employment for students with financial need. Overall, two-thirds of full-time, matriculated undergraduate students who complete the Free Application for Federal Student Aid (FAFSA) receive some type of assistance through loans and/or grants. The college directly administers its own institutional grants and scholarships, which are provided by the FIT Foundation.

College-administered funding includes Federal Pell Grants, Federal Perkins Loans, Federal Supplemental Educational Opportunity Grants, Federal Work-Study, and the Federal Family Educational Loan Program, which includes student and parent loans. New York State residents who meet eligibility guidelines may also receive grants from the Tuition Assistance Program (TAP) and/or Educational Opportunity Program (EOP). To be considered for need-based federal financial aid, U.S. citizens and permanent residents must file the FAFSA prior to February 15 for fall admission or November 1 for spring admission. Additional documentation may be requested by Financial Aid Services.

## Faculty

FIT's faculty is drawn from top professionals in academia, art, design, communications, and business, providing a curriculum rich in real-world experience and traditional educational values. Student-instructor interaction is encouraged, with a maximum class size of 25, and courses are structured to foster collaboration, independent thinking, and self-expression.

## Student Body Profile

Fall 2017 enrollment was 8,846 with 8,251 students enrolled in degree programs. Forty percent of degree-seeking students are enrolled in the School of Art and Design; 54 percent were in the Baker School of Business and Technology. The average age of full-time degree seekers was 23. Thirty-seven percent of FIT's students were New York City residents, 25 percent were New York State (non–New York City) residents, and 37 percent were out-of-state residents or international students. The ethnic/racial makeup of the student body was approximately 11 percent Asian; 9 percent black; 19 percent Hispanic; 3 percent multiracial; and 44 percent white. There were 1,051 international students.

## Student Activities

Participation in campus life is encouraged, and the college is home to more than sixty student organizations, societies, athletic teams, major-related groups, and special-interest clubs. Student-run publications include a campus newspaper, a fashion and beauty magazine, and a literary and art magazine. Each organization is open to all students who have paid their activity fee.

**Student Government:** The FIT Student Government Association grants all students the privileges and responsibilities of citizens in a self-governing college community. Faculty committees often include student representatives, and the president of the student government sits on FIT's Board of Trustees.

**Athletics:** FIT has intercollegiate teams in cross-country and half marathon, track and field, table tennis, women's tennis, women's soccer, swimming and diving, and women's volleyball; there is also a coed dance company. Athletics and Recreation offers a full array of group fitness classes, including aerobics, dance, spin, and yoga at no extra cost. Students can also work out on their own in a 5,000-square-foot fitness center. Open gym activities allow students to participate in both team and individual sports.

**Events:** Concerts, dances, field trips, films, flea markets, and other events are planned by the FIT Student Government Association and Programming Board and various clubs.

## Facilities and Resources

FIT's campus provides its students with classrooms, laboratories, and studios that reflect the most advanced educational and industry practices. The Fred P. Pomerantz Art and Design Center houses drawing, painting, photography, printmaking, and sculpture studios; display and exhibition design rooms; a model-making workshop; and a graphics printing service bureau. The Peter G. Scotese Computer-Aided Design and Communications Center provides the latest technology in computer graphics, design, photography, and animation.

Other cutting-edge facilities include a professionally equipped fragrance-development laboratory—the only one of its kind on a U.S. college campus—cutting and sewing labs, a design/research lighting laboratory, knitting lab, broadcasting studio, multimedia foreign languages laboratory, and forty-six computer labs containing Mac and PC workstations.

The Museum at FIT, New York City's only museum dedicated to fashion, contains one of the most important collections of fashion and textiles in the world. The museum, which is accredited by the American Alliance of Museums, operates year-round, and its exhibitions are free and open to the public. The Gladys Marcus Library provides more than 300,000 volumes of print, nonprint, and digital materials. The periodicals collection includes over 500 current subscriptions, with a specialization in international design and trade publications; online resources include more than 90 searchable databases. Students also have access to the library's Special Collections, a highly specialized repository of primary-source research materials related to fashion and design.

The David Dubinsky Student Center offers student lounges, a game room, a student radio station, the Style Shop (a student-run boutique), a full-service dining hall and Starbucks, student government and club offices, disability services, comprehensive health services and a counseling center, two gyms, a state-of-the-art fitness center, and a dance studio.

## Location

Occupying an entire block in Manhattan's Chelsea neighborhood, FIT makes extensive use of the city's creative, commercial, and cultural resources, providing students with unrivaled internship opportunities and professional connections. A wide range of cultural and entertainment options are available within a short walk of the campus, as is convenient access to several subway and bus lines and the city's major rail and bus transportation hubs.

## Admission Requirements

Applicants for admission must be either candidates for or recipients of a high school diploma or a General Educational Development (GED) certificate. Admission is based on performance in college-preparatory coursework and the student essay. A portfolio evaluation is required for art and design majors. Specific portfolio requirements are explained on FIT's website. SAT and ACT scores are required for placement in math and English classes and students applying to the Presidential Scholars honors program. International applicants whose native language is not English must submit scores from either the TOEFL, PTE, or IELTS examinations.

Transfer applicants must submit official transcripts for all coursework previously taken at an accredited college/university. Transfer applicants may qualify either for the one-year A.A.S. program if they hold a bachelor's degree or have a minimum of 30 transferable college credits, including 24 credits equivalent to FIT's liberal arts degree requirements.

Students seeking admission to a B.F.A. or B.S. program must hold an A.A.S. degree from FIT or an equivalent college degree and must meet the prerequisites for the specific major. A portfolio is required for applicants to B.F.A. programs. Any student who applies for baccalaureate-level transfer to FIT from a four-year bachelor's-level program must have completed a minimum of 60 credits, including the requisite art or technical courses and the liberal arts requirements.

## Application and Information

Prospective students wishing to visit FIT are encouraged to attend an admissions information session and a student-led tour of FIT's campus. The visit schedule, including open houses, portfolio review days, and Junior Days for high school juniors, is available online at fitnyc.edu/visitfit. A virtual tour of the campus can be found at fitnyc.edu/virtualtour. Candidates may apply for undergraduate admission online at fitnyc.edu/admissions. More information is available by contacting:
Undergraduate Admissions
FIT
227 West 27th Street, Room C139
New York, New York 10001-5992
Phone: 212-217-3760
E-mail: fitinfo@fitnyc.edu
Website:  http://www.fitnyc.edu/admissions
http://www.facebook.com/FashionInstituteofTechnology
http://www.instagram.com/fitnyc
http://www.twitter.com/fit

# MIAMI DADE COLLEGE
## MIAMI, FLORIDA

Miami Dade College

★ To read more about this school, visit http://petersons.to/miami-dade-college

## The College and Its Mission

With 165,000 students currently enrolled and more than 2 million students admitted, Miami Dade College (MDC) is the largest campus-based institution of higher education in the United States. MDC's eight campuses are located in and around Miami, Florida, and include the Hialeah, Homestead, InterAmerican, Kendall, Medical, North, West and Wolfson campuses. In addition, MDC has a major outreach center: The Carrie P. Meek Entrepreneurial Education Center.

The College's multiple locations across Miami-Dade County allow it to offer students highly flexible scheduling options for more than 300 study pathways. Students may pursue four-year bachelor's degrees and two-year associate degrees, as well as various professional and college credit certificates. MDC offers evening and weekend courses and many online through MDC's Virtual College at http://www.mdc.edu/virtual/. With numerous special industry partnerships, MDC programs are the backbone of the region's workforce which provides its graduates immediate employment in emerging and in-demand fields.

Miami Dade College, its students, faculty, and staff, have been recognized through numerous prestigious awards and honors. Recent examples include the 2017 Leah Meyer Austin Award from Achieving the Dream, the 2016 Higher Education Excellence in Diversity award from Insight into Diversity, and the Presidential Medal of Freedom, which was presented to MDC President Eduardo J. Padrón by former U.S. President Barack Obama, among many others.

In addition to being one of the most respected colleges in the nation, MDC has long served as the anchor of South Florida's cultural scene. The College produces and hosts nationally acclaimed artistic events, such as the Miami Book Fair and Miami Film Festival, and operates cultural venues including the Museum of Art and Design at MDC, Tower Theater, Koubek Center, the National Historic Landmark Freedom Tower and Teatro Prometeo.

Graduates from MDC include many notable professionals, artists, political figures and other celebrities, including: U.S. Rep. Ileana Ros-Lehtinen, Emilio Estefan, Andy Garcia, Oscar-winning playwright Tarell Alvin McCraney, Pulitzer Prize-winning journalist Mirta Ojito, The Related Group co-founder and CEO Jorge M. Perez, National Baseball Hall of Fame inductee Mike Piazza, Miami-Dade County State Attorney Katherine Fernández Rundle, Sylvester Stallone and *Miami Herald* president and publisher Alexandra Villoch, among many others.

## Academic Programs

**Associate Degree Programs:** Two-year associate degree programs at Miami Dade College prepare students to enter into junior-year studies at universities or immediate employment in certain career fields. MDC offers hundreds of associate degree pathways in areas such as accounting, architecture, biology, computer science, criminal justice, dietetics, education, fashion, hospitality, interior design, journalism, paralegal studies, social work and sociology. MDC awards more associate degrees to Hispanics than any other institution of higher education in the United States.

A student graduating with an associate degree from MDC is guaranteed admission into any public university in Florida, as well as many other universities nationwide with which MDC has articulation agreements. Graduates of Miami Dade College have often transferred to top-ranking institutions such as Harvard, Yale, Georgetown, Columbia and Boston University.

**Specialized Training and Certificate Options:** Miami Dade College offers several options for students looking to start new careers, improve their job skills, or learn a trade. MDC's technical certification programs prepare students for specific vocations in more than 40 areas, including electronic technology, firefighting, massage therapy, medical assisting, pharmacy technician and television production.

The College also offers more than 80 college credit certificates that focus on a unique industry or a specific job. Credits earned may be applied toward a related Associate in Science degree. In 2018, MDC launched several trailblazing certificate programs, including cybersecurity, digital forensics, mechatronics and visual and augmented reality.

Non-credit and alternative education options at MDC include GED preparation, English as a second language (ESL) courses, and dual enrollment courses open to accelerated high school students.

**Bachelor's Degree Programs:** Miami Dade College offers bachelor's degree programs in select majors, including biological sciences, data analytics, education, electronics engineering technology, film, TV and digital production, information systems technology, nursing, physician assistant studies, public safety management, supervision and management, and supply chain management. All bachelor's degree programs at MDC are workforce driven and coursework is designed to prepare students for a specific career.

Students considering MDC have the option to apply to The Honors College, a division of Miami Dade College that is open to high school graduates with exceptional GPA and SAT scores. Benefits of admission to The Honors College include small classes, study-abroad opportunities, development of capstone projects for potential publication and personalized educational planning.

## Study-Abroad Opportunities

Students at MDC can study abroad in other countries while earning credits toward an MDC degree. The College sponsors study-abroad programs as well as numerous faculty-led programs to destinations around the world. As a member of the

College Consortium for International Students (CCIS), MDC students also are able to participate in study-abroad programs sponsored by other CCIS partner institutions.

## Costs

For the 2018–19 academic year, the full time (24 credits) associate degree cost for in-state students is $2,837.28 and $9,660.24 for out-of-state students. Career and Technical Education Programs cost $1,092.96 per term (12 credits) for in-state students and $4,263.72 for out-of-state students. Up-to-date tuition and fees information can be found online at http://www.mdc.edu/tuition/.

To pay in-state tuition rates, prospective students need to provide proof of Florida residency. More information is available at www.mdc.edu/main/flresidency/.

## Financial Aid and Scholarships

Ample financial aid opportunities are available based on financial need and/or academic record, and include direct loan programs, scholarships, federal student aid, Pell Grants, the Florida Bright Futures Scholarship Program and MDC's American Dream Scholarship, which covers two years of tuition for qualified high-achieving students.

## Student Activities

Each MDC campus has a culture that is as diverse its student body. Each offers an opportunity for teamwork and leader-ship. All club and organization information can be found on SharkNet, MDC's virtual connection to Student Life (http://sharknet.mdc.edu). Here students can browse existing organizations, create a new organization, submit event requests and more.

Miami Dade College is home to five intercollegiate athletic teams: women's basketball, softball and volleyball, as well as men's basketball and baseball. Since 1961, the Miami Dade College Sharks have won multiple championships and various recognitions and honors. MDC is a member of the National Junior College Athletic Association and the Florida Community College Activities Association's Southern Conference.

## Facilities and Resources

Learning Resources at Miami Dade College provides a stimulating learning environment that enhances the classroom experience through a variety of services such as face-to-face tutoring, information literacy instruction and informative workshops. Its facilities enable students to study collaboratively as well as individually and access MDC's specialized collections of print and electronic resources.

MDC's Learning Resources Labs and Courtyards offer students and faculty a wide array of supplemental assistance to ensure academic success, from state-of-the-art technology and software to knowledgeable tutors who can provide instruction in a variety of courses such as math, writing, reading, business, natural science, health sciences, speech and test preparation, and more.

Library liaisons work with discipline faculty to ensure that resources needed to support the curriculum are available collegewide. These resources may include such things as LibGuides, books, online databases or eBooks. In addition, the library liaison can design instructional sessions or work with faculty to design assignments that teach students information-literacy skills.

## Location

Miami Dade College has eight Florida campuses: Hialeah, Homestead, InterAmerican (Miami), Kendall (Miami), Medical (Miami), North (Miami), West (Doral) and Wolfson (Miami), along with its Carrie P. Meek Entrepreneurial Education Center (Miami).

Details on each of the campuses can be found at www.mdc.edu/about/campuses.aspx.

## Application and Information

The online application is the fastest, easiest way to apply for admission to Miami Dade College, which has rolling admissions and an acceptance rate of 100 percent. In addition to a $30 application fee, a high school transcript is required. Additional information, including the link to apply online, can be found at http://www.mdc.edu/admissions/.

For more information, prospective students should contact:

Ms. Ferne Creary, Interim College Registrar
Miami Dade College
300 N.E. Second Avenue
Miami, Florida 33132
United States
Phone: 305-237-2206
Fax: 305-237-2532
E-mail: fcreary@mdc.edu

Miami Dade College Kendall Campus

# MIRACOSTA COLLEGE
## OCEANSIDE, CALIFORNIA

### The College and Its Mission

MiraCosta College offers a friendly and safe suburban environment within easy driving distance of world famous attractions in Southern California. The sunny climate and ocean views make the campus a great place to study. Facilities include library and technology center, student computer labs, free academic tutoring and writing center, cafeteria and patio, an outdoor amphitheater, tennis courts, track, gymnasium, and fitness center.

The MiraCosta Community College District is located in North San Diego County, along the Southern California coast between Orange County to the north and the metropolitan area of San Diego to the south. Classes and resources are available in four separate locations within the district.

The MiraCosta Community College District's mission is to provide superior educational opportunities and student support services to a diverse population of learners with a focus on their success. MiraCosta offers associate degrees, university transfer courses, career and technical education, certificate programs, basic skills education, and lifelong learning opportunities that strengthen the economic, cultural, social, and educational well-being of the communities it serves.

### Academic Programs

MiraCosta Community College offers students a wide range of subjects to pursue. Most classes are also available online. Academic programs include:

Accounting
Administration of justice
Anthropology
Art
Astronomy
Athletics
Automotive technology
Biology
Biotechnology
Business administration
Business office technology
Career and life planning
Chemistry
Child development
Chinese
Communication
Computer studies and
    information technology
Computer science
Counseling
Dance
Design
Dramatic arts
Earth science
Economics
English
English as a second
    language
Film
French
Geography
Geology
German
Gerontology
Health education
History
Horticulture
Hospitality management
Humanities
Internship studies and
    cooperative education
Italian
Japanese
Kinesiology
Linguistics
Literature
Mathematics
Media arts and
    technologies
Medical administrative
    professional
Massage therapy
Music
Nursing
Nutrition
Oceanography
Philosophy
Physical science
Physics
Political science
Psychology
Reading
Real estate
Religious studies
Sociology
Spanish
Surgical technology

### Costs

For the 2017–18 academic year, tuition at MiraCosta College is $46 per credit unit for California residents and $280 per credit unit for nonresident and international students.

### Financial Aid

In fiscal year 2014, a total of $11,321,677 in financial aid was distributed to 11,330 students.

### Faculty

The College has 178 full-time faculty members and 540 part-time faculty members.

### Student Body Profile

There are approximately 18,500 students enrolled at MiraCosta College. The diverse student body includes people from a variety of ages, ethnicities, and cultural backgrounds. Fifty-six percent of the students are women and 44 percent are men; 64 percent are age 24 or younger, while 36 percent are 25 and older. Ethnicity of the student body is 46 percent white, 34 percent Hispanic, 8 percent Asian/Pacific Islander, 4 percent African American, and 8 percent multiethnic or other.

### Student Activities

The Offices of Student Activities supports a wide range of activities and events, provides information and resources centers, and serves as a focal point for service and leadership development programs. MiraCosta has more than forty active student clubs including the Accounting and Business

Club, the International Club, the Black Student Union, the Dance Club, the Martial Arts Club, the Performance Writers Club, and many others.

## Facilities and Resources

*Advisement/Counseling:* MiraCosta College offers individualized academic, career, and personal counseling to assist both prospective and current students develop their educational programs; coordinate their career and academic goals; and understand graduation, major, certificate, and transfer requirements.

*Specialized Services:* With an average class size of about 30 to 45, MiraCosta students rave about their professors and the personal attention they receive. Both students and staff enjoy a friendly atmosphere and a shared belief in helping one another.

*Career Planning/Placement:* The mission of the Center for Career Studies and Services is to empower students to make informed, intentional career decisions. Career Center resources include a computer lab, resource library, workshops, and career counseling by appointment.

*Library and Audiovisual Services:* Maintaining thousands of academic research databases, periodicals, reference materials, and professional research guides, the Library and Information Hub is the center for learning and academic support for MiraCosta students. The Library is also home to the Academic Tutoring Center, the Math Learning Center, the Writing Center, and a large computer lab. All services are free to MiraCosta students.

## Location

MiraCosta College's district is coastal North San Diego County, approximately 35 miles north of San Diego and 90 miles south of Los Angeles. The Oceanside Campus is a 121-acre hilltop location with coastal and mountain views; the San Elijo Campus is on 42 acres in Cardiff facing the San Elijo Lagoon and Nature Preserve.

Students enjoy MiraCosta's friendly and safe environment. MiraCosta is within driving distance of Los Angeles, Mexico, Disneyland, Hollywood, La Jolla, San Diego Zoo, SeaWorld, and other world famous attractions in Southern California. Facilities include a new library and technology center, student computer labs, cafeteria and patio, an outdoor amphitheater, tennis courts, track, gymnasium, and fitness center.

## Admission Requirements

U.S. adults and high school students (sophomore level and higher) are able to enroll. International students who are at least 18 years old with a high school diploma and English proficiency can apply with a written application and supporting documents. International students should contact the International Office for application procedures. MiraCosta College also offers intensive English language training for students seeking to improve their English skills.

## Application and Information

For more information, prospective students should contact:

Admissions Office
MiraCosta College
1 Barnard Drive
Oceanside, California 92056
Phone: 760-757-2121
Website: www.miracosta.edu
    www.miracosta.edu/iip (for international students)
    www.facebook.com/MiraCostaCC
    www.twitter.com/MiraCosta
    https://www.instagram.com/miracostacollege
    https://www.youtube.com/user/MiraCostaCC

Students at MiraCosta College enjoying the first day of fall semester.

# Indexes

# Associate Degree Programs at Two-Year Colleges

## ACCOUNTING
Adirondack Comm Coll (NY)
Alexandria Tech and Comm Coll (MN)
Alvin Comm Coll (TX)
Amarillo Coll (TX) .
American Samoa Comm Coll (AS)
Arizona Western Coll (AZ)
Asheville-Buncombe Tech Comm Coll (NC)
Austin Comm Coll District (TX)
Barton County Comm Coll (KS)
Beal Coll (ME)
Black Hawk Coll, Moline (IL)
Blue Ridge Comm and Tech Coll (WV)
Bristol Comm Coll (MA)
Brookhaven Coll (TX)
Bunker Hill Comm Coll (MA)
Caldwell Comm Coll and Tech Inst (NC)
Cedar Valley Coll (TX)
Central Lakes Coll (MN)
Central Maine Comm Coll (ME)
Central New Mexico Comm Coll (NM)
Central Ohio Tech Coll (OH)
Central Oregon Comm Coll (OR)
Century Coll (MN)
Chandler-Gilbert Comm Coll (AZ)
Chipola Coll (FL)
Chippewa Valley Tech Coll (WI)
Cleveland Comm Coll (NC)
Coll of Eastern Idaho (ID)
Coll of the Ouachitas (AR)
The Coll of Westchester (NY)
Colorado Northwestern Comm Coll (CO)
Comm Coll of Philadelphia (PA)
Copiah-Lincoln Comm Coll (MS)
Craven Comm Coll (NC)
De Anza Coll (CA)
Del Mar Coll (TX)
Des Moines Area Comm Coll (IA)
Dutchess Comm Coll (NY)
Eastern Gateway Comm Coll (OH)
Edison State Comm Coll (OH)
El Paso Comm Coll (TX)
Fayetteville Tech Comm Coll (NC)
Fox Valley Tech Coll (WI)
Frederick Comm Coll (MD)
Gateway Tech Coll (WI)
Genesee Comm Coll (NY)
George C. Wallace Comm Coll (AL)
Great Falls Coll Montana State U (MT)
Greenville Tech Coll (SC)
Harford Comm Coll (MD)
Harper Coll (IL)
Hawkeye Comm Coll (IA)
Haywood Comm Coll (NC)
Highland Comm Coll (IL)
Hill Coll (TX)
Housatonic Comm Coll (CT)
Houston Comm Coll (TX)
Howard Comm Coll (MD)
Hudson County Comm Coll (NJ)
Illinois Central Coll (IL)
Illinois Eastern Comm Colls, Olney Central College (IL)
Illinois Valley Comm Coll (IL)
Independence Comm Coll (KS)
Iowa Central Comm Coll (IA)
James Sprunt Comm Coll (NC)
Jefferson Comm Coll (NY)
Johnston Comm Coll (NC)
Kaskaskia Coll (IL)
Kingsborough Comm Coll of the City U of New York (NY)

Lackawanna Coll (PA)
Lakeland Comm Coll (OH)
Lakeshore Tech Coll (WI)
Lakes Region Comm Coll (NH)
Lake Superior Coll (MN)
Laramie County Comm Coll (WY)
LDS Business Coll (UT)
Lenoir Comm Coll (NC)
Lorain County Comm Coll (OH)
Los Angeles City Coll (CA)
Macomb Comm Coll (MI)
Manchester Comm Coll (CT)
Manor Coll (PA)
Massachusetts Bay Comm Coll (MA)
McHenry County Coll (IL)
McLennan Comm Coll (TX)
Mid-State Tech Coll (WI)
Minnesota State Comm and Tech Coll (MN)
Minnesota West Comm and Tech Coll (MN)
Mission Coll (CA)
Mitchell Comm Coll (NC)
Mohave Comm Coll (AZ)
Monroe Comm Coll (NY)
Monroe County Comm Coll (MI)
Morton Coll (IL)
Mt. San Antonio Coll (CA)
Muskegon Comm Coll (MI)
Nassau Comm Coll (NY)
National Park Coll (AR)
Navarro Coll (TX)
New River Comm Coll (VA)
Niagara County Comm Coll (NY)
Northcentral Tech Coll (WI)
Northeast Comm Coll (NE)
Northeastern Jr Coll (CO)
Northeastern Tech Coll (SC)
Northeast Iowa Comm Coll (IA)
Northern Essex Comm Coll (MA)
Northern Maine Comm Coll (ME)
North Hennepin Comm Coll (MN)
North Iowa Area Comm Coll (IA)
North Shore Comm Coll (MA)
NorthWest Arkansas Comm Coll (AR)
Northwest Coll (WY)
Northwest Vista Coll (TX)
Odessa Coll (TX)
Oklahoma State U–Oklahoma City (OK)
Orange Coast Coll (CA)
Paris Jr Coll (TX)
Pasadena City Coll (CA)
Pennsylvania Highlands Comm Coll (PA)
Pensacola State Coll (FL)
Piedmont Comm Coll (NC)
Piedmont Virginia Comm Coll (VA)
Queensborough Comm Coll of the City U of New York (NY)
Randolph Comm Coll (NC)
Rappahannock Comm Coll (VA)
Richland Coll (TX)
Richmond Comm Coll (NC)
Ridgewater Coll (MN)
Rock Valley Coll (IL)
Rowan-Cabarrus Comm Coll (NC)
St. Louis Comm Coll (MO)
San Jacinto Coll District (TX)
San Joaquin Delta Coll (CA)
Sauk Valley Comm Coll (IL)
Scottsdale Comm Coll (AZ)
Seminole State Coll (OK)
Seminole State Coll of Florida (FL)
Shawnee Comm Coll (IL)
Sisseton-Wahpeton Coll (SD)
Southeast Tech Inst (SD)
Southern U at Shreveport (LA)

South Suburban Coll (IL)
Southwestern Coll (CA)
Southwestern Comm Coll (NC)
Springfield Tech Comm Coll (MA)
Stark State Coll (OH)
Sullivan County Comm Coll (NY)
Tarrant County Coll District (TX)
Three Rivers Comm Coll (CT)
Tidewater Comm Coll (VA)
Tri-County Comm Coll (NC)
Trident Tech Coll (SC)
Trinity Valley Comm Coll (TX)
Waukesha County Tech Coll (WI)
Wayne Comm Coll (NC)
Westchester Comm Coll (NY)
Western Dakota Tech Inst (SD)
Western Iowa Tech Comm Coll (IA)
Western Texas Coll (TX)
Western Wyoming Comm Coll (WY)
White Mountains Comm Coll (NH)
Wisconsin Indianhead Tech Coll (WI)
Wytheville Comm Coll (VA)
York County Comm Coll (ME)

## ACCOUNTING AND BUSINESS/MANAGEMENT
CollAmerica–Denver (CO)
Des Moines Area Comm Coll (IA)
LDS Business Coll (UT)
Mitchell Tech Inst (SD)
Renton Tech Coll (WA)

## ACCOUNTING AND FINANCE
Oklahoma City Comm Coll (OK)
Stark State Coll (OH)

## ACCOUNTING RELATED
John Tyler Comm Coll (VA)
J. Sargeant Reynolds Comm Coll (VA)
Mesalands Comm Coll (NM)
Raritan Valley Comm Coll (NJ)
Southwest Virginia Comm Coll (VA)

## ACCOUNTING TECHNOLOGY AND BOOKKEEPING
Adirondack Comm Coll (NY)
Alamance Comm Coll (NC)
Anne Arundel Comm Coll (MD)
Antelope Valley Coll (CA)
Austin Comm Coll District (TX)
Bucks County Comm Coll (PA)
Camden County Coll (NJ)
Carroll Comm Coll (MD)
Cayuga County Comm Coll (NY)
Chandler-Gilbert Comm Coll (AZ)
Chesapeake Coll (MD)
Clark Coll (WA)
Coll of Central Florida (FL)
Coll of Marin (CA)
Coll of the Canyons (CA)
Coll of the Desert (CA)
Columbia-Greene Comm Coll (NY)
Comm Coll of Allegheny County (PA)
Comm Coll of Baltimore County (MD)
Copiah-Lincoln Comm Coll (MS)
Danville Area Comm Coll (IL)
Daytona State Coll (FL)
Del Mar Coll (TX)
Des Moines Area Comm Coll (IA)
Dutchess Comm Coll (NY)
East Central Coll (MO)
Feather River Coll (CA)
Fiorello H. LaGuardia Comm Coll of the City U of New York (NY)
Front Range Comm Coll (CO)
Fullerton Coll (CA)
Gulf Coast State Coll (FL)
Hagerstown Comm Coll (MD)

Harford Comm Coll (MD)
Harrisburg Area Comm Coll (PA)
Haywood Comm Coll (NC)
H. Councill Trenholm State Comm Coll (AL)
Hinds Comm Coll (MS)
Holyoke Comm Coll (MA)
Hudson County Comm Coll (NJ)
Ivy Tech Comm Coll–Bloomington (IN)
Ivy Tech Comm Coll–Central Indiana (IN)
Ivy Tech Comm Coll–Columbus (IN)
Ivy Tech Comm Coll–East Central (IN)
Ivy Tech Comm Coll–Kokomo (IN)
Ivy Tech Comm Coll–Lafayette (IN)
Ivy Tech Comm Coll–North Central (IN)
Ivy Tech Comm Coll–Northeast (IN)
Ivy Tech Comm Coll–Northwest (IN)
Ivy Tech Comm Coll–Richmond (IN)
Ivy Tech Comm Coll–Sellersburg (IN)
Ivy Tech Comm Coll–Southeast (IN)
Ivy Tech Comm Coll–Southwest (IN)
Ivy Tech Comm Coll–Wabash Valley (IN)
Jamestown Comm Coll (NY)
Jefferson Comm Coll (NY)
Jefferson State Comm Coll (AL)
Kellogg Comm Coll (MI)
Kennebec Valley Comm Coll (ME)
Kent State U at Ashtabula (OH)
Kent State U at East Liverpool (OH)
Kent State U at Salem (OH)
Kent State U at Trumbull (OH)
Kent State U at Tuscarawas (OH)
Kirtland Comm Coll (MI)
LDS Business Coll (UT)
Lehigh Carbon Comm Coll (PA)
Los Angeles City Coll (CA)
Merced Coll (CA)
Miami Dade Coll (FL)
Mohawk Valley Comm Coll (NY)
Montgomery Coll (MD)
Montgomery County Comm Coll (PA)
Mott Comm Coll (MI)
Nassau Comm Coll (NY)
Naugatuck Valley Comm Coll (CT)
Northampton Comm Coll (PA)
North Hennepin Comm Coll (MN)
North Iowa Area Comm Coll (IA)
Northland Comm and Tech Coll (MN)
Northwest-Shoals Comm Coll (AL)
Northwest Vista Coll (TX)
Oakton Comm Coll (IL)
Orange Coast Coll (CA)
Ozarks Tech Comm Coll (MO)
Palomar Coll (CA)
Pasadena City Coll (CA)
Pensacola State Coll (FL)
Pueblo Comm Coll (CO)
Queensborough Comm Coll of the City U of New York (NY)
Raritan Valley Comm Coll (NJ)
St. Charles Comm Coll (MO)
St. Philip's (TX)
Salt Lake Comm Coll (UT)
San Juan Coll (NM)
Schenectady County Comm Coll (NY)
Schoolcraft Coll (MI)
Southeast Tech Inst (SD)
Southern U at Shreveport (LA)
South Suburban Coll (IL)
Southwestern Coll (CA)
Southwestern Comm Coll (IA)
Southwestern Indian Polytechnic Inst (NM)

Southwestern Michigan Coll (MI)
Sowela Tech Comm Coll (LA)
State U of New York Coll of Technology at Alfred (NY)
Tallahassee Comm Coll (FL)
Three Rivers Coll (MO)
Three Rivers Comm Coll (CT)
Tompkins Cortland Comm Coll (NY)
Tulsa Comm Coll (OK)
Union County Coll (NJ)
Vincennes U (IN)
Wayne County Comm Coll District (MI)
Westchester Comm Coll (NY)
Western Iowa Tech Comm Coll (IA)
Williston State Coll (ND)

## ACTING
KD Conservatory Coll of Film and Dramatic Arts (TX)
Montgomery County Comm Coll (PA)
Northampton Comm Coll (PA)

## ADMINISTRATIVE ASSISTANT AND SECRETARIAL SCIENCE
Alvin Comm Coll (TX)
Amarillo Coll (TX)
Antelope Valley Coll (CA)
Austin Comm Coll District (TX)
Barton County Comm Coll (KS)
Beal Coll (ME)
Bevill State Comm Coll (AL)
Black Hawk Coll, Moline (IL)
Bossier Parish Comm Coll (LA)
Camden County Coll (NJ)
Carroll Comm Coll (MD)
Cecil Coll (MD)
Central Lakes Coll (MN)
Central Louisiana Tech Comm Coll (LA)
Central Maine Comm Coll (ME)
Central New Mexico Comm Coll (NM)
Central Texas Coll (TX)
Century Coll (MN)
Chippewa Valley Tech Coll (WI)
Cleveland State Comm Coll (TN)
Cloud County Comm Coll (KS)
Cochise County Comm Coll District (AZ)
Coll of Eastern Idaho (ID)
Coll of The Albemarle (NC)
Coll of the Canyons (CA)
Coll of the Ouachitas (AR)
Collin County Comm Coll District (TX)
Comm Coll of Allegheny County (PA)
Comm Coll of Baltimore County (MD)
Copiah-Lincoln Comm Coll (MS)
Crowder Coll (MO)
Dabney S. Lancaster Comm Coll (VA)
De Anza Coll (CA)
Del Mar Coll (TX)
Eastern Gateway Comm Coll (OH)
El Paso Comm Coll (TX)
Fiorello H. LaGuardia Comm Coll of the City U of New York (NY)
Fox Valley Tech Coll (WI)
Fullerton Coll (CA)
Gateway Tech Coll (WI)
George C. Wallace Comm Coll (AL)
Greenville Tech Coll (SC)
Harper Coll (IL)
Harrisburg Area Comm Coll (PA)
H. Councill Trenholm State Comm Coll (AL)
Highland Comm Coll (IL)
Hill Coll (TX)

Hinds Comm Coll (MS)
Holyoke Comm Coll (MA)
Hopkinsville Comm Coll (KY)
Housatonic Comm Coll (CT)
Hutchinson Comm Coll (KS)
Illinois Central Coll (IL)
Independence Comm Coll (KS)
Iowa Central Comm Coll (IA)
Ivy Tech Comm Coll–Bloomington (IN)
Ivy Tech Comm Coll–Columbus (IN)
Ivy Tech Comm Coll–East Central (IN)
Ivy Tech Comm Coll–Kokomo (IN)
Ivy Tech Comm Coll–Sellersburg (IN)
Ivy Tech Comm Coll–Southeast (IN)
Ivy Tech Comm Coll–Southwest (IN)
Jamestown Comm Coll (NY)
Jefferson Comm Coll (NY)
Jefferson State Comm Coll (AL)
Johnston Comm Coll (NC)
Kellogg Comm Coll (MI)
Kent State U at Ashtabula (OH)
Kent State U at Salem (OH)
Kent State U at Trumbull (OH)
Kent State U at Tuscarawas (OH)
Kingsborough Comm Coll of the City U of New York (NY)
Kishwaukee Coll (IL)
Lackawanna Coll (PA)
Lakeland Comm Coll (OH)
Lakeshore Tech Coll (WI)
LDS Business Coll (UT)
Lehigh Carbon Comm Coll (PA)
Los Angeles City Coll (CA)
Lurleen B. Wallace Comm Coll (AL)
Macomb Comm Coll (MI)
Manchester Comm Coll (CT)
McHenry County Coll (IL)
McLennan Comm Coll (TX)
Merced Coll (CA)
Meridian Comm Coll (MS)
Mesa Comm Coll (AZ)
Mid-Plains Comm Coll, North Platte (NE)
Mid-State Tech Coll (WI)
Minnesota State Comm and Tech Coll (MN)
Minnesota West Comm and Tech Coll (MN)
Mission Coll (CA)
Mohawk Valley Comm Coll (NY)
Monroe Comm Coll (NY)
Monroe County Comm Coll (MI)
Montgomery County Comm Coll (PA)
Morton Coll (IL)
Mt. San Antonio Coll (CA)
Muskegon Comm Coll (MI)
Nassau Comm Coll (NY)
National Park Coll (AR)
Navarro Coll (TX)
New Mexico State U–Alamogordo (NM)
New River Comm Coll (VA)
Niagara County Comm Coll (NY)
Northampton Comm Coll (PA)
Northcentral Tech Coll (WI)
North Central Texas Coll (TX)
Northeast Comm Coll (NE)
Northeastern Tech Coll (SC)
Northeast Iowa Comm Coll (IA)
Northeast State Comm Coll (TN)
North Iowa Area Comm Coll (IA)
Northland Comm and Tech Coll (MN)
North Shore Comm Coll (MA)
Northwest-Shoals Comm Coll (AL)
Northwest Vista Coll (TX)
Oakton Comm Coll (IL)
Odessa Coll (TX)
Otero Jr Coll (CO)
Palomar Coll (CA)
Panola Coll (TX)
Pasadena City Coll (CA)
Pensacola State Coll (FL)
Potomac State Coll of West Virginia U (WV)
Queensborough Comm Coll of the City U of New York (NY)
Rainy River Comm Coll (MN)
Rappahannock Comm Coll (VA)
Raritan Valley Comm Coll (NJ)
Reid State Tech Coll (AL)
Rend Lake Coll (IL)
Richland Coll (TX)
Ridgewater Coll (MN)
Rock Valley Coll (IL)
St. Philip's Coll (TX)
San Jacinto Coll District (TX)
Sauk Valley Comm Coll (IL)
Scottsdale Comm Coll (AZ)

Seminole State Coll of Florida (FL)
Southeast Kentucky Comm and Tech Coll (KY)
Southeast Tech Inst (SD)
Southwestern Coll (CA)
Sowela Tech Comm Coll (LA)
Springfield Tech Comm Coll (MA)
Stark State Coll (OH)
Sullivan County Comm Coll (NY)
Tarrant County Coll District (TX)
Texarkana Coll (TX)
Three Rivers Coll (MO)
Tidewater Comm Coll (VA)
Trident Tech Coll (SC)
Vincennes U (IN)
Waukesha County Tech Coll (WI)
Westchester Comm Coll (NY)
Western Iowa Tech Comm Coll (IA)
Western Texas Coll (TX)
Western Wyoming Comm Coll (WY)
Williamsburg Tech Coll (SC)
Wisconsin Indianhead Tech Coll (WI)
Wor-Wic Comm Coll (MD)
Wytheville Comm Coll (VA)

### ADULT AND CONTINUING EDUCATION
Cochise County Comm Coll District (AZ)

### ADULT DEVELOPMENT AND AGING
El Paso Comm Coll (TX)
Fiorello H. LaGuardia Comm Coll of the City U of New York (NY)
Wayne County Comm Coll District (MI)

### ADVERTISING
Central Ohio Tech Coll (OH)
Coll of Central Florida (FL)
Fashion Inst of Technology (NY)
Mohawk Valley Comm Coll (NY)
Mt. San Antonio Coll (CA)
Muskegon Comm Coll (MI)
Palomar Coll (CA)
Tidewater Comm Coll (VA)

### AERONAUTICAL/AEROSPACE ENGINEERING TECHNOLOGY
Daytona State Coll (FL)
Lenoir Comm Coll (NC)
Mohawk Valley Comm Coll (NY)
Tulsa Comm Coll (OK)

### AERONAUTICS/AVIATION/ AEROSPACE SCIENCE AND TECHNOLOGY
Alvin Comm Coll (TX)
Cecil Coll (MD)
Comm Coll of Baltimore County (MD)
Hesston Coll (KS)
Hinds Comm Coll (MS)
Lehigh Carbon Comm Coll (PA)
Miami Dade Coll (FL)
Naugatuck Valley Comm Coll (CT)

### AEROSPACE, AERONAUTICAL AND ASTRONAUTICAL/SPACE ENGINEERING
Kent State U at Ashtabula (OH)

### AESTHETICIAN/ESTHETICIAN AND SKIN CARE
Southeastern Coll–West Palm Beach (FL)

### AFRICAN AMERICAN/BLACK STUDIES
Nassau Comm Coll (NY)

### AGRIBUSINESS
American Samoa Comm Coll (AS)
Coll of Central Florida (FL)
Coll of the Desert (CA)
Copiah-Lincoln Comm Coll (MS)
Crowder Coll (MO)
Harford Comm Coll (MD)
Hinds Comm Coll (MS)
James Sprunt Comm Coll (NC)
Laramie County Comm Coll (WY)
Merced Coll (CA)
Minnesota West Comm and Tech Coll (MN)
Mitchell Comm Coll (NC)
Northcentral Tech Coll (WI)
Northeast Comm Coll (NE)
Northeast Iowa Comm Coll (IA)
Northwest Coll (WY)
The Ohio State U Ag Tech Inst (OH)

Ridgewater Coll (MN)
San Jacinto Coll District (TX)
Southwestern Comm Coll (IA)
State U of New York Coll of Technology at Alfred (NY)
Wayne Comm Coll (NC)

### AGRICULTURAL AND DOMESTIC ANIMAL SERVICES RELATED
Mesalands Comm Coll (NM)

### AGRICULTURAL AND EXTENSION EDUCATION
Potomac State Coll of West Virginia U (WV)

### AGRICULTURAL AND FOOD PRODUCTS PROCESSING
Minnesota State Comm and Tech Coll (MN)
Minnesota West Comm and Tech Coll (MN)
Northeast Iowa Comm Coll (IA)

### AGRICULTURAL BUSINESS AND MANAGEMENT
American Samoa Comm Coll (AS)
Arizona Western Coll (AZ)
Barton County Comm Coll (KS)
Cloud County Comm Coll (KS)
Cochise County Comm Coll District (AZ)
Copiah-Lincoln Comm Coll (MS)
County Coll of Morris (NJ)
Danville Area Comm Coll (IL)
Dawson Comm Coll (MT)
Hill Coll (TX)
Illinois Central Coll (IL)
Illinois Eastern Comm Colls, Wabash Valley College (IL)
Lake Area Tech Inst (SD)
Lake Region State Coll (ND)
Lamar Comm Coll (CO)
Mesalands Comm Coll (NM)
Mt. San Antonio Coll (CA)
North Dakota State Coll of Science (ND)
Northeastern Jr Coll (CO)
Northwest Mississippi Comm Coll (MS)
The Ohio State U Ag Tech Inst (OH)
Otero Jr Coll (CO)
Pensacola State Coll (FL)
Potomac State Coll of West Virginia U (WV)
Rend Lake Coll (IL)
San Joaquin Delta Coll (CA)
Santa Rosa Jr Coll (CA)
Sauk Valley Comm Coll (IL)
Shawnee Comm Coll (IL)
Treasure Valley Comm Coll (OR)
Vincennes U (IN)

### AGRICULTURAL BUSINESS AND MANAGEMENT RELATED
Copiah-Lincoln Comm Coll (MS)
Penn State DuBois (PA)
Penn State Fayette, The Eberly Campus (PA)
Penn State Mont Alto (PA)

### AGRICULTURAL BUSINESS TECHNOLOGY
Laramie County Comm Coll (WY)
North Dakota State Coll of Science (ND)
The Ohio State U Ag Tech Inst (OH)

### AGRICULTURAL COMMUNICATION/ JOURNALISM
Northwest Coll (WY)
The Ohio State U Ag Tech Inst (OH)
Santa Rosa Jr Coll (CA)

### AGRICULTURAL ECONOMICS
Copiah-Lincoln Comm Coll (MS)
North Iowa Area Comm Coll (IA)
The Ohio State U Ag Tech Inst (OH)
Treasure Valley Comm Coll (OR)

### AGRICULTURAL/FARM SUPPLIES RETAILING AND WHOLESALING
Cloud County Comm Coll (KS)
Copiah-Lincoln Comm Coll (MS)
Des Moines Area Comm Coll (IA)
Fox Valley Tech Coll (WI)
Hawkeye Comm Coll (IA)
Illinois Central Coll (IL)

Minnesota West Comm and Tech Coll (MN)
North Iowa Area Comm Coll (IA)
Western Iowa Tech Comm Coll (IA)

### AGRICULTURAL MECHANICS AND EQUIPMENT TECHNOLOGY
Black Hawk Coll, Moline (IL)
Hutchinson Comm Coll (KS)
Illinois Central Coll (IL)
Merced Coll (CA)
Mitchell Tech Inst (SD)
North Dakota State Coll of Science (ND)
Northland Comm and Tech Coll (MN)
Rend Lake Coll (IL)

### AGRICULTURAL MECHANIZATION
Crowder Coll (MO)
Fox Valley Tech Coll (WI)
Ivy Tech Comm Coll–Wabash Valley (IN)
Kishwaukee Coll (IL)
Navarro Coll (TX)
North Central Texas Coll (TX)
Northwest Mississippi Comm Coll (MS)
The Ohio State U Ag Tech Inst (OH)
Paris Jr Coll (TX)
Rend Lake Coll (IL)
San Joaquin Delta Coll (CA)
Southwest Texas Jr Coll (TX)
Three Rivers Coll (MO)

### AGRICULTURAL MECHANIZATION RELATED
Hinds Comm Coll (MS)

### AGRICULTURAL POWER MACHINERY OPERATION
Hawkeye Comm Coll (IA)
Northeast Iowa Comm Coll (IA)
The Ohio State U Ag Tech Inst (OH)

### AGRICULTURAL PRODUCTION
Black Hawk Coll, Moline (IL)
Chesapeake Coll (MD)
Cloud County Comm Coll (KS)
Hopkinsville Comm Coll (KY)
Illinois Eastern Comm Colls, Wabash Valley College (IL)
Laramie County Comm Coll (WY)
Minnesota West Comm and Tech Coll (MN)
Mitchell Tech Inst (SD)
Northeast Iowa Comm Coll (IA)
North Iowa Area Comm Coll (IA)
Northwest Coll (WY)
Owensboro Comm and Tech Coll (KY)
Rend Lake Coll (IL)
Ridgewater Coll (MN)
Southwestern Michigan Coll (MI)

### AGRICULTURAL TEACHER EDUCATION
Northeastern Jr Coll (CO)
Northwest Coll (WY)
The Ohio State U Ag Tech Inst (OH)
Trinity Valley Comm Coll (TX)
Western Texas Coll (TX)

### AGRICULTURE
American Samoa Comm Coll (AS)
Ancilla Coll (IN)
Arizona Western Coll (AZ)
Barton County Comm Coll (KS)
Black Hawk Coll, Moline (IL)
Central Texas Coll (TX)
Chipola Coll (FL)
Coll of Central Florida (FL)
Coll of the Desert (CA)
Copiah-Lincoln Comm Coll (MS)
Crowder Coll (MO)
Dyersburg State Comm Coll (TN)
Feather River Coll (CA)
Harford Comm Coll (MD)
Hill Coll (TX)
Hutchinson Comm Coll (KS)
Ivy Tech Comm Coll–Columbus (IN)
Ivy Tech Comm Coll–East Central (IN)
Ivy Tech Comm Coll–Kokomo (IN)
Ivy Tech Comm Coll–Lafayette (IN)
Ivy Tech Comm Coll–Northeast (IN)
Ivy Tech Comm Coll–Richmond (IN)
Ivy Tech Comm Coll–Southwest (IN)
Ivy Tech Comm Coll–Wabash Valley (IN)

Minnesota West Comm and Tech Coll (MN)
North Iowa Area Comm Coll (IA)
Western Iowa Tech Comm Coll (IA)

Kaskaskia Coll (IL)
Laramie County Comm Coll (WY)
Macomb Comm Coll (MI)
Merced Coll (CA)
Miami Dade Coll (FL)
Minnesota West Comm and Tech Coll (MN)
Missouri State U–West Plains (MO)
Mt. San Antonio Coll (CA)
Northeast Comm Coll (NE)
Northeastern Jr Coll (CO)
Northland Comm and Tech Coll (MN)
Odessa Coll (TX)
Panola Coll (TX)
Paris Jr Coll (TX)
Pensacola State Coll (FL)
Potomac State Coll of West Virginia U (WV)
Ridgewater Coll (MN)
San Jacinto Coll District (TX)
San Joaquin Delta Coll (CA)
Sauk Valley Comm Coll (IL)
State U of New York Coll of Technology at Alfred (NY)
Texarkana Coll (TX)
Tillamook Bay Comm Coll (OR)
Treasure Valley Comm Coll (OR)
U of Wisconsin–Baraboo/Sauk County (WI)
U of Wisconsin–Barron County (WI)
U of Wisconsin–Fond du Lac (WI)
U of Wisconsin–Fox Valley (WI)
U of Wisconsin–Manitowoc (WI)
U of Wisconsin–Marathon County (WI)
U of Wisconsin–Marinette (WI)
U of Wisconsin–Marshfield/Wood County (WI)
U of Wisconsin–Richland (WI)
U of Wisconsin–Rock County (WI)
U of Wisconsin–Sheboygan (WI)
U of Wisconsin–Washington County (WI)
U of Wisconsin–Waukesha (WI)
Western Texas Coll (TX)
Williston State Coll (ND)

### AGRICULTURE AND AGRICULTURE OPERATIONS RELATED
Potomac State Coll of West Virginia U (WV)

### AGROECOLOGY AND SUSTAINABLE AGRICULTURE
Kennebec Valley Comm Coll (ME)
Lenoir Comm Coll (NC)
Lorain County Comm Coll (OH)
Mesa Comm Coll (AZ)
Santa Rosa Jr Coll (CA)
Tompkins Cortland Comm Coll (NY)
Wayne Comm Coll (NC)

### AGRONOMY AND CROP SCIENCE
Chipola Coll (FL)
Chippewa Valley Tech Coll (WI)
Merced Coll (CA)
Minnesota West Comm and Tech Coll (MN)
Northcentral Tech Coll (WI)
Northeast Comm Coll (NE)
Northeastern Jr Coll (CO)
The Ohio State U Ag Tech Inst (OH)
Potomac State Coll of West Virginia U (WV)
Ridgewater Coll (MN)
Treasure Valley Comm Coll (OR)

### AIR AND SPACE OPERATIONS TECHNOLOGY
Cochise County Comm Coll District (AZ)

### AIRCRAFT POWERPLANT TECHNOLOGY
Antelope Valley Coll (CA)
Colorado Northwestern Comm Coll (CO)
Lake Area Tech Inst (SD)
Northeast State Comm Coll (TN)
Orange Coast Coll (CA)
St. Philip's Coll (TX)
Somerset Comm Coll (KY)
Sowela Tech Comm Coll (LA)
State Tech Coll of Missouri (MO)
Texas State Tech Coll (TX)
Vincennes U (IN)
Wayne County Comm Coll District (MI)

## AIRFRAME MECHANICS AND AIRCRAFT MAINTENANCE TECHNOLOGY
Amarillo Coll (TX)
Central New Mexico Comm Coll (NM)
Craven Comm Coll (NC)
Hinds Comm Coll (MS)
Ivy Tech Comm Coll–Wabash Valley (IN)
Lake Superior Coll (MN)
Mohawk Valley Comm Coll (NY)
Mt. San Antonio Coll (CA)
Northland Comm and Tech Coll (MN)
Orange Coast Coll (CA)
St. Philip's Coll (TX)
State Tech Coll of Missouri (MO)
Texas State Tech Coll (TX)
Trident Tech Coll (SC)
Wayne Comm Coll (NC)
Wayne County Comm Coll District (MI)

## AIRLINE FLIGHT ATTENDANT
Orange Coast Coll (CA)

## AIRLINE PILOT AND FLIGHT CREW
Central Oregon Comm Coll (OR)
Central Texas Coll (TX)
Chandler-Gilbert Comm Coll (AZ)
Cochise County Comm Coll District (AZ)
Colorado Northwestern Comm Coll (CO)
Comm Coll of Allegheny County (PA)
Comm Coll of Baltimore County (MD)
County Coll of Morris (NJ)
Dutchess Comm Coll (NY)
Fox Valley Tech Coll (WI)
Gateway Tech Coll (WI)
Hesston Coll (KS)
Iowa Central Comm Coll (IA)
Kishwaukee Coll (IL)
Lake Superior Coll (MN)
Lehigh Carbon Comm Coll (PA)
Lenoir Comm Coll (NC)
Miami Dade Coll (FL)
Mt. San Antonio Coll (CA)
North Shore Comm Coll (MA)
Northwest Coll (WY)
Pennsylvania Highlands Comm Coll (PA)
Salt Lake Comm Coll (UT)
San Jacinto Coll District (TX)
Texas State Tech Coll (TX)
Treasure Valley Comm Coll (OR)
Vincennes U (IN)

## AIR TRAFFIC CONTROL
Cecil Coll (MD)
Comm Coll of Baltimore County (MD)
Hesston Coll (KS)
Miami Dade Coll (FL)
Mt. San Antonio Coll (CA)
Texas State Tech Coll (TX)
Tulsa Comm Coll (OK)

## AIR TRANSPORTATION RELATED
Cloud County Comm Coll (KS)
Cochise County Comm Coll District (AZ)

## ALLIED HEALTH AND MEDICAL ASSISTING SERVICES RELATED
Blue Ridge Comm and Tech Coll (WV)
Bowling Green State U–Firelands Coll (OH)
Mount Wachusett Comm Coll (MA)
Northern Maine Comm Coll (ME)
Northwest Coll (WY)
Oklahoma City Comm Coll (OK)
Pennsylvania Inst of Technology (PA)
Raritan Valley Comm Coll (NJ)

## ALLIED HEALTH DIAGNOSTIC, INTERVENTION, AND TREATMENT PROFESSIONS RELATED
Gateway Comm and Tech Coll (KY)

## ALTERNATIVE AND COMPLEMENTARY MEDICAL SUPPORT SERVICES RELATED
Mount Wachusett Comm Coll (MA)

## ALTERNATIVE FUEL VEHICLE TECHNOLOGY
Coll of the Desert (CA)

## AMERICAN GOVERNMENT AND POLITICS
St. Philip's Coll (TX)

## AMERICAN INDIAN/NATIVE AMERICAN STUDIES
Arizona Western Coll (AZ)
Nebraska Indian Comm Coll (NE)
Saginaw Chippewa Tribal Coll (MI)
San Juan Coll (NM)
Sisseton-Wahpeton Coll (SD)

## AMERICAN SIGN LANGUAGE (ASL)
Antelope Valley Coll (CA)
Bristol Comm Coll (MA)
Montgomery Coll (MD)
Oklahoma State U–Oklahoma City (OK)
Santa Rosa Jr Coll (CA)
Vincennes U (IN)
Wayne County Comm Coll District (MI)

## AMERICAN STUDIES
Miami Dade Coll (FL)

## ANESTHESIOLOGIST ASSISTANT
Oklahoma City Comm Coll (OK)
Renton-Tech Coll (WA)
Wayne County Comm Coll District (MI)

## ANIMAL/LIVESTOCK HUSBANDRY AND PRODUCTION
Chippewa Valley Tech Coll (WI)
Hawkeye Comm Coll (IA)
Hinds Comm Coll (MS)
Illinois Central Coll (IL)
James Sprunt Comm Coll (NC)
Jefferson Comm Coll (NY)
Merced Coll (CA)
Mt. San Antonio Coll (CA)
North Central Texas Coll (TX)
The Ohio State U Ag Tech Inst (OH)
Ridgewater Coll (MN)
Wayne Comm Coll (NC)

## ANIMAL PHYSIOLOGY
Massachusetts Bay Comm Coll (MA)

## ANIMAL SCIENCES
Alamance Comm Coll (NC)
Ancilla Coll (IN)
Coll of Central Florida (FL)
James Sprunt Comm Coll (NC)
Kaskaskia Coll (IL)
Mt. San Antonio Coll (CA)
Niagara County Comm Coll (NY)
North Dakota State Coll of Science (ND)
Northeast Comm Coll (NE)
Northeastern Jr Coll (CO)
Northwest Coll (WY)
Northwest Mississippi Comm Coll (MS)
The Ohio State U Ag Tech Inst (OH)
Potomac State Coll of West Virginia U (WV)
San Joaquin Delta Coll (CA)
Santa Rosa Jr Coll (CA)
Treasure Valley Comm Coll (OR)
Trinity Valley Comm Coll (TX)
Westchester Comm Coll (NY)

## ANIMAL TRAINING
Lamar Comm Coll (CO)

## ANIMATION, INTERACTIVE TECHNOLOGY, VIDEO GRAPHICS AND SPECIAL EFFECTS
Antelope Valley Coll (CA)
Austin Comm Coll District (TX)
Cecil Coll (MD)
Century Coll (MN)
Coll of Marin (CA)
Coll of the Canyons (CA)
Front Range Comm Coll (CO)
Hagerstown Comm Coll (MD)
Houston Comm Coll (TX)
Kellogg Comm Coll (MI)
Lakes Region Comm Coll (NH)
Lehigh Carbon Comm Coll (PA)
McHenry County Coll (IL)
Miami Dade Coll (FL)
Missouri State U–West Plains (MO)
Montgomery Coll (MD)
New Mexico State U–Alamogordo (NM)

## AMERICAN STUDIES
Miami Dade Coll (FL)

## ANTHROPOLOGY
Antelope Valley Coll (CA)
Austin Comm Coll District (TX)
Barton County Comm Coll (KS)
Central New Mexico Comm Coll (NM)
Coll of the Desert (CA)
Eastern Arizona Coll (AZ)
Feather River Coll (CA)
Fullerton Coll (CA)
Harford Comm Coll (MD)
Houston Comm Coll (TX)
Laramie County Comm Coll (WY)
Merced Coll (CA)
Miami Dade Coll (FL)
Muskegon Comm Coll (MI)
Northeastern Jr Coll (CO)
Northwest Coll (WY)
Orange Coast Coll (CA)
Pasadena City Coll (CA)
San Joaquin Delta Coll (CA)
Santa Rosa Jr Coll (CA)
Southwestern Coll (CA)
Truckee Meadows Comm Coll (NV)
Western Wyoming Comm Coll (WY)

## APPAREL AND ACCESSORIES MARKETING
Des Moines Area Comm Coll (IA)

## APPAREL AND TEXTILE MANUFACTURING
Fashion Inst of Technology (NY)
Orange Coast Coll (CA)

## APPAREL AND TEXTILE MARKETING MANAGEMENT
FIDM/Fashion Inst of Design & Merchandising, Orange County Campus (CA)
Fullerton Coll (CA)
Orange Coast Coll (CA)
Palomar Coll (CA)

## APPAREL AND TEXTILES
Antelope Valley Coll (CA)
Fullerton Coll (CA)
Mt. San Antonio Coll (CA)

## APPLIANCE INSTALLATION AND REPAIR TECHNOLOGY
Renton Tech Coll (WA)

## APPLIED BEHAVIOR ANALYSIS
Montgomery County Comm Coll (PA)

## APPLIED HORTICULTURE/ HORTICULTURAL BUSINESS SERVICES RELATED
Chippewa Valley Tech Coll (WI)
Des Moines Area Comm Coll (IA)
Hinds Comm Coll (MS)
Northeast Comm Coll (NE)

## APPLIED HORTICULTURE/ HORTICULTURE OPERATIONS
Alamance Comm Coll (NC)
Antelope Valley Coll (CA)
Black Hawk Coll, Moline (IL)
Cecil Coll (MD)
Central Lakes Coll (MN)
Century Coll (MN)
Coll of the Desert (CA)
Comm Coll of Allegheny County (PA)
Comm Coll of Baltimore County (MD)
Fayetteville Tech Comm Coll (NC)
Front Range Comm Coll (CO)
Fullerton Coll (CA)
Gateway Tech Coll (WI)
Haywood Comm Coll (NC)
Houston Comm Coll (TX)
Illinois Central Coll (IL)
J. Sargeant Reynolds Comm Coll (VA)
Kaskaskia Coll (IL)
Kishwaukee Coll (IL)
Lenoir Comm Coll (NC)

## ANTHROPOLOGY (cont.)
Orange Coast Coll (CA)
Palomar Coll (CA)
Pasadena City Coll (CA)
Pueblo Comm Coll (CO)
Raritan Valley Comm Coll (NJ)
Southeast Tech Inst (SD)
Southwestern Coll (CA)
Springfield Tech Comm Coll (MA)
State U of New York Coll of Technology at Alfred (NY)
Tyler Jr Coll (TX)
Western Iowa Tech Comm Coll (IA)
West Kentucky Comm and Tech Coll (KY)
York County Comm Coll (ME)

## [column 4]
McHenry County Coll (IL)
Merced Coll (CA)
Montgomery Coll (MD)
Mt. San Antonio Coll (CA)
Orange Coast Coll (CA)
Southeast Tech Inst (SD)
Tulsa Comm Coll (OK)
Vincennes U (IN)
Western Texas Coll (TX)

## APPLIED MATHEMATICS
Muskegon Comm Coll (MI)

## APPLIED PSYCHOLOGY
Northampton Comm Coll (PA)

## AQUACULTURE
Carteret Comm Coll (NC)

## ARABIC
Austin Comm Coll District (TX)

## ARCHEOLOGY
Austin Comm Coll District (TX)
Northwest Coll (WY)
Palomar Coll (CA)
Western Wyoming Comm Coll (WY)

## ARCHITECTURAL AND BUILDING SCIENCES
J. Sargeant Reynolds Comm Coll (VA)
Springfield Tech Comm Coll (MA)

## ARCHITECTURAL DRAFTING AND CAD/CADD
American Samoa Comm Coll (AS)
Anne Arundel Comm Coll (MD)
Carroll Comm Coll (MD)
Central New Mexico Comm Coll (NM)
Central Ohio Tech Coll (OH)
Coll of the Canyons (CA)
Comm Coll of Allegheny County (PA)
Comm Coll of Baltimore County (MD)
Des Moines Area Comm Coll (IA)
Harper Coll (IL)
Hutchinson Comm Coll (KS)
Johnson Coll (PA)
Kaskaskia Coll (IL)
Lake Superior Coll (MN)
Macomb Comm Coll (MI)
Merced Coll (CA)
Mesa Comm Coll (AZ)
Miami Dade Coll (FL)
Minnesota State Comm and Tech Coll (MN)
Montgomery Coll (MD)
Northeast Comm Coll (NE)
Northland Comm and Tech Coll (MN)
Oakton Comm Coll (IL)
Oklahoma City Comm Coll (OK)
Oklahoma State U–Oklahoma City (OK)
Palomar Coll (CA)
Pennsylvania Highlands Comm Coll (PA)
Rend Lake Coll (IL)
South Suburban Coll (IL)
Three Rivers Comm Coll (CT)
Truckee Meadows Comm Coll (NV)
Vincennes U (IN)
Waukesha County Tech Coll (WI)

## ARCHITECTURAL ENGINEERING TECHNOLOGY
Amarillo Coll (TX)
Coll of The Albemarle (NC)
Del Mar Coll (TX)
Dutchess Comm Coll (NY)
Erie Comm Coll, South Campus (NY)
Fayetteville Tech Comm Coll (NC)
Front Range Comm Coll (CO)
Gateway Tech Coll (WI)
Greenville Tech Coll (SC)
Harper Coll (IL)
Harrisburg Area Comm Coll (PA)
Hinds Comm Coll (MS)
Independence Comm Coll (KS)
Miami Dade Coll (FL)
Monroe County Comm Coll (MI)
Mott Comm Coll (MI)
Mt. San Antonio Coll (CA)
New River Comm Coll (VA)
Northampton Comm Coll (PA)
Northcentral Tech Coll (WI)
North Dakota State Coll of Science (ND)
Oklahoma State U–Oklahoma City (OK)
Penn State Fayette, The Eberly Campus (PA)
Salt Lake Comm Coll (UT)

## ARCHITECTURAL TECHNOLOGY
Arizona Western Coll (AZ)
Coll of Marin (CA)
Coll of the Desert (CA)
Dunwoody Coll of Technology (MN)
Fullerton Coll (CA)
Grand Rapids Comm Coll (MI)
John Tyler Comm Coll (VA)
Miami Dade Coll (FL)
Orange Coast Coll (CA)
Palomar Coll (CA)
Pensacola State Coll (FL)
Southwestern Coll (CA)
Thaddeus Stevens Coll of Technology (PA)

## ARCHITECTURE
Barton County Comm Coll (KS)
Coll of Central Florida (FL)
Copiah-Lincoln Comm Coll (MS)
Daytona State Coll (FL)
Grand Rapids Comm Coll (MI)
Harrisburg Area Comm Coll (PA)
Panola Coll (TX)
Pasadena City Coll (CA)
Truckee Meadows Comm Coll (NV)

## ARCHITECTURE RELATED
LDS Business Coll (UT)

## AREA STUDIES RELATED
Fullerton Coll (CA)

## ART
Alvin Comm Coll (TX)
Amarillo Coll (TX)
American Samoa Comm Coll (AS)
Antelope Valley Coll (CA)
Austin Comm Coll District (TX)
Barton County Comm Coll (KS)
Black Hawk Coll, Moline (IL)
Bunker Hill Comm Coll (MA)
Carroll Comm Coll (MD)
Cayuga County Comm Coll (NY)
Central New Mexico Comm Coll (NM)
Central Oregon Comm Coll (OR)
Chipola Coll (FL)
Cochise County Comm Coll District (AZ)
Coll of Central Florida (FL)
Coll of Marin (CA)
Coll of The Albemarle (NC)
Coll of the Canyons (CA)
Coll of the Desert (CA)
Columbia-Greene Comm Coll (NY)
Comm Coll of Allegheny County (PA)
Comm Coll of Philadelphia (PA)
Crowder Coll (MO)
Danville Area Comm Coll (IL)
De Anza Coll (CA)
Del Mar Coll (TX)
Dutchess Comm Coll (NY)
Edison State Comm Coll (OH)
Frederick Comm Coll (MD)
Fullerton Coll (CA)
Gordon State Coll (GA)
Grand Rapids Comm Coll (MI)
Harper Coll (IL)
Hill Coll (TX)
Holyoke Comm Coll (MA)
Housatonic Comm Coll (CT)
Howard Comm Coll (MD)
Independence Comm Coll (KS)
Kingsborough Comm Coll of the City U of New York (NY)
Kishwaukee Coll (IL)
Laramie County Comm Coll (WY)
Lehigh Carbon Comm Coll (PA)
Los Angeles City Coll (CA)
Merced Coll (CA)
Miami Dade Coll (FL)
Minnesota State Comm and Tech Coll (MN)
Mission Coll (CA)
Mohave Comm Coll (AZ)
Mohawk Valley Comm Coll (NY)
Monroe Coll (NY)
Monroe County Comm Coll (MI)
Montgomery Coll (MD)
Montgomery County Comm Coll (PA)
Morton Coll (IL)
Mount Wachusett Comm Coll (MA)

Muskegon Comm Coll (MI)
Nassau Comm Coll (NY)
National Park Coll (AR)
Naugatuck Valley Comm Coll (CT)
Navarro Coll (TX)
Northeast Comm Coll (NE)
Northeastern Jr Coll (CO)
Northwest Coll (WY)
Odessa Coll (TX)
Oklahoma City Comm Coll (OK)
Orange Coast Coll (CA)
Palomar Coll (CA)
Panola Coll (TX)
Paris Jr Coll (TX)
Pasadena City Coll (CA)
Pensacola State Coll (FL)
Piedmont Virginia Comm Coll (VA)
Queensborough Comm Coll of the
  City U of New York (NY)
St. Philip's Coll (TX)
San Jacinto Coll District (TX)
San Joaquin Delta Coll (CA)
Santa Rosa Jr Coll (CA)
Sauk Valley Comm Coll (IL)
Seminole State Coll (OK)
Southwestern Coll (CA)
Texarkana Coll (TX)
Trinity Valley Comm Coll (TX)
Tyler Jr Coll (TX)
Vincennes U (IN)
Westchester Comm Coll (NY)
Western Texas Coll (TX)
Western Wyoming Comm Coll (WY)

**ART HISTORY, CRITICISM AND CONSERVATION**
Bucks County Comm Coll (PA)
De Anza Coll (CA)
Muskegon Comm Coll (MI)
Northeastern Jr Coll (CO)
Santa Rosa Jr Coll (CA)

**ARTIFICIAL INTELLIGENCE**
Richland Coll (TX)

**ARTS, ENTERTAINMENT, AND MEDIA MANAGEMENT RELATED**
Hinds Comm Coll (MS)

**ART TEACHER EDUCATION**
Copiah-Lincoln Comm Coll (MS)
Danville Area Comm Coll (IL)
Del Mar Coll (TX)
McLennan Comm Coll (TX)
Muskegon Comm Coll (MI)
Pensacola State Coll (FL)
Vincennes U (IN)
Western Texas Coll (TX)

**ART THERAPY**
Vincennes U (IN)

**ASIAN STUDIES**
Miami Dade Coll (FL)

**ASTRONOMY**
Fullerton Coll (CA)
Gordon State Coll (GA)
Palomar Coll (CA)
Southwestern Coll (CA)

**ATHLETIC TRAINING**
Barton County Comm Coll (KS)
Coll of the Canyons (CA)
Coll of the Desert (CA)
Comm Coll of Allegheny County (PA)
Independence Comm Coll (KS)
Northampton Comm Coll (PA)
Northeast Comm Coll (NE)
Northwest Coll (WY)
Odessa Coll (TX)
Sauk Valley Comm Coll (IL)
Tyler Jr Coll (TX)
Westchester Comm Coll (NY)

**AUDIOLOGY AND SPEECH-LANGUAGE PATHOLOGY**
Miami Dade Coll (FL)
Orange Coast Coll (CA)
Pasadena City Coll (CA)

**AUDIOVISUAL COMMUNICATIONS TECHNOLOGIES RELATED**
Bossier Parish Comm Coll (LA)
Northeast Comm Coll (NE)

**AUTOBODY/COLLISION AND REPAIR TECHNOLOGY**
American Samoa Comm Coll (AS)

Antelope Valley Coll (CA)
Arkansas State U–Newport (AR)
Austin Comm Coll District (TX)
Central Texas Coll (TX)
Coll of Marin (CA)
Crowder Coll (MO)
Des Moines Area Comm Coll (IA)
Dunwoody Coll of Technology (MN)
Erie Comm Coll, South Campus
  (NY)
Fayetteville Tech Comm Coll (NC)
Fox Valley Tech Coll (WI)
George C. Wallace Comm Coll (AL)
Greenville Tech Coll (SC)
Hawkeye Comm Coll (IA)
Haywood Comm Coll (NC)
Highland Comm Coll (IL)
Hill Coll (TX)
Hutchinson Comm Coll (KS)
Illinois Eastern Comm Colls, Olney
  Central College (IL)
Kishwaukee Coll (IL)
Lake Area Tech Inst (SD)
Laramie County Comm Coll (WY)
Lenoir Comm Coll (NC)
Merced Coll (CA)
Mid-Plains Comm Coll, North Platte
  (NE)
Minnesota State Comm and Tech
  Coll (MN)
North Dakota State Coll of Science
  (ND)
Northeast Comm Coll (NE)
Northern Maine Comm Coll (ME)
Northland Comm and Tech Coll (MN)
Ohio Tech Coll (OH)
Oklahoma State U Inst of
  Technology (OK)
Ozarks Tech Comm Coll (MO)
Palomar Coll (CA)
Pueblo Comm Coll (CO)
Randolph Comm Coll (NC)
Renton Tech Coll (WA)
Ridgewater Coll (MN)
St. Philip's Coll (TX)
Salt Lake Comm Coll (UT)
San Jacinto Coll District (TX)
San Juan Coll (NM)
Southeast Tech Inst (SD)
Southwestern Comm Coll (IA)
Southwest Texas Jr Coll (TX)
State Tech Coll of Missouri (MO)
State U of New York Coll of
  Technology at Alfred (NY)
Texas State Tech Coll (TX)
Thaddeus Stevens Coll of
  Technology (PA)
U of Arkansas Comm Coll at
  Morrilton (AR)
Vincennes U (IN)
Wayne Comm Coll (NC)
Wayne County Comm Coll District
  (MI)
Western Iowa Tech Comm Coll (IA)

**AUTOMATION ENGINEER TECHNOLOGY**
Alexandria Tech and Comm Coll
  (MN)
Blue Ridge Comm and Tech Coll
  (WV)
Cleveland Comm Coll (NC)
Dyersburg State Comm Coll (TN)
Fox Valley Tech Coll (WI)
Gateway Tech Coll (WI)
Gulf Coast State Coll (FL)
Hawkeye Comm Coll (IA)
Hutchinson Comm Coll (KS)
Miami Dade Coll (FL)
Mitchell Tech Inst (SD)
Mott Comm Coll (MI)
Northland Comm and Tech Coll (MN)
Southwestern Michigan Coll (MI)
Vincennes U (IN)
Waukesha County Tech Coll (WI)
Wisconsin Indianhead Tech Coll (WI)

**AUTOMOBILE/AUTOMOTIVE MECHANICS TECHNOLOGY**
Alamance Comm Coll (NC)
Alvin Comm Coll (TX)
Amarillo Coll (TX)
American Samoa Comm Coll (AS)
Antelope Valley Coll (CA)
Arizona Western Coll (AZ)
Arkansas State U–Newport (AR)
Asheville-Buncombe Tech Comm
  Coll (NC)
Austin Comm Coll District (TX)
Barton County Comm Coll (KS)

Black Hawk Coll, Moline (IL)
Brookhaven Coll (TX)
Caldwell Comm Coll and Tech Inst
  (NC)
Cedar Valley Coll (TX)
Central Maine Comm Coll (ME)
Central Oregon Comm Coll (OR)
Central Texas Coll (TX)
City Colls of Chicago, Olive-Harvey
  College (IL)
Clark Coll (WA)
Cochise County Comm Coll District
  (AZ)
Coll of Eastern Idaho (ID)
Coll of Marin (CA)
Coll of the Canyons (CA)
Coll of the Desert (CA)
Colorado Northwestern Comm Coll
  (CO)
Columbia-Greene Comm Coll (NY)
Comm Coll of Allegheny County (PA)
Comm Coll of Baltimore County
  (MD)
Comm Coll of Philadelphia (PA)
Copiah-Lincoln Comm Coll (MS)
Craven Comm Coll (NC)
Crowder Coll (MO)
Danville Area Comm Coll (IL)
De Anza Coll (CA)
Del Mar Coll (TX)
Des Moines Area Comm Coll (IA)
Dunwoody Coll of Technology (MN)
East Central Coll (MO)
Eastern Arizona Coll (AZ)
El Paso Comm Coll (TX)
Erie Comm Coll, South Campus
  (NY)
Fayetteville Tech Comm Coll (NC)
Fox Valley Tech Coll (WI)
Front Range Comm Coll (CO)
Fullerton Coll (CA)
Gateway Tech Coll (WI)
George C. Wallace Comm Coll (AL)
Grand Rapids Comm Coll (MI)
Greenville Tech Coll (SC)
Harrisburg Area Comm Coll (PA)
Hawkeye Comm Coll (IA)
Haywood Comm Coll (NC)
Highland Comm Coll (IL)
Hill Coll (TX)
Houston Comm Coll (TX)
Hutchinson Comm Coll (KS)
Illinois Central Coll (IL)
Illinois Eastern Comm Colls, Frontier
  Community College (IL)
Illinois Eastern Comm Colls, Olney
  Central College (IL)
Illinois Valley Comm Coll (IL)
Iowa Central Comm Coll (IA)
Ivy Tech Comm Coll–Central Indiana
  (IN)
Ivy Tech Comm Coll–Columbus (IN)
Ivy Tech Comm Coll–East Central
  (IN)
Ivy Tech Comm Coll–Kokomo (IN)
Ivy Tech Comm Coll–Lafayette (IN)
Ivy Tech Comm Coll–Northeast (IN)
Ivy Tech Comm Coll–Northwest (IN)
Ivy Tech Comm Coll–Richmond (IN)
Ivy Tech Comm Coll–Sellersburg (IN)
Ivy Tech Comm Coll–Southwest (IN)
Ivy Tech Comm Coll–Wabash Valley
  (IN)
Johnson Coll (PA)
J. Sargeant Reynolds Comm Coll
  (VA)
Kaskaskia Coll (IL)
Kirtland Comm Coll (MI)
Kishwaukee Coll (IL)
Lake Area Tech Inst (SD)
Lake Region State Coll (ND)
Lakes Region Comm Coll (NH)
Lake Superior Coll (MN)
Laramie County Comm Coll (WY)
Lenoir Comm Coll (NC)
Macomb Comm Coll (MI)
Massachusetts Bay Comm Coll (MA)
Merced Coll (CA)
Mesa Comm Coll (AZ)
Mesalands Comm Coll (NM)
Mid-Plains Comm Coll, North Platte
  (NE)
Minnesota State Comm and Tech
  Coll (MN)
Minnesota West Comm and Tech
  Coll (MN)
Mohave Comm Coll (AZ)
Monroe Comm Coll (NY)
Montgomery Coll (MD)
Montgomery County Comm Coll (PA)

Morton Coll (IL)
Mott Comm Coll (MI)
Mount Wachusett Comm Coll (MA)
Muskegon Comm Coll (MI)
Naugatuck Valley Comm Coll (CT)
New Mexico State U–Alamogordo
  (NM)
New River Comm Coll (VA)
Northampton Comm Coll (PA)
Northcentral Tech Coll (WI)
North Central Texas Coll (TX)
North Dakota State Coll of Science
  (ND)
Northeast Comm Coll (NE)
Northeastern Jr Coll (CO)
Northeast Iowa Comm Coll (IA)
Northern Maine Comm Coll (ME)
North Iowa Area Comm Coll (IA)
Northland Comm and Tech Coll (MN)
Oakton Comm Coll (IL)
Odessa Coll (TX)
Ohio Tech Coll (OH)
Oklahoma City Comm Coll (OK)
Oklahoma State U Inst of
  Technology (OK)
Owensboro Comm and Tech Coll
  (KY)
Ozarks Tech Comm Coll (MO)
Palomar Coll (CA)
Pasadena City Coll (CA)
Pueblo Comm Coll (CO)
Quinsigamond Comm Coll (MA)
Randolph Comm Coll (NC)
Rend Lake Coll (IL)
Renton Tech Coll (WA)
Ridgewater Coll (MN)
Rock Valley Coll (IL)
Rowan-Cabarrus Comm Coll (NC)
St. Louis Comm Coll (MO)
St. Philip's Coll (TX)
San Jacinto Coll District (TX)
San Joaquin Delta Coll (CA)
San Juan Coll (NM)
Santa Rosa Jr Coll (CA)
Seminole State Coll of Florida (FL)
Shawnee Comm Coll (IL)
Southcentral Kentucky Comm and
  Tech Coll (KY)
Southeast Tech Inst (SD)
Southwestern Coll (CA)
Southwestern Comm Coll (IA)
Southwestern Comm Coll (NC)
Southwestern Michigan Coll (MI)
Southwest Texas Jr Coll (TX)
Springfield Tech Comm Coll (MA)
State Tech Coll of Missouri (MO)
State U of New York Coll of
  Technology at Alfred (NY)
Tarrant County Coll District (TX)
Texarkana Coll (TX)
Texas State Tech Coll (TX)
Tidewater Comm Coll (VA)
Tri-County Comm Coll (NC)
Trident Tech Coll (SC)
Trinity Valley Comm Coll (TX)
Truckee Meadows Comm Coll (NV)
Tyler Jr Coll (TX)
Union County Coll (NJ)
U of Arkansas Comm Coll at
  Morrilton (AR)
Vincennes U (IN)
Waukesha County Tech Coll (WI)
Wayne Comm Coll (NC)
Wayne County Comm Coll District
  (MI)
Western Iowa Tech Comm Coll (IA)
Western Wyoming Comm Coll (WY)
West Kentucky Comm and Tech Coll
  (KY)
White Mountains Comm Coll (NH)

**AUTOMOTIVE ENGINEERING TECHNOLOGY**
American Samoa Comm Coll (AS)
Arizona Western Coll (AZ)
Camden County Coll (NJ)
Comm Coll of Allegheny County (PA)
George C. Wallace Comm Coll (AL)
H. Councill Trenholm State Comm
  Coll (AL)
Macomb Comm Coll (MI)
New Castle School of Trades (PA)
Raritan Valley Comm Coll (NJ)
Thaddeus Stevens Coll of
  Technology (PA)

**AVIATION/AIRWAY MANAGEMENT**
Comm Coll of Allegheny County (PA)

Comm Coll of Baltimore County
  (MD)
Dutchess Comm Coll (NY)
Hinds Comm Coll (MS)
Iowa Central Comm Coll (IA)
Lake Superior Coll (MN)
Miami Dade Coll (FL)
Orange Coast Coll (CA)

**AVIONICS MAINTENANCE TECHNOLOGY**
Cochise County Comm Coll District
  (AZ)
Fox Valley Tech Coll (WI)
Housatonic Comm Coll (CT)
Mt. San Antonio Coll (CA)
North Central Inst (TN)
Rock Valley Coll (IL)
Salt Lake Comm Coll (UT)
Schenectady County Comm Coll
  (NY)
Southern U at Shreveport (LA)
Tarrant County Coll District (TX)
Texas State Tech Coll (TX)

**BAKING AND PASTRY ARTS**
Asheville-Buncombe Tech Comm
  Coll (NC)
Blue Ridge Comm and Tech Coll
  (WV)
Bristol Comm Coll (MA)
Bucks County Comm Coll (PA)
Carteret Comm Coll (NC)
Clark Coll (WA)
Collin County Comm Coll District
  (TX)
Culinary Inst LeNotre (TX)
Hudson County Comm Coll (NJ)
J. Sargeant Reynolds Comm Coll
  (VA)
Montgomery County Comm Coll (PA)
Mott Comm Coll (MI)
Niagara County Comm Coll (NY)
St. Louis Comm Coll (MO)
St. Philip's Coll (TX)
San Jacinto Coll District (TX)
Sullivan County Comm Coll (NY)
Waukesha County Tech Coll (WI)
White Mountains Comm Coll (NH)

**BANKING AND FINANCIAL SUPPORT SERVICES**
Alamance Comm Coll (NC)
Barton County Comm Coll (KS)
Bristol Comm Coll (MA)
Cleveland Comm Coll (NC)
Comm Coll of Allegheny County (PA)
Craven Comm Coll (NC)
Fox Valley Tech Coll (WI)
Harper Coll (IL)
Hinds Comm Coll (MS)
Houston Comm Coll (TX)
Illinois Central Coll (IL)
Lackawanna Coll (PA)
Lake Area Tech Inst (SD)
Los Angeles City Coll (CA)
Miami Dade Coll (FL)
Minnesota State Comm and Tech
  Coll (MN)
Mohawk Valley Comm Coll (NY)
Oakton Comm Coll (IL)
Seminole State Coll of Florida (FL)
Southeast Tech Inst (SD)
Southwestern Coll (CA)
Three Rivers Comm Coll (CT)

**BARBERING**
Rend Lake Coll (IL)

**BEHAVIORAL SCIENCES**
Amarillo Coll (TX)
Ancilla Coll (IN)
De Anza Coll (CA)
Galveston Coll (TX)
Hill Coll (TX)
Miami Dade Coll (FL)
Monroe Comm Coll (NY)
Naugatuck Valley Comm Coll (CT)
St. Louis Comm Coll (MO)
San Jacinto Coll District (TX)
Santa Rosa Jr Coll (CA)
Seminole State Coll (OK)
Vincennes U (IN)

**BIBLICAL STUDIES**
Amarillo Coll (TX)
Hesston Coll (KS)

**BIOCHEMISTRY**
Pasadena City Coll (CA)
Pensacola State Coll (FL)

## BIOCHEMISTRY AND MOLECULAR BIOLOGY

Minnesota State Comm and Tech Coll (MN)

## BIOENGINEERING AND BIOMEDICAL ENGINEERING

Bunker Hill Comm Coll (MA)
Quinsigamond Comm Coll (MA)

## BIOINFORMATICS

Massachusetts Bay Comm Coll (MA)

## BIOLOGICAL AND BIOMEDICAL SCIENCES RELATED

Massachusetts Bay Comm Coll (MA)
Seminole State Coll (OK)
Vincennes U (IN)

## BIOLOGICAL AND PHYSICAL SCIENCES

Ancilla Coll (IN)
Antelope Valley Coll (CA)
Black Hawk Coll, Moline (IL)
Caldwell Comm Coll and Tech Inst (NC)
Central Oregon Comm Coll (OR)
Chipola Coll (FL)
City Colls of Chicago, Olive-Harvey College (IL)
Coll of Marin (CA)
Coll of the Canyons (CA)
Coll of the Desert (CA)
Comm Coll of Baltimore County (MD)
Copiah-Lincoln Comm Coll (MS)
Dabney S. Lancaster Comm Coll (VA)
Danville Area Comm Coll (IL)
Eastern Shore Comm Coll (VA)
Fullerton Coll (CA)
Galveston Coll (TX)
Highland Comm Coll (IL)
Howard Comm Coll (MD)
Hudson County Comm Coll (NJ)
Illinois Eastern Comm Colls, Frontier Community College (IL)
Illinois Eastern Comm Colls, Lincoln Trail College (IL)
Illinois Eastern Comm Colls, Olney Central College (IL)
Illinois Eastern Comm Colls, Wabash Valley College (IL)
Illinois Valley Comm Coll (IL)
Iowa Central Comm Coll (IA)
J. Sargeant Reynolds Comm Coll (VA)
Kaskaskia Coll (IL)
Kishwaukee Coll (IL)
Laramie County Comm Coll (WY)
Los Angeles City Coll (CA)
McHenry County Coll (IL)
Monroe Comm Coll (NY)
Morton Coll (IL)
Mt. San Antonio Coll (CA)
Navarro Coll (TX)
New River Comm Coll (VA)
Niagara County Comm Coll (NY)
North Central Texas Coll (TX)
Oakton Comm Coll (IL)
Otero Jr Coll (CO)
Palomar Coll (CA)
Paris Jr Coll (TX)
Pasadena City Coll (CA)
Penn State DuBois (PA)
Penn State Fayette, The Eberly Campus (PA)
Rainy River Comm Coll (MN)
Rappahannock Comm Coll (VA)
Rend Lake Coll (IL)
Shawnee Comm Coll (IL)
South Suburban Coll (IL)
Southwestern Coll (CA)
Southwest Texas Jr Coll (TX)
Tidewater Comm Coll (VA)
Trident Tech Coll (SC)
U of South Carolina Union (SC)
Western Wyoming Comm Coll (WY)
Wor-Wic Comm Coll (MD)
Wytheville Comm Coll (VA)

## BIOLOGY/BIOLOGICAL SCIENCES

Alvin Comm Coll (TX)
Amarillo Coll (TX)
Arizona Western Coll (AZ)
Austin Comm Coll District (TX)
Barton County Comm Coll (KS)
Bristol Comm Coll (MA)
Bunker Hill Comm Coll (MA)
Carl Albert State Coll (OK)
Carroll Comm Coll (MD)
Cecil Coll (MD)

Central Maine Comm Coll (ME)
Central New Mexico Comm Coll (NM)
Central Oregon Comm Coll (OR)
Central Texas Coll (TX)
Century Coll (MN)
Chesapeake Coll (MD)
Cochise County Comm Coll District (AZ)
Coll of Central Florida (FL)
Coll of Marin (CA)
Coll of the Desert (CA)
Comm Coll of Allegheny County (PA)
Comm Coll of Philadelphia (PA)
Copiah-Lincoln Comm Coll (MS)
Crowder Coll (MO)
De Anza Coll (CA)
Del Mar Coll (TX)
Eastern Arizona Coll (AZ)
Edison State Comm Coll (OH)
Feather River Coll (CA)
Fiorello H. LaGuardia Comm Coll of the City U of New York (NY)
Frederick Comm Coll (MD)
Fullerton Coll (CA)
Genesee Comm Coll (NY)
Georgia Military Coll (GA)
Harford Comm Coll (MD)
Harper Coll (IL)
Harrisburg Area Comm Coll (PA)
Hill Coll (TX)
Holyoke Comm Coll (MA)
Houston Comm Coll (TX)
Hutchinson Comm Coll (KS)
Independence Comm Coll (KS)
Kingsborough Comm Coll of the City U of New York (NY)
Lackawanna Coll (PA)
Laramie County Comm Coll (WY)
Lehigh Carbon Comm Coll (PA)
Macomb Comm Coll (MI)
Merced Coll (CA)
Miami Dade Coll (FL)
Minnesota State Comm and Tech Coll (MN)
Monroe Comm Coll (NY)
Monroe County Comm Coll (MI)
Mott Comm Coll (MI)
Mount Wachusett Comm Coll (MA)
Navarro Coll (TX)
Northampton Comm Coll (PA)
Northeast Comm Coll (NE)
Northeastern Jr Coll (CO)
Northern Essex Comm Coll (MA)
North Hennepin Comm Coll (MN)
Northwest Coll (WY)
Odessa Coll (TX)
Oklahoma City Comm Coll (OK)
Orange Coast Coll (CA)
Otero Jr Coll (CO)
Ozarks Tech Comm Coll (MO)
Palomar Coll (CA)
Panola Coll (TX)
Paris Jr Coll (TX)
Pasadena City Coll (CA)
Pensacola State Coll (FL)
Potomac State Coll of West Virginia U (WV)
Quinsigamond Comm Coll (MA)
Ridgewater Coll (MN)
St. Charles Comm Coll (MO)
St. Philip's Coll (TX)
Salt Lake Comm Coll (UT)
San Jacinto Coll District (TX)
San Joaquin Delta Coll (CA)
San Juan Coll (NM)
Santa Rosa Jr Coll (CA)
Sauk Valley Comm Coll (IL)
Seminole State Coll (OK)
Southern U at Shreveport (LA)
Southwestern Coll (CA)
Springfield Tech Comm Coll (MA)
State U of New York Coll of Technology at Alfred (NY)
Texarkana Coll (TX)
Trinity Valley Comm Coll (TX)
Truckee Meadows Comm Coll (NV)
Tyler Jr Coll (TX)
Union County Coll (NJ)
U of Wisconsin–Baraboo/Sauk County (WI)
U of Wisconsin–Barron County (WI)
U of Wisconsin–Fond du Lac (WI)
U of Wisconsin–Fox Valley (WI)
U of Wisconsin–Manitowoc (WI)
U of Wisconsin–Marathon County (WI)
U of Wisconsin–Marinette (WI)
U of Wisconsin–Marshfield/Wood County (WI)
U of Wisconsin–Richland (WI)
U of Wisconsin–Rock County (WI)

U of Wisconsin–Sheboygan (WI)
U of Wisconsin–Washington County (WI)
U of Wisconsin–Waukesha (WI)
Western Texas Coll (TX)
Western Wyoming Comm Coll (WY)

## BIOLOGY/BIOTECHNOLOGY LABORATORY TECHNICIAN

Asheville-Buncombe Tech Comm Coll (NC)
Austin Comm Coll District (TX)
Bucks County Comm Coll (PA)
Camden County Coll (NJ)
Cloud County Comm Coll (KS)
County Coll of Morris (NJ)
East Central Coll (MO)
Fox Valley Tech Coll (WI)
Genesee Comm Coll (NY)
Hagerstown Comm Coll (MD)
Houston Comm Coll (TX)
Hutchinson Comm Coll (KS)
Jamestown Comm Coll (NY)
Kennebec Valley Comm Coll (ME)
Lackawanna Coll (PA)
Massachusetts Bay Comm Coll (MA)
Mesa Comm Coll (AZ)
Minnesota West Comm and Tech Coll (MN)
Monroe Comm Coll (NY)
Montgomery Coll (MD)
Montgomery County Comm Coll (PA)
Muskegon Comm Coll (MI)
North Shore Comm Coll (MA)
Northwest Vista Coll (TX)
The Ohio State U Ag Tech Inst (OH)
Salt Lake Comm Coll (UT)
Southwestern Coll (CA)
Tompkins Cortland Comm Coll (NY)
Wayne Comm Coll (NC)

## BIOLOGY TEACHER EDUCATION

Bucks County Comm Coll (PA)

## BIOMEDICAL TECHNOLOGY

Austin Comm Coll District (TX)
Caldwell Comm Coll and Tech Inst (NC)
Des Moines Area Comm Coll (IA)
Fullerton Coll (CA)
Howard Comm Coll (MD)
Johnson Coll (PA)
Merced Coll (CA)
Miami Dade Coll (FL)
Muskegon Comm Coll (MI)
New Mexico State U–Alamogordo (NM)
Ozarks Tech Comm Coll (MO)
Penn State DuBois (PA)
Penn State Fayette, The Eberly Campus (PA)
Pennsylvania Inst of Technology (PA)
Quinsigamond Comm Coll (MA)
Rend Lake Coll (IL)
St. Philip's Coll (TX)
Schoolcraft Coll (MI)
Southwestern Coll (CA)
Stark State Coll (OH)
Texas State Tech Coll (TX)
Wayne County Comm Coll District (MI)
Western Iowa Tech Comm Coll (IA)

## BIOTECHNOLOGY

Alamance Comm Coll (NC)
Bunker Hill Comm Coll (MA)
Cecil Coll (MD)
Central New Mexico Comm Coll (NM)
Cleveland Comm Coll (NC)
Coll of The Albemarle (NC)
Comm Coll of Allegheny County (PA)
Erie Comm Coll, North Campus (NY)
Genesee Comm Coll (NY)
Holyoke Comm Coll (MA)
Howard Comm Coll (MD)
Humacao Comm Coll (PR)
Ivy Tech Comm Coll–Bloomington (IN)
Ivy Tech Comm Coll–Central Indiana (IN)
Ivy Tech Comm Coll–Lafayette (IN)
Ivy Tech Comm Coll–North Central (IN)
Ivy Tech Comm Coll–Southwest (IN)
Lakeland Comm Coll (OH)
Lehigh Carbon Comm Coll (PA)
Miami Dade Coll (FL)
Montgomery County Comm Coll (PA)
Mount Wachusett Comm Coll (MA)
Northampton Comm Coll (PA)
Piedmont Virginia Comm Coll (VA)

Queensborough Comm Coll of the City U of New York (NY)
Quinsigamond Comm Coll (MA)
St. Louis Comm Coll (MO)
St. Philip's Coll (TX)
Springfield Tech Comm Coll (MA)
Tulsa Comm Coll (OK)

## BOILERMAKING

Ivy Tech Comm Coll–Southwest (IN)

## BOTANY/PLANT BIOLOGY

Pensacola State Coll (FL)

## BROADCAST JOURNALISM

Amarillo Coll (TX)
Iowa Central Comm Coll (IA)
Kingsborough Comm Coll of the City U of New York (NY)
Oklahoma City Comm Coll (OK)
Palomar Coll (CA)
Pasadena City Coll (CA)
San Joaquin Delta Coll (CA)

## BUILDING/CONSTRUCTION FINISHING, MANAGEMENT, AND INSPECTION RELATED

Comm Coll of Baltimore County (MD)
Fayetteville Tech Comm Coll (NC)
Frederick Comm Coll (MD)
Haywood Comm Coll (NC)
Hudson County Comm Coll (NJ)
Mid-Plains Comm Coll, North Platte (NE)
Mohave Comm Coll (AZ)
Montgomery Coll (MD)
Mt. San Antonio Coll (CA)
Nebraska Indian Comm Coll (NE)
Northeast Comm Coll (NE)
Oakton Comm Coll (IL)
Salt Lake Comm Coll (UT)
Seminole State Coll of Florida (FL)
Springfield Tech Comm Coll (MA)
Vincennes U (IN)

## BUILDING/CONSTRUCTION SITE MANAGEMENT

Coll of the Canyons (CA)
Coll of the Desert (CA)
Comm Coll of Baltimore County (MD)
Dunwoody Coll of Technology (MN)
Erie Comm Coll, North Campus (NY)
Fox Valley Tech Coll (WI)
Fullerton Coll (CA)
Ivy Tech Comm Coll–Kokomo (IN)
J. Sargeant Reynolds Comm Coll (VA)
Lehigh Carbon Comm Coll (PA)
Lorain County Comm Coll (OH)
Mesa Comm Coll (AZ)
Minnesota State Comm and Tech Coll (MN)
The Ohio State U Ag Tech Inst (OH)
Southwestern Coll (CA)

## BUILDING CONSTRUCTION TECHNOLOGY

Central Maine Comm Coll (ME)
Central New Mexico Comm Coll (NM)
Cochise County Comm Coll District (AZ)
Comm Coll of Allegheny County (PA)
Kennebec Valley Comm Coll (ME)
Lake Area Tech Inst (SD)
Lake Superior Coll (MN)
Mitchell Tech Inst (SD)
North Dakota State Coll of Science (ND)

## BUILDING/HOME/ CONSTRUCTION INSPECTION

Coll of the Desert (CA)
Fullerton Coll (CA)
Johnson Coll (PA)
Oklahoma State U–Oklahoma City (OK)
Palomar Coll (CA)
Pasadena City Coll (CA)
South Suburban Coll (IL)
Southwestern Coll (CA)

## BUILDING/PROPERTY MAINTENANCE

Asheville-Buncombe Tech Comm Coll (NC)
Central Texas Coll (TX)
Century Coll (MN)
Comm Coll of Allegheny County (PA)
Del Mar Coll (TX)
Erie Comm Coll (NY)
Ivy Tech Comm Coll–Bloomington (IN)

Ivy Tech Comm Coll–East Central (IN)
Ivy Tech Comm Coll–Kokomo (IN)
Ivy Tech Comm Coll–Lafayette (IN)
Ivy Tech Comm Coll–North Central (IN)
Ivy Tech Comm Coll–Northeast (IN)
Ivy Tech Comm Coll–Northwest (IN)
Ivy Tech Comm Coll–Richmond (IN)
Ivy Tech Comm Coll–Sellersburg (IN)
Ivy Tech Comm Coll–Southwest (IN)
Ivy Tech Comm Coll–Wabash Valley (IN)
Pensacola State Coll (FL)
Renton Tech Coll (WA)
Rowan-Cabarrus Comm Coll (NC)
Wayne County Comm Coll District (MI)

## BUSINESS ADMINISTRATION AND MANAGEMENT

Adirondack Comm Coll (NY)
Alamance Comm Coll (NC)
Alexandria Tech and Comm Coll (MN)
Alvin Comm Coll (TX)
Amarillo Coll (TX)
American Samoa Comm Coll (AS)
Ancilla Coll (IN)
Anne Arundel Comm Coll (MD)
Antelope Valley Coll (CA)
Arizona Western Coll (AZ)
Asheville-Buncombe Tech Comm Coll (NC)
Austin Comm Coll District (TX)
Barton County Comm Coll (KS)
Blue Ridge Comm and Tech Coll (WV)
Bowling Green State U–Firelands Coll (OH)
Bristol Comm Coll (MA)
Brookhaven Coll (TX)
Bucks County Comm Coll (PA)
Bunker Hill Comm Coll (MA)
Caldwell Comm Coll and Tech Inst (NC)
Camden County Coll (NJ)
Carl Albert State Coll (OK)
Carroll Comm Coll (MD)
Carteret Comm Coll (NC)
Cayuga County Comm Coll (NY)
Cecil Coll (MD)
Cedar Valley Coll (TX)
Central Lakes Coll (MN)
Central Maine Comm Coll (ME)
Central New Mexico Comm Coll (NM)
Central Ohio Tech Coll (OH)
Central Oregon Comm Coll (OR)
Central Texas Coll (TX)
Central Virginia Comm Coll (VA)
Century Coll (MN)
Chandler-Gilbert Comm Coll (AZ)
Chesapeake Coll (MD)
Chipola Coll (FL)
Chippewa Valley Tech Coll (WI)
City Colls of Chicago, Olive-Harvey College (IL)
Clark Coll (WA)
Cleveland Comm Coll (NC)
Cleveland State Comm Coll (TN)
Cloud County Comm Coll (KS)
Cochise County Comm Coll District (AZ)
Coll of Business and Technology– Cutler Bay Campus (FL)
Coll of Business and Technology– Flagler Campus (FL)
Coll of Business and Technology– Main Campus (FL)
Coll of Business and Technology– Miami Gardens (FL)
Coll of Central Florida (FL)
Coll of Marin (CA)
Coll of The Albemarle (NC)
Coll of the Canyons (CA)
Coll of the Desert (CA)
Coll of the Ouachitas (AR)
The Coll of Westchester (NY)
Collin County Comm Coll District (TX)
Columbia-Greene Comm Coll (NY)
Comm Coll of Allegheny County (PA)
Comm Coll of Baltimore County (MD)
Comm Coll of Philadelphia (PA)
Copiah-Lincoln Comm Coll (MS)
County Coll of Morris (NJ)
Craven Comm Coll (NC)
Crowder Coll (MO)
Dabney S. Lancaster Comm Coll (VA)
Daytona State Coll (FL)

De Anza Coll (CA)
Del Mar Coll (TX)
Des Moines Area Comm Coll (IA)
Dutchess Comm Coll (NY)
Dyersburg State Comm Coll (TN)
Eastern Arizona Coll (AZ)
Eastern Gateway Comm Coll (OH)
Eastern Shore Comm Coll (VA)
Edison State Comm Coll (OH)
El Paso Comm Coll (TX)
Erie Comm Coll (NY)
Erie Comm Coll, North Campus (NY)
Erie Comm Coll, South Campus (NY)
Fayetteville Tech Comm Coll (NC)
Fiorello H. LaGuardia Comm Coll of the City U of New York (NY)
Florida Keys Comm Coll (FL)
Fox Valley Tech Coll (WI)
Frederick Comm Coll (MD)
Front Range Comm Coll (CO)
Fullerton Coll (CA)
Galveston Coll (TX)
Gateway Comm and Tech Coll (KY)
Gateway Tech Coll (WI)
Genesee Comm Coll (NY)
George C. Wallace Comm Coll (AL)
Gordon State Coll (GA)
Grand Rapids Comm Coll (MI)
Greenville Tech Coll (SC)
Gulf Coast State Coll (FL)
Hagerstown Comm Coll (MD)
Halifax Comm Coll (NC)
Harford Comm Coll (MD)
Harper Coll (IL)
Harrisburg Area Comm Coll (PA)
Haywood Comm Coll (NC)
Hesston Coll (KS)
Highland Comm Coll (IL)
Hill Coll (TX)
Hinds Comm Coll (MS)
Holyoke Comm Coll (MA)
Hopkinsville Comm Coll (KY)
Housatonic Comm Coll (CT)
Houston Comm Coll (TX)
Howard Comm Coll (MD)
Hudson County Comm Coll (NJ)
Illinois Central Coll (IL)
Illinois Eastern Comm Colls, Olney Central College (IL)
Illinois Eastern Comm Colls, Wabash Valley College (IL)
Illinois Valley Comm Coll (IL)
Independence Comm Coll (KS)
Iowa Central Comm Coll (IA)
Ivy Tech Comm Coll–Bloomington (IN)
Ivy Tech Comm Coll–Central Indiana (IN)
Ivy Tech Comm Coll–Columbus (IN)
Ivy Tech Comm Coll–East Central (IN)
Ivy Tech Comm Coll–Kokomo (IN)
Ivy Tech Comm Coll–Lafayette (IN)
Ivy Tech Comm Coll–North Central (IN)
Ivy Tech Comm Coll–Northeast (IN)
Ivy Tech Comm Coll–Northwest (IN)
Ivy Tech Comm Coll–Richmond (IN)
Ivy Tech Comm Coll–Sellersburg (IN)
Ivy Tech Comm Coll–Southeast (IN)
Ivy Tech Comm Coll–Southwest (IN)
Ivy Tech Comm Coll–Wabash Valley (IN)
James Sprunt Comm Coll (NC)
Jamestown Comm Coll (NY)
Jefferson Comm Coll (NY)
Johnston Comm Coll (NC)
John Tyler Comm Coll (VA)
J. Sargeant Reynolds Comm Coll (VA)
Kellogg Comm Coll (MI)
Kingsborough Comm Coll of the City U of New York (NY)
Kirtland Comm Coll (MI)
Kishwaukee Coll (IL)
Lackawanna Coll (PA)
Lakeland Comm Coll (OH)
Lake Region State Coll (ND)
Lake Superior Coll (MN)
Laramie County Comm Coll (WY)
LDS Business Coll (UT)
Lehigh Carbon Comm Coll (PA)
Lenoir Comm Coll (NC)
Lorain County Comm Coll (OH)
Los Angeles City Coll (CA)
Louisiana State U at Eunice (LA)
Macomb Comm Coll (MI)
Manchester Comm Coll (CT)
Massachusetts Bay Comm Coll (MA)
Maysville Comm and Tech Coll, Maysville (KY)
McHenry County Coll (IL)
McLennan Comm Coll (TX)
Merced Coll (CA)
Mesa Comm Coll (AZ)
Mesalands Comm Coll (NM)
Miami Dade Coll (FL)
Mid-Plains Comm Coll, North Platte (NE)
Mid-State Tech Coll (WI)
Minnesota State Comm and Tech Coll (MN)
Minnesota West Comm and Tech Coll (MN)
Mission Coll (CA)
Mitchell Comm Coll (NC)
Mohave Comm Coll (AZ)
Mohawk Valley Comm Coll (NY)
Monroe Comm Coll (NY)
Monroe County Comm Coll (MI)
Montgomery Comm Coll (NC)
Montgomery County Comm Coll (PA)
Morton Coll (IL)
Motlow State Comm Coll (TN)
Mott Comm Coll (MI)
Mt. San Antonio Coll (CA)
Mount Wachusett Comm Coll (MA)
Muskegon Comm Coll (MI)
Nassau Comm Coll (NY)
National Park Coll (AR)
Naugatuck Valley Comm Coll (CT)
Navarro Coll (TX)
Nebraska Indian Comm Coll (NE)
New River Comm Coll (VA)
Niagara County Comm Coll (NY)
Northampton Comm Coll (PA)
Northcentral Tech Coll (WI)
North Central Texas Coll (TX)
North Dakota State Coll of Science (ND)
Northeast Comm Coll (NE)
Northeastern Jr Coll (CO)
Northeastern Tech Coll (SC)
Northeast Iowa Comm Coll (IA)
Northeast State Comm Coll (TN)
Northern Essex Comm Coll (MA)
Northern Maine Comm Coll (ME)
North Hennepin Comm Coll (MN)
North Iowa Area Comm Coll (IA)
Northland Comm and Tech Coll (MN)
North Shore Comm Coll (MA)
NorthWest Arkansas Comm Coll (AR)
Northwest Coll (WY)
Odessa Coll (TX)
Oklahoma State U–Oklahoma City (OK)
Orange Coast Coll (CA)
Otero Jr Coll (CO)
Owensboro Comm and Tech Coll (KY)
Palomar Coll (CA)
Panola Coll (TX)
Paris Jr Coll (TX)
Pasadena City Coll (CA)
Pennsylvania Inst of Technology (PA)
Pensacola State Coll (FL)
Piedmont Comm Coll (NC)
Piedmont Virginia Comm Coll (VA)
Pittsburgh Tech Coll (PA)
Potomac State Coll of West Virginia U (WV)
Pueblo Comm Coll (CO)
Queensborough Comm Coll of the City U of New York (NY)
Quinsigamond Comm Coll (MA)
Rainy River Comm Coll (MN)
Randolph Comm Coll (NC)
Rappahannock Comm Coll (VA)
Raritan Valley Comm Coll (NJ)
Richland Coll (TX)
Richmond Comm Coll (NC)
Ridgewater Coll (MN)
Rock Valley Coll (IL)
Rowan-Cabarrus Comm Coll (NC)
St. Louis Comm Coll (MO)
St. Philip's Coll (TX)
Salt Lake Comm Coll (UT)
San Jacinto Coll District (TX)
San Joaquin Delta Coll (CA)
San Juan Coll (NM)
Santa Rosa Jr Coll (CA)
Sauk Valley Comm Coll (IL)
Schenectady County Comm Coll (NY)
Schoolcraft Coll (MI)
Scottsdale Comm Coll (AZ)
Seminole State Coll (OK)
Seminole State Coll of Florida (FL)
Shawnee Comm Coll (IL)
Sisseton-Wahpeton Coll (SD)
Somerset Comm Coll (KY)
Southcentral Kentucky Comm and Tech Coll (KY)
Southeast Kentucky Comm and Tech Coll (KY)
Southeast Tech Inst (SD)
Southwestern Coll (CA)
Southwestern Comm Coll (IA)
Southwestern Comm Coll (NC)
Southwestern Indian Polytechnic Inst (NM)
Southwestern Michigan Coll (MI)
Southwest Texas Jr Coll (TX)
Springfield Tech Comm Coll (MA)
Stark State Coll (OH)
State U of New York Coll of Technology at Alfred (NY)
Sullivan County Comm Coll (NY)
Tarrant County Coll District (TX)
Texarkana Coll (TX)
Tidewater Comm Coll (VA)
Tohono O'odham Comm Coll (AZ)
Tompkins Cortland Comm Coll (NY)
Treasure Valley Comm Coll (OR)
Tri-County Comm Coll (NC)
Trident Tech Coll (SC)
Trinity Valley Comm Coll (TX)
Tulsa Comm Coll (OK)
Tyler Jr Coll (TX)
Union County Coll (NJ)
U of South Carolina Lancaster (SC)
Victoria Coll (TX)
Vincennes U (IN)
Volunteer State Comm Coll (TN)
Walters State Comm Coll (TN)
Waukesha County Tech Coll (WI)
Wayne Comm Coll (NC)
Wayne County Comm Coll District (MI)
Westchester Comm Coll (NY)
Western Dakota Tech Inst (SD)
Western Iowa Tech Comm Coll (IA)
Western Texas Coll (TX)
Western Wyoming Comm Coll (WY)
West Kentucky Comm and Tech Coll (KY)
White Mountains Comm Coll (NH)
Wisconsin Indianhead Tech Coll (WI)
Wor-Wic Comm Coll (MD)
Wytheville Comm Coll (VA)
York County Comm Coll (ME)

**BUSINESS ADMINISTRATION, MANAGEMENT AND OPERATIONS RELATED**
Ancilla Coll (IN)
Anne Arundel Comm Coll (MD)
Blue Ridge Comm and Tech Coll (WV)
Bunker Hill Comm Coll (MA)
Chandler-Gilbert Comm Coll (AZ)
Coll of Central Florida (FL)
Genesee Comm Coll (NY)
John Tyler Comm Coll (VA)
Lackawanna Coll (PA)
LDS Business Coll (UT)
Northern Essex Comm Coll (MA)
Northwest Vista Coll (TX)
Rappahannock Comm Coll (VA)
Rowan-Cabarrus Comm Coll (NC)
Southwest Virginia Comm Coll (VA)
Waukesha County Tech Coll (WI)
Williston State Coll (ND)

**BUSINESS AND PERSONAL/ FINANCIAL SERVICES MARKETING**
Hutchinson Comm Coll (KS)
North Central Texas Coll (TX)

**BUSINESS AUTOMATION/ TECHNOLOGY/DATA ENTRY**
Clark Coll (WA)
Comm Coll of Allegheny County (PA)
Copiah-Lincoln Comm Coll (MS)
Crowder Coll (MO)
Danville Area Comm Coll (IL)
El Paso Comm Coll (TX)
Houston Comm Coll (TX)
Illinois Eastern Comm Colls, Frontier Community College (IL)
Illinois Eastern Comm Colls, Lincoln Trail College (IL)
Illinois Eastern Comm Colls, Olney Central College (IL)
Illinois Eastern Comm Colls, Wabash Valley College (IL)
Illinois Valley Comm Coll (IL)
Ivy Tech Comm Coll–Bloomington (IN)
Ivy Tech Comm Coll–Central Indiana (IN)
Ivy Tech Comm Coll–Columbus (IN)
Ivy Tech Comm Coll–Lafayette (IN)
Ivy Tech Comm Coll–North Central (IN)
Ivy Tech Comm Coll–Northeast (IN)
Ivy Tech Comm Coll–Northwest (IN)
Ivy Tech Comm Coll–Richmond (IN)
Ivy Tech Comm Coll–Sellersburg (IN)
Ivy Tech Comm Coll–Southeast (IN)
Ivy Tech Comm Coll–Southwest (IN)
Kaskaskia Coll (IL)
Lakes Region Comm Coll (NH)
Lake Superior Coll (MN)
Lamar Comm Coll (CO)
Macomb Comm Coll (MI)
Miami Dade Coll (FL)
Minnesota State Comm and Tech Coll (MN)
Mitchell Tech Inst (SD)
Northeast Iowa Comm Coll (IA)
Panola Coll (TX)
Paris Jr Coll (TX)
Pasadena City Coll (CA)
Potomac State Coll of West Virginia U (WV)
Pueblo Comm Coll (CO)
Renton Tech Coll (WA)
Schoolcraft Coll (MI)
Shawnee Comm Coll (IL)
Southwest Texas Jr Coll (TX)
Western Iowa Tech Comm Coll (IA)

**BUSINESS/COMMERCE**
Alexandria Tech and Comm Coll (MN)
Alvin Comm Coll (TX)
Anne Arundel Comm Coll (MD)
Antelope Valley Coll (CA)
Arkansas State U–Newport (AR)
Austin Comm Coll District (TX)
Bossier Parish Comm Coll (LA)
Bristol Comm Coll (MA)
Brookhaven Coll (TX)
Bucks County Comm Coll (PA)
Carl Albert State Coll (OK)
Cecil Coll (MD)
Cedar Valley Coll (TX)
Central Texas Coll (TX)
Central Virginia Comm Coll (VA)
Century Coll (MN)
Chandler-Gilbert Comm Coll (AZ)
Chesapeake Coll (MD)
Coll of Central Florida (FL)
Coll of Marin (CA)
Coll of the Desert (CA)
Coll of the Ouachitas (AR)
Collin County Comm Coll District (TX)
Colorado Northwestern Comm Coll (CO)
Columbia-Greene Comm Coll (NY)
Comm Coll of Baltimore County (MD)
Dawson Comm Coll (MT)
Del Mar Coll (TX)
East Central Coll (MO)
El Paso Comm Coll (TX)
Feather River Coll (CA)
Georgia Military Coll (GA)
Hagerstown Comm Coll (MD)
Harford Comm Coll (MD)
Harrisburg Area Comm Coll (PA)
Hill Coll (TX)
Humacao Comm Coll (PR)
Hutchinson Comm Coll (KS)
Kaskaskia Coll (IL)
Kent State U at Ashtabula (OH)
Kent State U at East Liverpool (OH)
Kent State U at Salem (OH)
Kent State U at Trumbull (OH)
Kent State U at Tuscarawas (OH)
Lackawanna Coll (PA)
Lakes Region Comm Coll (NH)
Laramie County Comm Coll (WY)
Lehigh Carbon Comm Coll (PA)
Macomb Comm Coll (MI)
Massachusetts Bay Comm Coll (MA)
Merced Coll (CA)
Mesa Comm Coll (AZ)
Minnesota State Comm and Tech Coll (MN)
Minnesota West Comm and Tech Coll (MN)
Missouri State U–West Plains (MO)
Montgomery Coll (MD)
Montgomery County Comm Coll (PA)
Mott Comm Coll (MI)
Mount Wachusett Comm Coll (MA)
Naugatuck Valley Comm Coll (CT)
New Mexico State U–Alamogordo (NM)
Northampton Comm Coll (PA)
Northeast Comm Coll (NE)
Northern Essex Comm Coll (MA)
Northwest Coll (WY)
Nunez Comm Coll (LA)
Oklahoma City Comm Coll (OK)
Oklahoma State U Inst of Technology (OK)
Orange Coast Coll (CA)
Palomar Coll (CA)
Paris Jr Coll (TX)
Penn State DuBois (PA)
Penn State Fayette, The Eberly Campus (PA)
Penn State Mont Alto (PA)
Pennsylvania Highlands Comm Coll (PA)
Pensacola State Coll (FL)
Quinsigamond Comm Coll (MA)
Raritan Valley Comm Coll (NJ)
Rend Lake Coll (IL)
Saginaw Chippewa Tribal Coll (MI)
San Jacinto Coll District (TX)
Schoolcraft Coll (MI)
Seminole State Coll (OK)
Southeast Arkansas Coll (AR)
Southeast Tech Inst (SD)
Southern U at Shreveport (LA)
Southwestern Coll (CA)
Southwestern Indian Polytechnic Inst (NM)
Sowela Tech Comm Coll (LA)
Spartanburg Methodist Coll (SC)
Springfield Tech Comm Coll (MA)
Texarkana Coll (TX)
Three Rivers Comm Coll (CT)
Truckee Meadows Comm Coll (NV)
Tulsa Comm Coll (OK)
Tyler Jr Coll (TX)
Union County Coll (NJ)
U of Arkansas Comm Coll at Morrilton (AR)
U of Wisconsin–Baraboo/Sauk County (WI)
U of Wisconsin–Barron County (WI)
U of Wisconsin–Fond du Lac (WI)
U of Wisconsin–Fox Valley (WI)
U of Wisconsin–Manitowoc (WI)
U of Wisconsin–Marathon County (WI)
U of Wisconsin–Marinette (WI)
U of Wisconsin–Marshfield/Wood County (WI)
U of Wisconsin–Richland (WI)
U of Wisconsin–Rock County (WI)
U of Wisconsin–Sheboygan (WI)
U of Wisconsin–Washington County (WI)
U of Wisconsin–Waukesha (WI)
Vincennes U (IN)
Williamsburg Tech Coll (SC)
Wor-Wic Comm Coll (MD)

**BUSINESS/CORPORATE COMMUNICATIONS**
Cecil Coll (MD)
Houston Comm Coll (TX)

**BUSINESS MACHINE REPAIR**
Comm Coll of Allegheny County (PA)
De Anza Coll (CA)
Del Mar Coll (TX)
Muskegon Comm Coll (MI)

**BUSINESS, MANAGEMENT, AND MARKETING RELATED**
Bristol Comm Coll (MA)
Chandler-Gilbert Comm Coll (AZ)
Cloud County Comm Coll (KS)
Coll of the Desert (CA)
County Coll of Morris (NJ)
Eastern Arizona Coll (AZ)
Genesee Comm Coll (NY)
LDS Business Coll (UT)
Manor Coll (PA)
Niagara County Comm Coll (NY)
Queensborough Comm Coll of the City U of New York (NY)
Schenectady County Comm Coll (NY)
Southeastern Coll–West Palm Beach (FL)
Tulsa Comm Coll (OK)

## BUSINESS OPERATIONS SUPPORT AND SECRETARIAL SERVICES RELATED
Bristol Comm Coll (MA)
Bunker Hill Comm Coll (MA)
Central Virginia Comm Coll (VA)
Eastern Arizona Coll (AZ)
Genesee Comm Coll (NY)
Southwest Virginia Comm Coll (VA)

## BUSINESS TEACHER EDUCATION
Amarillo Coll (TX)
Eastern Arizona Coll (AZ)
Iowa Central Comm Coll (IA)
Mt. San Antonio Coll (CA)
Northern Essex Comm Coll (MA)
Paris Jr Coll (TX)
Rio Hondo Coll (CA)
Trinity Valley Comm Coll (TX)
Vincennes U (IN)

## CABINETMAKING AND MILLWORK
Bucks County Comm Coll (PA)
George C. Wallace Comm Coll (AL)
Ivy Tech Comm Coll–Bloomington (IN)
Ivy Tech Comm Coll–Central Indiana (IN)
Ivy Tech Comm Coll–Columbus (IN)
Ivy Tech Comm Coll–Lafayette (IN)
Ivy Tech Comm Coll–North Central (IN)
Ivy Tech Comm Coll–Northeast (IN)
Ivy Tech Comm Coll–Northwest (IN)
Ivy Tech Comm Coll–Richmond (IN)
Ivy Tech Comm Coll–Sellersburg (IN)
Ivy Tech Comm Coll–Southwest (IN)
Ivy Tech Comm Coll–Wabash Valley (IN)
Johnson Coll (PA)
Macomb Comm Coll (MI)
Palomar Coll (CA)
Thaddeus Stevens Coll of Technology (PA)

## CAD/CADD DRAFTING/DESIGN TECHNOLOGY
Arizona Western Coll (AZ)
Asheville-Buncombe Tech Comm Coll (NC)
Central Ohio Tech Coll (OH)
Central Oregon Comm Coll (OR)
Century Coll (MN)
Comm Coll of Allegheny County (PA)
Danville Area Comm Coll (IL)
Dunwoody Coll of Technology (MN)
Erie Comm Coll, South Campus (NY)
Front Range Comm Coll (CO)
Gulf Coast State Coll (FL)
Harford Comm Coll (MD)
Illinois Valley Comm Coll (IL)
Kellogg Comm Coll (MI)
Kent State U at Tuscarawas (OH)
Kishwaukee Coll (IL)
Lake Superior Coll (MN)
Miami Dade Coll (FL)
Mohawk Valley Comm Coll (NY)
Morrison Inst of Technology (IL)
Morton Coll (IL)
Northampton Comm Coll (PA)
Northwest Coll (WY)
Oklahoma City Comm Coll (OK)
South Suburban Coll (IL)
Tallahassee Comm Coll (FL)
Thaddeus Stevens Coll of Technology (PA)
Wayne County Comm Coll District (MI)

## CARDIOVASCULAR SCIENCE
Lackawanna Coll (PA)

## CARDIOVASCULAR TECHNOLOGY
Bunker Hill Comm Coll (MA)
Harper Coll (IL)
Harrisburg Area Comm Coll (PA)
Houston Comm Coll (TX)
Howard Comm Coll (MD)
Kirtland Comm Coll (MI)
Minnesota State Comm and Tech Coll (MN)
Northeast State Comm Coll (TN)
Oklahoma State U–Oklahoma City (OK)
Orange Coast Coll (CA)
St. Philip's Coll (TX)
San Jacinto Coll District (TX)
Southeast Arkansas Coll (AR)
Southeast Tech Inst (SD)

## CARPENTRY
Alamance Comm Coll (NC)
American Samoa Comm Coll (AS)
Arizona Western Coll (AZ)
Austin Comm Coll District (TX)
Comm Coll of Allegheny County (PA)
Fullerton Coll (CA)
George C. Wallace Comm Coll (AL)
Hawkeye Comm Coll (IA)
Hutchinson Comm Coll (KS)
Iowa Central Comm Coll (IA)
Ivy Tech Comm Coll–Central Indiana (IN)
Ivy Tech Comm Coll–East Central (IN)
Ivy Tech Comm Coll–Lafayette (IN)
Ivy Tech Comm Coll–North Central (IN)
Ivy Tech Comm Coll–Northwest (IN)
Ivy Tech Comm Coll–Sellersburg (IN)
Ivy Tech Comm Coll–Southwest (IN)
Ivy Tech Comm Coll–Wabash Valley (IN)
Johnson Coll (PA)
Kaskaskia Coll (IL)
Lake Superior Coll (MN)
Minnesota State Comm and Tech Coll (MN)
Mohawk Valley Comm Coll (NY)
Northern Maine Comm Coll (ME)
North Iowa Area Comm Coll (IA)
Palomar Coll (CA)
Ridgewater Coll (MN)
San Juan Coll (NM)
Southwestern Comm Coll (IA)
Southwestern Michigan Coll (MI)
Thaddeus Stevens Coll of Technology (PA)
Treasure Valley Comm Coll (OR)
Vincennes U (IN)
Western Iowa Tech Comm Coll (IA)

## CERAMIC ARTS AND CERAMICS
De Anza Coll (CA)
Palomar Coll (CA)

## CHEMICAL ENGINEERING
Monroe Comm Coll (NY)
Muskegon Comm Coll (MI)

## CHEMICAL TECHNOLOGY
Alvin Comm Coll (TX)
Amarillo Coll (TX)
Bucks County Comm Coll (PA)
Comm Coll of Allegheny County (PA)
County Coll of Morris (NJ)
Del Mar Coll (TX)
Fullerton Coll (CA)
Houston Comm Coll (TX)
Humacao Comm Coll (PR)
Ivy Tech Comm Coll–Lafayette (IN)
Ivy Tech Comm Coll–Wabash Valley (IN)
Lehigh Carbon Comm Coll (PA)
Mohawk Valley Comm Coll (NY)
Niagara County Comm Coll (NY)
Ozarks Tech Comm Coll (MO)
Pensacola State Coll (FL)
San Jacinto Coll District (TX)
Southwestern Coll (CA)
Sowela Tech Comm Coll (LA)
Texas State Tech Coll (TX)
Victoria Coll (TX)

## CHEMISTRY
Amarillo Coll (TX)
Arizona Western Coll (AZ)
Austin Comm Coll District (TX)
Barton County Comm Coll (KS)
Bunker Hill Comm Coll (MA)
Cecil Coll (MD)
Central New Mexico Comm Coll (NM)
Central Texas Coll (TX)
Cochise County Comm Coll District (AZ)
Coll of Central Florida (FL)
Coll of Marin (CA)
Coll of the Desert (CA)
Comm Coll of Allegheny County (PA)
Comm Coll of Philadelphia (PA)
Copiah-Lincoln Comm Coll (MS)
Del Mar Coll (TX)
Eastern Arizona Coll (AZ)
Frederick Comm Coll (MD)
Fullerton Coll (CA)
Genesee Comm Coll (NY)
Gordon State Coll (GA)
Grand Rapids Comm Coll (MI)
Harford Comm Coll (MD)
Harper Coll (IL)
Harrisburg Area Comm Coll (PA)
Hill Coll (TX)

Holyoke Comm Coll (MA)
Houston Comm Coll (TX)
Kingsborough Comm Coll of the City U of New York (NY)
Laramie County Comm Coll (WY)
Lehigh Carbon Comm Coll (PA)
Los Angeles City Coll (CA)
Macomb Comm Coll (MI)
Merced Coll (CA)
Miami Dade Coll (FL)
Minnesota State Comm and Tech Coll (MN)
Monroe Comm Coll (NY)
Mount Wachusett Comm Coll (MA)
Navarro Coll (TX)
Northampton Comm Coll (PA)
Northeast Comm Coll (NE)
Northeastern Jr Coll (CO)
North Hennepin Comm Coll (MN)
Northwest Coll (WY)
Odessa Coll (TX)
Oklahoma City Comm Coll (OK)
Orange Coast Coll (CA)
Ozarks Tech Comm Coll (MO)
Palomar Coll (CA)
Panola Coll (TX)
Paris Jr Coll (TX)
Pasadena City Coll (CA)
Pensacola State Coll (FL)
Potomac State Coll of West Virginia U (WV)
Queensborough Comm Coll of the City U of New York (NY)
Quinsigamond Comm Coll (MA)
Ridgewater Coll (MN)
St. Charles Comm Coll (MO)
St. Philip's Coll (TX)
Salt Lake Comm Coll (UT)
San Jacinto Coll District (TX)
San Joaquin Delta Coll (CA)
San Juan Coll (NM)
Santa Rosa Jr Coll (CA)
Sauk Valley Comm Coll (IL)
Southwestern Coll (CA)
Springfield Tech Comm Coll (MA)
Texarkana Coll (TX)
Trinity Valley Comm Coll (TX)
Truckee Meadows Comm Coll (NV)
Tyler Jr Coll (TX)
Union County Coll (NJ)
U of Wisconsin–Baraboo/Sauk County (WI)
U of Wisconsin–Barron County (WI)
U of Wisconsin–Fond du Lac (WI)
U of Wisconsin–Fox Valley (WI)
U of Wisconsin–Manitowoc (WI)
U of Wisconsin–Marathon County (WI)
U of Wisconsin–Marinette (WI)
U of Wisconsin–Marshfield/Wood County (WI)
U of Wisconsin–Richland (WI)
U of Wisconsin–Rock County (WI)
U of Wisconsin–Sheboygan (WI)
U of Wisconsin–Washington County (WI)
U of Wisconsin–Waukesha (WI)
Western Wyoming Comm Coll (WY)

## CHEMISTRY RELATED
Vincennes U (IN)

## CHEMISTRY TEACHER EDUCATION
Anne Arundel Comm Coll (MD)
Carroll Comm Coll (MD)
Chesapeake Coll (MD)
Comm Coll of Baltimore County (MD)
Daytona State Coll (FL)
Harford Comm Coll (MD)
Montgomery Coll (MD)
Vincennes U (IN)

## CHILD-CARE AND SUPPORT SERVICES MANAGEMENT
Anne Arundel Comm Coll (MD)
Barton County Comm Coll (KS)
Bevill State Comm Coll (AL)
Carroll Comm Coll (MD)
Cayuga County Comm Coll (NY)
Cecil Coll (MD)
Central Lakes Coll (MN)
Central Oregon Comm Coll (OR)
Chesapeake Coll (MD)
Cloud County Comm Coll (KS)
Coll of the Desert (CA)
Coll of the Ouachitas (AR)
Comm Coll of Baltimore County (MD)
Dutchess Comm Coll (NY)
East Central Coll (MO)
Eastern Gateway Comm Coll (OH)
El Paso Comm Coll (TX)

Erie Comm Coll (NY)
George C. Wallace Comm Coll (AL)
Grand Rapids Comm Coll (MI)
Greenville Tech Coll (SC)
Hagerstown Comm Coll (MD)
Haywood Comm Coll (NC)
H. Councill Trenholm State Comm Coll (AL)
Holyoke Comm Coll (MA)
Hutchinson Comm Coll (KS)
Independence Comm Coll (KS)
Ivy Tech Comm Coll–North Central (IN)
Ivy Tech Comm Coll–Northwest (IN)
Jefferson Comm Coll (NY)
Jefferson State Comm Coll (AL)
Kellogg Comm Coll (MI)
Kishwaukee Coll (IL)
Lurleen B. Wallace Comm Coll (AL)
Macomb Comm Coll (MI)
Minnesota West Comm and Tech Coll (MN)
Mitchell Comm Coll (NC)
Montgomery County Comm Coll (PA)
Mount Wachusett Comm Coll (MA)
Nebraska Indian Comm Coll (NE)
Northwest-Shoals Comm Coll (AL)
Orange Coast Coll (CA)
Palomar Coll (CA)
Pennsylvania Highlands Comm Coll (PA)
Pensacola State Coll (FL)
Piedmont Comm Coll (NC)
St. Charles Comm Coll (MO)
Southeast Tech Inst (SD)
Texarkana Coll (TX)
Three Rivers Coll (MO)
Three Rivers Comm Coll (CT)
Tompkins Cortland Comm Coll (NY)
Vincennes U (IN)
Wayne County Comm Coll District (MI)
Westchester Comm Coll (NY)
Williamsburg Tech Coll (SC)
Wisconsin Indianhead Tech Coll (WI)
Wor-Wic Comm Coll (MD)

## CHILD-CARE PROVISION
Antelope Valley Coll (CA)
Black Hawk Coll, Moline (IL)
Bossier Parish Comm Coll (LA)
Bucks County Comm Coll (PA)
City Colls of Chicago, Olive-Harvey College (IL)
Coll of Marin (CA)
Coll of the Canyons (CA)
Coll of the Desert (CA)
Collin County Comm Coll District (TX)
Comm Coll of Allegheny County (PA)
Copiah-Lincoln Comm Coll (MS)
Danville Area Comm Coll (IL)
Dawson Comm Coll (MT)
Des Moines Area Comm Coll (IA)
Feather River Coll (CA)
Fullerton Coll (CA)
Gulf Coast State Coll (FL)
Harper Coll (IL)
Hawkeye Comm Coll (IA)
Highland Comm Coll (IL)
Hill Coll (TX)
Hinds Comm Coll (MS)
Hopkinsville Comm Coll (KY)
Hudson County Comm Coll (NJ)
Illinois Central Coll (IL)
Illinois Valley Comm Coll (IL)
John Tyler Comm Coll (VA)
J. Sargeant Reynolds Comm Coll (VA)
Kaskaskia Coll (IL)
Kishwaukee Coll (IL)
Lackawanna Coll (PA)
Lakeland Comm Coll (OH)
Lake Region State Coll (ND)
Louisiana State U at Eunice (LA)
Maysville Comm and Tech Coll, Maysville (KY)
McHenry County Coll (IL)
Merced Coll (CA)
Meridian Comm Coll (MS)
Mesalands Comm Coll (NM)
Miami Dade Coll (FL)
Montgomery Coll (MD)
Morton Coll (IL)
Mott Comm Coll (MI)
Nunez Comm Coll (LA)
Oakton Comm Coll (IL)
Orange Coast Coll (CA)
Owensboro Comm and Tech Coll (KY)
Ozarks Tech Comm Coll (MO)

Palomar Coll (CA)
Pensacola State Coll (FL)
Raritan Valley Comm Coll (NJ)
Rend Lake Coll (IL)
San Juan Coll (NM)
Shawnee Comm Coll (IL)
Somerset Comm Coll (KY)
Southeast Arkansas Coll (AR)
Southeast Tech Inst (SD)
South Suburban Coll (IL)
Southwestern Coll (CA)
Southwest Virginia Comm Coll (VA)
Trident Tech Coll (SC)
Western Iowa Tech Comm Coll (IA)
Western Texas Coll (TX)
West Kentucky Comm and Tech Coll (KY)

## CHILD DEVELOPMENT
Alvin Comm Coll (TX)
Amarillo Coll (TX)
Austin Comm Coll District (TX)
Brookhaven Coll (TX)
Carl Albert State Coll (OK)
Cleveland State Comm Coll (TN)
Cloud County Comm Coll (KS)
Collin County Comm Coll District (TX)
Comm Coll of Allegheny County (PA)
Copiah-Lincoln Comm Coll (MS)
De Anza Coll (CA)
Del Mar Coll (TX)
Dyersburg State Comm Coll (TN)
Edison State Comm Coll (OH)
El Paso Comm Coll (TX)
Frederick Comm Coll (MD)
Houston Comm Coll (TX)
Howard Comm Coll (MD)
Illinois Eastern Comm Colls, Wabash Valley College (IL)
Illinois Valley Comm Coll (IL)
Ivy Tech Comm Coll–Central Indiana (IN)
James Sprunt Comm Coll (NC)
Jefferson Comm Coll (NY)
Kennebec Valley Comm Coll (ME)
Los Angeles City Coll (CA)
Miami Dade Coll (FL)
Monroe County Comm Coll (MI)
Mt. San Antonio Coll (CA)
Mount Wachusett Comm Coll (MA)
Muskegon Comm Coll (MI)
National Park Coll (AR)
New River Comm Coll (VA)
Northeastern Jr Coll (CO)
Northeast State Comm Coll (TN)
North Shore Comm Coll (MA)
Northwest-Shoals Comm Coll (AL)
Odessa Coll (TX)
Oklahoma City Comm Coll (OK)
Pasadena City Coll (CA)
Rock Valley Coll (IL)
St. Louis Comm Coll (MO)
St. Philip's Coll (TX)
San Jacinto Coll District (TX)
Santa Rosa Jr Coll (CA)
Schoolcraft Coll (MI)
Seminole State Coll (OK)
Seminole State Coll of Florida (FL)
Southwestern Coll (CA)
Southwestern Comm Coll (NC)
Southwest Texas Jr Coll (TX)
Texarkana Coll (TX)
Tohono O'odham Comm Coll (AZ)
Trinity Valley Comm Coll (TX)
Tulsa Comm Coll (OK)
Tyler Jr Coll (TX)
U of Arkansas Comm Coll at Morrilton (AR)
Volunteer State Comm Coll (TN)
Walters State Comm Coll (TN)

## CHINESE
Austin Comm Coll District (TX)
Los Angeles City Coll (CA)

## CHIROPRACTIC ASSISTANT
Barton County Comm Coll (KS)

## CINEMATOGRAPHY AND FILM/VIDEO PRODUCTION
Bucks County Comm Coll (PA)
Camden County Coll (NJ)
Central New Mexico Comm Coll (NM)
Century Coll (MN)
Coll of Marin (CA)
Coll of the Canyons (CA)
Coll of the Desert (CA)
El Paso Comm Coll (TX)
Houston Comm Coll (TX)
Los Angeles City Coll (CA)
Miami Dade Coll (FL)

Mott Comm Coll (MI)
Northcentral Tech Coll (WI)
Oklahoma City Comm Coll (OK)
Orange Coast Coll (CA)
Pasadena City Coll (CA)
Piedmont Comm Coll (NC)
Western Iowa Tech Comm Coll (IA)

### CIVIL DRAFTING AND CAD/CADD
Central Ohio Tech Coll (OH)
Comm Coll of Allegheny County (PA)
Genesee Comm Coll (NY)
Renton Tech Coll (WA)

### CIVIL ENGINEERING
American Samoa Comm Coll (AS)
Fiorello H. LaGuardia Comm Coll of the City U of New York (NY)
Potomac State Coll of West Virginia U (WV)
Tidewater Comm Coll (VA)
Truckee Meadows Comm Coll (NV)

### CIVIL ENGINEERING TECHNOLOGY
Arizona Western Coll (AZ)
Asheville-Buncombe Tech Comm Coll (NC)
Bristol Comm Coll (MA)
Central Maine Comm Coll (ME)
Central Ohio Tech Coll (OH)
Chippewa Valley Tech Coll (WI)
Comm Coll of Allegheny County (PA)
Copiah-Lincoln Comm Coll (MS)
Des Moines Area Comm Coll (IA)
Dunwoody Coll of Technology (MN)
Eastern Arizona Coll (AZ)
Erie Comm Coll, North Campus (NY)
Fayetteville Tech Comm Coll (NC)
Gulf Coast State Coll (FL)
Harrisburg Area Comm Coll (PA)
Hawkeye Comm Coll (IA)
Lakeland Comm Coll (OH)
Lake Superior Coll (MN)
Macomb Comm Coll (MI)
Miami Dade Coll (FL)
Mid-State Tech Coll (WI)
Minnesota State Comm and Tech Coll (MN)
Mohawk Valley Comm Coll (NY)
Monroe Comm Coll (NY)
Mt. San Antonio Coll (CA)
Nassau Comm Coll (NY)
North Dakota State Coll of Science (ND)
Northern Essex Comm Coll (MA)
Northwest Mississippi Comm Coll (MS)
Pensacola State Coll (FL)
San Joaquin Delta Coll (CA)
Santa Rosa Jr Coll (CA)
Seminole State Coll of Florida (FL)
Southeast Tech Inst (SD)
Springfield Tech Comm Coll (MA)
Stark State Coll (OH)
State Tech Coll of Missouri (MO)
Trident Tech Coll (SC)
Westchester Comm Coll (NY)
Wytheville Comm Coll (VA)

### CLASSICS AND CLASSICAL LANGUAGES
Pasadena City Coll (CA)

### CLINICAL LABORATORY SCIENCE/MEDICAL TECHNOLOGY
Amarillo Coll (TX)
Chipola Coll (FL)
Coll of Central Florida (FL)
Del Mar Coll (TX)
Howard Comm Coll (MD)
Monroe County Comm Coll (MI)
National Park Coll (AR)
St. Louis Comm Coll (MO)
Tarrant County Coll District (TX)

### CLINICAL/MEDICAL LABORATORY ASSISTANT
Somerset Comm Coll (KY)

### CLINICAL/MEDICAL LABORATORY SCIENCE AND ALLIED PROFESSIONS RELATED
Houston Comm Coll (TX)
Southeast Tech Inst (SD)

### CLINICAL/MEDICAL LABORATORY TECHNOLOGY
Alamance Comm Coll (NC)
Alexandria Tech and Comm Coll (MN)
Anne Arundel Comm Coll (MD)
Asheville-Buncombe Tech Comm Coll (NC)
Austin Comm Coll District (TX)
Barton County Comm Coll (KS)
Blue Ridge Comm and Tech Coll (WV)
Bristol Comm Coll (MA)
Bunker Hill Comm Coll (MA)
Camden County Coll (NJ)
Central New Mexico Comm Coll (NM)
Central Texas Coll (TX)
Chippewa Valley Tech Coll (WI)
Coll of the Canyons (CA)
Comm Coll of Allegheny County (PA)
Comm Coll of Baltimore County (MD)
Comm Coll of Philadelphia (PA)
Copiah-Lincoln Comm Coll (MS)
Del Mar Coll (TX)
Des Moines Area Comm Coll (IA)
Dutchess Comm Coll (NY)
Edison State Comm Coll (OH)
El Paso Comm Coll (TX)
Erie Comm Coll, North Campus (NY)
Fox Valley Tech Coll (WI)
Genesee Comm Coll (NY)
George C. Wallace Comm Coll (AL)
Greenville Tech Coll (SC)
Halifax Comm Coll (NC)
Harrisburg Area Comm Coll (PA)
Hawkeye Comm Coll (IA)
Hinds Comm Coll (MS)
Houston Comm Coll (TX)
Hutchinson Comm Coll (KS)
Illinois Central Coll (IL)
Iowa Central Comm Coll (IA)
Ivy Tech Comm Coll–Lafayette (IN)
Ivy Tech Comm Coll–North Central (IN)
Ivy Tech Comm Coll–Sellersburg (IN)
Ivy Tech Comm Coll–Wabash Valley (IN)
Jefferson State Comm Coll (AL)
J. Sargeant Reynolds Comm Coll (VA)
Kaskaskia Coll (IL)
Lake Area Tech Inst (SD)
Lakeland Comm Coll (OH)
Lake Superior Coll (MN)
Lorain County Comm Coll (OH)
Manchester Comm Coll (CT)
Maysville Comm and Tech Coll, Maysville (KY)
McLennan Comm Coll (TX)
Meridian Comm Coll (MS)
Miami Dade Coll (FL)
Mid-Plains Comm Coll, North Platte (NE)
Minnesota State Comm and Tech Coll (MN)
Minnesota West Comm and Tech Coll (MN)
Mitchell Tech Inst (SD)
Montgomery County Comm Coll (PA)
Mount Wachusett Comm Coll (MA)
Nassau Comm Coll (NY)
National Park Coll (AR)
Navarro Coll (TX)
Northcentral Tech Coll (WI)
Northeast Iowa Comm Coll (IA)
North Hennepin Comm Coll (MN)
North Iowa Area Comm Coll (IA)
Oakton Comm Coll (IL)
Odessa Coll (TX)
Orange Coast Coll (CA)
Panola Coll (TX)
Queensborough Comm Coll of the City U of New York (NY)
St. Philip's Coll (TX)
Salt Lake Comm Coll (UT)
San Jacinto Coll District (TX)
San Juan Coll (NM)
Seminole State Coll (OK)
Shawnee Comm Coll (IL)
Southeast Kentucky Comm and Tech Coll (KY)
Southeast Tech Inst (SD)
Southern U at Shreveport (LA)
Southwestern Comm Coll (NC)
Spencerian Coll (KY)
Springfield Tech Comm Coll (MA)
Stark State Coll (OH)

Tarrant County Coll District (TX)
Three Rivers Coll (MO)
Trident Tech Coll (SC)
Tulsa Comm Coll (OK)
Tyler Jr Coll (TX)
Volunteer State Comm Coll (TN)
Western Dakota Tech Inst (SD)
West Kentucky Comm and Tech Coll (KY)
Wytheville Comm Coll (VA)

### CLINICAL/MEDICAL SOCIAL WORK
Asheville-Buncombe Tech Comm Coll (NC)
Central Texas Coll (TX)
Dawson Comm Coll (MT)
Nebraska Indian Comm Coll (NE)

### CLINICAL RESEARCH COORDINATOR
Oklahoma City Comm Coll (OK)

### COMMERCIAL AND ADVERTISING ART
Alamance Comm Coll (NC)
Alexandria Tech and Comm Coll (MN)
Amarillo Coll (TX)
Bucks County Comm Coll (PA)
Central Lakes Coll (MN)
Central Texas Coll (TX)
Coll of the Desert (CA)
Collin County Comm Coll District (TX)
Comm Coll of Allegheny County (PA)
Comm Coll of Baltimore County (MD)
De Anza Coll (CA)
Des Moines Area Comm Coll (IA)
Dutchess Comm Coll (NY)
East Central Coll (MO)
Eastern Arizona Coll (AZ)
El Paso Comm Coll (TX)
Fashion Inst of Technology (NY)
Fayetteville Tech Comm Coll (NC)
Hagerstown Comm Coll (MD)
Halifax Comm Coll (NC)
Hill Coll (TX)
Housatonic Comm Coll (CT)
James Sprunt Comm Coll (NC)
Kingsborough Comm Coll of the City U of New York (NY)
Lakeland Comm Coll (OH)
Macomb Comm Coll (MI)
Manchester Comm Coll (CT)
Miami Dade Coll (FL)
Mid-Plains Comm Coll, North Platte (NE)
Mission Coll (CA)
Mohawk Valley Comm Coll (NY)
Monroe Comm Coll (NY)
Montgomery Coll (MD)
Mt. San Antonio Coll (CA)
Muskegon Comm Coll (MI)
Nassau Comm Coll (NY)
National Park Coll (AR)
Navarro Coll (TX)
Northern Essex Comm Coll (MA)
NorthWest Arkansas Comm Coll (AR)
Northwest Coll (WY)
Northwest Mississippi Comm Coll (MS)
Orange Coast Coll (CA)
Palomar Coll (CA)
Pensacola State Coll (FL)
Randolph Comm Coll (NC)
St. Charles Comm Coll (MO)
San Jacinto Coll District (TX)
San Joaquin Delta Coll (CA)
San Juan Coll (NM)
School of Advertising Art (OH)
Southwestern Comm Coll (NC)
Sowela Tech Comm Coll (LA)
Springfield Tech Comm Coll (MA)
Sullivan County Comm Coll (NY)
Tallahassee Comm Coll (FL)
Tidewater Comm Coll (VA)
Tompkins Cortland Comm Coll (NY)
Trident Tech Coll (SC)
Truckee Meadows Comm Coll (NV)
Vincennes U (IN)
Westchester Comm Coll (NY)

### COMMERCIAL PHOTOGRAPHY
Austin Comm Coll District (TX)
Bucks County Comm Coll (PA)
Cecil Coll (MD)
Century Coll (MN)

Collin County Comm Coll District (TX)
Fashion Inst of Technology (NY)
Fiorello H. LaGuardia Comm Coll of the City U of New York (NY)
Hawkeye Comm Coll (IA)
Houston Comm Coll (TX)
McHenry County Coll (IL)
Mohawk Valley Comm Coll (NY)
Montgomery Coll (MD)
Northwest Coll (WY)
Randolph Comm Coll (NC)
Ridgewater Coll (MN)
Springfield Tech Comm Coll (MA)
Trinity Valley Comm Coll (TX)
Western Iowa Tech Comm Coll (IA)

### COMMUNICATION
Arizona Western Coll (AZ)
Central New Mexico Comm Coll (NM)
Northeastern Jr Coll (CO)
Pennsylvania Inst of Technology (PA)
Potomac State Coll of West Virginia U (WV)
Santa Rosa Jr Coll (CA)
Sauk Valley Comm Coll (IL)
Tulsa Comm Coll (OK)
U of Wisconsin–Baraboo/Sauk County (WI)
U of Wisconsin–Barron County (WI)
U of Wisconsin–Fond du Lac (WI)
U of Wisconsin–Fox Valley (WI)
U of Wisconsin–Manitowoc (WI)
U of Wisconsin–Marathon County (WI)
U of Wisconsin–Marinette (WI)
U of Wisconsin–Marshfield/Wood County (WI)
U of Wisconsin–Richland (WI)
U of Wisconsin–Rock County (WI)
U of Wisconsin–Sheboygan (WI)
U of Wisconsin–Washington County (WI)
U of Wisconsin–Waukesha (WI)

### COMMUNICATION AND JOURNALISM RELATED
Cayuga County Comm Coll (NY)
Harford Comm Coll (MD)
Harrisburg Area Comm Coll (PA)
Ivy Tech Comm Coll–Kokomo (IN)
Queensborough Comm Coll of the City U of New York (NY)

### COMMUNICATION AND MEDIA RELATED
County Coll of Morris (NJ)
Lackawanna Coll (PA)
Manor Coll (PA)
Raritan Valley Comm Coll (NJ)

### COMMUNICATIONS SYSTEMS INSTALLATION AND REPAIR TECHNOLOGY
Cayuga County Comm Coll (NY)
Des Moines Area Comm Coll (IA)
Dutchess Comm Coll (NY)
Southwestern Coll (CA)

### COMMUNICATIONS TECHNOLOGIES AND SUPPORT SERVICES RELATED
Anne Arundel Comm Coll (MD)
Bowling Green State U–Firelands Coll (OH)
Comm Coll of Allegheny County (PA)
Comm Coll of Baltimore County (MD)
Harford Comm Coll (MD)
Montgomery Coll (MD)
Vincennes U (IN)

### COMMUNICATIONS TECHNOLOGY
Gulf Coast State Coll (FL)
Hutchinson Comm Coll (KS)
Mott Comm Coll (MI)
Ozarks Tech Comm Coll (MO)
Pensacola State Coll (FL)
Pueblo Comm Coll (CO)

### COMMUNITY HEALTH AND PREVENTIVE MEDICINE
Arizona Western Coll (AZ)
Massachusetts Bay Comm Coll (MA)
Northwest Vista Coll (TX)
Quinsigamond Comm Coll (MA)

### COMMUNITY HEALTH SERVICES COUNSELING
Comm Coll of Allegheny County (PA)
Daytona State Coll (FL)
Dutchess Comm Coll (NY)
Kingsborough Comm Coll of the City U of New York (NY)
Lake Area Tech Inst (SD)
Miami Dade Coll (FL)
Mott Comm Coll (MI)
Northern Essex Comm Coll (MA)
Santa Rosa Jr Coll (CA)

### COMMUNITY ORGANIZATION AND ADVOCACY
Del Mar Coll (TX)
Iowa Central Comm Coll (IA)
Jefferson Comm Coll (NY)
Kellogg Comm Coll (MI)
New River Comm Coll (VA)
Schenectady County Comm Coll (NY)
Westchester Comm Coll (NY)

### COMMUNITY PSYCHOLOGY
Dawson Comm Coll (MT)

### COMPARATIVE LITERATURE
Miami Dade Coll (FL)
Otero Jr Coll (CO)
San Joaquin Delta Coll (CA)

### COMPUTER AND INFORMATION SCIENCES
Ancilla Coll (IN)
Anne Arundel Comm Coll (MD)
Arizona Western Coll (AZ)
Austin Comm Coll District (TX)
Bevill State Comm Coll (AL)
Bristol Comm Coll (MA)
Bucks County Comm Coll (PA)
Camden County Coll (NJ)
Carl Albert State Coll (OK)
Cayuga County Comm Coll (NY)
Central New Mexico Comm Coll (NM)
Central Virginia Comm Coll (VA)
Chandler-Gilbert Comm Coll (AZ)
Cleveland State Comm Coll (TN)
Coll of Central Florida (FL)
Coll of the Ouachitas (AR)
Collin County Comm Coll District (TX)
Columbia-Greene Comm Coll (NY)
Comm Coll of Baltimore County (MD)
Dawson Comm Coll (MT)
Dyersburg State Comm Coll (TN)
Edison State Comm Coll (OH)
El Paso Comm Coll (TX)
Erie Comm Coll, North Campus (NY)
Front Range Comm Coll (CO)
Gateway Comm and Tech Coll (KY)
George C. Wallace Comm Coll (AL)
Grand Rapids Comm Coll (MI)
Hagerstown Comm Coll (MD)
Harford Comm Coll (MD)
Harper Coll (IL)
Harrisburg Area Comm Coll (PA)
H. Councill Trenholm State Comm Coll (AL)
Hill Coll (TX)
Hopkinsville Comm Coll (KY)
Hudson County Comm Coll (NJ)
Hutchinson Comm Coll (KS)
Independence Comm Coll (KS)
Ivy Tech Comm Coll–Bloomington (IN)
Ivy Tech Comm Coll–Central Indiana (IN)
Ivy Tech Comm Coll–Columbus (IN)
Ivy Tech Comm Coll–East Central (IN)
Ivy Tech Comm Coll–Kokomo (IN)
Ivy Tech Comm Coll–Lafayette (IN)
Ivy Tech Comm Coll–North Central (IN)
Ivy Tech Comm Coll–Northeast (IN)
Ivy Tech Comm Coll–Northwest (IN)
Ivy Tech Comm Coll–Richmond (IN)
Ivy Tech Comm Coll–Sellersburg (IN)
Ivy Tech Comm Coll–Southeast (IN)
Ivy Tech Comm Coll–Southwest (IN)
Ivy Tech Comm Coll–Wabash Valley (IN)
Jamestown Comm Coll (NY)
Jefferson Comm Coll (NY)
Jefferson State Comm Coll (AL)
John Tyler Comm Coll (VA)

J. Sargeant Reynolds Comm Coll (VA)
Kingsborough Comm Coll of the City U of New York (NY)
Lakes Region Comm Coll (NH)
LDS Business Coll (UT)
Lehigh Carbon Comm Coll (PA)
Lurleen B. Wallace Comm Coll (AL)
Maysville Comm and Tech Coll, Maysville (KY)
Mesa Comm Coll (AZ)
Mesalands Comm Coll (NM)
Mid-Plains Comm Coll, North Platte (NE)
Mohawk Valley Comm Coll (NY)
Montgomery Coll (MD)
Mt. San Antonio Coll (CA)
Mount Wachusett Comm Coll (MA)
Nassau Comm Coll (NY)
North Dakota State Coll of Science (ND)
Northeast Comm Coll (NE)
Northern Essex Comm Coll (MA)
Northwest Coll (WY)
Northwest-Shoals Comm Coll (AL)
Northwest Vista Coll (TX)
Odessa Coll (TX)
Owensboro Comm and Tech Coll (KY)
Paris Jr Coll (TX)
Pennsylvania Highlands Comm Coll (PA)
Pensacola State Coll (FL)
Piedmont Virginia Comm Coll (VA)
Potomac State Coll of West Virginia U (WV)
Pueblo Comm Coll (CO)
Queensborough Comm Coll of the City U of New York (NY)
Quinsigamond Comm Coll (MA)
Raritan Valley Comm Coll (NJ)
Salt Lake Comm Coll (UT)
San Jacinto Coll District (TX)
Somerset Comm Coll (KY)
Southcentral Kentucky Comm and Tech Coll (KY)
Southwestern Coll (CA)
Southwest Texas Jr Coll (TX)
Southwest Virginia Comm Coll (VA)
Stark State Coll (OH)
State U of New York Coll of Technology at Alfred (NY)
Texarkana Coll (TX)
Tompkins Cortland Comm Coll (NY)
Treasure Valley Comm Coll (OR)
U of Wisconsin–Baraboo/Sauk County (WI)
U of Wisconsin–Barron County (WI)
U of Wisconsin–Fond du Lac (WI)
U of Wisconsin–Fox Valley (WI)
U of Wisconsin–Manitowoc (WI)
U of Wisconsin–Marathon County (WI)
U of Wisconsin–Marinette (WI)
U of Wisconsin–Marshfield/Wood County (WI)
U of Wisconsin–Richland (WI)
U of Wisconsin–Rock County (WI)
U of Wisconsin–Sheboygan (WI)
U of Wisconsin–Washington County (WI)
U of Wisconsin–Waukesha (WI)
Volunteer State Comm Coll (TN)
Walters State Comm Coll (TN)
Westchester Comm Coll (NY)
Western Texas Coll (TX)
Western Wyoming Comm Coll (WY)
West Kentucky Comm and Tech Coll (KY)
White Mountains Comm Coll (NH)
Wor-Wic Comm Coll (MD)

**COMPUTER AND INFORMATION SCIENCES AND SUPPORT SERVICES RELATED**
Bowling Green State U–Firelands Coll (OH)
Bunker Hill Comm Coll (MA)
Cayuga County Comm Coll (NY)
Chandler-Gilbert Comm Coll (AZ)
Chesapeake Coll (MD)
Coll of the Desert (CA)
Del Mar Coll (TX)
Des Moines Area Comm Coll (IA)
Eastern Shore Comm Coll (VA)
Fiorello H. LaGuardia Comm Coll of the City U of New York (NY)
Jefferson Comm Coll (NY)
LDS Business Coll (UT)
Los Angeles City Coll (CA)
Massachusetts Bay Comm Coll (MA)
Mohawk Valley Comm Coll (NY)
Monroe Comm Coll (NY)
Northcentral Tech Coll (WI)
North Central Texas Coll (TX)
Northwest Vista Coll (TX)
Seminole State Coll of Florida (FL)
Southeastern Coll–West Palm Beach (FL)
Southeast Tech Inst (SD)
Thaddeus Stevens Coll of Technology (PA)
Tulsa Comm Coll (OK)
Union County Coll (NJ)
Westchester Comm Coll (NY)

**COMPUTER AND INFORMATION SCIENCES RELATED**
Bristol Comm Coll (MA)
Central Oregon Comm Coll (OR)
Chipola Coll (FL)
Dawson Comm Coll (MT)
Del Mar Coll (TX)
Genesee Comm Coll (NY)
Howard Comm Coll (MD)
Lakeshore Tech Coll (WI)
LDS Business Coll (UT)
Los Angeles City Coll (CA)
Mid-State Tech Coll (WI)
Mohave Comm Coll (AZ)
Monroe Comm Coll (NY)
Monroe County Comm Coll (MI)
Nassau Comm Coll (NY)
North Shore Comm Coll (MA)
Pensacola State Coll (FL)
Sauk Valley Comm Coll (IL)
Seminole State Coll of Florida (FL)
Tulsa Comm Coll (OK)

**COMPUTER AND INFORMATION SYSTEMS SECURITY**
Anne Arundel Comm Coll (MD)
Asheville-Buncombe Tech Comm Coll (NC)
Blue Ridge Comm and Tech Coll (WV)
Bunker Hill Comm Coll (MA)
Carroll Comm Coll (MD)
Central Texas Coll (TX)
Century Coll (MN)
Chesapeake Coll (MD)
Cochise County Comm Coll District (AZ)
Collin County Comm Coll District (TX)
Comm Coll of Baltimore County (MD)
Craven Comm Coll (NC)
Donnelly Coll (KS)
Dyersburg State Comm Coll (TN)
Edison State Comm Coll (OH)
Fox Valley Tech Coll (WI)
Georgia Military Coll (GA)
Grand Rapids Comm Coll (MI)
Hagerstown Comm Coll (MD)
Harford Comm Coll (MD)
Harrisburg Area Comm Coll (PA)
Hinds Comm Coll (MS)
Hudson County Comm Coll (NJ)
LDS Business Coll (UT)
Lehigh Carbon Comm Coll (PA)
Massachusetts Bay Comm Coll (MA)
Minnesota State Comm and Tech Coll (MN)
Minnesota West Comm and Tech Coll (MN)
Mohawk Valley Comm Coll (NY)
Montgomery Coll (MD)
Northampton Comm Coll (PA)
Northwest Vista Coll (TX)
Oklahoma City Comm Coll (OK)
Pensacola State Coll (FL)
Piedmont Virginia Comm Coll (VA)
Pittsburgh Tech Coll (PA)
Quinsigamond Comm Coll (MA)
Rowan-Cabarrus Comm Coll (NC)
St. Louis Comm Coll (MO)
St. Philip's Coll (TX)
Seminole State Coll of Florida (FL)
Southeast Tech Inst (SD)
Springfield Tech Comm Coll (MA)
Texas State Tech Coll (TX)
Waukesha County Tech Coll (WI)
Westchester Comm Coll (NY)

**COMPUTER ENGINEERING**
Carroll Comm Coll (MD)
Comm Coll of Baltimore County (MD)
Pensacola State Coll (FL)

**COMPUTER ENGINEERING RELATED**
Eastern Gateway Comm Coll (OH)
Monroe Comm Coll (NY)
Seminole State Coll of Florida (FL)

**COMPUTER ENGINEERING TECHNOLOGIES RELATED**
Lorain County Comm Coll (OH)

**COMPUTER ENGINEERING TECHNOLOGY**
Alvin Comm Coll (TX)
Amarillo Coll (TX)
Asheville-Buncombe Tech Comm Coll (NC)
Brookhaven Coll (TX)
Carteret Comm Coll (NC)
Coll of The Albemarle (NC)
Comm Coll of Allegheny County (PA)
Daytona State Coll (FL)
Des Moines Area Comm Coll (IA)
Houston Comm Coll (TX)
Hudson County Comm Coll (NJ)
Iowa Central Comm Coll (IA)
Lakeland Comm Coll (OH)
Lenoir Comm Coll (NC)
Lorain County Comm Coll (OH)
Los Angeles City Coll (CA)
McLennan Comm Coll (TX)
Miami Dade Coll (FL)
Mid-State Tech Coll (WI)
Minnesota State Comm and Tech Coll (MN)
Minnesota West Comm and Tech Coll (MN)
Mission Coll (CA)
Monroe Comm Coll (NY)
Monroe County Comm Coll (MI)
Mt. San Antonio Coll (CA)
Naugatuck Valley Comm Coll (CT)
New River Comm Coll (VA)
North Central Texas Coll (TX)
North Shore Comm Coll (MA)
Paris Jr Coll (TX)
Queensborough Comm Coll of the City U of New York (NY)
Quinsigamond Comm Coll (MA)
Richmond Comm Coll (NC)
Rock Valley Coll (IL)
Seminole State Coll of Florida (FL)
Southeast Kentucky Comm and Tech Coll (KY)
South Florida State Coll (FL)
Southwestern Comm Coll (NC)
Southwest Texas Jr Coll (TX)
Springfield Tech Comm Coll (MA)
State U of New York Coll of Technology at Alfred (NY)
Three Rivers Comm Coll (CT)
Trident Tech Coll (SC)
Western Texas Coll (TX)

**COMPUTER GRAPHICS**
AIC Coll of Design (OH)
Antelope Valley Coll (CA)
Arizona Western Coll (AZ)
Carroll Comm Coll (MD)
Central Ohio Tech Coll (OH)
Coll of the Desert (CA)
Daytona State Coll (FL)
De Anza Coll (CA)
Genesee Comm Coll (NY)
Howard Comm Coll (MD)
Hudson County Comm Coll (NJ)
Kellogg Comm Coll (MI)
Miami Dade Coll (FL)
Monroe County Comm Coll (MI)
Mt. San Antonio Coll (CA)
Nassau Comm Coll (NY)
National Park Coll (AR)
Navarro Coll (TX)
New River Comm Coll (VA)
North Central Texas Coll (TX)
North Shore Comm Coll (MA)
Orange Coast Coll (CA)
Palomar Coll (CA)
Pensacola State Coll (FL)
Pittsburgh Tech Coll (PA)
Quinsigamond Comm Coll (MA)
Schoolcraft Coll (MI)
Seminole State Coll of Florida (FL)
Sullivan County Comm Coll (NY)
Tallahassee Comm Coll (FL)
Trident Tech Coll (SC)

**COMPUTER HARDWARE ENGINEERING**
Seminole State Coll of Florida (FL)

**COMPUTER/INFORMATION TECHNOLOGY SERVICES ADMINISTRATION RELATED**
Barton County Comm Coll (KS)
Bossier Parish Comm Coll (LA)
Bunker Hill Comm Coll (MA)
Daytona State Coll (FL)
Dutchess Comm Coll (NY)
Eastern Shore Comm Coll (VA)
Hawkeye Comm Coll (IA)
Hesston Coll (KS)
Howard Comm Coll (MD)
Jefferson Comm Coll (NY)
LDS Business Coll (UT)
Massachusetts Bay Comm Coll (MA)
North Central Texas Coll (TX)
Northwest Vista Coll (TX)
Panola Coll (TX)
Pasadena City Coll (CA)
Schenectady County Comm Coll (NY)
Seminole State Coll of Florida (FL)
Southeast Kentucky Comm and Tech Coll (KY)
Trident Tech Coll (SC)
Vincennes U (IN)
Western Iowa Tech Comm Coll (IA)

**COMPUTER INSTALLATION AND REPAIR TECHNOLOGY**
Fiorello H. LaGuardia Comm Coll of the City U of New York (NY)
Genesee Comm Coll (NY)
Hinds Comm Coll (MS)
Lake Region State Coll (ND)
Merced Coll (CA)
Miami Dade Coll (FL)
Orange Coast Coll (CA)
Queensborough Comm Coll of the City U of New York (NY)
Southwestern Coll (CA)
Tulsa Comm Coll (OK)

**COMPUTER NUMERICALLY CONTROLLED (CNC) MACHINIST TECHNOLOGY**
Dunwoody Coll of Technology (MN)
Greenville Tech Coll (SC)
Lake Superior Coll (MN)
Wayne County Comm Coll District (MI)

**COMPUTER PROGRAMMING**
Alvin Comm Coll (TX)
Amarillo Coll (TX)
Antelope Valley Coll (CA)
Austin Comm Coll District (TX)
Bristol Comm Coll (MA)
Brookhaven Coll (TX)
Bunker Hill Comm Coll (MA)
Caldwell Comm Coll and Tech Inst (NC)
Cedar Valley Coll (TX)
Central Ohio Tech Coll (OH)
Central Texas Coll (TX)
Chandler-Gilbert Comm Coll (AZ)
Chippewa Valley Tech Coll (WI)
Clark Coll (WA)
Cochise County Comm Coll District (AZ)
Coll of The Albemarle (NC)
Coll of the Desert (CA)
Copiah-Lincoln Comm Coll (MS)
Dabney S. Lancaster Comm Coll (VA)
Daytona State Coll (FL)
De Anza Coll (CA)
Del Mar Coll (TX)
Edison State Comm Coll (OH)
El Paso Comm Coll (TX)
Feather River Coll (CA)
Fiorello H. LaGuardia Comm Coll of the City U of New York (NY)
Florida Keys Comm Coll (FL)
Fox Valley Tech Coll (WI)
Gateway Tech Coll (WI)
Grand Rapids Comm Coll (MI)
Great Falls Coll Montana State U (MT)
Gulf Coast State Coll (FL)
Harper Coll (IL)
Hill Coll (TX)
Hinds Comm Coll (MS)
Houston Comm Coll (TX)
Illinois Central Coll (IL)
Illinois Valley Comm Coll (IL)
Independence Comm Coll (KS)
J. Sargeant Reynolds Comm Coll (VA)
Kellogg Comm Coll (MI)
Lakeshore Tech Coll (WI)
Laramie County Comm Coll (WY)
LDS Business Coll (UT)
Lehigh Carbon Comm Coll (PA)
Louisiana State U at Eunice (LA)
Macomb Comm Coll (MI)
Miami Dade Coll (FL)
Minnesota State Comm and Tech Coll (MN)
Mission Coll (CA)
Mitchell Comm Coll (NC)
Mohawk Valley Comm Coll (NY)
Montgomery County Comm Coll (PA)
Mott Comm Coll (MI)
Navarro Coll (TX)
New Mexico State U–Alamogordo (NM)
Northampton Comm Coll (PA)
North Central Texas Coll (TX)
Northeastern Tech Coll (SC)
Northern Essex Comm Coll (MA)
North Shore Comm Coll (MA)
NorthWest Arkansas Comm Coll (AR)
Northwest Vista Coll (TX)
Oakton Comm Coll (IL)
Oklahoma City Comm Coll (OK)
Orange Coast Coll (CA)
Ozarks Tech Comm Coll (MO)
Palomar Coll (CA)
Pensacola State Coll (FL)
Pittsburgh Tech Coll (PA)
Quinsigamond Comm Coll (MA)
Raritan Valley Comm Coll (NJ)
Rend Lake Coll (IL)
Richland Coll (TX)
Ridgewater Coll (MN)
Rowan-Cabarrus Comm Coll (NC)
St. Charles Comm Coll (MO)
St. Philip's Coll (TX)
Schenectady County Comm Coll (NY)
Schoolcraft Coll (MI)
Seminole State Coll of Florida (FL)
Southeast Tech Inst (SD)
South Florida State Coll (FL)
Southwestern Coll (CA)
Southwestern Michigan Coll (MI)
Sowela Tech Comm Coll (LA)
State Tech Coll of Missouri (MO)
Tallahassee Comm Coll (FL)
Tarrant County Coll District (TX)
Texas State Tech Coll (TX)
Tidewater Comm Coll (VA)
Vincennes U (IN)
Waukesha County Tech Coll (WI)
Wayne County Comm Coll District (MI)
Wisconsin Indianhead Tech Coll (WI)

**COMPUTER PROGRAMMING RELATED**
Del Mar Coll (TX)
Genesee Comm Coll (NY)
Lakeshore Tech Coll (WI)
LDS Business Coll (UT)
Lorain County Comm Coll (OH)
Mid-State Tech Coll (WI)
North Central Texas Coll (TX)
Northern Essex Comm Coll (MA)
Seminole State Coll of Florida (FL)

**COMPUTER PROGRAMMING (SPECIFIC APPLICATIONS)**
Barton County Comm Coll (KS)
Bunker Hill Comm Coll (MA)
Coll of The Albemarle (NC)
Craven Comm Coll (NC)
Danville Area Comm Coll (IL)
Daytona State Coll (FL)
Del Mar Coll (TX)
Des Moines Area Comm Coll (IA)
Grand Rapids Comm Coll (MI)
Harper Coll (IL)
Holyoke Comm Coll (MA)
Houston Comm Coll (TX)
Humacao Comm Coll (PR)
Kellogg Comm Coll (MI)
Kent State U at Ashtabula (OH)
Kent State U at East Liverpool (OH)
Kent State U at Salem (OH)
Kent State U at Trumbull (OH)
Kent State U at Tuscarawas (OH)
Lakeland Comm Coll (OH)
LDS Business Coll (UT)
Lehigh Carbon Comm Coll (PA)
Macomb Comm Coll (MI)
Manor Coll (PA)
Miami Dade Coll (FL)
Mid-State Tech Coll (WI)
Mitchell Comm Coll (NC)
Mohave Comm Coll (AZ)
Monroe County Comm Coll (MI)
Mott Comm Coll (MI)

North Central Texas Coll (TX)
Northeast Iowa Comm Coll (IA)
Northern Essex Comm Coll (MA)
North Shore Comm Coll (MA)
Northwest Mississippi Comm Coll (MS)
Pensacola State Coll (FL)
Quinsigamond Comm Coll (MA)
Schoolcraft Coll (MI)
Seminole State Coll of Florida (FL)
Springfield Tech Comm Coll (MA)
Stark State Coll (OH)
Sullivan County Comm Coll (NY)
Tallahassee Comm Coll (FL)
Trident Tech Coll (SC)
Truckee Meadows Comm Coll (NV)
Western Iowa Tech Comm Coll (IA)
Western Wyoming Comm Coll (WY)

### COMPUTER PROGRAMMING (VENDOR/PRODUCT CERTIFICATION)
Chandler-Gilbert Comm Coll (AZ)
Del Mar Coll (TX)
Gulf Coast State Coll (FL)
Miami Dade Coll (FL)
North Central Texas Coll (TX)
Pensacola State Coll (FL)
Seminole State Coll of Florida (FL)

### COMPUTER SCIENCE
Adirondack Comm Coll (NY)
Amarillo Coll (TX)
Barton County Comm Coll (KS)
Bristol Comm Coll (MA)
Bunker Hill Comm Coll (MA)
Central New Mexico Comm Coll (NM)
Central Oregon Comm Coll (OR)
Century Coll (MN)
Chesapeake Coll (MD)
Chipola Coll (FL)
Cochise County Comm Coll District (AZ)
Coll of Marin (CA)
Coll of the Canyons (CA)
Coll of the Desert (CA)
Comm Coll of Philadelphia (PA)
County Coll of Morris (NJ)
De Anza Coll (CA)
Del Mar Coll (TX)
Dutchess Comm Coll (NY)
Fiorello H. LaGuardia Comm Coll of the City U of New York (NY)
Frederick Comm Coll (MD)
Fullerton Coll (CA)
Galveston Coll (TX)
Genesee Comm Coll (NY)
George C. Wallace Comm Coll (AL)
Georgia Military Coll (GA)
Gordon State Coll (GA)
Harford Comm Coll (MD)
Harper Coll (IL)
Harrisburg Area Comm Coll (PA)
Houston Comm Coll (TX)
Howard Comm Coll (MD)
Independence Comm Coll (KS)
Ivy Tech Comm Coll–Bloomington (IN)
Ivy Tech Comm Coll–Central Indiana (IN)
Ivy Tech Comm Coll–Columbus (IN)
Ivy Tech Comm Coll–East Central (IN)
Ivy Tech Comm Coll–Kokomo (IN)
Ivy Tech Comm Coll–Lafayette (IN)
Ivy Tech Comm Coll–Northeast (IN)
Ivy Tech Comm Coll–Richmond (IN)
Ivy Tech Comm Coll–Sellersburg (IN)
Ivy Tech Comm Coll–Southeast (IN)
Ivy Tech Comm Coll–Southwest (IN)
Ivy Tech Comm Coll–Wabash Valley (IN)
Jefferson Comm Coll (NY)
Kingsborough Comm Coll of the City U of New York (NY)
Lake Area Tech Inst (SD)
Laramie County Comm Coll (WY)
LDS Business Coll (UT)
Los Angeles City Coll (CA)
Massachusetts Bay Comm Coll (MA)
Merced Coll (CA)
Miami Dade Coll (FL)
Minnesota West Comm and Tech Coll (MN)
Mohave Comm Coll (AZ)
Monroe Comm Coll (NY)
Montgomery County Comm Coll (PA)
Mt. San Antonio Coll (CA)
Nassau Comm Coll (NY)

Navarro Coll (TX)
Niagara County Comm Coll (NY)
Northampton Comm Coll (PA)
North Central Texas Coll (TX)
Northeast Comm Coll (NE)
Northeastern Tech Coll (SC)
Northern Essex Comm Coll (MA)
North Hennepin Comm Coll (MN)
North Shore Comm Coll (MA)
Northwest Vista Coll (TX)
Odessa Coll (TX)
Oklahoma City Comm Coll (OK)
Orange Coast Coll (CA)
Panola Coll (TX)
Pasadena City Coll (CA)
Pennsylvania Highlands Comm Coll (PA)
Pennsylvania Inst of Technology (PA)
Pensacola State Coll (FL)
Quinsigamond Comm Coll (MA)
Renton Tech Coll (WA)
Ridgewater Coll (MN)
Rock Valley Coll (IL)
St. Philip's Coll (TX)
Salt Lake Comm Coll (UT)
San Joaquin Delta Coll (CA)
Santa Rosa Jr Coll (CA)
Seminole State Coll (OK)
Southern U at Shreveport (LA)
Southwestern Coll (CA)
Springfield Tech Comm Coll (MA)
Tarrant County Coll District (TX)
Treasure Valley Comm Coll (OR)
Trinity Valley Comm Coll (TX)
Tulsa Comm Coll (OK)
Tyler Jr Coll (TX)
Union County Coll (NJ)
Western Texas Coll (TX)
Western Wyoming Comm Coll (WY)
York County Comm Coll (ME)

### COMPUTER SOFTWARE AND MEDIA APPLICATIONS RELATED
Asheville-Buncombe Tech Comm Coll (NC)
Carteret Comm Coll (NC)
The Coll of Westchester (NY)
Genesee Comm Coll (NY)
Seminole State Coll of Florida (FL)

### COMPUTER SOFTWARE ENGINEERING
LDS Business Coll (UT)
Oklahoma City Comm Coll (OK)
St. Louis Comm Coll (MO)
Seminole State Coll of Florida (FL)

### COMPUTER SOFTWARE TECHNOLOGY
Miami Dade Coll (FL)

### COMPUTER SUPPORT SPECIALIST
Central Ohio Tech Coll (OH)
Fox Valley Tech Coll (WI)
Gateway Tech Coll (WI)
Genesee Comm Coll (NY)
Grand Rapids Comm Coll (MI)
LDS Business Coll (UT)
Miami Dade Coll (FL)
Mitchell Tech Inst (SD)
Morton Coll (IL)
Northampton Comm Coll (PA)
Northland Comm and Tech Coll (MN)
Oklahoma City Comm Coll (OK)
Tompkins Cortland Comm Coll (NY)
Waukesha County Tech Coll (WI)
Wisconsin Indianhead Tech Coll (WI)

### COMPUTER SYSTEMS ANALYSIS
Amarillo Coll (TX)
Bristol Comm Coll (MA)
Chandler-Gilbert Comm Coll (AZ)
Crowder Coll (MO)
Florida Keys Comm Coll (FL)
Hutchinson Comm Coll (KS)
Lakeland Comm Coll (OH)
Lakeshore Tech Coll (WI)
Lehigh Carbon Comm Coll (PA)
Mesa Comm Coll (AZ)
Mitchell Comm Coll (NC)
Northcentral Tech Coll (WI)
Oklahoma City Comm Coll (OK)
Pensacola State Coll (FL)
Quinsigamond Comm Coll (MA)
Tohono O'odham Comm Coll (AZ)
Wor-Wic Comm Coll (MD)

### COMPUTER SYSTEMS NETWORKING AND TELECOMMUNICATIONS
Adirondack Comm Coll (NY)
Alexandria Tech and Comm Coll (MN)
Anne Arundel Comm Coll (MD)
Antelope Valley Coll (CA)
Asheville-Buncombe Tech Comm Coll (NC)
Austin Comm Coll District (TX)
Barton County Comm Coll (KS)
Bowling Green State U–Firelands Coll (OH)
Bristol Comm Coll (MA)
Bucks County Comm Coll (PA)
Bunker Hill Comm Coll (MA)
Carteret Comm Coll (NC)
Cedar Valley Coll (TX)
Central Lakes Coll (MN)
Central Oregon Comm Coll (OR)
Century Coll (MN)
Chandler-Gilbert Comm Coll (AZ)
Chippewa Valley Tech Coll (WI)
Clark Coll (WA)
Cochise County Comm Coll District (AZ)
Coll of Business and Technology–Flagler Campus (FL)
Coll of Business and Technology–Miami Gardens (FL)
Coll of Eastern Idaho (ID)
Coll of Marin (CA)
Coll of the Canyons (CA)
Collin County Comm Coll District (TX)
Comm Coll of Allegheny County (PA)
Comm Coll of Baltimore County (MD)
Copiah-Lincoln Comm Coll (MS)
Craven Comm Coll (NC)
Crowder Coll (MO)
Danville Area Comm Coll (IL)
Del Mar Coll (TX)
Dunwoody Coll of Technology (MN)
East Central Coll (MO)
Edison State Comm Coll (OH)
Fiorello H. LaGuardia Comm Coll of the City U of New York (NY)
Fox Valley Tech Coll (WI)
Front Range Comm Coll (CO)
Gateway Tech Coll (WI)
Genesee Comm Coll (NY)
Grand Rapids Comm Coll (MI)
Great Falls Coll Montana State U (MT)
Gulf Coast State Coll (FL)
Harrisburg Area Comm Coll (PA)
Hawkeye Comm Coll (IA)
Haywood Comm Coll (NC)
Hinds Comm Coll (MS)
Houston Comm Coll (TX)
Howard Comm Coll (MD)
Hutchinson Comm Coll (KS)
Illinois Central Coll (IL)
Illinois Eastern Comm Colls, Lincoln Trail College (IL)
Illinois Valley Comm Coll (IL)
Independence Comm Coll (KS)
Ivy Tech Comm Coll–Bloomington (IN)
Ivy Tech Comm Coll–East Central (IN)
Ivy Tech Comm Coll–Kokomo (IN)
Ivy Tech Comm Coll–Lafayette (IN)
Ivy Tech Comm Coll–Sellersburg (IN)
Ivy Tech Comm Coll–Wabash Valley (IN)
J. Sargeant Reynolds Comm Coll (VA)
Lakeland Comm Coll (OH)
LDS Business Coll (UT)
Lehigh Carbon Comm Coll (PA)
Lorain County Comm Coll (OH)
McHenry County Coll (IL)
Mesa Comm Coll (AZ)
Miami Dade Coll (FL)
Minnesota State Comm and Tech Coll (MN)
Minnesota West Comm and Tech Coll (MN)
Mott Comm Coll (MI)
Nassau Comm Coll (NY)
Northampton Comm Coll (PA)
Northcentral Tech Coll (WI)
North Dakota State Coll of Science (ND)
Northern Essex Comm Coll (MA)
Northern Maine Comm Coll (ME)
Northland Comm and Tech Coll (MN)

Odessa Coll (TX)
Ozarks Tech Comm Coll (MO)
Palomar Coll (CA)
Randolph Comm Coll (NC)
Renton Tech Coll (WA)
Ridgewater Coll (MN)
Rock Valley Coll (IL)
Schoolcraft Coll (MI)
Seminole State Coll of Florida (FL)
Southeast Arkansas Coll (AR)
Southeastern Coll–West Palm Beach (FL)
Southeast Tech Inst (SD)
Southwestern Coll (CA)
Southwestern Comm Coll (IA)
Southwestern Michigan Coll (MI)
Sowela Tech Comm Coll (LA)
Stark State Coll (OH)
State Tech Coll of Missouri (MO)
Tallahassee Comm Coll (FL)
Three Rivers Coll (MO)
Trident Tech Coll (SC)
Truckee Meadows Comm Coll (NV)
Tyler Jr Coll (TX)
Vincennes U (IN)
Waukesha County Tech Coll (WI)
Western Dakota Tech Inst (SD)
Wisconsin Indianhead Tech Coll (WI)

### COMPUTER TECHNOLOGY/ COMPUTER SYSTEMS TECHNOLOGY
American Samoa Comm Coll (AS)
Arkansas State U–Newport (AR)
Brookhaven Coll (TX)
Central Lakes Coll (MN)
Central Texas Coll (TX)
Century Coll (MN)
Comm Coll of Allegheny County (PA)
Erie Comm Coll, South Campus (NY)
ITI Tech Coll (LA)
Jefferson Comm Coll (NY)
Kellogg Comm Coll (MI)
Kent State U at Ashtabula (OH)
Lakeland Comm Coll (OH)
Lake Superior Coll (MN)
Lorain County Comm Coll (OH)
Miami Dade Coll (FL)
Minnesota State Comm and Tech Coll (MN)
Minnesota West Comm and Tech Coll (MN)
Montgomery Coll (MD)
Montgomery County Comm Coll (PA)
Northern Essex Comm Coll (MA)
Pasadena City Coll (CA)
Piedmont Virginia Comm Coll (VA)
Rend Lake Coll (IL)
Ridgewater Coll (MN)
St. Philip's Coll (TX)
Southeast Tech Inst (SD)
Texas State Tech Coll (TX)
U of Arkansas Comm Coll at Morrilton (AR)

### COMPUTER TYPOGRAPHY AND COMPOSITION EQUIPMENT OPERATION
Del Mar Coll (TX)
Paris Jr Coll (TX)

### CONSERVATION BIOLOGY
Central Lakes Coll (MN)

### CONSTRUCTION ENGINEERING
Bossier Parish Comm Coll (LA)

### CONSTRUCTION ENGINEERING TECHNOLOGY
Arizona Western Coll (AZ)
Bossier Parish Comm Coll (LA)
Coll of Central Florida (FL)
Comm Coll of Allegheny County (PA)
Comm Coll of Philadelphia (PA)
Crowder Coll (MO)
Daytona State Coll (FL)
De Anza Coll (CA)
Greenville Tech Coll (SC)
Gulf Coast State Coll (FL)
Harrisburg Area Comm Coll (PA)
Houston Comm Coll (TX)
Illinois Central Coll (IL)
Jefferson State Comm Coll (AL)
Lake Area Tech Inst (SD)
Lorain County Comm Coll (OH)
Macomb Comm Coll (MI)
Miami Dade Coll (FL)

Mid-Plains Comm Coll, North Platte (NE)
Monroe Comm Coll (NY)
Morrison Inst of Technology (IL)
New Castle School of Trades (PA)
North Dakota State Coll of Science (ND)
Odessa Coll (TX)
The Ohio State U Ag Tech Inst (OH)
Oklahoma State U–Oklahoma City (OK)
Panola Coll (TX)
Pensacola State Coll (FL)
Raritan Valley Comm Coll (NJ)
Rock Valley Coll (IL)
St. Philip's Coll (TX)
San Jacinto Coll District (TX)
San Joaquin Delta Coll (CA)
Seminole State Coll of Florida (FL)
Southeast Tech Inst (SD)
South Suburban Coll (IL)
State U of New York Coll of Technology at Alfred (NY)
Sullivan County Comm Coll (NY)
Tallahassee Comm Coll (FL)
Tarrant County Coll District (TX)
Three Rivers Coll (MO)
Tompkins Cortland Comm Coll (NY)

### CONSTRUCTION/HEAVY EQUIPMENT/EARTHMOVING EQUIPMENT OPERATION
Copiah-Lincoln Comm Coll (MS)
Ivy Tech Comm Coll–Southwest (IN)
Ivy Tech Comm Coll–Wabash Valley (IN)
Lake Area Tech Inst (SD)
Mesa Comm Coll (AZ)

### CONSTRUCTION MANAGEMENT
Arizona Western Coll (AZ)
Central New Mexico Comm Coll (NM)
ITI Tech Coll (LA)
Kaskaskia Coll (IL)
McHenry County Coll (IL)
Minnesota State Comm and Tech Coll (MN)
Northampton Comm Coll (PA)
North Hennepin Comm Coll (MN)
The Ohio State U Ag Tech Inst (OH)
Oklahoma State U–Oklahoma City (OK)
Renton Tech Coll (WA)
State U of New York Coll of Technology at Alfred (NY)
Three Rivers Comm Coll (CT)

### CONSTRUCTION TRADES
American Samoa Comm Coll (AS)
Coll of The Albemarle (NC)
Comm Coll of Allegheny County (PA)
Crowder Coll (MO)
East Central Coll (MO)
Harrisburg Area Comm Coll (PA)
Illinois Eastern Comm Colls, Frontier Community College (IL)
Illinois Eastern Comm Colls, Lincoln Trail College (IL)
Ivy Tech Comm Coll–East Central (IN)
Ivy Tech Comm Coll–Northeast (IN)
Ivy Tech Comm Coll–Northwest (IN)
Ivy Tech Comm Coll–Richmond (IN)
Lamar Comm Coll (CO)
Lehigh Carbon Comm Coll (PA)
Northeast Iowa Comm Coll (IA)
Oklahoma State U Inst of Technology (OK)
Oklahoma State U–Oklahoma City (OK)
Orange Coast Coll (CA)
Ozarks Tech Comm Coll (MO)
Pasadena City Coll (CA)
Southwest Texas Jr Coll (TX)
Texas State Tech Coll (TX)

### CONSTRUCTION TRADES RELATED
Central Maine Comm Coll (ME)
Comm Coll of Allegheny County (PA)
Dutchess Comm Coll (NY)
Fullerton Coll (CA)
Ivy Tech Comm Coll–East Central (IN)
Ivy Tech Comm Coll–Kokomo (IN)
Ivy Tech Comm Coll–Northeast (IN)
Ivy Tech Comm Coll–Richmond (IN)
Mitchell Tech Inst (SD)

Northern Maine Comm Coll (ME)
Palomar Coll (CA)
State U of New York Coll of Technology at Alfred (NY)
York County Comm Coll (ME)

**CONSUMER MERCHANDISING/ RETAILING MANAGEMENT**
Del Mar Coll (TX)
J. Sargeant Reynolds Comm Coll (VA)
Monroe Comm Coll (NY)
Navarro Coll (TX)
Niagara County Comm Coll (NY)
Sullivan County Comm Coll (NY)
Tarrant County Coll District (TX)
Westchester Comm Coll (NY)

**CONSUMER SERVICES AND ADVOCACY**
Pensacola State Coll (FL)

**COOKING AND RELATED CULINARY ARTS**
Adirondack Comm Coll (NY)
Central Oregon Comm Coll (OR)
Coll of the Desert (CA)
Copiah-Lincoln Comm Coll (MS)
Feather River Coll (CA)
Hinds Comm Coll (MS)
J. Sargeant Reynolds Comm Coll (VA)
Kennebec Valley Comm Coll (ME)
Kingsborough Comm Coll of the City U of New York (NY)
Merced Coll (CA)
Miami Dade Coll (FL)
Minnesota State Comm and Tech Coll (MN)
Mitchell Comm Coll (NC)
Orange Coast Coll (CA)
Pensacola State Coll (FL)
Pittsburgh Tech Coll (PA)
Pueblo Comm Coll (CO)
Southwestern Coll (CA)
Truckee Meadows Comm Coll (NV)

**CORRECTIONS**
Alvin Comm Coll (TX)
Amarillo Coll (TX)
Austin Comm Coll District (TX)
Barton County Comm Coll (KS)
Cayuga County Comm Coll (NY)
Comm Coll of Allegheny County (PA)
Danville Area Comm Coll (IL)
De Anza Coll (CA)
Eastern Gateway Comm Coll (OH)
El Paso Comm Coll (TX)
Grand Rapids Comm Coll (MI)
Hill Coll (TX)
Illinois Eastern Comm Colls, Frontier Community College (IL)
Illinois Eastern Comm Colls, Lincoln Trail College (IL)
Illinois Valley Comm Coll (IL)
Kellogg Comm Coll (MI)
Lakeland Comm Coll (OH)
Laramie County Comm Coll (WY)
Lorain County Comm Coll (OH)
Miami Dade Coll (FL)
Mid-State Tech Coll (WI)
Monroe Comm Coll (NY)
Mott Comm Coll (MI)
Mt. San Antonio Coll (CA)
Mount Wachusett Comm Coll (MA)
Navarro Coll (TX)
Northeast Comm Coll (NE)
Pennsylvania Highlands Comm Coll (PA)
San Joaquin Delta Coll (CA)
Sauk Valley Comm Coll (IL)
Tallahassee Comm Coll (FL)
Trinity Valley Comm Coll (TX)
Wayne County Comm Coll District (MI)
Westchester Comm Coll (NY)
Western Texas Coll (TX)
Wytheville Comm Coll (VA)

**CORRECTIONS AND CRIMINAL JUSTICE RELATED**
Chesapeake Coll (MD)
El Paso Comm Coll (TX)
Feather River Coll (CA)
Genesee Comm Coll (NY)
Hill Coll (TX)
Hinds Comm Coll (MS)
Miami Dade Coll (FL)
Pennsylvania Inst of Technology (PA)

**COSMETOLOGY**
Caldwell Comm Coll and Tech Inst (NC)
Central New Mexico Comm Coll (NM)
Century Coll (MN)
Colorado Northwestern Comm Coll (CO)
Copiah-Lincoln Comm Coll (MS)
Del Mar Coll (TX)
Eastern Arizona Coll (AZ)
Fayetteville Tech Comm Coll (NC)
Fullerton Coll (CA)
Haywood Comm Coll (NC)
Hill Coll (TX)
Houston Comm Coll (TX)
Hutchinson Comm Coll (KS)
Independence Comm Coll (KS)
James Sprunt Comm Coll (NC)
Kaskaskia Coll (IL)
Kirtland Comm Coll (MI)
Lamar Comm Coll (CO)
Lenoir Comm Coll (NC)
Minnesota State Comm and Tech Coll (MN)
Northeastern Jr Coll (CO)
Northeast Iowa Comm Coll (IA)
Odessa Coll (TX)
Paris Jr Coll (TX)
Pasadena City Coll (CA)
Pueblo Comm Coll (CO)
Randolph Comm Coll (NC)
Rend Lake Coll (IL)
Ridgewater Coll (MN)
Rowan-Cabarrus Comm Coll (NC)
San Jacinto Coll District (TX)
San Juan Coll (NM)
Southwestern Comm Coll (NC)
Southwest Texas Jr Coll (TX)
Texarkana Coll (TX)
Trinity Valley Comm Coll (TX)
Vincennes U (IN)

**COSMETOLOGY AND PERSONAL GROOMING ARTS RELATED**
Comm Coll of Allegheny County (PA)
LDS Business Coll (UT)

**COSMETOLOGY, BARBER/ STYLING, AND NAIL INSTRUCTION**
Copiah-Lincoln Comm Coll (MS)
Hill Coll (TX)
Pasadena City Coll (CA)
San Jacinto Coll District (TX)

**COSTUME DESIGN**
Vincennes U (IN)

**COURT REPORTING**
Alvin Comm Coll (TX)
Coll of Marin (CA)
Comm Coll of Allegheny County (PA)
Del Mar Coll (TX)
El Paso Comm Coll (TX)
Fox Valley Tech Coll (WI)
Hinds Comm Coll (MS)
Houston Comm Coll (TX)
Lakeshore Tech Coll (WI)
Miami Dade Coll (FL)
South Suburban Coll (IL)
Stark State Coll (OH)
State U of New York Coll of Technology at Alfred (NY)

**CRAFTS, FOLK ART AND ARTISANRY**
Coll of The Albemarle (NC)
Haywood Comm Coll (NC)
Southwestern Coll (CA)

**CREATIVE WRITING**
Adirondack Comm Coll (NY)
Austin Comm Coll District (TX)
Coll of the Desert (CA)
North Hennepin Comm Coll (MN)
Tompkins Cortland Comm Coll (NY)

**CRIMINALISTICS AND CRIMINAL SCIENCE**
Alvin Comm Coll (TX)
Central Lakes Coll (MN)
Tyler Jr Coll (TX)

**CRIMINAL JUSTICE/LAW ENFORCEMENT ADMINISTRATION**
Amarillo Coll (TX)
Anne Arundel Comm Coll (MD)
Arizona Western Coll (AZ)
Arkansas State U–Newport (AR)
Beal Coll (ME)

Brookhaven Coll (TX)
Bunker Hill Comm Coll (MA)
Carteret Comm Coll (NC)
Central Maine Comm Coll (ME)
Central New Mexico Comm Coll (NM)
Central Ohio Tech Coll (OH)
Central Virginia Comm Coll (VA)
Coll of Central Florida (FL)
Coll of The Albemarle (NC)
Collin County Comm Coll District (TX)
Columbia-Greene Comm Coll (NY)
Comm Coll of Philadelphia (PA)
Craven Comm Coll (NC)
Dabney S. Lancaster Comm Coll (VA)
Daytona State Coll (FL)
De Anza Coll (CA)
Del Mar Coll (TX)
Des Moines Area Comm Coll (IA)
Eastern Arizona Coll (AZ)
Erie Comm Coll (NY)
Erie Comm Coll, North Campus (NY)
Erie Comm Coll, South Campus (NY)
Frederick Comm Coll (MD)
Gateway Comm and Tech Coll (KY)
Genesee Comm Coll (NY)
Georgia Military Coll (GA)
Grand Rapids Comm Coll (MI)
Gulf Coast State Coll (FL)
Harper Coll (IL)
Harrisburg Area Comm Coll (PA)
Haywood Comm Coll (NC)
Hill Coll (TX)
Hopkinsville Comm Coll (KY)
Housatonic Comm Coll (CT)
Howard Comm Coll (MD)
Illinois Valley Comm Coll (IL)
Jamestown Comm Coll (NY)
Jefferson Comm Coll (NY)
John Tyler Comm Coll (VA)
J. Sargeant Reynolds Comm Coll (VA)
Kaskaskia Coll (IL)
Kingsborough Comm Coll of the City U of New York (NY)
Kirtland Comm Coll (MI)
Lackawanna Coll (PA)
Laramie County Comm Coll (WY)
Lehigh Carbon Comm Coll (PA)
Los Angeles City Coll (CA)
Macomb Comm Coll (MI)
Manchester Comm Coll (CT)
Manor Coll (PA)
Massachusetts Bay Comm Coll (MA)
Maysville Comm and Tech Coll, Maysville (KY)
McLennan Comm Coll (TX)
Miami Dade Coll (FL)
Mitchell Comm Coll (NC)
Mohawk Valley Comm Coll (NY)
Monroe Comm Coll (NY)
Mount Wachusett Comm Coll (MA)
Muskegon Comm Coll (MI)
Nassau Comm Coll (NY)
National Park Coll (AR)
Navarro Coll (TX)
New River Comm Coll (VA)
Niagara County Comm Coll (NY)
North Central Texas Coll (TX)
North Shore Comm Coll (MA)
NorthWest Arkansas Comm Coll (AR)
Odessa Coll (TX)
Owensboro Comm and Tech Coll (KY)
Pasadena City Coll (CA)
Pennsylvania Highlands Comm Coll (PA)
Pensacola State Coll (FL)
Pueblo Comm Coll (CO)
Queensborough Comm Coll of the City U of New York (NY)
Rappahannock Comm Coll (VA)
Raritan Valley Comm Coll (NJ)
Rio Hondo Coll (CA)
Rock Valley Coll (IL)
Rowan-Cabarrus Comm Coll (NC)
Salt Lake Comm Coll (UT)
Santa Rosa Jr Coll (CA)
Sauk Valley Comm Coll (IL)
Schenectady County Comm Coll (NY)
Scottsdale Comm Coll (AZ)
Seminole State Coll (OK)
Seminole State Coll of Florida (FL)
Somerset Comm Coll (KY)
Southeast Arkansas Coll (AR)
Southern U at Shreveport (LA)
South Florida State Coll (FL)
Southwest Texas Jr Coll (TX)

Southwest Virginia Comm Coll (VA)
Spartanburg Methodist Coll (SC)
Tallahassee Comm Coll (FL)
Tarrant County Coll District (TX)
Texarkana Coll (TX)
Tillamook Bay Comm Coll (OR)
Tompkins Cortland Comm Coll (NY)
Trident Tech Coll (SC)
Trinity Valley Comm Coll (TX)
Union County Coll (NJ)
U of Arkansas Comm Coll at Morrilton (AR)
U of South Carolina Lancaster (SC)
Western Texas Coll (TX)
Western Wyoming Comm Coll (WY)
West Kentucky Comm and Tech Coll (KY)
Wytheville Comm Coll (VA)

**CRIMINAL JUSTICE/POLICE SCIENCE**
Adirondack Comm Coll (NY)
Alexandria Tech and Comm Coll (MN)
Alvin Comm Coll (TX)
Amarillo Coll (TX)
Anne Arundel Comm Coll (MD)
Antelope Valley Coll (CA)
Austin Comm Coll District (TX)
Barton County Comm Coll (KS)
Black Hawk Coll, Moline (IL)
Bunker Hill Comm Coll (MA)
Camden County Coll (NJ)
Carroll Comm Coll (MD)
Cayuga County Comm Coll (NY)
Cecil Coll (MD)
Central Lakes Coll (MN)
Central Louisiana Tech Comm Coll (LA)
Central Ohio Tech Coll (OH)
Century Coll (MN)
Chippewa Valley Tech Coll (WI)
Cleveland State Comm Coll (TN)
Cloud County Comm Coll (KS)
Cochise County Comm Coll District (AZ)
Coll of Marin (CA)
Coll of the Canyons (CA)
Coll of the Desert (CA)
Comm Coll of Allegheny County (PA)
Comm Coll of Baltimore County (MD)
Copiah-Lincoln Comm Coll (MS)
County Coll of Morris (NJ)
Danville Area Comm Coll (IL)
Dawson Comm Coll (MT)
De Anza Coll (CA)
Del Mar Coll (TX)
Dutchess Comm Coll (NY)
Dyersburg State Comm Coll (TN)
Eastern Arizona Coll (AZ)
Eastern Gateway Comm Coll (OH)
Edison State Comm Coll (OH)
El Paso Comm Coll (TX)
Erie Comm Coll, North Campus (NY)
Fox Valley Tech Coll (WI)
Fullerton Coll (CA)
Gateway Tech Coll (WI)
Genesee Comm Coll (NY)
George C. Wallace Comm Coll (AL)
Grand Rapids Comm Coll (MI)
Hagerstown Comm Coll (MD)
Harford Comm Coll (MD)
Harrisburg Area Comm Coll (PA)
Hawkeye Comm Coll (IA)
Houston Comm Coll (TX)
Hudson County Comm Coll (NJ)
Hutchinson Comm Coll (KS)
Illinois Central Coll (IL)
Illinois Valley Comm Coll (IL)
Iowa Central Comm Coll (IA)
Jamestown Comm Coll (NY)
Jefferson State Comm Coll (AL)
Johnston Comm Coll (NC)
Kirtland Comm Coll (MI)
Kishwaukee Coll (IL)
Lackawanna Coll (PA)
Lake Area Tech Inst (SD)
Lakeland Comm Coll (OH)
Lake Region State Coll (ND)
Lakeshore Tech Coll (WI)
Lorain County Comm Coll (OH)
Los Angeles City Coll (CA)
Louisiana State U at Eunice (LA)
Macomb Comm Coll (MI)
McHenry County Coll (IL)
McLennan Comm Coll (TX)
Merced Coll (CA)
Mesa Comm Coll (AZ)
Mesalands Comm Coll (NM)
Miami Dade Coll (FL)
Mid-State Tech Coll (WI)

Minnesota West Comm and Tech Coll (MN)
Missouri State U–West Plains (MO)
Mohave Comm Coll (AZ)
Mohawk Valley Comm Coll (NY)
Monroe Comm Coll (NY)
Monroe County Comm Coll (MI)
Montgomery Coll (MD)
Montgomery County Comm Coll (PA)
Morton Coll (IL)
Mott Comm Coll (MI)
Mt. San Antonio Coll (CA)
Naugatuck Valley Comm Coll (CT)
Navarro Coll (TX)
New River Comm Coll (VA)
Northcentral Tech Coll (WI)
North Central Texas Coll (TX)
Northeast Comm Coll (NE)
Northeastern Jr Coll (CO)
Northern Essex Comm Coll (MA)
North Hennepin Comm Coll (MN)
North Iowa Area Comm Coll (IA)
Northland Comm and Tech Coll (MN)
Northwest-Shoals Comm Coll (AL)
Oakton Comm Coll (IL)
Odessa Coll (TX)
Oklahoma State U–Oklahoma City (OK)
Piedmont Virginia Comm Coll (VA)
Quinsigamond Comm Coll (MA)
Rappahannock Comm Coll (VA)
Rend Lake Coll (IL)
Ridgewater Coll (MN)
St. Charles Comm Coll (MO)
St. Louis Comm Coll (MO)
San Jacinto Coll District (TX)
San Joaquin Delta Coll (CA)
San Juan Coll (NM)
Sauk Valley Comm Coll (IL)
Schoolcraft Coll (MI)
Seminole State Coll (OK)
Southeast Kentucky Comm and Tech Coll (KY)
Southeast Tech Inst (SD)
Southwestern Coll (CA)
Southwestern Comm Coll (NC)
Southwest Texas Jr Coll (TX)
Springfield Tech Comm Coll (MA)
Sullivan County Comm Coll (NY)
Three Rivers Comm Coll (MO)
Three Rivers Comm Coll (CT)
Tompkins Cortland Comm Coll (NY)
Treasure Valley Comm Coll (OR)
Trinity Valley Comm Coll (TX)
Truckee Meadows Comm Coll (NV)
Tulsa Comm Coll (OK)
Victoria Coll (TX)
Vincennes U (IN)
Volunteer State Comm Coll (TN)
Walters State Comm Coll (TN)
Waukesha County Tech Coll (WI)
Wayne Comm Coll (NC)
Wayne County Comm Coll District (MI)
Western Dakota Tech Inst (SD)
Western Iowa Tech Comm Coll (IA)
Western Texas Coll (TX)
Wor-Wic Comm Coll (MD)
Wytheville Comm Coll (VA)

**CRIMINAL JUSTICE/SAFETY**
Alamance Comm Coll (NC)
Alvin Comm Coll (TX)
American Samoa Comm Coll (AS)
Ancilla Coll (IN)
Asheville-Buncombe Tech Comm Coll (NC)
Blue Ridge Comm and Tech Coll (WV)
Bossier Parish Comm Coll (LA)
Bowling Green State U–Firelands Coll (OH)
Bristol Comm Coll (MA)
Bucks County Comm Coll (PA)
Cedar Valley Coll (TX)
Central Lakes Coll (MN)
Central Maine Comm Coll (ME)
Central Texas Coll (TX)
Century Coll (MN)
Chandler-Gilbert Comm Coll (AZ)
City Colls of Chicago, Olive-Harvey College (IL)
Cleveland Comm Coll (NC)
Coll of the Ouachitas (AR)
Craven Comm Coll (NC)
Dyersburg State Comm Coll (TN)
El Paso Comm Coll (TX)
Fayetteville Tech Comm Coll (NC)
Fiorello H. LaGuardia Comm Coll of the City U of New York (NY)

Galveston Coll (TX)
Genesee Comm Coll (NY)
Gordon State Coll (GA)
Greenville Tech Coll (SC)
Halifax Comm Coll (NC)
Haywood Comm Coll (NC)
Holyoke Comm Coll (MA)
Ivy Tech Comm Coll–Bloomington (IN)
Ivy Tech Comm Coll–Central Indiana (IN)
Ivy Tech Comm Coll–Columbus (IN)
Ivy Tech Comm Coll–East Central (IN)
Ivy Tech Comm Coll–Kokomo (IN)
Ivy Tech Comm Coll–Lafayette (IN)
Ivy Tech Comm Coll–North Central (IN)
Ivy Tech Comm Coll–Northeast (IN)
Ivy Tech Comm Coll–Northwest (IN)
Ivy Tech Comm Coll–Richmond (IN)
Ivy Tech Comm Coll–Southeast (IN)
Ivy Tech Comm Coll–Southwest (IN)
Ivy Tech Comm Coll–Wabash Valley (IN)
James Sprunt Comm Coll (NC)
Kellogg Comm Coll (MI)
Kent State U at Ashtabula (OH)
Kent State U at East Liverpool (OH)
Kent State U at Trumbull (OH)
Kent State U at Tuscarawas (OH)
Kishwaukee Coll (IL)
Lackawanna Coll (PA)
Lehigh Carbon Comm Coll (PA)
Lenoir Comm Coll (NC)
Mesa Comm Coll (AZ)
Mesalands Comm Coll (NM)
Minnesota State Comm and Tech Coll (MN)
Monroe County Comm Coll (MI)
Montgomery Comm Coll (NC)
Nassau Comm Coll (NY)
New Mexico State U–Alamogordo (NM)
Northampton Comm Coll (PA)
Northeast State Comm Coll (TN)
North Hennepin Comm Coll (MN)
NorthWest Arkansas Comm Coll (AR)
Northwest Coll (WY)
Northwest Vista Coll (TX)
Paris Jr Coll (TX)
Piedmont Comm Coll (NC)
Potomac State Coll of West Virginia U (WV)
Randolph Comm Coll (NC)
Richmond Comm Coll (NC)
St. Philip's Coll (TX)
Southeast Arkansas Coll (AR)
South Suburban Coll (IL)
Southwestern Michigan Coll (MI)
Southwest Texas Jr Coll (TX)
Sowela Tech Comm Coll (LA)
Texarkana Coll (TX)
Truckee Meadows Comm Coll (NV)
Tyler Jr Coll (TX)
Volunteer State Comm Coll (TN)
Walters State Comm Coll (TN)
Wayne Comm Coll (NC)
Western Dakota Tech Inst (SD)
White Mountains Comm Coll (NH)
Wisconsin Indianhead Tech Coll (WI)
York County Comm Coll (ME)

## CRIMINOLOGY
Central New Mexico Comm Coll (NM)
Coll of Central Florida (FL)
Genesee Comm Coll (NY)
Panola Coll (TX)
Paris Jr Coll (TX)
Potomac State Coll of West Virginia U (WV)
State U of New York Coll of Technology at Alfred (NY)
Western Wyoming Comm Coll (WY)

## CRISIS/EMERGENCY/DISASTER MANAGEMENT
Erie Comm Coll (NY)
Fayetteville Tech Comm Coll (NC)
Lenoir Comm Coll (NC)
Montgomery Coll (MD)
Raritan Valley Comm Coll (NJ)
Sullivan County Comm Coll (NY)
Wayne Comm Coll (NC)
Western Iowa Tech Comm Coll (IA)

## CRITICAL INFRASTRUCTURE PROTECTION
Bucks County Comm Coll (PA)
Comm Coll of Allegheny County (PA)

## CROP PRODUCTION
Arizona Western Coll (AZ)
Barton County Comm Coll (KS)
Black Hawk Coll, Moline (IL)
Cloud County Comm Coll (KS)
Cochise County Comm Coll District (AZ)
Coll of the Desert (CA)
Illinois Central Coll (IL)
Merced Coll (CA)
Northeast Iowa Comm Coll (IA)
Northwest Coll (WY)
The Ohio State U Ag Tech Inst (OH)
Ridgewater Coll (MN)
San Joaquin Delta Coll (CA)

## CULINARY ARTS
Alamance Comm Coll (NC)
Alvin Comm Coll (TX)
Arizona Western Coll (AZ)
Asheville-Buncombe Tech Comm Coll (NC)
Austin Comm Coll District (TX)
Blue Ridge Comm and Tech Coll (WV)
Bossier Parish Comm Coll (LA)
Bucks County Comm Coll (PA)
Bunker Hill Comm Coll (MA)
Caldwell Comm Coll and Tech Inst (NC)
Carteret Comm Coll (NC)
Central New Mexico Comm Coll (NM)
Central Ohio Tech Coll (OH)
Central Virginia Comm Coll (VA)
Clark Coll (WA)
Cochise County Comm Coll District (AZ)
Coll of The Albemarle (NC)
Coll of the Desert (CA)
Collin County Comm Coll District (TX)
Comm Coll of Allegheny County (PA)
Comm Coll of Philadelphia (PA)
County Coll of Morris (NJ)
Culinary Inst LeNotre (TX)
Daytona State Coll (FL)
Del Mar Coll (TX)
Des Moines Area Comm Coll (IA)
East Central Coll (MO)
El Paso Comm Coll (TX)
Erie Comm Coll (NY)
Erie Comm Coll, North Campus (NY)
Fayetteville Tech Comm Coll (NC)
Fox Valley Tech Coll (WI)
Galveston Coll (TX)
Gateway Tech Coll (WI)
Grand Rapids Comm Coll (MI)
Greenville Tech Coll (SC)
Harrisburg Area Comm Coll (PA)
H. Councill Trenholm State Comm Coll (AL)
Houston Comm Coll (TX)
Hudson County Comm Coll (NJ)
Illinois Central Coll (IL)
Illinois Eastern Comm Colls, Olney Central College (IL)
Kaskaskia Coll (IL)
Lackawanna Coll (PA)
Lakes Region Comm Coll (NH)
Lenoir Comm Coll (NC)
Lorain County Comm Coll (OH)
Macomb Comm Coll (MI)
Maysville Comm and Tech Coll, Maysville (KY)
Miami Dade Coll (FL)
Mitchell Tech Inst (SD)
Mohave Comm Coll (AZ)
Mohawk Valley Comm Coll (NY)
Monroe County Comm Coll (MI)
Montgomery County Comm Coll (PA)
Mott Comm Coll (MI)
Niagara County Comm Coll (NY)
Northampton Comm Coll (PA)
Northcentral Tech Coll (WI)
North Dakota State Coll of Science (ND)
North Shore Comm Coll (MA)
NorthWest Arkansas Comm Coll (AR)
Odessa Coll (TX)
Orange Coast Coll (CA)
Ozarks Tech Comm Coll (MO)
Piedmont Virginia Comm Coll (VA)
Rend Lake Coll (IL)
Renton Tech Coll (WA)
St. Louis Comm Coll (MO)
St. Philip's Coll (TX)
Salt Lake Comm Coll (UT)
San Jacinto Coll District (TX)
San Joaquin Delta Coll (CA)
Santa Rosa Jr Coll (CA)
Schoolcraft Coll (MI)
Scottsdale Comm Coll (AZ)
Somerset Comm Coll (KY)
Southcentral Kentucky Comm and Tech Coll (KY)
Southwestern Comm Coll (NC)
Sowela Tech Comm Coll (LA)
State U of New York Coll of Technology at Alfred (NY)
Sullivan County Comm Coll (NY)
Texarkana Coll (TX)
Texas State Tech Coll (TX)
Tompkins Cortland Comm Coll (NY)
Trident Tech Coll (SC)
Vincennes U (IN)
West Kentucky Comm and Tech Coll (KY)
White Mountains Comm Coll (NH)
York County Comm Coll (ME)

## CULINARY ARTS RELATED
Ancilla Coll (IN)
Bristol Comm Coll (MA)
Oklahoma State U Inst of Technology (OK)

## CUSTOMER SERVICE MANAGEMENT
Central Oregon Comm Coll (OR)

## CUSTOMER SERVICE SUPPORT/CALL CENTER/TELESERVICE OPERATION
Miami Dade Coll (FL)

## CYBER/COMPUTER FORENSICS AND COUNTERTERRORISM
Century Coll (MN)
Comm Coll of Baltimore County (MD)
Harper Coll (IL)
Pensacola State Coll (FL)

## CYBER/ELECTRONIC OPERATIONS AND WARFARE
Lorain County Comm Coll (OH)

## CYTOTECHNOLOGY
Barton County Comm Coll (KS)

## DAIRY HUSBANDRY AND PRODUCTION
Northeast Iowa Comm Coll (IA)
The Ohio State U Ag Tech Inst (OH)
Ridgewater Coll (MN)

## DAIRY SCIENCE
Mt. San Antonio Coll (CA)
The Ohio State U Ag Tech Inst (OH)

## DANCE
Austin Comm Coll District (TX)
Barton County Comm Coll (KS)
Coll of Marin (CA)
Fullerton Coll (CA)
Miami Dade Coll (FL)
Montgomery County Comm Coll (PA)
Nassau Comm Coll (NY)
Orange Coast Coll (CA)
Palomar Coll (CA)
Pasadena City Coll (CA)
Queensborough Comm Coll of the City U of New York (NY)
Raritan Valley Comm Coll (NJ)
San Jacinto Coll District (TX)
San Joaquin Delta Coll (CA)
Santa Rosa Jr Coll (CA)
Southwestern Coll (CA)
Trinity Valley Comm Coll (TX)
Tyler Jr Coll (TX)
Western Wyoming Comm Coll (WY)

## DANCE RELATED
Orange Coast Coll (CA)

## DATA ENTRY/MICROCOMPUTER APPLICATIONS
Antelope Valley Coll (CA)
Arizona Western Coll (AZ)
Bunker Hill Comm Coll (MA)
Chandler-Gilbert Comm Coll (AZ)
Clark Coll (WA)
Coll of The Albemarle (NC)

Del Mar Coll (TX)
Mid-State Tech Coll (WI)
Montgomery Coll (MD)
North Shore Comm Coll (MA)
St. Philip's Coll (TX)
Seminole State Coll of Florida (FL)
Sullivan County Comm Coll (NY)
Western Wyoming Comm Coll (WY)

## DATA ENTRY/MICROCOMPUTER APPLICATIONS RELATED
Blue Ridge Comm and Tech Coll (WV)
Pasadena City Coll (CA)
Potomac State Coll of West Virginia U (WV)
Seminole State Coll of Florida (FL)
Southwestern Coll (CA)

## DATA MODELING/WAREHOUSING AND DATABASE ADMINISTRATION
Chandler-Gilbert Comm Coll (AZ)
Coll of Marin (CA)
Ivy Tech Comm Coll–Bloomington (IN)
Ivy Tech Comm Coll–Central Indiana (IN)
Ivy Tech Comm Coll–Columbus (IN)
Ivy Tech Comm Coll–East Central (IN)
Ivy Tech Comm Coll–Kokomo (IN)
Ivy Tech Comm Coll–Lafayette (IN)
Ivy Tech Comm Coll–Northeast (IN)
Ivy Tech Comm Coll–Richmond (IN)
Ivy Tech Comm Coll–Sellersburg (IN)
Ivy Tech Comm Coll–Southeast (IN)
Ivy Tech Comm Coll–Southwest (IN)
Ivy Tech Comm Coll–Wabash Valley (IN)
LDS Business Coll (UT)
Quinsigamond Comm Coll (MA)
Seminole State Coll of Florida (FL)
Waukesha County Tech Coll (WI)
Wayne County Comm Coll District (MI)

## DATA PROCESSING AND DATA PROCESSING TECHNOLOGY
Bristol Comm Coll (MA)
Cedar Valley Coll (TX)
Century Coll (MN)
Copiah-Lincoln Comm Coll (MS)
Dabney S. Lancaster Comm Coll (VA)
Eastern Gateway Comm Coll (OH)
Greenville Tech Coll (SC)
Hudson County Comm Coll (NJ)
Illinois Valley Comm Coll (IL)
Iowa Central Comm Coll (IA)
Kingsborough Comm Coll of the City U of New York (NY)
Louisiana State U at Eunice (LA)
Mission Coll (CA)
Monroe Comm Coll (NY)
Monroe County Comm Coll (MI)
Morton Coll (IL)
Mt. San Antonio Coll (CA)
Muskegon Comm Coll (MI)
Nassau Comm Coll (NY)
National Park Coll (AR)
Navarro Coll (TX)
North Central Texas Coll (TX)
Northeastern Tech Coll (SC)
Northern Essex Comm Coll (MA)
NorthWest Arkansas Comm Coll (AR)
Odessa Coll (TX)
Queensborough Comm Coll of the City U of New York (NY)
Richland Coll (TX)
San Juan Coll (NM)
Schenectady County Comm Coll (NY)
Seminole State Coll of Florida (FL)
Southeast Kentucky Comm and Tech Coll (KY)
Southwest Texas Jr Coll (TX)
Trinity Valley Comm Coll (TX)
Walters State Comm Coll (TN)
Western Wyoming Comm Coll (WY)

## DEAF STUDIES
Quinsigamond Comm Coll (MA)

## DENTAL ASSISTING
Camden County Coll (NJ)
Central Oregon Comm Coll (OR)
Century Coll (MN)

Coll of Central Florida (FL)
Coll of Marin (CA)
Eastern Gateway Comm Coll (OH)
El Paso Comm Coll (TX)
H. Councill Trenholm State Comm Coll (AL)
Hinds Comm Coll (MS)
Humacao Comm Coll (PR)
Ivy Tech Comm Coll–Columbus (IN)
Ivy Tech Comm Coll–East Central (IN)
Ivy Tech Comm Coll–Kokomo (IN)
Ivy Tech Comm Coll–Lafayette (IN)
Kaskaskia Coll (IL)
Lake Area Tech Inst (SD)
Manor Coll (PA)
Mid-Plains Comm Coll, North Platte (NE)
Minnesota State Comm and Tech Coll (MN)
Minnesota West Comm and Tech Coll (MN)
Mohave Comm Coll (AZ)
Mott Comm Coll (MI)
North Dakota State Coll of Science (ND)
Northern Essex Comm Coll (MA)
Orange Coast Coll (CA)
Ozarks Tech Comm Coll (MO)
Palomar Coll (CA)
Pasadena City Coll (CA)
Pueblo Comm Coll (CO)
Renton Tech Coll (WA)
Tallahassee Comm Coll (FL)
Truckee Meadows Comm Coll (NV)
Western Iowa Tech Comm Coll (IA)

## DENTAL HYGIENE
Amarillo Coll (TX)
Asheville-Buncombe Tech Comm Coll (NC)
Austin Comm Coll District (TX)
Barton County Comm Coll (KS)
Bristol Comm Coll (MA)
Camden County Coll (NJ)
Century Coll (MN)
Chippewa Valley Tech Coll (WI)
Clark Coll (WA)
Collin County Comm Coll District (TX)
Colorado Northwestern Comm Coll (CO)
Comm Coll of Baltimore County (MD)
Comm Coll of Philadelphia (PA)
Daytona State Coll (FL)
Del Mar Coll (TX)
Des Moines Area Comm Coll (IA)
El Paso Comm Coll (TX)
Erie Comm Coll, North Campus (NY)
Fayetteville Tech Comm Coll (NC)
Fox Valley Tech Coll (WI)
Georgia Highlands Coll (GA)
Grand Rapids Comm Coll (MI)
Great Falls Coll Montana State U (MT)
Greenville Tech Coll (SC)
Gulf Coast State Coll (FL)
Hagerstown Comm Coll (MD)
Halifax Comm Coll (NC)
Harper Coll (IL)
Harrisburg Area Comm Coll (PA)
Hawkeye Comm Coll (IA)
Illinois Central Coll (IL)
Ivy Tech Comm Coll–East Central (IN)
Ivy Tech Comm Coll–Kokomo (IN)
Kellogg Comm Coll (MI)
Lakeland Comm Coll (OH)
Lakeshore Tech Coll (WI)
Lake Superior Coll (MN)
Laramie County Comm Coll (WY)
Lenoir Comm Coll (NC)
Lorain County Comm Coll (OH)
Manor Coll (PA)
Meridian Comm Coll (MS)
Mesa Comm Coll (AZ)
Miami Dade Coll (FL)
Minnesota State Comm and Tech Coll (MN)
Mohave Comm Coll (AZ)
Monroe Comm Coll (NY)
Montgomery County Comm Coll (PA)
Mott Comm Coll (MI)
Mount Wachusett Comm Coll (MA)
Northampton Comm Coll (PA)
Northcentral Tech Coll (WI)
North Dakota State Coll of Science (ND)
Ozarks Tech Comm Coll (MO)

Pasadena City Coll (CA)
Pensacola State Coll (FL)
Pueblo Comm Coll (CO)
Quinsigamond Comm Coll (MA)
Raritan Valley Comm Coll (NJ)
Rock Valley Coll (IL)
St. Louis Comm Coll (MO)
Salt Lake Comm Coll (UT)
San Juan Coll (NM)
Santa Rosa Jr Coll (CA)
Southern U at Shreveport (LA)
South Florida State Coll (FL)
Southwestern Coll (CA)
Springfield Tech Comm Coll (MA)
Stark State Coll (OH)
Tallahassee Comm Coll (FL)
Tarrant County Coll District (TX)
Trident Tech Coll (SC)
Truckee Meadows Comm Coll (NV)
Tulsa Comm Coll (OK)
Tyler Jr Coll (TX)
Union County Coll (NJ)
Waukesha County Tech Coll (WI)
Wayne Comm Coll (NC)
Wayne County Comm Coll District (MI)
Wytheville Comm Coll (VA)

### DENTAL LABORATORY TECHNOLOGY
Erie Comm Coll, South Campus (NY)
J. Sargeant Reynolds Comm Coll (VA)
Los Angeles City Coll (CA)
Pasadena City Coll (CA)

### DENTAL SERVICES AND ALLIED PROFESSIONS RELATED
Gordon State Coll (GA)
Quinsigamond Comm Coll (MA)

### DESIGN AND APPLIED ARTS RELATED
County Coll of Morris (NJ)
Del Mar Coll (TX)
Howard Comm Coll (MD)
Kingsborough Comm Coll of the City U of New York (NY)
LDS Business Coll (UT)
Muskegon Comm Coll (MI)
Niagara County Comm Coll (NY)
Odessa Coll (TX)
Vincennes U (IN)
Westchester Comm Coll (NY)

### DESIGN AND VISUAL COMMUNICATIONS
Adirondack Comm Coll (NY)
Austin Comm Coll District (TX)
Black Hawk Coll, Moline (IL)
Bristol Comm Coll (MA)
Brookhaven Coll (TX)
Bunker Hill Comm Coll (MA)
Cecil Coll (MD)
Central Virginia Comm Coll (VA)
Coll of Marin (CA)
FIDM/Fashion Inst of Design & Merchandising, Orange County Campus (CA)
FIDM/Fashion Inst of Design & Merchandising, San Diego Campus (CA)
Harford Comm Coll (MD)
Harrisburg Area Comm Coll (PA)
Hutchinson Comm Coll (KS)
Ivy Tech Comm Coll–Central Indiana (IN)
Ivy Tech Comm Coll–Columbus (IN)
Ivy Tech Comm Coll–Kokomo (IN)
Ivy Tech Comm Coll–North Central (IN)
Ivy Tech Comm Coll–Sellersburg (IN)
Ivy Tech Comm Coll–Southwest (IN)
Ivy Tech Comm Coll–Wabash Valley (IN)
Mesa Comm Coll (AZ)
Nassau Comm Coll (NY)
Palomar Coll (CA)
St. Philip's Coll (TX)
Salt Lake Comm Coll (UT)

### DESKTOP PUBLISHING AND DIGITAL IMAGING DESIGN
Alvin Comm Coll (TX)
Antelope Valley Coll (CA)
Camden County Coll (NJ)
Des Moines Area Comm Coll (IA)
Dunwoody Coll of Technology (MN)
Hawkeye Comm Coll (IA)
Houston Comm Coll (TX)
Northeast Iowa Comm Coll (IA)
North Iowa Area Comm Coll (IA)

---

Palomar Coll (CA)
Pasadena City Coll (CA)
Ridgewater Coll (MN)
Southeast Tech Inst (SD)
Western Iowa Tech Comm Coll (IA)

### DEVELOPMENTAL AND CHILD PSYCHOLOGY
Central Lakes Coll (MN)
De Anza Coll (CA)
McLennan Comm Coll (TX)
Muskegon Comm Coll (MI)
Navarro Coll (TX)
Tarrant County Coll District (TX)
Trinity Valley Comm Coll (TX)

### DIAGNOSTIC MEDICAL SONOGRAPHY AND ULTRASOUND TECHNOLOGY
Alvin Comm Coll (TX)
Asheville-Buncombe Tech Comm Coll (NC)
Austin Comm Coll District (TX)
Bowling Green State U–Firelands Coll (OH)
Bunker Hill Comm Coll (MA)
Caldwell Comm Coll and Tech Inst (NC)
Central New Mexico Comm Coll (NM)
Central Ohio Tech Coll (OH)
Chippewa Valley Tech Coll (WI)
Collin County Comm Coll District (TX)
Comm Coll of Allegheny County (PA)
Del Mar Coll (TX)
El Paso Comm Coll (TX)
Greenville Tech Coll (SC)
Gulf Coast State Coll (FL)
Gurnick Academy of Medical Arts (CA)
Harper Coll (IL)
Harrisburg Area Comm Coll (PA)
H. Councill Trenholm State Comm Coll (AL)
Hinds Comm Coll (MS)
Howard Comm Coll (MD)
Lackawanna Coll (PA)
Laramie County Comm Coll (WY)
Lorain County Comm Coll (OH)
Lurleen B. Wallace Comm Coll (AL)
Merced Coll (CA)
Miami Dade Coll (FL)
Montgomery Coll (MD)
Northampton Comm Coll (PA)
Orange Coast Coll (CA)
Pensacola State Coll (FL)
Piedmont Virginia Comm Coll (VA)
St. Philip's Coll (TX)
San Jacinto Coll District (TX)
Southeast Tech Inst (SD)
Springfield Tech Comm Coll (MA)
State U of New York Coll of Technology at Alfred (NY)
Tallahassee Comm Coll (FL)
Tulsa Comm Coll (OK)
Tyler Jr Coll (TX)
Union County Coll (NJ)
West Kentucky Comm and Tech Coll (KY)

### DIESEL MECHANICS TECHNOLOGY
Alexandria Tech and Comm Coll (MN)
Asheville-Buncombe Tech Comm Coll (NC)
Central Lakes Coll (MN)
Central Texas Coll (TX)
City Colls of Chicago, Olive-Harvey College (IL)
Clark Coll (WA)
Coll of Eastern Idaho (ID)
Copiah-Lincoln Comm Coll (MS)
Des Moines Area Comm Coll (IA)
Eastern Arizona Coll (AZ)
Florida Keys Comm Coll (FL)
Fox Valley Tech Coll (WI)
Gateway Tech Coll (WI)
Hawkeye Comm Coll (IA)
Hinds Comm Coll (MS)
Illinois Central Coll (IL)
Illinois Eastern Comm Colls, Wabash Valley College (IL)
Johnson Coll (PA)
Johnston Comm Coll (NC)
Kishwaukee Coll (IL)
Lake Area Tech Inst (SD)
Laramie County Comm Coll (WY)
Lurleen B. Wallace Comm Coll (AL)
Mesalands Comm Coll (NM)
Mid-Plains Comm Coll, North Platte (NE)

---

Minnesota State Comm and Tech Coll (MN)
Minnesota West Comm and Tech Coll (MN)
New Castle School of Trades (PA)
Northcentral Tech Coll (WI)
North Dakota State Coll of Science (ND)
Northeast Comm Coll (NE)
Ohio Tech Coll (OH)
Oklahoma City Comm Coll (OK)
Oklahoma State U Inst of Technology (OK)
Owensboro Comm and Tech Coll (KY)
Palomar Coll (CA)
St. Louis Comm Coll (MO)
St. Philip's Coll (TX)
Salt Lake Comm Coll (UT)
San Jacinto Coll District (TX)
San Juan Coll (NM)
Santa Rosa Jr Coll (CA)
Southeast Tech Inst (SD)
Southwest Texas Jr Coll (TX)
State U of New York Coll of Technology at Alfred (NY)
Texarkana Coll (TX)
Texas State Tech Coll (TX)
Truckee Meadows Comm Coll (NV)
Vincennes U (IN)
Waukesha County Tech Coll (WI)
Western Wyoming Comm Coll (WY)
White Mountains Comm Coll (NH)
Williston State Coll (ND)

### DIETETICS
Central Oregon Comm Coll (OR)
El Paso Comm Coll (TX)
Harper Coll (IL)
Harrisburg Area Comm Coll (PA)
Los Angeles City Coll (CA)
Miami Dade Coll (FL)
Northeast Comm Coll (NE)
Pensacola State Coll (FL)
Tarrant County Coll District (TX)
Truckee Meadows Comm Coll (NV)
Vincennes U (IN)

### DIETETICS AND CLINICAL NUTRITION SERVICES RELATED
Oklahoma State U–Oklahoma City (OK)

### DIETETIC TECHNOLOGY
Camden County Coll (NJ)
Chandler-Gilbert Comm Coll (AZ)
Coll of the Desert (CA)
Fiorello H. LaGuardia Comm Coll of the City U of New York (NY)
Harper Coll (IL)
Los Angeles City Coll (CA)
Miami Dade Coll (FL)
Mohawk Valley Comm Coll (NY)
Northland Comm and Tech Coll (MN)
Orange Coast Coll (CA)
Santa Rosa Jr Coll (CA)

### DIETITIAN ASSISTANT
Barton County Comm Coll (KS)
Chandler-Gilbert Comm Coll (AZ)
Comm Coll of Allegheny County (PA)
Erie Comm Coll, North Campus (NY)
Lenoir Comm Coll (NC)
Westchester Comm Coll (NY)

### DIGITAL ARTS
Fiorello H. LaGuardia Comm Coll of the City U of New York (NY)
Genesee Comm Coll (NY)
Gulf Coast State Coll (FL)
Harford Comm Coll (MD)
Mohawk Valley Comm Coll (NY)
Queensborough Comm Coll of the City U of New York (NY)
Volunteer State Comm Coll (TN)
Westchester Comm Coll (NY)

### DIGITAL COMMUNICATION AND MEDIA/MULTIMEDIA
Chippewa Valley Tech Coll (WI)
Cochise County Comm Coll District (AZ)
Daytona State Coll (FL)
Gulf Coast State Coll (FL)
Hawkeye Comm Coll (IA)
Laramie County Comm Coll (WY)
Naugatuck Valley Comm Coll (CT)
Oklahoma City Comm Coll (OK)
Pasadena City Coll (CA)
Ridgewater Coll (MN)
San Jacinto Coll District (TX)

---

Santa Rosa Jr Coll (CA)
Tompkins Cortland Comm Coll (NY)
Tulsa Comm Coll (OK)
Wayne County Comm Coll District (MI)
Westchester Comm Coll (NY)

### DIRECTING AND THEATRICAL PRODUCTION
Quinsigamond Comm Coll (MA)

### DIVING, PROFESSIONAL AND INSTRUCTION
Florida Keys Comm Coll (FL)

### DIVINITY/MINISTRY
The Salvation Army Coll for Officer Training at Crestmont (CA)

### DRAFTING AND DESIGN TECHNOLOGY
Alvin Comm Coll (TX)
Amarillo Coll (TX)
Antelope Valley Coll (CA)
Austin Comm Coll District (TX)
Bossier Parish Comm Coll (LA)
Camden County Coll (NJ)
Cayuga County Comm Coll (NY)
Central Oregon Comm Coll (OR)
Central Texas Coll (TX)
Coll of Central Florida (FL)
Coll of the Desert (CA)
Collin County Comm Coll District (TX)
Comm Coll of Allegheny County (PA)
Comm Coll of Philadelphia (PA)
Copiah-Lincoln Comm Coll (MS)
Crowder Coll (MO)
Dabney S. Lancaster Comm Coll (VA)
Daytona State Coll (FL)
Del Mar Coll (TX)
Eastern Arizona Coll (AZ)
Eastern Gateway Comm Coll (OH)
El Paso Comm Coll (TX)
Frederick Comm Coll (MD)
Fullerton Coll (CA)
Genesee Comm Coll (NY)
George C. Wallace Comm Coll (AL)
Greenville Tech Coll (SC)
H. Councill Trenholm State Comm Coll (AL)
Hill Coll (TX)
Hinds Comm Coll (MS)
Houston Comm Coll (TX)
Hutchinson Comm Coll (KS)
Illinois Valley Comm Coll (IL)
Independence Comm Coll (KS)
Iowa Central Comm Coll (IA)
ITI Tech Coll (LA)
Ivy Tech Comm Coll–Bloomington (IN)
Ivy Tech Comm Coll–Central Indiana (IN)
Ivy Tech Comm Coll–Columbus (IN)
Ivy Tech Comm Coll–East Central (IN)
Ivy Tech Comm Coll–Kokomo (IN)
Ivy Tech Comm Coll–Lafayette (IN)
Ivy Tech Comm Coll–Northeast (IN)
Ivy Tech Comm Coll–Northwest (IN)
Ivy Tech Comm Coll–Sellersburg (IN)
Ivy Tech Comm Coll–Southeast (IN)
Ivy Tech Comm Coll–Southwest (IN)
Ivy Tech Comm Coll–Wabash Valley (IN)
Kellogg Comm Coll (MI)
Laramie County Comm Coll (WY)
Lehigh Carbon Comm Coll (PA)
Macomb Comm Coll (MI)
Meridian Comm Coll (MS)
Miami Dade Coll (FL)
Mission Coll (CA)
Mohave Comm Coll (AZ)
Monroe County Comm Coll (MI)
Montgomery County Comm Coll (PA)
Morrison Inst of Technology (IL)
Morton Coll (IL)
Mott Comm Coll (MI)
Mt. San Antonio Coll (CA)
Muskegon Comm Coll (MI)
Navarro Coll (TX)
New River Comm Coll (VA)
Niagara County Comm Coll (NY)
North Central Texas Coll (TX)
NorthWest Arkansas Comm Coll (AR)
Northwest-Shoals Comm Coll (AL)
Odessa Coll (TX)
Ozarks Tech Comm Coll (MO)
Palomar Coll (CA)
Paris Jr Coll (TX)

---

Pasadena City Coll (CA)
Pensacola State Coll (FL)
Pittsburgh Tech Coll (PA)
Renton Tech Coll (WA)
St. Charles Comm Coll (MO)
Salt Lake Comm Coll (UT)
San Jacinto Coll District (TX)
San Juan Coll (NM)
Schoolcraft Coll (MI)
Seminole State Coll of Florida (FL)
Southeast Arkansas Coll (AR)
Southwestern Coll (CA)
Sowela Tech Comm Coll (LA)
State Tech Coll of Missouri (MO)
State U of New York Coll of Technology at Alfred (NY)
Tallahassee Comm Coll (FL)
Tarrant County Coll District (TX)
Texarkana Coll (TX)
Texas State Tech Coll (TX)
Tidewater Comm Coll (VA)
Treasure Valley Comm Coll (OR)
Trinity Valley Comm Coll (TX)
Truckee Meadows Comm Coll (NV)
Tyler Jr Coll (TX)
U of Arkansas Comm Coll at Morrilton (AR)
Westchester Comm Coll (NY)
Western Dakota Tech Inst (SD)
Wytheville Comm Coll (VA)
York County Comm Coll (ME)

### DRAFTING/DESIGN ENGINEERING TECHNOLOGIES RELATED
Asheville-Buncombe Tech Comm Coll (NC)
Coll of The Albemarle (NC)
Comm Coll of Allegheny County (PA)
Dabney S. Lancaster Comm Coll (VA)
De Anza Coll (CA)
Genesee Comm Coll (NY)
Illinois Valley Comm Coll (IL)
Kennebec Valley Comm Coll (ME)
Lakeshore Tech Coll (WI)
Macomb Comm Coll (MI)
Mesa Comm Coll (AZ)
Mid-State Tech Coll (WI)
Mt. San Antonio Coll (CA)
Niagara County Comm Coll (NY)
Northeastern Tech Coll (SC)
Richland Coll (TX)
Rock Valley Coll (IL)

### DRAMA AND DANCE TEACHER EDUCATION
Hutchinson Comm Coll (KS)

### DRAMATIC/THEATER ARTS
Alvin Comm Coll (TX)
Amarillo Coll (TX)
American Academy of Dramatic Arts–Los Angeles (CA)
American Academy of Dramatic Arts–New York (NY)
Arizona Western Coll (AZ)
Austin Comm Coll District (TX)
Barton County Comm Coll (KS)
Bossier Parish Comm Coll (LA)
Bunker Hill Comm Coll (MA)
Central Texas Coll (TX)
Chandler-Gilbert Comm Coll (AZ)
Cochise County Comm Coll District (AZ)
Coll of Central Florida (FL)
Coll of Marin (CA)
Coll of The Albemarle (NC)
Coll of the Canyons (CA)
Coll of the Desert (CA)
Comm Coll of Allegheny County (PA)
Crowder Coll (MO)
De Anza Coll (CA)
Del Mar Coll (TX)
Eastern Arizona Coll (AZ)
Edison State Comm Coll (OH)
Fiorello H. LaGuardia Comm Coll of the City U of New York (NY)
Fullerton Coll (CA)
Galveston Coll (TX)
Genesee Comm Coll (NY)
Gordon State Coll (GA)
Harrisburg Area Comm Coll (PA)
Hill Coll (TX)
Howard Comm Coll (MD)
Independence Comm Coll (KS)
KD Conservatory Coll of Film and Dramatic Arts (TX)
Kingsborough Comm Coll of the City U of New York (NY)
Los Angeles City Coll (CA)
Manchester Comm Coll (CT)

Merced Coll (CA)
Mesa Comm Coll (AZ)
Miami Dade Coll (FL)
Mount Wachusett Comm Coll (MA)
Nassau Comm Coll (NY)
Navarro Coll (TX)
Niagara County Comm Coll (NY)
Northeast Comm Coll (NE)
Northeastern Jr Coll (CO)
North Hennepin Comm Coll (MN)
Oklahoma City Comm Coll (OK)
Orange Coast Coll (CA)
Otero Jr Coll (CO)
Owensboro Comm and Tech Coll (KY)
Palomar Coll (CA)
Panola Coll (TX)
Paris Jr Coll (TX)
Pasadena City Coll (CA)
Pensacola State Coll (FL)
Queensborough Comm Coll of the City U of New York (NY)
St. Philip's Coll (TX)
San Jacinto Coll District (TX)
San Joaquin Delta Coll (CA)
Santa Rosa Jr Coll (CA)
Sauk Valley Comm Coll (IL)
Scottsdale Comm Coll (AZ)
Texarkana Coll (TX)
Trinity Valley Comm Coll (TX)
Tulsa Comm Coll (OK)
Tyler Jr Coll (TX)
Vincennes U (IN)
Western Texas Coll (TX)
Western Wyoming Comm Coll (WY)

## DRAMATIC/THEATER ARTS AND STAGECRAFT RELATED
Bristol Comm Coll (MA)
Genesee Comm Coll (NY)
Lackawanna Coll (PA)

## DRAWING
Cecil Coll (MD)
De Anza Coll (CA)
Palomar Coll (CA)

## DRYWALL INSTALLATION
Palomar Coll (CA)

## EARLY CHILDHOOD EDUCATION
Alexandria Tech and Comm Coll (MN)
Alvin Comm Coll (TX)
Ancilla Coll (IN)
Anne Arundel Comm Coll (MD)
Arizona Western Coll (AZ)
Asheville-Buncombe Tech Comm Coll (NC)
Austin Comm Coll District (TX)
Barton County Comm Coll (KS)
Bucks County Comm Coll (PA)
Bunker Hill Comm Coll (MA)
Caldwell Comm Coll and Tech Inst (NC)
Camden County Coll (NJ)
Carroll Comm Coll (MD)
Carteret Comm Coll (NC)
Central Maine Comm Coll (ME)
Central New Mexico Comm Coll (NM)
Central Ohio Tech Coll (OH)
Central Oregon Comm Coll (OR)
Central Texas Coll (TX)
Chesapeake Coll (MD)
Chippewa Valley Tech Coll (WI)
Clark Coll (WA)
Cleveland Comm Coll (NC)
Cochise County Comm Coll District (AZ)
Coll of Central Florida (FL)
Coll of the Ouachitas (AR)
Collin County Comm Coll District (TX)
Colorado Northwestern Comm Coll (CO)
Comm Coll of Baltimore County (MD)
Craven Comm Coll (NC)
Daytona State Coll (FL)
Eastern Arizona Coll (AZ)
Fayetteville Tech Comm Coll (NC)
Fox Valley Tech Coll (WI)
Frederick Comm Coll (MD)
Front Range Comm Coll (CO)
Gateway Tech Coll (WI)
Georgia Military Coll (GA)
Gulf Coast State Coll (FL)
Hagerstown Comm Coll (MD)

Halifax Comm Coll (NC)
Harford Comm Coll (MD)
Harper Coll (IL)
Harrisburg Area Comm Coll (PA)
Haywood Comm Coll (NC)
Hesston Coll (KS)
Highland Comm Coll (IL)
Houston Comm Coll (TX)
Illinois Valley Comm Coll (IL)
Ivy Tech Comm Coll–Bloomington (IN)
Ivy Tech Comm Coll–Central Indiana (IN)
Ivy Tech Comm Coll–Columbus (IN)
Ivy Tech Comm Coll–East Central (IN)
Ivy Tech Comm Coll–Kokomo (IN)
Ivy Tech Comm Coll–Lafayette (IN)
Ivy Tech Comm Coll–North Central (IN)
Ivy Tech Comm Coll–Northeast (IN)
Ivy Tech Comm Coll–Northwest (IN)
Ivy Tech Comm Coll–Richmond (IN)
Ivy Tech Comm Coll–Sellersburg (IN)
Ivy Tech Comm Coll–Southeast (IN)
Ivy Tech Comm Coll–Southwest (IN)
Ivy Tech Comm Coll–Wabash Valley (IN)
James Sprunt Comm Coll (NC)
Jefferson Comm Coll (NY)
Johnston Comm Coll (NC)
Kingsborough Comm Coll of the City U of New York (NY)
Lakes Region Comm Coll (NH)
Laramie County Comm Coll (WY)
Lehigh Carbon Comm Coll (PA)
Lorain County Comm Coll (OH)
Massachusetts Bay Comm Coll (MA)
Miami Dade Coll (FL)
Mitchell Comm Coll (NC)
Montgomery Coll (MD)
Montgomery Comm Coll (NC)
Morton Coll (IL)
Mott Comm Coll (MI)
Naugatuck Valley Comm Coll (CT)
New Mexico State U–Alamogordo (NM)
Northampton Comm Coll (PA)
Northcentral Tech Coll (WI)
Northeast Comm Coll (NE)
NorthWest Arkansas Comm Coll (AR)
Northwest Coll (WY)
Oklahoma State U–Oklahoma City (OK)
Paris Jr Coll (TX)
Pennsylvania Highlands Comm Coll (PA)
Pennsylvania Inst of Technology (PA)
Pensacola State Coll (FL)
Piedmont Comm Coll (NC)
Potomac State Coll of West Virginia U (WV)
Pueblo Comm Coll (CO)
Quinsigamond Comm Coll (MA)
Randolph Comm Coll (NC)
Renton Tech Coll (WA)
Richmond Comm Coll (NC)
Ridgewater Coll (MN)
Rowan-Cabarrus Comm Coll (NC)
Santa Rosa Jr Coll (CA)
Sauk Valley Comm Coll (IL)
Southwestern Indian Polytechnic Inst (NM)
Southwestern Michigan Coll (MI)
Springfield Tech Comm Coll (MA)
Tallahassee Comm Coll (FL)
Tohono O'odham Comm Coll (AZ)
Tri-County Comm Coll (NC)
Urban Coll of Boston (MA)
Vincennes U (IN)
Waukesha County Tech Coll (WI)
Wayne Comm Coll (NC)
Western Texas Coll (TX)
Western Wyoming Comm Coll (WY)
White Mountains Comm Coll (NH)
Wor-Wic Comm Coll (MD)
York County Comm Coll (ME)

## E-COMMERCE
Brookhaven Coll (TX)
Century Coll (MN)
Del Mar Coll (TX)
Genesee Comm Coll (NY)
Lackawanna Coll (PA)
Southwestern Coll (CA)
Wayne County Comm Coll District (MI)

## ECONOMICS
Austin Comm Coll District (TX)
Barton County Comm Coll (KS)
Cochise County Comm Coll District (AZ)
Coll of Central Florida (FL)
Coll of the Desert (CA)
Copiah-Lincoln Comm Coll (MS)
De Anza Coll (CA)
Edison State Comm Coll (OH)
Fullerton Coll (CA)
Hill Coll (TX)
Laramie County Comm Coll (WY)
Miami Dade Coll (FL)
Muskegon Comm Coll (MI)
Northeastern Jr Coll (CO)
Orange Coast Coll (CA)
Palomar Coll (CA)
Potomac State Coll of West Virginia U (WV)
St. Philip's Coll (TX)
Salt Lake Comm Coll (UT)
San Joaquin Delta Coll (CA)
Santa Rosa Jr Coll (CA)
Sauk Valley Comm Coll (IL)
Southwestern Coll (CA)
Tyler Jr Coll (TX)
U of Wisconsin–Baraboo/Sauk County (WI)
U of Wisconsin–Barron County (WI)
U of Wisconsin–Fond du Lac (WI)
U of Wisconsin–Fox Valley (WI)
U of Wisconsin–Manitowoc (WI)
U of Wisconsin–Marathon County (WI)
U of Wisconsin–Marinette (WI)
U of Wisconsin–Marshfield/Wood County (WI)
U of Wisconsin–Richland (WI)
U of Wisconsin–Rock County (WI)
U of Wisconsin–Sheboygan (WI)
U of Wisconsin–Washington County (WI)
U of Wisconsin–Waukesha (WI)
Western Wyoming Comm Coll (WY)

## EDUCATION
American Samoa Comm Coll (AS)
Bossier Parish Comm Coll (LA)
Bowling Green State U–Firelands Coll (OH)
Bunker Hill Comm Coll (MA)
Caldwell Comm Coll and Tech Inst (NC)
Carroll Comm Coll (MD)
Cecil Coll (MD)
Cedar Valley Coll (TX)
Central Oregon Comm Coll (OR)
Central Virginia Comm Coll (VA)
Century Coll (MN)
Chesapeake Coll (MD)
Chipola Coll (FL)
Coll of The Albemarle (NC)
Comm Coll of Baltimore County (MD)
Comm Coll of Philadelphia (PA)
Copiah-Lincoln Comm Coll (MS)
Crowder Coll (MO)
Dabney S. Lancaster Comm Coll (VA)
Del Mar Coll (TX)
Dyersburg State Comm Coll (TN)
East Central Coll (MO)
Eastern Shore Comm Coll (VA)
Edison State Comm Coll (OH)
Frederick Comm Coll (MD)
Galveston Coll (TX)
Genesee Comm Coll (NY)
Hagerstown Comm Coll (MD)
Harford Comm Coll (MD)
Hutchinson Comm Coll (KS)
Illinois Valley Comm Coll (IL)
Independence Comm Coll (KS)
Iowa Central Comm Coll (IA)
Ivy Tech Comm Coll–Bloomington (IN)
Ivy Tech Comm Coll–Central Indiana (IN)
Ivy Tech Comm Coll–Columbus (IN)
Ivy Tech Comm Coll–East Central (IN)
Ivy Tech Comm Coll–Kokomo (IN)
Ivy Tech Comm Coll–Lafayette (IN)
Ivy Tech Comm Coll–Richmond (IN)
Ivy Tech Comm Coll–Sellersburg (IN)
Ivy Tech Comm Coll–Southeast (IN)
Ivy Tech Comm Coll–Southwest (IN)
Ivy Tech Comm Coll–Wabash Valley (IN)

Kingsborough Comm Coll of the City U of New York (NY)
Lackawanna Coll (PA)
Laramie County Comm Coll (WY)
Lehigh Carbon Comm Coll (PA)
Mesalands Comm Coll (NM)
Miami Dade Coll (FL)
Mohave Comm Coll (AZ)
Motlow State Comm Coll (TN)
Muskegon Comm Coll (MI)
National Park Coll (AR)
Navarro Coll (TX)
New Mexico State U–Alamogordo (NM)
New River Comm Coll (VA)
Northeast Comm Coll (NE)
Northeast State Comm Coll (TN)
Northern Essex Comm Coll (MA)
North Hennepin Comm Coll (MN)
NorthWest Arkansas Comm Coll (AR)
Nunez Comm Coll (LA)
Odessa Coll (TX)
Oklahoma City Comm Coll (OK)
Palomar Coll (CA)
Panola Coll (TX)
Paris Jr Coll (TX)
Pennsylvania Highlands Comm Coll (PA)
Pensacola State Coll (FL)
Piedmont Virginia Comm Coll (VA)
St. Louis Comm Coll (MO)
Sauk Valley Comm Coll (IL)
Schenectady County Comm Coll (NY)
Schoolcraft Coll (MI)
Southwest Texas Jr Coll (TX)
Three Rivers Comm Coll (CT)
Tidewater Comm Coll (VA)
Trinity Valley Comm Coll (TX)
Tulsa Comm Coll (OK)
U of Wisconsin–Baraboo/Sauk County (WI)
U of Wisconsin–Barron County (WI)
U of Wisconsin–Fond du Lac (WI)
U of Wisconsin–Fox Valley (WI)
U of Wisconsin–Manitowoc (WI)
U of Wisconsin–Marathon County (WI)
U of Wisconsin–Marinette (WI)
U of Wisconsin–Marshfield/Wood County (WI)
U of Wisconsin–Richland (WI)
U of Wisconsin–Rock County (WI)
U of Wisconsin–Sheboygan (WI)
U of Wisconsin–Washington County (WI)
U of Wisconsin–Waukesha (WI)
Vincennes U (IN)
Volunteer State Comm Coll (TN)
Walters State Comm Coll (TN)
Western Wyoming Comm Coll (WY)
White Mountains Comm Coll (NH)
Wor-Wic Comm Coll (MD)
Wytheville Comm Coll (VA)
York County Comm Coll (ME)

## EDUCATIONAL/INSTRUCTIONAL TECHNOLOGY
Bossier Parish Comm Coll (LA)
Ivy Tech Comm Coll–North Central (IN)
Tarrant County Comm Coll District (TX)
Texas State Tech Coll (TX)

## EDUCATIONAL LEADERSHIP AND ADMINISTRATION
J. Sargeant Reynolds Comm Coll (VA)

## EDUCATION (MULTIPLE LEVELS)
Arkansas State U–Newport (AR)
Brookhaven Coll (TX)
Camden County Coll (NJ)
Cayuga County Comm Coll (NY)
Central New Mexico Comm Coll (NM)
Genesee Comm Coll (NY)
Houston Comm Coll (TX)
Kishwaukee Coll (IL)
Lorain County Comm Coll (OH)
Oklahoma State U Inst of Technology (OK)
Paris Jr Coll (TX)
St. Philip's Coll (TX)
Three Rivers Coll (MO)
Tyler Jr Coll (TX)
Westchester Comm Coll (NY)

Western Wyoming Comm Coll (WY)

## EDUCATION RELATED
Genesee Comm Coll (NY)
Kent State U at Salem (OH)
Kent State U at Tuscarawas (OH)
Miami Dade Coll (FL)

## EDUCATION (SPECIFIC LEVELS AND METHODS) RELATED
Comm Coll of Allegheny County (PA)
Harford Comm Coll (MD)
Manor Coll (PA)
Miami Dade Coll (FL)
Pensacola State Coll (FL)

## EDUCATION (SPECIFIC SUBJECT AREAS) RELATED
Comm Coll of Allegheny County (PA)
Harford Comm Coll (MD)
Ozarks Tech Comm Coll (MO)
St. Charles Comm Coll (MO)
Three Rivers Coll (MO)

## ELECTRICAL AND ELECTRONIC ENGINEERING TECHNOLOGIES RELATED
American Samoa Comm Coll (AS)
Blue Ridge Comm and Tech Coll (WV)
Fox Valley Tech Coll (WI)
Kent State U at Trumbull (OH)
Kent State U at Tuscarawas (OH)
Lake Region State Coll (ND)
Massachusetts Bay Comm Coll (MA)
Miami Dade Coll (FL)
Minnesota State Comm and Tech Coll (MN)
North Dakota State Coll of Science (ND)
Owensboro Comm and Tech Coll (KY)
Ozarks Tech Comm Coll (MO)
Pasadena City Coll (CA)
Somerset Comm Coll (KY)
Southcentral Kentucky Comm and Tech Coll (KY)
Thaddeus Stevens Coll of Technology (PA)

## ELECTRICAL AND ELECTRONICS ENGINEERING
Anne Arundel Comm Coll (MD)
Caldwell Comm Coll and Tech Inst (NC)
Carroll Comm Coll (MD)
Comm Coll of Baltimore County (MD)
Fiorello H. LaGuardia Comm Coll of the City U of New York (NY)
Humacao Comm Coll (PR)
Montgomery County Comm Coll (PA)
Pasadena City Coll (CA)
Potomac State Coll of West Virginia U (WV)
St. Louis Comm Coll (MO)

## ELECTRICAL AND POWER TRANSMISSION INSTALLATION
Ivy Tech Comm Coll–Columbus (IN)
Minnesota West Comm and Tech Coll (MN)
Mohawk Valley Comm Coll (NY)
Oklahoma State U Inst of Technology (OK)
Oklahoma State U–Oklahoma City (OK)
Piedmont Comm Coll (NC)
Richmond Comm Coll (NC)
San Jacinto Coll District (TX)
State U of New York Coll of Technology at Alfred (NY)

## ELECTRICAL AND POWER TRANSMISSION INSTALLATION RELATED
Minnesota West Comm and Tech Coll (MN)
Oklahoma State U–Oklahoma City (OK)
Vincennes U (IN)

## ELECTRICAL, ELECTRONIC AND COMMUNICATIONS ENGINEERING TECHNOLOGY
Adirondack Comm Coll (NY)
Alamance Comm Coll (NC)
Alvin Comm Coll (TX)
Amarillo Coll (TX)
American Samoa Comm Coll (AS)
Anne Arundel Comm Coll (MD)

Arizona Western Coll (AZ)
Asheville-Buncombe Tech Comm Coll (NC)
Austin Comm Coll District (TX)
Camden County Coll (NJ)
Career Coll of Northern Nevada (NV)
Cayuga County Comm Coll (NY)
Cecil Coll (MD)
Central Ohio Tech Coll (OH)
Central Oregon Comm Coll (OR)
Clark Coll (WA)
Cleveland Comm Coll (NC)
Cleveland State Comm Coll (TN)
Cochise County Comm Coll District (AZ)
Collin County Comm Coll District (TX)
Comm Coll of Allegheny County (PA)
Copiah-Lincoln Comm Coll (MS)
County Coll of Morris (NJ)
Craven Comm Coll (NC)
Crowder Coll (MO)
Dabney S. Lancaster Comm Coll (VA)
Daytona State Coll (FL)
Del Mar Coll (TX)
Des Moines Area Comm Coll (IA)
Dunwoody Coll of Technology (MN)
Dutchess Comm Coll (NY)
Eastern Gateway Comm Coll (OH)
Eastern Shore Comm Coll (VA)
Edison State Comm Coll (OH)
El Paso Comm Coll (TX)
Erie Comm Coll, North Campus (NY)
Fayetteville Tech Comm Coll (NC)
Fox Valley Tech Coll (WI)
Gateway Tech Coll (WI)
George C. Wallace Comm Coll (AL)
Grand Rapids Comm Coll (MI)
Greenville Tech Coll (SC)
Gulf Coast State Coll (FL)
Harper Coll (IL)
Harrisburg Area Comm Coll (PA)
Hawkeye Comm Coll (IA)
Haywood Comm Coll (NC)
Hinds Comm Coll (MS)
Hopkinsville Comm Coll (KY)
Howard Comm Coll (MD)
Hudson County Comm Coll (NJ)
Hutchinson Comm Coll (KS)
Illinois Central Coll (IL)
Illinois Valley Comm Coll (IL)
Iowa Central Comm Coll (IA)
ITI Tech Coll (LA)
Ivy Tech Comm Coll–Bloomington (IN)
Ivy Tech Comm Coll–Central Indiana (IN)
Ivy Tech Comm Coll–Columbus (IN)
Ivy Tech Comm Coll–East Central (IN)
Ivy Tech Comm Coll–Kokomo (IN)
Ivy Tech Comm Coll–Lafayette (IN)
Ivy Tech Comm Coll–North Central (IN)
Ivy Tech Comm Coll–Northeast (IN)
Ivy Tech Comm Coll–Northwest (IN)
Ivy Tech Comm Coll–Richmond (IN)
Ivy Tech Comm Coll–Sellersburg (IN)
Ivy Tech Comm Coll–Southeast (IN)
Ivy Tech Comm Coll–Southwest (IN)
Ivy Tech Comm Coll–Wabash Valley (IN)
Johnson Coll (PA)
Kaskaskia Coll (IL)
Kennebec Valley Comm Coll (ME)
Kirtland Comm Coll (MI)
Kishwaukee Coll (IL)
Lake Area Tech Inst (SD)
Lakeland Comm Coll (OH)
Lakeshore Tech Coll (WI)
Lake Superior Coll (MN)
Lehigh Carbon Comm Coll (PA)
Lorain County Comm Coll (OH)
Macomb Comm Coll (MI)
Massachusetts Bay Comm Coll (MA)
Meridian Comm Coll (MS)
Mesa Comm Coll (AZ)
Miami Dade Coll (FL)
Mid-State Tech Coll (WI)
Minnesota State Comm and Tech Coll (MN)
Mission Coll (CA)
Mitchell Comm Coll (NC)
Mohawk Valley Comm Coll (NY)
Monroe Comm Coll (NY)
Monroe County Comm Coll (MI)
Montgomery County Comm Coll (PA)
Mott Comm Coll (MI)
Mt. San Antonio Coll (CA)
Muskegon Comm Coll (MI)

National Park Coll (AR)
Naugatuck Valley Comm Coll (CT)
New Castle School of Trades (PA)
New Mexico State U–Alamogordo (NM)
New River Comm Coll (VA)
Northampton Comm Coll (PA)
North Central Texas Coll (TX)
Northeastern Tech Coll (SC)
Northeast Iowa Comm Coll (IA)
Northeast State Comm Coll (TN)
Northern Essex Comm Coll (MA)
Northern Maine Comm Coll (ME)
North Iowa Area Comm Coll (IA)
NorthWest Arkansas Comm Coll (AR)
Oakton Comm Coll (IL)
Odessa Coll (TX)
Oklahoma State U–Oklahoma City (OK)
Paris Jr Coll (TX)
Penn State DuBois (PA)
Penn State Fayette, The Eberly Campus (PA)
Pennsylvania Inst of Technology (PA)
Pensacola State Coll (FL)
Pittsburgh Tech Coll (PA)
Pueblo Comm Coll (CO)
Queensborough Comm Coll of the City U of New York (NY)
Quinsigamond Comm Coll (MA)
Reid State Tech Coll (AL)
Richland Coll (TX)
Richmond Comm Coll (NC)
Ridgewater Coll (MN)
Rock Valley Coll (IL)
Rowan-Cabarrus Comm Coll (NC)
Salt Lake Comm Coll (UT)
San Jacinto Coll District (TX)
San Joaquin Delta Coll (CA)
San Juan Coll (NM)
Santa Rosa Jr Coll (CA)
Sauk Valley Comm Coll (IL)
Schenectady County Comm Coll (NY)
Schoolcraft Coll (MI)
Scottsdale Comm Coll (AZ)
Seminole State Coll of Florida (FL)
Sisseton-Wahpeton Coll (SD)
Southeast Tech Inst (SD)
South Suburban Coll (IL)
Southwestern Comm Coll (NC)
Southwest Virginia Comm Coll (VA)
Springfield Tech Comm Coll (MA)
State Tech Coll of Missouri (MO)
State U of New York Coll of Technology at Alfred (NY)
Sullivan County Comm Coll (NY)
Tarrant County Coll District (TX)
Texarkana Coll (TX)
Texas State Tech Coll (TX)
Thaddeus Stevens Coll of Technology (PA)
Three Rivers Comm Coll (CT)
Tidewater Comm Coll (VA)
Tri-County Comm Coll (NC)
Trident Tech Coll (SC)
Tulsa Comm Coll (OK)
Victoria Coll (TX)
Vincennes U (IN)
Waukesha County Tech Coll (WI)
Wayne Comm Coll (NC)
Wayne County Comm Coll District (MI)
Westchester Comm Coll (NY)
Western Wyoming Comm Coll (WY)
Wytheville Comm Coll (VA)

### ELECTRICAL, ELECTRONICS AND COMMUNICATIONS ENGINEERING RELATED
American Samoa Comm Coll (AS)

### ELECTRICAL/ELECTRONICS DRAFTING AND CAD/CADD
Dunwoody Coll of Technology (MN)
Mission Coll (CA)
Palomar Coll (CA)

### ELECTRICAL/ELECTRONICS EQUIPMENT INSTALLATION AND REPAIR
Antelope Valley Coll (CA)
Fullerton Coll (CA)
Hinds Comm Coll (MS)
Hutchinson Comm Coll (KS)
Lakes Region Comm Coll (NH)
Los Angeles City Coll (CA)
Macomb Comm Coll (MI)
Merced Coll (CA)
Orange Coast Coll (CA)
Pittsburgh Tech Coll (PA)

Southeast Tech Inst (SD)
Southwestern Coll (CA)
State Tech Coll of Missouri (MO)
Western Wyoming Comm Coll (WY)

### ELECTRICAL/ELECTRONICS MAINTENANCE AND REPAIR TECHNOLOGY RELATED
Bunker Hill Comm Coll (MA)
Kennebec Valley Comm Coll (ME)
Mohawk Valley Comm Coll (NY)

### ELECTRICIAN
Adirondack Comm Coll (NY)
Antelope Valley Coll (CA)
Asheville-Buncombe Tech Comm Coll (NC)
Bevill State Comm Coll (AL)
Central New Mexico Comm Coll (NM)
Cleveland Comm Coll (NC)
Coll of Business and Technology–Cutler Bay Campus (FL)
Coll of Business and Technology–Flagler Campus (FL)
Coll of Business and Technology–Hialeah Campus (FL)
Coll of Business and Technology–Miami Gardens (FL)
Coll of Eastern Idaho (ID)
Coll of the Ouachitas (AR)
Dunwoody Coll of Technology (MN)
Fayetteville Tech Comm Coll (NC)
George C. Wallace Comm Coll (AL)
Harrisburg Area Comm Coll (PA)
Haywood Comm Coll (NC)
H. Councill Trenholm State Comm Coll (AL)
Hinds Comm Coll (MS)
Illinois Valley Comm Coll (IL)
Ivy Tech Comm Coll–Bloomington (IN)
Ivy Tech Comm Coll–Central Indiana (IN)
Ivy Tech Comm Coll–East Central (IN)
Ivy Tech Comm Coll–Kokomo (IN)
Ivy Tech Comm Coll–Lafayette (IN)
Ivy Tech Comm Coll–North Central (IN)
Ivy Tech Comm Coll–Northeast (IN)
Ivy Tech Comm Coll–Northwest (IN)
Ivy Tech Comm Coll–Richmond (IN)
Ivy Tech Comm Coll–Sellersburg (IN)
Ivy Tech Comm Coll–Southwest (IN)
Ivy Tech Comm Coll–Wabash Valley (IN)
Johnson Coll (PA)
John Tyler Comm Coll (VA)
Kellogg Comm Coll (MI)
Kennebec Valley Comm Coll (ME)
Lake Superior Coll (MN)
Merced Coll (CA)
Miami Dade Coll (FL)
Minnesota West Comm and Tech Coll (MN)
Mitchell Comm Coll (NC)
Mitchell Tech Inst (SD)
Montgomery Comm Coll (NC)
Northampton Comm Coll (PA)
Northeast Comm Coll (NE)
Northeast Iowa Comm Coll (IA)
Northwest Coll (WY)
Palomar Coll (CA)
Panola Coll (TX)
Piedmont Comm Coll (NC)
Randolph Comm Coll (NC)
Ridgewater Coll (MN)
Rock Valley Coll (IL)
Rowan-Cabarrus Comm Coll (NC)
St. Philip's Coll (TX)
Southcentral Kentucky Comm and Tech Coll (KY)
Southeast Tech Inst (SD)
Southwestern Comm Coll (IA)
State Tech Coll of Missouri (MO)
Vincennes U (IN)
Western Dakota Tech Inst (SD)
Western Iowa Tech Comm Coll (IA)
Western Wyoming Comm Coll (WY)
West Kentucky Comm and Tech Coll (KY)

### ELECTROCARDIOGRAPH TECHNOLOGY
Oklahoma State U–Oklahoma City (OK)
Orange Coast Coll (CA)

### ELECTROMECHANICAL AND INSTRUMENTATION AND

### MAINTENANCE TECHNOLOGIES RELATED
Asheville-Buncombe Tech Comm Coll (NC)
Fayetteville Tech Comm Coll (NC)
Greenville Tech Coll (SC)
Halifax Comm Coll (NC)
Haywood Comm Coll (NC)
Hinds Comm Coll (MS)
Lenoir Comm Coll (NC)
Mitchell Comm Coll (NC)
Montgomery Comm Coll (NC)
Piedmont Comm Coll (NC)
Pueblo Comm Coll (CO)
Richmond Comm Coll (NC)
Wayne Comm Coll (NC)

### ELECTROMECHANICAL TECHNOLOGY
Bristol Comm Coll (MA)
Camden County Coll (NJ)
Central Maine Comm Coll (ME)
Chandler-Gilbert Comm Coll (AZ)
Chippewa Valley Tech Coll (WI)
Cleveland State Comm Coll (TN)
Coll of the Ouachitas (AR)
Craven Comm Coll (NC)
Edison State Comm Coll (OH)
Fox Valley Tech Coll (WI)
Galveston Coll (TX)
Gateway Tech Coll (WI)
Hawkeye Comm Coll (IA)
Kirtland Comm Coll (MI)
Lakeshore Tech Coll (WI)
Macomb Comm Coll (MI)
Maysville Comm and Tech Coll, Maysville (KY)
Mesa Comm Coll (AZ)
Muskegon Comm Coll (MI)
Northampton Comm Coll (PA)
Northcentral Tech Coll (WI)
Northeast Comm Coll (NE)
Paris Jr Coll (TX)
Quinsigamond Comm Coll (MA)
Randolph Comm Coll (NC)
Richmond Comm Coll (NC)
Ridgewater Coll (MN)
Southcentral Kentucky Comm and Tech Coll (KY)
Southeast Tech Inst (SD)
Springfield Tech Comm Coll (MA)
Tarrant County Coll District (TX)
Texas State Tech Coll (TX)
Tyler Jr Coll (TX)
Union County Coll (NJ)
Volunteer State Comm Coll (TN)

### ELECTRONEURODIAGNOSTIC/ ELECTROENCEPHALOGRAPHIC TECHNOLOGY
Alvin Comm Coll (TX)
Collin County Comm Coll District (TX)
Comm Coll of Allegheny County (PA)
Fox Valley Tech Coll (WI)
Harford Comm Coll (MD)
Orange Coast Coll (CA)
Southeast Tech Inst (SD)

### ELEMENTARY EDUCATION
Amarillo Coll (TX)
American Samoa Comm Coll (AS)
Ancilla Coll (IN)
Arizona Western Coll (AZ)
Asheville-Buncombe Tech Comm Coll (NC)
Barton County Comm Coll (KS)
Bristol Comm Coll (MA)
Carl Albert State Coll (OK)
Carroll Comm Coll (MD)
Cecil Coll (MD)
Chandler-Gilbert Comm Coll (AZ)
Chesapeake Coll (MD)
Cleveland Comm Coll (NC)
Cochise County Comm Coll District (AZ)
Coll of Central Florida (FL)
Comm Coll of Allegheny County (PA)
Comm Coll of Baltimore County (MD)
Copiah-Lincoln Comm Coll (MS)
Craven Comm Coll (NC)
Crowder Coll (MO)
Del Mar Coll (TX)
Eastern Arizona Coll (AZ)
Fayetteville Tech Comm Coll (NC)
Frederick Comm Coll (MD)
Genesee Comm Coll (NY)
Grand Rapids Comm Coll (MI)
Hagerstown Comm Coll (MD)
Harford Comm Coll (MD)
Harper Coll (IL)
Haywood Comm Coll (NC)

Hill Coll (TX)
Howard Comm Coll (MD)
Illinois Valley Comm Coll (IL)
James Sprunt Comm Coll (NC)
Kellogg Comm Coll (MI)
Kingsborough Comm Coll of the City U of New York (NY)
Manor Coll (PA)
Massachusetts Bay Comm Coll (MA)
Mesa Comm Coll (AZ)
Miami Dade Coll (FL)
Missouri State U–West Plains (MO)
Mitchell Comm Coll (NC)
Monroe County Comm Coll (MI)
Montgomery Coll (MD)
Montgomery County Comm Coll (PA)
Mount Wachusett Comm Coll (MA)
Muskegon Comm Coll (MI)
National Park Coll (AR)
Navarro Coll (TX)
Niagara County Comm Coll (NY)
Northeast Comm Coll (NE)
Northeastern Jr Coll (CO)
Northern Essex Comm Coll (MA)
Northwest Coll (WY)
Orange Coast Coll (CA)
Otero Jr Coll (CO)
Paris Jr Coll (TX)
Pensacola State Coll (FL)
Potomac State Coll of West Virginia U (WV)
Quinsigamond Comm Coll (MA)
Richmond Comm Coll (NC)
Rowan-Cabarrus Comm Coll (NC)
San Juan Coll (NM)
Sauk Valley Comm Coll (IL)
Seminole State Coll (OK)
Springfield Tech Comm Coll (MA)
Sullivan County Comm Coll (NY)
Treasure Valley Comm Coll (OR)
Trinity Valley Comm Coll (TX)
Truckee Meadows Comm Coll (NV)
Vincennes U (IN)
Wayne Comm Coll (NC)
Wayne County Comm Coll District (MI)
Western Wyoming Comm Coll (WY)
Wor-Wic Comm Coll (MD)

### EMERGENCY CARE ATTENDANT (EMT AMBULANCE)
Barton County Comm Coll (KS)
Hudson County Comm Coll (NJ)
Illinois Eastern Comm Colls, Frontier Community College (IL)
Mohawk Valley Comm Coll (NY)

### EMERGENCY MEDICAL TECHNOLOGY (EMT PARAMEDIC)
Alvin Comm Coll (TX)
Amarillo Coll (TX)
Arizona Western Coll (AZ)
Arkansas State U–Newport (AR)
Asheville-Buncombe Tech Comm Coll (NC)
Austin Comm Coll District (TX)
Barton County Comm Coll (KS)
Bevill State Comm Coll (AL)
Black Hawk Coll, Moline (IL)
Blue Ridge Comm and Tech Coll (WV)
Bossier Parish Comm Coll (LA)
Brookhaven Coll (TX)
Bunker Hill Comm Coll (MA)
Caldwell Comm Coll and Tech Inst (NC)
Camden County Coll (NJ)
Carroll Comm Coll (MD)
Carteret Comm Coll (NC)
Cecil Coll (MD)
Central New Mexico Comm Coll (NM)
Central Ohio Tech Coll (OH)
Central Oregon Comm Coll (OR)
Central Texas Coll (TX)
Central Virginia Comm Coll (VA)
Century Coll (MN)
Chesapeake Coll (MD)
Chippewa Valley Tech Coll (WI)
Clark Coll (WA)
Cleveland Comm Coll (NC)
Cleveland State Comm Coll (TN)
Cochise County Comm Coll District (AZ)
Coll of Central Florida (FL)
Collin County Comm Coll District (TX)
Colorado Northwestern Comm Coll (CO)
Comm Coll of Allegheny County (PA)
Comm Coll of Baltimore County (MD)

Crowder Coll (MO)
Daytona State Coll (FL)
Del Mar Coll (TX)
Dutchess Comm Coll (NY)
Dyersburg State Comm Coll (TN)
East Central Coll (MO)
Eastern Arizona Coll (AZ)
Eastern Gateway Comm Coll (OH)
El Paso Comm Coll (TX)
Erie Comm Coll, South Campus (NY)
Fayetteville Tech Comm Coll (NC)
Fiorello H. LaGuardia Comm Coll of the City U of New York (NY)
Frederick Comm Coll (MD)
Galveston Coll (TX)
Gateway Tech Coll (WI)
George C. Wallace Comm Coll (AL)
Great Falls Coll Montana State U (MT)
Greenville Tech Coll (SC)
Gulf Coast State Coll (FL)
Hagerstown Comm Coll (MD)
Harper Coll (IL)
Harrisburg Area Comm Coll (PA)
Hawkeye Comm Coll (IA)
H. Councill Trenholm State Comm Coll (AL)
Highland Comm Coll (IL)
Hill Coll (TX)
Hinds Comm Coll (MS)
Houston Comm Coll (TX)
Howard Comm Coll (MD)
Hudson County Comm Coll (NJ)
Hutchinson Comm Coll (KS)
Illinois Central Coll (IL)
Ivy Tech Comm Coll–Bloomington (IN)
Ivy Tech Comm Coll–Columbus (IN)
Ivy Tech Comm Coll–Kokomo (IN)
Ivy Tech Comm Coll–North Central (IN)
Ivy Tech Comm Coll–Richmond (IN)
Ivy Tech Comm Coll–Southwest (IN)
Ivy Tech Comm Coll–Wabash Valley (IN)
Jefferson Comm Coll (NY)
Jefferson State Comm Coll (AL)
John Tyler Comm Coll (VA)
J. Sargeant Reynolds Comm Coll (VA)
Kaskaskia Coll (IL)
Kellogg Comm Coll (MI)
Kennebec Valley Comm Coll (ME)
Kent State U at Trumbull (OH)
Kingsborough Comm Coll of the City U of New York (NY)
Kirtland Comm Coll (MI)
Kishwaukee Coll (IL)
Lackawanna Coll (PA)
Lake Area Tech Inst (SD)
Laramie County Comm Coll (WY)
Lenoir Comm Coll (NC)
Lurleen B. Wallace Comm Coll (AL)
Macomb Comm Coll (MI)
McHenry County Coll (IL)
Merced Coll (CA)
Meridian Comm Coll (MS)
Mesa Comm Coll (AZ)
Miami Dade Coll (FL)
Mohave Comm Coll (AZ)
Mott Comm Coll (MI)
Mt. San Antonio Coll (CA)
National Park Coll (AR)
New Mexico State U–Alamogordo (NM)
Northcentral Tech Coll (WI)
North Central Texas Coll (TX)
North Dakota State Coll of Science (ND)
Northeast Comm Coll (NE)
Northeastern Jr Coll (CO)
Northeast Iowa Comm Coll (IA)
Northeast State Comm Coll (TN)
Northern Essex Comm Coll (MA)
Northern Maine Comm Coll (ME)
North Iowa Area Comm Coll (IA)
Northland Comm and Tech Coll (MN)
NorthWest Arkansas Comm Coll (AR)
Northwest-Shoals Comm Coll (AL)
Odessa Coll (TX)
Oklahoma City Comm Coll (OK)
Oklahoma State U–Oklahoma City (OK)
Owensboro Comm and Tech Coll (KY)
Ozarks Tech Comm Coll (MO)
Palomar Coll (CA)
Paris Jr Coll (TX)

Pennsylvania Highlands Comm Coll (PA)
Pensacola State Coll (FL)
Piedmont Virginia Comm Coll (VA)
Pueblo Comm Coll (CO)
Quinsigamond Comm Coll (MA)
Rend Lake Coll (IL)
St. Charles Comm Coll (MO)
St. Louis Comm Coll (MO)
San Jacinto Coll District (TX)
San Juan Coll (NM)
Santa Rosa Jr Coll (CA)
Schoolcraft Coll (MI)
Seminole State Coll of Florida (FL)
Somerset Comm Coll (KY)
Southeast Arkansas Coll (AR)
Southeastern Coll–West Palm Beach (FL)
South Florida State Coll (FL)
Southwestern Coll (CA)
Southwestern Comm Coll (NC)
Southwest Virginia Comm Coll (VA)
Tallahassee Comm Coll (FL)
Tarrant County Coll District (TX)
Texarkana Coll (TX)
Three Rivers Coll (MO)
Trinity Valley Comm Coll (TX)
Tyler Jr Coll (TX)
Union County Coll (NJ)
Victoria Coll (TX)
Vincennes U (IN)
Waukesha County Tech Coll (WI)
Wayne County Comm Coll District (MI)
Westchester Comm Coll (NY)
Western Dakota Tech Inst (SD)
Western Iowa Tech Comm Coll (IA)
West Kentucky Comm and Tech Coll (KY)
Wisconsin Indianhead Tech Coll (WI)
Wor-Wic Comm Coll (MD)

## ENERGY MANAGEMENT AND SYSTEMS TECHNOLOGY
Century Coll (MN)
Comm Coll of Allegheny County (PA)
Crowder Coll (MO)
Danville Area Comm Coll (IL)
Fiorello H. LaGuardia Comm Coll of the City U of New York (NY)
Front Range Comm Coll (CO)
Gateway Comm and Tech Coll (KY)
Hawkeye Comm Coll (IA)
Houston Comm Coll (TX)
Illinois Central Coll (IL)
Illinois Eastern Comm Colls, Wabash Valley College (IL)
Ivy Tech Comm Coll–East Central (IN)
Ivy Tech Comm Coll–Sellersburg (IN)
Ivy Tech Comm Coll–Southwest (IN)
Ivy Tech Comm Coll–Wabash Valley (IN)
Lakeland Comm Coll (OH)
Lamar Comm Coll (CO)
Laramie County Comm Coll (WY)
Lenoir Comm Coll (NC)
Lorain County Comm Coll (OH)
Macomb Comm Coll (MI)
Minnesota West Comm and Tech Coll (MN)
Mitchell Tech Inst (SD)
Northeast Comm Coll (NE)
Northeast Iowa Comm Coll (IA)
Oklahoma State U–Oklahoma City (OK)
Quinsigamond Comm Coll (MA)
Rock Valley Coll (IL)
Truckee Meadows Comm Coll (NV)
Walters State Comm Coll (TN)
Wayne Comm Coll (NC)
Western Iowa Tech Comm Coll (IA)

## ENGINEERING
Adirondack Comm Coll (NY)
Amarillo Coll (TX)
Anne Arundel Comm Coll (MD)
Arizona Western Coll (AZ)
Austin Comm Coll District (TX)
Bossier Parish Comm Coll (LA)
Bristol Comm Coll (MA)
Bucks County Comm Coll (PA)
Bunker Hill Comm Coll (MA)
Carl Albert State Coll (OK)
Central Lakes Coll (MN)
Central Oregon Comm Coll (OR)
Central Texas Coll (TX)
Central Virginia Comm Coll (VA)
Cochise County Comm Coll District (AZ)

Coll of Central Florida (FL)
Coll of Marin (CA)
Collin County Comm Coll District (TX)
Comm Coll of Baltimore County (MD)
Comm Coll of Philadelphia (PA)
Copiah-Lincoln Comm Coll (MS)
Danville Area Comm Coll (IL)
De Anza Coll (CA)
Dutchess Comm Coll (NY)
East Central Coll (MO)
El Paso Comm Coll (TX)
Erie Comm Coll, North Campus (NY)
Frederick Comm Coll (MD)
Fullerton Coll (CA)
Genesee Comm Coll (NY)
Gordon State Coll (GA)
Grand Rapids Comm Coll (MI)
Hagerstown Comm Coll (MD)
Harford Comm Coll (MD)
Harper Coll (IL)
Harrisburg Area Comm Coll (PA)
Highland Comm Coll (IL)
Hill Coll (TX)
Holyoke Comm Coll (MA)
Howard Comm Coll (MD)
Hutchinson Comm Coll (KS)
Illinois Central Coll (IL)
Illinois Eastern Comm Colls, Frontier Community College (IL)
Illinois Eastern Comm Colls, Olney Central College (IL)
Illinois Eastern Comm Colls, Wabash Valley College (IL)
Illinois Valley Comm Coll (IL)
Jamestown Comm Coll (NY)
Jefferson Comm Coll (NY)
John Tyler Comm Coll (VA)
J. Sargeant Reynolds Comm Coll (VA)
Kaskaskia Coll (IL)
Kishwaukee Coll (IL)
Laramie County Comm Coll (WY)
Lehigh Carbon Comm Coll (PA)
Los Angeles City Coll (CA)
McHenry County Coll (IL)
Miami Dade Coll (FL)
Missouri State U–West Plains (MO)
Mohawk Valley Comm Coll (NY)
Montgomery Coll (MD)
Nassau Comm Coll (NY)
Navarro Coll (TX)
New River Comm Coll (VA)
Northampton Comm Coll (PA)
Northeast Comm Coll (NE)
Northwest Coll (WY)
Oakton Comm Coll (IL)
Oklahoma City Comm Coll (OK)
Ozarks Tech Comm Coll (MO)
Paris Jr Coll (TX)
Pensacola State Coll (FL)
Piedmont Virginia Comm Coll (VA)
Queensborough Comm Coll of the City U of New York (NY)
Rend Lake Coll (IL)
Richland Coll (TX)
St. Philip's Coll (TX)
Salt Lake Comm Coll (UT)
San Jacinto Coll District (TX)
San Joaquin Delta Coll (CA)
San Juan Coll (NM)
Santa Rosa Jr Coll (CA)
Schoolcraft Coll (MI)
Seminole State Coll (OK)
Southwestern Coll (CA)
Southwestern Indian Polytechnic Inst (NM)
Southwest Texas Jr Coll (TX)
Springfield Tech Comm Coll (MA)
State U of New York Coll of Technology at Alfred (NY)
Texarkana Coll (TX)
Tidewater Comm Coll (VA)
Tompkins Cortland Comm Coll (NY)
Truckee Meadows Comm Coll (NV)
Tyler Jr Coll (TX)
Union County Coll (NJ)
U of Wisconsin–Baraboo/Sauk County (WI)
U of Wisconsin–Barron County (WI)
U of Wisconsin–Fond du Lac (WI)
U of Wisconsin–Fox Valley (WI)
U of Wisconsin–Manitowoc (WI)
U of Wisconsin–Marathon County (WI)
U of Wisconsin–Marinette (WI)
U of Wisconsin–Marshfield/Wood County (WI)
U of Wisconsin–Richland (WI)

U of Wisconsin–Rock County (WI)
U of Wisconsin–Sheboygan (WI)
U of Wisconsin–Washington County (WI)
U of Wisconsin–Waukesha (WI)
Westchester Comm Coll (NY)
Western Texas Coll (TX)

## ENGINEERING/INDUSTRIAL MANAGEMENT
LDS Business Coll (UT)
Mitchell Comm Coll (NC)

## ENGINEERING RELATED
Bristol Comm Coll (MA)
Macomb Comm Coll (MI)
Miami Dade Coll (FL)
San Joaquin Delta Coll (CA)

## ENGINEERING-RELATED TECHNOLOGIES
Chesapeake Coll (MD)
Thaddeus Stevens Coll of Technology (PA)
Tulsa Comm Coll (OK)
Wayne County Comm Coll District (MI)

## ENGINEERING SCIENCE
Bristol Comm Coll (MA)
Camden County Coll (NJ)
Comm Coll of Allegheny County (PA)
County Coll of Morris (NJ)
Genesee Comm Coll (NY)
Houston Comm Coll (TX)
Hudson County Comm Coll (NJ)
Jefferson Comm Coll (NY)
Kingsborough Comm Coll of the City U of New York (NY)
Manchester Comm Coll (CT)
Monroe Comm Coll (NY)
Montgomery County Comm Coll (PA)
Naugatuck Valley Comm Coll (CT)
Northern Essex Comm Coll (MA)
North Shore Comm Coll (MA)
Queensborough Comm Coll of the City U of New York (NY)
Raritan Valley Comm Coll (NJ)
St. Louis Comm Coll (MO)
Three Rivers Comm Coll (CT)
Vincennes U (IN)

## ENGINEERING TECHNOLOGIES AND ENGINEERING RELATED
Bristol Comm Coll (MA)
Camden County Coll (NJ)
Carl Albert State Coll (OK)
Chesapeake Coll (MD)
Coll of the Desert (CA)
Comm Coll of Allegheny County (PA)
Comm Coll of Baltimore County (MD)
County Coll of Morris (NJ)
Hagerstown Comm Coll (MD)
Harford Comm Coll (MD)
Harrisburg Area Comm Coll (PA)
Massachusetts Bay Comm Coll (MA)
Mesalands Comm Coll (NM)
Montgomery County Comm Coll (PA)
Mott Comm Coll (MI)
Orange Coast Coll (CA)
Pennsylvania Highlands Comm Coll (PA)
Raritan Valley Comm Coll (NJ)
Truckee Meadows Comm Coll (NV)
Union County Coll (NJ)

## ENGINEERING TECHNOLOGY
Antelope Valley Coll (CA)
Barton County Comm Coll (KS)
Bucks County Comm Coll (PA)
Central Virginia Comm Coll (VA)
Century Coll (MN)
Cleveland State Comm Coll (TN)
Coll of Central Florida (FL)
Coll of Marin (CA)
Comm Coll of Philadelphia (PA)
Daytona State Coll (FL)
De Anza Coll (CA)
Gateway Comm and Tech Coll (KY)
Gulf Coast State Coll (FL)
Ivy Tech Comm Coll–Bloomington (IN)
Ivy Tech Comm Coll–Columbus (IN)
Ivy Tech Comm Coll–East Central (IN)
Ivy Tech Comm Coll–Kokomo (IN)
Ivy Tech Comm Coll–Richmond (IN)
Ivy Tech Comm Coll–Sellersburg (IN)
Ivy Tech Comm Coll–Southwest (IN)

Ivy Tech Comm Coll–Wabash Valley (IN)
Jefferson State Comm Coll (AL)
Massachusetts Bay Comm Coll (MA)
Maysville Comm and Tech Coll, Maysville (KY)
Merced Coll (CA)
Miami Dade Coll (FL)
Morrison Inst of Technology (IL)
Mt. San Antonio Coll (CA)
Muskegon Comm Coll (MI)
Naugatuck Valley Comm Coll (CT)
North Central Texas Coll (TX)
Oklahoma City Comm Coll (OK)
Oklahoma State U Inst of Technology (OK)
Oklahoma State U–Oklahoma City (OK)
Pasadena City Coll (CA)
Pennsylvania Inst of Technology (PA)
Pensacola State Coll (FL)
Pueblo Comm Coll (CO)
Rappahannock Comm Coll (VA)
Salt Lake Comm Coll (UT)
San Joaquin Delta Coll (CA)
San Juan Coll (NM)
Somerset Comm Coll (KY)
Southcentral Kentucky Comm and Tech Coll (KY)
South Florida State Coll (FL)
Southwestern Michigan Coll (MI)
Three Rivers Comm Coll (CT)
Trident Tech Coll (SC)
Western Wyoming Comm Coll (WY)

## ENGINE MACHINIST
Lake Area Tech Inst (SD)
Tri-County Comm Coll (NC)

## ENGLISH
Amarillo Coll (TX)
Ancilla Coll (IN)
Antelope Valley Coll (CA)
Arizona Western Coll (AZ)
Austin Comm Coll District (TX)
Barton County Comm Coll (KS)
Bucks County Comm Coll (PA)
Bunker Hill Comm Coll (MA)
Carl Albert State Coll (OK)
Central New Mexico Comm Coll (NM)
Cochise County Comm Coll District (AZ)
Coll of Central Florida (FL)
Coll of Marin (CA)
Coll of the Canyons (CA)
Coll of the Desert (CA)
Comm Coll of Allegheny County (PA)
Comm Coll of Philadelphia (PA)
Copiah-Lincoln Comm Coll (MS)
De Anza Coll (CA)
Del Mar Coll (TX)
Edison State Comm Coll (OH)
Feather River Coll (CA)
Fiorello H. LaGuardia Comm Coll of the City U of New York (NY)
Fullerton Coll (CA)
Galveston Coll (TX)
Georgia Military Coll (GA)
Grand Rapids Comm Coll (MI)
Harford Comm Coll (MD)
Harper Coll (IL)
Hill Coll (TX)
Houston Comm Coll (TX)
Hutchinson Comm Coll (KS)
Illinois Valley Comm Coll (IL)
Independence Comm Coll (KS)
Laramie County Comm Coll (WY)
Los Angeles City Coll (CA)
Massachusetts Bay Comm Coll (MA)
Merced Coll (CA)
Miami Dade Coll (FL)
Mohave Comm Coll (AZ)
Monroe County Comm Coll (MI)
Navarro Coll (TX)
Northeast Comm Coll (NE)
Northeastern Jr Coll (CO)
Northwest Coll (WY)
Odessa Coll (TX)
Palomar Coll (CA)
Panola Coll (TX)
Paris Jr Coll (TX)
Pensacola State Coll (FL)
Potomac State Coll of West Virginia U (WV)
Quinsigamond Comm Coll (MA)
Raritan Valley Comm Coll (NJ)
St. Philip's Coll (TX)
Salt Lake Comm Coll (UT)
San Jacinto Coll District (TX)

San Joaquin Delta Coll (CA)
Santa Rosa Jr Coll (CA)
Sauk Valley Comm Coll (IL)
Seminole State Coll (OK)
Southwestern Coll (CA)
Trinity Valley Comm Coll (TX)
Truckee Meadows Comm Coll (NV)
Union County Coll (NJ)
U of Wisconsin–Baraboo/Sauk County (WI)
U of Wisconsin–Barron County (WI)
U of Wisconsin–Fond du Lac (WI)
U of Wisconsin–Fox Valley (WI)
U of Wisconsin–Manitowoc (WI)
U of Wisconsin–Marathon County (WI)
U of Wisconsin–Marinette (WI)
U of Wisconsin–Marshfield/Wood County (WI)
U of Wisconsin–Richland (WI)
U of Wisconsin–Rock County (WI)
U of Wisconsin–Sheboygan (WI)
U of Wisconsin–Washington County (WI)
U of Wisconsin–Waukesha (WI)
Vincennes U (IN)
Western Wyoming Comm Coll (WY)

**ENGLISH AS A SECOND/FOREIGN LANGUAGE (TEACHING)**
Gordon State Coll (GA)

**ENGLISH LANGUAGE AND LITERATURE RELATED**
Mt. San Antonio Coll (CA)

**ENGLISH/LANGUAGE ARTS TEACHER EDUCATION**
Anne Arundel Comm Coll (MD)
Carroll Comm Coll (MD)
Cecil Coll (MD)
Chesapeake Coll (MD)
Comm Coll of Baltimore County (MD)
Hagerstown Comm Coll (MD)
Harford Comm Coll (MD)
Montgomery Coll (MD)

**ENTREPRENEURIAL AND SMALL BUSINESS RELATED**
LDS Business Coll (UT)
Truckee Meadows Comm Coll (NV)

**ENTREPRENEURSHIP**
Anne Arundel Comm Coll (MD)
Bristol Comm Coll (MA)
Bunker Hill Comm Coll (MA)
Cayuga County Comm Coll (NY)
Central Oregon Comm Coll (OR)
Cleveland Comm Coll (NC)
Comm Coll of Allegheny County (PA)
Craven Comm Coll (NC)
Genesee Comm Coll (NY)
Harford Comm Coll (MD)
Haywood Comm Coll (NC)
Independence Comm Coll (KS)
Laramie County Comm Coll (WY)
LDS Business Coll (UT)
Lorain County Comm Coll (OH)
Miami Dade Coll (FL)
Mott Comm Coll (MI)
Nassau Comm Coll (NY)
Northcentral Tech Coll (WI)
North Dakota State Coll of Science (ND)
North Hennepin Comm Coll (MN)
North Iowa Area Comm Coll (IA)
Richmond Comm Coll (NC)
Salt Lake Comm Coll (UT)
Tallahassee Comm Coll (FL)
Tompkins Cortland Comm Coll (NY)

**ENVIRONMENTAL BIOLOGY**
Eastern Arizona Coll (AZ)

**ENVIRONMENTAL CONTROL TECHNOLOGIES RELATED**
Holyoke Comm Coll (MA)
Massachusetts Bay Comm Coll (MA)
Westchester Comm Coll (NY)
Western Dakota Tech Inst (SD)

**ENVIRONMENTAL DESIGN/ARCHITECTURE**
Central New Mexico Comm Coll (NM)
Queensborough Comm Coll of the City U of New York (NY)
Scottsdale Comm Coll (AZ)

**ENVIRONMENTAL ENGINEERING TECHNOLOGY**
Austin Comm Coll District (TX)

Bristol Comm Coll (MA)
Comm Coll of Allegheny County (PA)
Crowder Coll (MO)
El Paso Comm Coll (TX)
Erie Comm Coll, North Campus (NY)
Harford Comm Coll (MD)
Kent State U at Trumbull (OH)
Miami Dade Coll (FL)
Naugatuck Valley Comm Coll (CT)
Northwest-Shoals Comm Coll (AL)
Queensborough Comm Coll of the City U of New York (NY)
Salt Lake Comm Coll (UT)
Schoolcraft Coll (MI)
State U of New York Coll of Technology at Alfred (NY)
Texas State Tech Coll (TX)
Three Rivers Comm Coll (CT)

**ENVIRONMENTAL/ENVIRONMENTAL HEALTH ENGINEERING**
Coll of the Desert (CA)

**ENVIRONMENTAL HEALTH**
Amarillo Coll (TX)
Queensborough Comm Coll of the City U of New York (NY)
St. Charles Comm Coll (MO)
Three Rivers Coll (MO)

**ENVIRONMENTAL SCIENCE**
Arizona Western Coll (AZ)
Austin Comm Coll District (TX)
Bucks County Comm Coll (PA)
Central Texas Coll (TX)
Chesapeake Coll (MD)
Coll of the Desert (CA)
Daytona State Coll (FL)
Erie Comm Coll, North Campus (NY)
Fiorello H. LaGuardia Comm Coll of the City U of New York (NY)
Gordon State Coll (GA)
Harrisburg Area Comm Coll (PA)
Humacao Comm Coll (PR)
Jamestown Comm Coll (NY)
Lackawanna Coll (PA)
Lake Area Tech Inst (SD)
Lehigh Carbon Comm Coll (PA)
Miami Dade Coll (FL)
Northampton Comm Coll (PA)
NorthWest Arkansas Comm Coll (AR)
The Ohio State U Ag Tech Inst (OH)
Ozarks Tech Comm Coll (MO)
Quinsigamond Comm Coll (MA)
San Jacinto Coll District (TX)
Tallahassee Comm Coll (FL)
Truckee Meadows Comm Coll (NV)
Tulsa Comm Coll (OK)
Westchester Comm Coll (NY)
Western Wyoming Comm Coll (WY)

**ENVIRONMENTAL STUDIES**
Ancilla Coll (IN)
Bristol Comm Coll (MA)
Coll of Central Florida (FL)
Coll of the Desert (CA)
Columbia-Greene Comm Coll (NY)
De Anza Coll (CA)
Feather River Coll (CA)
Fullerton Coll (CA)
Harford Comm Coll (MD)
Harper Coll (IL)
Howard Comm Coll (MD)
Hudson County Comm Coll (NJ)
Minnesota State Comm and Tech Coll (MN)
Monroe Comm Coll (NY)
Montgomery County Comm Coll (PA)
Mt. San Antonio Coll (CA)
Mount Wachusett Comm Coll (MA)
Santa Rosa Jr Coll (CA)
Southwestern Comm Coll (NC)
Sullivan County Comm Coll (NY)
Tompkins Cortland Comm Coll (NY)
Vincennes U (IN)
Westchester Comm Coll (NY)
White Mountains Comm Coll (NH)

**EQUESTRIAN STUDIES**
Black Hawk Coll, Moline (IL)
Cochise County Comm Coll District (AZ)
Coll of Central Florida (FL)
Colorado Northwestern Comm Coll (CO)
Highland Comm Coll (IL)
Laramie County Comm Coll (WY)
Minnesota State Comm and Tech Coll (MN)
North Central Texas Coll (TX)

Northeastern Jr Coll (CO)
Northwest Coll (WY)
The Ohio State U Ag Tech Inst (OH)
Scottsdale Comm Coll (AZ)

**ETHNIC, CULTURAL MINORITY, GENDER, AND GROUP STUDIES RELATED**
Coll of Marin (CA)
Fullerton Coll (CA)
New Mexico State U–Alamogordo (NM)
Southwestern Coll (CA)

**EXECUTIVE ASSISTANT/EXECUTIVE SECRETARY**
Alamance Comm Coll (NC)
Alvin Comm Coll (TX)
Brookhaven Coll (TX)
Cedar Valley Coll (TX)
Clark Coll (WA)
Crowder Coll (MO)
Danville Area Comm Coll (IL)
Edison State Comm Coll (OH)
Hawkeye Comm Coll (IA)
Hopkinsville Comm Coll (KY)
Humacao Comm Coll (PR)
Illinois Eastern Comm Colls, Frontier Community College (IL)
Illinois Eastern Comm Colls, Wabash Valley College (IL)
Ivy Tech Comm Coll–Bloomington (IN)
Ivy Tech Comm Coll–Central Indiana (IN)
Ivy Tech Comm Coll–Columbus (IN)
Ivy Tech Comm Coll–East Central (IN)
Ivy Tech Comm Coll–Kokomo (IN)
Ivy Tech Comm Coll–Lafayette (IN)
Ivy Tech Comm Coll–North Central (IN)
Ivy Tech Comm Coll–Northeast (IN)
Ivy Tech Comm Coll–Northwest (IN)
Ivy Tech Comm Coll–Richmond (IN)
Ivy Tech Comm Coll–Sellersburg (IN)
Ivy Tech Comm Coll–Southeast (IN)
Ivy Tech Comm Coll–Southwest (IN)
Ivy Tech Comm Coll–Wabash Valley (IN)
Kaskaskia Coll (IL)
Maysville Comm and Tech Coll, Maysville (KY)
Mitchell Comm Coll (NC)
Owensboro Comm and Tech Coll (KY)
Quinsigamond Comm Coll (MA)
Shawnee Comm Coll (IL)
Somerset Comm Coll (KY)
South Suburban Coll (IL)
Thaddeus Stevens Coll of Technology (PA)

**FAMILY AND COMMUNITY SERVICES**
Merced Coll (CA)
Palomar Coll (CA)

**FAMILY AND CONSUMER ECONOMICS RELATED**
American Samoa Comm Coll (AS)

**FAMILY AND CONSUMER SCIENCES/HOME ECONOMICS TEACHER EDUCATION**
Copiah-Lincoln Comm Coll (MS)
Vincennes U (IN)

**FAMILY AND CONSUMER SCIENCES/HUMAN SCIENCES**
Antelope Valley Coll (CA)
Arizona Western Coll (AZ)
Coll of Central Florida (FL)
Hill Coll (TX)
Hutchinson Comm Coll (KS)
Monroe Comm Coll (NY)
Mt. San Antonio Coll (CA)
Orange Coast Coll (CA)
Palomar Coll (CA)
San Joaquin Delta Coll (CA)
Tyler Jr Coll (TX)
Vincennes U (IN)

**FAMILY SYSTEMS**
Maysville Comm and Tech Coll, Maysville (KY)

**FARM AND RANCH MANAGEMENT**
Central Texas Coll (TX)
Copiah-Lincoln Comm Coll (MS)
Crowder Coll (MO)

Hutchinson Comm Coll (KS)
North Central Texas Coll (TX)
Northeast Comm Coll (NE)
Northeastern Jr Coll (CO)
Northwest Coll (WY)
Panola Coll (TX)
Southwest Texas Jr Coll (TX)
Treasure Valley Comm Coll (OR)
Trinity Valley Comm Coll (TX)

**FASHION AND FABRIC CONSULTING**
Harper Coll (IL)

**FASHION/APPAREL DESIGN**
El Paso Comm Coll (TX)
Fashion Inst of Technology (NY)
FIDM/Fashion Inst of Design & Merchandising, Orange County Campus (CA)
FIDM/Fashion Inst of Design & Merchandising, San Diego Campus (CA)
Fullerton Coll (CA)
Genesee Comm Coll (NY)
Harper Coll (IL)
Houston Comm Coll (TX)
Lehigh Carbon Comm Coll (PA)
Monroe Comm Coll (NY)
Nassau Comm Coll (NY)
Orange Coast Coll (CA)
Palomar Coll (CA)
Pasadena City Coll (CA)
Santa Rosa Jr Coll (CA)
Wade Coll (TX)

**FASHION MERCHANDISING**
Alexandria Tech and Comm Coll (MN)
Fashion Inst of Technology (NY)
FIDM/Fashion Inst of Design & Merchandising, Orange County Campus (CA)
FIDM/Fashion Inst of Design & Merchandising, San Diego Campus (CA)
Genesee Comm Coll (NY)
Grand Rapids Comm Coll (MI)
Harper Coll (IL)
Hinds Comm Coll (MS)
Houston Comm Coll (TX)
Kingsborough Comm Coll of the City U of New York (NY)
Minnesota State Comm and Tech Coll (MN)
Monroe Comm Coll (NY)
Mt. San Antonio Coll (CA)
Nassau Comm Coll (NY)
Pasadena City Coll (CA)
San Joaquin Delta Coll (CA)
Santa Rosa Jr Coll (CA)
Scottsdale Comm Coll (AZ)
Tarrant County Coll District (TX)
Trinity Valley Comm Coll (TX)
Vincennes U (IN)
Wayne County Comm Coll District (MI)

**FASHION MODELING**
Fashion Inst of Technology (NY)

**FIBER, TEXTILE AND WEAVING ARTS**
Haywood Comm Coll (NC)

**FILM/CINEMA/VIDEO STUDIES**
Coll of Marin (CA)
De Anza Coll (CA)
Fashion Inst of Technology (NY)
KD Conservatory Coll of Film and Dramatic Arts (TX)
Palomar Coll (CA)

**FINANCE**
Bunker Hill Comm Coll (MA)
Chipola Coll (FL)
Del Mar Coll (TX)
Harper Coll (IL)
Lakeshore Tech Coll (WI)
Los Angeles City Coll (CA)
Macomb Comm Coll (MI)
McLennan Comm Coll (TX)
Miami Dade Coll (FL)
Monroe County Comm Coll (MI)
Morton Coll (IL)
Mt. San Antonio Coll (CA)
Muskegon Comm Coll (MI)
National Park Coll (AR)
Naugatuck Valley Comm Coll (CT)
Northeast Comm Coll (NE)
North Hennepin Comm Coll (MN)

NorthWest Arkansas Comm Coll (AR)
Salt Lake Comm Coll (UT)
Scottsdale Comm Coll (AZ)
Seminole State Coll of Florida (FL)
Stark State Coll (OH)
Tidewater Comm Coll (VA)
Trinity Valley Comm Coll (TX)
Western Iowa Tech Comm Coll (IA)
Wisconsin Indianhead Tech Coll (WI)

**FINANCE AND FINANCIAL MANAGEMENT SERVICES RELATED**
Bristol Comm Coll (MA)

**FINANCIAL PLANNING AND SERVICES**
Barton County Comm Coll (KS)
Cecil Coll (MD)
Howard Comm Coll (MD)
Lackawanna Coll (PA)
Minnesota State Comm and Tech Coll (MN)

**FINE ARTS RELATED**
Bunker Hill Comm Coll (MA)
County Coll of Morris (NJ)
Mid-Plains Comm Coll, North Platte (NE)
Schoolcraft Coll (MI)
Seminole State Coll (OK)
Truckee Meadows Comm Coll (NV)

**FINE/STUDIO ARTS**
Amarillo Coll (TX)
Arizona Western Coll (AZ)
Bristol Comm Coll (MA)
Caldwell Comm Coll and Tech Inst (NC)
Camden County Coll (NJ)
Cayuga County Comm Coll (NY)
Cecil Coll (MD)
Central Texas Coll (TX)
Century Coll (MN)
Chandler-Gilbert Comm Coll (AZ)
Cottey Coll (MO)
Del Mar Coll (TX)
East Central Coll (MO)
Erie Comm Coll (NY)
Erie Comm Coll, North Campus (NY)
Erie Comm Coll, South Campus (NY)
Fashion Inst of Technology (NY)
Fiorello H. LaGuardia Comm Coll of the City U of New York (NY)
Genesee Comm Coll (NY)
Harford Comm Coll (MD)
Harper Coll (IL)
Houston Comm Coll (TX)
Hudson County Comm Coll (NJ)
Ivy Tech Comm Coll–Bloomington (IN)
Jamestown Comm Coll (NY)
Kishwaukee Coll (IL)
Lakes Region Comm Coll (NH)
Lake Superior Coll (MN)
Manchester Comm Coll (CT)
McHenry County Coll (IL)
Mesa Comm Coll (AZ)
Morton Coll (IL)
New Mexico State U–Alamogordo (NM)
Niagara County Comm Coll (NY)
Northampton Comm Coll (PA)
Northeastern Jr Coll (CO)
North Hennepin Comm Coll (MN)
Owensboro Comm and Tech Coll (KY)
Queensborough Comm Coll of the City U of New York (NY)
Raritan Valley Comm Coll (NJ)
Rend Lake Coll (IL)
St. Philip's Coll (TX)
South Suburban Coll (IL)
Springfield Tech Comm Coll (MA)
Three Rivers Comm Coll (CT)
Tidewater Comm Coll (VA)
Tulsa Comm Coll (OK)
West Kentucky Comm and Tech Coll (KY)

**FIRE PREVENTION AND SAFETY TECHNOLOGY**
Anne Arundel Comm Coll (MD)
Antelope Valley Coll (CA)
Asheville-Buncombe Tech Comm Coll (NC)
Austin Comm Coll District (TX)
Bunker Hill Comm Coll (MA)
Camden County Coll (NJ)
Cleveland Comm Coll (NC)
Coll of the Canyons (CA)

Coll of the Desert (CA)
Collin County Comm Coll District (TX)
Comm Coll of Allegheny County (PA)
County Coll of Morris (NJ)
Daytona State Coll (FL)
Del Mar Coll (TX)
Des Moines Area Comm Coll (IA)
El Paso Comm Coll (TX)
Fayetteville Tech Comm Coll (NC)
Gulf Coast State Coll (FL)
Houston Comm Coll (TX)
Jefferson Comm Coll (NY)
Lakeland Comm Coll (OH)
Lakes Region Comm Coll (NH)
Lake Superior Coll (MN)
Macomb Comm Coll (MI)
Merced Coll (CA)
Miami Dade Coll (FL)
Montgomery Coll (MD)
Montgomery County Comm Coll (PA)
Mott Comm Coll (MI)
Mount Wachusett Comm Coll (MA)
Northland Comm and Tech Coll (MN)
Palomar Coll (CA)
Pasadena City Coll (CA)
Pensacola State Coll (FL)
South Florida State Coll (FL)
Southwestern Coll (CA)
Springfield Tech Comm Coll (MA)
Sullivan County Comm Coll (NY)
Treasure Valley Comm Coll (OR)
Truckee Meadows Comm Coll (NV)
Tyler Jr Coll (TX)
Union County Coll (NJ)
Wayne County Comm Coll District (MI)

**FIRE PROTECTION RELATED**
St. Louis Comm Coll (MO)

**FIRE SCIENCE/FIREFIGHTING**
Amarillo Coll (TX)
Arizona Western Coll (AZ)
Barton County Comm Coll (KS)
Bristol Comm Coll (MA)
Cecil Coll (MD)
Central New Mexico Comm Coll (NM)
Central Ohio Tech Coll (OH)
Central Oregon Comm Coll (OR)
Cochise County Comm Coll District (AZ)
Coll of Central Florida (FL)
Coll of Eastern Idaho (ID)
Coll of the Desert (CA)
Collin County Comm Coll District (TX)
Comm Coll of Philadelphia (PA)
Crowder Coll (MO)
Danville Area Comm Coll (IL)
Del Mar Coll (TX)
East Central Coll (MO)
Eastern Arizona Coll (AZ)
Fox Valley Tech Coll (WI)
Frederick Comm Coll (MD)
Gateway Comm and Tech Coll (KY)
Greenville Tech Coll (SC)
Harper Coll (IL)
Harrisburg Area Comm Coll (PA)
Hawkeye Comm Coll (IA)
Hill Coll (TX)
Hutchinson Comm Coll (KS)
Illinois Central Coll (IL)
Illinois Eastern Comm Colls, Frontier Community College (IL)
J. Sargeant Reynolds Comm Coll (VA)
Lakes Region Comm Coll (NH)
Laramie County Comm Coll (WY)
Lorain County Comm Coll (OH)
Louisiana State U at Eunice (LA)
McHenry County Coll (IL)
Meridian Comm Coll (MS)
Miami Dade Coll (FL)
Mid-Plains Comm Coll, North Platte (NE)
Mission Coll (CA)
Mohave Comm Coll (AZ)
Monroe Comm Coll (NY)
Morton Coll (IL)
Mt. San Antonio Coll (CA)
National Park Coll (AR)
Navarro Coll (TX)
Northampton Comm Coll (PA)
Northeast Iowa Comm Coll (IA)
North Shore Comm Coll (MA)
Oakton Comm Coll (IL)
Odessa Coll (TX)

Oklahoma State U–Oklahoma City (OK)
Owensboro Comm and Tech Coll (KY)
Ozarks Tech Comm Coll (MO)
Pueblo Comm Coll (CO)
Rock Valley Coll (IL)
San Jacinto Coll District (TX)
San Joaquin Delta Coll (CA)
San Juan Coll (NM)
Santa Rosa Jr Coll (CA)
Sauk Valley Comm Coll (IL)
Schenectady County Comm Coll (NY)
Schoolcraft Coll (MI)
Seminole State Coll of Florida (FL)
Southcentral Kentucky Comm and Tech Coll (KY)
Southwestern Coll (CA)
Southwestern Michigan Coll (MI)
Tallahassee Comm Coll (FL)
Tarrant County Coll District (TX)
Three Rivers Coll (MO)
Vincennes U (IN)
Volunteer State Comm Coll (TN)
Waukesha County Tech Coll (WI)
Western Dakota Tech Inst (SD)
Western Iowa Tech Comm Coll (IA)
West Kentucky Comm and Tech Coll (KY)

**FIRE SERVICES ADMINISTRATION**
Black Hawk Coll, Moline (IL)
Bucks County Comm Coll (PA)
Camden County Coll (NJ)
Central Texas Coll (TX)
Dutchess Comm Coll (NY)
Erie Comm Coll, South Campus (NY)
Jefferson Comm Coll (NY)
Jefferson State Comm Coll (AL)
Lake Superior Coll (MN)
Minnesota State Comm and Tech Coll (MN)
Mohawk Valley Comm Coll (NY)
Naugatuck Valley Comm Coll (CT)
Northampton Comm Coll (PA)
NorthWest Arkansas Comm Coll (AR)
Quinsigamond Comm Coll (MA)
Schoolcraft Coll (MI)
Tulsa Comm Coll (OK)

**FISHING AND FISHERIES SCIENCES AND MANAGEMENT**
Central Oregon Comm Coll (OR)
Florida Keys Comm Coll (FL)

**FLORICULTURE/FLORISTRY MANAGEMENT**
Danville Area Comm Coll (IL)
J. Sargeant Reynolds Comm Coll (VA)
The Ohio State U Ag Tech Inst (OH)
Santa Rosa Jr Coll (CA)
Southwestern Coll (CA)

**FOOD SCIENCE**
Miami Dade Coll (FL)
Missouri State U–West Plains (MO)

**FOOD SERVICE AND DINING ROOM MANAGEMENT**
Kaskaskia Coll (IL)
LDS Business Coll (UT)
Montgomery County Comm Coll (PA)
Pasadena City Coll (CA)

**FOOD SERVICE SYSTEMS ADMINISTRATION**
Bucks County Comm Coll (PA)
Comm Coll of Allegheny County (PA)
Harper Coll (IL)
Mesa Comm Coll (AZ)
Mott Comm Coll (MI)
Pensacola State Coll (FL)
Wayne County Comm Coll District (MI)
Westchester Comm Coll (NY)

**FOODS, NUTRITION, AND WELLNESS**
Bossier Parish Comm Coll (LA)
Carl Albert State Coll (OK)
Coll of the Desert (CA)
Fullerton Coll (CA)
North Shore Comm Coll (MA)
Orange Coast Coll (CA)
Pensacola State Coll (FL)
Truckee Meadows Comm Coll (NV)

**FOOD TECHNOLOGY AND PROCESSING**
Adirondack Comm Coll (NY)
Copiah-Lincoln Comm Coll (MS)
Genesee Comm Coll (NY)
Mission Coll (CA)
Monroe Comm Coll (NY)
Tarrant County Coll District (TX)

**FOREIGN LANGUAGES AND LITERATURES**
Bunker Hill Comm Coll (MA)
Central Oregon Comm Coll (OR)
Central Texas Coll (TX)
Coll of Central Florida (FL)
Coll of Marin (CA)
Comm Coll of Allegheny County (PA)
Eastern Arizona Coll (AZ)
Fullerton Coll (CA)
Gordon State Coll (GA)
Grand Rapids Comm Coll (MI)
Hill Coll (TX)
Hutchinson Comm Coll (KS)
Orange Coast Coll (CA)
Palomar Coll (CA)
Panola Coll (TX)
Paris Jr Coll (TX)
St. Philip's Coll (TX)
San Jacinto Coll District (TX)
Texarkana Coll (TX)
Tyler Jr Coll (TX)
Vincennes U (IN)

**FOREIGN LANGUAGES RELATED**
Genesee Comm Coll (NY)
Sauk Valley Comm Coll (IL)
Tulsa Comm Coll (OK)

**FORENSIC SCIENCE AND TECHNOLOGY**
American Samoa Comm Coll (AS)
Arkansas State U–Newport (AR)
Carroll Comm Coll (MD)
Central Ohio Tech Coll (OH)
Fayetteville Tech Comm Coll (NC)
Fox Valley Tech Coll (WI)
Gulf Coast State Coll (FL)
Illinois Valley Comm Coll (IL)
Kishwaukee Coll (IL)
Macomb Comm Coll (MI)
Miami Dade Coll (FL)
New River Comm Coll (VA)
Palomar Coll (CA)
Pensacola State Coll (FL)
Potomac State Coll of West Virginia U (WV)
Queensborough Comm Coll of the City U of New York (NY)
Shawnee Comm Coll (IL)
Southeast Arkansas Coll (AR)
Southwestern Coll (CA)
Sullivan County Comm Coll (NY)
U of Arkansas Comm Coll at Morrilton (AR)
Wayne Comm Coll (NC)

**FOREST/FOREST RESOURCES MANAGEMENT**
Three Rivers Coll (MO)
Tyler Jr Coll (TX)

**FOREST RESOURCES PRODUCTION AND MANAGEMENT**
Potomac State Coll of West Virginia U (WV)

**FORESTRY**
Barton County Comm Coll (KS)
Central Oregon Comm Coll (OR)
Coll of Central Florida (FL)
Copiah-Lincoln Comm Coll (MS)
Eastern Arizona Coll (AZ)
Gordon State Coll (GA)
Grand Rapids Comm Coll (MI)
Miami Dade Coll (FL)
Monroe Comm Coll (NY)
Panola Coll (TX)
Western Wyoming Comm Coll (WY)

**FOREST TECHNOLOGY**
Central Oregon Comm Coll (OR)
Dabney S. Lancaster Comm Coll (VA)
Haywood Comm Coll (NC)
Lurleen B. Wallace Comm Coll (AL)
Montgomery Comm Coll (NC)
Mt. San Antonio Coll (CA)
Penn State Mont Alto (PA)
Three Rivers Coll (MO)

Wayne Comm Coll (NC)

**FRENCH**
Austin Comm Coll District (TX)
Coll of Marin (CA)
Coll of the Canyons (CA)
Coll of the Desert (CA)
Los Angeles City Coll (CA)
Merced Coll (CA)
Miami Dade Coll (FL)
Oklahoma City Comm Coll (OK)
Palomar Coll (CA)
Santa Rosa Jr Coll (CA)
Southwestern Coll (CA)

**FUNERAL SERVICE AND MORTUARY SCIENCE**
Amarillo Coll (TX)
Barton County Comm Coll (KS)
Comm Coll of Baltimore County (MD)
Dallas Inst of Funeral Service (TX)
Des Moines Area Comm Coll (IA)
Fayetteville Tech Comm Coll (NC)
FINE Mortuary Coll, LLC (MA)
Ivy Tech Comm Coll–Northwest (IN)
Jefferson State Comm Coll (AL)
John Tyler Comm Coll (VA)
Miami Dade Coll (FL)
Monroe County Comm Coll (MI)
Nassau Comm Coll (NY)
Northampton Comm Coll (PA)
Northeast Comm Coll (NE)
St. Louis Comm Coll (MO)
Vincennes U (IN)

**FURNITURE DESIGN AND MANUFACTURING**
Northcentral Tech Coll (WI)

**GAME AND INTERACTIVE MEDIA DESIGN**
Cayuga County Comm Coll (NY)
Collin County Comm Coll District (TX)
Comm Coll of Allegheny County (PA)
Fayetteville Tech Comm Coll (NC)
Hinds Comm Coll (MS)
Lehigh Carbon Comm Coll (PA)
Miami Dade Coll (FL)
Montgomery County Comm Coll (PA)
Quinsigamond Comm Coll (MA)
Texas State Tech Coll (TX)
Wayne Comm Coll (NC)
Wayne County Comm Coll District (MI)
Western Iowa Tech Comm Coll (IA)

**GENERAL STUDIES**
Alvin Comm Coll (TX)
Amarillo Coll (TX)
Ancilla Coll (IN)
Arizona Western Coll (AZ)
Arkansas State U–Newport (AR)
Asheville-Buncombe Tech Comm Coll (NC)
Austin Comm Coll District (TX)
Barton County Comm Coll (KS)
Bevill State Comm Coll (AL)
Black Hawk Coll, Moline (IL)
Blue Ridge Comm and Tech Coll (WV)
Bossier Parish Comm Coll (LA)
Bristol Comm Coll (MA)
Brookhaven Coll (TX)
Bunker Hill Comm Coll (MA)
Carroll Comm Coll (MD)
Cayuga County Comm Coll (NY)
Cecil Coll (MD)
Cedar Valley Coll (TX)
Central New Mexico Comm Coll (NM)
Central Texas Coll (TX)
Chandler-Gilbert Comm Coll (AZ)
Chesapeake Coll (MD)
City Colls of Chicago, Olive-Harvey College (IL)
Cleveland Comm Coll (NC)
Cleveland State Comm Coll (TN)
Cochise County Comm Coll District (AZ)
Colorado Northwestern Comm Coll (CO)
Columbia-Greene Comm Coll (NY)
Comm Coll of Allegheny County (PA)
Craven Comm Coll (NC)
Crowder Coll (MO)
Danville Area Comm Coll (IL)
Dutchess Comm Coll (NY)
Dyersburg State Comm Coll (TN)

East Central Coll (MO)
Eastern Arizona Coll (AZ)
El Paso Comm Coll (TX)
Erie Comm Coll (NY)
Erie Comm Coll, North Campus (NY)
Erie Comm Coll, South Campus (NY)
Fayetteville Tech Comm Coll (NC)
Frederick Comm Coll (MD)
Front Range Comm Coll (CO)
Galveston Coll (TX)
Gateway Comm and Tech Coll (KY)
Genesee Comm Coll (NY)
George C. Wallace Comm Coll (AL)
Georgia Military Coll (GA)
Gordon State Coll (GA)
Harford Comm Coll (MD)
Harrisburg Area Comm Coll (PA)
H. Councill Trenholm State Comm Coll (AL)
Hesston Coll (KS)
Highland Comm Coll (IL)
Hill Coll (TX)
Hinds Comm Coll (MS)
Houston Comm Coll (TX)
Howard Comm Coll (MD)
Illinois Central Coll (IL)
Illinois Eastern Comm Colls, Frontier Community College (IL)
Illinois Eastern Comm Colls, Lincoln Trail College (IL)
Illinois Eastern Comm Colls, Olney Central College (IL)
Illinois Eastern Comm Colls, Wabash Valley College (IL)
Illinois Valley Comm Coll (IL)
Ivy Tech Comm Coll–Bloomington (IN)
Ivy Tech Comm Coll–Central Indiana (IN)
Ivy Tech Comm Coll–Columbus (IN)
Ivy Tech Comm Coll–East Central (IN)
Ivy Tech Comm Coll–Kokomo (IN)
Ivy Tech Comm Coll–Lafayette (IN)
Ivy Tech Comm Coll–North Central (IN)
Ivy Tech Comm Coll–Northwest (IN)
Ivy Tech Comm Coll–Richmond (IN)
Ivy Tech Comm Coll–Sellersburg (IN)
Ivy Tech Comm Coll–Southeast (IN)
Ivy Tech Comm Coll–Southwest (IN)
Ivy Tech Comm Coll–Wabash Valley (IN)
James Sprunt Comm Coll (NC)
Jamestown Comm Coll (NY)
Jefferson State Comm Coll (AL)
John Tyler Comm Coll (VA)
Kaskaskia Coll (IL)
Kellogg Comm Coll (MI)
Kirtland Comm Coll (MI)
Lakes Region Comm Coll (NH)
Laramie County Comm Coll (WY)
LDS Business Coll (UT)
Lehigh Carbon Comm Coll (PA)
Lenoir Comm Coll (NC)
Louisiana State U at Eunice (LA)
Lurleen B. Wallace Comm Coll (AL)
Macomb Comm Coll (MI)
Manchester Comm Coll (CT)
Marion Military Inst (AL)
Massachusetts Bay Comm Coll (MA)
McHenry County Coll (IL)
Mesa Comm Coll (AZ)
Miami Dade Coll (FL)
Missouri State U–West Plains (MO)
Mitchell Comm Coll (NC)
Mohawk Valley Comm Coll (NY)
Motlow State Comm Coll (TN)
Mott Comm Coll (MI)
Mount Wachusett Comm Coll (MA)
Nassau Comm Coll (NY)
Naugatuck Valley Comm Coll (CT)
New River Comm Coll (VA)
Niagara County Comm Coll (NY)
Northampton Comm Coll (PA)
Northcentral Tech Coll (WI)
Northeast Comm Coll (NE)
Northeast State Comm Coll (TN)
Northern Essex Comm Coll (MA)
Northern Maine Comm Coll (ME)
Northwest Coll (WY)
Northwest-Shoals Comm Coll (AL)
Nunez Comm Coll (LA)
Oklahoma City Comm Coll (OK)
Oklahoma State U–Oklahoma City (OK)
Panola Coll (TX)
Paris Jr Coll (TX)

Pennsylvania Highlands Comm Coll (PA)
Pennsylvania Inst of Technology (PA)
Piedmont Comm Coll (NC)
Piedmont Virginia Comm Coll (VA)
Pueblo Comm Coll (CO)
Queensborough Comm Coll of the City U of New York (NY)
Quinsigamond Comm Coll (MA)
Rowan-Cabarrus Comm Coll (NC)
St. Charles Comm Coll (MO)
St. Louis Comm Coll (MO)
Salt Lake Comm Coll (UT)
San Jacinto Coll District (TX)
San Juan Coll (NM)
Schoolcraft Coll (MI)
Seminole State Coll (OK)
Shawnee Comm Coll (IL)
Southeast Arkansas Coll (AR)
Southern U at Shreveport (LA)
Southwestern Coll (CA)
Southwestern Michigan Coll (MI)
Southwest Texas Jr Coll (TX)
Sowela Tech Comm Coll (LA)
State U of New York Coll of Technology at Alfred (NY)
Three Rivers Comm Coll (CT)
Tillamook Bay Comm Coll (OR)
Treasure Valley Comm Coll (OR)
Truckee Meadows Comm Coll (NV)
Tulsa Comm Coll (OK)
Tyler Jr Coll (TX)
U of Arkansas Comm Coll at Morrilton (AR)
U of Arkansas Rich Mountain (AR)
Volunteer State Comm Coll (TN)
Walters State Comm Coll (TN)
Western Wyoming Comm Coll (WY)
White Mountains Comm Coll (NH)

**GEOGRAPHIC INFORMATION SCIENCE AND CARTOGRAPHY**
Austin Comm Coll District (TX)
Brookhaven Coll (TX)
Central New Mexico Comm Coll (NM)
Collin County Comm Coll District (TX)
Front Range Comm Coll (CO)
Harrisburg Area Comm Coll (PA)
Hinds Comm Coll (MS)
Lehigh Carbon Comm Coll (PA)
Mitchell Tech Inst (SD)
Oklahoma City Comm Coll (OK)
Southwestern Indian Polytechnic Inst (NM)

**GEOGRAPHY**
Antelope Valley Coll (CA)
Austin Comm Coll District (TX)
Cayuga County Comm Coll (NY)
Central New Mexico Comm Coll (NM)
Coll of Marin (CA)
Coll of the Canyons (CA)
Coll of the Desert (CA)
Del Mar Coll (TX)
Fullerton Coll (CA)
Merced Coll (CA)
Mesa Comm Coll (AZ)
Montgomery Coll (MD)
Northeastern Jr Coll (CO)
Orange Coast Coll (CA)
Palomar Coll (CA)
Southwestern Coll (CA)
U of Wisconsin–Baraboo/Sauk County (WI)
U of Wisconsin–Barron County (WI)
U of Wisconsin–Fond du Lac (WI)
U of Wisconsin–Fox Valley (WI)
U of Wisconsin–Manitowoc (WI)
U of Wisconsin–Marathon County (WI)
U of Wisconsin–Marinette (WI)
U of Wisconsin–Marshfield/Wood County (WI)
U of Wisconsin–Richland (WI)
U of Wisconsin–Rock County (WI)
U of Wisconsin–Sheboygan (WI)
U of Wisconsin–Washington County (WI)
U of Wisconsin–Waukesha (WI)

**GEOGRAPHY RELATED**
Palomar Coll (CA)

**GEOLOGICAL AND EARTH SCIENCES/GEOSCIENCES RELATED**
Potomac State Coll of West Virginia U (WV)

**GEOLOGY/EARTH SCIENCE**
Amarillo Coll (TX)

Antelope Valley Coll (CA)
Arizona Western Coll (AZ)
Austin Comm Coll District (TX)
Barton County Comm Coll (KS)
Central Texas Coll (TX)
Coll of Marin (CA)
Coll of the Canyons (CA)
Coll of the Desert (CA)
Del Mar Coll (TX)
Eastern Arizona Coll (AZ)
Edison State Comm Coll (OH)
Fullerton Coll (CA)
Grand Rapids Comm Coll (MI)
Hill Coll (TX)
Merced Coll (CA)
Miami Dade Coll (FL)
Northeastern Jr Coll (CO)
Odessa Coll (TX)
Orange Coast Coll (CA)
Palomar Coll (CA)
Panola Coll (TX)
Pensacola State Coll (FL)
Potomac State Coll of West Virginia U (WV)
Salt Lake Comm Coll (UT)
San Jacinto Coll District (TX)
San Joaquin Delta Coll (CA)
San Juan Coll (NM)
Southwestern Coll (CA)
Trinity Valley Comm Coll (TX)
Truckee Meadows Comm Coll (NV)
Tyler Jr Coll (TX)
Western Wyoming Comm Coll (WY)

**GERMAN**
Austin Comm Coll District (TX)
Merced Coll (CA)
Miami Dade Coll (FL)

**GERONTOLOGY**
Anne Arundel Comm Coll (MD)
Genesee Comm Coll (NY)
Lakes Region Comm Coll (NH)
North Shore Comm Coll (MA)
Wisconsin Indianhead Tech Coll (WI)
York County Comm Coll (ME)

**GOLF COURSE OPERATION AND GROUNDS MANAGEMENT**
Coll of the Desert (CA)
Hawkeye Comm Coll (IA)

**GRAPHIC AND PRINTING EQUIPMENT OPERATION/ PRODUCTION**
Central Maine Comm Coll (ME)
Central Texas Coll (TX)
Erie Comm Coll, South Campus (NY)
Fullerton Coll (CA)
Lakes Region Comm Coll (NH)
Macomb Comm Coll (MI)
Mission Coll (CA)
Monroe Comm Coll (NY)
Palomar Coll (CA)
Pasadena City Coll (CA)
Rock Valley Coll (IL)
Tarrant County Coll District (TX)
Tulsa Comm Coll (OK)

**GRAPHIC COMMUNICATIONS**
Central Maine Comm Coll (ME)
Clark Coll (WA)
Hutchinson Comm Coll (KS)
Northcentral Tech Coll (WI)
Ozarks Tech Comm Coll (MO)
Piedmont Comm Coll (NC)
St. Louis Comm Coll (MO)

**GRAPHIC COMMUNICATIONS RELATED**
H. Councill Trenholm State Comm Coll (AL)
Thaddeus Stevens Coll of Technology (PA)

**GRAPHIC DESIGN**
Anne Arundel Comm Coll (MD)
Barton County Comm Coll (KS)
Bristol Comm Coll (MA)
Brookhaven Coll (TX)
Cayuga County Comm Coll (NY)
Cedar Valley Coll (TX)
Century Coll (MN)
Cloud County Comm Coll (KS)
Coll of the Canyons (CA)
Collin County Comm Coll District (TX)
Comm Coll of Allegheny County (PA)
County Coll of Morris (NJ)
Dunwoody Coll of Technology (MN)
Eastern Arizona Coll (AZ)

FIDM/Fashion Inst of Design & Merchandising, Orange County Campus (CA)
Fullerton Coll (CA)
Gateway Tech Coll (WI)
Genesee Comm Coll (NY)
Harford Comm Coll (MD)
Harrisburg Area Comm Coll (PA)
Highland Comm Coll (IL)
Hinds Comm Coll (MS)
Illinois Central Coll (IL)
Illinois Valley Comm Coll (IL)
Kellogg Comm Coll (MI)
Kirtland Comm Coll (MI)
Lehigh Carbon Comm Coll (PA)
Lenoir Comm Coll (NC)
Los Angeles City Coll (CA)
Minnesota State Comm and Tech Coll (MN)
Montgomery County Comm Coll (PA)
Mott Comm Coll (MI)
New Mexico State U–Alamogordo (NM)
Northampton Comm Coll (PA)
Northeast Comm Coll (NE)
North Hennepin Comm Coll (MN)
Oakton Comm Coll (IL)
Oklahoma City Comm Coll (OK)
Oklahoma State U Inst of Technology (OK)
Palomar Coll (CA)
Pasadena City Coll (CA)
Pensacola State Coll (FL)
Rend Lake Coll (IL)
Salt Lake Comm Coll (UT)
Santa Rosa Jr Coll (CA)
Southwestern Coll (CA)
Southwestern Michigan Coll (MI)
State U of New York Coll of Technology at Alfred (NY)
Texas State Tech Coll (TX)
Three Rivers Comm Coll (CT)
Tidewater Comm Coll (VA)
Tyler Jr Coll (TX)
Waukesha County Tech Coll (WI)

**GREENHOUSE MANAGEMENT**
Comm Coll of Allegheny County (PA)
The Ohio State U Ag Tech Inst (OH)

**GUNSMITHING**
Fayetteville Tech Comm Coll (NC)
Lenoir Comm Coll (NC)
Montgomery Comm Coll (NC)

**HAZARDOUS MATERIALS MANAGEMENT AND WASTE TECHNOLOGY**
Barton County Comm Coll (KS)
Fullerton Coll (CA)
Odessa Coll (TX)
Pensacola State Coll (FL)
Southwestern Coll (CA)

**HEALTH AIDE**
Ivy Tech Comm Coll–Kokomo (IN)
Ivy Tech Comm Coll–Lafayette (IN)
Ivy Tech Comm Coll–Wabash Valley (IN)
Texarkana Coll (TX)

**HEALTH AIDES/ATTENDANTS/ ORDERLIES RELATED**
Barton County Comm Coll (KS)

**HEALTH AND MEDICAL ADMINISTRATIVE SERVICES RELATED**
Barton County Comm Coll (KS)
Copiah-Lincoln Comm Coll (MS)
Hinds Comm Coll (MS)
Kent State U at Ashtabula (OH)
Kent State U at Salem (OH)
Owensboro Comm and Tech Coll (KY)

**HEALTH AND PHYSICAL EDUCATION/FITNESS**
Alvin Comm Coll (TX)
Anne Arundel Comm Coll (MD)
Antelope Valley Coll (CA)
Arizona Western Coll (AZ)
Austin Comm Coll District (TX)
Central New Mexico Comm Coll (NM)
Central Oregon Comm Coll (OR)
Cochise County Comm Coll District (AZ)
Coll of Marin (CA)
Coll of the Desert (CA)
Comm Coll of Allegheny County (PA)
Eastern Arizona Coll (AZ)
Erie Comm Coll (NY)

Erie Comm Coll, North Campus (NY)
Erie Comm Coll, South Campus (NY)
Feather River Coll (CA)
Fullerton Coll (CA)
Genesee Comm Coll (NY)
Gordon State Coll (GA)
Harrisburg Area Comm Coll (PA)
Hill Coll (TX)
Holyoke Comm Coll (MA)
Houston Comm Coll (TX)
Hudson County Comm Coll (NJ)
Illinois Central Coll (IL)
Jamestown Comm Coll (NY)
McHenry County Coll (IL)
Merced Coll (CA)
Mesa Comm Coll (AZ)
Montgomery County Comm Coll (PA)
Mt. San Antonio Coll (CA)
Northeast Comm Coll (NE)
Northern Essex Comm Coll (MA)
North Hennepin Comm Coll (MN)
Northwest Coll (WY)
Orange Coast Coll (CA)
Paris Jr Coll (TX)
San Jacinto Coll District (TX)
San Juan Coll (NM)
Santa Rosa Jr Coll (CA)
Southwestern Coll (CA)
Tyler Jr Coll (TX)
Vincennes U (IN)
Western Texas Coll (TX)

**HEALTH AND PHYSICAL EDUCATION RELATED**
Chesapeake Coll (MD)
Fayetteville Tech Comm Coll (NC)
Genesee Comm Coll (NY)
Kingsborough Comm Coll of the City U of New York (NY)

**HEALTH AND WELLNESS**
Erie Comm Coll (NY)
Erie Comm Coll, North Campus (NY)
Erie Comm Coll, South Campus (NY)

**HEALTH/HEALTH-CARE ADMINISTRATION**
Des Moines Area Comm Coll (IA)
Harrisburg Area Comm Coll (PA)
Kent State U at Trumbull (OH)
Manor Coll (PA)
National Park Coll (AR)
Oklahoma State U–Oklahoma City (OK)
Pennsylvania Inst of Technology (PA)
Pensacola State Coll (FL)

**HEALTH INFORMATION/ MEDICAL RECORDS ADMINISTRATION**
Amarillo Coll (TX)
Barton County Comm Coll (KS)
Bunker Hill Comm Coll (MA)
Camden County Coll (NJ)
Career Coll of Northern Nevada (NV)
Central New Mexico Comm Coll (NM)
The Coll of Westchester (NY)
El Paso Comm Coll (TX)
Humacao Comm Coll (PR)
Illinois Eastern Comm Colls, Lincoln Trail College (IL)
LDS Business Coll (UT)
McLennan Comm Coll (TX)
Miami Dade Coll (FL)
Monroe Comm Coll (NY)
Mount Wachusett Comm Coll (MA)
National Park Coll (AR)
North Central Texas Coll (TX)
Northern Essex Comm Coll (MA)
Oakton Comm Coll (IL)
Pensacola State Coll (FL)
Southcentral Kentucky Comm and Tech Coll (KY)
Southern U at Shreveport (LA)
Southwestern Comm Coll (NC)
Stark State Coll (OH)
Tarrant County Coll District (TX)

**HEALTH INFORMATION/ MEDICAL RECORDS TECHNOLOGY**
Anne Arundel Comm Coll (MD)
Austin Comm Coll District (TX)
Beal Coll (ME)
Black Hawk Coll, Moline (IL)
Bristol Comm Coll (MA)
Carroll Comm Coll (MD)
Central New Mexico Comm Coll (NM)
Central Oregon Comm Coll (OR)
Chippewa Valley Tech Coll (WI)
Coll of Business and Technology– Cutler Bay Campus (FL)

Coll of Business and Technology– Miami Gardens (FL)
Coll of Central Florida (FL)
Collin County Comm Coll District (TX)
Comm Coll of Allegheny County (PA)
Craven Comm Coll (NC)
Crowder Coll (MO)
Danville Area Comm Coll (IL)
Daytona State Coll (FL)
Del Mar Coll (TX)
Dyersburg State Comm Coll (TN)
East Central Coll (MO)
Erie Comm Coll, North Campus (NY)
Fox Valley Tech Coll (WI)
Front Range Comm Coll (CO)
Gateway Tech Coll (WI)
Great Falls Coll Montana State U (MT)
Greenville Tech Coll (SC)
Highland Comm Coll (IL)
Hinds Comm Coll (MS)
Houston Comm Coll (TX)
Hudson County Comm Coll (NJ)
Hutchinson Comm Coll (KS)
Illinois Eastern Comm Colls, Frontier Community College (IL)
Ivy Tech Comm Coll–Central Indiana (IN)
Ivy Tech Comm Coll–East Central (IN)
Ivy Tech Comm Coll–Kokomo (IN)
Ivy Tech Comm Coll–Lafayette (IN)
Ivy Tech Comm Coll–Wabash Valley (IN)
Jamestown Comm Coll (NY)
Kaskaskia Coll (IL)
Kennebec Valley Comm Coll (ME)
Kirtland Comm Coll (MI)
Lackawanna Coll (PA)
Lehigh Carbon Comm Coll (PA)
Miami Dade Coll (FL)
Minnesota State Comm and Tech Coll (MN)
Mohawk Valley Comm Coll (NY)
Montgomery Coll (MD)
Morton Coll (IL)
North Dakota State Coll of Science (ND)
Northeast Comm Coll (NE)
Northeast Iowa Comm Coll (IA)
NorthWest Arkansas Comm Coll (AR)
Ozarks Tech Comm Coll (MO)
Panola Coll (TX)
Paris Jr Coll (TX)
Pennsylvania Highlands Comm Coll (PA)
Pennsylvania Inst of Technology (PA)
Pensacola State Coll (FL)
Quinsigamond Comm Coll (MA)
Raritan Valley Comm Coll (NJ)
Rend Lake Coll (IL)
Richmond Comm Coll (NC)
Ridgewater Coll (MN)
St. Charles Comm Coll (MO)
St. Louis Comm Coll (MO)
St. Philip's Coll (TX)
San Jacinto Coll District (TX)
San Juan Coll (NM)
Schoolcraft Coll (MI)
Southern U at Shreveport (LA)
Southwestern Comm Coll (NC)
Southwestern Michigan Coll (MI)
Springfield Tech Comm Coll (MA)
State U of New York Coll of Technology at Alfred (NY)
Tallahassee Comm Coll (FL)
Tulsa Comm Coll (OK)
Tyler Jr Coll (TX)
U of Arkansas Rich Mountain (AR)
Vincennes U (IN)
Volunteer State Comm Coll (TN)
Walters State Comm Coll (TN)
Waukesha County Tech Coll (WI)
Wisconsin Indianhead Tech Coll (WI)
York County Comm Coll (ME)

**HEALTH/MEDICAL PREPARATORY PROGRAMS RELATED**
Ancilla Coll (IN)
Arkansas State U–Newport (AR)
Coll of Central Florida (FL)
Coll of the Desert (CA)
Edison State Comm Coll (OH)
Fullerton Coll (CA)
Gordon State Coll (GA)
Manor Coll (PA)
Merced Coll (CA)
Miami Dade Coll (FL)

Missouri State U–West Plains (MO)
Northeast Comm Coll (NE)
Northwest Coll (WY)
Southwestern Coll (CA)
Three Rivers Coll (MO)
Tulsa Comm Coll (OK)
Western Wyoming Comm Coll (WY)

## HEALTH PROFESSIONS RELATED

Bowling Green State U–Firelands Coll (OH)
Bucks County Comm Coll (PA)
Carl Albert State Coll (OK)
Carroll Comm Coll (MD)
Comm Coll of Allegheny County (PA)
Comm Coll of Philadelphia (PA)
Gateway Comm and Tech Coll (KY)
Genesee Comm Coll (NY)
Harrisburg Area Comm Coll (PA)
Lackawanna Coll (PA)
Lakeland Comm Coll (OH)
LDS Business Coll (UT)
Manor Coll (PA)
Miami Dade Coll (FL)
Mission Coll (CA)
Mitchell Comm Coll (NC)
National Park Coll (AR)
Northeast State Comm Coll (TN)
North Shore Comm Coll (MA)
Ozarks Tech Comm Coll (MO)
Panola Coll (TX)
Pennsylvania Highlands Comm Coll (PA)
Piedmont Comm Coll (NC)
Queensborough Comm Coll of the City U of New York (NY)
Richmond Comm Coll (NC)
Salt Lake Comm Coll (UT)
Southeastern Coll–West Palm Beach (FL)
Volunteer State Comm Coll (TN)

## HEALTH SERVICES ADMINISTRATION

Harrisburg Area Comm Coll (PA)

## HEALTH SERVICES/ALLIED HEALTH/HEALTH SCIENCES

Alvin Comm Coll (TX)
American Samoa Comm Coll (AS)
Ancilla Coll (IN)
Bucks County Comm Coll (PA)
Camden County Coll (NJ)
Carl Albert State Coll (OK)
Cayuga County Comm Coll (NY)
Cecil Coll (MD)
Central New Mexico Comm Coll (NM)
Central Ohio Tech Coll (OH)
Century Coll (MN)
Coll of Central Florida (FL)
Coll of the Desert (CA)
Collin County Comm Coll District (TX)
Dyersburg State Comm Coll (TN)
Georgia Military Coll (GA)
Gulf Coast State Coll (FL)
Holyoke Comm Coll (MA)
Houston Comm Coll (TX)
Hudson County Comm Coll (NJ)
Lake Superior Coll (MN)
Lehigh Carbon Comm Coll (PA)
Miami Dade Coll (FL)
Missouri State U–West Plains (MO)
New Mexico State U–Alamogordo (NM)
North Hennepin Comm Coll (MN)
Northland Comm and Tech Coll (MN)
Oklahoma State U Inst of Technology (OK)
Orange Coast Coll (CA)
Paris Jr Coll (TX)
Pennsylvania Inst of Technology (PA)
Queensborough Comm Coll of the City U of New York (NY)
Quinsigamond Comm Coll (MA)
Rainy River Comm Coll (MN)
Raritan Valley Comm Coll (NJ)
St. Philip's Coll (TX)
Schoolcraft Coll (MI)
Southeast Tech Inst (SD)
Union County Coll (NJ)
U of Wisconsin–Baraboo/Sauk County (WI)
U of Wisconsin–Barron County (WI)
U of Wisconsin–Fond du Lac (WI)
U of Wisconsin–Fox Valley (WI)
U of Wisconsin–Manitowoc (WI)

U of Wisconsin–Marathon County (WI)
U of Wisconsin–Marinette (WI)
U of Wisconsin–Marshfield/Wood County (WI)
U of Wisconsin–Richland (WI)
U of Wisconsin–Rock County (WI)
U of Wisconsin–Sheboygan (WI)
U of Wisconsin–Washington County (WI)
U of Wisconsin–Waukesha (WI)
Western Dakota Tech Inst (SD)
Western Wyoming Comm Coll (WY)
West Kentucky Comm and Tech Coll (KY)
White Mountains Comm Coll (NH)
York County Comm Coll (ME)

## HEALTH TEACHER EDUCATION

Copiah-Lincoln Comm Coll (MS)
Del Mar Coll (TX)
Georgia Military Coll (GA)
Harper Coll (IL)
Howard Comm Coll (MD)
South Florida State Coll (FL)
Vincennes U (IN)

## HEALTH UNIT COORDINATOR/ WARD CLERK

Comm Coll of Allegheny County (PA)
Southeast Tech Inst (SD)

## HEARING INSTRUMENT SPECIALIST

Ozarks Tech Comm Coll (MO)

## HEATING, AIR CONDITIONING, VENTILATION AND REFRIGERATION MAINTENANCE TECHNOLOGY

Amarillo Coll (TX)
Antelope Valley Coll (CA)
Arizona Western Coll (AZ)
Arkansas State U–Newport (AR)
Asheville-Buncombe Tech Comm Coll (NC)
Cedar Valley Coll (TX)
Central New Mexico Comm Coll (NM)
Central Texas Coll (TX)
Century Coll (MN)
Coll of the Desert (CA)
Comm Coll of Allegheny County (PA)
Copiah-Lincoln Comm Coll (MS)
Craven Comm Coll (NC)
Des Moines Area Comm Coll (IA)
Dunwoody Coll of Technology (MN)
East Central Coll (MO)
El Paso Comm Coll (TX)
Fayetteville Tech Comm Coll (NC)
Galveston Coll (TX)
Gateway Tech Coll (WI)
George C. Wallace Comm Coll (AL)
Grand Rapids Comm Coll (MI)
Harper Coll (IL)
Harrisburg Area Comm Coll (PA)
Hill Coll (TX)
Hinds Comm Coll (MS)
Illinois Central Coll (IL)
Ivy Tech Comm Coll–Bloomington (IN)
Ivy Tech Comm Coll–Central Indiana (IN)
Ivy Tech Comm Coll–Columbus (IN)
Ivy Tech Comm Coll–Kokomo (IN)
Ivy Tech Comm Coll–Lafayette (IN)
Ivy Tech Comm Coll–North Central (IN)
Ivy Tech Comm Coll–Northeast (IN)
Ivy Tech Comm Coll–Northwest (IN)
Ivy Tech Comm Coll–Richmond (IN)
Ivy Tech Comm Coll–Sellersburg (IN)
Ivy Tech Comm Coll–Southwest (IN)
Ivy Tech Comm Coll–Wabash Valley (IN)
Johnson Coll (PA)
Johnston Comm Coll (NC)
Kaskaskia Coll (IL)
Kellogg Comm Coll (MI)
Kirtland Comm Coll (MI)
Laramie County Comm Coll (WY)
Lehigh Carbon Comm Coll (PA)
Macomb Comm Coll (MI)
Miami Dade Coll (FL)
Mid-Plains Comm Coll, North Platte (NE)
Mitchell Tech Inst (SD)
Mohave Comm Coll (AZ)
Mohawk Valley Comm Coll (NY)

Monroe Comm Coll (NY)
Montgomery Comm Coll (NC)
Morton Coll (IL)
Mt. San Antonio Coll (CA)
Northampton Comm Coll (PA)
North Dakota State Coll of Science (ND)
Northeast Comm Coll (NE)
Northern Maine Comm Coll (ME)
North Iowa Area Comm Coll (IA)
Northland Comm and Tech Coll (MN)
Northwest Mississippi Comm Coll (MS)
Odessa Coll (TX)
Oklahoma State U Inst of Technology (OK)
Owensboro Comm and Tech Coll (KY)
Paris Jr Coll (TX)
Pittsburgh Tech Coll (PA)
Renton Tech Coll (WA)
Richmond Comm Coll (NC)
Salt Lake Comm Coll (UT)
San Jacinto Coll District (TX)
San Joaquin Delta Coll (CA)
Sauk Valley Comm Coll (IL)
Southcentral Kentucky Comm and Tech Coll (KY)
Southeast Tech Inst (SD)
Southwest Texas Jr Coll (TX)
Springfield Tech Comm Coll (MA)
State Tech Coll of Missouri (MO)
State U of New York Coll of Technology at Alfred (NY)
Tarrant County Coll District (TX)
Texarkana Coll (TX)
Thaddeus Stevens Coll of Technology (PA)
Trinity Valley Comm Coll (TX)
Truckee Meadows Comm Coll (NV)
Tyler Jr Coll (TX)
U of Arkansas Comm Coll at Morrilton (AR)
Vincennes U (IN)
Wayne County Comm Coll District (MI)
Western Dakota Tech Inst (SD)
Western Iowa Tech Comm Coll (IA)

## HEATING, VENTILATION, AIR CONDITIONING AND REFRIGERATION ENGINEERING TECHNOLOGY

Alamance Comm Coll (NC)
Antelope Valley Coll (CA)
Arizona Western Coll (AZ)
Austin Comm Coll District (TX)
Bevill State Comm Coll (AL)
Chippewa Valley Tech Coll (WI)
Coll of Business and Technology–Flagler Campus (FL)
Coll of Business and Technology–Hialeah Campus (FL)
Coll of the Desert (CA)
Collin County Comm Coll District (TX)
Comm Coll of Baltimore County (MD)
Dunwoody Coll of Technology (MN)
Front Range Comm Coll (CO)
George C. Wallace Comm Coll (AL)
H. Councill Trenholm State Comm Coll (AL)
Humacao Comm Coll (PR)
Kennebec Valley Comm Coll (ME)
Macomb Comm Coll (MI)
Merced Coll (CA)
Miami Dade Coll (FL)
Minnesota State Comm and Tech Coll (MN)
Mott Comm Coll (MI)
New Castle School of Trades (PA)
North Dakota State Coll of Science (ND)
Oakton Comm Coll (IL)
Ozarks Tech Comm Coll (MO)
Raritan Valley Comm Coll (NJ)
St. Philip's Coll (TX)
Texas State Tech Coll (TX)

## HEAVY EQUIPMENT MAINTENANCE TECHNOLOGY

Amarillo Coll (TX)
Del Mar Coll (TX)
Highland Comm Coll (IL)
The Ohio State U Ag Tech Inst (OH)
Ozarks Tech Comm Coll (MO)
Rend Lake Coll (IL)
State Tech Coll of Missouri (MO)
Western Wyoming Comm Coll (WY)

## HEAVY/INDUSTRIAL EQUIPMENT MAINTENANCE TECHNOLOGIES RELATED

East Central Coll (MO)
Ozarks Tech Comm Coll (MO)
State U of New York Coll of Technology at Alfred (NY)

## HIGH PERFORMANCE AND CUSTOM ENGINE TECHNOLOGY

Ohio Tech Coll (OH)

## HISPANIC-AMERICAN, PUERTO RICAN, AND MEXICAN-AMERICAN/CHICANO STUDIES

San Jacinto Coll District (TX)

## HISTOLOGIC TECHNICIAN

Houston Comm Coll (TX)
Miami Dade Coll (FL)
Mott Comm Coll (MI)
North Hennepin Comm Coll (MN)
Pennsylvania Highlands Comm Coll (PA)

## HISTOLOGIC TECHNOLOGY/ HISTOTECHNOLOGIST

Miami Dade Coll (FL)

## HISTORIC PRESERVATION AND CONSERVATION

Piedmont Comm Coll (NC)

## HISTORY

Alvin Comm Coll (TX)
Amarillo Coll (TX)
Ancilla Coll (IN)
Antelope Valley Coll (CA)
Arizona Western Coll (AZ)
Austin Comm Coll District (TX)
Barton County Comm Coll (KS)
Bucks County Comm Coll (PA)
Bunker Hill Comm Coll (MA)
Central New Mexico Comm Coll (NM)
Coll of Central Florida (FL)
Coll of Marin (CA)
Coll of the Canyons (CA)
Coll of the Desert (CA)
Copiah-Lincoln Comm Coll (MS)
De Anza Coll (CA)
Del Mar Coll (TX)
Eastern Arizona Coll (AZ)
Edison State Comm Coll (OH)
Feather River Coll (CA)
Fullerton Coll (CA)
Galveston Coll (TX)
Georgia Military Coll (GA)
Harford Comm Coll (MD)
Harper Coll (IL)
Hill Coll (TX)
Laramie County Comm Coll (WY)
Merced Coll (CA)
Miami Dade Coll (FL)
Mohave Comm Coll (AZ)
Monroe Comm Coll (NY)
Mount Wachusett Comm Coll (MA)
Northeastern Jr Coll (CO)
Northwest Coll (WY)
Odessa Coll (TX)
Oklahoma City Comm Coll (OK)
Orange Coast Coll (CA)
Otero Jr Coll (CO)
Panola Coll (TX)
Paris Jr Coll (TX)
Pasadena City Coll (CA)
Pensacola State Coll (FL)
Potomac State Coll of West Virginia U (WV)
Quinsigamond Comm Coll (MA)
St. Philip's Coll (TX)
Salt Lake Comm Coll (UT)
San Jacinto Coll District (TX)
San Joaquin Delta Coll (CA)
Santa Rosa Jr Coll (CA)
Sauk Valley Comm Coll (IL)
Southwestern Coll (CA)
Texarkana Coll (TX)
Trinity Valley Comm Coll (TX)
Truckee Meadows Comm Coll (NV)
Tyler Jr Coll (TX)
Union County Coll (NJ)
U of Wisconsin–Baraboo/Sauk County (WI)
U of Wisconsin–Barron County (WI)
U of Wisconsin–Fond du Lac (WI)
U of Wisconsin–Fox Valley (WI)
U of Wisconsin–Manitowoc (WI)

U of Wisconsin–Marathon County (WI)
U of Wisconsin–Marinette (WI)
U of Wisconsin–Marshfield/Wood County (WI)
U of Wisconsin–Richland (WI)
U of Wisconsin–Rock County (WI)
U of Wisconsin–Sheboygan (WI)
U of Wisconsin–Washington County (WI)
U of Wisconsin–Waukesha (WI)
Vincennes U (IN)
Western Wyoming Comm Coll (WY)

## HISTORY TEACHER EDUCATION

Bucks County Comm Coll (PA)

## HOLISTIC HEALTH

Front Range Comm Coll (CO)

## HOME HEALTH AIDE/HOME ATTENDANT

Barton County Comm Coll (KS)

## HOMELAND SECURITY

Arizona Western Coll (AZ)
Georgia Military Coll (GA)
Harper Coll (IL)
Palomar Coll (CA)

## HOMELAND SECURITY, LAW ENFORCEMENT, FIREFIGHTING AND PROTECTIVE SERVICES RELATED

Barton County Comm Coll (KS)
Century Coll (MN)
El Paso Comm Coll (TX)
Lakeland Comm Coll (OH)
Laramie County Comm Coll (WY)
Pittsburgh Tech Coll (PA)
Schoolcraft Coll (MI)
Southeast Arkansas Coll (AR)
West Kentucky Comm and Tech Coll (KY)

## HOMELAND SECURITY RELATED

Fox Valley Tech Coll (WI)
Pensacola State Coll (FL)
Tallahassee Comm Coll (FL)

## HORSE HUSBANDRY/EQUINE SCIENCE AND MANAGEMENT

Black Hawk Coll, Moline (IL)
Cecil Coll (MD)
Feather River Coll (CA)
Merced Coll (CA)
Minnesota State Comm and Tech Coll (MN)
Mt. San Antonio Coll (CA)
The Ohio State U Ag Tech Inst (OH)
Potomac State Coll of West Virginia U (WV)
Santa Rosa Jr Coll (CA)
Treasure Valley Comm Coll (OR)

## HORTICULTURAL SCIENCE

Central Lakes Coll (MN)
Century Coll (MN)
Miami Dade Coll (FL)
Mt. San Antonio Coll (CA)
Naugatuck Valley Comm Coll (CT)
The Ohio State U Ag Tech Inst (OH)
Oklahoma State U–Oklahoma City (OK)
Potomac State Coll of West Virginia U (WV)
St. Louis Comm Coll (MO)
Southeast Tech Inst (SD)
South Florida State Coll (FL)
Tarrant County Coll District (TX)
Tidewater Comm Coll (VA)
Treasure Valley Comm Coll (OR)
Trident Tech Coll (SC)
Trinity Valley Comm Coll (TX)

## HOSPITAL AND HEALTH-CARE FACILITIES ADMINISTRATION

Bossier Parish Comm Coll (LA)
Minnesota West Comm and Tech Coll (MN)

## HOSPITALITY ADMINISTRATION

Adirondack Comm Coll (NY)
Arizona Western Coll (AZ)
Austin Comm Coll District (TX)
Bristol Comm Coll (MA)
Bucks County Comm Coll (PA)
Bunker Hill Comm Coll (MA)

Camden County Coll (NJ)
Central New Mexico Comm Coll (NM)
Central Texas Coll (TX)
Chesapeake Coll (MD)
Coll of the Canyons (CA)
Coll of the Desert (CA)
Collin County Comm Coll District (TX)
Copiah-Lincoln Comm Coll (MS)
County Coll of Morris (NJ)
Daytona State Coll (FL)
Des Moines Area Comm Coll (IA)
Florida Keys Comm Coll (FL)
Fox Valley Tech Coll (WI)
Front Range Comm Coll (CO)
Gateway Tech Coll (WI)
Genesee Comm Coll (NY)
Gulf Coast State Coll (FL)
Harper Coll (IL)
Hawkeye Comm Coll (IA)
Highland Comm Coll (IL)
Hinds Comm Coll (MS)
Hudson County Comm Coll (NJ)
Ivy Tech Comm Coll–Bloomington (IN)
Ivy Tech Comm Coll–Columbus (IN)
Ivy Tech Comm Coll–East Central (IN)
Ivy Tech Comm Coll–North Central (IN)
Ivy Tech Comm Coll–Northeast (IN)
Ivy Tech Comm Coll–Northwest (IN)
Ivy Tech Comm Coll–Southwest (IN)
Jefferson Comm Coll (NY)
Jefferson State Comm Coll (AL)
J. Sargeant Reynolds Comm Coll (VA)
Lackawanna Coll (PA)
Lakeland Comm Coll (OH)
Lakes Region Comm Coll (NH)
Massachusetts Bay Comm Coll (MA)
Miami Dade Coll (FL)
Muskegon Comm Coll (MI)
Naugatuck Valley Comm Coll (CT)
Niagara County Comm Coll (NY)
North Shore Comm Coll (MA)
Pasadena City Coll (CA)
Pensacola State Coll (FL)
Potomac State Coll of West Virginia U (WV)
Quinsigamond Comm Coll (MA)
St. Louis Comm Coll (MO)
Scottsdale Comm Coll (AZ)
Sisseton-Wahpeton Coll (SD)
Southern U at Shreveport (LA)
Southwestern Coll (CA)
Sullivan County Comm Coll (NY)
Three Rivers Comm Coll (CT)
Union County Coll (NJ)
Waukesha County Tech Coll (WI)
Wor-Wic Comm Coll (MD)
York County Comm Coll (ME)

## HOSPITALITY ADMINISTRATION RELATED

Ancilla Coll (IN)
Bunker Hill Comm Coll (MA)
Chesapeake Coll (MD)
Holyoke Comm Coll (MA)
Ivy Tech Comm Coll–Central Indiana (IN)
Ivy Tech Comm Coll–East Central (IN)
Ivy Tech Comm Coll–Northeast (IN)
J. Sargeant Reynolds Comm Coll (VA)

## HOSPITALITY AND RECREATION MARKETING

Iowa Central Comm Coll (IA)
Montgomery County Comm Coll (PA)
Muskegon Comm Coll (MI)

## HOTEL/MOTEL ADMINISTRATION

Anne Arundel Comm Coll (MD)
Asheville-Buncombe Tech Comm Coll (NC)
Austin Comm Coll District (TX)
Carl Albert State Coll (OK)
Central Oregon Comm Coll (OR)
Coll of the Canyons (CA)
Comm Coll of Allegheny County (PA)
Comm Coll of Philadelphia (PA)
Del Mar Coll (TX)
El Paso Comm Coll (TX)
Frederick Comm Coll (MD)
Genesee Comm Coll (NY)
Houston Comm Coll (TX)
J. Sargeant Reynolds Comm Coll (VA)
Lackawanna Coll (PA)

Manchester Comm Coll (CT)
Miami Dade Coll (FL)
Mid-State Tech Coll (WI)
Mohawk Valley Comm Coll (NY)
Monroe Comm Coll (NY)
Montgomery Coll (MD)
Mt. San Antonio Coll (CA)
Muskegon Comm Coll (MI)
Nassau Comm Coll (NY)
Naugatuck Valley Comm Coll (CT)
Northampton Comm Coll (PA)
Northern Essex Comm Coll (MA)
Northwest Mississippi Comm Coll (MS)
Orange Coast Coll (CA)
Pensacola State Coll (FL)
Pittsburgh Tech Coll (PA)
St. Philip's Coll (TX)
Schenectady County Comm Coll (NY)
Scottsdale Comm Coll (AZ)
Southwestern Coll (CA)
Trident Tech Coll (SC)
Vincennes U (IN)

## HOTEL, MOTEL, AND RESTAURANT MANAGEMENT

Caldwell Comm Coll and Tech Inst (NC)
Carteret Comm Coll (NC)
Craven Comm Coll (NC)
Fayetteville Tech Comm Coll (NC)
Pensacola State Coll (FL)
Tompkins Cortland Comm Coll (NY)

## HOUSING AND HUMAN ENVIRONMENTS RELATED

Comm Coll of Allegheny County (PA)

## HUMAN DEVELOPMENT AND FAMILY STUDIES

Central New Mexico Comm Coll (NM)
Coll of the Desert (CA)
Missouri State U–West Plains (MO)
Penn State DuBois (PA)
Penn State Fayette, The Eberly Campus (PA)
Penn State Mont Alto (PA)
Salt Lake Comm Coll (UT)

## HUMAN DEVELOPMENT AND FAMILY STUDIES RELATED

Comm Coll of Allegheny County (PA)

## HUMANITIES

Antelope Valley Coll (CA)
Bristol Comm Coll (MA)
Brookhaven Coll (TX)
Cayuga County Comm Coll (NY)
Central Oregon Comm Coll (OR)
Cochise County Comm Coll District (AZ)
Coll of Central Florida (FL)
Coll of Marin (CA)
Coll of the Canyons (CA)
Coll of the Desert (CA)
Columbia-Greene Comm Coll (NY)
Comm Coll of Allegheny County (PA)
De Anza Coll (CA)
Dutchess Comm Coll (NY)
Erie Comm Coll (NY)
Erie Comm Coll, North Campus (NY)
Erie Comm Coll, South Campus (NY)
Feather River Coll (CA)
Fullerton Coll (CA)
Galveston Coll (TX)
Genesee Comm Coll (NY)
Harper Coll (IL)
Housatonic Comm Coll (CT)
Jamestown Comm Coll (NY)
Jefferson Comm Coll (NY)
John Tyler Comm Coll (VA)
Laramie County Comm Coll (WY)
Los Angeles City Coll (CA)
Merced Coll (CA)
Miami Dade Coll (FL)
Mohawk Valley Comm Coll (NY)
Mt. San Antonio Coll (CA)
Niagara County Comm Coll (NY)
Oklahoma City Comm Coll (OK)
Orange Coast Coll (CA)
Otero Jr Coll (CO)
Palomar Coll (CA)
Pasadena City Coll (CA)
Salt Lake Comm Coll (UT)
San Joaquin Delta Coll (CA)
Santa Rosa Jr Coll (CA)
Seminole State Coll (OK)
State U of New York Coll of Technology at Alfred (NY)
Texarkana Coll (TX)
Tompkins Cortland Comm Coll (NY)

Westchester Comm Coll (NY)
Western Wyoming Comm Coll (WY)

## HUMAN RESOURCES MANAGEMENT

Asheville-Buncombe Tech Comm Coll (NC)
Barton County Comm Coll (KS)
Beal Coll (ME)
Cecil Coll (MD)
Chippewa Valley Tech Coll (WI)
Clark Coll (WA)
Comm Coll of Allegheny County (PA)
Edison State Comm Coll (OH)
Fox Valley Tech Coll (WI)
Harford Comm Coll (MD)
Hawkeye Comm Coll (IA)
Illinois Eastern Comm Colls, Olney Central College (IL)
Lehigh Carbon Comm Coll (PA)
Lorain County Comm Coll (OH)
Minnesota State Comm and Tech Coll (MN)
Santa Rosa Jr Coll (CA)
Tulsa Comm Coll (OK)
Waukesha County Tech Coll (WI)
Western Iowa Tech Comm Coll (IA)
Wisconsin Indianhead Tech Coll (WI)

## HUMAN RESOURCES MANAGEMENT AND SERVICES RELATED

Barton County Comm Coll (KS)

## HUMAN SERVICES

Alexandria Tech and Comm Coll (MN)
American Samoa Comm Coll (AS)
Bowling Green State U–Firelands Coll (OH)
Bunker Hill Comm Coll (MA)
Central Maine Comm Coll (ME)
Central Ohio Tech Coll (OH)
Century Coll (MN)
Coll of Central Florida (FL)
Columbia-Greene Comm Coll (NY)
Comm Coll of Philadelphia (PA)
Dutchess Comm Coll (NY)
Frederick Comm Coll (MD)
Genesee Comm Coll (NY)
Georgia Highlands Coll (GA)
Greenville Tech Coll (SC)
Harper Coll (IL)
Harrisburg Area Comm Coll (PA)
Hopkinsville Comm Coll (KY)
Housatonic Comm Coll (CT)
Ivy Tech Comm Coll–Bloomington (IN)
Ivy Tech Comm Coll–Central Indiana (IN)
Ivy Tech Comm Coll–Columbus (IN)
Ivy Tech Comm Coll–East Central (IN)
Ivy Tech Comm Coll–Kokomo (IN)
Ivy Tech Comm Coll–Lafayette (IN)
Ivy Tech Comm Coll–North Central (IN)
Ivy Tech Comm Coll–Northeast (IN)
Ivy Tech Comm Coll–Northwest (IN)
Ivy Tech Comm Coll–Richmond (IN)
Ivy Tech Comm Coll–Sellersburg (IN)
Ivy Tech Comm Coll–Southeast (IN)
Ivy Tech Comm Coll–Southwest (IN)
Ivy Tech Comm Coll–Wabash Valley (IN)
Jamestown Comm Coll (NY)
Jefferson Comm Coll (NY)
Kingsborough Comm Coll of the City U of New York (NY)
Lackawanna Coll (PA)
Lake Area Tech Inst (SD)
Lakes Region Comm Coll (NH)
Laramie County Comm Coll (WY)
Lehigh Carbon Comm Coll (PA)
Los Angeles City Coll (CA)
Manchester Comm Coll (CT)
Massachusetts Bay Comm Coll (MA)
Merced Coll (CA)
Miami Dade Coll (FL)
Minnesota West Comm and Tech Coll (MN)
Mitchell Tech Inst (SD)
Mohawk Valley Comm Coll (NY)
Monroe Comm Coll (NY)
Mount Wachusett Comm Coll (MA)
New Mexico State U–Alamogordo (NM)
Niagara County Comm Coll (NY)
Northeast Comm Coll (NE)
Northern Essex Comm Coll (MA)
North Hennepin Comm Coll (MN)
Odessa Coll (TX)

Owensboro Comm and Tech Coll (KY)
Pennsylvania Highlands Comm Coll (PA)
Quinsigamond Comm Coll (MA)
Randolph Comm Coll (NC)
Raritan Valley Comm Coll (NJ)
Rock Valley Coll (IL)
St. Charles Comm Coll (MO)
St. Louis Comm Coll (MO)
Santa Rosa Jr Coll (CA)
Southern U at Shreveport (LA)
Southwestern Coll (CA)
Stark State Coll (OH)
State U of New York Coll of Technology at Alfred (NY)
Sullivan County Comm Coll (NY)
Tohono O'odham Comm Coll (AZ)
Tompkins Cortland Comm Coll (NY)
Trident Tech Coll (SC)
Union County Coll (NJ)
Urban Coll of Boston (MA)
Western Wyoming Comm Coll (WY)
White Mountains Comm Coll (NH)
York County Comm Coll (ME)

## HYDRAULICS AND FLUID POWER TECHNOLOGY

Comm Coll of Allegheny County (PA)
Comm Coll of Baltimore County (MD)
Minnesota West Comm and Tech Coll (MN)
The Ohio State U Ag Tech Inst (OH)

## ILLUSTRATION

Collin County Comm Coll District (TX)
Fashion Inst of Technology (NY)

## INDUSTRIAL AND PRODUCT DESIGN

Comm Coll of Allegheny County (PA)
Fiorello H. LaGuardia Comm Coll of the City U of New York (NY)
Mt. San Antonio Coll (CA)
Rock Valley Coll (IL)

## INDUSTRIAL ELECTRONICS TECHNOLOGY

Career Coll of Northern Nevada (NV)
Central Lakes Coll (MN)
Danville Area Comm Coll (IL)
Des Moines Area Comm Coll (IA)
Dyersburg State Comm Coll (TN)
Eastern Arizona Coll (AZ)
Hill Coll (TX)
Johnson Coll (PA)
Lehigh Carbon Comm Coll (PA)
Lenoir Comm Coll (NC)
Lurleen B. Wallace Comm Coll (AL)
Northampton Comm Coll (PA)
Northwest-Shoals Comm Coll (AL)
Pasadena City Coll (CA)
Southeast Arkansas Coll (AR)
Tyler Jr Coll (TX)
Western Wyoming Comm Coll (WY)

## INDUSTRIAL ENGINEERING

Central Lakes Coll (MN)
Manchester Comm Coll (CT)

## INDUSTRIAL MECHANICS AND MAINTENANCE TECHNOLOGY

Bevill State Comm Coll (AL)
Bossier Parish Comm Coll (LA)
Career Coll of Northern Nevada (NV)
Chippewa Valley Tech Coll (WI)
Danville Area Comm Coll (IL)
Des Moines Area Comm Coll (IA)
Dyersburg State Comm Coll (TN)
Eastern Arizona Coll (AZ)
George C. Wallace Comm Coll (AL)
H. Councill Trenholm State Comm Coll (AL)
Hill Coll (TX)
Illinois Eastern Comm Colls, Olney Central College (IL)
Ivy Tech Comm Coll–East Central (IN)
Johnson Coll (PA)
Kaskaskia Coll (IL)
Kennebec Valley Comm Coll (ME)
Lackawanna Coll (PA)
Macomb Comm Coll (MI)
Maysville Comm and Tech Coll, Maysville (KY)
Minnesota State Comm and Tech Coll (MN)
New Castle School of Trades (PA)
North Central Texas Coll (TX)
Northwest-Shoals Comm Coll (AL)

Oklahoma State U Inst of Technology (OK)
Owensboro Comm and Tech Coll (KY)
Rend Lake Coll (IL)
Renton Tech Coll (WA)
San Juan Coll (NM)
Somerset Comm Coll (KY)
Southcentral Kentucky Comm and Tech Coll (KY)
Southeast Arkansas Coll (AR)
Southwestern Comm Coll (IA)
Southwestern Michigan Coll (MI)
Texarkana Coll (TX)
Tillamook Bay Comm Coll (OR)
U of Arkansas Comm Coll at Morrilton (AR)
Western Iowa Tech Comm Coll (IA)
Western Wyoming Comm Coll (WY)
West Kentucky Comm and Tech Coll (KY)

## INDUSTRIAL PRODUCTION TECHNOLOGIES RELATED

Antelope Valley Coll (CA)
Barton County Comm Coll (KS)
Camden County Coll (NJ)
Dawson Comm Coll (MT)
Ivy Tech Comm Coll–Central Indiana (IN)
Ivy Tech Comm Coll–East Central (IN)
Ivy Tech Comm Coll–Kokomo (IN)
Ivy Tech Comm Coll–Lafayette (IN)
Ivy Tech Comm Coll–North Central (IN)
Ivy Tech Comm Coll–Northeast (IN)
Ivy Tech Comm Coll–Richmond (IN)
Ivy Tech Comm Coll–Southwest (IN)
Ivy Tech Comm Coll–Wabash Valley (IN)
Kellogg Comm Coll (MI)
Kent State U at Trumbull (OH)
Missouri State U–West Plains (MO)
North Dakota State Coll of Science (ND)
Sowela Tech Comm Coll (LA)

## INDUSTRIAL RADIOLOGIC TECHNOLOGY

Amarillo Coll (TX)
Copiah-Lincoln Comm Coll (MS)
Del Mar Coll (TX)
Eastern Gateway Comm Coll (OH)
Iowa Central Comm Coll (IA)
Los Angeles City Coll (CA)
McLennan Comm Coll (TX)
Monroe Comm Coll (NY)
Mt. San Antonio Coll (CA)
National Park Coll (AR)
Northern Essex Comm Coll (MA)
Odessa Coll (TX)
Salt Lake Comm Coll (UT)
Tarrant County Coll District (TX)

## INDUSTRIAL SAFETY TECHNOLOGY

Fox Valley Tech Coll (WI)
Southwestern Coll (CA)

## INDUSTRIAL TECHNOLOGY

Arizona Western Coll (AZ)
Bossier Parish Comm Coll (LA)
Bowling Green State U–Firelands Coll (OH)
Central Louisiana Tech Comm Coll (LA)
Central Oregon Comm Coll (OR)
Central Virginia Comm Coll (VA)
Cleveland State Comm Coll (TN)
Coll of the Ouachitas (AR)
Comm Coll of Allegheny County (PA)
Crowder Coll (MO)
De Anza Coll (CA)
Eastern Gateway Comm Coll (OH)
Edison State Comm Coll (OH)
Erie Comm Coll, North Campus (NY)
Gateway Comm and Tech Coll (KY)
Grand Rapids Comm Coll (MI)
Hagerstown Comm Coll (MD)
Highland Comm Coll (IL)
Hopkinsville Comm Coll (KY)
Illinois Central Coll (IL)
Illinois Eastern Comm Colls, Wabash Valley College (IL)
Illinois Valley Comm Coll (IL)
Ivy Tech Comm Coll–Bloomington (IN)
Ivy Tech Comm Coll–Central Indiana (IN)
Ivy Tech Comm Coll–Columbus (IN)

Ivy Tech Comm Coll–East Central (IN)
Ivy Tech Comm Coll–Kokomo (IN)
Ivy Tech Comm Coll–Lafayette (IN)
Ivy Tech Comm Coll–North Central (IN)
Ivy Tech Comm Coll–Northeast (IN)
Ivy Tech Comm Coll–Northwest (IN)
Ivy Tech Comm Coll–Richmond (IN)
Ivy Tech Comm Coll–Sellersburg (IN)
Ivy Tech Comm Coll–Southeast (IN)
Ivy Tech Comm Coll–Southwest (IN)
Ivy Tech Comm Coll–Wabash Valley (IN)
John Tyler Comm Coll (VA)
Kellogg Comm Coll (MI)
Kent State U at Trumbull (OH)
Kent State U at Tuscarawas (OH)
Lackawanna Coll (PA)
Lenoir Comm Coll (NC)
Macomb Comm Coll (MI)
Manchester Comm Coll (CT)
Miami Dade Coll (FL)
Mid-State Tech Coll (WI)
Monroe Comm Coll (NY)
Monroe County Comm Coll (MI)
Muskegon Comm Coll (MI)
Navarro Coll (TX)
Northeast State Comm Coll (TN)
Nunez Comm Coll (LA)
The Ohio State U Ag Tech Inst (OH)
Panola Coll (TX)
Piedmont Comm Coll (NC)
Richland Coll (TX)
Rock Valley Coll (IL)
Rowan-Cabarrus Comm Coll (NC)
St. Charles Comm Coll (MO)
San Juan Coll (NM)
Seminole State Coll of Florida (FL)
Stark State Coll (OH)
Treasure Valley Comm Coll (OR)
Trident Tech Coll (SC)
Victoria Coll (TX)
Walters State Comm Coll (TN)

**INFORMATICS**
Ivy Tech Comm Coll–Bloomington (IN)
Ivy Tech Comm Coll–Central Indiana (IN)
Ivy Tech Comm Coll–Columbus (IN)
Ivy Tech Comm Coll–East Central (IN)
Ivy Tech Comm Coll–Kokomo (IN)
Ivy Tech Comm Coll–Lafayette (IN)
Ivy Tech Comm Coll–Richmond (IN)
Ivy Tech Comm Coll–Sellersburg (IN)
Ivy Tech Comm Coll–Southeast (IN)
Ivy Tech Comm Coll–Southwest (IN)
Ivy Tech Comm Coll–Wabash Valley (IN)

**INFORMATION RESOURCES MANAGEMENT**
U of Arkansas Rich Mountain (AR)

**INFORMATION SCIENCE/ STUDIES**
Alamance Comm Coll (NC)
Alexandria Tech and Comm Coll (MN)
Amarillo Coll (TX)
Asheville-Buncombe Tech Comm Coll (NC)
Barton County Comm Coll (KS)
Bossier Parish Comm Coll (LA)
Bristol Comm Coll (MA)
Brookhaven Coll (TX)
Bucks County Comm Coll (PA)
Cayuga County Comm Coll (NY)
Century Coll (MN)
Cochise County Comm Coll District (AZ)
Coll of The Albemarle (NC)
Dabney S. Lancaster Comm Coll (VA)
De Anza Coll (CA)
Del Mar Coll (TX)
Dutchess Comm Coll (NY)
Dyersburg State Comm Coll (TN)
Eastern Arizona Coll (AZ)
Genesee Comm Coll (NY)
Harford Comm Coll (MD)
Howard Comm Coll (MD)
ITI Tech Coll (LA)
Ivy Tech Comm Coll–Bloomington (IN)
Ivy Tech Comm Coll–Central Indiana (IN)
Ivy Tech Comm Coll–Columbus (IN)

Ivy Tech Comm Coll–East Central (IN)
Ivy Tech Comm Coll–Kokomo (IN)
Ivy Tech Comm Coll–Lafayette (IN)
Ivy Tech Comm Coll–Richmond (IN)
Ivy Tech Comm Coll–Sellersburg (IN)
Ivy Tech Comm Coll–Southeast (IN)
Ivy Tech Comm Coll–Southwest (IN)
Ivy Tech Comm Coll–Wabash Valley (IN)
Jamestown Comm Coll (NY)
Jefferson Comm Coll (NY)
Manchester Comm Coll (CT)
McLennan Comm Coll (TX)
Miami Dade Coll (FL)
Mid-State Tech Coll (WI)
Mission Coll (CA)
Mitchell Comm Coll (NC)
Monroe Comm Coll (NY)
Muskegon Comm Coll (MI)
National Park Coll (AR)
New River Comm Coll (VA)
Niagara County Comm Coll (NY)
North Central Texas Coll (TX)
North Shore Comm Coll (MA)
Odessa Coll (TX)
Oklahoma State U–Oklahoma City (OK)
Panola Coll (TX)
Paris Jr Coll (TX)
Penn State DuBois (PA)
Pensacola State Coll (FL)
Queensborough Comm Coll of the City U of New York (NY)
Rappahannock Comm Coll (VA)
Rowan-Cabarrus Comm Coll (NC)
Salt Lake Comm Coll (UT)
Scottsdale Comm Coll (AZ)
Seminole State Coll of Florida (FL)
Sisseton-Wahpeton Coll (SD)
Southwestern Comm Coll (NC)
State U of New York Coll of Technology at Alfred (NY)
Sullivan County Comm Coll (NY)
Tompkins Cortland Comm Coll (NY)
Westchester Comm Coll (NY)
Western Wyoming Comm Coll (WY)
Wytheville Comm Coll (VA)

**INFORMATION TECHNOLOGY**
Adirondack Comm Coll (NY)
Antelope Valley Coll (CA)
Asheville-Buncombe Tech Comm Coll (NC)
Beal Coll (ME)
Black Hawk Coll, Moline (IL)
Blue Ridge Comm and Tech Coll (WV)
Caldwell Comm Coll and Tech Inst (NC)
Carteret Comm Coll (NC)
Chandler-Gilbert Comm Coll (AZ)
City Colls of Chicago, Olive-Harvey College (IL)
Cleveland Comm Coll (NC)
Coll of Central Florida (FL)
Coll of The Albemarle (NC)
Coll of the Desert (CA)
Columbia-Greene Comm Coll (NY)
County Coll of Morris (NJ)
Craven Comm Coll (NC)
Daytona State Coll (FL)
Del Mar Coll (TX)
Des Moines Area Comm Coll (IA)
Dyersburg State Comm Coll (TN)
Erie Comm Coll, South Campus (NY)
Fayetteville Tech Comm Coll (NC)
Florida Keys Comm Coll (FL)
Frederick Comm Coll (MD)
Fullerton Coll (CA)
Georgia Military Coll (GA)
Gordon State Coll (GA)
Great Falls Coll Montana State U (MT)
Halifax Comm Coll (NC)
Haywood Comm Coll (NC)
Highland Comm Coll (IL)
Howard Comm Coll (MD)
Illinois Eastern Comm Colls, Frontier Community College (IL)
Illinois Eastern Comm Colls, Olney Central College (IL)
Illinois Valley Comm Coll (IL)
ITI Tech Coll (LA)
Ivy Tech Comm Coll–Bloomington (IN)
Ivy Tech Comm Coll–Central Indiana (IN)
Ivy Tech Comm Coll–Columbus (IN)

Ivy Tech Comm Coll–East Central (IN)
Ivy Tech Comm Coll–Kokomo (IN)
Ivy Tech Comm Coll–Lafayette (IN)
Ivy Tech Comm Coll–Richmond (IN)
Ivy Tech Comm Coll–Sellersburg (IN)
Ivy Tech Comm Coll–Southeast (IN)
Ivy Tech Comm Coll–Southwest (IN)
Ivy Tech Comm Coll–Wabash Valley (IN)
James Sprunt Comm Coll (NC)
Jamestown Comm Coll (NY)
Johnson Coll (PA)
John Tyler Comm Coll (VA)
Kishwaukee Coll (IL)
LDS Business Coll (UT)
Lenoir Comm Coll (NC)
Los Angeles City Coll (CA)
McHenry County Coll (IL)
Merced Coll (CA)
Miami Dade Coll (FL)
Minnesota State Comm and Tech Coll (MN)
Minnesota West Comm and Tech Coll (MN)
Mitchell Comm Coll (NC)
Mohave Comm Coll (AZ)
Monroe Comm Coll (NY)
Monroe County Comm Coll (MI)
Montgomery Comm Coll (NC)
Montgomery County Comm Coll (PA)
Morton Coll (IL)
New Mexico State U–Alamogordo (NM)
Northeast State Comm Coll (TN)
Oakton Comm Coll (IL)
Oklahoma State U Inst of Technology (OK)
Oklahoma State U–Oklahoma City (OK)
Palomar Coll (CA)
Panola Coll (TX)
Pensacola State Coll (FL)
Piedmont Comm Coll (NC)
Piedmont Virginia Comm Coll (VA)
Queensborough Comm Coll of the City U of New York (NY)
Randolph Comm Coll (NC)
Raritan Valley Comm Coll (NJ)
Richmond Comm Coll (NC)
Rowan-Cabarrus Comm Coll (NC)
Salt Lake Comm Coll (UT)
Seminole State Coll of Florida (FL)
Shawnee Comm Coll (IL)
Southeast Kentucky Comm and Tech Coll (KY)
South Suburban Coll (IL)
Southwestern Coll (CA)
Tallahassee Comm Coll (FL)
Tidewater Comm Coll (VA)
Tri-County Comm Coll (NC)
Union County Coll (NJ)
Vincennes U (IN)
Volunteer State Comm Coll (TN)
Wade Coll (TX)
Wayne Comm Coll (NC)
Western Wyoming Comm Coll (WY)

**INSTITUTIONAL FOOD WORKERS**
El Paso Comm Coll (TX)
James Sprunt Comm Coll (NC)
Southwestern Indian Polytechnic Inst (NM)

**INSTRUMENTATION TECHNOLOGY**
Amarillo Coll (TX)
Bevill State Comm Coll (AL)
Hagerstown Comm Coll (MD)
Houston Comm Coll (TX)
ITI Tech Coll (LA)
Lakeland Comm Coll (OH)
Merced Coll (CA)
Mid-State Tech Coll (WI)
Monroe Comm Coll (NY)
Nassau Comm Coll (NY)
New River Comm Coll (VA)
Ridgewater Coll (MN)
St. Philip's Coll (TX)
Salt Lake Comm Coll (UT)
San Jacinto Coll District (TX)
San Juan Coll (NM)
Sowela Tech Comm Coll (LA)
Texas State Tech Coll (TX)
Western Wyoming Comm Coll (WY)

**INSURANCE**
Comm Coll of Allegheny County (PA)
Mesa Comm Coll (AZ)

Nassau Comm Coll (NY)
Palomar Coll (CA)
Southeast Tech Inst (SD)
Southwestern Coll (CA)
Trinity Valley Comm Coll (TX)

**INTELLIGENCE**
Cochise County Comm Coll District (AZ)

**INTERDISCIPLINARY STUDIES**
Bowling Green State U–Firelands Coll (OH)
Del Mar Coll (TX)
Gateway Tech Coll (WI)
Maysville Comm and Tech Coll, Maysville (KY)
Northeast State Comm Coll (TN)
North Shore Comm Coll (MA)
Oklahoma State U Inst of Technology (OK)
Schenectady County Comm Coll (NY)
U of Wisconsin–Baraboo/Sauk County (WI)
U of Wisconsin–Barron County (WI)
U of Wisconsin–Fond du Lac (WI)
U of Wisconsin–Fox Valley (WI)
U of Wisconsin–Manitowoc (WI)
U of Wisconsin–Marathon County (WI)
U of Wisconsin–Marinette (WI)
U of Wisconsin–Marshfield/Wood County (WI)
U of Wisconsin–Richland (WI)
U of Wisconsin–Rock County (WI)
U of Wisconsin–Sheboygan (WI)
U of Wisconsin–Washington County (WI)
U of Wisconsin–Waukesha (WI)
Victoria Coll (TX)
Western Dakota Tech Inst (SD)
Williamsburg Tech Coll (SC)
Wisconsin Indianhead Tech Coll (WI)

**INTERIOR ARCHITECTURE**
Coll of Central Florida (FL)

**INTERIOR DESIGN**
Alexandria Tech and Comm Coll (MN)
Amarillo Coll (TX)
Antelope Valley Coll (CA)
Century Coll (MN)
Coll of Marin (CA)
Coll of the Canyons (CA)
Collin County Comm Coll District (TX)
Daytona State Coll (FL)
El Paso Comm Coll (TX)
Fashion Inst of Technology (NY)
FIDM/Fashion Inst of Design & Merchandising, Orange County Campus (CA)
Fox Valley Tech Coll (WI)
Front Range Comm Coll (CO)
Fullerton Coll (CA)
Gateway Tech Coll (WI)
Harper Coll (IL)
Houston Comm Coll (TX)
Ivy Tech Comm Coll–Columbus (IN)
Ivy Tech Comm Coll–East Central (IN)
Ivy Tech Comm Coll–North Central (IN)
Ivy Tech Comm Coll–Southwest (IN)
LDS Business Coll (UT)
Lehigh Carbon Comm Coll (PA)
Mesa Comm Coll (AZ)
Miami Dade Coll (FL)
Monroe Comm Coll (NY)
Montgomery Coll (MD)
Mt. San Antonio Coll (CA)
Nassau Comm Coll (NY)
Northampton Comm Coll (PA)
Orange Coast Coll (CA)
Palomar Coll (CA)
Randolph Comm Coll (NC)
Raritan Valley Comm Coll (NJ)
St. Louis Comm Coll (MO)
San Jacinto Coll District (TX)
Santa Rosa Jr Coll (CA)
Scottsdale Comm Coll (AZ)
Seminole State Coll of Florida (FL)
State U of New York Coll of Technology at Alfred (NY)
Tidewater Comm Coll (VA)
Tulsa Comm Coll (OK)
Wade Coll (TX)
Waukesha County Tech Coll (WI)

Western Iowa Tech Comm Coll (IA)

**INTERMEDIA/MULTIMEDIA**
Bristol Comm Coll (MA)
Oklahoma State U Inst of Technology (OK)

**INTERNATIONAL BUSINESS/ TRADE/COMMERCE**
Austin Comm Coll District (TX)
Bunker Hill Comm Coll (MA)
El Paso Comm Coll (TX)
Fullerton Coll (CA)
Harper Coll (IL)
Houston Comm Coll (TX)
Massachusetts Bay Comm Coll (MA)
Monroe Comm Coll (NY)
Orange Coast Coll (CA)
Palomar Coll (CA)
Pasadena City Coll (CA)
Richland Coll (TX)
San Jacinto Coll District (TX)
Southwestern Coll (CA)
Tompkins Cortland Comm Coll (NY)
Tulsa Comm Coll (OK)
Waukesha County Tech Coll (WI)
Westchester Comm Coll (NY)
White Mountains Comm Coll (NH)

**INTERNATIONAL/GLOBAL STUDIES**
Jamestown Comm Coll (NY)
Macomb Comm Coll (MI)
Massachusetts Bay Comm Coll (MA)
Northampton Comm Coll (PA)
Northwest Vista Coll (TX)
Pasadena City Coll (CA)
Salt Lake Comm Coll (UT)
Tompkins Cortland Comm Coll (NY)

**INTERNATIONAL RELATIONS AND AFFAIRS**
Coll of Marin (CA)
De Anza Coll (CA)
Harford Comm Coll (MD)
Harrisburg Area Comm Coll (PA)
Merced Coll (CA)
Miami Dade Coll (FL)
Northwest Coll (WY)
Salt Lake Comm Coll (UT)

**IRONWORKING**
Ivy Tech Comm Coll–North Central (IN)
Ivy Tech Comm Coll–Northeast (IN)
Ivy Tech Comm Coll–Northwest (IN)
Ivy Tech Comm Coll–Southwest (IN)
Ivy Tech Comm Coll–Wabash Valley (IN)

**ITALIAN**
Austin Comm Coll District (TX)
Coll of the Desert (CA)
Miami Dade Coll (FL)
Southwestern Coll (CA)

**JAPANESE**
Austin Comm Coll District (TX)
Fiorello H. LaGuardia Comm Coll of the City U of New York (NY)
Los Angeles City Coll (CA)

**JAZZ/JAZZ STUDIES**
Santa Rosa Jr Coll (CA)

**JOURNALISM**
Amarillo Coll (TX)
Austin Comm Coll District (TX)
Barton County Comm Coll (KS)
Bucks County Comm Coll (PA)
Central Texas Coll (TX)
Cloud County Comm Coll (KS)
Cochise County Comm Coll District (AZ)
Coll of Central Florida (FL)
Coll of the Canyons (CA)
Coll of the Desert (CA)
Comm Coll of Allegheny County (PA)
Copiah-Lincoln Comm Coll (MS)
De Anza Coll (CA)
Del Mar Coll (TX)
Fullerton Coll (CA)
Grand Rapids Comm Coll (MI)
Illinois Valley Comm Coll (IL)
Iowa Central Comm Coll (IA)
Kingsborough Comm Coll of the City U of New York (NY)
Los Angeles City Coll (CA)
Manchester Comm Coll (CT)
Mesa Comm Coll (AZ)
Miami Dade Coll (FL)

Monroe County Comm Coll (MI)
Mt. San Antonio Coll (CA)
Northampton Comm Coll (PA)
Northeastern Jr Coll (CO)
Northern Essex Comm Coll (MA)
Oklahoma City Comm Coll (OK)
Orange Coast Coll (CA)
Palomar Coll (CA)
Panola Coll (TX)
Paris Jr Coll (TX)
Pensacola State Coll (FL)
Potomac State Coll of West Virginia U (WV)
San Jacinto Coll District (TX)
San Joaquin Delta Coll (CA)
Southwestern Coll (CA)
Texarkana Coll (TX)
Trinity Valley Comm Coll (TX)
Tyler Jr Coll (TX)
Vincennes U (IN)
Westchester Comm Coll (NY)
Western Wyoming Comm Coll (WY)

### JUVENILE CORRECTIONS
Danville Area Comm Coll (IL)
Illinois Valley Comm Coll (IL)
Kaskaskia Coll (IL)

### KINDERGARTEN/PRESCHOOL EDUCATION
Alamance Comm Coll (NC)
Bristol Comm Coll (MA)
Central Lakes Coll (MN)
Comm Coll of Philadelphia (PA)
County Coll of Morris (NJ)
Del Mar Coll (TX)
El Paso Comm Coll (TX)
Genesee Comm Coll (NY)
Hesston Coll (KS)
Howard Comm Coll (MD)
Manchester Comm Coll (CT)
McLennan Comm Coll (TX)
Mesa Comm Coll (AZ)
Miami Dade Coll (FL)
Mitchell Comm Coll (NC)
Mt. San Antonio Coll (CA)
Nassau Comm Coll (NY)
Northern Essex Comm Coll (MA)
Northern Maine Comm Coll (ME)
North Shore Comm Coll (MA)
Nunez Comm Coll (LA)
Odessa Coll (TX)
Otero Jr Coll (CO)
Quinsigamond Comm Coll (MA)
Raritan Valley Comm Coll (NJ)
Sisseton-Wahpeton Coll (SD)
Southern U at Shreveport (LA)
Sullivan County Comm Coll (NY)
Tidewater Comm Coll (VA)
Trinity Valley Comm Coll (TX)
Truckee Meadows Comm Coll (NV)

### KINESIOLOGY AND EXERCISE SCIENCE
Ancilla Coll (IN)
Antelope Valley Coll (CA)
Austin Comm Coll District (TX)
Barton County Comm Coll (KS)
Bucks County Comm Coll (PA)
Carroll Comm Coll (MD)
Central Oregon Comm Coll (OR)
Central Texas Coll (TX)
Chandler-Gilbert Comm Coll (AZ)
Coll of the Canyons (CA)
Coll of the Desert (CA)
County Coll of Morris (NJ)
Feather River Coll (CA)
Hudson County Comm Coll (NJ)
Ivy Tech Comm Coll–East Central (IN)
Ivy Tech Comm Coll–Sellersburg (IN)
Laramie County Comm Coll (WY)
Lehigh Carbon Comm Coll (PA)
Merced Coll (CA)
Mount Wachusett Comm Coll (MA)
Northeast Comm Coll (NE)
Orange Coast Coll (CA)
Palomar Coll (CA)
Raritan Valley Comm Coll (NJ)
St. Philip's Coll (TX)
Salt Lake Comm Coll (UT)
San Jacinto Coll District (TX)
Santa Rosa Jr Coll (CA)
South Suburban Coll (IL)
Three Rivers Comm Coll (CT)
Western Wyoming Comm Coll (WY)

### KOREAN
Los Angeles City Coll (CA)

### LABOR AND INDUSTRIAL RELATIONS
Kingsborough Comm Coll of the City U of New York (NY)

### LANDSCAPE ARCHITECTURE
Caldwell Comm Coll and Tech Inst (NC)
Chesapeake Coll (MD)
Monroe Comm Coll (NY)
Mt. San Antonio Coll (CA)
Truckee Meadows Comm Coll (NV)
Western Texas Coll (TX)

### LANDSCAPING AND GROUNDSKEEPING
Antelope Valley Coll (CA)
Coll of Central Florida (FL)
Coll of Marin (CA)
Comm Coll of Allegheny County (PA)
Fullerton Coll (CA)
Grand Rapids Comm Coll (MI)
Hawkeye Comm Coll (IA)
Hinds Comm Coll (MS)
Kishwaukee Coll (IL)
Miami Dade Coll (FL)
The Ohio State U Ag Tech Inst (OH)
Pensacola State Coll (FL)
San Juan Coll (NM)
Santa Rosa Jr Coll (CA)
Southeast Tech Inst (SD)
South Florida State Coll (FL)
Southwestern Coll (CA)
Springfield Tech Comm Coll (MA)

### LANGUAGE INTERPRETATION AND TRANSLATION
Century Coll (MN)
Cleveland Comm Coll (NC)
Des Moines Area Comm Coll (IA)
Lake Region State Coll (ND)
Southwestern Coll (CA)

### LASER AND OPTICAL TECHNOLOGY
Amarillo Coll (TX)
Monroe Comm Coll (NY)
Quinsigamond Comm Coll (MA)
Springfield Tech Comm Coll (MA)
Texas State Tech Coll (TX)
Three Rivers Comm Coll (CT)

### LATIN
Austin Comm Coll District (TX)

### LATIN AMERICAN STUDIES
Central New Mexico Comm Coll (NM)
Miami Dade Coll (FL)
Santa Rosa Jr Coll (CA)

### LAW ENFORCEMENT INVESTIGATION AND INTERVIEWING
Arizona Western Coll (AZ)
Mohawk Valley Comm Coll (NY)

### LEGAL ADMINISTRATIVE ASSISTANT/SECRETARY
Alamance Comm Coll (NC)
Alexandria Tech and Comm Coll (MN)
Alvin Comm Coll (TX)
Amarillo Coll (TX)
Central Lakes Coll (MN)
Cleveland Comm Coll (NC)
Comm Coll of Allegheny County (PA)
Craven Comm Coll (NC)
Crowder Coll (MO)
Dabney S. Lancaster Comm Coll (VA)
Del Mar Coll (TX)
Eastern Gateway Comm Coll (OH)
Fullerton Coll (CA)
Harper Coll (IL)
Howard Comm Coll (MD)
Kellogg Comm Coll (MI)
Los Angeles City Coll (CA)
Manchester Comm Coll (CT)
McLennan Comm Coll (TX)
Miami Dade Coll (FL)
Minnesota State Comm and Tech Coll (MN)
Monroe Comm Coll (NY)
Monroe County Comm Coll (MI)
Morton Coll (IL)
Mt. San Antonio Coll (CA)
Muskegon Comm Coll (MI)
Nassau Comm Coll (NY)
Navarro Coll (TX)
North Central Texas Coll (TX)
North Iowa Area Comm Coll (IA)
North Shore Comm Coll (MA)

Odessa Coll (TX)
Pensacola State Coll (FL)
Renton Tech Coll (WA)
Ridgewater Coll (MN)
Sauk Valley Comm Coll (IL)
Southwestern Coll (CA)
Stark State Coll (OH)
Trinity Valley Comm Coll (TX)
Western Wyoming Comm Coll (WY)

### LEGAL ASSISTANT/PARALEGAL
Alexandria Tech and Comm Coll (MN)
Alvin Comm Coll (TX)
Anne Arundel Comm Coll (MD)
Arizona Western Coll (AZ)
Austin Comm Coll District (TX)
Blue Ridge Comm and Tech Coll (WV)
Bristol Comm Coll (MA)
Bunker Hill Comm Coll (MA)
Caldwell Comm Coll and Tech Inst (NC)
Camden County Coll (NJ)
Carteret Comm Coll (NC)
Central Texas Coll (TX)
Chesapeake Coll (MD)
Chippewa Valley Tech Coll (WI)
Cloud County Comm Coll (KS)
Coll of Central Florida (FL)
Coll of Eastern Idaho (ID)
Coll of the Canyons (CA)
Collin County Comm Coll District (TX)
Comm Coll of Allegheny County (PA)
Comm Coll of Baltimore County (MD)
Daytona State Coll (FL)
De Anza Coll (CA)
Des Moines Area Comm Coll (IA)
Dutchess Comm Coll (NY)
Edison State Comm Coll (OH)
El Paso Comm Coll (TX)
Erie Comm Coll (NY)
Fayetteville Tech Comm Coll (NC)
Fiorello H. LaGuardia Comm Coll of the City U of New York (NY)
Fox Valley Tech Coll (WI)
Frederick Comm Coll (MD)
Front Range Comm Coll (CO)
Fullerton Coll (CA)
Genesee Comm Coll (NY)
Georgia Military Coll (GA)
Greenville Tech Coll (SC)
Halifax Comm Coll (NC)
Harford Comm Coll (MD)
Harper Coll (IL)
Harrisburg Area Comm Coll (PA)
Hinds Comm Coll (MS)
Houston Comm Coll (TX)
Hutchinson Comm Coll (KS)
Illinois Central Coll (IL)
Illinois Eastern Comm Colls, Wabash Valley College (IL)
Ivy Tech Comm Coll–Bloomington (IN)
Ivy Tech Comm Coll–Central Indiana (IN)
Ivy Tech Comm Coll–Columbus (IN)
Ivy Tech Comm Coll–East Central (IN)
Ivy Tech Comm Coll–Kokomo (IN)
Ivy Tech Comm Coll–Lafayette (IN)
Ivy Tech Comm Coll–North Central (IN)
Ivy Tech Comm Coll–Northeast (IN)
Ivy Tech Comm Coll–Northwest (IN)
Ivy Tech Comm Coll–Richmond (IN)
Ivy Tech Comm Coll–Sellersburg (IN)
Ivy Tech Comm Coll–Southeast (IN)
Ivy Tech Comm Coll–Southwest (IN)
Ivy Tech Comm Coll–Wabash Valley (IN)
Jefferson Comm Coll (NY)
Johnston Comm Coll (NC)
J. Sargeant Reynolds Comm Coll (VA)
Kent State U at East Liverpool (OH)
Kent State U at Trumbull (OH)
Lackawanna Coll (PA)
Lakeland Comm Coll (OH)
Lakeshore Tech Coll (WI)
Lake Superior Coll (MN)
Laramie County Comm Coll (WY)
Lehigh Carbon Comm Coll (PA)
Los Angeles City Coll (CA)
Macomb Comm Coll (MI)
Manchester Comm Coll (CT)
Manor Coll (PA)
Massachusetts Bay Comm Coll (MA)
McLennan Comm Coll (TX)
Miami Dade Coll (FL)

Minnesota State Comm and Tech Coll (MN)
Mohave Comm Coll (AZ)
Montgomery Coll (MD)
Mt. San Antonio Coll (CA)
Mount Wachusett Comm Coll (MA)
Nassau Comm Coll (NY)
Naugatuck Valley Comm Coll (CT)
Navarro Coll (TX)
New Mexico State U–Alamogordo (NM)
Northampton Comm Coll (PA)
North Central Texas Coll (TX)
North Hennepin Comm Coll (MN)
North Shore Comm Coll (MA)
NorthWest Arkansas Comm Coll (AR)
Northwest Mississippi Comm Coll (MS)
Nunez Comm Coll (LA)
Pasadena City Coll (CA)
Pensacola State Coll (FL)
Raritan Valley Comm Coll (NJ)
St. Louis Comm Coll (MO)
Salt Lake Comm Coll (UT)
San Jacinto Coll District (TX)
San Juan Coll (NM)
Santa Rosa Jr Coll (CA)
Seminole State Coll of Florida (FL)
Southeast Arkansas Coll (AR)
South Suburban Coll (IL)
Southwestern Coll (CA)
Southwestern Comm Coll (NC)
Sullivan County Comm Coll (NY)
Tallahassee Comm Coll (FL)
Tarrant County Coll District (TX)
Tidewater Comm Coll (VA)
Tompkins Cortland Comm Coll (NY)
Trident Tech Coll (SC)
Truckee Meadows Comm Coll (NV)
Tulsa Comm Coll (OK)
Tyler Jr Coll (TX)
Union County Coll (NJ)
Vincennes U (IN)
Volunteer State Comm Coll (TN)
Wayne County Comm Coll District (MI)
Westchester Comm Coll (NY)
Western Iowa Tech Comm Coll (IA)

### LEGAL PROFESSIONS AND STUDIES RELATED
Bristol Comm Coll (MA)
Bucks County Comm Coll (PA)

### LEGAL STUDIES
Alvin Comm Coll (TX)
Carroll Comm Coll (MD)
Del Mar Coll (TX)
Harford Comm Coll (MD)
Macomb Comm Coll (MI)
Navarro Coll (TX)
Palomar Coll (CA)
Trident Tech Coll (SC)

### LIBERAL ARTS AND SCIENCES AND HUMANITIES RELATED
Anne Arundel Comm Coll (MD)
Bossier Parish Comm Coll (LA)
Bucks County Comm Cbll (PA)
Chandler-Gilbert Comm Coll (AZ)
Chesapeake Coll (MD)
Cleveland Comm Coll (NC)
Coll of Central Florida (FL)
Comm Coll of Baltimore County (MD)
Craven Comm Coll (NC)
Dutchess Comm Coll (NY)
Erie Comm Coll (NY)
Fayetteville Tech Comm Coll (NC)
Frederick Comm Coll (MD)
Front Range Comm Coll (CO)
Genesee Comm Coll (NY)
Georgia Highlands Coll (GA)
Great Falls Coll Montana State U (MT)
Hagerstown Comm Coll (MD)
Halifax Comm Coll (NC)
Harford Comm Coll (MD)
Haywood Comm Coll (NC)
Holyoke Comm Coll (MA)
Ivy Tech Comm Coll–Richmond (IN)
James Sprunt Comm Coll (NC)
Jamestown Comm Coll (NY)
J. Sargeant Reynolds Comm Coll (VA)
Kellogg Comm Coll (MI)
Kent State U at Ashtabula (OH)
Kent State U at East Liverpool (OH)
Kent State U at Salem (OH)
Kent State U at Trumbull (OH)
Kent State U at Tuscarawas (OH)
Lackawanna Coll (PA)

Lenoir Comm Coll (NC)
Louisiana State U at Eunice (LA)
Minnesota West Comm and Tech Coll (MN)
Mitchell Comm Coll (NC)
Mohawk Valley Comm Coll (NY)
Montgomery Coll (MD)
Northampton Comm Coll (PA)
Northern Maine Comm Coll (ME)
Nunez Comm Coll (LA)
Ozarks Tech Comm Coll (MO)
Panola Coll (TX)
Piedmont Comm Coll (NC)
Piedmont Virginia Comm Coll (VA)
Pueblo Comm Coll (CO)
Randolph Comm Coll (NC)
Ridgewater Coll (MN)
Southern U at Shreveport (LA)
South Florida State Coll (FL)
Sowela Tech Comm Coll (LA)
State U of New York Coll of Technology at Alfred (NY)
Tompkins Cortland Comm Coll (NY)
Vincennes U (IN)
Wayne Comm Coll (NC)
Wor-Wic Comm Coll (MD)

### LIBERAL ARTS AND SCIENCES/LIBERAL STUDIES
Adirondack Comm Coll (NY)
Alamance Comm Coll (NC)
Alexandria Tech and Comm Coll (MN)
Alvin Comm Coll (TX)
Amarillo Coll (TX)
American Samoa Comm Coll (AS)
Anne Arundel Comm Coll (MD)
Antelope Valley Coll (CA)
Asheville-Buncombe Tech Comm Coll (NC)
Barton County Comm Coll (KS)
Bevill State Comm Coll (AL)
Black Hawk Coll, Moline (IL)
Blue Ridge Comm and Tech Coll (WV)
Bossier Parish Comm Coll (LA)
Bowling Green State U–Firelands Coll (OH)
Bristol Comm Coll (MA)
Brookhaven Coll (TX)
Bucks County Comm Coll (PA)
Caldwell Comm Coll and Tech Inst (NC)
Camden County Coll (NJ)
Carroll Comm Coll (MD)
Carteret Comm Coll (NC)
Cayuga County Comm Coll (NY)
Cecil Coll (MD)
Central Lakes Coll (MN)
Central Maine Comm Coll (ME)
Central New Mexico Comm Coll (NM)
Central Ohio Tech Coll (OH)
Central Oregon Comm Coll (OR)
Central Texas Coll (TX)
Central Virginia Comm Coll (VA)
Century Coll (MN)
Chandler-Gilbert Comm Coll (AZ)
Chesapeake Coll (MD)
Chipola Coll (FL)
Chippewa Valley Tech Coll (WI)
City Colls of Chicago, Olive-Harvey College (IL)
Clark Coll (WA)
Cleveland Comm Coll (NC)
Cleveland State Comm Coll (TN)
Cloud County Comm Coll (KS)
Coll of Central Florida (FL)
Coll of Marin (CA)
Coll of The Albemarle (NC)
Coll of the Canyons (CA)
Coll of the Desert (CA)
Coll of the Ouachitas (AR)
Collin County Comm Coll District (TX)
Colorado Northwestern Comm Coll (CO)
Columbia-Greene Comm Coll (NY)
Comm Coll of Allegheny County (PA)
Comm Coll of Baltimore County (MD)
Comm Coll of Philadelphia (PA)
Copiah-Lincoln Comm Coll (MS)
County Coll of Morris (NJ)
Craven Comm Coll (NC)
Crowder Coll (MO)
Dabney S. Lancaster Comm Coll (VA)
Danville Area Comm Coll (IL)
Dawson Comm Coll (MT)
Daytona State Coll (FL)
De Anza Coll (CA)
Del Mar Coll (TX)

Des Moines Area Comm Coll (IA)
Donnelly Coll (KS)
Dutchess Comm Coll (NY)
Dyersburg State Comm Coll (TN)
Eastern Arizona Coll (AZ)
Eastern Shore Comm Coll (VA)
Edison State Comm Coll (OH)
El Paso Comm Coll (TX)
Erie Comm Coll (NY)
Erie Comm Coll, North Campus (NY)
Erie Comm Coll, South Campus (NY)
Fayetteville Tech Comm Coll (NC)
Feather River Coll (CA)
Fiorello H. LaGuardia Comm Coll of the City U of New York (NY)
Florida Keys Comm Coll (FL)
Frederick Comm Coll (MD)
Front Range Comm Coll (CO)
Fullerton Coll (CA)
Galveston Coll (TX)
Gateway Comm and Tech Coll (KY)
Genesee Comm Coll (NY)
George C. Wallace Comm Coll (AL)
Gordon State Coll (GA)
Grand Rapids Comm Coll (MI)
Greenville Tech Coll (SC)
Gulf Coast State Coll (FL)
Hagerstown Comm Coll (MD)
Halifax Comm Coll (NC)
Harford Comm Coll (MD)
Harper Coll (IL)
Hawaii Tokai International Coll (HI)
Hawkeye Comm Coll (IA)
Haywood Comm Coll (NC)
H. Councill Trenholm State Comm Coll (AL)
Hesston Coll (KS)
Highland Comm Coll (IL)
Holyoke Comm Coll (MA)
Hopkinsville Comm Coll (KY)
Housatonic Comm Coll (CT)
Howard Comm Coll (MD)
Hudson County Comm Coll (NJ)
Hutchinson Comm Coll (KS)
Illinois Central Coll (IL)
Illinois Eastern Comm Colls, Frontier Community College (IL)
Illinois Eastern Comm Colls, Lincoln Trail College (IL)
Illinois Eastern Comm Colls, Olney Central College (IL)
Illinois Eastern Comm Colls, Wabash Valley College (IL)
Illinois Valley Comm Coll (IL)
Independence Comm Coll (KS)
Iowa Central Comm Coll (IA)
Ivy Tech Comm Coll–Bloomington (IN)
Ivy Tech Comm Coll–Central Indiana (IN)
Ivy Tech Comm Coll–Columbus (IN)
Ivy Tech Comm Coll–East Central (IN)
Ivy Tech Comm Coll–Kokomo (IN)
Ivy Tech Comm Coll–Lafayette (IN)
Ivy Tech Comm Coll–North Central (IN)
Ivy Tech Comm Coll–Northeast (IN)
Ivy Tech Comm Coll–Northwest (IN)
Ivy Tech Comm Coll–Richmond (IN)
Ivy Tech Comm Coll–Sellersburg (IN)
Ivy Tech Comm Coll–Southeast (IN)
Ivy Tech Comm Coll–Wabash Valley (IN)
James Sprunt Comm Coll (NC)
Jamestown Comm Coll (NY)
Jefferson Comm Coll (NY)
Jefferson State Comm Coll (AL)
Johnston Comm Coll (NC)
Kaskaskia Coll (IL)
Kellogg Comm Coll (MI)
Kennebec Valley Comm Coll (ME)
Kingsborough Comm Coll of the City U of New York (NY)
Kirtland Comm Coll (MI)
Kishwaukee Coll (IL)
Lackawanna Coll (PA)
Lakeland Comm Coll (OH)
Lake Region State Coll (ND)
Lakes Region Comm Coll (NH)
Lake Superior Coll (MN)
Lamar Comm Coll (CO)
Lehigh Carbon Comm Coll (PA)
Lenoir Comm Coll (NC)
Lorain County Comm Coll (OH)
Los Angeles City Coll (CA)
Lurleen B. Wallace Comm Coll (AL)
Macomb Comm Coll (MI)
Manchester Comm Coll (CT)
Manor Coll (PA)
Marion Military Inst (AL)
Massachusetts Bay Comm Coll (MA)
Maysville Comm and Tech Coll, Maysville (KY)
McHenry County Coll (IL)
McLennan Comm Coll (TX)
Merced Coll (CA)
Mesa Comm Coll (AZ)
Mesalands Comm Coll (NM)
Miami Dade Coll (FL)
Mid-Plains Comm Coll, North Platte (NE)
Minnesota State Comm and Tech Coll (MN)
Minnesota West Comm and Tech Coll (MN)
Mission Coll (CA)
Mitchell Comm Coll (NC)
Mohave Comm Coll (AZ)
Mohawk Valley Comm Coll (NY)
Monroe Comm Coll (NY)
Monroe County Comm Coll (MI)
Montgomery Coll (MD)
Montgomery Comm Coll (NC)
Montgomery County Comm Coll (PA)
Morton Coll (IL)
Motlow State Comm Coll (TN)
Mott Comm Coll (MI)
Mount Wachusett Comm Coll (MA)
Muskegon Comm Coll (MI)
Nassau Comm Coll (NY)
National Park Coll (AR)
Naugatuck Valley Comm Coll (CT)
Nebraska Indian Comm Coll (NE)
New River Comm Coll (VA)
Niagara County Comm Coll (NY)
Northampton Comm Coll (PA)
North Central Texas Coll (TX)
North Dakota State Coll of Science (ND)
Northeast Comm Coll (NE)
Northeastern Jr Coll (CO)
Northeastern Tech Coll (SC)
Northeast Iowa Comm Coll (IA)
Northeast State Comm Coll (TN)
Northern Essex Comm Coll (MA)
North Hennepin Comm Coll (MN)
North Iowa Area Comm Coll (IA)
Northland Comm and Tech Coll (MN)
North Shore Comm Coll (MA)
NorthWest Arkansas Comm Coll (AR)
Northwest Mississippi Comm Coll (MS)
Northwest-Shoals Comm Coll (AL)
Northwest Vista Coll (TX)
Oakton Comm Coll (IL)
Odessa Coll (TX)
Oklahoma City Comm Coll (OK)
Orange Coast Coll (CA)
Otero Jr Coll (CO)
Owensboro Comm and Tech Coll (KY)
Palomar Coll (CA)
Paris Jr Coll (TX)
Pasadena City Coll (CA)
Penn State DuBois (PA)
Penn State Fayette, The Eberly Campus (PA)
Penn State Mont Alto (PA)
Pensacola State Coll (FL)
Piedmont Comm Coll (NC)
Potomac State Coll of West Virginia U (WV)
Pueblo Comm Coll (CO)
Queensborough Comm Coll of the City U of New York (NY)
Quinsigamond Comm Coll (MA)
Rainy River Comm Coll (MN)
Randolph Comm Coll (NC)
Rappahannock Comm Coll (VA)
Raritan Valley Comm Coll (NJ)
Rend Lake Coll (IL)
Richland Coll (TX)
Richmond Comm Coll (NC)
Ridgewater Coll (MN)
Rio Hondo Coll (CA)
Rock Valley Coll (IL)
Rowan-Cabarrus Comm Coll (NC)
Saginaw Chippewa Tribal Coll (MI)
St. Charles Comm Coll (MO)
St. Philip's Coll (TX)
San Joaquin Delta Coll (CA)
San Juan Coll (NM)
Santa Rosa Jr Coll (CA)
Schenectady County Comm Coll (NY)
Seminole State Coll (OK)
Seminole State Coll of Florida (FL)
Sisseton-Wahpeton Coll (SD)
Somerset Comm Coll (KY)
Southcentral Kentucky Comm and Tech Coll (KY)
Southeast Arkansas Coll (AR)
Southeast Kentucky Comm and Tech Coll (KY)
South Suburban Coll (IL)
Southwestern Coll (CA)
Southwestern Comm Coll (IA)
Southwestern Comm Coll (NC)
Southwestern Indian Polytechnic Inst (NM)
Southwestern Michigan Coll (MI)
Southwest Texas Jr Coll (TX)
Southwest Virginia Comm Coll (VA)
Spartanburg Methodist Coll (SC)
Springfield Tech Comm Coll (MA)
State U of New York Coll of Technology at Alfred (NY)
Sullivan County Comm Coll (NY)
Tallahassee Comm Coll (FL)
Tarrant County Coll District (TX)
Texarkana Coll (TX)
Three Rivers Coll (MO)
Three Rivers Comm Coll (CT)
Tidewater Comm Coll (VA)
Tillamook Bay Comm Coll (OR)
Tohono O'odham Comm Coll (AZ)
Tompkins Cortland Comm Coll (NY)
Treasure Valley Comm Coll (OR)
Tri-County Comm Coll (NC)
Trident Tech Coll (SC)
Trinity Valley Comm Coll (TX)
Truckee Meadows Comm Coll (NV)
Union County Coll (NJ)
U of Arkansas Comm Coll at Morrilton (AR)
U of Arkansas Rich Mountain (AR)
U of South Carolina Lancaster (SC)
U of South Carolina Union (SC)
U of Wisconsin–Baraboo/Sauk County (WI)
U of Wisconsin–Barron County (WI)
U of Wisconsin–Fond du Lac (WI)
U of Wisconsin–Fox Valley (WI)
U of Wisconsin–Manitowoc (WI)
U of Wisconsin–Marathon County (WI)
U of Wisconsin–Marinette (WI)
U of Wisconsin–Marshfield/Wood County (WI)
U of Wisconsin–Richland (WI)
U of Wisconsin–Rock County (WI)
U of Wisconsin–Sheboygan (WI)
U of Wisconsin–Washington County (WI)
U of Wisconsin–Waukesha (WI)
Urban Coll of Boston (MA)
Vincennes U (IN)
Volunteer State Comm Coll (TN)
Walters State Comm Coll (TN)
Wayne Comm Coll (NC)
Wayne County Comm Coll District (MI)
Westchester Comm Coll (NY)
Western Iowa Tech Comm Coll (IA)
Western Texas Coll (TX)
Western Wyoming Comm Coll (WY)
West Kentucky Comm and Tech Coll (KY)
White Mountains Comm Coll (NH)
Williamsburg Tech Coll (SC)
Williston State Coll (ND)
Wisconsin Indianhead Tech Coll (WI)
Wor-Wic Comm Coll (MD)
Wytheville Comm Coll (VA)
York County Comm Coll (ME)

### LIBRARY AND ARCHIVES ASSISTING
Coll of the Canyons (CA)
Illinois Central Coll (IL)
Ivy Tech Comm Coll–Bloomington (IN)
Ivy Tech Comm Coll–Columbus (IN)
Ivy Tech Comm Coll–East Central (IN)
Ivy Tech Comm Coll–Kokomo (IN)
Ivy Tech Comm Coll–Lafayette (IN)
Ivy Tech Comm Coll–North Central (IN)
Ivy Tech Comm Coll–Northeast (IN)
Ivy Tech Comm Coll–Northwest (IN)
Ivy Tech Comm Coll–Richmond (IN)
Ivy Tech Comm Coll–Sellersburg (IN)
Ivy Tech Comm Coll–Southwest (IN)
Ivy Tech Comm Coll–Wabash Valley (IN)
Kaskaskia Coll (IL)
Northeast Comm Coll (NE)
Palomar Coll (CA)
Pueblo Comm Coll (CO)
Western Dakota Tech Inst (SD)

### LIBRARY AND INFORMATION SCIENCE
Chippewa Valley Tech Coll (WI)
Coll of Central Florida (FL)
Copiah-Lincoln Comm Coll (MS)
Grand Rapids Comm Coll (MI)
Northeast Comm Coll (NE)
Southwestern Comm Coll (IA)

### LIBRARY SCIENCE RELATED
Pasadena City Coll (CA)

### LICENSED PRACTICAL/ VOCATIONAL NURSE TRAINING
Alvin Comm Coll (TX)
Amarillo Coll (TX)
Barton County Comm Coll (KS)
Carroll Comm Coll (MD)
Central Maine Comm Coll (ME)
Central Ohio Tech Coll (OH)
Central Oregon Comm Coll (OR)
Central Texas Coll (TX)
Coll of The Albemarle (NC)
Coll of the Desert (CA)
Comm Coll of Allegheny County (PA)
Copiah-Lincoln Comm Coll (MS)
De Anza Coll (CA)
Des Moines Area Comm Coll (IA)
Eastern Gateway Comm Coll (OH)
Feather River Coll (CA)
Fiorello H. LaGuardia Comm Coll of the City U of New York (NY)
George C. Wallace Comm Coll (AL)
Grand Rapids Comm Coll (MI)
Great Falls Coll Montana State U (MT)
Howard Comm Coll (MD)
Hudson County Comm Coll (NJ)
Iowa Central Comm Coll (IA)
J. Sargeant Reynolds Comm Coll (VA)
Mid-Plains Comm Coll, North Platte (NE)
Minnesota State Comm and Tech Coll (MN)
Mission Coll (CA)
Mitchell Tech Inst (SD)
Navarro Coll (TX)
New River Comm Coll (VA)
North Dakota State Coll of Science (ND)
Northeastern Jr Coll (CO)
North Iowa Area Comm Coll (IA)
Northwest Mississippi Comm Coll (MS)
Ozarks Tech Comm Coll (MO)
Pasadena City Coll (CA)
San Joaquin Delta Coll (CA)
Santa Rosa Jr Coll (CA)
Southeastern Coll–West Palm Beach (FL)
Southeast Tech Inst (SD)
Southwestern Coll (CA)
Texarkana Coll (TX)
Trinity Valley Comm Coll (TX)
Western Dakota Tech Inst (SD)
Western Iowa Tech Comm Coll (IA)
Western Wyoming Comm Coll (WY)
Williston State Coll (ND)

### LINEWORKER
Chandler-Gilbert Comm Coll (AZ)
Ivy Tech Comm Coll–Lafayette (IN)
Kennebec Valley Comm Coll (ME)
Minnesota State Comm and Tech Coll (MN)
Minnesota West Comm and Tech Coll (MN)
Mitchell Tech Inst (SD)
Northeast Comm Coll (NE)
Pennsylvania Highlands Comm Coll (PA)
Raritan Valley Comm Coll (NJ)
State Tech Coll of Missouri (MO)
Vincennes U (IN)

### LITERATURE
Tyler Jr Coll (TX)

### LITERATURE RELATED
Cayuga County Comm Coll (NY)

### LIVESTOCK MANAGEMENT
Barton County Comm Coll (KS)
James Sprunt Comm Coll (NC)
North Dakota State Coll of Science (ND)
The Ohio State U Ag Tech Inst (OH)

### LOGISTICS, MATERIALS, AND SUPPLY CHAIN MANAGEMENT
Ancilla Coll (IN)
Arizona Western Coll (AZ)
Austin Comm Coll District (TX)
Barton County Comm Coll (KS)
Cecil Coll (MD)
City Colls of Chicago, Olive-Harvey College (IL)
Cochise County Comm Coll District (AZ)
Collin County Comm Coll District (TX)
Edison State Comm Coll (OH)
Fayetteville Tech Comm Coll (NC)
Fox Valley Tech Coll (WI)
Georgia Military Coll (GA)
Hinds Comm Coll (MS)
Houston Comm Coll (TX)
Hudson County Comm Coll (NJ)
Ivy Tech Comm Coll–Bloomington (IN)
Ivy Tech Comm Coll–Central Indiana (IN)
Ivy Tech Comm Coll–Columbus (IN)
Ivy Tech Comm Coll–East Central (IN)
Ivy Tech Comm Coll–Richmond (IN)
Ivy Tech Comm Coll–Sellersburg (IN)
Ivy Tech Comm Coll–Southeast (IN)
Ivy Tech Comm Coll–Southwest (IN)
Ivy Tech Comm Coll–Wabash Valley (IN)
Lenoir Comm Coll (NC)
Miami Dade Coll (FL)
Northcentral Tech Coll (WI)
Northern Essex Comm Coll (MA)
Shawnee Comm Coll (IL)
Southwestern Coll (CA)
Union County Coll (NJ)
Vincennes U (IN)
West Kentucky Comm and Tech Coll (KY)

### MACHINE SHOP TECHNOLOGY
Asheville-Buncombe Tech Comm Coll (NC)
Comm Coll of Allegheny County (PA)
Craven Comm Coll (NC)
Eastern Arizona Coll (AZ)
Fayetteville Tech Comm Coll (NC)
Haywood Comm Coll (NC)
Ivy Tech Comm Coll–Central Indiana (IN)
Ivy Tech Comm Coll–East Central (IN)
Ivy Tech Comm Coll–Kokomo (IN)
Ivy Tech Comm Coll–Richmond (IN)
Ivy Tech Comm Coll–Wabash Valley (IN)
Johnson Coll (PA)
Lenoir Comm Coll (NC)
Maysville Comm and Tech Coll, Maysville (KY)
Mitchell Comm Coll (NC)
North Central Texas Coll (TX)
Owensboro Comm and Tech Coll (KY)
Pasadena City Coll (CA)
Pueblo Comm Coll (CO)
Randolph Comm Coll (NC)
Southcentral Kentucky Comm and Tech Coll (KY)
State U of New York Coll of Technology at Alfred (NY)
Thaddeus Stevens Coll of Technology (PA)
U of Arkansas Comm Coll at Morrilton (AR)
Wayne Comm Coll (NC)
West Kentucky Comm and Tech Coll (KY)

### MACHINE TOOL TECHNOLOGY
Alamance Comm Coll (NC)
Amarillo Coll (TX)
Central Lakes Coll (MN)
Central Maine Comm Coll (ME)
Central New Mexico Comm Coll (NM)
Clark Coll (WA)
Coll of Marin (CA)
Copiah-Lincoln Comm Coll (MS)
De Anza Coll (CA)
Del Mar Coll (TX)
Des Moines Area Comm Coll (IA)

East Central Coll (MO)
El Paso Comm Coll (TX)
George C. Wallace Comm Coll (AL)
Greenville Tech Coll (SC)
Hawkeye Comm Coll (IA)
H. Councill Trenholm State Comm Coll (AL)
Hutchinson Comm Coll (KS)
Illinois Eastern Comm Colls, Wabash Valley College (IL)
Iowa Central Comm Coll (IA)
Ivy Tech Comm Coll–Bloomington (IN)
Ivy Tech Comm Coll–Central Indiana (IN)
Ivy Tech Comm Coll–Columbus (IN)
Ivy Tech Comm Coll–East Central (IN)
Ivy Tech Comm Coll–Kokomo (IN)
Ivy Tech Comm Coll–Lafayette (IN)
Ivy Tech Comm Coll–North Central (IN)
Ivy Tech Comm Coll–Northwest (IN)
Ivy Tech Comm Coll–Richmond (IN)
Ivy Tech Comm Coll–Sellersburg (IN)
Ivy Tech Comm Coll–Southwest (IN)
Ivy Tech Comm Coll–Wabash Valley (IN)
Johnson Coll (PA)
Kellogg Comm Coll (MI)
Kennebec Valley Comm Coll (ME)
Lake Area Tech Inst (SD)
Macomb Comm Coll (MI)
Meridian Comm Coll (MS)
Mesa Comm Coll (AZ)
Mt. San Antonio Coll (CA)
Muskegon Comm Coll (MI)
New Castle School of Trades (PA)
New River Comm Coll (VA)
North Central Texas Coll (TX)
North Dakota State Coll of Science (ND)
Northeastern Tech Coll (SC)
Northern Essex Comm Coll (MA)
Northern Maine Comm Coll (ME)
Northwest Mississippi Comm Coll (MS)
Odessa Coll (TX)
Orange Coast Coll (CA)
Ozarks Tech Comm Coll (MO)
Renton Tech Coll (WA)
Ridgewater Coll (MN)
St. Philip's Coll (TX)
San Joaquin Delta Coll (CA)
State Tech Coll of Missouri (MO)
Tarrant County Coll District (TX)
Trident Tech Coll (SC)
Western Dakota Tech Inst (SD)
Wytheville Comm Coll (VA)
York County Comm Coll (ME)

**MAGNETIC RESONANCE IMAGING (MRI) TECHNOLOGY**
Gurnick Academy of Medical Arts (CA)
Mitchell Tech Inst (SD)

**MANAGEMENT INFORMATION SYSTEMS**
Anne Arundel Comm Coll (MD)
Camden County Coll (NJ)
Carl Albert State Coll (OK)
Carroll Comm Coll (MD)
Cecil Coll (MD)
Central Maine Comm Coll (ME)
Central Oregon Comm Coll (OR)
Comm Coll of Allegheny County (PA)
Comm Coll of Baltimore County (MD)
County Coll of Morris (NJ)
Del Mar Coll (TX)
Georgia Military Coll (GA)
Gulf Coast State Coll (FL)
Hagerstown Comm Coll (MD)
Harford Comm Coll (MD)
Kennebec Valley Comm Coll (ME)
Lackawanna Coll (PA)
Lakeland Comm Coll (OH)
Lake Region State Coll (ND)
Lake Superior Coll (MN)
Manchester Comm Coll (CT)
Miami Dade Coll (FL)
Nassau Comm Coll (NY)
North Hennepin Comm Coll (MN)
Panola Coll (TX)
Pensacola State Coll (FL)
Raritan Valley Comm Coll (NJ)
St. Louis Comm Coll (MO)
San Jacinto Coll District (TX)
Southeast Arkansas Coll (AR)
Southeast Kentucky Comm and Tech Coll (KY)
State Tech Coll of Missouri (MO)
Three Rivers Comm Coll (CT)
Treasure Valley Comm Coll (OR)

**MANAGEMENT INFORMATION SYSTEMS AND SERVICES RELATED**
Anne Arundel Comm Coll (MD)
Bowling Green State U–Firelands Coll (OH)
Pensacola State Coll (FL)
Seminole State Coll (OK)
Truckee Meadows Comm Coll (NV)

**MANAGEMENT SCIENCE**
Central Virginia Comm Coll (VA)
Lakeshore Tech Coll (WI)
LDS Business Coll (UT)
Oklahoma State U–Oklahoma City (OK)
Pensacola State Coll (FL)
Piedmont Virginia Comm Coll (VA)
Sauk Valley Comm Coll (IL)

**MANUFACTURING ENGINEERING**
Bristol Comm Coll (MA)
Mesa Comm Coll (AZ)
Mitchell Comm Coll (NC)
Penn State Fayette, The Eberly Campus (PA)
St. Louis Comm Coll (MO)

**MANUFACTURING ENGINEERING TECHNOLOGY**
Arizona Western Coll (AZ)
Bevill State Comm Coll (AL)
Black Hawk Coll, Moline (IL)
Central Ohio Tech Coll (OH)
Central Oregon Comm Coll (OR)
Chippewa Valley Tech Coll (WI)
Clark Coll (WA)
Comm Coll of Allegheny County (PA)
Comm Coll of Baltimore County (MD)
Copiah-Lincoln Comm Coll (MS)
Crowder Coll (MO)
Danville Area Comm Coll (IL)
Edison State Comm Coll (OH)
Fox Valley Tech Coll (WI)
Gulf Coast State Coll (FL)
H. Councill Trenholm State Comm Coll (AL)
Houston Comm Coll (TX)
Hutchinson Comm Coll (KS)
Illinois Central Coll (IL)
Illinois Eastern Comm Colls, Wabash Valley College (IL)
ITI Tech Coll (LA)
Ivy Tech Comm Coll–Bloomington (IN)
Ivy Tech Comm Coll–Central Indiana (IN)
Ivy Tech Comm Coll–Columbus (IN)
Ivy Tech Comm Coll–East Central (IN)
Ivy Tech Comm Coll–Kokomo (IN)
Ivy Tech Comm Coll–Lafayette (IN)
Ivy Tech Comm Coll–Richmond (IN)
Ivy Tech Comm Coll–Southeast (IN)
Ivy Tech Comm Coll–Southwest (IN)
Ivy Tech Comm Coll–Wabash Valley (IN)
John Tyler Comm Coll (VA)
Lake Area Tech Inst (SD)
Lehigh Carbon Comm Coll (PA)
Lorain County Comm Coll (OH)
Macomb Comm Coll (MI)
Mesa Comm Coll (AZ)
Miami Dade Coll (FL)
Minnesota State Comm and Tech Coll (MN)
Minnesota West Comm and Tech Coll (MN)
Mitchell Comm Coll (NC)
Northcentral Tech Coll (WI)
North Dakota State Coll of Science (ND)
Northland Comm and Tech Coll (MN)
Oakton Comm Coll (IL)
Ozarks Tech Comm Coll (MO)
Pueblo Comm Coll (CO)
Quinsigamond Comm Coll (MA)
Raritan Valley Comm Coll (NJ)
Rend Lake Coll (IL)
St. Charles Comm Coll (MO)
Schoolcraft Coll (MI)
State Tech Coll of Missouri (MO)
Tallahassee Comm Coll (FL)
Texas State Tech Coll (TX)
Three Rivers Coll (MO)
Three Rivers Comm Coll (CT)
Truckee Meadows Comm Coll (NV)
U of Arkansas Rich Mountain (AR)
Vincennes U (IN)
Waukesha County Tech Coll (WI)

**MARINE MAINTENANCE AND SHIP REPAIR TECHNOLOGY**
Coll of The Albemarle (NC)
Kingsborough Comm Coll of the City U of New York (NY)
Lakes Region Comm Coll (NH)
Minnesota State Comm and Tech Coll (MN)

**MARINE SCIENCE/MERCHANT MARINE OFFICER**
American Samoa Comm Coll (AS)
San Jacinto Coll District (TX)

**MARINE SCIENCES**
American Samoa Comm Coll (AS)

**MARINE TRANSPORTATION RELATED**
Orange Coast Coll (CA)
West Kentucky Comm and Tech Coll (KY)

**MARKETING/MARKETING MANAGEMENT**
Adirondack Comm Coll (NY)
Alvin Comm Coll (TX)
Asheville-Buncombe Tech Comm Coll (NC)
Austin Comm Coll District (TX)
Barton County Comm Coll (KS)
Bristol Comm Coll (MA)
Brookhaven Coll (TX)
Camden County Coll (NJ)
Cecil Coll (MD)
Cedar Valley Coll (TX)
Central Lakes Coll (MN)
Central Oregon Comm Coll (OR)
Century Coll (MN)
Chippewa Valley Tech Coll (WI)
Cleveland Comm Coll (NC)
Coll of Central Florida (FL)
Coll of Eastern Idaho (ID)
Comm Coll of Allegheny County (PA)
Copiah-Lincoln Comm Coll (MS)
De Anza Coll (CA)
Des Moines Area Comm Coll (IA)
Edison State Comm Coll (OH)
Fox Valley Tech Coll (WI)
Gateway Tech Coll (WI)
Genesee Comm Coll (NY)
Harford Comm Coll (MD)
Harper Coll (IL)
Hinds Comm Coll (MS)
Houston Comm Coll (TX)
Illinois Valley Comm Coll (IL)
Kennebec Valley Comm Coll (ME)
Kingsborough Comm Coll of the City U of New York (NY)
Lake Area Tech Inst (SD)
Lakeland Comm Coll (OH)
Lakeshore Tech Coll (WI)
Lamar Comm Coll (CO)
LDS Business Coll (UT)
Lenoir Comm Coll (NC)
Los Angeles City Coll (CA)
Macomb Comm Coll (MI)
Manchester Comm Coll (CT)
Manor Coll (PA)
Meridian Comm Coll (MS)
Mesa Comm Coll (AZ)
Miami Dade Coll (FL)
Mid-State Tech Coll (WI)
Minnesota State Comm and Tech Coll (MN)
Mission Coll (CA)
Monroe Comm Coll (NY)
Monroe County Comm Coll (MI)
Morton Coll (IL)
Mott Comm Coll (MI)
Mt. San Antonio Coll (CA)
Muskegon Comm Coll (MI)
Nassau Comm Coll (NY)
Naugatuck Valley Comm Coll (CT)
Navarro Coll (TX)
New River Comm Coll (VA)
Northampton Comm Coll (PA)
Northcentral Tech Coll (WI)
North Dakota State Coll of Science (ND)
Northeastern Jr Coll (CO)
Northeastern Tech Coll (SC)
Northern Essex Comm Coll (MA)
North Hennepin Comm Coll (MN)
North Shore Comm Coll (MA)
Oakton Comm Coll (IL)
Ozarks Tech Comm Coll (MO)
Pasadena City Coll (CA)
Ridgewater Coll (MN)
Rock Valley Coll (IL)
Rowan-Cabarrus Comm Coll (NC)
St. Charles Comm Coll (MO)
Salt Lake Comm Coll (UT)
Sauk Valley Comm Coll (IL)
Schoolcraft Coll (MI)
Seminole State Coll of Florida (FL)
Southeast Tech Inst (SD)
Springfield Tech Comm Coll (MA)
Stark State Coll (OH)
Sullivan County Comm Coll (NY)
Tarrant County Coll District (TX)
Texarkana Coll (TX)
Three Rivers Coll (MO)
Three Rivers Comm Coll (CT)
Tidewater Comm Coll (VA)
Trident Tech Coll (SC)
Trinity Valley Comm Coll (TX)
Tulsa Comm Coll (OK)
Union County Coll (NJ)
Vincennes U (IN)
Waukesha County Tech Coll (WI)
Western Texas Coll (TX)
Western Wyoming Comm Coll (WY)

**MARKETING RELATED**
Westchester Comm Coll (NY)

**MASONRY**
Ivy Tech Comm Coll–Central Indiana (IN)
Ivy Tech Comm Coll–Columbus (IN)
Ivy Tech Comm Coll–East Central (IN)
Ivy Tech Comm Coll–Lafayette (IN)
Ivy Tech Comm Coll–Northeast (IN)
Ivy Tech Comm Coll–Northwest (IN)
Ivy Tech Comm Coll–Southwest (IN)
Ivy Tech Comm Coll–Wabash Valley (IN)
Palomar Coll (CA)
State U of New York Coll of Technology at Alfred (NY)
Tallahassee Comm Coll (FL)
Thaddeus Stevens Coll of Technology (PA)

**MASSAGE THERAPY**
Arizona Western Coll (AZ)
Camden County Coll (NJ)
Carteret Comm Coll (NC)
Central Oregon Comm Coll (OR)
Chandler-Gilbert Comm Coll (AZ)
Comm Coll of Baltimore County (MD)
Illinois Valley Comm Coll (IL)
Ivy Tech Comm Coll–Northeast (IN)
Lenoir Comm Coll (NC)
Miami Dade Coll (FL)
Morton Coll (IL)
Niagara County Comm Coll (NY)
Queensborough Comm Coll of the City U of New York (NY)
Renton Tech Coll (WA)
Schoolcraft Coll (MI)
Southeastern Coll–West Palm Beach (FL)
Southwestern Comm Coll (NC)
Spencerian Coll (KY)
Williston State Coll (ND)

**MASS COMMUNICATION/ MEDIA**
Amarillo Coll (TX)
Ancilla Coll (IN)
Bunker Hill Comm Coll (MA)
Chipola Coll (FL)
Coll of Marin (CA)
Coll of the Desert (CA)
Crowder Coll (MO)
De Anza Coll (CA)
Fullerton Coll (CA)
Genesee Comm Coll (NY)
Georgia Military Coll (GA)
Gordon State Coll (GA)
Harford Comm Coll (MD)
Iowa Central Comm Coll (IA)
Laramie County Comm Coll (WY)
Miami Dade Coll (FL)
Monroe Comm Coll (NY)
Monroe County Comm Coll (MI)
Mount Wachusett Comm Coll (MA)
Nassau Comm Coll (NY)
Niagara County Comm Coll (NY)
Northeast Comm Coll (NE)
Orange Coast Coll (CA)
Salt Lake Comm Coll (UT)
Union County Coll (NJ)
Western Texas Coll (TX)
Wytheville Comm Coll (VA)

**MATERIALS SCIENCE**
Mt. San Antonio Coll (CA)
Northern Essex Comm Coll (MA)

**MATHEMATICS**
Alvin Comm Coll (TX)
Amarillo Coll (TX)
Anne Arundel Comm Coll (MD)
Antelope Valley Coll (CA)
Arizona Western Coll (AZ)
Austin Comm Coll District (TX)
Barton County Comm Coll (KS)
Bucks County Comm Coll (PA)
Bunker Hill Comm Coll (MA)
Carl Albert State Coll (OK)
Cecil Coll (MD)
Central New Mexico Comm Coll (NM)
Central Oregon Comm Coll (OR)
Central Texas Coll (TX)
Cochise County Comm Coll District (AZ)
Coll of Central Florida (FL)
Coll of Marin (CA)
Coll of the Canyons (CA)
Coll of the Desert (CA)
Comm Coll of Allegheny County (PA)
Crowder Coll (MO)
De Anza Coll (CA)
Del Mar Coll (TX)
Eastern Arizona Coll (AZ)
Edison State Comm Coll (OH)
Feather River Coll (CA)
Frederick Comm Coll (MD)
Fullerton Coll (CA)
Galveston Coll (TX)
Genesee Comm Coll (NY)
Georgia Military Coll (GA)
Harford Comm Coll (MD)
Harper Coll (IL)
Harrisburg Area Comm Coll (PA)
Hill Coll (TX)
Holyoke Comm Coll (MA)
Housatonic Comm Coll (CT)
Houston Comm Coll (TX)
Hutchinson Comm Coll (KS)
Independence Comm Coll (KS)
Jefferson Comm Coll (NY)
J. Sargeant Reynolds Comm Coll (VA)
Kingsborough Comm Coll of the City U of New York (NY)
Laramie County Comm Coll (WY)
Lehigh Carbon Comm Coll (PA)
Los Angeles City Coll (CA)
Macomb Comm Coll (MI)
Massachusetts Bay Comm Coll (MA)
Merced Coll (CA)
Miami Dade Coll (FL)
Mission Coll (CA)
Mohave Comm Coll (AZ)
Monroe Comm Coll (NY)
Monroe County Comm Coll (MI)
Montgomery County Comm Coll (PA)
Mt. San Antonio Coll (CA)
Nassau Comm Coll (NY)
Navarro Coll (TX)
Niagara County Comm Coll (NY)
Northampton Comm Coll (PA)
Northeast Comm Coll (NE)
Northeastern Jr Coll (CO)
North Hennepin Comm Coll (MN)
Northwest Coll (WY)
Odessa Coll (TX)
Oklahoma City Comm Coll (OK)
Orange Coast Coll (CA)
Otero Jr Coll (CO)
Palomar Coll (CA)
Panola Coll (TX)
Paris Jr Coll (TX)
Pasadena City Coll (CA)
Pensacola State Coll (FL)
Potomac State Coll of West Virginia U (WV)
St. Philip's Coll (TX)
San Jacinto Coll District (TX)
San Joaquin Delta Coll (CA)
San Juan Coll (NM)
Santa Rosa Jr Coll (CA)
Sauk Valley Comm Coll (IL)
Scottsdale Comm Coll (AZ)
Seminole State Coll (OK)
Southern U at Shreveport (LA)
Southwestern Coll (CA)
Springfield Tech Comm Coll (MA)
Sullivan County Comm Coll (NY)
Texarkana Coll (TX)
Trinity Valley Comm Coll (TX)
Truckee Meadows Comm Coll (NV)
Tulsa Comm Coll (OK)
Tyler Jr Coll (TX)
Union County Coll (NJ)
U of Wisconsin–Baraboo/Sauk County (WI)

U of Wisconsin–Barron County (WI)
U of Wisconsin–Fond du Lac (WI)
U of Wisconsin–Fox Valley (WI)
U of Wisconsin–Manitowoc (WI)
U of Wisconsin–Marathon County (WI)
U of Wisconsin–Marinette (WI)
U of Wisconsin–Marshfield/Wood County (WI)
U of Wisconsin–Richland (WI)
U of Wisconsin–Rock County (WI)
U of Wisconsin–Sheboygan (WI)
U of Wisconsin–Washington County (WI)
U of Wisconsin–Waukesha (WI)
Western Texas Coll (TX)
Western Wyoming Comm Coll (WY)

**MATHEMATICS AND COMPUTER SCIENCE**
Crowder Coll (MO)

**MATHEMATICS AND STATISTICS RELATED**
Bristol Comm Coll (MA)

**MATHEMATICS RELATED**
Cayuga County Comm Coll (NY)
Genesee Comm Coll (NY)

**MATHEMATICS TEACHER EDUCATION**
Anne Arundel Comm Coll (MD)
Bucks County Comm Coll (PA)
Carroll Comm Coll (MD)
Chesapeake Coll (MD)
Comm Coll of Baltimore County (MD)
Frederick Comm Coll (MD)
Harford Comm Coll (MD)
Highland Comm Coll (IL)
Montgomery Coll (MD)
Vincennes U (IN)

**MECHANICAL DRAFTING AND CAD/CADD**
Alexandria Tech and Comm Coll (MN)
Central Lakes Coll (MN)
Chippewa Valley Tech Coll (WI)
Cleveland Comm Coll (NC)
Comm Coll of Allegheny County (PA)
Des Moines Area Comm Coll (IA)
Edison State Comm Coll (OH)
Fox Valley Tech Coll (WI)
Gateway Tech Coll (WI)
Greenville Tech Coll (SC)
Hutchinson Comm Coll (KS)
Macomb Comm Coll (MI)
Merced Coll (CA)
Minnesota State Comm and Tech Coll (MN)
Mitchell Comm Coll (NC)
Morrison Inst of Technology (IL)
Northcentral Tech Coll (WI)
Queensborough Comm Coll of the City U of New York (NY)
Ridgewater Coll (MN)
Vincennes U (IN)
Waukesha County Tech Coll (WI)
Western Iowa Tech Comm Coll (IA)

**MECHANICAL ENGINEERING**
Bristol Comm Coll (MA)
Cayuga County Comm Coll (NY)
Fiorello H. LaGuardia Comm Coll of the City U of New York (NY)
Montgomery County Comm Coll (PA)
Pasadena City Coll (CA)
Potomac State Coll of West Virginia U (WV)
St. Philip's Coll (TX)

**MECHANICAL ENGINEERING/ MECHANICAL TECHNOLOGY**
Alamance Comm Coll (NC)
Bowling Green State U–Firelands Coll (OH)
Bristol Comm Coll (MA)
Caldwell Comm Coll and Tech Inst (NC)
Camden County Coll (NJ)
Cayuga County Comm Coll (NY)
Central Ohio Tech Coll (OH)
County Coll of Morris (NJ)
Craven Comm Coll (NC)
Eastern Gateway Comm Coll (OH)
Erie Comm Coll, North Campus (NY)
Fullerton Coll (CA)
Greenville Tech Coll (SC)
Hagerstown Comm Coll (MD)

Harrisburg Area Comm Coll (PA)
Illinois Central Coll (IL)
Illinois Eastern Comm Colls, Lincoln Trail College (IL)
Illinois Valley Comm Coll (IL)
Ivy Tech Comm Coll–Lafayette (IN)
Jamestown Comm Coll (NY)
Kent State U at Trumbull (OH)
Kent State U at Tuscarawas (OH)
Lakeland Comm Coll (OH)
Lehigh Carbon Comm Coll (PA)
Lenoir Comm Coll (NC)
Macomb Comm Coll (MI)
Massachusetts Bay Comm Coll (MA)
Merced Coll (CA)
Mitchell Comm Coll (NC)
Mohawk Valley Comm Coll (NY)
Monroe Comm Coll (NY)
Montgomery County Comm Coll (PA)
Mott Comm Coll (MI)
Oakton Comm Coll (IL)
Oklahoma State U Inst of Technology (OK)
Penn State DuBois (PA)
Queensborough Comm Coll of the City U of New York (NY)
Richland Coll (TX)
Richmond Comm Coll (NC)
San Joaquin Delta Coll (CA)
Southeast Tech Inst (SD)
Springfield Tech Comm Coll (MA)
Stark State Coll (OH)
State U of New York Coll of Technology at Alfred (NY)
Tarrant County Coll District (TX)
Texas State Tech Coll (TX)
Three Rivers Comm Coll (CT)
Trident Tech Coll (SC)
Wayne Comm Coll (NC)
Westchester Comm Coll (NY)
Wytheville Comm Coll (VA)

**MECHANICAL ENGINEERING TECHNOLOGIES RELATED**
Asheville-Buncombe Tech Comm Coll (NC)
Camden County Coll (NJ)
Florida Keys Comm Coll (FL)
Jefferson Comm Coll (NY)
John Tyler Comm Coll (VA)
Mohawk Valley Comm Coll (NY)

**MECHANIC AND REPAIR TECHNOLOGIES RELATED**
Chandler-Gilbert Comm Coll (AZ)
Cloud County Comm Coll (KS)
Greenville Tech Coll (SC)
Ivy Tech Comm Coll–Bloomington (IN)
Ivy Tech Comm Coll–Columbus (IN)
Ivy Tech Comm Coll–Kokomo (IN)
Ivy Tech Comm Coll–Lafayette (IN)
Ivy Tech Comm Coll–North Central (IN)
Ivy Tech Comm Coll–Northwest (IN)
Ivy Tech Comm Coll–Southwest (IN)
Laramie County Comm Coll (WY)
Macomb Comm Coll (MI)
Ohio Tech Coll (OH)
Three Rivers Coll (MO)
West Kentucky Comm and Tech Coll (KY)

**MECHANICS AND REPAIR**
Ivy Tech Comm Coll–Bloomington (IN)
Ivy Tech Comm Coll–Central Indiana (IN)
Ivy Tech Comm Coll–Columbus (IN)
Ivy Tech Comm Coll–Kokomo (IN)
Ivy Tech Comm Coll–Lafayette (IN)
Ivy Tech Comm Coll–North Central (IN)
Ivy Tech Comm Coll–Northeast (IN)
Ivy Tech Comm Coll–Northwest (IN)
Ivy Tech Comm Coll–Richmond (IN)
Ivy Tech Comm Coll–Sellersburg (IN)
Ivy Tech Comm Coll–Southwest (IN)
Ivy Tech Comm Coll–Wabash Valley (IN)
Western Wyoming Comm Coll (WY)

**MECHATRONICS, ROBOTICS, AND AUTOMATION ENGINEERING**
Anne Arundel Comm Coll (MD)
Cochise County Comm Coll District (AZ)
Comm Coll of Allegheny County (PA)
Harrisburg Area Comm Coll (PA)

Lorain County Comm Coll (OH)
Mitchell Comm Coll (NC)
Randolph Comm Coll (NC)
Schoolcraft Coll (MI)

**MEDICAL ADMINISTRATIVE ASSISTANT AND MEDICAL SECRETARY**
Alamance Comm Coll (NC)
Alexandria Tech and Comm Coll (MN)
Alvin Comm Coll (TX)
Amarillo Coll (TX)
Anne Arundel Comm Coll (MD)
Barton County Comm Coll (KS)
Bristol Comm Coll (MA)
Bunker Hill Comm Coll (MA)
Carteret Comm Coll (NC)
Central Lakes Coll (MN)
Central Texas Coll (TX)
Century Coll (MN)
Clark Coll (WA)
Coll of Marin (CA)
Coll of The Albemarle (NC)
Coll of the Ouachitas (AR)
Comm Coll of Allegheny County (PA)
Comm Coll of Baltimore County (MD)
Craven Comm Coll (NC)
Crowder Coll (MO)
Dabney S. Lancaster Comm Coll (VA)
Danville Area Comm Coll (IL)
Del Mar Coll (TX)
Des Moines Area Comm Coll (IA)
Eastern Gateway Comm Coll (OH)
Edison State Comm Coll (OH)
Erie Comm Coll, North Campus (NY)
Frederick Comm Coll (MD)
Galveston Coll (TX)
Genesee Comm Coll (NY)
Grand Rapids Comm Coll (MI)
Gulf Coast State Coll (FL)
Halifax Comm Coll (NC)
Harper Coll (IL)
Hawkeye Comm Coll (IA)
Howard Comm Coll (MD)
Humacao Comm Coll (PR)
Illinois Eastern Comm Colls, Olney Central College (IL)
Jefferson Comm Coll (NY)
Kellogg Comm Coll (MI)
Kennebec Valley Comm Coll (ME)
Lackawanna Coll (PA)
Lakeshore Tech Coll (WI)
Lake Superior Coll (MN)
LDS Business Coll (UT)
Los Angeles City Coll (CA)
Manchester Comm Coll (CT)
Maysville Comm and Tech Coll, Maysville (KY)
McLennan Comm Coll (TX)
Merced Coll (CA)
Minnesota State Comm and Tech Coll (MN)
Minnesota West Comm and Tech Coll (MN)
Monroe County Comm Coll (MI)
Morton Coll (IL)
Mt. San Antonio Coll (CA)
Muskegon Comm Coll (MI)
Nassau Comm Coll (NY)
National Park Coll (AR)
Northampton Comm Coll (PA)
Northeast Comm Coll (NE)
Northern Essex Comm Coll (MA)
North Iowa Area Comm Coll (IA)
Northland Comm and Tech Coll (MN)
North Shore Comm Coll (MA)
Owensboro Comm and Tech Coll (KY)
Palomar Coll (CA)
Piedmont Comm Coll (NC)
Quinsigamond Comm Coll (MA)
Renton Tech Coll (WA)
Ridgewater Coll (MN)
Scottsdale Comm Coll (AZ)
Somerset Comm Coll (KY)
Spencerian Coll (KY)
Springfield Tech Comm Coll (MA)
Treasure Valley Comm Coll (OR)
Trident Tech Coll (SC)
Tyler Jr Coll (TX)
Westchester Comm Coll (NY)
Western Iowa Tech Comm Coll (IA)
Western Wyoming Comm Coll (WY)
West Kentucky Comm and Tech Coll (KY)
Wisconsin Indianhead Tech Coll (WI)
Wytheville Comm Coll (VA)

**MEDICAL/CLINICAL ASSISTANT**
Alamance Comm Coll (NC)
Antelope Valley Coll (CA)
Barton County Comm Coll (KS)
Beal Coll (ME)
Blue Ridge Comm and Tech Coll (WV)
Bossier Parish Comm Coll (LA)
Bucks County Comm Coll (PA)
Caldwell Comm Coll and Tech Inst (NC)
Career Coll of Northern Nevada (NV)
Carteret Comm Coll (NC)
Central Maine Comm Coll (ME)
Central Oregon Comm Coll (OR)
Central Virginia Comm Coll (VA)
Clark Coll (WA)
Cleveland Comm Coll (NC)
Coll of Eastern Idaho (ID)
Coll of Marin (CA)
The Coll of Westchester (NY)
Columbia-Greene Comm Coll (NY)
Comm Coll of Allegheny County (PA)
Craven Comm Coll (NC)
De Anza Coll (CA)
Des Moines Area Comm Coll (IA)
East Central Coll (MO)
Eastern Gateway Comm Coll (OH)
Edison State Comm Coll (OH)
El Paso Comm Coll (TX)
Frederick Comm Coll (MD)
George C. Wallace Comm Coll (AL)
Great Falls Coll Montana State U (MT)
Harford Comm Coll (MD)
Harper Coll (IL)
Harrisburg Area Comm Coll (PA)
Haywood Comm Coll (NC)
H. Councill Trenholm State Comm Coll (AL)
Highland Comm Coll (IL)
Hinds Comm Coll (MS)
Hudson County Comm Coll (NJ)
Illinois Eastern Comm Colls, Lincoln Trail College (IL)
Iowa Central Comm Coll (IA)
Ivy Tech Comm Coll–Central Indiana (IN)
Ivy Tech Comm Coll–Columbus (IN)
Ivy Tech Comm Coll–East Central (IN)
Ivy Tech Comm Coll–Kokomo (IN)
Ivy Tech Comm Coll–Lafayette (IN)
Ivy Tech Comm Coll–North Central (IN)
Ivy Tech Comm Coll–Northeast (IN)
Ivy Tech Comm Coll–Northwest (IN)
Ivy Tech Comm Coll–Richmond (IN)
Ivy Tech Comm Coll–Sellersburg (IN)
Ivy Tech Comm Coll–Southeast (IN)
Ivy Tech Comm Coll–Southwest (IN)
Ivy Tech Comm Coll–Wabash Valley (IN)
Johnston Comm Coll (NC)
Kennebec Valley Comm Coll (ME)
Kirtland Comm Coll (MI)
Lake Area Tech Inst (SD)
Lehigh Carbon Comm Coll (PA)
Lenoir Comm Coll (NC)
Lorain County Comm Coll (OH)
Macomb Comm Coll (MI)
Miami Dade Coll (FL)
Minnesota West Comm and Tech Coll (MN)
Mitchell Comm Coll (NC)
Mitchell Tech Inst (SD)
Mohave Comm Coll (AZ)
Mohawk Valley Comm Coll (NY)
Montgomery Comm Coll (NC)
Mount Wachusett Comm Coll (MA)
Niagara County Comm Coll (NY)
North Iowa Area Comm Coll (IA)
Northwest-Shoals Comm Coll (AL)
Oklahoma City Comm Coll (OK)
Orange Coast Coll (CA)
Owensboro Comm and Tech Coll (KY)
Panola Coll (TX)
Pasadena City Coll (CA)
Pennsylvania Highlands Comm Coll (PA)
Piedmont Comm Coll (NC)
Potomac State Coll of West Virginia U (WV)
Queensborough Comm Coll of the City U of New York (NY)
Randolph Comm Coll (NC)
Raritan Valley Comm Coll (NJ)
Rend Lake Coll (IL)

Renton Tech Coll (WA)
Richmond Comm Coll (NC)
Ridgewater Coll (MN)
Salt Lake Comm Coll (UT)
San Jacinto Coll District (TX)
Santa Rosa Jr Coll (CA)
Southeastern Coll–West Palm Beach (FL)
Southwestern Coll (GA)
Southwestern Michigan Coll (MI)
Spencerian Coll (KY)
Springfield Tech Comm Coll (MA)
Stark State Coll (OH)
Sullivan County Comm Coll (NY)
Treasure Valley Comm Coll (OR)
Tri-County Comm Coll (NC)
Wayne Comm Coll (NC)
Western Dakota Tech Inst (SD)
Western Iowa Tech Comm Coll (IA)
Western Wyoming Comm Coll (WY)
White Mountains Comm Coll (NH)
York County Comm Coll (ME)

**MEDICAL/HEALTH MANAGEMENT AND CLINICAL ASSISTANT**
CollAmerica–Denver (CO)
Ivy Tech Comm Coll–Bloomington (IN)
Ivy Tech Comm Coll–Central Indiana (IN)
Ivy Tech Comm Coll–East Central (IN)
Ivy Tech Comm Coll–Lafayette (IN)
Ivy Tech Comm Coll–Richmond (IN)
Ivy Tech Comm Coll–Sellersburg (IN)
Ivy Tech Comm Coll–Southeast (IN)
Ivy Tech Comm Coll–Southwest (IN)
Ivy Tech Comm Coll–Wabash Valley (IN)
Pittsburgh Tech Coll (PA)

**MEDICAL INFORMATICS**
Cleveland State Comm Coll (TN)
Comm Coll of Baltimore County (MD)
Harrisburg Area Comm Coll (PA)
Volunteer State Comm Coll (TN)

**MEDICAL INSURANCE CODING**
Barton County Comm Coll (KS)
Bucks County Comm Coll (PA)
Central Texas Coll (TX)
Collin County Comm Coll District (TX)
Hawkeye Comm Coll (IA)
Laramie County Comm Coll (WY)
Minnesota West Comm and Tech Coll (MN)
Northland Comm and Tech Coll (MN)
Ozarks Tech Comm Coll (MO)
Paris Jr Coll (TX)
Renton Tech Coll (WA)
Southeastern Coll–West Palm Beach (FL)
Southeast Tech Inst (SD)
Southwestern Coll (CA)
Spencerian Coll (KY)
Springfield Tech Comm Coll (MA)

**MEDICAL INSURANCE/ MEDICAL BILLING**
Northcentral Tech Coll (WI)
Pasadena City Coll (CA)
Southeastern Coll–West Palm Beach (FL)
Spencerian Coll (KY)

**MEDICAL OFFICE ASSISTANT**
Barton County Comm Coll (KS)
Beal Coll (ME)
Front Range Comm Coll (CO)
Harford Comm Coll (MD)
Mitchell Tech Inst (SD)
Pasadena City Coll (CA)
Pittsburgh Tech Coll (PA)
Sauk Valley Comm Coll (IL)
Western Wyoming Comm Coll (WY)
White Mountains Comm Coll (NH)

**MEDICAL OFFICE COMPUTER SPECIALIST**
Carteret Comm Coll (NC)
Richmond Comm Coll (NC)
Western Wyoming Comm Coll (WY)

**MEDICAL OFFICE MANAGEMENT**
Caldwell Comm Coll and Tech Inst (NC)
Cleveland Comm Coll (NC)

Coll of the Ouachitas (AR)
Craven Comm Coll (NC)
Fayetteville Tech Comm Coll (NC)
Fox Valley Tech Coll (WI)
Halifax Comm Coll (NC)
Haywood Comm Coll (NC)
Johnston Comm Coll (NC)
Lenoir Comm Coll (NC)
Montgomery Comm Coll (NC)
Montgomery County Comm Coll (PA)
Pennsylvania Inst of Technology (PA)
Piedmont Comm Coll (NC)
Pueblo Comm Coll (CO)
Queensborough Comm Coll of the
  City U of New York (NY)
Randolph Comm Coll (NC)
Richmond Comm Coll (NC)
Rowan-Cabarrus Comm Coll (NC)
Wayne Comm Coll (NC)
Western Iowa Tech Comm Coll (IA)

**MEDICAL RADIOLOGIC
TECHNOLOGY**
Anne Arundel Comm Coll (MD)
Bowling Green State U–Firelands
  Coll (OH)
Bunker Hill Comm Coll (MA)
Chesapeake Coll (MD)
Chippewa Valley Tech Coll (WI)
Coll of Central Florida (FL)
Comm Coll of Allegheny County (PA)
Comm Coll of Baltimore County (MD)
Comm Coll of Philadelphia (PA)
Daytona State Coll (FL)
Del Mar Coll (TX)
Dunwoody Coll of Technology (MN)
East Central Coll (MO)
El Paso Comm Coll (TX)
Erie Comm Coll (NY)
Fiorello H. LaGuardia Comm Coll of
  the City U of New York (NY)
Galveston Coll (TX)
George C. Wallace Comm Coll (AL)
Greenville Tech Coll (SC)
Gulf Coast State Coll (FL)
Hagerstown Comm Coll (MD)
Holyoke Comm Coll (MA)
Hutchinson Comm Coll (KS)
Illinois Eastern Comm Colls, Olney
  Central College (IL)
Ivy Tech Comm Coll–Bloomington
  (IN)
Ivy Tech Comm Coll–Central Indiana
  (IN)
Ivy Tech Comm Coll–Columbus (IN)
Ivy Tech Comm Coll–East Central
  (IN)
Ivy Tech Comm Coll–Richmond (IN)
Ivy Tech Comm Coll–Southeast (IN)
Ivy Tech Comm Coll–Wabash Valley
  (IN)
Johnson Coll (PA)
Kellogg Comm Coll (MI)
Kent State U at Ashtabula (OH)
Kent State U at Salem (OH)
Lakeland Comm Coll (OH)
Lorain County Comm Coll (OH)
Miami Dade Coll (FL)
Mitchell Tech Inst (SD)
Mohawk Valley Comm Coll (NY)
Montgomery Coll (MD)
Mott Comm Coll (MI)
Nassau Comm Coll (NY)
Naugatuck Valley Comm Coll (CT)
Niagara County Comm Coll (NY)
Northcentral Tech Coll (WI)
Northeast Comm Coll (NE)
Northern Essex Comm Coll (MA)
North Shore Comm Coll (MA)
Pensacola State Coll (FL)
Rend Lake Coll (IL)
Salt Lake Comm Coll (UT)
Somerset Comm Coll (KY)
Southcentral Kentucky Comm and
  Tech Coll (KY)
Southeast Arkansas Coll (AR)
Southeast Kentucky Comm and Tech
  Coll (KY)
Southern U at Shreveport (LA)
South Florida State Coll (FL)
Southwestern Comm Coll (NC)
Tallahassee Comm Coll (FL)
Truckee Meadows Comm Coll (NV)
Tulsa Comm Coll (OK)
Vincennes U (IN)
Volunteer State Comm Coll (TN)
Westchester Comm Coll (NY)
Wor-Wic Comm Coll (MD)

**MEDICAL STAFF SERVICES
TECHNOLOGY**
Rend Lake Coll (IL)

**MEDICAL TRANSCRIPTION**
Barton County Comm Coll (KS)
Hudson County Comm Coll (NJ)
Northern Essex Comm Coll (MA)
Treasure Valley Comm Coll (OR)
Western Dakota Tech Inst (SD)

**MEDICATION AIDE**
Barton County Comm Coll (KS)

**MEDIUM/HEAVY VEHICLE AND
TRUCK TECHNOLOGY**
Edison State Comm Coll (OH)
James Sprunt Comm Coll (NC)
Williston State Coll (ND)

**MEETING AND EVENT
PLANNING**
Bucks County Comm Coll (PA)
Fox Valley Tech Coll (WI)
Northampton Comm Coll (PA)
Raritan Valley Comm Coll (NJ)

**MENTAL AND SOCIAL HEALTH
SERVICES AND ALLIED
PROFESSIONS RELATED**
Carteret Comm Coll (NC)
Chesapeake Coll (MD)
Halifax Comm Coll (NC)
John Tyler Comm Coll (VA)
J. Sargeant Reynolds Comm Coll
  (VA)
Kennebec Valley Comm Coll (ME)
Lackawanna Coll (PA)
Lenoir Comm Coll (NC)
Montgomery Comm Coll (NC)
New River Comm Coll (VA)
Northcentral Tech Coll (WI)
Piedmont Comm Coll (NC)
Richmond Comm Coll (NC)
Southwest Virginia Comm Coll (VA)
Wayne Comm Coll (NC)

**MENTAL HEALTH
COUNSELING**
Alvin Comm Coll (TX)
Austin Comm Coll District (TX)
Del Mar Coll (TX)
Kingsborough Comm Coll of the City
  U of New York (NY)
Macomb Comm Coll (MI)
McLennan Comm Coll (TX)
Mt. San Antonio Coll (CA)
North Shore Comm Coll (MA)
Orange Coast Coll (CA)
Southwestern Comm Coll (NC)
Tarrant County Coll District (TX)
Truckee Meadows Comm Coll (NV)

**MERCHANDISING**
Mesa Comm Coll (AZ)
North Central Texas Coll (TX)

**MERCHANDISING, SALES, AND
MARKETING OPERATIONS
RELATED (GENERAL)**
Lake Region State Coll (ND)
Minnesota State Comm and Tech
  Coll (MN)
Northcentral Tech Coll (WI)
Orange Coast Coll (CA)

**MERCHANDISING, SALES, AND
MARKETING OPERATIONS
RELATED (SPECIALIZED)**
Wade Coll (TX)

**METAL AND JEWELRY ARTS**
Coll of The Albemarle (NC)
Fashion Inst of Technology (NY)
Haywood Comm Coll (NC)
Palomar Coll (CA)
Paris Jr Coll (TX)

**METAL FABRICATOR**
Waukesha County Tech Coll (WI)

**METALLURGICAL
TECHNOLOGY**
Macomb Comm Coll (MI)
Penn State DuBois (PA)
Penn State Fayette, The Eberly
  Campus (PA)
Schoolcraft Coll (MI)

**MICROBIOLOGY**
Fullerton Coll (CA)
Humacao Comm Coll (PR)

**MIDDLE SCHOOL EDUCATION**
Alvin Comm Coll (TX)
Arkansas State U–Newport (AR)
Austin Comm Coll District (TX)

Collin County Comm Coll District
  (TX)
Comm Coll of Allegheny County (PA)
El Paso Comm Coll (TX)
Georgia Military Coll (GA)
Miami Dade Coll (FL)
Montgomery County Comm Coll (PA)
Northampton Comm Coll (PA)
Panola Coll (TX)
Tyler Jr Coll (TX)
U of Arkansas Comm Coll at
  Morrilton (AR)

**MILITARY STUDIES**
Barton County Comm Coll (KS)

**MILITARY TECHNOLOGIES AND
APPLIED SCIENCES RELATED**
Copiah-Lincoln Comm Coll (MS)

**MINING TECHNOLOGY**
Eastern Arizona Coll (AZ)
Illinois Eastern Comm Colls, Wabash
  Valley College (IL)
Vincennes U (IN)
Western Wyoming Comm Coll (WY)

**MODELING, VIRTUAL
ENVIRONMENTS AND
SIMULATION**
Raritan Valley Comm Coll (NJ)

**MODERN LANGUAGES**
Amarillo Coll (TX)
Barton County Comm Coll (KS)
Odessa Coll (TX)
Oklahoma City Comm Coll (OK)
Otero Jr Coll (CO)
Potomac State Coll of West Virginia
  U (WV)

**MORTUARY SCIENCE AND
EMBALMING**
Gupton-Jones Coll of Funeral
  Service (GA)
Wayne County Comm Coll District
  (MI)

**MOTORCYCLE MAINTENANCE
AND REPAIR TECHNOLOGY**
State Tech Coll of Missouri (MO)
State U of New York Coll of
  Technology at Alfred (NY)
Western Iowa Tech Comm Coll (IA)

**MULTI/INTERDISCIPLINARY
STUDIES RELATED**
Alexandria Tech and Comm Coll
  (MN)
Anne Arundel Comm Coll (MD)
Arkansas State U–Newport (AR)
Austin Comm Coll District (TX)
Blue Ridge Comm and Tech Coll
  (WV)
Bucks County Comm Coll (PA)
Carroll Comm Coll (MD)
Cedar Valley Coll (TX)
Central Maine Comm Coll (ME)
Century Coll (MN)
Chippewa Valley Tech Coll (WI)
Cloud County Comm Coll (KS)
Coll of the Desert (CA)
Coll of the Ouachitas (AR)
County Coll of Morris (NJ)
Eastern Arizona Coll (AZ)
El Paso Comm Coll (TX)
Fox Valley Tech Coll (WI)
Greenville Tech Coll (SC)
Harford Comm Coll (MD)
Hawkeye Comm Coll (IA)
Hinds Comm Coll (MS)
Hopkinsville Comm Coll (KY)
Kennebec Valley Comm Coll (ME)
Lackawanna Coll (PA)
Lake Superior Coll (MN)
LDS Business Coll (UT)
Minnesota State Comm and Tech
  Coll (MN)
Northcentral Tech Coll (WI)
North Hennepin Comm Coll (MN)
Northwest-Shoals Comm Coll (AL)
Oklahoma State U Inst of Technology
  (OK)
Owensboro Comm and Tech Coll
  (KY)
Raritan Valley Comm Coll (NJ)
Somerset Comm Coll (KY)
Southcentral Kentucky Comm and
  Tech Coll (KY)
Southeast Arkansas Coll (AR)
Tulsa Comm Coll (OK)
U of Arkansas Rich Mountain (AR)

Waukesha County Tech Coll (WI)
Western Iowa Tech Comm Coll (IA)
West Kentucky Comm and Tech Coll
  (KY)
Williston State Coll (ND)
Wisconsin Indianhead Tech Coll (WI)
York County Comm Coll (ME)

**MUSEUM STUDIES**
Queensborough Comm Coll of the
  City U of New York (NY)

**MUSIC**
Adirondack Comm Coll (NY)
Alvin Comm Coll (TX)
Amarillo Coll (TX)
American Samoa Comm Coll (AS)
Antelope Valley Coll (CA)
Arizona Western Coll (AZ)
Austin Comm Coll District (TX)
Barton County Comm Coll (KS)
Bossier Parish Comm Coll (LA)
Brookhaven Coll (TX)
Bucks County Comm Coll (PA)
Bunker Hill Comm Coll (MA)
Carroll Comm Coll (MD)
Central Texas Coll (TX)
Century Coll (MN)
Cochise County Comm Coll District
  (AZ)
Coll of Central Florida (FL)
Coll of Marin (CA)
Coll of The Albemarle (NC)
Coll of the Canyons (CA)
Coll of the Desert (CA)
Collin County Comm Coll District
  (TX)
Comm Coll of Allegheny County (PA)
Comm Coll of Philadelphia (PA)
Crowder Coll (MO)
Dawson Comm Coll (MT)
De Anza Coll (CA)
Del Mar Coll (TX)
East Central Coll (MO)
Eastern Arizona Coll (AZ)
El Paso Comm Coll (TX)
Fullerton Coll (CA)
Galveston Coll (TX)
Gordon State Coll (GA)
Grand Rapids Comm Coll (MI)
Harford Comm Coll (MD)
Harper Coll (IL)
Hill Coll (TX)
Holyoke Comm Coll (MA)
Howard Comm Coll (MD)
Independence Comm Coll (KS)
Jamestown Comm Coll (NY)
Kaskaskia Coll (IL)
Kingsborough Comm Coll of the City
  U of New York (NY)
Laramie County Comm Coll (WY)
Los Angeles City Coll (CA)
Manchester Comm Coll (CT)
McHenry County Coll (IL)
McLennan Comm Coll (TX)
Merced Coll (CA)
Mesa Comm Coll (AZ)
Miami Dade Coll (FL)
Minnesota State Comm and Tech
  Coll (MN)
Monroe Comm Coll (NY)
Morton Coll (IL)
Mt. San Antonio Coll (CA)
Navarro Coll (TX)
Niagara County Comm Coll (NY)
Northeastern Jr Coll (CO)
Northern Essex Comm Coll (MA)
North Hennepin Comm Coll (MN)
Northwest Coll (WY)
Oakton Comm Coll (IL)
Odessa Coll (TX)
Oklahoma City Comm Coll (OK)
Orange Coast Coll (CA)
Palomar Coll (CA)
Panola Coll (TX)
Paris Jr Coll (TX)
Pensacola State Coll (FL)
Piedmont Virginia Comm Coll (VA)
Quinsigamond Comm Coll (MA)
Raritan Valley Comm Coll (NJ)
Rend Lake Coll (IL)
St. Charles Comm Coll (MO)
St. Philip's Coll (TX)
Salt Lake Comm Coll (UT)
San Jacinto Coll District (TX)
San Joaquin Delta Coll (CA)
Sauk Valley Comm Coll (IL)
Southwestern Coll (CA)
Southwestern Comm Coll (IA)
Texarkana Coll (TX)
Tidewater Comm Coll (VA)
Trinity Valley Comm Coll (TX)

Truckee Meadows Comm Coll (NV)
Tulsa Comm Coll (OK)
Tyler Jr Coll (TX)
Vincennes U (IN)
Western Wyoming Comm Coll (WY)

**MUSICAL INSTRUMENT
FABRICATION AND REPAIR**
Queensborough Comm Coll of the
  City U of New York (NY)
Renton Tech Coll (WA)
Western Iowa Tech Comm Coll (IA)

**MUSICAL THEATER**
Coll of the Canyons (CA)
KD Conservatory Coll of Film and
  Dramatic Arts (TX)

**MUSIC HISTORY, LITERATURE,
AND THEORY**
Queensborough Comm Coll of the
  City U of New York (NY)

**MUSIC MANAGEMENT**
Austin Comm Coll District (TX)
Cedar Valley Coll (TX)
Chandler-Gilbert Comm Coll (AZ)
Collin County Comm Coll District
  (TX)
Harrisburg Area Comm Coll (PA)
Houston Comm Coll (TX)
Mesa Comm Coll (AZ)
Northeast Comm Coll (NE)
Southwestern Coll (CA)

**MUSIC PERFORMANCE**
Adirondack Comm Coll (NY)
Cedar Valley Coll (TX)
Cleveland State Comm Coll (TN)
Houston Comm Coll (TX)
Macomb Comm Coll (MI)
Miami Dade Coll (FL)
Nassau Comm Coll (NY)
Northeast Comm Coll (NE)
Truckee Meadows Comm Coll (NV)
Volunteer State Comm Coll (TN)
Walters State Comm Coll (TN)

**MUSIC RELATED**
Cayuga County Comm Coll (NY)
County Coll of Morris (NJ)
Santa Rosa Jr Coll (CA)

**MUSIC TEACHER EDUCATION**
Amarillo Coll (TX)
Coll of Central Florida (FL)
Copiah-Lincoln Comm Coll (MS)
Del Mar Coll (TX)
Grand Rapids Comm Coll (MI)
Miami Dade Coll (FL)
Montgomery County Comm Coll (PA)
Northeast Comm Coll (NE)
Pensacola State Coll (FL)

**MUSIC TECHNOLOGY**
Daytona State Coll (FL)
Gulf Coast State Coll (FL)
Miami Dade Coll (FL)
Mott Comm Coll (MI)
Northwest Coll (WY)

**MUSIC THEORY AND
COMPOSITION**
Cedar Valley Coll (TX)
Houston Comm Coll (TX)

**NANOTECHNOLOGY**
Comm Coll of Allegheny County (PA)
Erie Comm Coll, North Campus (NY)
Genesee Comm Coll (NY)
Harper Coll (IL)
Lehigh Carbon Comm Coll (PA)
Montgomery County Comm Coll (PA)

**NATURAL RESOURCES AND
CONSERVATION RELATED**
Southwestern Indian Polytechnic Inst
  (NM)

**NATURAL RESOURCES/
CONSERVATION**
American Samoa Comm Coll (AS)
Central Lakes Coll (MN)
Central Oregon Comm Coll (OR)
Coll of the Desert (CA)
Feather River Coll (CA)
Fox Valley Tech Coll (WI)
Niagara County Comm Coll (NY)
Santa Rosa Jr Coll (CA)
Treasure Valley Comm Coll (OR)
Truckee Meadows Comm Coll (NV)
U of Wisconsin–Baraboo/Sauk
  County (WI)

U of Wisconsin–Barron County (WI)
U of Wisconsin–Fond du Lac (WI)
U of Wisconsin–Fox Valley (WI)
U of Wisconsin–Manitowoc (WI)
U of Wisconsin–Marathon County (WI)
U of Wisconsin–Marinette (WI)
U of Wisconsin–Marshfield/Wood County (WI)
U of Wisconsin–Richland (WI)
U of Wisconsin–Rock County (WI)
U of Wisconsin–Sheboygan (WI)
U of Wisconsin–Washington County (WI)
U of Wisconsin–Waukesha (WI)
Vincennes U (IN)

**NATURAL RESOURCES MANAGEMENT AND POLICY**
Hawkeye Comm Coll (IA)
Hutchinson Comm Coll (KS)
Northwest Coll (WY)
The Ohio State U Ag Tech Inst (OH)
Pensacola State Coll (FL)
San Joaquin Delta Coll (CA)

**NATURAL RESOURCES MANAGEMENT AND POLICY RELATED**
The Ohio State U Ag Tech Inst (OH)

**NATURAL SCIENCES**
Amarillo Coll (TX)
Arkansas State U–Newport (AR)
Bossier Parish Comm Coll (LA)
Galveston Coll (TX)
Miami Dade Coll (FL)
Northeastern Jr Coll (CO)
San Joaquin Delta Coll (CA)
Santa Rosa Jr Coll (CA)
Sisseton-Wahpeton Coll (SD)
Tyler Jr Coll (TX)

**NETWORK AND SYSTEM ADMINISTRATION**
Bucks County Comm Coll (PA)
Career Coll of Northern Nevada (NV)
The Coll of Westchester (NY)
Collin County Comm Coll District (TX)
Daytona State Coll (FL)
Del Mar Coll (TX)
Genesee Comm Coll (NY)
Gulf Coast State Coll (FL)
Houston Comm Coll (TX)
Illinois Valley Comm Coll (IL)
Ivy Tech Comm Coll–Bloomington (IN)
Ivy Tech Comm Coll–Central Indiana (IN)
Ivy Tech Comm Coll–East Central (IN)
Ivy Tech Comm Coll–Kokomo (IN)
Ivy Tech Comm Coll–Richmond (IN)
Ivy Tech Comm Coll–Sellersburg (IN)
Ivy Tech Comm Coll–Southeast (IN)
Ivy Tech Comm Coll–Southwest (IN)
Ivy Tech Comm Coll–Wabash Valley (IN)
Kaskaskia Coll (IL)
Kishwaukee Coll (IL)
Lake Superior Coll (MN)
LDS Business Coll (UT)
Massachusetts Bay Comm Coll (MA)
Miami Dade Coll (FL)
Mitchell Tech Inst (SD)
Montgomery County Comm Coll (PA)
Pittsburgh Tech Coll (PA)
Ridgewater Coll (MN)
St. Louis Comm Coll (MO)
Seminole State Coll of Florida (FL)
Southeast Tech Inst (SD)
South Florida State Coll (FL)
Southwestern Coll (CA)
Texas State Tech Coll (TX)
York County Comm Coll (ME)

**NEUROSCIENCE**
Bucks County Comm Coll (PA)

**NONPROFIT MANAGEMENT**
Miami Dade Coll (FL)

**NUCLEAR MEDICAL TECHNOLOGY**
Amarillo Coll (TX)
Caldwell Comm Coll and Tech Inst (NC)
Comm Coll of Allegheny County (PA)
Del Mar Coll (TX)
Frederick Comm Coll (MD)

Galveston Coll (TX)
Gulf Coast State Coll (FL)
Harrisburg Area Comm Coll (PA)
Houston Comm Coll (TX)
Howard Comm Coll (MD)
Lakeland Comm Coll (OH)
Miami Dade Coll (FL)

**NUCLEAR/NUCLEAR POWER TECHNOLOGY**
George C. Wallace Comm Coll (AL)
State Tech Coll of Missouri (MO)
Texas State Tech Coll (TX)
Three Rivers Comm Coll (CT)

**NURSING ADMINISTRATION**
Paris Jr Coll (TX)
South Suburban Coll (IL)

**NURSING ASSISTANT/AIDE AND PATIENT CARE ASSISTANT/AIDE**
Barton County Comm Coll (KS)
Central New Mexico Comm Coll (NM)
Comm Coll of Allegheny County (PA)
North Iowa Area Comm Coll (IA)
Pensacola State Coll (FL)
Spencerian Coll (KY)
Tallahassee Comm Coll (FL)
Western Iowa Tech Comm Coll (IA)
Western Wyoming Comm Coll (WY)

**NURSING EDUCATION**
American Samoa Comm Coll (AS)

**NURSING PRACTICE**
Genesee Comm Coll (NY)

**NURSING SCIENCE**
Gurnick Academy of Medical Arts (CA)
Piedmont Virginia Comm Coll (VA)
St. Louis Comm Coll (MO)
Spencerian Coll (KY)

**NUTRITION SCIENCES**
Santa Rosa Jr Coll (CA)
Sisseton-Wahpeton Coll (SD)
Tulsa Comm Coll (OK)

**OCCUPATIONAL HEALTH AND INDUSTRIAL HYGIENE**
Niagara County Comm Coll (NY)

**OCCUPATIONAL SAFETY AND HEALTH TECHNOLOGY**
Anne Arundel Comm Coll (MD)
Comm Coll of Baltimore County (MD)
Del Mar Coll (TX)
Houston Comm Coll (TX)
Ivy Tech Comm Coll–Central Indiana (IN)
Ivy Tech Comm Coll–Northwest (IN)
Ivy Tech Comm Coll–Wabash Valley (IN)
Mt. San Antonio Coll (CA)
NorthWest Arkansas Comm Coll (AR)
San Jacinto Coll District (TX)
San Juan Coll (NM)
Texas State Tech Coll (TX)
Three Rivers Coll (MO)

**OCCUPATIONAL THERAPIST ASSISTANT**
Austin Comm Coll District (TX)
Bossier Parish Comm Coll (LA)
Bristol Comm Coll (MA)
Camden County Coll (NJ)
Cayuga County Comm Coll (NY)
Comm Coll of Allegheny County (PA)
County Coll of Morris (NJ)
Crowder Coll (MO)
Daytona State Coll (FL)
Del Mar Coll (TX)
East Central Coll (MO)
Erie Comm Coll, North Campus (NY)
Fiorello H. LaGuardia Comm Coll of the City U of New York (NY)
Fox Valley Tech Coll (WI)
Greenville Tech Coll (SC)
Hawkeye Comm Coll (IA)
Houston Comm Coll (TX)
Illinois Central Coll (IL)
Jamestown Comm Coll (NY)
Kaskaskia Coll (IL)
Kennebec Valley Comm Coll (ME)
Kent State U at Ashtabula (OH)
Kent State U at East Liverpool (OH)

Lake Area Tech Inst (SD)
Lehigh Carbon Comm Coll (PA)
Lorain County Comm Coll (OH)
Macomb Comm Coll (MI)
Manchester Comm Coll (CT)
McHenry County Coll (IL)
Mott Comm Coll (MI)
North Dakota State Coll of Science (ND)
Northland Comm and Tech Coll (MN)
Oklahoma City Comm Coll (OK)
Ozarks Tech Comm Coll (MO)
Panola Coll (TX)
Penn State DuBois (PA)
Penn State Mont Alto (PA)
Pueblo Comm Coll (CO)
Quinsigamond Comm Coll (MA)
Raritan Valley Comm Coll (NJ)
Rowan-Cabarrus Comm Coll (NC)
St. Charles Comm Coll (MO)
St. Louis Comm Coll (MO)
St. Philip's Coll (TX)
Salt Lake Comm Coll (UT)
San Juan Coll (NM)
Shawnee Comm Coll (IL)
South Suburban Coll (IL)
Springfield Tech Comm Coll (MA)
Three Rivers Coll (MO)
Tyler Jr Coll (TX)
Walters State Comm Coll (TN)
Wisconsin Indianhead Tech Coll (WI)
Wor-Wic Comm Coll (MD)

**OCCUPATIONAL THERAPY**
Amarillo Coll (TX)
Barton County Comm Coll (KS)
Coll of Central Florida (FL)
Comm Coll of Baltimore County (MD)
Iowa Central Comm Coll (IA)
Navarro Coll (TX)
North Central Texas Coll (TX)
North Shore Comm Coll (MA)
San Jacinto Coll District (TX)
Sauk Valley Comm Coll (IL)
Stark State Coll (OH)
Trident Tech Coll (SC)
Tulsa Comm Coll (OK)
Vincennes U (IN)

**OFFICE MANAGEMENT**
Alexandria Tech and Comm Coll (MN)
Asheville-Buncombe Tech Comm Coll (NC)
Brookhaven Coll (TX)
Carteret Comm Coll (NC)
Cecil Coll (MD)
Cleveland Comm Coll (NC)
Coll of Central Florida (FL)
Coll of Marin (CA)
Coll of the Desert (CA)
Coll of the Ouachitas (AR)
Comm Coll of Allegheny County (PA)
Craven Comm Coll (NC)
Daytona State Coll (FL)
Des Moines Area Comm Coll (IA)
Erie Comm Coll, North Campus (NY)
Fayetteville Tech Comm Coll (NC)
Fox Valley Tech Coll (WI)
Gateway Tech Coll (WI)
Gulf Coast State Coll (FL)
Halifax Comm Coll (NC)
Howard Comm Coll (MD)
James Sprunt Comm Coll (NC)
Jefferson Comm Coll (NY)
Jefferson State Comm Coll (AL)
Johnston Comm Coll (NC)
Lake Superior Coll (MN)
Lenoir Comm Coll (NC)
Merced Coll (CA)
Miami Dade Coll (FL)
Minnesota State Comm and Tech Coll (MN)
Mitchell Comm Coll (NC)
Montgomery Comm Coll (NC)
Northwest Mississippi Comm Coll (MS)
Pensacola State Coll (FL)
Piedmont Comm Coll (NC)
Renton Tech Coll (WA)
Richmond Comm Coll (NC)
Rowan-Cabarrus Comm Coll (NC)
St. Charles Comm Coll (MO)
South Florida State Coll (FL)
South Suburban Coll (IL)
Tallahassee Comm Coll (FL)
Treasure Valley Comm Coll (OR)
Waukesha County Tech Coll (WI)
Wayne Comm Coll (NC)

Wayne County Comm Coll District (MI)
White Mountains Comm Coll (NH)
Wisconsin Indianhead Tech Coll (WI)

**OFFICE OCCUPATIONS AND CLERICAL SERVICES**
Alamance Comm Coll (NC)
Alvin Comm Coll (TX)
American Samoa Comm Coll (AS)
Caldwell Comm Coll and Tech Inst (NC)
Cloud County Comm Coll (KS)
Del Mar Coll (TX)
ITI Tech Coll (LA)
Jefferson Comm Coll (NY)
Mesalands Comm Coll (NM)
New Mexico State U–Alamogordo (NM)
Northeast Comm Coll (NE)
Southeast Tech Inst (SD)

**OPERATIONS MANAGEMENT**
Blue Ridge Comm and Tech Coll (WV)
Bunker Hill Comm Coll (MA)
Chippewa Valley Tech Coll (WI)
Cleveland Comm Coll (NC)
Daytona State Coll (FL)
LDS Business Coll (UT)
Lenoir Comm Coll (NC)
Macomb Comm Coll (MI)
McHenry County Coll (IL)
Miami Dade Coll (FL)
Mitchell Comm Coll (NC)
Mohawk Valley Comm Coll (NY)
Northcentral Tech Coll (WI)
Oakton Comm Coll (IL)
Pennsylvania Highlands Comm Coll (PA)
Pensacola State Coll (FL)
South Florida State Coll (FL)
Stark State Coll (OH)
Wayne Comm Coll (NC)

**OPHTHALMIC TECHNOLOGY**
Lakeland Comm Coll (OH)
Miami Dade Coll (FL)
Renton Tech Coll (WA)
Volunteer State Comm Coll (TN)

**OPTICIANRY**
Camden County Coll (NJ)
El Paso Comm Coll (TX)
Erie Comm Coll, North Campus (NY)
J. Sargeant Reynolds Comm Coll (VA)
Miami Dade Coll (FL)
Raritan Valley Comm Coll (NJ)
Southwestern Indian Polytechnic Inst (NM)

**OPTOMETRIC TECHNICIAN**
Barton County Comm Coll (KS)
El Paso Comm Coll (TX)
Raritan Valley Comm Coll (NJ)
San Jacinto Coll District (TX)

**ORGANIZATIONAL BEHAVIOR**
Chandler-Gilbert Comm Coll (AZ)
Lackawanna Coll (PA)
Mesa Comm Coll (AZ)

**ORNAMENTAL HORTICULTURE**
Coll of the Desert (CA)
Comm Coll of Allegheny County (PA)
Kishwaukee Coll (IL)
Mesa Comm Coll (AZ)
Miami Dade Coll (FL)
Mt. San Antonio Coll (CA)
Pensacola State Coll (FL)
Richland Coll (TX)
San Joaquin Delta Coll (CA)
Southwestern Coll (CA)
Walters State Comm Coll (TN)

**ORTHOTICS/PROSTHETICS**
Century Coll (MN)
Oklahoma State U Inst of Technology (OK)

**PAINTING AND WALL COVERING**
Comm Coll of Allegheny County (PA)
Ivy Tech Comm Coll–Central Indiana (IN)
Ivy Tech Comm Coll–East Central (IN)
Ivy Tech Comm Coll–Lafayette (IN)

Ivy Tech Comm Coll–North Central (IN)
Ivy Tech Comm Coll–Northeast (IN)
Ivy Tech Comm Coll–Northwest (IN)
Ivy Tech Comm Coll–Southwest (IN)
Ivy Tech Comm Coll–Wabash Valley (IN)

**PALEONTOLOGY**
Mesalands Comm Coll (NM)

**PARKS, RECREATION AND LEISURE**
Coll of Central Florida (FL)
Coll of the Canyons (CA)
Coll of the Desert (CA)
Del Mar Coll (TX)
Feather River Coll (CA)
Florida Keys Comm Coll (FL)
Fullerton Coll (CA)
Kingsborough Comm Coll of the City U of New York (NY)
Mesa Comm Coll (AZ)
Miami Dade Coll (FL)
Monroe Comm Coll (NY)
Mt. San Antonio Coll (CA)
Muskegon Comm Coll (MI)
National Park Coll (AR)
Niagara County Comm Coll (NY)
Northern Essex Comm Coll (MA)
Northwest Coll (WY)
Palomar Coll (CA)
San Juan Coll (NM)
Southwestern Coll (CA)
Sullivan County Comm Coll (NY)
Tompkins Cortland Comm Coll (NY)

**PARKS, RECREATION AND LEISURE FACILITIES MANAGEMENT**
Adirondack Comm Coll (NY)
Arizona Western Coll (AZ)
Coll of the Desert (CA)
Mohawk Valley Comm Coll (NY)
Mt. San Antonio Coll (CA)
National Park Coll (AR)
Potomac State Coll of West Virginia U (WV)
Santa Rosa Jr Coll (CA)
Tompkins Cortland Comm Coll (NY)
Western Texas Coll (TX)

**PARKS, RECREATION, LEISURE, AND FITNESS STUDIES RELATED**
Coll of the Desert (CA)
Comm Coll of Baltimore County (MD)
Genesee Comm Coll (NY)
Southwestern Comm Coll (NC)

**PASTORAL STUDIES/COUNSELING**
Hesston Coll (KS)

**PERIOPERATIVE/OPERATING ROOM AND SURGICAL NURSING**
Comm Coll of Allegheny County (PA)

**PERSONAL AND CULINARY SERVICES RELATED**
Mohave Comm Coll (AZ)

**PETROLEUM TECHNOLOGY**
Bossier Parish Comm Coll (LA)
Houston Comm Coll (TX)
Lackawanna Coll (PA)
Oklahoma State U Inst of Technology (OK)
Panola Coll (TX)
Rend Lake Coll (IL)
Western Texas Coll (TX)
Williston State Coll (ND)

**PHARMACY**
Barton County Comm Coll (KS)
Mount Wachusett Comm Coll (MA)
Navarro Coll (TX)

**PHARMACY TECHNICIAN**
Alvin Comm Coll (TX)
Austin Comm Coll District (TX)
Barton County Comm Coll (KS)
Bossier Parish Comm Coll (LA)
Comm Coll of Allegheny County (PA)
Eastern Arizona Coll (AZ)
El Paso Comm Coll (TX)
Fayetteville Tech Comm Coll (NC)
Humacao Comm Coll (PR)
Hutchinson Comm Coll (KS)

J. Sargeant Reynolds Comm Coll (VA)
Miami Dade Coll (FL)
Minnesota State Comm and Tech Coll (MN)
Mohave Comm Coll (AZ)
North Dakota State Coll of Science (ND)
Northland Comm and Tech Coll (MN)
Pennsylvania Inst of Technology (PA)
Pensacola State Coll (FL)
Renton Tech Coll (WA)
San Jacinto Coll District (TX)
Santa Rosa Jr Coll (CA)
Southeastern Coll–West Palm Beach (FL)
Southeast Tech Inst (SD)
Tallahassee Comm Coll (FL)
Texarkana Coll (TX)
Vincennes U (IN)
Wayne County Comm Coll District (MI)
Western Dakota Tech Inst (SD)
Western Iowa Tech Comm Coll (IA)

## PHILOSOPHY
Antelope Valley Coll (CA)
Arizona Western Coll (AZ)
Austin Comm Coll District (TX)
Barton County Comm Coll (KS)
Cochise County Comm Coll District (AZ)
Coll of Central Florida (FL)
Coll of the Canyons (CA)
Coll of the Desert (CA)
De Anza Coll (CA)
Fiorello H. LaGuardia Comm Coll of the City U of New York (NY)
Fullerton Coll (CA)
Harford Comm Coll (MD)
Harper Coll (IL)
Harrisburg Area Comm Coll (PA)
Hill Coll (TX)
Merced Coll (CA)
Miami Dade Coll (FL)
Northeastern Jr Coll (CO)
Orange Coast Coll (CA)
Pensacola State Coll (FL)
San Jacinto Coll District (TX)
San Joaquin Delta Coll (CA)
Santa Rosa Jr Coll (CA)
Southwestern Coll (CA)
Truckee Meadows Comm Coll (NV)
U of Wisconsin–Baraboo/Sauk County (WI)
U of Wisconsin–Barron County (WI)
U of Wisconsin–Fond du Lac (WI)
U of Wisconsin–Fox Valley (WI)
U of Wisconsin–Manitowoc (WI)
U of Wisconsin–Marathon County (WI)
U of Wisconsin–Marinette (WI)
U of Wisconsin–Marshfield/Wood County (WI)
U of Wisconsin–Richland (WI)
U of Wisconsin–Rock County (WI)
U of Wisconsin–Sheboygan (WI)
U of Wisconsin–Washington County (WI)
U of Wisconsin–Waukesha (WI)
Vincennes U (IN)

## PHILOSOPHY AND RELIGIOUS STUDIES RELATED
Edison State Comm Coll (OH)

## PHLEBOTOMY TECHNOLOGY
Barton County Comm Coll (KS)
Miami Dade Coll (FL)
Spencerian Coll (KY)

## PHOTOGRAPHIC AND FILM/VIDEO TECHNOLOGY
Antelope Valley Coll (CA)
Austin Comm Coll District (TX)
Carteret Comm Coll (NC)
Central Lakes Coll (MN)
Daytona State Coll (FL)
Eastern Arizona Coll (AZ)
Hinds Comm Coll (MS)
Los Angeles City Coll (CA)
Miami Dade Coll (FL)
Mohawk Valley Comm Coll (NY)
Orange Coast Coll (CA)
Palomar Coll (CA)
Randolph Comm Coll (NC)
Salt Lake Comm Coll (UT)
Southwestern Coll (CA)
Tompkins Cortland Comm Coll (NY)

## PHOTOGRAPHY
Amarillo Coll (TX)

Antelope Valley Coll (CA)
Cecil Coll (MD)
Coll of the Canyons (CA)
Comm Coll of Philadelphia (PA)
County Coll of Morris (NJ)
Daytona State Coll (FL)
De Anza Coll (CA)
Harford Comm Coll (MD)
Harrisburg Area Comm Coll (PA)
Howard Comm Coll (MD)
LDS Business Coll (UT)
Merced Coll (CA)
Miami Dade Coll (FL)
Mott Comm Coll (MI)
Mt. San Antonio Coll (CA)
Nassau Comm Coll (NY)
Odessa Coll (TX)
Oklahoma City Comm Coll (OK)
Oklahoma State U Inst of Technology (OK)
Orange Coast Coll (CA)
Pasadena City Coll (CA)
Pensacola State Coll (FL)
St. Louis Comm Coll (MO)
San Joaquin Delta Coll (CA)
Scottsdale Comm Coll (AZ)
Southwestern Coll (CA)
Sullivan County Comm Coll (NY)
Western Wyoming Comm Coll (WY)

## PHOTOJOURNALISM
Pasadena City Coll (CA)
Randolph Comm Coll (NC)
Vincennes U (IN)

## PHYSICAL EDUCATION TEACHING AND COACHING
Alvin Comm Coll (TX)
Amarillo Coll (TX)
Barton County Comm Coll (KS)
Bucks County Comm Coll (PA)
Carl Albert State Coll (OK)
Coll of Central Florida (FL)
Copiah-Lincoln Comm Coll (MS)
Crowder Coll (MO)
De Anza Coll (CA)
Del Mar Coll (TX)
Dutchess Comm Coll (NY)
Galveston Coll (TX)
Genesee Comm Coll (NY)
Grand Rapids Comm Coll (MI)
Harper Coll (IL)
Laramie County Comm Coll (WY)
McLennan Comm Coll (TX)
Miami Dade Coll (FL)
Mohawk Valley Comm Coll (NY)
Monroe Comm Coll (NY)
Montgomery County Comm Coll (PA)
Navarro Coll (TX)
Niagara County Comm Coll (NY)
Northeastern Jr Coll (CO)
Northern Essex Comm Coll (MA)
North Hennepin Comm Coll (MN)
Odessa Coll (TX)
Panola Coll (TX)
Potomac State Coll of West Virginia U (WV)
San Joaquin Delta Coll (CA)
Sauk Valley Comm Coll (IL)
Seminole State Coll (OK)
Trinity Valley Comm Coll (TX)
Tyler Jr Coll (TX)
U of Wisconsin–Baraboo/Sauk County (WI)
U of Wisconsin–Barron County (WI)
U of Wisconsin–Fond du Lac (WI)
U of Wisconsin–Fox Valley (WI)
U of Wisconsin–Manitowoc (WI)
U of Wisconsin–Marathon County (WI)
U of Wisconsin–Marinette (WI)
U of Wisconsin–Marshfield/Wood County (WI)
U of Wisconsin–Richland (WI)
U of Wisconsin–Rock County (WI)
U of Wisconsin–Sheboygan (WI)
U of Wisconsin–Washington County (WI)
U of Wisconsin–Waukesha (WI)
Vincennes U (IN)

## PHYSICAL FITNESS TECHNICIAN
Alexandria Tech and Comm Coll (MN)
Central Maine Comm Coll (ME)
Lake Region State Coll (ND)
Orange Coast Coll (CA)
Pensacola State Coll (FL)
Schoolcraft Coll (MI)
Southwestern Coll (CA)
Tallahassee Comm Coll (FL)

Western Iowa Tech Comm Coll (IA)

## PHYSICAL SCIENCES
Alvin Comm Coll (TX)
Amarillo Coll (TX)
Antelope Valley Coll (CA)
Barton County Comm Coll (KS)
Carl Albert State Coll (OK)
Central Oregon Comm Coll (OR)
Chandler-Gilbert Comm Coll (AZ)
Coll of Marin (CA)
Crowder Coll (MO)
Feather River Coll (CA)
Harper Coll (IL)
Harrisburg Area Comm Coll (PA)
Howard Comm Coll (MD)
Hutchinson Comm Coll (KS)
Independence Comm Coll (KS)
Lehigh Carbon Comm Coll (PA)
Mesa Comm Coll (AZ)
Miami Dade Coll (FL)
Montgomery County Comm Coll (PA)
Mount Wachusett Comm Coll (MA)
National Park Coll (AR)
Navarro Coll (TX)
Northeastern Jr Coll (CO)
Paris Jr Coll (TX)
Queensborough Comm Coll of the City U of New York (NY)
Salt Lake Comm Coll (UT)
San Jacinto Coll District (TX)
San Joaquin Delta Coll (CA)
San Juan Coll (NM)
Seminole State Coll (OK)
Southwestern Coll (CA)
Trinity Valley Comm Coll (TX)
Tulsa Comm Coll (OK)

## PHYSICAL SCIENCES RELATED
Mt. San Antonio Coll (CA)
Naugatuck Valley Comm Coll (CT)

## PHYSICAL SCIENCE TECHNOLOGIES RELATED
Northern Essex Comm Coll (MA)

## PHYSICAL THERAPY
Amarillo Coll (TX)
Barton County Comm Coll (KS)
Bossier Parish Comm Coll (LA)
Central Oregon Comm Coll (OR)
Chesapeake Coll (MD)
Coll of Central Florida (FL)
De Anza Coll (CA)
Genesee Comm Coll (NY)
Gurnick Academy of Medical Arts (CA)
Hill Coll (TX)
Housatonic Comm Coll (CT)
Iowa Central Comm Coll (IA)
Kingsborough Comm Coll of the City U of New York (NY)
McLennan Comm Coll (TX)
Monroe County Comm Coll (MI)
Morton Coll (IL)
NorthWest Arkansas Comm Coll (AR)
Odessa Coll (TX)
Oklahoma City Comm Coll (OK)
St. Louis Comm Coll (MO)
Seminole State Coll of Florida (FL)
Stark State Coll (OH)
Tarrant County Coll District (TX)
Trident Tech Coll (SC)
Wytheville Comm Coll (VA)

## PHYSICAL THERAPY TECHNOLOGY
Anne Arundel Comm Coll (MD)
Austin Comm Coll District (TX)
Barton County Comm Coll (KS)
Black Hawk Coll, Moline (IL)
Blue Ridge Comm and Tech Coll (WV)
Bossier Parish Comm Coll (LA)
Caldwell Comm Coll and Tech Inst (NC)
Carl Albert State Coll (OK)
Carroll Comm Coll (MD)
Central New Mexico Comm Coll (NM)
Chesapeake Coll (MD)
Chippewa Valley Tech Coll (WI)
Coll of Central Florida (FL)
Comm Coll of Allegheny County (PA)
Craven Comm Coll (NC)
Daytona State Coll (FL)
Edison State Comm Coll (OH)
El Paso Comm Coll (TX)
Fayetteville Tech Comm Coll (NC)
Fiorello H. LaGuardia Comm Coll of the City U of New York (NY)
Gateway Tech Coll (WI)

Genesee Comm Coll (NY)
George C. Wallace Comm Coll (AL)
Great Falls Coll Montana State U (MT)
Greenville Tech Coll (SC)
Gulf Coast State Coll (FL)
Hawkeye Comm Coll (IA)
Hinds Comm Coll (MS)
Houston Comm Coll (TX)
Howard Comm Coll (MD)
Hutchinson Comm Coll (KS)
Illinois Central Coll (IL)
Ivy Tech Comm Coll–East Central (IN)
Ivy Tech Comm Coll–Kokomo (IN)
Ivy Tech Comm Coll–Sellersburg (IN)
Jefferson State Comm Coll (AL)
Kaskaskia Coll (IL)
Kellogg Comm Coll (MI)
Kennebec Valley Comm Coll (ME)
Kent State U at Ashtabula (OH)
Kent State U at East Liverpool (OH)
Kingsborough Comm Coll of the City U of New York (NY)
Lackawanna Coll (PA)
Lake Area Tech Inst (SD)
Lake Superior Coll (MN)
Laramie County Comm Coll (WY)
Lehigh Carbon Comm Coll (PA)
Lorain County Comm Coll (OH)
Macomb Comm Coll (MI)
Manchester Comm Coll (CT)
Miami Dade Coll (FL)
Mohave Comm Coll (AZ)
Montgomery Coll (MD)
Morton Coll (IL)
Mott Comm Coll (MI)
Mount Wachusett Comm Coll (MA)
Nassau Comm Coll (NY)
Naugatuck Valley Comm Coll (CT)
Niagara County Comm Coll (NY)
Northeast Comm Coll (NE)
Northland Comm and Tech Coll (MN)
North Shore Comm Coll (MA)
Oakton Comm Coll (IL)
Ozarks Tech Comm Coll (MO)
Penn State DuBois (PA)
Penn State Mont Alto (PA)
Pennsylvania Inst of Technology (PA)
Pensacola State Coll (FL)
Pueblo Comm Coll (CO)
St. Philip's Coll (TX)
Salt Lake Comm Coll (UT)
San Jacinto Coll District (TX)
San Juan Coll (NM)
Somerset Comm Coll (KY)
Southeast Kentucky Comm and Tech Coll (KY)
Southern U at Shreveport (LA)
Southwestern Comm Coll (NC)
Springfield Tech Comm Coll (MA)
State Tech Coll of Missouri (MO)
Tulsa Comm Coll (OK)
Tyler Jr Coll (TX)
Union County Coll (NJ)
Victoria Coll (TX)
Vincennes U (IN)
Volunteer State Comm Coll (TN)
Walters State Comm Coll (TN)
Western Iowa Tech Comm Coll (IA)
West Kentucky Comm and Tech Coll (KY)
Wor-Wic Comm Coll (MD)

## PHYSICIAN ASSISTANT
Barton County Comm Coll (KS)
Miami Dade Coll (FL)
Wayne County Comm Coll District (MI)

## PHYSICS
Amarillo Coll (TX)
Antelope Valley Coll (CA)
Arizona Western Coll (AZ)
Austin Comm Coll District (TX)
Barton County Comm Coll (KS)
Bunker Hill Comm Coll (MA)
Cecil Coll (MD)
Central New Mexico Comm Coll (NM)
Cochise County Comm Coll District (AZ)
Coll of Central Florida (FL)
Coll of Marin (CA)
Coll of the Canyons (CA)
Coll of the Desert (CA)
Comm Coll of Allegheny County (PA)
De Anza Coll (CA)
Del Mar Coll (TX)
Eastern Arizona Coll (AZ)
Fullerton Coll (CA)
Gordon State Coll (GA)
Harford Comm Coll (MD)

Hill Coll (TX)
Holyoke Comm Coll (MA)
Houston Comm Coll (TX)
Kingsborough Comm Coll of the City U of New York (NY)
Los Angeles City Coll (CA)
Merced Coll (CA)
Miami Dade Coll (FL)
Monroe Comm Coll (NY)
Mount Wachusett Comm Coll (MA)
Navarro Coll (TX)
Northampton Comm Coll (PA)
Northeast Comm Coll (NE)
Northwest Coll (WY)
Odessa Coll (TX)
Oklahoma City Comm Coll (OK)
Orange Coast Coll (CA)
Panola Coll (TX)
Paris Jr Coll (TX)
Pensacola State Coll (FL)
Potomac State Coll of West Virginia U (WV)
Salt Lake Comm Coll (UT)
San Jacinto Coll District (TX)
San Juan Coll (NM)
Santa Rosa Jr Coll (CA)
Sauk Valley Comm Coll (IL)
Southwestern Coll (CA)
Springfield Tech Comm Coll (MA)
Texarkana Coll (TX)
Truckee Meadows Comm Coll (NV)
Tyler Jr Coll (TX)

## PHYSICS TEACHER EDUCATION
Anne Arundel Comm Coll (MD)
Chesapeake Coll (MD)
Comm Coll of Baltimore County (MD)
Harford Comm Coll (MD)
Montgomery Coll (MD)

## PIPEFITTING AND SPRINKLER FITTING
Ivy Tech Comm Coll–Bloomington (IN)
Ivy Tech Comm Coll–Central Indiana (IN)
Ivy Tech Comm Coll–Columbus (IN)
Ivy Tech Comm Coll–East Central (IN)
Ivy Tech Comm Coll–Lafayette (IN)
Ivy Tech Comm Coll–North Central (IN)
Ivy Tech Comm Coll–Northeast (IN)
Ivy Tech Comm Coll–Northwest (IN)
Ivy Tech Comm Coll–Richmond (IN)
Ivy Tech Comm Coll–Sellersburg (IN)
Ivy Tech Comm Coll–Wabash Valley (IN)
Kellogg Comm Coll (MI)
Miami Dade Coll (FL)
Vincennes U (IN)

## PLANT NURSERY MANAGEMENT
Coll of Marin (CA)
Comm Coll of Allegheny County (PA)
Fullerton Coll (CA)
Miami Dade Coll (FL)
The Ohio State U Ag Tech Inst (OH)
Southwestern Coll (CA)

## PLANT PROTECTION AND INTEGRATED PEST MANAGEMENT
Hinds Comm Coll (MS)

## PLANT SCIENCES
Arizona Western Coll (AZ)

## PLASTICS AND POLYMER ENGINEERING TECHNOLOGY
El Paso Comm Coll (TX)
Grand Rapids Comm Coll (MI)
Macomb Comm Coll (MI)
Mount Wachusett Comm Coll (MA)
Schoolcraft Coll (MI)

## PLATEMAKING/IMAGING
Illinois Central Coll (IL)

## PLUMBING TECHNOLOGY
Arizona Western Coll (AZ)
Hinds Comm Coll (MS)
Macomb Comm Coll (MI)
Miami Dade Coll (FL)
Minnesota State Comm and Tech Coll (MN)
Minnesota West Comm and Tech Coll (MN)
Northeast Iowa Comm Coll (IA)
Southeast Tech Inst (SD)

Thaddeus Stevens Coll of
   Technology (PA)
Vincennes U (IN)

**POLITICAL SCIENCE AND GOVERNMENT**
American Samoa Comm Coll (AS)
Antelope Valley Coll (CA)
Arizona Western Coll (AZ)
Austin Comm Coll District (TX)
Barton County Comm Coll (KS)
Coll of Marin (CA)
Coll of the Canyons (CA)
Coll of the Desert (CA)
De Anza Coll (CA)
Del Mar Coll (TX)
Eastern Arizona Coll (AZ)
Feather River Coll (CA)
Frederick Comm Coll (MD)
Fullerton Coll (CA)
Georgia Military Coll (GA)
Gordon State Coll (GA)
Harford Comm Coll (MD)
Hill Coll (TX)
Laramie County Comm Coll (WY)
Los Angeles City Coll (CA)
Miami Dade Coll (FL)
Monroe Comm Coll (NY)
Northeastern Jr Coll (CO)
Northern Essex Comm Coll (MA)
Northwest Coll (WY)
Odessa Coll (TX)
Oklahoma City Comm Coll (OK)
Orange Coast Coll (CA)
Otero Jr Coll (CO)
Paris Jr Coll (TX)
Potomac State Coll of West Virginia
   U (WV)
Salt Lake Comm Coll (UT)
San Jacinto Coll District (TX)
San Joaquin Delta Coll (CA)
Santa Rosa Jr Coll (CA)
Sauk Valley Comm Coll (IL)
Southwestern Coll (CA)
Texarkana Coll (TX)
Trinity Valley Comm Coll (TX)
Tyler Jr Coll (TX)
U of Wisconsin–Baraboo/Sauk
   County (WI)
U of Wisconsin–Barron County (WI)
U of Wisconsin–Fond du Lac (WI)
U of Wisconsin–Fox Valley (WI)
U of Wisconsin–Manitowoc (WI)
U of Wisconsin–Marathon County
   (WI)
U of Wisconsin–Marinette (WI)
U of Wisconsin–Marshfield/Wood
   County (WI)
U of Wisconsin–Richland (WI)
U of Wisconsin–Rock County (WI)
U of Wisconsin–Sheboygan (WI)
U of Wisconsin–Washington County
   (WI)
U of Wisconsin–Waukesha (WI)
Western Wyoming Comm Coll (WY)

**POLYMER/PLASTICS ENGINEERING**
Central Oregon Comm Coll (OR)

**POLYSOMNOGRAPHY**
Genesee Comm Coll (NY)
Kingsborough Comm Coll of the City
   U of New York (NY)
Lenoir Comm Coll (NC)

**PORTUGUESE**
Miami Dade Coll (FL)

**POULTRY SCIENCE**
Hinds Comm Coll (MS)

**PRACTICAL NURSING, VOCATIONAL NURSING AND NURSING ASSISTANTS RELATED**
American Samoa Comm Coll (AS)
Pennsylvania Inst of Technology (PA)
Westchester Comm Coll (NY)

**PRE-CHIROPRACTIC**
Eastern Arizona Coll (AZ)

**PRECISION PRODUCTION RELATED**
East Central Coll (MO)
Mott Comm Coll (MI)
Ozarks Tech Comm Coll (MO)
St. Charles Comm Coll (MO)

**PRECISION PRODUCTION TRADES**
Johnson Coll (PA)

**PRE-DENTISTRY STUDIES**
Barton County Comm Coll (KS)
Hill Coll (TX)
Northeast Comm Coll (NE)
Oklahoma City Comm Coll (OK)
Panola Coll (TX)
Pensacola State Coll (FL)
Potomac State Coll of West Virginia
   U (WV)
St. Philip's Coll (TX)
Western Wyoming Comm Coll (WY)

**PRE-ENGINEERING**
Alexandria Tech and Comm Coll
   (MN)
Amarillo Coll (TX)
Antelope Valley Coll (CA)
Barton County Comm Coll (KS)
Central New Mexico Comm Coll
   (NM)
Century Coll (MN)
Chipola Coll (FL)
Coll of the Canyons (CA)
Coll of the Desert (CA)
Craven Comm Coll (NC)
Crowder Coll (MO)
De Anza Coll (CA)
Del Mar Coll (TX)
Fayetteville Tech Comm Coll (NC)
Gordon State Coll (GA)
Haywood Comm Coll (NC)
Illinois Valley Comm Coll (IL)
Ivy Tech Comm Coll–Columbus (IN)
Ivy Tech Comm Coll–Lafayette (IN)
Ivy Tech Comm Coll–Southwest (IN)
Lenoir Comm Coll (NC)
Macomb Comm Coll (MI)
Merced Coll (CA)
Miami Dade Coll (FL)
Minnesota State Comm and Tech
   Coll (MN)
Mission Coll (CA)
Monroe County Comm Coll (MI)
Montgomery Comm Coll (NC)
Mt. San Antonio Coll (CA)
Navarro Coll (TX)
New Mexico State U–Alamogordo
   (NM)
North Central Texas Coll (TX)
Northeastern Jr Coll (CO)
North Hennepin Comm Coll (MN)
North Shore Comm Coll (MA)
Northwest Vista Coll (TX)
Odessa Coll (TX)
Orange Coast Coll (CA)
Otero Jr Coll (CO)
Palomar Coll (CA)
Quinsigamond Comm Coll (MA)
Rainy River Comm Coll (MN)
Rock Valley Coll (IL)
St. Charles Comm Coll (MO)
Seminole State Coll (OK)
Three Rivers Coll (MO)
Trinity Valley Comm Coll (TX)
Tulsa Comm Coll (OK)
Wayne County Comm Coll District
   (MI)
Western Wyoming Comm Coll (WY)

**PRE-LAW STUDIES**
American Samoa Comm Coll (AS)
Anne Arundel Comm Coll (MD)
Barton County Comm Coll (KS)
Carl Albert State Coll (OK)
Central New Mexico Comm Coll
   (NM)
Central Oregon Comm Coll (OR)
Coll of Central Florida (FL)
Hill Coll (TX)
Laramie County Comm Coll (WY)
Northeast Comm Coll (NE)
Panola Coll (TX)
Paris Jr Coll (TX)
Pensacola State Coll (FL)
Potomac State Coll of West Virginia
   U (WV)
Vincennes U (IN)
Western Texas Coll (TX)
Western Wyoming Comm Coll (WY)

**PREMEDICAL STUDIES**
Austin Comm Coll District (TX)
Barton County Comm Coll (KS)
Central Oregon Comm Coll (OR)
Coll of Central Florida (FL)
Eastern Arizona Coll (AZ)

Hill Coll (TX)
Howard Comm Coll (MD)
Mesalands Comm Coll (NM)
Northeast Comm Coll (NE)
Oklahoma City Comm Coll (OK)
Paris Jr Coll (TX)
Pensacola State Coll (FL)
Potomac State Coll of West Virginia
   U (WV)
St. Philip's Coll (TX)
San Juan Coll (NM)
Sauk Valley Comm Coll (IL)
Springfield Tech Comm Coll (MA)
Western Texas Coll (TX)
Western Wyoming Comm Coll (WY)

**PRENURSING STUDIES**
Arizona Western Coll (AZ)
Cochise County Comm Coll District
   (AZ)
Edison State Comm Coll (OH)
Georgia Military Coll (GA)
Hill Coll (TX)
Lenoir Comm Coll (NC)
Manor Coll (PA)
Northeast Comm Coll (NE)
Oklahoma City Comm Coll (OK)
Paris Jr Coll (TX)
Pensacola State Coll (FL)
Potomac State Coll of West Virginia
   U (WV)
St. Philip's Coll (TX)
Three Rivers Coll (MO)
Tulsa Comm Coll (OK)
Western Wyoming Comm Coll (WY)

**PRE-OCCUPATIONAL THERAPY**
Gordon State Coll (GA)
Manor Coll (PA)
Potomac State Coll of West Virginia
   U (WV)

**PRE-OPTOMETRY**
Northwest Coll (WY)
Three Rivers Coll (MO)

**PRE-PHARMACY STUDIES**
Amarillo Coll (TX)
Central Oregon Comm Coll (OR)
Coll of Central Florida (FL)
Eastern Arizona Coll (AZ)
Gordon State Coll (GA)
Hill Coll (TX)
Howard Comm Coll (MD)
Laramie County Comm Coll (WY)
Manor Coll (PA)
Monroe Comm Coll (NY)
Northeast Comm Coll (NE)
Northwest Coll (WY)
Oklahoma City Comm Coll (OK)
Ozarks Tech Comm Coll (MO)
Panola Coll (TX)
Paris Jr Coll (TX)
Pensacola State Coll (FL)
Potomac State Coll of West Virginia
   U (WV)
Quinsigamond Comm Coll (MA)
St. Charles Comm Coll (MO)
St. Philip's Coll (TX)
Schoolcraft Coll (MI)
Three Rivers Coll (MO)
Tulsa Comm Coll (OK)
Western Wyoming Comm Coll (WY)

**PRE-PHYSICAL THERAPY**
Eastern Arizona Coll (AZ)
Gordon State Coll (GA)
Manor Coll (PA)
Potomac State Coll of West Virginia
   U (WV)
Sauk Valley Comm Coll (IL)

**PRE-VETERINARY STUDIES**
Barton County Comm Coll (KS)
Coll of Central Florida (FL)
Hill Coll (TX)
Northeast Comm Coll (NE)
Panola Coll (TX)
Pensacola State Coll (FL)
Potomac State Coll of West Virginia
   U (WV)
Western Wyoming Comm Coll (WY)

**PRINTMAKING**
De Anza Coll (CA)

**PROFESSIONAL, TECHNICAL, BUSINESS, AND SCIENTIFIC WRITING**
Austin Comm Coll District (TX)

De Anza Coll (CA)
Fox Valley Tech Coll (WI)
Gateway Tech Coll (WI)

**PROJECT MANAGEMENT**
LDS Business Coll (UT)

**PSYCHIATRIC/MENTAL HEALTH SERVICES TECHNOLOGY**
Alvin Comm Coll (TX)
Anne Arundel Comm Coll (MD)
Comm Coll of Allegheny County (PA)
Comm Coll of Baltimore County
   (MD)
El Paso Comm Coll (TX)
Fiorello H. LaGuardia Comm Coll of
   the City U of New York (NY)
Gateway Tech Coll (WI)
Hagerstown Comm Coll (MD)
Harford Comm Coll (MD)
Houston Comm Coll (TX)
Ivy Tech Comm Coll–Bloomington
   (IN)
Ivy Tech Comm Coll–Central Indiana
   (IN)
Ivy Tech Comm Coll–Columbus (IN)
Ivy Tech Comm Coll–Lafayette (IN)
Ivy Tech Comm Coll–Northeast (IN)
Ivy Tech Comm Coll–Northwest (IN)
Ivy Tech Comm Coll–Richmond (IN)
Ivy Tech Comm Coll–Sellersburg (IN)
Ivy Tech Comm Coll–Southeast (IN)
Ivy Tech Comm Coll–Southwest (IN)
Kingsborough Comm Coll of the City
   U of New York (NY)
Montgomery Coll (MD)
Montgomery County Comm Coll (PA)
Naugatuck Valley Comm Coll (CT)
Northern Essex Comm Coll (MA)
Pennsylvania Inst of Technology (PA)
Pueblo Comm Coll (CO)
San Jacinto Coll District (TX)
Three Rivers Comm Coll (CT)
Waukesha County Tech Coll (WI)
Wayne County Comm Coll District
   (MI)
Williston State Coll (ND)
Wisconsin Indianhead Tech Coll (WI)

**PSYCHOLOGY**
Alvin Comm Coll (TX)
Amarillo Coll (TX)
Arizona Western Coll (AZ)
Austin Comm Coll District (TX)
Barton County Comm Coll (KS)
Bucks County Comm Coll (PA)
Bunker Hill Comm Coll (MA)
Carroll Comm Coll (MD)
Central New Mexico Comm Coll
   (NM)
Chandler-Gilbert Comm Coll (AZ)
Coll of Central Florida (FL)
Coll of Marin (CA)
Coll of the Canyons (CA)
Coll of the Desert (CA)
Comm Coll of Allegheny County (PA)
Comm Coll of Philadelphia (PA)
Crowder Coll (MO)
De Anza Coll (CA)
Del Mar Coll (TX)
Eastern Arizona Coll (AZ)
Edison State Comm Coll (OH)
Fiorello H. LaGuardia Comm Coll of
   the City U of New York (NY)
Frederick Comm Coll (MD)
Fullerton Coll (CA)
Genesee Comm Coll (NY)
Georgia Military Coll (GA)
Gordon State Coll (GA)
Harford Comm Coll (MD)
Harper Coll (IL)
Harrisburg Area Comm Coll (PA)
Hill Coll (TX)
Hutchinson Comm Coll (KS)
Lackawanna Coll (PA)
Laramie County Comm Coll (WY)
Lehigh Carbon Comm Coll (PA)
Manor Coll (PA)
Merced Coll (CA)
Miami Dade Coll (FL)
Mohave Comm Coll (AZ)
Monroe County Comm Coll (MI)
Navarro Coll (TX)
Northeast Comm Coll (NE)
Northeastern Jr Coll (CO)
Northern Essex Comm Coll (MA)
Northwest Coll (WY)
Odessa Coll (TX)
Oklahoma City Comm Coll (OK)

Orange Coast Coll (CA)
Otero Jr Coll (CO)
Palomar Coll (CA)
Panola Coll (TX)
Paris Jr Coll (TX)
Pasadena City Coll (CA)
Pennsylvania Highlands Comm Coll
   (PA)
Pensacola State Coll (FL)
Potomac State Coll of West Virginia
   U (WV)
Quinsigamond Comm Coll (MA)
St. Philip's Coll (TX)
Salt Lake Comm Coll (UT)
San Jacinto Coll District (TX)
San Joaquin Delta Coll (CA)
San Juan Coll (NM)
Santa Rosa Jr Coll (CA)
Sauk Valley Comm Coll (IL)
Southwestern Coll (CA)
Sullivan County Comm Coll (NY)
Trinity Valley Comm Coll (TX)
Truckee Meadows Comm Coll (NV)
Tyler Jr Coll (TX)
U of Wisconsin–Baraboo/Sauk
   County (WI)
U of Wisconsin–Barron County (WI)
U of Wisconsin–Fond du Lac (WI)
U of Wisconsin–Fox Valley (WI)
U of Wisconsin–Manitowoc (WI)
U of Wisconsin–Marathon County
   (WI)
U of Wisconsin–Marinette (WI)
U of Wisconsin–Marshfield/Wood
   County (WI)
U of Wisconsin–Richland (WI)
U of Wisconsin–Rock County (WI)
U of Wisconsin–Sheboygan (WI)
U of Wisconsin–Washington County
   (WI)
U of Wisconsin–Waukesha (WI)
Western Wyoming Comm Coll (WY)

**PSYCHOLOGY RELATED**
Cayuga County Comm Coll (NY)
Genesee Comm Coll (NY)
Lackawanna Coll (PA)
Seminole State Coll (OK)

**PUBLIC ADMINISTRATION**
Barton County Comm Coll (KS)
Central Texas Coll (TX)
County Coll of Morris (NJ)
Del Mar Coll (TX)
Houston Comm Coll (TX)
Laramie County Comm Coll (WY)
Lehigh Carbon Comm Coll (PA)
Lorain County Comm Coll (OH)
Mesalands Comm Coll (NM)
Miami Dade Coll (FL)
National Park Coll (AR)
Palomar Coll (CA)
Scottsdale Comm Coll (AZ)
Southwestern Coll (CA)
Tyler Jr Coll (TX)

**PUBLIC ADMINISTRATION AND SOCIAL SERVICE PROFESSIONS RELATED**
Cleveland State Comm Coll (TN)
Oklahoma State U–Oklahoma City
   (OK)
Schenectady County Comm Coll
   (NY)
Southwestern Coll (CA)

**PUBLIC HEALTH**
Anne Arundel Comm Coll (MD)
County Coll of Morris (NJ)
Montgomery County Comm Coll (PA)
Northern Essex Comm Coll (MA)
Oklahoma City Comm Coll (OK)
Queensborough Comm Coll of the
   City U of New York (NY)

**PUBLIC HEALTH/COMMUNITY NURSING**
American Samoa Comm Coll (AS)

**PUBLIC HEALTH EDUCATION AND PROMOTION**
Northampton Comm Coll (PA)

**PUBLIC HEALTH RELATED**
Salt Lake Comm Coll (UT)

**PUBLIC POLICY ANALYSIS**
Del Mar Coll (TX)

## PUBLIC RELATIONS, ADVERTISING, AND APPLIED COMMUNICATION

Chippewa Valley Tech Coll (WI)
Oklahoma City Comm Coll (OK)

## PUBLIC RELATIONS, ADVERTISING, AND APPLIED COMMUNICATION RELATED

Harper Coll (IL)

## PUBLIC RELATIONS/IMAGE MANAGEMENT

Amarillo Coll (TX)
Crowder Coll (MO)
Mesa Comm Coll (AZ)
Vincennes U (IN)

## PURCHASING, PROCUREMENT/ ACQUISITIONS AND CONTRACTS MANAGEMENT

Cecil Coll (MD)
De Anza Coll (CA)
Greenville Tech Coll (SC)

## QUALITY CONTROL AND SAFETY TECHNOLOGIES RELATED

Ivy Tech Comm Coll–Lafayette (IN)
Ivy Tech Comm Coll–Wabash Valley (IN)
Macomb Comm Coll (MI)

## QUALITY CONTROL TECHNOLOGY

Comm Coll of Allegheny County (PA)
Grand Rapids Comm Coll (MI)
Illinois Eastern Comm Colls, Lincoln Trail College (IL)
Lakeland Comm Coll (OH)
Lakeshore Tech Coll (WI)
Macomb Comm Coll (MI)
Mid-State Tech Coll (WI)
Monroe Comm Coll (NY)
Mt. San Antonio Coll (CA)
Northampton Comm Coll (PA)
Rock Valley Coll (IL)
Salt Lake Comm Coll (UT)
Tarrant County Coll District (TX)

## RADIO AND TELEVISION

Alvin Comm Coll (TX)
Amarillo Coll (TX)
Austin Comm Coll District (TX)
Central Texas Coll (TX)
Coll of the Desert (CA)
Daytona State Coll (FL)
De Anza Coll (CA)
Del Mar Coll (TX)
Fullerton Coll (CA)
Genesee Comm Coll (NY)
Illinois Eastern Comm Colls, Wabash Valley College (IL)
Iowa Central Comm Coll (IA)
Los Angeles City Coll (CA)
Miami Dade Coll (FL)
Mt. San Antonio Coll (CA)
Palomar Coll (CA)
Pasadena City Coll (CA)
Southwestern Coll (CA)
Sullivan County Comm Coll (NY)
Tyler Jr Coll (TX)
Western Texas Coll (TX)

## RADIO AND TELEVISION BROADCASTING TECHNOLOGY

Adirondack Comm Coll (NY)
Arizona Western Coll (AZ)
Camden County Coll (NJ)
Cedar Valley Coll (TX)
Cleveland Comm Coll (NC)
Cloud County Comm Coll (KS)
Genesee Comm Coll (NY)
Hinds Comm Coll (MS)
Houston Comm Coll (TX)
Hutchinson Comm Coll (KS)
Lehigh Carbon Comm Coll (PA)
Miami Dade Coll (FL)
Mount Wachusett Comm Coll (MA)
Northampton Comm Coll (PA)
Pasadena City Coll (CA)
Salt Lake Comm Coll (UT)
San Jacinto Coll District (TX)
Schoolcraft Coll (MI)
Springfield Tech Comm Coll (MA)
Tompkins Cortland Comm Coll (NY)
Vincennes U (IN)

## RADIOLOGIC TECHNOLOGY/ SCIENCE

Amarillo Coll (TX)
Antelope Valley Coll (CA)

Arizona Western Coll (AZ)
Asheville-Buncombe Tech Comm Coll (NC)
Austin Comm Coll District (TX)
Barton County Comm Coll (KS)
Black Hawk Coll, Moline (IL)
Brookhaven Coll (TX)
Bucks County Comm Coll (PA)
Caldwell Comm Coll and Tech Inst (NC)
Carteret Comm Coll (NC)
Central New Mexico Comm Coll (NM)
Central Ohio Tech Coll (OH)
Central Oregon Comm Coll (OR)
Central Virginia Comm Coll (VA)
Century Coll (MN)
CHI Health School of Radiologic Technology (NE)
Cleveland Comm Coll (NC)
Comm Coll of Allegheny County (PA)
Copiah-Lincoln Comm Coll (MS)
County Coll of Morris (NJ)
Danville Area Comm Coll (IL)
El Paso Comm Coll (TX)
Fayetteville Tech Comm Coll (NC)
Galveston Coll (TX)
George C. Wallace Comm Coll (AL)
Gordon State Coll (GA)
Gurnick Academy of Medical Arts (CA)
Harper Coll (IL)
Harrisburg Area Comm Coll (PA)
H. Councill Trenholm State Comm Coll (AL)
Hinds Comm Coll (MS)
Houston Comm Coll (TX)
Hudson County Comm Coll (NJ)
Hutchinson Comm Coll (KS)
Illinois Central Coll (IL)
Jefferson State Comm Coll (AL)
Kaskaskia Coll (IL)
Kennebec Valley Comm Coll (ME)
Kishwaukee Coll (IL)
Lakeshore Tech Coll (WI)
Lake Superior Coll (MN)
Laramie County Comm Coll (WY)
Lenoir Comm Coll (NC)
Los Angeles City Coll (CA)
Louisiana State U at Eunice (LA)
Maine Coll of Health Professions (ME)
Massachusetts Bay Comm Coll (MA)
Merced Coll (CA)
Miami Dade Coll (FL)
Minnesota State Comm and Tech Coll (MN)
Minnesota West Comm and Tech Coll (MN)
Mitchell Tech Inst (SD)
Montgomery County Comm Coll (PA)
National Park Coll (AR)
Northampton Comm Coll (PA)
Northeast Iowa Comm Coll (IA)
Northern Essex Comm Coll (MA)
Northland Comm and Tech Coll (MN)
Oklahoma State U–Oklahoma City (OK)
Owensboro Comm and Tech Coll (KY)
Paris Jr Coll (TX)
Pasadena City Coll (CA)
Pennsylvania Highlands Comm Coll (PA)
Piedmont Virginia Comm Coll (VA)
Pueblo Comm Coll (CO)
Quinsigamond Comm Coll (MA)
Randolph Comm Coll (NC)
Ridgewater Coll (MN)
Rowan-Cabarrus Comm Coll (NC)
St. Louis Comm Coll (MO)
St. Luke's Coll (IA)
St. Philip's Coll (TX)
San Jacinto Coll District (TX)
Santa Rosa Jr Coll (CA)
Sauk Valley Comm Coll (IL)
Somerset Comm Coll (KY)
Southern U at Shreveport (LA)
South Suburban Coll (IL)
Southwest Texas Jr Coll (TX)
Southwest Virginia Comm Coll (VA)
Spencerian Coll (KY)
Springfield Tech Comm Coll (MA)
State U of New York Coll of Technology at Alfred (NY)
Tyler Jr Coll (TX)
Union County Coll (NJ)
West Kentucky Comm and Tech Coll (KY)

## RADIO, TELEVISION, AND DIGITAL COMMUNICATION RELATED

Cayuga County Comm Coll (NY)
Fox Valley Tech Coll (WI)
Genesee Comm Coll (NY)
Montgomery County Comm Coll (PA)
Pennsylvania Highlands Comm Coll (PA)
Sullivan County Comm Coll (NY)

## RANGE SCIENCE AND MANAGEMENT

Northwest Coll (WY)
Treasure Valley Comm Coll (OR)
Trinity Valley Comm Coll (TX)

## REAL ESTATE

Amarillo Coll (TX)
Antelope Valley Coll (CA)
Austin Comm Coll District (TX)
Bristol Comm Coll (MA)
Cedar Valley Coll (TX)
Coll of Marin (CA)
Coll of the Canyons (CA)
Collin County Comm Coll District (TX)
Comm Coll of Allegheny County (PA)
De Anza Coll (CA)
Del Mar Coll (TX)
Eastern Gateway Comm Coll (OH)
El Paso Comm Coll (TX)
Fullerton Coll (CA)
Hinds Comm Coll (MS)
Houston Comm Coll (TX)
Lorain County Comm Coll (OH)
Los Angeles City Coll (CA)
McLennan Comm Coll (TX)
Merced Coll (CA)
Mesa Comm Coll (AZ)
Miami Dade Coll (FL)
Mission Coll (CA)
Montgomery County Comm Coll (PA)
Mt. San Antonio Coll (CA)
Nassau Comm Coll (NY)
North Central Texas Coll (TX)
Oakton Comm Coll (IL)
Orange Coast Coll (CA)
Palomar Coll (CA)
Richland Coll (TX)
San Jacinto Coll District (TX)
Santa Rosa Jr Coll (CA)
Scottsdale Comm Coll (AZ)
Southwestern Coll (CA)
Tidewater Comm Coll (VA)
Trinity Valley Comm Coll (TX)
Waukesha County Tech Coll (WI)

## RECEPTIONIST

Bristol Comm Coll (MA)

## RECORDING ARTS TECHNOLOGY

Bossier Parish Comm Coll (LA)
Comm Coll of Philadelphia (PA)
Fiorello H. LaGuardia Comm Coll of the City U of New York (NY)
Front Range Comm Coll (CO)
Fullerton Coll (CA)
Grand Rapids Comm Coll (MI)
Illinois Eastern Comm Colls, Wabash Valley College (IL)
Lehigh Carbon Comm Coll (PA)
Mesa Comm Coll (AZ)
Miami Dade Coll (FL)
Montgomery County Comm Coll (PA)
Northeast State Comm Coll (TN)
Northwest Vista Coll (TX)
Orange Coast Coll (CA)
Queensborough Comm Coll of the City U of New York (NY)
Ridgewater Coll (MN)
Schoolcraft Coll (MI)
Springfield Tech Comm Coll (MA)
Vincennes U (IN)
Western Iowa Tech Comm Coll (IA)

## REGISTERED NURSING, NURSING ADMINISTRATION, NURSING RESEARCH AND CLINICAL NURSING RELATED

Genesee Comm Coll (NY)
Harford Comm Coll (MD)
St. Joseph School of Nursing (NH)

## REGISTERED NURSING/ REGISTERED NURSE

Adirondack Comm Coll (NY)
Alamance Comm Coll (NC)
Alexandria Tech and Comm Coll (MN)
Alvin Comm Coll (TX)

Amarillo Coll (TX)
Ancilla Coll (IN)
Anne Arundel Comm Coll (MD)
Antelope Valley Coll (CA)
Arizona Western Coll (AZ)
Arkansas State U–Newport (AR)
Asheville-Buncombe Tech Comm Coll (NC)
Austin Comm Coll District (TX)
Barton County Comm Coll (KS)
The Belanger School of Nursing (NY)
Bevill State Comm Coll (AL)
Black Hawk Coll, Moline (IL)
Blue Ridge Comm and Tech Coll (WV)
Bossier Parish Comm Coll (LA)
Bowling Green State U–Firelands Coll (OH)
Bristol Comm Coll (MA)
Brookhaven Coll (TX)
Bucks County Comm Coll (PA)
Bunker Hill Comm Coll (MA)
Caldwell Comm Coll and Tech Inst (NC)
Camden County Coll (NJ)
Carl Albert State Coll (OK)
Carroll Comm Coll (MD)
Carteret Comm Coll (NC)
Cayuga County Comm Coll (NY)
Cecil Coll (MD)
Central Lakes Coll (MN)
Central Maine Comm Coll (ME)
Central New Mexico Comm Coll (NM)
Central Ohio Tech Coll (OH)
Central Oregon Comm Coll (OR)
Central Texas Coll (TX)
Century Coll (MN)
Chandler-Gilbert Comm Coll (AZ)
Chesapeake Coll (MD)
Chipola Coll (FL)
Chippewa Valley Tech Coll (WI)
Clark Coll (WA)
Cleveland Comm Coll (NC)
Cleveland State Comm Coll (TN)
Cloud County Comm Coll (KS)
Cochise County Comm Coll District (AZ)
Cochran School of Nursing (NY)
Coll of Central Florida (FL)
Coll of Eastern Idaho (ID)
Coll of Marin (CA)
Coll of The Albemarle (NC)
Coll of the Canyons (CA)
Coll of the Desert (CA)
Coll of the Ouachitas (AR)
Collin County Comm Coll District (TX)
Colorado Northwestern Comm Coll (CO)
Columbia-Greene Comm Coll (NY)
Comm Coll of Allegheny County (PA)
Comm Coll of Baltimore County (MD)
Copiah-Lincoln Comm Coll (MS)
County Coll of Morris (NJ)
Craven Comm Coll (NC)
Crowder Coll (MO)
Dabney S. Lancaster Comm Coll (VA)
Danville Area Comm Coll (IL)
Daytona State Coll (FL)
De Anza Coll (CA)
Del Mar Coll (TX)
Des Moines Area Comm Coll (IA)
Dutchess Comm Coll (NY)
Dyersburg State Comm Coll (TN)
East Central Coll (MO)
Eastern Arizona Coll (AZ)
Eastern Shore Comm Coll (VA)
Edison State Comm Coll (OH)
El Paso Comm Coll (TX)
Erie Comm Coll (NY)
Erie Comm Coll, North Campus (NY)
Fayetteville Tech Comm Coll (NC)
Fiorello H. LaGuardia Comm Coll of the City U of New York (NY)
Florida Keys Comm Coll (FL)
Fox Valley Tech Coll (WI)
Frederick Comm Coll (MD)
Front Range Comm Coll (CO)
Galveston Coll (TX)
Gateway Comm and Tech Coll (KY)
Gateway Tech Coll (WI)
Genesee Comm Coll (NY)
George C. Wallace Comm Coll (AL)
Georgia Highlands Coll (GA)
Gordon State Coll (GA)
Grand Rapids Comm Coll (MI)
Great Falls Coll Montana State U (MT)
Greenville Tech Coll (SC)
Hagerstown Comm Coll (MD)

Halifax Comm Coll (NC)
Harford Comm Coll (MD)
Harper Coll (IL)
Harrisburg Area Comm Coll (PA)
Hawkeye Comm Coll (IA)
Haywood Comm Coll (NC)
Hesston Coll (KS)
Highland Comm Coll (IL)
Hill Coll (TX)
Hinds Comm Coll (MS)
Holyoke Comm Coll (MA)
Hopkinsville Comm Coll (KY)
Houston Comm Coll (TX)
Howard Comm Coll (MD)
Hudson County Comm Coll (NJ)
Hutchinson Comm Coll (KS)
Illinois Central Coll (IL)
Illinois Eastern Comm Colls, Frontier Community College (IL)
Illinois Eastern Comm Colls, Olney Central College (IL)
Illinois Valley Comm Coll (IL)
Iowa Central Comm Coll (IA)
Ivy Tech Comm Coll–Bloomington (IN)
Ivy Tech Comm Coll–Central Indiana (IN)
Ivy Tech Comm Coll–East Central (IN)
Ivy Tech Comm Coll–Kokomo (IN)
Ivy Tech Comm Coll–Lafayette (IN)
Ivy Tech Comm Coll–North Central (IN)
Ivy Tech Comm Coll–Northeast (IN)
Ivy Tech Comm Coll–Northwest (IN)
Ivy Tech Comm Coll–Richmond (IN)
Ivy Tech Comm Coll–Sellersburg (IN)
Ivy Tech Comm Coll–Southeast (IN)
Ivy Tech Comm Coll–Southwest (IN)
Ivy Tech Comm Coll–Wabash Valley (IN)
James Sprunt Comm Coll (NC)
Jamestown Comm Coll (NY)
Jefferson Comm Coll (NY)
Jefferson State Comm Coll (AL)
Johnston Comm Coll (NC)
John Tyler Comm Coll (VA)
Kaskaskia Coll (IL)
Kellogg Comm Coll (MI)
Kennebec Valley Comm Coll (ME)
Kent State U at Ashtabula (OH)
Kent State U at East Liverpool (OH)
Kent State U at Tuscarawas (OH)
Kingsborough Comm Coll of the City U of New York (NY)
Kirtland Comm Coll (MI)
Kishwaukee Coll (IL)
Lake Area Tech Inst (SD)
Lakeland Comm Coll (OH)
Lake Region State Coll (ND)
Lakeshore Tech Coll (WI)
Lakes Region Comm Coll (NH)
Lake Superior Coll (MN)
Lamar Comm Coll (CO)
Laramie County Comm Coll (WY)
Lehigh Carbon Comm Coll (PA)
Lenoir Comm Coll (NC)
Lorain County Comm Coll (OH)
Los Angeles City Coll (CA)
Louisiana State U at Eunice (LA)
Lurleen B. Wallace Comm Coll (AL)
Macomb Comm Coll (MI)
Massachusetts Bay Comm Coll (MA)
Maysville Comm and Tech Coll, Maysville (KY)
McHenry County Coll (IL)
McLennan Comm Coll (TX)
Merced Coll (CA)
Meridian Comm Coll (MS)
Mesa Comm Coll (AZ)
Miami Dade Coll (FL)
Mid-Plains Comm Coll, North Platte (NE)
Mid-State Tech Coll (WI)
Minnesota State Comm and Tech Coll (MN)
Minnesota West Comm and Tech Coll (MN)
Missouri State U–West Plains (MO)
Mitchell Comm Coll (NC)
Mohave Comm Coll (AZ)
Mohawk Valley Comm Coll (NY)
Monroe Comm Coll (NY)
Monroe County Comm Coll (MI)
Montgomery Coll (MD)
Montgomery County Comm Coll (PA)
Morton Coll (IL)
Motlow State Comm Coll (TN)
Mott Comm Coll (MI)
Mt. San Antonio Coll (CA)
Mount Wachusett Comm Coll (MA)

Muskegon Comm Coll (MI)
Nassau Comm Coll (NY)
National Park Coll (AR)
Naugatuck Valley Comm Coll (CT)
Navarro Coll (TX)
New River Comm Coll (VA)
Niagara County Comm Coll (NY)
Northampton Comm Coll (PA)
Northcentral Tech Coll (WI)
North Central Texas Coll (TX)
North Dakota State Coll of Science (ND)
Northeast Comm Coll (NE)
Northeastern Jr Coll (CO)
Northeastern Tech Coll (SC)
Northeast Iowa Comm Coll (IA)
Northeast State Comm Coll (TN)
Northern Essex Comm Coll (MA)
Northern Maine Comm Coll (ME)
North Hennepin Comm Coll (MN)
North Iowa Area Comm Coll (IA)
Northland Comm and Tech Coll (MN)
North Shore Comm Coll (MA)
NorthWest Arkansas Comm Coll (AR)
Northwest Coll (WY)
Northwest Mississippi Comm Coll (MS)
Northwest-Shoals Comm Coll (AL)
Oakton Comm Coll (IL)
Odessa Coll (TX)
Oklahoma City Comm Coll (OK)
Oklahoma State U Inst of Technology (OK)
Oklahoma State U–Oklahoma City (OK)
Otero Jr Coll (CO)
Owensboro Comm and Tech Coll (KY)
Ozarks Tech Comm Coll (MO)
Palomar Coll (CA)
Panola Coll (TX)
Paris Jr Coll (TX)
Pasadena City Coll (CA)
Penn State Fayette, The Eberly Campus (PA)
Penn State Mont Alto (PA)
Pensacola State Coll (FL)
Piedmont Comm Coll (NC)
Pittsburgh Tech Coll (PA)
Pueblo Comm Coll (CO)
Queensborough Comm Coll of the City U of New York (NY)
Quinsigamond Comm Coll (MA)
Randolph Comm Coll (NC)
Rappahannock Comm Coll (VA)
Raritan Valley Comm Coll (NJ)
Rend Lake Coll (IL)
Renton Tech Coll (WA)
Richmond Comm Coll (NC)
Ridgewater Coll (MN)
Rio Hondo Coll (CA)
Rock Valley Coll (IL)
Rowan-Cabarrus Comm Coll (NC)
St. Charles Comm Coll (MO)
St. Luke's Coll (IA)
St. Philip's Coll (TX)
Salt Lake Comm Coll (UT)
San Jacinto Coll District (TX)
San Joaquin Delta Coll (CA)
San Juan Coll (NM)
Santa Rosa Jr Coll (CA)
Sauk Valley Comm Coll (IL)
Schoolcraft Coll (MI)
Scottsdale Comm Coll (AZ)
Seminole State Coll (OK)
Seminole State Coll of Florida (FL)
Shawnee Comm Coll (IL)
Sisseton-Wahpeton Coll (SD)
Somerset Comm Coll (KY)
Southcentral Kentucky Comm and Tech Coll (KY)
Southeast Arkansas Coll (AR)
Southeast Kentucky Comm and Tech Coll (KY)
Southeast Tech Inst (SD)
Southern U at Shreveport (LA)
South Florida State Coll (FL)
Southwestern Coll (CA)
Southwestern Comm Coll (IA)
Southwestern Comm Coll (NC)
Southwestern Michigan Coll (MI)
Southwest Texas Jr Coll (TX)
Southwest Virginia Comm Coll (VA)
Sowela Tech Comm Coll (LA)
Spencerian Coll (KY)
Springfield Tech Comm Coll (MA)
Stark State Coll (OH)
State U of New York Coll of Technology at Alfred (NY)

Sullivan County Comm Coll (NY)
Tallahassee Comm Coll (FL)
Tarrant County Coll District (TX)
Texarkana Coll (TX)
Three Rivers Coll (MO)
Three Rivers Comm Coll (CT)
Tidewater Comm Coll (VA)
Tompkins Cortland Comm Coll (NY)
Treasure Valley Comm Coll (OR)
Tri-County Comm Coll (NC)
Trident Tech Coll (SC)
Trinity Valley Comm Coll (TX)
Truckee Meadows Comm Coll (NV)
Tulsa Comm Coll (OK)
Tyler Jr Coll (TX)
Union County Coll (NJ)
U of Arkansas Comm Coll at Morrilton (AR)
U of Arkansas Rich Mountain (AR)
U of South Carolina Lancaster (SC)
Victoria Coll (TX)
Vincennes U (IN)
Walters State Comm Coll (TN)
Waukesha County Tech Coll (WI)
Wayne Comm Coll (NC)
Wayne County Comm Coll District (MI)
Westchester Comm Coll (NY)
Western Iowa Tech Comm Coll (IA)
West Kentucky Comm and Tech Coll (KY)
White Mountains Comm Coll (NH)
Williston State Coll (ND)
Wisconsin Indianhead Tech Coll (WI)
Wor-Wic Comm Coll (MD)
Wytheville Comm Coll (VA)

## REHABILITATION AND THERAPEUTIC PROFESSIONS RELATED

Camden County Coll (NJ)
Nassau Comm Coll (NY)
Raritan Valley Comm Coll (NJ)
Union County Coll (NJ)
Vincennes U (IN)

## RELIGIOUS STUDIES

Amarillo Coll (TX)
Barton County Comm Coll (KS)
Coll of Central Florida (FL)
Fullerton Coll (CA)
Hill Coll (TX)
Laramie County Comm Coll (WY)
Orange Coast Coll (CA)
San Joaquin Delta Coll (CA)
Santa Rosa Jr Coll (CA)
Trinity Valley Comm Coll (TX)

## RELIGIOUS STUDIES RELATED

Ancilla Coll (IN)
Spartanburg Methodist Coll (SC)

## RESORT MANAGEMENT

Coll of the Desert (CA)
Lehigh Carbon Comm Coll (PA)
White Mountains Comm Coll (NH)

## RESPIRATORY CARE THERAPY

Alvin Comm Coll (TX)
Amarillo Coll (TX)
Antelope Valley Coll (CA)
Barton County Comm Coll (KS)
Bossier Parish Comm Coll (LA)
Bowling Green State U–Firelands Coll (OH)
Carteret Comm Coll (NC)
Central New Mexico Comm Coll (NM)
Central Virginia Comm Coll (VA)
Chippewa Valley Tech Coll (WI)
Cochise County Comm Coll District (AZ)
Collin County Comm Coll District (TX)
Comm Coll of Allegheny County (PA)
Comm Coll of Baltimore County (MD)
Comm Coll of Philadelphia (PA)
Copiah-Lincoln Comm Coll (MS)
County Coll of Morris (NJ)
Daytona State Coll (FL)
Del Mar Coll (TX)
Des Moines Area Comm Coll (IA)
Eastern Gateway Comm Coll (OH)
El Paso Comm Coll (TX)
Erie Comm Coll, North Campus (NY)
Fayetteville Tech Comm Coll (NC)
Frederick Comm Coll (MD)
Genesee Comm Coll (NY)
George C. Wallace Comm Coll (AL)

Great Falls Coll Montana State U (MT)
Greenville Tech Coll (SC)
Gulf Coast State Coll (FL)
Harrisburg Area Comm Coll (PA)
Hawkeye Comm Coll (IA)
H. Councill Trenholm State Comm Coll (AL)
Hinds Comm Coll (MS)
Houston Comm Coll (TX)
Hutchinson Comm Coll (KS)
Illinois Central Coll (IL)
Ivy Tech Comm Coll–Central Indiana (IN)
Ivy Tech Comm Coll–Lafayette (IN)
Ivy Tech Comm Coll–Northeast (IN)
Ivy Tech Comm Coll–Northwest (IN)
Ivy Tech Comm Coll–Richmond (IN)
Ivy Tech Comm Coll–Sellersburg (IN)
Ivy Tech Comm Coll–Wabash Valley (IN)
J. Sargeant Reynolds Comm Coll (VA)
Kaskaskia Coll (IL)
Kent State U at Ashtabula (OH)
Lakeland Comm Coll (OH)
Lake Superior Coll (MN)
Louisiana State U at Eunice (LA)
Macomb Comm Coll (MI)
Manchester Comm Coll (CT)
Maysville Comm and Tech Coll, Maysville (KY)
McLennan Comm Coll (TX)
Meridian Comm Coll (MS)
Miami Dade Coll (FL)
Mid-State Tech Coll (WI)
Missouri State U–West Plains (MO)
Mohawk Valley Comm Coll (NY)
Monroe County Comm Coll (MI)
Mott Comm Coll (MI)
Mt. San Antonio Coll (CA)
Nassau Comm Coll (NY)
Naugatuck Valley Comm Coll (CT)
Northeast Comm Coll (NE)
Northeast Iowa Comm Coll (IA)
Northern Essex Comm Coll (MA)
Northland Comm and Tech Coll (MN)
North Shore Comm Coll (MA)
NorthWest Arkansas Comm Coll (AR)
Oklahoma City Comm Coll (OK)
Orange Coast Coll (CA)
Ozarks Tech Comm Coll (MO)
Pueblo Comm Coll (CO)
Quinsigamond Comm Coll (MA)
Raritan Valley Comm Coll (NJ)
Rock Valley Coll (IL)
St. Louis Comm Coll (MO)
St. Luke's Coll (IA)
St. Philip's Coll (TX)
San Jacinto Coll District (TX)
San Juan Coll (NM)
Seminole State Coll of Florida (FL)
Somerset Comm Coll (KY)
Southeast Arkansas Coll (AR)
Southeast Kentucky Comm and Tech Coll (KY)
Southern U at Shreveport (LA)
Southwestern Comm Coll (NC)
Spencerian Coll (KY)
Springfield Tech Comm Coll (MA)
Stark State Coll (OH)
Sullivan County Comm Coll (NY)
Tallahassee Comm Coll (FL)
Tarrant County Coll District (TX)
Thaddeus Stevens Coll of Technology (PA)
Trident Tech Coll (SC)
Tulsa Comm Coll (OK)
Tyler Jr Coll (TX)
Union County Coll (NJ)
Victoria Coll (TX)
Volunteer State Comm Coll (TN)
Walters State Comm Coll (TN)
Westchester Comm Coll (NY)

## RESPIRATORY THERAPY TECHNICIAN

Bunker Hill Comm Coll (MA)
Hutchinson Comm Coll (KS)
Miami Dade Coll (FL)
Northern Essex Comm Coll (MA)
Southcentral Kentucky Comm and Tech Coll (KY)

## RESTAURANT, CULINARY, AND CATERING MANAGEMENT

Arizona Western Coll (AZ)
Blue Ridge Comm and Tech Coll (WV)

Coll of Central Florida (FL)
Coll of the Canyons (CA)
Comm Coll of Allegheny County (PA)
Culinary Inst LeNotre (TX)
Daytona State Coll (FL)
Florida Keys Comm Coll (FL)
Grand Rapids Comm Coll (MI)
Gulf Coast State Coll (FL)
Lakeland Comm Coll (OH)
Miami Dade Coll (FL)
Missouri State U–West Plains (MO)
Mohawk Valley Comm Coll (NY)
Orange Coast Coll (CA)
Ozarks Tech Comm Coll (MO)
Pensacola State Coll (FL)
Raritan Valley Comm Coll (NJ)
St. Philip's Coll (TX)
San Jacinto Coll District (TX)
Southwestern Coll (CA)
Vincennes U (IN)
Waukesha County Tech Coll (WI)
Westchester Comm Coll (NY)

## RESTAURANT/FOOD SERVICES MANAGEMENT

Central Texas Coll (TX)
Erie Comm Coll, North Campus (NY)
Fiorello H. LaGuardia Comm Coll of the City U of New York (NY)
J. Sargeant Reynolds Comm Coll (VA)
Lakes Region Comm Coll (NH)
Miami Dade Coll (FL)
Naugatuck Valley Comm Coll (CT)
Northampton Comm Coll (PA)
North Dakota State Coll of Science (ND)
Quinsigamond Comm Coll (MA)
Santa Rosa Jr Coll (CA)
Schenectady County Comm Coll (NY)

## RETAILING

Alamance Comm Coll (NC)
Black Hawk Coll, Moline (IL)
Central Oregon Comm Coll (OR)
Clark Coll (WA)
Comm Coll of Allegheny County (PA)
Holyoke Comm Coll (MA)
Hutchinson Comm Coll (KS)
Illinois Central Coll (IL)
Nassau Comm Coll (NY)
North Central Texas Coll (TX)
Westchester Comm Coll (NY)
Western Iowa Tech Comm Coll (IA)

## RETAIL MANAGEMENT

Collin County Comm Coll District (TX)
Orange Coast Coll (CA)

## RHETORIC AND COMPOSITION

Amarillo Coll (TX)
Austin Comm Coll District (TX)
Carl Albert State Coll (OK)
De Anza Coll (CA)
Del Mar Coll (TX)
Hill Coll (TX)
Monroe County Comm Coll (MI)
Navarro Coll (TX)
Odessa Coll (TX)
Paris Jr Coll (TX)
St. Philip's Coll (TX)
San Jacinto Coll District (TX)
San Joaquin Delta Coll (CA)
Southwestern Coll (CA)
Trinity Valley Comm Coll (TX)

## ROBOTICS TECHNOLOGY

Central Lakes Coll (MN)
Comm Coll of Allegheny County (PA)
Dunwoody Coll of Technology (MN)
Illinois Central Coll (IL)
Kaskaskia Coll (IL)
Kirtland Comm Coll (MI)
Lake Area Tech Inst (SD)
Macomb Comm Coll (MI)
McHenry County Coll (IL)
Minnesota West Comm and Tech Coll (MN)
Texas State Tech Coll (TX)

## RUSSIAN

Austin Comm Coll District (TX)

## SALES, DISTRIBUTION, AND MARKETING OPERATIONS

Alexandria Tech and Comm Coll (MN)
Antelope Valley Coll (CA)

Coll of the Canyons (CA)
Des Moines Area Comm Coll (IA)
Fullerton Coll (CA)
Greenville Tech Coll (SC)
Harper Coll (IL)
Harrisburg Area Comm Coll (PA)
Hawkeye Comm Coll (IA)
Johnson Coll (PA)
LDS Business Coll (UT)
Merced Coll (CA)
Minnesota State Comm and Tech Coll (MN)
Montgomery County Comm Coll (PA)
North Central Texas Coll (TX)
Northeast Iowa Comm Coll (IA)
North Iowa Area Comm Coll (IA)
Northland Comm and Tech Coll (MN)
Oakton Comm Coll (IL)
Orange Coast Coll (CA)
Ridgewater Coll (MN)
Southwestern Coll (CA)
State U of New York Coll of Technology at Alfred (NY)
Western Iowa Tech Comm Coll (IA)

## SALON/BEAUTY SALON MANAGEMENT

Mott Comm Coll (MI)
Northwest-Shoals Comm Coll (AL)
Schoolcraft Coll (MI)

## SCIENCE TEACHER EDUCATION

Iowa Central Comm Coll (IA)
San Jacinto Coll District (TX)
Vincennes U (IN)

## SCIENCE TECHNOLOGIES

Central Virginia Comm Coll (VA)
Northern Essex Comm Coll (MA)

## SCIENCE TECHNOLOGIES RELATED

Blue Ridge Comm and Tech Coll (WV)
Cayuga County Comm Coll (NY)
Cleveland State Comm Coll (TN)
Comm Coll of Allegheny County (PA)
Frederick Comm Coll (MD)
Front Range Comm Coll (CO)
Lamar Comm Coll (CO)
Montgomery County Comm Coll (PA)
Pueblo Comm Coll (CO)
Schenectady County Comm Coll (NY)
Sullivan County Comm Coll (NY)

## SCIENCE, TECHNOLOGY AND SOCIETY

Southeast Arkansas Coll (AR)
Truckee Meadows Comm Coll (NV)

## SCULPTURE

De Anza Coll (CA)
Mesalands Comm Coll (NM)
Palomar Coll (CA)

## SECONDARY EDUCATION

Alvin Comm Coll (TX)
Ancilla Coll (IN)
Arizona Western Coll (AZ)
Austin Comm Coll District (TX)
Barton County Comm Coll (KS)
Brookhaven Coll (TX)
Carl Albert State Coll (OK)
Cecil Coll (MD)
Coll of Central Florida (FL)
Collin County Comm Coll District (TX)
Eastern Arizona Coll (AZ)
Georgia Military Coll (GA)
Gordon State Coll (GA)
Grand Rapids Comm Coll (MI)
Harrisburg Area Comm Coll (PA)
Hill Coll (TX)
Houston Comm Coll (TX)
Howard Comm Coll (MD)
Montgomery County Comm Coll (PA)
Northampton Comm Coll (PA)
Northeast Comm Coll (NE)
Northwest Coll (WY)
Paris Jr Coll (TX)
Potomac State Coll of West Virginia U (WV)
San Jacinto Coll District (TX)
San Juan Coll (NM)
Sauk Valley Comm Coll (IL)
Springfield Tech Comm Coll (MA)
Tyler Jr Coll (TX)
Vincennes U (IN)
Western Texas Coll (TX)

Western Wyoming Comm Coll (WY)

**SECURITIES SERVICES ADMINISTRATION**
Montgomery County Comm Coll (PA)
Vincennes U (IN)
Western Iowa Tech Comm Coll (IA)

**SECURITY AND LOSS PREVENTION**
Hill Coll (TX)
Miami Dade Coll (FL)
Tallahassee Comm Coll (FL)

**SELLING SKILLS AND SALES**
Clark Coll (WA)
Danville Area Comm Coll (IL)
Illinois Valley Comm Coll (IL)
McHenry County Coll (IL)
Ridgewater Coll (MN)

**SEMICONDUCTOR MANUFACTURING TECHNOLOGY**
Mohawk Valley Comm Coll (NY)

**SHEET METAL TECHNOLOGY**
Comm Coll of Allegheny County (PA)
Ivy Tech Comm Coll–Central Indiana (IN)
Ivy Tech Comm Coll–Lafayette (IN)
Ivy Tech Comm Coll–North Central (IN)
Ivy Tech Comm Coll–Northeast (IN)
Ivy Tech Comm Coll–Northwest (IN)
Ivy Tech Comm Coll–Sellersburg (IN)
Ivy Tech Comm Coll–Southwest (IN)
Ivy Tech Comm Coll–Wabash Valley (IN)
Lake Superior Coll (MN)
Macomb Comm Coll (MI)
Miami Dade Coll (FL)
Palomar Coll (CA)
Rock Valley Coll (IL)
Shawnee Comm Coll (IL)
Thaddeus Stevens Coll of Technology (PA)
Vincennes U (IN)

**SIGNAL/GEOSPATIAL INTELLIGENCE**
Northland Comm and Tech Coll (MN)

**SIGN LANGUAGE INTERPRETATION AND TRANSLATION**
Antelope Valley Coll (CA)
Austin Comm Coll District (TX)
Camden County Coll (NJ)
Coll of the Canyons (CA)
Collin County Comm Coll District (TX)
Comm Coll of Allegheny County (PA)
Comm Coll of Baltimore County (MD)
Comm Coll of Philadelphia (PA)
Del Mar Coll (TX)
El Paso Comm Coll (TX)
Front Range Comm Coll (CO)
Hinds Comm Coll (MS)
Houston Comm Coll (TX)
Illinois Central Coll (IL)
J. Sargeant Reynolds Comm Coll (VA)
Lakeland Comm Coll (OH)
McLennan Comm Coll (TX)
Miami Dade Coll (FL)
Minnesota State Comm and Tech Coll (MN)
Mohawk Valley Comm Coll (NY)
Mott Comm Coll (MI)
Mt. San Antonio Coll (CA)
Northcentral Tech Coll (WI)
Northern Essex Comm Coll (MA)
Oklahoma State U–Oklahoma City (OK)
Palomar Coll (CA)
St. Louis Comm Coll (MO)
Salt Lake Comm Coll (UT)
Tarrant County Coll District (TX)
Tulsa Comm Coll (OK)
Tyler Jr Coll (TX)

**SMALL BUSINESS ADMINISTRATION**
Antelope Valley Coll (CA)
Black Hawk Coll, Moline (IL)
Bristol Comm Coll (MA)
Bucks County Comm Coll (PA)
Coll of the Canyons (CA)
Colorado Northwestern Comm Coll (CO)
Eastern Arizona Coll (AZ)

Fullerton Coll (CA)
Harper Coll (IL)
Independence Comm Coll (KS)
J. Sargeant Reynolds Comm Coll (VA)
LDS Business Coll (UT)
Merced Coll (CA)
Raritan Valley Comm Coll (NJ)
Schoolcraft Coll (MI)
Southeast Tech Inst (SD)
South Suburban Coll (IL)
Springfield Tech Comm Coll (MA)
Westchester Comm Coll (NY)

**SMALL ENGINE MECHANICS AND REPAIR TECHNOLOGY**
Mitchell Tech Inst (SD)
North Dakota State Coll of Science (ND)
Southwestern Coll (CA)

**SOCIAL PSYCHOLOGY**
Macomb Comm Coll (MI)

**SOCIAL SCIENCES**
Amarillo Coll (TX)
Antelope Valley Coll (CA)
Arizona Western Coll (AZ)
Bristol Comm Coll (MA)
Bucks County Comm Coll (PA)
Carl Albert State Coll (OK)
Central Oregon Comm Coll (OR)
Central Texas Coll (TX)
Cochise County Comm Coll District (AZ)
Coll of Central Florida (FL)
Coll of Marin (CA)
Coll of the Canyons (CA)
Coll of the Desert (CA)
Comm Coll of Allegheny County (PA)
De Anza Coll (CA)
Feather River Coll (CA)
Frederick Comm Coll (MD)
Galveston Coll (TX)
Genesee Comm Coll (NY)
Harrisburg Area Comm Coll (PA)
Howard Comm Coll (MD)
Hutchinson Comm Coll (KS)
Independence Comm Coll (KS)
J. Sargeant Reynolds Comm Coll (VA)
Laramie County Comm Coll (WY)
Massachusetts Bay Comm Coll (MA)
Merced Coll (CA)
Miami Dade Coll (FL)
Mission Coll (CA)
Monroe Comm Coll (NY)
Montgomery County Comm Coll (PA)
Mt. San Antonio Coll (CA)
Navarro Coll (TX)
Niagara County Comm Coll (NY)
Northeast Comm Coll (NE)
Northeastern Jr Coll (CO)
Northwest Coll (WY)
Odessa Coll (TX)
Orange Coast Coll (CA)
Otero Jr Coll (CO)
Palomar Coll (CA)
Paris Jr Coll (TX)
San Jacinto Coll District (TX)
San Joaquin Delta Coll (CA)
Santa Rosa Jr Coll (CA)
Seminole State Coll (OK)
Texarkana Coll (TX)
Tulsa Comm Coll (OK)
Western Texas Coll (TX)
Western Wyoming Comm Coll (WY)

**SOCIAL SCIENCES RELATED**
Genesee Comm Coll (NY)

**SOCIAL WORK**
Amarillo Coll (TX)
Austin Comm Coll District (TX)
Barton County Comm Coll (KS)
Bowling Green State U–Firelands Coll (OH)
Bristol Comm Coll (MA)
Bucks County Comm Coll (PA)
Camden County Coll (NJ)
Chandler-Gilbert Comm Coll (AZ)
Chipola Coll (FL)
Coll of Central Florida (FL)
Comm Coll of Allegheny County (PA)
Del Mar Coll (TX)
Edison State Comm Coll (OH)
El Paso Comm Coll (TX)
Galveston Coll (TX)
Genesee Comm Coll (NY)
Georgia Military Coll (GA)
Gordon State Coll (GA)
Harford Comm Coll (MD)

Harrisburg Area Comm Coll (PA)
Holyoke Comm Coll (MA)
Hopkinsville Comm Coll (KY)
Hudson County Comm Coll (NJ)
Illinois Eastern Comm Colls, Wabash Valley College (IL)
Illinois Valley Comm Coll (IL)
Iowa Central Comm Coll (IA)
Lakeland Comm Coll (OH)
Lehigh Carbon Comm Coll (PA)
Lorain County Comm Coll (OH)
Manchester Comm Coll (CT)
Mesalands Comm Coll (NM)
Miami Dade Coll (FL)
Monroe County Comm Coll (MI)
Northampton Comm Coll (PA)
Northeast Iowa Comm Coll (IA)
Oakton Comm Coll (IL)
Paris Jr Coll (TX)
Potomac State Coll of West Virginia U (WV)
St. Philip's Coll (TX)
Salt Lake Comm Coll (UT)
San Juan Coll (NM)
Sauk Valley Comm Coll (IL)
Shawnee Comm Coll (IL)
South Suburban Coll (IL)
Southwestern Michigan Coll (MI)
Tulsa Comm Coll (OK)
Tyler Jr Coll (TX)
Vincennes U (IN)
Wayne County Comm Coll District (MI)
Western Wyoming Comm Coll (WY)

**SOCIAL WORK RELATED**
Genesee Comm Coll (NY)

**SOCIOLOGY**
Alvin Comm Coll (TX)
Antelope Valley Coll (CA)
Arizona Western Coll (AZ)
Austin Comm Coll District (TX)
Barton County Comm Coll (KS)
Bunker Hill Comm Coll (MA)
Central New Mexico Comm Coll (NM)
Coll of Central Florida (FL)
Coll of the Canyons (CA)
Coll of the Desert (CA)
Comm Coll of Allegheny County (PA)
De Anza Coll (CA)
Del Mar Coll (TX)
Eastern Arizona Coll (AZ)
Feather River Coll (CA)
Fullerton Coll (CA)
Georgia Military Coll (GA)
Gordon State Coll (GA)
Harford Comm Coll (MD)
Hill Coll (TX)
Iowa Central Comm Coll (IA)
Laramie County Comm Coll (WY)
Merced Coll (CA)
Miami Dade Coll (FL)
Mohave Comm Coll (AZ)
Navarro Coll (TX)
Northeastern Jr Coll (CO)
Northwest Coll (WY)
Odessa Coll (TX)
Oklahoma City Comm Coll (OK)
Orange Coast Coll (CA)
Palomar Coll (CA)
Panola Coll (TX)
Paris Jr Coll (TX)
Pasadena City Coll (CA)
Pensacola State Coll (FL)
Potomac State Coll of West Virginia U (WV)
St. Philip's Coll (TX)
Salt Lake Comm Coll (UT)
San Jacinto Coll District (TX)
San Joaquin Delta Coll (CA)
Santa Rosa Jr Coll (CA)
Sauk Valley Comm Coll (IL)
Southwestern Coll (CA)
Trinity Valley Comm Coll (TX)
Tyler Jr Coll (TX)
U of Wisconsin–Baraboo/Sauk County (WI)
U of Wisconsin–Barron County (WI)
U of Wisconsin–Fond du Lac (WI)
U of Wisconsin–Fox Valley (WI)
U of Wisconsin–Manitowoc (WI)
U of Wisconsin–Marathon County (WI)
U of Wisconsin–Marinette (WI)
U of Wisconsin–Marshfield/Wood County (WI)
U of Wisconsin–Richland (WI)
U of Wisconsin–Rock County (WI)
U of Wisconsin–Sheboygan (WI)
U of Wisconsin–Washington County (WI)

U of Wisconsin–Waukesha (WI)
Western Wyoming Comm Coll (WY)

**SOCIOLOGY AND ANTHROPOLOGY**
Harper Coll (IL)

**SOIL SCIENCE AND AGRONOMY**
The Ohio State U Ag Tech Inst (OH)
Treasure Valley Comm Coll (OR)

**SOLAR ENERGY TECHNOLOGY**
Arizona Western Coll (AZ)
Comm Coll of Allegheny County (PA)
Crowder Coll (MO)
Lorain County Comm Coll (OH)
Texas State Tech Coll (TX)
Treasure Valley Comm Coll (OR)

**SPANISH**
Arizona Western Coll (AZ)
Austin Comm Coll District (TX)
Coll of Marin (CA)
Coll of the Canyons (CA)
Coll of the Desert (CA)
De Anza Coll (CA)
Fiorello H. LaGuardia Comm Coll of the City U of New York (NY)
Laramie County Comm Coll (WY)
Los Angeles City Coll (CA)
Merced Coll (CA)
Miami Dade Coll (FL)
Northwest Coll (WY)
Oklahoma City Comm Coll (OK)
Orange Coast Coll (CA)
Pasadena City Coll (CA)
Santa Rosa Jr Coll (CA)
Southwestern Coll (CA)
Trinity Valley Comm Coll (TX)
Western Wyoming Comm Coll (WY)

**SPANISH LANGUAGE TEACHER EDUCATION**
Anne Arundel Comm Coll (MD)
Carroll Comm Coll (MD)
Comm Coll of Baltimore County (MD)
Frederick Comm Coll (MD)
Harford Comm Coll (MD)
Montgomery Coll (MD)

**SPECIAL EDUCATION**
Coll of Central Florida (FL)
Craven Comm Coll (NC)
Harford Comm Coll (MD)
Highland Comm Coll (IL)
Hill Coll (TX)
Lehigh Carbon Comm Coll (PA)
McHenry County Coll (IL)
Miami Dade Coll (FL)
Pensacola State Coll (FL)
San Juan Coll (NM)
Sauk Valley Comm Coll (IL)
Vincennes U (IN)

**SPECIAL EDUCATION–EARLY CHILDHOOD**
Harford Comm Coll (MD)
Merced Coll (CA)
Mitchell Comm Coll (NC)
Motlow State Comm Coll (TN)
Orange Coast Coll (CA)
Palomar Coll (CA)

**SPECIAL EDUCATION– ELEMENTARY SCHOOL**
Harford Comm Coll (MD)

**SPECIAL EDUCATION– INDIVIDUALS WITH HEARING IMPAIRMENTS**
Miami Dade Coll (FL)

**SPECIAL PRODUCTS MARKETING**
Copiah-Lincoln Comm Coll (MS)
Del Mar Coll (TX)
Mission Coll (CA)
Monroe Comm Coll (NY)
Muskegon Comm Coll (MI)
Northland Comm and Tech Coll (MN)
Scottsdale Comm Coll (AZ)
Tompkins Cortland Comm Coll (NY)

**SPEECH COMMUNICATION AND RHETORIC**
Ancilla Coll (IN)
Antelope Valley Coll (CA)
Barton County Comm Coll (KS)
Bristol Comm Coll (MA)
Brookhaven Coll (TX)
Bucks County Comm Coll (PA)
Bunker Hill Comm Coll (MA)

Central Oregon Comm Coll (OR)
Cochise County Comm Coll District (AZ)
Coll of Marin (CA)
Coll of the Canyons (CA)
Coll of the Desert (CA)
Collin County Comm Coll District (TX)
Dutchess Comm Coll (NY)
Eastern Arizona Coll (AZ)
Edison State Comm Coll (OH)
El Paso Comm Coll (TX)
Erie Comm Coll, South Campus (NY)
Fiorello H. LaGuardia Comm Coll of the City U of New York (NY)
Fullerton Coll (CA)
Harper Coll (IL)
Hill Coll (TX)
Houston Comm Coll (TX)
Hutchinson Comm Coll (KS)
Jamestown Comm Coll (NY)
Laramie County Comm Coll (WY)
Lehigh Carbon Comm Coll (PA)
Los Angeles City Coll (CA)
Macomb Comm Coll (MI)
Manchester Comm Coll (CT)
Merced Coll (CA)
Montgomery Coll (MD)
Montgomery County Comm Coll (PA)
Nassau Comm Coll (NY)
Northampton Comm Coll (PA)
Northeast Comm Coll (NE)
Northwest Coll (WY)
Oklahoma City Comm Coll (OK)
Orange Coast Coll (CA)
Palomar Coll (CA)
Panola Coll (TX)
Pasadena City Coll (CA)
Salt Lake Comm Coll (UT)
Sauk Valley Comm Coll (IL)
Tompkins Cortland Comm Coll (NY)
Tyler Jr Coll (TX)
Westchester Comm Coll (NY)
Western Wyoming Comm Coll (WY)

**SPEECH-LANGUAGE PATHOLOGY**
Lake Region State Coll (ND)
Williston State Coll (ND)

**SPEECH-LANGUAGE PATHOLOGY ASSISTANT**
Alexandria Tech and Comm Coll (MN)
Caldwell Comm Coll and Tech Inst (NC)
Fayetteville Tech Comm Coll (NC)
Mitchell Tech Inst (SD)
Oklahoma City Comm Coll (OK)

**SPORT AND FITNESS ADMINISTRATION/ MANAGEMENT**
Adirondack Comm Coll (NY)
Arizona Western Coll (AZ)
Barton County Comm Coll (KS)
Bucks County Comm Coll (PA)
Bunker Hill Comm Coll (MA)
Camden County Coll (NJ)
Cayuga County Comm Coll (NY)
Central Oregon Comm Coll (OR)
Des Moines Area Comm Coll (IA)
Fullerton Coll (CA)
Holyoke Comm Coll (MA)
Howard Comm Coll (MD)
Hutchinson Comm Coll (KS)
Illinois Eastern Comm Colls, Frontier Community College (IL)
Illinois Eastern Comm Colls, Lincoln Trail College (IL)
Illinois Eastern Comm Colls, Wabash Valley College (IL)
Jefferson Comm Coll (NY)
Kingsborough Comm Coll of the City U of New York (NY)
Lehigh Carbon Comm Coll (PA)
Lorain County Comm Coll (OH)
Manor Coll (PA)
Niagara County Comm Coll (NY)
Northampton Comm Coll (PA)
North Iowa Area Comm Coll (IA)
Rock Valley Coll (IL)
Salt Lake Comm Coll (UT)
Southwestern Michigan Coll (MI)
State U of New York Coll of Technology at Alfred (NY)
Sullivan County Comm Coll (NY)
Three Rivers Comm Coll (CT)
Tompkins Cortland Comm Coll (NY)
Tulsa Comm Coll (OK)
Union County Coll (NJ)

## SPORTS COMMUNICATION
Illinois Eastern Comm Colls, Wabash Valley College (IL)

## SPORTS STUDIES
Genesee Comm Coll (NY)

## STATISTICS
Coll of Central Florida (FL)

## STRUCTURAL ENGINEERING
Bristol Comm Coll (MA)
Harrisburg Area Comm Coll (PA)

## SUBSTANCE ABUSE/ ADDICTION COUNSELING
Adirondack Comm Coll (NY)
Alvin Comm Coll (TX)
Amarillo Coll (TX)
Anne Arundel Comm Coll (MD)
Austin Comm Coll District (TX)
Beal Coll (ME)
Camden County Coll (NJ)
Central Oregon Comm Coll (OR)
Century Coll (MN)
Chippewa Valley Tech Coll (WI)
Clark Coll (WA)
Coll of the Desert (CA)
Comm Coll of Allegheny County (PA)
Comm Coll of Baltimore County (MD)
Dawson Comm Coll (MT)
El Paso Comm Coll (TX)
Erie Comm Coll (NY)
Fox Valley Tech Coll (WI)
Genesee Comm Coll (NY)
Howard Comm Coll (MD)
Illinois Central Coll (IL)
Jamestown Comm Coll (NY)
J. Sargeant Reynolds Comm Coll (VA)
Los Angeles City Coll (CA)
Miami Dade Coll (FL)
Mohave Comm Coll (AZ)
Mohawk Valley Comm Coll (NY)
Montgomery County Comm Coll (PA)
Naugatuck Valley Comm Coll (CT)
Northcentral Tech Coll (WI)
North Shore Comm Coll (MA)
Oakton Comm Coll (IL)
Odessa Coll (TX)
Oklahoma State U–Oklahoma City (OK)
Palomar Coll (CA)
Sisseton-Wahpeton Coll (SD)
Southwestern Comm Coll (NC)
Stark State Coll (OH)
Texarkana Coll (TX)
Tompkins Cortland Comm Coll (NY)
Treasure Valley Comm Coll (OR)
Tyler Jr Coll (TX)
Westchester Comm Coll (NY)
Wor-Wic Comm Coll (MD)

## SURGICAL TECHNOLOGY
Anne Arundel Comm Coll (MD)
Asheville-Buncombe Tech Comm Coll (NC)
Austin Comm Coll District (TX)
Black Hawk Coll, Moline (IL)
Central New Mexico Comm Coll (NM)
Central Ohio Tech Coll (OH)
Coll of Eastern Idaho (ID)
Collin County Comm Coll District (TX)
Comm Coll of Allegheny County (PA)
El Paso Comm Coll (TX)
Fayetteville Tech Comm Coll (NC)
Frederick Comm Coll (MD)
Front Range Comm Coll (CO)
Gateway Tech Coll (WI)
Great Falls Coll Montana State U (MT)
Gulf Coast State Coll (FL)
Harrisburg Area Comm Coll (PA)
Hinds Comm Coll (MS)
Hutchinson Comm Coll (KS)
Illinois Central Coll (IL)
Ivy Tech Comm Coll–Central Indiana (IN)
Ivy Tech Comm Coll–Columbus (IN)
Ivy Tech Comm Coll–East Central (IN)
Ivy Tech Comm Coll–Kokomo (IN)
Ivy Tech Comm Coll–Lafayette (IN)
Ivy Tech Comm Coll–Northwest (IN)
Ivy Tech Comm Coll–Southwest (IN)
Ivy Tech Comm Coll–Wabash Valley (IN)

Kingsborough Comm Coll of the City U of New York (NY)
Kirtland Comm Coll (MI)
Lackawanna Coll (PA)
Lakeland Comm Coll (OH)
Lake Superior Coll (MN)
Laramie County Comm Coll (WY)
Lorain County Comm Coll (OH)
Macomb Comm Coll (MI)
Manchester Comm Coll (CT)
Minnesota State Comm and Tech Coll (MN)
Minnesota West Comm and Tech Coll (MN)
Mohave Comm Coll (AZ)
Montgomery Coll (MD)
Montgomery County Comm Coll (PA)
Nassau Comm Coll (NY)
Niagara County Comm Coll (NY)
Northeast Comm Coll (NE)
Northeast State Comm Coll (TN)
Northland Comm and Tech Coll (MN)
Oklahoma City Comm Coll (OK)
Owensboro Comm and Tech Coll (KY)
Ozarks Tech Comm Coll (MO)
Paris Jr Coll (TX)
Pittsburgh Tech Coll (PA)
Pueblo Comm Coll (CO)
Renton Tech Coll (WA)
Rock Valley Coll (IL)
St. Louis Comm Coll (MO)
St. Philip's Coll (TX)
San Jacinto Coll District (TX)
San Juan Coll (NM)
Somerset Comm Coll (KY)
Southcentral Kentucky Comm and Tech Coll (KY)
Southeast Arkansas Coll (AR)
Southeastern Coll–West Palm Beach (FL)
Southeast Tech Inst (SD)
Southern U at Shreveport (LA)
Southwestern Coll (CA)
Spencerian Coll (KY)
Springfield Tech Comm Coll (MA)
Stark State Coll (OH)
Tallahassee Comm Coll (FL)
Tarrant County Coll District (TX)
Trinity Valley Comm Coll (TX)
Tulsa Comm Coll (OK)
Tyler Jr Coll (TX)
Vincennes U (IN)
Walters State Comm Coll (TN)
Waukesha County Tech Coll (WI)
Wayne County Comm Coll District (MI)
Western Dakota Tech Inst (SD)
Western Iowa Tech Comm Coll (IA)
West Kentucky Comm and Tech Coll (KY)

## SURVEYING ENGINEERING
Central New Mexico Comm Coll (NM)
Des Moines Area Comm Coll (IA)

## SURVEYING TECHNOLOGY
Asheville-Buncombe Tech Comm Coll (NC)
Austin Comm Coll District (TX)
Clark Coll (WA)
Coll of the Canyons (CA)
Comm Coll of Baltimore County (MD)
Fayetteville Tech Comm Coll (NC)
Gateway Tech Coll (WI)
Macomb Comm Coll (MI)
Morrison Inst of Technology (IL)
Mt. San Antonio Coll (CA)
Oklahoma State U–Oklahoma City (OK)
Rend Lake Coll (IL)
Renton Tech Coll (WA)
Salt Lake Comm Coll (UT)
Santa Rosa Jr Coll (CA)
Southeast Tech Inst (SD)
State U of New York Coll of Technology at Alfred (NY)
Texas State Tech Coll (TX)
Tyler Jr Coll (TX)
U of Arkansas Comm Coll at Morrilton (AR)
Vincennes U (IN)

## SYSTEM, NETWORKING, AND LAN/WAN MANAGEMENT
Blue Ridge Comm and Tech Coll (WV)
Cloud County Comm Coll (KS)

Collin County Comm Coll District (TX)
Craven Comm Coll (NC)
El Paso Comm Coll (TX)
Hill Coll (TX)
Lamar Comm Coll (CO)
Mesa Comm Coll (AZ)
Paris Jr Coll (TX)
Rowan-Cabarrus Comm Coll (NC)
St. Philip's Coll (TX)
Southwestern Comm Coll (NC)
Southwestern Indian Polytechnic Inst (NM)
Texas State Tech Coll (TX)
Tyler Jr Coll (TX)
Williston State Coll (ND)

## TEACHER ASSISTANT/AIDE
Alamance Comm Coll (NC)
Antelope Valley Coll (CA)
Century Coll (MN)
Cloud County Comm Coll (KS)
Coll of The Albemarle (NC)
Comm Coll of Allegheny County (PA)
Danville Area Comm Coll (IL)
Fiorello H. LaGuardia Comm Coll of the City U of New York (NY)
Gateway Comm and Tech Coll (KY)
Gateway Tech Coll (WI)
Genesee Comm Coll (NY)
Harford Comm Coll (MD)
Highland Comm Coll (IL)
Hill Coll (TX)
Illinois Eastern Comm Colls, Lincoln Trail College (IL)
Illinois Valley Comm Coll (IL)
Jamestown Comm Coll (NY)
Jefferson Comm Coll (NY)
Kaskaskia Coll (IL)
Kingsborough Comm Coll of the City U of New York (NY)
Kishwaukee Coll (IL)
Lehigh Carbon Comm Coll (PA)
Manchester Comm Coll (CT)
Mesa Comm Coll (AZ)
Miami Dade Coll (FL)
Minnesota State Comm and Tech Coll (MN)
Mitchell Comm Coll (NC)
Montgomery County Comm Coll (PA)
Nebraska Indian Comm Coll (NE)
Northampton Comm Coll (PA)
Northcentral Tech Coll (WI)
Northland Comm and Tech Coll (MN)
Odessa Coll (TX)
Ridgewater Coll (MN)
St. Charles Comm Coll (MO)
Salt Lake Comm Coll (UT)
Schenectady County Comm Coll (NY)
Somerset Comm Coll (KY)
Southern U at Shreveport (LA)
Southwest Texas Jr Coll (TX)
Waukesha County Tech Coll (WI)
Westchester Comm Coll (NY)
Western Iowa Tech Comm Coll (IA)

## TECHNICAL TEACHER EDUCATION
East Central Coll (MO)

## TECHNOLOGY/INDUSTRIAL ARTS TEACHER EDUCATION
Central New Mexico Comm Coll (NM)
Fullerton Coll (CA)
Vincennes U (IN)

## TELECOMMUNICATIONS TECHNOLOGY
Amarillo Coll (TX)
Carl Albert State Coll (OK)
Cayuga County Comm Coll (NY)
Clark Coll (WA)
Collin County Comm Coll District (TX)
County Coll of Morris (NJ)
Hinds Comm Coll (MS)
Howard Comm Coll (MD)
Illinois Eastern Comm Colls, Lincoln Trail College (IL)
Iowa Central Comm Coll (IA)
Ivy Tech Comm Coll–Lafayette (IN)
Ivy Tech Comm Coll–North Central (IN)
Ivy Tech Comm Coll–Northwest (IN)
Ivy Tech Comm Coll–Sellersburg (IN)
Ivy Tech Comm Coll–Southwest (IN)
Meridian Comm Coll (MS)
Miami Dade Coll (FL)

Minnesota State Comm and Tech Coll (MN)
Mitchell Tech Inst (SD)
Monroe Comm Coll (NY)
Northern Essex Comm Coll (MA)
Penn State DuBois (PA)
Penn State Fayette, The Eberly Campus (PA)
Pensacola State Coll (FL)
Queensborough Comm Coll of the City U of New York (NY)
Quinsigamond Comm Coll (MA)
Ridgewater Coll (MN)
Salt Lake Comm Coll (UT)
Seminole State Coll of Florida (FL)
Springfield Tech Comm Coll (MA)
Texas State Tech Coll (TX)
Trident Tech Coll (SC)
Western Iowa Tech Comm Coll (IA)

## THEATER DESIGN AND TECHNOLOGY
Carroll Comm Coll (MD)
Genesee Comm Coll (NY)
Harford Comm Coll (MD)
Howard Comm Coll (MD)
Miami Dade Coll (FL)
Nassau Comm Coll (NY)
Pasadena City Coll (CA)
San Juan Coll (NM)
Vincennes U (IN)
Western Wyoming Comm Coll (WY)

## THEATER LITERATURE, HISTORY AND CRITICISM
Piedmont Virginia Comm Coll (VA)

## THEATER/THEATER ARTS MANAGEMENT
Genesee Comm Coll (NY)
Harper Coll (IL)

## THEOLOGY AND RELIGIOUS VOCATIONS RELATED
Ancilla Coll (IN)

## THERAPEUTIC RECREATION
Austin Comm Coll District (TX)
Comm Coll of Allegheny County (PA)
Ridgewater Coll (MN)

## TOOL AND DIE TECHNOLOGY
Bevill State Comm Coll (AL)
Craven Comm Coll (NC)
Des Moines Area Comm Coll (IA)
George C. Wallace Comm Coll (AL)
Ivy Tech Comm Coll–Bloomington (IN)
Ivy Tech Comm Coll–Central Indiana (IN)
Ivy Tech Comm Coll–Columbus (IN)
Ivy Tech Comm Coll–East Central (IN)
Ivy Tech Comm Coll–Kokomo (IN)
Ivy Tech Comm Coll–North Central (IN)
Ivy Tech Comm Coll–Northeast (IN)
Ivy Tech Comm Coll–Northwest (IN)
Ivy Tech Comm Coll–Richmond (IN)
Ivy Tech Comm Coll–Sellersburg (IN)
Ivy Tech Comm Coll–Southwest (IN)
Ivy Tech Comm Coll–Wabash Valley (IN)
Macomb Comm Coll (MI)
North Iowa Area Comm Coll (IA)
Ridgewater Coll (MN)
Rock Valley Coll (IL)
Vincennes U (IN)

## TOURISM AND TRAVEL SERVICES MANAGEMENT
Adirondack Comm Coll (NY)
Amarillo Coll (TX)
Austin Comm Coll District (TX)
Bunker Hill Comm Coll (MA)
El Paso Comm Coll (TX)
Fiorello H. LaGuardia Comm Coll of the City U of New York (NY)
Genesee Comm Coll (NY)
Hinds Comm Coll (MS)
Houston Comm Coll (TX)
Kingsborough Comm Coll of the City U of New York (NY)
Lakeland Comm Coll (OH)
Lorain County Comm Coll (OH)
Miami Dade Coll (FL)
Monroe Comm Coll (NY)
Niagara County Comm Coll (NY)
North Shore Comm Coll (MA)
St. Philip's Coll (TX)
Sullivan County Comm Coll (NY)

## TOURISM AND TRAVEL SERVICES MARKETING
Montgomery County Comm Coll (PA)
Orange Coast Coll (CA)
Southwestern Coll (CA)

## TOURISM PROMOTION
Comm Coll of Allegheny County (PA)
Genesee Comm Coll (NY)
Jefferson Comm Coll (NY)

## TRADE AND INDUSTRIAL TEACHER EDUCATION
Copiah-Lincoln Comm Coll (MS)
Del Mar Coll (TX)
Lenoir Comm Coll (NC)
National Park Coll (AR)
Quinsigamond Comm Coll (MA)
Southwestern Comm Coll (NC)

## TRANSPORTATION AND HIGHWAY ENGINEERING
Gateway Tech Coll (WI)

## TRANSPORTATION AND MATERIALS MOVING RELATED
Cecil Coll (MD)
Mid-Plains Comm Coll, North Platte (NE)
Mt. San Antonio Coll (CA)
Muskegon Comm Coll (MI)
Nassau Comm Coll (NY)
Schenectady County Comm Coll (NY)
Southwestern Coll (CA)

## TRANSPORTATION/MOBILITY MANAGEMENT
Cecil Coll (MD)
City Colls of Chicago, Olive-Harvey College (IL)
Comm Coll of Baltimore County (MD)
Del Mar Coll (TX)
Gulf Coast State Coll (FL)
Hagerstown Comm Coll (MD)
Ivy Tech Comm Coll–Central Indiana (IN)
South Florida State Coll (FL)

## TRUCK AND BUS DRIVER/ COMMERCIAL VEHICLE OPERATION/INSTRUCTION
Copiah-Lincoln Comm Coll (MS)
Mitchell Tech Inst (SD)
Mohave Comm Coll (AZ)

## TURF AND TURFGRASS MANAGEMENT
Coll of the Desert (CA)
Comm Coll of Allegheny County (PA)
Danville Area Comm Coll (IL)
Houston Comm Coll (TX)
The Ohio State U Ag Tech Inst (OH)
Ozarks Tech Comm Coll (MO)
Southeast Tech Inst (SD)
Southwestern Coll (CA)
State Tech Coll of Missouri (MO)
Texas State Tech Coll (TX)
Wayne Comm Coll (NC)
Western Texas Coll (TX)

## URBAN FORESTRY
Gateway Tech Coll (WI)
Kent State U at Trumbull (OH)

## VEHICLE MAINTENANCE AND REPAIR TECHNOLOGIES
Bevill State Comm Coll (AL)
Coll of the Desert (CA)
Ohio Tech Coll (OH)

## VEHICLE MAINTENANCE AND REPAIR TECHNOLOGIES RELATED
Central New Mexico Comm Coll (NM)
North Dakota State Coll of Science (ND)
State U of New York Coll of Technology at Alfred (NY)
Western Dakota Tech Inst (SD)

## VETERINARY/ANIMAL HEALTH TECHNOLOGY
Asheville-Buncombe Tech Comm Coll (NC)
Austin Comm Coll District (TX)
Black Hawk Coll, Moline (IL)
Bristol Comm Coll (MA)
Camden County Coll (NJ)

Cedar Valley Coll (TX)
Central New Mexico Comm Coll (NM)
Coll of Central Florida (FL)
Comm Coll of Baltimore County (MD)
Crowder Coll (MO)
Des Moines Area Comm Coll (IA)
Fiorello H. LaGuardia Comm Coll of the City U of New York (NY)
Front Range Comm Coll (CO)
Gateway Tech Coll (WI)
Genesee Comm Coll (NY)
Hinds Comm Coll (MS)
Holyoke Comm Coll (MA)
Independence Comm Coll (KS)
Jefferson State Comm Coll (AL)
Johnson Coll (PA)
Kaskaskia Coll (IL)
Kent State U at Tuscarawas (OH)
Lehigh Carbon Comm Coll (PA)
Macomb Comm Coll (MI)
Manor Coll (PA)
Mesa Comm Coll (AZ)
Miami Dade Coll (FL)
Mount Wachusett Comm Coll (MA)
Northampton Comm Coll (PA)
Northeast Comm Coll (NE)
North Shore Comm Coll (MA)
Northwest Coll (WY)
Oklahoma State U–Oklahoma City (OK)
Owensboro Comm and Tech Coll (KY)
Pensacola State Coll (FL)
Ridgewater Coll (MN)
San Juan Coll (NM)
Shawnee Comm Coll (IL)
State U of New York Coll of Technology at Alfred (NY)
Trident Tech Coll (SC)
Truckee Meadows Comm Coll (NV)
Tulsa Comm Coll (OK)
Tyler Jr Coll (TX)
Volunteer State Comm Coll (TN)
Western Iowa Tech Comm Coll (IA)
York County Comm Coll (ME)

**VISUAL AND PERFORMING ARTS**
Amarillo Coll (TX)
Antelope Valley Coll (CA)
Bucks County Comm Coll (PA)
Chandler-Gilbert Comm Coll (AZ)
Coll of the Desert (CA)
Comm Coll of Baltimore County (MD)
Dutchess Comm Coll (NY)
Feather River Coll (CA)
Fiorello H. LaGuardia Comm Coll of the City U of New York (NY)
Gordon State Coll (GA)
Harford Comm Coll (MD)
Harrisburg Area Comm Coll (PA)
Hutchinson Comm Coll (KS)
KD Conservatory Coll of Film and Dramatic Arts (TX)
Mesa Comm Coll (AZ)
Mott Comm Coll (MI)
Mt. San Antonio Coll (CA)
Nassau Comm Coll (NY)
Queensborough Comm Coll of the City U of New York (NY)
Schenectady County Comm Coll (NY)
Spartanburg Methodist Coll (SC)
U of Wisconsin–Baraboo/Sauk County (WI)
U of Wisconsin–Barron County (WI)
U of Wisconsin–Fond du Lac (WI)
U of Wisconsin–Fox Valley (WI)
U of Wisconsin–Manitowoc (WI)
U of Wisconsin–Marathon County (WI)
U of Wisconsin–Marinette (WI)
U of Wisconsin–Marshfield/Wood County (WI)
U of Wisconsin–Richland (WI)
U of Wisconsin–Rock County (WI)
U of Wisconsin–Sheboygan (WI)

U of Wisconsin–Washington County (WI)
U of Wisconsin–Waukesha (WI)
Westchester Comm Coll (NY)
Western Wyoming Comm Coll (WY)

**VISUAL AND PERFORMING ARTS RELATED**
Bossier Parish Comm Coll (LA)
Comm Coll of Allegheny County (PA)
John Tyler Comm Coll (VA)

**VITICULTURE AND ENOLOGY**
Harrisburg Area Comm Coll (PA)
James Sprunt Comm Coll (NC)
Kent State U at Ashtabula (OH)
Missouri State U–West Plains (MO)
Santa Rosa Jr Coll (CA)
Texas State Tech Coll (TX)

**VOICE AND OPERA**
Alvin Comm Coll (TX)
Del Mar Coll (TX)
Navarro Coll (TX)

**WATCHMAKING AND JEWELRYMAKING**
Austin Comm Coll District (TX)
Oklahoma State U Inst of Technology (OK)
Paris Jr Coll (TX)

**WATER QUALITY AND WASTEWATER TREATMENT MANAGEMENT AND RECYCLING TECHNOLOGY**
Arizona Western Coll (AZ)
Coll of the Canyons (CA)
Northern Maine Comm Coll (ME)
Northwest Vista Coll (TX)
Palomar Coll (CA)
Thaddeus Stevens Coll of Technology (PA)

**WATER RESOURCES ENGINEERING**
Gateway Tech Coll (WI)

**WEB/MULTIMEDIA MANAGEMENT AND WEBMASTER**
City Colls of Chicago, Olive-Harvey College (IL)
Clark Coll (WA)
Del Mar Coll (TX)
Fox Valley Tech Coll (WI)
Gateway Tech Coll (WI)
Illinois Central Coll (IL)
Kaskaskia Coll (IL)
Monroe County Comm Coll (MI)
Montgomery County Comm Coll (PA)
Morton Coll (IL)
Northern Essex Comm Coll (MA)
Seminole State Coll of Florida (FL)
Southwestern Coll (CA)
Trident Tech Coll (SC)
Vincennes U (IN)
Waukesha County Tech Coll (WI)
Wayne County Comm Coll District (MI)
Western Wyoming Comm Coll (WY)

**WEB PAGE, DIGITAL/ MULTIMEDIA AND INFORMATION RESOURCES DESIGN**
Bucks County Comm Coll (PA)
Bunker Hill Comm Coll (MA)
Camden County Coll (NJ)
Cecil Coll (MD)
Central Ohio Tech Coll (OH)
Century Coll (MN)
Cloud County Comm Coll (KS)
Coll of Eastern Idaho (ID)
The Coll of Westchester (NY)
Collin County Comm Coll District (TX)

County Coll of Morris (NJ)
Daytona State Coll (FL)
Del Mar Coll (TX)
Dunwoody Coll of Technology (MN)
Genesee Comm Coll (NY)
Gulf Coast State Coll (FL)
Hagerstown Comm Coll (MD)
Harper Coll (IL)
Harrisburg Area Comm Coll (PA)
Hawkeye Comm Coll (IA)
Highland Comm Coll (IL)
Hutchinson Comm Coll (KS)
Illinois Central Coll (IL)
Illinois Eastern Comm Colls, Frontier Community College (IL)
Independence Comm Coll (KS)
J. Sargeant Reynolds Comm Coll (VA)
Lake Superior Coll (MN)
Lehigh Carbon Comm Coll (PA)
Lorain County Comm Coll (OH)
Mesa Comm Coll (AZ)
Miami Dade Coll (FL)
Minnesota State Comm and Tech Coll (MN)
Mohawk Valley Comm Coll (NY)
Monroe County Comm Coll (MI)
Montgomery Coll (MD)
Montgomery County Comm Coll (PA)
Motlow State Comm Coll (TN)
Mount Wachusett Comm Coll (MA)
Niagara County Comm Coll (NY)
Northampton Comm Coll (PA)
North Dakota State Coll of Science (ND)
Northern Essex Comm Coll (MA)
North Shore Comm Coll (MA)
Northwest Vista Coll (TX)
Oklahoma City Comm Coll (OK)
Palomar Coll (CA)
Pensacola State Coll (FL)
Pittsburgh Tech Coll (PA)
Pueblo Comm Coll (CO)
Quinsigamond Comm Coll (MA)
Ridgewater Coll (MN)
Schoolcraft Coll (MI)
Seminole State Coll of Florida (FL)
Southwestern Coll (CA)
Southwestern Comm Coll (IA)
Stark State Coll (OH)
Tallahassee Comm Coll (FL)
Texas State Tech Coll (TX)
Trident Tech Coll (SC)
Walters State Comm Coll (TN)
Western Iowa Tech Comm Coll (IA)
Western Wyoming Comm Coll (WY)

**WELDING ENGINEERING TECHNOLOGY**
Arizona Western Coll (AZ)
Mitchell Tech Inst (SD)

**WELDING TECHNOLOGY**
Alamance Comm Coll (NC)
American Samoa Comm Coll (AS)
Antelope Valley Coll (CA)
Asheville-Buncombe Tech Comm Coll (NC)
Austin Comm Coll District (TX)
Beal Coll (ME)
Central Lakes Coll (MN)
Central New Mexico Comm Coll (NM)
Central Texas Coll (TX)
Clark Coll (WA)
Cochise County Comm Coll District (AZ)
Coll of Eastern Idaho (ID)
Coll of the Canyons (CA)
Collin County Comm Coll District (TX)
Comm Coll of Allegheny County (PA)
Copiah-Lincoln Comm Coll (MS)
Craven Comm Coll (NC)
Crowder Coll (MO)
Dawson Comm Coll (MT)
Del Mar Coll (TX)
Dunwoody Coll of Technology (MN)

East Central Coll (MO)
Eastern Arizona Coll (AZ)
Fox Valley Tech Coll (WI)
Front Range Comm Coll (CO)
Galveston Coll (TX)
George C. Wallace Comm Coll (AL)
Grand Rapids Comm Coll (MI)
Great Falls Coll Montana State U (MT)
Halifax Comm Coll (NC)
Hawkeye Comm Coll (IA)
Haywood Comm Coll (NC)
Highland Comm Coll (IL)
Hill Coll (TX)
Hutchinson Comm Coll (KS)
Illinois Central Coll (IL)
Iowa Central Comm Coll (IA)
Jamestown Comm Coll (NY)
Kaskaskia Coll (IL)
Kellogg Comm Coll (MI)
Kennebec Valley Comm Coll (ME)
Kirtland Comm Coll (MI)
Lake Area Tech Inst (SD)
Lake Superior Coll (MN)
Lenoir Comm Coll (NC)
Lorain County Comm Coll (OH)
Macomb Comm Coll (MI)
Maysville Comm and Tech Coll, Maysville (KY)
Merced Coll (CA)
Mesa Comm Coll (AZ)
Mid-Plains Comm Coll, North Platte (NE)
Mohave Comm Coll (AZ)
Mohawk Valley Comm Coll (NY)
Monroe County Comm Coll (MI)
Mt. San Antonio Coll (CA)
Muskegon Comm Coll (MI)
New River Comm Coll (VA)
Northampton Comm Coll (PA)
North Central Texas Coll (TX)
North Dakota State Coll of Science (ND)
North Iowa Area Comm Coll (IA)
Northwest Coll (WY)
Odessa Coll (TX)
Ohio Tech Coll (OH)
Orange Coast Coll (CA)
Owensboro Comm and Tech Coll (KY)
Ozarks Tech Comm Coll (MO)
Palomar Coll (CA)
Panola Coll (TX)
Paris Jr Coll (TX)
Pasadena City Coll (CA)
Pennsylvania Highlands Comm Coll (PA)
Pittsburgh Tech Coll (PA)
Pueblo Comm Coll (CO)
Rend Lake Coll (IL)
Renton Tech Coll (WA)
Ridgewater Coll (MN)
Rock Valley Coll (IL)
St. Charles Comm Coll (MO)
St. Philip's Coll (TX)
Salt Lake Comm Coll (UT)
San Jacinto Coll District (TX)
San Juan Coll (NM)
Schoolcraft Coll (MI)
Southcentral Kentucky Comm and Tech Coll (KY)
Southeast Tech Inst (SD)
Southwestern Comm Coll (IA)
State Tech Coll of Missouri (MO)
State U of New York Coll of Technology at Alfred (NY)
Tallahassee Comm Coll (FL)
Tarrant County Coll District (TX)
Texarkana Coll (TX)
Thaddeus Stevens Coll of Technology (PA)
Three Rivers Coll (MO)
Treasure Valley Comm Coll (OR)
Tri-County Comm Coll (NC)
Trinity Valley Comm Coll (TX)
Truckee Meadows Comm Coll (NV)
Tyler Jr Coll (TX)

Vincennes U (IN)
Wayne County Comm Coll District (MI)
Western Dakota Tech Inst (SD)
Western Iowa Tech Comm Coll (IA)
Western Texas Coll (TX)
Western Wyoming Comm Coll (WY)
Williston State Coll (ND)

**WILDLAND/FOREST FIREFIGHTING AND INVESTIGATION**
Antelope Valley Coll (CA)
Fox Valley Tech Coll (WI)

**WILDLIFE BIOLOGY**
Eastern Arizona Coll (AZ)

**WILDLIFE, FISH AND WILDLANDS SCIENCE AND MANAGEMENT**
Barton County Comm Coll (KS)
Feather River Coll (CA)
Florida Keys Comm Coll (FL)
Front Range Comm Coll (CO)
Haywood Comm Coll (NC)
Laramie County Comm Coll (WY)
Mt. San Antonio Coll (CA)
Penn State DuBois (PA)
Potomac State Coll of West Virginia U (WV)
Shawnee Comm Coll (IL)
Southwest Texas Jr Coll (TX)
Treasure Valley Comm Coll (OR)
Western Wyoming Comm Coll (WY)

**WINE STEWARD/SOMMELIER**
Cayuga County Comm Coll (NY)
Niagara County Comm Coll (NY)

**WOMEN'S STUDIES**
Palomar Coll (CA)
Santa Rosa Jr Coll (CA)
Southwestern Coll (CA)

**WOOD SCIENCE AND WOOD PRODUCTS/PULP AND PAPER TECHNOLOGY**
Dabney S. Lancaster Comm Coll (VA)
Potomac State Coll of West Virginia U (WV)

**WORD PROCESSING**
Del Mar Coll (TX)
Monroe County Comm Coll (MI)
North Central Texas Coll (TX)
Seminole State Coll of Florida (FL)
Western Wyoming Comm Coll (WY)

**WRITING**
Cayuga County Comm Coll (NY)
Eastern Arizona Coll (AZ)

**YOUTH MINISTRY**
Hesston Coll (KS)

**ZOOLOGY/ANIMAL BIOLOGY**
U of Wisconsin–Baraboo/Sauk County (WI)
U of Wisconsin–Barron County (WI)
U of Wisconsin–Fond du Lac (WI)
U of Wisconsin–Fox Valley (WI)
U of Wisconsin–Manitowoc (WI)
U of Wisconsin–Marathon County (WI)
U of Wisconsin–Marinette (WI)
U of Wisconsin–Marshfield/Wood County (WI)
U of Wisconsin–Richland (WI)
U of Wisconsin–Rock County (WI)
U of Wisconsin–Sheboygan (WI)
U of Wisconsin–Washington County (WI)
U of Wisconsin–Waukesha (WI)

# Associate Degree Programs at Four-Year Colleges

**ACCOUNTING**
Academy Coll (MN)
California U of Pennsylvania (PA)
Calumet Coll of Saint Joseph (IN)
Caribbean U (PR)
Central Methodist U (MO)
Central Penn Coll (PA)
Champlain Coll (VT)
Colegio Universitario de San Juan, San Juan (PR)
Davenport U, Grand Rapids (MI)
Hobe Sound Bible Coll (FL)
Husson U (ME)
Immaculata U (PA)
Indiana Tech (IN)
Indiana Wesleyan U (IN)
Inter American U of Puerto Rico, Aguadilla Campus (PR)
Inter American U of Puerto Rico, Barranquitas Campus (PR)
Inter American U of Puerto Rico, Bayamón Campus (PR)
Inter American U of Puerto Rico, Fajardo Campus (PR)
Inter American U of Puerto Rico, Metropolitan Campus (PR)
Inter American U of Puerto Rico, San Germán Campus (PR)
Keiser U, Fort Lauderdale (FL)
Liberty U (VA)
Mount Aloysius Coll (PA)
Mount Marty Coll (SD)
Muhlenberg Coll (PA)
Oakland City U (IN)
Palm Beach State Coll (FL)
Point U (GA)
Post U (CT)
Rasmussen Coll Bloomington (MN)
Rasmussen Coll Brooklyn Park (MN)
Rasmussen Coll Eagan (MN)
Rasmussen Coll Mankato (MN)
Rasmussen Coll New Port Richey (FL)
Rasmussen Coll Ocala (FL)
Rasmussen Coll St. Cloud (MN)
Rogers State U (OK)
Saint Francis U (PA)
Saint Mary-of-the-Woods Coll (IN)
Shawnee State U (OH)
Southern Adventist U (TN)
Tiffin U (OH)
Trine U (IN)
Union Coll (NE)
The U of Findlay (OH)
U of the Potomac (DC)
Utah Valley U (UT)
Walsh U (OH)
Webber International U (FL)
Youngstown State U (OH)

**ACCOUNTING AND BUSINESS/ MANAGEMENT**
Kansas State U (KS)

**ACCOUNTING AND FINANCE**
Ohio Christian U (OH)

**ACCOUNTING RELATED**
Florida National U (FL)
Montana State U Billings (MT)

**ACCOUNTING TECHNOLOGY AND BOOKKEEPING**
American Public U System (WV)
Ferris State U (MI)
Florida National U (FL)
Hilbert Coll (NY)
Kent State U at Geauga (OH)
Montana State U Billings (MT)

Montana Tech of The U of Montana (MT)
Pennsylvania Coll of Technology (PA)
Polk State Coll (FL)
State U of New York Coll of Agriculture and Technology at Cobleskill (NY)
State U of New York Coll of Technology at Canton (NY)
State U of New York Coll of Technology at Delhi (NY)
Sullivan U (KY)
Trine U (IN)
The U of Akron (OH)
U of Alaska Fairbanks (AK)
U of Montana (MT)
The U of Toledo (OH)
Valencia Coll (FL)

**ACTING**
Academy of Art U (CA)

**ADMINISTRATIVE ASSISTANT AND SECRETARIAL SCIENCE**
Arkansas Tech U (AR)
Ball State U (IN)
Black Hills State U (SD)
Campbellsville U (KY)
Clarion U of Pennsylvania (PA)
Colegio Universitario de San Juan, San Juan (PR)
Columbia Central U, Caguas (PR)
Concordia Coll–New York (NY)
Dickinson State U (ND)
EDP U of Puerto Rico (PR)
EDP U of Puerto Rico–San Sebastian (PR)
Hobe Sound Bible Coll (FL)
Idaho State U (ID)
Inter American U of Puerto Rico, San Germán Campus (PR)
Montana State U Billings (MT)
Montana Tech of The U of Montana (MT)
Northern Michigan U (MI)
Palm Beach State Coll (FL)
The U of Akron (OH)
U of Montana (MT)
Weber State U (UT)
Welch Coll (TN)

**ADULT AND CONTINUING EDUCATION ADMINISTRATION**
Concordia Coll–New York (NY)

**ADULT DEVELOPMENT AND AGING**
Madonna U (MI)

**ADVERTISING**
Academy of Art U (CA)
Fashion Inst of Technology (NY)

**AERONAUTICAL/AEROSPACE ENGINEERING TECHNOLOGY**
Idaho State U (ID)
Purdue U (IN)
Vaughn Coll of Aeronautics and Technology (NY)

**AERONAUTICS/AVIATION/ AEROSPACE SCIENCE AND TECHNOLOGY**
Embry-Riddle Aeronautical U– Daytona (FL)
Ohio U (OH)
Vaughn Coll of Aeronautics and Technology (NY)

**AGRIBUSINESS**
Southern Arkansas U–Magnolia (AR)
State U of New York Coll of Agriculture and Technology at Cobleskill (NY)
Vermont Tech Coll (VT)

**AGRICULTURAL BUSINESS AND MANAGEMENT**
Colorado Mesa U (CO)
North Carolina State U (NC)
State U of New York Coll of Agriculture and Technology at Cobleskill (NY)
U of New Hampshire (NH)
Washington State U (WA)

**AGRICULTURAL BUSINESS AND MANAGEMENT RELATED**
Penn State Abington (PA)
Penn State Altoona (PA)
Penn State Beaver (PA)
Penn State Berks (PA)
Penn State Brandywine (PA)
Penn State Erie, The Behrend Coll (PA)
Penn State Greater Allegheny (PA)
Penn State Hazleton (PA)
Penn State Lehigh Valley (PA)
Penn State New Kensington (PA)
Penn State Schuylkill (PA)
Penn State Shenango (PA)
Penn State Wilkes-Barre (PA)
Penn State Worthington Scranton (PA)
Penn State York (PA)
U of Guelph (ON, Canada)

**AGRICULTURAL PRODUCTION**
Eastern New Mexico U (NM)
U of the Fraser Valley (BC, Canada)
Western Kentucky U (KY)

**AGRICULTURE**
North Carolina State U (NC)
State U of New York Coll of Agriculture and Technology at Cobleskill (NY)
U of Guelph (ON, Canada)

**AGRICULTURE AND AGRICULTURE OPERATIONS RELATED**
Murray State U (KY)

**AGRONOMY AND CROP SCIENCE**
State U of New York Coll of Agriculture and Technology at Cobleskill (NY)

**AIRCRAFT POWERPLANT TECHNOLOGY**
Hallmark U (TX)
Idaho State U (ID)
Liberty U (VA)
Midland Coll (TX)
Pennsylvania Coll of Technology (PA)
U of Alaska Fairbanks (AK)

**AIRFRAME MECHANICS AND AIRCRAFT MAINTENANCE TECHNOLOGY**
Hallmark U (TX)
Lewis U (IL)
Middle Georgia State U (GA)
Midland Coll (TX)
Northern Michigan U (MI)

**AIRLINE FLIGHT ATTENDANT**
Liberty U (VA)

**AIRLINE PILOT AND FLIGHT CREW**
Academy Coll (MN)
Colorado Mesa U (CO)
Lewis U (IL)
Palm Beach State Coll (FL)
Polk State Coll (FL)
Purdue U (IN)
Southern Illinois U Carbondale (IL)
Southern Utah U (UT)
U of Alaska Fairbanks (AK)
Utah Valley U (UT)

**AIR TRAFFIC CONTROL**
LeTourneau U (TX)
Lewis U (IL)
Middle Georgia State U (GA)

**ALLIED HEALTH AND MEDICAL ASSISTING SERVICES RELATED**
Clarion U of Pennsylvania (PA)
Eastern U (PA)
Florida National U (FL)
Thomas Edison State U (NJ)
Widener U (PA)

**ALLIED HEALTH DIAGNOSTIC, INTERVENTION, AND TREATMENT PROFESSIONS RELATED**
Ball State U (IN)
Cameron U (OK)

**ALTERNATIVE AND COMPLEMENTARY MEDICINE**
American Coll of Healthcare Sciences (OR)

**ALTERNATIVE AND COMPLEMENTARY MEDICINE RELATED**
American Coll of Healthcare Sciences (OR)

**AMERICAN INDIAN/NATIVE AMERICAN STUDIES**
Inst of American Indian Arts (NM)

**AMERICAN NATIVE/NATIVE AMERICAN LANGUAGES**
Idaho State U (ID)
U of Alaska Fairbanks (AK)

**AMERICAN SIGN LANGUAGE (ASL)**
Bethel Coll (IN)
Idaho State U (ID)
Madonna U (MI)
Weber State U (UT)

**ANCIENT NEAR EASTERN AND BIBLICAL LANGUAGES**
Bethel Coll (IN)

**ANIMAL/LIVESTOCK HUSBANDRY AND PRODUCTION**
North Carolina State U (NC)
Southern Utah U (UT)
U of the Fraser Valley (BC, Canada)

**ANIMAL SCIENCES**
State U of New York Coll of Agriculture and Technology at Cobleskill (NY)
U of New Hampshire (NH)

**ANIMAL TRAINING**
Becker Coll (MA)

**ANIMATION, INTERACTIVE TECHNOLOGY, VIDEO GRAPHICS AND SPECIAL EFFECTS**
Academy of Art U (CA)
Ferris State U (MI)
New England Inst of Technology (RI)

**ANTHROPOLOGY**
U of Nevada, Reno (NV)

**APPAREL AND ACCESSORIES MARKETING**
U of Montana (MT)

**APPAREL AND TEXTILE MANUFACTURING**
Academy of Art U (CA)
Fashion Inst of Technology (NY)

**APPAREL AND TEXTILE MARKETING MANAGEMENT**
Academy of Art U (CA)

**APPAREL AND TEXTILES**
Academy of Art U (CA)
Palm Beach State Coll (FL)

**APPLIED HORTICULTURE/ HORTICULTURAL BUSINESS SERVICES RELATED**
U of Massachusetts Amherst (MA)

**APPLIED HORTICULTURE/ HORTICULTURE OPERATIONS**
State U of New York Coll of Technology at Delhi (NY)
U of Massachusetts Amherst (MA)
U of New Hampshire (NH)
U of the Fraser Valley (BC, Canada)

**APPLIED MATHEMATICS**
Central Methodist U (MO)

**APPLIED PSYCHOLOGY**
Christian Brothers U (TN)

**ARCHEOLOGY**
Weber State U (UT)

**ARCHITECTURAL DRAFTING AND CAD/CADD**
Academy of Art U (CA)

**ARCHITECTURAL ENGINEERING TECHNOLOGY**
Brigham Young U–Idaho (ID)
Ferris State U (MI)
New England Inst of Technology (RI)
Northern Kentucky U (KY)
Penn State Worthington Scranton (PA)
Purdue U Northwest (IN)
State U of New York Coll of Technology at Delhi (NY)
Vermont Tech Coll (VT)

**ARCHITECTURAL TECHNOLOGY**
New York Inst of Technology (NY)

**ARCHITECTURE RELATED**
Abilene Christian U (TX)

**ARMY ROTC/MILITARY SCIENCE**
Brigham Young U–Idaho (ID)

## ART
Arcadia U (PA)
Eastern New Mexico U (NM)
Felician U (NJ)
Hannibal-LaGrange U (MO)
Indiana Wesleyan U (IN)
Northern Michigan U (MI)
Northern Vermont U–Lyndon (VT)
Oakland City U (IN)
Palm Beach State Coll (FL)
State U of New York Empire State
  Coll (NY)
Union Coll (NE)
Villa Maria Coll (NY)
Weber State U (UT)

## ART HISTORY, CRITICISM AND CONSERVATION
John Cabot U (Italy)
Palm Beach State Coll (FL)

## ARTS, ENTERTAINMENT, AND MEDIA MANAGEMENT RELATED
Northern Vermont U–Lyndon (VT)

## ATHLETIC TRAINING
Dean Coll (MA)
Limestone Coll (SC)
Shawnee State U (OH)
The U of Akron (OH)

## AUTOBODY/COLLISION AND REPAIR TECHNOLOGY
Academy of Art U (CA)
Idaho State U (ID)
Montana State U Billings (MT)
New England Inst of Technology (RI)
Pennsylvania Coll of Technology
  (PA)
Utah Valley U (UT)

## AUTOMATION ENGINEER TECHNOLOGY
ECPI U, Virginia Beach (VA)
Weber State U (UT)

## AUTOMOBILE/AUTOMOTIVE MECHANICS TECHNOLOGY
Arkansas Tech U (AR)
Brigham Young U–Idaho (ID)
Colorado Mesa U (CO)
Ferris State U (MI)
Idaho State U (ID)
Midland Coll (TX)
Montana State U Billings (MT)
Montana Tech of The U of Montana
  (MT)
New England Inst of Technology (RI)
Northern Michigan U (MI)
Pennsylvania Coll of Technology
  (PA)
Pittsburg State U (KS)
Southern Adventist U (TN)
State U of New York Coll of
  Technology at Canton (NY)
State U of New York Coll of
  Technology at Delhi (NY)
Utah Valley U (UT)
Weber State U (UT)

## AUTOMOTIVE ENGINEERING TECHNOLOGY
Farmingdale State Coll (NY)
The U of West Alabama (AL)
Vermont Tech Coll (VT)

## AVIATION/AIRWAY MANAGEMENT
Academy Coll (MN)
Lynn U (FL)
Polk State Coll (FL)
Purdue U (IN)
Vaughn Coll of Aeronautics and
  Technology (NY)

## AVIONICS MAINTENANCE TECHNOLOGY
Hallmark U (TX)
Middle Georgia State U (GA)
Vaughn Coll of Aeronautics and
  Technology (NY)

## BAKING AND PASTRY ARTS
Colorado Mesa U (CO)
The Culinary Inst of America (NY)
ECPI U, Virginia Beach (VA)
Keiser U, Fort Lauderdale (FL)
Pennsylvania Coll of Technology
  (PA)
Sullivan U (KY)

Valencia Coll (FL)

## BANKING AND FINANCIAL SUPPORT SERVICES
Brescia U (KY)
Hilbert Coll (NY)
Northern State U (SD)

## BEHAVIORAL ASPECTS OF HEALTH
Point U (GA)

## BEHAVIORAL SCIENCES
Granite State Coll (NH)
Loyola U Chicago (IL)
Lynn U (FL)

## BIBLICAL STUDIES
Alaska Bible Coll (AK)
Appalachian Bible Coll (WV)
Barclay Coll (KS)
Beulah Heights U (GA)
Calvary U (MO)
Campbellsville U (KY)
Carolina Christian Coll (NC)
Carson-Newman U (TN)
Charlotte Christian Coll and
  Theological Seminary (NC)
Coll of Biblical Studies–Houston (TX)
Corban U (OR)
Covenant Coll (GA)
Crowley's Ridge Coll (AR)
Dallas Baptist U (TX)
Eastern Mennonite U (VA)
Emmaus Bible Coll (IA)
Horizon U (CA)
Howard Payne U (TX)
Johnson U (TN)
Johnson U Florida (FL)
Kentucky Mountain Bible Coll (KY)
Lincoln Christian U (IL)
Mid-Atlantic Christian U (NC)
Nyack Coll (NY)
Point U (GA)
Southern Adventist U (TN)
Southwestern Assemblies of God U
  (TX)
Trinity Coll of Florida (FL)
U of Valley Forge (PA)
Welch Coll (TN)

## BIOINFORMATICS
Coleman U, San Diego (CA)

## BIOLOGICAL AND BIOMEDICAL SCIENCES RELATED
Roberts Wesleyan Coll (NY)

## BIOLOGICAL AND PHYSICAL SCIENCES
Ferris State U (MI)
Penn State Altoona (PA)
Penn State Beaver (PA)
Penn State Greater Allegheny (PA)
Penn State New Kensington (PA)
Penn State Schuylkill (PA)
Penn State Shenango (PA)
Thomas Edison State U (NJ)
Trine U (IN)
Valparaiso U (IN)
Welch Coll (TN)

## BIOLOGY/BIOLOGICAL SCIENCES
Bryn Athyn Coll of the New Church
  (PA)
Dallas Baptist U (TX)
Dean Coll (MA)
Immaculata U (PA)
Indiana Wesleyan U (IN)
Palm Beach State Coll (FL)
Pine Manor Coll (MA)
Rogers State U (OK)
Shawnee State U (OH)
State U of New York Coll of
  Agriculture and Technology at
  Cobleskill (NY)
Utah Valley U (UT)
Welch Coll (TN)
Wright State U (OH)
Wright State U–Lake Campus (OH)
York Coll of Pennsylvania (PA)

## BIOLOGY/BIOTECHNOLOGY LABORATORY TECHNICIAN
State U of New York Coll of
  Agriculture and Technology at
  Cobleskill (NY)
Valencia Coll (FL)
Weber State U (UT)

## BIOMEDICAL TECHNOLOGY
Indiana U–Purdue U Indianapolis
  (IN)
Penn State Altoona (PA)
Penn State Berks (PA)
Penn State Erie, The Behrend Coll
  (PA)
Penn State Hazleton (PA)
Penn State New Kensington (PA)
Penn State Schuylkill (PA)
Penn State Shenango (PA)
Penn State York (PA)

## BIOTECHNOLOGY
EDP U of Puerto Rico (PR)
Keiser U, Fort Lauderdale (FL)
Northern State U (SD)

## BLOOD BANK TECHNOLOGY
Rasmussen Coll St. Cloud (MN)

## BOTANY/PLANT BIOLOGY
Palm Beach State Coll (FL)

## BROADCAST JOURNALISM
Evangel U (MO)

## BUILDING/CONSTRUCTION FINISHING, MANAGEMENT, AND INSPECTION RELATED
Palm Beach State Coll (FL)
Pratt Inst (NY)

## BUILDING/CONSTRUCTION SITE MANAGEMENT
State U of New York Coll of
  Technology at Canton (NY)
Wentworth Inst of Technology (MA)

## BUILDING CONSTRUCTION TECHNOLOGY
Southern Utah U (UT)
Wentworth Inst of Technology (MA)

## BUILDING/HOME/ CONSTRUCTION INSPECTION
Utah Valley U (UT)

## BUILDING/PROPERTY MAINTENANCE
Southern Adventist U (TN)
Utah Valley U (UT)

## BUSINESS ADMINISTRATION AND MANAGEMENT
Academy Coll (MN)
Alaska Pacific U (AK)
Anderson U (IN)
Bay Path U (MA)
Beacon Coll (FL)
Benedictine U (IL)
Bethel Coll (IN)
Bryan Coll (TN)
Calumet Coll of Saint Joseph (IN)
Cameron U (OK)
Campbellsville U (KY)
Caribbean U (PR)
Carroll Coll (MT)
Cazenovia Coll (NY)
Chaminade U of Honolulu (HI)
Coll of Saint Mary (NE)
Columbia Southern U (AL)
Concordia Coll–New York (NY)
Corban U (OR)
Cornerstone U (MI)
Dakota State U (SD)
Dallas Baptist U (TX)
Dean Coll (MA)
Defiance Coll (OH)
EDP U of Puerto Rico (PR)
EDP U of Puerto Rico–San
  Sebastian (PR)
Endicott Coll (MA)
Excelsior Coll (NY)
Faulkner U (AL)
Felician U (NJ)
Ferris State U (MI)
Fisher Coll (MA)
Florida National U (FL)
Geneva Coll (PA)
Granite State Coll (NH)
Gwynedd Mercy U (PA)
Hallmark U (TX)
Hampton U (VA)
Hawai`i Pacific U (HI)
Hilbert Coll (NY)
Husson U (ME)
Immaculata U (PA)
Indiana Tech (IN)
Indiana Wesleyan U (IN)

Inter American U of Puerto Rico,
  Aguadilla Campus (PR)
Inter American U of Puerto Rico,
  Barranquitas Campus (PR)
Inter American U of Puerto Rico,
  Bayamón Campus (PR)
Inter American U of Puerto Rico,
  Fajardo Campus (PR)
Inter American U of Puerto Rico, San
  Germán Campus (PR)
John Cabot U (Italy)
Keiser U, Fort Lauderdale (FL)
Lincoln Coll of New England,
  Southington (CT)
Lock Haven U of Pennsylvania (PA)
Long Island U–LIU Brooklyn (NY)
Loyola U Chicago (IL)
Madonna U (MI)
Marian U (IN)
Marietta Coll (OH)
Medgar Evers Coll of the City U of
  New York (NY)
MidAmerica Nazarene U (KS)
Missouri Baptist U (MO)
Montana State U Billings (MT)
Mount Aloysius Coll (PA)
Mount Marty Coll (SD)
Mount Saint Mary's U (CA)
Mount Vernon Nazarene U (OH)
Muhlenberg Coll (PA)
National U (CA)
New England Inst of Technology (RI)
Newman U (KS)
New Mexico Inst of Mining and
  Technology (NM)
New York Inst of Technology (NY)
Niagara U (NY)
Northern State U (SD)
Northern Vermont U–Lyndon (VT)
Nyack Coll (NY)
Oakland City U (IN)
Ohio Christian U (OH)
Ohio Dominican U (OH)
Peirce Coll (PA)
Pennsylvania Coll of Technology
  (PA)
Pine Manor Coll (MA)
Point U (GA)
Post U (CT)
Providence Coll (RI)
Rasmussen Coll Bloomington (MN)
Rasmussen Coll Brooklyn Park (MN)
Rasmussen Coll Eagan (MN)
Rasmussen Coll Mankato (MN)
Rasmussen Coll New Port Richey
  (FL)
Rasmussen Coll Ocala (FL)
Rasmussen Coll St. Cloud (MN)
Regent U (VA)
Robert Morris U Illinois (IL)
Rogers State U (OK)
Rust Coll (MS)
Saint Augustine's U (NC)
Saint Francis U (PA)
St. John's U (NY)
Saint Joseph's U (PA)
Saint Leo U (FL)
Saint Peter's U (NJ)
St. Thomas Aquinas Coll (NY)
Shawnee State U (OH)
Southern Adventist U (TN)
Southwestern Assemblies of God U
  (TX)
State U of New York Coll of
  Agriculture and Technology at
  Cobleskill (NY)
State U of New York Coll of
  Technology at Canton (NY)
State U of New York Coll of
  Technology at Delhi (NY)
Stevens–The Inst of Business & Arts
  (MO)
Sullivan U (KY)
Taylor U (IN)
Thomas Edison State U (NJ)
Tiffin U (OH)
Toccoa Falls Coll (GA)
Trevecca Nazarene U (TN)
Tulane U (LA)
Union Coll (NE)
The U of Akron (OH)
U of Alaska Fairbanks (AK)
U of Cincinnati (OH)
U of Maine at Fort Kent (ME)
U of Maine at Presque Isle (ME)
U of Management and Technology
  (VA)
The U of Montana Western (MT)
U of New Haven (CT)
U of Pennsylvania (PA)

U of Pikeville (KY)
The U of Scranton (PA)
U of Sioux Falls (SD)
U of Southern Indiana (IN)
U of the Fraser Valley (BC, Canada)
U of the Incarnate Word (TX)
U of the Potomac (DC)
Upper Iowa U (IA)
Utah Valley U (UT)
Vermont Tech Coll (VT)
Villa Maria Coll (NY)
Waldorf U (IA)
Walsh U (OH)
Warner Pacific U (OR)
Wayland Baptist U (TX)
Webber International U (FL)
Welch Coll (TN)
Western Kentucky U (KY)
Wright State U (OH)
Wright State U–Lake Campus (OH)
York Coll of Pennsylvania (PA)
Youngstown State U (OH)

## BUSINESS ADMINISTRATION, MANAGEMENT AND OPERATIONS RELATED
Bay Path U (MA)
Columbia Central U, Caguas (PR)
Eastern Oregon U (OR)

## BUSINESS AUTOMATION/ TECHNOLOGY/DATA ENTRY
Colorado Mesa U (CO)
Hallmark U (TX)
Montana State U Billings (MT)
Northern Michigan U (MI)
Point U (GA)
The U of Akron (OH)
Utah Valley U (UT)

## BUSINESS/COMMERCE
Academy Coll (MN)
Adams State U (CO)
American Public U System (WV)
Bethel Coll (IN)
Brescia U (KY)
Bryn Athyn Coll of the New Church
  (PA)
Champlain Coll (VT)
Christian Brothers U (TN)
Coll of Staten Island of the City U of
  New York (NY)
Columbia Coll (MO)
Davenport U, Grand Rapids (MI)
Delaware Valley U (PA)
Eastern Nazarene Coll (MA)
Gannon U (PA)
Hawai`i Pacific U (HI)
Idaho State U (ID)
Indiana U Southeast (IN)
Kent State U at Geauga (OH)
Liberty U (VA)
Limestone Coll (SC)
Metropolitan Coll of New York (NY)
MidAmerica Nazarene U (KS)
Midland Coll (TX)
Montana State U Billings (MT)
Murray State U (KY)
New Mexico State U (NM)
New York U (NY)
Niagara U (NY)
Nichols Coll (MA)
Northern Kentucky U (KY)
Northern Michigan U (MI)
Northern Vermont U–Lyndon (VT)
Penn State Abington (PA)
Penn State Altoona (PA)
Penn State Beaver (PA)
Penn State Berks (PA)
Penn State Brandywine (PA)
Penn State Erie, The Behrend Coll
  (PA)
Penn State Greater Allegheny (PA)
Penn State Harrisburg (PA)
Penn State Hazleton (PA)
Penn State Lehigh Valley (PA)
Penn State New Kensington (PA)
Penn State Schuylkill (PA)
Penn State Shenango (PA)
Penn State Wilkes-Barre (PA)
Penn State Worthington Scranton
  (PA)
Penn State York (PA)
Saint Mary-of-the-Woods Coll (IN)
Southeastern U (FL)
Southern Arkansas U–Magnolia
  (AR)
Southern Utah U (UT)
Southwest Baptist U (MO)

Southwestern Assemblies of God U
  (TX)
State U of New York Empire State
  Coll (NY)
Tabor Coll (KS)
Thomas U (GA)
Trine U (IN)
Tulane U (LA)
U of Bridgeport (CT)
U of Maine at Fort Kent (ME)
U of Massachusetts Lowell (MA)
The U of Toledo (OH)
Villa Maria Coll (NY)
Waldorf U (IA)
Wright State U (OH)
Youngstown State U (OH)

**BUSINESS/CORPORATE
COMMUNICATIONS**
Waldorf U (IA)

**BUSINESS, MANAGEMENT, AND
MARKETING RELATED**
Florida National U (FL)

**BUSINESS/MANAGERIAL
ECONOMICS**
Campbellsville U (KY)
Niagara U (NY)
Saint Peter's U (NJ)
Weber State U (UT)

**BUSINESS OPERATIONS
SUPPORT AND SECRETARIAL
SERVICES RELATED**
Thomas Edison State U (NJ)

**CABINETMAKING AND
MILLWORK**
Utah Valley U (UT)

**CAD/CADD DRAFTING/DESIGN
TECHNOLOGY**
Academy of Art U (CA)
Ferris State U (MI)
Idaho State U (ID)
Keiser U, Fort Lauderdale (FL)
Montana Tech of The U of Montana
  (MT)
Northern Michigan U (MI)
Shawnee State U (OH)
Southern Utah U (UT)

**CARDIOPULMONARY
TECHNOLOGY**
Inter American U of Puerto Rico,
  Barranquitas Campus (PR)

**CARDIOVASCULAR
TECHNOLOGY**
Arkansas Tech U (AR)
Gwynedd Mercy U (PA)
Molloy Coll (NY)
Nebraska Methodist Coll (NE)
Pennsylvania Coll of Health Sciences
  (PA)
Polk State Coll (FL)
Sentara Coll of Health Sciences (VA)
Valencia Coll (FL)

**CARPENTRY**
Montana State U Billings (MT)
Montana Tech of The U of Montana
  (MT)
New England Inst of Technology (RI)
Southern Utah U (UT)
State U of New York Coll of
  Technology at Delhi (NY)
U of Alaska Fairbanks (AK)

**CELL BIOLOGY AND
ANATOMICAL SCIENCES
RELATED**
National U (CA)

**CERAMIC ARTS AND CERAMICS**
Palm Beach State Coll (FL)

**CHEMICAL ENGINEERING**
Brigham Young U–Idaho (ID)

**CHEMICAL PROCESS
TECHNOLOGY**
Pennsylvania Coll of Technology (PA)

**CHEMICAL TECHNOLOGY**
Ferris State U (MI)
Lawrence Technological U (MI)
State U of New York Coll of
  Agriculture and Technology at
  Cobleskill (NY)
U of Puerto Rico–Humacao (PR)
U of South Dakota (SD)

Weber State U (UT)

**CHEMISTRY**
Central Methodist U (MO)
Indiana Wesleyan U (IN)
Lindsey Wilson Coll (KY)
Ohio Dominican U (OH)
Palm Beach State Coll (FL)
Southern Arkansas U–Magnolia (AR)
U of Saint Francis (IN)
Utah Valley U (UT)
Wright State U (OH)
Wright State U–Lake Campus (OH)
York Coll of Pennsylvania (PA)

**CHILD-CARE AND SUPPORT
SERVICES MANAGEMENT**
Eastern New Mexico U (NM)
Ferris State U (MI)
Idaho State U (ID)
Polk State Coll (FL)
Post U (CT)
Purdue U Northwest (IN)
Southeast Missouri State U (MO)
State U of New York Coll of
  Agriculture and Technology at
  Cobleskill (NY)
State U of New York Coll of
  Technology at Canton (NY)
U of the Fraser Valley (BC, Canada)
Youngstown State U (OH)

**CHILD-CARE PROVISION**
American Public U System (WV)
Pennsylvania Coll of Technology (PA)

**CHILD DEVELOPMENT**
Arkansas Tech U (AR)
Evangel U (MO)
Madonna U (MI)
Midland Coll (TX)
Northern Michigan U (MI)
Ohio U (OH)
Point U (GA)
Polk State Coll (FL)
Southern Utah U (UT)
U of Sioux Falls (SD)
Weber State U (UT)
Youngstown State U (OH)

**CHINESE**
Brigham Young U–Idaho (ID)
Weber State U (UT)

**CHRISTIAN STUDIES**
Messenger Coll (TX)
Oklahoma Baptist U (OK)
Ouachita Baptist U (AR)
Regent U (VA)
Southwestern Assemblies of God U
  (TX)

**CINEMATOGRAPHY AND FILM/
VIDEO PRODUCTION**
Academy of Art U (CA)
Clayton State U (GA)
Compass Coll of Cinematic Arts (MI)
FIDM/Fashion Inst of Design &
  Merchandising, Los Angeles
  Campus (CA)
Inst of American Indian Arts (NM)
Keiser U, Fort Lauderdale (FL)
New England Inst of Technology (RI)
Valencia Coll (FL)

**CIVIL ENGINEERING
TECHNOLOGY**
Ferris State U (MI)
Idaho State U (ID)
Montana Tech of The U of Montana
  (MT)
Murray State U (KY)
New England Inst of Technology (RI)
Pennsylvania Coll of Technology (PA)
State U of New York Coll of
  Technology at Canton (NY)
U of Massachusetts Lowell (MA)
U of New Hampshire (NH)
Valencia Coll (FL)
Vermont Tech Coll (VT)
Youngstown State U (OH)

**CLASSICS AND CLASSICAL
LANGUAGES**
John Cabot U (Italy)

**CLINICAL LABORATORY
SCIENCE/MEDICAL
TECHNOLOGY**
New England Inst of Technology (RI)
Shawnee State U (OH)
U of Wisconsin–Parkside (WI)

**CLINICAL/MEDICAL
LABORATORY ASSISTANT**
Brigham Young U–Idaho (ID)
New England Inst of Technology (RI)
U of Alaska Fairbanks (AK)
U of Maine at Presque Isle (ME)

**CLINICAL/MEDICAL
LABORATORY SCIENCE AND
ALLIED PROFESSIONS RELATED**
State U of New York Coll of
  Agriculture and Technology at
  Cobleskill (NY)
Youngstown State U (OH)

**CLINICAL/MEDICAL
LABORATORY TECHNOLOGY**
Colorado Mesa U (CO)
Farmingdale State Coll (NY)
The George Washington U (DC)
Keiser U, Fort Lauderdale (FL)
Marshall U (WV)
Mount Aloysius Coll (PA)
Penn State Hazleton (PA)
Penn State Schuylkill (PA)
Rasmussen Coll Mankato (MN)
Rasmussen Coll St. Cloud (MN)
Tarleton State U (TX)
U of Maine at Presque Isle (ME)
U of Saint Francis (IN)
Weber State U (UT)
Youngstown State U (OH)

**COMMERCIAL AND
ADVERTISING ART**
Academy of Art U (CA)
California U of Pennsylvania (PA)
Fashion Inst of Technology (NY)
Mount Saint Mary's U (CA)
Northern State U (SD)
Nossi Coll of Art (TN)
Palm Beach State Coll (FL)
Pennsylvania Coll of Technology (PA)
Pratt Inst (NY)
Robert Morris U Illinois (IL)
Southern Adventist U (TN)
State U of New York Coll of
  Agriculture and Technology at
  Cobleskill (NY)

**COMMERCIAL PHOTOGRAPHY**
Fashion Inst of Technology (NY)
Nossi Coll of Art (TN)

**COMMUNICATION**
Central Penn Coll (PA)
John Cabot U (Italy)

**COMMUNICATION AND
JOURNALISM RELATED**
Immaculata U (PA)
Madonna U (MI)
Tulane U (LA)
Valparaiso U (IN)

**COMMUNICATION AND MEDIA
RELATED**
Waldorf U (IA)

**COMMUNICATION DISORDERS
SCIENCES AND SERVICES
RELATED**
Granite State Coll (NH)

**COMMUNICATIONS
TECHNOLOGIES AND SUPPORT
SERVICES RELATED**
Southern Adventist U (TN)

**COMMUNICATIONS
TECHNOLOGY**
Colorado Mesa U (CO)
U of Puerto Rico–Humacao (PR)

**COMMUNITY HEALTH AND
PREVENTIVE MEDICINE**
Alaska Pacific U (AK)
Utah Valley U (UT)

**COMMUNITY ORGANIZATION
AND ADVOCACY**
Metropolitan Coll of New York (NY)
State U of New York Empire State
  Coll (NY)
The U of Akron (OH)
U of Alaska Fairbanks (AK)
U of New Hampshire (NH)
Wright State U (OH)
Wright State U–Lake Campus (OH)

**COMPARATIVE LITERATURE**
John Cabot U (Italy)

Palm Beach State Coll (FL)

**COMPUTER AND
INFORMATION SCIENCES**
Beacon Coll (FL)
Black Hills State U (SD)
Coleman U, San Diego (CA)
Columbia Coll (MO)
Faulkner U (AL)
Husson U (ME)
Indiana Wesleyan U (IN)
Inter American U of Puerto Rico,
  Barranquitas Campus (PR)
Inter American U of Puerto Rico,
  Fajardo Campus (PR)
Lincoln U (MO)
Manchester U (IN)
Montana State U Billings (MT)
New England Inst of Technology (RI)
Penn State Schuylkill (PA)
Rogers State U (OK)
St. John's U (NY)
Southeastern Oklahoma State U
  (OK)
State U of New York Coll of
  Agriculture and Technology at
  Cobleskill (NY)
Troy U (AL)
Tulane U (LA)
Union Coll (NE)
The U of Toledo (OH)
Utah Valley U (UT)
Webber International U (FL)
Youngstown State U (OH)

**COMPUTER AND
INFORMATION SCIENCES AND
SUPPORT SERVICES RELATED**
Montana State U Billings (MT)
New York U (NY)
Pace U (NY)
Pace U, Pleasantville Campus (NY)
Palm Beach State Coll (FL)
Purdue U Northwest (IN)
U of the Potomac (DC)

**COMPUTER AND
INFORMATION SCIENCES
RELATED**
Limestone Coll (SC)
Lindsey Wilson Coll (KY)
Madonna U (MI)

**COMPUTER AND
INFORMATION SYSTEMS
SECURITY**
Arkansas Tech U (AR)
Coleman U, San Diego (CA)
Davenport U, Grand Rapids (MI)
Ferris State U (MI)
St. John's U (NY)
Sullivan U (KY)
U of Maine at Fort Kent (ME)
U of the Potomac (DC)

**COMPUTER ENGINEERING**
The U of Scranton (PA)

**COMPUTER ENGINEERING
TECHNOLOGY**
California U of Pennsylvania (PA)
Northern Michigan U (MI)
Penn State New Kensington (PA)
Polk State Coll (FL)
U of Hartford (CT)
Valencia Coll (FL)
Vermont Tech Coll (VT)
Weber State U (UT)

**COMPUTER GRAPHICS**
Academy of Art U (CA)
Coleman U, San Diego (CA)
EDP U of Puerto Rico (PR)
Indiana Tech (IN)
Purdue U (IN)
Valencia Coll (FL)

**COMPUTER/INFORMATION
TECHNOLOGY SERVICES
ADMINISTRATION RELATED**
Limestone Coll (SC)
Pennsylvania Coll of Technology (PA)

**COMPUTER INSTALLATION
AND REPAIR TECHNOLOGY**
Inter American U of Puerto Rico,
  Aguadilla Campus (PR)
Inter American U of Puerto Rico,
  Bayamón Campus (PR)
Inter American U of Puerto Rico,
  Fajardo Campus (PR)
U of Alaska Fairbanks (AK)

**COMPUTER PROGRAMMING**
Black Hills State U (SD)
Caribbean U (PR)
Champlain Coll (VT)
Coll of Staten Island of the City U of
  New York (NY)
Columbia Central U, Caguas (PR)
ECPI U, Virginia Beach (VA)
EDP U of Puerto Rico (PR)
Limestone Coll (SC)
Medgar Evers Coll of the City U of
  New York (NY)
Midland Coll (TX)
New England Inst of Technology (RI)
Palm Beach State Coll (FL)
Polk State Coll (FL)
Rasmussen Coll Fargo (ND)
Saint Francis U (PA)
The U of Toledo (OH)
Youngstown State U (OH)

**COMPUTER PROGRAMMING
RELATED**
Inter American U of Puerto Rico,
  Metropolitan Campus (PR)

**COMPUTER PROGRAMMING
(SPECIFIC APPLICATIONS)**
Academy of Art U (CA)
Central Penn Coll (PA)
Kent State U at Geauga (OH)
Palm Beach State Coll (FL)
Valencia Coll (FL)

**COMPUTER SCIENCE**
Black Hills State U (SD)
Carroll Coll (MT)
Central Methodist U (MO)
Creighton U (NE)
Endicott Coll (MA)
Faulkner U (AL)
Felician U (NJ)
Florida National U (FL)
Hawai`i Pacific U (HI)
Inter American U of Puerto Rico,
  Aguadilla Campus (PR)
Inter American U of Puerto Rico,
  Barranquitas Campus (PR)
Inter American U of Puerto Rico,
  Bayamón Campus (PR)
Inter American U of Puerto Rico, San
  Germán Campus (PR)
Madonna U (MI)
New England Inst of Technology (RI)
Northern Vermont U–Lyndon (VT)
Palm Beach State Coll (FL)
Southwest Baptist U (MO)
The U of Findlay (OH)
U of Maine at Fort Kent (ME)
U of Management and Technology
  (VA)
U of the Virgin Islands (VI)
Utah Valley U (UT)
Walsh U (OH)
Weber State U (UT)

**COMPUTER SOFTWARE AND
MEDIA APPLICATIONS
RELATED**
Academy of Art U (CA)
Champlain Coll (VT)
Hobe Sound Bible Coll (FL)
Pace U (NY)
Pace U, Pleasantville Campus (NY)
Polytechnic U of Puerto Rico (PR)

**COMPUTER SOFTWARE
ENGINEERING**
Rasmussen Coll Bloomington (MN)
Rasmussen Coll Brooklyn Park (MN)
Rasmussen Coll Eagan (MN)
Rasmussen Coll Fargo (ND)
Rasmussen Coll Mankato (MN)
Rasmussen Coll New Port Richey
  (FL)
Rasmussen Coll Ocala (FL)
Rasmussen Coll St. Cloud (MN)
Vermont Tech Coll (VT)

**COMPUTER SOFTWARE
TECHNOLOGY**
Oregon Inst of Technology (OR)

**COMPUTER SUPPORT
SPECIALIST**
Sullivan U (KY)
U of Alaska Fairbanks (AK)

**COMPUTER SYSTEMS
ANALYSIS**
Caribbean U (PR)
Davenport U, Grand Rapids (MI)

The U of Akron (OH)

## COMPUTER SYSTEMS NETWORKING AND TELECOMMUNICATIONS
Coleman U, San Diego (CA)
Colorado Mesa U (CO)
Davenport U, Grand Rapids (MI)
Idaho State U (ID)
Indiana Tech (IN)
Montana Tech of The U of Montana (MT)
Pace U (NY)
Pace U, Pleasantville Campus (NY)
Robert Morris U Illinois (IL)
The U of Akron (OH)
Weber State U (UT)

## COMPUTER TECHNOLOGY/ COMPUTER SYSTEMS TECHNOLOGY
ECPI U, Virginia Beach (VA)
Excelsior Coll (NY)
New England Inst of Technology (RI)

## CONCRETE FINISHING
Pennsylvania Coll of Technology (PA)

## CONSTRUCTION ENGINEERING TECHNOLOGY
Ferris State U (MI)
Lawrence Technological U (MI)
Pennsylvania Coll of Technology (PA)
Southern Utah U (UT)
State U of New York Coll of Technology at Delhi (NY)
The U of Akron (OH)
U of Montana (MT)
Valencia Coll (FL)
Vermont Tech Coll (VT)

## CONSTRUCTION MANAGEMENT
John Brown U (AR)
U of Alaska Fairbanks (AK)
Utah Valley U (UT)
Vermont Tech Coll (VT)
Weber State U (UT)
Wentworth Inst of Technology (MA)

## CONSTRUCTION TRADES
Colorado Mesa U (CO)
Liberty U (VA)
Northern Michigan U (MI)

## CONSUMER MERCHANDISING/ RETAILING MANAGEMENT
Academy of Art U (CA)

## COOKING AND RELATED CULINARY ARTS
Colorado Mesa U (CO)
Southern Utah U (UT)

## CORRECTIONS
California U of Pennsylvania (PA)
Langston U (OK)
Mount Aloysius Coll (PA)
Youngstown State U (OH)

## CORRECTIONS AND CRIMINAL JUSTICE RELATED
Cameron U (OK)
EDP U of Puerto Rico (PR)
EDP U of Puerto Rico–San Sebastian (PR)
Inter American U of Puerto Rico, Aguadilla Campus (PR)
Inter American U of Puerto Rico, Metropolitan Campus (PR)
Rasmussen Coll Bloomington (MN)
Rasmussen Coll Brooklyn Park (MN)
Rasmussen Coll Eagan (MN)
Rasmussen Coll Mankato (MN)
Rasmussen Coll New Port Richey (FL)
Rasmussen Coll Ocala (FL)
Rasmussen Coll Rockford (IL)
Rasmussen Coll St. Cloud (MN)

## COSMETOLOGY
Midland Coll (TX)

## COSTUME DESIGN
FIDM/Fashion Inst of Design & Merchandising, Los Angeles Campus (CA)

## COUNSELING PSYCHOLOGY
Hobe Sound Bible Coll (FL)

## CREATIVE WRITING
Inst of American Indian Arts (NM)
John Cabot U (Italy)
National U (CA)
Trevecca Nazarene U (TN)

## CRIMINALISTICS AND CRIMINAL SCIENCE
Faulkner U (AL)
Keiser U, Fort Lauderdale (FL)

## CRIMINAL JUSTICE/LAW ENFORCEMENT ADMINISTRATION
Anderson U (IN)
Arkansas Tech U (AR)
Bemidji State U (MN)
Campbellsville U (KY)
Clarion U of Pennsylvania (PA)
Colorado Mesa U (CO)
Columbia Coll (MO)
Excelsior Coll (NY)
Hannibal-LaGrange U (MO)
Hawai'i Pacific U (HI)
Husson U (ME)
Inter American U of Puerto Rico, Barranquitas Campus (PR)
Keiser U, Fort Lauderdale (FL)
Lincoln Coll of New England, Southington (CT)
Lincoln U (MO)
Lock Haven U of Pennsylvania (PA)
Mansfield U of Pennsylvania (PA)
New England Inst of Technology (RI)
Northern Michigan U (MI)
Palm Beach State Coll (FL)
Peirce Coll (PA)
Polk State Coll (FL)
Regent U (VA)
Roger Williams U (RI)
St. John's U (NY)
Salve Regina U (RI)
Thomas U (GA)
Tiffin U (OH)
Toccoa Falls Coll (GA)
Trevecca Nazarene U (TN)
Trine U (IN)
U of Maine at Fort Kent (ME)
U of Maine at Presque Isle (ME)
U of Management and Technology (VA)
Utah Valley U (UT)
Valencia Coll (FL)
Webber International U (FL)
York Coll of Pennsylvania (PA)
Youngstown State U (OH)

## CRIMINAL JUSTICE/POLICE SCIENCE
Caribbean U (PR)
Columbia Southern U (AL)
Farmingdale State Coll (NY)
Ferris State U (MI)
Georgia Southern U–Armstrong Campus (GA)
Hilbert Coll (NY)
Idaho State U (ID)
Inter American U of Puerto Rico, Barranquitas Campus (PR)
Inter American U of Puerto Rico, Metropolitan Campus (PR)
Midland Coll (TX)
Missouri Western State U (MO)
Palm Beach State Coll (FL)
Rasmussen Coll Bloomington (MN)
Rasmussen Coll Brooklyn Park (MN)
Rasmussen Coll Eagan (MN)
Rasmussen Coll Mankato (MN)
Rasmussen Coll St. Cloud (MN)
Rogers State U (OK)
Southern Utah U (UT)
State U of New York Coll of Technology at Canton (NY)
Sullivan U (KY)
The U of Akron (OH)
U of New Haven (CT)
U of the Virgin Islands (VI)
Youngstown State U (OH)

## CRIMINAL JUSTICE/SAFETY
American Public U System (WV)
Arkansas Tech U (AR)
Ball State U (IN)
Bethel Coll (IN)
Calumet Coll of Saint Joseph (IN)
Cazenovia Coll (NY)
Central Penn Coll (PA)

Chaminade U of Honolulu (HI)
Colegio Universitario de San Juan, San Juan (PR)
Columbus State U (GA)
Dean Coll (MA)
Defiance Coll (OH)
Eastern Nazarene Coll (MA)
Endicott Coll (MA)
Fisher Coll (MA)
Florida National U (FL)
Gannon U (PA)
Hilbert Coll (NY)
Husson U (ME)
Idaho State U (ID)
Indiana Tech (IN)
Indiana Wesleyan U (IN)
Inter American U of Puerto Rico, Aguadilla Campus (PR)
Inter American U of Puerto Rico, Barranquitas Campus (PR)
Inter American U of Puerto Rico, Fajardo Campus (PR)
Kansas Wesleyan U (KS)
Keiser U, Fort Lauderdale (FL)
Kent State U at Stark (OH)
Liberty U (VA)
Madonna U (MI)
Manchester U (IN)
New Mexico State U (NM)
Northern Michigan U (MI)
Oakland City U (IN)
Penn State Altoona (PA)
Point U (GA)
Post U (CT)
State U of New York Coll of Technology at Delhi (NY)
U of Pikeville (KY)
U of Saint Francis (IN)
The U of Scranton (PA)
U of the Fraser Valley (BC, Canada)
Waldorf U (IA)
Weber State U (UT)
Youngstown State U (OH)

## CRIMINOLOGY
LeTourneau U (TX)

## CRISIS/EMERGENCY/DISASTER MANAGEMENT
Eastern New Mexico U (NM)
Waldorf U (IA)

## CRITICAL INFRASTRUCTURE PROTECTION
Idaho State U (ID)

## CROP PRODUCTION
North Carolina State U (NC)
U of Massachusetts Amherst (MA)

## CULINARY ARTS
Bob Jones U (SC)
Coll of Coastal Georgia (GA)
The Culinary Inst of America (NY)
Eastern New Mexico U (NM)
ECPI U, Virginia Beach (VA)
Inter American U of Puerto Rico, Barranquitas Campus (PR)
Keiser U, Fort Lauderdale (FL)
Pennsylvania Coll of Technology (PA)
Robert Morris U Illinois (IL)
Southern Adventist U (TN)
State U of New York Coll of Agriculture and Technology at Cobleskill (NY)
State U of New York Coll of Technology at Delhi (NY)
Sullivan U (KY)
The U of Akron (OH)
U of Alaska Fairbanks (AK)
Utah Valley U (UT)
Valencia Coll (FL)

## CULINARY ARTS RELATED
U of New Hampshire (NH)

## CYBER/COMPUTER FORENSICS AND COUNTERTERRORISM
Sullivan U (KY)

## DAIRY SCIENCE
Vermont Tech Coll (VT)

## DANCE
Dean Coll (MA)
U of Saint Francis (IN)
Utah Valley U (UT)

## DATA ENTRY/ MICROCOMPUTER APPLICATIONS
Davenport U, Grand Rapids (MI)

## DATA MODELING/ WAREHOUSING AND DATABASE ADMINISTRATION
American Public U System (WV)
Limestone Coll (SC)

## DATA PROCESSING AND DATA PROCESSING TECHNOLOGY
American Public U System (WV)
Campbellsville U (KY)
Hallmark U (TX)
Montana State U Billings (MT)
Pace U, Pleasantville Campus (NY)
Palm Beach State Coll (FL)
Youngstown State U (OH)

## DENTAL ASSISTING
ECPI U, Virginia Beach (VA)
Lincoln Coll of New England, Southington (CT)
U of Alaska Fairbanks (AK)
U of Southern Indiana (IN)

## DENTAL HYGIENE
Farmingdale State Coll (NY)
Ferris State U (MI)
Florida National U (FL)
Indiana U–Purdue U Indianapolis (IN)
Lincoln Coll of New England, Southington (CT)
New York U (NY)
Palm Beach State Coll (FL)
Pennsylvania Coll of Technology (PA)
Rutgers U–New Brunswick (NJ)
Shawnee State U (OH)
Southern Adventist U (TN)
State U of New York Coll of Technology at Canton (NY)
U of Alaska Fairbanks (AK)
U of Bridgeport (CT)
U of New Haven (CT)
U of Pittsburgh (PA)
Utah Valley U (UT)
Valencia Coll (FL)
Vermont Tech Coll (VT)
Weber State U (UT)
Western Kentucky U (KY)

## DENTAL LABORATORY TECHNOLOGY
Florida National U (FL)
Louisiana State U Health Sciences Center (LA)

## DENTAL SERVICES AND ALLIED PROFESSIONS RELATED
Valdosta State U (GA)

## DESIGN AND APPLIED ARTS RELATED
Bethel Coll (IN)
U of Maine at Presque Isle (ME)

## DESIGN AND VISUAL COMMUNICATIONS
FIDM/Fashion Inst of Design & Merchandising, Los Angeles Campus (CA)
FIDM/Fashion Inst of Design & Merchandising, San Francisco Campus (CA)
Keiser U, Fort Lauderdale (FL)
U of Saint Francis (IN)
Utah Valley U (UT)

## DESKTOP PUBLISHING AND DIGITAL IMAGING DESIGN
New England Inst of Technology (RI)

## DIAGNOSTIC MEDICAL SONOGRAPHY AND ULTRASOUND TECHNOLOGY
Adventist U of Health Sciences (FL)
ECPI U, Virginia Beach (VA)
Ferris State U (MI)
Florida National U (FL)
Keiser U, Fort Lauderdale (FL)
Midland Coll (TX)
Nebraska Methodist Coll (NE)
Pennsylvania Coll of Health Sciences (PA)
Polk State Coll (FL)
St. Catherine U (MN)

The U of Findlay (OH)
Valencia Coll (FL)

## DIESEL MECHANICS TECHNOLOGY
Idaho State U (ID)
Midland Coll (TX)
Montana State U Billings (MT)
Pennsylvania Coll of Technology (PA)
State U of New York Coll of Agriculture and Technology at Cobleskill (NY)
U of Montana (MT)
Utah Valley U (UT)
Vermont Tech Coll (VT)
Weber State U (UT)

## DIETETICS
Ferris State U (MI)
Northwest Missouri State U (MO)

## DIETETIC TECHNOLOGY
Youngstown State U (OH)

## DIETITIAN ASSISTANT
Youngstown State U (OH)

## DIGITAL ARTS
Academy of Art U (CA)
Oakland City U (IN)

## DIGITAL COMMUNICATION AND MEDIA/MULTIMEDIA
Lynn U (FL)
Vaughn Coll of Aeronautics and Technology (NY)

## DIRECT ENTRY MIDWIFERY
Midwives Coll of Utah (UT)

## DISPUTE RESOLUTION
Life U (GA)

## DIVINITY/MINISTRY
The Baptist Coll of Florida (FL)
Johnson U (TN)
Messenger Coll (TX)
Nebraska Christian Coll of Hope International U (NE)
Ohio Christian U (OH)
Southeastern U (FL)
U of Valley Forge (PA)

## DRAFTING AND DESIGN TECHNOLOGY
Academy of Art U (CA)
Black Hills State U (SD)
California U of Pennsylvania (PA)
Caribbean U (PR)
Langston U (OK)
LeTourneau U (TX)
Lincoln U (MO)
Montana State U Billings (MT)
Palm Beach State Coll (FL)
The U of Akron (OH)
U of Alaska Fairbanks (AK)
Utah Valley U (UT)
Valencia Coll (FL)
Weber State U (UT)
Youngstown State U (OH)

## DRAFTING/DESIGN ENGINEERING TECHNOLOGIES RELATED
Pennsylvania Coll of Technology (PA)
Weber State U (UT)

## DRAMATIC/THEATER ARTS
Adams State U (CO)
Dean Coll (MA)
Palm Beach State Coll (FL)
Pine Manor Coll (MA)
U of the Fraser Valley (BC, Canada)
Utah Valley U (UT)

## DRAWING
Pratt Inst (NY)

## EARLY CHILDHOOD EDUCATION
Adams State U (CO)
Becker Coll (MA)
Bethel Coll (IN)
Bob Jones U (SC)
Chaminade U of Honolulu (HI)
Clarion U of Pennsylvania (PA)
Coll of Saint Mary (NE)
Cornerstone U (MI)
Dean Coll (MA)

Eastern Nazarene Coll (MA)
Fisher Coll (MA)
Gannon U (PA)
Granite State Coll (NH)
Liberty U (VA)
Lindsey Wilson Coll (KY)
Manchester U (IN)
Maranatha Baptist U (WI)
Mount Aloysius Coll (PA)
Mount Saint Mary's U (CA)
Nova Southeastern U (FL)
Oakland City U (IN)
Pine Manor Coll (MA)
Rasmussen Coll Bloomington (MN)
Rasmussen Coll Brooklyn Park (MN)
Rasmussen Coll Eagan (MN)
Rasmussen Coll Fargo (ND)
Rasmussen Coll Mankato (MN)
Rasmussen Coll New Port Richey (FL)
Rasmussen Coll Ocala (FL)
Rasmussen Coll Rockford (IL)
Rasmussen Coll St. Cloud (MN)
Rust Coll (MS)
Southwestern Assemblies of God U (TX)
U of Alaska Fairbanks (AK)
U of Cincinnati (OH)
The U of Montana Western (MT)
U of Providence (MT)
U of the Virgin Islands (VI)
U of Valley Forge (PA)
Utah Valley U (UT)
Wayland Baptist U (TX)
Western Kentucky U (KY)
Wilmington U (DE)

**E-COMMERCE**
Limestone Coll (SC)

**ECONOMICS**
Bethel Coll (IN)
John Cabot U (Italy)
Palm Beach State Coll (FL)
U of Wisconsin–Parkside (WI)

**EDUCATION**
Corban U (OR)
Eastern Oregon U (OR)
Florida National U (FL)
Lincoln Christian U (IL)
Montana State U Billings (MT)
Ohio Christian U (OH)
Palm Beach State Coll (FL)
Saint Francis U (PA)
Southwestern Assemblies of God U (TX)
State U of New York Empire State Coll (NY)
Touro U Worldwide (CA)

**EDUCATION (MULTIPLE LEVELS)**
Coll of Coastal Georgia (GA)
Midland Coll (TX)

**EDUCATION RELATED**
Colorado Christian U (CO)
Liberty U (VA)
The U of Akron (OH)
Weber State U (UT)

**EDUCATION (SPECIFIC SUBJECT AREAS) RELATED**
Penn State U Park (PA)
U of New Hampshire (NH)

**ELECTRICAL AND ELECTRONIC ENGINEERING TECHNOLOGIES RELATED**
Colegio Universitario de San Juan, San Juan (PR)
Northern Michigan U (MI)
Rochester Inst of Technology (NY)
Thomas Edison State U (NJ)
Vaughn Coll of Aeronautics and Technology (NY)
Youngstown State U (OH)

**ELECTRICAL AND ELECTRONICS ENGINEERING**
New England Inst of Technology (RI)
The U of Scranton (PA)

**ELECTRICAL AND POWER TRANSMISSION INSTALLATION**
Colorado Mesa U (CO)
Polk State Coll (FL)
State U of New York Coll of Technology at Delhi (NY)

**ELECTRICAL, ELECTRONIC AND COMMUNICATIONS ENGINEERING TECHNOLOGY**
Brigham Young U–Idaho (ID)
California U of Pennsylvania (PA)
Colegio Universitario de San Juan, San Juan (PR)
Hallmark U (TX)
Idaho State U (ID)
Inter American U of Puerto Rico, Aguadilla Campus (PR)
Inter American U of Puerto Rico, San Germán Campus (PR)
Langston U (OK)
Northern Michigan U (MI)
Palm Beach State Coll (FL)
Penn State Altoona (PA)
Penn State Berks (PA)
Penn State Brandywine (PA)
Penn State Erie, The Behrend Coll (PA)
Penn State Hazleton (PA)
Penn State New Kensington (PA)
Penn State Schuylkill (PA)
Penn State Shenango (PA)
Penn State Wilkes-Barre (PA)
Penn State Worthington Scranton (PA)
Penn State York (PA)
Pennsylvania Coll of Technology (PA)
Purdue U (IN)
State U of New York Coll of Technology at Canton (NY)
State U of New York Coll of Technology at Delhi (NY)
The U of Akron (OH)
U of Hartford (CT)
U of Massachusetts Lowell (MA)
U of Montana (MT)
U of Puerto Rico–Humacao (PR)
Vermont Tech Coll (VT)
Weber State U (UT)
Youngstown State U (OH)

**ELECTRICAL/ELECTRONICS EQUIPMENT INSTALLATION AND REPAIR**
Colegio Universitario de San Juan, San Juan (PR)
New England Inst of Technology (RI)
Pittsburg State U (KS)

**ELECTRICAL/ELECTRONICS MAINTENANCE AND REPAIR TECHNOLOGY RELATED**
Colegio Universitario de San Juan, San Juan (PR)

**ELECTRICIAN**
Pennsylvania Coll of Technology (PA)
Weber State U (UT)

**ELECTROCARDIOGRAPH TECHNOLOGY**
Pennsylvania Coll of Health Sciences (PA)

**ELECTROMECHANICAL AND INSTRUMENTATION AND MAINTENANCE TECHNOLOGIES RELATED**
Excelsior Coll (NY)

**ELECTROMECHANICAL TECHNOLOGY**
Excelsior Coll (NY)
John Brown U (AR)
Midland Coll (TX)
Northern Michigan U (MI)
Pennsylvania Coll of Technology (PA)
Shawnee State U (OH)
State U of New York Coll of Technology at Delhi (NY)

**ELEMENTARY EDUCATION**
Adams State U (CO)
Brenau U (GA)
Bryn Athyn Coll of the New Church (PA)
Ferris State U (MI)
Lynn U (FL)
New Mexico Highlands U (NM)
Palm Beach State Coll (FL)
Rogers State U (OK)
Saint Mary-of-the-Woods Coll (IN)
Vanguard U of Southern California (CA)

**EMERGENCY MEDICAL TECHNOLOGY (EMT PARAMEDIC)**
Arkansas Tech U (AR)

Colorado Mesa U (CO)
Creighton U (NE)
ECPI U, Virginia Beach (VA)
EDP U of Puerto Rico (PR)
EDP U of Puerto Rico–San Sebastian (PR)
Idaho State U (ID)
Indiana U–Purdue U Indianapolis (IN)
Midland Coll (TX)
Montana State U Billings (MT)
New England Inst of Technology (RI)
Oregon Inst of Technology (OR)
Pennsylvania Coll of Technology (PA)
Polk State Coll (FL)
Purdue U Northwest (IN)
Rogers State U (OK)
Shawnee State U (OH)
Southwest Baptist U (MO)
State U of New York Coll of Agriculture and Technology at Cobleskill (NY)
The U of Akron (OH)
U of Alaska Fairbanks (AK)
U of New Haven (CT)
U of Sioux Falls (SD)
The U of West Alabama (AL)
Valencia Coll (FL)
Weber State U (UT)
Youngstown State U (OH)

**ENERGY MANAGEMENT AND SYSTEMS TECHNOLOGY**
Idaho State U (ID)
Montana State U Billings (MT)
U of Montana (MT)

**ENGINEERING**
Brescia U (KY)
Brigham Young U–Idaho (ID)
Cameron U (OK)
Coll of Staten Island of the City U of New York (NY)
Geneva Coll (PA)
Lindsey Wilson Coll (KY)
Southern Adventist U (TN)
State U of New York Coll of Technology at Canton (NY)
Union Coll (NE)
Weber State U (UT)

**ENGINEERING/INDUSTRIAL MANAGEMENT**
U of Management and Technology (VA)

**ENGINEERING SCIENCE**
Rochester Inst of Technology (NY)

**ENGINEERING TECHNOLOGIES AND ENGINEERING RELATED**
Excelsior Coll (NY)
Rogers State U (OK)
State U of New York Coll of Agriculture and Technology at Cobleskill (NY)
State U of New York Coll of Technology at Canton (NY)
State U of New York Maritime Coll (NY)

**ENGINEERING TECHNOLOGY**
Austin Peay State U (TN)
Brescia U (KY)
Brigham Young U–Idaho (ID)
Kansas State U (KS)
Lawrence Technological U (MI)
Lincoln U (MO)
Michigan Technological U (MI)
Morehead State U (KY)
National U (CA)
Northwestern State U of Louisiana (LA)
Polk State Coll (FL)
Trine U (IN)
Wentworth Inst of Technology (MA)
Wright State U (OH)
Wright State U–Lake Campus (OH)
Youngstown State U (OH)

**ENGLISH**
Bryn Athyn Coll of the New Church (PA)
Calumet Coll of Saint Joseph (IN)
Carroll Coll (MT)
Central Methodist U (MO)
Dean Coll (MA)
Felician U (NJ)
Hannibal-LaGrange U (MO)
Immaculata U (PA)
Indiana Wesleyan U (IN)
John Cabot U (Italy)
Madonna U (MI)

Palm Beach State Coll (FL)
Pine Manor Coll (MA)
Southwestern Assemblies of God U (TX)
Utah Valley U (UT)

**ENGLISH AS A SECOND/ FOREIGN LANGUAGE (TEACHING)**
Cornerstone U (MI)
Southwestern Assemblies of God U (TX)
Suffolk U (MA)

**ENGLISH LANGUAGE AND LITERATURE RELATED**
John Cabot U (Italy)
State U of New York Empire State Coll (NY)

**ENTREPRENEURSHIP**
Central Penn Coll (PA)
Inter American U of Puerto Rico, Barranquitas Campus (PR)
John Cabot U (Italy)
Missouri Valley Coll (MO)
The U of Findlay (OH)

**ENVIRONMENTAL CONTROL TECHNOLOGIES RELATED**
Montana Tech of The U of Montana (MT)

**ENVIRONMENTAL SCIENCE**
Georgia Gwinnett Coll (GA)
Madonna U (MI)
U of Saint Francis (IN)

**ENVIRONMENTAL STUDIES**
Columbia Coll (MO)
Dean Coll (MA)
State U of New York Coll of Agriculture and Technology at Cobleskill (NY)

**EQUESTRIAN STUDIES**
Delaware Valley U (PA)
Saint Mary-of-the-Woods Coll (IN)
The U of Findlay (OH)
U of Massachusetts Amherst (MA)
The U of Montana Western (MT)

**EXECUTIVE ASSISTANT/ EXECUTIVE SECRETARY**
Sullivan U (KY)

**EXPLOSIVE ORDINANCE/BOMB DISPOSAL**
American Public U System (WV)

**FAMILY AND CONSUMER SCIENCES/HUMAN SCIENCES**
Eastern New Mexico U (NM)
Palm Beach State Coll (FL)

**FASHION AND FABRIC CONSULTING**
Academy of Art U (CA)

**FASHION/APPAREL DESIGN**
Academy of Art U (CA)
EDP U of Puerto Rico (PR)
EDP U of Puerto Rico–San Sebastian (PR)
Fashion Inst of Technology (NY)
FIDM/Fashion Inst of Design & Merchandising, San Francisco Campus (CA)
Palm Beach State Coll (FL)
Parsons School of Design (NY)

**FASHION MERCHANDISING**
Academy of Art U (CA)
Fashion Inst of Technology (NY)
FIDM/Fashion Inst of Design & Merchandising, Los Angeles Campus (CA)
Fisher Coll (MA)
Immaculata U (PA)
LIM Coll (NY)
Palm Beach State Coll (FL)
Parsons School of Design (NY)
The U of Akron (OH)
U of Bridgeport (CT)

**FASHION MODELING**
Fashion Inst of Technology (NY)

**FILM/CINEMA/VIDEO STUDIES**
Fashion Inst of Technology (NY)
Southeastern U (FL)

Palm Beach State Coll (FL)
Pine Manor Coll (MA)
Southwestern Assemblies of God U (TX)
Utah Valley U (UT)

**FINANCE**
Davenport U, Grand Rapids (MI)
Hawai`i Pacific U (HI)
Indiana Wesleyan U (IN)
John Cabot U (Italy)
Palm Beach State Coll (FL)
Saint Peter's U (NJ)
The U of Findlay (OH)
Youngstown State U (OH)

**FINE ARTS RELATED**
Academy of Art U (CA)
Bryn Athyn Coll of the New Church (PA)
Pennsylvania Coll of Technology (PA)
Saint Francis U (PA)

**FINE/STUDIO ARTS**
Academy of Art U (CA)
Adams State U (CO)
Beacon Coll (FL)
Bryn Athyn Coll of the New Church (PA)
Fashion Inst of Technology (NY)
Illinois State U (IL)
Inst of American Indian Arts (NM)
Lindsey Wilson Coll (KY)
Pratt Inst (NY)
U of Saint Francis (IN)
Villa Maria Coll (NY)
York Coll of Pennsylvania (PA)

**FIRE PREVENTION AND SAFETY TECHNOLOGY**
Montana State U Billings (MT)
Polk State Coll (FL)
The U of Akron (OH)
U of New Haven (CT)
Valencia Coll (FL)

**FIRE SCIENCE/FIREFIGHTING**
American Public U System (WV)
Columbia Southern U (AL)
Idaho State U (ID)
Keiser U, Fort Lauderdale (FL)
Madonna U (MI)
Midland Coll (TX)
Palm Beach State Coll (FL)
Polk State Coll (FL)
Southwestern Adventist U (TX)
U of Alaska Fairbanks (AK)
U of Cincinnati (OH)
Utah Valley U (UT)
Vermont Tech Coll (VT)

**FIRE SERVICES ADMINISTRATION**
Columbia Coll (MO)
Waldorf U (IA)

**FISHING AND FISHERIES SCIENCES AND MANAGEMENT**
State U of New York Coll of Agriculture and Technology at Cobleskill (NY)

**FOODS AND NUTRITION RELATED**
U of Guelph (ON, Canada)

**FOOD SERVICE AND DINING ROOM MANAGEMENT**
U of Montana (MT)

**FOOD SERVICE SYSTEMS ADMINISTRATION**
Inter American U of Puerto Rico, Aguadilla Campus (PR)
Northern Michigan U (MI)
Wright State U (OH)
Wright State U–Lake Campus (OH)

**FOODS, NUTRITION, AND WELLNESS**
Huntington Coll of Health Sciences (TN)
Madonna U (MI)
The New School for Public Engagement (NY)
Palm Beach State Coll (FL)
Southern Adventist U (TN)
Youngstown State U (OH)

**FOREIGN LANGUAGES AND LITERATURES**
Bryn Athyn Coll of the New Church (PA)

**FOREIGN LANGUAGES RELATED**
U of Alaska Fairbanks (AK)

## FORENSIC SCIENCE AND TECHNOLOGY
Keiser U, Fort Lauderdale (FL)

## FOREST TECHNOLOGY
Pennsylvania Coll of Technology (PA)
State U of New York Coll of Environmental Science and Forestry (NY)
U of Maine at Fort Kent (ME)
U of New Hampshire (NH)

## FRENCH
Weber State U (UT)

## FUNERAL SERVICE AND MORTUARY SCIENCE
Ferris State U (MI)
Lincoln Coll of New England, Southington (CT)

## GAME AND INTERACTIVE MEDIA DESIGN
Academy of Art U (CA)
New England Inst of Technology (RI)

## GENERAL STUDIES
Adventist U of Health Sciences (FL)
Alverno Coll (WI)
American Baptist Coll (TN)
American Public U System (WV)
Arkansas Tech U (AR)
Asbury U (KY)
The Baptist Coll of Florida (FL)
Barclay Coll (KS)
Belhaven U (MS)
Bethel Coll (IN)
Black Hills State U (SD)
Bluefield Coll (VA)
Brandman U (CA)
Brenau U (GA)
Brewton-Parker Coll (GA)
California Christian Coll (CA)
Cameron U (OK)
Cardinal Stritch U (WI)
Carson-Newman U (TN)
Chaminade U of Honolulu (HI)
Christian Brothers U (TN)
Colorado Christian U (CO)
Columbia Coll (MO)
Columbia Southern U (AL)
Concordia U, St. Paul (MN)
Criswell Coll (TX)
Crowley's Ridge Coll (AR)
Dakota State U (SD)
Dean Coll (MA)
Eastern Mennonite U (VA)
Ferris State U (MI)
Fisher Coll (MA)
Franciscan Missionaries of Our Lady U (LA)
Geneva Coll (PA)
Granite State Coll (NH)
Hampton U (VA)
Hawai`i Pacific U (HI)
Hope International U (CA)
Idaho State U (ID)
Indiana Tech (IN)
Indiana Wesleyan U (IN)
John Brown U (AR)
King U (TN)
Langston U (OK)
La Salle U (PA)
Lawrence Technological U (MI)
Lincoln Christian U (IL)
Lincoln Coll (IL)
Lipscomb U (TN)
Madonna U (MI)
McNeese State U (LA)
Mercy Coll of Ohio (OH)
Mid-Atlantic Christian U (NC)
Midland Coll (TX)
Montana State U Billings (MT)
Morehead State U (KY)
Mount Aloysius Coll (PA)
Mount Marty Coll (SD)
Mount Vernon Nazarene U (OH)
National U (CA)
New Mexico Inst of Mining and Technology (NM)
Northern Kentucky U (KY)
Northern Michigan U (MI)
Northern State U (SD)
Northern Vermont U–Lyndon (VT)
Northwest Christian U (OR)
Northwestern State U of Louisiana (LA)
Oakland City U (IN)

The Ohio State U at Lima (OH)
The Ohio State U at Mansfield (OH)
The Ohio State U at Marion (OH)
The Ohio State U at Newark (OH)
Ouachita Baptist U (AR)
Pace U (NY)
Pace U, Pleasantville Campus (NY)
Peirce Coll (PA)
Point U (GA)
Regent U (VA)
Rider U (NJ)
Sacred Heart U (CT)
Shawnee State U (OH)
Shorter U (GA)
Southeastern U (FL)
Southern Arkansas U–Magnolia (AR)
Southern Utah U (UT)
Southwest Baptist U (MO)
Southwestern Adventist U (TX)
Southwestern Assemblies of God U (TX)
Southwestern Coll (KS)
State U of New York Coll of Technology at Canton (NY)
State U of New York Coll of Technology at Delhi (NY)
Tiffin U (OH)
Toccoa Falls Coll (GA)
Trevecca Nazarene U (TN)
U of Bridgeport (CT)
U of Central Arkansas (AR)
U of Hartford (CT)
U of La Verne (CA)
U of Louisiana at Monroe (LA)
U of Maine at Fort Kent (ME)
U of Management and Technology (VA)
U of Mobile (AL)
U of Montana (MT)
U of Saint Francis (IN)
U of South Florida Sarasota-Manatee (FL)
U of the Fraser Valley (BC, Canada)
U of the Incarnate Word (TX)
The U of Toledo (OH)
U of Wisconsin–Superior (WI)
Utah State U (UT)
Utah Valley U (UT)
Warner Pacific U (OR)
Wayland Baptist U (TX)
Weber State U (UT)
Western Kentucky U (KY)
Widener U (PA)
Wilmington U (DE)
York Coll of Pennsylvania (PA)

## GEOGRAPHIC INFORMATION SCIENCE AND CARTOGRAPHY
The U of Akron (OH)

## GEOGRAPHY
Wright State U (OH)
Wright State U–Lake Campus (OH)

## GEOGRAPHY RELATED
Adams State U (CO)

## GEOLOGY/EARTH SCIENCE
Wright State U (OH)
Wright State U–Lake Campus (OH)

## GERMAN
Weber State U (UT)

## GERONTOLOGY
Madonna U (MI)
Manchester U (IN)
Ohio Dominican U (OH)

## GOLF COURSE OPERATION AND GROUNDS MANAGEMENT
Keiser U, Fort Lauderdale (FL)

## GRAPHIC AND PRINTING EQUIPMENT OPERATION/ PRODUCTION
Chowan U (NC)

## GRAPHIC COMMUNICATIONS
Ferris State U (MI)
New England Inst of Technology (RI)

## GRAPHIC DESIGN
Academy of Art U (CA)
Brescia U (KY)
California U of Pennsylvania (PA)
Columbia Central U, Caguas (PR)
Creative Center (NE)
Defiance Coll (OH)

FIDM/Fashion Inst of Design & Merchandising, Los Angeles Campus (CA)
FIDM/Fashion Inst of Design & Merchandising, San Francisco Campus (CA)
Inter American U of Puerto Rico, San Germán Campus (PR)
Lynn U (FL)
Madonna U (MI)
Northern State U (SD)
Parsons School of Design (NY)
Pratt Inst (NY)
Southeastern U (FL)
State U of New York Coll of Agriculture and Technology at Cobleskill (NY)
Stevens–The Inst of Business & Arts (MO)
Union Coll (NE)
U of South Dakota (SD)
U of the Fraser Valley (BC, Canada)
Villa Maria Coll (NY)
Wright State U (OH)
Wright State U–Lake Campus (OH)

## HEALTH AND PHYSICAL EDUCATION/FITNESS
Dean Coll (MA)
Lincoln Coll (IL)
Robert Morris U Illinois (IL)
State U of New York Coll of Technology at Delhi (NY)
Utah Valley U (UT)

## HEALTH AND PHYSICAL EDUCATION RELATED
Dean Coll (MA)
Pennsylvania Coll of Technology (PA)

## HEALTH AND WELLNESS
American Coll of Healthcare Sciences (OR)
Dean Coll (MA)
Tulane U (LA)
U of Wisconsin–Superior (WI)

## HEALTH/HEALTH-CARE ADMINISTRATION
LeTourneau U (TX)
Mount Saint Mary's U (CA)
Regent U (VA)
The U of Scranton (PA)
Waldorf U (IA)
Warner Pacific U (OR)

## HEALTH INFORMATION/ MEDICAL RECORDS ADMINISTRATION
Keiser U, Fort Lauderdale (FL)
Lincoln Coll of New England, Southington (CT)
Montana State U Billings (MT)

## HEALTH INFORMATION/ MEDICAL RECORDS TECHNOLOGY
Dakota State U (SD)
Davenport U, Grand Rapids (MI)
ECPI U, Virginia Beach (VA)
Ferris State U (MI)
Fisher Coll (MA)
Gwynedd Mercy U (PA)
Idaho State U (ID)
Indiana U Northwest (IN)
Keiser U, Fort Lauderdale (FL)
Lincoln Coll of New England, Southington (CT)
Mercy Coll of Ohio (OH)
Midland Coll (TX)
Northern Michigan U (MI)
Peirce Coll (PA)
Pennsylvania Coll of Technology (PA)
Rasmussen Coll Bloomington (MN)
Rasmussen Coll Brooklyn Park (MN)
Rasmussen Coll Eagan (MN)
Rasmussen Coll Mankato (MN)
Rasmussen Coll New Port Richey (FL)
Rasmussen Coll Ocala (FL)
Rasmussen Coll Rockford (IL)
Rasmussen Coll St. Cloud (MN)
St. Catherine U (MN)
Valencia Coll (FL)
Weber State U (UT)
Western Kentucky U (KY)

## HEALTH/MEDICAL PREPARATORY PROGRAMS RELATED
Cornerstone U (MI)
Mount Saint Mary's U (CA)
Northwest U (WA)

## HEALTH PROFESSIONS RELATED
American Public U System (WV)
Caribbean U (PR)
Ferris State U (MI)
Fisher Coll (MA)
Hawai`i Pacific U (HI)
Life U (GA)
Lock Haven U of Pennsylvania (PA)
Newman U (KS)
New York U (NY)
Northwest U (WA)
Saint Peter's U (NJ)
U of Hartford (CT)

## HEALTH SERVICES ADMINISTRATION
Florida National U (FL)
Keiser U, Fort Lauderdale (FL)

## HEALTH SERVICES/ALLIED HEALTH/HEALTH SCIENCES
Aultman Coll of Nursing and Health Sciences (OH)
Cameron U (OK)
Central Penn Coll (PA)
Excelsior Coll (NY)
Fisher Coll (MA)
Howard Payne U (TX)
Lindsey Wilson Coll (KY)
Middle Georgia State U (GA)
Nebraska Methodist Coll (NE)
Ohio Dominican U (OH)
Pine Manor Coll (MA)
Southwestern Assemblies of God U (TX)
State U of New York Coll of Agriculture and Technology at Cobleskill (NY)
U of Hartford (CT)
U of Maine at Fort Kent (ME)
U of the Incarnate Word (TX)
Weber State U (UT)

## HEALTH TEACHER EDUCATION
Palm Beach State Coll (FL)

## HEATING, AIR CONDITIONING, VENTILATION AND REFRIGERATION MAINTENANCE TECHNOLOGY
Arkansas Tech U (AR)
Montana State U Billings (MT)
New England Inst of Technology (RI)
State U of New York Coll of Technology at Delhi (NY)

## HEATING, VENTILATION, AIR CONDITIONING AND REFRIGERATION ENGINEERING TECHNOLOGY
Ferris State U (MI)
Midland Coll (TX)
Northern Michigan U (MI)
Pennsylvania Coll of Technology (PA)
State U of New York Coll of Technology at Canton (NY)

## HEAVY EQUIPMENT MAINTENANCE TECHNOLOGY
Ferris State U (MI)
Pennsylvania Coll of Technology (PA)

## HEAVY/INDUSTRIAL EQUIPMENT MAINTENANCE TECHNOLOGIES RELATED
State U of New York Coll of Technology at Canton (NY)

## HIGHER EDUCATION/HIGHER EDUCATION ADMINISTRATION
Dallas Baptist U (TX)

## HISTOLOGIC TECHNICIAN
Indiana U–Purdue U Indianapolis (IN)
Northern Michigan U (MI)
Tarleton State U (TX)

## HISTOLOGIC TECHNOLOGY/ HISTOTECHNOLOGIST
Keiser U, Fort Lauderdale (FL)

## HISTORIC PRESERVATION AND CONSERVATION
Montana Tech of The U of Montana (MT)

## HISTORY
American Public U System (WV)
Bryn Athyn Coll of the New Church (PA)
Dean Coll (MA)
Immaculata U (PA)
Indiana Wesleyan U (IN)
John Cabot U (Italy)
Lindsey Wilson Coll (KY)
Palm Beach State Coll (FL)
Regent U (VA)
Rogers State U (OK)
State U of New York Empire State Coll (NY)
Utah Valley U (UT)
Wright State U (OH)
Wright State U–Lake Campus (OH)

## HOMELAND SECURITY
Hawai`i Pacific U (HI)
Keiser U, Fort Lauderdale (FL)
U of Management and Technology (VA)
Waldorf U (IA)

## HOMELAND SECURITY, LAW ENFORCEMENT, FIREFIGHTING AND PROTECTIVE SERVICES RELATED
Idaho State U (ID)

## HORSE HUSBANDRY/EQUINE SCIENCE AND MANAGEMENT
Southern Utah U (UT)
U of Guelph (ON, Canada)

## HORTICULTURAL SCIENCE
Andrews U (MI)
Temple U (PA)
U of Guelph (ON, Canada)
U of New Hampshire (NH)

## HOSPITALITY ADMINISTRATION
Coll of Coastal Georgia (GA)
Colorado Mesa U (CO)
Endicott Coll (MA)
Florida National U (FL)
Keiser U, Fort Lauderdale (FL)
The U of Akron (OH)
U of Montana (MT)
Utah Valley U (UT)
Valencia Coll (FL)
Webber International U (FL)
Youngstown State U (OH)

## HOSPITALITY ADMINISTRATION RELATED
Penn State Beaver (PA)
Penn State Berks (PA)

## HOTEL/MOTEL ADMINISTRATION
Palm Beach State Coll (FL)
State U of New York Coll of Agriculture and Technology at Cobleskill (NY)
The U of Akron (OH)
Valencia Coll (FL)

## HOTEL, MOTEL, AND RESTAURANT MANAGEMENT
Sullivan U (KY)

## HUMAN DEVELOPMENT AND FAMILY STUDIES
Bethel Coll (IN)
Penn State Abington (PA)
Penn State Altoona (PA)
Penn State Berks (PA)
Penn State Brandywine (PA)
Penn State Erie, The Behrend Coll (PA)
Penn State New Kensington (PA)
Penn State Schuylkill (PA)
Penn State Shenango (PA)
Penn State Worthington Scranton (PA)
Penn State York (PA)

**HUMAN DEVELOPMENT AND FAMILY STUDIES RELATED**
Utah State U (UT)

**HUMANITIES**
Bryn Athyn Coll of the New Church (PA)
Fisher Coll (MA)
John Cabot U (Italy)
Long Island U–LIU Brooklyn (NY)
Michigan Technological U (MI)
Ohio U (OH)
Purdue U Northwest (IN)
Saint Mary-of-the-Woods Coll (IN)
Saint Peter's U (NJ)
State U of New York Coll of Agriculture and Technology at Cobleskill (NY)
State U of New York Coll of Technology at Delhi (NY)
U of Cincinnati (OH)
Utah Valley U (UT)
Valparaiso U (IN)

**HUMAN RESOURCES MANAGEMENT**
Madonna U (MI)
Montana State U Billings (MT)
Rasmussen Coll Bloomington (MN)
Rasmussen Coll Brooklyn Park (MN)
Rasmussen Coll Eagan (MN)
Rasmussen Coll Fargo (ND)
Rasmussen Coll Mankato (MN)
Rasmussen Coll New Port Richey (FL)
Rasmussen Coll Ocala (FL)
Tulane U (LA)
U of Cincinnati (OH)
The U of Findlay (OH)
The U of Scranton (PA)
Waldorf U (IA)

**HUMAN RESOURCES MANAGEMENT AND SERVICES RELATED**
Oakland City U (IN)

**HUMAN SERVICES**
Arkansas Tech U (AR)
Beacon Coll (FL)
Bethel Coll (IN)
Brescia U (KY)
Calumet Coll of Saint Joseph (IN)
Caribbean U (PR)
The Catholic U of America (DC)
Cazenovia Coll (NY)
Columbia Coll (MO)
Cornerstone U (MI)
Excelsior Coll (NY)
Geneva Coll (PA)
Hilbert Coll (NY)
Lincoln Coll of New England, Southington (CT)
Mount Saint Mary's U (CA)
Ohio Christian U (OH)
Rasmussen Coll Bloomington (MN)
Rasmussen Coll Brooklyn Park (MN)
Rasmussen Coll Eagan (MN)
Rasmussen Coll Fargo (ND)
Rasmussen Coll Mankato (MN)
Rasmussen Coll New Port Richey (FL)
Rasmussen Coll Ocala (FL)
Rasmussen Coll St. Cloud (MN)
Southwestern Assemblies of God U (TX)
Thomas Edison State U (NJ)
U of Maine at Fort Kent (ME)
U of Providence (MT)
The U of Scranton (PA)
U of Valley Forge (PA)
Walsh U (OH)
Wayland Baptist U (TX)

**ILLUSTRATION**
Academy of Art U (CA)
Fashion Inst of Technology (NY)
Pratt Inst (NY)

**INDUSTRIAL AND PRODUCT DESIGN**
Academy of Art U (CA)

**INDUSTRIAL ELECTRONICS TECHNOLOGY**
Ferris State U (MI)
Pennsylvania Coll of Technology (PA)

**INDUSTRIAL ENGINEERING**
Indiana Tech (IN)

**INDUSTRIAL MECHANICS AND MAINTENANCE TECHNOLOGY**
Northern Michigan U (MI)
Pennsylvania Coll of Technology (PA)
The U of West Alabama (AL)

**INDUSTRIAL PRODUCTION TECHNOLOGIES RELATED**
California U of Pennsylvania (PA)
Clarion U of Pennsylvania (PA)
U of Alaska Fairbanks (AK)

**INDUSTRIAL RADIOLOGIC TECHNOLOGY**
Franciscan Missionaries of Our Lady U (LA)
The George Washington U (DC)
Palm Beach State Coll (FL)
Widener U (PA)

**INDUSTRIAL TECHNOLOGY**
Arkansas Tech U (AR)
Millersville U of Pennsylvania (PA)
Murray State U (KY)
Penn State York (PA)
Pittsburg State U (KS)
Southeastern Louisiana U (LA)

**INFORMATION RESOURCES MANAGEMENT**
Rasmussen Coll New Port Richey (FL)
Rasmussen Coll Ocala (FL)

**INFORMATION SCIENCE/ STUDIES**
Campbellsville U (KY)
Clayton State U (GA)
Colegio Universitario de San Juan, San Juan (PR)
Dakota State U (SD)
Immaculata U (PA)
Mansfield U of Pennsylvania (PA)
Newman U (KS)
Penn State Abington (PA)
Penn State Altoona (PA)
Penn State Berks (PA)
Penn State Erie, The Behrend Coll (PA)
Penn State Hazleton (PA)
Penn State Lehigh Valley (PA)
Penn State New Kensington (PA)
Penn State Schuylkill (PA)
Penn State U Park (PA)
Saint Peter's U (NJ)
State U of New York Coll of Agriculture and Technology at Cobleskill (NY)
State U of New York Coll of Technology at Canton (NY)
State U of New York Coll of Technology at Delhi (NY)
Tulane U (LA)
U of Management and Technology (VA)
U of Massachusetts Lowell (MA)
U of Pittsburgh at Bradford (PA)
The U of Scranton (PA)

**INFORMATION TECHNOLOGY**
Arkansas Tech U (AR)
Cameron U (OK)
EDP U of Puerto Rico–San Sebastian (PR)
Ferris State U (MI)
Florida National U (FL)
Golden Gate U (CA)
Hallmark U (TX)
Keiser U, Fort Lauderdale (FL)
Liberty U (VA)
Life U (GA)
Limestone Coll (SC)
New England Inst of Technology (RI)
Peirce Coll (PA)
Purdue U (IN)
Regent U (VA)
Southern Utah U (UT)
Tiffin U (OH)
Trevecca Nazarene U (TN)
U of Management and Technology (VA)
U of Montana (MT)
U of the Incarnate Word (TX)
The U of Toledo (OH)
Valencia Coll (FL)
Vermont Tech Coll (VT)
Youngstown State U (OH)

**INSTITUTIONAL FOOD WORKERS**
ECPI U, Virginia Beach (VA)

**INSTRUMENTATION TECHNOLOGY**
Idaho State U (ID)

**INSURANCE**
Inter American U of Puerto Rico, Metropolitan Campus (PR)

**INTERCULTURAL/ MULTICULTURAL AND DIVERSITY STUDIES**
Baptist U of the Americas (TX)
Nyack Coll (NY)
Waldorf U (IA)

**INTERDISCIPLINARY STUDIES**
Central Methodist U (MO)
Doane U (NE)
Keiser U, Fort Lauderdale (FL)
Lesley U (MA)
Ohio Christian U (OH)
Ohio Dominican U (OH)
Pennsylvania Coll of Technology (PA)
U of North Florida (FL)
U of Valley Forge (PA)

**INTERIOR DESIGN**
Academy of Art U (CA)
Bay Path U (MA)
Chaminade U of Honolulu (HI)
EDP U of Puerto Rico (PR)
EDP U of Puerto Rico–San Sebastian (PR)
Fashion Inst of Technology (NY)
FIDM/Fashion Inst of Design & Merchandising, Los Angeles Campus (CA)
FIDM/Fashion Inst of Design & Merchandising, San Francisco Campus (CA)
Indiana U–Purdue U Indianapolis (IN)
New England Inst of Technology (RI)
Palm Beach State Coll (FL)
Parsons School of Design (NY)
Robert Morris U Illinois (IL)
Stevens–The Inst of Business & Arts (MO)
Villa Maria Coll (NY)
Weber State U (UT)

**INTERNATIONAL BUSINESS/ TRADE/COMMERCE**
John Cabot U (Italy)
Saint Peter's U (NJ)
U of the Potomac (DC)

**INTERNATIONAL/GLOBAL STUDIES**
Sacred Heart U (CT)

**INTERNATIONAL RELATIONS AND AFFAIRS**
John Cabot U (Italy)

**ITALIAN STUDIES**
John Cabot U (Italy)

**JAPANESE**
Weber State U (UT)

**JOURNALISM**
Academy of Art U (CA)
Manchester U (IN)
Palm Beach State Coll (FL)

**JOURNALISM RELATED**
Adams State U (CO)

**KINDERGARTEN/PRESCHOOL EDUCATION**
Brigham Young U–Idaho (ID)
Eastern Nazarene Coll (MA)
Fisher Coll (MA)
Mount Saint Mary's U (CA)
Palm Beach State Coll (FL)
Shawnee State U (OH)
U of Cincinnati (OH)
U of Providence (MT)

**KINESIOLOGY AND EXERCISE SCIENCE**
Dean Coll (MA)
Southwestern Adventist U (TX)

**LABOR AND INDUSTRIAL RELATIONS**
State U of New York Empire State Coll (NY)

**LABOR STUDIES**
Indiana U Bloomington (IN)
Indiana U Northwest (IN)
Indiana U–Purdue U Indianapolis (IN)

Indiana U South Bend (IN)

**LANDSCAPE ARCHITECTURE**
Academy of Art U (CA)

**LANDSCAPING AND GROUNDSKEEPING**
Pennsylvania Coll of Technology (PA)
State U of New York Coll of Technology at Delhi (NY)
U of Massachusetts Amherst (MA)
Valencia Coll (FL)
Vermont Tech Coll (VT)

**LASER AND OPTICAL TECHNOLOGY**
Colegio Universitario de San Juan, San Juan (PR)

**LAY MINISTRY**
Bethel Coll (IN)
Howard Payne U (TX)
Maranatha Baptist U (WI)
Southwestern Assemblies of God U (TX)
U of Saint Francis (IN)

**LEGAL ADMINISTRATIVE ASSISTANT/SECRETARY**
Clarion U of Pennsylvania (PA)
Palm Beach State Coll (FL)
Shawnee State U (OH)
Sullivan U (KY)

**LEGAL ASSISTANT/PARALEGAL**
American Public U System (WV)
Bay Path U (MA)
Central Penn Coll (PA)
Champlain Coll (VT)
Clayton State U (GA)
Coll of Saint Mary (NE)
Davenport U, Grand Rapids (MI)
Elms Coll (MA)
Excelsior Coll (NY)
Ferris State U (MI)
Florida National U (FL)
Gannon U (PA)
Hilbert Coll (NY)
Husson U (ME)
Idaho State U (ID)
Keiser U, Fort Lauderdale (FL)
Liberty U (VA)
Madonna U (MI)
Marian U (IN)
McNeese State U (LA)
Midland Coll (TX)
Missouri Western State U (MO)
Mount Aloysius Coll (PA)
National Paralegal Coll (AZ)
National U (CA)
Newman U (KS)
Peirce Coll (PA)
Rasmussen Coll Bloomington (MN)
Rasmussen Coll Brooklyn Park (MN)
Rasmussen Coll Eagan (MN)
Rasmussen Coll Fargo (ND)
Rasmussen Coll Mankato (MN)
Rasmussen Coll New Port Richey (FL)
Rasmussen Coll Ocala (FL)
Rasmussen Coll Rockford (IL)
Rasmussen Coll St. Cloud (MN)
Robert Morris U Illinois (IL)
Saint Mary-of-the-Woods Coll (IN)
Shawnee State U (OH)
Southern Utah U (UT)
Stevens–The Inst of Business & Arts (MO)
Suffolk U (MA)
Sullivan U (KY)
Tulane U (LA)
The U of Akron (OH)
U of Alaska Fairbanks (AK)
U of Cincinnati (OH)
U of Hartford (CT)
U of Louisville (KY)
U of North Georgia (GA)
U of Providence (MT)
Utah Valley U (UT)
Valencia Coll (FL)
Western Kentucky U (KY)
Widener U (PA)

**LEGAL STUDIES**
Faulkner U (AL)
Post U (CT)
St. John's U (NY)
U of Hartford (CT)
U of Montana (MT)
U of New Haven (CT)

**LIBERAL ARTS AND SCIENCES AND HUMANITIES RELATED**
Adams State U (CO)
Anderson U (IN)
Ball State U (IN)
Coll of Saint Mary (NE)
Colorado Mesa U (CO)
Ferris State U (MI)
Florida National U (FL)
Gwynedd Mercy U (PA)
Kent State U at Geauga (OH)
Kent State U at Stark (OH)
King U (TN)
Long Island U–LIU Post (NY)
Marymount California U (CA)
Mount Aloysius Coll (PA)
New York U (NY)
Southern Vermont Coll (VT)
State U of New York Coll of Technology at Delhi (NY)
Talladega Coll (AL)
Taylor U (IN)
U of Maryland U Coll (MD)
U of Wisconsin–La Crosse (WI)
Walsh U (OH)
Wayland Baptist U (TX)
Wichita State U (KS)
William Penn U (IA)

**LIBERAL ARTS AND SCIENCES/ LIBERAL STUDIES**
Adams State U (CO)
Adelphi U (NY)
Alverno Coll (WI)
American International Coll (MA)
American U (DC)
Amridge U (AL)
Aquinas Coll (MI)
Arizona Christian U (AZ)
Austin Peay State U (TN)
Averett U (VA)
Bard Coll (NY)
Bay Path U (MA)
Beacon Coll (FL)
Becker Coll (MA)
Bemidji State U (MN)
Bethel Coll (IN)
Bethel U (MN)
Boise State U (ID)
Brenau U (GA)
Brescia U (KY)
Brigham Young U–Idaho (ID)
Bryan Coll (TN)
California U of Pennsylvania (PA)
Carson-Newman U (TN)
Cazenovia Coll (NY)
Charter Oak State Coll (CT)
Chestnut Hill Coll (PA)
Christendom Coll (VA)
Clarke U (IA)
Clayton State U (GA)
Coll of Coastal Georgia (GA)
Coll of Staten Island of the City U of New York (NY)
Colorado Mesa U (CO)
Columbia Coll (MO)
Columbus State U (GA)
Concordia Coll–New York (NY)
Concordia U Irvine (CA)
Corban U (OR)
Dean Coll (MA)
Dickinson State U (ND)
Dominican Coll (NY)
Eastern New Mexico U (NM)
Eastern U (PA)
Emmanuel Coll (GA)
Endicott Coll (MA)
Excelsior Coll (NY)
Fairleigh Dickinson U, Metropolitan Campus (NJ)
Farmingdale State Coll (NY)
Faulkner U (AL)
Felician U (NJ)
Fisher Coll (MA)
Florida Atlantic U (FL)
Florida Coll (FL)
Franklin U Switzerland (Switzerland)
Gannon U (PA)
Georgia Southern U–Armstrong Campus (GA)
Hilbert Coll (NY)
Hobe Sound Bible Coll (FL)
Huston-Tillotson U (TX)
Indiana U of Pennsylvania (PA)
Judson U (IL)
Kentucky State U (KY)
Limestone Coll (SC)
Long Island U–LIU Brooklyn (NY)
Loyola U Chicago (IL)
Mansfield U of Pennsylvania (PA)
Maria Coll (NY)

Marian U (IN)
Marietta Coll (OH)
Marymount California U (CA)
Medgar Evers Coll of the City U of
  New York (NY)
Mercy Coll (NY)
Mid-America Christian U (OK)
MidAmerica Nazarene U (KS)
Middle Georgia State U (GA)
Minnesota State U Moorhead (MN)
Missouri Valley Coll (MO)
Molloy Coll (NY)
Montana State U Billings (MT)
Mount Aloysius Coll (PA)
Mount Marty Coll (SD)
Mount Saint Mary's U (CA)
Murray State U (KY)
Neumann U (PA)
Newman U (KS)
New Saint Andrews Coll (ID)
New York U (NY)
Niagara U (NY)
Northern Kentucky U (KY)
Northwest U (WA)
Nyack Coll (NY)
The Ohio State U at Mansfield (OH)
The Ohio State U at Marion (OH)
The Ohio State U at Newark (OH)
Ohio U (OH)
Palm Beach State Coll (FL)
Penn State Abington (PA)
Penn State Altoona (PA)
Penn State Beaver (PA)
Penn State Berks (PA)
Penn State Brandywine (PA)
Penn State Erie, The Behrend Coll
  (PA)
Penn State Greater Allegheny (PA)
Penn State Harrisburg (PA)
Penn State Hazleton (PA)
Penn State Lehigh Valley (PA)
Penn State New Kensington (PA)
Penn State Schuylkill (PA)
Penn State Shenango (PA)
Penn State U Park (PA)
Penn State Wilkes-Barre (PA)
Penn State Worthington Scranton
  (PA)
Penn State York (PA)
Pine Manor Coll (MA)
Polk State Coll (FL)
Providence Coll (RI)
Rivier U (NH)
Rocky Mountain Coll (MT)
Rogers State U (OK)
St. Catherine U (MN)
St. John's U (NY)
Saint Joseph's U (PA)
Saint Leo U (FL)
St. Thomas Aquinas Coll (NY)
Salve Regina U (RI)
Schreiner U (TX)
Shiloh U (IA)
Southern Adventist U (TN)
State U of New York Coll of
  Agriculture and Technology at
  Cobleskill (NY)
State U of New York Coll of
  Technology at Delhi (NY)
Suffolk U (MA)
Syracuse U (NY)
Tabor Coll (KS)
Thomas Edison State U (NJ)
Thomas Jefferson U (PA)
Thomas U (GA)
Trine U (IN)
Troy U (AL)
Unity Coll (ME)
The U of Akron (OH)
U of Alaska Fairbanks (AK)
U of Dubuque (IA)
U of Hartford (CT)
U of Maine at Fort Kent (ME)
U of Maine at Presque Isle (ME)
The U of Montana Western (MT)
U of North Georgia (GA)
U of Pittsburgh at Bradford (PA)
U of Saint Francis (IN)
U of Sioux Falls (SD)
U of South Dakota (SD)
U of South Florida, St. Petersburg
  (FL)
U of the Fraser Valley (BC, Canada)
U of the Incarnate Word (TX)
U of Wisconsin–Eau Claire (WI)
U of Wisconsin–Parkside (WI)
U of Wisconsin–Superior (WI)
U of Wisconsin–Whitewater (WI)
Upper Iowa U (IA)
Valdosta State U (GA)

Valencia Coll (FL)
Villa Maria Coll (NY)
Waldorf U (IA)
Western Connecticut State U (CT)
Western New England U (MA)
Wichita State U (KS)
William Woods U (MO)
Winona State U (MN)
Youngstown State U (OH)

## LIBRARY AND ARCHIVES ASSISTING
U of the Fraser Valley (BC, Canada)

## LICENSED PRACTICAL/ VOCATIONAL NURSE TRAINING
Arkansas Tech U (AR)
Campbellsville U (KY)
Dickinson State U (ND)
Inter American U of Puerto Rico,
  Aguadilla Campus (PR)
Inter American U of Puerto Rico,
  Barranquitas Campus (PR)
Inter American U of Puerto Rico,
  Bayamón Campus (PR)
Inter American U of Puerto Rico,
  Metropolitan Campus (PR)
Inter American U of Puerto Rico, San
  Germán Campus (PR)
Maria Coll (NY)
Medgar Evers Coll of the City U of
  New York (NY)
Montana State U Billings (MT)
Pennsylvania Coll of Technology
  (PA)
U of Montana (MT)
U of the Fraser Valley (BC, Canada)

## LINEWORKER
Colorado Mesa U (CO)

## LINGUISTIC AND COMPARATIVE LANGUAGE STUDIES RELATED
Northwest U (WA)

## LOGISTICS, MATERIALS, AND SUPPLY CHAIN MANAGEMENT
Arkansas Tech U (AR)
FIDM/Fashion Inst of Design &
  Merchandising, Los Angeles
  Campus (CA)
Polytechnic U of Puerto Rico (PR)
Sullivan U (KY)

## MACHINE TOOL TECHNOLOGY
Colorado Mesa U (CO)
Idaho State U (ID)
Pennsylvania Coll of Technology
  (PA)

## MANAGEMENT INFORMATION SYSTEMS
Liberty U (VA)
Lindsey Wilson Coll (KY)
Morehead State U (KY)
Shawnee State U (OH)
The U of Findlay (OH)
U of the Incarnate Word (TX)
Weber State U (UT)
Wright State U (OH)
Wright State U–Lake Campus (OH)

## MANAGEMENT INFORMATION SYSTEMS AND SERVICES RELATED
Mount Aloysius Coll (PA)
Rasmussen Coll Bloomington (MN)
Rasmussen Coll Brooklyn Park (MN)
Rasmussen Coll Eagan (MN)
Rasmussen Coll Fargo (ND)
Rasmussen Coll Mankato (MN)
Rasmussen Coll New Port Richey
  (FL)
Rasmussen Coll Ocala (FL)
Rasmussen Coll Rockford (IL)
Rasmussen Coll St. Cloud (MN)

## MANUFACTURING ENGINEERING
Penn State Greater Allegheny (PA)
Penn State Hazleton (PA)
Penn State Wilkes-Barre (PA)
Penn State York (PA)

## MANUFACTURING ENGINEERING TECHNOLOGY
Colorado Mesa U (CO)
Idaho State U (ID)
Lawrence Technological U (MI)

Missouri Western State U (MO)
New England Inst of Technology (RI)
Pennsylvania Coll of Technology
  (PA)
The U of Akron (OH)
U of Cincinnati (OH)
Weber State U (UT)

## MARINE MAINTENANCE AND SHIP REPAIR TECHNOLOGY
New England Inst of Technology (RI)

## MARKETING/MARKETING MANAGEMENT
Central Penn Coll (PA)
Ferris State U (MI)
FIDM/Fashion Inst of Design &
  Merchandising, Los Angeles
  Campus (CA)
John Cabot U (Italy)
Madonna U (MI)
Palm Beach State Coll (FL)
Post U (CT)
Rasmussen Coll Bloomington (MN)
Rasmussen Coll Brooklyn Park (MN)
Rasmussen Coll Eagan (MN)
Rasmussen Coll Fargo (ND)
Rasmussen Coll Mankato (MN)
Rasmussen Coll New Port Richey
  (FL)
Rasmussen Coll Ocala (FL)
Rasmussen Coll St. Cloud (MN)
Saint Peter's U (NJ)
Tulane U (LA)
The U of Akron (OH)
Walsh U (OH)
Webber International U (FL)
Youngstown State U (OH)

## MASONRY
Pennsylvania Coll of Technology
  (PA)

## MASSAGE THERAPY
Columbia Central U, Caguas (PR)
ECPI U, Virginia Beach (VA)
Idaho State U (ID)
Keiser U, Fort Lauderdale (FL)

## MASS COMMUNICATION/ MEDIA
Adams State U (CO)
Black Hills State U (SD)
Dean Coll (MA)
John Cabot U (Italy)
Palm Beach State Coll (FL)
Southern Adventist U (TN)
Wright State U–Lake Campus (OH)
York Coll of Pennsylvania (PA)

## MATHEMATICS
Bryn Athyn Coll of the New Church
  (PA)
Creighton U (NE)
Dean Coll (MA)
Hawai'i Pacific U (HI)
Idaho State U (ID)
Indiana Wesleyan U (IN)
Northern Vermont U–Lyndon (VT)
Palm Beach State Coll (FL)
Shawnee State U (OH)
State U of New York Coll of
  Agriculture and Technology at
  Cobleskill (NY)
Taylor U (IN)
Thomas U (GA)
Trevecca Nazarene U (TN)
U of Providence (MT)
Utah Valley U (UT)
Weber State U (UT)

## MECHANICAL DRAFTING AND CAD/CADD
Midland Coll (TX)

## MECHANICAL ENGINEERING
New England Inst of Technology (RI)

## MECHANICAL ENGINEERING/ MECHANICAL TECHNOLOGY
Brigham Young U–Idaho (ID)
Colorado Mesa U (CO)
ECPI U, Virginia Beach (VA)
Farmingdale State Coll (NY)
Ferris State U (MI)
Idaho State U (ID)
Lawrence Technological U (MI)
Penn State Altoona (PA)
Penn State Berks (PA)
Penn State Erie, The Behrend Coll
  (PA)

Penn State Hazleton (PA)
Penn State New Kensington (PA)
Penn State Shenango (PA)
Penn State York (PA)
Purdue U (IN)
State U of New York Coll of
  Agriculture and Technology at
  Cobleskill (NY)
State U of New York Coll of
  Technology at Canton (NY)
The U of Akron (OH)
U of Cincinnati (OH)
Vermont Tech Coll (VT)
Weber State U (UT)
Youngstown State U (OH)

## MECHANICAL ENGINEERING TECHNOLOGIES RELATED
Polytechnic U of Puerto Rico (PR)
U of Massachusetts Lowell (MA)

## MECHANIC AND REPAIR TECHNOLOGIES RELATED
Pennsylvania Coll of Technology
  (PA)
Thomas Edison State U (NJ)

## MECHANICS AND REPAIR
Idaho State U (ID)
Utah Valley U (UT)
Weber State U (UT)

## MECHATRONICS, ROBOTICS, AND AUTOMATION ENGINEERING
U of the Fraser Valley (BC, Canada)
Utah Valley U (UT)

## MEDICAL ADMINISTRATIVE ASSISTANT AND MEDICAL SECRETARY
Arkansas Tech U (AR)
Hallmark U (TX)
Montana State U Billings (MT)
Rasmussen Coll Bloomington (MN)
Rasmussen Coll Brooklyn Park (MN)
Rasmussen Coll Eagan (MN)
Rasmussen Coll Fargo (ND)
Rasmussen Coll Mankato (MN)
Rasmussen Coll New Port Richey
  (FL)
Rasmussen Coll Ocala (FL)
Rasmussen Coll Rockford (IL)
Rasmussen Coll St. Cloud (MN)
U of Montana (MT)

## MEDICAL/CLINICAL ASSISTANT
Arkansas Tech U (AR)
Brigham Young U–Idaho (ID)
Central Penn Coll (PA)
Colorado Mesa U (CO)
Davenport U, Grand Rapids (MI)
ECPI U, Virginia Beach (VA)
Fisher Coll (MA)
Hallmark U (TX)
Idaho State U (ID)
Keiser U, Fort Lauderdale (FL)
Montana State U Billings (MT)
Montana Tech of The U of Montana
  (MT)
Mount Aloysius Coll (PA)
New England Inst of Technology (RI)
Rasmussen Coll Bloomington (MN)
Rasmussen Coll Brooklyn Park (MN)
Rasmussen Coll Eagan (MN)
Rasmussen Coll Mankato (MN)
Rasmussen Coll New Port Richey
  (FL)
Rasmussen Coll Ocala (FL)
Rasmussen Coll Rockford (IL)
Rasmussen Coll St. Cloud (MN)
Robert Morris U Illinois (IL)
Sullivan U (KY)
The U of Akron (OH)
U of Alaska Fairbanks (AK)
Youngstown State U (OH)

## MEDICAL/HEALTH MANAGEMENT AND CLINICAL ASSISTANT
Florida National U (FL)

## MEDICAL INFORMATICS
Montana Tech of The U of Montana
  (MT)
Oregon Inst of Technology (OR)

## MEDICAL INSURANCE CODING
Columbia Southern U (AL)
Davenport U, Grand Rapids (MI)

Fisher Coll (MA)
U of Montana (MT)

## MEDICAL OFFICE ASSISTANT
Liberty U (VA)
Sullivan U (KY)

## MEDICAL OFFICE MANAGEMENT
The U of Akron (OH)

## MEDICAL RADIOLOGIC TECHNOLOGY
Ball State U (IN)
Cameron U (OK)
Coll of Coastal Georgia (GA)
Drexel U (PA)
Ferris State U (MI)
Inter American U of Puerto Rico,
  Aguadilla Campus (PR)
Inter American U of Puerto Rico, San
  Germán Campus (PR)
Keiser U, Fort Lauderdale (FL)
La Roche Coll (PA)
Morehead State U (KY)
Mount Aloysius Coll (PA)
Newman U (KS)
Penn State New Kensington (PA)
Penn State Schuylkill (PA)
Pennsylvania Coll of Health
  Sciences (PA)
Pennsylvania Coll of Technology
  (PA)
Polk State Coll (FL)
St. Catherine U (MN)
Shawnee State U (OH)
The U of Akron (OH)
U of Charleston (WV)
U of New Mexico (NM)
U of Sioux Falls (SD)

## MEETING AND EVENT PLANNING
Sullivan U (KY)

## MENTAL AND SOCIAL HEALTH SERVICES AND ALLIED PROFESSIONS RELATED
Clarion U of Pennsylvania (PA)
U of Alaska Fairbanks (AK)

## MENTAL HEALTH COUNSELING
Stephen F. Austin State U (TX)

## MERCHANDISING
The U of Akron (OH)

## MERCHANDISING, SALES, AND MARKETING OPERATIONS RELATED (GENERAL)
Inter American U of Puerto Rico,
  Aguadilla Campus (PR)
State U of New York Coll of
  Technology at Delhi (NY)

## METAL AND JEWELRY ARTS
Academy of Art U (CA)
Fashion Inst of Technology (NY)
FIDM/Fashion Inst of Design &
  Merchandising, Los Angeles
  Campus (CA)

## METAL FABRICATOR
Pennsylvania Coll of Technology
  (PA)

## METALLURGICAL TECHNOLOGY
Penn State Altoona (PA)
Penn State Berks (PA)
Penn State Erie, The Behrend Coll
  (PA)
Penn State Hazleton (PA)
Penn State New Kensington (PA)
Penn State Schuylkill (PA)
Penn State Shenango (PA)
Penn State Wilkes-Barre (PA)
Penn State York (PA)

## MICROBIOLOGY
Weber State U (UT)

## MIDDLE SCHOOL EDUCATION
East Stroudsburg U of Pennsylvania
  (PA)

## MILITARY HISTORY
American Public U System (WV)

## MILITARY TECHNOLOGIES AND APPLIED SCIENCES RELATED
Lynn U (FL)
Thomas Edison State U (NJ)

## MINING AND PETROLEUM TECHNOLOGIES RELATED
U of the Virgin Islands (VI)

## MISSIONARY STUDIES AND MISSIOLOGY
Charlotte Christian Coll and Theological Seminary (NC)
Hobe Sound Bible Coll (FL)
Ohio Christian U (OH)
Southeastern U (FL)
Southwestern Assemblies of God U (TX)

## MULTI/INTERDISCIPLINARY STUDIES RELATED
Arkansas Tech U (AR)
Dallas Baptist U (TX)
John Brown U (AR)
Liberty U (VA)
Montana Tech of The U of Montana (MT)
Ohio U (OH)
Pennsylvania Coll of Technology (PA)
State U of New York Empire State Coll (NY)
Thomas Edison State U (NJ)
The U of Akron (OH)
U of Alaska Fairbanks (AK)
The U of Montana Western (MT)
Utah Valley U (UT)
Wright State U (OH)
Wright State U–Lake Campus (OH)

## MUSEUM STUDIES
Inst of American Indian Arts (NM)
U of Saint Francis (IN)

## MUSIC
Hannibal-LaGrange U (MO)
Marian U (IN)
Mount Vernon Nazarene U (OH)
Nyack U (NY)
Palm Beach State Coll (FL)
Southwestern Assemblies of God U (TX)
Utah Valley U (UT)
York Coll of Pennsylvania (PA)

## MUSICAL INSTRUMENT FABRICATION AND REPAIR
Indiana U Bloomington (IN)

## MUSIC HISTORY, LITERATURE, AND THEORY
Cairn U (PA)

## MUSIC MANAGEMENT
U of Central Oklahoma (OK)

## MUSIC PERFORMANCE
Inter American U of Puerto Rico, Metropolitan Campus (PR)
Trevecca Nazarene U (TN)
U of Central Oklahoma (OK)

## MUSIC RELATED
Alverno Coll (WI)
American Baptist Coll (TN)
Hobe Sound Bible Coll (FL)
Trevecca Nazarene U (TN)

## MUSIC TECHNOLOGY
U of Central Oklahoma (OK)
U of Saint Francis (IN)

## NANOTECHNOLOGY
Lock Haven U of Pennsylvania (PA)

## NATURAL RESOURCES/ CONSERVATION
State U of New York Coll of Environmental Science and Forestry (NY)

## NATURAL RESOURCES MANAGEMENT AND POLICY
U of Alaska Fairbanks (AK)

## NATURAL RESOURCES MANAGEMENT AND POLICY RELATED
U of Guelph (ON, Canada)

## NATURAL SCIENCES
Gwynedd Mercy U (PA)
Madonna U (MI)
Roberts Wesleyan Coll (NY)
U of Alaska Fairbanks (AK)

## NETWORK AND SYSTEM ADMINISTRATION
Academy Coll (MN)
Central Penn Coll (PA)
ECPI U, Virginia Beach (VA)
Florida National U (FL)
Palm Beach State Coll (FL)
Polk State Coll (FL)
Valencia Coll (FL)

## NUCLEAR ENGINEERING TECHNOLOGY
Arkansas Tech U (AR)
Idaho State U (ID)

## NUCLEAR MEDICAL TECHNOLOGY
Ball State U (IN)
The George Washington U (DC)
Keiser U, Fort Lauderdale (FL)
Molloy Coll (NY)
Pennsylvania Coll of Health Sciences (PA)
The U of Findlay (OH)

## NUCLEAR/NUCLEAR POWER TECHNOLOGY
Excelsior Coll (NY)

## NURSING SCIENCE
EDP U of Puerto Rico (PR)
EDP U of Puerto Rico–San Sebastian (PR)
Emmaus Bible Coll (IA)
Inter American U of Puerto Rico, Barranquitas Campus (PR)

## NUTRITION SCIENCES
U of the Incarnate Word (TX)

## OCCUPATIONAL SAFETY AND HEALTH TECHNOLOGY
Columbia Southern U (AL)
Waldorf U (IA)

## OCCUPATIONAL THERAPIST ASSISTANT
Adventist U of Health Sciences (FL)
Arkansas Tech U (AR)
California U of Pennsylvania (PA)
Central Penn Coll (PA)
Idaho State U (ID)
Jefferson Coll of Health Sciences (VA)
Keiser U, Fort Lauderdale (FL)
Lincoln Coll of New England, Southington (CT)
Maria Coll (NY)
Mercy Coll (NY)
Middle Georgia State U (GA)
New England Inst of Technology (RI)
Newman U (KS)
Penn State Berks (PA)
Pennsylvania Coll of Technology (PA)
Polk State Coll (FL)
Rutgers U–New Brunswick (NJ)
St. Catherine U (MN)
U of Charleston (WV)
U of Louisiana at Monroe (LA)
U of Puerto Rico–Humacao (PR)
U of Southern Indiana (IN)
Villa Maria Coll (NY)

## OCCUPATIONAL THERAPY
Palm Beach State Coll (FL)
Shawnee State U (OH)
Southern Adventist U (TN)

## OFFICE MANAGEMENT
Emmanuel Coll (GA)
Inter American U of Puerto Rico, Aguadilla Campus (PR)
Inter American U of Puerto Rico, Barranquitas Campus (PR)
Inter American U of Puerto Rico, Bayamón Campus (PR)
Inter American U of Puerto Rico, Fajardo Campus (PR)
Inter American U of Puerto Rico, Metropolitan Campus (PR)
Inter American U of Puerto Rico, San Germán Campus (PR)
Maranatha Baptist U (WI)
Shawnee State U (OH)
The U of Akron (OH)
Valencia Coll (FL)

## OFFICE OCCUPATIONS AND CLERICAL SERVICES
Bob Jones U (SC)
Midland Coll (TX)

## OPERATIONS MANAGEMENT
Polk State Coll (FL)

## OPTOMETRIC TECHNICIAN
Indiana U Bloomington (IN)

## ORGANIZATIONAL BEHAVIOR
Waldorf U (IA)

## ORGANIZATIONAL COMMUNICATION
Creighton U (NE)

## ORGANIZATIONAL LEADERSHIP
Beulah Heights U (GA)
Hawai'i Pacific U (HI)
Point U (GA)
Purdue U (IN)
Southeastern U (FL)

## ORNAMENTAL HORTICULTURE
Farmingdale State Coll (NY)
State U of New York Coll of Agriculture and Technology at Cobleskill (NY)
U of the Fraser Valley (BC, Canada)
Vermont Tech Coll (VT)

## PAINTING
Pratt Inst (NY)

## PALLIATIVE CARE NURSING
Madonna U (MI)

## PARKS, RECREATION AND LEISURE
Eastern New Mexico U (NM)

## PARKS, RECREATION AND LEISURE FACILITIES MANAGEMENT
Indiana Tech (IN)
State U of New York Coll of Technology at Delhi (NY)

## PASTORAL STUDIES/ COUNSELING
Indiana Wesleyan U (IN)
Marian U (IN)

## PETROLEUM TECHNOLOGY
Mansfield U of Pennsylvania (PA)
Montana State U Billings (MT)
U of Pittsburgh at Bradford (PA)

## PHARMACY, PHARMACEUTICAL SCIENCES, AND ADMINISTRATION RELATED
EDP U of Puerto Rico (PR)
EDP U of Puerto Rico–San Sebastian (PR)

## PHARMACY TECHNICIAN
Columbia Central U, Caguas (PR)
Inter American U of Puerto Rico, Aguadilla Campus (PR)
Inter American U of Puerto Rico, Metropolitan Campus (PR)
Rasmussen Coll Bloomington (MN)
Rasmussen Coll Brooklyn Park (MN)
Rasmussen Coll Eagan (MN)
Rasmussen Coll Mankato (MN)
Rasmussen Coll New Port Richey (FL)
Rasmussen Coll Ocala (FL)
Rasmussen Coll Rockford (IL)
Rasmussen Coll St. Cloud (MN)
Robert Morris U Illinois (IL)
Sullivan U (KY)

## PHILOSOPHY
Carroll Coll (MT)
John Cabot U (Italy)
Palm Beach State Coll (FL)
Utah Valley U (UT)

## PHILOSOPHY AND RELIGIOUS STUDIES
Bryn Athyn Coll of the New Church (PA)

## PHOTOGRAPHIC AND FILM/ VIDEO TECHNOLOGY
St. John's U (NY)
Villa Maria Coll (NY)

## PHOTOGRAPHY
Northern Vermont U–Lyndon (VT)
Paier Coll of Art, Inc. (CT)
Palm Beach State Coll (FL)

## PHYSICAL EDUCATION TEACHING AND COACHING
Palm Beach State Coll (FL)

## PHYSICAL FITNESS TECHNICIAN
The U of Findlay (OH)

## PHYSICAL SCIENCES
Coll of Staten Island of the City U of New York (NY)
Palm Beach State Coll (FL)
Roberts Wesleyan Coll (NY)
U of the Fraser Valley (BC, Canada)
Utah Valley U (UT)

## PHYSICAL SCIENCES RELATED
Lock Haven U of Pennsylvania (PA)
State U of New York Empire State Coll (NY)
U of Cincinnati (OH)

## PHYSICAL THERAPY
Louisiana Coll (LA)
Palm Beach State Coll (FL)
Southern Adventist U (TN)

## PHYSICAL THERAPY TECHNOLOGY
Arkansas Tech U (AR)
California U of Pennsylvania (PA)
Central Penn Coll (PA)
ECPI U, Virginia Beach (VA)
EDP U of Puerto Rico (PR)
EDP U of Puerto Rico–San Sebastian (PR)
Florida National U (FL)
Franciscan Missionaries of Our Lady U (LA)
Idaho State U (ID)
Jefferson Coll of Health Sciences (VA)
Keiser U, Fort Lauderdale (FL)
Louisiana Coll (LA)
Missouri Western State U (MO)
Mount Aloysius Coll (PA)
Nebraska Methodist Coll (NE)
New England Inst of Technology (RI)
Penn State Hazleton (PA)
Penn State Shenango (PA)
Pennsylvania Coll of Technology (PA)
Polk State Coll (FL)
St. Catherine U (MN)
Shawnee State U (OH)
Southern Illinois U Carbondale (IL)
State U of New York Coll of Technology at Canton (NY)
U of Cincinnati (OH)
U of Evansville (IN)
U of Maine at Presque Isle (ME)
U of Puerto Rico–Humacao (PR)
U of Saint Francis (IN)
Villa Maria Coll (NY)

## PHYSICS
Idaho State U (ID)
Rogers State U (OK)
U of the Virgin Islands (VI)
U of Wisconsin–Parkside (WI)
Utah Valley U (UT)
York Coll of Pennsylvania (PA)

## PIPEFITTING AND SPRINKLER FITTING
New England Inst of Technology (RI)
State U of New York Coll of Technology at Delhi (NY)

## PLANT SCIENCES
State U of New York Coll of Agriculture and Technology at Cobleskill (NY)

## PLASTICS AND POLYMER ENGINEERING TECHNOLOGY
Ferris State U (MI)
Penn State Erie, The Behrend Coll (PA)
Pennsylvania Coll of Technology (PA)
Shawnee State U (OH)

## POLITICAL SCIENCE AND GOVERNMENT
Immaculata U (PA)
John Cabot U (Italy)
Liberty U (VA)
Palm Beach State Coll (FL)

## POLYSOMNOGRAPHY
Oregon Inst of Technology (OR)

## POULTRY SCIENCE
State U of New York Coll of Agriculture and Technology at Cobleskill (NY)

## PRACTICAL NURSING, VOCATIONAL NURSING AND NURSING ASSISTANTS RELATED
Caribbean U (PR)

## PRECISION METAL WORKING RELATED
Montana Tech of The U of Montana (MT)

## PRE-DENTISTRY STUDIES
Concordia U Wisconsin (WI)

## PRE-ENGINEERING
Columbia Coll (MO)
Newman U (KS)
Palm Beach State Coll (FL)
Southern Utah U (UT)
Utah Valley U (UT)

## PRE-LAW STUDIES
Florida National U (FL)
Wayland Baptist U (TX)

## PREMEDICAL STUDIES
Concordia U Wisconsin (WI)

## PRENURSING STUDIES
Concordia U Wisconsin (WI)
Cornerstone U (MI)
Dean Coll (MA)
Eastern New Mexico U (NM)
Lincoln Christian U (IL)
Lincoln Coll (IL)
Missouri Baptist U (MO)

## PRE-PHARMACY STUDIES
Ferris State U (MI)
Madonna U (MI)

## PRE-THEOLOGY/PRE- MINISTERIAL STUDIES
Eastern Mennonite U (VA)
Tabor Coll (KS)
Theological U of the Caribbean (PR)

## PSYCHIATRIC/MENTAL HEALTH SERVICES TECHNOLOGY
Pennsylvania Coll of Technology (PA)

## PSYCHOLOGY
Beacon Coll (FL)
Bryn Athyn Coll of the New Church (PA)
Calumet Coll of Saint Joseph (IN)
Central Methodist U (MO)
Dean Coll (MA)
Eastern New Mexico U (NM)
Ferris State U (MI)
Fisher Coll (MA)
Inter American U of Puerto Rico, Metropolitan Campus (PR)
John Cabot U (Italy)
Liberty U (VA)
Life U (GA)
Marian U (IN)
Montana State U Billings (MT)
Muhlenberg Coll (PA)
Palm Beach State Coll (FL)
Point U (GA)
Regent U (VA)
Southwestern Assemblies of God U (TX)
State U of New York Empire State Coll (NY)
Utah Valley U (UT)
Waldorf U (IA)
Wright State U (OH)
Wright State U–Lake Campus (OH)

## PUBLIC ADMINISTRATION
Central Methodist U (MO)
Florida National U (FL)

## PUBLIC ADMINISTRATION AND SOCIAL SERVICE PROFESSIONS RELATED
Metropolitan Coll of New York (NY)
Northern Vermont U–Lyndon (VT)
Trevecca Nazarene U (TN)
The U of Akron (OH)

## PUBLIC HEALTH
American Public U System (WV)
U of Alaska Fairbanks (AK)

## PUBLIC POLICY ANALYSIS
Saint Peter's U (NJ)

## PUBLIC RELATIONS, ADVERTISING, AND APPLIED COMMUNICATION
Lynn U (FL)

## PUBLIC RELATIONS, ADVERTISING, AND APPLIED COMMUNICATION RELATED
Tulane U (LA)
U of Maine at Presque Isle (ME)

## PURCHASING, PROCUREMENT/ ACQUISITIONS AND CONTRACTS MANAGEMENT
Trevecca Nazarene U (TN)

## QUALITY CONTROL AND SAFETY TECHNOLOGIES RELATED
Madonna U (MI)

## RADIATION BIOLOGY
Suffolk U (MA)

## RADIATION PROTECTION/ HEALTH PHYSICS TECHNOLOGY
Keiser U, Fort Lauderdale (FL)

## RADIO AND TELEVISION
Lawrence Technological U (MI)
Ohio U–Zanesville (OH)

## RADIO AND TELEVISION BROADCASTING TECHNOLOGY
New England Inst of Technology (RI)
Northern Vermont U–Lyndon (VT)

## RADIOLOGIC TECHNOLOGY/ SCIENCE
Adventist U of Health Sciences (FL)
Allen Coll (IA)
Aultman Coll of Nursing and Health Sciences (OH)
Charles R. Drew U of Medicine and Science (CA)
Coll of Coastal Georgia (GA)
Colorado Mesa U (CO)
ECPI U, Virginia Beach (VA)
Fairleigh Dickinson U, Metropolitan Campus (NJ)
Florida National U (FL)
Gannon U (PA)
Holy Family U (PA)
Indiana U Kokomo (IN)
Indiana U Northwest (IN)
Indiana U–Purdue U Indianapolis (IN)
Indiana U South Bend (IN)
Inter American U of Puerto Rico, Barranquitas Campus (PR)
Mansfield U of Pennsylvania (PA)
Mercy Coll of Ohio (OH)
Missouri Baptist U (MO)
Montana Tech of The U of Montana (MT)
Nebraska Methodist Coll (NE)
Newman U (KS)
Northern Michigan U (MI)
Pennsylvania Coll of Health Sciences (PA)
Pennsylvania Coll of Technology (PA)
Sacred Heart U (CT)
U of Montana (MT)
U of Saint Francis (IN)
Weber State U (UT)
Widener U (PA)

## RADIO, TELEVISION, AND DIGITAL COMMUNICATION RELATED
Madonna U (MI)

## REAL ESTATE
American Public U System (WV)
Saint Francis U (PA)

## RECORDING ARTS TECHNOLOGY
Academy of Art U (CA)
Columbia Central U, Caguas (PR)
Indiana U Bloomington (IN)
New England Inst of Technology (RI)

## REGIONAL STUDIES
Arkansas Tech U (AR)

## REGISTERED NURSING/ REGISTERED NURSE
Alcorn State U (MS)
Arkansas Tech U (AR)
Aultman Coll of Nursing and Health Sciences (OH)
Becker Coll (MA)
Bethel Coll (IN)
Brigham Young U–Idaho (ID)
California U of Pennsylvania (PA)
Campbellsville U (KY)
Clarion U of Pennsylvania (PA)
Colegio Universitario de San Juan, San Juan (PR)
Coll of Coastal Georgia (GA)
Coll of Staten Island of the City U of New York (NY)
Colorado Mesa U (CO)
Columbia Central U, Caguas (PR)
Columbia Coll (MO)
ECPI U, Virginia Beach (VA)
Excelsior Coll (NY)
Florida National U (FL)
Franciscan Missionaries of Our Lady U (LA)
Gwynedd Mercy U (PA)
Hannibal-LaGrange U (MO)
Idaho State U (ID)
Inter American U of Puerto Rico, Barranquitas Campus (PR)
Keiser U, Fort Lauderdale (FL)
Kent State U at Geauga (OH)
Kentucky State U (KY)
La Roche Coll (PA)
Lincoln Memorial U (TN)
Lincoln U (MO)
Lock Haven U of Pennsylvania (PA)
Maria Coll (NY)
Marshall U (WV)
Mercy Coll of Ohio (OH)
Middle Georgia State U (GA)
Midland Coll (TX)
Montana State U Billings (MT)
Morehead State U (KY)
Mount Aloysius Coll (PA)
Mount Saint Mary's U (CA)
New England Inst of Technology (RI)
Northwestern State U of Louisiana (LA)
Palm Beach State Coll (FL)
Penn State Altoona (PA)
Penn State Berks (PA)
Penn State Erie, The Behrend Coll (PA)
Penn State Worthington Scranton (PA)
Pennsylvania Coll of Health Sciences (PA)
Pennsylvania Coll of Technology (PA)
Polk State Coll (FL)
Rivier U (NH)
Rogers State U (OK)
Sacred Heart U (CT)
Shawnee State U (OH)
Southern Adventist U (TN)
Southern Arkansas U–Magnolia (AR)
Southwest Baptist U (MO)
State U of New York Coll of Technology at Canton (NY)
State U of New York Coll of Technology at Delhi (NY)
Thomas Jefferson U (PA)
Thomas U (GA)
Troy U (AL)
U of Charleston (WV)
U of Guam (GU)
U of Montana (MT)
U of Pikeville (KY)
U of Pittsburgh at Bradford (PA)
U of Saint Francis (IN)
U of South Dakota (SD)
The U of West Alabama (AL)
Utah Valley U (UT)
Valencia Coll (FL)
Vermont Tech Coll (VT)
Weber State U (UT)
Western Kentucky U (KY)

## REHABILITATION AND THERAPEUTIC PROFESSIONS RELATED
Rutgers U–Newark (NJ)
Rutgers U–New Brunswick (NJ)

## RELIGIOUS EDUCATION
Dallas Baptist U (TX)
Marian U (IN)

## RELIGIOUS/SACRED MUSIC
The Baptist Coll of Florida (FL)
Bethel Coll (IN)
Calvary U (MO)
Indiana Wesleyan U (IN)
Mount Vernon Nazarene U (OH)
Nebraska Christian Coll of Hope International U (NE)
Ohio Christian U (OH)
Southeastern U (FL)
Trevecca Nazarene U (TN)

## RELIGIOUS STUDIES
Beulah Heights U (GA)
Bryn Athyn Coll of the New Church (PA)
Concordia Coll–New York (NY)
Corban U (OR)
Inter American U of Puerto Rico, Metropolitan Campus (PR)
Liberty U (VA)
Madonna U (MI)
Mount Marty Coll (SD)
Mount Vernon Nazarene U (OH)
Northwest U (WA)
Oakland City U (IN)
Palm Beach State Coll (FL)
Southern Adventist U (TN)

## RESORT MANAGEMENT
State U of New York Coll of Technology at Delhi (NY)

## RESPIRATORY CARE THERAPY
Clarion U of Pennsylvania (PA)
Dakota State U (SD)
Ferris State U (MI)
Florida National U (FL)
Gannon U (PA)
Gwynedd Mercy U (PA)
Idaho State U (ID)
Keiser U, Fort Lauderdale (FL)
Mansfield U of Pennsylvania (PA)
Middle Georgia State U (GA)
Midland Coll (TX)
Molloy Coll (NY)
Morehead State U (KY)
Nebraska Methodist Coll (NE)
New England Inst of Technology (RI)
Newman U (KS)
Pennsylvania Coll of Health Sciences (PA)
Polk State Coll (FL)
Rutgers U–New Brunswick (NJ)
Shawnee State U (OH)
U of Montana (MT)
U of Southern Indiana (IN)
Valencia Coll (FL)
Vermont Tech Coll (VT)
Weber State U (UT)
York Coll of Pennsylvania (PA)

## RESPIRATORY THERAPY TECHNICIAN
Florida National U (FL)
Keiser U, Fort Lauderdale (FL)
Northern Michigan U (MI)
U of the Incarnate Word (TX)

## RESTAURANT, CULINARY, AND CATERING MANAGEMENT
Arkansas Tech U (AR)
Ferris State U (MI)
State U of New York Coll of Agriculture and Technology at Cobleskill (NY)
State U of New York Coll of Technology at Delhi (NY)

## RESTAURANT/FOOD SERVICES MANAGEMENT
American Public U System (WV)
Pennsylvania Coll of Technology (PA)
The U of Akron (OH)
Valencia Coll (FL)

## RETAILING
American Public U System (WV)
Stevens–The Inst of Business & Arts (MO)
The U of Findlay (OH)
Weber State U (UT)

## RHETORIC AND COMPOSITION
Ferris State U (MI)

## ROBOTICS TECHNOLOGY
Idaho State U (ID)
Pennsylvania Coll of Technology (PA)

Utah Valley U (UT)

## RUSSIAN
Idaho State U (ID)

## SALES, DISTRIBUTION, AND MARKETING OPERATIONS
Inter American U of Puerto Rico, Aguadilla Campus (PR)
Southern Adventist U (TN)
Sullivan U (KY)

## SCIENCE TEACHER EDUCATION
Wright State U (OH)
Wright State U–Lake Campus (OH)

## SCIENCE TECHNOLOGIES RELATED
Madonna U (MI)
Maria Coll (NY)
State U of New York Coll of Agriculture and Technology at Cobleskill (NY)
U of Alaska Fairbanks (AK)

## SECONDARY EDUCATION
Ferris State U (MI)
McMurry U (TX)
Rogers State U (OK)

## SELLING SKILLS AND SALES
Inter American U of Puerto Rico, San Germán Campus (PR)
The U of Akron (OH)

## SHEET METAL TECHNOLOGY
Montana State U Billings (MT)

## SIGN LANGUAGE INTERPRETATION AND TRANSLATION
Mount Aloysius Coll (PA)
St. Catherine U (MN)

## SMALL BUSINESS ADMINISTRATION
Central Penn Coll (PA)
The U of Akron (OH)

## SOCIAL SCIENCES
Campbellsville U (KY)
Long Island U–LIU Brooklyn (NY)
Marymount Manhattan Coll (NY)
Ohio U–Zanesville (OH)
Palm Beach State Coll (FL)
Rogers State U (OK)
Saint Peter's U (NJ)
Shawnee State U (OH)
Southwestern Assemblies of God U (TX)
State U of New York Empire State Coll (NY)
Trine U (IN)
Tulane U (LA)
U of Cincinnati (OH)
U of Sioux Falls (SD)
U of Southern Indiana (IN)
Valparaiso U (IN)
Warner Pacific U (OR)
Wayland Baptist U (TX)

## SOCIAL SCIENCES RELATED
U of Wisconsin–Parkside (WI)

## SOCIAL WORK
Aultman Coll of Nursing and Health Sciences (OH)
Ferris State U (MI)
Palm Beach State Coll (FL)
State U of New York Coll of Agriculture and Technology at Cobleskill (NY)
U of the Fraser Valley (BC, Canada)
Youngstown State U (OH)

## SOCIAL WORK RELATED
Middle Georgia State U (GA)
The U of Akron (OH)

## SOCIOLOGY
Dean Coll (MA)
Middle Georgia State U (GA)
Montana State U Billings (MT)
U of California, San Diego (CA)
The U of Scranton (PA)
Wright State U (OH)
Wright State U–Lake Campus (OH)

## SPANISH
Bethel Coll (IN)

## SPECIAL EDUCATION
Montana State U Billings (MT)
U of Maine at Presque Isle (ME)

## SPECIAL EDUCATION– INDIVIDUALS WHO ARE DEVELOPMENTALLY DELAYED
Saint Mary-of-the-Woods Coll (IN)

## SPECIAL EDUCATION– INDIVIDUALS WITH SPEECH/ LANGUAGE IMPAIRMENTS
The U of Toledo (OH)

## SPECIAL EDUCATION RELATED
Minot State U (ND)

## SPECIAL PRODUCTS MARKETING
Palm Beach State Coll (FL)

## SPEECH COMMUNICATION AND RHETORIC
American Public U System (WV)
Dean Coll (MA)
Indiana Wesleyan U (IN)
State U of New York Coll of Agriculture and Technology at Cobleskill (NY)
Trevecca Nazarene U (TN)
Tulane U (LA)
Utah Valley U (UT)
Waldorf U (IA)
Weber State U (UT)
Wright State U (OH)
Wright State U–Lake Campus (OH)

## SPEECH-LANGUAGE PATHOLOGY
Elms Coll (MA)
Southern Adventist U (TN)

## SPORT AND FITNESS ADMINISTRATION/ MANAGEMENT
Dean Coll (MA)
Keiser U, Fort Lauderdale (FL)
Mount Vernon Nazarene U (OH)
Southwestern Adventist U (TX)
State U of New York Coll of Technology at Delhi (NY)
Waldorf U (IA)
Webber International U (FL)
William Paterson U of New Jersey (NJ)

## STRATEGIC STUDIES
U of Wisconsin–Parkside (WI)

## SUBSTANCE ABUSE/ ADDICTION COUNSELING
Indiana Wesleyan U (IN)
Midland Coll (TX)
National U (CA)
Southwestern Assemblies of God U (TX)
U of Providence (MT)

## SURGICAL TECHNOLOGY
Colorado Mesa U (CO)
ECPI U, Virginia Beach (VA)
Jefferson Coll of Health Sciences (VA)
Keiser U, Fort Lauderdale (FL)
Montana State U Billings (MT)
Mount Aloysius Coll (PA)
Nebraska Methodist Coll (NE)
New England Inst of Technology (RI)
Northern Michigan U (MI)
Pennsylvania Coll of Health Sciences (PA)
Pennsylvania Coll of Technology (PA)
Rasmussen Coll Brooklyn Park (MN)
Rasmussen Coll St. Cloud (MN)
Robert Morris U Illinois (IL)
Sentara Coll of Health Sciences (VA)
The U of Akron (OH)
U of Montana (MT)
U of Saint Francis (IN)

## SURVEYING TECHNOLOGY
Palm Beach State Coll (FL)
Penn State Wilkes-Barre (PA)
Pennsylvania Coll of Technology (PA)
Polytechnic U of Puerto Rico (PR)

State U of New York Coll of
  Environmental Science and
  Forestry (NY)
The U of Akron (OH)
Utah Valley U (UT)

**SUSTAINABILITY STUDIES**
Lock Haven U of Pennsylvania (PA)

**SYSTEM, NETWORKING, AND
LAN/WAN MANAGEMENT**
Dakota State U (SD)
Midland Coll (TX)

**TEACHER ASSISTANT/AIDE**
Alverno Coll (WI)
Eastern Mennonite U (VA)
Johnson U (TN)
Saint Mary-of-the-Woods Coll (IN)
State U of New York Coll of
  Agriculture and Technology at
  Cobleskill (NY)
U of Maine at Presque Isle (ME)
Valparaiso U (IN)
Waldorf U (IA)

**TECHNICAL TEACHER
EDUCATION**
Western Kentucky U (KY)

**TELECOMMUNICATIONS
TECHNOLOGY**
Pace U (NY)
Penn State Hazleton (PA)
Penn State New Kensington (PA)
Penn State Schuylkill (PA)
Penn State Shenango (PA)
Penn State Wilkes-Barre (PA)
Penn State York (PA)
St. John's U (NY)

**TERRORISM AND
COUNTERTERRORISM
OPERATIONS**
American Public U System (WV)

**THEATER DESIGN AND
TECHNOLOGY**
Northern Vermont U–Lyndon (VT)
Utah Valley U (UT)

**THEOLOGICAL AND
MINISTERIAL STUDIES
RELATED**
Bob Jones U (SC)
California Christian Coll (CA)
Lincoln Christian U (IL)
Northwest U (WA)

**THEOLOGY**
Appalachian Bible Coll (WV)
Calvary U (MO)
Creighton U (NE)
Immaculata U (PA)
Mid-America Baptist Theological
  Seminary (TN)
Ohio Dominican U (OH)

**THEOLOGY AND RELIGIOUS
VOCATIONS RELATED**
Missouri Baptist U (MO)
Trevecca Nazarene U (TN)
U of Valley Forge (PA)

**TOOL AND DIE TECHNOLOGY**
Ferris State U (MI)

**TOURISM AND TRAVEL
SERVICES MANAGEMENT**
Black Hills State U (SD)

**TOURISM AND TRAVEL
SERVICES MARKETING**
State U of New York Coll of
  Agriculture and Technology at
  Cobleskill (NY)
State U of New York Coll of
  Technology at Delhi (NY)

**TRADE AND INDUSTRIAL
TEACHER EDUCATION**
Murray State U (KY)

**TRANSPORTATION/MOBILITY
MANAGEMENT**
Polk State Coll (FL)

**TURF AND TURFGRASS
MANAGEMENT**
North Carolina State U (NC)
State U of New York Coll of
  Technology at Delhi (NY)
U of Guelph  (ON, Canada)
U of Massachusetts Amherst (MA)

**URBAN MINISTRY**
Charlotte Christian Coll and
  Theological Seminary (NC)
Tabor Coll (KS)

**URBAN STUDIES/AFFAIRS**
Saint Peter's U (NJ)

**VEHICLE AND VEHICLE PARTS
AND ACCESSORIES
MARKETING**
Pennsylvania Coll of Technology (PA)

**VETERINARY/ANIMAL HEALTH
TECHNOLOGY**
Becker Coll (MA)
Brigham Young U–Idaho (ID)
Lincoln Memorial U (TN)
Morehead State U (KY)
New England Inst of Technology (RI)
Northwestern State U of Louisiana
  (LA)
Purdue U (IN)
State U of New York Coll of
  Technology at Canton (NY)
State U of New York Coll of
  Technology at Delhi (NY)
U of Guelph  (ON, Canada)
U of New Hampshire  (NH)
Vermont Tech Coll (VT)

**VISUAL AND PERFORMING
ARTS**
Pine Manor Coll (MA)

**VITICULTURE AND ENOLOGY**
Colorado Mesa U (CO)

**WATER QUALITY AND
WASTEWATER TREATMENT
MANAGEMENT AND
RECYCLING TECHNOLOGY**
Colorado Mesa U (CO)

**WEAPONS OF MASS
DESTRUCTION**
American Public U System (WV)

**WEB/MULTIMEDIA
MANAGEMENT AND
WEBMASTER**
American Public U System (WV)
Indiana Tech (IN)
Montana Tech of The U of Montana
  (MT)

**WEB PAGE, DIGITAL/
MULTIMEDIA AND
INFORMATION RESOURCES
DESIGN**
Academy of Art U (CA)
Beacon Coll (FL)
Brigham Young U–Idaho (ID)
Dakota State U (SD)
Florida National U (FL)
Limestone Coll (SC)
New England Inst of Technology (RI)
Palm Beach State Coll (FL)
Polk State Coll (FL)
Rasmussen Coll Bloomington (MN)
Rasmussen Coll Brooklyn Park (MN)
Rasmussen Coll Eagan (MN)
Rasmussen Coll Fargo (ND)
Rasmussen Coll Mankato (MN)
Rasmussen Coll New Port Richey
  (FL)
Rasmussen Coll Ocala (FL)
Rasmussen Coll St. Cloud (MN)
Tulane U  (LA)
Utah Valley U (UT)

Weber State U (UT)
Wilmington U (DE)

**WELDING ENGINEERING
TECHNOLOGY**
New England Inst of Technology (RI)

**WELDING TECHNOLOGY**
Arkansas Tech U (AR)
Brigham Young U–Idaho (ID)
Ferris State U (MI)
Idaho State U (ID)
Midland Coll (TX)
Pennsylvania Coll of Technology (PA)
State U of New York Coll of
  Technology at Delhi (NY)
U of Montana (MT)

**WILDLAND/FOREST
FIREFIGHTING AND
INVESTIGATION**
Colorado Mesa U (CO)

**WILDLIFE, FISH AND
WILDLANDS SCIENCE AND
MANAGEMENT**
State U of New York Coll of
  Agriculture and Technology at
  Cobleskill (NY)

**WORD PROCESSING**
Palm Beach State Coll (FL)

**WRITING**
Carroll Coll  (MT)

**YOUTH MINISTRY**
Calvary U (MO)
U of Valley Forge (PA)

**ZOOLOGY/ANIMAL BIOLOGY**
Palm Beach State Coll (FL)

# Alphabetical Listing of Two-Year Colleges

**NOTES**

**NOTES**

**NOTES**

**NOTES**

**NOTES**

**NOTES**

**NOTES**

# NOTES